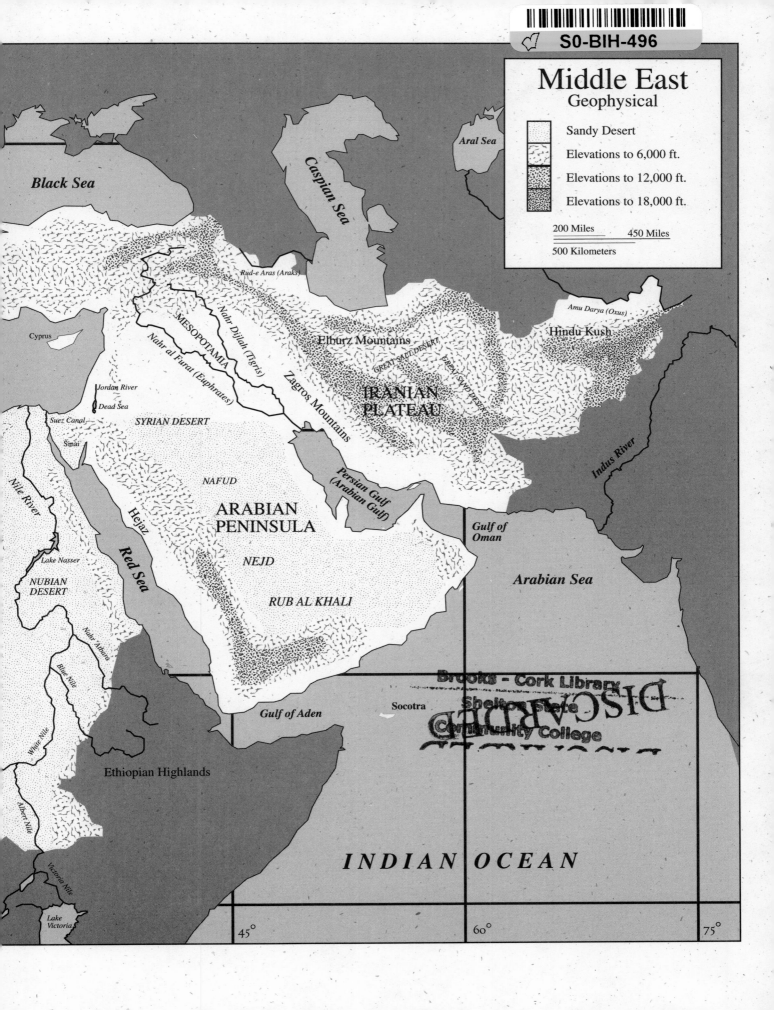

Middle East
Geophysical

Sandy Desert
Elevations to 6,000 ft.
Elevations to 12,000 ft.
Elevations to 18,000 ft.

200 Miles   450 Miles
500 Kilometers

Black Sea

Caspian Sea

Aral Sea

Cyprus

Rud-e Aras (Araks)

Amu Darya (Oxus)

MESOPOTAMIA

Nahr Dijlah (Tigris)

Nahr al Furat (Euphrates)

Elburz Mountains

Hindu Kush

GREAT SALT DESERT

GREAT SAND DESERT

Jordan River

Dead Sea

Zagros Mountains

IRANIAN
PLATEAU

Suez Canal

SYRIAN DESERT

Sinai

Nile River

NAFUD

Persian Gulf
(Arabian Gulf)

Indus River

Lake Nasser

Hejaz

ARABIAN
PENINSULA

Gulf of
Oman

NUBIAN
DESERT

Red Sea

NEJD

Arabian Sea

Nahr Atbara

RUB AL KHALI

Blue Nile

White Nile

Gulf of Aden

Socotra

Ethiopian Highlands

Albert Nile

Victoria Nile

INDIAN OCEAN

Lake
Victoria

45°   60°   75°

ENCYCLOPEDIA
OF THE
MODERN
MIDDLE EAST

ENCYCLOPEDIA

OF THE

MODERN

MIDDLE EAST

VOLUME 1

Edited by

Reeva S. Simon
Philip Mattar
Richard W. Bulliet

MACMILLAN REFERENCE USA
SIMON & SCHUSTER MACMILLAN
NEW YORK

SIMON & SCHUSTER AND PRENTICE HALL INTERNATIONAL
LONDON   MEXICO CITY   NEW DELHI   SINGAPORE   SYDNEY   TORONTO

Simon & Schuster Macmillan
1633 Broadway
New York, NY 10019-6785

PRINTED IN THE UNITED STATES OF AMERICA

printing number

2   3   4   5   6   7   8   9   10

LIBRARY OF CONGRESS CATALOGING-IN-PUBLICATION DATA

Encyclopedia of the Modern Middle East / edited by Reeva S. Simon,
    Philip Mattar, Richard W. Bulliet.
        p.   cm.
        Includes bibliographical references (p.   ) and index.
        ISBN 0-02-896011-4 (set : lib. bdg. : alk. paper). — ISBN
    0-02-897061-6 (v. 1 : lib. bdg. : alk. paper). — ISBN 0-02-897062-4
    (v. 2 : lib. bdg. : alk. paper). — ISBN 0-02-897063-2 (v. 3 : lib.
    bdg. : alk. paper). — ISBN 0-02-897064-0 (v. 4 : lib. bdg. : alk.
    paper).
        1. Middle East—Encyclopedias.   2. Africa, North—Encyclopedias.
    I. Simon, Reeva S.   II. Mattar, Philip, 1944–   III. Bulliet,
    Richard W.
    DS43.E53   1996
    956′.003—dc20   96-11800
                                                             CIP

This paper meets the requirements of ANSI/NISO Z39.48-1992
(Permanence of Paper)

Contents

Editorial and Production Staff

Project Editors

Martha Imber-Goldstein
Thomas McCarthy
Jean-Marc Ran Oppenheim

Editorial Assistants

Debra Alpern
Brian Kinsey
Karin Vanderveer

Manuscript Editors

Jonathan Amith
Patricia Brecht
Mary Grace Butler
Julie Marsh
Shirley Marshall
Suzanne Martinucci
Thomas F. McDow
Sara Simon Diamond
Estelle Silbermann
Ingrid Sterner
Beth Wilson
Nancy G. Wright

Proofreaders

Evangeline Legones
Edward G. McLeroy
Donald Spanel
Jillian Schwedler
Seija Tupasela

Illustration Editor

Scott Kurtz

Cartographer

Donald S. Frazier

Indexer

AEIOU, Inc.

Production Manager

Rose Capozzelli

MACMILLAN REFERENCE

Elly Dickason, *Publisher*
Paul Bernabeo, *Editor in Chief*

Preface

When Dr. Philip Mattar and Dr. Reeva S. Simon conceived this encyclopedia over a dozen years ago, their twofold concern was to make available to the general public a reference work that would, on the one hand, contain scholarly, balanced, and proportionate coverage of the conflict between Arabs and Israelis that has so strongly marked the history of the Middle East over the past century and, on the other hand, integrate that issue into the fabric of Middle East politics and culture. Both then and now, most reference works dealing specifically with the Middle East have concentrated on a single national or religious tradition, thereby slighting the multifaceted nature of Middle East history, culture, and society in the nineteenth and twentieth centuries.

Few would have imagined more than a decade ago that, by the time the project came to fruition, there would have been two major wars in the region—the Iran–Iraq War and the Gulf War—important breakthroughs in negotiations between Israel and the PLO, and a military coup d'état in Algeria that would suspend the results of democratic elections or that an assassin would have taken the life of an Israeli prime minister. Each of these events, and many more, convinced the editors—now including Prof. Richard W. Bulliet, director of the Middle East Institute of Columbia University—that a reference work for schools and the general public that embodied the inclusive perspective described above was desperately needed. This *Encyclopedia of the Modern Middle East* is the product of that conviction.

For the first time in a compendium of this scope and scale, the history and culture of Israel and Zionism are included with those of the Arab and Islamic countries of the region. Included herein is information about groups often given scanty coverage in works focusing on Islam, such as Christians and Baha'is. Likewise, information about the Kurds, Armenians, Berbers, and other minority groups sometimes omitted from reference works devoted to the numerically dominant peoples of the region—Arabs, Iranians, and Turks—will also be found.

The encyclopedia encompasses the interaction of political, historical, social, economic, and cultural movements as well as relevant persons (both living and dead), places, and events. Concepts that have been important in analyzing the historical and cultural development of the Middle East—such as nationalism, modernization, and feminism—receive attention, as do specifically theological and philosophical terms that bear a significant relation to life in the Middle East today. Thus, Islamic terms such as *hajj* and *molla* are included because of their relevance to the resurgent role of religion in contemporary politics.

The work is designed to be a ready reference tool, a compendium of knowledge about the Middle East since 1800. Spanning the geographical area from Afghanistan to Morocco, it provides easy identification of and immediate access to information about the region from the perspectives of many disciplines and approaches. It covers a broad range of topics drawn from many fields—politics, economics, religion, history, literature, the arts, and more—in articles that range from detailed country surveys to short definitions of terms.

Most of the nearly four thousand articles have been written by scholars known for their specialization in Middle East matters. The editors have also made a concerted effort to assign articles to scholars from the region itself and to permit the encyclopedia to represent a rich variety of views. All articles are signed by their authors.

The editors are deeply grateful to the Board of Consultants, a body of highly distinguished scholars with special expertise in various aspects of the Middle East. They have helped review lists of articles and solve problems of many different sorts. We are also grateful to the members of the Macmillan publishing and editorial staff for sticking with the project through innumerable delays and devoting to it their extraordinary talents.

Coverage

Fewer than half as many people live in Israel, Jordan, and the territories overseen in 1996 by an autonomous Palestinian governing authority as live in Yemen. However, the ratio of coverage between the first three political units and the last in this encyclopedia is close to one hundred to one. The governing principle behind the editors' choice of what to include and how much space to devote to a given topic was concern for usefulness and accessibility of information to the reader. Though the editors were determined that each of the twenty-four countries in the area embraced by the encyclopedia—that is, every country from Morocco to Afghanistan—should receive sufficient treatment, they recognized that the most likely audience for their work would be English-speaking readers interested in finding out more about names and places in the news, the cultural backgrounds of Middle Eastern peoples, and topics related to business or governmental concerns. Accordingly, the editors prepared a scheme of coverage that allotted the greatest amount of space to Egypt, Israel, and Turkey (including the Ottoman Empire). A large general category was devised for topics such as petroleum, agriculture, and matters dealing with the involvement of the European powers and the United States in modern Middle Eastern history. A second category of countries included Iran, Iraq, Syria, Morocco, Tunisia, Algeria, and Lebanon; a third, Afghanistan, Saudi Arabia, Palestine, Libya, Sudan, and Jordan; and a fourth, Cyprus, Mauritania, and the smaller countries of the Persian/Arabian Gulf region. Within the limits of articles of various lengths, the editors sought to cover cultural, economic, and social topics as well as historical events and personalities and major geographic locales.

While the editors are fully aware that no criteria for allotment of space will please all readers, they hope that the utility of the encyclopedia as a whole will compensate for any dissatisfaction.

Spelling and Transliteration

Middle East scholars prefer precision and consistency in spelling and transliteration. Their objective is to make it possible for a reader familiar with the non-Roman scripts in use in the Middle East—Arabic, Hebrew, and Armenian—to determine how a particular word or name is spelled in one of those scripts on the basis of the Roman letters, with accompanying diacritical marks, chosen to represent it. The transliteration systems underlying usage in this encyclopedia are those of the *International Journal of Middle East Studies* and, in modified form, that of the *Encyclopedia Judaica*. Yet the editors have elected not to apply these systems in a consistent fashion for several reasons:

(1) Many historical personalities and place-names are so familiar to readers of English in conventional but, in terms of a strict transliteration system, inaccurate form that it seemed best to stick with the convention in the interest of being friendly to the user of the encyclopedia. Thus, we retain Cairo for al-Qāhira, Gamal Abdel Nasser for Jamal ʿAbd al-Nāṣir, and Beirut for Bayrūt.

(2) Many Middle Eastern personalities of the twentieth century have adopted Roman-letter spellings of their own names. It seems presumptuous to suggest that these individuals are mistaken. If a Daʾud wishes to be known as Daoud or an Antun as Antoine, it should be that person's decision.

(3) People in areas under strong French influence or colonial occupation became accustomed to seeing personal names and place-names in French rather than English transliteration. While we have opted for an English transliteration for some place-names, personal names (particularly of North African origin) have more often been retained in their French form. Thus, we use Boumédienne.

(4) Pronunciation of Arabic differs from region to region within the Arab world. In Egypt, for example, the letter pronounced as English *j* is pronounced as hard *g* (as in *get*) in most other regions. Hence the disagreement over whether Nasser's first name should be rendered as Jamal or Gamal. In general, North Africa is the only area where we have accommodated local pronunciations, in part because they are the basis of common French renditions of personal names. The name Belkacem, for example, is a French rendering of Buʾl-Qasim in North African Arabic. This, in turn, is a local variant of what would be rendered as Abū al-Qāsim in standardized transliteration.

(5) The Turkish Republic established after World War I adopted the Roman alphabet in a completely consistent fashion. We have generally followed that system. In words and names from the period of the Turkish Republic, therefore, the letter *c* should be pronounced as *j* (e.g., Cumhuriyet = Jumhuriyet), *ç* should be pronounced as *ch*, *ş* should be pronounced as *sh*, and *ğ* should be pronounced as a slight glide between vowels or as a lengthening of the previous vowel. The undotted *ı* is a distinctive Turkish vowel pronounced toward the back of the mouth.

(6) Strict application of a transliteration system for Ottoman Turkish would closely resemble the current system used in the Turkish Republic. Thus, as a general principle, we have retained the Turkish transliteration for those Ottoman names and terms primarily associated with the central government since, under Ottoman rule, official personnel were recruited from all parts of the sultan's culturally diverse realm, and the use of Arabic script was empirewide. However, because most Ottoman given names, and many Ottoman technical terms, are of Arabic origin, we have adopted the Arabic forms for those officials who played crucial roles in the national histories of the Arab provinces. Thus, the quasi-independent governor of Egypt under Ottoman suzerainty early in the nineteenth century is referred to as Muhammad Ali Pasha instead of Mehmet Ali Paşa because he plays a more important role in Egyptian history than in Ottoman or Turkish history.

(7) Diacritical marks—mainly macrons above letters and dots below—are meaningless to anyone who does not know the language in question even though they are sometimes essential for determining which of two words is intended (e.g., Sa'īd and Ṣā'id are completely different names, though the latter is quite rare). We think these marks are confusing for the general reader and have chosen to exclude them.

(8) The Arabic alphabet contains two consonants that are not represented by characters in the Roman alphabet. Instead, they are represented by what look like punctuation marks: ' for the *hamza,* a glottal stop, and ' for the *'ayn,* a consonant pronounced in the back of the throat. We have decided generally to omit these marks when they occur at the beginning or end of a word because English speakers as a rule have no idea what the marks mean. However, we have generally retained them within a word so that the reader will realize that there should be a clear distinction made between the letters on either side of the mark. In other words, the mark for the *'ayn* should tell the reader that the name Sa'id should not be pronounced as the past tense of the verb *to say.* Rather, each vowel should be given full weight: Sa-eed. The phonetic distinction in pronunciation between the *hamza* and the *'ayn* is inconsequential for everyday English usage.

(9) Iranian and Afghan names and terms of Arabic origin have short vowels that are consistent with pronunciation in the Persian language (Farsi). Thus, the Arabic short *i* is rendered as *e,* and the Arabic short *u* is rendered as *o.* Persons named after the Prophet of Islam, for example, have their names rendered as Muhammad if they are Arabs and as Mohammad if they are Iranians or Afghans.

As is obvious, we have sacrificed precision and consistency for ease of use and practical convenience. To be sure, both goals might have been met by using an enormous number of cross-references, but this option would have cluttered the text and confused the general reader.

Order of entries and cross-references

Entry terms are alphabetized in letter-by-letter rather than word-by-word order, with very few exceptions. Thus, "National Guidance Committee, Palestinian" is followed by "Nationalism," "Nationalist Action Party," "Nationalist Democracy Party," and then by "National Liberal Party." Exceptions include a few rulers with nearly identical names that incorporate roman numerals. Where necessary, identical entry terms are placed in conventional person-place-thing order.

Letters with accents or diacritical marks are alphabetized as if the letters appeared unmarked; occasional characters not common to the English language are treated in the same way. Thus, *ü* is alphabetized as *u,* and undotted *ı* as *i.* Marks of punctuation, such as hyphens, are ignored for purposes of alphabetization.

Numerous cross-references appear throughout run of text in small capital letters. Others appear at the ends of articles and in the index as a means to direct readers to related discussions.

Reeva S. Simon

Philip Mattar

Richard W. Bulliet

List of Maps

Maps accompany the following entries.

Aba

A type of dress used by Arabs.

Reaching the knees or ankles and made of coarse wool, cotton, or silk, the dress may be embroidered around the edges and is usually held together around the waist by a cloth belt with fringes (*shamli*). Sleeves are optional, but in general the aba serves as an outer protective garment that is worn over the *gullabiyya* (djellabah).

Cyrus Moshaver

Abadan

A city with large oil refineries and an island in the province of Khuzistan in southwest Iran at the entrance of the Persian Gulf.

The island of Abadan is forty miles (64 km) long and from two to twelve miles (3 to 30 km) wide. The island is bounded by the Shatt-al-Arab river on the west, the Karun river on the north and the Persian Gulf on the south.

The city, nine miles (15 km) from the north-western tip of the island, was first mentioned by Muslim geographers in the mid-ninth century. In medieval times it was of importance to travelers and navigators as a source of woven straw mats, supplier of salt, and center of shipping and navigation. The growth of other commercial cities, such as BASRA (now part of Iraq), reduced Abadan to a small village by the end of the Middle Ages.

The city that developed after 1910 owed its growth to the discovery of Khuzistan oil fields. The first oil refinery, which was opened by the Anglo-Persian Oil Company in 1912 with an annual capacity of 120,000 tons (109,000 mt), grew into one of the world's largest refineries by the 1960s.

Abadan's population grew with its economic development. In 1948 refinery employees formed one-third of the city population of about 100,000. By the 1950s, however, due to natural increase and, especially, to immigration, the city's population reached about 220,000. The Iran–Iraq war heavily damaged the refinery as well as the city in the mid-1980s. Whereas in 1955 Abadan had formed the fifth largest city in Iran, after the war it ranked only seventh.

Because it is an industrial islet heavily influenced by foreign capitalist enterprise that uses the country's unskilled labor and raw material, Abadan's social structure is strongly segregated ethnically and economically.

BIBLIOGRAPHY

YARSHATER, EHSAN, ed. *Encyclopaedia Iranica,* vol. 1. London, 1985, pp. 51–57.

Parvaneh Pourshariati

Abalioğlu, Yunus Nadi   [1880–1945]

Turkish newspaperman.

Yunus Nadi Abalioğlu was born in Fethiye into a family of local notables and studied law in Istanbul. In 1900, he began his journalism career as a writer for the newspaper *Malumat* (Information). One year later, he was accused of being a member of a secret society opposed to ABDÜLMECIT II and sentenced to three years in prison. In 1908, he returned to Istanbul where he contributed to the newspapers *Ikdam* and *Tasvir-i Efkar*. In 1910, he was the head writer for a Committee of Union and Progress journal, *Rumeli Gazetisi,* and became a member of parliament from Aydın. In 1918, he founded the newspaper *Yedi Gün* (Seven Days). In 1924, he established the newspaper CUMHURIYET (The Republic), one of the most important newspapers of the Turkish republic to the present day. After his death, his sons, Doğan Nadi and Nadir Nadi, continued to publish *Cumhuriyet.*

BIBLIOGRAPHY

ORAL, FUAT SÜREYYA. *Turk Basım Tarihi, 1728–1922.* Ankara, p. 272.
Yeni Türk Ansiklopedisi. Vol. 12. Istanbul, 1985, p. 4821.

David Waldner

Abane, Ramdane   [1920–1957]

Controversial Algerian Front de Libération Nationale (FLN) leader.

Born in Azouza, Algeria, this Kabyle (BERBER) was fervently for nationalism with experience in Ahmed Messali's PARTI DU PEUPLE ALGÉRIEN (PPA) and Organisation Spéciale (OS) before emerging as the dominant leader of the FRONT DE LIBÉRATION NATIONALE in the early years of the Algerian War of Independence (1954–1962). Abane was at the height of his influence during the FLN's Soummam Conference (August 1956). His insistence that the civilian elite operating within Algeria determine revolutionary policy alienated the "external" elite and the military. Abane's fiery disposition led to his murder, which symbolized the tragedy of the intra-elite rivalry. Recent Algerian historiography has reassessed and rehabilitated his contribution to the revolution.

BIBLIOGRAPHY

NAYLOR, PHILLIP C., and ALF HEGGOY. *Historical Dictionary of Algeria,* 2nd ed. Metuchen, N.J., 1994.

Phillip C. Naylor

Abasiyanik, Sait Faik   [1906–1954]

Outstanding master of Turkish short-story writing, an honorary member of the International Mark Twain Society, elected in 1953 for services to twentieth-century literature.

The son of a prosperous merchant, Mehmet Faik (Abasizoğlu), Sait Faik was born in Adapazarı and died in Istanbul. The Greek occupation of Adapazarı during the war of independence interrupted his education and uprooted the family, which finally relocated in Istanbul. After graduation from the Bursa Lycée (1928), he attended Istanbul University for a short period, then spent several years in Europe traveling and studying literature. He wrote poems and short stories while still at the lycée. His first short story appeared in 1929, and his name started to be known when the literary journal *Varlık* began publishing his stories (1934).

Returning to Turkey in 1935, he tried teaching, business, and journalism. However, professing "becoming nothing" to be his goal in life, after 1942 he restricted himself to writing, dividing his time between his family's home on the island of Burgaz in the sea of Marmara and wandering about Istanbul.

A keen observer of scene and character and one who wrote easily and without revision, he was preoccupied with "social outcasts and marginal groups" on the fringes of society (fishermen, waiters, bootblacks, street vendors, streetwalkers, thieves, drunks, gamblers, etc.), vividly describing their lives in the colloquial langauge. Like many other writers of his period, he may be described as a social realist but one who takes a "sympathetic and tolerant view of life," a humanist and romantic who empathizes with those he describes, upholding their dignity and inherent rights.

BIBLIOGRAPHY

HALMAN, TALÂT SAIT, ed. *Sait Faik: A Dot on the Map.* Bloomington, Ind., 1983.
KARPAT, KEMAL H. *The Literary Review* 4, no. 2: 298–299.
"The Man Who Did Calisthenics." *Literature East and West* 22 (March 1973): 35–39.

Kathleen R. F. Burrill

Abbas, Ferhat   [1899–1985]

Leading Algerian nationalist and statesman.

Abbas was born in Taher to a family identified with French colonial rule. His father was a member of the Legion of Honor and served as a QA'ID or *caid* (administrator under the French). In 1909, Abbas entered the *lycée* at Philippeville (now Skikda) in ALGERIA. Following three years in the French army medical service, he enrolled in the pharmacy school at the University of Algiers.

Abbas's political career evolved from an earnest assimilationist to a reluctant revolutionary. In his first book, *Le jeune Algérien: De la colonie vers la province* (1931), he criticized the failure of French colonialism to live up to its assimilationist ideals. Along with Dr. Mohammed Saleh Bendjelloul, Abbas led the Fédération des Elus indigènes (founded in 1927), which continued to espouse the moderate reforms called for by the Jeunes Algériens (YOUNG ALGERIANS). Abbas embraced the ill-fated BLUM–VIOLLETTE PLAN, which would have granted full French citizenship to twenty to thirty thousand assimilated Algerians. The failure of the Blum–Viollette Plan split the moderates as Bendjelloul founded the Rassemblement Franco-Musulman Algérien (Assembly of French-Muslim Algerians), while Abbas organized the Union Populaire Algérien (Algerian People's Union, UPA), a party that began to affirm a separate Algerian identity while calling for full citizenship for all Muslims. This marked the redefinition of Abbas's position that he had presented in the federation's newspaper, *Entente,* where he wrote that he was unable to locate a historical Algerian nation and therefore tied Algeria's future to France.

Abbas volunteered at the beginning of World War II, but he was alienated by the Nazi occupation of France, Vichy government administration, and then by Free French general Henri Giraud's disinterest in reform while concurrently exhorting Muslims to enlist (though not on an equal basis) and sacrifice their lives. Abbas reacted by presenting the "Manifeste du peuple algérien" (Manifesto of the Algerian People) in February 1943, followed by a more explicit supplement called the "Projet de réformes faisant suite au Manifeste" (Project of Reforms Made Following the Manifesto) in May. These documents called for an autonomous Algerian state that was still closely associated with France.

Charles de Gaulle's ordinance of March 7, 1944, went beyond the provisions of the Blum-Viollette Plan, but it no longer corresponded to the aspirations of the nationalist elite. In March 1944, Abbas organized the Association des AMIS DU MANIFESTE ET DE LA LIBERTÉ (Friends of the Manifesto and of Liberty, AML), which briefly unified the Muslim nationalist movements under the leadership of Messali HADJ. Under Messalist pressures, the AML took a more radical position, calling for an Algerian government that reduced the attachment with France.

The deportation of Messali in April 1945 contributed to the bloody uprising at SÉTIF and Guelma in May. Abbas was placed under house arrest. After being freed, he founded the UNION DÉMOCRATIQUE DU MANIFESTE ALGÉRIEN (Democratic Union of the Algerian Manifesto, UDMA) in 1946. The UDMA sought a sovereign Algerian state responsible for internal affairs while being a member of the French union. Abbas was also elected to the Second French Constituent Assembly. He served as a member of the Muslim College of the Algerian Assembly from 1947 to 1955.

During the first eighteen months of the Algerian War of Independence (1954–1962), Abbas attempted to act as an intermediary between the FRONT DE LIBÉRATION NATIONAL (National Liberation Front, FLN) and the French, but in April 1956 he joined the FLN with other moderates and declared that it was the only representative force for the liberation of the country.

Appreciating his international prestige, on September 19, 1958, the FLN appointed Abbas president of the Gouvernement Provisoire de la République Algérienne (Provisional Government of the Algerian Republic, GPRA). In January 1961, he participated in a continental conference to establish an African Charter. Abbas signed an agreement with King HASSAN II of Morocco in July 1961 to settle border disputes after the end of the war of independence. In August, he was replaced by the more radical Ben Youssef BEN KHEDDA as president of the GPRA. The ouster of Abbas and the moderates signaled an important change in the FLN.

In fall 1962, Abbas was elected president of Algeria's National Constituent Assembly. He envisioned a democratic parliamentary form of government, which permitted political pluralism. His liberal democratic ideals were anachronistic compared to the revolutionary objectives of the younger elite (e.g., Premier Ahmed BEN BELLA), which were based on those of Egypt's President Gamal Abdel NASSER. The construction of a constitution that ignored the Constituent Assembly and the growing authoritarianism of Ben Bella led to Abbas's resignation in August 1963. He was subsequently removed from the FLN. This was a symbolic repudiation of a revolutionary heritage that had aimed at liberal reform and close ties with France.

Abbas's opposition to Ben Bella led to his arrest in 1964. After Houari BOUMÉDIENNE took over the government in June 1965, Abbas was released, but he refused to serve the military government. In March 1976, he joined Ben Khedda, Hocine LAHOUEL, and Mohamed Kheireddine in signing a manifesto entitled "New Appeal to the Algerian People." This courageous act condemned the lack of democratic institutions in Algeria, opposed the growing hostility between Algeria and Morocco over the decolonization of western Sahara and called for MAGHREB (North African) unity. Abbas was again placed under house arrest.

Ferhat Abbas's contributions to the creation of the Algerian state were publicly acknowledged in the "enhanced" National Center of 1986, which was published about two weeks after his death. Besides *Le jeune Algérien* (1931), Abbas authored several important works: *Guerre de Révolution d'Algérie: La nuit coloniale* (1962) and *Autopsie d'une guerre: L'aurore* (1980) reflect upon the war years. In *L'indépendance confisquée, 1962–1978* (1984), Abbas expressed his disillusionment with postcolonial Algeria, but he also dedicated the book to the emerging new generation. In some ways, his call for youth to restore the true meaning of the revolution has been heard since the October 1988 riots.

BIBLIOGRAPHY

"Abbas, Ferhat." *Current Biography,* 1961.
AGERON, CHARLES-ROBERT. *Histoire de l'Algérie contemporaine: De l'insurrection de 1871 au déclenchement de la guerre de libération (1954).* Paris, 1979.
KADDACHE, MAHFOUD. *Histoire du nationalisme algérien.* Algiers, 1981.
NAYLOR, PHILLIP C., and ALF A. HEGGOY. *The Historical Dictionary of Algeria,* 2nd ed. Metuchen, N.J., 1994.

Phillip C. Naylor

Abbas, Mahmud   [1937–   ]

Palestinian politician; a founder of Fath.

Mahmud Abbas (also called Abu Mazin) was born in Safad (Hebrew, Zefat), now in northern Israel but then in the British mandate of Palestine. He became the principal architect of the 1993 peace accords concluded between Israel and the PALESTINE LIBERATION ORGANIZATION (PLO). He had been organizing Palestinians in Saudi Arabia and in Qatar in the 1950s before joining Yasir ARAFAT, Khalil al-WAZIR, Salah KHALAF, and others in forming the group al-FATH after suffering the disappointment of the Egyptian and Palestinian defeat by Israel in the Arab–Israel War of 1956.

Since Israel's assassination of Khalil al-Wazir (known as Abu Jihad) in 1988, Abbas has been Arafat's closest political strategist. He, along with Israel's Foreign Minister Shimon Peres, signed the September 13, 1993, accord in Washington, D.C.

BIBLIOGRAPHY

SMITH, PAMELA ANN. "Palestine and the Palestinians." *Washington Post,* September 8, 1993, p. 21.

Steve Tamari

Abbas Hilmi I   [1812–1854]

Viceroy of Egypt, 1848–1854.

Son of Tusun and grandson of MUHAMMAD ALI, Abbas was born in Alexandria (or, some sources say, Jidda) and reared in Cairo. A cavalry officer, he accompanied his uncle, IBRAHIM Pasha, on his Syrian campaign, served as temporary governor-general of Egypt when Muhammad Ali went to the Sudan in 1839, and succeeded Ibrahim as viceroy upon his death in November 1848.

Abbas was viewed by many Europeans as a reactionary because he dismantled some of his grandfather's westernizing reforms and dismissed most of the French advisers to the Egyptian government (his policies tended to be pro-British and anti-French), but he reduced taxes on the peasants. He awarded a concession to an English company to build Egypt's first railroad, connecting Cairo and Alexandria. The land route from Cairo to Suez was also improved. He sought the support of the ULAMA (Islamic clergy) and the Sufi orders. He laid the cornerstone for the Sayyida Zaynab Mosque, a popular shrine, in Cairo. Abbas sent troops to fight on the side of the Ottoman Empire against Russia in the Crimea, where they suffered heavy casualties. His policies antagonized many members of the Muhammad Ali dynasty, and he died in Banha in 1854 under mysterious circumstances.

BIBLIOGRAPHY

Encyclopaedia of Islam, 2nd ed.
FAHMI, ZAKI. *Safwat al-asr fi tarikh wa rusum akabir rijal Misr.* Vol. 1. Cairo, 1926, pp. 40f.
TOLEDANO, EHUD R. *State and Society in Mid-Nineteenth Century Egypt.* Cambridge, Mass., 1990.

Arthur Goldschmidt, Jr.

Abbas Hilmi II   [1874–1944]

Egypt's khedive (viceroy), 1892–1914.

Born in Cairo, Abbas was the seventh member of the MUHAMMAD ALI dynasty to serve as viceroy of Egypt but the first whose whole term of office coincided with Britain's military occupation of the country. A high-spirited youth inclined to nationalism when he succeeded his father, TAWFIQ, Abbas soon clashed with the British consul-general, Lord Cromer, over the appointment of Egypt's new prime minister. The two men agreed finally on a compromise premier, Mustafa al-RIYAD, but Cromer had persuaded his government to enlarge the British occupation force.

In 1894 Abbas, while on an inspection tour of Upper Egypt, quarreled with the commander of the Egyptian army, Sir Herbert (later Lord) Kitchener, over what he viewed as the poor performance of the British-officered units. Kitchener offered to resign, but Cromer made Abbas issue a statement expressing his satisfaction with all the units of his army—a public admission of surrender. Unable to confront Britain directly, he formed a secret society that evolved into the National party, which initially placed its hopes on French support.

When France's challenge to Britain's predominance in the Nile valley waned after the 1898 Fashoda incident, Khedive Abbas moved away from the Nationalists, who were turning to pan-Islam and to appeals for constitutional government. After the Dinshaway incident, he briefly resumed his opposition to the British by helping the Nationalists to publish daily newspapers in French and English. After Cromer retired, however, he was lured away from nationalism by the friendlier policies pursued by the new British consul, JOHN ELDON GORST. In 1908, he named a new cabinet headed by Butros Ghali, a Copt (Christian) who favored the British. Abbas adopted a policy increasingly hostile to the Nationalists, reviving the 1881 Press Law, prosecuting the editor of al-Liwa, and promulgating the Exceptional Laws after the 1910 assassination of Butros Ghali by a Nationalist. When Gorst died and was succeeded by Lord Kitchener, Abbas again broke with the British. His hope of using the 1913 Organic Law to bring his supporters into the new Legislative Assembly was only partly successful, since S'ad ZAGHLUL, an old enemy, emerged as its leading spokesman.

When World War I broke out in 1914, he was in the Ottoman capital of Istanbul recovering from an assassination attempt. The British forbade him to return to Egypt, using the entry into war of the Ottoman Empire on their enemy's side as a pretext to depose him and sever Egypt's residual Ottoman ties. The former khedive spent most of the war years in Switzerland—plotting at first with the Nationalists to engineer an uprising in Egypt against the British; then with the Germans to buy shares in several Paris newspapers to influence their policies in a pacifist direction; and then with the British to secure the succession of his son to what had become the sultanate of Egypt.

After all these intrigues failed, Abbas returned to Istanbul and cooperated with the Central Powers (Germany, Austria-Hungry, and the Ottoman Empire) until their final defeat. (1918). He tried for several years to regain control of his properties in Egypt, but finally accepted a cash settlement and went into business in Europe. He attempted to mediate the Palestine question and supported a Muslim organization. He then backed the Axis powers (Germany, Japan, and Italy) early in World War II, (1939). Although energetic and patriotic, he failed to stem British moves to strengthen their military occupation of Egypt.

BIBLIOGRAPHY

BEAMAN, ARDERN HULME. *The Dethronement of the Khedive*. London, 1929.
CROMER, LORD. *Abbas II*. London, 1915.
AL-JAMI'I, ABD AL-MUN'IM. *Al-Khidiwi Abbas Hilmi wa al-Hizb al-Watani*. Cairo, 1982.
AL-ZIRIKLI, KHAYR AL-DIN. *Al-A'lam*, 4th ed. Beirut, 1980.

Arthur Goldschmidt, Jr.

Abbas Mirza, Na'eb al-Saltaneh
[1789–1833]

Crown prince and heir apparent of Persia's second monarch of the Qajar dynasty; military leader of Persia's forces against Russia; governor of Azerbaijan.

Abbas Mirza died before his father, and in 1834 succession went to his eldest son, Mohammad Mirza, who became MOHAMMAD ALI Shah. In 1799, Abbas Mirza had been made crown prince and governor of Azerbaijan, with Mirza Bozorg Qa'em Maqam as his minister and mentor. From 1804, however, Persia was involved in a long, disastrous war with Russia in the Caucasus, an area that had once been under Persia's rule. The first war lasted until 1813, ending with the Treaty of Golestan; but by 1824, war was renewed over boundaries and was concluded in 1828, with Persia losing, according to the Treaty of Turkmanchai.

Abbas Mirza led the Persian forces, and although he was personally courageous and valiant, he was defeated. His forces were no match for the Russians, and the shah had withheld funds. Under the Treaty of Golestan, the British were mediators; Persia ceded Georgia, Darband, Baku, Shirvan,

Ganjeh, Karabagh, and Moghan. Boundary limits had not been well defined, thus giving a pretext for the renewal of war by 1824. Although the Russians provoked the Persians, Abbas Mirza has been blamed for this resumption of war, allegedly to avenge his earlier defeat. Religious feelings had also been provoked, though, with claims that Muslims should not be ruled by infidels. Encouraged by Mirza Bozorg's son, Mirza Abu al-Qasem Qa'em Maqam, pamphlets calling for a holy war (jihad) were prepared and distributed to stir the public.

Persia was defeated after a short time, and Tabriz, the prince's capital in Azerbaijan, was occupied. The Treaty of Turkmanchai had dire consequences for Persia and Iran in the years to come. Not only was Persia expected to cede all the areas north of the Aras river but also to accept indemnity and capitulatory clauses; five million *tuman* had to be paid Russia before Tabriz was evacuated. As a result, not only was Persia's economy undermined, but the indemnity and capitulatory clauses served as a model for all future treaties with European nations.

In the years that followed the treaty, Abbas Mirza tried to pacify southern Persia, where rebellion was undermining governmental authority. He also set out to reestablish Persia's rule over Herat, now in northwest Afghanistan. He died during the second expedition, and his son Mohammad Mirza was declared heir apparent by the shah. This was in accord with the Treaty of Turkmanchai and approved by the British, who guaranteed the succession to the descendants of the crown prince.

Abbas Mirza came into contact with many European envoys, who sought Persia's alliance. He often carried out diplomatic negotiations for the shah and came to realize that Persia needed to modernize its army and governmental administration. Military advisers were employed toward this end, first from France, then from Britain. Persian students were also sent to Britain to study such subjects as medicine, arms manufacture, languages, and the arts, and useful books were translated. The untimely death of the crown prince ended any positive results from this pursuit.

BIBLIOGRAPHY

AVERY, P. *Modern Iran.* London, 1965.
CURZON, G. *Persia and the Persian Question.* 1892. Reprint, London, 1966.
PAKRAVAN, A. *'Abbas Mirza.* Tehran, 1958.
WATSON, R. G. *A History of Persia from the Beginning of the Nineteenth Century to the Year 1852.* London, 1866.

Mansoureh Ettehadieh

Abbud, Ibrahim [1900–?]

Ruler of the Sudan, 1958–1964.

Born in a village on the Red Sea and educated in Khartoum at Gordon Memorial College (now Khartoum University) and the military college, Abbud joined the Egyptian army in 1918 and later served with the Sudan Defense Force. During World War II he became the highest-ranking Sudanese officer. In 1956, he became commander-in-chief of the armed forces, when the Sudan became an independent republic.

After he engineered the coup d'état with the support of senior politicians in 1958, he headed the Supreme Council of the Armed Forces, which ruled the country for six years. Abbud suspended the constitution, closed parliament, and banned political parties and trade unions. He negotiated an accord with Egypt to reapportion the use of the Nile waters, but his hardline policy toward the south, which included the forced Arabization of schools and government offices and the placement of restrictions on Christian institutions, led to an escalation in fighting in that region, an overall deterioration in the economy, and protests in northern cities. He was overthrown in 1964 during mass demonstrations, led by students, professionals, and trade unions, which sought a return to democracy and the undertaking of diplomatic efforts to resolve the civil war in the south. Abbud was not forced into exile or even arrested; he was allowed to resign and to receive his pension.

BIBLIOGRAPHY

LESCH, ANN MOSELY. "Military Disengagement from Politics: The Sudan." In *Military Disengagement from Politics,* ed. by Constantine P. Danopoulos. New York, 1988.

Ann M. Lesch

Abbud, Marun [1886–?]

Lebanese journalist, author, and educator.

Abbud was born in Ayn Kfa. He attended school at Mar Yuhanna in Batrun and graduated from the al-Hikmah School. He then studied theology, planning to become a priest, like his grandfather. Having decided on a secular life instead, Abbud ran the famous high school at Alay known as the National University and taught Arabic literature. He also wrote for three newspapers: *al-Rawdah, al-Nasir,* and *al-Hikma.*

Abbud, a prolific writer, produced numerous books, especially novels and works of literary criticism. His novels usually depicted peasant life in the mountains. He also wrote historical novels. Abbud's literary style is original because, in the tradition of Ahmad Faris al-SHIDYAQ, he called for the simplification of the Arabic language and did not oppose the use of colloquialisms in classical Arabic novels.

Abbud is considered one of the voices of secular enlightenment. He abhorred sectarianism to such an extent that he named his son Muhammed in defiance of Christian practice.

As'ad AbuKhalil

Abd al-Aziz Abd al-Ghani

Yemeni economist and politician.

The U.S.-educated economist and technocrat of modest origins from the Shafii south of North Yemen served both as minister of economics and as founding head of the Central Bank of Yemen in the late 1960s through the mid-1970s. He went on to serve as prime minister of the Yemen Arab Republic under three presidents during all but three years between early 1975 and Yemeni unification in 1990. During 1980–1983 Abd al-Aziz was vice president, and during 1990–1994 he was a member of the five-man presidential council of the new Republic of Yemen. He became prime minister again in 1994.

Robert D. Burrowes

Abd al-Aziz al-Maqalih [1937–]

Yemeni nationalist and poet.

Born in the village of Maqalih in the central part of Yemen, al-Maqalih was educated at local schools and worked briefly as a teacher before going to Egypt where he received his Ph.D. in Arabic literature. His years in Egypt hastily came to an end when Anwar al-SADAT ordered his expulsion because of al-Maqalih's opposition to his policies. As a young writer and an Arab nationalist with passionately held socialist ideals, al-Maqalih played a crucial role in creating the intellectual and cultural climate that prepared the way for the Yemen Civil War of 1962, which ended the rule of the imams and inaugurated the Yemen Arab Republic.

In the early phase of the revolution in Yemen, al-Maqalih occupied important diplomatic and political positions, after which he consistently refrained from running for political office. However, his influence as a member of the Presidential Council and as president of the University of San'a has been immense. He is also the director of the Centre for Yemeni Studies and has been active in the Writers' Union.

Al-Maqalih has published eight volumes of poetry, nineteen volumes of literary, cultural, and historical research, and numerous articles. His work has received considerable critical attention. In 1990 he was awarded the prestigious Lotus Prize for poetry; he is considered one of the outstanding poets of his generation in the Arab world and is the best-known Yemeni intellectual and writer outside Yemen. His most distinctive characteristic is perhaps his totally uncompromising devotion to the cause of the revolution, social justice, the unity of Yemen, and Arab nationalism. For these reasons, al-Maqalih has been the target of vehement attacks by Islamic fundamentalists and royalist forces, not only in Yemen but also in other parts of the Arabian peninsula.

[*See also*: Literature, Arabic]

Kamal Abu-Deeb

Abd al-Aziz ibn al-Hassan

Sultan of Morocco, 1894–1908.

A young boy at the death of his father, HASSAN I, in 1894, Abd al-Aziz assumed the powers of sultan in 1900 upon the death of the regent, Ahmad ibn Musa. Under Ibn Musa, the modernizing reforms of Hassan had been undermined by social and economic changes, and Morocco became increasingly vulnerable to European imperialist ambitions. In 1900, France annexed the Saharan oasis of In Salah, previously claimed by Morocco, as well as territory along the Algeria–Morocco frontier.

This inaugurated the MOROCCAN QUESTION, a period of rising European imperialist ambitions (1900–1912). Abd al-Aziz's lack of experience and penchant for European ways permitted European speculators and business interests to take advantage of the situation. It also contributed to undermining his legitimacy. More important was the incompetent way a new universal tax on agriculture, the *tartib,* was introduced, which provoked revolts in several districts. The most important of these was the 1902 rebellion led by ABU HIMARA, whose victories enabled him to pose a long-term challenge to the regime. Following Moroccan attacks on Europeans, there were several important diplomatic crises.

The Moroccan crisis deepened in 1904 when, after complex French diplomatic maneuvers, Spain, Italy, and Britain renounced their claims to Morocco (although Spain's renunciation did not last). France sought rapidly to capitalize on the situation. It negotiated a major loan agreement with the bankrupt Moroccan government, thus gaining a dominant position in Moroccan finances. It also issued an ultimatum that Morocco adopt a French reform proposal, which would have amounted to a virtual protectorate. Seeking to stave off the French proposals, Abd al-Aziz referred them to an assembly of notables, or MAJLES, in 1905, while seeking diplomatic support from Germany.

Despite German intervention and the convening of the international ALGECIRAS CONFERENCE (1905–1906), however, Morocco was forced to accept the substance of France's proposals. Eventually Abd al-Aziz was compelled to sign the Act of Algeciras (1906) over the vociferous objections of the Moroccan elite. By doing this, he fatally undermined his regime.

In the post-Algeciras period, a new French aggressiveness, and the breakdown of rural security gave rise to attacks on French citizens. The landing of French troops at Oujda and Casablanca (1907) led to uprisings in both districts. More importantly, in August 1907, it provoked the rebellion of his brother, ABD AL-HAFID, the governor of Marrakech, in alliance with Madani and Tahami Glawi and other rural magnates of southern Morocco. Despite French support, Abd al-Aziz was eventually defeated after a year-long civil war and compelled to abdicate his throne. Thereafter, he lived in retirement in Tangier.

BIBLIOGRAPHY

BURKE, EDMUND, III. *Prelude to Protectorate in Morocco: Precolonial Protest and Resistance, 1860–1912.* Chicago, 1976.

HARRIS, WALTER BURTON. *The Morocco That Was.* Edinburgh and London, 1921.

LAROUI, ABDULLAH. *Les origines sociales et culturelles du nationalisme marocain (1830–1912).* Paris, 1977.

Edmund Burke III

Abd al-Aziz ibn Sa'ud Al Sa'ud
[1880–1953]

Muslim leader and founder of Saudi Arabia.

Abd al-Aziz ibn Sa'ud Al Sa'ud (known as Ibn Sa'ud) became the greatest of all Saudi rulers, restoring the Arabian empire of his ancestors in the early years of the twentieth century. In his reign of more than a half century he not only recovered the lost patrimony of the House of Sa'ud but laid the foundations for the economically powerful Saudi Arabia, over

The library in the King Abd al-Aziz Museum in Riyadh, Saudi Arabia. (Richard Bulliet)

which his sons continue to rule. Along with his ancestors Sa'ud ibn Abd al-Aziz and Abd al-Aziz ibn Muhammad (rulers of the Saudi state at the turn of the nineteenth century), he was the only Arabian ruler since the early Islamic era to unify most of the Arabian peninsula under a single political authority.

As he was growing up in Riyadh, the Saudi capital, where he received a traditional education centered on the memorization of the QUR'AN, he witnessed the last act in the decline of the second Saudi state and its submission to the AL SA'UD family's central Arabian rivals and former vassals, the AL RASHID of Hail, a town to the north of Riyadh. His father, Abd al-Rahman, failed in the attempt to reassert Saudi independence and the ten year old Abd al-Aziz fled into exile in Kuwait with the rest of the family. In 1902, he led a band of forty companions on a dramatic raid that seized Riyadh from its Rashidi overlords. Over the next quarter century bold military, political, and diplomatic initiatives brought all of Arabia except for Yemen, Oman, and the Gulf shaykhdoms under his rule.

In reestablishing Saudi authority, Abd al-Aziz self-consciously re-created the religio-political state of his Wahhabi ancestors. It was based on adherence to the strict beliefs and practices of Muhammad ibn Abd al-Wahhab, the eighteenth-century Islamic reformer whose 1744 alliance with Muhammad ibn Sa'ud had created the Saudi state of 1745. Indeed, he looked back to the first Islamic community under the Prophet Muhammad in creating, from 1912 on, a series of communities called *hujar* (pl.) (echoing the *hijra*—the migration of the Prophet and his early followers to Medina). Here unruly Bedouin tribesmen were settled as IKHWAN, brethren under the command of preacher/warriors who formed the core of Abd al-Aziz's military force. In addition to the crucial legitimacy provided by identification with Wahhabi Islam, he was able to draw on the established loyalty of many central Arabians, which derived from the significant history of rule by the House of Sa'ud. Moreover, Abd al-Aziz and the Saudi clan enjoyed the advantage of membership in the great Anaza tribal federation, conferring noble (sharifian) lineage, thus joining a critical aristocracy of blood to their religious credentials. Abd al-Aziz was brilliantly adept in his management of tribal relations, utilizing disbursement of material benefits, application of military force, and the establishment of marital ties to build the alliances necessary to secure his power. He made astute use of the bedouin magnanimity, for which he was famous, as when he carefully contrived to avoid casualties in his capture of Hail, last stronghold of the Al Rashid, then arranged for the comfortable confinement of his defeated rivals in Riyadh. Patient and generous treatment of his rebellious cousin Sa'ud al-Kabir served to deflect a challenge from within the Al Sa'ud and secured the line of succession for the direct descendants of Abd al-Rahman.

If mastery of traditional sources of power in Arabian statecraft carried Abd al-Aziz through the initial phases of reconquest, it was his capacity to utilize Western inventions and techniques as well as to adjust to new international realities that enabled him to establish a state that could endure. The source of this aptitude is not obvious and may be largely traceable simply to his superior intuitive abilities. It is likely, however, that it had something to do with his youthful exile in Kuwait, where the (by Arabian standards) cosmopolitan atmosphere meant exposure to information, ideas, and people not usually encountered in the xenophobic isolation of his native Najd. Early in his career of reconquest he met the British political resident in Kuwait, Captain William Shakespear, and developed an admiring friendship for him. Sir Percy Cox, senior British representative in the Gulf just before World War I, had a very strong influence on Abd al-Aziz, and Harry St. J. PHILBY, a British civil servant who left his government's service to live in Saudi Arabia, provided Abd al-Aziz with advice (not always taken) and a window on the outside world. Abd al-Aziz also relied heavily on a coterie of advisers from Syria, Egypt, and other Arab countries. This awareness of the outside world helped to induce a certain pragmatism, evident early on in his search for British protection and in his 1915 treaty with Great Britain that recognized his independence and guaranteed him against aggression. Similarly, after the 1924/25 conquest of the Hejaz (western Arabia, with

the holy cities of Mecca and Medina), he restrained his zealous warriors and assured his retention of that key province by demonstrating to the world Muslim community that he could provide a more efficient and secure administration of the territory than the Hashimite regime that he had defeated. In 1935, he granted generous terms to the imam of Yemen, whom he had defeated in a border war, doing so both to avert possible European intervention and to avoid inclusion in his kingdom of a population whose cultural distinctiveness would have made its assimilation very difficult.

In 1928, the pragmatic realism of Abd al-Aziz came into conflict with the tribal aggression and religious militancy of the ikhwan forces he had unleashed. The ikhwan's revolt followed his acceptance of the British-drawn borders of Trans-Jordan and Iraq to the north—for the first time imposing the constraints of explicit state frontiers on a society to which such notions were alien. By 1930, Abd al-Aziz had surmounted this threat, the gravest to his rule, making effective use of automobiles, machine guns, and radio communications to crush the revolt. The passions that drove it, however, remained alive and shook the Saudi kingdom a half century later, in November 1979, when Islamic extremists and disaffected members of the Utaiba tribe, from which many ikhwan rebels had come, seized the Great Mosque at Mecca in an effort to overthrow the rule of the Al Sa'ud.

With the ikhwan revolt behind him, Abd al-Aziz moved to draw together the disparate parts of his extensive realm. Since Sharif HUSAYN IBN ALI had assumed the title King of the Hejaz, Abd al-Aziz adopted the same title after conquering that province; he coupled it somewhat incongruously with the title Sultan of Najd and Its Dependencies in 1926. In the following year, he elevated the second title as well to monarchical status, in effect creating a dual monarchy. In 1932, Abd al-Aziz abandoned this arrangement and explicitly identified the country with the Al Sa'ud family by naming it the Kingdom of Saudi Arabia. The two earlier Saudi states had been Wahhabi commonwealths, largely isolated from the outside world and ruled by a Saudi imam, the title emphasizing religious authority and obligations. The new kingdom, while remaining committed to its original religious purpose, was a nation-state that developed an expanding network of relations with other nations, including the establishment of close ties with secular states beyond the Arab-Islamic world.

To secure the future stability of the state he had created and to preserve the continued rule of his line, in 1933, Abd al-Aziz formally designated his eldest surviving son, Sa'ud, to succeed him. This action, which senior princes, religious leaders, and tribal chiefs publicly endorsed, departed from the usual practice of Arabian tribal society. In addition to guaranteeing that future kings would come from Abd al-Aziz's branch of the Al Saud, it was doubtless also intended to avert the fratricidal conflict that had destroyed the second Saudi state at the end of the nineteenth century. It was understood that FAISAL (IBN ABD AL-AZIZ AL SA'UD), the next eldest brother, who possessed a much more impressive intellect and had, as foreign minister and viceroy for the Hejaz, exhibited a much greater capacity for public affairs, would succeed Sa'ud. Abd al-Aziz may have had several reasons for favoring Sa'ud as his immediate successor, but the establishment of seniority as the determining factor in succession was clearly preeminent. Sa'ud and Faisal became rivals, but Sa'ud's incompetence eventually drove the senior princes and religious leaders to depose him in favor of Faisal. Nevertheless, the principle that Abd al-Aziz established has, with certain qualifications, been preserved and served to maintain the stability of the kingdom.

The crucial economic and security relationships with the United States, a central pillar of the kingdom's foreign policy, grew from decisions that Abd al-Aziz took in the latter phase of his rule. In 1933, he granted the first oil concession to a U.S. company; he signed a petroleum exploration agreement with Standard Oil of California (Socal), choosing it over its British rival, the Iraq Petroleum Company. He did so largely because Socal could offer more money for his impoverished treasury but also because he saw an advantage in counterbalancing his close relationship with Great Britain with ties to a faraway country having no political involvement (as yet) in the Middle East. There followed the creation of the Arabian American Oil Company (Aramco) consortium and the exploitation of the world's largest oil reserves, bringing staggering wealth to the companies and the kingdom, and the creation of an intimate alignment with U.S. industry that largely determined the course of Saudi Arabia's economic modernization and development. From this time on—especially on radio, in newsreels, and in newspapers—he became known as King Ibn Sa'ud.

Equally significant for Saudi Arabia's future were the agreements that Ibn Sa'ud made with the United States to assure his country's external security. The king's meeting with President Franklin D. Roosevelt on a U.S. Navy cruiser in Egypt's Great Bitter Lake, in February 1945, prefigured the close, if informal, U.S.–Saudi security alliance that developed after World War II, as British power declined. In 1947, the king waved aside the suggestion of his son Prince Faisal, the foreign minister, that Saudi Arabia break diplomatic relations with the United States over the Truman Administration's support for the UN partition plan for Palestine—which paved the way for the creation of an independent Israel and contravened a pledge that Roosevelt had made to Ibn Sa'ud. The king, however, expected the United States to offer him something in exchange and, between 1947 and 1950, secret U.S. undertakings gave the king the assurances he sought without a formal treaty. Thus the foundations were laid for the far-reaching security relationship—embracing arms sales, military training, and the massive defense infrastructure whose scope was revealed only forty years later, in the course of the Desert Shield/Desert Storm operation of the Gulf Crisis of 1990/91.

The last years of the long rule of Ibn Sa'ud, when his physical health was in decline, were an unhappy coda to an extraordinary career. As massive oil income began to flow in the early 1950s, the king displayed little understanding of the economic or social implications of vast wealth—and some of the ostentation that became the hallmark of his reign was apparent before his death. Politically, he was no longer able to master the novel and complex challenges of a very different world than the one he had earlier dominated. The government of Saudi Arabia remained the simple affair that suited a largely traditional desert monarchy, with a small retinue of advisers and a handful of rudimentary ministries that had been established in an ad hoc manner. Somewhat ironically, the last significant governmental act of the old king was to create the Council of Ministers, until today the source of executive and legislative authority in the kingdom.

In November 1953, King Ibn Sa'ud died at Taif in the Hejaz. He was buried with his ancestors in Riyadh.

BIBLIOGRAPHY

ALMANA, MOHAMMED. *Arabia Unified: A Portrait of Ibn Saud.* London, 1980.
BESSON, YVES. *Ibn Saud, roi bedouin: La naissance du royaume d'arabie saoudite.* Lausanne, 1980.
BLIGH, ALEXANDER. *From Prince to King: Royal Succession in the House of Saud in the Twentieth Century.* New York, 1984.
HOLDEN, DAVID, and RICHARD JOHNS. *The House of Saud: The Rise and Rule of the Most Powerful Dynasty in the Arab World.* New York, 1981.
LACEY, ROBERT. *The Kingdom: Arabia & and the House of Sa'ud.* New York, 1981.
PHILBY, H. ST. J. B. *Arabian Jubilee.* London, 1952.
———. *Saudi Arabia.* London, 1955.
TROELLER, GARY. *The Birth of Saudi Arabia: The Rise of the House of Saud.* London, 1976.

Malcolm C. Peck

Abd al-Hadi, Awni   [1889–1970]

Liberal Palestinian and Arab nationalist active in politics and diplomacy.

Born in Nablus to a prominent landowning family, Awni Abd al-Hadi was educated in Istanbul, where he was influenced by the Arab revivalist Literary Club, and in Paris, where he received his law degree. Awni helped found the al-Fatat (Young Arab Society) secret society in 1911 in Paris, which agitated for the administrative independence of the Arab provinces from Ottoman rule and denounced Istanbul's Turkification policies. He participated in the Arab Congress in Paris in 1913, which called for Arab independence. Toward the end of World War I, Awni became personal secretary to Emir FAISAL, son of the Sharif Husayn of Mecca, who ruled Syria from 1918 to July 1920. Awni served as legal adviser to Husayn's delegation to the Versailles peace conference in 1919.

When Faisal's kingdom was destroyed by French forces in July 1920, Awni returned to Palestine and opened a law office in Jerusalem. He soon became a leading Palestinian political figure, who supported the basic national demands for abrogation of the Balfour Declaration and establishment of an independent state. However, he also sought dialogue with British officials and Jewish spokesmen—he urged the British to form an elected body to control education in 1923; urged the establishment of an elected legislative council in 1927; and participated in discussions with British officials and Jewish leaders just prior to the riots in Jerusalem at the Western (Wailing) Wall in August 1929, in an effort to negotiate an accord on Jewish and Muslim rights at holy places. Awni had already become a secretary of the Arab Executive that was reconstituted after the Arab congress in June 1928, and then participated in the fourth Arab delegation to London in spring 1930, which requested the stoppage of Jewish immigration and land purchases until a national government could be formed.

Known as a leading liberal pan-Arab, Awni established the Hizb al-Istiqlal (Independence party) in 1932 as a branch of the pan-Arab party. That party called for complete independence and the strengthening of ties with Arab states. Awni became more militant in the early 1930s, arguing that the Palestinians should focus on opposing the British, since the Zionist movement was merely its tool; he urged the Arab Executive to boycott the government, helped sponsor demonstrations in the main cities in 1933, and encouraged political debate in newspapers and clubs that stressed the links between Palestinian independence and pan-Arabism. The activities of the party were disrupted by the death of Faisal (who was

then king of Iraq) in 1933, but its ideological influence was pervasive among the young intelligentsia and youth movements.

Awni became the secretary of the Arab Higher Committee, formed on April 25, 1936, and was arrested by the British on June 7. He was released after the general strike ended in October 1936. He then presented evidence to the Peel Commission in January 1937. When the British cracked down again in October 1937, Awni was abroad on a diplomatic mission and thus avoided arrest. He was instrumental in convening the World Inter-Parliamentary Congress of the Arab and Muslim Countries for the Defense of Palestine, in Cairo, October 1938; he then participated in the Palestinian delegation to the London conference in the spring of 1939. The British allowed Awni to return to Palestine in July 1941. Starting in 1943, he and other members of the Independence party encouraged renewed nationalist activities, such as the national conference of Arab chambers of commerce in November 1943, the revival of the Arab Higher Committee, and the Arab National Bank. The latter promoted the Arab National Fund which sought to help villages stem the sale of land to Jewish land-purchasing companies. Awni criticized the dominance of the Husayni family over the national movement, but shared the basic demand for Palestinian independence.

In the 1948-Palestine War, Awni lost his home in west Jerusalem. Although he was allotted a ministerial post in the short-lived All-Palestine Government, formed in Gaza, he chose to stay in exile in Damascus, Syria, until 1951. He then accepted the post of ambassador to Cairo for the Hashimite Kingdom of Jordan, ruled by King ABDULLAH, the brother of his patron, Faisal. He served as ambassador until 1955, when he returned to Amman and served briefly as foreign minister in 1956. Ill health precluded his holding other ministerial appointments, although they were offered to him. He retired to Egypt in 1964, where he remained until his death in 1970.

BIBLIOGRAPHY

HUREWITZ, J. C. *The Struggle for Palestine.* New York, 1950. Reprint, 1976.
MUSLIH, MUHAMMAD Y. *The Origins of Palestinian Nationalism.* New York, 1988.

Ann M. Lesch

Abd al-Hadi Family

Prominent Palestinian Arab family.

The Abd al-Hadis were a leading landowning family in the Palestinian districts of Afula, Baysan, Jenin, and Nablus. Already well established in the seventeenth century, by the nineteenth century the family supported the 1830s rule of Ibrahim Pasha, which reduced the power of the Ottoman Empire. Later members of the family were prominent in Ottoman political, diplomatic, and military circles; some participated in the Ottoman parliament in 1908 and 1914. Ruhi Abd al-Hadi (born 1885) served for fifteen years in the Ottoman foreign office, including consular and diplomatic posts in the Balkans, Greece, and Switzerland. Rushdi Abd al-Hadi fought for the Ottman army in World War I and remained in Turkey to serve the new republic, whereas Ra'uf Abd al-Hadi was taken prisoner by the British forces and then joined Faisal's Arab army to fight the Ottoman army. Awni Abd al-Hadi supported the Arab national movement from 1910 and worked closely with FAISAL in Damascus until the Arab regime fell to the French in July 1920.

After World War I, when the British mandate was imposed on Palestine, members of the Abd al-Hadi family had divergent responses. Ruhi Abd al-Hadi joined the British administrative service in 1921, serving initially as a district officer and rising to the post of assistant senior secretary in 1944. Majid Abd al-Hadi served as a judge on the supreme court, Amin Abd al-Hadi was appointed to the Supreme Muslim Council in 1929, and Tahsin Abd al-Hadi was mayor of Jenin. Some members of the family secretly sold their shares of Zirin village to the Jewish National Fund in July 1930, despite nationalist opposition to such land sales; but others sold land to the Development Department to resettle landless Arab peasants.

Several Abd al-Hadis were active in the pan-Arab movement of 1918 to 1920, which sought to link Palestine to an independent Syria. They participated in the Palestinian Arab congresses in those years, criticized the fall of Faisal's Syrian kingdom to the French, and the imposition of separate mandates on Syria (France) and Palestine (Britain). Even at the Arab congress in Nablus in August 1922, Ibrahim Abd al-Hadi called for Palestine to be linked to Syria. With the establishment of the State of Israel in 1948, the Abd al-Hadis lost substantial agricultural lands, while retaining important—although gradually diminishing—influence in Jenin and Nablus during Jordanian rule.

BIBLIOGRAPHY

MA'OZ, MOSHE. *Ottoman Reform in Syria and Palestine, 1840–1861.* Oxford, 1968.

MUSLIH, MUHAMMAD Y. *The Origins of Palestinian Nationalism.* New York, 1988.

STEIN, KENNETH W. *The Land Question in Palestine, 1917–1939.* Chapel Hill, N.C., 1984.

Ann M. Lesch

Abd al-Hafid ibn al-Hassan   [1876–1937]

Sultan of Morocco, 1908–1912.

The fourth son of Sultan HASSAN I, he served as *khalifa* (royal governor) of Tiznit (1897–1901) and Marrakech (1901–1907) under his younger brother, ABD AL-AZIZ IBN AL-HASSAN, who was the sultan of Morocco from 1894 to 1908. In the politically tense period of the Moroccan Question (1901–1912), Abd al-Hafid (also Abd al-Hafiz) found himself increasingly opposed to the policies of his brother. Following the latter's acceptance of the Act of Algeciras in 1906 and acquiescence in France's military landings at Oujda and Casablanca in 1907, Abd al-Hafid joined with Madani and Tuhami Glawi in a rebellion aimed at deposing Abd al-Aziz. A civil war between the two brothers lasted from August 1907 to August 1908. Despite French support for Abd al-Aziz, in 1908 Abd al-Hafid was able to defeat him and take the throne.

Abd al-Hafid was an intellectual, poet, and author of numerous books. He favored the introduction of the ideas of the Salafiyya Movement to the Qarawiyyin mosque university in Fez. After becoming sultan in 1908, he appointed Abu Shu'ayb al-Dukkali (later known as "the Moroccan Abduh") to his Royal Learned Council. He sought to suppress heterodox Moroccan brotherhoods of Sufism, notably the Tijaniyya and the Kattaniya.

As sultan, Abd al-Hafid sought to recover Moroccan political and financial independence from France through a policy of alliances with the Ottoman Empire and Germany, and a program of governmental reforms. He cracked down on political dissidents, like Muhammad ibn Abd al-Kabir al-KATTANI and ABU HIMARA. In 1910, however, he was compelled to enter into a major loan agreement with France, the terms of which ended Moroccan financial independence. The loss of political independence came soon thereafter.

A rebellion of the tribes around Fez and Meknes in 1911 led to the occupation of the Moroccan interior by a French expeditionary force. On March 28, 1912, his authority weakened irreparably, Abd al-Hafid signed the Treaty of FES, thereby establishing the French protectorate. On August 12, 1912, Abd al-Hafid abdicated as sultan and was succeeded by a French-imposed successor, his brother Yusuf (1912–1927). The protectorates of France and Spain were to last until 1956.

The last sultan of independent Morocco, Abd al-Hafid died in 1937 at Tangier. His legacy is a mixed one—he came to the throne on a program of opposition to the Act of Algeciras and a French protectorate; however, he faced an impossible task, and his defeat was most probable. His support of pan-Islam and of Salafiyya ideas for regenerating Morocco were undermined by the corruption and brutality of his rule, notably the actions of his close collaborators, the Glawi brothers. His shameless bargaining with the French over the terms of his abdication and his willingness to sign the Treaty of Fes earned him the enmity of a later generation of Moroccan nationalists.

BIBLIOGRAPHY

BURKE, EDMUND, III. *Prelude to Protectorate in Morocco.* Chicago, 1976.
CAGNE, JACQUES. *Nation et nationalisme au Maroc: Aux racines de la nation marocaine.* Rabat, 1988.
LAROUI, ABDULLAH. *Les origines sociales et culturelles du nationalisme marocain (1830–1912).* Paris, 1977.

Edmund Burke III

Abd al-Huda   [1894–1956]

Prime minister of Jordan between 1938 and 1954.

Abd al-Huda (also, Tawfiq Abul-Huda) formed Jordan's first cabinet of ministers in August 1949; until then, the government was an executive council under the terms of the British mandate and the Anglo–Jordanian Treaty. He was part of the delegation that negotiated with Britain on amendments that led to new government structures, including a cabinet responsible to the head of state and a legislative council. He was leader of the Executive Council or prime minister twelve times between 1938 and 1954.

Abd al-Huda helped King ABDULLAH IBN HUSAYN steer through the political maze during the Arab-Israel War of 1948 and the union between central Palestine and Transjordan. When King Abdullah was assassinated, al-Huda was chosen by his peers, on 25 July 1951, to form the cabinet that saw Jordan through those troubled times. Paradoxically, he presided over the enactment of the very liberal constitution of 1952 under an impetus from King TALAL. Yet, during this two-year period, which ended with King HUSSEIN IBN TALAL ascending the throne, there was a shift of power from the king to the prime minister. As a consequence, Abd al-Huda exercised more power than any other prime minister in the history of Jordan.

When Fawzi al-MULKI's cabinet, the first under King Hussein, was shaken by disturbances following border clashes with Israel, the king turned to the veteran al-Huda to form the new cabinet. He convinced the king to dissolve parliament on 22 June 1954 as an assertion of executive dominance over the legislature. He issued the Defense Regulations of 1954, empowering the cabinet to deny licenses to political parties, dissolve existing parties, prohibit public meetings, and censor the press. The opposition charged that the new elections were fixed, and al-Huda's measures encouraged the opposition to seek extraparliamentary forms of dissent. Popular opposition forced his last cabinet to resign.

BIBLIOGRAPHY

ABIDI, AQIL HYDER HASAN. *Jordan: A Political Study, 1948–1957.* New Delhi, 1965.
MADI, MUNIB, and SULAYMAN MUSA. *Tarikh al-Urdun fi al-qarn al-ʿishrin, 1900–1959.* Amman, 1988.

Jenab Tutunji

Abd al-Ilah ibn Ali   [1913–1958]

Regent of Iraq for the child king Faisal II.

The son of Ali, king of the Hijaz, and grandson of the sharif of Mecca, Abd al-Ilah was brought up in Mecca. He came to Iraq at the age of thirteen, after his father lost the Hijazi throne in 1926. He had no strong roots in Iraq and was, or at least became, heavily dependent on British support. Abd al-Ilah came to prominence somewhat unexpectedly in 1939 following the accidental death of his cousin, King GHAZI (ibn Faisal) I. Ghazi's son, FAISAL II, was only three years old, and Abd al-Ilah, who was also the child's maternal uncle, was made regent. He became crown prince in 1943, and although formally relinquishing the regency after Faisal reached his majority in 1953, he was always known in Iraq as "the regent" (al-Wasi).

His friend and mentor at the time of his rise to power was Nuri al-SAʿID, another faithful servant of Britain, who would eventually serve as prime minister fourteen times under the mandate and monarchy. It was Abd al-Ilah's misfortune to come to prominence at a time when the central institutions of the new Iraqi state were extremely weak, the result of a combination of several factors, including the premature death of his uncle FAISAL I in 1933, the dominant role in politics being played by the officer corps, and the tide of anti-British sentiment flooding over Iraq and the rest of the Middle East at the end of the 1930s.

Although Iraq followed Britain's lead and declared war on Germany in September 1939, the Arab nationalist army officers, led by a group of four colonels known as the Golden Square, were soon able to make their influence felt, and an anti-British and more or less pro-Axis cabinet was formed under Rashid Ali al-KAYLANI in March 1940. After a brief reversal of fortune in the early months of 1941, Rashid Ali returned to power on April 12, and he and the Golden Square set in motion a somewhat quixotic but immensely popular revolt against Britain. Although the outcome was a foregone conclusion, the episode showed how little support there was in Iraq for Britain or for Britain's Iraqi partners; Nuri and Abd al-Ilah fled to Jordan in April with British assistance and did not return until after the Iraqi army had been crushed in June. All four of the colonels were eventually tried by Iraqi authorities and hanged in public in Baghdad, apparently on the express instructions of the regent and Nuri.

In 1947/48, the regent managed to alienate himself further from mainstream political sentiment by his support for the renegotiation of the terms of the Anglo–Iraqi Treaty. This time the opposition was more organized, and the demonstrations against the new treaty (signed in Portsmouth in January 1948) were so massive and so vehement that it had to be dropped. Over the next ten years there were frequent displays of mass discontent, which were usually countered by fierce repression and the imposition of martial law.

By the mid-1950s, the political situation in Iraq had deteriorated to the point that it was widely understood that it was a question of when, rather than if, the regime would fall. Although not always on the best of terms during this time, Nuri and Abd al-Ilah were widely regarded as embodying many of the evils and shortcomings of the regime, especially its almost slavish dependence on the West. But if the end was long expected, the actual occasion was sudden; a group of Free Officers led by Abd al-Karim KASSEM and Abd al-Salam ARIF managed to take control of a number of key military units and staged a coup on July 14, 1958. The royal palace and Nuri's house were surrounded; Nuri evaded capture until the following day, but the king, the regent, and other members of the royal family were shot in the courtyard of the palace on the morning of the revolution, thus bringing the Iraqi monarchy to an abrupt, violent, and largely unlamented end.

Peter Sluglett

Abd al-Karim

See Khattabi, Muhammad ibn Abd al-Karim al-

Abd al-Karim, Ahmad

Syrian politician.

An Alawi army officer who was loyal to the powerful military leader Adib Shishakli, Abd al-Karim was an anti-Ba'thist and was considered part of the so-called independent group, a loose coalition of politicians. He was head of the army investigations department in 1962 and minister of municipal and rural affairs in 1964.

BIBLIOGRAPHY

Who's Who in the Middle East, 1967–1968.

Charles U. Zenzie

Abd-Allah ibn Yahya Hamid al-Din

Political figure of North Yemen.

During a coup in 1955, Abd-Allah proclaimed himself imam after an attempt to oust his brother, Imam AHMAD IBN YAHYA HAMID AL-DIN, as Muslim spiritual leader. But Ahmad forcefully thwarted the attempt and had Abd-Allah put to death. Whether Abd-Allah participated in the conspiracy, he appeared to act hastily in taking his brother's title. Abd-Allah served as North Yemen's foreign minister, having previously served his father, Imam Yahya Hamid al-Din, as governor of Hodeida.

Robert D. Burrowes

Abd al-Masih, Georges

Syrian politician.

Georges Abd al-Masih assumed effective leadership of the Syrian National Social party (PPS), after the execution of party founder Antun SA'ADA in July 1949. He was most likely the head conspirator in the assassination of Lieutenant Colonel Adnan al-Malki on April 22, 1955, then the army deputy chief of staff with whom Abd al-Masih had had a personal feud. Secretly meeting in Beirut, under sentence of death for their involvement in this incident, the PPS leaders orchestrated an ill-fated plan to restore Adib SHISHAKLI to power in Syria.

BIBLIOGRAPHY

SEALE, PATRICK. *The Struggle for Syria: A Study of Post-War Arab Politics, 1945–1958.* London, 1958.

Charles U. Zenzie

Abd al-Nasir, Jamal

See Nasser, Gamal Abdel

Abd al-Qadir   [1807–1883]

Algerian leader who resisted initial French colonialism.

Abd al-Qadir (also spelled Abd el-Kader, Abdul Qader) was born in Guetna Oued al-Hammam, near Mascara, Western Algeria. His father, Muhyi al-Din, was spiritual head of the Qadiriyya order of Islam; his education was guided by Qadi Ahmad ibn Tahir of Azrou and Sidi Ahmad ibn Khoja of Oran. He pursued religious studies while traveling with his father within the Ottoman Empire, in Syria and Iraq and at al-Azhar in Egypt.

As the leader of Algerian tribal resistance to French colonialism between 1833 and 1847, Abd al-Qadir earned a reputation far beyond Algeria. It was only partly for military leadership, since his skill in founding alliances between hinterland tribes, especially in the western province of Oran and, for a time, as far east as Constantine, presented a political feat of no small consequence.

Abd al-Qadir's father had carried out several raids against the French in the Oran region in spring of 1832. The French had become enraged by the CORSAIRS, pirates, and slave trade of the Barbary coast and wanted to end the taking and selling of Christian sailors from Mediterranean shipping. By this date two figures, neither Algerian, had played roles in reacting to the French presence in the former beylicate of Oran. The only serious previous attempt to defend Oran came between November 1830 and April 1832, when Ali ibn Sulayman of Morocco intervened unsuccessfully in Algeria. Meanwhile, between February and August 1831, a token Tunisian force had come and gone from Oran following an agreement between the bey of Tunis and the French government. According to its terms, the French promised to recognize ill-defined Tunisian responsibility to govern the Algerian west in their name.

By 1833, it was clear that the unorganized Algerian forces under Abd al-Qadir's father could do little more than harass the French in Oran. The decision was made to recognize Abd al-Qadir's leadership, both of the Qadiriyya order and of provincial tribal resistance. This decision proved fateful, since Abd al-Qadir clearly viewed his mission in terms that went beyond mere military leadership. An early sign of this was his insistence that his followers swear allegiance according to the *bay'a* (the pledge) to the caliphs who succeeded the Prophet Muhammad. A good portion of Abd al-Qadir's military and political career—beyond his relations with the French—involved attempts to impose legitimizing symbols of rule on neighboring tribes. Such struggles to command allegiance in Islamic as well as tribal terms were complicated by the fact that some key local tribes were traditionally *makhzanis* (mercenaries), which meant they were willing to receive pay from secular executive authorities. Before 1830, such tribes would have been in the service of the Algerian beys; after 1830, the French tried to recruit makhzanis to their service, thus creating a dilemma in them between Islamic and opportunistic loyalties.

In February 1834, soon after the French opened formal diplomatic contact with the Algerian resistance forces, two treaties, one containing essential French conditions, the second with additional Algerian conditions, were signed between France and Abd al-Qadir. These provided for mutual recognition of two different types of polities in the west: three French enclaves on the coast and Abd al-Qadir's emirate with its capital at Mascara. Thus he was recognized as dey of Mascara.

During this brief truce, Abd al-Qadir may have benefited from French help to defeat Mustafa ibn Isma'il, his primary rival for political and religious ascendancy over the western tribes. Another rival, Shaykh al-Ghumari, was also captured and hanged. Had Franco-Algerian peace continued, Abd al-Qadir might have succeeded in extending his unprecedented tax levy (the *mu'uwna*) to more and more subordinates of his emirate. As it was, hostilities resumed in 1835 (after the Ottomans had sent a new governor to Tripoli), and the French were repeatedly defeated by Abd al-Qadir. In 1837, the French signed the Treaty of Tafna, with Marshal Thomas-Robert BUGEAUD granting most of the Algerian hinterland to Abd al-Qadir.

Perhaps the Tafna treaty was meant to keep Abd al-Qadir from objecting to French advances against the eastern beylicate of Constantine—which fell only four months after the Tafna accords. Once it fell, however, the French were never able to make deals with Abd al-Qadir again.

From late 1837 to 1847, intermittent hostilities with forces under Abd al-Qadir brought clashes as far east as Constantine and as far west as Morocco. It was only after Marshal Bugeaud led a large French expeditionary force into Algeria that systematic subjugation of the interior began. At this point Abd al-Qadir's crossings into Morocco involved refuge rather than tactics; and the major battle of Isly in 1844 dissuaded the Moroccans from offering him refuge again. Although the Algerians tried to reverse the inevitable tide, his fate became as insecure in Morocco as it was in Algeria. After his decision to surrender in December of 1847, Abd al-Qadir was promised exile but was sent a prisoner to France. He was released in 1852 by Napoleon III and finally granted his requested exile in Syria. He died in Damascus in 1883. Some eighty-five years later and six years after Algeria's independence, Abd al-Qadir's remains were reinterred in his native land in 1968.

His contribution to the history of North Africa may be viewed from several perspectives. Within the closest political and cultural context, his leadership reflected intertribal dynamics in what was eventually to become the entity of Algeria. His efforts to unify disparate tribes included a certain number of institutional innovations, suggesting rudiments of governmental responsibility that surpassed anything that had preceded this key period. Among these, formal executive appointments, regular decision-making councils, and taxation figured most prominently. One cannot escape the fact, however, that hinterland submission to Abd al-Qadir's ascendancy, both military and political, often came only after successful imposition of his will by force.

By contrast, those who emphasize the nationalist implications of Algerian resistance to French Colonialism would interpret Abd al-Qadir in ways that reflect more on the twentieth-century context of mass political movements than the highly fragmented setting of nineteenth-century Algeria. For the nationalist school, he represents a first stage in a process that became a model for the Algerian National Liberation Front at the end of the colonial era.

The third point of view combines speculation on what actual mid-nineteenth-century appraisals of Abd al-Qadir's leadership were with twentieth-century reflections on the living heritage of the past. This view would emphasize Islamic religious and cultural values embodied—then and thereafter—in resistance to foreign domination in any form. Seen from this perspective, a culturewide hero model like Abd al-Qadir represents a heritage that can be chronologically continuous and spatially all-encompassing. His actions not only had the effect of legitimizing his call to carry out a general *jihad* (holy war) against the French in the name of Islam but also gave him the assumed responsibility of overseeing the welfare of the entire *umma* (community of believers) in a responsible way that had not been effectively present in Algeria for centuries.

BIBLIOGRAPHY

ABUN-NASR, JAMIL M. *A History of the Maghrib in the Islamic Period.* Cambridge and New York, 1987.

LANGER, WILLIAM L. *An Encyclopedia of World History.* Boston, 1948.

Byron Cannon

Abd al-Quddus, Ihsan   [1918–1990]

Egyptian journalist, novelist, and short-story writer.

Abd al-Quddus began his literary career as an editor and writer for the leading Egyptian weekly *Ruz al-Yusuf*, which was founded in 1925 by his mother, Fatma al-Yusuf, a former actress. These writings made him well known throughout the Arab world. In the 1960s and 1970s, he was the editor of the newspapers AKHBAR AL-YAWM and the influential *al-Ahram*. In his column, "At a Cafe on Politics Street," he created fictional dialogues between customers at a cafe to discuss contemporary issues.

Abd al-Quddus authored more than sixty novels and collections of short stories, many of which were made into films. His works of Arabic literature were characterized by psychological studies of political and social behavior. Among his works translated into English are *I Am Free, The Bus Thief,* and *A Boy's Best Friend.*

BIBLIOGRAPHY

New York Times. January 1, 1990.

David Waldner

Abd al-Rahman, Aisha

See Bint al-Shati

Abd al-Rahman al-Mahdi   [1885–1959]

Leader in the Sudan after World War I.

Born after the death of his father, Muhammad AHMAD, in June 1885, Abd al-Rahman al-Mahdi was reared in Omdurman under the rule of the Khalifa Abdullahi. Upon the conquest of the Sudan by Anglo–Egyptian forces in 1898, he, as the eldest surviving son of the Mahdi (and consequently his spiritual and legal heir), was kept under close scrutiny by the British authorities until the outbreak of World War I, when they sought his assistance to counter any call for a jihad by the Ottoman Turks, who were allies of the Germans. Sayyid Abd al-Rahman unstintingly supported the British and in return received the freedom to enhance his wealth and his influence among the followers of his father, the Ansar; thus he emerged as the leading religious and political figure in the Anglo–Egyptian Sudan. Despite tensions between him and the British, who feared a revival of Muslim fanaticism in the guise of neo-Mahdism, the sayyid continued to prove his loyalty to the government. He used his abundant resources to acquire a loyal following among the Ansar, whom he converted into the UMMA political party. After World War II he remained the most influential Sudanese in the emerging political system. Like his father, he frustrated Egyptian claims in the Sudan and for a time regarded himself as a possible king of an independent Sudan. This was unacceptable to the vast majority of Sudanese, who did not wish to be dominated by the Ansar as they had been in the last two decades of the nineteenth century. Until his death Abd al-Rahman continued to pursue his ambitions to ensure that the Ansar and the Umma would remain preeminent in an independent Sudan.

Robert O. Collins

Abd al-Rahman ibn Hisham   [1789–1859]

Sultan of Morocco, 1822–1859.

During his reign, MOROCCO lost its international standing and suffered economic decline and social and political unrest.

A major problem was how to respond to the invasion of Algeria by France in 1830. Abd al-Rahman first tacitly supported Algerian resistance forces, then sought to avoid a confrontation. In August 1844, this policy failed when a Moroccan army was beaten at Isly by General Thomas-Robert BUGEAUD de la Piconnerie and Moroccan ports were bombarded by the French navy. Morocco's defeat opened the door to increased European political and economic intervention.

The economic policies pursued by Abd al-Rahman became disastrous as well. The signing of an Anglo–Moroccan commercial agreement in 1856 gave most-favored-nation status to Britain, and its provisions were soon extended to other European powers.

Finally, a major conflict with Spain erupted into war in August 1859.

BIBLIOGRAPHY

ABUN-NASR, JAMIL M. *A History of the Maghrib,* 2nd ed. Cambridge, Mass., 1975.
SCHROETER, DANIEL. *Merchants of Essaouira: Urban Society and Imperialism in Southwestern Morocco, 1844–1886.* Cambridge, Mass., 1988.

Edmund Burke III

Abd al-Rahman Khan   [1844–1910]

Ruler of Afghanistan.

Abd al-Rahman Khan Barakzai (also known as Abd er-Rahman) ascended the Afghan throne during the second British invasion of Afghanistan. Embarking on a relentless policy of centralization of power, he weathered four civil wars and a hundred rebellions during his reign (1880–1910).

He was the grandson of DOST MOHAMMAD (ruled 1826–1839; 1842–1863), the founder of the BARAKZAI DYNASTY. At the age of thirteen, he was given his first appointment, and he showed his talent when assigned, later on, to command the army of the northern region, of which his father was governor. Playing an active role in the five-year war of succession, he twice won the throne for his father and an uncle before being defeated by yet another uncle, Sher Ali (ruled 1863–1866; 1869–1879). Forced to leave, Abd al-Rahman spent eleven years in exile in the Asiatic colonies of Russia. His opportunity came in 1880, when Britain's invading forces, shaken by the intensity of Afghan resistance, were casting for a candidate acceptable both to them and to the resistance. In return for British control over Afghanistan's foreign relations, he was recognized as the ruler, in July 1880, and assigned a subsidy by Britain.

In the wake of Britain's invasion, multiple centers of power had emerged in Afghanistan, with two of Abd al-Rahman's cousins controlling major portions of the country. He rejected offers to share power, defeating one cousin in 1880 and the other in 1885, and emerged as the undisputed ruler of the country. His next challenge was to overcome the clans, whom he subdued, in a series of campaigns between 1880 and 1896. He imposed taxation, conscription, and adjudication on the defeated clans. His policies encompassed all linguistic and religious groups but took a particularly brutal form in the case of the Hazaras.

To establish his centralizing policies, he transformed the state apparatus. The army, chief vehicle of his policies, was reorganized and expanded, and the bulk of the state revenue was spent on its upkeep. Administrative and judicial practices were bureaucratized, with emphasis on record keeping and the separation of home and office. He justified these policies on religious grounds, making *shari'a* (the law of Islam) the law of the land, and nonetheless turning all judges into paid servants of the state.

Abd al-Rahman was able to concentrate on consolidating his rule at home because of Britain's and Russia's desire to avoid direct confrontation with each other. Afghanistan became a buffer state between the two empires; they imposed its present boundaries. Playing on their rivalry, Abd al-Rahman refused to allow European railways, which were touching on his eastern, southern, and northern borders, to expand within Afghanistan, and he resisted British attempts to station European representatives in his country. Toward the end of his reign, he felt secure enough to inform the viceroy of India that treaty obligations did not allow British representatives even to comment on his internal affairs.

When he died, he was succeeded by his son and heir apparent, HABIBOLLAH KHAN, who ruled until 1919.

BIBLIOGRAPHY

GHANI, ASHRAF. "Islam and State-Building in a Tribal Society: Afghanistan 1880–1901." *Modern Asian Studies* 12 (1978): 269–284.
KAKAR, HASSAN. *Afghanistan: A Study in Internal Development, 1880–1896.* Lahore, 1971.
———. *Government and Society in Afghanistan.* Austin, Tex., 1979.

Ashraf Ghani

Abd al-Rashid Doestam   [1954–   ]

Afghani military leader.

Abd al-Rashid Doestam, born in Jowzjan province of northern Afghanistan, commanded the largest paramilitary force in the Afghan Communist regime of President NAJIBULLAH. In January 1992, Doestam, an Uzbek, led his mainly Uzbek forces in a mutiny that led to the formation of an alliance of non-Pakhtun former government and Islamic resistance forces that captured Kabul. Doestam formed his followers into the Islamic National Movement and emerged as the premier warlord of northern Afghanistan and a regional ally of President Islam Karimov of Uzbekistan.

Barnett R. Rubin

Abd al-Raziq, Ali   [1888–1966]

Egyptian Islamic judge, writer, and politician.

Ali Abd al-Raziq, who came from a family of large landowners in southern EGYPT, was educated at al-Azhar in Cairo and in England and became an Islamic court judge in Mansura. In 1925, he published a controversial book on the secularization of power in the Muslim state, *Al-Islam wa usul al-hukm* (Islam and the Bases of Rule), in which he argued for separating Islamic from political authority, on the grounds that the Qur'an and biographies of Muham-

mad show that God called on the Prophet to be a religious counselor to his people, not a head of state, and that the caliphate as a political institution was a post-Qur'anic innovation not essential to Islam. The publication of this book aroused controversy among Muslims, especially Egyptians, because in the new Republic of Turkey, Mustafa Kemal (Atatürk) had recently abolished the Islamic caliphate, because many Muslims wanted to elect or appoint a new caliph in a country other than Turkey, and because King FU'AD I of Egypt had proposed himself as a candidate for the caliphate. Abd al-Raziq was accused of promoting atheism and was censured by the *ulama* (Islamic scholars) of al-Azhar, deprived of his title of shaykh, and relieved of his duties as a religious judge. He was, however, backed by many liberal writers, including Taha HUSAYN and Muhammad Husayn HAYKAL.

He continued to defend his ideas in articles written for *al-Siyasa,* the weekly journal of the Constitutional Liberal party, and in lectures delivered in Cairo University's faculties of law and of letters. He later served twice as *waqfs* (Muslim endowment) minister and was elected to membership in the Arabic Language Academy. Following the 1952 revolution, he practiced law and published a collection of writings by his brother, Mustafa Abd al-Raziq, including a detailed biography. He is often cited by Egyptian and foreign writers as a leading secularist thinker and an opponent of King's Fu'ad's religious pretensions.

BIBLIOGRAPHY

ADAMS, C. C. *Islam and Modernism in Egypt.* London, 1933.
BINDER, LEONARD. "Ali Abd al Raziq and Islamic Liberalism." *Asian and African Studies* 10 (March 1982): 31–67.
MORABIA, A. "Des rapports entre religion et état selon un théologien égyptien d'al-Azhar." *Orient* 32/33 (1964/65): 257–303.
ROSENTHAL, ERWIN I. J. *Islam in the Modern National State.* Cambridge, U.K., 1965.

Arthur Goldschmidt, Jr.

Abd al-Razzaq, Arif   [1921–   ]

Iraqi military leader and politician.

Born in the town of Kubaisa in the governorate of al-Ramadi Muhafazah, Arif Abd al-Razzaq graduated from the Military College of Iraq as an air force officer and later from the Staff College, after which he became the pilot of the royal family. He was an ardent supporter of President Nasser of Egypt. After the coup of 1958, Prime Minister Abd al-Karim Kassem appointed him commander of Habbaniyah Base. Later, he became commander of the Iraqi air force and minister of agriculture. After the downfall of Kassem, he was appointed prime minister. He attempted to lead a coup d'état to expedite unification with Egypt, but his attempt was foiled and he fled to Cairo.

Mamoon A. Zaki

Abd al-Sabur, Salah   [1931–1981]

Egyptian author, journalist, and poet.

Abd al-Sabur was born in the Egyptian countryside but grew up in Cairo. Originally writing poetry in traditional styles, Abd al-Sabur later wrote in free verse and is considered the leader of Egyptian modernists. In all of his works, Abd al-Sabur draws upon contemporary life for his subjects and his symbolism, expressing themes of existentialism, the search for new values, and the longing for youth and for rural life. Among his volumes of poetry are *Al-Nass fi Biladi* (The People of My Country), published in 1957, and *Aqulu Lakum* (I Say to You), published in 1961. Abd al-Sabur also wrote plays, including *Misafir Layl* (Nocturnal Pilgrims) and *Layla wa Majnun,* and several volumes of literary criticism, including *Hayati fi al-Shi'r* (My Life in Poetry), published in 1969, and *Qira'a Jadida li al-Shi'rna al-Qadim* (A New Reading of Our Old Poetry), published in 1968. In addition, Abd al-Sabur translated the drama of Ibsen into Arabic, as well as articles and essays that covered a broad range of subjects from British politics to atomic submarines.

BIBLIOGRAPHY

ALLEN, ROGER, ed. *Modern Arabic Literature: A Library of Literary Criticism.* New York, 1987, pp. 5–11.
BECKA, JIRI, ed. *Dictionary of Oriental Literatures.* Vol. 3, *West Asia and North Africa.* New York, 1974, p. 2.

David Waldner

Abdelghani, Benhamed Mohammed   [1927–   ]

Algerian officer and government minister.

Abdelghani was appointed commander of Algeria's first (1962), fourth (1965), and fifth (1967) military regions. In October 1973, he was charged with

dispatching Algerian troops to the Arab–Israel War. Abdelghani supported Colonel Houari BOUMÉDIENNE's coup against Ahmed BEN BELLA's government (1965) and joined the council of the revolution. After the death of Ahmed Medeghri, Abdelghani was rewarded for his loyalty with the portfolio of minister of interior (1975). President Chadli BENJEDID selected Abdelghani as his first prime minister (1979–1984), a strategic political choice to satisfy the Boumédienne faction. Abdelghani then served as a minister of state to the presidency.

BIBLIOGRAPHY

Les élites algériennes. Paris, 1985.

Phillip C. Naylor

Abdesselam, Belaid   [1928–   ]

Algerian prime minister, 1992–1993, minister of industry and energy, 1965–1977.

Termed the father of Algerian industrialization, Abdesselam was born in Ayn el-Kebira to a landed family. As a student leader, he supported independence for Algeria and a leader in that movement, Messali al-HADJ. During the Algerian War of Independence (1954–1962), he joined the Front de Libération Nationale (National Liberation Front, FLN) and politicized Algerian students in France. Later he served under ministries of the Gouvernement Provisoire de la République Algérienne (Provisional Government of the Republic of Algeria, GPRA). President Ahmed BEN BELLA had Abdesselam head SONATRACH, the Algerian hydrocarbon enterprise, until he was charged by Colonel Houari BOUMÉDIENNE with organizing development policy as minister of industry and energy. Under Abdesselam's direction, hydrocarbon revenues fueled impressive industrial capitalization. From 1977 to 1979, he was the minister of light industry, but then he was removed from power and was eventually accused of mismanagement.

Abdesselam resumed a public political role in 1989 with his election to the enlarged central committee of the FLN. Protesting the FLN's leadership, he resigned from the central committee in July 1991. Abdesselam was particularly critical of the government's hydrocarbon policy and teamed with other ex-Boumédienne ministers in opposition to President Chadli BENJEDID. In July 1992, the High Council of State appointed Abdesselam prime minister. His policies aimed at stopping Islamist assaults and stabilizing the collapsing economy. Continuing violence and economic deterioration, however, led to his dismissal in August 1993.

BIBLIOGRAPHY

NAYLOR, PHILLIP C., and ALF A. HEGGOY. *The Historical Dictionary of Algeria*, 2nd ed. Metuchen, N.J., 1994.
STORA, BENJAMIN. *Dictionnaire biographique de militants nationalistes algériens*. Paris, 1985.

Phillip C. Naylor

Abduh, Muhammad   [1849–1905]

Islamic reformer and author.

Born in a village in Gharbiyya province, Egypt, his family moved to Mahallat Nasr in Buhayra province, where he was reared. Educated at the Ahmadi Mosque in Tanta and at al-Azhar University, Muhammad Abduh became interested in philosophy and SUFISM. During the sojourn of Jamal al-Din al-AFGHANI in Cairo, Abduh came to know him and became his most loyal disciple. He taught for a while, then became editor of *al-Waqa'i al-Misriyya*, the Egyptian government newspaper, from 1880 to 1882. Although more moderate than his mentor, Abduh nevertheless backed the Urabi revolution. After its collapse he was imprisoned briefly and then was exiled to Beirut.

In 1884 Abduh went to Paris, where he collaborated with Afghani in forming a society called *al-Urwa al-Wuthqa* (The Indissoluble Bond), that published a journal by the same name which, although it lasted only eight months, stimulated the rise of Nationalism in many parts of the Muslim world. After it was banned, he returned to Beirut to teach and write, also translating into Arabic Afghani's *al-Radd ala al-dahriyyin* (Refutation of the Materialists).

In 1889 he was allowed to return to Egypt, where he became a judge, then a chancellor in the appeals court, and in 1899 the chief *mufti* (canon lawyer) of Egypt. In 1894 he became a member of the governing council of al-Azhar, for which he proposed far-reaching reforms. He was named to the legislative council in 1899.

His best-known theological work, *Risalat al-Tawhid* (Treatise on Unity), based on lectures he had given in Beirut, was published in 1897. He also wrote *al-Islam wa al-Nasraniyya ma'a al-ilm wa al-madaniyya*, published in 1902 in *al-Manar*, a journal edited by his disciple, Muhammad Rashid RIDA. Abduh also began writing a commentary on the Qur'an, completed by Rida after his death. He advocated reforming Islam by restoring it to what he believed had been its original condition, modernizing the Arabic language, and

upholding people's rights in relation to their rulers. He was among the first ulama (Islamic scholars) to favor nationalism, and one of his political disciples was Sa'd ZAGHLUL. His efforts to reconcile Islam with modernization have not fully survived the test of time, but Abduh remains a towering figure in Egypt's intellectual history.

BIBLIOGRAPHY

ADAMS, C. C. *Islam and Modernism in Egypt*. Oxford, 1933; New York, 1968.
AHMED, J. M. *Intellectual Origins of Egyptian Nationalism*. London, 1960.
AMIN, AHMAD. *Zu'ama al-Islah fi al-'asr al-hadith*. Cairo, 1948.
AMIN, OSMAN. *Muhammad 'Abduh*. Tr. by Charles Wendell. Washington, D.C., 1953.
Encyclopaedia of Islam, 2nd ed.
HOURANI, ALBERT. *Arabic Thought in the Liberal Age, 1798–1939*. London, 1962.
KERR, MALCOLM H. *Islamic Reform: The Political and Legal Theories of Muhammad 'Abduh and Rashid Rida*. Berkeley, Calif., 1966.

Arthur Goldschmidt, Jr.

Abdülaziz   [1830–1876]

Ottoman sultan, 1861–1876.

Administratively, the reign of Abdülaziz divides into two eras. During the first (1861–1871), real power was in the hands of the reformist ministers Ali and Fu'ad, protégés of the leader of the TANZIMAT reforms, Mustafa Reşit Paşa. Although Abdülaziz was not a figurehead, his powers were limited by his ministers; the bureaucracy ruled. Reforms continued to centralize and rationalize the Ottoman administrative system. Provincial borders were redrawn, and provincial governments were reformed by the Vilayet Law of 1867. The General Education Law of 1869 set a national curriculum stressing "modern" subjects such as the sciences, engineering, and geography. Specialized higher schools were created in the provinces, and in Constantinople (now Istanbul) a university (at least in concept) was established.

The second era (1871–1876) began upon the death of Ali in 1871 (Fu'ad had died in 1869) when Abdülaziz took personal charge of the government. The centralization of power, one of the pillars of Tanzimat reform, was especially attractive to him; he planned to transfer power to himself. To avoid concentrating power in the hands of the bureaucracy, the sultan changed ministers of state often. Grand viziers (the most famous being MAHMUD NEDIM Paşa) averaged well under a year in office. Serving at the pleasure of the sultan, the bureaucrats adapted themselves to carrying out his wishes and protecting their own careers. Some reformist measures were passed, particularly improvements in central administration and taxation. The thrust of reform, however, was weakened.

The military was greatly improved after 1871. Under Grand Vizier Hüseyin Avni Paşa (1874–1875), the government invested in military hardware, including up-to-date rifles and artillery from Germany. It rebuilt and improved fortresses on the Asian border with Russia and reorganized the Ottoman army corps. Previously garrisoned to face a now-unlikely internal rebellion, they were shifted to meet foreign threats. The Anatolian army, for example, was transferred from Sivas to Erzurum. The Turkish Straits were fortified. Unfortunately, the Ottoman Empire could not support even these most necessary expenditures.

Militarily, Abdülaziz's reign was relatively quiet. He and his successor, Murad V, who reigned for three months, were the only nineteenth-century sultans who did not fight a major war with Russia. Bloody uprisings in Bosnia-Herzegovina and Bulgaria, which were to result in the Russo–Turkish War of 1877–1878, began in Abdülaziz's reign. A revolt in Crete (1866–1869) resulted in administrative reforms on the island.

Russia remained the primary enemy of the Ottomans. Balanced in international affairs by the generally pro-Ottoman diplomacy of Great Britain, Russia nevertheless managed to upset the Ottoman Empire. Most damaging was Russia's policy in the Caucasus. When it conquered Circassia in 1864 and Abkhazia in 1867, Russia forced approximately 1.2 million Muslims from their homes. Robbed of their belongings by the Russians, the refugees were herded to Black Sea ports. The Ottomans were forced either to transport them to the Ottoman Empire or to let them die. The Ottomans settled the refugees in Anatolia and the Balkans. There was little but land to give them, so thefts by the starving Caucasians were widespread. Conflicts between refugees and villagers disrupted the empire for a decade.

In the face of Russia's threat and despite a good record of military preparedness, the foreign policy of Abdülaziz's later years was more than odd. The government took Russia's ambassador, Count Nicholas Ignatiev, as adviser and accommodated Ottoman policy to Russian wishes. Mahmud Nedim, twice grand vizir and Abdülaziz's main counselor, was widely, and probably correctly, viewed as being in the pay of Ignatiev. If pro-Russia policies were designed to avoid war, they were surely misguided, as Russia's attack in 1877 demonstrated.

Finances were Abdülaziz's undoing. Since the Crimean War, the Ottoman government had existed on a series of European loans. Because of vast defense needs, the costs of reform—advisers, teachers, economic infrastructure—could be paid only through borrowing. The expectation that reform would lead to economic improvement, greater tax revenues, and easy repayment of loans was never realized. The bill came due under Abdülaziz. Famine in Anatolia in 1873–1874 greatly reduced tax revenues, and the bureaucrats were not adept at collecting even what could be paid. Abdülaziz exacerbated the problem with personal expenditures on palaces and luxuries. By the end of his reign, debt payments theoretically took more than 40 percent of state income. European bankers, previously willing to cover Ottoman interest payments with further loans, had suffered from the general stock market crash of 1873 and were unwilling to oblige. The Ottoman government was forced to default on its loans.

Financial disaster turned European governments, always protective of bondholders, against Abdülaziz. Restive bureaucrats, reformers, and those who feared the effects of subservience to Russia already were against him. Popular resentment at weak Ottoman responses to the slaughter of Muslims by Serbian rebels in Bosnia added to the sultan's difficulties. On May 30, 1876, Abdülaziz was deposed in favor of Murad V. On June 5 he committed suicide.

BIBLIOGRAPHY

BROWN, L. CARL. *Imperial Legacy: The Ottoman Imprint on the Balkans and the Middle East.* New York, 1996.

DAVISON, RODERIC. *Essays in Ottoman and Turkish History, 1774–1923.* Austin, Tex., 1990.

FINDLEY, CARTER V. *Bureaucratic Reform in the Ottoman Empire: The Sublime Porte, 1789–1922.* Princeton, N.J., 1980.

LEWIS, BERNARD. *The Emergence of Modern Turkey.* Oxford, 1965.

SHAW, STANFORD, and EZEL KURAL SHAW. *History of the Ottoman Empire and Modern Turkey.* Vol. 2, *Reform, Revolution, and Republic, 1808–1975.* Cambridge, U.K., 1977.

Justin McCarthy

Abdülhamit II [1842–1918]

Ottoman sultan, 1876–1909.

Abdülhamit II assumed the Ottoman throne in perilous times. The two previous sultans, Abdülaziz and Murad V, had been deposed—the former primarily for financial incompetence, the latter for mental incompetence. The Ottoman Empire was at war with Serbia and Montenegro, and war with Russia threatened.

In international affairs, the main disaster of Abdülhamit's reign came at its beginning—the Russo–Turkish War of 1877–1878. In addition to the loss of more than 250,000 dead and the influx of more than 500,000 refugees into the empire, the war resulted in the largest loss of Ottoman territory since 1699. Under the terms of the Treaty of Berlin of 1878, the Ottomans lost the Kars-Ardahan region of northeastern Anatolia to the Russians, Serbia's and Montenegro's borders were extended at Ottoman expense, Romania and Serbia became independent, northern Bulgaria was made an independent kingdom, southern Bulgaria (Eastern Rumelia) became autonomous, and Austria's occupation of Bosnia-Herzegovina was sanctioned.

Losses of territory and administrative control over his empire might have been greater had Abdülhamit and his ministers not acted resolutely. Ceding Cyprus to Britain ensured that the British supported the Ottomans at the Congress of Berlin. The congress overturned the terms of the Treaty of San Stefano, under which almost all of Ottoman Europe was to have been lost. Instead, the Ottomans retained Thrace, Macedonia, and Albania.

The only other war fought by Abdülhamit's army, in 1897 with Greece, was a success, although the European powers forced the Ottomans to renounce their territorial gains. The powers also obliged the Ottomans to make Crete autonomous under a high commissioner, Prince George of Greece, in effect putting the island under Greek control.

Abdülhamit accepted losses that were blows to Ottoman prestige while retaining the empire's core territory. France seized Tunisia in 1881; Britain, Egypt in 1882. Although neither territory had been under Ottoman control, the losses indicated the empire's weakness to both the Europeans and the Ottomans. In 1886 that weakness forced the Ottomans to accept the de facto unification of Bulgaria and Eastern Rumelia. The European powers also compelled administrative changes in Macedonia and eastern Anatolia.

In eastern Anatolia, the powers did not bring about significant changes, despite strong sentiment in the West in favor of Armenian independence. From 1894 to 1896, Armenians in eastern Anatolia rebelled, killing Muslims and Ottoman officials. Ottoman troops and local Muslims responded in kind. However, diplomatic conflict among Britain, France, and Russia forestalled any European intervention, and Ottoman offers of administrative changes were accepted by the powers.

Like the Tanzimat reformers, Abdülhamit was concerned with the centralization of authority, the regularization of the state system, and the development of the economy. He blended these goals with the traditional ideal of Ottoman rule—an Islamic state in which all power emanated from the sultan. Although at first he accepted limited democracy, a constitution (1876), and a parliament (1877), he prorogued the Parliament within a year and ruled personally. His concept of reform was improvement of finances, infrastructure, administration, and education, not a transition to democracy.

Abdülhamit was more financially adept than his predecessors. Upon taking power, he inherited the debts that had led the empire into bankruptcy under Abdülaziz. He convinced the European bankers to accept partial payment, so nearly half of the Ottoman debt was forgiven (the Decree of Muharram, 1881). However, the price was the loss of financial independence. Valuable sources of state revenue (taxes on silk, fishing, alcoholic spirits, official stamps needed for all legal documents, and tobacco, as well as the tribute from Eastern Rumelia, Cyprus, Greece, Bulgaria, and Montenegro) were ceded to the European-controlled Public Debt Administration. In effect, Europeans became tax collectors in the Ottoman Empire. The empire was left with too few financial resources, and as a result, borrowing resumed.

Economic development of the empire was a first priority of Abdülhamit's rule. Improved roads increased almost sixfold. Many government-sponsored enterprises thrived—such as mining and agricultural exports. Local industry developed as well, although European manufactures and the Ottomans' inability to levy protective tariffs slowed growth considerably. The telegraph and railroad systems experienced major growth. Less than three hundred kilometers of railroad track had been laid in Ottoman Asia before Abdülaziz's reign, and trackage grew threefold under Abdülhamit. By the end of Abdülhamit's reign, feeder lines ran to major ports, and trunk lines (the Baghdad Railway and the Hijaz Railroad) were under construction. The length of telegraph line nearly tripled. In education, the number of teachers and schools approximately doubled. However, the increase was mainly in provincial capitals and, especially, Constantinople (now Istanbul).

Abdülhamit was vilified in the European and American press as the Red Sultan, an image primarily based on press accounts of events in eastern Anatolia, Crete, and Macedonia. He also was known as no friend of liberal democracy, an accurate assertion. In his concern for his personal rule and the continuation of a powerful sultanate, he took action against all manifestations of democratic reform. All publications were censored. His secret police spied on bureaucrats and intellectuals, on the lookout for revolution as well as malfeasance.

Abdülhamit was extremely concerned with his position (historically inaccurate) as caliph of the Muslims. Expenditures from his privy purse included donations to Islamic groups in Asia and Africa, as well as to Islamic revolutionaries against Christian rule. His view of the Ottoman Empire was traditional—a Muslim empire, not a Turkish state. This naturally put him at odds with the Turkish nationalism that developed during his reign.

A combination of economic pressures, foreign interference in the empire, and his own autocracy led to the demise of Abdülhamit's sultanate. In 1907, Bulgarian and Greek revolutionaries in Ottoman Macedonia were fighting guerrilla wars against Ottoman troops and each other. Russia and Austria had forced the sultan to accept European "controllers" over Macedonia. Officers of the Ottoman army in Macedonia felt, with justification, that Abdülhamit had placated the Europeans instead of punishing the guerrillas who were killing Muslim civilians, and that fear of the army had caused the sultan to keep needed support and supplies from them. Abdülhamit's fears were largely justified; army officers had been organized into revolutionary cells since their days at the military academy. They had opened communication with revolutionary groups in western Europe, and some had organized their own rebel bands. A poor harvest in 1907 reduced tax revenues, and salaries were in arrears, causing further disaffection.

However, Abdülhamit defused the threat of revolution in 1908 by reinstating Parliament and calling elections, deciding to rule as a constitutional monarch. Those who opposed his rule, known as the COMMITTEE OF UNION AND PROGRESS, became a major force in the Parliament. Abdülhamit's mistake came in 1909. Conservative reaction against the new Parliament led to a revolt in Constantinople and the expulsion of the Committee of Union and Progress's parliamentary delegates and officials. Abdülhamit associated himself with the revolt to regain power. However, the Macedonian army proved more powerful than the rebels. They converged on Constantinople, took control, and reinstated the Parliament. On April 27, 1909, Abdülhamit was deposed and exiled to Salonika. At the onset of the First Balkan War in 1912, he was moved to the Beylerbeyi Palace on the Bosporus, where he died in 1918.

BIBLIOGRAPHY

BROWN, L. CARL. *Imperial Legacy: The Ottoman Imprint on the Balkans and the Middle East.* New York, 1996.

DAVISON, RODERIC. *Essays in Ottoman and Turkish History, 1774–1923.* Austin, Tex., 1990.

FINDLEY, CARTER V. *Bureaucratic Reform in the Ottoman Empire: The Sublime Porte, 1789–1922.* Princeton, N.J., 1980.

LEWIS, BERNARD. *The Emergence of Modern Turkey.* Oxford, 1965.

SHAW, STANFORD, and EZEL KURAL SHAW. *History of the Ottoman Empire and Modern Turkey.* Vol. 2, *Reform, Revolution, and Republic, 1808–1975.* Cambridge, U.K., 1977.

Justin McCarthy

Abdullahi, Muhammad Turshain
[1846–1899]

Commander of the Mahdist forces and ruler of the Mahdist domains in the Sudan, 1885–1898.

Known in Western literature as Khalifa Abdullahi, Abdullahi was born at Turdat in southwestern Darfur, one of four sons of a holy man of the Ta'aisha Baqqara. Upon hearing of Muhammad AHMAD al-Mahdi, he went east to join him at Aba Island in the Bahr al-Abyad; he was the first to recognize him as the Mahdi. The Mahdi recognized his military abilities and made him a principal military commander. In 1881 Abdullahi was appointed a caliph, given the name Abu Bakr al-Siddiq, and placed in command of the prestigious black flag division of the Madhist army.

Abdullahi retired with the Mahdi to Kordofan and there organized a series of crushing defeats of the government forces that gave the Mahdist movement the reputation of invincibility. He fought in the Jazira and oversaw the siege of Khartoum, which, after long resistance, fell in January 1885. On the death of the Mahdi in June 1885, Abdullahi assumed the temporal functions of government as dictator of an empire that extended from Dar Mahas to the Upper Nile and from the Red Sea to Darfur. Except at Omdurman in 1898, when he was overthrown, he did not personally lead his armies, preferring to leave operational details to his field commanders.

Abdullahi ruled harshly and arbitrarily in order to maintain his large military establishment. His genius for organization was revealed in his system of taxation and his attempts to establish factories to manufacture steamers and ammunition, as well as mints to produce coins. He insisted on the strict observance of Islamic law. He was hostile to the religious brotherhoods, suppressing them where the Mahdi had only discountenanced them. His merciless rule at length aroused the opposition of most tribal peoples except his own *baqqara,* to whom he gave a privileged position in the state in return for their loyalty.

After the advance of the army of Egypt and Britain into Dongola in 1896, Abdullahi's prestige suffered. Numerous defeats of the incompetent general Amir al-Umara Mahmud Ahmad and Abdullahi's defeat at Atbara culminated in the battle of Omdurman in September 1898. Fleeing south, he and several companions were killed at Umm Dibaikarat in 1899. He was buried on the battlefield, several miles southeast of Tendelti on the Kordofan railway. His tomb is venerated.

Robert O. Collins

Abdullah ibn Husayn   [1882–1951]

King of Jordan, 1946–1951.

Abdullah, born in Mecca, was a son of HUSAYN IBN ALI. On his eleventh birthday, he went to Constantinople (now Istanbul) to join his father, who had been summoned by the sultan. In 1908 Husayn was appointed Sharif of Mecca, over the objections of the Committee of Union and Progress (the Young Turks). Between 1910 and 1914, Abdullah represented Mecca in the Ottoman Parliament.

The Turkish authorities tried to strip Husayn of his administrative (but not religious) duties when the construction of railroad and telegraph lines made direct rule from Constantinople possible. Husayn resisted, and he was in danger of dismissal when the dispute was shelved due to the outbreak of World War I.

Portrait of King Abdullah ibn Husayn on an overprinted Palestine postage stamp. (Richard Bulliet)

In February 1914, Abdullah met Lord KITCHENER, then minister plenipotentiary to Egypt, and asked him if Britain would aid Sharif Husayn in case of a dispute with the Turks. Abdullah also met with Ronald STORRS, the Oriental secretary at Britain's consulate in Cairo. This meeting led to a subsequent correspondence between Storrs and Abdullah that later developed into the HUSAYN–MCMAHON CORRESPONDENCE, an exchange in which certain pledges were made by Britain to the sharif concerning an independent Arab kingdom (with ambiguous boundaries) in the Fertile Crescent.

The Turks tried to persuade Husayn to endorse the call for jihad against the Allies, but he delayed until 10 June 1916, when the ARAB REVOLT was declared. Abdullah was entrusted with the siege of the Turkish garrisons in Taif and Medina. His brother FAISAL, meanwhile, scored quick victories in Syria. Faisal set up an independent Arab kingdom with its capital at Damascus toward the end of 1918; the French drove him out two years later. Meanwhile, Abdullah was defeated in an important battle with the Wahhabi followers of IBN SAʿUD. Britain placed Faisal on the throne of Iraq, which had been slated for Abdullah.

One key to understanding Abdullah is his deep loyalty to Islam, which in his mind was linked to the notion that God had favored the Arabs with a unique position as the carriers of culture and faith. For him, Arabism was inseparable from Islam and meaningless without it. His family, which claimed a direct line of descent from the Prophet Muhammad, provided the crucial link between the two.

Another key to an understanding of Abdullah's personality is that, as a rule, he sought cooperation, even in the midst of conflict. He preferred bargaining to fighting, and he constantly formulated value-maximizing strategies in which he compromised with his adversaries so that all sides might stand to gain from the outcome.

Although Abdullah strove for unity, he engaged in nation-building on a limited scale when unity was unattainable. When he appeared with a small band of armed followers in Madaba, after the French had ousted his brother Faisal from the throne of Syria in 1920, he was intent on leading Syrian political refugees, members of the ISTIQLAL PARTY still loyal to Faisal, and the bedouins he could muster in a bid to wrest Arab rights in Syria from the French. With T. E. LAWRENCE acting as a go-between, he negotiated a deal with the new British colonial secretary, Winston CHURCHILL, under which Abdullah agreed to administer Transjordan for six months, beginning on 1 April 1921, and was granted a subsidy by Britain. One consequence of this was to remove Transjordan from the sphere of applicability of the Balfour Declaration.

Abdullah took over the administration of an arid plateau with a population of about 235,000, largely bedouin, poor, and uneducated, a land with some two hundred villages, half a dozen towns, and no major cities. Governmental services were virtually nonexistent. When he died, he left a nation-state comparable with others in the Middle East, although lacking in financial independence. The period from 1924 to 1940 was one in which central administration was developed, with Palestinians gradually replacing Syrians. An exemplary land program gave farmers property security unmatched in the Fertile Crescent. In 1925 the Ma'an and Aqaba regions were effectively incorporated into Transjordan (they had technically formed part of the Hijaz). In the same period, the bedouins, who had preyed on the sedentary population, were successfully integrated into the state, for which John Bagot GLUBB, the organizer of the Desert Patrol, was largely responsible.

In 1928, Transjordan acquired an organic law under which Abdullah gained recognition in international law. It also provided for constitutional government and a legislative council, but Abdullah had wide authority to rule by decree, under the guidance of Britain. Although Transjordan remained militarily dependent on Britain, on 22 March 1946 a treaty was concluded whereby Britain recognized Transjordan "as a fully independent state and His Highness the Amir as the sovereign thereof." Following a name change, the Hashimite kingdom of Jordan concluded a new treaty with Britain in 1948.

Through years of dependency on Britain, Abdullah fell behind the times, continuing to reflect the Ottoman Empire in which he had grown up: dynastic and theocratic, Arabs accepting foreign suzerainty under compulsion. He was out of step with Palestinian and secular Arab nationalism as well as Zionism. He sought to use British influence to forge Arab unity rather than to get rid of the British as a first step toward unity. British residents, notably St. John Philby and Percy Cox, drove a wedge between him and Syrian members of the Istiqlal party, who had perceived the Hashimites as champions of Syria's independence from France. When Abd al-Rahman SHAHBANDAR, a nationalist Syrian leader who had been a longtime supporter of Abdullah, was assassinated in July 1940, Abdullah's base of support in Syria died with him.

Abdullah could accept a Jewish homeland only in the context of the old millet system: as a minority with a large degree of autonomy within a kingdom that he ruled. Zionists found this totally unacceptable but valued his accommodating approach to the prob-

lem. Yet he was a pioneer of Arab–Jewish understanding. He accepted the Peel Commission Report of 1937, which recommended partition of Palestine, even if he did not embrace a Jewish state. He also publicly accepted the 1939 white paper on Palestine, which was favorable to the Arabs. It has been said that he was driven by personal ambition, hoping to incorporate the Arab portion of Palestine within his domain, yet it is clear that he saw himself as an Arab acting for the Arabs. As his grandson King HUSSEIN pointed out, Abdullah realized that the Jewish community in Palestine was only the tip of the iceberg and that the balance of forces dictated compromise. Abdullah met with Golda MEIR, who was acting on behalf of the political department of the Jewish Agency, on 17 November 1947, and it was agreed that Abdullah would annex the Arab part of Palestine under the UN partition plan but would not invade the Jewish part.

When the British mandate ended on 14 May 1948, the Jews declared the creation of a Jewish state, and war broke out with the Arabs. The Arab Legion (Jordanian army) occupied what came to be known as the WEST BANK; Britain accepted this as long as Abdullah kept out of the Jewish zone; when Jewish forces and the Arab Legion clashed over Jerusalem, which was to have been designated an international zone, Britain cut off arms supplies and spare parts, and ordered all of its officers to return to Amman. The Arabs held on to East Jerusalem, but the Arab Legion had to withdraw from the towns of Lydda and Ramle, which laid Abdullah open to charges of betrayal. In the final analysis, his strategy salvaged territory for the Arabs that may one day serve as the basis for a Palestinian state.

Abdullah initiated a conference in Jericho at which the Palestinian participants expressed a wish to join in one country with Jordan. Parliamentary elections were subsequently held in the west and east banks, with twenty seats assigned to each. Parliament convened on 24 April 1950, at which time Palestinian deputies tabled a motion to unite both banks of the Jordan. This was unanimously adopted. Abdullah became king of a country that now included the holy places in Palestine, with a population of 1.5 million, triple the population of Transjordan alone.

Abdullah was assassinated at the Aqsa Mosque on 20 July 1951 by a handful of disgruntled Palestinians believed to be working with Egypt's intelligence service.

BIBLIOGRAPHY

ABDULLAH, KING OF JORDAN. *Memoirs of King Abdullah of Transjordan*. New York, 1950.
———. *My Memoirs Completed*. London, 1978.

DANN, URIEL. *Studies in the History of Transjordan, 1920–1949: The Making of a State.* Boulder, Colo., 1984.
KIRKBRIDE, SIR ALEC. *From the Wings: Amman Memoirs 1947–1951.* London, 1976.
SHLAIM, AVI. *Collusion across the Jordan.* New York, 1988.
WILSON, MARY C. *King Abdullah, Britain and the Making of Jordan.* Cambridge, U.K., 1987.

Jenab Tutunji

Abdülmecit I [1823–1861]

Thirty-first Ottoman sultan, reigned 1839–1861; initiated reform program based on proclaimed principles.

Oldest surviving son of the westernizing sultan MAHMUD II, Abdülmecit had a good education with a strong European component. He knew French well, subscribed to French publications, and admired European music. Abdülmecit was also well-versed in Ottoman Islamic culture: his mother, Bezmiâlem, a formidable lady, had a great influence on his upbringing and may have encouraged him to follow the reformist (*müceddidî*) Naqshbandi teaching of her Sufi spiritual adviser.

When Abdülmecit succeeded to the throne upon his father's death on 1 July 1839 at age seventeen, the empire was in a crisis, her army defeated, and her navy surrendered to the rebellious governor of Egypt, Muhammad Ali Pasha. The conflict was resolved only by the intervention of the great powers and their imposition of a settlement to define the position of Muhammad Ali Pasha as hereditary viceroy and to limit his territories. Henceforth Ottoman government was forced to recognize that the empire's internal affairs were to remain a concern for the Concert of Europe.

Within a few months of his accession, Abdülmecit brought to power a group of young reformist ministers, who seem to have been motivated as much by the ideals of the Naqshbandi movement as by a strong commitment to Europeanization. The leader of this group, Mustafa Reşid Pasha, prepared and publicly proclaimed, in the form of an imperial decree, the TANZIMAT reform program, limiting the sultan's arbitrary power and setting forth principles of fiscal, military, and religious reorganization. The young sultan stood fast to this program and left political power in the hands of Mustafa Reşid Pasha and others of similar conviction, though factionalism among ministers continued among reformists as well.

The Crimean War (1853–56) illustrates Great Power involvement in Ottoman affairs; it was also the occasion for Ottoman borrowing from European capital markets for military expenditures. These loans, obtained at unfavorable rates, were also spent on Abdülmecit's new and totally European-style palace, Dolmabahçe, and other features of material Europeanization, economically unproductive while symbolically significant. British and French alliance with the Ottomans during the Crimean War was promoted in Europe as aiding valiant Ottoman attempts at westernization, and Queen Victoria made Abdülmecit an honorary knight of the Garter, while the sultan proclaimed a second reform decree (Islahat) to promote equality for his non-Muslim subjects as requested by his allies at the conclusion of the war. In the longer run, however, foreign loans led to bankruptcy and submission to European financial domination.

Though leaving government to his ministers, Abdülmecit did take an interest in the course of reforms in his domains, visiting new military and civilian projects and touring some provinces. Hailed abroad as a sensitive and intelligent ruler, his program was less popular among his Muslim subjects, who perceived little immediate benefit but much greater political and economic foreign intervention helping non-Muslim Ottomans. Resentment broke out in violent risings in Jidda, Damascus, and Beirut in 1860, but they occasioned only greater European involvement. Nor were Tanzimat reforms sufficient to quell non-Muslim discontent in the Balkans.

Abdülmecit died young, of tuberculosis aggravated by a dissolute private life. His Muslim subjects looked to his vigorous brother and successor ABDÜLAZIZ to champion their rights. Among his many children were the last four sultans of the dynasty.

BIBLIOGRAPHY

ALDERSON, A. D. *The Structure of the Ottoman Dynasty.* Oxford, 1956.
DAVISON, RODERIC H. *Reform in the Ottoman Empire, 1856–1876.* Princeton, N.J., 1963.

I. Metin Kunt

Abdülmecit II [1868–1944]

Last Ottoman caliph.

The son of Sultan Abdülaziz, Abdülmecit II (also Abdülmecid) was known as a mild and scholarly man. He was elected caliph November 18, 1922, by the Grand National Assembly in Ankara, which, under the leadership of Mustafa Kemal (ATATÜRK), had abolished the Ottoman sultanate on November 1. As caliph, Abdülmecit encouraged the loyalty of Muslims in Turkey and elsewhere, particularly India. His growing influence was seen as a threat to the new

Turkish republic, and on March 3, 1924, the assembly abolished the Ottoman caliphate and sent Abdülmecit into exile aboard the Orient Express.

BIBLIOGRAPHY

LEWIS, BERNARD. *The Emergence of Modern Turkey.* New York, 1961.
SHAW, STANFORD J., and EZEL KURAL SHAW. *History of the Ottoman Empire and Modern Turkey.* Vol. 2. Cambridge, U.K., 1977.

Elizabeth Thompson

Ab Gusht

A popular Iranian meat-based stew.

Ab gusht (literally, water meat) is made of lamb, vegetables, and some seasoning. Although regional variations exist in the choice of ingredients, the standard variety today is made of lamb, dried chickpeas, white beans, and potato, with turmeric and dried lime for seasoning. The dish was not known under this name prior to the last decades of the nineteenth century. The most traditional type of ab gusht is *ab gusht-e dizi,* prepared in a clay pot (*dizi*) and cooked slowly over an open fire.

BIBLIOGRAPHY

RAMAZANI, N., et al. "Āb-Gŭšt." *Encyclopaedia Iranica,* vol. 1. London, 1985, pp. 47–48.

Neguin Yavari

Abha

Medium-sized city in the highlands of southwestern Saudi Arabia.

Occupied by Ottoman forces in 1871, Abha came briefly under the control of the local Al Ayid and al-Idrisi families. The city fell into Saudi hands in 1922 and was made the seat of the Saudi province of Asir in 1926.

John E. Peterson

Abidin, Dino   [1913–   ]

Turkish painter.

Dino Abidin was born in the Ottoman Empire but spent most of his life in Paris. He was one of the founders of the New Group, an artistic movement of the 1940s that favored socially conscious art, often exhibiting the life of laborers, villagers, and fishermen. Abidin's art is characterized by efforts to forge compromise between seemingly contradictory elements. In addition, Abidin is a prolific author of articles on subjects from philosophy to contemporary cinema.

BIBLIOGRAPHY

BASKAN, SEYFI. *Ondokuzuncu Yüzyıldan Günümüze Türk Ressamları.* Ankara, 1991.
RENDA, GÜNSEL. "Modern Trends in Turkish Painting." In *The Transformation of Turkish Culture: The Ataturk Legacy,* ed. by Günsel Renda and C. Max Kortepeter. Princeton, N.J., 1986.

David Waldner

Abi Shahla, Habib

Greek Orthodox politician in Lebanon.

Abi Shahla served in high government posts both before and after the independence of Lebanon. He is best known for his activities in November 1943, when the top government officials were arrested by French troops. At the time, Abi Shahla was minister of justice and national education as well as deputy prime minister. He assumed the prime ministership and helped rally public opinion against French mandate authorities.

Abi Shahla became the symbol of the Chamoun government, the temporary government that was established to assume the responsibilities that the French wanted to retain. Known for moderate views, he was associated with the Arab orientations of Riyad al-Sulh and Bishara al-KHURI. In the 1951 parliamentary election he received more than eleven thousand votes in the Beirut district. A city circle and a street in Beirut are named for him.

BIBLIOGRAPHY

AL-NAHAR. *Parliamentary Archives.*

As'ad AbuKhalil

Aboulker Family

An elite Jewish family in Algeria.

Descendants of Isaac ben Samuel I, a Spanish scholar, who came to Algiers via Italy after 1492, the Aboulker family (in Arabic, Abu al-Khayr) produced numerous rabbis and communal leaders. Rabbi Isaac ben Samuel II was one of six notables executed in 1815 for their opposition to the abuses of the dey's financier and courtier Joseph Baqri. Professor Henri (Samuel) Aboulker (1876–1957), son of Rabbi Isaac III, was a decorated war hero in World War I and a physician. In 1917, he founded the Algerian Committee for Social Studies (Comité juif algérien d'études sociales), a sort of antidefamation league to combat rampant *pied noir* ANTI-SEMITISM.

During World War II, he and other members of his family organized underground resistance to the Vichy Government after the fall of France to Germany. His son José (1920–   ) led two hundred fellow students and discharged army officers, including several other members of the family, in a bold putsch that paralyzed communications and captured strategic points in Algiers on November 7/8, 1942, the night Allied forces landed in French North Africa under General Dwight D. Eisenhower.

BIBLIOGRAPHY

STILLMAN, NORMAN A. *The Jews of Arab Lands in Modern Times.* Philadelphia, 1991.

Norman Stillman

Abovian, Khachatur   [1809–1848?]

Armenian author and educator.

Abovian was born in Kanaker, a village in the vicinity of Erevan (later Yerevan), which at the time was the seat of an Iranian khanate. He was a student at the Echmiadsin seminary and continued his education at the Nersesian Academy in Tbilisi. Abovian witnessed the conquest of the province of Erevan by Russian troops in 1828. The following year found him serving as secretary and translator at the Catholicosate of Echmiadsin. He also acted as guide and interpreter for Professor Friedrich Parrot of the University of Dorpat when the latter made a scientific expedition to the area and scaled the peak of Mount Ararat in 1829. Impressed by the young man's abilities, Parrot arranged for Abovian to attend the University of Dorpat, thus making him the first Armenian known to have reached the summit of the "sacred" mountain of the Armenians as well as the first Armenian known to have attended a European university, at least in the Russian Empire. Exposed to German and French Enlightenment literature, Abovian devoted himself to writing and educating upon his return to the Caucasus in 1836. He was not, however, well-received by the Armenian clergy who

were responsible for education in the region, and most of his writing never saw the light during his lifetime. He vanished in 1848. Speculation on his disappearance has included the suggestion of suicide for his chagrin at the rejection by an Armenian society unprepared yet to listen to his advocation of modern education, while another theory advanced the notion of a secret arrest and banishment by czarist police for espousing seemingly radical ideas at a time of revolutionary ferment elsewhere in Europe.

Abovian wrote pedagogical works and poetry, and prepared translations of Enlightenment writers. He is best remembered, however, as the author of the first Armenian novel, *Verk Hayastani* (The Wounds of Armenia), written in 1841. It was published in 1858, ten years after his disappearance. *Verk Hayastani* is also regarded as the primary example of Armenian patriotic literature wherein the virtues of national self-esteem are lauded and the price for the submission to foreign rule is critiqued. To convey his ideas and his message to fellow Armenians, Abovian also became the first figure in Armenian literature to write most of his oeuvre in the vernacular. With his efforts then begins the cultivation of the eastern Armenian dialect as a literary language, a matter of considerable historical significance and not just from the standpoint of cultural modernization. The emergence of an Armenian state in eastern Armenia resulted in the formalization of this dialect as the state language of the Armenian Republic. Abovian today is celebrated as a major figure in Armenian culture, with schools, streets, a town, and even an entire district of Armenia named after him.

Rouben P. Adalian

Abu

Form of the Arabic word "Ab" (father).

"Abu" is the form which designates the following word as a possession, state, or property. In some cases "Abu," followed by a name, is used to distinguish between brothers, while in others a man is called after his son. Arab masculine names compounded with "Abu" are sometimes abbreviated to "Bu."

Cyrus Moshaver

Abu Alaa

See Qurai, Ahmad Sulaiman

Abu al-Timman, Ja'far   [1881–1945]

Iraqi nationalist leader.

Ja'far Abu al-Timman was born in Baghdad to a rich Shiite merchant family. He contributed generously to support troops of the Ottoman Empire who were fighting the British occupation of Iraq during World War I. After the war, he was instrumental in organizing the 1920 Iraqi armed uprising against the British, who had created for themselves a mandate through the League of Nations. By 1922, the British recognized IRAQ as a kingdom, under their nominee for king, FAISAL I IBN HUSAYN, but they continued controlling the country. They ended the mandate in 1932, and Iraq was then admitted into the League of Nations. A treaty of alliance, however, had been signed between the two countries in 1930.

Throughout his life, Abu al-Timman focused on two main goals: (1) forging a national union between the two largest Islamic communities, the Sunni and the Shi'ite; (2) struggling to end British control. Upon his formation of the National party in 1922, the British authorities exiled him to the island of Henjam in the Persian/Arabian Gulf for a year. In 1928, during the early years of the kingdom, he was elected a deputy of Baghdad in Iraq's parliament. He and the majority in the National party boycotted the elections of both 1930 and 1933, objecting to the abuse of the democratic process by the governments in power. Abu al-Timman halted his political activities from 1933 to 1935; in late 1935, he started publishing the newspaper *al-Mabda* (The Principle) and allied himself with the leftist group called *al-*AHALI (The People's Group). From 1935 to 1939 he served as president of Baghdad's Chamber of Commerce and encouraged national industry as a way toward national independence. He supported the military coup led by Bakr SIDQI in October 1936 and served as minister of finance in the coup cabinet formed by Hikmat SULAYMAN. He worked for an egalitarian policy and for a larger role for the state in the economy of Iraq. Political infighting prompted him to resign this post in June 1937.

World War II began in 1939. In 1941, he supported the coup led by pro-Axis Premier Rashid Ali al-KAYLANI, which attempted unsuccessfully to end the British presence in Iraq (based on the 1930 treaty of alliance).

BIBLIOGRAPHY

BATATU, HANNA. *The Old Social Classes and Revolutionary Movements of Iraq: A Study of Iraq's Old Landed and Commercial Classes and Its Communists, Ba'thists, and Free Officers.* Princeton, N.J., 1978.

Mahmoud Haddad

Abu Amar

See Arafat, Yasir

Abu Asaf, Amin

Syrian military officer.

Of Druze heritage, Amin Abu Asaf commanded the First Armored Brigade of the Syrian army with Captain Fadlallah Abu Mansur. The two leaders were instrumental in carrying out the August 14, 1949, coup against President Husni al-ZA'IM. Colonel Abu Asaf was also involved in overthrowing the authoritarian ruler Adib SHISHAKLI in 1954.

BIBLIOGRAPHY

SEALE, PATRICK. *The Struggle for Syria: A Study of Post-War Arab Politics, 1945–1958.* London, 1958.

Charles U. Zenzie

Abu Da'ud   [1937–   ]

Palestine Liberation Organization (PLO) commando leader in Jordan and member of Fath.

Abu Da'ud (also Muhammad Daud Mahmud Audeh) was one of FATH's main military commanders during the Jordanian Civil War, the showdown with Jordanian forces that started in Amman in September 1970 and ended in the battle of AJLUN in April 1971. He was captured and tried in Jordan in February 1972, allegedly telling interrogators that there was no such organization as BLACK SEPTEMBER, a group he helped organize. He further said that it was a name used by Fath when it did not want to appear as the direct executor of a particular operation. Abu Da'ud was sentenced to death, but his sentence was commuted by King Hussein ibn Talal in 1973 to life imprisonment. He was released in 1979 when relations between Jordan and the PLO were resumed. He is reported to have been shot and wounded soon after his release but has not appeared in public since.

BIBLIOGRAPHY

LIVINGSTONE, NEIL C., and DAVID HALEVY. *Inside the PLO.* New York, 1990.

Jenab Tutunji

Abu Dhabi

The largest, wealthiest, and most powerful of the seven shaykhdoms that make up the United Arab Emirates (UAE).

Abu Dhabi's 28,000 square miles (72,500 sq km) make up 87 percent of the federation's area. It is mostly an eastward extension of the great RUB AL-KHALI (Empty Quarter); the coastal areas comprise a sandy plain and large salt flats called *sabkhas* (Arabic, *sabakh*; pl., *sibakh*). Abu Dhabi's 250 miles (400 km) of coastline slope at a very slight gradient, with extremely shallow water extending well out into the Persian/Arabian Gulf. Numerous islands dot the coast, including the one occupied by Abu Dhabi City, the capital of the emirate and the federation. The name Abu Dhabi (father of the gazelle) is derived from the island's shape. The summer weather is harsh, with temperatures reaching over 120°F (49°C) in the interior, and high humidity combined with only slightly lower temperatures on the coast. Winters are mild and pleasant. In the eastern part of the emirate, rainfall runoff from the Hajar Mountains has created the al-AYN oasis, and to the west, slight rainfall collects in depressions to create the arc of oases called al-LIWA. Abu Dhabi possesses 90 percent of the UAE's approximately 100 billion barrels of oil reserves and 60 percent of its significant gas reserves. The emirate's population of 798,000 (1991 official estimate), virtually all of it in the capital city of Abu Dhabi and al-Ayn, is about 42 percent of the UAE's

The palace and garden at al-Ayn oasis in Abu Dhabi. (D.W. Lockhard)

total. At least 80 percent are expatriate workers and their dependents, the great majority from South Asia.

The history of Abu Dhabi is largely that of the BANU YAS tribal confederation and its leading clan, the al-NAHAYYAN. From their early seat of power in al-Liwa, they expanded to the coast in the seventeenth and eighteenth centuries, settling in 1761 on Abu Dhabi Island, which became their capital in 1790. Thus Abu Dhabi had become a maritime power by the early nineteenth century, when the British intervened against the naval power of their Qawasim rivals in SHARJA and RA'S AL-KHAYMA and instituted a maritime peace. The largely land-based

The al-Ayn oasis in Abu Dhabi as viewed from a hotel window, 1972. (D.W. Lockhard)

View of the city of Abu Dhabi, 1982. (Richard Bulliet)

Banu Yas were the principal beneficiaries of the new situation in the lower Gulf and, under the strong leadership of Zayid the Great in the late nineteenth and early twentieth centuries, consolidated their pre-eminent position there. In the interior, control of the al-Ayn area was contested with the Saudis through much of the nineteenth century and again in the twentieth. In 1833 the Al Bu Falasa group of the Banu Yas seceded to establish its own shaykhdom in DUBAI. A keen rivalry still exists between the two emirates.

In 1966 Zayid ibn Sultan al-NAHAYYAN seized power from his brother, Shakhbut, in a bloodless coup and initiated the rapid creation of a welfare state with one of the highest per capita incomes in the world. Following the 1968 British announcement of impending withdrawal of military and political protection, Shaykh Zayid worked with his rival, Dubai's ruler, Shaykh Rashid ibn Sa'id al-MAKTUM, to launch the United Arab Emirates as an independent federal union in 1971. Zayid has served since then as president, using Abu Dhabi's wealth to promote the economic development of the poorer emirates.

BIBLIOGRAPHY

PECK, MALCOLM C. *The United Arab Emirates: A Venture in Unity.* Boulder, Colo., 1986.
ZAHLAN, ROSEMARIE SAID. *The Origins of the United Arab Emirates: A Political and Social History of the Trucial States.* London, 1978.

Malcolm C. Peck

Abu Dhabi National Oil Company

Firm that controls and coordinates Abu Dhabi's state oil investments.

The Abu Dhabi National Oil Company (ADNOC) was established in November 1971. Its initial holdings were acquired through "participation," a phased-in nationalization plan developed by the ORGANIZATION OF PETROLEUM EXPORTING COUNTRIES in the early 1970s that enabled member countries to purchase equity in the operating companies producing oil and gas within their territories. ADNOC also took over the domestic marketing of petroleum products, and acquired additional downstream interests in refining, gas liquefaction, and petrochemicals manufacturing, as well as upstream investments in exploration and drilling. ADNOC has discovered new oil and natural gas reserves. It markets crude oil and products of its own refineries to customers around the world.

[*See also:* Natural Gas; Petrochemicals; Petroleum, Oil, and Natural Gas.]

BIBLIOGRAPHY

Middle East Economic Survey. Nicosia, Cyprus.
ORGANIZATION OF PETROLEUM EXPORTING COUNTRIES. *OPEC Member Country Profiles.* Vienna, 1980.
SKEET, IAN. *OPEC: Twenty-five Years of Prices and Politics.* New York, 1988.

Mary Ann Tétreault

Abu Fadel, Munir   [1912?–   ]

Lebanese politician and soldier.

A Greek Orthodox, born in Ein Enoub, Abu Fadel earned degrees from the National College in Choueifat and the law school of Jerusalem. He fought against the Vichy French forces in 1941 and held a command under the Arab Higher Committee during the 1948 Arab–Israel War. Elected to the Lebanese parliament from Aley for four terms beginning in 1957, Abu Fadel served as vice-speaker of the chamber of deputies from July 1960 to February 1964, and again from October 1968 to October 1969.

BIBLIOGRAPHY

International Who's Who of the Arab World. London, 1978.

Mark Mechler

Abuhatzeira, Aharon   [1938–   ]

Israeli politician, member of the Knesset.

Born in Morocco, Abuhatzeira was elected to the KNESSET (Israel's parliament) in 1974 and 1977 as a NATIONAL RELIGIOUS PARTY member and served as minister of religious affairs in the first government of Menachem Begin. In 1981, he founded and chaired TAMI, a party identified with Israel's Moroccan community. He was elected to the Knesset with TAMI in 1981 and 1984. He subsequently joined the LIKUD and served as minister of labor, welfare and absorption.

Martin Malin

Abu Himara

Arabic for "the man on the she-ass," a nickname of the leader of the 1902–1909 Moroccan rebellion that helped discredit the governments of the sultans Abd al-Aziz and his successor Abd al-Hafid.

Jilali ibn Idris al-Yusufi al-Zarhuni, the real name of the leader of the rebellion, was a minor Moroccan official and former engineering student with a talent for mimicry and some skills as a thaumaturge. Following a 1902 incident, he declared himself to be the MAHDI (legendary imam who returned to restore justice) and launched a rebellion among the tribes to the northeast of FEZ. Subsequently he declared himself to be the sultan's elder brother Muhammad, a claim which, although false, was generally accepted by his supporters.

Between 1902 and his eventual defeat in 1909 Abu Himara (also called Bu or Bou Hmara) ruled much of northeastern Morocco from his base at Salwan, near Mellila. His rebellion derailed a 1901 British-sponsored reform program, and opened the way for the French colonial offensive. The inability of Sultan ABD AL-AZIZ and his successor, ABD AL-HAFID, to defeat him played a significant role in the MOROCCAN QUESTION.

His unusual sobriquet derives from a precolonial Moroccan tradition, according to which recaptured army deserters would be paraded around camp mounted sitting backwards on a she-ass, to the jeers of the troops. The cultural referent is obscure, but may be a satiric inversion of the Maghrebi (North African) tradition that states that the *mahdi* would appear from the west, mounted on a she-ass.

BIBLIOGRAPHY

BURKE, EDMUND, III. *Prelude to Protectorate in Morocco: Precolonial Protest and Resistance, 1860–1912.* Chicago, 1976.
DUNN, ROSS E. "The Bu Himara Rebellion in Northeast Morocco: Phase I." *Middle Eastern Studies* 17 (1981): 31–48.
MALDONADO, EDUARDO. *El Roghi.* Tetuan, 1952.

Edmund Burke III

Abu Iyad

See Khalaf, Salah

Abu Jihad

See Wazir, Khalil al-

Abulafia, Hayyim Nissim   [1775–1861]

Chief rabbi of Jerusalem and Palestine.

Abulafia was born in Tiberias, Palestine, then a province of the Ottoman Empire. He succeeded his father as the leader of the Jews of Tiberias but then became chief rabbi of Damascus (now capital of Syria). After moving to Jerusalem, where a community of Jewish scholars lived and worked, he helped protect the Jews of Palestine during the chaotic years of Ottoman rule that followed the defeat in 1840 of IBRAHIM PASHA (son of Muhammad Ali Pasha of Egypt), who had captured Jerusalem in an effort to break with the Ottoman state. In 1854, Abulafia was elected chief rabbi of Jerusalem.

BIBLIOGRAPHY

Encyclopedia Judaica. New York, 1971.

Zachary Karabell

Abulafia, Itzhaq Moshe   [c. 1830–1909]

Important Jewish religious leader during the Ottoman Empire.

Born in Tiberius, Palestine, into a distinguished family of rabbis, Abulafia was one of the leading rabbinic authorities in the Levant provinces of the OTTOMAN EMPIRE during the nineteenth century. He served as the head of the Rabbinic Tribunal of Damascus from about 1877. He was also the official chief rabbi (*haham bashi*) of Damascus and of the Ottoman province of Damascus (now Syria). He later served in Tyre, moved to Jerusalem, and then back to Tiberius, where he died.

BIBLIOGRAPHY

ZOHAR, ZVI. "Twentieth-Century Rabbinate-Karaite Intermarriage." In *The Jews of Egypt: A Mediterranean Society in Modern Times,* ed. by Shimon Shamir. Boulder, Colo., 1987.

David Waldner

Abu Lutf

See Qaddumi, Faruq

Abu Mansur, Fadlallah

Syrian military officer and politician.

Of Druze descent, Fadlallah Abu Mansur was a member of the Syrian National Social party (PPS) and a devoted follower of its founder, Antun Sa'ada. Co-leader of the First Armored Brigade, Captain Abu Mansur not only carried out the August 1949 coup against Husni al-ZA'IM but was the first in the president's house to confront and charge Za'im of betraying Sa'ada—and actually pulled the trigger on the president. He subsequently wrote a detailed account of the events. He was also involved in a 1952 plot against Adib SHISHAKLI.

BIBLIOGRAPHY

SEALE, PATRICK. The Struggle for Syria: A Study of Post-War Arab Politics, 1945–1958. London, 1958.

Charles U. Zenzie

Abu Mazin

See Abbas, Mahmud

Abu Musa Island

Small island at the entrance to the Gulf, belonging to Sharja.

At the entrance to the Gulf are two small islands—Abu Musa and Sirri. Abu Musa is nearer to Sharja, now part of the United Arab Emirates, than it is to Lingeh in Iran (formerly Persia).

At the end of the nineteenth century, the issue of sovereignty over the islands caused a dispute between Sharja and Persia; it began when Persia occupied the island of Sirri in 1887.

In 1906, when the ruler of Sharja granted a concession to a German company for the red-oxide deposits, Britain objected and the ruler canceled it. Britain had exercised a protectorate over the Gulf region since the nineteenth century but withdrew in 1971. At that time, Sharja signed an ambiguous agreement with Iran permitting the stationing of Iranian troops on the island. Neither party acknowledged the other's title but agreed to divide the income from any petroleum that was discovered. The United Arab Emirates and the other Arab states condemned Iranian occupation of half of Abu Musa on November 30, 1971, the last day of the British protectorate in the Gulf.

BIBLIOGRAPHY

ABDULLAH, M. MORSY. The United Arab Emirates. London and New York, 1978.
KELLY, J. B. Britain and the Persian Gulf. London, 1968.

M. Morsy Abdullah

Abu Naddara

See Sanu, Ya'qub

Abu Nidal

See Banna, Sabri al-

Abu Nuwwar, Ali   [1925–1991]

Chief of staff of the Jordanian Arab army and leader of pro-Egyptian and pro-Ba'thist officers who conspired to overthrow King Hussein in April 1957.

Although it was unclear at first that Ali Abu Nuwwar was involved, his leadership role in the conspiracy to overthrow Jordan's King HUSSEIN IBN TALAL emerged when a loyal officer gained access to the king and informed him of Abu Nuwwar's plot. Abu Nuwwar had been the king's protégé when he was appointed chief of staff of the force that replaced the British-led ARAB LEGION. This was two months after the legion's commander, General Sir John Bagot Glubb, had been expelled from Jordan on March 2, 1956. The attempted coup occurred at the same time that Sulayman al-NABULSI, who was prime minister at the head of a leftist cabinet, was purging government officials loyal to the king. As a result, suspicions arose that Abu Nuwwar and Nabulsi were coconspirators, although both denied this. Abu Nuwwar was not tried for his actions but was allowed to flee to Syria. He remained in self-imposed exile in Egypt and was eventually pardoned by the king.

BIBLIOGRAPHY

DANN, URIEL. King Hussein and the Challenge of Arab Radicalism: Jordan, 1955–1967. New York, 1989.
GUBSER, PETER. Jordan: Crossroads of Middle Eastern Events. Boulder, Colo., 1983.
MADI, MUNIB, and SULAYMAN MUSA. Tarikh al-Urdun fi al-qarn al-'ishrin, 1900–1959. Amman, 1988.

Jenab Tutunji

Abu Qir, Battle of

Naval battle in which the English destroyed the French fleet in Egyptian waters.

Abu Qir is a bay located between the Rosetta branch of the Nile River and Alexandria, Egypt. After capturing the island of Malta in the Mediterranean Sea in April 1798, the fleet of Napoléon, then commander of the army of France, avoided the swifter fleet of Britain, commanded by Admiral Horatio Nelson. After French troops landed in Alexandria on July 1, 1798, the French fleet took shelter in Abu Qir bay. On August 1, Nelson's fleet located and destroyed the French fleet.

BIBLIOGRAPHY

GOLDSCHMIDT, ARTHUR, JR. *Modern Egypt: The Formation of a Nation-State.* Boulder, Colo., 1988, p. 15.

David Waldner

Abu Risha, Umar

Syrian poet.

One of the most influential literary figures in the Arab world, Umar Abu Risha was born in Aleppo. He studied at the American University of Beirut. He held several senior positions, including director of the National Library in Aleppo and ambassador of Syria to Brazil, India, and the United States. His literary talent earned him numerous orders of merit from Syria, Brazil, Argentina, Lebanon, and Vienna. Abu Risha's exquisite poetry echoes the beauty of nature and expresses a passion for freedom.

Muhammad Muslih

Abu Safa

Offshore oil field located between Bahrain and Saudi Arabia, which extends below waters claimed by Bahrain.

In the late 1960s, Bahrain and Saudi Arabia agreed to share PETROLEUM production and revenues from Abu Safa, which began operating in 1966. By the mid-1970s, Bahrain's income from the oil field amounted to some 50 percent of its revenues. Abu Safa's production has been steadily decreasing in recent years.

BIBLIOGRAPHY

The Middle East and North Africa, 1991, 37th ed. London, 1991.

Emile A. Nakhleh

Abu Sa'id

See Hasan, Khalid al-

Abu Simbel

Ancient Egyptian temple complex along the Nile.

Located about 175 miles (280 km) south of Aswan, Egypt, are two temples that were cut into the rock of the cliff along the NILE river during the reign of Ramses II (c. 1250 B.C.E.). They were discovered by

Pharaonic Temple at Abu Simbel. (Laura Mendelson and David Rewcastle)

Europeans in 1812 and opened for viewing in 1817. The large temple was dedicated to Amun-Re of Thebes, the main god of Upper Egypt, and to the sun god Re-Harakhty of Heliopolis, the main god of Lower Egypt. The smaller temple was dedicated to the goddess Hathor. Ramses II's favorite wife, Nefertari, was also deified here.

When the ASWAN HIGH DAM was planned for the Nile, it was known that the enormous reservoir created would flood the sites. UNESCO (the United Nations Educational, Scientific, and Cultural Organization) mounted an operation to move them to safety, to the top of the cliff overlooking what would become Lake NASSER. From 1964 to 1966, the four colossal figures of the larger temple (over 65 feet [6 m] high) were cut apart and reassembled before the dam began flooding the area; the temples are underwater, however, since there was not enough time to complete the enormous project. International archeological survey teams worked along the two banks of the Nile, from 1960 to 1966, to map and excavate any other ancient remains that would also be flooded.

BIBLIOGRAPHY

Baedeker's Egypt. New York, 1987.

David Waldner

Abyan Development Board

Administrative body for an agricultural project in South Yemen.

The agricultural project was located in Abyan, the fertile coastal delta in South Yemen, twenty-five miles (40 km) northeast of ADEN. Developed by the British during World War II to grow cereals for Aden, the project was used after the war for the cultivation of highly prized long-staple cotton.

Robert D. Burrowes

Accari, Nazim   [1902–?]

Lebanese politician.

Educated at the Ottoman school in his birthplace, Beirut, Accari entered politics in 1932 and, from 1939 to 1943, served as governor of Zahleh. From 1943 to 1971 Accari was director, then secretary-general, of the council of ministers. During that time he also briefly held posts as interior minister and foreign affairs minister.

BIBLIOGRAPHY

Who's Who of Lebanon, 1977–1978. Beirut, 1977.

Mark Mechler

Acheson, Dean   [1893–1971]

U.S. statesman.

As undersecretary of state (1945–1947), Acheson was one of the main proponents of the Truman Doctrine (1947), aiding Greece and Turkey. He is often associated with the U.S. containment policy for communism and promoted the foundation of NATO (1949). As secretary of state (1949–1953), he was concerned primarily with the USSR and Korea, although he had been involved in the early negotiations with Iran's prime minister (1951–1953) Mohammad Mossadegh. He won a Pulitzer Prize in 1969 for *Present at the Creation.*

BIBLIOGRAPHY

FINDLING, JOHN, ed. *Dictionary of American Diplomatic History.* New York, 1989.
SPIEGEL, STEVEN. *The Other Arab–Israeli Conflict.* Chicago, 1985.

Zachary Karabell

Achille Lauro

Ship commandeered by Palestinian terrorists.

On October 7, 1985, the Italian cruise ship *Achille Lauro* was seized off the coast of Egypt by four mem-

bers of the Palestine Liberation Front (PLF), who murdered a crippled American passenger, Leon Klinghoffer. Egypt's government convinced them to end the two-day standoff and fly to Tunisia; U.S. military jets intercepted the plane and forced it to land in Italy, whereupon the terrorists were imprisoned. Italian authorities, however, released PLF leader Muhammad Abu al-Abbas, who had been involved in the planning of the seizure.

Michael R. Fischbach

Achour, Habib   [1913–   ]

Tunisian labor leader.

A native of the Kerkenna islands, off the coast of central Tunisia, Achour (also called Ashur) founded the Tunisian General Labor Union, which merged with the General Union of Tunisian Workers (Union Générale des Travailleurs Tunisiens, UGTT) in 1957. His appointment to the political bureau of the DESTOUR PARTY (PSD) in 1964 reflected broad cooperation between the union and the PSD. In the mid-1970s, this cooperation gave way to tension as the union leadership grew critical of state policies. In January 1978, Achour resigned from the bureau and, following the events of BLACK THURSDAY, he and other leaders of the UGTT were arrested. Achour was pardoned by Tunisian President Habib BOURGUIBA in 1981 and elected president of the union, a newly created post. In 1984, in a successful power play, he wrested control of the post of secretary-general. The next year, with tensions high between the union and the government of Mohammed Mzali, Achour and other labor leaders were again imprisoned.

BIBLIOGRAPHY

PERKINS, KENNETH. *Tunisia: Crossroads of the Islamic and European Worlds.* Boulder, Colo., 1986.
TOUMI, MOHSEN. *Tunisie: Pouvoirs et luttes.* Paris, 1978.
Tunisia: A Country Survey. Washington, D.C., 1988.

Matthew S. Gordon

Adalat-Khaneh

Iran's ministry of justice, founded in 1927.

In Persia, judicial reform began during the ministry of Mirza Taqi Khan AMIR KABIR, 1848–1852, and was revived during the ministry of Mirza Hoseyn Khan, 1870–1873, but none had any lasting effect. Persia had two types of judicial law: religious laws, those of the *Shari'a,* based on the Qur'an and dispensed by the *ulama* (the body of mullahs); and the law of *urf* (common law), based on practice, which was neither written nor uniformly applied. Not only was the administration of justice chaotic, but the common people had little recourse to it. Many nineteenth-century Persian reformers had pointed to the need for state law (*qanun*), but all efforts had been unsuccessful.

In 1904, when groups of dissatisfied merchants and ulama took *bast* (sanctuary) in the shrine of Shah Abd al-Azim, one of the major demands was for a House of Justice (Adalat-Khaneh or Edalat Khaneh). The shah, MOZAFFAR AL-DIN, accepted their demands but no action was taken. In 1906, demonstrations began—taking the life of a religious student, followed by the exodus of the ulama to Qom and the bast of many merchants at the British embassy.

The demand for a House of Justice was overshadowed by the fundamental need for a national constituent assembly, a *majles-e shura-ye melli*. After the MAJLES was constituted, people still addressed their representatives with their complaints for law and demands for justice, so they announced that the majles was not a house of justice but an assembly for the making of laws. Complaints were directed to the ministry of interior. The need for judicial reform and the organization of a ministry of justice were pursued, and in 1907, provisions were made for them in the Supplementary Fundamental Laws. This process took some time and many attempts before a modern ministry of justice was founded in 1927, during the reign of Iran's new ruler, Reza Shah PAHLAVI.

BIBLIOGRAPHY

BROWNE, E. G. *The Persian Revolution, 1905–1909.* Cambridge, 1910.
FLOOR, M. "Change and Development in the Judicial System of Qajar Iran, 1800–1925." In *Qajar Iran, 1800–1925: Political, Social, and Cultural Change,* ed. by C. E. Bosworth and C. Hillenbrand. Edinburgh, 1983.

Mansoureh Ettehadieh

Adalat Party

An Iranian political party that unsuccessfully planned a Communist takeover of Iran.

The Adalat party was established in Iran by veteran Social Democrats, sympathetic to the Russian Bolsheviks, almost immediately after the Russian Revolution of 1917. The leadership of the party consisted mainly of Iranian intellectuals from Azerbaijan who were closely tied to the Bolsheviks. The Adalat founded a bilingual Azeri-Persian newspaper called *Hürriyet* (or Freedom) and was very active among the Iranian workers in the Baku oilfields. The party's membership, according to the party's own estimate, was primarily composed of workers and apprentices, but also included office employees, craftsmen, and tradesmen. After its first major congress at Baku in June 1920, the party changed its name to the Communist Party of Iran (Firqeh-ye Komunist-e Iran) and created a program that included land reforms, formation of trade unions, and self-determination for minorities. Clergymen, landowners, and merchants were barred from its ranks. Most importantly, together with the JANGALI in Gilan, the party announced the formation of a Soviet Socialist Republic of Iran, based in Rasht. By the end of 1920, the party, together with the Red Army, was preparing a march into Tehran. The activities of the party at this time greatly contributed to the crisis that paved the way for the emergence of Colonel Reza Khan, who became Iran's ruler as Reza Shah PAHLAVI and founded the Pahlavi dynasty.

BIBLIOGRAPHY

ABRAHAMIAN, E. *Iran between Two Revolutions.* Princeton, N.J., 1982.

Parvaneh Pourshariati

Adamiyat, Abbasquli [1861–1939]

A pioneer of the constitutional and freedom movement in Iran.

Mirza Abbasquli Khan Qazvini, later surnamed Adamiyat (humanity), was born in Qazvin, Persia. His political activism started about 1885, in cooperation with Mirza MALKOM KHAN and Mirza Yousuf Khan Mostashar al-Dowleh. He was involved in the publication of the underground *Qanun* (Law) that was sent to his country from Europe, and he was one of the organizers of the Society of Humanity (Majma-el Adamiyat). The society was the organizational expression of liberal and humanist throught in turn-of-the-century Iran; it fought for the formation of a parliamentary government (which was actually drawn up in 1906—but political events intervened until the CONSTITUTIONAL REVOLUTION of 1909).

Adamiyat is the author of several articles, including "Precept of the Human Being" (Farizeh-ye Adam) and "The Sound of Awakening" (Bung-i Bidari).

BIBLIOGRAPHY

ADAMIYAT, FEREYDOUN. *Fikr-i azadi va mogaddameh-ye nahzat-i mashrutiyat-i Iran* (The Idea of Freedom and the

Beginnings of the Constitutional Movement in Iran). Tehran, 1961.

KERMANI, NAZIM ABU-ISLAM. *Tarikh-i bidari-ye Iranian* (History of the Awakening of the Iranians). Tehran, 1967.

Mansoor Moaddel

Adamiyat, Fereydun   [1920–   ]

A leading social historian of contemporary Iran.

Fereydoun was born in Tehran in 1920; he is the son of Abbasquli ADAMIYAT, a pioneer of the constitutional movement. Fereydun Adamiyat received his B.A. from the University of Tehran and his Ph.D. in diplomatic history from the University of London. He is known for his original works on various aspects of the social and political history of Persia (Iran from 1935), most of them dealing with the ideological foundations of the CONSTITUTIONAL REVOLUTION— the movement and reform in turn-of-the-century Persia. Although predominantly published in Persian, he is often cited by Western academicians. Adamiyat has also been a diplomat and has served, *inter alia,* as Iran's ambassador to the Netherlands and India. He has worked as well for the United Nations in various capacities.

Mansoor Moaddel

Adana

Capital of Adana province, Turkey.

Adana is the leading COTTON, cotton-textile, and citrus-producing region of Turkey. Known since Hittite times, it was a minor town until the U.S. Civil War (1861–1865), when worldwide cotton shortages induced a boom in Adana's region. Nearby Incirlik Air Base is the largest NATO facility in the eastern Mediterranean. Adana's 1990 population was 931,555; the province's was 1,945,565.

BIBLIOGRAPHY

Yearbook of the Province of Adana. Adana, 1968.

John R. Clark

Adana Conference

Meeting of Turkish president and British prime minister, 1943.

During World War II, Turkey was faced with a dilemma; for reasons of security, it remained officially neutral for much of the war, but its sympathies lay with the Allies. In the early stages of the war, Turkey stayed out of the conflict and even signed a nonaggression pact with Germany (1941), to forestall a German attack. However, Turkish neutrality was assailed by the USSR as opportunistic and hypocritical.

On January 30 and 31, 1943, Britain's Prime Minister Winston Churchill met with Turkey's President Ismet İNÖNÜ in Adana, Turkey. Churchill assured İnönü that the Allies, under the Anglo-Turkish agreement of 1939, would continue to guarantee Turkish security. In addition, Churchill agreed to supply Turkey with supplies necessary for self-defense; henceforth, Turkey was eligible for the U.S. LEND–LEASE PROGRAM and received significant amounts of such aid until 1945. Although Churchill did not extract any binding commitment from İnönü, he was assured that Turkey would do all it could to aid the Allies without violating its neutrality.

BIBLIOGRAPHY

SHAW, STANFORD, and EZEL KURAL SHAW. *History of the Ottoman Empire and Modern Turkey.* New York, 1977.

Zachary Karabell

Aden

Seaport city in the Republic of Yemen.

Located on the southeastern tip of the Arabian peninsula, Aden is the second largest city in the Republic of Yemen and one of the best natural ports on the Arabian Sea. From 1829 to 1967, Aden was a British colony; from 1967 to 1990, it was the capital of the People's Democratic Republic of Yemen.

F. Gregory Gause, III

Aden Association

An organization that advocated the independence of Aden.

One of the first modern political organizations in South Yemen, the Aden Association called for the independence of the city of Aden within the British Commonwealth. The association was created in the early 1950s and led by the prominent family of Muhammad Ali LUQMAN. Its existence became moot when its call for the creation of a Singapore-like city-state ceased to be a viable political option by the late 1950s.

Robert D. Burrowes

Adenauer, Konrad   [1876–1967]

German statesman and first chancellor of the German Federal Republic (West Germany), 1949–1963.

Adenauer began his political career during the Weimar Republic, but was dismissed from his several political posts by the Nazis to live in seclusion until 1944—when he was sent to a concentration camp in a political purge. After the Allied occupation of a defeated Germany in 1945, Adenauer became a founder of the Christian Democratic Union—a supradenominational party aimed at a centrist position and a rebuilding of Germany in the Christian spirit. He became party leader (1946–1966), president of the parliamentary council (1949) that drafted the new constitution for the German Federal Republic (West Germany), and first chancellor (1949–1963). He tied his country to the Christian West, opposing the antireligious Communist USSR, and encouraged German business development away from political controls.

From 1953 to 1965, he oversaw collective indemnification to the State of Israel and the Jewish people for property stolen under the Nazi administration (1933–1945); he admitted Germany's guilt without pressure from the West, and his Federal Republic assumed responsibility for the crimes of the Third Reich. In Israel, reparations became controversial, since they were seen as a political means for Germany to rejoin the West—by buying off Jewish survivors. After a vote in the Knesset, Adenauer and Israel's Foreign Minister Moshe SHARETT signed the Reparations Agreement in 1952, but the threat of an Arab boycott kept the German government from approving the protocols until 1953. Until 1964, payment was made by Adenauer's government in goods and monies; the agreement was carried out fully and Israel's economy received a firm financial base for the development of water resources, a merchant fleet, and the mechanization of agriculture and industry.

BIBLIOGRAPHY

BALABKINS, N. *West German Reparations to Israel.* New Brunswick, N.J., 1971.

SAGI, NANA. *German Reparations: A History of the Negotiations.* New York, 1986.

Zachary Karabell

Adıvar, Abdulhak Adnan   [1881–1955]

Turkish doctor, historian, and writer.

Born in Gallipoli to a prominent family of Ottoman *ulama* (Islamic clergy), Adıvar graduated from the Imperial School of Medicine in 1905. Suspected of

working against the regime, he left for Europe and became an assistant at the Berlin Faculty of Medicine. Returning to Constantinople (now Istanbul) upon the restoration of the constitution, he taught at and became dean of the School of Medicine (1909–1911). He worked with the Red Crescent Society during the Tripoli War and with the Ottoman Department of Public Health in World War I, being credited with contributing substantially to the reorganization of both institutions.

At the armistice, Adıvar became a member of the last Ottoman parliament but avoided British arrest and deportation, escaping to Anatolia with his wife Halid Edip ADIVAR and becoming one of ATATÜRK's inner circle. During the war of independence, he served in various ministerial positions and was vice-president of the TURKISH GRAND NATIONAL ASSEMBLY. After the armistice, he served in the national government's delegation in Istanbul. He supported the short-lived Progressive Republican Party but was in Europe when news broke of a conspiracy against Atatürk (June 1926).

Tried in absentia for complicity, he was acquitted but chose to remain in exile until 1939, at first in England, then Paris, teaching at the Ecole des Langues Orientales and engaged in scholarly research and writing. Upon his return, Adıvar fostered the teaching and practice of science and was a founder and first president of the International Society for Oriental Research.

He directed publication of the Turkish edition of the *Encyclopaedia of Islam,* contributing its introduction and a number of articles. His other works include *La Science chez les Turks Ottomans* (Paris, 1939), a Turkish translation of Bertrand Russell's *Philosophical Matters* (1936), a two-volume work in Turkish on science and religion through history, and many essays and articles on cultural and scientific topics. He served a final period as deputy for Istanbul (1946–1950).

BIBLIOGRAPHY

SHAW, STANFORD J., and EZEL KURAL SHAW. *History of the Ottoman Empire and Modern Turkey,* vol. 2. Cambridge, U.K., 1977.

TOYNBEE, ARNOLD S. *Acquaintances.* London, 1967.

Kathleen R. F. Burrill

Adıvar, Halide Edip   [1884–1964]

Prolific Turkish author (best known as a novelist), journalist, pioneer feminist, nationalist, and educator.

Born in Constantinople (now Istanbul), Halide Edip Adıvar lost her mother early in life. Her father (a first secretary to the sultan's privy purse) remarried, and she spent much of her childhood in her maternal grandmother's traditional Muslim household, where she learned to read, write, and recite the Qur'an. She also came in touch with Christianity and learned Greek (attending a Greek-run kindergarten), and her Anglophile father provided her with English governesses and later with various private tutors. She had spent a year at the American College for Girls when she was eleven but withdrew on orders of the sultan. Reentering in 1899, she was the first Turk to graduate from the college (1901). The same year, she married one of her tutors, mathematician Salih Zeki. They had two sons but were divorced in 1910 when he took a second wife. She later married Dr. Abdülhak Adnan Adıvar.

Halide Edip Adıvar began writing at the time of the Second Constitution (1908), contributing articles to Tanin that urged educational and social reforms. Vulnerable as a progressive, she left the country during the 1909 counterrevolution. On her return, she taught for a while then served as inspector of schools under the Ministry of Religious Foundations. Believing in democracy and the social responsibilities of the educated toward the people at large, she was a member of the first Women's Club in Turkey, addressing protest meetings on the treatment of women, and was active in relief and nursing activities during the Balkan War. Like other prominent intellectuals, she fell under the influence of Ziya GÖKALP and participated in the activities of the Turkish Hearth Association, addressing public demonstrations after the Greek landing at İzmir in particular that of May 23, 1919, in Sultan Ahmed Square. First advocating an American mandate for Turkey, when the British started to deport members of the last Ottoman parliament to Malta, she and Adnan Adıvar escaped to Anatolia to join the nationalists (March 1920).

She played an important role during the war of independence in Ankara as one of ATATÜRK's inner circle and as "Corporal Halide" at the front. Disillusioned after the founding of the republic, she left Turkey with her husband (1926) and, apart from one short visit, returned only after Atatürk's death. She spent the intervening period mainly in London and Paris but also toured India and visited the United States to lecture. Back in Turkey, she held the chair of English language and literature at Istanbul University and served as deputy in the Grand National Assembly (1950–1954).

Halide Edip Adıvar's novels fall into three main categories: psychological novels, sagas of the war of independence, and panoramas of city life or period novels. She denied that she herself is the woman behind her heroines—whom she subjects to keen psychological analysis. However, their experiences frequently reflect her own, as in *Yeni Turan* (New Turan, 1912) in which the heroine sacrifices herself for PAN-TURKISM, a cause then espoused by the author. Her most famous war of independence novel is *Ateşten Gömlek* (Shirt of Fire). Serialized in the press before publication in book form (1923), it portrays the popular support for the national movement. *Sinekli Bakkal* (1923), a panorama of Constantinople life in the Abdülhamit II period is a highpoint of her novel writing. Published first in English as *The Clown and His Daughter* (London, 1935), it received the Turkish Republican People's Party Prize for Best Novel (1943). Also serialized, it became a best-seller and was made into a film.

In addition to novels and many articles, she produced translations (including Orwell's *Animal Farm*), a three-volume history of English literature, numerous short stories, and three works in English containing her impressions of India and lectures delivered in India and the United States. Her language and style (influenced by her English-American education) have been criticized by Turks. However, she proved popular with the reading public, her Turkish being close to the spoken word of her day. Moreover, her works, which reflect her acute powers of observation and understanding of people, are extremely strong in descriptive passages and bring the Turkish scene alive in a manner not previously achieved.

BIBLIOGRAPHY

BOMBACI, ALESSIO. *Storia della Letteratura Turca*. Milan, 1962, pp. 434–437. French translation by I. Melikoff. *Histoire de la littérature turque*. Paris, 1968.
EDIP, HALIDE. *Memoirs*. London, 1926.
———. *The Turkish Ordeal*. New York, 1928.
WOODSMALL, RUTH FRANCIS. *Moslem Women Enter a New World*. New York, 1936.

Kathleen R. F. Burrill

Adli   [1864–1933]

Egyptian official, cabinet minister, and politician who served as prime minister three times between 1919 and 1930.

Descended from a family of large landowners and related to the Muhammad Ali royal family, Adli split from the popular Wafdist movement, led by Sa'd Zaghlul beginning in 1919. Adli became prime minister in 1921, but the Wafd undercut his efforts to negotiate an independence treaty with Britain. After Britain unilaterally declared Egypt independent (but with significant restrictions) in 1922, Adli's supporters—large landlords and a handful of reformist intellectuals—formed the LIBERAL CONSTITUTIONALIST PARTY. The Wafd won the parliamentary elections in 1926, but the British regarded Zaghlul as an extremist and refused to let him return to the prime ministry. Adli therefore headed a coalition cabinet with the Wafd. Forced to maneuver between the Wafd, the British, and the palace, neither Adli nor his party ever felt at home in the world of mass politics.

BIBLIOGRAPHY

DEEB, MARIUS. *Party Politics in Egypt: The Wafd and Its Rivals, 1919–1939.* London, 1979.

Donald Malcolm Reid

Adonis [1930–]

Pen name of Ali Ahmad Sa'id, Syrian-Lebanese modernist poet.

Born in Qassabin, Syria, Adonis was educated at Damascus University and St. Joseph University in Beirut, Lebanon. His critiques of orthodoxy in Islam and of conventional writing made him highly controversial. In poetry and prose, he opposes what he sees as the static and conservative tradition of Arabic literature and culture. His revolutionary ideas were shaped by involvement in the PARTI POPULAIRE SYRIEN, which resulted in his imprisonment in 1956. On release, he escaped to Lebanon, later becoming a Lebanese citizen.

In 1957, his *Qasa'id Ula* (First Poems) was published, and he co-founded *Shi'r* (Poetry) magazine, later starting his own magazine, *Mawaqif* (Attitudes).

Adonis taught Arabic literature at Lebanese University until 1985 when he moved to France, where he held teaching and research posts; he now teaches in Geneva, Switzerland. *Orbits of Desire,* a selection of his poetry translated by Kamal Abu-Deeb, was published in London in 1992.

BIBLIOGRAPHY

ADONIS. "This Is My Name." Tr. by Kamal Abu-Deeb. *Grand Street* (1992): 40.
BOULLATA, ISSA, ed. *Modern Arab Poets, 1950–1975.* Washington, D.C., and London, 1976.
AL-JAYYUSI, SALMA AL-KHADRA, ed. *Modern Arabic Poetry: An Anthology.* New York, 1988.

Kamal Abu-Deeb

Adrianople

See Edirne

Advisory Council, Palestine

An advisory body in Palestine to the British high commissioner during the British mandate.

In October 1920, shortly after taking office as the first British high commissioner of Palestine, Sir Herbert Samuel set up a nominated advisory council (AC) pending the establishment of a legislative body. The AC was composed of ten Palestinian officials: four Muslims, three Christians, and three Jewish members of the YISHUV. In August 1922 Samuel proposed, as a first step to self-government in Palestine, a constitution that called for the replacement of the AC with a LEGISLATIVE COUNCIL (LC). The Jews reluctantly accepted, but the Muslims and the Christians rejected the proposed constitution and boycotted the elections for the LC in February 1923. Sir Herbert therefore returned to the 1920 system of an AC, which was, however, to be composed now of twenty-three members, eleven of whom (including the high commissioner) would be officials, the remaining twelve being eight Muslims, two Christians, and two Jews.

The Muslim and Christian Palestinians had not objected to the AC in 1920 because it was considered a temporary measure until a legislative body could be established and because the appointees, who were prominent individuals, did not claim to represent the community. But in May 1923 although they had accepted the government's invitation to join the new council, all but three withdrew when the high commissioner associated it with the LC, which had been repudiated by the non-Jewish Palestinians, who considered participation in it a tacit endorsement of the British mandate and the pro-Zionist Balfour policy. Consequently, the high commissioner abandoned the idea of nonofficial participation in the Palestine government, and Palestine was run, from 1923 until the end of the mandate in 1948, by the high commissioner in consultation with an AC composed only of officials.

BIBLIOGRAPHY

ESCO. *Palestine: A Study of Jewish, Arab, and British Policies.* 2 vols. New Haven, Conn., 1947.
Great Britain and Palestine, 1915–1945. Information Papers 20. London, 1946.
LESCH, ANN MOSELY. *Arab Politics in Palestine, 1917–1939: The Frustrations of a Nationalist Movement.* Ithaca, N.Y., 1979.
PALESTINE GOVERNMENT. *A Survey of Palestine for the Information of the Anglo-American Committee of Inquiry.* 2 vols. Jerusalem, 1946. Reprint, 1991.

Philip Mattar

Aegean Sea

Arm of the Mediterranean between Greece and Turkey.

The Aegean contains more than three thousand islands and is considered the home of the earliest European civilization (formerly the Mycenean-Minoan, now called the Aegean), from about 3000 to 1100 B.C.E. Crete is the largest island, lying almost equidistant from both Greece and Turkey, at the southern end of the Aegean, with the Ionian Sea to its west. Since the Aegean is the only breach in the mountainous belt to the north of the Mediterranean, it has been extremely important as a trading area and trade route; control of this sea has been the cause of wars since early Near Eastern civilization clashed with early European.

In 1820, all the shores and islands of the Aegean belonged to the Ottoman Empire, but the western shore and practically all the islands have since gradually gone to Greece, a cause of Turkish resentment. Two islands, İmroz (Greek, Imbros) and Bozca (Greek, Tenedos), are still Turkish. Greece claims the Aegean as a territorial sea, which Turkey disputes, in hopes of sharing benthic minerals. Petroleum was discovered on the sea bottom east of Thasos in 1970, which has sharpened the dispute.

BIBLIOGRAPHY

DRYSDALE, ALASDAIR, and GERALD H. BLAKE. *The Middle East and North Africa.* New York, 1985.

John R. Clark

Afaqi

Arabic, "from over the horizon."

Afaqi is used especially in the Maghreb (North Africa) to refer pejoratively to a nonurban person or one not from the capital city—outsider, bedouin.

Laurence Michalak

Afghani, Jamal al-Din al-   [c. 1838–1896]

Influential and charismatic Muslim leader.

One of the most seminal figures of the nineteenth-century Islamic world, Jamal al-Din al-Afghani, although not a major philosophical thinker, spoke and wrote effectively on such subjects as anti-imperialism and the strengthening of the self; these themes were to become increasingly central to the Muslim world.

Much of what Afghani and his followers said about his life was myth, and many myths about him persist, even now when a more accurate picture can be drawn.

Ample evidence now indicates that Jamal al-Din was born and raised in northwest Iran (not in Afghanistan, as he usually claimed). It also appears that he got his higher education in the Shi'a shrine cities of Iraq, where treatises in his possession show that he was attracted to the innovative, philosophical Shaikhi school of SHI'ISM. From Iraq he went to India (c. 1857), and it seems likely that in India (and possibly in Bushehr in south Iran, which was under British wartime occupation around the time of his stop there) he developed his lifelong hatred for the British. After travels, apparently to Mecca and the Levant, he went across Iran to Afghanistan, where documents show he claimed to be a Turk from Anatolia. He soon entered into the counsels of the Afghan emir, whom he advised to fight the British, but he lost favor and was expelled when a new pro-British emir assumed power. After a brief stop in India, he went to Istanbul (1869–1871).

In Istanbul, he showed the reformist, self-strengthening part of his persona by entering the Council of Higher Education and signing up to give a public lecture at the new university. This lecture in which Afghani said that philosophy and prophecy were both crafts got him and the university and its director (the real targets of the *ulama*) in trouble.

Jamal al-Din al-Afghani as shown on an Iranian postage stamp. (Richard Bulliet)

(This view accords with the teachings of the medieval philosophers, who are still taught in Iran today, although they are anathema in western Islam.) Afghani was expelled and went to Cairo, where he had stopped briefly on his way to Istanbul.

In Cairo, Afghani did his most important work (1871–1879), educating and inspiring a group of young thinkers and activists, many of whom (such as Muhammad ABDUH, Sa'd ZAGHLUL, Abdullah Naqim, and Ibrahim al-Laqqani) continued to be important influences in later Egyptian political and intellectual life. The Muslim philosophers constituted the subject of Afghani's teachings; he stressed their belief in natural law, in reason, and in speaking one way to the religious masses and a different way to the intellectual elite. In the late 1870s, when government debt thrust Egypt into an international crisis, Afghani and many of his followers ventured more openly into politics. He encouraged his followers, who included Syrian immigrants as well as Egyptians, to found newspapers, some of which published his lectures. He also gave talks to, secretly joined, and became the leader of a Masonic lodge, which he used as a political vehicle.

He and his chief disciple Abduh favored the deposition of Khedive ISMA'IL and the accession of his son TAWFIQ, whom he expected to influence. When Tawfiq became khedive (1879), however, the deposition and accession were accomplished by the British and French, to whom Tawfiq was beholden. Tawfiq opposed Afghani's fiery anti-British speeches and activities, and soon had Afghani deported. There is no evidence that the British had a hand in this deportation.

Afghani went back to India, via Iran, and from 1880 to 1882 he chose to stay in the south-central Indian state of Hyderabad, which was ruled by a Muslim prince. During these years, Afghani wrote his most important articles and the short treatise known in English as "Refutation of the Materialists." In 1883, Afghani went to Paris, where Abduh rejoined him. Using funds that probably came from the Briton Wilfrid BLUNT and a Tunisian general, they founded the newspaper AL-URWA AL-WUTHQA (*The Firmest Bond*), which was sent free throughout the Muslim world. The paper, which primarily printed theoretical articles and critiques of British policy in Egypt, Sudan, and elsewhere, was one of the chief sources of fame for its two editors.

In Paris, Afghani also wrote a response to an article by Joseph Ernest Renan in which Renan had asserted that religion, and particularly the Semitic Muslim religion, was hostile to science. Afghani's response, frequently misrepresented as a defense of Islam, in fact agreed that all religions were hostile to science; it differed only in saying that Islam was no more hostile to science than Christianity, and that since Islam was several hundred years younger, it might evolve, as had Christianity. Renan then voiced his essential agreemenet with Afghani, who, he noted, was not a Semite.

After stopping publication of *al-Urwa al-Wuthqa*, probably for financial reasons, Afghani went to London (1885), where he joined Blunt in the latter's schemes to negotiate British withdrawal from Egypt and Sudan. There is no evidence for Afghani's claim that he was at the time an envoy of the Sudanese Mahdi. Although it was the only occasion when he cooperated with the British (and even then it was with the goal of removing them from Egypt and Sudan), this period and Blunt's books about it accounted for the reputation Afghani acquired in some quarters of being a British agent.

Afghani then accepted an invitation from the anti-British Russian publicist Mikhail Katkov to go to Russia, but on the way he stopped in Tehran for several months. His plotting against the British in Russia came to nothing, but both in Iran and Russia, as usual, he won contacts with men in high places by dint of his personality. When the shah's party came to St. Petersburg on its way west, Afghani was snubbed, but he caught up with them in Europe and believed he had been given a mission in Russia by the prime minister. He returned first to Russia and then to Iran, but the prime minister, AMIN AL-SOLTAN, refused to see him. Amin al-Soltan planned to expel him, but Afghani avoided banishment by going to a shrine south of Tehran, where he continued to see his followers. A letter attacking concessions to Europeans, including the tobacco concession to the British, was attributed to Afghani, and he was forced to leave Iran for Iraq in midwinter.

From Iraq and then also from Britain, Afghani helped influence the movement against the tobacco concession (1891–1892). An invitation from the Ottoman sultan, ABDÜLHAMIT II, brought him to Istanbul, where he soon was forbidden to write or speak publicly. When one of his Iranian followers killed Naser al-Din Shah in 1896, the Iranians tried unsuccessfully to gain Afghani's extradition, but his death from cancer (1897) made the issue moot.

Although Afghani is known mainly as a pan-Islamist, the characterization applies to him only from the year 1883 or so. He was primarily concerned with awakening and strengthening the Muslim world, especially against the encroachment by the British, and for this purpose he sometimes stressed political reform, sometimes local nationalism, and sometimes a pan-Islamic approach. He was a charismatic speaker and teacher, but his writings do not measure up to the standard set by the writings of many of his contemporaries. Despite many facets of his life that underscore his unorthodoxy, he remains for many a model figure of modern Islam. Because he voiced so many of the ideas then in the air among politically minded Muslims, the potency of his influence and especially the myths surrounding him have remained strong.

Nikki Keddie

Afghanistan

Central Asian country, formerly the Republic of Afghanistan, was renamed the Islamic State of Afghanistan in April 1992.

According to the only official census (allegedly taken in 1979, a year of expanding civil war), Afghanistan's total population slightly exceeds 15.5 million. The United Nations High Commissioner for Refugees (UNHCR) estimated Afghanistan's population fig-ures for 1986/87 to be 16.7 million—with 11 million living in Afghanistan and 5.7 million refugees (2.4 million in Iran, 3.2 million in Pakistan, and 0.1 million elsewhere), the world's largest refugee population.

In 1978, pro-Soviet leftists took power in a violent coup and concluded an economic and military treaty with the former Soviet Union. Late in December 1979, Soviet troops moved into KABUL, the capital, fanning out into the countryside to fight the Islamist rebels (MOJAHEDIN). This guerrilla warfare lasted until a U.N.-mediated withdrawal of Soviet troops in 1988/89. After the collapse of the Soviet Union (1991), the communist regime in Kabul fell (April 1992), but the new Islamic government that took over is yet to consolidate its power due to continued factional infighting.

Geography. Afghanistan is landlocked, comprising some 251,773 square miles (647,500 sq km). It shares borders with Iran, Pakistan, the Xinjiang province of China, and the newly independent successor Central

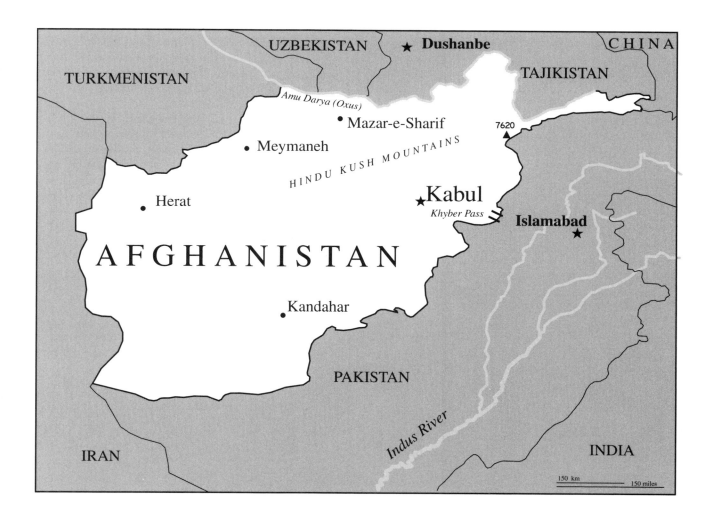

The Citadel of Herat in Afghanistan. (Richard Bulliet)

Scene in a Pakhtun village, 1966. (Richard Bulliet)

Asian states of Turkmenistan, Uzbekistan, and Tajikistan. Kabul remains Afghanistan's capital and its largest city, with more than 1.5 million, including internal refugees. Cities of 50,000 to 200,000 people include Qandahar, Herat, Mazar-i-Sharif, Jalalabad, and Kunduz.

The HINDU KUSH MOUNTAINS (rising to 24,000 feet [7,315 m]) stretch diagonally from the northeast, through the center, to the Herat region in the west, dominating the country's topography, ecology, and economy. Deep narrow valleys, many of them impenetrable, cover much of the central, northeastern, eastern, and south-central areas, surrounded by the fertile Turkistan plain and foothills in the north and northwest, the Herat-Farah lowlands, the Sistan basin and Helmand valley in the west, and the deserts of the southwest. Four major river systems drain the Hindu Kush—the AMU DARYA (Oxus) drains the northern slopes and marks much of the former Afghan–Soviet border; the HARI RUD drains the northwest; the HELMAND-Arghandab, the southwest;

and the KABUL, the east. Communications and road systems between these valleys are poor, although a few difficult passes connect them with Central Asia and the subcontinent of India. Temperatures and the amount and form of precipitation are directly dependent on altitude. Summers are very hot and dry, the temperatures reaching 120° F (49° C) in the desert south and southwest. Winters are bitterly cold, the temperatures falling to −15° F (−26° C), with heavy snow cover in the mountains. Precipitation is low, two to six inches (50–150 mm) in the south and southwest, and twelve to fourteen inches (300–350 mm) in the north.

Economy. Afghanistan has thirty provinces (*wilayat*), divided into districts (*woluswali*) and subdistricts (*alaqadari*). According to government figures, the per-capita income in 1986/87 was 160 U.S. dollars. Although rich in natural resources, mineral extractions benefit investors or remain undeveloped. For example, in 1985/86, of the annual production of

Overlooking Herat. (Richard Bulliet)

City street in Kabul. (Richard Bulliet)

natural gas (estimated reserves of over 100,000 million cubic meters), 97 percent was exported to the Soviet Union at a rate of 2.6 billion cubic meters a year. Deposits of petroleum, coal, copper, high-grade iron ore, talc, barite, sulphur, lead, zinc, salt, lapis lazuli and other semiprecious and precious gemstones exist; some are extracted.

Before 1978, 85 percent of the population lived in 22,000 villages; they farmed or were Nomads. Their major subsistence crops are wheat, maize, barley, and rice; major cash crops are cotton, sugar beet, oilseeds, fruits, nuts, and vegetables. Sheep (including Karakul/Persian lamb), goats, and cattle are the main sources of milk, meat, wool, hides, and pelts, while camels, horses, and donkeys serve as means of transportation in the difficult terrain. Livestock become the vital buffer during poor harvests. Since 1978, the civil war has seriously damaged more than half the villages and much of the agriculture infrastructure. Reports show that 1987 wheat production was reduced by 50 percent, sheep and goats to 30 percent, and cattle to 52 percent of 1978 levels.

Industries include rugs, carpets, and textiles, chemical fertilizers, sugar, plastics, leather goods, soap, cement, natural gas, oil, coal, and hydroelectric power. Government figures for 1986/87 show industrial production accounted for 23.87 percent of gross domestic product. Exports, primarily to the former Soviet Union and Eastern Europe, India, and Pakistan, included natural gas, cotton, livestock products, rugs, medicinal herbs, fruits, and nuts, with reported earnings in 1988 of 512 million U.S. dollars. Imports of wheat, foods, textiles, vehicles, machinery, and petroleum products, at a cost of 996 million U.S. dollars in 1988, came mostly from the Soviet Union and Japan.

Language and Ethnic Groups. Two major ethnolinguistic communities, Indo-Iranian and Turko-Mongol, live in Afghanistan. The Indo-Iranians include the dominant Pakhtu-speaking PAKHTUN (or Pashtun, traditionally estimated at 45–50%); the Afghan-Persian or Dari-speaking TAJIK (25–30%); and minority Nuristani, Gujar, Baluch, Wakhi, Sheghni, and Zebaki. The Hazara, who have a Mongol appearance, speak Hazaragi, a Persian dialect, and are estimated at 12 to 15 percent of the population. The Turkic speakers include the UZBEKS (about 10%), TURKMEN, Kazakh, and Kirghiz. Persian (most widely spoken) and Pakhtu are the official government languages. Islam is the religion of more than 99 percent of Afghans—about 80 percent are hanafi Sunni and about 20 percent Shi'a (mostly Imami and some Isma'ili). Also present are very small numbers of Hindus, Sikhs, Jews, and Christians.

Education. Primary education, grades one through eight, is compulsory for ages seven to fifteen. Secondary school continues for an additional four years (voluntary). Most schools in rural areas were destroyed during the early years of the civil war. Resistance organizations and international aid agencies have, in recent years, tried to reestablish schools in the liberated areas. Some poorly equipped and poorly run schools for Afghan refugee children in host countries also exist. Since 1979, the execution, imprisonment, and departure of many teachers badly disrupted institutions of higher education. In 1987, an estimated fifteen thousand Afghans received training and education in the Soviet Union. In 1988, the Kabul government claimed eight vocational colleges, fifteen technical colleges, and five universities in operation. Losses of previously trained manpower, along with the damage to educational, health-care, and cultural facilities and the lack of training opportunities for the new generation of Afghans during the 1980s and 1990s leave prospects for the future reconstruction of Afghanistan extremely challenging.

Government. On the basis of the 1987 constitution, the government structure consists of a bicameral legislature called the *Melli Shura.* It consists of a 192-member *Sena* (Senate) and a 234-member *Wolusi Jirga* (House of Representative). Members are elected by the *Watan* (PDPA) party, except for a few members of the Sena and fifty members of the Wolusi Jirga reserved for opposition parties. The president is elected for a seven-year term by the majority vote of a *Loya Jirga* (Grand Assembly) as head of the executive branch—who appoints the prime minister, who in turn appoints the cabinet (the council of ministers). The judicial branch is headed by the supreme court.

History. The emergence of Afghanistan in 1747 as a separate political entity is credited to Ahmad Shah DURRANI, who made the city of Qandahar his capital and created a great empire stretching from Khurasan to Kashmir and Punjab; and from the Oxus river (Amu Darya) to the Indian Ocean. His son Timur Shah (1773–1793) shifted the capital to Kabul and held his patrimony together. By the turn of the nineteenth century, the Durrani empire had declined because of fraternal feuds over royal succession. Between 1800 and 1880, Afghanistan became a battleground during the rivalry between Britain and Russia for control of Central Asia. Afghanistan emerged as a buffer state, with its present boundaries demarcated entirely by Britain and Russia—and with Britain in control of Afghanistan's foreign affairs. The Afghan wars fought against the British by DOST MO-

HAMMAD BARAKZAI, his son, and his grandson (1838–1842; 1878–1880) had ended in defeat.

With British military and financial help, a member of the Barakzai Pakhtun clan—Emir Abd al-Rahman, the so-called Iron Emir—consolidated direct central government rule by brutally suppressing tribal and rural leaders to lay the foundation of a modern state (1880–1901). His son, HABIBOLLAH KHAN, who ruled from 1901 to 1919, relaxed some of the harsher measures of the previous rule and in 1903 established the first modern school, HABIBIA. Later, the first significant newspaper, *Siraj al-Akhbar,* was published in Kabul (1911–1918). When Habibullah was assassinated, his son AMANOLLAH took the title of king (1919–1929) and declared Afghanistan's independence from Britain, which was granted after a brief war in 1919 (see RAWALPINDI, Treaty of). King Amanullah, impressed by the secular sociopolitical experiments of Mustafa Kemal ATATÜRK in the new Republic of Turkey, launched a series of secular, liberal constitutional reforms and modernization programs, which led to a rebellion—justified as jihad (religious war) against his rule—forcing his abdication. After nine months of rule by a non-Pashtun (Emir Habibullah II), a member of the MUSAHIBAN family of the Barakzai clan, Muhammad NADIR (1929–1933), reclaimed the monarchy. Following Nadir's assassination, his son of nineteen, Mohammad ZAHIR (1933–1973), became king.

From 1933 to 1963, Zahir reigned while two of his uncles and a cousin ruled as prime ministers. Concerned primarily with preserving their family's position, the Musahiban adopted a cautious approach toward modernization, with highly autocratic domestic and xenophobic foreign policies until about 1935. During Sardar (Prince) Muhammad DAUD's term as prime minister (1953–1963), with substantial military and economic aid, initially from the Soviet Union and later from the West, a series of five-year modernization plans was begun, focusing on the expansion of educational and communications systems. In 1963, Daud resigned because of disagreements over his hostile policies toward Pakistan and his favoring of greater dependence on the Soviet Union. King Zahir then appointed Dr. Muhammad Yusuf, a commoner, as prime minister.

King Zahir's last decade (1963–1973) was a period of experimentation in democracy, which failed—mostly due to his reluctance to sign legislation legalizing political parties and his unwillingness to curb interference in democratic processes by his family and friends. The Communist party and Islamist-opposition movements were formed during this period; they agitated against both the government and each other. In July 1973, Daud, the former prime minister (and king's cousin and brother-in-law), overthrew the monarchy with assistance from the pro-Soviet PARCHAM wing of the Communist party in a military coup, to become the president of the Republic of Afghanistan (1973–1978). Daud returned autocratic rule and persecuted his perceived enemies, especially members of the Islamist movements. He relied heavily on his old networks and began to distance himself from the pro-Soviet communists whom he had protected and nurtured. In an environment of growing discontent, in April 1978, a communist coup ousted and killed Daud.

Nur Muhammad Taraki, the head of the People's Democratic party of Afghanistan (PDPA), was installed as president of the revolutionary council and prime minister (1978/79). He renamed the country the Democratic Republic of Afghanistan (DRA), abolished the constitution, and banned all opposition movements. Less than two months later, the coalition of two warring factions of PDPA—Khalq (People) and Parcham (Banner)—that had joined to gain power then fell apart. Khalq monopolized all power, offering Parcham leaders ambassadorial posts overseas, and began purging Parcham members from military and civilian posts. Supported by the Soviets, Taraki attempted to create a Marxist state, but by the spring of 1979 a nationwide rebellion began—led by Islamist-opposition groups and Muslim religious leaders. Brutal retaliation by government in rural areas forced the flight of thousands of refugees to Iran and Pakistan. In September 1979, Hafizullah AMIN, then deputy prime minister and minister of foreign affairs and an advocate of hardline communist policies, suspecting a plot against himself, killed President Taraki and assumed Taraki's duties. During Christmas 1979, the Soviet army invaded Afghanistan with eighty thousand troops. They killed Hafizullah Amin and installed Babrak KARMAL, leader of the Parcham, as the new head of state. Soviet intervention intensified factionalism between the Parcham and Khalq parties, which resulted in riots and strikes in the major cities. It turned anticommunist rebellions into a *jihad* for the cause of Islam and national liberation.

From 1980 to 1986, Karmal tried but failed to consolidate his power, reduce factional strife, and promote national unity. In 1986, Dr. Najibullah Ahmadzai, the former head of the state security forces (KHAD) and a member of Parcham, assumed power, relieving Karmal of all party and government duties. He adopted a shrewd policy of unilateral cease-fires, offers of negotiation and power sharing with his opponents, and the formation of a coalition government of national unity. He also adopted a new constitution in 1987, allowing the formation of a multiparty political system and a bicameral legislature. He won some support from his internal leftist opponent, but the seven-party alliance of mojahedin (Islamic Unity of Afghan Mojahedin) remained defiant, calling for unconditional Soviet withdrawal and the abolition of communist rule.

The failure of a Soviet military victory and the ever increasing outside military and financial support from the mojahedin (from 1984 to 1988) led to the signing of the Geneva accords on April 14, 1988, under United Nations auspices. The accords called for the withdrawal of 120,000 Soviet troops, which was completed on February 15, 1989. After Soviet troop withdrawal, the continuing civil war in Afghanistan was overshadowed by the events of the democratization of Eastern Europe (1989) and what became the former Soviet Union (1991). The collapse of the Soviet Union, the end of their military and financial support to Dr. Najibullah's communist government, and the desertion of his militia forces to the Islamist resistance all resulted in Najibullah's ouster from power on April 16, 1992. A coalition of Islamist forces from northern Afghanistan led by Commander Ahmad Shah Mas'ud surrounded Kabul. In Peshawar, a fifty-member Interim Council of the Islamist resistance groups was formed and dispatched to assume power in Kabul from the communists. Following two days (April 26–27, 1992) of factional fighting that resulted in dislodging Golbuddin HEKMATYAR's forces from Kabul, Sebghatullah Mujaddedi, the president of the Interim Council— later called *Shura-i qiyadi* (Leadership Council)— took power on April 28, 1992, as the Head of the Islamic State of Afghanistan for a period of two months. Professor Burhanuddin RABBANI succeeded him as the interim president of the country on June 28, 1992, for four months. During his tenure Rabbani and the Leadership Council were to organize and convene the *Shura-i Hall wa Aqd* or the *Loya Jirgah* (the Council of Resolution and Settlement or the Grand National Assembly) representing all the peoples of Afghanistan, including those living in exile, to choose the next president for a term of eighteen months. The new president would then oversee the drafting of a new constitution and the first general election.

In opposition to Rabbani's government, Gulbuddin Hekmatyar's forces launched a rocket attack in late August 1992 destroying much of Kabul. Other forms of factional fighting along sectarian, ethnic, and regional lines have plagued the new Islamist regime, seriously hampering repatriation of the refugees, reconstruction, and the return of law and order in the war-ravaged country. At the end of December 1992, a *shura* (assembly) of some 1,335 members

convened and elected the sole candidate, Burhanuddin Rabbani, the interim president for two years. Five of the nine Islamist factions reportedly boycotted the assembly, disputing the validity of Rabbani's election. The possibility of all-out civil war looms large while the suffering of millions of ordinary Afghans continues.

BIBLIOGRAPHY

ARNOLD, ANTHONY. *Afghanistan's Two-Party Communism: Parcham and Khalq.* Stanford, Calif., 1983.
BRADSHER, HENRY S. *Afghanistan and the Soviet Union.* Durham, N.C., 1985.
DUPREE, LOUIS. *Afghanistan.* Princeton, N.J., 1980.
GREGORIAN, VARTAN. *The Emergence of Modern Afghanistan: Politics of Reform and Modernization, 1880–1946.* Stanford, Calif., 1969.
ROY, OLIVIER. *Islam and Resistance in Afghanistan,* 2nd ed. Cambridge, Mass., 1991.
SHAHRANI, M. NAZIF, and ROBERT L. CANFIELD, eds. *Revolutions & Rebellions in Afghanistan: Anthropological Perspectives.* Berkeley, Calif., 1984.

M. Nazif Shahrani

Afghanistan, Islamic Movements in

Ideologically based politically motivated, organized Islamic movements.

These movements (in Arabic Janbush-i Islami or Nahzat-i Islami) formed when Afghanistan established official *madrasas* (Muslim colleges) and the Faculty of *Shari'yat* (Islamic law; see SHARI'A) at Kabul University to train modern Islamic scholars and functionaries during the 1940s and 1950s. The government sent a group of young faculty to al-AZHAR in Egypt for graduate training in Islamic studies and law. By the early 1960s, they returned home impressed by the Islamist ideals and political goals of Egypt's Ikhwan al-Muslimin (MUSLIM BROTHERHOOD) and its struggles against Egypt's President Gamal Abdel NASSER. This small group of *ustazan* (professors), meeting clandestinely, began to translate, disseminate, and discuss the writings of Hasan al-BANNA, Sayyid QUTB, Mawdudi, and other Islamist thinkers. The patron and guide of this emergent movement was Professor Ghulam Muhammad Niyazi, who later became dean of the Faculty of Shari'yat in Kabul. Led by Islamic intellectuals and reformist *ulama* (Minhajuddin Gahiz, Mowlana Khalis, Mowlawi Faizani, and others), groups also formed outside the university.

After the adoption of Afghanistan's 1964 liberal constitution and the unsanctioned establishment of the Khalq communist party on January 1, 1965, the pace of political activities quickened. Agitation, demonstrations against the government, and violent confrontations among members of the Islamic movements and the communist parties marked the years from 1965 to 1972. The student branch of the Islamic movement Sazman-i Javanani Musalman (Organization of Muslim Youth), nicknamed the Ikhwan-i-ha (the Brothers), became increasingly active. In 1972, the "professors" also formally, but secretly, organized themselves as Jam'iat-i Islami Afghanistan (Islamic Association of Afghanistan). Its fifteen member executive council (shura-i ali) composed of students and faculty, primarily of rural and provincial origins, recognized Professor Niyazi as founder and unofficial leader and appointed Burhanuddin RABBANI as "amir" of the movement.

The declared goals were establishment of a completely Islamic political order, which would oppose communism, atheism, corruption, and all forms of social and economic discrimination, internal oppression, external domination, and exploitation. The movement's initial strategy was to work methodically and peacefully against the government and the communists. After Sardar Muhammad DAUD overthrew the monarchy (July 17, 1973), aided by PARCHAM, the pro-Soviet Communist party, Professor Niyazi and 180 members of the movement were jailed and eventually executed (May 29, 1978) by the Khalq and Parcham communists when they took power.

Only a few leaders, among them Rabbani and Golbuddin HEKMATYAR, managed to escape to Pakistan during Daud's regime. In 1975, they failed at a revolt against Daud. Their efforts proved more effective when they organized the JIHAD (religious war) against the Khalq/Parcham communist coalition following the coup. Four of the seven major mojahedin parties (the so-called fundamentalists) participating in the current struggle are splinter groups from the original Jami'ati Islami movement. Their objectives are similar, although their strategies and organizational styles differ. Several Afghan Shia Islamic organizations and three traditionalist Islamic groups were also formed following the 1978 communist coup.

The Islamist opposition fought effectively, defeated the communist regime in April 1992, and assumed power to establish the Islamic State of Afghanistan. The Islamists are unable to reconcile their political differences, however, and their factional fighting plagues the new government headed by Professor Burhanuddin Rabbani. Therefore, slim prospects exist for peaceful rule, reconstruction, and the repatriation of millions of Afghan refugees.

BIBLIOGRAPHY

ROY, OLIVIER. Islam and Resistance in Afghanistan. Cambridge, U.K., 1986.
SHAHRANI, M. NAZIF. "Introduction: Marxist 'Revolution' and Islamic Resistance in Afghanistan." In Revolutions & Rebellions in Afghanistan: Anthropological Perspectives, ed. by M. Nazif Shahrani and Robert Canfield. Berkeley, Calif., 1984.

M. Nazif Shahrani

Afghanistan, Political Parties in

The development of mature political parties in Afghanistan did not occur until the 1960s, during the period of constitutional reform under Mohammad Zahir Shah, 1963–1973.

Earlier, a number of factors had worked against the formation of political parties. For one, Afghans had strong ties and allegiances to tribal, kin, religious, or ethnic groups that precluded membership in political parties. In addition, the lack of class awareness and the very small size of the intelligentsia limited the formation of political parties. Also, true parliamentary elections were not held until 1965, and therefore political parties did not have a direct role in national politics until that date.

There were political societies as early as 1911, during the reign of Amir Habibullah (1901–1919). A small group of young nobles and intellectuals, including future King Amanullah, formed a group called the Young Afghan Party. It centered around the personality of Mahmud Tarzi, a major political thinker and poet, and his weekly journal *Siraj al-Akhbar*. This protoparty was largely a discussion and literary group that advocated the rapid modernization of Afghanistan and was strongly anti-British. Its members were much impressed by the YOUNG TURKS in Turkey, for whom they named themselves, and advocated that Afghanistan side with Turkey in World War I.

In 1947, a similar organization called the AWAKENED YOUTH (Wish Zalmayan in Pakhtun) was formed in Kandahar by members of the Pakhtun upper class. It also became popular with the Kabul intelligentsia. It began as a progressive party, favoring national development and modernization, and was strongly pro-Pakhtun, especially with regard to the Pakhtunistan issue. With the establishment of liberal press laws in 1951, the party was able to publish in a number of newly created opposition newspapers in Kabul. With the end of the liberal Seventh National Assembly under Prime Minister Shah Mahmud in 1953, official toleration of opposition groups ended, the liberal press law was abolished, and a number of the party members were either jailed or sent abroad as diplomats. For the next ten years, Sardar Daoud was prime minister of Afghanistan, and no political parties were allowed.

Political parties arose in earnest during the constitutional reforms that began in 1963, and especially with the liberalization of the press laws in 1964. In this period parties of three types emerged, each representing sentiments of a relatively small educated class. One type of party was based on the European socialist model, particularly on the German Social Democratic party. Afghanistan had had a warm relationship with Germany, in part because of Afghanistan's long and vitriolic relationship with Britain, and in part because many Afghans believe that they are the true Aryans. Many members of Afghanistan's upper class had been trained in Germany and spoke German. These political parties include the Jam'iat-e Social Demokrat (the Social Democratic Society), usually called the Afghan Millat (Afghan Nation), led by Ghulum Mohammad Farhad. This strong Pakhtun party led to several spin-off parties, including the Millat (Nation). The other major party of this type was the Jam'iat Demokrate-ye Mottaraqi (Progressive Democratic Party), founded by the popular prime minister Mohammad Hashim MAIWANDWAL (1965–1967). It advocated evolutionary socialism and parliamentary democracy. By 1973 these parties had ceased to play a major role in Afghanistan's politics, even though remnants still existed, largely because political forces from the right and left forced out the parties of the middle. After 1973, politics became dominated by the conflict between the parties of the religious right and parties of the radical left.

The parties on the left also arose in the mid-1960s. They include the PEOPLE'S DEMOCRATIC PARTY OF AFGHANISTAN (PDPA), which was founded in 1965 by Babrak KARMAL, Hafizullah AMIN, and Mohammad Taraki. It was pro-Soviet and had a Marxist-Leninist ideology. In 1967, the party split into two factions, the Khalq (People's) faction, led by Taraki and Amin, and the PARCHAM (Banner), led by Karmal. In April 1978, the factions temporarily united and the PDPA led a successful coup to take over the government. It ruled Afghanistan until 1992.

Other parties on the left included the Setem-e Melli (National Oppression), led by Taher Badakhshi. This party had a Marxist-Leninist orientation but also contained Maoist elements, and was strongly anti-Pakhtun. Sholay-e Jawid (Eternal Flame), another popular Marxist party, was led by Dr. Rahim Mahmudi. Both were popular among minorities (non-Pakhtuns), especially among the Shi'a, and the

ethnic groups in northern Afghanistan. The leftist parties dominated campus politics at Kabul University and were influential in the Daoud government that took over Afghanistan in 1973.

The Islamic parties appeared in Afghanistan in the late 1960s, partly as a reaction to the increased secularization of Afghan politics, and particularly the influence of the leftist parties and the growing friendship with the Soviet Union. Islam had played an important role in national politics in earlier periods, often as a means of mobilizing national sentiment against an outside force, usually the British. The Islamic parties that formed in the 1960s were of two types: those of the traditional *ulama,* or religious scholars, and those hostile to the *ulama* and advocating a new and more radical Islam. The new and more radical parties had their origins on the campus of Kabul University and were centered in the Faculty of Islamic Law. A number of professors in this faculty had studied at al-Azhar University in Cairo, and had established contacts with the Muslim Brotherhood (al-Ikhwan al-Muslimin). They brought this Islamic fundamentalist message back to Afghanistan. In 1970 they established the Javanan-e Muslimin (Islamic Youth) movement on campus; that year the party won the student elections after years of leftist control. In 1971 the movement formed a party called JAMI'AT-E ISLAMI (Islamic Society), led by Burhanuddin RABBANI and Abdul Rasul Sayyaf, which was the main party of the new Islamic thinkers.

In 1973 Daoud took over Afghanistan in a political coup, ending the democratic experiment. He incorporated many of the leftist parties into his government, but the Islamic parties were forced underground or into exile. Rabbani and Sayyaf fled to Peshawar, Pakistan, and with the aid of the government of Pakistan, they began an armed insurrection against the government in Kabul. By 1990, counting Jam'iat, there were four parties; the three others were HEZB-E ISLAMI (Islamic Party), led by Golbuddin HEKMATYAR; another Hezb-e Islami, led by Mohammad Unis KHALIS, and Ittihad-e Islami (Islamic Union), led by Sayyaf. Each of the leaders had been in the Jam'iat at one time.

The traditional clergy also fled to Pakistan, where they formed parties to lead an armed resistance against the Kabul government. These parties were Harakat-e Inqilab-e Islami (Islamic Revolutionary Movement), led by Maulawi Mohammad Nabi MOHAMMADI; Jebhe-ye Nejat Milli (National Liberation Front), led by Sufi Pir Sebghatullah MUJADDEDI; and Mahaz-e Islami (Islamic Front) led by Sufi Pir Sayyid Ahmad GAILANI.

These seven parties formed a loose coalition during the 1980s to coordinate their war efforts and to attempt to form an Afghan government in exile. In February 1989 they formed an Afghan Interim Government (AIG) in Pakistan and elected Mujaddedi president. Very soon, however, conflicts arose, and the Hezb-e Islami led by Hekmatyar withdrew from the AIG.

Other religious parties were excluded from the AIG. These were primarily the Shi'a parties. Shi'a make up between 15 and 20 percent of the population of Afghanistan and are mostly HAZARA. They have several political parties, most with ties to Iran. The first Shi'a parties, founded in 1979, were the Shura-ye Ittifagh-e Islami (Islamic Council), led by Sayyed Beheshti, and the Harakat-e Islami (Islamic Union), led by Shaykh Asaf Mohseni. The Shura was formed as a quasi government of the HAZARAJAT, and in the early 1980s it operated as such. However, by the mid-1980s the Shi'a areas of Afghanistan, primarily the Hazarajat, were taken over by Iranian-based parties, especially the Nasr (Victory) and the Pasdaran (REVOLUTIONARY GUARDS). These parties, imbued with Islamic fervor resulting from the Iranian Revolution, ruthlessly pushed out the more moderate Shi'a parties. In the late 1980s, these parties united into a political front called the Wahadat (Unity), which represents most of the Shi'a parties and is led by Khalili.

In 1992, the Islamic political parties returned to Kabul to form a government. By late 1993, however, any unity that might have existed among them had disappeared, and there was bitter fighting between rival Islamic parties in Kabul and other major cities for the control of Afghanistan.

BIBLIOGRAPHY

ARNOLD, ANTHONY. *Afghanistan's Two-Party Communism: Parcham and Khalq*. Stanford, Calif., 1983.
DUPREE, LOUIS. *Afghanistan*. Princeton, N.J., 1980.
FARR, GRANT. "The New Middle Class as Refugees and Insurgents." In *Afghanistan Resistance: The Politics of Survival*, ed. by Grant Farr and John Merriam. Boulder, Colo., 1984.
POULLADA, LEON. *Reform and Rebellion in Afghanistan, 1919–1929*. Ithaca, N.Y., 1973.
ROY, OLIVIER. *Islam and Resistance in Afghanistan*. New York, 1986.

Grant Farr

Afghanistan, Soviet Intervention in

Soviet troops invaded Afghanistan in December 1979 to preserve a shaky Communist government, but after failing to quell guerrilla resistance, they withdrew in February 1989. A cutoff of military and economic aid from the collapsing Soviet Union led to the Afghan government's fall to a resistance coalition in April 1992.

The Union of Soviet Socialist Republics (USSR) secretly encouraged and financed Afghan communists from before the formation of their People's Democratic Party of Afghanistan (PDPA) in 1965 until the party unexpectedly came to power through a military coup d'état on April 27, 1978. There was no evidence that the USSR organized or controlled the coup, but it rushed advisers to Kabul to help consolidate the new regime under the PDPA leader, Nur Mohammed Taraki. When popular opposition to the regime's economic and social changes provoked armed resistance, Moscow supplied weapons and military advisers who took unofficial command of the Afghan armed forces. In mid-1979, the Soviets sought the removal of Taraki's deputy, Hafizullah AMIN. They blamed Amin for antagonizing the Afghan people into rebellion.

Soviet President Leonid I. BREZHNEV was angered by Amin's overthrow of Taraki on September 14, 1979, and Amin's later order to murder Taraki. Brezhnev and other Soviet officials also feared that Afghanistan's communist regime might be defeated by strengthening Muslim guerrillas, that such a defeat of a client would damage Soviet prestige worldwide, and the adjacent Muslim areas of the USSR would be destabilized. Without consulting military and political specialists on possible repercussions or observing constitutional requirements for the Soviet government to make decisions, Brezhnev's clique of about five Communist party leaders decided on December 12, 1979, to send the Soviet army into Afghanistan. Soviet professional soldiers later insisted that they had recognized the difficulties of coping with Afghan guerrillas and opposed the invasion but were overruled by the clique's politically appointed defense minister, Dmitriy Ustinov.

The Soviet army seized control of Kabul on December 27, killing Amin and installing Babrak KARMAL as president. Moscow claimed its army had been officially invited into Afghanistan. It never produced proof of this or justified killing the supposed inviter. Through advisers, the USSR ran Karmal's government until Moscow decided he was a failure and replaced him in May 1986 with another puppet, Mohammed NAJIBULLAH.

The Soviet invasion turned what had been a civil war into a defense of nationalism and the Islamic religion against foreign atheists and their Afghan puppets. A Soviet force that reached about 118,000 men fought an estimated 200,000 or more *mojahedin* (Islamic holy warriors). The Soviet army was not trained or equipped for counterinsurgency warfare, and it never mastered the situation. Although it could mount offensives that temporarily seized control of any desired part of the Texas-sized country, it and the weak Afghan army were unable to maintain lasting control of much more than main towns and key communications lines. Soviet military operations drove some 5 million Afghans into refuge in Pakistan and Iran, and another 2 million sought shelter in towns from Soviet devastation of rural areas. Soviet soldiers slaughtered unarmed civilians in retaliation for guerrilla attacks; unproven reports said they used poison gas on unprotected villagers; and they spread millions of land mines that continued to kill and maim long after the war ended.

The mojahedin, armed by the United States and its allies, and trained and directed by Pakistan's military intelligence service, ambushed roads and harassed garrisons. Soviet adaptations for more mobile warfare, including sending raiding teams into guerrilla territory to interrupt supply lines, had only limited success. The guerrillas' introduction in September 1986 of American-supplied Stinger antiaircraft missiles curtailed the Soviet advantage of air power to attack guerrillas and move troops over the rugged terrain. The military advantage began shifting to the resistance as the Soviets lost heart.

The war exacerbated more general Soviet problems. At home, corruption increased in the military conscription system, veterans were denied promised benefits while war invalids were given little help, efforts to censor knowledge of the war undercut official credibility, and war costs strained the economy. Abroad, nonaligned nations voted in the United Nations against the Soviet troop presence in Afghanistan, and Western countries restricted ties with the USSR.

After becoming the Soviet leader in March 1985, Mikhail Gorbachev decided the economically staggering USSR needed to improve relations with the West to reduce its military spending burden and obtain technical aid. He recognized the Afghanistan war as an obstacle to better Western relations as well as a source of Soviet public malaise. Therefore, Moscow coerced Afghanistan into signing agreements—under UN auspices in Geneva April 14, 1988—that the Soviet army would withdraw from Afghanistan (Pakistan was also a signatory). After the withdrawal was completed on February 15, 1989, the USSR said 14,453 of its personnel had been killed in Afghanistan and 11,600 had been left invalids. The number of Afghans killed—among the regime, mojahedin, and noncombatants—was estimated between 1 and 1.5 million, with tens of thousands of others crippled.

The Soviet Union continued to arm and finance the Najibullah regime after the withdrawal, enabling its survival against disunited mojahedin groups. But the military and secret police officials who had been Kabul's staunchest Soviet supporters led the unsuccessful attempt in August 1991 to overthrow Gorbachev. After they were imprisoned, the USSR agreed with the United States to halt—by January 1, 1992—aid to both sides in the continuing civil war. Deprived of aid, Najibullah's regime lost support and collapsed. The mojahedin who had fought the Soviet Union took control of Kabul on April 28, 1992.

The USSR's bitter Afghanistan experience created an "Afghan syndrome" that Moscow commentators compared with the "Vietnam syndrome" of American wariness about foreign commitments after 1975. As a result, the Soviet Union was unwilling to get involved in the GULF CRISIS in 1991, and later some Russian soldiers wanted to avoid commitment to regional conflicts in republics of the former USSR. Soviet soldiers who had served in Afghanistan, known as "Afghantsy," became prominent in military and civilian positions in the republics.

Henry S. Bradsher

Aflaq, Michel [1910–1989]

Syrian Christian pan-Arab nationalist; intellectual, teacher, journalist, and politician; one of the founders of the Ba'th party.

Michel (also Mishayl) Aflaq was born the son of a Greek Orthodox grain merchant in the Maydan quarter of Damascus. During the French mandate over Syria, he began his secondary education in the Greek Orthodox lyceneum in Damascus (1922–1926), but after long-standing disagreements with students and teachers, he transferred in his final year to the Damascus state secondary school (*al-tajhiz*). He studied at the University of Paris (1928–1934), where he took the licentiate in law. After returning to Damascus, he taught history in the state secondary school and in the French lay secondary school. He participated in Arab nationalism in Damascus and Paris, but after returning to Damascus devoted himself to literary activities, writing short stories, a novel, and a play. Social reform was his preoccupation in his earliest political action—articles published in *al-Tali,* a weekly that he and Salah al-Din al-BITAR, a fellow student and friend in Paris, and others published for six months in 1935/36. Aflaq and Bitar were attracted by Marxism and were friendly with communists in Paris and in Syria, but they never joined the party. The French author André Gide (1869–1951) was their greatest influence; the two friends became disillusioned by communist support for the 1936 Franco–Syrian treaty and the denunciation of the communists by intellectuals like Gide.

With the start of World War II, Aflaq and Bitar organized a group of pan-Arab students, but the group's principal activity before 1943 was the distribution of occasional handbills. These circulars were identified simply as from al-Ihya al-Arabi (the Arab Awakening) or, from the later half of 1941 on, al-Ba'th al-Arabi (the Arab Resurrection), a term that Zaki al-ARSUZI had used to designate a similar group of students formed by him in 1940. Meanwhile, in May 1941, Aflaq and Bitar organized a group to send arms and volunteers to assist Rashid Ali al-Kaylani against the British.

Aflaq's literary activity won him a substantial reputation, and his teaching had a great impact on some students. Aflaq and Bitar were of middle economic status, but their families were considered notable and aristocratic. Nevertheless, with fewer than ten members in 1943, growth was slow and organization weak until two better positioned notables, Jalal al-Sayyid of Deir-ez-Zor and Midhat al-Bitar of Damascus, joined the leadership during 1942/43. Thereafter, the undefined group without a fixed name became in 1943 the movement (haraka), in 1944 the party of the Arab Resurrection (al-Ba'th al-Arab), with a permanent office, and in 1946 a newspaper. The followers of Arsuzi—now led by Wahib GHANIM—then joined, and a congress of 247 members met in Damascus to adopted a constitution, April 4, 1947.

Aflaq was elected the first amid (dean) and thereafter held, at least nominally, the leading position in the BA'TH party, as well as the editorship of the newspaper. Yet he was soon the focus of unending controversy. The most detailed information is provided by self-interested sources other than Aflaq, but these are consistent with each other and the public actions of the party. Aflaq possessed both ambition and envy. He ran without success for the Syrian parliament in 1943 and 1947. He was minister of education during the HINNAWI period but resigned when he failed to be elected to the constituent assembly; then when Sayyid was offered a place in the cabinet, Aflaq and Bitar foreclosed the appointment by demanding two positions. Unlike Sayyid, Aflaq had no power base of his own. Consequently, he was neither willing nor able to prevent the appropriation of the party by Akram al-HAWRANI (also spelled Hurani, Hourani). Although party rules forbade membership by the military, Aflaq cooperated with Hawrani, whose greatest strength was a following in the officers corps.

Despite the opposition of Sayyid, the Ba'th and Hawrani's Arab Socialist party cooperated and merged in November 1952 to form the Arab Socialist Ba'th party. Aflaq and Hawrani became political exiles from January to October of 1953, but in 1954 their party numbered 2,500 in contrast to the 500 of premerger Ba'th in 1952. Hawrani's military friends and his political strength and skill kept the party at the center of power until Syria's union with Egypt in 1958—the formation of the United Arab Republic (UAR). Aflaq and Hawrani had been instrumental in this, but they defected at the end of 1959 and moved to Beirut (Lebanon). The party organization had been amended in 1954 to reflect its pan-Arab character, which was based on its growth outside Syria. Aflaq had been reelected secretary general and a member of the National Command (the executive body composed of representatives from the various regions [countries]), and he had retained these positions even though the party had been dissolved in Syria. As a strong pan-Arab, he broke with Hawrani, who took a Syrianist line, especially after Syria's secession from the UAR in 1961.

Aflaq's position in the party enabled him to take an active part in both Iraqi and Syrian politics after their Ba'thist coups in early 1963, but as the military Ba'thists gained control in Syria, Aflaq's influence waned until finally, following the coup of February 23, 1966, he fled Syria and was expelled from the party. During the rivalry between the Syria Ba'th and the Iraqi Ba'th, which came to power in 1968, the Iraqis continued to recognize Afaq as secretary general of the party. In Syria, he was sentenced to death in absentia in 1971, and Arsuzi was accorded the honor of being the true founder of the Ba'th. Aflaq moved to Baghdad around 1980 and died there in 1989. At his death the Iraqi Ba'th announced that he had long been a secret convert to Islam.

Aflaq's version of Arabism is idealistic and metaphysical; it presents the ideology that became standard by the 1930s—Islamic modernism is combined with the historical vision of the Arab nation that holds that from the time of the earliest-known Arabs, the ancient Semitic peoples, they have been in perpetual conflict with aggressive neighbors—notably the Aryans—including the Europeans. Periods of Arab power and glory have been followed by corruption and disunion due to foreign influences and abasement by imperialism, from which the nation has recovered by returning to its true culture. The greatest of these awakenings was engendered by the gift of Islam, which, in Aflaq's version, was induced or earned by the Prophet Muhammad's acting for the nation. To regain the lost greatness, according to Aflaq, every Arab must act as Muhammad did.

BIBLIOGRAPHY

The theological term *ba'th* had been used by others to designate not only God's sending of Muhammad but also the resulting revival or resurrection of the nation; in other contexts, these writers usually used synonyms for *awakening* or *revival* (*yaqza, nahda*). Aflaq virtually replaced these terms with *ba'th*. Aflaq's many speeches and essays have been collected in *Ma'raka al-masir al-wahid* (The Battle of the Sole Destiny, Beirut, 1958; 2nd ed., 1963); *Fi sabil al-ba'th* (In the Path of Resurrection, Beirut, 1959; 2nd ed. 1963); and *Nuqtat al-bidaya: Ahadith ba'd al-khamis min haziran* (The Beginning Point: Talks after the Fifth of June, Beirut, 1971).

No full critical biography has been published. There is much material on Aflaq in John Devlin, *The Ba'th Party: A History from Its Origins to 1966* (Stanford, Calif., 1976). Norma Salem-Babikian, "A Partial Reconstruction of Michel Aflaq's Thought," in *The Muslim World* (vol. 67, October 1977, pp. 280–294), is informative and innovative.

C. Ernest Dawn

Agadir Crisis

Known as the second Moroccan crisis.

It erupted as the almost inevitable outgrowth on the 1906 ALGECIRAS CONFERENCE, which allowed for Spanish and French control over nominally independent Morocco. In 1911, local opposition culminated in revolts against the French. France responded by sending an occupation force to Fez (Morocco) in May 1911, and Germany concluded it would not permit any revision of the Algeciras Act without some compensation. In July, under the pretext of protecting German citizens, the Germans then ordered the gunboat *Panther* to proceed to Agadir (Morocco) to pressure the French to negotiate. In November, after a brief war scare amid Britain's promises of support for France (Prime Minister Lloyd George's Mansion House speech), a Franco–German accord was signed, granting a French protectorate over Morocco in return for some French sub-Saharan territories to be ceded to Germany. This end to Morocco's nominal independence contributed directly to the outbreak of the 1911 Tripolitanian War and, thus, the BALKAN WARS (1912–1913).

BIBLIOGRAPHY

TAYLOR, A. J. P. *The Struggle for the Mastery of Europe, 1848–1918*. Oxford, England, 1954.

Jon Jucovy

Agal

The name for a circular band or coil.

The agal, made of wool or goat's hair wound tightly about a cotton cord which, going twice around the head, fastens the protective head cloth (*kafiyya*) in place. Generally black, the agal is worn exclusively by Arab men; its varied manufacture, girth, length of tail, and other distinctions identify territorial or tribal affiliations.

Cyrus Moshaver

Agam, Yaacov   [1928–   ]

Israeli artist and sculptor.

The son of a rabbi, Agam was born in Rishon le-Zion and studied at the Bezalel Academy of Arts and Design in Jerusalem, at the Johannes Ittan School in Zurich, and at the Academy of Abstract Art in Paris. Since 1951, he has spent most of his time in Paris, where he became widely recognized for his optic and kinetic art and sculpture. Agam achieves motion in his works by endowing his creations with mobile segments or by giving the impression of movement through the viewer's changing position. His works also include religious objects such as the menorah, mezuzah or Star of David. President Georges Pompidou of France commissioned him to decorate a room in the Elysée Palace. Agam's works are displayed in many public buildings and areas including the president's house in Jerusalem, the Juilliard School of Music in New York, the Elysée Palace, and the Defense Quarters in Paris.

Ann Kahn

Agnon, Shmuel Yosef   [1888–1970]

Hebrew writer who won the Nobel Prize for literature in 1966.

Born in Buczacz (Buchach), Galicia, Agnon emigrated to Palestine in 1907. In 1913 he went to Germany, where he married Ester Marx and started a family. In 1924 he returned to Palestine and settled in Jerusalem.

Agnon was influenced by a variety of social, cultural, and literary sources. The pious milieu of the small Jewish town where he grew up and the Jewish scholarly traditions in which he was steeped from an early age had a deep and lasting effect on his writing. The development of Hebrew literature at the end of the nineteenth century and the beginning of the twentieth also had a formative influence on him. In 1908, after his arrival in Palestine, Agnon became involved with the literary world of the Zionist pioneers, whose ideals and way of life remained important to him throughout his life. The horrors of World War I, which Agnon witnessed in Germany, were influential for his development as a writer. He saw the world he knew disappear before his eyes.

In his works Agnon examines the psychological and philosophical repercussions of the great historical changes that occurred during his lifetime. In particular, he writes about the demise of traditional Jewish culture in Eastern Europe after World War I and the development of a new Jewish center in Palestine. Although he uses the archaic language and pious style of earlier generations, Agnon gives full expression to the vicissitudes of modern human existence: the disintegration of traditional ways of life, the loss of faith, and the loss of identity.

Agnon published four novels, each of which represents a stage in his literary development. The first, *The Bridal Canopy,* was written in Germany between 1920 and 1921. The novel tells about a pious Jew who travels across Galicia to collect money for his daughters' wedding. The novel evokes a bygone world of faith and superstition through a complex blend of nostalgia and irony. The second novel, *A Guest for the Night,* is an account of a writer's visit to his hometown shortly after the end of World War I. The account is an attempt to grapple with the devastating impact the war had on traditional Jewish life in Eastern Europe and with the responsibility of the artist as witness. Written in the 1930s, the novel eerily foreshadows the destruction of European Jewry during the Holocaust. The third novel, published in 1945, is called *Only Yesterday* and takes place in Palestine during the 1920s. It revolves around the unsuccessful attempt of its hero, an idealistic pioneer who came to settle the land, to live up to his ideals. The novel is a harsh account of one of the most important periods in the development of Zionism. The fourth novel, *Shira,* explores the social forces in Palestine during the 1920s and 1940s through the life of a Jerusalem academic who is torn between his petit bourgeois world and his desire to live his life to the fullest.

In addition to his novels, Agnon published many parables, short stories, novellas, and other works in varying genres, including psychological love stories (*The Doctor's Divorce, Fahrenheim*), social satires (*Young and Old*), grotesque tales (*The Frogs, Pisces*), and pious fables about Hassidic sages (*The Story of Rabbi Gadiel the Baby*). Their polished exterior and detached tone hide a deep sense of pathos and pervasive irony. Agnon's frequent use of ancient Jewish sources, and the new ways in which he interprets them, create a tension between style and content that enhances the meaning of both.

Agnon had greatly influenced several generations of Hebrew writers, who found in his works a link between the Jewish world that vanished after the world wars and the existential concerns of their own time. Admired by readers and critics alike, he is one of the most acclaimed Hebrew writers and among the most widely translated. *The Collected Works of S. Y. Agnon,* which includes twenty-four volumes of his fiction, was published in eight volumes between 1953 and 1962. Many of his works have been published posthumously.

BIBLIOGRAPHY

AGNON, S. Y. *The Collected Works of S. Y. Agnon.* 8 vols. 1953–1962. In Hebrew.
BAND, ARNOLD. *Nostalgia and Nightmare.* Berkeley, Calif., 1968.
MINTZ, ALAN, and ANNE GOLOMB HOFFMAN, eds. *A Book That Was Lost and Other Stories by S. Y. Agnon.* New York, 1995.
SHAKED, GERSHON. *Hebrew Narrative Fiction, 1880–1980,* vol. 2. Tel Aviv, 1988. In Hebrew.
———. *S. Y. Agnon—A Revolutionary Traditionalist.* New York, 1993.

Yarom Peleg

Agop, Gullu   [1840–1891]

Early Turkish theater director and actor.

Gullu Agop was born in Constantinople as Gulluyan Hagop Vartovyan, to Armenian parents. He began working in theater in 1862 and, in 1867, founded the first Turkish language theater in the Ottoman Empire, called the Ottoman Theater. In 1870, he obtained a government monopoly on Turkish-language theater for fifteen years. He was known for innovation, producing in 1873 the first modern play written originally in Turkish: *Vatan Yahut Silistre* (The Motherland Silistre [a Bulgarian province and city on the Danube that was part of the Ottoman Empire from 1420 to 1878]) by NAMIK KEMAL.

In 1884, Sultan ABDÜLHAMIT II labeled the theater subversive and had it burned down in 1885. Ironically, Agop then spent his last years as state director at the sultan's palace.

BIBLIOGRAPHY

SHAW, STANFORD, and EZEL KURAL SHAW. *History of the Ottoman Empire and Modern Turkey.* New York, 1977.

Elizabeth Thompson

Agriculture

Soil cultivation for the production of crops first began in the ancient Near East during the Neolithic era, c. 10,000 B.C.E.

The Middle East, including North Africa, has become the least food self-sufficient area of the world's major populated regions. Although the differences among Middle Eastern countries are great (for example, Turkey is an occasional exporter of wheat, but Sudan repeatedly experienced famine in the 1980s and early 1990s), some regional generalizations may be made. Rapidly increasing demand for food has outpaced the domestic supply, because of (1) rapid population increase and (2) considerable expansion of per capita incomes during the period of the petroleum boom (roughly 1973–1985). Supply response has been significant though constrained by nature, history, and public policy—but the agricultural systems of the region have undergone considerable transformation as a result of recent efforts to increase domestic food supplies.

During the 1980s, population grew in the Middle East at just under 3 percent each year. Only sub-Saharan African populations are growing more swiftly. Nevertheless, food production has kept pace with population growth in Egypt, Morocco, Tunisia, Saudi Arabia, Yemen, Algeria, Libya, Iraq, Israel, and Jordan—and has nearly done so in Iran. From 1965 to 1988, however, per capita incomes were also growing at about 3 percent each year.

Middle Easterners spend a substantial fraction of their additional income on food, especially on "luxury" foods, such as meat and fresh produce. Accordingly, demand for all food rose at about 4 to 5 percent each year—and demand for meat, milk, vegetables,

Cattle in fields near Jonglei Canal in Sudan. (© Chris Kutschera)

and fruits grew at roughly 6 percent each year in the same period.

Few agricultural sectors could have met this increased demand from domestic supply alone; the countries of the Middle East could not, and they became increasingly dependent on food imports. Most countries in the region now import at least 200 pounds (100 kg) of grain per person per year, and many import far more. In 1988, Libya imported 755 pounds (342 kg), and Israel, 900 pounds (409 kg); these are similar to the amounts needed by the non-agricultural city-state of Singapore, 890 pounds (405 kg). In the Middle East, food imports typically declined, however, as a proportion of total imports between 1965 and 1988. Over the decades, such increasing food dependency has led many national planners in the region to try to accelerate agricultural growth—but they have had to deal with significant natural and social constraints.

Egyptian agricultural worker using a shadoof, *an irrigation device, with the Hadum pyramid visible in the background, c. 1940.* (D.W. Lockhard)

Plowing the Gaza Strip (mid-1950s). (D.W. Lockhard)

Dikes constructed between irrigated fields in northeast Iran, 1966. (Richard Bulliet)

The scarcity of fresh water is the main natural obstacle to greater food production in the region. Many areas receive less than 20 inches (50 cm) of rain per year, making unirrigated agriculture extremely risky. Rainfall is also highly variable as to seasonal pattern; only the shores of the Caspian and Black seas receive rainfall year round. Elsewhere, precipitation follows one of two seasonal patterns: (1) a winter maximum along the Mediterranean shore, the FERTILE CRESCENT, and central and southern Iran, or (2) a summer monsoonal maximum in Southern Arabia and Sudan. Precipitation within these areas of climate often varies considerably, and rain may even fall at the wrong time during the planting cycle.

Irrigated land area was increased from about 30 million acres (12 million ha), some 15 percent of arable land in the early 1960s, to about 42 million acres (17 million ha), some 17 percent of arable land in 1985. Irrigation resources are unequally distributed across countries. Roughly 34 percent of all irrigated land in the region is in Iran; in descending order, the four countries with the largest amount of irrigated land are Iran, Egypt, Turkey, and Iraq. Likewise, irrigated land as a percentage of the arable land varies widely by country. At one extreme, virtually all (97%) of Egypt's farmland is irrigated, as is 65 percent of Israel's. By contrast, only 8 percent of Turkey's and 7 percent of Morocco's arable land is irrigated. Iran and Iraq have roughly 33 to 40 percent of their arable land irrigated. Since irrigated land produces much more per acre than nonirrigated land, with higher value crops such as fruits and vegetables (as opposed to grains), these numbers actually understate the economic contribution of irrigated farming in the Middle East.

Unfortunately, irrigation development has too often neglected long-run environmental issues, thereby jeopardizing the sustainability of the considerable short-term output gains from irrigation expansion. Two problems predominate—the neglect of drainage and the overexploitation of groundwater. Irrigation without drainage raises soil salinity, which reduces crop yields; because irrigation raises output immediately, while neglect of drainage reduces it only after a time (10–20 years), governments short of cash have often sacrificed the future by underinvesting in drainage. This problem has plagued all irrigation systems in the region, and in fact, throughout the world. Overexploitation of groundwater is another example of heavily discounting the future—in many cases, this is "fossil water," which is not replenishable (particularly in the Arabian peninsula). In time, these ancient stores of water (similar to underground pools of petroleum) will be depleted and the farms that depend on such water will have to be abandoned.

Since water is currently *free* to farmers, they have no incentive to economize it. The water problem can only grow more serious throughout the region, and it can only be mitigated through intelligent water-use efficiency, which requires a great investment in both physical and human capital. Drip irrigation, pioneered in Israel and California, which delivers precisely calibrated amounts of water to individual fruit trees, costs at least three times as much to install as conventional flow irrigation. Drip techniques also require literature and technically trained personnel to operate them effectively. Future water-conservation imperatives will also likely reduce the allocation of land to water-intensive crops such as alfalfa, rice, and cotton. In addition, few legal mechanisms have been established for trading water rights. The allocation of ever scarcer water must increasingly concern all farmers and governments in the Middle East.

Rain-fed farming systems may be divided into two general types: (1) the "Mediterranean dry-farming" system, in which winter wheat or barley alternates with fallow and the grazing of sheep, goats, cattle, and/or camels, and (2) the dry-farming techniques of Sudan. Slow progress is being made in relying on increasingly sophisticated methods for conserving soil moisture and raising the productivity of the first system. Sudanese rain-fed agriculture in the central zone of the country must be differentiated along two axes: north/south, which corresponds to the rainfall gradient, and east/west, which has two very different soil types, heavy clay and sandy soils. The heavy clay soils are the most productive, especially when farmed by mechanized labor. Such mechanization, however, has caused some social conflicts—by exacerbating existing problems between semi-migratory cattle herders and more sedentary farmers.

Cereal grains are the dominant crop in the Middle East, occupying over 40 percent of the arable land. Wheat, which is indigenous to the region (specifically, to the northern Fertile Crescent) constitutes more than 50 percent of all regional cereal production; it is planted on about 25 percent of the farmed area in any year. Barley, also indigenous, is especially well-suited to drier areas and is a distant second. About 34 percent of all land planted in wheat in less developed countries is found in the Middle East. Because of natural and social constraints, grain production has grown less rapidly than population in the region. Increasingly, greater output of grains and all other foodstuffs will require a shift—from bringing additional land into cultivation to raising the output per unit of land. (The only country with significant un- or underexploited areas of land is Sudan.) Such intensive agricultural growth is, however, constrained not merely by water resources but by social conditions and economic policies.

The principal social constraints to agricultural development have been unequal access to land and other problems concerning property rights, unfavorable terms of trade facing farmers, and low levels of investment and/or technical difficulties, such as those with irrigation mentioned above.

Despite considerable differences between countries and regions, the following generalizations on land tenure may be made: (1) prereform land tenure was "bimodal," with a small number of farmers owning large areas of land and a large number of others holding small parcels; (2) states were and are very active in shaping land-tenure patterns; (3) LAND REFORM has reduced but not eliminated unequal distributions of land; (4) governments usually intervened largely for political reasons, specifically, to destroy their enemies, but (5) states also often had development strategies or programs that involved trying to transfer resources from agriculture to industry and/or urban areas; thus (6) states tried to monopolize the distribution of farm inputs and output, and (7) states throughout the region have retreated from land reforms as part of a more general regional-economic trend toward an increasingly expanded scope for the private sector.

Governments often created state marketing monopolies as part of land-reform programs—eventually allowing them to tax farmers, by reducing the price of outputs below world-market levels and raising those of inputs above world-market levels. Such price policies combined with macroeconomic and trade policies that distorted foreign exchange rates, weakened the incentives for farmers to produce the taxed crops. Not all crops were taxed, but grains and major export goods (e.g., cotton) usually were.

These unfavorable pricing policies help to explain the sluggish growth of grain output until the early 1980s. After that, governments increasingly recognized the need to offer farmers adequate incentives if food-security goals were to be met; they also understood that only private farms produce effectively, since far too many risks and critical daily decisions must be made to entrust farming to unwieldy state bureaucracies. The taxation on farming has been reduced in many countries, and price policies have been improved. Less success has been achieved in improving macroeconomic policies that affect agriculture, however, such as inflation control and exchange-rate management.

Increased output per land unit is usually associated with greater use of higher-yielding varieties (HYVs), which have been specially bred to be more responsive to fertilizer. The adoption rate for HYV wheat has been constrained by both limited water supplies and pricing policies. Only about 30 percent of Middle East wheat fields are planted with HYVs, compared with nearly 80 percent in Latin America and Asia. By contrast, farm mechanization, especially tractor use, has diffused rapidly, especially for such power-intensive tasks as land preparation. For example, in 1960, there were some 2,500 acres (1000 ha) for every tractor in Iran, but only some 250 acres (100 ha) per tractor in 1985. The use of harvesting machinery, such as combines, has spread more slowly than tractors. The pattern of mechanization indicates that machines were substituted for animal labor as opposed to being substituted for human labor; animals had become far more valuable as producers of meat and milk, whereas governments in the region often subsidized fuel.

Mechanized techniques also economize on human labor, since recent emigration from the countryside has negatively affected the agricultural sector in many Middle East countries. Everywhere the proportion of agricultural laborers has declined. From 1960 to 1985, the number of farm workers fell in Algeria, Jordan, and Syria, though remaining roughly stable in Egypt, Iraq, Tunisia, and Turkey. Labor MIGRATION—from rural areas to cities and from non-oil to oil-exporting countries within the region—accounts for most of the additions to the rural population. Education in the countryside has raised skill levels and expectations, leading many young people to abandon farming. Only if the educated youth are given the technology and incentives to succeed in agriculture will the Middle East be able to mitigate water scarcity and even partially meet the growing demand for food.

Alan R. Richards

Agudat Israel

Organization of Orthodox Jewry; political party of Orthodox Jews in Israel.

The organization was founded in Katowice (Upper Silesia, now in the southwestern part of Poland), in 1912, as a worldwide movement of Orthodox Jews. It established the Council of Torah Sages as its religious authority on all political matters. Opposed to secular Zionism and the World Zionist Organization (the settlement of Jews in Palestine; a return to Palestine), it consisted of three major groups: German Orthodox followers of Rabbi Samson Raphael Hirsch; the Lithuanian yeshiva (religious school) community; and Polish Hasidic rabbis and their followers—especially the Gur Hasidic group. The major objective was to provide a range of religion-based communal services to strengthen the Orthodox community.

In Palestine, Agudat Israel was established to be independent of the organized Jewish community (the Yishuv). Despite its ideological opposition to secular Zionism, in 1933 it entered into an agreement with the Jewish Agency there (which represented the Yishuv to the British mandate authority), according to which Agudat Israel would receive 6.5 percent of the immigration permits. In 1947, just before Israel's independence, it entered into an even more comprehensive agreement, which has come to be known as the status quo letter. This purported to guarantee basic religious interests in Israel and served to legitimize Agudat Israel's joining the government-in-information and the initial 1949–1951 government coalition. At this point, it bolted—opposing the government's decision to draft women into the military. In 1977, Agudat Israel supported the Likud-led coalition; it joined Israel's national unity government in 1984 and has since remained part of the government, although it has refused a ministry.

Agudat Israel experienced a number of internal rifts that came to a head in the 1980s and have resulted in the emergence of a group of ultra-Orthodox, or *haredi*, parties. In 1983, due to long-simmering anger over the absence of Sephardic leadership in the party, the Jerusalem *sephardi* members of Agudat Israel broke away and established the Sephardi Torah Guardians party, SHAS; it was so successful in the municipal elections in Jerusalem during October 1983 that it ran a national slate of candidates in 1984 and became an impressive force. At the same time, an old conflict between the Hasidic and Lithuanian-type yeshiva elements within Agudat Israel—represented by the Hasidic rabbis of Gur and Vizhnitz, on one side, and the head of the Ponevez yeshiva in B'nai Brak, Rabbi Eliezer Shach, on the other—reached new heights and culminated in the formation of Shach's Degel HaTorah (Torah Flag) party for the 1988 national elections.

Agudat Israel, like the other *haredi* parties, is generally moderate on foreign-policy issues, including the administered territories; but it is concerned with all matters of domestic policy, those it perceives as affecting religion, in general, and especially its own educational institutions.

BIBLIOGRAPHY

DON-YEHIYA, ELIEZER. "Origin and Development of the Aguda and Mafdal Parties." *Jerusalem Quarterly* 20 (1981): 49–64.

FRIEDMAN, MENACHEM. *Dat ve-hevrah. Religion and Society: Non-Zionist Orthodoxy in Eretz Israel, 1918–1936.* Jerusalem, 1977.

FUND, YOSEF. "Agudat Israel Confronting Zionism and the State of Israel—Theology and Policy." Ph.D. diss., Bar-Ilan University, 1989 (Hebrew with English summary).

GREILSAMMER, ILAN. "The Religious Parties." In *Israel's Odd Couple: The 1984 Knesset Elections and the National Unity Government,* ed. by Daniel J. Elazar and Shmuel Sandler. Detroit, 1990.

Chaim I. Waxman

Ahad Ha-Am   [1856–1927]

Early Zionist author; pen name of Asher Ginzberg.

Born in Skvire in the Ukraine, Ha-Am (in Hebrew, One of the People) was moved to a rural estate in 1868, rented by his wealthy father, a follower of the mystical Hasidic movement. There he was educated in Jewish topics by private tutors, while teaching himself Russian, German, French, and English. He became a devotee of the English positivists, of which Herbert Spencer was his key inspiration. Ginzberg broke with traditional Judaism and, in 1886, settled in Odessa, a center of progressive Jewish life. There he quickly rose to prominence in the emerging Zionist movement, then spearheaded by the Odessa-based Hovevei Zion. He worked as an editor of several periodicals and founded *Ha-Shiloach,* a pioneering Hebrew-language journal when Hebrew was being transformed into a modern idiom. In 1908, he moved to London, where he was employed by a tea firm and became a close adviser to Chaim WEIZMANN during the negotiations leading to the BALFOUR DECLARATION of 1917. Ginzberg settled in Palestine in 1922; he died there at the age of 70.

For several decades after 1889, when he first published his major article "This Is Not the Way" (*Lo zeh ha-derekh*), Ahad Ha-Am became prominent in

Hebrew letters. His ironic spare prose set new standards for the Hebrew essay. His stand on Jewish nationalism was based on two interlinked themes—the perils of Jewish assimilation and the role of Palestine as a spiritual center. He saw not mounting anti-Semitism but the threat of assimilation as the spur for Zionism: He saw the return of Jews to their homeland accompanied by a return to their original language and by a rebirth of political institutions—which had been supplanted by adherence to theology and ritual after the Roman conquest of Palestine in the first century C.E. In his view, before the HASKALA (enlightenment) movement of the late eighteenth century, Jewry had been sustained by commitment to community, to collective life—but modernism and citizenship or the prospect of citizenship in European states was isolating Jews from their natural community and from each other. He championed the Russian-based Hovevei Zion movement as the natural heir to the Jewish people's legacy of exile and the focal point of Jewish identity in a world where both the refusal to assimilate outside influences and an unchecked eagerness to do so could result in the disappearance of Jewry. Herzlian Zionism, which came to dominate Jewish nationalist circles following the First Zionist Congress in 1897, was, he contended, shortsighted in its stress on diplomacy and politics—and its indifference to the slow deliberate but essential colonizing efforts of the Hovevei Zion.

As an alternative both to philanthropic and to diplomatic Zionism, Ahad Ha-Am promoted his concept of "spiritual center"—since, in the past, Jewry had owed its collective existence to an ability to concentrate its spiritual resources on the rebuilding of its future. Martin BUBER, Mordecai Kaplan, Judah MAGNES, and Zionist socialists read his work and respected his views, in part, while at the same time others criticized his politics as elitist, apolitical, and impractical.

A key to his abiding reputation was based on his being the first Zionist to see the darker side to the Arab-Jewish relationship in Palestine, insisting that what others believed to be merely skirmishes, were, in fact, threats to the Jewish national enterprise. As early as 1891, in his essay "The Truth from the Land of Israel" (*Emet me-eretz yisrael*), he argued that the brutal recent treatment of Arabs by some Jews was a tragic reaction to a history of Jewish subjugation in the DIASPORA. The weight he gave to the issue of Arab retaliation to Jewish settlement activity placed it, however tenuously, on the Zionist agenda. In the last years of his life he argued that Palestine would face its greatest test in how it treated the "strangers" in its midst. While on one level, success would be determined by the ability to galvanize the Jewish people so as to make Arabs into a minority in Palestine, on another, failure to create a society in which Arabs (Palestinians) could live with dignity would traduce the Jewish past and mean defilement to Zion.

Ahad Ha-Am's reputation declined after the establishment of the State of Israel in 1948. His caution appeared misguided, his pessimism idiosyncratic rather than prescient; his gradualism was at odds with the new state's heroic prerequisites. After the election of Menachem BEGIN in 1977, however, he was put to use by some intellectuals on Israel's liberal-left who were frustrated by the ability of the right-wing Revisionist Zionists to win not only control of the government but to usurp classical Jewish nationalism as well.

BIBLIOGRAPHY

HERTZBERG, ARTHUR. *The Zionist Idea.* New York, 1959.
LUZ, EHUD. *Parallels Meet.* Philadelphia, 1988.
ZIMON, LEON. *Ahad Ha-am: A Biography.* Philadelphia, 1960.
ZIPPERSTEIN, STEVEN J. *Elusive Prophet: Ahad Ha'am and the Origins of Zionism.* Berkeley, Calif., 1993.

Steven Zipperstein

Ahaggar Mountains

Mountainous plateau in the central Sahara.

The Ahaggar (also called Hoggar) range is approximately 1,000 miles (1,600 km) south of Algiers, in southern Algeria. Its extinct volcanoes rise to nearly 9,900 feet (3,020 m), and its higher rainfall levels than the surrounding desert support light pastoral nomadism by the Tuareg. The principal oasis, Tamanrasset, is strategically located along the trans-Saharan route, midway between Algiers and Kano (in northern Nigeria).

Will D. Swearingen

Ahali, al-

Egyptian newspaper.

Al-Ahali (The Masses, or The People), is a leftist newspaper founded in Cairo in February 1978 by the NATIONAL PROGRESSIVE UNIONIST PARTY (Tagammu) of Khalid Muhyi al-Din. Banned later that year for its criticism of Anwar al-Sadat's domestic policies and his rapprochement with Israel, the paper reappeared in 1984. The views of *al-Ahali* and the Tagammu range from Marxist to Nasserist. Lately it has muted its criticism of the Mubarak regime and made common cause with the government in resisting Islamist politics.

BIBLIOGRAPHY

BAKER, RAYMOND WILLIAMS. *Sadat and After.* Cambridge, Mass., 1990.

Donald Malcolm Reid

Ahali Group

Political group in Iraq, 1930–1958.

At the group's forefront in early 1930 were several young intellectuals imbued with liberal ideals and a strong desire to reform the economic, political, and social conditions of Iraq. Four of them stand out: Hussain Jamil, Abd al-Qadir ISMA'IL, Muhammad HADID, and Fatah Ibrahim. The first two were Sunni Muslims from Baghdad who were classmates in high school and briefly at Baghdad Law College. Both were active in the opposition politics of the 1920s and were suspended from school. Muhammad Hadid was a Sunni Muslim who belonged to a wealthy conservative family from Mosul. He studied at the American University of Beirut and did a year of graduate work at Columbia University. Both Hadid and Ibrahim were influenced by liberal and socialist thought while studying abroad.

These four young men and other individuals decided to publish a newspaper to express their ideas and philosophy. They chose the name *Ahali* to stress their ties and unity with the people—this name has since been applied to the whole group. The first issue of the newspaper, dated January 2, 1932, appeared under the slogan "People's Benefit Is Above All Benefits." *Ahali* quickly gained popularity and became the most influential paper in Baghdad. It served as a mouthpiece for the most constructive, the most modern, and the most progressive minds in Iraq. *Al-Ahali* was distinguished for its coverage and analysis of the social and economic conditions of the country and for its sharp attack on government policies. Consequently, it had difficulties with government officials and publication was repeatedly suspended.

Initially, the members of the Ahali Group were united by their anti-British sentiment, their critical stand against the government, and their desire for reform. They advocated ideas of the French Revolution and called for a strengthening of the parliamentary system. In 1933, Kamil CHADIRCHI, a young liberal lawyer from an aristocratic family in Baghdad, joined the group. Chadirchi was a member of the opposition group who in the 1920s became disenchanted with the IKHA AL-WATANI PARTY headed by Yasin al-HASHIMI. In 1934, the Ahali Group adopted a more socialist agenda. They called their new emphasis "Shabiya" populism to avoid the misunderstanding surrounding the word "socialism." Shabiya, a doctrine that seeks welfare for all people regardless of gender, class, race, or religion, stresses the importance of human rights, equal opportunity, and freedom from tyranny. It emphasizes the state as provider of health care and education for its people, and recognizes the importance of religion, family, and the parliamentary system.

In 1933, the Ahali Group established the Baghdad Club and the Campaign Against Illiteracy Association. Both organizations had cultural objectives but were designed to broaden popular support for the Ahali Group. In 1934, under the leadership of Chadirchi, the group was able to influence and recruit Ja'far Abu al-Timman to head the Campaign Against Illiteracy Association and later to join the Ahali Group. Al-Timman was formerly the leader of the national al-Watani Party. He was a well-respected national figure in Iraq and a believer in democratic institutions. His accession to Ahali enhanced the status of the group. Moreover, Chadirchi was able to recruit Hikmat SULAYMAN, a former member of the Ikha Party who left because of disagreements with its leader.

In 1935, the Ikha came to power and inspired the Ahali Group to work more actively toward achieving power. At this juncture it was decided to deemphasize the Shabiya ideas and adopt a broader program of liberal reform to gain wider support. Through Sulayman's influence the Ahali Group recruited a few army officers; chief among them was General Bakr SIDQI. Sulayman persuaded Sidqi to conduct a coup against the Ikha government. On 29 October 1936, the coup was successfully executed, the first in the modern history of Iraq and in the Arab world. The Ahali Group was a reluctant participant. Al-Timan, Chadirchi, and Hadid opposed the idea, fearing it could lead to tyranny and military dictatorship. However, Sulayman's opinion prevailed. Ahali received the lion's share of cabinet positions in the new government and organized the Popular Reform Society to propagate the group's reform ideals. The group, however, soon discovered that the real power was in the hands of Sidqi and Sulayman. Even though Sulayman was a member of Ahali, he abandoned its ideas in favor of "politics as usual." Unable to push for reform, the Ahali ministers resigned from the government on 19 June 1937. The Popular Reform Society and al-*Ahali* ceased to exist. The members of the group were scattered, exiled, or imprisoned.

In the 1940s and 1950s, Ahali's members and supporters continued to play an active role in Iraq's national politics. In 1946, three influential members of the group—Chadirchi, Hadid, Jamil—formed the NATIONAL DEMOCRATIC PARTY, which advocated democracy and moderate socialism. It functioned both openly and secretly, taking an active part in opposition politics of the 1940s and 1950s. It participated in the uprisings against the government in 1948, 1952, and 1956, and supported the revolution of 1958. The party eventually split into two factions because of internal disagreement over the regime of Abd al-Karim KASSEM. In the 1960s and 1970s, Ahali's influence faded as other ideologies and groups, such as the al-BA'TH Party, replaced it in the political spotlight.

BIBLIOGRAPHY

KHADDURI, MAJID. *Independent Iraq 1932–1958: A Study in Iraqi Politics.* London, 1960.
———. *Republican Iraq: A Study in Iraqi Politics Since the Revolution of 1958.* London, 1969.

Ayad al-Qazzaz

Ahardane, Majoub   [1921–   ]

Moroccan political leader.

Born into a Middle Atlas BERBER family, Majoub Ahardane served in the French army during World War II and then supported Moroccan nationalism. After independence from French Colonialism in 1956, he led the effort to form the primarily Berber-based Popular Movement (MOUVEMENT POPULAIRE; MP) in 1957. Following a difficult period when Ahardane and other party leaders were imprisoned for their activities, the party was recognized in 1959. As secretary-general of the MP until 1986, Ahardane remained closely tied to the throne, serving King Hassan II as minister of defense twice (1961–1964 and 1966–1967) and in other cabinet posts during the 1970s and 1980s.

BIBLIOGRAPHY

WATERBURY, JOHN. *The Commander of the Faithful.* New York, 1970.
Who's Who in the Arab World, 1990–1991.

Matthew S. Gordon

Aharonian, Avetis   [1866–1948]

Armenian writer, educator, and political figure.

Aharonian was born in the town of Igdir, then in Erevan province of the Russian Empire. He received his primary education at the Echmiadsin seminary and became a teacher in his native town before pursuing higher education in Lausanne and Paris. After his return he joined the ARF (DASHNAK PARTY) and became associated with its main organ *Droshak* while gaining recognition as the author of works of romantic nationalism. He served as headmaster of the Nersesian Academy in Tbilisi from 1907 to 1909, then faced arrest, imprisonment, and exile at the hands of the czarist police. He escaped from prison in 1911 and fled to Switzerland. Returning to the Caucasus in 1916, Aharonian became one of the organizers of the Armenian National Congress, which convened in October 1917 to provide representation for the Armenian population in democratic Russia. The Armenian National Congress, dominated by the Dashnaks, elected an executive body called the Armenian National Council with Aharonian as its chairman. In the wake of the breakup of the Russian Empire after the Bolshevik Revolution, this same council, still under the chairmanship of Aharonian, assumed responsibility for the declaration of an independent Armenian state in the area of Erevan province in May 1918.

Without prior diplomatic experience, but trusting his commitment, penmanship, and knowledge of the French language, the Armenian Republic relied upon Aharonian as its most visible envoy on the international scene. First he led a delegation to Constantinople (now Istanbul) in June 1918 to negotiate a settlement of the Armenian border with the Ottoman Empire which had been at war against Russia in the Transcaucasus. The assignment required meeting with the Young Turk government leaders, including then Prime Minister Talat and Minister of War EN-VER, both held responsible by Armenians for the deportations and mass killings instituted against the Ottoman Armenian population in 1915. In December 1918 the Armenian Parliament named Aharonian as president of the permanent delegation to the Paris Peace Conference. Aharonian arrived in Paris to discover that the Republic of Armenia was denied a seat at the conference. He stayed to sign the Treaty of Sèvres on behalf of the Republic of Armenia in August 1920. The agreement, which finally extended international recognition to the Republic of Armenia two years after its formation, became a dead letter with the sovietization of Armenia at the end of November 1920. Aharonian remained in France and continued to represent Armenian interests until the question of Armenia was resolved by the Treaty of Lausanne in 1923 by avoiding all mention of such a country. Aharonian spent the rest of his life in Marseilles.

BIBLIOGRAPHY

HOVANNISIAN, RICHARD. *Armenia on the Road to Independence, 1918.* Berkeley, Calif., 1967.
————. *The Republic of Armenia: The First Year, 1918–1919.* Berkeley, Calif., 1971.
WALKER, CHRISTOPHER J. *Armenia: The Survival of a Nation.* New York, 1980.

Rouben P. Adalian

Ahd, al-

A secret Arab nationalist society composed of Iraqi and Syrian officers in the Ottoman army in 1913.

Al-Ahd (literally, The Covenant) was headed by Aziz Ali al-Masri, an Egyptian officer. There is very little information on the society and how it was formed; however, it is significant that it was formed after the Ottoman Empire lost Tripolitania to Italy in 1911/12 and was defeated in the first Balkan Wars in 1912/13. Apparently, member Arab officers were fearful that the Arab Ottoman Asiatic provinces were about to face a destiny similar to that of Tripolitania or the Balkans. The Arab officers may have had some grievances also against the ruling government of the COMMITTEE OF UNION AND PROGRESS (CUP). While al-Ahd called for Arab autonomy within a federated Ottoman state, it also spoke of Arab–Turkish cooperation to defend the East from the West and insisted on keeping the Islamic caliphate (religious leadership) under Ottoman control.

The most prominent members of al-Ahd were: Taha al-HASHIMI, Yasin al-HASHIMI, Nuri al-SA'ID, Mawlud Mukhlis, Ali Jawdat al-AYYUBI, Jamil Madfa'i, Abdallah al-Dulimi, Tahsin Ali, Muhammad Hilmi, Ali Rida al-Ghazali, Muwafaq Kamil, Abd al-Ghafur al-Badri (Iraqis); Salim al-Jazairi, Awni Qadamani, Muhammad Bek Ismail, Mustafa Wasfi, Yahya Kazim Abu al-Khair, Muhi al-Din al-Jabban, Ali al-Nashashibi, and Amin Lufti al-Hafiz (Syrians).

According to some sources, the society had some local branches. The Mosul branch in northern Iraq was said to have been led by Yasin al-Hashimi and included Mawlud Mukhlis, Ali Jawdat, Abd al-Rahman Sharaf, Abdallah al-Dulymi, Sharif al-Faruqi, Majid Hassun (Iraqis), and Tawfiq al-Mahmud, Hassan Fahmi, Sadiq al-Jundi, and Mukhtar al-Tarabulsi (Syrians).

BIBLIOGRAPHY

KHADDURI, MAJID. "Aziz Ali Misri and the Arab Nationalist Movement." *Middle Eastern Affairs,* no. 4, *St. Antony's Papers,* no. 17, ed. by Albert Hourani. London, 1965.
QAYSI, SAMI ABD AL-HAFIZ AL-. *Yasin al-Hashimi wa dawruhu fi al-siyasah al-iraqiyya bayn ami, 1922–1936.* Basra, Iraq, 1975.
RAWI, IBRAM AL-. *Min al-thawra al-arabiyya al-kubra ila al-iraq al-hadith: Dhikarayat.* Beirut, 1969.

Mahmoud Haddad

Ahdut ha-Avodah

An Israeli socialist party founded in 1919 by veterans of the Jewish Legion and other Palestine pioneers.

With strong support in the Kibbutz ha-Me'uhad movement, Ahdut ha-Avodah (also Achdut Ha'-Avodah; The Unity of Labor) worked for the unification of Jewish labor movements and the development of new forms of settlement and labor units. It rejected Marxist doctrines of class warfare in favor of social democracy. In 1930, it joined with others in founding the MAPAI party. Becoming independent from that party in 1944, Ahdut ha-Avodah joined with ha-SHOMER HA-TZA'IR, a Zionist socialist youth movement, to found the more radical left-wing MAPAM in 1948. It split with MAPAM in 1954, formed an alignment with MAPAI in 1965, and in 1968 merged again with MAPAI and the RAFI PARTY to form the Israeli LABOR PARTY. Among those closely associated with it were David BEN-GURION, Yizhak BEN-ZVI, Yitzhak TABENKIN, Moshe David REMEZ, and Berl KATZNELSON.

BIBLIOGRAPHY

ROLEF, SUSAN, ed. *Political Dictionary of Israel.*

Walter F. Weiker

Ahidous

Line dance of Middle Atlas Berber-speaking people.

At festive gatherings, drummers surround a bonfire and dancers form two lines. One of the dancers calls a phrase that is refined and repeated by others in his or her group, to the accompaniment of the drums and clapping. Then the other group intones a phrase, often a response to the first. In the Middle Atlas Mountains men and women form both lines. In southern Morocco, where the dance is often called *ahwash,* women form a separate line. Movements—shuffling, bending the body forward and back, lifting and dropping the arms—are in unison.

Thomas G. Penchoen

Ahmad, Muhammad   [c. 1840–1885]

Islamic politico-religious leader, called al-Mahdi, known as the father of Sudanese nationalism.

Born Muhammad Ahmad ibn Abdallah, he was the son of a boat builder on Labab island, in the Nile, south of Dongola, Sudan. His father, also a boat builder, claimed descent from the family of the Prophet. The family moved to Karari, north of Omdurman, and then Khartoum, while Muhammad Ahmad was a child. He was enrolled in Qur'anic schools and then pursued advanced studies under Shaykh Muhammad al-Dikar in Barbara and then under Shaykh al-Quashi wad al-Zain in the Sammaniyya *tariqah* (religious order) school in Khartoum. An ascetic person, who sought a puritanic, meditative lifestyle, he broke with his religious teacher in 1881, soon after he moved to Aba island in the White Nile.

In June 1881, he dispatched letters to religious leaders throughout the Sudan, informing them that he was the "expected Mahdi," the divine leader chosen by God to fill the earth with justice and equity at the end of time. After emissaries from the Turko–Egyptian government tried to dissuade him, an armed force was dispatched to capture him and his small band of followers. His three hundred adherents, armed only with swords and spears, defeated the expedition on Aba island, August 12, 1881. Following that seemingly miraculous victory, the Mahdi led his followers to Qadir mountain in the region of Kurdufan. Their migration imitated the Prophet Muhammad's *hijra* (holy flight) from Mecca to Medina. The move to Kurdufan also enabled him to recruit adherents from the Nuba and *baqqara* (cattle-herding Arab) tribes of the west, who had long defied the control of the central government. The *Ansar* (helpers or followers) defeated government expeditions in December 1881, June 1882, and November 1883.

By then, the Mahdi had flooded the country with letters that explained the politico-religious significance of his mission: his task was to reverse the socioreligious abuses of the Turko–Egyptian regime, which had departed from God's path, and to revive the simple and just practices of early Islam. Since his mission was divinely ordained, those who opposed him were termed infidels. Efforts by the government and established clergy to denounce him as an im-

poster had diminishing effect, as growing numbers of tribes and religious leaders rallied to his banner. By the time that the Mahdi besieged Khartoum in late 1884, some 100,000 Ansar were camped outside. The Mahdi captured Khartoum on January 26, 1885, and established his capital across the White Nile at Omdurman. Muhammad Ahmad al-Mahdi died of a sudden illness on June 22, 1885, and was succeeded by his principal baqqara follower, Abdullahi ibn Muhammad, who converted Mahdi's religious state into a military dictatorship and ruled until the Anglo–Egyptian conquest in 1898. Under the leadership of his son Abd al-Rahman al-Mahdi, the Mahdi's followers formed a brotherhood to continue his teachings.

Sudanese nationalists later viewed the Mahdi as "the father of independence," who united the tribes, drove out the foreign rulers, and founded the Sudanese nation-state; he saw himself, rather, as "a renewer of the Muslim Faith, come to purge Islam of faults and accretions" (Holt and Daly, 1979, p. 87). Moreover, as the successor to the prophet, he was restoring the community of the faithful: That belief justified his political role. Finally, his belief that he was the "expected Mahdi" emphasized the ecstatic dimension and the idea that his coming foretold the end of time. The combining of those elements—political, religious, and social—produced a powerful, popularly based movement that swept away the decaying Turko–Egyptian regime. The Mahdi's death, immediately after gaining control over almost all of northern Sudan, made it impossible to assess whether he had the ability to craft an Islamic polity on the basis of his charismatic authority.

BIBLIOGRAPHY

HOLT, P. M. *The Mahdist State in the Sudan, 1881–1898.* Oxford, 1970.
HOLT, P. M., and M. W. DALY. *The History of the Sudan.* Boulder, Colo., 1979.
SHEBEIKA, MEKKI. *The Independent Sudan.* New York, 1959.

Ann M. Lesch

Ahmad, Muhammad Sulayman al-
[1908–?]

Syrian politician and poet.

The son of Sulayman al-Ahmad, Muhammad was born in Lattakia, where he served as deputy in 1943, 1947, and 1954. A member of the Damascus and the Arab scientific academies, he became minister of health in 1954 and minister of state in 1956. Using his (perhaps more widely recognized) pen name Badawy al-Jabal, he wrote a collection of poetry, entitled *Diwan Badawy al-Jabal*.

BIBLIOGRAPHY

Who's Who in the Middle East, 1967–1968.

Charles U. Zenzie

Ahmad al-Jazzar   [1735–1804]

Mamluk governor of Acre, Syria, and Lebanon; known as the Butcher (Arabic, al-Jazzar) for his harshness.

Bosnian by birth, Ahmad Pasha al-Jazzar started his military and political career as part of a MAMLUK household in Egypt. In 1768, he went to Syria and was appointed governor of Sidon (Lebanon) in 1775. Ahmad Pasha ruled southeastern Syria and Lebanon at a time when local forces posed serious threats to the Ottoman government. Although nominally subservient to the Ottoman Empire, Ahmad al-Jazzar, like Zahir al-Umar in Galilee, the AZM FAMILY of Damascus, the CHEHAB FAMILY of Mount Lebanon, and the Mamluks of Egypt, virtually ruled his territory independently.

Ahmad Pasha made concerted efforts to weaken the control of the Chehabs of Mount Lebanon and, by the end of his tenure, he had reduced them to subservience. Ahmad al-Jazzar's control over Lebanon interrupted economic ties between Beirut and Western Europe for a quarter century. He was appointed governor of Damascus in 1785, though Acre (in today's Israel) always remained the base of his power. With British help, he repulsed Napoleon Bonaparte, who invaded Palestine in 1799.

BIBLIOGRAPHY

HOLT, P. M. *Egypt and the Fertile Crescent: 1516–1922.* Ithaca, N.Y., 1966.
SALIBI, KAMAL. *House of Many Mansions: The History of Lebanon Reconsidered.* Berkeley, Calif., 1988.

Steve Tamari

Ahmad Bey Husayn   [1806–1855]

Bey, 1837–1855, who attempted to Westernize Tunisia and detach it from the Ottoman Empire.

Ahmad Bey's mother was a Sardinian slave captured in a raid on San Pietro in 1798; his father was Mustafa ibn Mahmud (bey of Tunis, 1835–1837). Ah-mad was the tenth bey of the Husaynid dynasty. From his mother, he acquired a knowledge of conversational Italian. He also knew some Turkish and could speak the Tunisian Arabic dialect. Ahmad Bey received a traditional education, learning the Qur'an by heart. His father took a personal interest in his education and charged Ramadan Bash Mamluk, and later Sahib al-Tabi Mustafa, to ensure that he was taught well. Besides studying the traditional Qur'anic sciences and Turkish, Ahmad learned European history and geography. The latter knowledge influenced his efforts to modernize Tunisian society and turned his foreign policy orientation away from the Ottoman Empire and closer to Europe.

Ahmad Bey's upbringing introduced him to palace intrigues and political disputations. A month before his ascension to power, he participated in the execution of a prominent MAMLUK official, Shakir Sahib al-Tabi, keeper of the seal. He had been the most powerful official in the bey's court. When Ahmad Bey assumed the throne in October 1837, he quickly consolidated his authority. The patronage and support system of Shakir Sahib al-Tabi had to be dismantled, and Ahmad Bey had to build his own patron-client political machine. To do so, he appointed his own clique of friends, mamluks, and clients to key positions. By 1840, the new network of alliances was in place, and he could stamp the regime with his own outlook.

Upon becoming bey, Ahmad had two primary goals: to maintain Tunisia's relative independence vis-à-vis the Ottoman Empire and France's colonial regime in Algeria, and to strengthen Tunisia's internal political order. To accomplish the first, he avoided implementing the Ottoman TANZIMAT reform program that had begun in 1837. He also sought international legitimacy through recognition by nations of Europe (especially France). To placate the Ottomans, he continued to send the obligatory annual gift in exchange for the *firman* (decree) of investiture while avoiding implementation of the *tanzimat* by pleading Tunisia's lack of resources to do so. Ahmad Bey maintained good relations with France, and continued to seek France's guarantees of Tunisian independence and to deny Ottoman claims of sovereignty. In the 1850s, he sent troops to the Crimea to show support for the Ottomans rather than to reflect their sovereignty.

Ahmad Bey's goal of reforming the fabric of the state has been criticized for attempting too much and accomplishing too little. Inspiration for his reform efforts came from Napoleon's France, Muhammad Ali's Egypt, and the tanzimat program. All of these taught him that military strength was paramount. Wedged between France's colonial regime in Algeria and a resurgent Ottoman Empire in Libya, Ahmad saw modernizing the military as one way to maintain Tunisia's territorial integrity against the aspirations of its powerful neighbors.

In 1831, Husayn Bey had begun reforming the military by inviting Europeans to train a *nizami* corps of infantry based on the latest European and Ottoman models. The term nizami was borrowed from the Ottoman designation *nizami jadid* (new order), applied by Sultan MAHMUD II to Ottoman military modernization efforts. The Tunisian nizamis wore European uniforms and Tunisian *shashiyas* (small red hats with tassels).

Mustafa Bey accelerated the expansion of the *nizami* corps by developing a conscription system. An attempt to draft soldiers in the capital of Tunis was abandoned after popular disturbances. Thereafter, only provincials were recruited, often through press-gang methods on an irregular basis. An informal system of recruiting troops (in exchnage for returning an earlier batch to the same area as reserves) was developed in order to minimize friction between recruiters and the local populace. To avoid antagonizing the Turkish military elite, the bey maintained Turkish-Mamluk domination of the upper ranks. The army thus remained top-heavy in inefficient higher-rank officers who were traditional in outlook and ill-suited to the disciplinary codes of modern armies. The lower ranks and noncommissioned officers were reasonably motivated but poorly led. As a result, although the reforms looked good on paper, they largely failed to produce the desired results.

From a small contingent of about 1,800 men at the beginning of his reign, by 1850 Ahmad Bey had expanded the nizami forces to between 26,000 and 36,000, with 16,000 actually in service at any one time. Seven regiments of infantry, two of artillery, and a partial one of cavalry comprised the corps. In the last two years of his reign, financial constraints forced Ahmad Bey to drastically reduce the size of the military. A brief attempt to develop a navy failed, largely because the harbor chosen for its headquarters, Porto Farina (Ghar al-Milh), kept silting up.

A critical step in Ahmad Bey's military reform efforts was the establishment in 1840 of a military academy (*maktab harbi*) adjacent to the Bey's Palace at Bardo (a suburb of Tunis), to train young Mamluks, Turks, and sons of prestigious Arab families in the military arts. Forty to sixty students at a time studied at the academy for a period of six to nine years. The school prepared an elite cadre of graduates who later led reform efforts in the 1870s, during the administration of Prime Minister KHAYR AL-DIN al-

Tunisi (1873–1877). It set the precedent for SADIQI COLLEGE (established in 1875), which trained Tunisians in modern subjects. Its graduates were members of the YOUNG TUNISIANS in the 1890s and early 1900s. Most Tunisian nationalists who formed the DESTOUR and Neo Destour political movements studied at Sadiqi, including independent Tunisia's first president, Habib BOURGUIBA.

Seeking to make Tunisia self-sufficient in military-related goods, Ahmad ordered the construction of a cannon foundry, a small arms factory, powder mills, tanneries, saddle/leather factories, a textile factory, and other industries. He imported European technicians to train Tunisian workers in modern manufacturing techniques. These efforts provided the Tunisian elite and some workers with a rudimentary understanding of European industrialization practices.

Between 1841 and 1846, Ahmad Bey abolished slavery, initiated with the closing of the slave market in Tunis (the Suq al-Birka) and culminating with the January 1846 decree officially abolishing slavery in Tunisia. At al-Muhammadiya, about ten miles southwest of Tunis, he built a magnificent governmental complex, which he intended to serve as Tunisia's Versailles. Europeans designed and furnished this complex with the latest European gadgets, such as a telegraph system linking Al-Muhammadiya with the palaces at Bardo and La Goulette (now Halq al-Wadi).

The last five years of Ahmad's reign were a period of financial chaos, declining agricultural production, his poor health, and overall ruin of his accomplishments. His need for money to finance his military reforms led him to depend on a ruthless tax farmer, Mahmud ibn Ayad. Ahmad Bey tolerated the financial oppression of his subjects so long as ibn Ayad increased the state revenues. The decline of those state revenues between 1849 and 1852 culminated in the flight of ibn Ayad to Paris and his subsequent attempts to sue Tunisia's government. Khayr al-Din arbitrated the matter in Paris, but recovered none of the funds ibn Ayad had taken.

In July 1852, Ahmad Bey suffered a stroke; this and subsequent strokes seriously impaired his ability to rule. In 1853, he was forced to disband his army due to financial problems. Ahmad Bey died in May 1855, at age forty-eight. He had sought to modernize a backward and traditional state and society through emphasis on military reforms. He established positive precedents in the Bardo military academy and the conscription of native Tunisians, and negative ones in the lack of accountability of his leading ministers and in his own financial irresponsibility.

BIBLIOGRAPHY

ANDERSON, LISA. *The State and Social Transformation in Tunisia and Libya, 1830–1980.* Princeton, N.J., 1986.

BROWN, L. CARL. *The Tunisia of Ahmad Bey, 1837–1855.* Princeton, N.J., 1974.

KRAIEM, MUSTAPHA. *La Tunisie précoloniale.* 2 vols. Tunis, 1973.

NELSON, HAROLD D., ed. *Tunisia: A Country Study.* 3rd ed. Washington, D.C., 1986.

PERKINS, KENNETH J. *Historical Dictionary of Tunisia.* Metuchen, N.J., 1989.

Larry A. Barrie

Ahmad Bey of Constantine   [c. 1784–1850]

Commander of the province of Constantine in eastern Algeria, 1826–1837.

When the French conquered Algiers in 1830, ending Ottoman rule, al-Hajj Ahmad assumed direct authority in the name of the sultan. However, the latter was unable to provide support, and after an initial victory over the French (1836), Ahmad was forced to abandon Constantine (1837) and eventually to surrender (1848). Nationalists today consider him, together with Abd al-Qadir, one of the heroes of resistance.

BIBLIOGRAPHY

TEMIMI, ABDELJELIL. *Le Beylik de Constantine et Hadj Ahmed Bey (1830–1837).* Tunis, 1978.

Peter von Sivers

Ahmad Durrani   [c. 1722–1772]

Ruler of Afghanistan; founder of the Durrani dynasty.

Ahmad Durrani was elected ruler by an assembly of PAKHTUN elders in KANDAHAR in 1747, at a time when the Moghul empire in India was disintegrating and the recent Afshar dynasty in Persia was collapsing. He united the Pakhtun clans and led them to create an empire that went from Meshed to Punjab. This Durrani empire did not outlast him by long, but Afghanistan did become a polity with Pakhtuns playing the dominant role in the country's politics.

Born in Herat around 1722, Ahmad belonged to the Saddozai lineage of the Abdali clan. His ancestors had led the clan since 1588. In 1717, the Abdalis proclaimed HERAT an independent state but were de-feated by Nadir Afshar in 1732 and relocated in Khorasan (in Persia). Then in 1736, they were permitted to go to Kandahar. That year Nadir became king of Persia and Ahmad joined Nadir's army, rising to prominence. When Nadir was assassinated in 1747, the Abdali contingent serving in his army returned to Kandahar. In a *loya jirga* (grand assembly) of clan elders, it was decided to create a Pakhtun kingdom, and Ahmad was elected leader.

Ahmad spent most of his reign campaigning in India and Persia (Iran). His most memorable encounter took place in the field of Panipat, near Delhi, on January 14, 1761, when he destroyed a Mahratta army and briefly became the master of Northern India. The Pakhtuns were unable to consolidate their hold, but the destruction of Mahratta power paved the way for the conquest of India by the British. Booty and revenue from the provinces of Punjab, Kashmir, and Sind provided the riches to consolidate Ahmad's rule at home and to keep content the Pakhtun, Baluchi, Uzbek, and Kizilbash clans that constituted his army. As his reign drew to a close, Sikh resistance in the Punjab made campaigning in India less and less profitable.

By then, an Afghan polity was already in place. To incorporate the various clans within the structure of the state, Ahmad systematically assigned to each clan a Khan (leader) who was allowed to farm taxes (IL-TIZAM) in the newly conquered territories or was granted a regular stipend. Ahmad's own clansmen were given even more privileges—the khans among them controlled most key positions in the state, while the rest were exempted from taxation and paid salaries during their campaigns in India. Investing their newly found wealth in land, they became the dominant power in southern Afghanistan and acquired land elsewhere. To reflect their enhanced status, Ahmad changed their name from Abdali to Durrani (Persian, *dur,* or pearl).

A poet and a patron of SUFIS (Muslim mystics and scholars of Islam), Ahmad justified his campaigns in India in Islamic terms. During his reign, SUNNI ISLAM flourished in Afghanistan; mosques, shrines and Islamic schools enjoyed the financial support of the state. He died in the mountains east of Kandahar, and his son Timur Shah succeeded him (1772–1793).

BIBLIOGRAPHY

DUPREE, LOUIS. *Afghanistan.* Princeton, N.J., 1980.

RAWLINSON, H. "Report on the Durranis." In *Historical and Political Gazetteer of Afghanistan,* ed. by Ludwig Adamec. Graz, Austria, 1980.

Ashraf Ghani

Ahmad Hibat Allah   [c. 1870–c. 1920]

Moroccan resistance leader against the French, 1912–1920.

Ahmad Hibat Allah (also known as El Hiba) was the son of the noted scholar of Islam and patriot Ma al-Aynayn. He led an important millenarian movement in the Sous valley, which was able to capture Marrakech in August 1912, following the abdication of ABD AL-HAFID as sultan. After his defeat in September 1912, he withdrew into southern Morocco and established his headquarters at Tiznit.

During World War I, Hibat Allah was a major beneficiary of a pan-Islamic Turco-German effort to support Moroccan resistance from Spain. Together with his brother Murabbih Rabbuh, who suceeded him upon his death about 1920, he sought with little success to organize attacks on the French positions in the Sous valley.

BIBLIOGRAPHY

BURKE, EDMUND, III. "Moroccan Resistance, Pan-Islam and German War Strategy, 1914–1918." *Francia* 3 (1975): 434–464.
———. *Prelude to Protectorate in Morocco: Precolonial Protest and Resistance, 1860–1912.* Chicago, 1976.

Edmund Burke III

Ahmadi, al-

Petroleum center in Kuwait.

Al-Ahmadi (or Mina al-Ahmadi), on the Persian/Arabian Gulf coast south of Kuwait Bay, is the center of operations for the KUWAIT OIL COMPANY. It is adjacent to the massive al-Burgan field from which oil flows by gravity to the coast. The city gives its name to one of the country's four governorates.

BIBLIOGRAPHY

HELD, COLBERT C. *Middle East Patterns: Places, Peoples, and Politics.* Boulder, Colo., 1989.

Malcolm C. Peck

Ahmad ibn Abd al-Karim

See Abd al-Karim, Ahmad

Ahmad ibn Muhammad al-Raysuni

Political figure in Morocco from 1900 until his death in 1926.

A descendant of the SHARIFIAN lineage of Bani Arus and a charismatic personality, al-Raysuni (also called al-Raysuli or El Raisuni) parlayed his position as a rural power broker in MOROCCO and leader of local anti-European feelings to rise to prominence in the period 1903–1906. By organizing a series of political kidnappings, the most celebrated of which was of the American Ian Perdicaris, he helped to undermine the regime of Sultan Abd al-Aziz.

Following the establishment of the protectorates of France and Spain in 1912, al-Raysuni became an official in the Spanish protectorate. Following the rebellion of ABD AL-KARIM against the Spanish authorities (1921), he came briefly to prominence again by playing off the two sides and enhancing his own position. In this, his career resembles those of other Moroccan regional figures of the period.

BIBLIOGRAPHY

FORBES, ROSITA. *El Raisuni.* London, 1924.
WOOLMAN, DAVID. *Rebels in the Rif.* Stanford, 1968.

Edmund Burke III

Ahmad ibn Rashid al-Mualla

Member of the ruling family of Al Ali, the main tribe in the emirate of Umm al-Qaywayn.

In the 1950s, the inhabitants of this GULF shaykhdom were mainly pearl divers, fishermen, or nomadic camel herders who traveled around their wells and oases in the interior of Falaj Ali. Ahmad ibn Rashid's father, Rashid ibn Ahmad (1904–1922), was, on accession, a young and forceful leader. He was successful in encouraging some tribes to seek his protection, thus expanding the territories of his emirate.

Shaykh Ahmad has been known for his strict observance of Islam. He came to power in 1929 and encouraged modern education, became a member of the Trucial States Rulers' Council in 1952, and joined the United Arab Emirates in December 1971. His eldest son, Rashid, succeeded him in 1981 as ruler of Umm al-Qaywayn and has become a member of the Supreme Council of the United Arab Emirates.

BIBLIOGRAPHY

ANTHONY, J. DUKE. *Arab States of the Lower Gulf.* Washington, D.C., 1975.
REICH, BERNARD, ed. *Political Leaders of the Contemporary Middle East and North Africa.* London and New York, 1990.

M. Morsy Abdullah

Ahmad ibn Yahya Hamid al-Din

[1891–1962]

The second of the three Hamid al-Din imams to govern Yemen after independence in 1918, from March 15, 1948 to September 18, 1962.

During his father's tenure as imam, from 1904 to 1948, and as king of Yemen, from 1918 to 1948, Ahmad was apprentice to and an important supporter of his father. Ahmad was also the governor of Ta'izz province, Yemen's primary military commander, and the designated successor to his father as both imam and king.

After Imam YAHYA's assassination in 1948, and the effort at major reforms, Ahmad organized important tribal elements to overthrow the usurpers and became imam and king. Although he had earlier established some tenuous links with reform elements, he introduced very few changes to the autocratic and highly centralized system established by his father. By the early 1960s, the extent of opposition to his rule had resulted in numerous revolts and assassination attempts, even by some of the tribal elements that had earlier supported him. He died in September 1962, and was succeeded by his son Muhammad al-BADR who, however, was deposed one week later in the revolution which turned Yemen into a republic.

Manfred W. Wenner

Ahmadiyya School, al-

School built in the emirate of Dubai in 1912.

The school was built by the rich pearl merchant Ahmad ibn Dalmuk in the Gulf emirate of Dubai, which is now a member of the United Arab Emirates. Its teachers were originally brought from al-Hasa (Arabia) and al-Zubayr (Iraq). In 1950, a modern curriculum was added to the traditional religious studies of Islam; its old building has become a teacher-training center and new buildings have been added.

M. Morsy Abdullah

Ahmad Qajar   [1869–1929]

Sixth and last monarch of Persia's Qajar dynasty.

He was the son of Mohammad Ali Shah and Malekeh Jahan (daughter of Kamran Mirza, a son of Naser al-Din Shah, the fourth QAJAR monarch). Ahmad Shah (also called Soltan Ahmad Shah) ascended to the throne at age eleven, when his father was deposed in 1909. Care was taken with his education; besides the traditional studies, he had a French professor who taught him political science and administrative law. A regent was appointed until he reached his majority, and the second *majles* (assembly) was called by him.

Ahmad Shah's reign coincided with a change in rivalry between Britain and Russia. The Convention of 1907 had divided Persia into three zones: Russia in the north, Britain in the southeast, and a neutral zone. The old rivalry between Russia and Britain, which had guaranteed Persia's independence, became an alliance that threatened to control. Russia issued an ultimatum that they would occupy Tehran unless Persia dismissed Morgan SHUSTER, an American financier, employed with the approval of the *majles* to reform Persia's financial administration. This was done and the regent closed the *majles* for three years, until Ahmad Shah came of age in 1914 and had to take his oath of office in the *majles* before he could be crowned. The coronation actually preceded the opening, on the eve of World War I.

At the outbreak of war, Persia declared neutrality, but the belligerents disregarded it and soon turned the country into a battleground. Nationalists and the *majles* favored the Germans and Turks—who opposed Persia's traditional enemies, Britain and Russia. When the Russians threatened to advance on Tehran, Ahmad Shah was persuaded that were he to go he would forfeit his throne.

Until the Russian Revolution in 1917, the Allies controlled Persia, with financial aid and military occupation. The Russian Revolution left the British in sole control. They tried to take advantage of the new situation by negotiating a treaty to keep financial and military control—and Ahmad Shah signed it, reluctantly, since it was opposed by the nationalists, who eventually defeated it.

A succession of weak governments, civil war, and communist infiltration from the newly formed Soviet Union caused a coup d'état in 1921, partly planned and inspired by the British occupying forces, which were soon to evacuate the country. The coup was carried out by Reza Khan, commander of the Persian Cossack Brigade, and a pro-British journalist, Sayyid Ziya al-Din. Overcome by the turn of events, Ahmad Shah installed them in power—Sayyid Ziya as prime minister and Reza as minister of war. Reza ousted Sayyid Ziya and became prime minister, controlling the new army he had formed. His modernization policy also won him the support of the young nationalists.

In 1923, Ahmad Shah left Iran, appointing his brother to be in charge. A movement to establish a republic with Reza as president was defeated, especially by the *ulama* (body of mullahs), who feared secularization, as was established in Turkey. In 1925, the Qajar dynasty was deposed by the fifth *majles*, which voted to give the monarchy to the PAHLAVI DYNASTY, with Reza Khan becoming Reza Shah Pahlavi, the founder. Ahmad Shah has been maligned by the historians of the Pahlavi era, shown as weak and vacillating; recent historians have emphasized his democratic nature, his wish to reign and not to rule. He lived and died in exile and was buried in Karbala, a holy Shi'ite city in southern Iraq.

BIBLIOGRAPHY

AVERY, P. *Modern Iran*. London, 1965.
Documents on British Foreign Policy, 1919–1939. First series, vol. 13. London, 1963.
MAKKI, H. *Zendegani-ye Soltan Ahmad Shah* (The Life of Sultan Ahmad Shah). Tehran, 1967.

Mansoureh Ettehadieh

Ahmad Rasim [1825–1897]

Ottoman administrator.

Served in the foreign and health ministries and in the provincial administration from 1844 to 1896. As Governor of Tripolitania (1881–1896), Ahmad Rasim Pasha improved communications, modernized Tripoli's water supply and sewage system, introduced modern hospitals and schools, tried to recultivate disused lands, and was instrumental in the suppression of the slave trade.

BIBLIOGRAPHY

HACOHEN, MORDEKHAI. *Higgid Mordecai*. Jerusalem, 1978.
MARTIN, B. G. "Ahmad Rasim Pasha and the Suppression of the Fezzan Slave Trade, 1881–1896." *Africa* 38 (December 1983): 545–579.

Rachel Simon

Ahmad Shah Mas'ud [1953–]

Afghan nationalist, government official.

Ahmad Shah Mas'ud, born in the Panjsher valley, northeast Afghanistan, became the most powerful field commander of the Islamic resistance (*mojahedin*) to Soviet forces. Mas'ud joined the Islamic movement at the university and chose the Islamic Society

led by Burhanuddin RABBANI, after the movement split on largely ethnic lines in exile in Pakistan. In 1979 he returned to Panjsher. Adopting the guerrilla strategy of China's Mao Tse-tung, he built up a guerrilla army across northeastern Afghanistan, while he served as amir of the Supervisory Council of the North. In April 1992 Mas'ud, in temporary alliance with Abdal-Rashid Doestam, commanded the military forces that took control of Kabul after the flight of President Najibullah. As defense minister of the Islamic State of Afghanistan, he resisted repeated offenses from his longtime rival in the Islamic movement, Golbuddin HEKMATYAR.

Barnett R. Rubin

Ahmar, Abdullah ibn Husayn al-
[1916–]

A leader of the Hashid tribal federation, 1950–1980; president of Yemen, 1973–1974.

Abdullah ibn Husayn al-Ahmar was a very influential leader of the Hashid tribal federation in northern YEMEN. His was one of the two most powerful tribal federations of the central and northern plateaus of Yemen—the other being the Bakil. Both practically dictated national politics in the San'a region as long ago as the 1890s. In the early 1960s, al-Ahmar broke with the royalists, partly because Yemen's ruler Imam Ahmad had executed his father and brother; he then supported the republican forces, who deposed Imam al-BADR within a month of inheriting the imamate and the rule of Yemen.

In 1965, al-Ahmar was appointed a cabinet member by Prime Minister Shaykh Ahmad Muhammad al Nu'man. By this time the YEMEN CIVIL WAR was raging, with no end until 1970. In 1971, al-Ahmar was elected speaker of the advisory council (*majles al-shura*) as the government of the late 1960s and early 1970s became increasingly dependent on him. In 1973, following the resignation of President Qadi Abd al-Rahman al-Iryani, the presidency was filled by al-Ahmar.

Lt. Colonel Ibrahim al-HAMDI became president in 1974, and in 1976, al-Ahmar broke with him over the budget, threatening to mobilize his Hasid tribes for military action against the government. In 1978, one of the first tasks of the newly elected President Ali Abdallah SALIH was to make peace with al-Ahmar and his tribal federation. In the early 1980s, his political influence began to diminish; however, al-Ahmar and his party—Yemen Grouping for Reform and Islah—supported the merger into one Yemen on May 22, 1990.

BIBLIOGRAPHY

BIDWELL, ROBIN. *The Two Yemens.* Boulder, Colo., 1983.
WENNER, MANFRED. *The Yemen Arab Republic.* Boulder, Colo., 1991.

Emile A. Nakhleh

Ahmet İhsan To'kgoz   [1868–1942]

Ottoman Turkish publisher.

Ahmet İhsan To'kgoz was born in Erzurum, where his father was a civil servant, and graduated from the Mulkiye civil service school in Istanbul, where he studied literature with RECAIZADE MAHMUD EKREM. Upon graduation, he began to work as a French translator in the foreign ministry and to publish a journal, *Ümran* (Prosperity). In 1891, he began to publish the journal *Servet-i Fünun* (The Wealth of Sciences), which was the main medium for the literary movement known as the new literature. Disputes between Ahmet İhsan To'kgoz and his editor, TEVFIK FIKRET, hastened the downfall of *Servet-i Fünun,* which was ordered closed in 1897. Ahmet İhsan To'kgoz joined the Committee of Union and Progress in 1907, and, following the revolution, began to publish *Servet-i Fünun* as a daily political paper. Tiring of politics, he turned it into a weekly literary digest, the organ of the FECR-I ATI literary movement. In 1931, he became a member of parliament representing Ordu.

BIBLIOGRAPHY

SHAW, STANFORD J., and EZEL KURAL SHAW. *Reform, Revolution, and Republic: The Rise of Modern Turkey, 1808–1975,* vol. 2 of *History of the Ottoman Empire and Modern Turkey.* Cambridge, U.K., 1977, pp. 254–255.
Yeni Türk Ansiklopedisi, vol. 11. Istanbul, 1985, pp. 4135–4136.

David Waldner

Ahmet İzzet   [1864–1937]

Ottoman general and grand vizier.

Ahmet İzzet rose to prominence in 1893 as an influential second scribe of Abdülhamit II. After the 1908 revolution, he became chief of general staff under the Young Turks and commander of the Caucasus front during World War I. During his brief tenure as grand vizier (October–November 1918), he negotiated the MUDROS ARMISTICE with the British, formally ending Ottoman participation in World War I. He closed his career as minister of war in the early years of the Turkish Republic.

BIBLIOGRAPHY

LEWIS, BERNARD. *The Emergence of Modern Turkey.* New York, 1961, pp. 239–240, 464–465.
SHAW, STANFORD J., and EZEL KURAL SHAW. *History of the Ottoman Empire and Modern Turkey,* vol. 2. Cambridge, U.K., 1977.

Elizabeth Thompson

Ahmet Rasim   [1864?–1932]

Turkish journalist and short-story writer.

Born in Istanbul during the Ottoman Empire, Rasim grew up in poverty after his father, a Cypriot postal official, divorced his mother. Forced to attend school at an orphanage, he graduated at the head of his class. After a short period as a postal worker, he began to work as a journalist; for the next forty-eight years, he wrote in the major Istanbul newspapers. He was also an elected member of the Turkish Grand National Assembly from 1927 to 1932 in ATATÜRK's new Republic of Turkey.

Rasim's writings are characterized by his incorporation of the folklore and anecdotes of daily life in Istanbul. Using sparse language, he captured the vitality of the different neighborhoods of the city, making him an important source of information about the daily existence of Old Turkey. Rasim's contributions to Turkish literature also include memoirs, travelogues, historical accounts, and articles on various subjects.

BIBLIOGRAPHY

MITLER, LOUIS. *Ottoman Turkish Writers: A Bibliographical Dictionary of Significant Figures in Pre-Republican Turkish Literature.* New York, 1988.

David Waldner

Ahmet Rıza   (1859–1930)

Young Turk leader and educator.

Born in Istanbul to an Austrian mother and to a father who was an Anglophile Ottoman bureaucrat, Ahmet Rıza grew up among the wealthy elite. He attended the prestigious Galatasaray Lycée in Istanbul and studied agriculture in France. As an idealistic young man, he sought to improve the condition of the Ottoman peasantry, first at the Ministry of Agriculture, then at the Ministry of Education, where he served as the director of education in the city of Bursa.

At the age of thirty, Ahmet Rıza returned to France, where he became an early leader of the YOUNG TURKS. In 1894 he published a series of tracts demanding a constitutional regime in the Ottoman Empire based on Islamic and Ottoman traditions of consultation. In 1895, he began publishing a bimonthly newspaper, Meşveret, which soon became a locus of the exile Young Turk movement. The newspaper was also smuggled into the empire and ciculated among liberal intellectuals there. Ahmet Rıza's chief rival was the more radical Prince Sabahettin, who founded a separate Young Turk group and newspaper in Paris. Ahmet Rıza opposed the prince's calls for revolution and European intervention in the empire at the 1902 Congress of Ottoman Liberals in Paris. At the Second Young Turk Congress in 1907, Ahmet Rıza at first reluctantly endorsed the use of violence to depose the sultan, but later reversed his position.

Ahmet Rıza returned to Istanbul after the 1908 revolution and headed the Unionist party, which was backed by the COMMITTEE OF UNION AND PROGRESS (CUP) and which opposed Prince Sabahettin's Ottoman Liberal Union party and Islamist groups. The Unionists were successful in the elections, and Ahmet Rıza became president of the Chamber of Deputies. However, in April 1909 leaders of a mass demonstration at the Sultan Ahmet mosque organized by the Society of Islamic Unity called for Ahmet Rıza's resignation and for his replacement by a "true Muslim." Two deputies were killed, apparently mistaken for Ahmet Rıza, when the crowd entered the Parliament buildings. Ahmet Rıza was deposed, and Isma'il Kemal was elected the new president of the Chamber in the ensuing reorganization of government.

Ahmet Rıza remained loyal to the CUP during his years in government. But, in 1919 he founded a new party, the National Unity Party, and allied himself with Sultan Vahidettin against the Kemalists. He spent the years of the Independence War in Paris, then returned to Istanbul, where he was an instructor at the prestigious Dar al-Fonun school until his death.

Rıza's contribution to the Young Turk movement went beyond his organizational abilities. As a follower of the French sociologist Auguste Comte, he first formulated the principles that would influence the development of secularist reform in Turkey. For example, the slogan heading his magazine Meşveret, "order and progress," was drawn from French positivist ideas and is probably linked to the simultaneous naming of an Istanbul opposition group, Union and Progress.

BIBLIOGRAPHY

Aksın, Sına. 100 Soruda Jön Türkler ve Ittihat ve Terakki. Istanbul, 1980.
Inönü Ansiklopedisi, vol. 1, Ankara, 1946, p. 268.
Lewis, Bernard. The Emergence of Modern Turkey. New York, 1961.
Shaw, Stanford J., and Ezel Kural Shaw. History of the Ottoman Empire and Modern Turkey, vol. 2. Cambridge, U.K., 1977.

Elizabeth Thompson

Ahmet Vefik [1823–1891]

Ottoman administrator and scholar.

Like his father and grandfather, Ahmet Vefik entered government service and soon rose to positions of great importance during the TANZIMAT period of the Ottoman Empire. He served twice as minister of education (1872 and 1877) and helped to reform the Ottoman educational system. In 1877, Sultan Abdülhamit II appointed him president of the first Ottoman parliament, and when it was dissolved less than a year later, Ahmet Vefik served as the sultan's grand vizier for several months in early 1878, as governor of Bursa (1878–1882), and briefly as grand vizier once more at the end of 1882.

Ahmet Vefik as depicted on a commemorative stamp from Turkey. (Richard Bulliet)

In spite of his illustrious political career, Ahmet Vefik is better remembered for his work as a writer, translator, and educator. Having served as ambassador to France, he translated Molière into Turkish. He also edited the first modern dictionary of the Turkish language, published in 1876, and he compiled a history of the Ottoman Empire that became the standard text in the Ottoman *ruşdiye* (adolescence) schools.

BIBLIOGRAPHY

LEWIS, BERNARD. *The Emergence of Modern Turkey.* New York, 1961.

SHAW, STANFORD J., and EZEL KURAL SHAW. *History of the Ottoman Empire and Modern Turkey.* New York, 1977.

Zachary Karabell

Ahram Center for Political and Strategic Studies, al-

A policy research institute founded in 1968.

The center is part of the publishing empire that Muhammad Hasanayn HAYKAL built up around the famous newspaper *al-Ahram,* and is showcased in a dazzling steel-and-glass 12-story building. The center for Political Studies's original name—Center for Zionist and Palestine Studies—is revealing. In the wake of Egypt's devastating defeat by Israel in the 1967 Arab–Israel War, Nasser and Haykal agreed that Egyptians could no longer afford to remain ignorant of Israeli social and political dynamics. As Nasser's closest journalist confidant, Haykal offered the center's researchers protection from outside interference. Boutros Boutrus-Ghali, the respected academic who has since become secretary general of the United Nations, became general supervisor of the center, with a son-in-law of Nasser's as director.

The center's privileged young social scientists set to work to analyze as dispassionately as possible such topics as the reasons for Egypt's defeat, the sources of Israel's strengths, and the nature of U.S.–Israel relations. The center's seminars and publications series soon branched out into far-ranging social, economic, and political analyses, probing possible options as Egypt moved from the age of Nasser to that of Sadat and then on to Mubarak. The center also invited in foreign scholars to make scholarly presentations.

Haykal fell out with Sadat and was dismissed from *al-Ahram* in 1974, and Nasser's son-in-law lost his post. The center drifted briefly, having lost its facile access to the top political elite. Sayyid Yasin, from the National Institute for Criminological Research,

gave the center new direction. With the help of such talented social scientists as Ali al-Din Hilal and Sa'd al-Din Ibrahim, he directed the center's efforts toward the educated elite in Egypt and the Arab world. The center's scholars could often get away with limited yet pointed criticisms of regime policies which would not have been tolerated in the regular press or other political forums. In place of Sadat's effusions about the new era of Egyptian-Israeli and Egyptian-American relations, for example, the center's scholars offered cold-blooded, detached analyses of Egyptian national interest.

BIBLIOGRAPHY

BAKER, RAYMOND WILLIAMS. "Thinking in the National Interest: The Ahram Center for Political and Strategic Studies." In *Sadat and After.* Cambridge, Mass., 1990, pp. 179–204.

Donald Malcolm Reid

Ahrar, al-

Egyptian daily newspaper.

Founded in November 1977, *al-Ahrar* is the newspaper of Egypt's Socialist Liberal Party, the right-center party that proved to be less tame than Anwar al-Sadat had hoped. *Al-Ahrar* pushed for an expanded scope for free enterprise, but its ideological slant was often vague.

BIBLIOGRAPHY

RUGH, WILLIAM A. *The Arab Press: News Media and Political Process in the Arab World,* 2nd ed. Syracuse, 1987.

Donald Malcolm Reid

Ahsa'i, Ahmad al-   [1753–1826]

Innovative Shi'ite thinker.

Ahmad al-Ahsa'i was born in 1753 in al-Hasa or al-Ahsa, then nominally an Arabian/Persian Gulf province of the Ottoman Empire with a largely Shi'ite population. Ahmad may well have been from an artisan family, since he knew metalworking and carpentry, but a series of visions of the Shi'a imams led him to study the seminary subjects of Islam. Around 1792, he went to Iraq for higher studies, staying in Najaf and Karbala for four years, and afterward lived in Bahrain. From 1800 to 1806 he was based in Basra and journeyed in southern Iraq. From 1806 to 1814 he lived in Yazd, and from 1814 to 1824 in Kermanshah, although he continued to travel widely. He was in Karbala in 1825 and died in 1826 on his way to Medina.

His move to Persia (Iran) had come at the invitation of the shah and of Qajar princes who offered him patronage to adorn their cities. In 1808, Fath-Ali Shah summoned Ahmad to Tehran and attempted to convince him to stay in the capital, but the shaykh declined for fear that he would eventually come into conflict with the shah. Ahmad claimed authority not only as a trained jurisprudent (*mujtahid*) but also as the recipient of intuitive knowledge from the imams (the holy figures of SHI'ISM); he emphasized the esoteric, gnostic heritage within Twelver Shi'ism, writing about letter/number symbolism (numerology) and other cabalistic subjects. He innovated in Shi'a theology both in his doctrine of God's attributes and his positing of two sorts of body, the ethereal and the physical, allowing him to suggest that the resurrection would be of the ethereal type. He appears to have been influenced by the medieval Iranian illuminationist Suhravardi and wrote original commentaries on the metaphysical works of Safavid thinkers like Mulla Sadra Shirazi and Mulla Muhsin Fayz, criticizing their monistic tendencies but accepting many of their other premises and technical terms. Only very late in life, from 1823, was Ahmad denounced by some of his colleagues as heterodox, and this appears to have been a minority position in his lifetime. His followers coalesced in the SHAYKHI school, which for a time contended with the scholastic USULI school for dominance of Twelver Shi'ism in the nineteenth century.

BIBLIOGRAPHY

CORBIN, HENRY. "L'Ecole shaykhie en théologie shī'ite." *Annuaire de l'École Pratique des Hautes Études, Section des Sciences Religieuses* (1960–1961): 1–59.

NICOLAS, A. L. M. *Essai sur le cheïkhisme,* vol. 1: *Cheïkh Ahmad Lahçahi.* Paris, 1910.

Juan R. I. Cole

Ahvaz

Capital of the province of Khuzistan in southwestern Iran, the town of Ahvaz lies on the only navigable river in Iran, the Karun.

A flourishing pre-Islamic city, Ahvaz became the capital of the province of Khuzistan in the late tenth century. It was a commercial center and the entrepot for Fars and Isfahan, as navigation on the river Karun was very important. Its silk textile and sugar production were highly regarded. By the time of the medieval geographers, the prosperity of Ahvaz had somewhat declined, and by the twelfth century its population was greatly reduced.

By the nineteenth century, Ahvaz had dwindled to a small borough. But the opening of the Karun river in 1888 to international navigation, the beginning of oil exploration in 1908 at Masjed Suleyman—which made Ahvaz a center for exploration and the place from which a pipeline to Abadan was built and, finally, the construction of the Trans-Iranian railroad, which reached the town in 1929, all stimulated the growth of the city. By the 1950s the population of Ahvaz had reached over 100,000. The primary causes of growth during this period were commerce and port activity. But industrial activity, such as the construction of a weaving and spinning factory, and a refinery of beet sugar, and the exploitation of nearby oil fields, also contributed to the growth of the city. The population was 579,826 in the 1986 census.

BIBLIOGRAPHY

YARSHATER, EHSAN, ed. *Encyclopaedia Iranica,* vol. 1. London, 1985, pp. 688–691.

Parvaneh Pourshariati

AIOC

See Anglo–Iranian Oil Company

AIPAC

See American Israel Political Affairs Committee

Airlines

Country	Airlines	Year Established
Algeria	Air Algérie	1963
Bahrain	Gulf Air	1950
Cyprus	Cyprus Airways	1964
	Kıbrıs Türk Hava Yolları	1974
Egypt	EgyptAir	1932
	Zas Passenger Service	—
	Zarkani Air Services	—
Iran	Iran Air	1962
	Iran Asseman Airlines	—
	Kish Air	1991
	Saha Airline	1990

Country	Airlines	Year Established
Iraq	Iraqi Airways	1948
Israel	El Al Israel Airlines	1948
	Arkia Israeli Airlines	1980
Jordan	Royal Jordanian Airlines	1963
	Arab Wings	1975
Kuwait	Kuwait Airways	1954
Lebanon	Middle East Airlines	1945
	Trans-Mediterranean Airways	1989
Morocco	Royal Air Maroc	1953
Oman	Gulf Air	1950
	Oman Aviation Service	1981
Qatar	Gulf Air	1950
	Gulf Helicopters	1974
Saudi Arabia	Saudia–Saudi Arabian Airlines	1947
Syria	Syrian Arab Airlines	1946
Tunisia	Tunis Air	1947
	Air Liberté Tunisie	1990
	Tunisavia	1974
Turkey	Türk Hava Yolları	1933
	Birgen Hava Yolları	1989
	Green Air	1990
	Istanbul Hava Yolları	1985
	Onur Air	1992
	Pegasus Hava Taşımacılığı	1990
	Sultan Hava Yolları	1989
	Sun Express	1990
	TUR European Airways	1988
United Arab Emirates	Gulf Air	1950
	Emirates Air Service	1976
	Emirates (EK) Dubai	1988
	Gulf Air Dubai	1985
	Abu Dhabi Aviation	—
Yemen	Yemen Airways (Yemenia)	1963
	Alyemda	1961

Michael R. Fischbach

Ait Ahmed, Hocine [1926–   ]

Algerian revolutionary and Kabyle (Berber) leader.

Though his father served France as a colonial *caïd* (*qa'id*), Ait Ahmed joined Messali Hadj's Parti du Peuple Algérien and its successor, the Mouvement pour le Triomphe des Libertés Démocratiques. In 1947 he became the first director of the paramilitary Organisation Spéciale. He left Algeria in 1951 and became one of the planners ("historic chiefs") of the revolution.

During the Algerian War of Independence (1954–1962) he served the FRONT DE LIBÉRATION NATIONALE's (FLN) "external" delegation and attended the Bandung Conference of 1955. Though not at the FLN's Soummam Conference (August 1956), he was elected to the Conseil National de la Révolution Algérienne. Along with Ahmed ben Bella and other historic chiefs (Mohamed Boudiaf, Mohamed Khider, and Rabah Bitat), he was skyjacked by the French in October 1956 and spent the rest of the war in prison.

After independence, Ait Ahmed organized the Front des Forces Socialistes (FFS) in 1963 and led the Berbers of Kabylia in revolt against Ben Bella's government. He was captured but escaped from prison in 1966 and fled to exile in France and then Switzerland. After the October 1988 riots, he returned to Algeria in December 1989. The FFS was legalized as an opposition party. He boycotted the June 1990 regional elections; this boycott was regarded by many as a mistake. Ait Ahmed and the Kabyles were particularly upset over the December 1990 Arabization law. In 1991 he actively campaigned in the national parliamentary elections. After the forced deposition of President Chadli Benjedid (January 1992), Ait Ahmed criticized the suspension of the democratic process by the military-civilian High State Council, even though it probably prevented the Islamist and Arabist Islamic Salvation Front from winning a stunning electoral victory. He is the author of *La Guerre et l'après guerre* (1964) and *Mémoires d'un combattant* (1983).

BIBLIOGRAPHY

HEGGOY, ALF ANDREW. *Historical Dictionary of Algeria.* Metuchen, N.J., 1981.
STORA, BENJAMIN. *Dictionnaire biographique des militants nationalistes algériens.* Paris, 1985.

Phillip C. Naylor

Aix-la-Chapelle, Congress of

Meeting of Holy Alliance that agreed to stop Barbary piracy.

Though primarily concerned with the question of France and the European balance of power, the congress did include a resolution to end once and for all Barbary piracy. The European powers agreed to coordinate their naval activities in order to force the pirates, or Corsairs, to stop raiding ships along the North African coast of the Mediterranean Sea.

BIBLIOGRAPHY

HUREWITZ, J. C., ed. *The Middle East and North Africa in World Politics.* New Haven, Conn., 1975.

Zachary Karabell

Ajlani, Munir al-   [1905–   ]

Syrian journalist and politician.

Born in Damascus during the Ottoman Empire to a prominent landowning family, Munir al-Ajlani was educated in law at the Arab Law Institute of the Syrian University in Damascus and at the Sorbonne in Paris. While in Paris, during the 1920s, his writings and activities with Arab cultural organizations earned him a brief exile to Switzerland. Upon his return to Syria, he became involved with anticolonial nationalist youth movements—the NATIONAL BLOC and Fakhr al-BARONDI's Steel Shirts.

He was elected parliamentary deputy for Damascus in 1936, 1947, 1950, and 1954; and he served as Syria's minister of propaganda and youth in 1942, of social affairs in 1943, of education in 1947 and 1954, and of justice in 1956. Ajlani was a faculty member at the Syrian University from 1946 through 1957 and was a frequent contributor to the newspapers *al-Qabas, al-*JAZIRA, and *al-Nidal.*

BIBLIOGRAPHY

KHOURY, PHILIP S. *Syria and the French Mandate: The Politics of Arab Nationalism, 1920–1945.* Princeton, N.J., 1987.

Charles U. Zenzie

Ajlun, Battle of

Last battle between Jordanian troops and Palestinian resistance fighters, July 13–19, 1971.

After the ARAB–ISRAEL WAR of 1967, Palestinians who had fled their homes in the West Bank were given refuge in Jordan. Palestinian resistance organizations, which had begun striking at Israel in 1965, now made Jordan their main base of operations. Increasingly, armed Palestinian groups became a threat to Jordan, where they established a state within a state, jeopardizing the authority of the Hashimite crown. Palestinians, in turn, were angered by Jordan's acceptance of the U.S. diplomatic initiative called the Rogers Plan of 1970, which ignored Palestinian nationalist aspirations.

These tensions culminated in September 1970 when the Jordanian army attacked Palestinian fight-

ers. In July 1971 at the Battle of Ajlun in northern Jordan, the Jordanian army defeated Palestinian forces, ending what had become the JORDANIAN CIVIL WAR.

BIBLIOGRAPHY

HIRST, DAVID. *The Gun and the Olive Branch.* London, 1977.

Steve Tamari

Ajman Tribe

A large sharif tribe in Saudi Arabia.

Centered in the al-Hasa region of Saudi Arabia, near Kuwait, the Ajman tribe traces its origin to the mythical ancestor Yam. Formerly camel-breeding, the tribe is currently almost completely settled, with many of its men employed in the Saudi National Guard.

Eleanor Abdella Doumato

Akbulut, Ahmet Ziya   [1869–1938]

Ottoman Turkish painter.

Istanbul-born Akbulut graduated from the Ottoman Empire's military academy in 1877 and spent the next fifteen years painting in the art studio of the General Staff. A student of Hoca Ali Riza, Akbulut was known for his close attention to perspective, about which he wrote articles. He taught painting at the Fine Arts Academy and at the military school.

BIBLIOGRAPHY

Yeni Türk ansiklopedisi (New Turkish Encyclopedia). Istanbul, 1985.

David Waldner

Akçura, Yusuf   [1876–1935]

Turkish nationalist and writer.

Born Yusuf Akçurin in the Russian city of Simbirsk (Ulyanovsk), on the Volga river, Akçura migrated to Istanbul, capital of the Ottoman Empire, with his family at an early age. He studied at a military school there and then at the Institut des Sciences Politiques in Paris, where he met several YOUNG TURKS. In 1904, Akçura wrote the first manifesto of Turkish nationalism, "Uç Tarz-i Siyaset" (Three Ways of Government), in which he considered Ottomanism and pan-Islam to be impractical routes for Turkish political development. Akçura soon became one of the most influential nationalists—promoting PAN-TURKISM before World War I. He spent a number of years in Russia spreading Turkish nationalist ideas, returning to Istanbul after the Young Turk revolution of 1908.

Akçura was a cofounder of the Türk Yurdu Cemiyati (Turkish Homeland Society) in 1911, with Ziya GÖKALP, publisher of its famous periodical TÜRK YURDU. The group campaigned to simplify the Turkish language, to adopt the customs of Western civilization, and to promote the interests of Turks inside and outside the Ottoman Empire. He joined the Kemalist movement in 1921, but maintained that it was the embodiment of pan-Turkism, and continued to write on Turkism for Russian Turks.

BIBLIOGRAPHY

ARAI, MASAMI. *Turkish Nationalism in the Young Turk Era.* New York, 1991.

Elizabeth Thompson

Akhavan-Saless, Mehdi   [1928–1991]

Iranian poet and literary critic who wrote under the pen name Mim Omid, or Omid.

Born in Mashhad, Akhavan later lived in Khorramshahr and Tehran. During his youth, he was politically active and was imprisoned briefly after the coup d'état of 1953.

His first published collection of verse, *Zemestan* (Winter; 1956), expresses a nostalgia for love by using nature imagery. His later verse at times reflects a deep cynicism and sarcasm, and at times is lively and witty. Akhavan is known for his long narrative poetry, which captures the reader's attention with its flowing dialogues. In addition to poetry, Akhavan has written a book for children, *Derakht-e Pir va Jangal* (The Old Tree and the Jungle), and articles on literary criticism brought together as *Majmu'a-ye Maqalat* (Collection of Articles).

BIBLIOGRAPHY

KARIMI-HAKKAK, AHMAD, ed. *An Anthology of Modern Persian Poetry.* Boulder, Colo., 1978.

Pardis Minuchehr

Akhbar, al- (Egypt)

Popular Cairo daily newspaper.

Founded in 1920 by Amin al-Rafi'i and purchased by Mustafa and Ali Amin in 1949, the present daily was established in 1952 as *al-Akhbar al-Jadida* (The New *Akhbar*) and soon became Egypt's most widely read newspaper, with an estimated circulation of 160,000 in 1962 and 790,000 in 1992.

BIBLIOGRAPHY

RUGH, WILLIAM A. *The Arab Press,* 2nd ed. Syracuse, N.Y., 1987.

Arthur Goldschmidt, Jr.

Akhbar, al- (Jordan)

Short-lived Jordanian newspaper.

Al-Akhbar was founded in 1976 by Rakkan al-Majali, who was head of Jordan Radio, as a pro-establishment newspaper. The publisher was the Arab Press Company, who claimed a circulation of 15,000. Editorial policy emphasized the Jordanian, as opposed to the Palestinian, point of view. The paper never achieved much prominence and ceased publishing within a few months.

Jenab Tutunji

Akhbar al-Yawm

Egyptian weekly newspaper and publishing house.

Akhbar al-Yawm, the weekly edition of *al-Akhbar* (published on Saturdays) was founded in 1944 by Mustafa and Ali Amin. Akhbar al-Yawm is also the name of the publishing house that produces *al-Akhbar* and several other weeklies, including *al-Ithnayn*. Privately owned until 1960, it was placed under the control of the National Union and, later, the Arab Socialist Union, thus effectively subjecting it to state control. This system was slightly changed in 1975, when Sadat's government established the Higher Press Council, which was empowered to issue publishing licenses and was assigned ownership of 49 percent of all publishing companies.

BIBLIOGRAPHY

RUGH, WILLIAM A. *The Arab Press,* 2nd ed. Syracuse, N.Y., 1987.

Arthur Goldschmidt, Jr.

Akhbari

The school of Shi'a jurisprudence.

Origins of the Akhbari can be traced to the twelfth century. It firmly rejected IJTIHAD, or the power of *ulama* to interpret the Qur'an and the teachings of the Prophet of Islam. Rather, it emphasized the supremacy of the teachings of God, the Prophet, and the infallible imams of Twelver Shi'ism, arguing that Islamic law can be derived directly from the *akhbar,* or traditions of the imams and the Prophet.

Akhbari traditionalism reemerged in the seventeenth and eighteenth centuries in Safavi Iran. Undermining the position of an independent clergy, the Akhbari school, at least by extension, advocated a fusion between government and religion by rejecting all forms of intercession between believers and the Prophet, plus his twelve infallible progeny. From the ascendancy of the Safavis to the nineteenth century, most Akhbari clerics resided in the shrine cities of Iraq. In Iran, the Akhbaris were eventually defeated by the rival *Usuli* camp, which favored a hegemonic clerical hierarchy. In Bahrain, however, Akhbarism triumphed by the end of the eighteenth century. During the Iranian constitutional revolution from 1905 to 1911, elements of Akhbari teachings were drawn upon by pro-constitutionalist *ulama* in refuting challenges by more conservative clergymen who objected to the un-Islamic nature of constitutionalism.

BIBLIOGRAPHY

ARJOMAND, SAID AMIR. *The Shadow of God and the Hidden Imam.* Chicago, 1984.
HAIRI, ABDUL HADI. *Shi'ism and Constitutionalism in Iran.* Leiden, 1977.

Neguin Yavari

Akhir Sa'a

Egyptian magazine.

Established in 1934, *Akhir Sa'a* is an independent weekly magazine published by the Dar Akhbar al-Yawm publishing house. It has an estimated circulation of 150,000.

Michael R. Fischbach

Akhondzadeh, Mirza Fath Ali   [1812–1878]

Azerbaijani playwright, propagator of atheism, and proponent of alphabet reform.

After an early education in Azerbaijan along traditional lines, Akhondzadeh entered a Russian school in Tiflis (Tbilisi, Russian Georgia), where he swiftly mastered the Russian language and became acquainted with European literature and ideas. He was soon a pronounced Russophile, and from 1834 until the end of his life, he was continuously in the employ of the Russian government. His most important literary works were six satirical comedies, written in Azerbaijani Turkish (AZERI), intended to discredit the traditional classes of the Muslim world and their beliefs and to propagate a positivist world view. Important for the development of modern Azerbaijani literature, these plays were also widely circulated in Persia (now Iran), in Persian translation.

Akhondzadeh expressed his hostility to ISLAM more systematically in a series of fictitious letters attributed to two princes, one Persian and the other Indian, in which the criticisms of Islam current in Christian nineteenth-century Europe were fully reflected. Among the Persian politicians and reformers with whom he was in contact, the most significant was Mirza MALKOM KHAN (Malkum Khan), with whom he shared not only a belief in the need for unconditional Westernization but also an enthusiasm for reforming the Arabic alphabet in its application to the Persian and Turkish languages by introducing letters to indicate vowels.

BIBLIOGRAPHY

ADAMIYAT, FERIDUN. *Andisha-haye Mirza Fath Ali Akhondzadeh* (Ideas of Mirza Fath Ali Akhondzadeh). Tehran, 1970.

Hamid Algar

Akkar Plain

Area north of Tripoli, Lebanon.

The Akkar plain, the area north of Tripoli, is a *qada,* the administrative unit within a governorate (province). Its diverse population is preponderantly Sunni (Muslims) and Maronites (Christians). The extreme poverty of its peasants stems from the strong feudal social structure, which has allowed a few families to control the region's wealth and power for much of its history.

Akkar experienced important changes in the 1960s and 1970s when more people from peasant backgrounds earned university degrees and were exposed to ideas and ideologies of change and revolution. The Lebanese army was historically the only institution that provided an opportunity for the peasants of Akkar to escape the stifling feudal structure. With the opening of the public Lebanese University, poorer Lebanese had an alternative to the inaccessible class-conscious, private American and Jesuit universities.

In the 1970s educated Akkaris were receptive to ideas of the Left, and many joined radical Palestinian and Lebanese organizations. Even Talal al-Mir'ibi, a member of an elite family who has represented Akkar in the Lebanese parliament since 1972, joined the al-Fath movement in his youth to earn radical credentials. Peasant uprisings, instigated by leftist organizations, were not uncommon in the early 1970s. The Lebanese state responded ruthlessly.

BIBLIOGRAPHY

MUSAWI, RASHAD. *Lebanon: A Country Study*.

As'ad AbuKhalil

Akl, Sa'id   [1912–   ]

Lebanese poet, philosopher, and professor.

Educated at the Frères Maristes College in his hometown of Zahleh, Akl became known for his lyric poems about nationalist subjects and for his plays about the Phoenician era, written in the style of seventeenth-century French playwrights. Akl's writings revolutionized the language and alphabet; he is considered the father of written Lebanese and is regarded as an architect of Lebanonism. The author of about thirty books, Akl is also the founder of the weekly *Lubnan*.

BIBLIOGRAPHY

Who's Who in Lebanon, 1988–1989. Beirut, 1988.

Mark Mechler

Akrad, Hayy al-

Kurdish quarter on the slopes of the mountain of Qasiyun, overlooking Damascus, Syria; the other two quarters are the Muhajirin and the Salihiyya.

The three quarters owe their existence to the water of the river Yazid, a tributary of the Barada river, which splits from it in the gorge of al-Rabweh. While al-Muhajirin was created by the municipality of Damascus, capital of Syria, and the Salihiyya is almost a replica of Damascus, Hayy al-Akrad has been described as a sheer fantasy. Its streets, though wide, are irregular and do not present a defensive aspect like those of Damascus because its inhabitants, the KURDS, were feared and not attacked.

Still inhabited mostly by Kurds, Hayy al-Akrad was originally a village for Kurds, starting in the time of Saladin in the twelfth century, and attracted a new wave of Kurdish immigrants in the nineteenth century. Engaged primarily in livestock trade and serving in the military and as aides in tax-farming, the Kurds polarized around their clan leaders, who played major roles in the life of Damascus as notables, landowners, military chieftains, and also Communists. The head of the Communist party since its early years has been the octogenarian Khalid Bakdash, who comes from Hayy al-Akrad and has the support of many of its Kurdish inhabitants.

BIBLIOGRAPHY

THOUMIN, R. "Deux quartiers de Damas, le Quartier Chrétien de Bab Musalla et le Quartier Kurde". *Bulletin d'Études Orientales* 1 (1931): 99–135.

Abdul-Karim Rafeq

Aksariyat

See Feda'iyan-e Khalq

al-

For the numerous Arabic names beginning with the definite article *al-*, see under the following part of the name.

Ala, Hoseyn   [1883–1964]

Iranian statesman.

Hoseyn Ala, son of Mirza Mohammad Ali Khan ALA AL-SALTANEH, was also known as the Mu'in al-Wizara. Similar to many political dignitaries of Pahlavi Iran, his father had served the Qajars as prime minister, minister, and ambassador, and was a main actor in the constitutional revolution from 1905 to 1911. Hoseyn Ala filled cabinet posts in the Ministries of Foreign Affairs, Finance, Agriculture, Trade, Court, and Public Welfare. He served as a delegate to the Paris Peace Conference following World War I, was Iran's chief delegate to the United Nations after World War II, and served as ambassador to the United States, Spain, and England.

Considered a royalist, Hoseyn Ala was appointed as prime minister by the monarch Mohammad Reza Pahlavi in 1951, following the assassination of Prime Minister Razmara by an Islamic group, the Feda'iyan-e Islam. During his tenure as prime minister, the Iranian Parliament passed the Oil Nationalization Bill of 1951. Unable to withstand public pressure in favor of nationalization, Ala resigned his position in 1952, and resumed his duties as Minister of Court. He was appointed as prime minister for a second time in 1955, and headed Iran's delegation to the first meeting of the Baghdad Pact, held in Iraq in 1955. Political dissatisfaction with the Baghdad Pact was manifested in an assassination attempt on Ala's life, before his departure to Baghdad, by a member of the Fedai'iyan-e Islam. In 1957, Ala was reappointed as Minister of Court, retaining his position until 1963, when he was demoted to senator because of his opposition to the Shah's policies in the quelling of the June 1963 uprisings.

BIBLIOGRAPHY

AQELI, BAQER. *Nakhost vaziran Iran az Moshir al-Dowleh ta Bakhtiar* (Iranian Prime Ministers from Moshir al-Dowleh to Bakhtiar). Tehran, 1991.

Neguin Yavari

Ala al-Saltaneh, Mirza Mohammad Ali Khan [1838–1918]

Iranian statesman.

Born in Baghdad, the son of the Iranian consul Mirza Ibrahim Khan, Mirza Mohammad Ali Khan followed his father into the foreign service. He was serving as general consul in Tbilisi when he met the Qajar monarch NASER AL-DIN SHAH (1889), during the latter's return trip to Persia. As a result of that encounter, he was appointed the ambassador to Britain by Naser al-Din Shah and received the title Ala al-Saltaneh. In 1913, after having held several other ministerial positions, Ala al-Saltaneh became prime minister and retained that position for seven months.

BIBLIOGRAPHY

BAMDAD, MEHDI. *Sharh-e Hal-e Rejal-e Iran dar Qarn-e 12, 13, va 14 Hejri* (Biographies of Iranian Notables in the Twelfth, Thirteenth, and Fourteenth Centuries), vol. 3. Tehran, 1979. In Persian.
" 'Alā' al-Salṭanah." In *Encyclopaedia Iranica,* vol. 2, ed. by E. Yarshater. New York, 1989.

Neguin Yavari

Alaini, Muhsin

See Ayni, Musin al-

Alam, Amir Asadollah [1919–1978]

Iranian politician of the Pahlavi period.

Amir Asadollah Alam was the son of Showkat al-Molk Alam, who was governor of Birjand under Mozaffar al-Din Shah of the Qajars and also a member of Reza Shah PAHLAVI's inner court. He was born in Birjand into a family that originally came from an Arab tribe of the southern region of Khuzistan. Patronized by Reza Shah from the start, Alam married Malektaj Qavam, the sister-in-law of Ashraf Pahlavi, the shah's daughter. His long-standing friendship with the crown prince was fostered in this period. Alam was one of the few members of Iran's traditional aristocracy who not only manifested his loyalty to the Pahlavi dynasty from the very start, but repeatedly did so in the course of an unusually long political career during which he held several gubernatorial and ministerial positions. A confidant of the new shah, Mohammad Reza Shah Pahlavi, he was ordered to found the MARDOM (People's) PARTY, which was envisioned as the party of loyal opposition. In 1962, Alam was appointed prime minister, to facilitate the implementation of the WHITE REVOLUTION, launched in 1963 by the shah. He was also prime minister at the time of the uprisings engineered by Ayatollah Khomeini in Qom (1963), in protest against the White Revolution. In 1964, he was appointed president of the Pahlavi University in Shiraz, and under his leadership it became Iran's model university. In 1966, he was appointed minister of court, and in this capacity he allegedly was one of the strongest influences on the shah. He retained this position until 1977, when he was forced to resign because of illness. He died in 1978 of leukemia.

BIBLIOGRAPHY

ALAM, AMIR ASSADOLLAH. *The Shah and I: The Confidential Diary of Iran's Royal Court, 1969–1977,* ed. by Alinaghi Alikhani. London, 1991.

Neguin Yavari

Alamayn, al-

Village in northwest Egypt, on the Mediterranean, northeast of the Qattara depression, site of the battle of El Alamein, where the British drove back the Germans in a pivotal battle of World War II, October 23–November 4, 1942.

General Bernard Law Montgomery's British and Commonwealth Eighth Army met and overcame General Erwin Rommel's German–Italian Afrika

British cemetery at al-Alamayn. (Mia Bloom)

Korps at al-Alamayn, approximately 80 miles (128.7 km) west of Alexandria. The retreat of Rommel's forces ended the Axis threat to conquer Egypt and seize the Suez Canal. Montgomery had some 195,000 men, 1,150 tanks, and 1,900 guns against Rommel's 100,000 men, 530 tanks, and 1,325 guns. Montgomery attacked at 9:30 P.M. on October 23, with an artillery barrage from 1,000 guns. The Afrika Korps held and counterattacked on October 27. Montgomery resumed the offensive the next day, with a week-long tank battle. British air superiority and force of numbers wore down the Afrika Korps, and Rommel withdrew a few miles to the west on November 1. Another attack on November 3 resulted in Rommel's ordering another withdrawal, at first countermanded by Hitler, but finally approved. Montgomery's pursuit on November 5 stalled because of a rainstorm, and Rommel was able to disengage his force and retreat to the Libyan border by November 7. The Afrika Korps had 59,000 men killed, wounded, and captured and lost some 500 tanks and 400 guns, against Eighth Army losses of 13,500 men, 500 tanks, and 100 guns. Moreover, most of the British tanks were reparable while Rommel had only twenty operational tanks at the end of the fighting.

BIBLIOGRAPHY

PITT, BARRIE. *The Crucible of War, Year of Alamein 1942.* London, 1982.

Daniel E. Spector

Alami, Musa al- [1897–?]

Prominent Palestinian nationalist.

Born in Jerusalem, Musa al-Alami received a law degree from Cambridge in England. He held senior positions in the Palestine government including private secretary to High Commissioner General Sir Arthur WAUCHOPE as well as government advocate. Musa's moderation, pragmatism, and the high respect he commanded in British circles did not endear him to many Arabs and Jews. In 1933, he proposed in vain, apparently in coordination with the *mufti* (canon lawyer) of Jerusalem, al-Hajj Muhammad Amin al-HUSAYNI, the establishment of an autonomous Jewish canton in coastal areas in Palestine within the framework of the MANDATE SYSTEM. In 1937, the British authorities charged Musa with fomenting disorder and deported him to Beirut. His deportation notwithstanding, Musa was a member of the Palestine delegation that participated in the LONDON (St. James) CONFERENCE, 1939, where he served on the conference committee, which examined the HUSAYN-MCMAHON CORRESPONDENCE. In 1944, three years after his return to Palestine, he served as Palestinian representative at an Alexandria meeting that drew up plans for the Arab League. One year later, the Arab League asked Musa to organize the Arab Information Offices and the ARAB DEVELOPMENT SOCIETY, whose purpose was to help Palestinian peasants. Musa's refusal to yield control over these institutions to al-Hajj Amin ended a long, but not always smooth, relationship between the two men. After the Disaster of 1948, Musa disengaged himself from all political activities and chose instead to devote himself to a communal farm located between Jericho and the Allenby Bridge. On the farm, needy Palestinian refugees were trained to become farmers and artisans.

BIBLIOGRAPHY

FURLONGE, GEOFFREY. *Palestine Is My Country: The Story of Musa Alami.* London, 1969.
Al-Mawsu'a al-Filastiniyya, vol. 4, p. 220.
PORATH, Y. *The Palestinian Arab National Movement 1929–1939: From Riots to Rebellion.* London, 1977.

Muhammad Muslih

Alami Family, al-

A leading Arab family in Jerusalem who claimed direct descent from Hassan, the grandson of the Prophet Muhammad.

The Alami ancestors migrated from Arabia to northern Morocco in the seventh century C.E., where they adopted the name Alam, from Mount Alam. In the twelfth century, Shaykh Muhammad al-Alami, head of both the family and a sufi order, assisted Salah al-Din in his effort to expel the Crusaders from Palestine and Lebanon in the twelfth century. In return, Salah al-Din (Saladin) granted the family substantial land, including most of the Mount of Olives in Jerusalem. Members of the family played a prominent role in the civil and religious life of the city during the following centuries.

Faydi al-Alami (died 1924) was the leading member of the family in the late Ottoman period. His father had been mayor of Jerusalem but died when Faydi was sixteen years old. He took over as head of the family, working in the finance department and later the judiciary as a tax assessor. The Ottoman government appointed him district officer (*mudir*) of Bethlehem in 1902 and then Jerusalem in 1904, where he served as mayor from 1906 to 1909. His term ended shortly after the Young Turk coup d'état in Istanbul, and he was elected to the administrative council for the Jerusalem district. In 1914, he became one of three residents of Jerusalem to serve as a member of the central parliament in Istanbul, where he was living when World War I began. He became increasingly disillusioned with the policies of the Young Turks, because of their pro-German foreign policy and their emphasis on Turkification. Faydi al-Alami returned to Palestine after the war, where he died in 1924.

Musa al-Alami (1897–1984), Faydi's son, was born on May 8, 1897, in Jerusalem and was drafted into the Ottoman army during World War I. During the final winter of the war, 1917/18, he hid in Damascus, where he contacted the Arab nationalist movement. Musa studied law at Cambridge University 1919–1924. There, he met British Zionists and began to recognize the relative weakness of the Palestinian political movement. On his return to Jerusalem, by then under the British mandate, the British administration appointed him junior legal adviser in 1925; assistant government advocate in 1929; private secretary to the high commissioner in 1932/33; then government advocate until 1937. During those years, Musa al-Alami quietly criticized the British tax policy that increased rural indebtedness and thereby encouraged land sales to Jewish land-purchasing organizations. As private secretary, he urged the high commissioner to balance the interests of the Arab and Jewish communities and enable the indigenous population to gain such political rights as representation in a legislative assembly. Under pressure from the Zionist Organization, the colonial office ordered the high commissioner to transfer Alami back to his judicial post. Nonetheless, he continued to express his views. In June 1936, the high commissioner allowed him to circulate a petition among the senior Arab government officials, which 137 signed, calling upon the

government to accept the Arab general-strike demand that London suspend Jewish immigration as a precondition for ending the strike.

Al-Alami was fired from the legal department in October 1937, in the wake of the Peel Commission report, which recommended that he be replaced by a British senior advocate. Alami was forced into exile in Lebanon, where he lived until the summer of 1939, when the French forced him to leave. He returned to Beirut after two years in Baghdad, shortly before the British seized Lebanon in June 1941. Alami was then allowed to return home. After he was dismissed from government service, Alami became directly active in political life. He urged the British to convene the London conference in 1939 and to allow prominent Palestinian politicians associated with the Arab Higher Committee (banned in October 1937) to participate in the Palestinian delegation.

Toward the end of World War II, Alami served as the Palestinian delegate to the Alexandria conference in the summer of 1944 that established the League of Arab States. British pressure on the Egyptian government prevented the league from seating him as an official delegate, but he persuaded the participants to accord him official status as the only representative of a community, rather than an independent state. Alami already had close relations with Arab leaders, particularly through his father-in-law, the Syrian nationalist Ihsan Jabri. Alami successfully urged the Alexandria conference to set up a fund to improve conditions in Palestinian villages and buy land from impoverished farmers, so that the land would not be bought by Jewish land-purchasing agents. He also urged the conference to set up information offices abroad that would promote Arab perspectives on the Palestine problem.

Alami then headed the London information office and organized the Constructive Scheme to help villages. The Arab governments, however, failed to contribute most of the money that they had pledged for those efforts and so the information offices in London, New York, and Washington had little with which to operate. In late 1945, Alami was forced to place his information efforts and Constructive Scheme under the authority of the reestablished Arab Higher Committee (AHC), rather than operate them independently. That led to mounting tension between Alami and his brother-in-law Jamal al-Husayni for control over those important activities. By December 1947, Alami and Husayni established rival information offices abroad, which epitomized the fissures in the Palestinian community and reduced the effectiveness of their efforts to attract international support.

Alami was in London during the Arab–Israel War of 1948/49 and lost his property in Jerusalem to Israel as well as his agricultural land in the Baysan and Jaffa districts. He used the balance in the Constructive Scheme funds, renamed the Arab Development Society, to reclaim land near Jericho, where he established an orphanage for refugee boys. Despite the difficulty of growing produce, raising poultry, and promoting dairy products in that saline environment, well below sea level, Alami turned the orphanage into a flourishing enterprise. He added a vocational training center and sold food to the expanding market in Saudi Arabia. During the 1967 war, the Israeli army overran the farm; most of its residents fled to Jordan, but the staff managed to keep it functioning. The farm has continued at a sharply reduced level since then. After Musa al-Alami's death in 1984, an international board of directors continued to maintain the project.

BIBLIOGRAPHY

FURLONGE, GEOFFREY. *Palestine Is My Country: The Story of Musa Alami*. London, 1969.
MUSLIH, MUHAMMAD Y. *The Origins of Palestinian Nationalism*. New York, 1988.

Ann M. Lesch

Alavi, Bozorg   [1904–   ]

Iran's most famous leftist writer.

Born in Tehran, Alavi was educated in Europe. After returning to Iran in the early 1930s, Alavi taught, published a volume of short stories called *The Suitcase*, and was arrested in 1937 for violation of a 1933 anti-Communist law. He and fifty-two others remained in jail until the Allied occupation of Iran in the fall of 1941. Afterward, Alavi wrote two books on his time in prison: *Fifty-Three Persons* and *Scraps of Paper from Prison*. In the World War II years, he was active in the formation and development of the TUDEH (Communist) party of Iran.

In 1952, Alavi published his most famous work in Persian, a novel called *Her Eyes,* as well as a collection of stories called *Letters and Other Stories,* which contained "The Man from Gilan," his most famous story.

When Mohammad Reza Shah PAHLAVI (ruled 1941–1979) returned to power in the coup d'état that bought Mohammad MOSSADEGH's nationalist government down in August 1953, Alavi was in East Germany, where he remained. He visited Iran briefly in 1979 and 1980. In the 1980s, he lectured widely as an elder statesman of anti-establishment literary intellectuals.

BIBLIOGRAPHY

"The Man from Gilan" appears in English translation in *Literature East & West,* volume 20 (1980), while a translation of ALAVI's novel *Her Eyes* was published in 1989. A biographical sketch and translations appear in D. RAFFAT's, *The Prison Papers of Bozorg Alavi* (1985).

Michael C. Hillmann

Alawi

Term applied to descendants, political domains, or sects most commonly connected with Ali ibn Abi Talib, the Prophet Muhammad's cousin and son-in-law.

In the early years of Islam, the Alawis founded and ruled many states in the Islamic world, including Amol, Andalusia, the Maghrib, Mecca, northern Persia, and Yemen. In modern times, *Alawi* and *Alawiyya* have been used to denote the sect widely dispersed in western Syria and southeastern present-day Turkey, the only branch of extreme Kufan SHI-'ISM that has survived. In Morocco in particular, Alawi refers to the descendants of the Prophet Muhammad who took over Morocco's throne in the 1600s and remain in power to this day.

Muslim heresiographers identify the Alawis of Syria and Turkey as the Numayriyya or Nusayriyya, a name derived from the group's eponym, Abu Su'ayb Muhammad ibn Nusayr al-Numayri, born in Basra in the ninth century. By the twelfth century the Nusayriyya were established in northwestern Syria, but not until 1920, under the French mandate, were they known as Alawis. At this time they claimed that this was their original name, but they had been prevented from using it since the Ottoman conquest of Syria.

According to various heresiographies, the Nusayris deify Ali, the first Shi'a imam. He is the axis of a Nusayriyya trinity whose two other members are the Prophet Muhammad and Salman Parsi; they correspond to the Christian Father, Son, and Holy Spirit. The Nusayris developed an elaborate belief in *tanasukh* (metempsychosis) and interpreted the pillars of Islam as symbols, an act that led to their abandonment of the performance of principal Islamic rituals. It also is said that the image of Christ as the Messiah plays an important role in the sect's doctrine.

As an extreme Shi'a sect within the body of an orthodox Sunni Islamic whole, the Nusayris were severely persecuted by the successive Sunni dynasties that ruled Syria. Nevertheless, they survived and remained active through the twilight of Ottoman rule in the region.

The collapse of the Ottoman Empire marked an important beginning for the Alawis. During the interwar mandate period and until Syrian independence in 1946, they took advantage of French colonial policy favoring minorities to begin to climb the socioeconomic ladder out of abject poverty. The French opened schools, introduced the rudiments of public administration, and brought law and order to unruly mountainous terrain. The French recruited young Alawis into the Special Forces of the Levant, a local force raised in 1921, in which they served under French officers together with other minorities. Service with the French laid the foundations of a tradition central to the community's later ascent. The export of tobacco to Europe from Latakia provided that city with a semblance of prosperity and established it as the "capital" of the Alawi homeland.

Independence and the eventual domination of the Syrian political landscape by the secular Arab nationalist Ba'th Party gave the ambitious Alawi a sense of opportunities never known before. The central role that a young Alawi officer, HAFIZ AL-ASAD, played in the 1963 revolution that brought the Ba'th to power ushered a new Alawi generation into the mainstream of Syrian life. With education as their tool, the Alawis became strongly represented in the professions, the party, and senior cadres of the state. With a tradition of self-reliance and military prowess, they grew into a formidable force in the army, Special Forces, and Presidential Guard. With Asad's rise to the pinnacle of Syrian power in 1970, the Alawis were represented in every institution across the land.

BIBLIOGRAPHY

SEALE, PATRICK. *Asad of Syria: The Struggle for the Middle East.* Berkeley, Calif., 1988.

Majed Halawi

Alawi, Mawlay al-Arabi al-

Early twentieth-century leader of the Salafiyya movement in Morocco.

His lessons at the Qarawiyyin mosque university in Fez in the 1920s and his attack on the Tijaniyya sufi *tariqa* brought ideas of the SALAFIYYA MOVEMENT to the attention of the emerging generation of Morocco's nationalists, among them Allal al-FASI.

BIBLIOGRAPHY

ABUN-NASR, JAMIL. "The Salafiyya Movement in Morocco: The Religious Bases of the Moroccan Nationalist Movement." In *Social Change: The Colonial Situation,* ed. by I. Wallerstein. New York, 1966.

AL-FASI, ALLAL. *Independence Movements in Arab North Africa,* trans. by H. Z. Nuseibeh. Washington, D.C., 1954.

Edmund Burke III

Alawite Dynasty

Moroccan rulers since 1666.

The Alawite dynasty has ruled Morocco continually since Mawlay Rashid conquered Fez in 1666. The challenges and achievements of the Alawites can best be discussed in two periods, from the onset of their rule to the French protectorate, and from independence in 1956 to the present time.

The founders of the Alawite dynasty, Mawlay Rashid (died 1672), who undertook the earlier conquests, and Mawlay Isma'il (died 1727), who consolidated the empire and established a new capital at Meknes, took on a badly divided nation following a century of political chaos and national disintegration. Their task was to unify a sufficient segment of the country to allow them to rule, to set up a national administration and workable taxation system, to guarantee the trade routes and defend against Christian incursions, and to establish an army that would be responsive to the Sultan, not to any local or tribal group. In response to these imperatives, Mawlay Isma'il established a centralized administration and a janissarylike national army of slaves (*abid*) loyal to the person of the sultan. Muhammad III (died 1790) emphasized the family's status as sharifs and attempted to establish the regime's legitimacy on a religious basis as defenders of the Muslim community against the encroaching European infidels. Weaker successors eventually capitulated to European demands and, in 1912, France established a protectorate over Morocco and gave Spain control over the northern sector. Sultan Muhammad ibn Yusuf (died 1961) played an instrumental role in the independence process.

Following Morocco's independence, the Alawite regime experienced a different set of challenges in building a postcolonial state. MUHAMMED V and his successor, HASSAN II, inherited a unified nation (despite Spanish possession of Ifni, the Western [Spanish] Sahara, Ceuta, and Melilla), a coherent administration, and a strong popular sense of the regime's legitimacy based on their defense of Moroccan nationalism and the king's position as imam of the Moroccan Muslim community as well as head of state. Their task was to build a modern developed state, ensure the loyalty of divided political and regional groups, deliver social services, and stimulate employment and economic development for a population with heightened expectations. A war in the Western Sahara to reclaim territory considered part of historical Morocco has proved extremely popular. The regime's greatest weaknesses during the time since independence in 1956 have been administrative corruption, periodic disaffection of segments of the armed forces, a limited national resource base, drought, and most important, a rapidly expanding population. The regime has been challenged by popular discontent, due in part to the severe strain on state resources as the regime has tried to meet the needs of a rapidly expanding population while, at the same time, satisfying vital interest groups. By the year 2000, the population of Morocco is expected to reach 31.4 million. King Hassan II has two sons, the crown prince, Sidi Muhammad (born 1963), and Rashid (born 1968), who are expected to carry on the succession.

The Alawite Dynasty

1.	al-Rashid	1664–1672
2.	Isma'il	1672–1727
3.	Ahmad al-Dhahabi *and*	1727–1728
4.	Abd al-Malik	[contested]
	Second reign of Ahmad	1728–1729
5.	Abd Allah	1729–1757
6.	Muhammad III	1757–1790
7.	Yazid	1790–1792
8.	Sulayman	1792–1822
9.	Abd al-Rahman	1822–1859
10.	Muhammad IV	1859–1873
11.	al-Hassan I	1873–1894
12.	Abd al-Aziz	1894–1908
13.	Abd al-Hafidh	1908–1912
14.	Yusuf	1912–1927
15.	Muhammad V	1927–1961
16.	Hassan II	1961–present

BIBLIOGRAPHY

ABUN-NASR, JAMIL M. *A History of the Maghrib*, 2nd ed. Cambridge, U.K., 1975.

CIGAR, NORMAN. *Muhammad al-Qadiri's Nashr al Mathani: The Chronicles*. London, 1981.

LAROUI, ABDALLAH. *The History of the Maghrib: An Interpretative Essay*, trans. by Ralph Manheim. Princeton, N.J., 1977.

POPULATION REFERENCE BUREAU. *Population Data Sheet*. Washington, D.C., 1990.

TERASSE, HENRI. "Alawis." In *Encyclopedia of Islam*, 2nd ed. Leiden, 1978.

———. *History of Morocco*. Casablanca, 1952.

Donna Lee Bowen

Albanians

An ethnic group of people native to Albania.

Three million Albanians live in Albania, which lies on the Balkan peninsula on the eastern shore of the Adriatic Sea, and another two million ethnic Albanians reside in Serbia, Macedonia, and Montenegro, and there are significant Albanian emigré communities in Turkey and the United States. Albanians are the descendants of the ancient Illyrians, and the Albanian language is Indo-European and not closely related to any other. There are two distinct groups of Albanians, the Ghegs in the north and the Tosks in the south. As a consequence of being part of the OTTOMAN EMPIRE from the fifteenth to the twentieth century, an estimated 70 percent of Albanians residing in Albania are Muslim; 20 percent are Orthodox Christians, and 10 percent Catholic. Agriculture, manufacturing, mining, and quarrying are the main occupations.

As European countries sought to dismantle the Ottoman Empire, Albania was eyed by Serbia as a prize in the BALKAN WARS (1912–1913). The Albanians successfully fended off this effort.

Major historical figures include Skanderbeg (Gjerj Kastrioti), who successfully resisted Turkish domination in the fifteenth century, King Zog I (Ahmet Zogu), a modernizer who ruled the country from 1925 to 1939, and Enver Hoxha, the Communist dictator from 1944 to 1985.

BIBLIOGRAPHY

BIBERAJ, ELEZ. *Albania: A Socialist Maverick*. Boulder, Colo., 1990.

John Micgiel

Albright Institute

See William Foxwell Albright Institute for Archeological Research in Jerusalem

Al Bu Sa'id, Faysal ibn Turki   [1864–1913]

Sultan of Oman from 1888 to 1913.

Faysal was born to Sultan Turki and an Abyssinian mother. His reign saw both the loss of the interior of OMAN to tribal and religious forces and British domination of affairs in MUSQAT. He was succeeded on his death by his son Taymur ibn Faysal AL BU SA'ID.

John E. Peterson

Al Bu Sa‘id, Qabus ibn Sa‘id [1940–]

Sultan of Oman since 1970 and the fourteenth member of the Al Bu Sa‘id dynasty to rule Oman.

Qabus was born in Salala, in the southern Omani province of Dhufar, on November 18, 1940. His father was Sultan Sa‘id ibn Taymur AL BU SA‘ID, while his mother came from the Bayt Ma‘shani tribe of the Dhufari mountains. In 1958, Qabus was sent to England for schooling, and he subsequently attended the Royal Military Academy at Sandhurst. Attached to the British Army of the Rhine for seven months, he then spent a short period studying local government in the English Midlands. A world tour in 1964 was followed by years of enforced inactivity back in Salala, studying Islamic law under the watchful eye of his father, who had not been to his capital at Musqat since 1958.

The late 1960s saw increasing unrest in Oman, due to Sultan Sa‘id's apparent refusal to spend his new oil revenues and because of the DHUFAR REBELLION against the sultan's paternalistic rule. By mid-1970, the situation had worsened and Qabus joined forces with his friends in Salala and British and Omani backers in Musqat to organize a coup d'état against his father on July 23, 1970.

In contrast to his father, Qabus threw the country open to development and welcomed back the thousands of Omanis working abroad. Within a week of his accession, the country's first true Council of Ministers was formed with Qabus' uncle, Tariq ibn Taymur AL BU SA‘ID, as prime minister. Two weeks after the coup, Sultan Qabus arrived in Musqat for the first time and took charge of the new government. Unfortunately, differences between the two men forced Tariq's resignation in 1971; Qabus has served as his own prime minister since then.

From the beginning of his reign, Qabus faced two primary challenges: economically transforming one of the world's most underdeveloped countries and dealing with the serious rebellion in Dhufar. In the early 1970s, development activity concentrated on providing education, health care, water, and electricity to the people and creating a modern infrastructure. By 1976, sufficient groundwork had been laid for implementing the country's first five-year development plan. At the same time, the course of the Dhufar rebellion was reversed with British, Jordanian, and Iranian assistance and through an intensive "hearts and minds" campaign, and the sultan was able to declare the war over in December 1975.

Qabus clearly stands at the apex of the political system of Oman. Decision making tends to bypass the Council of Ministers and flow directly up to the sultan. He has steered the country to a moderate path in international affairs, establishing diplomatic relations with China and the former Soviet Union while maintaining close political and security links with Britain and the United States. Qabus was one of the few Arab leaders not to break off relations with Egypt following the Camp David Accords. The sultan was careful to keep channels open to both sides during the Iran–Iraq War and permitted Western powers to use Omani facilities during the 1990/91 hostilities against Iraq (Gulf crisis). He also agreed to border treaties in the early 1990s with Yemen and Saudi Arabia.

Qabus has no direct heirs. A marriage arranged by his father to the daughter of an important tribal shaykh was never finalized. A marriage in 1976 to his cousin Kamila, a daughter of Tariq, ended in divorce.

John E. Peterson

Al Bu Sa‘id, Sa‘id ibn Sultan [c. 1788–1856]

Sultan of Oman and Zanzibar from about 1807 to 1856.

Sa‘id was born in Sama'il (Oman), the son of Sultan ibn Ahmad (reigned 1792–1804). He became ruler of Oman by assassinating his cousin. An alliance with the British enabled him to defeat the invading Saudi forces and to eliminate the threat posed by the Qawasim emirate of nearby Ra's al-Khayma. Building up his maritime power, Sa‘id turned his attention to the East African coastal region. His expansionist endeavors were so successful that eventually he moved his residence to Zanzibar. Able to relate with European powers on equal terms, he sent the first Arab envoy to the United States in 1840. On his death in 1856, his Arabian possessions, chiefly Oman, went to his eldest son Thuwayni, while another son Majid received Zanzibar. The Al Bu Sa‘id gradually evolved into separate ruling families and Omani fortunes subsequently declined.

John E. Peterson

Al Bu Sa‘id, Sa‘id ibn Taymur [1910–1972]

Sultan of Oman from 1932 to 1970.

Sa‘id was born in MUSQAT to Sultan Taymur ibn Faysal AL BU SA‘ID and an Al Bu Sa‘id mother. Like his father, Sa‘id was sent to Baghdad and India for education. Upon his return to Musqat at the age of 18, Sa'id effectively was made regent in the absence of his father and succeeded his father in 1932. By the end of World War II, Sultan Sa'id had pulled OMAN out of debt and reduced British influence in internal affairs. With British military assistance, he restored Al Bu Sa'id control over the interior in the 1950s. But his paternalistic rule led to growing discontent, especially after the discovery of oil in 1964. A rebellion in the southern province of Dhufar led to Sa'id's overthrow in July 1970 by his son Qabus ibn Sa'id AL BU SA'ID. Sa'id died in exile in London in October 1972.

John E. Peterson

Al Bu Sa'id, Tariq ibn Taymur
[1922–1980]

Omani prime minister.

Born in Constantinople (now Istanbul), Tariq's early years were spent in Turkey and Germany before study in India. He left Oman for exile in 1962. His nephew Qabus, after overthrowing Sultan Sa'id ibn Taymur AL BU SA'ID in 1970, appointed him prime minister, but differences led to Tariq's resignation a year later. His daughter married Qabus in 1976, and Tariq died a few years later.

John E. Peterson

Al Bu Sa'id, Taymur ibn Faysal
[1886–1965]

Sultan of Oman from 1913 to 1931.

Taymur was born in Musqat in 1886 to Sultan Faysal ibn Turki AL BU SA'ID and the daughter of a sultan of Zanzibar. He was educated in Baghdad and India. In 1920, he was forced to give autonomy to tribes of the Omani interior. Taymur abdicated in 1931 in favor of his son Sa'id ibn Taymur AL BU SA'ID and died in 1965.

John E. Peterson

Alcohol

An element of Middle Eastern life with a long and controversial history.

The drinking of alcoholic beverages has been a continuous feature of Middle Eastern life since the fourth millennium B.C.E. Beer played an important role in the Sumerian civilization of Mesopotamia, and the use of wild grapes to make wine originated in the region, where it became ritually important in Judaism and Christianity. In the medieval period, Muslim chemists pioneered the distillation process used to produce concentrated alcoholic beverages. Running counter to this historical tradition, however, are the clear strictures against wine drinking in Qur'anic verses 4:43, 2:219, and 5:90–91. Yet the QUR'AN also visualizes paradise as containing rivers of wine "delicious to the drinkers" (47:15).

Since *khamr*, normally translated as "grape wine," is the only beverage specifically mentioned in the Qur'an, Muslim legists long debated how broadly to interpret the prohibition against drinking it. All agreed to ban its sale to Muslims and to absolve anyone who destroyed wine in a Muslim's possession. They also held that the slightest taint of wine invalidated the ritual purity required for prayer. Shi'ite, Maliki, Shafi'i, and Hanbali jurists further agreed that any intoxicating beverage should be considered as belonging to the category of khamr. The Hanafis, whose legal interpretations were favored by the Ottoman government, disagreed; they maintained that *khamr* denoted only the fermentation of uncooked fruit such as grapes, dates, raisins. They thereby permitted the use of certain beverages fermented from cooked juices and from uncooked materials like honey, wheat, barley, millet, and figs. These, however, could only be consumed in "nonintoxicating" amounts. The legists, who also debated this limitation, produced definitions of intoxication that ranged from "giddy" and "boisterous" to "blind drunk."

Islamic legal variations, local custom, and the acknowledged right of non-Muslims living under Muslim rule to make, sell, and consume alcoholic beverages resulted in an almost continual presence of alcohol in Middle Eastern society throughout the Islamic period. Drinking songs, royal and aristocratic drinking sessions, drunkenness as a metaphor for love of God, and the breaking of wine jars as an expression of moral outrage are commonplaces in Islamic literature.

In the nineteenth century, alcoholic beverages were produced in many parts of the Middle East. Most of the vintners were non-Muslims, although some employed Muslims in their vineyards. In French-dominated Algeria, the alcoholic beverages produced were mostly designated for the European market. By World War I, Algerian grapes were yielding over 2 million metric tons (2.2 millon tons) of wine per year. The yield from the Ottoman Empire was more modest and local. The region of Bursa, for example, produced some 12.0 metric tons (13.2 tons) of grapes in 1880, of which around one-third—from Christian growers—was made into wine or *raki,* an anise-flavored spirit distilled from grape pulp and allowed to ferment after pressing. (In Arab lands, rakı is known as *araq.*)

The rise of secularism and socialism led to varying degrees of permissiveness and state control with respect to the production and sale of alcoholic beverages. In the Republic of Turkey, for example, a state monopoly (*tekel*) on tobacco and alcohol was established. After the Egyptian revolution of 1952, Greek-owned vineyards and European-owned breweries were nationalized, and the state became the primary producer. Algeria continued to produce wine for the French market after winning its war of independence in 1962. Regulations on importing alcohol in these countries varied according to the overall import policies of the country and its desire to protect profits from state enterprises.

Efforts to ban or sharply limit alcoholic beverages are often associated with states that favor a traditional way of life, often under an Islamic political ideology. Saudi Arabia and Libya strenuously enforce bans on both the production and importation of these beverages. Iran and Yemen strictly limit consumption to non-Muslims, although South Yemen (the former People's Democratic Republic of Yemen) once had a brewery that was destroyed by Muslim activists. Flogging (usually forty or eighty stripes) is the prescribed punishment for violating the religious proscription.

BIBLIOGRAPHY

HATTOX, RALPH S. *Coffee and Coffeehouses: The Origins of a Social Beverage in the Medieval Near East.* Seattle, 1985.

Richard W. Bulliet

Al-e Ahmad, Jalal   [1923–1969]

Iranian author; prominent nonestablishment intellectual.

The son of a Shiite Muslim cleric, Al-e Ahmad was educated at Tehran University and was the author of four volumes of short stories, four novels, and nearly a dozen volumes of essays. Al-e Ahmad focused on the present in his writing, concerned primarily with the negative influence of aspects of traditional Islam and of the modern West on Iran. His writings and life embody ongoing dilemmas for secular-minded Iranians, among them the values of the past versus the present, religion versus secularism, and West ver-

Iranian postage stamp honoring the author Jalal Al-e Ahmad. (Richard Bulliet)

sus East. His strident attacks on historical Western imperialism and post–World War II U.S involvement in Iran, together with his recognition of the unifying capacity of Islam, persuaded some Iranians to consider him influential in the success of the Iranian revolution of 1978/79. Consequently, in Persian literature, this most translated prose writer has suffered a loss of reputation among secular-minded Iranian intellectuals.

His best-known work of fiction is a realistic 1958 story about public education at the local elementary school level called *The School Principal,* available in two English translations (1974, 1986). Another of his longer fictions, a 1961 novel called *By the Pen,* available in a 1989 English translation featuring M. Hillmann's prefatory assessment of Al-e Ahmad's fiction in general, tells the story of an unsuccessful religious revolution.

BIBLIOGRAPHY

Iranian Society: An Anthology of Writings (1982) offers English translations of representative AL-E AHMAD short stories. Three translations of his polemical essay on Gharbzadegi are available: *Gharbzadegi (Weststruckness)* (1982), *Plagued by the West (Gharbzadegi)* (1982), and *Occidentosis: A Plague from the West* (1984). AL-E AHMAD's travel diary of his 1964 pilgrimage to Mecca has been translated as *Lost in the Crowd* (1985), a volume that included a biographical sketch and an extensive bibliography.

Michael C. Hillmann

Alemdar

See Bayrakdar, Mustafa

Aleppo

The principal city of northern Syria.

Syria's second largest metropolis after Damascus, Aleppo has long been a prominent economic, cultural, and political center, and, with a population of 1.8 million (1995 estimate), it ranks among the leading cities of the Middle East. Located about 70 miles inland from the Mediterranean Sea, at an elevation of 1,280 feet (390 m), Aleppo has a moderate climate, with short, cool, wet winters and long, dry, hot summers. Its surrounding region, parts of which are semi-arid, supports extensive agriculture as well as the raising of livestock.

The majority of Aleppo's townspeople are Sunni Muslims (*see* SUNNI ISLAM), but they live alongside substantial numbers of Christians affiliated with various churches. Tens of thousands of Armenian refugees from Anatolia settled in Aleppo during World War I and strengthened the traditionally prominent Christian presence. The local Jewish community, whose roots went back to pre-Islamic times, also grew during the modern period, but the Arab-Israeli hostilities caused most of its members to leave the country around 1948. The remaining Jewish presence, which continued to dwindle thereafter, came to a historic end with the departure of the last Jews in 1994.

During the period of Ottoman rule in Syria (1516–1918), Aleppo served as the administrative capital of a large province that extended over much of northern Syria as well as parts of southern Anatolia. Ottoman governors dispatched from Istanbul administered the affairs of the area with the cooperation of Aleppo's local Muslim elite. The city's politics were characterized by the competition for influence among local powerful figures and by periodic local clashes with the

The city of Aleppo and countryside as viewed from the Citadel. (Richard Bulliet)

Ottoman authorities. The unusually troubled years from 1770 to 1850 witnessed violent factional strife, popular unrest, and occupation by the Egyptian army (1832–1840). In the calmer period that followed, more orderly Ottoman control was restored, and the community began to experience the benefits of European-inspired innovations, including modern schools, improved sanitation and health care, street lighting, printing, newspapers, and wheeled transport. The local notable families integrated themselves more fully into the Ottoman provincial administration at this time and strengthened their power by acquiring large amounts of rural land.

With the establishment of modern Syria in 1920, Aleppo continued to serve as the seat of government for the surrounding region. Its Sunni landowning families, with their counterparts from Damascus, dominated national politics during the French mandate (1920–1946) and the first two decades of independence. As of the 1960s, however, the old landed notables began to be displaced by a new political elite composed of men of provincial and minority origins (particularly Alawi). Land-reform measures resulted in the expropriation of the great agricultural estates and helped to break the political back of the Sunni elite. In the 1970s and 1980s, opposition in Aleppo and other Sunni centers to the new political structure gave rise to clashes of Muslim organizations with Hafiz al-Asad's regime.

The modern period also transformed Aleppo's commercial role. Since the sixteenth century, the city had been a leading center of regional and international trade, with a network of markets that included cities in Anatolia, Iraq, Iran, Syria, Arabia, Egypt, Europe, and Asia. In the nineteenth century, however, much of the region's external trade, now oriented increasingly toward Europe, shifted from inland cities like Aleppo to the Mediterranean coastal

The citadel at Aleppo, in northern Syria. (David Rewcastle)

Old street and storehouse with sheep carcasses in Aleppo, 1965. (Richard Bulliet)

towns. The end of the Ottoman Empire (1918) cut Aleppo off from some of its traditional markets in the region and narrowed still further its commercial horizons. The city's manufacturing sector, however, remained strong, and today, as a major industrial center, Aleppo produces fine silk and cotton fabric, soaps and dyes, processed foods, leather goods, and articles of gold and silver.

Like other major Middle Eastern cities, Aleppo grew dramatically during the modern period, especially since around 1950, when the migration from rural regions to urban centers began to assume massive proportions. Its population, about 90,000 in 1800, had risen modestly to 110,000 in 1900 and to 320,000 in 1950, but it then increased sharply by 1.5 million in the next forty-five years.

With this population growth came a corresponding physical expansion. Beginning in the 1870s, vast new areas developed all around the old historic city, thereby giving birth to modern Aleppo. The new districts, built on a European model of apartment buildings and wide streets laid out in a regular grid pattern, contrasted sharply with the dense environment of courtyard houses and narrow, winding alleyways in the old parts. As the better-off townspeople gradually moved out of the old city, it deteriorated into an over-

crowded habitat for the urban poor and for rural migrants. This exodus represented the rejection of an environment that had come to be regarded as backward and unsuited to modern living. The old city has nevertheless remained among the best preserved and most handsome of the traditional Middle Eastern cities, and since the 1970s a movement to conserve its historic monuments and urban fabric has taken hold, although with still unresolved debates over proposed rehabilitation plans.

Aleppo, which has remained one of Syria's leading centers of cultural life, is particularly renowned, in the country and wider region, for its role as a creative center of traditional music. The *muwashshah,* a song traced back to Muslim Spain, has been a local specialty; hundreds of these vocal pieces—now known as *muwashshahat halabiyya*—were composed or preserved in the city and diffused from there throughout the region. Ottoman music has also been popular, and Turkish influences continue to distinguish local approaches to music theory. Many accomplished Arab musicians have hailed from Aleppo, among them the violin virtuosos Sami al-Shawwa (1887–1960) and Tawfiq al-Sabbagh (1890–1955) and the popular singer Sabah Fakhri (1933–   ). The most influential figure was Ali al-Darwish (1884–1952), whose encyclopedic knowledge of the Arab and Ottoman musical systems and repertoires, derived from thirty years of travel in the Middle East and North Africa, has profoundly marked the region's musical scene and scholarship.

BIBLIOGRAPHY

Gaube, Heinz, and Eugen Wirth. *Aleppo.* Wiesbaden, Germany, 1984.
Marcus, Abraham. *The Middle East on the Eve of Modernity: Aleppo in the Eighteenth Century.* New York, 1989.
Sauvaget, Jean. *Alep.* Paris, 1941.

Abraham Marcus

Alevi

The adherents of a belief system fitting loosely under a Shi'ite rubric.

Alevis constitute a significant minority in contemporary Turkey; though no reliable statistics enumerate them, estimates of their numbers are as high as 20 percent of Turkey's population, or somewhere in the region of 10–12 million. They variously are understood to be a religious sect, or an ethnic minority group. Be that as it may (and such endeavors at categorization ultimately prove futile) the term *Alevi* refers to a number of diverse groups all maintaining different levels of identification with Alevi-ness (*Alevilik,* in Turkish) and with each other.

Scholars interested in Alevi antinomian cosmology have posited numerous theories about influences and origins. Alevis are variously believed to be the descendants of neo-platonists, gnostics, Manicheanists, Zoroastrians, and early Anatolian Christian cults. Many Alevis living in the Kurdish regions of Eastern Anatolia speak one of the indigenous Kurdish languages, Zazaca (Demili) or Kurmancı; others in the southern portions of Anatolia, near the Syrian border speak Arabic, while large portions of Turkey's Alevi population in western Anatolia are monolingual Turkish speakers, such as the so-called Tahtacı (sedentarized, formerly transhumant woodcutters; Kehl-Bodgrogi, 1988), the Abdals, and the Çepni. Alevilik also resembles belief systems and practices of groups such as the Shabak of northern Iraq and the Ahl-i Haqq of Iran.

Most of these groups recognize a sacred hierarchy that includes a trinity consisting of Allah, Muhammad, and Ali; they also revere the twelve imams. After these, the next most important figure is the saint Haci Bektash Veli, said to be originally of Khorasan but who settled with his followers in the Kir Şehir region of Central Anatolia in the thirteenth century. A village bearing his name, Haci Bektash Köyü, became the center of this group of dervishes, and a large tekke—one that is still important today—was established there. Presumably he was part of a larger movement of Turkmen Babas practicing a mystical tradition influenced by Ahmet Yesevi, the Central Asian *sufi* (mystic), whose tomb remains an important pilgrimage site. Having won many followers whom he initiated in his ritual path during the course of his lifetime, Haci Bektash Veli instructed these disciples to spread the word, and he appointed apostles for this purpose.

The history and traditions of the followers of Haci Bektash Veli, the BEKTASHIS, overlap with Alevis in many areas. Among the Bektashis, there has been a distinction between *Yol Evladı* (Children of the Path) and *Bel Evladı* (natural descendants). The former believe that Haci Bektash was celibate, and membership in the order can only be accomplished through study with a murşit, or spiritual guide, and eventual initiation at an *ayın-i cem.* The *dedebaba,* the leader of the whole order, is elected by their *baba*s. The *Bel Evladı* segment believe that Haci Bektash married, begot a son, and that the order's leadership since that time should go to his descendants, the Çelebis. Çelebis need not go through initiation (though their followers, *talip*s, must be initiated) but are Bektashis through ascription. Many Alevis would affiliate with the *Bel Evladı* interpretation. This concurs with Norton's claim that *Bel Evladı* more often are found in rural areas, whereas *Yol Evladı* tend to be town and urban dwellers.

Many village-based Alevis were the talips, the client-disciples, of a Bektash effendi or çelebi, based in the tekke of Haci Bektash, who might visit them annually, collect tribute, officiate at an *ayın-i cem,* and mediate in disputes. Other Alevi villages maintained the talip relationship with *pir*s, members of holy lineages which were not directly related to the Bektashis.

The central communal ritual for Alevis, as for Bektashis, is the *ayın-i cem,* held, if in a village, in a *cem evi.* The pirs officiate, and during it the martyrdoms of Hasan, Hüseyin, and the twelve imams are symbolically reinacted by means of the dousing of twelve candles, accompanied by impassioned wailing. Some groups of Alevis include wine or *rakı* ceremonially as part of the *cem.* An essential component of a cem is the playing and singing of poetry and songs of early Alevi *aşık*s or *ozan*s (wandering minstrels) such as Yunus Emre and Pir Sultan Abdal. (The later was hanged by Sultan Süleyman in 1560.) The poetry can be understood on multiple levels; ostensible love songs also refer to mystical aspects of the relationship between humans and God, for example. Music is played on the *saz,* a plucked instrument resembling a long-necked lute, sometimes said to be the embodiment of Ali. The strumming and fingering can be complex, demanding a high level of technical virtuosity; many of the rhythms are repetitive, conducive to the *semah,* trance-inducing dancing performed in the ayın-i cem.

Other beliefs and practices of many Alevis include fasting during the first twelve days of Muharram and the celebration of Nevruz. The most well-known Alevi precept is *eline, diline, beline, sahip ol* (be the master of your hands, tongue, and loins). This guides behavior for Alevis. Many Alevis minimize the Sunni practices of making an outward show of their piety at the expense of inner purity. This is consonant with the belief and permitted practice of *taqiya* (dissimulation). Taqiya reflects the pervasive belief in esotericism privileging the internal, the unseen, the purity of one's heart. Many Alevi beliefs have been codified and inscribed in *Buyruk* (Decree), believed to be the collected sayings of Imam Çafer Sadik, the sixth of the twelve imams.

Other religious tenets include a belief in divine incarnations and the related belief in reincarnation. In addition, there are beliefs in spiritual guidance and in the hierarchy of the four gates of *şeriat, tarikat, hakikat,* and *marifet.*

As in the religious observances, Alevis are differentiated by their attitudes about the social and ritual place and status of women. An Alevi saying, *kadın, toplumun annesidir* (woman is the mother of society), summarizes the central role women are seen to play; women are integral to the cem ceremony. Furthermore, it is less common to see Alevi women wearing headscarves or veils. This is consistent with the belief system that would have the inner, esoteric aspects valued more highly than the external.

As a minority that explicitly opposed the hegemonic Sunni power of the Ottoman Empire, the Alevis have been seen as threatening, and subject to centuries of persecution. The pejorative sobriquet *kızılbaş* (red head) derives from an implication that they were traitors, in league with the Iranian Safavi Empire. Republican Turkey saw the closure in 1925 of all sufi orders, tarikats, and tekkes, the banning of the use of related titles, and the prohibition of certain practices.

A sense of victimization pervades the Alevi worldview. Subject to persecution and massacres throughout their history, Alevis revere and identify with ancestral martyrs. Twentieth-century massacres and oppression are conceptualized in mythohistorical terms, as part of the cultural logic of their own particular *longue durée*. More recent massacres in Malatya, Kahraman Maraş and in Çorum in the late 1970s, and Sivas in 1993, serve as proof for Alevis of the persistence of persecution. The massacres in the 1970s, perpetrated by right-wing Sunnis, were incited by the fascist National Movement Party, and depended on the collusion of local police and the army, who identified *Alevilik* with communism.

The late 1980s saw a resurgence of *Alevilik* in Turkey and in the west European diaspora. In Turkey, numerous publications appeared in bookstores, *Alevilik* was discussed in the national press, and there were efforts to establish a special Alevi desk at the Directorate of Religion in Ankara. No longer associated exclusively with the political left, some Alevis have moved to the right. In the 1980s the popular annual festival at Haci Bektash Köyu began to be patronized by politicians of all persuasions, eager to win over the Alevi electorate; the state now sponsors the festival. The lifting of government sanctions against Alevi self-expression has acted as a buffer against Kurdish nationalism.

BIBLIOGRAPHY

BIRGE, JOHN KINGSLY. *The Bektashi Order of Dervishes*. London, 1937.

BUMKE, PETER J. "Kizilbas Kurden in Dersim: Marginalität und Häresie." *Anthropos* 74(1979): 530–548.

KEHL-BODROGI, KRISZTINA. *Die Kizilibas/Aleviten: Untersuchungen eine esoterischen Glaubensgemeinschaft*. Berlin, 1988.

MELIKOFF, IRENE. *Sur les traces du soufism turc: Recherches sur l'Islam populaire en Anatolie*. Istanbul, 1992.

NORTON, J. D. "Bektashis in Turkey." In *Islam in the Modern World*, ed. by D. MacEoin and A. al-Shah. London, 1983.

Ruth Mandel

Alexander I [1777–1825]

Czar of Russia, 1801–1825.

Vacillating between territorial aggrandizement through war and grandiose designs for peace, Alexander sent troops against the OTTOMAN EMPIRE—in Turkey from 1806 to 1812 (Treaty of Bucharest) and in Persia from 1804 to 1813 (Treaty of Gulistan). Although tempted to aid the Greek revolution against the Ottomans, he was working with Britain to achieve a negotiated settlement at the time of his death.

BIBLIOGRAPHY

FLORINSKY, MICHAEL T. *Russia: A History and an Interpretation*, 2 vols. Toronto, 1970.

Jon Jucovy

Alexander II [1818–1881]

Czar of Russia, 1855–1881.

Alexander's reign was dominated by recovery from defeat in the CRIMEAN WAR (1853–1856). Expansion took place in East Asia, the Caucasus, and Central Asia. Although personally inimical to pan-Slavism, Alexander became embroiled in the nationalist revolts against the OTTOMAN EMPIRE's expansion into the Balkans. The revival of the EASTERN QUESTION led to war with the Ottomans, which was concluded by the 1878 treaties of San Stefano and Berlin.

BIBLIOGRAPHY

FLORINSKY, MICHAEL T. *Russia: A History and an Interpretation*, 2 vols. Toronto, 1970.

Jon Jucovy

Alexandretta

Mediterranean port city in Turkey (now called Iskenderun; also, Iskederun and Scanderum), founded by Alexander the Great, 333 B.C.E.

The ancient port city remained relatively small and unimportant and was called "little Alexandria" in late Roman times, hence Alexandretta, in contrast to the much larger Alexandria in Egypt. Alexandretta is located on the southeast shore of the Gulf of Iskenderun just north of Syria; it first became important as the main port for Aleppo (Syria) and the overland route to the Persian/Arabian Gulf in the 1590s. Because of rampant malaria, only its commercial functions kept it alive. With the agricultural boom that began around 1890, Alexandretta gained importance as an outlet for farm produce, but it was eclipsed by Tripoli and Beirut, since the railroad came to it only in 1913.

During World War I, the Sanjac of Alexandretta was assigned to France under the SYKES–PICOT AGREEMENT and was excluded from the area "said to be purely Arab" in the HUSAYN–MCMAHON CORRESPONDENCE. The Turks ceded it to France by the FRANKLIN–BOUILLON AGREEMENT of 1921, and it became part of the French mandate in Syria. Its population was an ethnic mix: In 1936, French authorities estimated that 39 percent were Turks, 28 percent Alawi, 11 percent Armenian, 10 percent Sunni Arab, and 8 percent various other Christians. In the 1930s, wishing to avoid Arab rule, the Turks sought an independent sanjak tied to Turkey. Alawis and Armenians, fearing both Turks and Arabs, desired an autonomous sanjak tied to Syria. Only the Sunni Arabs favored full integration with Syria. Thus began the Alexandretta crisis: In December 1937, Turkey denounced their 1926 treaty of friendship with Syria, and France sent a military mission to Ankara threatening war. By July, France and Turkey came to an agreement, that both would supervise elections in Alexandretta with 2,500 troops each. Fearing Italian expansionism, France had taken the Turkish side, arranging that twenty-two of the forty members of the new assembly would be Turkish.

In July, the troops arrived; in August, the election duly produced the twenty-two Turkish delegates. On September 2, the sanjak was voted the Republic of Hatay by the new assembly, to be coextensive with the former sanjak of Alexandretta. The Turks were evidently in control and the republic existed only pro forma. Almost immediately, 20 percent of the population—mostly Alawis, Armenians, and Sunni Arabs—became refugees in Syria. Hatay became part of Turkey on June 23, 1939, by agreement between France and Turkey.

Since annexation, Iskenderun (its Turkish name) has become strategically and commercially important to Turkey. During the Cold War, NATO planners assumed that the Turkish defense against a Soviet thrust into eastern Turkey could only be supplied through Iskenderun and Mersin. Consequently, a network of paved roads was built from the Gulf of Iskenderun into the eastern interior. Hostility between Iraq and Syria in the 1960s and 1970s threatened to close pipelines that brought Iraqi petroleum to Syrian ports. Iraq then arranged with Turkey to build pipelines from Iraq to the Gulf of Iskenderun, at Yumurtalik and near Dortyol, just north of the city of Iskenderun. The first oil arrived in 1977. Iskenderun's tidewater location at the point in Tur-

key nearest its major Middle Eastern markets led to the construction of a large steel plant. These investments have made Iskenderun one of Turkey's fastest growing cities, sustaining an average growth rate of more than 5 percent per year since 1970. The population in 1985 was 173,607.

BIBLIOGRAPHY

KHOURY, PHILIP S. *Syria and the French Mandate*. Princeton, N.J., 1987.
LANGER, WILLIAM L. *An Encyclopedia of World History*. Boston, 1948.

John R. Clark

Alexandria

Egypt's second largest city and main port.

Modern Alexandria stands on the site the ancient city of the same name, founded by Alexander the Great in 322 B.C.E. It is located on a narrow spit of land with the Mediterranean Sea to the north and Lake Mariut to the south and lies on an axis approximately five to seven miles long by three-quarters of a mile wide. The climate is temperate and averages 45 degrees Fahrenheit during the winter months. Summer weather, although not as hot as in Cairo, Egypt's capital and largest city, is significantly affected by sea-borne humidity and reaches 90 degrees Fahrenheit.

The current population stands at approximately 2.5 million but nearly doubles during the summer months, when Alexandria becomes a popular resort for Cairo residents. It is also the site of oil refineries, food processing plants, and car-assembly works. The port is the main point of export for cotton as well as other agricultural products and one of Egypt's major venues for imports. Because of its significance to the commercial activity of the city, the harbor underwent major expansions in the first quarter of the twentieth century. Indeed, its size and position made it the headquarters of the Royal Navy's Mediterranean squadron until the end of World War II.

The history of modern Alexandria begins in 1798 when the French occupied it until 1801 as part of Napoléon Bonaparte's Egyptian campaign. The city experienced a genuine revival in the early nineteenth century when Muhammad Ali connected it to the Nile river by the Mahmudiyya Canal, dredged its long-neglected harbor, and made it the site of his naval building program and arsenal. To staff these endeavors, he conscripted peasants, forcing them to live in Alexandria, hence swelling the original urban population of twelve thousand. By 1824, because of

Fort Qaitbay in Alexandria, Egypt. (Mia Bloom)

Muhammad Ali's agricultural policies, Egypt was experiencing the first of two significant cotton exporting booms. Both booms led to the arrival of numerous European entrepreneurs involved with cotton, a combination that was to govern Alexandria's commercial and political fortunes until the advent of Nasser and the Suez Crisis of October 1956. Alexandria's dynamism, however, was greatly curtailed when Muhammad Ali, under Anglo-French pressure in 1840, abandoned his expansionist policies vis-à-vis his suzerain, the Ottoman sultan.

During the U.S. Civil War and the ensuing Union naval blockade of the Confederacy, Alexandria experienced a recurrence of its commercial and urban fortunes as well as a population explosion reaching over 180,000 inhabitants. With the disappearance of southern American cotton, European, especially British, mills turned to Egypt as the closest source of acceptable cotton. Between 1861 and July 1864, Egypt's cotton earnings on the British market alone increased from 1.4 million pounds to a peak of 14 million pounds. This in turn led to feverish eco-

Panoramic view of the Alexandria harbor and skyline. (Mia Bloom)

nomic activity aimed at improving agriculture, increasing urban development, manufacturing, and transport, and culminated in the digging of the Suez Canal in 1869. The Egyptian viceroy had embarked on an ambitious program of modernization thus heavily indebting himself. European financiers and entrepreneurs settled in Alexandria transforming it from a marginal seaside town into the major entrepôt of the eastern Mediterranean for the next three-quarters of a century. The seaport also became the financial and political center of the country while Cairo remained the political capital of Egypt. By World War I, Alexandria's population had grown to nearly half a million and had reached a million when King Farouk abdicated in 1952.

Unable to repay or service the debt, in 1876 Egypt came under the supervision of Anglo-French financial advisers. This latest foreign jurisdiction, known as the Dual Control, led to the growth of nationalist sentiments culminating in the ministry of Ahmad Urabi Pasha. In 1882, the British fleet bombarded and then occupied Alexandria in order to crush a nationalist insurrection seeking, under his leadership, to curtail European domination of Egyptian affairs.

After the bombardment, the town was rebuilt along European lines with clearly demarcated areas for business, industry, and residence. The new city grew into nearly separate European and indigenous sections reflecting, like much colonial urbanism, the demographic dichotomies of its population. Today Alexandria still presents a unique mixture of architectural styles, blending Venetian rococo, turn-of-the-century Beaux Arts, Bauhaus, Mediterranean stucco and, more recently, post-Modernist high tech, although it lacks Cairo's rich Islamic architectural heritage.

The Suez Crisis and the ensuing ARAB–ISRAELI WAR of 1956 led to a mass exodus of Alexandria's foreign resident population. Those developments also encouraged Nasser to intensively Arabize and Egyptianize the city's ethos. This policy was undoubtedly motivated by the still vast and disproportionate wealth and commercial influence of the foreign population despite its reduction from about one-fifth of the total in 1917 to approximately one-thirteenth of the total in 1947. Not by coincidence did Nasser choose Alexandria, that most European of Egypt's cities, to deliver a speech in July 1956 announcing the nationalization of the SUEZ CANAL Company.

Thus from the middle of the nineteenth to the middle of the twentieth century, Alexandria was home to a polyglot population representing the Mediterranean litoral and comprising different national, ethnocultural, and religious backgrounds. While the booming economy led to relative harmony among the diverse population, serious nationalist disturbances aimed at the foreign presence required the intervention of the British army in 1882 and 1921, and the Egyptian military in 1947. Hence, along with its cosmopolitanism, Alexandria reflected the realities of Egyptian nationalist politics spanning the British occupation in 1882 to decolonization after World War II. After the Suez crisis, Nasser reduced the size and the scope of the foreign resident community at an accelerating tempo through expropriations and expulsions. By the time of the Six-Day War in 1967, Alexandria's foreign resident community was almost entirely eradicated.

BIBLIOGRAPHY

ACIMAN, ANDRÉ. *Out of Egypt: A Memoir*. New York, 1995.
BERQUE, JACQUES. *Egypt: Imperialism and Revolution*. New York, 1972.
FORSTER, E. M. *A History and a Guide*. New York, 1973.
OWEN, E. R. J. *Cotton and the Egyptian Economy, 1820–1914*. Oxford, 1969.
REIMER, MICHAEL J. "Colonial Bridgehead: Social and Spatial Change in Alexandria, 1850–1882." *International Journal of Middle East Studies* 20, no. 4 (1988).

Jean-Marc R. Oppenheim

Alexandria Conference of Arab States

Meeting in 1944 that laid the foundations of the Arab League.

Held in Alexandria, Egypt, September 25 to October 7, 1944, the conference was attended by representatives of Egypt, Iraq, Jordan, Lebanon, Saudi Arabia, Syria, Yemen, and Palestine Arabs. It issued the Alexandria Protocol announcing that the attending Arab states would form a league to ensure their cooperation in international matters and to protect their sovereignty. The Arab League is now the LEAGUE OF ARAB STATES. The protocol also stated that Palestinian rights concerned the entire Arab world.

BIBLIOGRAPHY

HUREWITZ, J. C. *The Struggle for Palestine*. New York, 1950, 1976.
MACDONALD, ROBERT W. *The League of Arab States*. Princeton, N.J., 1965.

Elizabeth Thompson

Alexandria Convention

Agreement made between the British and Muhammad Ali of Egypt to end Egypt's territorial aggression.

By the London Convention of July 1840, Muhammad Ali Pasha, ruler of Egypt, was given an ultimatum by the Ottoman Empire and its allies, to evacuate his troops from Anatolia and Syria. He refused, and Britain sent a naval squadron under Admiral Charles Napier to aid Syria. After the defeat of Egypt's forces in Syria, the British sailed to Egypt's port of Alexandria. Muhammad Ali recognized the weakness of his position and the strength of the forces arrayed against him; he sued for peace and signed the Alexandria Convention with Napier on November 27, 1840.

Under its terms, he renounced his claims to Syria and agreed to yield to the Ottoman sultan. In return, the sultan granted him hereditary possession of Egypt. When news of the Alexandria Convention reached Europe, there was some concern that the terms had been too light; it was months before the sultan fully endorsed the agreement, fearing additional empire-building on the part of Muhammad Ali. The convention was used to signify the end of Muhammad Ali as a threat to the integrity of the rest of the Ottoman Empire—an integrity that was thenceforth preserved with the aid of the European powers.

BIBLIOGRAPHY

ANDERSON, M. S. *The Eastern Question*. London, 1966.
HUREWITZ, J. C., ed. *The Middle East and North Africa in World Politics*. New Haven, Conn., 1975.

Zachary Karabell

Alexandria Protocol

Agreement to form the League of Arab States.

The fruition of years of planning, after a September to October meeting in Alexandria, Egypt, the protocol was signed on October 7, 1944, by Egypt, Transjordan (now Jordan), Yemen, Saudi Arabia, Iraq, Lebanon, Syria, and a representative of the Palestinian Arabs. They agreed to form a LEAGUE OF ARAB STATES (also called the Arab League), and special resolutions were passed supporting Lebanon's independence and the political aspirations of the Palestinian Arabs. These resolutions were embodied in the league's charter.

BIBLIOGRAPHY

HUREWITZ, J. C., ed. *The Middle East and North Africa in World Politics*. New Haven, Conn., 1979.

LENCZOWSKI, GEORGE. *The Middle East in World Affairs*, 4th ed. Ithaca, N.Y., 1980.

Zachary Karabell

Alexandria University

Egyptian institution of higher learning founded in 1942.

Originally named Farouk University after the country's ruling monarch, Alexandria University is Egypt's second oldest state university, after Cairo's which was founded in 1925. It was renamed following the 1952 Revolution that toppled the monarchy.

The construction of the university began in the mid-1930s but was not completed until 1942 due to the vagaries of Egyptian politics and the onset of World War II. Its opening ceremony led by the king was highly symbolic because the university addressed the needs of higher learning. More importantly, the occasion also served to remove the sting of a British ultimatum given to King Farouk on 4 February 1942 resulting in the appointment of a Wafd government sympathetic to British wartime policies in Egypt but anathema to Farouk himself.

The university, with a number of campuses throughout the city, offers undergraduate and graduate degrees in the humanities, the social and natural sciences, engineering, dentistry, medicine, veterinary science, and law. The language of instruction is Arabic although English is used for dentistry, medicine and some branches of engineering. As of the mid-1990s, the university enrolled over one hundred thousand students and had an instructor-student ratio of over 1:100. Like most Egyptian institutions of higher education, the quality of instruction is of low standard resulting from inadequate staff in both numbers and quality, lack of time for independent study and research, and a shortage of funds for library acquisitions and research facilities—particularly foreign exchange for the purchase of foreign publications. Nonetheless, the Alexandria University Press publishes scholarly works in English as well as in Arabic.

Islamist priorities at the university in the 1990s represent the direction of grass roots values and culture in Egypt, but also affect the dynamics necessary for critical thinking in an institution of advanced learning.

BIBLIOGRAPHY

COCHRAN, JUDITH. *Education in Egypt*. London, 1986.
HEYWORTH-DUNNE, JAMES. *An Introduction to the History of Education in Modern Egypt*. London, 1938.

HYDE, GEORGIE. *Education in Modern Egypt: Ideals and Realities.* Boston, 1978.

Jean-Marc R. Oppenheim

Algeciras Conference

Conference (January 16–April 7, 1906) convened in Algeciras, Spain, to resolve the first Moroccan crisis over German attempts to break up the Anglo–French entente cordiale that dated from April 1904.

Anglo–French agreements recognized France's paramount interests in Morocco and Britain's special position in Egypt. They also secretly provided for the future partition of Morocco between France and Spain. In 1905, German chancellor Prince Bernhard von Bülow believed that Germany should demonstrate its great-power status and its right to be consulted over such issues. He pressed Germany's Kaiser Wilhelm II to undertake a trip to Tangier (March 1905) to assure the sultan of German support for Moroccan independence. French Premier Théophile Delcassé resigned, and Germany appeared to have achieved its goal of disrupting French–British ties. Nevertheless, von Bülow insisted on pressing his advantage and forced the convening of an international conference at Algeciras in Spain to discuss France's reform program for Morocco.

The conference was a disaster for the Germans. Their policy of threats had so alienated governments and public opinion throughout Europe that Germany found itself all but isolated, with only the Austro-Hungarian Empire and Morocco itself siding with the Germans. On the surface, Germany appeared to have gained its goal, for the conference reaffirmed Moroccan independence. But it also approved French and Spanish control over the Moroccan police and banks, and it paved the way for France to further encroach on Moroccan independence. The first Moroccan crisis encouraged closer relations between France and Britain and revealed the weakness of Germany's diplomatic position. By permitting French penetration of Morocco, it practically guaranteed the rise of Moroccan nationalist opposition to the agreements. Such opposition was almost certain to lead to further French encroachments over Morocco's merely formal independence. The Algeciras Act was doomed from the outset, culminating in the AGADIR CRISIS of 1911.

BIBLIOGRAPHY

TAYLOR, A. J. P. *The Struggle for the Mastery of Europe, 1848–1918.* Oxford, 1954.

Jon Jucovy

Algeria

Arab republic situated in North Africa.

The Democratic and Popular Republic of Algeria comprises an area of some 920,000 square miles (2,381,741 sq km) in the Maghrib (North Africa). It is bounded by the Mediterranean Sea on the north, Morocco on the west, Mauritania on the southwest, Mali and Burkina Faso on the south, and Libya and Tunisia on the east. The 1992 population totaled about twenty-seven million people. Major cities include the capital ALGIERS (al-Jaza'ir), Oran, Constantine, and Annaba.

Algeria is divided into a relatively humid and mountainous north, which is part of the ATLAS MOUNTAIN system, and the lower desert in the south, which makes up the overwhelming part of the country and which belongs to the Saharan tableland. The Atlas mountain system itself consists of three separate parts: the Tell Atlas, the High Plateaus, and the Saharan Atlas that abuts the desert. The Sahara, stretching south for more than 930 miles (1,500 km), is interrupted by several plateaus and by the great massif of the Ahaggar mountains, which rise to a height of almost ten thousand feet (3,050 m) in a series of crystalline and volcanic peaks extending into neighboring Mali and Burkina Faso.

Climate. Northernmost Algeria enjoys a Mediterranean-type CLIMATE with warm, wet winters and hot, dry summers. Rainfall in the north varies between four and five inches (100–130 mm) per year, most of it accumulated during the winter months. The summer period includes a dry spell of three to four months during which hot winds blow in from the Sahara, winds known locally as the *chehili.* South of the Saharan Atlas, rainfall drops precipitously, making regular cultivation without irrigation impossible, particularly in the absence of permanent rivers in the area.

The Sahara, which extends more than 930 miles (1,500 km) south of the northern coastal area, is hot and extremely dry, with annual precipitation less than 5 inches (130 mm) per year and, in some parts, less than 0.5 inches (10 mm) per year. In addition this rainfall is highly erratic and unpredictable, often arriving in single downpours interrupted by several years of drought.

Government. Algeria's central government is augmented by subnational units at the *wilaya* level (provinces—48 at present) and at the local level by communes (1,540 at present). Each has executive and legislative assemblies. In addition, an intermediary unit, the *daira,* facilitates a number of adminis-

trative and legal issues that neither the wilaya nor the commune engages in.

The 1976 national constitution provides for a presidential system of government and a unicameral National Popular Assembly. The apparatus of government includes the conventional executive, legislative, and judicial branches. The president, as head of the executive branch, directs the affairs of the Council of Ministers and presides over joint meetings of party and government organs. The president also heads the Higher Judicial Council and is chairman of the Superior Security Council and of the advisory body on national security matters.

Economy. Algeria's economy is dominated by the hydrocarbon sector (oil and natural gas), which provides the overwhelming share of revenues for the country and contributes more than 35 percent of gross domestic product (GDP). Most of the country's heavy industry, particularly steel and PETRO-CHEMICALS, was linked to these revenues during the socialist phase after Algeria's independence from France (1962) in an intricate network of industrial plants along the country's coast.

As a result of the industrialization strategy, agriculture has suffered greatly since independence, now contributing only about 8 percent to GDP, even

The Ahaggar mountains in the Sahara desert of southern Algeria. (Richard Bulliet)

An aerial view of the Mzab oasis in central Algeria. (Richard Bulliet)

though 40 percent of the population remains connected to the agricultural sector. Almost 70 percent of domestic food consumption is now imported into Algeria and makes up the single largest foreign currency expenditure of the government. Despite more recent attention to the sector, agriculture continues to lag far behind.

Exports from Algeria—except for some industrial and consumer products that are sold to neighboring Maghrebi countries—consist exclusively of oil, petroleum products, and natural gas, which are sold primarily to the European and the U.S. market. Imports, in addition to substantial food purchases, concentrate on industrial and high-technology items obtained from the United States and Europe. Since the liberalization campaign that started during the presidency of Chadli BENJEDID (1978–1992), Algeria has turned away from intensive trade with Eastern bloc countries.

Population and Culture. Algerian Arabs constitute 80 percent of the population, the remaining group being mainly BERBER (primarily the Kabyles living in Kabylie and the Chaouias of the Awras mountains). In addition, there are small groups of MZAB living at the edge of the Sahara region and Twaregs in the southernmost part of the country. The Arabic, Berber (several dialects), and French languages are spoken, although an Arabization campaign has increasingly stressed the use of Arabic as the official language. Almost all Algerians are Sunni Muslims; the Mzab (population 80,000), however, are Ibadites, who adhere to a puritanical form of Islam.

Algeria possesses a well-developed structure of institutes of higher education and a number of technical institutes. In addition to universities in major cities, Algeria has an Islamic university in Constantine. Primary and high school education are, at least in theory, almost universal.

The northern edge of the Sahara desert, near Laghouat. (Richard Bulliet)

A typical modern petroleum complex in Algeria. (© Chris Kutschera)

Algerian workers constructing a pipeline at Hassi Messaoud. (© Chris Kutschera)

Port of Algiers. (© Chris Kutschera)

History. At the start of the nineteenth century, the Regency of Algiers formally still belonged to the Ottoman Empire. Despite the existence of formal administrative arrangements and internal division into several *beyliks* (provinces), the actual power of the Ottoman government and its local representatives varied across the territory—a territory that was increasingly desired by France, for a number of complex economic, social and ideological reasons, as a necessary extension of its own territory. The alleged insult of the French consul in Algiers in 1827 by the *dey* (a ruling official) provided the convenient excuse for a French invasion in July 1830.

For almost a quarter century, France pursued its conquest of Algeria—although it managed to pacify and control the coastal area by the mid-1840s—in part due to the tenacity and strategies of General Thomas-Robert Bugeaud de la Piconnerie, who became the architect of French rule in Algeria. In 1848,

The Constantine suspension bridge, also known as Pont Sidi M'Cid, in Algeria. (© Chris Kutschera)

Algeria was made a part of France. Under General Bugeaud, an intensive policy of colonization followed that transferred huge tracts of land to the French settler population, particularly after an unsuccessful Algerian rebellion in 1871. Shortly afterward, a French civil administration with the status of a French *département* (province or state) was installed, opening the road for further migration and the steady expansion of large-scale industrial and agricultural enterprises.

By 1900, the French in Algeria had secured administrative and financial autonomy for the country. As in other Maghrebi and Middle Eastern countries, a wave of nationalism wafted across Algeria in the early part of the century, headed by Messali Hadj and later by the more politically moderate Ferhat ABBAS. For a short while, France allowed this movement to develop, suggesting in the 1936 Blum–Viollette Plan that Algerians could gradually and in increasing numbers be granted full rights of citizenship. The proposal was however dropped after opposition emerged, particularly among French settlers and the Algerian civil service. Although in the years leading up to World War II the nationalist demands of the local elites were somewhat weakened, Messali Hadj managed to form the PARTI DU PEUPLE ALGÉRIEN (Party of the Algerian People, PPA), whose motto was "neither assimilation nor separation, but emancipation." At the same time, Ferhat Abbas also suggested post–World War II arrangements that would have given the Algerian population a greater say in their own affairs but, significantly, did not yet ask for independence outside any framework suggested by France. (During World War II, France was occupied by Nazi Germany, which sponsored the Vichy Government; the Free French joined with the Allies to overthrow Germany. Both Vichy colonial and German troops fought the Allies in North Africa until the Germans withdrew. Many nationalist groups took advantage of weakened colonial administrations to promote their own causes.)

Since France could not respond to Abbas, backed by a number of Algerian nationalists he issued the 1943 MANIFESTO OF THE ALGERIAN MUSLIM PEOPLE, which included a demand to the end of colonization. After a number of subterfuges, the Vichy French countered with a new statute for Algeria in 1944, which did not satisfy the Algerians, the settlers, or substantial parts of the French population. The SÉTIF REVOLT of May 1945, at the end of World War II, formed the catalyst for the ALGERIAN WAR OF INDE-PENDENCE (1954–1962) and marked the end of whatever unfruitful negotiations had been conducted on the future of Algeria and its citizens. On both sides, the recourse to force and violence increased exponentially and seemingly unhaltingly. Algeria's new constitution, introduced by France in 1947, answered most of the demands made by the Algerian nationalists prior to the war, but by this time they were already viewed as inadequate.

By the beginning of the war of independence, the willingness to compromise had vanished on both sides. On the Algerian side, moreover, the old division between Hadj and Abbas gave way to increasing fragmentation among a large number of Algerian factions that had temporarily, and often with several setbacks, worked together during World War II. The FRONT DE LIBÉRATION NATIONALE (National Libera-tion Front, FLN) emerged as the overarching insti-tutional body under which the different factions, both inside Algeria and those in exile, fought against the French. For eight years, the two sides fought each other in an increasingly gruesome and bitter war that eventually was solved as much by the fear of its effects within France as by the lingering and in-conclusive nature of the conflict itself. In a final ref-erendum on July 1, 1962, more than 90 percent of eligible voters approved independence for Algeria. Two days later, General Charles de Gaulle formally proclaimed that independence, after a colonial pres-ence that had lasted 132 years.

Independence left the Algerian leadership, only united in their wish for the end of French tutelage, with the challenge of accommodating the various factions, of establishing a political status quo that proved acceptable to all sides and of rebuilding the country's economy that had been devastated both by the war and by loss of further access to French mar-kets. Ahmed BEN BELLA was elected president on September 13, 1962, and quickly moved to consol-idate power around him by assuming not only the position as head of state, but as well the head of government and commander in chief of the armed

forces. Three years later he was replaced, on June 19, 1965, by one of his former collaborators—Houari Boumédienne, who sought to preserve the position of the army and who objected to the dictatorial lean-ings of Ben Bella. Boumédienne augured in a period of collegial leadership but with the Algerian army firmly in charge of events. He also became the ar-chitect of the country's socialist economic strategy that centralized all economic decision making among a small group of technocrats in charge of a relatively small number of state enterprises. Under this tech-nocratic/military alliance, Algeria sought to pursue an intensive industrialization effort, fueled by the rapidly growing revenues from the country's petro-leum and natural gas reserves. A further outcome was that the FLN, the country's single party, slowly lost the legitimacy and the mobilizational potential it had originally held. Almost imperceptibly at first, but gathering momentum as the economic and social dislocations inside the country grew, the link be-tween the rulers and those ruled in Algeria grew wider and more worrisome.

By 1978, the year Boumédienne died, Algeria's economic strategy was in question. Although his suc-cession was settled along lines spelled out in the con-stitution—but with sideline intervention by the military—growing conflicts between those who per-ferred the old economic strategy and those in favor of a new approach emerged openly. The new pres-ident, Chadli BENJEDID, opted for an economic lib-eralization that included increased attention to the private sector and fewer privileges or autonomy for state enterprises. The move toward a more market-oriented economy was fraught with danger in Alge-ria—not only because it could temporarily deny goods and services to a population already living in austerity but also because the country's political sys-tem relied heavily on the patronage maintained by its numerous powerful groups.

Despite increasingly draconian economic measures and accelerated, but often boycotted, liberalization efforts, Algeria's economic fortunes continued to de-cline. After several smaller popular demonstrations of discontent, major riots broke out in Algeria's biggest cities in October 1988. Although the disturbances were started by young demonstrators, the Islamists (political rule by religious leaders) quickly seized the opportunity to increase their own visibility. A state of emergency was proclaimed, and it took almost two weeks before calm was restored, at a price of several hundred dead Algerians. In the wake of the riots, President Benjedid announced a number of thoroughgoing political reforms that would eventu-ally lead, he insisted, to a system of multiparty pol-itics. Algeria's constitution was amended, and on July

2, 1989, the National Assembly approved new legislation that made the formation of political parties possible.

The first test of Algeria's move toward greater political freedom came on June 12, 1990, when local elections were held throughout the country. In the elections, the Islamists managed to secure 55 percent of the vote, while the FLN's fortunes dramatically declined. Although the victory for the Islamists may have been due as much to antipathy for the ruling party as to support for the religious party itself, the implications of their victory were not lost on the various participants in the elections. In effect, these elections, which were to be followed by national elections a few months later, had shown how polarized political opinion had become in Algeria and how all other secular oppositions had been eviscerated. In this climate, the first round of the National Assembly elections took place, it delivered a solid victory to the Islamists and raised the possibility of their control of the National Assembly once the second round of elections had taken place.

Within a climate of uncertainty and growing unease, Benjedid, seemingly at the urging of the military, dissolved the National Assembly in January 1992 and shortly afterward resigned as president. The second round of elections was cancelled, and a High Security Council took over the duties of government. Muhammed BOUDIAF, one of the country's leaders during the war of independence, was persuaded to head the council.

Violence erupted soon afterward; several prominent Islamists were incarcerated and their Islamist party dissolved. In June 1992, after exhibiting an autonomy that the Algerian military had clearly not expected, Boudiaf was gunned down in Annaba by unknown assassins. In the mid-1990s, Algeria remains torn by social and political conficts that were never resolved at the start of independence, exhibiting the tendency toward fractional politics and a recourse to violence that was only temporarily held in abeyance.

BIBLIOGRAPHY

ENTELIS, JOHN. *Algeria: The Revolution Institutionalized.* Boulder, Colo., 1986.
PFEIFER, KAREN. *Agrarian Reform under State Capitalism in Algeria.* Boulder, Colo., 1985.
RAFFINOT, MARC, and PIERRE JACQUEMOT. *Le capitalisme d'état algérien.* Paris, 1977.
RUEDY, JOHN. *Modern Algeria: The Origins and Development of a Nation.* Bloomington, Ind., 1992.
TLEMCANI, RACHID. *State and Revolution in Algeria.* Boulder, Colo., and London, 1986.

Dirk Vandewalle

Algerian People's Party

See Parti du Peuple Algérien

Algerian War of Independence

This war ended more than 130 years of French colonial rule over Algeria.

The Algerian war of independence began in the early hours of November 1, 1954, and ended officially July 3, 1962, when France's President Charles de Gaulle formally renounced his nation's sovereignty over Algeria and proclaimed its independence.

The French occupation of Algeria, begun in 1830, led to a colonial situation in which a minority of European settlers and their descendants dominated the Algerian economy. They maintained that domination through monopolies of political power and the means of coercion. During the first half of the twentieth century, a series of initiatives by various indigenous leaderships sought first to secure meaningful political participation for the Muslim majority within the colonial system and later to negotiate autonomy, confederation, or independence. When these efforts proved fruitless, a group of radical young nationalists founded the COMITÉ RÉVOLUTIONNAIRE D'UNITÉ ET D'ACTION (CRUA; Revolutionary Committee of Unity and Action), which began, in the spring or summer of 1952, to plan an insurrection. Six CRUA members, together with three political exiles, are considered the *chefs historiques* of the Algerian revolution. The CRUA chiefs, led by Mohamed BOUDIAF of M'sila, included Moustafa BEN BOULAID, Mourad DIDOUCHE, Belkacem KRIM, Rabah BITAT, and Larbi BEN M'HIDI. The external leaders were Hocine AIT AHMED, Mohamed KHIDER, and Ahmed BEN BELLA, who later became Algeria's first president.

Estimates of the number of militants taking part in the initial insurrection range from nine hundred to about three thousand. It began with attacks on French installations in several parts of the country, but the most effective actions took place in the Aurès region of the southeast. During the ensuing winter, the French managed to contain the insurrection, limiting its manifestations to distant and inaccessible regions. In August of 1955, the leadership, concerned that neither the bulk of Algerians nor the European community were taking the insurrection seriously, decided to begin targeting European civilians in some twenty-six localities in the eastern part of the country. As many as 123 people were killed in what were called the Philippeville massacres. In outraged reaction, French forces responded by taking a far larger number of Muslim lives. These events served to polarize the two communities in such a way that a narrowly based insurrection became a nationwide revolution; thousands of men joined guerrilla units, while France rapidly built its own forces into the hundreds of thousands.

In its initial proclamation, on October 31, 1954, the CRUA had announced the creation of a FRONT DE LIBÉRATION NATIONALE (FLN) to which it had invited Algerians of all political persuasions to rally. As a result of the polarization following the events of August 1955, Algerian political classes across a broad ideological spectrum gradually closed down their independent operations and joined the FLN in revolution. By the summer of 1956, only Messali HADJ, long leader of the most radical wing of the Algerian natinalist movement but now bypassed by events, remained outside of the FLN.

In order to accommodate the dramatically broadened movement, the revolutionaries organized a clandestine congress in the Soumamm valley of the KABYLIA during August and September 1956. It created a broad CONSEIL NATIONAL DE LA RÉVOLUTION ALGÉRIENNE (CNRA) to serve as a protoparliament and a COMITÉ DE COORDINATION ET D'EXÉCUTION (CCE; Committee of Coordination and Implementation) to bear the executive functions. One of the first decisions of the new executive was to initiate, at the end of September 1956, the urban warfare strategy that became known as the Battle of Algiers. A very visible phase of the war that the French managed to win by the middle of 1957, the recourse to urban warfare brought the war home in a physical way to the majority of COLONS, who were urban residents, and attracted the attention of metropolitan Frenchmen and the wider world for the first time to the Algerian situation. Another result of the Battle of Algiers was that the severe French repression drove the top FLN leadership out of the country to Tunis. This in turn generated problems in communications and orientation between the external leadership and the internal *mojahedin*. These problems caused troublesome divisions within the movement that lasted throughout the war and beyond.

Between the fall of 1957 and the spring of 1958, the French army, now grown to roughly 500,000 men, succeeded in bringing most of Algeria under its physical control and was concentrating on limiting cross-border raids by Algerian guerrillas from Morocco and Tunisia. But the military were apprehensive. They feared that their achievements might be undone by the divided political leadership at home, which was sensitive to the violence involved in pacification and to growing world pressure. Thus, the army, under the leadership of General Jacques Massu

and with the enthusiastic support of the colons, proclaimed the creation on May 13, 1958, of a Committee of Public Safety at Algiers. This challenge to government authority brought down the Fourth French Republic and propelled de Gaulle to power as head of the Fifth Republic, pledging an early resolution of the Algerian conflict. By the autumn of 1958, de Gaulle offered Algerians the opportunity of total integration as equals into the French republic, inaugurated a massive plan of economic renewal, and invited the revolutionary troops to join their French compatriots in a "paix des braves."

The CCE and the CNRA rejected these terms and, instead, created a Provisional Government of the Algerian Republic (Gouvernement Provisoir de la République Algérienne; GPRA) at Tunis, with Ferhat ABBAS at its head. From this point on, even though French forces remained in control of most of Algeria, the GPRA campaigned to win world support for Algerian independence. The campaign centered primarily on third-world and eastern bloc countries and upon the United Nations. Within a year, de Gaulle began speaking of Algerian self-determination. The war of independence might have ended soon afterward, but there were obstacles. Principal among these was the fate of the Sahara, in which French companies had recently discovered oil. Even more important was the resistance of the colon community, which increasingly found more in common with the military. During 1960 they created a Front de l'Algérie Française in order to fight against independence and in January 1961 the ORGANISATION ARMÉE SECRÈTE (OAS; Secret Army Organization), which eventually led an armed insurrection against French civil authority and launched a campaign of terror against Muslim Algerians.

After several abortive attempts at negotiations, the provisional government and France finally signed the Evian Agreement on March 18, 1962, which led to unequivocal independence in July. The war had caused the dislocation from their homes of about 3 million Algerians, the destruction of much social and economic infrastructure, and the deaths of several hundred thousand Algerians. The rebuilding tasks faced by independent Algeria would be formidable.

BIBLIOGRAPHY

COURRIÈRE, YVES. *La guerre d'Algérie,* 4 vols. Paris, 1968–1971.
HORNE, ALISTAIR. *A Savage War of Peace: Algeria 1954–1962.* London, 1977.
RUEDY, JOHN. *Modern Algeria. The Origins and Development of a Nation.* Bloomington, Ind., 1992.

John Ruedy

Algiers

Capital of the Democratic and Popular Republic of Algeria (population 2.1 million, 1990).

Algiers is located at the northwestern end of a large bay in the Mediterranean sea. To the south and east, on the plain of the Mitidja, most industrial activity is concentrated. The region contains 48 percent of the country's factories and 55 percent of its industrial workforce.

The city's origins reach back to the Phoenicians (possibly) and the Romans (first century C.E.). Berbers reestablished the city on the roman ruins in the ninth century, naming it al-Jaza'ir (islands) because of rock outcroppings in the bay. In the early sixteenth century Algiers was drawn into Castile's overseas expansion and the Ottoman reaction against it. After expelling the Spaniards in 1529, the Turks established a corsair principality. At its height in the 1600s, the city, with perhaps forty thousand inhabitants, held as many as twenty thousand Christians for ransom. In the eighteenth century Western states forced an end to corsair activities, and Algiers began to specialize in grain exports. A dispute over payment for grain deliveries to Napoléon led to the occupation of Algiers by the French (1830).

The army ruled Algeria until 1871. Both the military and the settlers initially erected their residential and commercial structures in the lower part of the CASBAH (*qasba,* citadel), as the pre-1830 part of Algiers was called, rather than build a separate European city center outside the walls.

The end of the nineteenth century was a time of rapid population increase (by 41 percent from 1886 to 1896 alone, to a total of 155,000 settlers and 45,000 Muslims by 1918) and considerable agricultural wealth (particularly from wine exports). Re-

Algiers as viewed from the Casbah. (© Chris Kutschera)

sulting public expenditures included a central train depot and a new harbor (both complete by 1896), streetcar lines (begun in 1896), and municipal and educational infrastructures (water, gas, hospitals, university). Ambitious plans to turn the entire lower Casbah into a city with wide boulevards were quashed by the military, but the incorporation of the suburb of Mustapha in 1904 at last opened the way for a more systematic southern expansions. Regional Algiers was born.

In the new city the French rejected the Arab architecture of the Casbah for French bourgeois classicism, while the residents of the wealthier suburbs opted for imitations of the "Turkish gardens" (*jinan*) architecture. After World War I, European monumental classicism took over, and in the 1930s, functional modernism began to emerge. Construction of a new waterfront neighborhood pushed the Casbah into the hills, where it was greatly reduced in size (1,700 houses versus 6,800 in 1830). The former corsair city was finally cut off from the sea.

A view of Algiers seen from the waterfront, 1983. (© Chris Kutschera)

Picture postcard showing French colons with an automobile on an Algiers street in 1935. (André Kaim)

During the interwar period Muslim agriculture had reached the productive limits possible within the framework of traditional farming practices on the less fertile lands that the colonists left for the indigenous population. The capital offered employment in the port, small-scale shipbuilding, mechanical industries, and trucking firms. In addition, there were small-scale construction firms, an industry for the processing of agricultural products, and a large administrative sector. French settlers, however, held most of these jobs; the Muslim rural immigrants, crowded into shantytowns in the hills or the Casbah (with twice as many people in one-quarter of the houses, compared with 1830) were left mostly to their own devices.

In 1954 overwhelming economic misery triggered the war of independence. The effects of the war hastened the rural exodus, and around 1956, for the first time, more Muslims than Europeans lived in Algiers. Also in 1956, the war reached the city, where it was fought in the Casbah's maze of cul-de-sacs. However, France's President Charles de Gaulle grew weary of the toll the war was exacting, and in 1962 he granted independence. Furious settlers scorched parts of downtown Algiers before leaving the city en masse (311,000 between 1960 and 1962).

In a mad rush, many of the 550,000 Muslims in town occupied the dwellings vacated by the settlers, but with the reestablishment of civil authority, housing was distributed according to employment and income. A new system of nationalization and rent control in 20 percent of the housing stock contributed much to a de facto continuation of the colonial pattern: a central city of mixed business and residential structures; the decaying, overpopulated Casbah; the well-off (uphill) and poorer (downhill) suburbs; and the shantytowns in the hillside ravines. Free-market rents continued to be charged in the traditionally Muslim quarters, composed of mostly low-grade dwellings. Furthermore, over the period 1960–1966, 362,000 new rural migrants quickly filled the vacated shantytowns or slums (for a total of 911,000 inhabitants in Algiers).

In 1966, Algiers had the highest literacy rate (85 percent, versus 47 percent in Algeria as a whole), the densest transportation network (private cars, taxis and buses), and the deepest urban infrastructure (hospitals, sports complexes, theaters, cinemas, libraries and museums). By the 1980s state industries in the Algiers region were particularly strong in the sectors of mechanical and electrical machinery, processed agricultural goods, building materials, textiles, wood, and paper. The government built 50,000 new apartments to accommodate as many of the 110,000 workers and managers in these industries as possible.

However, in the early 1980s it became obvious that the industrial and urban sprawl was destroying Algiers' rich agricultural belt. The government ordered a halt to expansion, moved large numbers of squatters to new quarters or back to their villages, enforced both existing and new building codes, and built freeways to relieve urban gridlock. However, a number of pressing needs—such as the relocation of the National Assembly, the National Library, and the Congress Palace, and construction of a subway system—have yet to be completed or even begun. The Casbah, a treasure of Islamic vernacular architecture, is in dire need of rehabilitation. Unfortunately, a severe financial crisis (resulting from low prices for oil and gas since 1986), the canceled elections of 1992, a de facto takeover by the military, and increased Islamist terrorism have called into question the entire postindependence development.

BIBLIOGRAPHY

BENATIA, FAROUK. *Alger, aggrégat ou cité: L'intégration citadine à Alger.* Algiers, 1980.

DELUZ, J. J. *L'urbanisme et l'architecture d'Alger: Aperçu critique.* Algiers, 1988.

KADDACHE, MAHFOUD. *La vie politique à Alger de 1919 à 1939.* Algiers, 1970.

LESBET, DJAFFAR. *La Casbah d'Alger: Gestion urbaine et vide social.* Algiers, 1985.

LESPÈS, RENÉ. *Alger: Esquisse de géographie urbaine.* Algiers, 1925.

Peter von Sivers

Algiers, Battle of

Events generally dated from September 1956 to May 1957 that marked an important turn in the 1954–1962 Algerian war for independence from France.

In Algeria, key developments led to the decision by the nationalist leadership of the FRONT DE LIBERATION NATIONAL (FLN), which had largely concentrated on organizing rural opposition to French rule, to bring the war to the capital, Algiers, and other urban centers. These included an increasingly effective French military response to the nationalist insurgency in the countryside as well as the desire on the part of the FLN leadership to both demonstrate its standing in Algerian society and to focus international attention on conditions in Algeria.

The decision to launch a coordinated campaign in Algiers was accompanied by the announcement by the FLN of an eight-day national strike. Organized by Muhammad Larbi BEN M'HIDI, a founding member of the executive leadership of the FLN, and Saadi Yacef, the military commander of Algiers, the campaign itself was launched with a series of bombings and assassinations carried out against both the French official and civilian populations. Targets included cafés, restaurants, and offices as well as the French police, soldiers, and civil officials. These acts of urban violence capped a series of similar events carried out by parties on both sides in the summer of 1956.

France's response was harsh. The French commander-in-chief, Raoul Salan, assigned command of operations to General Jacques Massu, commander of the Tenth Paratroop Regiment. Massu turned ruthlessly to the task—his troops broke the back of the general strike by rounding up strike participants and forcing open shops and businesses. More violent still were the measures taken to suppress the FLN network under Yacef and his lieutenant, Ali la Pointe (né Ali Amara). Adopting tactics used in the rural areas, Massu isolated the Arab Muslim quarters and subjected them to massive searches and military assaults. "Most notably he instituted widespread and systematic use of torture as an aid to interrogation" (Ruedy, p. 168). Among the large numbers of victims of interrogation was Ben M'hidi. In 1958, publication of *La Question,* a first-hand account of torture by French Communist editor Henri Alleg, brought home to many in France the nature of French activities in Algeria.

Massu's measures were in the short term effective; by the summer of 1957, Yacef was in prison and la Pointe dead, their network largely silenced. The level of seemingly indiscriminate violence had soured popular support for the FLN, while continued French suppression led to the flight of the surviving FLN leadership to Tunisia—hence the weakening of its command and contact with the movement within Algeria. In the long term, however, French policies and the nine-month-long conflict in Algiers generated considerable world attention and sparked heated debate within France over Algeria and French colonialism. Negative press outside France and growing disillusionment within France contributed in a significant manner to the ultimate decision by the administration of Charles de Gaulle to accept Algerian independence.

The events in Algiers were the subject of an important film by Gillo Pontecorvo, an Italian director. Released in 1966, the documentary-style dramatic *La Battaglia di Algeri,* contributed to the angry debate in France and, more significantly, brought home to a world audience sharp images of French policies in Algeria. Filmed in a grainy black and white and starring, among others, Saadi Yacef, the docudrama re-

mains widely shown on university campuses in the United States and Europe.

BIBLIOGRAPHY

HEGGOY, ALF ANDREW. *Insurgency and Counterinsurgency in Algeria.* Bloomington, Ind., 1972.
RUEDY, JOHN. *Modern Algeria.* Bloomington, Ind., 1992.
SOLINAS, PIER NICO, ed. *Gillo Pontecorvo's "The Battle of Algiers."* New York, 1973.

Matthew S. Gordon

Algiers Agreement

Treaty between Iraq and Iran.

On 6 March 1975, President Houari Boumédienne of Algeria negotiated an agreement between Iraq and Iran whereby Iraq would enter into a treaty with Iran that granted the latter sovereignty over half of the Shatt al-Arab following the thalweg (midpoint) principle. In return, Iran agreed to stop aiding the Kurdish insurgency, thus causing the rebellion in Iraq to break down. In September 1980, Iraq unilaterally abrogated the agreement.

BIBLIOGRAPHY

ISMAEL, TAREQ Y. *Iran and Iraq: Roots of Conflict.* Syracuse, N.Y., 1982.

Mia Bloom

Algiers Charter

The document that redefined the goals of Algeria's FLN after the country gained its independence.

The Algiers Charter is a 176-page document adopted by a congress of the FRONT DE LIBÉRATION NATIONALE (FLN; National Liberation Front) held in Algiers between April 16 and April 21, 1964. The processes of drafting and adoption were carefully managed by President Ahmed BEN BELLA and his followers. The charter's aims were to reshape the FLN, a wartime organization that had led Algeria to independence, into an avant-garde party that would become the motor of social and economic revolution and to sharpen the ideologies and strategies of that revolution.

The charter formalized the organization of the FLN and defined, at least in theory, its relationship to government. Highly populist in tone, it reaffirmed Algeria's socialist option and laid out plans for agrarian reform and for nationalization of most major sectors of the economy. The Algiers Charter remained until 1976 the official statement of Algeria's political and ideological orientation.

BIBLIOGRAPHY

OTTAWAY, DAVID and MARINA. *Algeria. The Politics of a Socialist Revolution.* Berkeley, Calif., 1970.

John Ruedy

Algiers Summit

Meeting in November 1973 of Arab heads of state to discuss the implications of the 1973 Arab–Israel War.

All members of the League of Arab States (Arab League), except Iraq and Libya, met in Algiers following the 1973 ARAB–ISRAEL WAR. They discussed economic and diplomatic issues, endorsing the idea of using Arab petroleum exports to pressure supporters of Israel into heeding the Arab demand for Israel's withdrawal from occupied Arab territory and the recognition of Palestinian demands for self-determination.

BIBLIOGRAPHY

New York Times, November 29, 1973, p. 16.

Steve Tamari

Ali

See Islam

Ali, Rashid

See Kaylani, Rashid Ali al-

Ali Nasir Muhammad al-Hasani

Yemeni politician and government official.

This forceful, but moderate, pragmatic politician served as head of state of the People's Democratic Republic of Yemen (PDRY) and head of the ruling YEMENI SOCIALIST PARTY (YSP) from late 1980 until 1986. This period was distinguished by a more relaxed, eclectic, nondogmatic approach to domestic policy and nonrevolutionary, broadly cooperative external relations, most notably with the PDRY's immediate neighbors, the Yemen Arab Republic, Oman, and Saudi Arabia. His bloody preemptive attack against his domestic enemies in early 1986 failed, and Ali Nasir was forced into exile. An early activist in the NATIONAL LIBERATION FRONT (NLF), Ali Nasir had served as the PDRY prime minister throughout the 1970s.

Robert D. Burrowes

Ali Rıza   [1858–1930]

Ottoman Turkish landscape painter.

The son of an army officer, Ali Rıza was born in ÜSKÜDAR, the district on the Asian shore of ISTANBUL. A pioneer of modern painting in Ottoman Turkey, Ali Rıza graduated from the OTTOMAN EMPIRE's military academy and taught art there for many years. Like other nineteenth-century Ottoman artists, he used new brush techniques to create color effects, especially in his scenic watercolors and oils depicting Istanbul and Üsküdar.

Through his teaching and his detailed ornamental landscapes, Ali Rıza was instrumental in the spread of secular concepts in painting in a culture long accustomed to nonrepresentational Islamic art forms.

BIBLIOGRAPHY

RENDA, GÜNSEL. "Modern Trends in Turkish Painting." In *The Transformation of Turkish Culture: The Atatürk Legacy,* ed. by Günsel Renda and C. Max Kortepeter. Princeton, N.J., 1986.

David Waldner

Alishan, Ghevond   [1820–1901]

Armenian writer and historian.

Alishan, baptized Kerovbe Alishanian, was born in Constantinople (now Istanbul) and attended an Armenian Catholic school before going to Venice to continue his education at the Mekhitarian monastery. He joined the Armenian Catholic order of monks known as the Mekhitarians in 1838 and later was ordained a priest. Although the author of a number of religious works, Alishan spent his adult years as a instructor in the educational institutions maintained by the Mekhitarians. Early on, he developed an interest in Armenian folklore and had turned to composing poetry. The last third of his life was devoted solely to scholarship.

Alishan gained fame as a prodigious writer of historical works. He published a twenty-two-volume series of Armenian primary sources from the manuscript collection in the Mekhitarian monastery. He also issued a set of large, illustrated volumes on various provinces of historical Armenia—*Shirak* (1881), *Sisvan* (1885), *Ayrarat* (1890), and *Sisakan* (1893)—containing therein all the geographical, topographical, historical, architectural, and other information culled from ancient and contemporary sources. These volumes provided the basis for the development of a strong sense of national identification with Armenia among Armenians in expatriate communities and among younger generations of Armenians. These people began to perceive of Armenia as a land imbued with history and creativity and not just desolation and oppression. In the last year of his life, on the occasion of the two-hundredth year of the founding of the Mekhitarian Order, Alishan issued his culminating work, called *Hayapatum* (Armenian History), in which he arranged selections from Armenian historians into a comprehensive narrative history.

While most Armenian translators put works from French and German literature into Armenian, Alishan was one the rare figures of the nineteenth-century Armenian cultural renaissance who also learned English. He traveled to England in 1852 and published that same year the translation, in Armenian, of a section of Milton's *Paradise Lost*. Subsequently he issued translations of Byron and Longfellow. In 1867 he published his *Armenian Popular Songs Translated into English,* believed to contain the first English renditions of Armenian poetry. Alishan died in Venice.

Rouben P. Adalian

Ali Suavi   [1838–1878]

Ottoman intellectual.

Born into a working class family in Istanbul, Ali Suavi became a teacher in *ruşdiye* schools (for adolescents) in Bursa and Filibe before being dismissed by an irate governor for his unorthodox ideas. He traveled to Paris and London and there joined such individuals as the poets NAMIK KEMAL and Ziya Paşa, members of the YOUNG OTTOMANS. In 1867, Ali Suavi became the editor of *Munbir,* a Young Ottoman newspaper devoted to issues of government reform.

Ali Suavi was deeply religious and passionately devoted to the unification of all Turkic-speaking peoples; he soon broke with the other Young Ottomans, who were more interested in the reform of the Ottoman empire along the lines of European liberalism. After opposing Midhat Paşa, grand vizier of the empire, and the Constitution of 1876, Suavi

gained the favor of the autocratic Sultan ABDÜLHAMIT II, and he was rewarded with an appointment as director of the Galatasaray School. But Ali Suavi soon became dissatisfied with the new sultan, and after the ignominious defeat of the Ottomans in the Russo-Ottoman War of 1877–1878, Suavi led a coup attempt to restore the deposed Murad V to the throne. The coup failed, and Ali Suavi was executed.

BIBLIOGRAPHY

LEWIS, BERNARD. *The Emergence of Modern Turkey.* New York, 1961.
SHAW, STANFORD, and EZEL KURAL SHAW. *History of the Ottoman Empire and Modern Turkey.* New York, 1977.

Zachary Karabell

Aliyah

Literally, an "ascending"; the return of Jews to Zion, to Eretz Yisrael, from their worldwide dispersal, called the Diaspora.

In the late nineteenth century, ZIONISM asserted the unconditional right of Jews to go home; to return to Eretz Yisrael (the Land of Israel), part of Palestine during the Ottoman Empire. Such a return would provide a population base for a new Jewish homeland, a nation, in the biblical region from which they had been dispersed during the Assyrian, Babylonian, Persian, and Roman empires. The Jews that returned would eventually shape a new social and political identity in the midst of a hostile Arab world.

A Jew's immigration to Palestine, now ISRAEL, is called an *aliyah,* an "ascending"; emigration is called a "descending." One of the fundamental laws of the State of Israel was the Law of Return, which grants every Jew the right to citizenship merely by stepping onto the land (although one must still apply for citizenship, which is almost always granted). Zionist ideology motivated a turn-of-the-century immigration to Palestine to create a modern Hebrew-based culture in the homeland; Zionists continue to encourage immigration to Israel, although the modern nation suffers from various sociopolitical problems, not all related to the defense of the nation against either the Arab nations or the Palestinians, who after more than forty years still claim the same land for their own state. Israel soon discovered that Jews from non-European nations had assimilated the surrounding cultures in a variety of ways that did not always suit the Zionist ideal; that different traditions, different prejudices, and different social structures had to be understood and respected before such Jewish immigrants could become Israelis.

The first aliyah (large-scale immigration) occurred after the 1881 pogroms in Russia and the tightening of discriminatory legislation in Russia and Romania. Some twenty thousand to thirty thousand Jews arrived in Ottoman Palestine between 1882 and 1903. Receiving some financial assistance from the organization Hovevei Zion (Lovers of Zion), immigrants from Russia and Romania established thirty agricultural settlements, although some were later abandoned. This group of immigrants created a basis for self-supporting Jewish agriculture but not without substantial external aid. Baron Edmond de Rothschild rescued many of the settlements by providing both funds and agronomists to manage the farms. While many appreciated the material help, few enjoyed the tutelage that accompanied it. Declining revenues persuaded the baron to transfer the administration of some of his colonies to the Jewish Colonization Association in 1900. In this period, Zionists also settled into the seaport city of Jaffa and established it as a center of modern European-style Jewish culture. Some immigrants had professional skills and commercial expertise, which started a small Jewish urban economy to develop in that city.

The second aliyah (1904–1914) included about thirty-five thousand Jews, mostly young, unmarried, and committed to the social and institutional transformation of the Jewish people. Calling themselves pioneers (halutzim), many planned their activities to serve as the foundation for the new Jewish society they wished to form: manual labor, return to the soil, self-defense, and rejuvenation of the Hebrew language. Although a large proportion of those who came in the second aliyah eventually left for other countries, those who remained exercised a profound influence during the British mandate years, during early statehood, and on ongoing Israeli politics. The second aliyah demanded that Jewish enterprises employ only Jewish labor—an aim for self-sufficiency denoted by the phrase "the conquest of labor"; this became the basis for their critique of the agricultural settlements founded by the first aliyah, which had employed local Arab labor. Many of Israel's distinctive institutions trace their origins to organizations begun by these immigrants.

The third aliyah began in 1919, after World War I and the British support that was stated in the so-called Balfour Declaration. Before the flow ebbed in 1923, another 35,000 Jews had arrived in British-mandated Palestine. Many of these had belonged to Zionist organizations in Europe and had been trained, before their arrival, for agricultural work. A substantial number of Russian Socialist Zionists immigrated—many influenced by Bolshevism—drawing on their wartime experience and

their familiarity with revolution for ideas on how to organize a new society and economy. Along with leaders from the second aliyah, and in cooperation with British mandate authorities, these immigrants elaborated an institutional framework for the Jewish National Home.

In the fourth aliyah of the 1920s and 1930s, some eighty-two thousand European Jews journeyed to Palestine, primarily to escape economic depression and the wave of discriminatory legislation in Nazi Germany and other countries aimed at squeezing out Jews from many businesses and professions. Restrictive immigration policies in Western Europe and the United States directed the flow of immigrants to Palestine. Many came with some capital and opened small businesses in towns and cities, contributing to dramatic economic growth and expansion. In Europe, national war debts, inflation, unstable governments, and the Great Depression affected international currencies; consequently, Palestine's prosperity waned, some businesses failed, and unemployment resulted. In 1928, more Jews left Palestine than arrived. The Yishuv (Jewish community) leaders blamed the Polish immigrants (whose currency had failed during the Pilsudski coup), saying they lacked commitment and steadfastness.

The fifth aliyah of the mid-1930s to 1944 comprised about 265,000 Jews who had fled Germany and Nazi-dominated Europe. At the outset, many arrived with some capital and invested in the urban economy. A large number of professionals from Germany helped expand the educational and music establishments and introduced new services.

At the end of World War II, Jewish immigration to Palestine had become problematical to the British, who realized that the Middle East's oil was crucial to postwar recovery and the industries of the future. Most of the oil was already in Arab-dominated lands and Palestinian Arabs were demanding their own nation just as Palestinian Jews were. The problem of bringing HOLOCAUST survivors to Palestine forced the British to turn to the United Nations to resolve the mounting dispute between Jews and Arabs. The partition resolution in November 1947 and the establishment of Israel in May 1948 as a sovereign Jewish state ended all impediments to Jewish immigration—except for the ensuing Arab attack on Israel, now called the 1948 Arab–Israel War (or the 1948 Independence War). Nevertheless, a relocation and settlement effort was made by Israel to accommodate all refugees from the Soviet Union, Europe, and the hostile Arab nations. Almost the entire Jewish population of Iraq, Yemen, Egypt, and, to a lesser extent, Morocco, Tunisia, Algeria, Syria, and Lebanon immigrated to Israel by 1958.

In recent years, Jews from the former Soviet Union, Romania, and Ethiopia have arrived in large numbers. From the United States, numerous educators, idealists, pietists, pioneers, technicians, romantics, and politicians have made an ongoing aliyah since the early 1900s (including one of Israel's leaders, Golda Meir).

[*See also:* Refugees, Jewish]

BIBLIOGRAPHY

EISENSTADT, S. N. *Israeli Society.* London, 1967.
ELON, AMOS. *The Israelis: Founders and Sons.* New York, 1971.
GVATI, CHAIM. *A Hundred Years of Settlement.* Jerusalem, 1985.
HALPERN, BEN, and JEHUDA REINHARZ. "The Cultural and Social Background of the Second Aliyah." *Middle Eastern Studies* 27 (July 1991): 487–517.

Donna Robinson Divine

Al Jiluwi

A branch of the Al Sa'ud, the ruling family of Saudi Arabia.

Abd Allah ibn Jiluwi was one of the closest companions of Abd al-Aziz (IBN SA'UD) in creating the state of SAUDI ARABIA in the early twentieth century. Abd Allah and his son Sa'ud were rewarded with the rule of al-HASA (the Eastern Province). They ruled autocratically, treating the large Shi'ite population with particular harshness.

BIBLIOGRAPHY

HOLDEN, DAVID, and RICHARD JOHNS. *The House of Saud: The Rise and Rule of the Most Powerful Arab Dynasty.* New York, 1981.

Malcolm C. Peck

Alkalai, Judah ben Solomon Hai
[1798–1878]

Precursor of modern Zionism.

Alkalai, a Sephardic rabbi who was born in Sarejevo and studied in Jerusalem, served as a rabbi in the Balkans and was influenced by Serbian Nationalism and the Damascus Affair (1840). Also, well-versed in the kabbalah, Alkalai believed that the era of messianic redemption was at hand. He asserted that redemption must be preceded by the return of the Jews to the land of Israel. In his books *Darkhei No'am* (1839) and *Shalom Yerushalayim* (1840), he called upon Jews to prepare for the coming redemption and to donate money to those already residing in the Land of Israel. In *Minhat Yehuda* (1843), he advocated the formation of an Assembly of Jewish Notables to represent the Jewish people in their appeals to other nations to permit their return to their homeland. Alkalai wrote numerous pamphlets and articles and, in 1851/52, toured several foreign countries to spread his ideas. In 1871, he visited Palestine and founded a settlement society there, which was unsuccessful. In 1874, he settled in Palestine.

BIBLIOGRAPHY

HERTZBERG, ARTHUR. *The Zionist Idea.* New York, 1979.

Martin Malin

Allah

The Arabic equivalent of the English word "God."

A likely etymology of the term is that it is an ancient contraction of *al-ilah* (Arabic for "*the* god") and was probably first used in Arabian cosmologies before ISLAM to refer to some kind of high deity who may have been considered the progenitor of a number of lesser divinities. The word *Allah* is best known in the West as the name Muslims ascribe to the one and only God whom they believe to be the transcendent and partnerless creator, lord, and judge of the universe. It is important to note that according to Muslim teaching, Allah is not only the God of the Prophet Muhammad but also the God of Moses and Jesus—and is therefore identical to the divine being of Jewish and Christian sacred history.

While Muslim tradition recognizes Allah to be the comprehensive name of God encompassing all the divine attributes, it also ascribes to the deity an additional ninety-nine "beautiful names" (*al-asma al-husna*), each of which evoke a distinct characteristic of the godhead. The most famous and most frequently referenced of these are "the Merciful" (*al-rahman*) and "the Compassionate" (*al-rahim*).

BIBLIOGRAPHY

GUILLAUME, ALFRED. *Islam.* Baltimore, 1962.

Scott Alexander

Allenby, Edmund Henry   [1861–1936]

British officer who commanded British forces in the Middle East during World War I; military governor of Palestine and high commissioner of Egypt.

Allenby's early career included extensive service in Africa, including the Boer War (1899–1902). Posted to France at the start of World War I, he was sent to the Middle East in June 1917, where he led Britain's Egyptian Expeditionary Force and took Beersheba and Gaza (1917); with the help of Colonel T. E. Lawrence (of Arabia) and Prince Faisal, he occupied Jerusalem in December 1917. He launched his final offensive in 1918, taking Megiddo from September 18 to 21. This classic of military strategy led to the collapse of Ottoman Empire forces and the British occupation of Syria.

At the peace conference in Paris, Allenby argued, as military governor of Palestine, that Britain should support Faisal as king of Syria, but the League of Nations awarded the French a mandate over Syria; they occupied the new kingdom and ousted Faisal. Created a viscount in 1919, Allenby was appointed high commissioner for Egypt (1919–1925). There he advocated accommodation with rising Arab Nationalism, thus clashing over policy with British Colonial Secretary Winston Churchill. His threat to resign persuaded the British government to issue the Allenby Declaration on February 28, 1922, which granted formal independence to Egypt but retained enormous rights for the British over Egyptian affairs.

BIBLIOGRAPHY

WAVELL, ARCHIBALD P. Allenby: A Study in Greatness, 2 vols. London, 1940.

Jon Jucovy

Allenby Bridge

Bridge across the Jordan river connecting the East Bank and the West Bank.

The Allenby Bridge (also the King Hussein Bridge) started as a pontoon bridge across the Jordan River, linking al-salt on the eastern side with Jericho and Jerusalem, to facilitate General Edmund Allenby's entrance to Jerusalem in 1917. It became the major crossing for people and goods between the two banks until 1967, when it was almost totally destroyed by Israeli shelling during the Arab–Israel War. Although partly collapsed, the bridge was heavily used by refugees fleeing the West Bank in 1967 towards Jordan. After the war, it became the major checkpoint between Jordan and the Israeli occupied territories, having been rebuilt to withstand both pedestrian and vehicular traffic. It is currently used exclusively for people, while goods are mainly transported across the Prince Mohammad bridge to the north.

Allenby (King Hussein) Bridge, spanning the Jordan river. (Bryan McBurney)

BIBLIOGRAPHY

GUBSER, PETER. Jordan: Crossroads of Middle Eastern Events. Boulder, Colo., 1983.

Jenab Tutunji

Alliance Israélite Universelle (AIU)

International Jewish organization created in Paris, 1860.

Until 1860, the Jews of France had been represented by the Consistoire Central des Israélites de France, headquartered in Paris, with branches throughout the country. The AIU was founded in Paris on May 17, 1860, by several idealistic French Jews—businessmen, political activists, and members of the free professions; they included Narcisse Leven, a lawyer who was actively involved in French municipal politics, Eugène Emmanuel, a celebrated poet, Charles Netter, a prominent merchant, and a dozen other young distinguished or rising professionals of mid-nineteenth century France. Certainly the most important member of the AIU was Adolphe Crémieux, who in 1870 became minister of justice while serving as AIU president, a post he held from 1863 until his death in 1880.

The decision to create the AIU, a move to diversify and extend Jewish political acitivities outside France, was partly hastened by the controversy over the Mortara Case, a case of the abduction of a Jewish child by Roman Catholic conversionists. On the night of June 23, 1858, Edgardo Mortara, the six-year-old son of a Jewish family in Bologna, Italy, was abducted by the papal police and taken to Rome. The boy had been secretly and unlawfully baptized five years earlier by a Chrstian domestic servant, who thought he was about to die. The parents vainly attempted to get their child back, and the case caused a universal outcry. Young French Jews then created the AIU two years later in the name of religious freedom.

The AIU's aim was to aid Jews and Judaism—mainly in the Ottoman, Sharifian (North African), and Qajar (Iran) empires—in three ways: The first was to "work toward the emancipation and moral progress of the Jews." While it did not state that education was the basic motivation behind emancipation and moral progress, the first aim defined the educational sphere. Moral progress meant the need to combat disease, poverty, and ignorance, and to acculturate Jews in the tradition of French secular education. Therefore, the AIU established schools that taught Jews in Mediterranean-basin countries the concepts of liberty, equality, and fraternity.

The most important schools were created between 1862 and 1914. They were situated in some cities of Morocco, Tunisia, Libya, Egypt, Syria, Turkey, Iran, and Iraq. The teachers dispatched to these countries were alumni of the AIU schools from the Ottoman Empire—Sephardim trained in Paris at the AIU teacher-training center: the École Normale Israélite Orientale (ENIO). Although the French language was used in AIU schools, nevertheless, the AIU did not advocate total emulation of French secular culture, for its leaders realized that blind imitation of ideas emanating from France would encounter fierce opposition among tradition-bound Jews. Therefore, from the outset, the AIU attempted to strike a balance between secular learning, embodying progressive Western ideas, and the sacred traditions and education of Jewish communities.

The second goal was to "lend effective support to all those who suffer because of their membership in the Jewish faith." It referred to allocation of funds necessary to help Jews in distress outside Europe—and more importantly, to inform European leaders and their diplomatic representatives in countries where Jews were harassed to urge that help be given. Further, this meant that the AIU had to alert the leaders of both Middle Eastern and North African countries when such injustice occurred, possibly wresting concessions from them to remedy the situation.

The third aim was to awaken Europe to the Jews' plight. It called for "encouraging all proper publications to bring an end to Jewish sufferings." Whereas the second category called for quiet negotiations and diplomatic action, the third stressed the utilization of AIU and other periodicals to influence public opinion. For example, it published the *Bulletin de l'Alliance Israélite Universelle* (1860–1913) and *Paix et Droit* for this purpose and utilized the French press and the London *Jewish Chronicle* to point out human rights violations, particularly in Iran and Morocco.

Information on the abuses perpetrated against Jews in Muslim lands was obtained by the AIU Central Committee in Paris through regional committees in countries where it had schools and personnel. These forces also alerted local European consuls and ministers plenipotentiary to the abuses by regional governors and chieftains. The AIU Central Committee then brought the problems before the Foreign Office in London or the French Foreign Ministry in Paris, which in turn pressured the Ottoman Porte, the Qajar Shahs, and the Moroccan *Makhzan* to protect their Jewish subjects (*dhimmis*).

In terms of its educational influence, the AIU survived from the Ottoman and precolonial eras into the colonial period and beyond—well into the decolonization stage. In 1956, the AIU had 143 schools and approximately 51,000 students in the Mediterranean-basin countries, mainly in Morocco, Iran, Israel, and Lebanon. In 1991, the AIU had 30 schools in Israel, Morocco, Iran, and Syria. Until the early or mid-1960s most AIU schools—primary, secondary, and vocational—were concentrated in the Mediterranean basin; since then, school expansion has taken place in Israel, France, Canada, Spain, and Belgium. Today, the trend is to expand the schools in Europe and Israel (in the wake of Soviet Jewish emigration). The AIU in France still helps to maintain the schools in the Muslim world—in Morocco, Iran, and Syria—because Jewish communities continue to exist there despite attempted emigration to Europe, the Americas, or Israel.

Since its inception, the AIU has been financed by membership fund-raising, conducted by the regional committees throughout the world. After World War I, however, as its school networks expanded in the Middle East, and especially in North Africa, a substantial portion of the AIU's budget was derived from the French government. Since the end of World War II, the AIU schools have also received subsidies from the American Jewish Joint Distribution Committee, which uses funds of the United Jewish Appeal.

BIBLIOGRAPHY

CHOURAQUI, ANDRÉ. *L'Alliance Israélite Universelle et la renaissance juive contemporaine, 1860–1960*. Paris, 1965.
LASKIER, MICHAEL M. *The Alliance Israélite Universelle and the Jewish Communities of Morocco: 1862–1962*. Albany, N.Y., 1983.
LEVEN, NARCISSE. *Cinquante ans l'histoire: L'Alliance Israélite Universelle*. Paris, 1911–1920.

RODRIQUE, ARON. *De l'instruction à l'emancipation: Les enseignants de l'Alliance Israélite Universelle et les Juifs d'Orient.* Paris, 1989.

———. *French Jews, Turkish Jews: The Alliance Israélite Universelle in Turkey: 1860–1925.* Bloomington, Ind., 1990.

Michael M. Laskier

Allied Middle East Command

Military administrative command of the World War II era, headquartered in Cairo, Egypt, created by the British government in 1939 to organize the war effort in the Middle East.

General Sir Archibald Wavell was the first commander, taking charge in June 1939. At first encompassing Egypt, the Sudan, Cyprus, and Transjordan, the command spanned two continents and encompassed an area 1,700 by 2,000 miles (2,735 to 3,218 km). After the beginning of World War II, the command was expanded to include Aden, British Somaliland, and the Persian/Arabian Gulf. Under Wavell's command, the British were successful in operations against the Italians but failed when the Germans, under General Erwin Rommel, counterattacked. Command passed to General Sir Claude Auchinleck in July 1941, and then to Geneal Sir Harold R.L.G. Alexander in August 1942. During this period, the British finally prevailed against German and Italian forces in North Africa. In August 1942, Iran and Iraq were detached from the command, and consideration was given by Prime Minister Winston S. Churchill to renaming it the Near Eastern Command. To preclude confusion, the Cabinet convinced Churchill to retain the original name for the command in Cairo. After the successful American and British invasion of North Africa in November 1942, under the leadership of General Dwight D. Eisenhower, the Middle East Command was primarily concerned with administrative and logistic problems.

BIBLIOGRAPHY

BARNET, CORRELLI. *The Desert Generals.* Bloomington, Ind., 1982.

Daniel E. Spector

Allon, Yigal [1918–1980]

Israeli politician; deputy prime minister, 1969–1974.

Born in Kfar Tabor, Palestine, Yigal Allon was originally named Yigal Paicovitch. The change to Allon—which means oak, to symbolize Allon's commitment to Israel—occurred in 1948, at the time the state of Israel was proclaimed. Allon's early education took place in Palestine, at the Kadoorie Agricultural School and the Hebrew University, but he subsequently attended St. Anthony's College in Oxford. In 1937, he was one of the cofounders of Kibbutz Ginossar, on the western shore of Lake Tiberias.

From 1937 to 1939 he served in the Haganah; at the same time, he was working for the British as an officer in the Jewish Settlement Police. Along with Moshe Dayan, Allon was one of the leading forces in the creation of the Palmach, the commando unit of the Haganah, and in 1945 he attained the rank of commander in the unit. During World War II, he fought with Allied forces to liberate Vichy-held Syria and Lebanon and in 1948 was made brigadier general. A senior officer in the Israel Defense Forces at the time of the Arab-Israel War of 1948, he fought in a number of campaigns in that conflict.

Allon was a member of Knesset throughout Israel's early years. In 1960, he resigned his seat in order to attend Oxford University for a year, but in 1961 he was reelected and continued to serve. He was minister of labor from 1961 to 1967, deputy prime minister from 1966 to 1968, minister of education and culture from 1969 to 1974, and minister of foreign affairs from 1974 to 1977. From February 26 to March 17, 1969, he served as acting prime minister, following the death of Prime Minister Levi Eshkol until Golda MEIR received a vote of confidence from the Knesset and took over the position of prime minister.

During Meir's term in office, Allon, who remained deputy prime minister, was an important adviser to the prime minister. The role he played during the period leading up to the Arab-Israel War of 1973, however, and his agreement with the position taken by Meir that Israel should never again engage in a preemptive strike against its Arab neighbors (even if they were threatening to attack) made him a nonviable candidate to succeed Meir when she resigned in 1974. Yitzhak Rabin, a war hero untainted with any part of the blame for the decision in 1973, was chosen by the Labor party to succeed Meir, and Allon was appointed foreign minister. In 1975, during the era of Kissinger's famous shuttle diplomacy, Allon actively participated in the peace talks, but his efforts were not repaid by substantive results.

Allon may best be remembered for suggesting, in discussions on Israeli defense, that since the Jewish people had a clear right to the lands on the West Bank of the Jordan River, it was necessary to act strategically to make sure Israel would be secure. The ALLON PLAN, as it became known, called for Israel to annex a strip of land along the Jordan river and through the middle of the Dead sea which would remain Israeli territory. In addition, Allon recommended that the territory, which became known as the GAZA STRIP, should also become part of Israel.

Although Allon did not reject the idea of a Palestinian state, he argued that it should not come about at the expense of Israel's security or its right to exist. His endorsement of the idea of a dense belt of Jewish villages along the Jordan river that would provide security for Israel continues to be cited to this day.

BIBLIOGRAPHY

ALLON, YIGAL. *My Father's House.* New York, 1976.
BEN-GURION, DAVID. *Israel: A Personal History.* New York, 1971.
SACHAR, HOWARD M. *A History of Israel: From the Rise of Zionism to Our Time.* New York, 1981.

Gregory S. Mahler

Allon Plan

Plan for Israel's new borders, after winning territory in the 1967 War; presented July 26, 1967, by Israel's Minister of Labor Yigal Allon to the national unity government headed by Levi Eshkol.

The main aim of the plan was to translate Israel's success in the recent (June 1967) war into a lasting settlement with the Arab states. The plan envisaged the annexation of the Gaza Strip to Israel and the return of about 70 percent of the West Bank to Jordan, with Israel keeping the Jordan river valley—as a security belt and strategic border—and keeping Jerusalem united under Israeli sovereignty.

Because of the profoundly differing views represented within the coalition government, the cabinet did not formally adopt the Allon Plan, nor did it reject it. The government did follow the operational aspects of the plan in its policy of establishing Jewish settlements on the West Bank. The plan was also repeatedly presented by Israel's leaders as the basis for a political settlement in secret meetings with King Hussein of Jordan, and it was repeatedly rejected by him. With the rise to power of the Likud party in 1977, the plan ceased to serve even as an unofficial guide to government policy.

Avi Shlaim

All-Palestine Government

Post–World War II concept for forming an Arab government for the whole of Palestine after the end of the British mandate, May 14, 1948.

The All-Palestine Government was the product of the complex relationship between the Palestinian national movement led by Hajj Amin al-Husayni, the Mufti of Jerusalem, and the Arab states loosely organized within the Arab League. After World War II, when the British mandate over Palestine was to expire and the struggle between the Arabs and the Jews was approaching its climax, the weakness of the Palestinian Arabs made them ever more dependent on the Arab League. Within the league, however, no one policy existed for the future of the region: The mufti's plan was maximalist, an independent Palestinian state throughout the whole of Palestine; King Abdullah of Transjordan's plan was to accept the partition of Palestine with the Jews and to incorporate the Arab part into his kingdom.

From December 1947, the mufti pleaded with the Arab League for the establishment of a Palestinian government to manage the affairs of the country and direct the struggle against the Jews, but his pleas fell on deaf ears. He and his colleagues on the Arab Higher Committee (AHC) were progressively marginalized. Thus, when the British mandate over Palestine expired and the State of Israel was proclaimed on May 15, 1948, the Arabs of Palestine had no government, no administrative regime, and no unified military command.

On July 8, 1948, the Arab League decided to set up a temporary civil administration in Palestine, to be directly responsible to the Arab League. This was a compromise proposal that failed to satisfy either of the two principal claimants. With strong opposition from King Abdullah, and only half-hearted support from the AHC, the new body was never properly established.

The Egyptian government, suspicious of King Abdullah's growing power in Palestine, put a proposal to the Arab League meeting that opened in Alexandria on September 6, 1948. The plan would turn the temporary civil administration, which had been agreed to in July, into an Arab government with a seat in Gaza for the whole of Palestine. The formal announcement of the Arab League's decision to form the Government of All-Palestine was issued on September 20. In the eyes of its Egyptian sponsors, the immediate purpose of this government was to provide a focal point of opposition to King Abdullah's ambition to federate the Arab part of Palestine with Transjordan. The other Arab governments supported the Egyptian proposal at least partly because it furnished them with a means for withdrawing their armies from Palestine with some protection against popular outcry.

Despite the unpopularity of the Mufti of Jerusalem in most Arab capitals, the AHC played a major part in the formation of the new government, which was headed by Ahmad Hilmi Abd al-Baqi. Hilmi's cabinet consisted largely of followers of the mufti but also included representatives of the other factions of the Palestinian ruling class. Jamal al-Husayni became foreign minister, Raja al-Husayni became defense minister, Michael Abcarius was finance minister, and Anwar Nusaybi was secretary of the cabinet. Twelve ministers in all, living in different Arab countries, headed for Gaza to take up their new positions.

During the first week of its life in Gaza, the All-Palestine Government revived the Holy War Army, with the declared aim of liberating Palestine; sought international recognition without much success; and issued several thousand Palestinian passports. To endow the government with legitimacy, a Palestinian National Council was convened in Gaza on September 30, 1948, under the chairmanship of the Mufti of Jerusalem. The council, in a mood of great elation, passed a series of resolutions culminating in a declaration of independence over the whole of Palestine. Although the new government claimed jurisdiction over the whole of Palestine, it had no administration, no civil service, no money, and no real army of its own. Even in the small enclave around the town of Gaza, its writ ran only by the grace of the Egyptian authorities. Taking advantage of the new government's dependence on them for funds and protection, the Egyptian paymasters manipulated it to undermine King Abdullah's claim to represent the Palestinians in the Arab League and international forums. Ostensibly the embryo for an independent Palestinian state, the new government was thus reduced to the unhappy role of a shuttlecock in the ongoing power struggle between Egypt and Jordan.

The Jordanian authorities were determined to stop the growth of the mufti's army. On October 3, Jordan gave the order to the Arab Legion to surround, and forcibly disarm, various units of the Holy War Army. This move effectively neutralized the All-Palestine Government's military power and checked the growth of public sentiment in favor of an autonomous Palestinian state.

Shortly afterward, on October 15, 1948, Israel launched an offensive against the Egyptian army, forcing it to retreat down the coast to Gaza. Ironically, mid-October was also when the Arab governments got around to recognizing the All-Palestine Government. Nothing is more indicative of their half-hearted support than the lateness of their formal recognition. By the time it was granted, the game was over.

The Egyptian defeat deprived the All-Palestine Government of its last and exceedingly tenuous hold on Palestinian soil, forcing it to transfer its seat from Gaza to Cairo. Its weakness was exposed for all to see, its prestige slumped, and its authority was undermined. In Cairo, the Government of All-Palestine gradually fell apart because of its impotence, ending up four years later as a department of the Arab League. Thereafter, it continued to exist in name only until Egypt's President Gamal Abdel Nasser closed its offices in 1959.

Although the All-Palestine Government was projected as the nucleus of Palestinian self-government, it was an Egyptian-led phantom deliberately created by the Arab states to meet their publics' opposition to partition and to challenge Transjordan's claim to the rest of Arab Palestine. It was for selfish reasons that the Arab states created it, and it was for selfish reasons that they abandoned it. True, in the first three weeks of its short life, this fledgling government did represent a genuine attempt by the Palestinians to assert their independence from their dubious sponsors—to assume control over their own destiny; but the attempt was short-lived. Born of inter-Arab rivalries, the All-Palestine Government soon foundered on the rocks of inter-Arab rivalries. Consequently, if there is one lesson that stands, it is the need for Palestinian self-reliance, especially for defending the Palestinian cause against control and manipulation by the Arab states.

BIBLIOGRAPHY

SHLAIM, AVI. "The Rise and Fall of the All-Palestine Government in Gaza." *Journal of Palestine Studies* 20, no. 1 (Autumn 1990).

SMITH, PAMELA ANN. *Palestine and the Palestinians.* London, 1984.

Avi Shlaim

Almog, Ruth   [1936–   ]

Israeli author.

Ruth Almog was born in Petah Tikva, Israel, to a Jewish orthodox family. She studied education, literature and philosophy in Jerusalem and at Tel Aviv University. She is currently the assistant literary editor of the Hebrew daily *Haaretz*.

Since the publication of her first short story in 1967, Almog has written fourteen books: four collections of short stories, four novels, and six children books. A recent book, *Artistic Emendation* (1993), includes six short stories and a novella. For the novel *Roots of Light* (1987) Almog was awarded the Brenner Prize for literature. *Death in the Rain* (1982) was translated into English (1993), and two collections of short stories were published in German: *The Blue Woman* (1992) and *The Silver Ball* (1993).

The protagonists of Almog's works tend to be women, often young and troubled by their quest for identity, space, or self-expression. Alienated and sensitive, they struggle with the traumas of their childhood, the crisis of adolescence and independence, and an unfulfilled yearning for spiritual transcendence. The heroine of *Don't Hurry the Journey* (1971) leaves Israel for Germany in serarch of her father's home. Her tragic world unravels in the poetic style that marks Almog's writing. Similarly, the young heroes of her short stories—victims of social, economic, and geographic marginalization, emotionally deprived children of immigrants and Holocaust survivors—search for redemption through imagination and art. Almog tells the stories of nonmainstream Israelis, the "others," as representatives of the universal human condition.

Zvia Ginor

Alphabet Reform

See Romanization

Al Rashid Family

Rulers of central Arabia from 1836 to 1921.

In 1836, Faysal Ibn Turki Al Sa'ud conquered Ha'il, the capital of Jabal Shammar, the north-central part of the Arabian peninsula's interior. He installed as governor his friend, ally, and fellow supporter of strict Wahhabi Islamic reform, Abdullah ibn Rashid. His family, the Al Rashid, then ruled there as vassals, rivals, or masters of the Al Sa'ud for the next eighty-five years.

Following the death of Faysal in 1865, the Al Rashid, taking advantage of internecine rivalries among the Al Sa'uds, established an independent state based on the powerful Shammar tribe. Muhammad ibn Rashid (ruled 1869–1897) was then the most powerful chief in all Arabia. He ruled Najd, the traditional power base of the AL SA'UD (House of Sa'ud); from its capital of Riyadh, in 1890, Abd al-Rahman Al Sa'ud had fled to Kuwait.

In January 1902, the son of Abd al-Rahman, Abd al-Aziz (known in the West as IBN SA'UD) reconquered Riyadh and, benefiting from divisions among the Al Rashid, reconquered Najd and Jabal Shammar. Ha'il finally fell in 1921 when the Al Rashid, weakened by their internal dissensions and the loss of their World War I Ottoman allies, opened the city gates to Abd al-Aziz.

BIBLIOGRAPHY

HOLDEN, DAVID, and RICHARD JOHNS. *The House of Saud: The Rise and Rule of the Most Powerful Dynasty in the Arab World.* New York, 1981.
SALIBI, KAMAL. *A History of Arabia.* Delmar, N.Y., 1980.

Malcolm C. Peck

Al Sabah, Abd Allah I   [?–1812]

Second ruler of Kuwait, from 1762 or 1764 to 1812.

Abd Allah was the youngest of the five children of Sabah ibn Jabir AL SABAH, the first ruler of KUWAIT. Although historians do not agree on his year of accession (or death), he ruled for some fifty years. His prosperous reign established relations with the British and the Wahhabis of Saudi Arabia, which became important for Kuwait's future.

BIBLIOGRAPHY

ABU-HAKIMA, AHMAD. *The Modern History of Kuwait.* London, 1983.

Emile A. Nakhleh

Al Sabah, Abd Allah II   [1816–1892]

Fifth ruler of Kuwait, from 1866 to 1892.

Abd Allah ibn Sabah ibn Jabir became ruler of KUWAIT at the age of fifty. He was considered humble, fair, and decent. He showed wisdom and courage in leading his people at a time when much regional instability prevailed—both regarding the Sa'ud family (of Saudi Arabia) and the expanding authority of the Ottoman Empire into eastern Arabia.

BIBLIOGRAPHY

ABU-HAKIMA, AHMAD. *The Modern History of Kuwait.* London, 1983.

Emile A. Nakhleh

Al Sabah, Jabir Ahmad   [1926–   ]

Thirteenth ruler of Kuwait, 1977–

Shaykh Jabir belongs to the Jabir branch, one of the two branches of the al-Sabah family that has ruled KUWAIT since the middle of the eighteenth century. The other branch is al-Salim. Jabir and Salim were the two sons of Shaykh Mubarak "the Great," who ruled Kuwait from 1896 to 1915. Jabir ruled from 1915 to 1917, and his son Ahmad ruled from 1921 to 1950. Ahmad's son, Jabir Ahmad, ascended to power on December 13, 1977. Mubarak's other son, Salim, ruled Kuwait from 1917 to 1921, and two of his sons also ruled—Abd Allah from 1950 to 1965 and Sabah from 1965 to 1977. Abd Allah's son, Shaykh Sa'd, is the current prime minister and crown prince, and he is expected to be the next ruler of Kuwait.

Many significant developments occurred in Kuwait during Shaykh Jabir's rule. On the positive side, in the late 1970s Kuwait became a financial giant, both regionally and internationally. In the late 1970s and early 1980s, he promoted democratization and free speech and assembly, resurrected the National Assembly in 1981 after its dissolution in 1976, and encouraged a free press. However, in response to the rise in terrorism in Kuwait in the mid-1980s, Shaykh Jabir dissolved the National Assembly in 1986, muzzled the press, and suspended the constitution. Also, in 1982 Kuwait experienced the crash of the unofficial stock market, the Suq Al-Manakh; the effects were felt in Kuwait throughout the 1980s.

During the Iran–Iraq War (1980–1989), Kuwait, under Shaykh Jabir's rule, walked a tightrope between the two combatants; it supported Iraq financially but was careful not to anger Iran excessively. Toward the end of the war, Kuwait felt seriously threatened by Iran, and Kuwaiti shipping began to be attacked by Iranian naval vessels and armed patrol boats. Kuwait sought U.S. help in protecting its oil tankers and other vessels. The U.S. Navy and Coast Guard provided protection by placing the U.S. flag on Kuwaiti ships. This reflagging operation brought the United States almost into a direct military confrontation with Iran.

Following the Iran–Iraq War, Kuwait became embroiled in a dispute with Iraq over several issues: the loans that Kuwait extended to Iraq during the war; the Iraq–Kuwait boundary; the Bubiyan and al-Warbah islands and access to the sea; the Rumaylan oil field; and the oil quota and pricing policies. Iraq refused to pay back the loans, claiming it fought the war against Iran on behalf of Kuwait and the rest of the Gulf shaykhdoms. Also, Iraq accused Kuwait of pumping more oil than the approved Organization of Petroleum Exporting Countries (OPEC) quota agreement in order to keep the prices low. Furthermore, Iraq accused Kuwait of "stealing" more oil than its share from the neutral zone. Iraq argued that Kuwait's activities were unacceptable and would not be al-lowed to continue. Attempts at reconciliation through Saudi Arabia in the late spring and early summer of 1990 failed; on August 2, 1990, Iraq invaded Kuwait.

Hours after the invasion, Shaykh Jabir and most of his family and government fled the country to Saudi Arabia, where he set up a government in exile. He and his government returned to Kuwait after liberation, in March 1991. Shaykh Jabir was criticized severely by many Kuwaitis, especially those who stayed in the country during its occupation by Iraq, for fleeing Kuwait so quickly and without any resistance. Leaders of the Kuwaiti resistance movement also criticized Kuwait's armed forces for their precipitous collapse in the face of the Iraqi invasion.

Shaykh Jabir and Crown Prince Shaykh Sa'd attempted to nullify the criticism by promising a return to democracy after liberation. This promise was made by the ruler and the crown prince at the Kuwaiti people's conference held in Jidda, Saudi Arabia, in October 1990. Upon his return to Kuwait, Shaykh Jabir announced that national elections would be held in October 1992.

BIBLIOGRAPHY

The Middle East and North Africa, 1991, 37th ed. London, 1991.

Emile A. Nakhleh

Al Sabah, Jabir al-Jabir ibn Mubarak al-Sabah

Amir of Kuwait, 1915–1917.

Jabir succeeded his father, the powerful Mubarak "The Great," generally regarded as the father of modern Kuwait. The son's rule lasted just over a year (1915–1917) and was uneventful. However, he and his brother Salim, who succeeded him (reigned 1917–1921), were indirectly important because a succession pattern was established by which only their descendants, the Al Jabir and the Al Salim, in alternation, could be selected as amir.

BIBLIOGRAPHY

Arabian Personalities of the Early Twentieth Century. Cambridge, U.K., 1986 (British documents originally compiled in 1917).
CRYSTAL, JILL. *Oil and Politics in the Gulf: Rulers and Merchants in Kuwait and Qatar.* New York, 1990.

Malcolm C. Peck

Al Sabah, Jabir I al-Sabah   [?–1859]

Third ruler of Kuwait, 1812–1859.

Jabir's long rule did not introduce any new direction in the policies of KUWAIT. During his reign, the British and the Ottoman Empire (through Egyptian expeditions) assumed influence in the affairs of the Gulf region, and both actively sought the establishment of closer relations with Kuwait. Jabir's relations with the British were generally friendly, since Kuwait did not engage in piracy or slavery, as did some other tribes (who preyed on British and all other shipping in their waters).

BIBLIOGRAPHY

ABU-HAKIMA, AHMAD. *The Modern History of Kuwait.* London, 1983.

Emile A. Nakhleh

Al Sabah, Mubarak

Ruler of Kuwait, 1896–1915.

Mubarak al-Sabah, often called "Mubarak the Great," has been called the most forceful ruler of KUWAIT. He is the only ruler in Kuwait's history to achieve his position as the result of a coup; he killed one of his brothers, Muhammad, the then ruler, and one of his sons killed another of Mubarak's brothers, Muhammad's close adviser, Jarrah. Apologists excuse these actions by pointing to Muhammad's pro-Turkish proclivities. Critics agree that Mubarak prevented the absorption of Kuwait into the Ottoman Empire but note that he did this not by keeping Kuwait independent but by making it a British client. The result of Mubarak's several secret treaties with Britain was to relinquish Kuwait's autonomy in foreign policy. This amounted to a larger concession of sovereignty than had been made to the Ottomans by Mubarak's predecessor. More important for the political development of Kuwait in the twentieth century, however, was Mubarak's use of British economic and military resources to attenuate the power of local notables, a process that was continued by his successors, who relied on oil revenues to insulate themselves from popular checks on their power.

Kuwait's economy thrived during Mubarak's reign. However, his domestic power rested on his close relationship to the bedouin tribes rather than to the urban merchants. Even after he became ruler, Mubarak spent time camping with the bedouins in the desert. Unlike the tradition established by most previous emirs of Kuwait, however, Mubarak publicly enjoyed a lavish life-style. His income from taxes, British payments and annuities, and family investments (including date gardens located in Iraq) enabled Mubarak to live well and to employ armed guards to protect himself from his subjects. Resentment of his high taxes and military levies provoked several leading pearl merchants to leave Kuwait for Bahrain in 1910. A delegation from the ruler that carried Mubarak's promise to rescind the burdensome taxes encouraged only some to return.

Mubarak's military campaigns against the al-Rashid shaykhs of the JABAL SHAMMAR were aimed at allies of the exiled relatives of Muhammad and Jarrah. In September 1902, British warships were sent against a force commanded by two of Mubarak's nephews who were seeking revenge for their fathers' deaths. But Mubarak's military adventures were also problematic for the British, who wanted to maintain their alliance with the Ottomans. Nevertheless, they continued to support him, and in 1905 the Turks abandoned their efforts to incorporate Kuwait into the vilayet of Basra.

Mubarak had confidence in the British as Kuwait's ultimate protectors against the Turks. But British rapprochement with the Sublime Porte prior to the outbreak of World War I produced the Anglo–Turkish Convention of 1913. This declared Kuwait to be a *kaza* (autonomous province) of the Ottoman Empire and recognized Turkey's right to have a political representative in Kuwait. Mubarak was shocked by what he saw as a betrayal of his interests. However, the convention never went into effect. On 3 November 1914, it was repudiated, and two centuries of diplomatic ties between Kuwait and the Ottomans were broken. One year later, Mubarak died. True to their promise to a leader who had become a staunch ally, the British planned to honor another of their pledges to Mubarak: that they would ensure that the next ruler of Kuwait would be his designated heir rather than a descendant of the brothers he had killed in 1896. In the event, no external intervention was necessary. Subsequent rulers of Kuwait have also been direct descendants of Mubarak.

BIBLIOGRAPHY

RUSH, ALAN DE LACY. *Al-Sabah: History and Genealogy of Kuwait's Ruling Family, 1752–1987.* London, 1987.
———, ed. *Records of Kuwait, 1899–1961.* Vol. 1, *Internal Affairs, 1899–1921.* London, 1989.
TÉTREAULT, MARY ANN. "Autonomy, Necessity, and the Small State: Ruling Kuwait in the Twentieth Century." *International Organization* 45 (Autumn 1991).

Mary Ann Tétreault

Al Sabah, Mubarak al-Abd Allah al-Jabir
[1934–   ]

Chief of staff of the Kuwaiti armed forces in the 1970s and 1980s.

Shaykh Mubarak was criticized for the performance of the armed forces in KUWAIT during the Iraqi invasion of August 1990. He resumed his position as chief of staff after liberation by the UN coalition forces in 1991.

Emile A. Nakhleh

Al Sabah, Muhammad al-Sabah   [?–1896]

Sixth ruler of Kuwait, 1892–1896.

Muhammad assumed the throne of KUWAIT on the death of his father Shaykh Abd Allah II AL SABAH. With his brother Jarrah, he managed the financial affairs of the shaykhdom; his other brother Mubarak was entrusted with keeping the peace among the desert tribes, who were his subjects. This kept Mubarak away from the center of power, but in 1896 Mubarak killed both his brothers and became the ruler.

BIBLIOGRAPHY

ABU-HAKIMA, AHMAD. *The Modern History of Kuwait.* London, 1983.

Emile A. Nakhleh

Al Sabah, Sabah al-Salim   [?–1977]

Ruler of Kuwait, 1965–1977.

In 1962 the emir of Kuwait, Shaykh Abdallah al-Salim, made his brother Sabah heir apparent, breaking the established pattern of alternation between the al-Salim and al-Jabir branches of the ruling Al Sabah family. The decision reflected Sabah's noncontroversial nature and represented a compromise acceptable to the senior Al Sabah.

When Sabah became ruler in November 1965 he brought to the position considerable experience in public affairs, dating from his appointment as head of the police in 1938. After Kuwait's independence in 1961 he was deputy prime minister and foreign minister. Sabah continued his brother's domestic policies, utilizing Kuwait's growing oil revenues to build an advanced welfare state. He sought new political allies, especially among the conservative bedouin population, to counter the Al Sabah's opponents in the National Assembly and, in 1976, dissolved the assembly when the opposition of the nationalist bloc became strident. In foreign affairs he sought to counter potential regional threats with generous economic aid to other Arab countries and support for Arab nationalist causes, especially that of the Palestinians. Before and during the Arab-Israel War of 1973, Sabah indicated his willingness to use the oil weapon to try to alter United States policy. When Sabah died in 1977 Shaykh Jabir al-Ahmad, who had long run the country's day-to-day affairs, succeeded him, restoring the ruling family's pattern of succession. Sabah's son Sa'd is the present heir apparent.

BIBLIOGRAPHY

CRYSTAL, JILL. *Oil and Politics in the Gulf: Rulers and Merchants in Kuwait and Qatar.* New York, 1990.
ZAHLAN, ROSEMARIE SAID. *The Making of the Modern Gulf States.* Boston, 1989.

Malcolm C. Peck

Al Sabah, Sabah ibn Jabir

First of the Al Sabah family to rule Kuwait, 1756–1762 or 1764.

Sabah ibn Jabir is considered the ancestor of Kuwait's ruling family. He was elected by the al-UTUB tribe as a leading shaykh and was, in effect, the first emir of KUWAIT. Before his rise, authority in eastern Arabia belonged to the Bani Khalid tribes. Sabah was chosen by the inhabitants of the town of Kuwait to administer justice there.

BIBLIOGRAPHY

ABU-HAKIMA, AHMAD. *The Modern History of Kuwait.* London, 1983.

Emile A. Nakhleh

Al Sabah, Salim al-Mubarak al-Jabir
[d. 1921]

Ninth ruler of Kuwait, 1917–1921, second son of Mubarak.

Salim assumed the leadership of KUWAIT upon the death of his brother Shaykh Jabir Ahmad Al Sabah, and ruled until his own death four years later. Although he had a difficult relationship with his father, Shaykh Mubarak Al Sabah, he led armies on the latter's behalf and served as his envoy to the pearl merchants who left Kuwait for BAHRAIN in 1910 in protest over Mubarak's high taxes. After he was installed as emir, Salim, a devout Muslim, resisted Britain's demands to enforce an embargo against the Ottoman Empire during World War I, assigning his son Abd Allah (later Abd Allah III) to work with the British while remaining in quiet contact with the Ottomans for the rest of the war.

After the war, Salim's personal feud with Ibn Sa'ud, which dated back to their childhood, when the AL SA'UD family were exiles in Kuwait, grew into a boundary dispute between Kuwait and Saudi Arabia. Fighting between Kuwait's forces and Wahhabi supporters of Ibn Sa'ud broke out in May 1920, and the former were soundly defeated. Within a few weeks, the citizens of Kuwait constructed a new wall to protect Kuwait City. At the end of the summer, Salim raised an army at Jahra. On 10 October, the Wahhabis attacked Salim and his forces, driving them to take shelter in the Red Fort (al-Qasr al-Ahmar). The inability of the Wahhabis to breach the Red Fort's defenses, plus the arrival of reinforcements from Kuwait City, brought about negotiations. Salim refused to accept Wahhabism as a condition of peace. Fearing a renewal of hostilities, Kuwait notables prevailed upon him to appeal for assistance to Britain. The British sent ships, armored cars, and warplanes, causing the Wahhabis to retreat.

Although Ibn Sa'ud proclaimed that his quarrels with Kuwait ended when Salim died, the Wahhabis continued to raid Kuwait for more than ten years, and Ibn Sa'ud himself sought British intervention, at the Uqayr Conference in 1922, to gain 60 percent of Kuwait's territory.

BIBLIOGRAPHY

DICKSON, H. R. P. *Kuwait and Her Neighbours*. London, 1956.

RUSH, ALAN DE LACY. *Al-Sabah: History and Genealogy of Kuwait's Ruling Family, 1752–1987*. London, 1987.

Mary Ann Tétreault

Al Saqr Family

Family prominent in the politics of Kuwait.

Members of the Al Saqr family were among the founders of KUWAIT in the eighteenth century. They made their money in shipping and trade and were reputed to be among the toughest dealmakers in the country. They acquired the first stock ticker in Kuwait, in the 1920s, and shortly afterward, they cornered local coffee supplies after learning that a storm had destroyed much of the year's crop.

Like other prominent merchant families, the Al Saqr participated in the democratization movements that recurred throughout the twentieth century. In 1921, Hamid Al Saqr led an organization of notables who petitioned the ruling family for the right to advise on the succession to the emirship. After Ahmad al-Jabir became emir, he refused to consult with the notables. Hamid Al Saqr became leader of the opposition and, upon his death in 1930, was succeeded by his son Abdullah Hamid.

The Al Saqr family founded the Ahliyya Library, where the opposition met to plan its strategy. Abdullah Hamid was a leader of the 1938/1939 *majles* movement. He was a member of both councils elected during this period and among those who refused to disband when the emir suspended the second council's activities. He was forced to flee the country when the movement failed. He died in India.

The merchants developed a close relationship to the emir's brother, Abdullah al-Salim, who had served as the president of the elected councils and attempted to mediate the many conflicts between the councils and the emir. After Abdullah al-Salim became emir in 1950, a group of five merchant families, including the Al Saqr, approached him about establishing a bank. He granted the National Bank of Kuwait a charter in 1952 and helped to capitalize the bank with a large interest-free deposit.

The Al Saqr family continued its political activities during the rule of Abdullah al-Salim and for some time after. Abd al-Aziz, another of Hamid Al Saqr's sons, was a wealthy trader and shipyard owner. He was a member of the Constitutional Assembly that was convened in 1961 to prepare Kuwait's first constitution and was elected to the first National Assembly. He became its president and the minister of health in the first cabinet. Abd al-Aziz was one of the leaders of Kuwait's 1989/1990 pro-democracy movement and, at the time, president of the Kuwait Chamber of Commerce and Industry. With Ahmad al-Sa'dun, the president of the 1985 National Assembly that had been suspended by the emir in 1986, Abd al-Aziz effected a reconciliation between the ruling family and the political opposition at an October 1990 meeting in Jidda, Saudi Arabia.

Another sibling, Jasim Hamid, served on the board of Kuwait University and was a private sector member of the board of the Kuwait National Petroleum Company before resigning, along with the other private members, in a 1960s dispute with the government representatives over selecting Hispanoil as a partner in an exploration concession. Jasim also served in the National Assembly and was its presiding officer when it was reorganized following the 1992 elections.

The Al Saqr family retains extensive business and financial interests in Kuwait and overseas. Economic retaliation against the family for its political activities by the current emir, Jabir al-Ahmad, may be responsible in part for the tendency of younger family members to focus their attention on business at the expense of politics.

[*See also:* Banks, Kuwait.]

BIBLIOGRAPHY

CRYSTAL, JILL. *Oil and Politics in the Gulf: Rulers and Merchants in Kuwait and Qatar.* New York, 1990.
RUSH, ALAN DE LACY, ed. *Records of Kuwait, 1899–1961.* Vol. 2, *Internal Affairs, 1921–1950.* London, 1989.
TÉTREAULT, MARY ANN. *The Kuwait Petroleum Corporation and the Economics of the New World Order.* Westport, Conn., 1995.

Mary Ann Tétreault

Al Sa'ud, Fawwaz ibn Abd al-Aziz

[1934–   ]

Member of the ruling family of Saudi Arabia.

Fawwaz was one of three Sa'ud princes who publicly called for a constitutional monarchy for SAUDI ARABIA in 1962. In 1971, King Faisal appointed him governor of Mecca. In November 1979, the leader of the seizure of the Grand Mosque of Mecca attacked Fawwaz for moral laxity; he resigned the governorship shortly afterward.

BIBLIOGRAPHY

HOLDEN, DAVID, and RICHARD JOHNS. *The House of Saud: The Rise and Rule of the Most Powerful Dynasty in the Arab World.* New York, 1981.

Malcolm C. Peck

Al Sa'ud, Khalid ibn Musa'id   [?–1965]

Member of the ruling family of Saudi Arabia.

Khalid was an unstable young man whose student debaucheries in the West yielded to intense Islamic piety on his return to SAUDI ARABIA. He led a group of zealots in 1965 to protest the introduction of television by King FAISAL IBN ABD AL-AZIZ AL SA'UD and was shot dead while resisting the police. It is likely that a desire for revenge prompted his brother Faysal to assassinate the king in March 1975.

BIBLIOGRAPHY

LACEY, ROBERT. *The Kingdom: Arabia and the House of Saud.* New York, 1981.

Malcolm C. Peck

Al Sa'ud, Muhammad ibn Abd al-Aziz

[1910–1990]

Member of the ruling family of Saudi Arabia.

Muhammad, sixth son of King Abd al-Aziz Al Sa'ud (known as Ibn Sa'ud in the West), held no official positions in his later years, although he played a key role in the affairs of the kingdom as a strong-willed senior prince. When still in his twenties, Muhammad served as deputy to Prince FAISAL IBN ABD AL-AZIZ AL SA'UD, then viceroy of Hijaz (later king of SAUDI ARABIA). Muhammad, however, lacked a natural power base in the family and was notorious for his ungovernable rages, which led in late 1963 to his renunciation of a place in the royal succession. His younger full brother Prince Khalid took his place. Khalid subsequently became king in 1975.

Muhammad strongly opposed his half brother Sa'ud ibn Abd al-Aziz AL SA'UD, the successor to their father Ibn Sa'ud, as unfit to rule. He was the only son not to swear allegiance, and from 1955 on, he led efforts to depose Sa'ud in favor of Prince Faisal, playing a major role in pressing the case to its conclusion in 1964. He gained international notoriety from the television production *Death of a Princess*, which was a dramatization of the execution—at his insistence—of his granddaughter, Princess Mishal, and her lover for adultery.

BIBLIOGRAPHY

HOLDEN, DAVID, and RICHARD JOHNS. *The House of Saud: The Rise and Rule of the Most Powerful Dynasty in the Arab World.* New York, 1981.

Malcolm C. Peck

Al Sa'ud, Nayif ibn Abd al-Aziz

[1933–   ]

A prince of Saudi Arabia.

Nayif, twenty-sixth son of King Abd al-Aziz Al Sa'ud (known in the West as Ibn Sa'ud), is a full brother of the present king of Saudi Arabia, Fahd. He is one of the six brothers of the Sudayri Seven (as they are generally known in the West), or Al Fahd, to hold a senior government position. He was governor of Riyadh, 1953/54, and in 1970 became deputy minister of the interior when Fahd headed that ministry. Since 1975, when Fahd became crown prince and relinquished the ministry, Nayif has been minister of the interior, and the youngest of the Al Fahd, Ahmad, has been his deputy.

Nayif is a pious and austere Muslim, though he has amassed a considerable fortune, and has been sympathetic to conservative demands for more extensive restrictions on both Saudi and foreign conduct in public. He has a special interest in the Gulf Arab states, with which he has developed close internal security ties. Fahd places special trust in Nayif and, after the 1979 seizure of the Grand Mosque in Mecca, directed him to head a committee to draft plans for a consultative council (MAJLES AL-SHURA) that was finally implemented in 1992.

BIBLIOGRAPHY

HOLDEN, DAVID, and RICHARD JOHNS. *The House of Saud: The Rise and Rule of the Most Powerful Dynasty in the Arab World.* New York, 1981.

Malcolm C. Peck

Al Sa'ud, Sa'ud ibn Abd al-Aziz

[1902–1969]

Succeeded his father, Ibn Sa'ud, as king of Saudi Arabia, 1953–1964.

Sa'ud's life appeared to begin auspiciously, since he was born on January 16, 1902—the same day that his father Abd al-Aziz reconquered Riyadh. In 1919, the death of the eldest son, Turki, made Sa'ud the eldest surviving son. He received the usual court education of memorizing the Qur'an, formal instruction in practical subjects, and more relevant lessons in court business.

In 1921, Sa'ud led troops in the final campaign against the Al Rashid, and in 1926, Abd al-Aziz appointed him viceroy of Najd, the Saudi heartland. In 1933 his father directed Sa'ud's designation as crown prince. Ibn Sa'ud was aware that Sa'ud's abilities were greatly inferior to those of FAISAL, his next son, or other potential candidates among the princes. What almost certainly led him to insist on Sa'ud's designation as his successor was the memory of the family's internal rivalries, which shortly before had brought their fortunes to their lowest ebb: also, there were potential challenges emerging to continued rule through Ibn Sa'ud's line

Despite a long tenure as viceroy and crown prince, Sa'ud had never exercised meaningful authority before becoming king of Saudi Arabia in 1953, and he lacked any understanding of modern state administration and finance. Rather than relying on the council of ministers, Sa'ud delegated authority to his sons and cronies. Self-indulgent and good-hearted, he regarded the country's oil wealth as his own, to be spent as he pleased. Serious physical infirmities were a major liability throughout his reign.

By 1958, debt and political crisis forced Sa'ud to yield power to his brother Faisal. The precipitating factor was Sa'ud's ill-considered attempt to challenge Egypt's president Gamal Abdel NASSER by acting as leader of the conservative Arab camp, supported by the United States. Once Faisal had restored the country's solvency and established a temporary modus vivendi with Nasser, Sa'ud thrust himself back into full power in alliance with Talal ibn Abd al-Aziz AL SA'UD and other brothers identified as the Free Princes, who called for a constitutional monarchy. But once more a conclave of senior princes forced Sa'ud to yield power to his brother Faisal.

In 1964, Sa'ud tried for a final time to reclaim the powers of his office. The senior princes, backed by the *ulama,* forced Sa'ud's abdication on November 2, 1964. The remainder of his life was passed in sybaritic exile, largely in Athens, Greece, where he died on February 23, 1969.

BIBLIOGRAPHY

BLIGH, ALEXANDER. *From Prince to King: Royal Succession in the House of Saud in the Twentieth Century.* New York, 1984.
HOLDEN, DAVID, and RICHARD JOHNS. *The House of Saud: The Rise and Rule of the Most Powerful Dynasty in the Arab World.* New York, 1981.

Malcolm C. Peck

Al Sa'ud, Sa'ud ibn Faisal   [1940–   ]

Saudi Arabia's foreign minister since 1975.

The fourth son of Saudi Arabia's King Faisal, Sa'ud is the eldest of the four born to the king's favorite wife, Iffat. Like his full brothers, he received a Western education, earning a bachelor's degree in economics at Princeton University. Sa'ud bears a striking physical resemblance to his late father and presents the same aristocratic bearing. His father's influence was strong as was that of his maternal uncle Kamal Adham, former head of Saudi intelligence. Doubtless his diplomatic polish and sophistication owe something to his 1971 to 1975 tenure as deputy to Minister of Petroleum and Mineral Resources Ahmad Zaki Yamani.

Following King Faisal's assassination in 1975, Sa'ud assumed the position of foreign minister that was previously held by his father for over forty years. Both as crown prince and king, FAHD IBN ABD AL-AZIZ AL SA'UD has valued his nephew Sa'ud's intelligence and skill in handling foreign assignments, but their relationship is not particularly warm. Based on his strong belief in nationalism, Sa'ud has seen the U.S.–Saudi relationship as excessively one-way, in

Washington's favor, and has argued for a nonaligned policy. He is probably the most likely candidate among the grandsons of King Abd al-Aziz Al Sa'ud (known in the West as Ibn Saud) to become king.

BIBLIOGRAPHY

MACKEY, SANDRA. *The Saudis: Inside the Desert Kingdom.* Boston, 1987.
QUANDT, WILLIAM B. *Saudi Arabia in the 1980s: Foreign Policy, Security, and Oil.* Washington, D.C., 1981.

Malcolm C. Peck

Al Sa'ud, Sultan ibn Abd al-Aziz
[1924–   ]

A deputy prime minister in Saudi Arabia since 1982 and an heir to the throne.

Sultan was born in Riyadh, SAUDI ARABIA, and is the next oldest full brother of King Fahd, a son of Hassa bint Ahmad AL SUDAYRI, the favorite wife of King Abd al-Aziz Al Sa'ud (known in the West as Ibn Sa'ud). He is a key part of the Al Fahd—the king and his six full brothers—often referred to in the Western press as the Sudayri Seven—who are the dominant grouping in the Saudi royal family.

Sultan and the other members of the Al Fahd are the first princes to build their careers through service in the bureaucracy. When Sultan was still in his early twenties, his father appointed him governor of the province of Riyadh. King Sa'ud named him minister of agriculture in the first Council of Ministers in 1954. In 1960, Sultan replaced his half brother Talal, one of the Free Princes, as minister of communications. In 1962, Crown Prince Faisal, then serving as King Sa'ud's prime minister, appointed Sultan defense minister—the position that he has since held for thirty years. Faisal gave Sultan great authority in determining Saudi Arabia's military needs and in filling them. He also relied extensively on his advice in general matters, in part to balance the views of conservatives in the AL SA'UD FAMILY with Sultan's progressive perspectives. After 1975, during the reign of Faisal's successor, King Khalid, Sultan became part of the inner circle of senior princes who direct the nation's course. In 1982, when Fahd became king, Sultan was made second deputy prime minister, de facto successor after Crown Prince Abdullah—and will certainly become king if he survives those two brothers.

The crucial importance of Saudi Arabia's security concerns in the 1980s and 1990s has reinforced the power Sultan enjoys from three decades of controlling the military establishment and presiding over the vast patronage opportunities of his ministry. In addition, he has exercised special responsibility for Saudi Arabia's problematic relations with the Yemens (since May 1990 united as the YEMEN ARAB REPUBLIC). His power base, were he to become king, would lack the strong support of the Islamic religious establishment that his predecessors, except Sa'ud and Fahd, enjoyed. He has also been denied the firm loyalty of the Arab tribes, which Abdullah has already secured. As with Fahd, his support derives from his mastery of the modern governmental structure, specifically the armed forces, as well as from being a member of the largest and most capable natural grouping of princes.

Saudi Arabia's reliance on the United States as its principal source of security assistance—weapons, training, and military infrastructure—has led Sultan to favor close relations with Washington. This has not precluded occasional strains growing out of Sultan's strong feelings on the ARAB–ISRAEL CONFLICT and from the several U.S. denials of advanced weaponry to Saudi Arabia because of the Israel lobby's influence in Congress. Sultan has not hesitated to turn elsewhere, for example, to Great Britain for the Tornado jet fighter in place of the U.S. F-15 and to the People's Republic of China for missiles to substitute for the disallowed Lance.

As second deputy prime minister, thus effectively next after Abdullah to succeed Fahd, as well as being minister of defense and aviation, Sultan is, next to them, the most senior and powerful prince in the government of Saudi Arabia. Throughout his long career, he has exhibited great energy and ambition. Though apparently reconciled to honoring Abdullah's selection to succeed Fahd, he has in the past tried to force the bypassing of his older half brother in the order of succession. This suggests that Fahd's death, if it precedes Abdullah's, might result in a succession less smooth than the previous two.

BIBLIOGRAPHY

BLIGH, ALEXANDER. *From Prince to King: Royal Succession in the House of Saud in the Twentieth Century.* New York, 1984.
HOLDEN, DAVID, and RICHARD JOHNS. *The House of Saud: The Rise and Rule of the Most Powerful Dynasty in the Arab World.* New York, 1981.

Malcolm C. Peck

Al Sa'ud, Talal ibn Abd al-Aziz   [1931–   ]

Member of the ruling family of Saudi Arabia; government official.

Talal was born in Riyadh, SAUDI ARABIA, the twenty-third son of King Abd al-Aziz Al Sa'ud (known in the West as Ibn Sa'ud). He received the usual princely training—rote memorization of the Qur'an and limited acquaintance with subjects of practical utility, as well as what education came from observing the conduct of political business in the court. Of Talal's mother, Munayyir, little is known except that she was a woman of unusual grace and beauty (probably a concubine of Armenian origin) and a favorite of her husband. Talal consequently grew up a spoiled child and adopted an opulent lifestyle as a young man.

At the age of nineteen, Talal became comptroller of the royal household and persuaded his father to permit him to establish a cement factory, one of the first princely ventures in entrepreneurship in Saudi Arabia. Talal also displayed early on a certain intellectual sophistication and, from a number of sources, drew ideas for liberal reforms that he intended to implement in Saudi Arabia. He may have assimilated some of these ideas from his first wife, the daughter of Lebanon's former premier, Riyad al-SULH. When his ties to dissident army elements led in 1955 to his dismissal as minister of communications in King Sa'ud's Council of Ministers, he went to Paris as ambassador (accredited both to France and Spain) and there further developed democratic constitutional concepts for Saudi Arabia.

In 1960, Sa'ud named Talal minister of finance and economy. The king, though not in sympathy with Talal's ideas, saw him and his several reformist brothers as useful allies in his attempt to regain and consolidate power. Earlier, Sa'ud had yielded most of his authority to Crown Prince Faisal in the monarchy's 1958 crisis. In this Talal saw an opportunity to implement his ideas for reform. Neither brother satisfied his expectations, and Sa'ud forced Talal out of the cabinet after less than a year.

Talal subsequently left Saudi Arabia for Beirut, Lebanon, where in the summer of 1962 he issued a manifesto titled "Letter to a Fellow Countryman." It called for a constitutional monarchy with a national assembly, two-thirds of its members to be elected, which could propose legislation, with the king retaining veto power. In the Saudi context, such notions were radical, and when Talal proceeded to criticize the Saudi government in public, to call for the freeing of slaves and concubines, and to introduce more extreme notions such as centralized "socialism," the king took his passport. Talal's full brother Nawwaf and his half brothers Badr and Fawwaz, collectively called the Free Princes outside Saudi Arabia but self-described as Young Najd (Najd al-Fatah), gave up their passports in sympathy and joined Talal in exile in Cairo. Egypt's President Gamal Abdel Nasser tried to use the situation to his advantage against Saudi Arabia, hoping that the defections by the princes could lead to the monarchy's collapse.

The episode shook the Saudi ruling family severely, especially as it immediately preceded a republican coup in neighboring YEMEN and the defection of officers from the Saudi Air Force to Nasser's Egypt. It strengthened the resolve of the Al Sa'ud never again to permit family differences to be aired in public. The exiled princes all eventually returned, Talal doing so in 1964 and making an "admission of guilt." He has resumed a respected place in the royal family and, since 1979, has served as a special envoy to the United Nations Educational, Scientific, and Cultural Organization (UNESCO).

BIBLIOGRAPHY

BLIGH, ALEXANDER. *From Prince to King: Royal Succession in the House of Saud in the Twentieth Century.* New York, 1984.
HOLDEN, DAVID, and RICHARD JOHNS. *The House of Saud: The Rise and Rule of the Most Powerful Dynasty in the Arab World.* New York, 1981.

Malcolm C. Peck

Al Sa'ud, Turki ibn Abd al-Aziz
[1934–   ]

Member of the ruling family of Saudi Arabia.

Turki is a full brother of Saudi Arabia's King FAHD ibn Abd al-Aziz Al Sa'ud and named for the early nineteenth-century father of the ruling dynasty as well as the first son born to King Abd al-Aziz (known in the West as Ibn Sa'ud), who died in his youth. Turki was deputy defense minister for his country from 1969 to 1978. The erratic behavior of his wife, which created unwelcome publicity, forced him to relinquish that post.

BIBLIOGRAPHY

HOLDEN, DAVID, and RICHARD JOHNS. *The House of Saud: The Rise and Rule of the Most Powerful Dynasty in the Arab World.* New York, 1981.

Malcolm C. Peck

Al Sa'ud, Turki ibn Faisal   [1945–   ]

Member of the ruling family of Saudi Arabia.

Turki is the youngest son of Saudi Arabia's King Faisal by Iffat, his third and favorite wife. He received his college education in the United States and did graduate studies in Islamic law at London University. Possessed of a keen analytical intelligence, Turki became deputy to the head of the General Intelligence Directorate, Kamal Adham, his uncle. In early 1979, Turki replaced Adham, who had taken much of the blame for failure to foresee Egypt's peace initiative with Israel succeed in the agreement called the CAMP DAVID ACCORDS.

In November 1979, Turki distinguished himself by taking charge of the operations to regain government control of the Grand Mosque in Mecca; Islamic extremists had seized it in an effort to promote the overthrow of the monarchy. Turki has acted as a polished spokesman for Saudi Arabia's international interests. Like his father, he combines a sophisticated knowledge of the contemporary world with genuine piety and a firm belief in his country's inherent moral superiority. Turki is clearly a leader among the young princes—the grandsons of King Abd al-Aziz (known in the West as Ibn Saʿud)—and he is almost certainly destined to hold high office.

BIBLIOGRAPHY

MACKEY, SANDRA. *The Saudis: Inside the Desert Kingdom.* Boston, 1987.
HOLDEN, DAVID, and RICHARD JOHNS. *The House of Saud: The Rise and Rule of the Most Powerful Dynasty in the Arab World.* New York, 1981.

Malcolm C. Peck

Al Saʿud Family

The ruling family of Saudi Arabia.

In reality a clan numbering well into the thousands, the Al Saʿud family dominates the country's political and economic life. The king, who is selected by the senior princes, with the approval of the senior religious leaders, is an authoritarian, patriarchal, but not absolute, monarch who must satisfy several constituencies to rule effectively. Although SAUDI ARABIA, as presently constituted, dates from 1932, the career of the Al Saʿud as a dominant force in Arabia goes back several centuries.

The first known leader of the clan, sixteen generations removed from the present king, was Mani al-Muraydi ibn Rabia who, at the invitation of a cousin, left his home near the Persian/Arabian Gulf in the area of al-Qatif in 1446 to take possession of two small fiefs in central Arabia, north of the present Saudi capital of RIYADH. For three centuries his successors gradually expanded their patrimony and came to be known by the title emir of Dirʿiya, the capital

that was named for the original home in eastern Arabia. They ruled one of several modest principalities in central Arabia, which had remained politically fragmented since the early period of Islam. From the beginning of their rule, the Al Saʿud were townsmen whose strength derived principally from the loyalty of other townsmen. At the same time, the clan enjoyed a crucial advantage for exercising leadership in Arabian tribal society—it belonged to the Masalikh subsection of the Anaza tribe, one of the great sharifian (noble) tribes (the same term also refers to descent from the Prophet Muhammad). To this day, the Al Saʿud are extremely solicitous of the aristocratic bloodlines of their lineage and guard them with great care.

What enabled these rulers of a small state unknown to the outside world to become masters of an Arabian empire was their identification with an expansive Islamic reform movement that, to this day, represents a key source of legitimacy for the Al Saʿud. This circumstance came about through the alliance in 1744 of Muhammad ibn Saʿud, whose father thus ranks as the eponymous founder of the dynasty, and Muhammad ibn Abd al-Wahhab, a religious reformer who preached the return to a strict and rigorous vision of Islam, one purged of innovations. His preaching emphasized the doctrine of *tawhid,* the absolute oneness of God unqualified by any anthropomorphic attributes, and his followers were called MUWAHHIDUN (unitarians), though generally known outside Arabia as Wahhabis. Rejected in his own settlement, he took refuge with Muhammad ibn Saʿud in Dirʿiya and made with him an alliance based consciously on the pact of the Prophet and the Medinans after the *hijra* (or hegira; the Prophet's flight to Medina from Mecca) of 622. During his lifetime, Abdul Wahhab remained the *imam* (Muslim spiritual leader) of the community, a title signifying religiopolitical authority; his Saudi partner remained the emir, a purely secular title. Since Ibn Abd al-Wahhab's death, the Al Saʿud have also taken on the position of imam for themselves.

The military brilliance of Abdul Aziz (son of Muhammad ibn Saʿud, sometimes referred to as Abd al-Aziz I) and his son Saʿud, harnessed to religious zeal, had created by 1811 a realm that extended to the outskirts of Aleppo and Basra in its northern reaches, stretched from the Red Sea to the Gulf, and reached into Oman and the Hadramawt.

In southeastern Arabia the Saudi forces and their Qawasim allies (rulers today of Sharja and Raʾs al-Khayma) came up against Oman's British allies and were checked. The end of the first Saudi state came, however, at the hands of MUHAMMAD ALI, ruler of Egypt and nominal vassal of the sultan of the Ottoman Empire. The sultan sought to harness Muhammad Ali's ambitions by deputizing him to drive the Wahhabis from the holy cities of MECCA and MEDINA. The Egyptian forces carried out a brutal seven-year campaign that ended with the razing of Dir'iya, whose ruins are preserved today as they were left then. Abdullah ibn Sa'ud, who had succeeded Sa'ud in 1814, was captured and taken to Istanbul, where he was beheaded in 1818. Najd was subjected to a harsh Egyptian occupation, then an abortive attempt to rule through local surrogates, until 1823 when Turki, son of Abdullah, set about restoring the fortunes of the House of Sa'ud in central Arabia. In 1824, he recaptured Dir'iya and made it the capital of Najd, as it remains to the present. During the next six years he extended Saudi rule once more to al-Hasa (today's eastern province) as well as to the areas north of Najd. Turki, who fully reestablished the Saudi–Wahhabi alliance that his great-grandfather had formed, was an impressive ruler but, after a brief rule, was assassinated by another member of the Al Sa'ud in 1834. Turki's son FAYSAL IBN TURKI succeeded him, ruling until 1838 when a second Egyptian invasion led to his capture and exile in Cairo. Five years later, Faysal made a dramatic escape from exile and, after overthrowing a cousin, Abdullah ibn Thunayyan who had seized Riyadh, embarked upon a reign of twenty-two years that represented the heyday of the second Saudi state. Faysal reconquered all of central and eastern Arabia and extended Saudi sway into Oman. One of the two or three greatest Saudi rulers, he brought prosperity and stability to a realm slightly less extensive than today's Saudi Arabia. The ruling branch of the contemporary state is the Al Faysal, the descendants of Faysal ibn Turki.

Faysal's death in 1865 ushered in a period of internal strife that brought an end to the second Saudi state. His sons Abdullah and Sa'ud contested the succession throughout the decade that followed and, after Sa'ud's death in 1875, Abdullah was imam for another decade, during which he presided over the disintegration of the weakened Saudi state. At that point, the rule of the Al Sa'ud ended, yielding to that of their former vassals, the AL RASHID.

The re-creation of the Saudi state in its third incarnation was the work of Abd al-Aziz ibn Abd al-Rahman, known also as King IBN SA'UD, a grandson of the great Faysal. As a young boy, he had fled with his father into exile in Kuwait when the latter had failed in an effort to reclaim Riyadh from its Rashidi overlords. The son began the process of reconquest with a dramatic raid on the city in 1902 and, over the next third of a century, restored the realm of his ancestors to its present limits. Like its predecessors, it

was a religiopolitical state. Its ideological base continued to be the stern Islamic reform of Muhammad ibn Abd al-Wahhab, carried forward by religious leaders who included his Al Shaykh descendants. While the rulers of the first and second Saudi states had styled themselves emirs of Najd and imams and protectors of the muwahiddun, Ibn Sa'ud became the king of the Kingdom of Saudi Arabia in 1932. Although Saudi Arabia's population became more settled under King Ibn Sa'ud, the king's relations with the tribes remained critical in preserving power. Before he could secure his rule over the Saudi state, he was obliged to crush a revolt led by tribal chiefs who were not prepared to accept the limitations of international borders that were imposed by British fiat. He and his successors have retained the title of imam. The present king, FAHD IBN ABD AL-AZIZ, has added and given primacy to the title Custodian of the Two Holy Mosques.

Early in the process of reconquest Ibn Sa'ud had faced a challenge from within the Al Sa'ud family. The family of one his uncles, under the leadership of Ibn Sa'ud's first cousin, Sa'ud ibn Abd al-Aziz, fomented a tribal revolt in an attempt to realize the claims of his family line to rule. With the revolt quashed, Ibn Sa'ud arranged for the marriage of his favorite sister Nura to that cousin Sa'ud, who renounced his claim in 1912 and was henceforth known as Sa'ud al-Kabir, distinguishing him from Ibn Sa'ud's son and successor of the same name. Sa'ud's offspring are now known as the Al Sa'ud al-Kabir—a collateral or cadet branch of the reigning Al Sa'ud. Other significant cadet branches are the Al Farhan and AL THUNAYYAN, deriving from sons of Muhammad ibn Sa'ud, founder of the first Saudi state. The Al Turki and Al Jiluwi lines date back to sons of Turki ibn Abdullah in the mid-nineteenth century, as does the main Al Faysal branch (within which the Al Sa'ud al-Kabir are included). Members of the cadet branches may hold significant government positions, although key posts tend to be reserved for the ruling line. Many have served in the armed forces, the most prominent among them Fahd ibn Abdullah, chief of Air Force Operations. Members of the ruling line may marry only within the Al Sa'ud and with members of two other families—the AL SHAYKH and the AL-SUDAYRI.

The defeat of the challenge of Sa'ud al-Kabir confined the succession to the line of Abd al-Rahman, father of Ibn Sa'ud. Khalid ibn Muhammad, the nephew of Ibn Sa'ud, defied the king's designation of his eldest surviving son Sa'ud as his successor and refused to swear the *bay'a*, the oath of loyalty, to Sa'ud in 1933. Khalid's death, in 1938, however, ended any challenge to the succession. Since the death of Ibn Sa'ud in 1953, the succession has been confined to his sons, even if among them rivalries have persisted. Both before and after Sa'ud's accession as king, he was in competition, at least implicitly, with his abler brother FAISAL IBN ABD AL-AZIZ. The latter became king in 1964, when the senior princes and religious leaders deposed the ailing Sa'ud, whose incompetence had endangered the kingdom's survival.

The successions of Sa'ud's brothers KHALID IBN ABD AL-AZIZ (following Faisal's assassination in 1975) and Fahd ibn Abd al-Aziz in 1982 (following Khalid's death by natural causes) were smooth. Yet, even after the promulgation of a basic law in 1992, there is no predetermined order of succession among the sons and grandsons of Ibn Sa'ud. The Al Fahd—comprising the king, his six full brothers, and their sons—have emerged as the strongest grouping within the family. Sultan, second eldest among the Al Fahd, has tried to supplant Abdullah, next in line in the succession. This effort has failed and it seems certain that, should Abdullah survive Fahd, he will succeed him. There remains, however, the complicating factor of the grandsons of Ibn Sa'ud, or the "nephews" as they are frequently referred to in the media. Prominent among these are the Al Faysal, the sons of King Faisal by "Queen" Iffat. Intelligent, energetic, and presumably not lacking monarchical ambition, they include Sa'ud ibn Faisal, foreign minister since his father's death, and Turki ibn Faisal, director of Royal Intelligence.

The great number of sons and grandsons of Ibn Sa'ud may complicate succession, and the enormous numbers within the Al Sa'ud clan, probably in the tens of thousands when all the cadet branches are included, may dilute its prestige. At the same time these prolific numbers have provided many capable royal princes, whose service in civilian and military capacities strengthens the Al Sa'ud's ruling position. Moreover, princes are to be found on various sides of domestic and foreign policy issues that split Saudi opinion, thus obviating the clan's identification with a single position. Even within the Al Fahd, Na'if and Ahmad, the minister and the deputy minister of the interior, represent a fairly conservative religious point of view, while King Fahd and Sultan, the minister of defense and aviation, are generally liberal and secular in their approach. Finally, the senior princes' skill in maintaining a dynamic balance between the various factions in the Al Sa'ud, and their keen awareness of the dangers of failing to maintain essential unity in confronting threats to their continued rule, make it likely that the third Saudi state will endure for some time to come.

BIBLIOGRAPHY

BLIGH, ALEXANDER. *From Prince to King: Royal Succession in the House of Saud in the Twentieth Century.* New York, 1984.
LEES, BRIAN. *A Handbook of the Al Sa'ud Ruling Family of Saudi Arabia.* London, 1980.
PHILBY, H. ST. J.B. *Arabia.* London, 1930.
———. *Saudi Arabia.* London, 1955.
RUSH, ALAN DE LACY. "The Monarchy of Saudi Arabia." In *Burke's Royal Families of the World.* Vol. 3, *Africa and the Middle East.* London, 1980.
WINDER, R. BAYLY. *Saudi Arabia in the Nineteenth Century.* New York, 1965.

Malcolm C. Peck

Al Shaykh Family

Important family or clan in Saudi Arabia; one of only two nonroyal families, the other being the Al Sudayri, with whom Al Sa'ud princes may marry.

The Al Shaykh, "the family of the SHAYKH," are descendants of MUHAMMAD IBN ABD AL-WAHHAB, the Islamic reformer who formed an alliance with Muhammad ibn Sa'ud in the mid-eighteenth century. This association has shaped their families' fortunes and those of most of the Arabian peninsula since. Ibn abd al-Wahhab was born in 1703 in the Najd, probably in the central Arabian town of Ayaina. Influenced by the strict teachings of Ibn Taymiya, a thirteenth–fourteenth century jurist of the conservative HANBALI LAW SCHOOL, he returned home from prolonged study to preach a simple, puritanical faith that eschewed theological innovations and aimed at countering the moral laxity of his Najdi contemporaries. Those who accepted his teaching and its emphasis on *tawhid,* the oneness of the Qur'anic God unchallenged and untainted by any earthly attributes, were MUWAHHIDUN (unitarians), known outside Arabia as Wahhabis. Unwelcome in Ayaina, the preacher moved to Dir'iya where Muhammad ibn Sa'ud was EMIR, ruler of a district in Najd. The latter's political leadership and the military abilities of his son, Abd al-Aziz, combined with the reformer's zeal, brought all of Najd under Saudi rule within thirty years. In 1803, the year of his death by assassination, Abd al-Aziz took Mecca, and his son Sa'ud expanded the first Saudi state over the course of the next decade to approximately its present limits.

During his lifetime, ibn Abd al-Wahhab was the Imam (Muslim spiritual leader) of the expanding Saudi state, a title conveying responsibility for enforcing norms of correct Islamic belief and behavior as well as carrying the Wahhabi interpretation of

Islam to the rest of the Islamic world and beyond. When he died, the title passed to the Al Sa'ud rulers. The shaykh's descendants did not directly exercise political power in the decades that followed, although they were accorded special respect. The Al Sa'ud have continued the practice of intermarriage with members of the Al Shaykh, begun when Abd al-Aziz ibn Muhammad married a daughter of Muhammad ibn Abd al-Wahhab. The late King Faisal's mother (IBN SA'UD's grandmother) was Tarfah bint Abdullah, daughter of a distinguished Al Shaykh scholar and jurist, making Faisal the great-great-great grandson of the original shaykh. Moreover, the family continued to produce religious leaders who exercised great influence on all decision making in a state whose essential legitimacy depended on adherence to and propagation of Wahhabi beliefs. Members of the Al Shaykh held the post of Qadi (judge) of Riyadh, the Saudi capital, and later the position of grand MUFTI, highest judicial office in the state.

In recent years the position of the Al Shaykh has changed in significant ways. In 1969, as part of his effort to create a more efficient government securely under Al Sa'ud control, King Faisal ibn abd al-Aziz Sa'ud abolished the office of grand mufti and replaced it with a ministry of justice. The Al Shaykh and other senior religious leaders were, in effect, co-opted, losing their former autonomy in exchange for a role within the government. While the first minister of justice was not an Al Shaykh, subsequent ministers have been. Moreover, from the early 1960s, members of the Al Shaykh have regularly held ministerial positions. As is usually the case, there are currently three who do so: minister of justice, Dr. Abdullah ibn Muhammad ibn Ibrahim; minister of agriculture and water, Dr. Abdul Rahman ibn Abd al-Aziz Al Shaykh; and minister of municipalities and rural affairs, Dr. Muhammad ibn Abd al-Aziz ibn Hasan Al Shaykh. Other members of the family serve in important military and civilian capacities. Although the Al Shaykh have lost some of their moral prestige through identification with the Saudi political establishment, the family alliance is still crucial to the Al Sa'ud in maintaining their legitimacy.

BIBLIOGRAPHY

HELMS, CHRISTINE MOSS. *The Cohesion of Saudi Arabia.* Baltimore, 1981.
HOLDEN, DAVID, and RICHARD JOHNS. *The House of Saud: The Rise and Rule of the Most Powerful Dynasty in the Arab World.* New York, 1981.
NYROP, RICHARD F., ed. *Saudi Arabia: A Country Study.* Washington, D.C., 1984.
PHILBY, H. ST. J. B. *Saudi Arabia.* London, 1955.

Malcolm C. Peck

Al Sudayri, Hassa bint Ahmad

Wife of Ibn Sa'ud, mother of Saudi kings.

Hassa bint Ahmad Al Sudayri was one of three Hassa cousins from a prominent clan in eastern SAUDI ARABIA who married King ABD AL-AZIZ IBN SA'UD AL SA'UD (known as Ibn Sa'ud). Her sons include King FAHD IBN ABD AL-AZIZ AL SA'UD and Defense Minister Sultan ibn Abd al-Aziz and constitute the most important bloc of senior places among the Al Sa'ud family.

BIBLIOGRAPHY

HOLDEN, DAVID, and RICHARD JOHNS. *The House of Saud: The Rise and Rule of the Most Powerful Dynasty in the Arab World.* New York, 1981.
LACEY, ROBERT. *The Kingdom: Arabia and the House of Saud.* New York, 1981.

Malcolm C. Peck

Al Sudayri Family

Important family or clan in Saudi Arabia, part of a tribe of the same name.

The Al Sudayri (also spelled Al Sudairi or al-Sudairi) family's origins may be traced to a branch of the DAWASIR TRIBE, which was a sharifian or noble tribe that lived on the edge of the Rub al-Khali desert about 1400. By about 1550, the Al Sudayri were situated at the town of Ghat in Sudayr, an area in NAJD to the northwest of Riyadh that took its name from the tribe. The main branch, whose fortunes have been closely linked with the fortunes of the AL SA'UD FAMILY of Saudi Arabia, comes into view in the early eighteenth century.

First to achieve special prominence among the Sudayri was Ahmad al-Kabir, whose life spanned the first two-thirds of the nineteenth century. He served the Al Sa'ud for fifty years in a number of civilian and military capacities, including the governorship of al-HASA, the country's eastern province. His daughter Sara was the mother of King Abd al-Aziz (also known as IBN SA'UD), and it was largely from her that he inherited his imposing physical stature. Ahmad al-Kabir's grandson and namesake, Ahmad bin Muhammad Al Sudayri (1869–1935) cemented further his family's ties to the Al Sa'ud. In the early twentieth century, he participated in the Al Sa'ud's military campaigns against their AL RASHID rivals. His daughter Hassa was a favorite wife of Abd al-Aziz, who also married two of Ahmad's nieces, Haya and Jawhara. The extent and significance of the Al

Sa'ud–Al Sudayri interrelationship is evident in the fact that nearly two dozen of Abd al-Aziz's sons or grandsons were Sudayris in the maternal line. The first wife of his son Faisal (reigned 1964–1975) was Sultana bint Ahmad Al Sudayri, younger sister of Hassa. Six of Ahmad's eight sons became governors of provinces. Moreover, other Sudayris have served as governors, especially in strategic border areas of the kingdom, and in other high-level government positions.

The impact of the Sudayri on the ruling family is most apparent in the dominant position of the sons of Abd al-Aziz by Hassa bint Ahmad AL SUDAYRI. These constitute a grouping of senior princes known as the Al Fahd, the present king and his six full brothers. (The term "Sudayri seven," sometimes used in the West to refer to this grouping, is not used in Saudi Arabia.) The Al Fahd are the largest group of full brothers among the sons of Abd al-Aziz, and all but one, Prince Turki (who earlier served as deputy minister of Defense and Aviation), now occupy key positions in the government. Sultan has been minister of Defense and Aviation for over three decades with Abd al Rahman currently the deputy minister, while Na'if is minister of the Interior and Ahmad is his deputy. Salman has been governor of Riyadh since 1962. Moreover, Sultan is second deputy prime minister and next after Crown Prince Abdullah to succeed Fahd as king.

While all the sons of Hassa bint Ahmad Al Sudayri are intelligent and ambitious, they differ significantly in personal character and political/philosophical outlook. Fahd and Sultan are the most secularly oriented and the most pro-American, while Na'if and Ahmad most notably embody traditional, conservative Islamic virtues. Ties of blood and a strong sense of self-interest, however, outweigh any differences. Moreover, the differences can help to gain support from different constituencies within the Al Sa'ud and in the country at large. It is likely that, after Abdullah, succession will continue through the Al Fahd. Should the Al Sa'ud find themselves divided over the succession, Salman, who commands broad support, would be a likely compromise candidate.

BIBLIOGRAPHY

HOLDEN, DAVID, and RICHARD JOHNS. *The House of Saud: The Rise and Rule of the Most Powerful Dynasty in the Arab World*. New York, 1981.

LEES, BRIAN. *A Handbook of the Al Sa'ud Ruling Family of Sa'udi Arabia*. London, 1980.

NYROP, RICHARD F., ed. *Saudi Arabia: A Country Study*. Washington, D.C., 1984.

PHILBY, H. ST. J. B. *Arabian Jubilee*. London, 1952.

Malcolm C. Peck

Altalena

Armed IZL ship sunk by the Israel Defense Forces on June 22, 1948 on Tel-Aviv's shore.

Purchased in America in 1947 by an official of the IRGUN ZVA'I LE'UMI (IZL) and renamed *Altalena,* Ze'ev JABOTINSKY's Italian pen name, the 1,820-ton landing craft was at first used to carry European refugees to Palestine. It became a transporter of arms for the Irgunists following the United Nation's partition resolution on November 29, 1947, which set off the first Arab-Israel War (1947–1948). On June 1, 1948, Menachem BEGIN, a leader of the Irgun, met with official military leaders of the newly independent state of Israel to sign an agreement for the incorporation of the Irgun battalions into the Israel Defense Forces (IDF) but did not let the government know of Irgun's negotiations with France, which had agreed to supply the Irgun with arms materiel from war overstock. The arms—including 5,000 British rifles, 4 million bullets, 300 Bren guns, 250 Stens, 150 Spandau rifles, and 50 eight-inch mortars—would be transported on the *Altalena,* also carrying 900 trained Irgun recruits from Europe.

The *Altalena* left Port du Bouc with its cargo of arms and men on June 11, 1948, the first day of a month-long UN-brokered peace that pledged Arabs and Jews not to import arms into Israel. In view of the truce and a newspaper article (June 10, 1948) and a BBC broadcast (June 11, 1948) that made Irgun's *Altalena* operation public, Begin notified the Israeli government of the ship's impending arrival. Prime Minister BEN-GURION considered the Irgun's actions a danger to the truce and a critical challenge to the authority of the state, but he conditionally permitted the ship to proceed because of the country's vital need for arms. In the ensuing negotiations between the Irgun high command and government representatives, which began on June 16, 1948, Irgunists agreed to hand over to the IDF half of the stock of arms, provided a considerable portion of the remaining supply would be apportioned to the incorporated Irgun units and that one-fifth would be allocated to the Irgun forces in Jerusalem (which, according to UN decree, had not become part of Israel). The Irgun leaders also agreed to dock the *Altalena* at Kfar Vitkin, a settlement north of Tel Aviv loyal to Ben-Gurion forces, to which the ship came on June 19, 1948. An unresolved difference as to where the arms would be warehoused resulted in the government issuing Irgun with the ultimatum to turn over the arms.

When the Irgun men ignored the ultimatum, government forces attacked disembarked Irgunists. Disregarding Begin's orders to stay and fight, the

Irgunists removed the *Altalena* to Tel Aviv, where they believed the government would not hazard starting a civil war. In the port of Tel Aviv, on June 22, 1948, Ben-Gurion ordered government forces to take all measures necessary to put down Irgun's "revolt." An initial Irgun advantage was overcome by reinforced IDF units, which hit the ship with shells from a cannon ("a blessed gun," according to Ben-Gurion). In spite of a call for a truce from the mayor of Tel Aviv and the raising of a white flag by the Irgunists, government forces continued to hit the *Altalena* until the ammunition below deck caught fire and the burning ship had to be evacuated. It sank with bombs and ammunition detonating. In the fighting, a total of twenty Irgunists were killed and eighty-seven wounded.

In the aftermath of the sinking of the *Altalena,* the Irgun accused Ben-Gurion of conspiring to get rid of his opponents, and the government accused the Irgun of planning a revolt against it. The extended conflict, which increased the tension between the two groups, represented the last physical confrontation between the organized YISHUV and the dissenters. Two cabinet ministers resigned in protest of the government's handling of the situation, and for many years the events surrounding the *Altalena*'s sinking cast a pall over Israeli politics.

BIBLIOGRAPHY

BRENNER, URI. *Altalena.* Tel Aviv. In Hebrew.
DUPUY, TREVOR. *Elusive Victory: The Arab-Israeli Wars, 1947–1974,* rev. ed. Fairfax, Va., 1984.
NAKDIMON, SHLOMO. *Altalena.* Jerusalem, 1978. In Hebrew.

Yaakov Shavit

Alterman, Natan   [1910–1970]

Israeli poet, playwright, essayist and translator.

A central author of modern Hebrew poetry and an influential cultural and political figure of the first decades of the State of Israel, Natan Alterman immigrated to Palestine in 1925 from Warsaw via France, where he had studied agronomy. The five volumes of his collected poetry, his plays, his satirical works, and his children's books are noted for their wit, their creative use of traditional form in modernist variations, and their manipulation of the language. Alterman is considered the most prominent poet of Hebrew literature since BIALIK.

Alterman's affinity with the Russian and French avant-garde shaped his Hebrew poetry and, in turn, filtered into the mainstream of Israeli poetry. He was the leading imagist of his time and an exponent of the well-wrought poem that employed symmetry and balanced stanza, meter, and structured rhyme schemes. These poetic characteristics were turned against him in the 1950s, when Anglo-American literary tastes—with their preference for concrete poetry, free verse, irony, and colloquialism—replaced the neoromanticism of the previous generation.

Much of his work is enigmatic and hermetic. Autobiographic materials are coded into symbolic and abstract terms, personal experiences are suppressed, and historical events allegorized. Yet the tensions and drama of personal anguish are transmitted through a virtuoso use of language and intellectual structure. In *Stars Outside* (1938), his first collection, Alterman created a world in which troubadours and wandering minstrels roam roads and frequent taverns as they worship a symbolic merciless lady who represents the universe or earth. This poetry suggests that the role of the poet is to be the lyric transmitter of the world as he subjectively experiences it. Similarly, Alterman refrained from extensive employment of intertextual references to traditional Hebrew sources, an otherwise dominant characteristic of Hebrew literature. He thus maintained a universal, existential poetic perception.

In 1943 Alterman began to publish a weekly satirical column, "The Seventh Column," in which he reflected in verse on the turbulent circumstances of the Jewish population in Palestine on the road to independence and statehood. This column both expressed and formed the mood of the many people who read and quoted it weekly. One such column, "The Silver Platter" (November 1947), was a mythic poem of foresight and somber fortitude anticipating the war of independence. This poem soon reached the status of a national hymn and is still recited and performed annually in Memorial Day ceremonies.

Many of Alterman's poems have been set to music, in addition to the songs, ballads, and verse plays he composed for the stage. He translated into Hebrew the major works of Shakespeare, Racine, and Molière, among others, as well as classics of Russian and Yiddish literature. Only a few of his works have been translated into English (*Selected Poems* [1978]; *Little Tel Aviv* [1981]).

Zvia Ginor

Al Thani, Ahmad ibn Ali

Ruler of Qatar, 1960–1972.

Ahmad succeeded his father, Ali, as ruler of QATAR when the latter abdicated in October 1960, even though Ali had earlier agreed to succession by his nephew, Khalifa ibn Hamad. Financial extravagances and failure to establish an effective, modernized government lost Ahmad the support of the Al Thani. Khalifa, who had assumed the bulk of the country's day-to-day administration, deposed and succeeded Ahmad in February 1972.

BIBLIOGRAPHY

ZAHLAN, ROSEMARIE SAID. *The Creation of Qatar.* New York, 1979.

Malcolm C. Peck

Al Thani, Hamad ibn Khalifa

Emir of Qatar, 1995–

Shaykh Hamad became the emir of Qatar on June 27, 1995 when he ousted his father in a bloodless palace coup. The eldest son of his predecessor Shaykh Khalifa, Hamad was born in Doha in 1950. He graduated from the Royal Military College in Sandhurst, England, in 1971, and in 1977 he was named heir apparent and defense minister by his father. In 1992 he took control of the day-to-day governing of Qatar when his father allowed him to appoint a cabinet of his own choice. In his first cabinet, appointed in July 1995, he retained for himself the positions of defense minister and commander of the Qatari armed forces and, in addition, appointed himself prime minister, a position previously held by his father.

F. Gregory Gause, III

Al Thani, Khalifa ibn Hamad   [1932–   ]

Ruler of Qatar, 1972–1995.

Shaykh Khalifa received a traditional Islamic education from tutors. Recognition of his abilities led to appointment as a civil court judge, then as director of education, and, in 1960, as finance minister. He has implemented major governmental reforms while presiding over the very large and often fractious Al Thani clan.

BIBLIOGRAPHY

GRAZ, LIESL. *The Turbulent Gulf: People, Politics and Power,* rev. ed. London, 1992.

Malcolm C. Peck

Al Thani, Qasim ibn Muhammad
[?–1913]

Major figure in the Al Thani clan of Qatar.

Qasim was instrumental in establishing Al Thani rule over an independent Qatar. He accepted limited Ottoman suzerainty, after the Turks' seizure of the al-Hasa province in eastern Arabia in 1871. He did so primarily to thwart reoccupation by the former overlords, the al-KHALIFA FAMILY of Bahrain, then played the Turks against Britain to secure Qatar's de facto independence. In the month that he died, July 1913, an Anglo–Turkish agreement (never ratified) formally ended all Ottoman claims of authority.

BIBLIOGRAPHY

CRYSTAL, JILL. *Oil and Politics in the Gulf: Rulers and Merchants in Kuwait and Qatar.* Cambridge, 1990.

Malcolm C. Peck

Al Thunayyan Family

A branch of the Al Sa'ud, the ruling family of Saudi Arabia.

The Al Thunayyan (also Al Thunayan, Al Thunaiyan) are descended from an eponymous ancestor who was the brother of the dynasty's founder, Muhammad ibn Sa'ud. That Thunayyan joined his brother in support of the teachings of Muhammad ibn Abd al-Wahhab, the Islamic reformer whose teachings (known as wahhabism outside Arabia) have provided the essential ideological legitimacy for the rule of the AL SA'UD FAMILY.

Abdullah ibn Thunayyan was briefly ruler of Najd (1841–1843), following the second Egyptian occupation of the Saudi state, then met defeat at the hands of FAYSAL IBN TURKI, who restored Saudi rule over both central and eastern Arabia. Subsequently, the family of Abdullah moved to Istanbul, acquiring there a certain cosmopolitanism that set them apart from their Najdi cousins. His great-grandson, Ahmad, returned to Arabia to serve as private secretary to Emir (later King) Abd al-Aziz, also known as IBN SA'UD, from before World War I until his death in 1921. Ahmad accompanied the young Prince (later King) FAISAL IBN ABD AL-AZIZ on the latter's diplomatic tour of Europe in 1919. Ahmad's intelligent and well-educated niece Iffat later became Faisal's very influential wife.

BIBLIOGRAPHY

DeGaury, Gerald. *Faisal: King of Saudi Arabia*. London, 1966.
Philby, H. St. J. B. *Arabia*. London, 1930.

Malcolm C. Peck

Altinay, Ahmed Refik [c. 1879–c. 1935]

Turkish historian, journalist, and poet.

Born in Istanbul, his father was an agha from Ürgüp who had migrated there to serve the government of the Ottoman Empire. Altinay joined the military in 1898 and later taught French and history at the war school. He worked as an official censor during the Balkan War and World War I, when he began writing history articles. Before and after the wars, he served on a government historical commission and in 1918 became a professor of Ottoman history at Istanbul University. He retired to his home on Büyük Ada island in the 1930s.

His vast output of popular histories was written in simplified Turkish. He had a flair for storytelling. He wrote on many eras—from the period of Alexander the Great to the rise of the Prussian state—but is best remembered for his evocations of daily life in Constantinople through the centuries. Throughout his life, he contributed articles, sketches, and poems to newspapers, and he wrote several children's history books.

BIBLIOGRAPHY

Gökman, Muzaffer. *Tarihi Sevdiren Adam: Ahmed Refik Altınay,* (A Man Who Made Others Love History: Ahmed Refik Altınay). Istanbul, 1978.

Elizabeth Thompson

Aluminium Bahrayn Company (ALBA)

Bahrain's major aluminum smelter and producer of aluminum ingots.

Established in Bahrain in 1972, ALBA's total annual production reached more than 200,000 tons (181,400 metric tons) by the late 1980s. Of the original four investors in the company, the government of Bahrain owns the largest percentage of shares. The raw alumina powder used to produce ingots comes from Australia (almost 500 million tons [453.5 million metric tons] per year).

BIBLIOGRAPHY

The Statesman's Year-Book, 1991–92, 128th ed. New York, 1991.

Emile A. Nakhleh

Alusi, Mahmud Shukri al- [1857–1924]

Iraqi historian, writer, and teacher; a Sunni reformer.

Alusi was born in Baghdad to a well-known but impoverished family of clerics. Educated in Islam by his father and uncle, he taught in Madrasa (Islamic schools) attached to mosques, wrote, and occasionally engaged in politics.

In 1889, the Ottoman Empire's governor (*wali*) of Baghdad named Alusi to be Arabic-language editor of the official journal *al-Zawra*; however, the next wali persecuted Alusi for his pro-Wahhabi inclinations—Alusi had attacked Ottoman innovations and so-called superstitious religious practices. Around 1905, he was exiled for a short period when the wali accused him of incitement against the Ottoman sultan.

Due to Alusi's great popularity with the Sunni Muslims, in 1911, the Ottoman wali Cemal Paşa asked him to join the administrative council of Baghdad's province. In November 1914, he was sent to convince the Saudi emir Ibn Sa'ud to support the Ottoman Empire in World War I, but he failed.

In his writings, Alusi defends Islamic reformists, such as Jamal al-Din al-Afghani, Muhammad Abduh, and Rashid Rida; he attacks deviationist practices in Sunni Islam, which he saw as a return to polytheism. More ferocious were his attacks against the Shi'ites. He branded them *rafida* (renegades) and accused them of rejoicing in the Ottoman's defeat by the Russians; he also issued legal opinions (*fatwa*). His histories deal with Baghdad, its *ulama* (body of Islamic scholars), and mosques; Islamic Spain; the Najd; Arab markets, eating and drinking habits, and punishments in the Jahili period; Arab games; and Baghdadi proverbs. He also wrote essays on Arabic philology.

BIBLIOGRAPHY

Basri, Mir. *A'lam al-yaqza al-fikriyya fi al-Iraq al-hadith*. Baghdad, 1970.

Amatzia Baram

Alwan, Jasim

Syrian military officer.

Born in Dayr al-Zawr, Alwan rose through the ranks to become a lieutenant colonel by 1961. As commander of the Aleppo garrison he led the "Free Officers" in resisting the coup of March and April 1962. Relieved of his post for this resistance, he was later arrested and sentenced to death for his participation in the pro-Nasser coup of July 1963. He received amnesty in 1964 and fled to Egypt.

BIBLIOGRAPHY

HOPKINS, ED. "Military Intervention in Syria and Iraq." M.A. thesis, American University of Beirut, 1970.

Charles U. Zenzie

Alya [1948–1977]

Third wife of King Hussein ibn Talal of Jordan.

The daughter of a Jordanian official of Palestinian origin, Alya Baha al-Din Tuqan married the king in December 1972. She then took the name Alya al-Hussein. She gave birth to a daughter (Haya) and a son (Ali) and adopted a second daughter (Abir) with the king before her death in a helicopter crash in February 1977.

BIBLIOGRAPHY

Who's Who in the Arab World, 4th ed. (1974/75) and 5th ed. (1978/79). Beirut.

Abla M. Amawi

AMAL

Resistance movement in Lebanon.

The AMAL movement was established in 1975 by Imam Musa SADR. In Arabic the name means hope; it is also the acronym for Afwaj al-Muqawimah al-Lubnaniyya (Lebanese Resistance Detachments). The name was originally used for the military arm of the Movement of the Disinherited, which was founded in 1974 by Sadr to promote the Shi'ite Lebanese cause. Although Sadr established his own militia, he later opposed a military solution to the Lebanese civil war, refusing to involve AMAL in the fighting during 1975 and 1976. This reluctance discredited the movement in the eyes of many Shi'ites, who chose instead to support the Palestine Liberation Organization (PLO), and members of the Lebanese National Movement. AMAL was also unpopular for endorsing Syria's military intervention in Lebanon in 1976.

Several factors caused AMAL to make a dramatic resurgence in the late 1970s. First, the Shi'ites became disillusioned with the conduct and policies of the PLO and its Lebanese allies. Second, the mysterious disappearance of Sadr while on a visit to Libya in 1978 made him symbolic of the Shi'ite heritage; the significance attached to his absence was not unlike the concealment/absence of the twelfth imam of the Shi'ite Twelvers. Third, the Iranian revolution revived hope among Lebanese Shi'ites and instilled a sense of growing communal solidarity. Moreover, when the PLO feared the increased power of AMAL, it tried to crack down on its cells by sheer military force. This strategy backfired and rallied an even greater number of Shi'ites around AMAL.

Husayn al-HUSAYN, former speaker of parliament, headed AMAL from 1979 until April 1980, when Nabi BERRI assumed the leadership and transformed the movement into one of the most powerful political and military forces in Lebanon. Although its charter expressed dedication to the Palestinian cause, the movement laid seige to Palestinian refugee camps in Lebanon and started the war of the camps that lasted from 1985 until 1988. In 1994 Berri was speaker of parliament, and AMAL's role had been enhanced by the 1992 landslide victory of Berri's slate of candidates in the South. The disarming of militias in the late 1980s forced AMAL into the political arena, and it remains a major force. Its success has been aided by Berri's political subservience to Syria.

AMAL's broad support in predominantly Shi'ite areas notwithstanding, neither AMAL's rank and file nor its leadership is cohesive. The movement has become a political tool for Berri, who uses his influential position in goverment to advance the cause. Many members and leaders of AMAL have been appointed to key government positions.

BIBLIOGRAPHY

AJAMI, FOUAD. *The Vanished Imam: Musa al-Sadr and the Shia of Lebanon.* Ithaca, N.Y., 1986.
NORTON, A. R. *Amal and the Shi'a: The Struggle for the Soul of Lebanon.* Austin, Tex., 1987.

As'ad AbuKhalil

Amal, al-

The principal daily newspaper of the Lebanese Phalange party, Hizb al-Kata'ib al-Lubnaniyya.

Between 1939 and 1946, *al-Amal* was published every two weeks in both Arabic and French (entitled

Action). Party leaders expressed their opinion on Lebanese politics at least once a week. Between 1946 and 1948, the bilingual weekly was replaced with the daily newspaper in Arabic. During the Lebanese Civil War (1975–1989), *al-Amal* was an important source of information on the thinking inside the Lebanese Phalange party.

BIBLIOGRAPHY

Tarikh Hizb al-Kata'ib al-Lubnaniyya (History of the Lebanese Phalange Party). Beirut, 1979.

George E. Irani

Amanollah Khan   [1892–1960]

King of Afghanistan, 1919–1929.

Amanollah (also called Amanullah Barakzai) launched a jihad (holy war) against Great Britain and declared AFGHANISTAN's independence from Britain in 1919. He embarked on an ambitious program of modernization, introducing secular reforms and education.

He was the third son of HABIBOLLAH KHAN (ruled 1901–1919), who was assassinated. Amanollah, then governor of Kabul, convinced the army and power elite to prefer his claim to the throne over his brothers and uncle. In May 1919, he went to war against the British administration and, at the end of a one-month campaign, was able to negotiate control of his country's foreign policy (which his grandfather Abd al-Rahman Khan had surrendered). He welcomed recognition of his regime by the then new and revolutionary government of the Soviet Union; however, he soon turned to countries without territorial designs on Central Asia, establishing ties with France, Germany, Italy, Japan, and the Ottoman Empire. He failed to initiate official relations with the United States.

Advised by Ottoman-educated Afghans and impressed by Ottoman Turkey's example, Amanullah embarked on his own scheme of development. First he promulgated a constitution and convened three *loya jirga* (grand assemblies, composed of various segments of the power elite) to ratify his important decisions. Second, he systematized the administrative divisions of the country into a territorial hierarchy of subdistricts, districts, and provinces. The centrally appointed administrators at each level were assisted by a locally elected consultative body. Third, he replaced ILTIZAM (tax farming) with directly collected taxes in cash. Fourth, he tolerated a free press, entrusted the intelligentsia with responsible positions in the government, and spent a major portion of the revenue of the state on the expansion of education.

These reforms proved to be enduring. However, he alienated his subjects with more symbolic policies such as the mandatory unveiling of Afghan women and the imposition of European attire on civil servants and schoolchildren. Simultaneously, he canceled the monetary and symbolic sinecures enjoyed by the leaders of the clans and the headmen of villages. Furthermore, his new tax policies weighed heavily on agricultural producers and were unpopular in the countryside. Opposition was organized under the symbolic defense of the values of Islam and spearheaded by leaders of the religious establishment. Leaders of clans and social bandits also played an important role. He might have overcome the challenge had he paid more attention to his army—but he had neglected its welfare and was unable to prevent soldiers from joining the several revolts that broke out simultaneously in 1928. He was forced to abdicate in May of 1929 and went into exile in Italy.

BIBLIOGRAPHY

ADAMEC, LUDWIG. *Afghanistan 1900–1923: A Diplomatic History.* Berkeley, 1967.

POULLADA, LEON. *Reform and Rebellion in Afghanistan 1919–29: King Amanullah's Failure to Transform a Tribal Society.* Ithaca, N.Y., 1973.

Ashraf Ghani

American Israel Political Affairs Committee

Umbrella organization (AIPAC), founded in 1954, to lobby the U.S. Congress in support of Israel.

AIPAC's board of directors includes representatives from other Jewish organizations, allowing it to utilize their grassroots resources for its lobbying efforts. Since its establishment, it has advocated increases in U.S. economic and military aid to Israel, resistance to military aid to Arab states, resistance to the Arab boycott of Israel and direct Arab–Israeli peace negotiations. AIPAC also produces and distributes to opinion makers books and articles favorable to Israel. Its official publication is *Near East Report*.

The extent of AIPAC's influence in Congress is a subject of controversy. It has dedicated significant resources, with considerable success, to both the reelection of candidates whose voting record is favorable to Israel and the defeat of candidates who are deemed to be unfriendly. The group has also succeeded at times in placing limits on U.S. foreign policy. It has not, however, been omnipotent. For example, despite strenuous efforts, it was unable to prevent the 1978 sale of F-15 aircraft to Saudi Arabia or the subsequent decision to supply the Saudis with AWACs in 1981.

BIBLIOGRAPHY

SPEIGEL, STEVEN. *The Other Arab–Israeli Conflict: Making America's Middle East Policy from Truman to Reagan.* Chicago, 1986.

Martin Malin

American Jewish Committee

Organization founded in 1906 to "prevent the infraction of the . . . rights of Jews . . . and secure for Jews equality of . . . opportunity."

At the beginning of World War I, the American Jewish Committee (AJC) joined with the Zionist Organization of America in extending emergency aid to Jews in Palestine. It fought for the retention of an open-door immigration policy in the United States and, when restrictive legislation was enacted, tried to mitigate the effects. During the Hitler period, the AJC exposed the aims of Nazism. Although the committee is non-Zionist, it has had a consistently favorable attitude toward Palestine and Israel. In 1990, it had about 40,000 members in over 500 cities throughout the United States. Its publications are the *American Jewish Year Book* and *Commentary,* a monthly magazine.

BIBLIOGRAPHY

COHEN, NAOMI WEINER. *Not Free to Desist: The American Jewish Committee 1906–1966.* Philadelphia, 1972.
GOLDSTEIN, JUDITH S. *Politics of Ethnic Pressure: The American Jewish Committee Fight against Immigration Restriction, 1906–1917.* New York, 1990.

Mia Bloom

American Jewish Congress

Organization founded in 1917 to secure Jewish civil, political, and religious rights in Central and Eastern Europe and in Palestine.

Funded by Zionists, the American Jewish Congress sent a delegation, headed by Julian W. Mack and Louis Marshall, to the Paris Peace Conference after World War I. After the conference, the congress adjourned sine die. Another organization was formed in 1922 under the same name. Subsequent presidents included Stephen S. Wise and Arthur Hertzberg. The congress played an important role in the fight against Nazism, in supporting Zionism, and in defending civil rights in the United States.

Mia Bloom

American University in Cairo

A small, international university founded in 1919 by Western-oriented educators.

The American University in Cairo (AUC) opened in 1920 under its founder/president Charles R. Watson, the Egyptian-born son of missionary parents. Although he had worked for the United Presbyterians' Board of Foreign Mission, nevertheless, he insisted that the university be independent of that organization; he wanted a Christian but nondenominational school.

The university opened modestly with a preparatory section (which closed in the early 1950s). There were also four other programs—characteristic of colleges throughout the United States—an undergraduate College of Arts and Sciences; a noncredit Extension (now Public Service) Division; a Department of Education; and a School of Oriental Studies to serve missionaries, businessmen, diplomats, and other Westerners. AUC also featured physical education, coeducation, an open-stack library, a journalism major, and extracurricular clubs.

After twenty-five years, Watson was succeeded by John Badeau (1945–1953), who brought AUC into the postcolonial era. Arabic-speaking and affable, he cultivated Egypt's President Gamal Abdel Nasser and other influential Egyptians. As U.S. ambassador to Egypt (1961–1964), he kept a friendly eye on the university.

Outdoor campus scene at the American University in Cairo. (David Rewcastle)

The students were drawn mainly from economic and cultural elites, including many foreigners and minorities—Jews, Greeks, and Armenians were numerous until their communities emigrated en masse during Nasser's regime. Egypt's Coptic Christians were part of the student mix, as were women. Muslims were few, especially during the 1930s, when it was charged that AUC was proselytizing them for Christianity. AUC dropped hymns and prayers from its assemblies, but it was not until the 1960s, when AUC began closing on the Muslim sabbath, Friday, and hired some full-time Muslim academics, that Muslim students returned in great numbers. Today they outnumber Christians.

Tiny beside Egyptian universities, AUC has sought distinctive offerings for both its Egyptian and foreign students. In 1961/62, when Cairo University had almost 30,000 students, AUC had only 360 enrolled; in the 1990s, enrollment had risen to about 3,000. Since 1950, graduate programs have been added, as well as the Social Research Center, English Language Institute, Center for Arabic Studies, Center for Arabic Studies Abroad (CASA), University Press, Management Extension Services, and Desert Development Center. In the late 1950s, the Ford Foundation and the U.S. government provided major funding, to replace funding once provided by private U.S. donors with missionary ideals. In the 1980s, a Saudi business alumnus was the largest private donor.

When the United States replaced Britain as the dominant foreign power in the Middle East, the highly visible AUC campus became the target of anti-American demonstrations. During the Arab–Israel war of 1967, the university was sequestered, but Nasser's personal interest (he had sent a daughter there) soon restored things to normal. Egypt's President Anwar Sadat (1970–1981) had pro-U.S. policies, which brought new opportunities to the university. In the 1990s, Egypt's President Hosni Mubarak (1981–   ) is married to an alumna of the university.

BIBLIOGRAPHY

Murphy, Lawrence R. *The American University in Cairo: 1919–1987.* Cairo, 1987.

Donald Malcolm Reid

American University of Beirut

Prominent institution of higher education in Lebanon.

The American University of Beirut (AUB) was established as the Syrian Protestant College by the American Protestant Evangelical Mission to Syria in

Main campus of the American University of Beirut. (American University of Beirut Archives)

1866. The AUB is run by the New York-based board of trustees, whose members are citizens of various countries. The university was incorporated under the laws of the state of New York.

The arts and sciences faculty awards bachelor's and master's degrees; the faculty of medicine awards bachelor's and master's degrees in science, master's degrees in public health, and certificates in undergraduate nursing and basic laboratory techniques; the faculty of engineering and architecture awards bachelor's and master's degrees in engineering and bachelor's degrees in architecture; the faculty of agriculture and food sciences awards master's degrees in all departments, as well as doctorates in agronomy. English is the language of instruction except in courses within the department of Arabic.

Initially most of the students at the university came from elite Christian families, but the reputation of the university as the best in the Middle East soon eliminated any sectarian label. Arabs from various countries besides Lebanon have been attracted to the university. Its admissions standards and its tuition made it, and continue to make it, inaccessible to most students from lower income groups. However, the student body has become more diversified through scholarships and grants for needy students.

While the university took its Christian message seriously in the early years, to the point of dismissing a popular professor for daring to teach Darwinism, its curricula became secularized during the twentieth century—perhaps to reflect the religious diversity of the Lebanese population.

AUB's medical school has been one of its most important divisions, training generations of physicians who practice throughout the Middle East. It was, and to a degree it remains, one of the most prestigious educational institutions in the region. The American University Hospital has become known as one of the best hospitals in the Middle East. The university has benefited from a relatively large endowment and from U.S. congressional support. The liberal atmosphere of Lebanon, at least before the LEBANESE CIVIL WARS, allowed the university to attract scholars, faculty, and staff from the world's best educational institutions.

The AUB has been criticized by many thinkers and political activists, including by such alumni as Dr. George HABASH of the Popular Front for the Liberation of Palestine (PFLP), for its close American association. It was seen by some as a bastion of "cultural pluralism," especially during the 1960s and 1970s, when the university administration responded firmly to student protests. For militant student leaders, the campus was considered no more than "an espionage den" and a recruiting center for the CIA. Yet militants and moderates, secularists and fundamentalists all wanted to be admitted. A degree from AUB provided the best financial prospects; in fact, until the 1970s, it almost always guaranteed a job for its holder. Political and economic changes in Lebanon, however, decreased its value, especially when some Lebanese were able to afford to attend far more prestigious foreign universities.

The university underwent tremendous changes because of the civil war. Despite extensive damage, it continued to function, even during repeated interruptions due to intense fighting. Some of its professors were threatened or kidnapped, and its president, Malcolm Kerr, was assassinated in 1984 by unknown gunmen. Its main administrative building, College Hall, bombed in the early 1990s, has been reconstructed. The division of the city of Beirut into eastern and western zones affected the life of the campus community, which became more divided along sectarian lines. The administration authorized the opening of an off-campus program in East Beirut during the war, for those who could not reach predominantly Muslim West Beirut.

The quality and standards of the AUB have clearly declined as a result of the war. Many of the foreign nationals on the faculty have had to leave, depriving the students of some of the most qualified teachers. The flight of many Lebanese and Palestinian professors has forced the administration to accept applicants who, in previous times, would have been considered underqualified. The shortage of professors in some departments has led the administration to accept those with an M.A. as teachers, which was uncommon before the war.

The declared end of the civil war promised improvements at the university, and the restoration of peace and normalcy increased the number of professors returning from exile. The new president, Dr. Robert Haddad, formerly of Smith College, announced that his goal was bringing AUB back to its former level of excellence.

BIBLIOGRAPHY

JESSUP, HENRY. *Thirty Years in Syria and Lebanon.* N.p., n.d.

As'ad AbuKhalil

Amery, Leopold Charles   [1873–1955]

British journalist and politician.

Amery was on the editorial staff of the London *Times* from 1899 to 1909, after covering the Boer War (1899–1900). From 1911 to 1945, he was a member of the British Parliament, where he was a staunch conservative. He became first lord of the admiralty (1922–1924), then secretary of state for colonies and for dominion affairs (1924–1929). He was sympathetic to Zionism and characterized the 1929/30 Passfield white papers as in conflict with the intention of the British mandate over Palestine (1922–1948), as well as with the Balfour Declaration of 1917. The white paper had called for the control of Jewish immigration to Palestine and land transfers there.

Amery is the author of *The Empire in the New Era* (1928), *The Forward View* (1935), and *My Political Life* (1953–55).

BIBLIOGRAPHY

STEIN, KENNETH. *The Land Question in Palestine: 1917–1939.* Chapel Hill, N.C., 1984.
WILLIAMS, E.T., and HELEN M. PALMER, eds. *Dictionary of National Biography 1951–1960.* London, 1971.

Steve Tamari

Amghar

Head of the djema'a in Berber-speaking areas.

Typically the *amghar* is selected on a rotating basis from the DJEMA'A members for a perod of one year. He speaks for the *djema'a* in intercommunity matters and has such decision-making powers as setting the agricultural calendar and, among nomadic groups, determining when and where to move camp.

Thomas G. Penchoen

Amichai, Yehuda   [1924–   ]

Hebrew poet, playwright, and novelist.

Amichai, born in Würzburg, Germany, emigrated with his family to Palestine in 1936. He grew up in an Orthodox Jewish home and was educated in religious schools where he absorbed sacred texts, especially the prayer book. He served in the Jewish Brigade of the British army during World War II, in the Palmach in Israel's War of Independence, and later in the Israel Defense Forces. Amichai studied Bible and literature at the Hebrew University of Jerusalem, then taught for decades, mostly in Jerusalem schools and colleges. He received the Israel Prize for poetry in 1982.

Amichai published his first poems in the late 1940s. His first book, *Akhshav Uvayamim Ha-'aherim* (Now and in Other Days, 1955) and his retrospective collection *Shirim 1948–1962* (Poems 1948–1962) mark a major turning point in Hebrew poetry. Amichai's lyrics introduced new sensibilities, a new worldview, and new values, as well as a lower diction and style along with a whimsical irreverence toward central beliefs and texts of Judaism. His poetry was a quintessential expression of the "Generation of the State" literary revolution of Israel in the 1960s.

The individual's happiness is, for Amichai, the yardstick for all things. National, social, and religious commands are inferior to intimate human relationships; love (not God) is the only, yet fragile, shelter in a world of war. "I want to die in my bed," Amichai says, rejecting heroism and glory in one poem; he portrays God as responsible for the shortage of mercy in the world in another.

Amichai achieves his unique, hallmark diction by absorbing and reworking prosaic materials (such as colloquialisms and technical, military, or legal terms), then combining them with fragments of prayers or biblical phrases. He has rejuvenated classical Hebrew, dismembered and rebuilt idioms, as though he were juggling. His playful inventiveness is manifest in his surprising figurative, conceitlike compositions.

Love, war, father, God, childhood, time, and land—Amichai's main themes—form a pseudoautobiographical diary that, together with his blend of the modern and conventional, has contributed to his great popularity. His poetry is at once deeply personal and a universal expression of the human condition. The long lyrical epic "Travels of a Latter-Day Benjamin of Tudela" (1968) stands out for its account of specific events.

Landmark collections of the 1970s and 1980s are *Time, Great Tranquility: Questions and Answers*, and *Of Man Thou Art, and Unto Man Shalt Thou Return*. Amichai's late poetry is looser in form and less sure of its stand. The placard statements are replaced with understatement, even resignation. Metaphors are fewer but are carefully wrought, suggestive, and intertextually loaded. Experience is more intimate, yet Amichai's awareness of the role of camouflage in his poetry grows.

Although Amichai is known mainly for his poetry, his works of fiction have a significant place in modern Hebrew literature. His novel *Not of This Time, Not of This Place* (1963), with its complex structure and its protagonist's double existence, is a precursor of postmodernist works. Amichai's works have been translated into more than twenty languages.

BIBLIOGRAPHY

ABRAMSON, GLENDA. *The Writing of Yehuda Amichai.* Albany, N.Y., 1994.
AMICHAI, YEHUDA. *A Man and His Poetry.* Tr. by Barbara Harshav and Benjamin Harshav. New York, 1994.
———. *Not of This Time, Not of This Place.* Tr. by Shlomo Katz. New York, 1968.
———. *Selected Poetry.* Ed. and tr. by Chana Mitchell and Stephen Mitchell. New York, 1986.
GOLD, NILI SCHARF. *Lo Kabrosh.* 1994.

Nili Gold

Amiens, Treaty of

Treaty that brought peace to Europe under Napoléon, as signed by England and France, March 27, 1802.

The Napoleonic wars had reached a point where France and England concluded that further fighting was useless. Under the terms of the treaty, all of England's conquests were surrendered to France, but Napoléon BONAPARTE delayed the signing because he still hoped to retain Egypt, which he had invaded in 1798; after his troops there capitulated to the British, however, he agreed to return Egypt to the Ottoman Empire and Malta to the Order of the Knights of Malta. Because of the treaty, peace was also concluded between France and the Ottomans. Napoléon became consul for life of the French Empire, with the right of appointing his successor, but his interlude was brief and Napoléon hinted at the possible reconquest of Egypt.

Britain, during this period, could not abide French control of Europe under Napoléon and refused to evacuate Malta. By 1803, war had resumed. Napoléon never managed to recover his position in the eastern Mediterranean.

BIBLIOGRAPHY

LEFEBVRE, GEORGES. *Napoleon: From Tilsit to Waterloo, 1807–1815.* New York, 1969.

Jon Jucovy

Amin, Abd al-Mutallib al-

Iraqi military officer.

Abd al-Mutallib al-Amin was sent to Damascus by the Baghdad regime in April 1949 to negotiate a defense pact with Syria. As Iraqi military attaché to Damascus in 1953, he reportedly masterminded Plan X, the secret plot for an Iraqi invasion of Syria (which was never carried out).

BIBLIOGRAPHY

SEALE, PATRICK. *The Struggle for Syria: A Study of Post-War Arab Politics, 1945–1958.* London, 1958.

Charles U. Zenzie

Amin, Ahmad   [1886–1954]

Egyptian Muslim educator and writer.

Born in Cairo, son of a shaykh at al-Azhar, his early education was in *kuttabs,* at a government primary school, and then at al-Azhar. In 1907 he entered Madrasat al-Qada, a mosque school, spending four years as a student and some ten as assistant to the director, who introduced him to Western and particularly English scholarship. After a few years as a *Shari'a* judge, he joined the faculty of the Egyptian University (now University of Cairo) in 1926 and remained there until retirement in 1946. He was dean of the Faculty of Arts from 1939 to 1941. From 1914 until his death, he chaired the Committee on Authorship, Translation, and Publication (*Lajnat al-Ta'lif wa al-Tarjama wa al-Nashr*), editing its weekly literary magazine, *al-Thaqafa,* from 1939 to 1953. He was also a member of the Arabic Language Academy, founded the Popular University (later, Foundation for Popular Culture), and served as director of the Cultural Department of the Arab League. Through these and other activities, he was a prominent participant in the intellectual life of Egypt.

The best known of his writings are his eight-volume series on early Islamic cultural history, *Fajr al-Islam* (The Dawn of Islam, 1929), *Duha al-Islam* (The Forenoon of Islam, 1933–1936), and *Zuhr al-Islam* (The Noon of Islam, 1945–1955), the first ef-

fort by an Arab Muslim writer to make use of Western scholarship in writing this history. He wrote over 600 articles on almost every conceivable topic except party politics for periodicals such as *al-Thaqafa, al-Risala* and *al-Hilal;* most of these were republished in ten volumes of *Fayd al-Khatir* (Overflowing Thoughts, 1938–1955) or in *Zu'ama al-Islah fi 'l-'Asr al-Hadith* (Leaders of Reform in the Modern Age, 1948). He collaborated in editing a number of classical Islamic texts and authored or co-authored books for schools and books on Western philosophy and literature. Other writings include *Yawm al-Islam* (The Day of Islam, 1952), *al-Sharq wa al-Gharb* (The East and the West, 1955), and his autobiography, *Hayati* (My Life, 1950, 1952).

He held opinions close to the secularist ones for which Ali ABD AL-RAZIQ and Taha HUSAYN were criticized but stated them more cautiously; he was particularly known for questioning the authenticity of the *hadith* (legends and traditions surrounding the Prophet Muhammad). He wanted his compatriots to learn from the West but at the same time affirm their own Arab–Islamic cultural personality. Thus, much of his work seeks to present the treasures of Islamic civilization to his readers. His series on Islamic cultural history uses Western scholarship to help make that history accessible to modern Muslims, while, by stressing the contribution of non-Muslim cultures to early Islamic culture, the series conveys the message that Muslims today can also learn from non-Muslims. Other writings also give a positive presentation of Western ideas and ways, although his criticism of Western colonialism and materialism could be harsh and angry, especially in some of his last writings.

BIBLIOGRAPHY

AMIN, AHMAD. *My Life.* Tr. by Issa J. Boullata. 1978.
SHEPARD, WILLIAM. *The Faith of a Modern Muslim Intellectual.* New Delhi, 1983.

William Shepard

Amin, Hafizullah   [1929–1979]

Prime minister and president of Afghanistan, 1979.

Hafizullah Amin was born in the Afghan province of Paghman near Kabul in a Gilzai Pushtun family, the youngest son of seven children. His father was a low-ranking civil servant, and Amin attended the local village school. He continued his education as a boarder at the Dar al-Mo'allamin Teachers Training

High School in Kabul and, after graduation, became a schoolteacher. His extensive connections with the United States included receiving a master's degree from the University of Wisconsin and serving as the cultural officer at the Embassy of the Royal Government of Afghanistan in Washington, D.C., from 1952 to 1953. He also worked for the United States Agency for International Development in Kabul from 1955 to 1958 and was a U.S. embassy translator in Kabul from May 1962 to September 1963. He was expelled from the United States in 1965 for his political activities among Afghan students while he was working on a doctorate at Teachers College, Columbia University.

Amin was a well-known teacher in Kabul and became active in leftist politics during the period of constitutional reforms by Zahir Shah (1963–1973). Amin was one of the founding members of the PEOPLE'S DEMOCRATIC PARTY OF AFGHANISTAN (PDPA), a Marxist organization with strong Leninist leanings that was founded in 1965. In 1967, the PDPA split into rival factions over issues of personality and ideology. Amin became a leader of the Khalq, or people's faction of the PDPA, which had strong Pushtun and rural ties.

When the PDPA gained control of Afghanistan in the Saur Revolution in April 1978, Taraki became president and prime minister and Amin became foreign minister and deputy prime minister. Amin subsequently became prime minister in March 1979 and, after a power struggle with Taraki, became president in September of the same year. As president, Amin inherited a government that was near collapse after the Marxist reforms instigated by the PDPA had led to massive revolt in the countryside. Amin sought to bring the revolt under control by imposing increasingly harsh measures that included arresting thousands of people and imposing conscription for military service.

Amin also sought to develop a foreign policy that would move Afghanistan away from dependence upon the Soviet Union. He was unsuccessful, and on December 23 and 24, 1979, a large Soviet military contingent occupied Kabul. Amin and his family were killed in a barrage of gunfire in the Tapi Tajbek Palace, where they had taken refuge on December 27, 1979.

Opinion is divided on Amin's place in history. Some see him as a Soviet puppet who was responsible for numerous killings—including the killing of Adolph Dubs, the U.S. Ambassador to Kabul—and who was ultimately responsible for the Soviet invasion that ironically led to his own death. Others liken him to Abd al-Rahman and consider him an Afghan nationalist with strong American sympathies who tried to steer Afghanistan away from its close reliance on the Soviet Union. His reign, either way it is viewed, was short and tragic.

BIBLIOGRAPHY

ARNOLD, ANTHONY. *Afghanistan's Two-Party Communism: Parcham and Khalq.* Stanford, Calif., 1983.
MALE, BEVERLEY. *Revolutionary Afghanistan.* New York, 1982.

Grant Farr

Amin, Qasim [1865–1908]

One of the first modern Arab writers to treat women's issues.

Qasim (also Kassim) Amin was the son of Muhammad Bey Amin Khan, an official of the Ottoman Empire who at one point served as governor of Kurdistan. When Kurdistan revolted, the sultan retired him with a land grant near Damanhur in Egypt. Qasim's father married into the family of Ahmad Bey Khattab and became a brigadier in the military of Isma'il Khedive in Egypt. Qasim was born in Alexandria, and he attended the aristocratic primary school in Ra's al-Tin. The family then moved to Cairo, where Qasim studied French in the Khedivial primary school. In 1881, he received a bachelor's degree from the School of Law and Administration. From 1881 to 1885 he studied law in Montpelier, France; he then began a career in the Egyptian judicial system.

In 1894, he married a daughter of the Turkish admiral Amin Tawfiq, who had been raised by an English nanny. Thus, his own daughters were given European nannies. Amin's first book on women's issues, *Les Égyptiens,* published in 1894, defended the treatment of women by Islam in the Middle East. He reversed himself in 1899 with *Tahrir al-Mar'a* (Liberation of Women), coauthored with Muhammad ABDUH and Ahmad Lutfi al-SAYYID. This tract was rooted in Islam, but it argued for a reform of women's position. In a third book, *Al-Mar'a al-Jadida* (The New Woman), Amin advanced an even more liberal, social Darwinist argument, jettisoning many of its Islamic arguments.

BIBLIOGRAPHY

AHMED, LEILA. *Women and Gender in Islam: Historical Roots of a Modern Debate.* New Haven, Conn., 1992.

Juan R. I. Cole

Amin al-Dowleh, Mirza Ali Khan

[1844–1904]

One of the most influential statesmen of the Qajar Dynasty.

Born in Tehran (Persia) to an important court official, Mirza Ali Khan was a proponent of Westernization and modern education and an opponent of the *ulama* (Islamic clergy). He is regarded as a reformer who tried to centralize revenue collection and cut expenditures. He held a succession of high posts under the QAJAR DYNASTY, under NASER AL-DIN SHAH, serving for twenty years as his private secretary. He enriched himself by managing the mint and the postal system. His arch-rival was Al-Asghar AMIN AL-SOLTAN.

In 1880, the shah granted him the title Amin al-Dowleh (Trusted of the State). In 1897, MOZAFFAR AL-DIN QAJAR named him prime minister. To alleviate the fiscal crisis, he encouraged the shah to contract foreign loans, a disastrous policy that contributed to the downfall of the dynasty. After failing to obtain a large loan from the British-owned Imperial Bank of Persia, to which he had promised significant concessions, including control of the southern customs, rivals at court helped to engineer his dismissal from office on June 5, 1898. Amin al-Dowleh, although noted for his personal pessimism over the country's prospects for reform, was later (especially during Iran's Constitutional Revolution) admired for his progressive policies.

BIBLIOGRAPHY

FARMAYAN, HAFEZ. "Portrait of a Nineteenth-Century Iranian Statesman: The Life and Times of Grand Vizier Amin ud-Dawlah, 1844–1904." *International Journal of Middle East Studies* 15 (1983): 337–351.

Lawrence G. Potter

Amin al-Dowleh, Mohammad Husayn

[?–1823]

Governor of Isfahan under Agha Mohammad Khan Qajar and prime minister of Persia under Fath Ali Shah.

Born in Isfahan, Persia, Hajji Mohammad Husayn Khan was originally an illiterate hay-seller, who, by dint of his abilities, was promoted from headman of a quarter of the city, to mayor of the city, and to tax collector of a nearby district. He eventually became governor of Isfahan. He worked closely with Isfahan's merchants to promote the city's commerce and became one of the richest men in Persia. In 1806, he became minister of finance and, from 1819 to 1823, served as prime minister under FATH ALI SHAH QAJAR.

BIBLIOGRAPHY

MORIER, JAMES J. *A Second Journey through Persia, Armenia and Asia Minor to Constantinople.* London, 1818.

Lawrence G. Potter

Amin al-Soltan, Ali-Asghar   [1858–1907]

One of the most influential politicians of late nineteenth-century Persia and prime minister to three Qajar shahs.

Ali-Asghar was notorious for surrendering Persian sovereignty to foreign interests in order to raise money for the king (shah). His father was reportedly a slave boy of Christian Circassian origin who rose from a lowly position in the shah's household to become his most trusted adviser. Upon his father's death in 1883, Ali-Asghar inherited his title, *amin al-soltan* (Trusted of the Sovereign), and many of his duties.

During his first period in power, until 1896, he was regarded as pro-British. He supported the granting of a monopoly on Iran's tobacco crop to a British subject (1890), a key event in Persian history that led to mass protests and the cancellation of the concession. He retained the confidence of the king and his own power, however, and was able to maintain order in Tehran after the assassination of NASER AL-DIN SHAH in 1896. He was briefly replaced by his arch-rival Mirza Ali Khan AMIN AL-DOWLEH, after which he enjoyed a second period as prime minister (1898–1903). During this time he was regarded as pro-Russian, having secured two large loans with conditions compromising his country's sovereignty. In 1900, he was granted the exceptional title, Atabak-e A'zam.

Before being forced to resign, he was supposedly excommunicated by the Shi'ite *ulama* (Islamic clergy) living in Iraq. Following a world tour, he returned in 1907 to head briefly a new government under Mohammad Ali Shah. The details of his assassination are still disputed.

BIBLIOGRAPHY

CALMARD, J. "Atabak-e A'zam," *Encyclopaedia Iranica* II.
KEDDIE, NIKKI R. "The Assassination of the Amin as-Sultan (Atabak-i A'zam), 31 August 1907." In *Iran and Islam,* ed. by C. E. Bosworth. Edinburgh, 1971.

Lawrence G. Potter

Amin al-Zarb, Mohammad Hasan
[1837–1898]

Custodian of the state mint under Shah Naser al-Din and the most prominent entrepreneur in late nineteenth-century Persia.

Born in Isfahan, Persia, to a family of modest traders, Mohammad Hasan had only an elementary education. He moved to Tehran in the 1860s and within two decades had achieved great success as a banker and as a leading trader with Western Europe.

In 1879, as master of the mint for the QAJAR DYNASTY, he instituted currency reforms. In the 1880s and 1890s, he was widely, and probably erroneously, believed to have enriched himself while debasing the Persian currency. After a rapid drop in the value of copper coinage used in local transactions, he was arrested in 1896, imprisoned, and given a large fine. He later regained government favor. Mohammad Hasan was an advocate of reform and was closely associated with Ali-Asghar AMIN AL-SOLTAN.

BIBLIOGRAPHY

AMIN AL-ZARB II, HAJ MUHAMMAD HUSAYN. "Memento of a Life." *Iran* 30 (1992): 107-121.
ENAYAT, A. "Amin (-e Dar)-al-Zarb." *Encyclopaedia Iranica* I.

Lawrence G. Potter

Amin Bey, al-

Head of the Husaynid beylicate of Tunisia, 1943–1957.

Al-Amin assumed power following the ouster by the Free French of Tayyib Brahim Munsif Bey. In 1942, Munsif Bey had acceded to power but was removed because of his nationalist stance against French control of Tunisia. Al-Amin, in his early sixties at the time of his accession, proved unable to rally nationalist support for the beylicate and to resist French demands on his government. The Neo-Destour movement headed by Habib BOURGUIBA and Salah ibn YUSUF dominated the movement for nationalism from that point forward. Following Tunisia's independence in March 1956 and the election of a constituent assembly, the beylicate was abolished. Al-Amin was formally deposed in August 1957.

BIBLIOGRAPHY

ABUN-NASR, JAMIL. *A History of the Maghrib.* Cambridge, U.K., 1976.
PERKINS, KENNETH. *Tunisia.* Boulder, Colo., 1986.

Matthew S. Gordon

Amini, Abu al-Qasem   [1910–   ]

Iranian minister of court, 1951–1953.

Brother of Ali Amini, Abu al-Qasem Amini was born to a traditional landowning Iranian family. After completing his education in France and returning to Iran, he founded the *Omid* magazine in 1942. During the critical years of Mohammad MOSSADEGH's premiership (1951–1953), Amini was made minister of court, but he fell from the shah's favor afterward and left the country.

BIBLIOGRAPHY

ECHO OF IRAN. *Iran Who's Who.* Tehran, 1972.

Neguin Yavari

Amini, Ali   [1905–1991]

Iranian statesman of the Pahlavi period.

Ali Amini was born in 1905 to Qajar aristocracy. His father was Amin al-Dowleh, prime minister in the Qajar period, and his mother was Fakhr al-Dowleh, daughter of Qajar monarch Mozaffar al-Din Shah. After being educated in France, Ali Amini returned to Iran and entered government service. By 1947, he was a member of the Iranian parliament and was known as a pro-American liberal. The shah, Mohammad Reza Pahlavi, distrusted Amini primarily because of the latter's support for a limited constitutional monarchy. In 1950, after the nationalization of Iranian oil, Mohammad MOSSADEGH, the premier, appointed Amini minister of finance, but he was dismissed in 1952. He was reinstalled as minister of finance in the cabinet of Gen. Fazlollah Zahedi, following the CIA-engineered coup against the government of Mossadegh. Amini was the main Iranian statesman to negotiate the Consortium Oil Agreement of 1954, whose signatories were made up of a number of foreign oil companies (several American companies with 40 percent of the shares, several British ones with another 40 percent, and a host of French and Dutch companies with the remaining 20 percent). According to the agreement, the companies would produce and market Iranian oil for twenty-five years, and the Iranian government would receive 50 percent of the proceeds. The agreement in effect annulled the nationalization of Iranian oil achieved under Mossadegh. In 1961, faced with popular unrest over the state of the economy and lack of political freedom, the shah reluctantly appointed Amini prime minister. In 1962, Amini was forced to resign because of the shah's refusal to curtail military expenditures in the national budget. As manifested in the tenets of the WHITE REVOLUTION of 1963 (renamed the Revolution of the Shah and the People after 1967), the shah appropriated Amini's pro-American, liberal, and land-reform policies. While not silent during the 1979 Islamic Revolution, Amini did not assume a prominent position in it. He left Iran shortly thereafter and died in Paris in 1991.

BIBLIOGRAPHY

KATOUZIAN, HOMA. *The Political Economy of Modern Iran, 1926–1979.* New York, 1981.

ZONIS, MARVIN. *The Political Elite of Iran.* Princeton, N.J., 1971.

Neguin Yavari

Amir

Honorific title.

Amir (or emir), from the Arabic verb for "command," is obtained by appointment or heredity, and denotes leadership, dominion, or command over a territory, army, justice, or faith. In general, the title bespeaks primacy or firstness in social or political positions. Common variations are *Amir al-Umara* (first Amir), *Amir al-Mu'minin* (leader and first in faith), *Amir-Dad* (first of justice).

Cyrus Moshaver

Amir, Abd al-Hakim   [1919–1967]

Egypt's minister of war, 1954–1967.

Gen. Abd al-Hakim Amir played a role in securing military support for Gamal Abdel NASSER as president of Egypt. He graduated from the military academy in 1938 and served in the Arab–Israel War of 1948. In 1964 he was appointed first vice president of Egypt but resigned after the Arab defeat in the Arab–Israel War of 1967. On 14 September 1967 Amir committed suicide after being arrested for allegedly plotting a military coup against President Nasser.

Karen A. Thornsvard

Amir, Eli   [1937–   ]

Israeli writer and civil servant.

Eli Amir was born in Baghdad and immigrated to Israel in 1950 at the age of twelve. As part of the systematic absorption process of the great immigration waves of the 1950s, Amir was separated from his family and sent to be educated on a kibbutz. He later studied the Arab language and literature and the history of the Middle East at the Hebrew University of Jerusalem. Following his studies he joined the Israeli civil service and served in various immigration absorption and educational capacities.

In 1984 Amir published his first novel, *Scapegoat.* Loosely based on his own life, the novel tells the bittersweet story of an Iraqi immigrant boy who is torn between the world he knew and loved in the old country and the new one he must adopt. The novel describes the clash between two different Jewish cultures—European and Middle Eastern—through the eyes of an innocent adolescent. Amir's novel brought back into national consciousness one of the most painful social conflicts in Israel's short history: an internal conflict that marked the beginning of the momentous social and cultural changes that shape Israeli society to this day. *Scapegoat* was an immediate success and established Amir as a promising writer and a keen critic of Israeli society.

Amir's second novel, *Farewell Baghdad,* is about the Jewish community in Baghdad on the eve of its mass immigration to Israel in the 1950s.

BIBLIOGRAPHY

SHAKED, GERSHON, ed. *Hebrew Writers: A General Directory,* Institute for the Translation of Hebrew Literature, 1993. In Hebrew.

Yarom Peleg

Amir-Entezam, Abbas   [1933–   ]

Iranian political activist.

Abbas Amir-Entezam graduated from Tehran University's Faculty of Engineering in 1955. He earned his master's degree from the University of California at Berkeley in 1966. As a student, he was active in the National Resistance Movement of Iran, formed after the nationalization of Iranian oil and the subsequent coup d'état against the premiership of Mohammad MOSSADEGH in 1953. While in the United States, he joined the Muslim Student Association and the Confederation of Iranian Students. Amir-Entezam, later became deputy to Prime Minister Bazargan in 1979, and one of the founding members of the Liberation Movement of Iran. Based on documents seized from the American Embassy in Tehran in November 1979, he was recalled as ambassador to Scandinavia, and arrested as a CIA spy. Amir-Entezam remains in prison.

BIBLIOGRAPHY

CHEHABI, HOUSHANG E. *Iranian Politics and Religious Modernism*. Ithaca, N.Y., 1990.

Neguin Yavari

Amir Kabir, Mirza Taqi Khan
[1807–1852]

Prime minister and the most famous reformer of nineteenth-century Persia.

Born the son of a cook in the Farahan district in western Persia, Mirza Taqi Khan joined the staff of the crown prince, ABBAS MIRZA, at Tabriz. He later held several positions in the army of Azerbaijan. In 1848, he accompanied NASER AL-DIN to Tehran upon his accession, and the new Shah of Persia's Qajar dynasty gave him the the titles *amir-e kabir* (the great amir) and *atabak-e a'zam,* which referred to his function as the shah's tutor (who was then only sixteen years old).

Before he went to Tehran, Mirza Taqi Khan had participated in several diplomatic missions to Russia and the Ottoman Empire, and he sought to institute in Persia some reforms he had observed abroad. One key to reform, he believed, was reducing the power of the *ulama* (Islamic clergy). Amir Kabir suppressed the Babi insurrection, a major challenge to central authority, and executed Sayyed Ali Mohammad, the BAB, in 1850.

During his four years as prime minister, Amir Kabir instituted numerous administrative and economic reforms and built up-to-date factories, often with the aim of strengthening the military. He was also active in building public works throughout the country. Particularly significant was his founding of Iran's first technical school, the DAR AL-FONUN (Abode of Sciences). In foreign affairs, he sought to avoid dependence on either of the predominant outside powers, England or Russia.

Amir Kabir made many enemies at court and alienated others because of his haughty manner and successful measures to extract revenue. Ultimately the shah turned against him, dismissed him from office in November 1851, and subsequently had him assassinated. By the twentieth century, Amir Kabir had become an idealized figure, regarded as the most enlightened statesman of his time who was regrettably prevented from modernizing the country. Modern critical scholars (Abbas Amanat, Hamid Algar, John Lorentz), however, regard his goal as improving the system to increase the power of the shah, not ushering in democratic government.

BIBLIOGRAPHY

AMANAT, ABBAS. "The Downfall of Mirza Taqi Khan Amir Kabir and the Problem of Ministerial Authority in Qajar Iran." *International Journal of Middle East Studies* 23 (1991): 577–599.
LORENTZ, JOHN H. "Iran's Great Reformer of the Nineteenth Century: An Analysis of Amir Kabir's Reforms." *Iranian Studies* 4 (1971): 85–103.

Lawrence G. Potter

Amir Kabir Publishers

Iranian commercial publishing company.

The Amir Kabir Publishing House, one of Iran's oldest and most prestigious commercial publishers, was founded in 1949 by Abd al-Rahim Ja'fari. Amir Kabir began by publishing translations from the famous French series, *Que Sais-Je?,* translations of Thomas Mann, Ernest Hemingway, and Pierre Rousseau's *History of Science.*

Amir Kabir was, in addition, one of the first Iranian houses to publish books exclusively for children. Amir Kabir was nationalized after the Islamic Revolution of 1979, and continues its activities today.

BIBLIOGRAPHY

"Amir Kabir and Abdolrahim Jafari: Interview with the Founder of Amir Kabir Publishing House." *Goftogu* 7, (Spring 1955) 65–79.

Neguin Yavari

Amis du Manifeste et de la Liberte

Algerian nationalist organization (usually called AML), 1944–1945 (in English, Friends of the Manifesto and of Liberty).

The AML represented a remarkable synthesis of Algerian groups dedicated to nationalism—moderates, followers of Messali HADJ (Messalists), and the *ulama* (Islamic scholars). It was chiefly organized by Ferhat ABBAS, a moderate nationalist who was increasingly pessimistic over the prospects of genuine colonial reform; he had authored the "Manifesto of the Algerian Muslim People" in February of 1943. Messali Hadj, the most radical nationalist, was recognized as the AML's titular head. In addition, the ASSOCIATION OF ALGERIAN MUSLIM ULAMA (or Reformist Ulama) supported the new nationalist front. The AML was blamed for the violence of the SETIF

REVOLT in May 1945. Its fragile unity, fissured before this tragedy, fractured afterward as the nationalists resumed their separate paths toward independence.

BIBLIOGRAPHY

AGERON, CHARLES-ROBERT. *Histoire de l'Algérie contemporaine: De l'insurrection de 1871 au déclenchement de la guerre de libération (1954)*. Paris, 1979.

Phillip C. Naylor

Amit, Meir   [1921–   ]

Israeli business executive, former member of the Knesset, and military commander.

Throughout the 1950s Amit Meir held high command posts in Israel's military, including commander of the Golani Brigade (1950), head of the Instruction Command (1951), head of operations on the General Staff (1951, 1956), commander of the Southern Command (1955), and commander of the Northern Command (1958). In 1959 he attended Columbia University's School of Business. He returned to Israel in 1963 to become head of the MOSSAD, a position he held until 1968. Amit then moved to industry, serving as managing director of the Histradrut's Koor industries until 1977. He was a founding member of the Democratic Movement for Change, a centrist party advocating electoral reform. He served briefly as minister of transportation in the first Begin government, then left in 1978 to form Shinui, another centrist liberal party. Since 1978 he has held senior managerial positions in various high-technology firms.

Martin Malin

Amman

Capital and largest city of Jordan.

Amman enjoys a special position in JORDAN because of its size and population composition, as well as its importance as the capital and the center of communication, commerce, banking, industry, and cultural life. Unlike the ancient capitals of other Arab countries, Amman is a relatively new city. Before 1875, what is now Amman consisted solely of the site of the long-forgotten biblical town of Rabbath Ammon; that later became the prosperous Roman city of Philadelphia, of which significant ruins, including an amphitheater, remain. Encouraged by the Ottoman Empire, the CIRCASSIANS started settling the area in the 1870s, and the Circassian village of Amman de-

Roman amphitheater at Amman, Jordan. (Richard Bulliet)

veloped with a minor reputation as a commercial center. In 1905, this role was considerably augmented by the construction of the Hijaz railroad, which reached the vicinity of the village, three miles (5 km) distant. This major communications link connected Amman with Damascus, Constantinople (Istanbul) and eventually the Hijaz—the western Arabian peninsula of Mecca and Medina. The official role of the budding town of Amman was established in 1921, when Emir ABDULLAH IBN HUSAYN, the head of the newly formed Hashimite Emirate (princedom) of Transjordan, made it his residence and his capital.

Although the departments and institutions of government were centered in Amman, its population growth was slow. It reached only about 20,000 in the early 1940s. After 1948, the establishment of the State of Israel and the influx of Palestinians caused the town to experience very rapid growth: 108,000 in 1952; 848,587 in 1979; and well over 1 million in 1992 if the greater Amman urban region is included. While the impetus and sustaining cause for this population growth was the arrival of the Palestinians, refugees and nonrefugees alike, it was also increased by rural-to-urban migration and a rising birth rate. (See REFUGEES, PALESTINIAN)

By the early 1990s, Amman possessed a well-developed infrastructure. From an original small town built on precipitous hills, called *jabals,* it has now spread to rolling plains in all directions from the city center. Throughout are found the royal palace, parliament, the courts, ministerial and government offices and institutions, numerous parks, sports facilities, schools, hospitals, colleges, and a major university (the UNIVERSITY OF JORDAN). Banking and commerce are a vibrant part of the city, including a stock exchange and the Amman central vegetable market, which sells as far afield as the United Arab Emirates and Iraq. Amman is served by a major international airport, a railroad, and major trunk roads to all parts of the nation and to neighboring countries. Radio has long been present; television was introduced in the late 1960s. Newspaper, magazine, and book publishing is part of the political and cultural life. Since the 1970s, with the increase in hotels and meeting facilities, Amman has become a much frequented center for both regional and international conferences.

BIBLIOGRAPHY

GUBSER, PETER. *Jordan: Crossroads of Middle Eastern Events.* Boulder, Colo., 1983.
HACKER, JAMES M. *Modern Amman.* Durham, England, 1960.

Peter Gubser

Amman Summit

Arab meeting precipitated by onset of Iran–Iraq War.

The Arab Summit of November 1980, hosted by Jordan in Amman, was boycotted by a Syrian-led bloc that included Libya, the Palestine Liberation Organization (PLO), Lebanon, Algeria, and South Yemen. The summit was convened about two months after the start of the IRAN–IRAQ WAR, with Jordan having thrown its support behind Iraq, while Syria and Libya supported Iran. This division reflected the growing hostility between Jordan and Syria that developed when Hafiz al-ASAD accused Jordan of abetting Muslim Brotherhood militancy in Syria.

BIBLIOGRAPHY

GUBSER, PETER. *Jordan: Crossroads of Middle Eastern Events.* Boulder, Colo., 1983.

Jenab Tutunji

Ammun, Dawud

Lebanese writer and politician.

Ammun was the son of the first Maronite member of the Administrative Council, which according to the Order of 1861 was assigned to run the domestic affairs of Lebanon under the authority of the Istanbul-appointed *mutasarrif.* Dawud (also Daud) was a member of the last elected Administrative Council, which was dissolved by CEMAL PAÇA in 1915. His loyalty to France did not further his political career because France favored his bitter rival, Habib al-SAAD who served as president before independence. Ammun founded the Democratic Union party in 1925. His presidential aspirations were never fulfilled.

BIBLIOGRAPHY

MURQUS, MICHEL. "Al-Jumhuriyyah qabla An Tanhar" (The Republic before It Collapsed). *Al-Nahar* (n.d.).

As'ad AbuKhalil

Amri, Hasan al-

North Yemen soldier.

This Yemen Arab Republic army officer, despite his long, close association with President Abdullah al-Sallal, managed to sidestep al-Sallal's overthrow in 1967. He became the military strongman during the first four years of the regime of President Abd al-Rahman al-Iryani, serving as either or both commander in chief and prime minister. Volatile, if not unstable, al-Amri was forced into permanent exile by al-Iryani over a bizarre shooting incident in 1971. His reputation rested mainly on his military leadership in the field during the YEMEN CIVIL WAR and especially during the siege of San'a in 1968. In 1936, along with al-Sallal, he had been in the first group of thirteen boys sent abroad by the imam for training.

Robert D. Burrowes

Amrouche, Jean   [1906–1962]

Algerian poet and essayist.

Amrouche's parents were Kabyle Christian converts. Though assimilated into French culture, Amrouche was deeply drawn by his native roots as he reflected: "France is the spirit of my soul, Algeria is the soul of my spirit." Among his poetic works are *Cendres* (1934) and *Etoile secrète* (1937); *L'éternel Jugurtha* (1943) is his renowned essay. He significantly influenced the Generation of 1954 writers (i.e., Mohammed DIB, Kateb YACINE, Malek HADDAD, Moulaoud MAMMERI, Mouloud FERAOUN). During the war of independence, Amrouche attempted to serve as an intermediary between Ferhat Abbas and

Charles de Gaulle. Taos (Marie-Louise) Amrouche (1913–1976), another prominent Algerian literary figure, was his sister.

BIBLIOGRAPHY

DÉJEUX, JEAN. *La littérature algérienne contemporaine.* Paris, 1975.

Phillip C. Naylor

Amu Darya

Afghan river.

The Amu Darya, also known in the past as the Oxus River, forms the principal boundary between Afghanistan and the Tajik and Uzbek republics, a distance of about 680 miles (1,094 km). The Amu Darya begins in the Pamir mountains, runs a total distance of about 1,500 miles (2,414 km), and eventually empties into the Aral Sea.

BIBLIOGRAPHY

DUPREE, LOUIS. *Afghanistan.* Princeton, N.J., 1980.

Grant Farr

Amuzegar, Jahangir   [1920–   ]

Iranian economist.

Amuzegar earned a doctorate degree from the University of California at Los Angeles. He held various high positions in the government of Iran including minister of commerce (1961–1962), minister of finance (1962), and chairman of the high council of the National Iranian Oil Company (1962). He also served as executive director of the International Monetary Fund (1973–1980).

Farhad Shirzad

Amuzegar, Jamshid

Iranian statesman, prime minister 1977–1978.

Amuzegar held various ministerial portfolios in Iran including labor, agriculture, health, treasury, state and representative to OPEC (Organization of Petroleum Exporting Countries). After Iran's economic downturn, he was chosen to replace Amir Abbas HOVEYDA as prime minister.

Farhad Shirzad

Anatolia

The Asian region of Turkey, called Anadolu in Turkish.

When the Byzantine Empire reorganized Asia Minor, about 650 C.E., they named it Phrygia Anatolicon for the legion stationed there, and the name now refers to the entire peninsula.

Crustal deformation following the collision of the Afro-Arabian tectonic plate with the Eurasian plate (c. 10 million years ago) created a peninsula with east–west faults demarcating parallel ranges and valleys. The continuing pressure of the collision causes fault slippage and frequent earthquakes. Associated vulcanism has built mountains (Mountain Ararat, Erciyes Daği) and produced numerous hot springs. One ridge forms the Kocaeli peninsula opposite Istanbul and the other ridges the mountain ranges of western Anatolia. Spaces between the ridges form fertile valleys and coves that provide good harbors. The sides of the peninsula are edged with high mountains—the Pontic in the north and the TAURUS MOUNTAINS in the south; they generally lack harbors, making the interior accessible only from the west and east, from where invasions have come historically.

The climate is varied—warm enough on the sheltered south coast to grow bananas near Anamur; cold enough for glaciers on Ararat. Summers in the southeast are hot, with temperatures of 114°F (46°C). The northeast interior is very cold, with winter temperatures falling below −60°F (−40°C). Southern and western Anatolia are Mediterranean, with hot dry summers and cool wet winters. The north coast has cooler moister winters and significant rainfall in summer. The driest regions are the southeast and the interior basin east of Konya, where precipitation averages thirteen inches (32.6 cm) per year. Rize on

Steppe in central Anatolia, 1939. (D.W. Lockhard)

Central Anatolia in the 1950s. (D.W. Lockhard)

the Black Sea is the wettest, with rainfall of some ninety inches (232 cm) per year.

Anatolia has been inhabited since the Paleolithic, and archaeological sites for the Mesolithic and Neolithic indicate the change in social order from hunting to collecting to settled farm communities—such as at Çatal Höyük and Hacılar—two of the earliest (8,000 B.C.E.) large Neolithic sites. Anatolian Hittite and Luvian are the oldest Indo-European languages yet discovered. The Hittite Empire flourished from 1800 to 1200 B.C.E., followed by the Phrygians and Lydians, the Persians (546 B.C.E.), the Macedonians (332 B.C.E.), succeeded by the Romans (133 B.C.E.) and Byzantines. By 500 C.E., Anatolia was Greek speaking and Christian. The Turks arrived from Central Asia about 1060, occupied Anatolia after victory at Malazgırt (Manzikert) in 1071, and gradually Anatolia became Muslim and Turkish. The OTTOMAN EMPIRE was founded in northwest Anatolia (c. 1300), but in 1453, Istanbul became the capital, making Anatolia a rural backwater.

Countryside of eastern Anatolia between Sivas and Erzurum. (Richard Bulliet)

After 1860, this changed, with railroad construction and European interest in Anatolia's resources. After the Ottoman Turks became allies of the Central powers in World War I, and lost, the empire was dismembered; Turkish nationalists under Mustafa Kemal (Atatürk) established their capital at Ankara in 1923. They started developing the interior of the new Republic of Turkey and, today, Anatolia produces coal in Zonguldak, iron ore in Divriği, chromium in the Muğla region, and copper in the southeast. The southeast also has some oil and abundant hydropower, mainly from the EUPHRATES river; it also produces citrus, cotton, olives, tobacco, grains, livestock, corn, and trees.

Of Anatolia's peoples, 82 percent speak Turkish, 15 percent Kurdish, and 3 percent Arabic; Greeks, Armenians, and Jews, once numerous, are now almost gone. About 80 percent of Anatolians are Sunni Muslim; most of the rest are Shi'ites (Alevi), who live within a triangle bounded by Amasya, Adıyaman, and Erzurum.

BIBLIOGRAPHY

NYROP, RICHARD F. *Turkey: A Country Study.* Washington, D.C., 1980.

John R. Clark

Anaza Tribe

Considered the most prestigious of Arabian tribes.

Members of this sharif Anaza tribe include the ruling families of Saudi Arabia (AL SA'UD), Kuwait (Al Sabah), and Bahrain (Al KHALIFA). Sections live in Najd, Iraq, and Syria. In the early twentieth century, the tribe, whose ruling members have been settled for generations, was the wealthiest and militarily the strongest of all tribal confederations. Currently many Anaza tribal members are among the most wealthy of the urban elite and hold important government positions.

Eleanor Abdella Doumato

Anderson, Terry   [1947–   ]

American journalist held hostage in Beirut, Lebanon, by the Islamic Jihad for almost seven years, longer than any other hostage.

Anderson was an Associated Press correspondent when he was taken hostage in Beirut, Lebanon, on March 16, 1985, by the Islamic Jihad—a group of militant Shi'ites. His capture followed the veto by the United States of a United Nations resolution condemning Israel's raids in southern Lebanon. Anderson spent the next 2,455 days in captivity, longer than any other hostage. In time, he became the most well-known of the American hostages, both because of the length of his captivity and because of the efforts of his sister, Peggy Say, to publicize his case. Throughout 1991, UN Secretary General Javier Pérez de Cuéllar negotiated for the release of hostages held in Beirut; at the end of the year his efforts bore fruit. On December 4, 1991, Terry Anderson was released.

BIBLIOGRAPHY

Time, December 16, 1991.

Zachary Karabell

Andranik, Ozanian   [1865–1927]

Leading figure in the Armenian resistance against Ottoman rule.

Ozanian Andranik is popularly known as General Andranik (Andranik Zoravar in Armenian). He was born in Shabin Karahisar in central Anatolia. He received only an elementary education and was trained as a carpenter. He became involved in revolutionary activities in 1888 and joined the DASHNAK PARTY (ARF) in 1892. Soon after, he emerged as the leader of a band of guerrilla fighters involved in the defense of Armenian villages in the region of Sasun and Moush during the 1895–1896 mass killings instituted against the Armenians in the Ottoman Empire. He gained legendary stature among provincial Armenians after breaking out of the Arakelots Monastery in the Moush area, in which he had been trapped by Turkish troops. Andranik retreated with his men into Iran, resigned from the ARF, and thereafter traveled to Europe, where he participated in the First Balkan War in 1912 at the head of a small group of Armenian volunteers fighting in the Bulgarian army.

With the outbreak of World War I, Andranik went to Transcaucasia and took command of a contingent of Armenian volunteers supporting the Russian army in the campaigns against the Ottomans. He was promoted to the rank of major general, and eventually placed in charge of a division consisting of Armenians, who were left to defend the front as the Russian army disintegrated in the wake of the Bolshevik Revolution. Forced to retreat against superior Ottoman forces, Andranik had a falling-out with the political leadership of the just-founded Republic of Armenia for submitting to Ottoman terms in the Treaty of Batum signed on June 4, 1918. Resigning his command, Andranik formed a new brigade consisting of Western Armenians. He took refuge in the Zangezur district of Eastern Armenia, where he continued fighting against local Muslim forces, and was about to march to relieve the Armenians of Karabagh when a telegram from General Thomson, the British commander in Baku, informed him of the end of the war and ordered him to cease hostilities. The moment proved fateful, as the British commander subsequently decided to place Karabagh under Azerbaijani jurisdiction. Forced by the British to disband his forces, Andranik left Transcaucasia in 1919 and traveled to Europe to plead the cause of the Western Armenians dispersed by the Ottomans. He eventually settled in the Armenian community of Fresno, Calif., where he spent his remaining years. Communist authorities in Armenia denied his remains entry while in transit; thus he was buried at Père Lachaise cemetery in Paris.

BIBLIOGRAPHY

HOVANNISIAN, RICHARD. *Armenia on the Road to Independence, 1918.* Berkeley, Calif., 1967.
WALKER, CHRISTOPHER J. *Armenia: The Survival of a Nation.* New York, 1980.

Rouben P. Adalian

Andrássy, Julius   [1823–1890]

Foreign minister of the Austro-Hungarian Empire, 1871–1879.

On December 30, 1875, Julius Andrássy sent to Europe's great powers a copy of a note that he had directed to the Ottoman court. He enlisted their diplomatic support. Although the Ottoman Turks accepted the note, they ignored it—it urged legal equality for Christians and Muslims, tax reforms, and representative self-government for the provinces of Bosnia and Herzegovina.

Following the Russian victory over the Ottomans in the Russo–Turkish War of 1877/78, Count Andrássy represented Austria-Hungary at the Congress of Berlin, which awarded Bosnia-Herzegovina to the protection of the Austro-Hungarian Empire.

BIBLIOGRAPHY

EVERSLEY, G. J. S. *The Turkish Empire from 1288 to 1914.* New York, 1969.

Arnold Blumberg

Andrews, Lewis   [1896–1937]

District commissioner of Galilee for the British government in Palestine.

Andrews was assassinated in 1937—possibly by followers of the politico-religious leader Izz al-Din al-Qassam, who initiated a revolt of Palestinian peasants in the Galilee in the early 1930s (and who had been killed in 1935). The assassination followed the publication of the findings of the 1937 Palestine Royal Commission Report (called the PEEL COMMISSION REPORT), which recommended the partition of Palestine into a Jewish and an Arab state.

Under the plan, Galilee was to be allotted to the Jewish state. The assassination of Andrews marked the beginning of the most violent phase of the PALESTINE ARAB REVOLT of 1936 to 1939.

BIBLIOGRAPHY

HIRST, DAVID. *The Gun and the Olive Branch.* London, 1977.

MILLER, YLANA. *Government and Society in Rural Palestine: 1920–48.* Austin, Tex., 1985.

Steve Tamari

Anglo–Afghan Treaty

Peace treaty favoring the British.

Signed in 1855 in Peshawar for the British by Sir John Lawrence, chief commissioner of the Punjab, and for the Afghans by Ghulam Haider, the eldest son and heir apparent to Dost Mohammad, king of Afghanistan, the Anglo–Afghan peace treaty emphasized three points: mutual peace and friendship, respect for each other's territorial integrity, and a recognition that the enemies and friends of one country would be regarded as the enemies and friends of the other.

Most historians now believe that the treaty favored the British, who wanted to maintain the status quo in their relationship with the Afghans. Since the British defeat by the Afghans in the war of 1838–1842, the British had rapidly expanded their control over the Indian subcontinent and by 1855 their controlled area extended to the Afghan border. They wished, therefore, to reach an accommodation with the Afghans on potentially problematic border issues so that they would be left free to pursue military campaigns elsewhere.

BIBLIOGRAPHY

FLETCHER, ARNOLD. *Afghanistan: Highway of Conquest.* Ithaca, N.Y., 1965.

Grant Farr

Anglo–Afghan Wars

Three wars (1838–1842; 1879–1880; 1919–1920) that defined the northernmost limit of British expansion in Central Asia, determining the present boundaries of Afghanistan.

The first two wars took place in the context of the GREAT GAME that pitted the empires of BRITAIN and RUSSIA against each other for the control of Central Asia and Persia (now IRAN). The backdrop for the third war was an increasingly assertive Asian NATIONALISM and a turbulent civil war in Russia following the revolution.

Interpreting a Persian attack on the city of HERAT in 1837 as inspired by Russia, British officials decided to intervene in AFGHANISTAN and restore a former ruler, Shah Shuja Durrani (ruled 1803–1809; 1839–1842). In November 1838, they assembled an army of 21,100 soldiers and 38,000 camp followers. The army entered Afghanistan on April 14, 1839. Kandahar fell without a struggle on April 20. Shuja was proclaimed king on May 8 and marched toward Kabul on June 27. The major confrontation took place in Ghazni on July 23, when British forces swiftly overpowered the Afghan garrison. Abandoned by his followers, DOST MOHAMMAD BARAKZAI (1826–1839; 1842–1863) the ruler of Kabul, fled to the northern region. Shuja entered Kabul on August 8.

British and Afghan perceptions of the events differed considerably. The British officials attributed the initial absence of resistance to their military might. Afghans attributed Shuja's success to his legitimate claims and his skills at forging alliances. The British role was viewed as one of assistance rather than domination of Shuja; but it soon became evident that Shuja was no more than a tool for British power and that the British were keen to gain direct control of the affairs of the country. Armed resistance followed, reaching its peak in 1841. On November 2, 1841, Afghan forces attacked the British garrison in Kabul. On January 6, 1842, a British force of 16,500 evacuated the city but was attacked on the road to Jalalabad. Only one officer made it safely to tell the story of the army's destruction. Having spent 8 million pounds sterling on the conquest of Afghanistan, Britain judged the cost of conquest too high and decided to abandon its plans. To restore prestige, however, Britain sent a punitive expedition in 1842 that looted the city of Kabul, then returned to India at the end of December 1842. Dost Mohammad regained power.

By 1876, the Russian empire had established itself as the paramount power in Central Asia. Alarmed at this expansion, Britain renewed plans to gain control of Afghanistan. Following a diplomatic squabble, British forces crossed into eastern Afghanistan on

November 21, 1878, and in a treaty signed on May 25, 1878, gained their key objectives—one of which was the posting of British officials in Kabul. Afghan resentment grew at the increasing power of the British envoy, who was killed when his embassy was burned down on September 3, 1879. British forces retaliated by taking over the city of Kabul on October 5, 1879, and unleashed a reign of terror in Kabul, Kandahar, and their surroundings. In December, the Afghan *ulama* (Islamic leaders) called for a *jihad* (holy war) against the British. By December 14, the 10,281-strong British army in Kabul had been forced to withdraw to its cantonment. Afghan resistance in other locations was equally intense.

Shaken by the intensity of the opposition, British officials decided to withdraw from Afghanistan, but not before attempting to dismember the country into a number of principalities. Extensive campaigns against Afghans were undertaken. But the Afghan victory at the battle of Maiwand of July 27, 1880, shook the foundation of this policy. British forces were withdrawn from Kabul and its surroundings on September 7, 1880, and from Kandahar and its surroundings on April 27, 1881.

To prepare for the evacuation of Afghanistan, British officials carried on intensive negotiations with Afghan leaders. On July 22, 1880, they recognized ABD AL-RAHMAN KHAN, a grandson of Dost Mohammad, as the ruler of Afghanistan. He agreed in return to cede control of his country's foreign relations to the British. Some districts were also annexed to British India.

Domestic and international conditions were quite different at the onset of the third Anglo–Afghan war. Internally, Abd al-Rahman had bequeathed his son and successor HABIBOLLAH KHAN a centralized state in 1901. During his rule (to 1919) a group of Afghan nationalists had also forged a conception of Afghan nationalism, emphasizing the need for full sovereignty. Britain appeared exhausted by its travails in World War I, and nationalists were actively challenging Britain's domination of India. The Russian empire had collapsed in revolution and was in the throes of civil war. And in Central Asia, independent Muslim governments were emerging.

Habibollah was assassinated on February 19, 1919. His son, AMANOLLAH KHAN (1919–1929), succeeded him, after thwarting an uncle's claim to the throne. On April 13, 1919, Amanollah officially declared his country independent. Britain, however, refused to accept the unilateral declaration of independence. On May 4, 1919, the undeclared third Anglo–Afghan War began when two Afghan columns crossed into the North-West Frontier province of British India. Afghan troops were initially victorious, but the British responded by using their air force to bomb Kabul and

Jalalabad. The duration of the clashes was brief, as both parties agreed on May 24 to end the hostilities. The willingness of the PAKHTUN tribes in the North-West Frontier province of India to join their Afghan kinsmen against the British troops was a major factor in driving British officials to the negotiating table.

Diplomatic negotiations started in earnest after the end of hostilities, but it took three conferences before an agreement could be reached. By December 8, 1921, Britain had agreed to recognize the full independence of Afghanistan. The brief war had cost the British empire some 16.5 million pounds. Persia, Turkey, and the Soviet Union were the first countries to recognize the fully independent Afghan state in 1920.

BIBLIOGRAPHY

ADAMEC, LUDWIG. *Afghanistan 1900–1923: A Diplomatic History.* Berkeley, Calif., 1967.

DUPREE, LOUIS. *Afghanistan.* Princeton, N.J., 1980.

NORRIS, J.A. *The First Afghan War 1838–1842.* Cambridge, U.K., 1967.

YAPP, M.E. *Strategies of British India.* Oxford, 1980.

Ashraf Ghani

Anglo–American Committee of Inquiry

Committee that examined the condition of European Jewry after World War II.

This committee was formed in 1946, following the revelation of the extent of Nazi atrocities against Jews in Europe during World War II. It looked into the problems of Jewish refugees in Europe and the possibility of Jewish immigration to Palestine. The committee's findings called for the granting of 100,000 immigration certificates to European Jewish refugees, the lifting of restrictions on land sales in Palestine to Jews, and the continuation of British rule over Palestine. The 1937 PEEL COMMISSION REPORT had recommended limiting Jewish immigration and restricting Palestinian land sales to Jews.

BIBLIOGRAPHY

SMITH, PAMELA ANN. *Palestine and the Palestinians.* New York, 1984.

Steve Tamari

Anglo–Iranian Oil Company

British-organized oil company, also called AIOC, based on a concession agreement with the shah of Persia, 1901; nationalized by Iran, 1951.

The history of the Anglo-Iranian Oil Company goes back to 1901 when a British engineer, William Knox D'ARCY, obtained a concession from Persia's shah giving him exclusive rights for the discovery, exploitation, and export of PETROLEUM in return for 16 percent of his annual profits and 20,000 pounds sterling in cash and another 20,000 pounds sterling in paid-up shares of stock in the venture enterprise. Oil was discovered in 1903. In 1905, D'Arcy became a part owner of the newly founded British Oil Company. In 1908, the British government bought D'Arcy's shares. In 1909, the Anglo-Persian Oil Company (APOC) was formed.

Because of its bias, the 1901 concession was not ratified by the parliament of the CONSTITUTIONAL REVOLUTION of 1905–1911. Moreover, APOC did not consistently follow the terms of the agreement. For example, during WORLD WAR I from 1914 to 1920, oil output had increased from 274,000 to 1,385,000 tons (250,000 to 1,255,000 t) annually; by 1933, the company had made a profit of 200 million pounds sterling. By contrast, Persia had received only some 10 million of the 32 million pounds sterling due contractually—less than one-third the share to which it was entitled by the concession.

In 1933, Reza PAHLAVI terminated the concession of 1901 and concluded a new agreement with the British that reduced the area of concession from 400,000 to 100,000 square miles (1,036,000 to 260,000 sq km), assured a minimum payment of 225,000 to 300,000 pounds sterling annually as a tax on the production of crude petroleum, and provided for a specific royalty of 4 shillings per ton of the oil sold. Iran was also to receive 20 percent of the net profit over and above a dividend guarantee of 671,250 pounds sterling. The agreement changed the company's name to the Anglo-Iranian Oil Company and, in 1935, Persia officially became IRAN.

For Britain, the new agreement had certain advantages over the 1901 concession. It extended British control over Iranian oil for an additional thirty-two years, until 1993, while the previous concession was due to expire in 1961. Unlike the concession of 1901, the 1933 agreement was not a contract between a private individual and the shah of Iran, which could be terminated without much difficulty. The 1933 agreement had the character of public law because it had been ratified by the Iranian parliament; it could not be annulled without entailing political complications. The 1933 agreement, however, was not as beneficial to Iran, and some of its terms were particularly disadvantageous. For example, prices for refined petroleum products in Iran were based upon average Romanian or Gulf of Mexico f.o.b. (free on board) prices—whichever was

lower—plus actual transportation and distribution costs, less a 10 percent discount. The bias of the agreement was argued based on the production cost of oil in the Middle East averaging only 1.2 U.S. dollars per ton compared to 12.45 dollars per ton in the United States. The AIOC's labor and housing policies were also less than satisfactory from the Iranian perspective.

The Anglo-Iranian oil disputes were not resolved amicably; they culminated in the nationalization of the British-run Iranian oil industry in 1951 under the premiership of Mohammad MOSSADEGH. AIOC then became the National Iranian Oil Company.

BIBLIOGRAPHY

MOADDEL, MANSOOR. "State-Centered vs. Class-Centered Perspectives in International Politics: The Case of U.S. and British Participation in the 1953 Coup against Premiere Mosaddeq in Iran." *Studies in Comparative International Development* (Summer 1989):3–22.

WALDEN, JERROLD L. "The International Petroleum Cartel in Iran—Private Power and the Public Interest." *Journal of Public Law* 11, no. 1 (Spring 1962):64–121.

Mansoor Moaddel

Anglo–Iraqi Treaties

Four treaties between Britain and Iraq, signed in 1922, 1926, 1930 and 1948.

As a result of the dispositions between the victorious allies after World War I, Iraq became a mandated state of the newly formed League of Nations; in April 1920, under the terms of the Treaty of San Remo, Britain was awarded the mandate for Iraq. By the end of 1920, Britain had decided to set up an Iraqi monarchy and had selected Faisal, the third son of Husayn ibn Ali, the Sharif of Mecca, as king. In the summer of 1921, before Faisal's coronation on August 23, Sir Percy COX, the high commissioner in Baghdad, suggested that the mandate might be made more palatable if its terms were to be embodied in a treaty between Britain and Iraq. This was the genesis of the treaty of 1922.

A long period of bargaining followed, during which the British were intent on having their powers fully defined, and Faisal tried to convince them of the importance of his not being made to appear too blatant a British puppet. The treaty itself covered such matters as the framing of a constitution, the number and duties of British officials employed in Iraq, British supervision of the judicial system, Iraqi diplomatic representation abroad, equality of access to Iraq for all foreign states, and agreements governing the financial and military arrangements between the two states. Iraq was eventually to take responsibility to defend itself against external aggression; at the same time, British imperial interests in and around Iraq had to be secured.

What all this implied was a change in the form without any change in the substance; Britain would, ultimately, force the government of Iraq to comply with the terms, and the treaty was widely unpopular in Iraq. The opposition was so persistent that its leaders had to be arrested, and the prime minister eventually coerced into signing the treaty, since Faisal had taken ill with appendicitis a few days before his signature was due. A protocol to the treaty was negotiated in 1923, reducing its operative period from twenty years to four years after the signature of the peace treaty with Turkey. Even so, ratification by the Chamber of Deputies in June 1924 was quite problematic; a bare quorum was obtained, with only 37 out of 59 deputies present (out of a chamber of 110) voting in favor.

The treaty of 1926 was less contentious, since its main function was to take account of the new circumstances that had come into being with the "final" settlement of the Turco–Iraqi frontier. Apart from guaranteeing a measure of local administration and Kurdish linguistic rights for the population of the area (mostly honored in the breach), this treaty extended the provisions of the 1922 treaty for twenty-five years, unless Iraq was admitted to the League of Nations before the end of that period.

The remaining six years of the mandate formed a period of general cooperation with Britain, in sharp contrast to the conflicts of earlier years. At the time of the first reconsideration of the treaty in 1927, it was suggested that Iraq should be considered for league membership in 1928; negotiations dragged on until September 1929 when the matter was dropped on the understanding that unreserved British support would be given for an application for 1932.

The Anglo–Iraqi Treaty of 1930 was concluded much more rapidly than its predecessors, largely because this time there was no real opposition. Apart from stipulations about the precedence to be given to the British representative, the employment of British officials, and the employment of a British military mission, the treaty declared that "responsibility for the maintenance of internal order rests with the King of Iraq," while Britain was bound to go to the aid of her ally in the event of invasion from outside. Air bases were to be maintained rent-free in Iraq for the (British) Royal Air Force, and the treaty was to last until 1957, twenty-five years from Iraq's entry into the league in 1932.

It was not until the late 1940s that Iraqi opposition became sufficiently articulate or organized to oppose continued British control and influence. In 1946/47, the British government expressed interest in extending the 1930 treaty under the guise of revising it. On the Iraqi side, the negotiations were masterminded by Nuri al-SAʿID and the regent, ABD AL-ILAH, but actually carried out by the Shiʿite prime minister, Salih JABR. Jabr and his colleagues spent late December 1947 and the first part of January 1948 in Britain working on a new Anglo–Iraqi treaty, the text of which was released on January 15; it turned out to be almost identical with the treaty of 1930 and was rejected out of hand by crowds in the streets of Baghdad—so vehemently, in fact, that the regent was forced to disavow it. Relations between Britain and Iraq remained governed by the treaty of 1930 until 1958, when it was repudiated by the revolutionary government.

Peter Sluglett

Anglo–Jewish Association

Organization established in 1871 by Jews in Great Britain to protect and aid other Jews.

The goals and activities of the Anglo–Jewish Association (AJA) paralleled those of the French ALLIANCE ISRAÉLITE UNIVERSELLE. The AJA funded schools that taught in English or included English-language instruction in the curriculum in Mogador (Essaouira), Morocco; in Tanta, Egypt; and in the Ottoman Empire.

BIBLIOGRAPHY

AJA Annual Report. 1870–present.

Norman Stillman

Anglo–Moroccan Treaty

Gave Britain most-favored-nation status and affirmed special rights for British subjects in Morocco.

In possession of the Mediterranean ports of Gibraltar and Minorca, Britain needed Morocco to be a source for provisioning troops. The two countries had signed five commercial agreements between 1721 and 1791, but the Anglo–Moroccan Treaty of June 14, 1801, solidified these earlier agreements and gave Britain most-favored-nation status. It also affirmed the capitulatory rights of British individuals when in Morocco, such as the right to be tried by the British consul and immunity from Moroccan taxes.

BIBLIOGRAPHY

HUREWITZ, J. C., ed. *The Middle East and North Africa in World Politics*. New Haven, Conn., 1975.

Zachary Karabell

Anglo–Omani Treaties

Agreements concluded by Oman's rulers and British India's local representatives that successively expanded British involvement in Omani affairs and culminated in Oman becoming a virtual British protectorate.

British interest in Oman and the Persian/Arabian GULF was based on the India trade. It became a political interest as the East India Company's focus shifted in the late eighteenth century from commerce to the administration of India as the British government's trustee. In addition, the Gulf's strategic significance increased, since communications linking Britain to India skirted the region. The consequences became apparent in 1798 when, after Napoleon annexed Egypt, French plans to invade India were countered by a British diplomatic offensive to protect India's frontiers. Among this effort's fruit was the first formal treaty between an Arab state of the Gulf and Britain, the Anglo–Omani *Qawl-nama* (agreement) signed October 12, 1798, by the Omani ruler, Sultan ibn Ahmad, and an East India Company representative. This excluded France and her allies, such as the Indian ruler, Tipu Sultan, from Omani territories and was amended in 1800 to permit stationing a British "agent" at Muscat. Since Oman was then a leading Indian Ocean maritime power, these engagements constituted an alliance between ostensible equals and implied no Omani dependency upon Britain.

Increased Omani subordination became apparent in the treaty of commerce signed May 31, 1839, by Omani and East India Company representatives. Concluded six years after the United States obtained a commercial agreement, and at a time when Muhammad Ali's Egypt seemingly threatened Gulf peace, this treaty placed Anglo–Omani relations on firmer legal footing. It also significantly diminished Omani sovereignty, by limiting the duty Oman could levy on British goods, by formalizing British extraterritorial jurisdiction over its subjects resident in Oman, and by permitting British warships to detain Omani vessels suspected of slave trading, thereby expanding an 1822 anti-slave-trade engagement.

The 1839 treaty was superseded by one signed March 19, 1891, by Sultan Faisal of Oman and Britain's Political Resident Sir Edward Ross. Although this treaty barely increased Britain's formal privileges, an accompanying secret declaration issued March 20, 1891, bound Oman's ruler and his successors never to "cede, sell, mortgage, or otherwise give for occupation" any part of his possessions except to Britain. Actually, these engagements were reached in lieu of formally declaring a British protectorate over Oman, an idea shelved because it conflicted with an 1862 Anglo-French guarantee of Oman's independence. Nevertheless, the 1891 declaration initiated a fifty-year period when Oman, albeit legally independent, functioned as a veiled British protectorate. The legal regime founded on these undertakings began eroding in 1939, when the 1891 treaty was renegotiated and, especially in 1951, when the present Anglo–Omani treaty was concluded and Oman resumed formal control over its foreign relations. It shattered completely between 1958—when the territorial nonalienation declaration of 1891 was mutually terminated—and 1967, when Britain's extraterritorial rights in Oman finally lapsed. Only an updated version of the original 1798 Anglo–Omani alliance endures.

BIBLIOGRAPHY

AITCHESON, C. U., compiler. *A Collection of Treaties, Documents, and Sanads Relating to India and Neighbouring Countries*. Vol. 11, 5th ed. Delhi, 1933. Reprint, 1973.

AL-BAHARNA, HUSAIN M. *The Arabian Gulf States: Their Legal and Political Status and Their International Problems*, 2nd ed. Beirut, 1975, 1978.

Robert G. Landen

Anglo–Persian Agreement

Contract to allow Britain to do business in Persia in return for compensation.

Signed at Tehran on August 9, 1919, the agreement obliged Britain to supply, at a cost to the Persian government, administrative advisers, officers, munitions, and equipment for the formation of a uniform force; to assist in the construction of railways and revision of custom tariff; to cooperate with Persia for the collection of war compensation from belligerent parties; and to grant Persia a loan of 2 million pounds sterling at 7 percent annual interest. In return, Britain obtained a monopoly in supplying administrative advisers as well as military experts and equipment, and the Persian customs office was pledged to repay the loan. The agreement produced bitter controversy. The Persian government believed that it would finance administrative and military reforms, avert social revolution, and assist in maintaining order. The opposition and most foreign observers believed that with the signing of the agreement "a virtual protectorate over Persia had been established, and that the British Empire had in effect received another extension" (MacDonald 1913, p. 371). The agreement was abrogated in 1921, since the Persian assembly (*majles*) refused to convene to ratify it.

BIBLIOGRAPHY

"Agreement between His Britannic Majesty's Government and the Persian Government." *British Parliamentary Papers*. 1919.
MACDONALD, WILLIAM. "Persian and British Honor." *The Nation* (September 1913):371–372.

Mansoor Moaddel

Anglo–Persian War

War occasioned by Iran's seizure of Herat.

In March 1856, the government of Iran's Qajar monarch, Nassir al-Din Shah (ruled 1848–1896), dispatched a military force to capture Herat, a city in western Afghanistan whose control had been a source of contention between the Afghans and Iranians since Afghanistan asserted its independence from Iran in the mid-eighteenth century. After a long siege, Herat surrendered to the Iranians in October 1856. The capture of Herat prompted Great Britain, which had long opposed Iran's claims to the city, to declare war. Actual hostilities between Iranian and British forces were limited, but Britain captured Kharg Island in the Persian Gulf and landed a military contingent at the port of Bushehr. Iran sued for peace, but the British captured the port of Khorramshahr before negotiations were completed. Under the terms of the Treaty of Paris of March 1857, Iran agreed to evacuate Herat, renounce all claims to the city, and recognize the independence of Afghanistan.

BIBLIOGRAPHY

RAWLINSON, SIR HENRY. *England and Persia in the East: a Series of Papers on the Political and Geographical Condition of Central Asia* (Denis Sinor, ed.). New York, 1970.

Eric J. Hooglund

Anglo–Russian Agreement

Accord that divided Iran into spheres of influence, 1907.

During the last third of the nineteenth century, Russian imperial advances into Central Asia and the con-

solidation of British imperial domination in south Asia led to intense rivalry between the two European empires. The conflicting interests centered on Afghanistan, Iran, and Tibet, three states that constituted buffers between Britain's and Russia's colonial possessions in Asia. The emergence of Germany as a world power and the humiliating defeat in 1905 of Russia by a nascent Asian power, Japan, helped to persuade some British and Russian officials of a need to resolve their respective differences in Asia. Consequently, in 1907, Britain and Russia signed an agreement to regulate their economic and political interests. With respect to Iran, the Anglo–Russian Agreement recognized the country's strict independence and integrity, but then divided it into three separate zones.

The agreement designated all of northern Iran, which bordered Russia's possessions in Transcaucasia and Central Asia, as an exclusive sphere of influence for Russian interests. This northern zone was defined as beginning at Qasr-e Shirin in the west, on the border with the Ottoman Empire, and running through Tehran, Isfahan, and Yazd to the eastern border, where the frontiers of Afghanistan, Iran, and Russia intersected. A smaller zone in southeastern Iran, which bordered Britain India, was recognized as an exclusive sphere for Britain. The British zone extended west as far as Kerman in the north and Bandar Abbas in the south. The area separating these two spheres, including part of central Iran and the entire southwest, was designated a neutral zone where both countries and their respective private citizens could compete for influence and commercial privileges. For Britain and Russia, the agreement was important in establishing a diplomatic alliance that endured until World War I. The government of Iran, however, had not been consulted about the agreement; it was informed after the fact. Although not in a position to prevent Britain and Russia from implementing the Anglo–Russian Agreement, the Iranian government refused to recognize the accord's legitimacy, since from an Iranian perspective, it threatened the country's integrity and independence. Iranian nationalists, in particular, felt betrayed by Britain, a country they had idealized as a democratic beacon during the CONSTITUTIONAL REVOLUTION (1905–1907). Thus, an important legacy of the agreement was the growth of anti-British sentiment specifically and anti-Western attitudes more generally as strong components of Iranian nationalism.

The Anglo–Russian Agreement did not eliminate all competition between the two powers with respect to their policies in Iran, but after 1907 it did foster broad cooperation, often to the detriment of Iranian interests. In particular, Britain and Russia intervened in Iran's domestic politics by supporting the royalists in their contest with the constitutionalists, and increasingly, their intervention assumed military dimensions. The agreement lapsed in 1918 after it was renounced by a new revolutionary government in Russia.

BIBLIOGRAPHY

KAZEMZADEH, FIRUZ. *Russia and Britain in Persia, 1864–1914: A Study in Imperialism.* New Haven, Conn., 1968.

Eric J. Hooglund

Anglo–Russian–French Agreement

See Sykes–Picot Agreement

Anglo–Russo–Persian Treaty of Alliance

Agreement for ending Allied occupation of Iran following World War II.

Following a dispute with Reza Shah PAHLAVI over the presence of an estimated two thousand Germans in the country, British and Soviet troops occupied Iran in August–September 1941. To assuage Iranian fears of permanent occupation, to legalize the occupation, and to secure Soviet guarantees of withdrawal after the war in 1942, Britain persuaded the Soviet Union to agree on the terms of a tripartite alliance. Iran was forced to accede but did manage to alter some of the terms of the agreement. Article 5, for example, was changed to oblige Allied withdrawal six months after the cessation of hostilities, not one year as originally proposed. In Article 1, the Allies pledged "to respect the territorial integrity, sovereignty and political independence of Iran."

BIBLIOGRAPHY

HUREWITZ, J.C. *The Middle East and North Africa in World Politics: A Documentary Record.* 2 vols, 2nd ed. New Haven, Conn., 1975–79.

David Waldner

Anglo–Tunisian Agreement

Agreement regarding British subjects in Tunisia.

The Anglo–Tunisian Agreement of 1863 sought to grant British subjects in Tunisia proprietary and other rights equal to those of Tunisians. It also represented a test of the FUNDAMENTAL PACT (1855) and the constitution of 1861, which provided for the extension of rights and privileges to Europeans and religious minorities. Bey MUHAMMAD AL-SADIQ and the English consul, Richard Woods, viewed this agreement as an important means to diminish the influence of France while maintaining the fiction of Ottoman suzerainty.

BIBLIOGRAPHY

GANIAGE, JEAN. *Les Origines du protectorat français en Tunisie (1861–1881).* Paris, 1959.

Larry A. Barrie

Ani, Yusuf al- [c. 1930–]

Iraqi playwright and actor, founder of Firqat al-Misrah al-Fanni al-Hadith (Modern Artistic Group Theater) of Baghdad.

Born in Iraq, al-Ani graduated from the Fine Arts Institute in Baghdad. His most successful play, *Al-Beg wa al-Saiq* (The Master and the Driver), influenced by Bertolt Brecht, has been performed in several Arab countries. His interest in Iraq's folk hero and his traditions led al-Ani to write and play the lead in *Mullah Aboud al-Karkhi,* about the twentieth-century Arab poet whose poetry has been set to music.

In 1973, the Egyptian director Ibrahim Abdul-Galil directed al-Ani's play *Aboud Irani* in Baghdad, and cast the playwright in the title role, a wise and honest man in a corrupt society.

Films in which Ani has acted include Yusuf Shaheen's *Al-Yawm al-Sadis* (The Sixth Day; 1987), about Napoleon's invasion of Egypt, and *Al-Mas'ala al-Kubra* (The Clash of Royalties), in which he played the Iraqi nationalist al-Basir.

Al-Ani's book *Cinema Arabia* remains the best source on the Iraqi film.

Hind Rassam Culhane

Animism

A generic term most commonly used to describe the religious beliefs of those who do not adhere to a recognized, recorded, and defined practice of spiritual devotion.

Although religious rituals regarded as animism vary widely, they all have a common doctrine that personal organic development is immaterial to the spirit. Consequently, spirits exist separate from the body and are frequently associated with natural objects or, more generally, nature. Animism is most widely practiced by communities that live close to the land from which they derive their sustenance; the vagaries of the natural environment condition the daily rhythm of their lives. The rituals that have evolved for worship of the spirits have remained a fundamental part of the cultural history of many peoples, and although some individuals may have accepted one of the more organized religions, they seldom entirely abandon their animistic rituals, preferring to integrate them into the traditional liturgy in a symbiotic relationship.

Robert O. Collins

Anjoman

Persian word for "assembly."

Used as far back as the eleventh century in Firdawsi's *Shah Namah* (*Book of Kings*) in the sense of "assembly" or "meeting," the term *anjoman* had come to refer to cultural, religious, political, administrative, and professional "associations" by the late nineteenth century. During the CONSTITUTIONAL REVOLUTION (1905–1912), a number of secret or open political groups that were often called anjoman played important roles. In the latter part of the twentieth century, a variety of Islamic associations, especially those formed among students in Iran and abroad, called themselves anjoman. Originally religious and cultural associations, these groups were politicized during the 1978–1979 Iranian revolution, when both Islamic and secular popular assemblies (called SHURA, or anjoman) appeared all over Iran, at all levels of society. With the consolidation of the new Islamic regime, however, these independent organizations were eliminated or else were turned into government organs. The notion of anjoman, or shura, as some ideal form of popular self-rule is nevertheless still current, especially in leftist political literature.

BIBLIOGRAPHY

ADAMIYAT, FEREYDUN. *Fekr-e demokrasi-ye ejtema'i dar nehzat-e mashrutiyat-e Iran.* Tehran, 1977.
BAYAT, ASSEF. *Workers and Revolution in Iran: A Third World Experience of Workers' Control.* 1987.
LAMBTON, A. K. S. "The Secret Societies and the Persian Revolution of 1905–1906." *St. Anthony's Papers* 4 (1958).

Nikki Keddie

Ankara

Capital of Ankara province and of the Republic of Turkey. The name was changed officially from Angora to Ankara in 1930, although it was made the Turkish capital in 1923.

Ankara (formerly Angora) was a Hittite settlement and remained a provincial city throughout its history, except when it was made capital of the Celtic kingdom of Galatia (284 B.C.E.–17 C.E.), which became dependent on the Romans in the second century B.C.E. As the capital of the Roman province of Galatia, after 25 B.C.E., baths and a temple were built. It was then conquered by Persians, Arabs, Seljuk Turks, Crusaders, and in 1360 by the Ottoman Turks. During the later Ottoman Empire, Ankara received a spur of the BERLIN–BAGHDAD RAILROAD. After the Ottoman defeat in World War I, Mustafa Kemal ATATÜRK chose Ankara as headquarters of the Nationalist resistance in 1920, because of these communications with the outside world. As part of an effort to give the new Republic of Turkey an Anatolian cast, he made Ankara the national capital in 1923.

The modern city was first built between the medieval citadel and the railroad station to its west. By 1930, a larger area was needed, and this new city was laid out on a plan by the Austrian architect Hermann Jansen, beginning in 1932. The plan provided only for the upper and middle classes; the masses of villagers who came to Ankara to become tradesmen and artisans had to fend for themselves. To avoid the authorities, they built houses by night to form districts of GECEKONDU that now ring the planned city and contain about 55 percent of Ankara's inhabitants. The plan envisioned a population

A view of Ankara with the citadel in background, 1965. (Richard Bulliet)

of 335,000 by 1985; in that year the population had reached 2.3 million.

Ankara is now the economic and transport center of the interior of Turkey. Railroads were extended eastward to Kayseri, Sivas, Erzurum and Diyarbakır in the 1920s and 1930s, and a network of paved roads connecting Ankara to all parts of the interior was built in the 1950s. The airport at Esenboğa has become the hub of Turkey's interior air network. Atatürk's goal of interior development has been largely realized with the growth of Ankara and of subsidiary industrial centers in Eskişehir, Kayseri, and Kırıkkale.

The government and the military are Ankara's major employers. Most service employment is directly related to government (education, legal services, support of the foreign community) or to the needs of running the metropolis (transportation, construction, general services). Industry is also concentrated in the government sector (armaments, official publishing). The burgeoning of ministerial bureaucracies has fueled the city's rapid growth, which has led to problems other than gecekondus. For example, serious air pollution has resulted from the burning of soft coal in central heating systems. Abatement plans have been proposed for decades, but the problem continues. Traffic congestion (and its hydrocarbon pollutants) led to plans for a subway system, now under construction.

BIBLIOGRAPHY

Rustow, D. A. *Turkey, America's Forgotten Ally.* New York, 1987.

Yearbook of the Province of Ankara. Ankara, 1973.

John R. Clark

Ankara, Treaty of

Treaty of friendship between Greece and Turkey, signed October 30, 1930, in Turkey's new capital.

The treaty affirmed the boundaries between Turkey and Greece, settled the property claims of exchanged populations, and agreed to naval equality in the eastern Mediterranean. The treaty was a remarkable rapprochement, despite bitter feeling left from the recent Turkish war of independence. The impetus for the treaty was the 1929 Turkish treaty with Britain—Greece's ally—and by fears of Bulgarian interest in reconquering Thrace. This and other friendship treaties in 1930 marked Turkey's entry into the family of nations—and eventually the League of Nations in 1932.

BIBLIOGRAPHY

Lenczowski, George. *The Middle East in World Affairs.* Ithaca, N.Y., 1982.

Elizabeth Thompson

Ankara University

A public university in the capital of Turkey.

Founded in 1946, it comprises faculties of letters, pharmacy, education, science, law, divinity, political science, medicine, veterinary science, agriculture, and dentistry, as well as schools of home economics, journalism, and justice, a College of Health Sciences, and vocational schools in neighboring Çankiri, Kastamonu, and Kirikkale provinces. In 1990, the university had about 2,500 teaching staff and 31,000 students (12,000 were female). Its 1991 budget, state-funded, amounted to 330 billion Turkish lire, of which 62 billion was for capital investment.

Ankara University came into being with the incorporation of three existing faculties. The first to be established in Ankara, the new capital of the Republic of Turkey, was the Faculty of Law, founded in 1925. Since Turkey's legal system was completely Europeanized with the adoption of the Swiss Civil Code to replace Islamic law, the Ankara Faculty of Law was envisaged as the academic safeguard of legal reform. In the same spirit, the Faculty of Language, History, and Geography was established in 1936 to establish and promote the recent language reform and the republican vision of history. Also in 1936, the Faculty of Political Science, originally established in Istanbul in 1859 to train civil servants of the Ottoman Empire in the first era of Europeanization, was moved to Ankara to identify it more securely with republican ideology. In 1949, the Faculty of Divinity was founded—partly as a reaction to the earlier extreme secular spirit of the republic, but also for the study of comparative religion, not just Islam.

From 1933 until after World War II, the three faculties that were to comprise Ankara University benefited in their early development from the influx of many well-established liberal European scholars, most of them German and many Jewish, escaping the Nazi regime. With the proliferation of universities in Ankara as well as in the rest of Turkey, Ankara University gradually lost its special identification with republican reform. In the 1970s, Ankara University and Istanbul University were highly politicized.

BIBLIOGRAPHY

Higher Education in Turkey. UNESCO, European Centre for Higher Education. December 1990.
World of Learning. 1990.

I. Metin Kunt

Annab, Radi

Jordanian military officer.

Annab was a senior officer in the ARAB LEGION when King Hussein of Jordan dismissed the British chief of the General Staff, Gen. John Bagot GLUBB, on March 1, 1956, replacing him with Annab. Annab retired soon thereafter and was replaced by Ali ABU NUWWAR. When Abu Nuwwar attempted a coup, King Hussein reappointed Annab chief of staff on April 20, 1957.

Jenab Tutunji

Annaba

Algerian seaport situated near the Tunisian border.

Called Bona (or Bône) before the independence of Algeria (1962), Annaba was one of North Africa's major trading posts prior to the French invasion in 1830. Bona itself, where France had obtained certain trading privileges prior to the invasion, was occupied in 1832. The city remained an important trading port throughout the nineteenth century. It was singled out by the French government in the 1950s for a number of major industrial projects, including Algeria's most important steel plant. These were part of the final effort by France—the so-called Constantine plan of 1958—to tie Algeria's postindependence economic development to the *métropole* (France itself).

After independence, Annaba emerged as an important harbor and industrial center. This was based in part on the earlier steel industry that had been started by the French and on heavy industries related to Algeria's socialist strategy adopted shortly after independence. Annaba's population is about 256,000 (1990).

BIBLIOGRAPHY

RUEDY, JOHN. *Modern Algeria: The Origins and Development of a Nation.* Bloomington, Ind., 1992.

Dirk Vandewalle

Ansar, al-

Disciples of Muhammad Ahmad ibn Abdallah, the self-declared Mahdi in the Sudan, who led the tribes to overthrow Turko–Egyptian rule in the early 1880s.

The Ansar (in Arabic, the Helpers or Followers) had three components during the Turko–Egyptian period in the Sudan: the religious disciples of the Mahdi, who joined him on Aba island in 1881 and followed him on his *hijra* (holy flight) to Kurdufan that summer; the *baqqara* (cattle-herding Arab) nomads of Kurdufan and Darfur, who traditionally opposed the authority of the central government and one of whose members, Abdallahi ibn Muhammad, succeeded the Mahdi as ruler; and members of the Ja'aliyyin and Danaqla tribes of north Sudan who had been dispersed to the southwest where they became traders. Others also joined the Ansar from the Nuba tribe in southern Kurdufan and the Hadendowa (Beja) near the Red Sea. The Ansar thus joined the Mahdi for a combination of religious and material motives: the belief in him as the heir to the Prophet Muhammad; and the benefit derived from him against government control and taxes.

When the Turko–Egyptian government was defeated in January 1885 and Abdallahi succeeded the Mahdi as ruler in June 1885, strains appeared among the Ansar. Those reflected tensions between the tribes that originated in the Nile valley (*awlad al-balad*) and those from the west (*awlad al-Arab*). Moreover, they reflected the tribes' resentment that the new government imposed taxes and control in a manner not dissimilar to the previous regime. Nonetheless, Abdallahi ruled the Sudan until 1898, when Anglo-Egyptian forces defeated the Ansar and Abdallahi died.

The Mahdi's posthumous son, Sayyid Abd al-Rahman, gradually regained authority in the traditional Mahdist areas during the 1920s and 1930s. Even in 1908, the Anglo–Egyptian government permitted him to cultivate land on Aba island, the Mahdi's original stronghold. During World War I, he won contracts from the government to supply wood from the island for river steamers and, in the early 1920s, he won government contracts to supply materials to construct the Sennar Dam. The government also allowed him to cultivate substantial areas distant from Aba island. Ansar from Kurdufan and Darfur worked on those projects, generally without pay. They received food and clothing from Sayyid Abd al-Rahman, who also conferred his blessing upon them. The economic and religious blessings were mutually reinforcing and helped provide the basis for his subsequent political strength.

The British authorities supported Sayyid Abd al-Rahman because he served as a counter to the nationalist politicians influenced by Egypt. He founded the Umma party in 1945, which pressed for the separation of the Sudan from Egypt. The Ansar underlined his power: when the Egyptian president came on March 1, 1954, for example, to inaugurate the parliament in Khartum, 40,000 Ansar demonstrated and the ceremony was postponed. When the Egyptians relinquished their claims to rule the Sudan, Umma participated in the first independent government (January 1956).

Sayyid Abd al-Rahman al-Mahdi died on March 24, 1959 and was succeeded by his son Sayyid Siddiq al-Mahdi as head of the Ansar and the Umma party. When he died in September 1961, his brother Sayyid al-Hadi al-Mahdi became *imam* (leader) of the Ansar and his son Sayyid al-Sadiq al-Mahdi headed the Umma party. That bifurcation weakened the movement, since al-Sadiq al-Mahdi challenged his uncle's authority. When Ja'far Muhammad al-Numairi seized power in a coup d'état in May 1969, he determined to destroy the power of the Ansar. After clashes between the army and the Ansar in Omdurman and Aba Island, Numairi launched an attack by the air force on Aba Island on March 27, 1970. Hundreds of Ansar died, Imam al-Hadi was killed as he escaped to Ethiopia, and al-Sadiq al-Mahdi fled into exile. Numairi confiscated the Mahdi family's holdings, to undermine their economic power.

Al-Sadiq al-Mahdi was a leader of the exiled opposition to Numairi and mounted a major attempt to overthrow the regime in July 1976. When he and Numairi reconciled in 1977, he returned to the Sudan and slowly rebuilt the economic and religious bases of the Ansar. When Numairi was overthrown, the Ansar-based Umma party won 38 percent of the vote in April 1986, and al-Sadiq al-Mahdi became Prime Minister. He, in turn, was overthrown by a coup d'état on June 30, 1989. By then, Ansar was no longer a formidable paramilitary force. Its 1–2 million members provided guaranteed votes for the Umma party but were not the cohesive movement that they had been in previous years.

BIBLIOGRAPHY

HOLT, P. M., and M. W. DALY. *The History of the Sudan.* Boulder, Colo., 1979.

NIBLOCK, TIM. *Class and Power in Sudan.* Albany, N.Y., 1987.

SHEBEIKA, MEKKI. *The Independent Sudan.* New York, 1959.

Ann M. Lesch

Ansar Detention Centers

Al-Ansar is the name of a town in southern Lebanon for which these prison camps are named.

The Israeli army established a large detention camp at al-Ansar to hold thousands of Palestinians and Lebanese following Israel's invasion of Lebanon in June 1982. Israel's military detention center of Katiba, located in the Gaza Strip, is known as Ansar II. Ansar III is the popular name for an Israeli prison camp established in March 1988 in the Negev desert, near the Egyptian border at Ketsyot, established to hold Palestinian political prisoners and administrative detainees from the occupied territories during the Palestinian uprising (INTIFADA), which had begun in December 1987.

The HUMAN RIGHTS organizations Amnesty International, the Lawyers Committee for Human Rights, and Human Rights Watch have condemned Israel's practice of administrative detention. In August 1988, the Red Cross stated that the detention of Palestinians inside Israel violates the Fourth Geneva Convention of 1949, which prohibits the transfer of populations.

BIBLIOGRAPHY

AL HAQ/LAW IN THE SERVICE OF MAN. *Punishing a Nation: Human Rights Violations during the Palestinian Uprising: December 1987–December 1988.* Boston, 1990.

AMNESTY INTERNATIONAL. *1989 Annual Report.* Jerusalem, 1989. Reprinted in *al-Fajr.*

LAWYERS COMMITTEE FOR HUMAN RIGHTS AND HUMAN RIGHTS WATCH REPORT. "The Reagan Administration's Record on Human Rights in 1988." Jerusalem, 1989. Reprinted in *al-Fajr.*

Steve Tamari

Antaki, Rizq Allah   [1908–?]

Syrian lawyer, professor, and author.

Born in Aleppo to Loutfallah Antaki, Rizq Allah received a licentiate of law from Damascus University and a doctorate from the Sorbonne. A politically active professor at Damascus University, he was arrested in Adib Shishakli's preemptive coup against the Ba'th-dominated coalition on the night of January 27/28 in 1954. He became minister of finances in 1955 and minister of national economy in 1956. His publications include *Al-Huquq al-Tijariya al-Bashriya.*

BIBLIOGRAPHY

Who's Who in the Middle East, 1967–1968.

Charles U. Zenzie

Antakya

Capital of Hatay province, Turkey.

Center of the cotton and citrus region, Antakya, as Antioch, was the capital of Hellenistic and Roman Syria. Part of the French mandate over Syria after World War I, it went to Turkey in 1938/39. Today, Antakya is a prosperous commercial center, with an excellent archeological museum and extensive ruins of its ancient walls. The population in 1985 was 109,233.

BIBLIOGRAPHY

DOWNEY, G. *A History of Antioch in Syria from Seleucus to the Arab Conquest.* Princeton, N.J., 1961.

John R. Clark

Antar, Ali Ahmad Nasser   [?–1986]

Yemeni politician and government official.

Ali Antar was a veteran of the Radfan Rebellion and member of the left wing of the ruling group in the PEOPLE'S DEMOCRATIC REPUBLIC OF YEMEN (PDRY). He held high government and party posts from the late 1960s through the mid-1980s—among them minister of defense and politburo member—and always seemed at the center of the political struggles during these years. Ali Antar was much involved in the intrigue that both brought ALI NASIR MUHAMMAD AL-HASANI to the top position in 1980 and aimed at reining him in from 1984 on. Ali Antar was killed in 1986 when Ali Nasir tried to save himself through a preemptive ambush. Ali Antar came from al-Dhala and enjoyed up-country support; he also found much support in the military.

Robert D. Burrowes

Anti-Semitism

Anti-Jewish sentiments and action.

Any analysis of the nature of anti-Jewish sentiment and anti-movements within the Islamic world must take into account the vastness and diversity of that world as well as the distinctive position of the Jews withinn it. Centuries of coexistence provide ample illustrations for almost any thesis of apologists for Islam or polemicists against it. In general, as long as the Muslim empire was dynamic and expanding, Jewish life tended to be fairly secure and stable (seventh through twelfth centuries); when the Muslim world entered an extended era of political and economic decline (thirteenth through the nineteenth centuries), Jewish life tended to be more precarious and demeaned. By and large, Jewish life under Islam has been characterized by low-level toleration with a good deal of humiliation. Persecution has been sporadic and generally localized. Islamic attitudes toward Jews have never displayed the violence and genocidal dimensions, nor the demonic stereotyping, that characterized the Christian world for much of its history.

Anti-Jewish sentiments have been rooted in Islam since its inception. Muhammad's words, as embodied in the Qur'an and the traditions of the Prophet, provide the paradigm for behavior toward Jews and toward believers everywhere. Early sources have a great deal to say about Jews and Judaism because Muhammad's career intersected forcefully with the Jews of Arabia. During the second, more public phase of his career in Medina (622–632), he engaged in frequent debates with the Jews. Although he drew upon many elements of Judaism, he sincerely believed himself to be the seal and perfection of prophecy and was dismayed that the Jews rejected his prophetic claims. Echoes of heated debates with the Jews are preserved in the Qur'an, and therefore are considered by Muslims to be the literal word of God as conveyed to the Prophet through the angel Gabriel. Whereas the ancient Jews were considered to be recipients of a divine message, their sinful nature had been revealed even in antiquity. They had disobeyed Moses (Sura 2:51), desecrated the Sabbath, broken the covenant (Sura 2:82–85), and killed their prophets (Sura 2:61). Even greater scorn and condemnation were meted out to the Jews of Muhammad's day; as the Prophet exclaimed, "Indeed, you will find that the most vehement of men in enmity to those who believe are the Jews and the polytheists" (Sura 5:82).

Muhammad condemned the Jews for their alleged perfidy and willful distortion of God's word. The Qur'an explains: "There is a group of them who distort the Scripture with their tongues that you might think it to be from the Scriptures, though it is not . . . the Scripture" (Sura 3:78). No wonder, according to the Qur'an, that the Jews have "wretchedness and baseness stamped upon them" (Sura 2:61). The hagiographic material on the life of the Prophet reinforced the negative Qur'anic descriptions of Jews. These traditions, too, are accorded deep respect by believers.

Yet Muhammad never questioned the basic validity of Judaism. Nor, since he was offering a separate and complete message to the Arabs of Arabia, did he need to convert the Jews to prove the veracity of his message. His message lacked the competitive edge and totalistic repudiation that made Jewish life so precarious in Christendom. Instead, subtle distinctions of toleration with humiliation were devised. Jews, like Christians, were considered to be "people of the book" (*ahl el-kitab*), who should be opposed until they surrendered. Thereafter, the imposition of tribute payments in the form of discriminatory taxes was one of several signs of humiliation and subordination. Although Jews were subjected to Islam, they were also to be protected (hence the term *ahl al-dhimma,* "protected people") and permitted to live humbly in the house of Islam (Sura 9:29).

The distinctive nature of Islamic toleration and anti-Semitism is contained in the Islamic notion of *dhimma* (humiliation/protection). Jews were permitted to live in the Islamic world and to practice their religion. At the same time, Muslim jurists devoted much time and attention to working out a system of humiliation. It included prohibitions on the public display of Judaism, the building of new synagogues or the repair of ones that had fallen into disrepair, the wearing of finery, and the bearing of arms. Jews should not exercise positions of authority over Muslims, nor could they ride horses. Their distinctive clothing should make them readily recognizable to any passersby. They should treat Muslims with deference and avoid anything that gave offense to Muslims. Over the course of time, discriminatory laws assumed outrageous forms, especially in Yemen, Morocco, and Iran from the seventeenth century on.

Islam's tolerance of Jews and Christians included a system of separation, subordination, and fiscal exploitation. Special payments for protection were only part of a complex relationship of Muslim superiority and DHIMMI inferiority. Collectively, the restrictions on dhimmis were known as the Pact of Umar. The fact that the Jews were not the only dissidents in the Muslim universe, as was the case of Jews in Christian Europe, made the burden and vulnerability of nonconformity more bearable. In addition, many of the strictures of the Pact of Umar were sporadically and unevenly applied. In medieval Spain and Egypt, for example, they were usually honored in the breach. Nevertheless, when the discrepancy between theory and practice became too great, or when a zealous ruler or preacher sensed that non–Muslims had risen too high, reformers insisted upon the restoration of discriminatory regulations. The Pact of Umar provided a potential source of inspiration for fundamentalist preachers and religious reformers, who could use its provisions to whip the populations to murderous passions at the spectacle of Jews exercising power as viziers and confidants of rulers.

In contrast to Europe, Jews in Muslim lands faced only sporadic official persecution. The violence of the twelfth-century Almohad persecution, which spread a wave of martyrdom and forced conversions through North Africa and Spain, was the exception to the general rule of low-level toleration. But with the decline of the world of Islam and the breakdown of public order, the burden of exploitation, political instability, and discrimination was compounded by the deleterious effects of ghettoization. Their ghettos were synonymous with misery and disease in North Africa and Iran. Jews were impoverished by indiscriminate extortionary taxes; their youth were forced to become artisans at a tender age. Scorn was heaped upon them by the Muslim majority, its members barely more fortunate than the Jews. By the late Middle Ages, most Christians had left the world of Western Islam, and the concept of dhimmi came to apply exclusively to Jews.

With the coming of the Western powers to the Middle East in the nineteenth century, anti-Jewish sentiments and actions assumed new and more menacing forms. The Ottoman Christian minorities, often with the active collaboration of Europeans, began to accuse Jews of murdering Christians for ritual purposes. The BLOOD LIBEL accusation appeared in the Middle East with great frequency and occasional virulence. Coupled with this accusation, the PROTOCOLS OF THE ELDERS OF ZION captured the popular Muslim imagination. These Western anti-semitic imports fell on receptive ears as the new movement of political Zionism entered the Middle East. Nationalists and fundamentalist preachers have exploited the traditional legacy of theological anti-Semitism in Islam, mixing it with ingredients from the ample arsenal of Western anti-Semitic materials. A voluminous anti-Semitic literature has emerged in the Arabic language in the twentieth century, replete with caricaturing of Jews that is quite reminiscent of Nazism. Thus Jews have become progressively more sinister and dehumanized. Since 1967, the line between anti-Zionism and anti-Semitism has become increasingly blurred in both serious literature and the popular press. Most recent trends have tended toward greater intolerance of Jews and Judaism, and the mixing of traditional Islamic and Western notions in a new and more hostile amalgam.

BIBLIOGRAPHY

COHEN, MARK R. *Under Crescent and Cross: The Jews in the Middle Ages.* Princeton, N.J., 1994.
GERBER, JANE S. "Anti-Semitism and the Muslim World." In *History and Hate: The Dimensions of Anti-Semitism,* ed. by David Berger. Philadelphia, 1986.

STILLMAN, NORMAN A. "Traditional Islamic Attitudes Toward Jews and Judaism." In *The Solomon Goldman Lectures,* vol. 4. 1985.

Jane Gerber

Antoine Bookstore

A major bookstore in Lebanon.

The Antoine Bookstore played an important intellectual role in prewar Lebanon; its main branch, in Bab Idris, served as a meeting place for writers, poets, and artists. After the Lebanese Civil War, its role was marginalized, although its branches in Ashrafiyya (in East Beirut) and in Hamra (in West Beirut) continued to serve customers. The shop was one of the first in Lebanon to sell foreign magazines and books.

As'ad AbuKhalil

Antonius, George [1891–1942]

Egyptian-born Christian Arab; member of the British Palestine Administration; political mediator between the Arabs and the British.

George Antonius was an author, administrator, and sometime intermediary between the British and the Arabs, whose only book, *The Arab Awakening* (1938), generated an ongoing debate over such issues as the origins of ARAB NATIONALISM, the significance of the ARAB REVOLT of 1916, and the machinations behind the post–World War I political settlement in the Middle East.

Born in Alexandria to a Greek Orthodox family of Lebanese origin, Antonius was raised as a privileged member of his native city's commercial upper class. His father, Habib, had emigrated to Egypt from the Lebanese village of Dayr al-Qamr. He speculated on the Alexandria cotton exchange, served as a *wakil* (agent) for prominent absentee landlords, and may have become a landowner himself. His business success insured that his four sons, Michael, George, Albert, and Constantine, could be educated at private schools and that he himself was able to retire to his native Lebanese village a prosperous man.

George Antonius attended Alexandria's elite Anglo-Arab public school, Victoria College, graduating as head of his class in 1910. He continued his education at King's College, Cambridge, earning a degree in engineering in 1913. The influence that he was later to exercise stemmed from his ability to function in two cultural environments—that of the Oxbridge-trained British elite and that of the Arab

notability. In circulating between these two elites, Antonius achieved the unique status of becoming recognized by each of them as its spokesman to the other. Despite his elegant use of the English language and his cultured manner, Antonius was never able completely to transcend the classification of "native" in the eyes of the British imperial administrators with whom he worked. Despite his command of Arabic and his disenchantment with British policy in Palestine, he was not regarded as a completely reliable colleague by Palestinian Arab Muslim leaders—who viewed him as something of an Anglophile.

During World War I, Antonius was employed in the censorship office of the British government in Egypt, stationed in Alexandria. As was to be the case throughout his life, his social and intellectual gifts enabled him to enjoy a diverse range of friendships, and he became a central figure in the literary and social circle that revolved around the British novelist E. M. Forster, the Greek poet Constantine Cavafy, and the bon vivants Demetrius Pericles and Robin Furness. Forster's published letters show that Antonius acted as his guide to Arab Alexandria, his traveling companion, and his confidant.

In 1921, Antonius accepted an appointment in the fledgling British Palestine Administration as assistant director of education. Jerusalem became his home for the rest of his life, and he came to regard himself as a Palestinian. Because of his administrative experience, his language abilities, and his interpersonal skills, however, Antonius was frequently ordered by British officials to undertake assignments outside Palestine. The most important of these required Antonius to spend much of the period from 1925 to 1928 on six arduous missions in Arabia and Yemen, five of them as first secretary to Sir Gilbert CLAYTON, the former head of the Arab Bureau. These missions found Antonius, the urbane Christian intellectual, serving as the principal negotiator between the British government and the Wahhabi tribal chieftain, Abd al-Aziz ibn al-Sa'ud (known later as King IBN SA'UD of Saudi Arabia). The missions achieved their objectives of satisfying ibn al-Sa'ud's desire to be recognized as the ruler of Arabia and Britain's wish to obtain agreement on the demarcation of the frontiers between ibn al-Sa'ud's domains and the British mandates in Iraq and Transjordan. In another instance of using his skills as a mediator, Antonius was called on by Lord Lloyd, the British high commissioner in Egypt, to play a crucial role in resolving the confrontation that became known as the Egyptian army crisis of 1927.

Although Antonius' service in Arabia earned him a commander of the British Empire, his lengthy absences from Jerusalem contributed to the ruin of his career in the Palestine government. Denied a promotion he thought he deserved and transferred against his will to the high commissioner's secretariat, he resigned in 1930.

From that point until shortly before his death, Antonius was employed as the Middle Eastern field representative of the Institute for Current World Affairs, a New York-based organization inspired and funded by the Chicago millionaire Charles Crane. In the course of his work for the institute, Antonius broadened his network of friends and acquaintances in high places and became a valued contact for many prominent foreigners visiting Jerusalem. His range of contacts was further expanded by his marriage in 1927 to Katy Nimr, the daughter of the wealthy Lebanese-Egyptian publisher and landowner, Faris NIMR. A vivacious and generous hostess, Katy Antonius made the Antonius home a focal point of Jerusalem social life, "a centre where people of all races could meet and talk and where a long succession of journalists, officials, officers and politicians were plunged, often for the first time, into a stimulating Arab intellectual milieu" ("Katy Antonius," obituary, *The Times* [London], December 8, 1984).

Once he resigned from government service, Antonius was able to associate freely with the Palestinian Arab community. He became an informal adviser to the Mufti of Jerusalem Hajj Amin al-HUSAYNI, and he endeavored to mediate a simmering dispute between the Arab members of the Greek Orthodox clergy in Jerusalem and the patriarch in Alexandria. Antonius's major triumph within the Palestinian movement occurred during the LONDON CONFERENCE of 1939, when he served as a member and secretary of the Palestinian delegation as well as secretary general of the entire Arab delegation. Antonius's book, *The Arab Awakening,* figured in the proceedings of the conference. The book contained the previously undisclosed HUSAYN–MCMAHON Correspondence, copies of which Antonius had acquired from Emir ABDULLAH IBN HUSAYN of Transjordan. By publishing the correspondence, Antonius compelled the British government to acknowledge its secret wartime pledges to the Arabs, to print an official version of the documents, and to address the question of the existence of potential contradictions between the pledges and the reality of the postwar settlement.

In addition to its immediate impact in British official circles, *The Arab Awakening* exercised a considerable influence on scholarship for many years. Although several of Antonius's interpretations have now been successfully challenged, his book remains an eloquent statement of the Arab perspective on the events that led to the division and occupation of Arab states after World War I.

Antonius was given little opportunity to bask in the acclaim accorded *The Arab Awakening.* He died in Jerusalem in 1942, during World War II, at the age of fifty-one, disillusioned by a warring world that had for the moment cast aside the need for mediators like himself.

BIBLIOGRAPHY

GEORGE ANTONIUS's influential work, *The Arab Awakening: The Story of the Arab National Movement,* was originally published in 1938 and has been reissued several times. The most compelling analysis of Antonius and his book is ALBERT HOURANI, "*The Arab Awakening* Forty Years Later" in Hourani, *The Emergence of the Modern Middle East* (London, 1981), pp. 193–215. An appreciation of Antonius's personal warmth and intellectual gifts is found in THOMAS HODGKIN, "Antonius, Palestine and the 1930s," *Gazelle Review of Literature on the Middle East* 10 (1982): 1–33. Volume 1 of *Selected Letters of E. M. Forster, 1879–1940,* edited by MARY LAGO and P. N. FURBANK (London, 1983), provides glimpses of Antonius's life in Alexandria during World War I. SIR GILBERT CLAYTON's account of his mission to Arabia in 1925, *An Arabian Diary,* edited by Robert O. Collins (Berkeley, 1969), offers an engaging portrait of Antonius and Clayton during their difficult journey. Antonius's administrative career in Palestine is examined in BERNARD WASSERSTEIN, *The British in Palestine: The Mandatory Government and the Arab–Jewish Conflict, 1917–1929,* 2nd ed. (Oxford, 1991). A poignant obituary of Katy Antonius appeared in *The Times* (London), December 8, 1984. Other sources consulted for this article include the Antonius papers in the Israeli State Archives (Jerusalem), the files of the Institute for Current World Affairs (Hanover, New Hampshire), and the Archives of St. Antony's College (Oxford).

William L. Cleveland

Antun, Farah   [1874–1922]

Lebanese intellectual.

Though originally from Tripoli in Lebanon, Antun spent much of his adult life in Cairo (Egypt) and in New York. He was the editor of the Arabic periodical *al-Jami'a* and the author of several books, including the famous *Ibn Rushd wa Falsafatuhu* (Ibn Rushd and His Philosophy).

As a Christian, and influenced by the French orientalist Ernest Renan, Antun addressed the question of religion and science in Islam. He concluded that neither can claim to be more true than the other. In Antun's view, the only solution to the dichotomy is to allow each its sphere; in the same vein, he believed in the separation of church and state. Antun was sensitive about the capacity of Islam to tolerate other creeds, be they different religious faiths or alternative world models, such as the one posited by Western science. Though Antun was at odds with individuals such as Muhammad ABDUH and Rashid RIDA over these questions, he deeply respected Islamic culture and strove to defend it against the intellectual onslaught of the West.

BIBLIOGRAPHY

HOURANI, ALBERT. *Arabic Thought in the Liberal Age 1798–1939.* New York, 1983.

Zachary Karabell

Aoun, Michel

Lebanese army officer.

Aoun (also Awn) was born in a suburb of Beirut, Lebanon, to a lower-middle-class MARONITE (Christian) family. He entered the military academy at Fayyadiyyah in 1955, and graduated as a lieutenant in the artillery corps. He attended advanced courses in the United States and France, and was promoted to commander of the artillery corps in 1976. Aoun, who rose through the ranks to general in the 1980s, sympathized with the Maronite-oriented militias in the Lebanese Civil War and staunchly opposed the Palestinians' presence in Lebanon. He supported the deployment of the army against the Palestine Liberation Organization (PLO) and its Lebanese allies.

In 1977, Aoun persuaded enlisted men and officers from different religious sects to join him in forming an integrated brigade, known later as the Eighth Brigade. He was appointed by President Amin JUMAYYIL (1982–1988) as commander in chief of the Lebanese army in June 1984. Just before the expiration of his term, and when the deep divisions in the country prevented the emergence of a national consensus to elect a president, Jumayyil appointed Aoun head of an interim government (in effect, as head of state). The appointment was rejected by many Lebanese. Aoun declared a "war of liberation" against the Syrian presence in Lebanon; Syrian forces intervened militarily and ousted him in October 1990. Aoun was forced into exile in France, where he remains as of 1994.

As'ad AbuKhalil

Aozou Strip

Disputed border land between Libya and Chad.

The Aozou Strip is disputed land along the common border between Libya and Chad some 310 miles (800 km) long and 40 miles (100 km) deep, encompassing at its northwestern end the Tibesti massif. The Strip was ceded by France from French Equatorial Africa to Italian Libya under the Mussolini–Laval Treaty in 1935. Although the treaty itself was ratified by both France and Italy, the instruments of ratification were never exchanged and, under the 1955 Franco–Libyan Treaty and the 1956 Franco–Libyan exchange of letters, the previous border, stemming from the 1899 Anglo–French Agreement over their respective spheres of influence in Africa, was generally regarded as being the appropriate international border—although not by Libya. In November 1972, Libya occupied the Aozou Strip and administered it until forced out of most of the region in March 1987. The dispute over the strip between Libya and Chad is now before the International Court of Justice at The Hague.

BIBLIOGRAPHY

JOFFE, E. G. H. "Frontiers in North Africa." In *Boundaries and State Territory in the Middle East and North Africa,* ed. by G. Blake and R. Schofield. Wisbech, U.K., 1987.

George Joffe

Apollo

Arab-language literary magazine, 1932–1934.

Founded by the poet Abu Shadi, this publication was the first of its kind in the Arabic language and had a significant impact on modern Arabic literature, even though it was only published for two years (for a total of twenty-five issues). The first issue appeared in September 1932 and the last in December 1934. *Apollo* magazine attempted to welcome all Arabic poets in Egypt (and elsewhere in the Arab world) to submit their work. The editors stressed poetic innovation and departure from traditional forms; special emphasis was placed on the authentic and artistic expression of emotions. The poets who contributed drew inspiration from such poetic trends as realism, romanticism, surrealism, and symbolism, as well as from the more traditional schools of Arabic poetry. *Apollo* was especially important as a forum for the discussion and debate of poetic theory; one of the most famous literary critics whose work appeared in *Apollo* was Isma'il Mazhar. The demise of the magazine is generally attributed to the disputes between Abu Shadi and Abbas Mahmud al-AQQAD and their followers; al-Aqqad favored a more radically avant-garde approach to poetry than did Abu Shadi.

Kenneth S. Mayers

Applefeld, Aharon   [1932–   ]

Hebrew writer and essayist.

Aharon Applefeld, born near Czernowvitz, Bukovina, grew up in a German speaking, affluent, assimilated Jewish home, close to Hasidic grandparents and Ukrainian caretakers. The Holocaust reached his family when he was eight: his mother and grandmother fell victim to it. Applefeld spent the subsequent four years in constant flight, battling hunger and fear in forests or villages, often with other hunted Jewish children. When World War II ended, he made his way to a displaced persons camp in Italy and, in 1946, finally made his way to Palestine. There he went to agricultural boarding schools, joined the army, and attended the Hebrew University of Jerusalem where, at last, he filled the gaps in his education.

Continuously searching for his roots, Applefeld delved into Hasidic, Yiddish, and mystical texts as well as into Kafka's works—all of these materials reverberate later in his own stories of uprootedness. Being a figure at the margins of the Israeli "generation of the state" writers, Applefeld struggles with the Jewish, rather than the strictly Israeli, experience. With an idiosyncratic diction—attempting to forge silence with words, his memory's black hole with details—Applefeld depicts the disintegrating pre-war central European Jewish milieu and its dislocated, fragmented, post-Holocaust remnants, be they in Israel or elsewhere.

The 1983 Israel Prize laureate and author of nearly twenty books, Applefeld published his first collection of short stories, *Ashan* (Smoke), in 1962 and a first novel, *The Skin and the Gown*, in 1970. These and other works like *Badenheim, 1939* (1980), *The Healer* (1985), and *Katerina* (1989) situate him among the foremost chroniclers of the impact of the Holocaust on the human psyche. He is a dispossessed writer whose protagonists, tongueless and homeless, are forever in exile. Applefeld teaches literature in the Ben-Gurion University of the Negev.

BIBLIOGRAPHY

EZRAHI, SIDRA DEKOVEN. *By Words Alone: The Holocaust in Literature.* Chicago, 1980.
RAMRAS-RAUCH, GILA. *Aharon Applefeld: The Holocaust and Beyond.* Bloomington, Ind., 1994.
ROSKIES, DAVID. *Against the Apocalypse: Responses to Catastrophe in Modern Jewish Culture.* Cambridge, Mass., 1984.
SCHWARTZ, YIGAL. *Eternity and the Tribe.* Jerusalem, 1996.

Nili Gold

View of Aqaba. (Laura Mendelson)

Aqaba

Seaport at the head of the Gulf of Aqaba, on the Red Sea, and just across the border from Eilat in Israel.

Aqaba was a small fishing village and site of an Ottoman fort when it became officially incorporated into the Emirate of Transjordan in 1924, giving Jordan its only outlet to the sea. In 1959, Aqaba's port became operational, and in 1976, a free trade zone was opened. The port experienced substantial development as a result of aid from Iraq, which needed safe access to a seaport during its war with Iran. By mid-1990, facilities at the port included twenty berths, one container terminal, two forty-ton (36 t) gantry cranes, and 358,000 square yards (299,000 m) of storage area. Iraqi aid also helped develop the country's roads and overland transportation systems. Cargo handled through Aqaba increased steadily throughout the 1980s, peaking in 1988 as trade with Iraq increased to 18.7 million tons (17 million t) of imports and exports handled in 1989. Cargo handling fell sharply to 10 million tons (9.07 million t) after the U.N. embargo against Iraq was imposed in 1990. In addition to the port, Aqaba is a popular tourist resort, known for its beaches and water sports, and is the sight of some of the most spectacular coral reefs that can be seen today.

BIBLIOGRAPHY

GUBSER, PETER. *Jordan: Crossroads of Middle Eastern Events.* Boulder, Colo., 1983.

Jenab Tutunji

Aqaba Incident

Border crisis in 1906 in the Sinai peninsula, also known as the Taba incident.

In 1906, Ottoman troops occupied Taba, an Egyptian town in the Sinai peninsula west of AQABA (in present-day Jordan), to enlarge Ottoman access to the Red Sea. The British, who occupied Egypt, forced them to withdraw. The two sides later agreed to cede to the Ottoman Empire a small area west of Aqaba, while retaining Taba in Egypt.

The Taba incident provoked a wave of secular nationalist agitation led by Mustafa Kamil and others who challenged Britain's right to negotiate Egyptian territory. Mustafa Kamil had started a newspaper, al-LIWA, to encourage nationalism.

BIBLIOGRAPHY

HOLT, P. M. *Egypt and the Fertile Crescent 1516–1922.* Ithaca, N.Y., 1966.
VATIKIOTIS, P. J. *The History of Modern Egypt,* 4th ed. London, 1991.

Elizabeth Thompson

Aqqad, Abbas Mahmud al-   [1889–1964]

Egyptian writer, critic and poet.

Born in Aswan, Egypt, to a middle-class, conservative Muslim family, al-Aqqad was educated in Aswan and worked there as a civil servant. Between 1913 and 1921, al-Aqqad published and wrote in *al-Diwan;* in these writings, he attacked traditional forms of poetry for their blind imitation of the past, while stressing the unity of an artistic work as an expression of the author's unique personality. During this time, Aqqad was an advocate of secular liberalism and the adoption of European culture. In the 1930s, however, he moved away from this strict modernist position and began to write volumes glorifying the Islamic past. Considered the main polemicist of the WAFD party in the 1920s, he later joined the Sa'dist party, writing regularly for its newspaper, *al-Asas.* Among his major works are two collections of verse, *Diwan* (Collection), published in 1916, and *Wahy al-Arba'in* (The Inspiration of Forty Years), published in 1933; a collection of essays entitled *Sa'at bayn al-Kutub* (Hours Spent with Books); a biography of Sa'd ZAGHLUL, *Sa'd Zaghlul: Sira wa Tahiyya* (Biography and Tribute); and an autobiography, *Ana* (I).

BIBLIOGRAPHY

ABDEL-MALEK, ANOUAR, ed. *Anthologie de la littérature arabe contemporaine.* Vol. 2, Les essais. Paris, 1965.
BECKA, JIRI. *Dictionary of Oriental Literatures.* Vol. 3, West Asia and North Africa. New York, 1974.

GERSHONI, ISRAEL, and JAMES P. JANKOWSKI. *Egypt, Islam, and the Arabs: The Search for Egyptian Nationhood, 1900–1930.* New York, 1986.
VATIKIOTIS, P. J. *A History of Modern Egypt,* 4th ed. London, 1991.

David Waldner

Aqqad, Umar Abd al-Fattah al-   [1927–   ]

Palestinian-Saudi engineer and banker.

Aqqad began his career as a director of the Saudi British Bank. He has subsequently directed the Saudi Bank and the Arab Investment Company of Luxembourg and Switzerland. Aqqad has been a major supporter of Palestinian educational institutions such as Bir Zeit University.

BIBLIOGRAPHY

Who's Who in the Arab World. Beirut, 1990–91.

Steve Tamari

Arab

The history, distribution, and culture of the Arab people, who originated in the Arabian peninsula.

For most of the recorded history, the term *Arabs* has denoted camel-breeding nomads (bedouin) living in the deserts of southwestern Asia and northern Africa and speaking one of several dialects of the Arabic language. During the twentieth century, the term has been broadened to include the native speakers of Arabic—city-dwellers and peasants as well as nomads—as well as to all who believed in the ideas and goals of Arab nationalism.

Politically, the term has at times been applied to all citizens of states in which Arabic is now the official language, even if some were not native Arabic speakers or did not identify themselves as Arabs. These states, listed from west to east, are Morocco, Algeria, Tunisia, Libya, Egypt, the Sudan, Saudi Arabia, Yemen, Lebanon, Syria, Jordan, Iraq, Kuwait, Bahrain, Qatar, the United Arab Emirates, and Oman. Culturally, the term has also been applied to persons of Arab descent living outside the states in which Arabic is the official language but still speaking a dialect of Arabic or otherwise involved in activities identified as Arab. In this case, Arabic speakers and their descendants in Europe, Africa, Asia, the Americas, and Australia might call themselves, or be regarded by others, as Arab. Definitions of "Arab" are various and much debated.

Arabs participated in most ancient Near Eastern civilizations as traders, auxiliary warriors, and providers of camels and other desert produce. They were usually organized into extended kinship units, for which Arabic has various words, depending on the size and cohesion of the unit, but the most frequently used term is *qawm*, commonly translated as "clan." For nomadic Arabs, the *qawm* was their main political, economic, and social organization. It determined where they led, watered, and grazed their camels, horses, and their flocks of sheep and goats, and with whom they fought or traded. Nomadism did not mean an aimless wandering through desert wastes, but rather a systematic migration of the *qawm*, its animals, and its belongings, following seasonal patterns of available water and vegetation, a sophisticated adaptation to their arid environment. Poetry, their main artistic expression, presented their most strongly held beliefs and values, summed up in the code known as the *muruwwa* (manly virtues): bravery in battle, patience in misfortune, persistence in revenge, protection of the weak, defiance toward the strong, hospitality to the guest, generosity to the needy, loyalty to the *qawm*, and fidelity in keeping promises. Most early Arabs were animists or ancestor-worshipers, but some adopted Judaism or Christianity before the advent of Islam.

The life and mission of Muhammad (570–632 C.E.) profoundly affected the Arabs, most of whom embraced Islam during or soon after the Prophet's lifetime. Many Arab clans took part in the early conquests to extend Islamic rule into the Fertile Crescent and across North Africa as far west as Morocco and Spain (711 C.E.) and eastward to the borders of India and China. The Arabic language and the Islamic religion were therefore widely adopted by non-Arab conquered peoples, some of whom intermarried with Arabs. Nevertheless, the Arab conquerors tended to maintain their clan ties and often reverted to nomadism when their military service was no longer required. All the early Muslim caliphs belonged to Muhammad's tribe, the QURAYSH, but the government of the caliphate depended on the bureaucratic skills of the Persians and other conquered non-Arabs; increasingly, the non-Arabs assumed political power as well. After the Turkish incursions of the ninth and tenth centuries and their assumption of power in the eleventh, the Arabs ceased to play a significant political role in Islam, except in the Arabian Peninsula, where they always held control. Arab *ulama* (clergy), mystics, and traders played a major role in spreading Islam to India, the spice islands of Southeast Asia, and eastern and western Africa.

In the late 1800s, some non-Arab thinkers, including Wilfrid Blunt, called for a revival of Arab political power. In the late Ottoman Empire, Arab nationalism emerged in some Beirut student societies. Some Arabs called for the restoration of the caliphate to an Arab ruler, as it was then claimed by the Ottoman sultans. In World War I, a family of Arabs (HASHIMITES) led by the sharif of Mecca—Amir Husayn, a descendant of Muhammad—undertook the Arab Revolt against Ottoman rule and succeeded in freeing parts of the Hejaz (Arabia), Palestine, and Syria from the Ottoman Turks. Aided during the war by Britain, these Arabs hoped that afterwards they might be allowed to form a united Arab state in the Arabian peninsula and the Fertile Crescent, but Britain honored other promises it had made to its allies (especially France) and to the Zionist movement. Husayn took but later lost control of the Hejaz; his son Faisal briefly ruled in Syria (until the French mandate took over in 1920) but was then made king of Iraq; another son, Abdallah, was given an emirate called Transjordan (now the Hashimite Kingdom of Jordan).

In the peace settlement that ended World War I, Arabs in Syria and Lebanon were placed under a League of Nations mandate administered by France; Britain held similar mandates in Palestine (initially including Transjordan) and Iraq. These mandates were intended to be temporary means for training the local inhabitants, most of whom were Arabs, to govern themselves. The Arabs themselves resented the Europeans, the rule by mandate, and the political divisions that were created in the Fertile Crescent, but the winning of independence from European control between 1932 and 1946 did not facilitate Arab unification. Most emirates and shaykhdoms in the Arabian Peninsula were under British military and diplomatic protection, but in 1932 the leader of the AL SA'UD FAMILY in Najd, Abd al-Aziz (known as IBN SA'UD) managed by conquest and diplomacy to unite most of the Peninsula Arabs in the Kingdom of Saudi Arabia. The predominantly Zaydi Shi'ite kingdom of Yemen also remained independent.

Because of European imperialism, Arab energies from 1900 to about 1950 were devoted mainly to achieving independence and to unifying the Arabic-speaking states. Unification efforts resulted in the creation of the League of Arab States in 1945, with Egypt assuming a leadership role for the first time, but this "Arab League," as it is called, tended to reinforce existing Arab states. It undermined Arab efforts to protect the Palestinians from the creation in 1948 of the State of ISRAEL, turning at least 500,000 into refugees. The protracted and costly Arab–Israel

Conflict led to Arab military defeats in 1949, 1956, 1967, and 1973.

Arab attempts to form organic unions, such as the United Arab Republic (1958–1961), have never succeeded. Arab federations, too, have failed, but inter-Arab pacts to create customs and telecommunications unions have been implemented. The Arabs' success at imposing an oil embargo (the OAPEC—Organization of Arab Petroleum Exporting countries—oil embargo) on the United States during and after the October 1973 war with Israel raised hopes for Arab unity, but Egypt's separate peace with Israel in 1979, the division of Arab countries over the Lebanese Civil War (1975–1990), the Iran–Iraq War (1980–1988), and Iraq's invasion of Kuwait (Gulf Crisis of 1990–1991) all pointed to deep-seated divisions among Arab governments and peoples. Petroleum revenues have enriched some Arab regimes—and public works, schools, roads, and so on make their people's lives better—but on the whole the Arabs have not prospered. The Islamist political movement is gaining momentum because of this.

If Arabs have been deeply frustrated by their failure to unite, they still take pride in their historical achievements, their culture, notably their language and literature, their role in the development and spread of Islam, and their keen family loyalty, generosity, and hospitality.

BIBLIOGRAPHY

ATIYAH, EDWARD S. *The Arabs.* Baltimore, 1958.
BERGER, MORROE. *The Arab World Today.* Garden City, N.Y., 1962.
BERQUE, JACQUES. *Arab Rebirth: Pain and Ecstasy.* London, 1983.
FISHER, SYDNEY N., and WILLIAM OCHSENWALD. *The Middle East: A History,* 4th ed. New York, 1990.
GOLDSCHMIDT, ARTHUR. *A Concise History of the Middle East,* 4th ed. Boulder, Colo., 1991.
HAMADY, SANIA. *Temperament and Character of the Arabs.* New York, 1960.
HITTI, PHILIP K. *History of the Arabs,* 10th ed. New York, 1970.
HOURANI, ALBERT. *History of the Arab Peoples.* Cambridge, Mass., 1991.
HUDSON, MICHAEL. *Arab Politics: The Search for Legitimacy.* New Haven, Conn., 1977.
IBRAHIM, SAAD EDDIN, and NICHOLAS HOPKINS, eds. *Arab Society: Social Science Perspectives.* Cairo, 1985.
LAMB, DAVID. *The Arabs: Journeys beyond the Mirage.* New York, 1987.
LEWIS, BERNARD. *The Arabs in History,* 6th ed. Oxford and New York, 1993.
MANSFIELD, PETER. *The Arabs,* 3d ed. New York, 1985.
MUSALLAM, BASIM. *The Arabs: A Living History.* London, 1983.
NYDELL, MARGARET. *Understanding Arabs: A Guide for Westerners.* Yarmouth, Maine, 1987.
PATAI, RAPHAEL. *The Arab Mind.* New York, 1973.
POLK, WILLIAM R. *The Arab World Today,* 5th ed. Cambridge, Mass., 1991.

Arthur Goldschmidt, Jr.

Arab Academy of Damascus

Center for Arabic studies.

Modeled on the Académie Française, the Academy of Arab Learning in Damascus (*al-Majma al-Ilmi al-Arabi bi Dimashq*) was established in June 1919 as a center for Arabic linguistics and studies in literature and the humanities. It was part of a concerted effort by the government of the newly established Kingdom of Syria to make Arabic the language of administration, the armed forces, high culture, and education within its boundaries. Its founders included Amin Suwaid, Anis Sallum, Sa'id al-Karmi, Abd al-Qadir al-Maghribi, Isa al-Ma'luf, Dimitri Qandalaft, Izz al-Din al-Tanuhi, and Muhammad Kurd Ali, who was its president. Influential nationalists such as Abd al-Rahman al-Shahbandar, Rashid Baqdunis, and Faris al-Khuri were early members.

The academy, headquartered in the historic Adiliyya School (*al-Madrasa al-Adiliyya*), sponsored public lectures on a wide range of cultural subjects and supervised the editing of important Arabic–language texts. In addition, it was responsible for overseeing the extensive collection of manuscripts and books that had been gathered by Shaykh Tahir al-Jaza'iri during the final decades of the nineteenth century in the adjacent Zahiriyya School (*al-Madrasa al-Zahiriyya*), as well as for administering the Syrian National Museum. By the spring of 1920, growing fiscal difficulties forced the government of King Faisal to cut back funding for the organization, which disbanded later that summer.

In early September 1920, Kurd Ali proposed to the French mandatory authorities that the academy reopen. The high commissioner, who saw the proposal as an opportunity to split Damascus's intelligentsia, immediately approved the proposal. Successive mandatory governors provided generous financial support for the organization, severely limiting its ability to serve either as a forum for open political debate or as an incubator of Arab nationalist sentiment. Nevertheless, the academy's cultural activities flourished under French patronage. A journal (*Majalla al-Majma al-Ilmi al-Arabi*) appeared in January 1921, along with a series of critical editions of writings by prominent Arab authors. The academy merged with the Syrian University in June 1923, and was reincorporated as a research institute for the study of formal Arabic language (*al-lugha al-fusha*) three years later. Throughout the 1930s and 1940s, the academy organized international festivals celebrating the contributions of major Arab literary figures. By the 1950s the circle of corresponding members had expanded to include such influential Western scholars as Carl Brockelmann, Ignaz Goldziher, Snouck Hurgronje, and Louis Massignon.

Fred H. Lawson

Arab Agency

British offer to Palestinian Arabs during mandate.

In 1923, British mandate authorities in Palestine offered to establish an Arab Agency to represent Palestinian Arab nationalist interests. The British effort was aimed at countering independent Palestinian political organizations that were opposed to their mandate (1922–1948) and to Zionism. Arab leaders rejected the British offer because they did not want to acknowledge the legality of the mandate.

BIBLIOGRAPHY

HUREWITZ, J. C. *The Struggle for Palestine.* New York, 1968.

Steve Tamari

Arab Boycott

Various measures of economic warfare against Israel by the League of Arab States.

Following Israel's creation in 1948 and the resultant displacement of hundreds of thousands of Palestinians the boycott has been the most long-lasting attempt at economic warfare in a region that has also seen oil embargoes against Western countries in 1973, American embargoes and boycotts aimed at Iran and Libya, and UN economic sanctions against Iraq.

On December 2, 1945, in pursuance of an idea dating from 1921, the League of Arab States Council called on all Arab states to prohibit the purchase of "products of Palestinian Jews" to prevent "the realization of Zionist political aims." After Israel's establishment in 1948, the boycott was greatly expanded with the aim of undermining the new state's viability.

The *primary boycott* barred Arab states, companies, and individuals from buying from or selling to Israel any goods or services and prohibited other commercial or financial relationships with the Jewish state. In 1950 a *secondary boycott* extended the prohibitions to dealings with companies anywhere in the world that contributed to Israeli economic or military strength. A subsequent *tertiary boycott* was aimed more broadly at individuals and organizations seen as supportive of Israel. The Central Boycott Office, established in 1951 in Damascus, administered boycott activities and maintained a roster of blacklisted companies. By 1976, sixty-three hundred firms from ninety-six countries had been blacklisted. However, the rulings of the office were only advisory. Many Arab states chose not to follow the secondary and tertiary boycotts or followed them only selectively.

In 1992 the Federation of Israeli Chambers of Commerce estimated that the boycott had reduced the exports by 10 percent and investments by 15 percent for a cumulative loss of forty-five billion dollars. Foreign reaction to the boycott ranged from repeated expressions of outrage and legal counteractions by the United States and some European countries to Japanese and Korean reluctance to engage in economic dealings with Israel at the risk of offending Arab countries.

Egypt ended participation in the boycott in 1979, and Jordan in 1994, following their peace treaties with Israel. Many other members of the League of Arab States initiated some degree of contact with Israel following the 1991 Gulf War and the subsequent agreements between Israel and the Palestine Liberation Organization. In February 1995 Egyptian, American, Israeli, Jordanian, and Palestinian trade representatives signed the Taba Declaration declaring support for ending the boycott in the interest of free and open markets.

BIBLIOGRAPHY

BARD, MITCHELL GEOFFREY. *The Water's Edge and Beyond: Defining the Limits of Domestic Influence on Middle East Policy* (esp. chapter 4, "The Antiboycott Bill," pp. 91–117). New Brunswick, N.J., 1991.
GRUEN, GEORGE E. "Breaking the Logjam on the Boycott." *Present Tense* 4 (Winter 1977): 44–51.
SARNA, AARON J. *Boycott and Blacklist: A History of Arab Economic Warfare against Israel.* Lanham, Md., 1986.
SCHÖPFLIN, JULIA. "The Arab Boycott of Israel: Can It Withstand the Peace Process?" *Institute of Jewish Affairs* [*London*] *Research Reports* 4 (March 1994).

George E. Gruen

Arab Bureau

See Bureaux Arabes

Arab Club

Early twentieth century organization that promoted Palestinian nationalism.

The Arab Club (al-Nadi al-Arabi), originally set up in Damascus as an offshoot of al-FATH by Palestinian nationalists who moved to the city after it fell to the armies of Field Marshal Viscount Edmund Allenby and Faisal I, king of Iraq, toward the end of World War I. The same organization emerged in Jerusalem in June 1918 and was dominated by younger members of the al-HUSAYNI FAMILY, most notably al-Hajj Amin, who became the president of the Palestine branch of the club. Real power rested in the hands of Damascus-based Palestinians from Nablus. Before the decline of its activities at the end of 1920, the club had over five hundred members, with branches in major Palestinian towns. Although al-Nadi was openly engaged in cultural and social activities, its overriding concerns were political. Under the direction of its Damascus central organization, the club opposed Zionism and called for the unification of Palestine with Syria. The club's principal instruments of mobilization were the mosques, the press, and political activists in Palestinian towns and villages. With the collapse of Faisal's Arab government in Syria in the summer of 1920 and the disintegration of its Arab nationalist lieutenants, the Arab Club lost the two most important sources of its support. It was eventually overtaken by the ARAB EXECUTIVE and the MUSLIM–CHRISTIAN ASSOCIATION.

BIBLIOGRAPHY

DARWAZA, MUHAMMAD IZZAT. "Tis'una Aman fi al-Hayat, 1888–1978," vol. 2 (unpublished autobiography).

AL-GHURI, EMILE. *Filastin Abra Sittina Aman,* vol. 1. Beirut, 1972.

PORATH, Y. *The Palestinian Arab National Movement, 1918–1929.* London, 1974.

Muhammad Muslih

Arab College of Jerusalem

One of the most important Arab educational institutions in Palestine during the period of the British mandate.

The Arab College of Jerusalem was officially established in 1926 in Bab al-Zahira (Herod's Gate) Jerusalem, on the premises of the Teacher Training Academy. In 1935, the Arab College was moved to Jabal al-Mukabhir (Hill of Evil Counsel) in Jerusalem, where it remained until 1948 when its activities were suspended after the creation of the State of Israel.

The Teacher Training Academy had been established by Britain, which in 1918 received a League of Nations mandate to rule Palestine and prepare it for independence. A number of Egyptian teachers were appointed to positions at the academy. In 1919, Khalil al-SAKAKINI, a Palestinian and well-known Arab literary figure, was named director. He remained in that office until 1922, when he resigned his post to protest the practice of Britain to use the academy teachers in activities that conflicted with their duties as educators, such as taking the census of Palestine.

Soon after, Khalil Tawtah, another Palestinian Arab educator, was appointed director of the academy. In 1925, he too resigned when the students and teachers went on strike to protest the BALFOUR DECLARATION of 1917—the strike coincided with the visit to Palestine of Britain's Arthur James, 1st Earl of Balfour himself.

Ahmad al-Samih al-KHALIDI then assumed the post of acting principal and was in 1926 officially appointed principal of the academy. Al-Khalidi introduced important changes in the curriculum that made the change of its name imperative. Henceforth, the name Teacher Training Academy (Dar al-Mu'allimin) was replaced by Arab College of Jerusalem (al-Kulliya al-Arabiya fi al-Quds). Al-Khalidi remained principal until its closing in 1948, when thousands of Palestinian Arabs fled or were expelled from the new State of Israel and took refuge in the neighboring Arab countries, many never to return or be allowed to return again.

The Arab College of Jerusalem, and its predecessor, the Teacher Training Academy, were open to both Arabs and Jews, but there were many schools for Jews that were preparing their teachers in a manner consistent with the short- and long-term objectives of ZIONISM. So Jews refrained from enrolling in the academy and in the college; of the twenty-three students at the academy in 1918, only one was Jewish. As the years went by, only Arab students attended the college; but the Arab students, although Muslim in majority, included Christians and Baha'is.

The total number of students in the college rarely exceeded one hundred, and each year's graduates usually numbered about twenty. With such small numbers, one would not expect the college to have a great impact on the cultural life of Palestine. In fact, however, the Arab College in Jerusalem acquired very wide fame in both Palestine and the neighboring Arab countries. This was due primarily to the quality of its students and of the education they received. It was a mark of outstanding performance for a student to be admitted to the college.

The principal of the college recruited his first-year students from the various Arab elementary schools in Palestine; he would choose the most brilliant who finished elementary, interview them, and then select from among them the *crème de la crème*. (There were rare exceptions to this rule: Prince Nayef, of the ruling Hashimite family in Transjordan, and Prince Abd al-Ilah, a Hashimite who became regent during the early 1930s in Iraq, were admitted to the college on the grounds of their social status.) Al-Khalidi was, in fact, the first educator in the Arab world to have applied intelligence tests to those who sought admission to the college.

Once admitted, the students were generally exempted from paying any tuition fees. They were taken as boarders, for which they paid a modest stipend. This was necessary, since most students came from poor villages; they could not afford to pay tuition or for food and lodging.

The curriculum of the college was unique in the Arab countries; it was conceived on the pattern of modern British schools with special emphasis on the English language and literature, Arabic, Latin, and practical training in teaching, in addition to history, geography, science, and mathematics. Upon graduation, the students who proved themselves worthy were sent to continue their education at British universities or at the AMERICAN UNIVERSITY OF BEIRUT. The remaining graduates continued their educations at Arab universities.

The teachers of the Arab College were outstanding in science, literature, and the arts. The English-language instructors were, in most cases, British. So fine was the college's reputation that it attracted numerous visitors from Arab countries and Britain, including Colonel Bertram THOMAS, the explorer of RUB AL-KHALI in the Arabian peninsula, and Rudyard Kipling (1865–1936), poet laureate of the British Empire and 1907 winner of the Nobel prize for literature. To this day, it is considered special to be a graduate of the Arab College of Jerusalem.

Hisham Nashabi

Arab Common Market

Middle East cooperative organization.

The Arab Common Market resolution of 13 August 1964 established regional economic integration among the nine signers of the Economic Unity Agreement (6 June 1962). It provided for the complete removal of customs duties and other barriers to free trade by 1974. Four Arab nations—Syria, Jordan, Iraq, and the United Arab Republic—ratified the resolution, and Kuwait participated without ratifying. This shortage of members, along with the protectionist policy of individual states, regional political conflicts, and economic changes, undermined progress on the agreement, which became of peripheral importance by the early 1970s.

BIBLIOGRAPHY

ALFRED G. MUSREY. *An Arab Common Market: A Study in Inter-Arab Trade Relations, 1920–67.* New York, 1969.

Charles U. Zenzie

Arab Constitution Party

Jordanian political party.

The Arab Constitution party (in Arabic, al-Hizb al-Arabi al-Dusturi) was established in 1956 by twenty-one members of parliament who supported the policies of the former prime minister, Tawfiq ABD AL-HUDA. The party's platform prescribed the subordination of foreign relations to the interests of the Arab nation (*al-*UMMA); working for Arab unity, liberation from foreign dominance, and the return of the seized portions of Palestine; raising the status of peasants and workers and defending the rights of farmers; and cooperating with all Arab countries. Membership remained limited to the founding members and never developed a popular following. The party was dissolved in 1957 when all political party activity in Jordan was suppressed.

BIBLIOGRAPHY

ABIDI, AQIL HYDER HASAN. *Jordan: A Political Study, 1948–1957.* New Delhi, 1965.

Jenab Tutunji

Arab Democratic Party

Lebanese nationalist party closely affiliated with the Syrian government.

The Arab Democratic party is aligned with Rif'at al-Asad, brother of Lebanon's President Hafiz al-Asad. Founded early during the LEBANESE CIVIL WAR, its nucleus was Rif'at's militia, Al-Fursan. It later developed into a full-fledged political party with a very small popular base. The ALAWITE deputy Ali Id, who in 1992 was elected from the north, had been secretary-general of the party since 1985. The other leader is a Shi'ite, Suhayl Hamadah, from Baalbek. Without direct Syrian military and political support, the party has no power. The decline of the fortunes of Rif'at diminished the influence of the party, which is associated by many Lebanese with the acts of thuggery that members were known to have committed during the civil war.

BIBLIOGRAPHY

TACHAU, FRANK, ed. *The Encyclopedia of Political Parties in the Middle East and North Africa.*

As'ad AbuKhalil

Arab Development Society (ADS)

Society founded in 1945 to aid Palestinian peasants.

Developed by the LEAGUE OF ARAB STATES (called the Arab League) immediately after its founding in 1945, the society (ADS) tried to help Palestinians increase agricultural production and resist temptation to sell their lands. It was headed by a Palestinian lawyer and politician, Musa al-ALAMI. After Israel was established in 1948, Alami used ADS funds to develop an experimental farm in the Jordan valley; the purpose was not production, but the training of peasants in the Jericho area. Reforestation was a priority.

BIBLIOGRAPHY

FURLONGE, GEOFFREY. *Palestine Is My Country: The Story of Musa Alami.* New York, 1969.

Steve Tamari

Arab Eastern Front Command

Joint Arab effort to defend the borders shared with Israel.

Formed by Jordan, Syria, and Iraq just prior to the outbreak of the 1967 Arab–Israel War, the front was concerned with the defense of the WEST BANK, Jordan, the GOLAN HEIGHTS, and Syria. According to the agreement, the armed forces of Jordan, Syria, and Iraq were to defend the eastern front under a unified command, headed by Lieutenant-General Abdel Mon'em Riyad of Egypt.

BIBLIOGRAPHY

GUBSER, PETER. *Jordan: Crossroads of Middle Eastern Events.* Boulder, Colo., 1983.

Jenab Tutunji

Arab Executive

Executive committee elected by the third Palestinian Arab Congress.

The Third PALESTINIAN ARAB CONGRESS, which convened in Haifa in December 1920, elected the Arab Executive to act as the executive committee of the Congress and coordinate its political activities with the help of a secretariat based in Jerusalem under the leadership of Jamal al-Husayni. An alliance of middle-aged Muslim and Christian men who hailed from upper class families, the Arab Executive became the most important Palestinian political organization from the date of its inception until its dissolution in August 1934, almost five months after the death of its octogenarian leader Musa Kazim Pasha al-Husayni in March 1934. The Palestinian nationalists who led the Arab Executive adhered to a system of ideas that formed the political orthodoxy of the Palestinians during the British mandate era. This system was cast in a nationalist program that rejected ZIONISM and called for the establishment of a Palestinian national government responsible to a representative assembly. The Arab Executive's very existence was predicated on struggle against Zionism, and therefore the organization's leaders had to win popular support by mobilizing the masses from above through the local Muslim–Christian associations and congresses, as well as the Jerusalem-based secretariat that drafted proposals and maintained contact with branch societies and other Palestinian political bodies.

The Arab Executive established an internal organization, including a secretariat and permanent committees with political, administrative, and economic responsibilities. Yet its organizational structure was rather feeble. Actually, the Arab Executive functioned on an informal basis through an elite of politicians, including many of the leading Muslim and Christian personalities. These politicians relied almost completely on a shared commitment to the nationalist cause and on ascriptive ties such as kinship, similar social backgrounds, and past participation in politics.

Despite the common threat of Zionism, the Arab Executive did not hold together as a cohesive front. Internal fissures were reflected in personal and family rivalries, most notably the Husayni-Nashashibi cleavage, as well as in disagreements over noncooperation against the British. Some prominent politicians, including Raghib Bey al-NASHASHIBI, Arif al-DAJANI, and the mayors of Acre, Gaza, and Nablus, favored in the early 1920s Palestinian participation in a legislative council in which the Palestinians would have a majority vote.

By contrast, the Husaynis and their supporters rejected participation in any political body based on the premises of the BALFOUR DECLARATION. Objectively, there was ambivalence in the position of the Husayni-dominated wing of the Arab Executive leadership. Jamal al-HUSAYNI and Awni ABD AL-HADI, for example, were willing to cooperate with the British government on administrative issues, but they rejected cooperation on issues related to constitutional matters; they particularly opposed elections to form a legislative council, in good part because Palestinian participation in such a council meant, in their view, the acceptance of the Zionist program.

In reality, the Arab Executive was far from being a revolutionary political movement. To promote the cause of Palestinian nationalism it relied primarily on traditional diplomatic methods, foremost among which was petitions to the British government.

In 1927, attempts were made to reunite the Arab Executive as an umbrella organization for the Palestinian nationalist movement. A new Arab Executive was formed, with forty-eight members, twelve of them Christian; the Husayni and Nashashibi camps were reunited. They struck a balance between the different Palestinian factions by giving senior positions within the Arab Executive to the Husaynis, the Nashashibis, and the neutral pan-Arab politicians, most notably Awni Abd al-Hadi. The main purpose behind this reunification was creation of a united Palestinian front that would effectively press the British authorities to establish representative institutions, including a reconstituted legislative council.

The reunification of the Arab Executive, however, was short-lived. The WESTERN (Wailing) WALL explosive incidents of August 1929 increased Jewish immigration, the emergence of new political and social forces, and a moribund and financially-strapped Arab Executive. All these factors led to the shaping of a new political climate, which contributed to a rearrangement of social and political forces in Palestine. By the early 1930s, the scale of politics was no longer restricted to the domain of the Arab Executive and its traditional leadership. More activist groups had already emerged by the end of the 1920s, including the Green Hand Gang and the underground cells of Shaykh Izz al-Din al-Qassam. Through strikes, demonstrations, and guerilla warfare in the countryside, these forces not only provided an alternative to the discredited style and methods of the Arab Executive, but they also set in motion the train of events that culminated in the Great Revolt of 1936–1939.

Muhammad Muslih

Arab Fund for Economic and Social Development

Established by the Arab League in 1969, in an attempt to deploy capital as a mechanism of economic integration.

In addition to funding infrastructural and developmental projects such as fertilizer plants, railroads, sewerage and water-supply systems, and crop-production programs, the fund has sought to promote Arab integration through three schemes. First is the development of an Arab communications satellite, the Pan-Arab Communications Network. Second was funding for the ARAB ORGANIZATION FOR INDUSTRIALIZATION, though this funding was terminated following the repercussions of Egypt's signing the CAMP DAVID ACCORDS. Finally, the fund established the Arab Authority for Agricultural Investment and Development, promoting the production of sugar and grain in the Sudan in order to reduce Arab dependence on imports of these goods. Though the fund's projects have not yet been profitable, this financial loss has been perceived as a necessary cost of regional food security, and the fund's financial backers, the oil-rich Arab countries, remain committed to these projects. It remains to be seen, however, how long this commitment will survive.

BIBLIOGRAPHY

RICHARDS, ALAN, and JOHN WATERBURY. *A Political Economy of the Middle East: State, Class and Economic Development.* Boulder, Colo., 1990.

David Waldner

Arab Higher Committee

An umbrella organization established in mandated Palestine on April 25, 1936, by six Arab political parties—the Palestine Arab party, the National Defense party, the Independence party, the Reform party, the National Bloc, and the Youth Congress.

Al-Hajj Amin al-Husayni, head of the Supreme Muslim Council, led the Arab Higher Committee (AHC), which sought to coordinate and represent the general strike that Palestinian Arabs had launched on April 15. The AHC articulated its nationalist demands to stop Jewish immigration and land purchase and to replace the British mandate with a national government responsible to an elected assembly. The strike ended on October 12, 1936, as a result of British military pressure and the threat of economic collapse, but the AHC did win the establishment of a Royal Commission to investigate the causes of and remedies for the disturbances. The AHC presented evidence before the commission but rejected its recommendation that Palestine be partitioned. Britain outlawed the AHC on October 1, 1937, and deported four of its members to the Seychelles. Nonetheless, AHC members participated in the London Conference in 1939, and the committee resumed its activities in late 1945. Although Britain then recognized the AHC as the official representative body for the Arab community in Palestine, the AHC failed to organize effectively as a political umbrella and became almost exclusively a vehicle for the HUSAYNI family. The AHC denounced United Nations plans to partition Palestine in the fall of 1947 as "absurd, impracticable and unjust" (Hurewitz, p. 299); it subsequently formed a short-lived Palestine government in Gaza in September 1948, after the new State of Israel defeated the attacking Arabs in the first of the Arab–Israel wars.

BIBLIOGRAPHY

GOVERNMENT OF PALESTINE. *A Survey of Palestine,* vol. 2. Jerusalem, 1946. Reprint, Washington, D.C., 1991.
HUREWITZ, J. C. *The Struggle for Palestine.* New York, 1976. Reprint of 1950 ed.

Ann M. Lesch

Arabia/Arabian Peninsula

Great peninsula of southwest Asia bounded by the Persian/Arabian Gulf to the east and the Red Sea to the west.

The Arabian peninsula is about thirteen hundred miles (2090 km) wide at its maximum breadth and about twelve hundred miles (1900 km) in length along the RED SEA. It is bounded at the north by Jordan and Iraq. It is fertile in some of the coastal regions, but the center is an arid plateau, called in ancient times Arabia Deserta (not to be confused with the Arabian Desert of Egypt, east of the Nile river to the Gulf of Suez). No rivers exist in the peninsula's arid region, but there are many short wadis and a few oases. The Arabian peninsula is an important region for PETROLEUM production, and the GULF states of the peninsula that produce petroleum include Bahrain (islands in the Gulf), KUWAIT, OMAN, QATAR, the UNITED ARAB EMIRATES (UAE), Yemen, and the large central kingdom of Saudi Arabia. The Arabian Sea is that part of the Indian Ocean between India on the east and the peninsula on the west.

The people of the peninsula belong to Semitic tribes; they are mainly ARAB whose consolidation was begun by the Prophet MUHAMMAD. The consolidation was extended after his death in 632 C.E. but collapsed into tribal warfare during the 700s, after the disintegration of the UMAYYAD caliphate (661–750). Arabia was then generally dominated by the Mamlukes until the early 1500s, then by the Ottoman Empire—but various parts were virtually independent—al-Hasa, Oman, Yemen, and Najd. The Wahhabi movement of Islam began in Arabia, centered in Najd, where resistance against the Ottoman Turks was organized in the eighteenth and nineteenth centuries. Reconquered for the Turks by Muhammad Ali Pasha of Egypt (1811–1820), the Wahhabi empire was reestablished from 1843 to 1865, but internal strife continued between tribes and Islamic sects. During World War I, the British officer T. E. Lawrence (of Arabia) directed a resistance effort here with Emir Faisal and his followers against the Ottoman Empire. In the early 1920s and 1930s, a gradual consolidation was effected by Ibn Sa'ud into the kingdom of SAUDI ARABIA.

BIBLIOGRAPHY

BRAWER, M., ed. *Atlas of the Middle East.* New York, 1988.

Martha Imber-Goldstein

Arabian American Oil Company

Petroleum partnership between American Firms and Saudi Arabia, 1933–1990.

The origins of the Arabian American Oil Company (ARAMCO) go back to the May 1933 signing of an oil concession agreement between Saudi Arabia's finance minister, Shaykh Abdullah Sulayman, and Lloyd N. Hamilton, an attorney representing Standard Oil of California (SOCAL, now Chevron). Oil exploration was begun three months later by CASOC, the SOCAL subsidiary established to operate the Saudi concession.

At that time, SOCAL was seeking a partner to market the oil it was producing in Bahrain and hoped to produce in Saudi Arabia. In 1936, it transferred 50 percent of the BAHRAIN PETROLEUM COMPANY (BAPCO) and 50 percent of CASOC to the Texas Company (Texaco), receiving in return 21 million U.S. dollars in cash and deferred payments, plus a half interest in Texaco's marketing facilities east of

ARAMCO airplane on a landing strip in Saudi Arabia, the 1950s. (D.W. Lockhard)

the Suez, which were reorganized as a subsidiary of BAPCO and named CALTEX. On 3 March 1938, CASOC brought in its first commercial oil well, Dammam no. 7. On 1 May 1939, King Abd al-Aziz was present when the first oil tanker was loaded with Saudi crude and sailed from RA'S TANURA.

The development of Saudi Arabia's oil fields was hampered, but not halted, by World War II. Italian aircraft bombed Dhahran, where CASOC was headquartered, in 1940, and the war at sea limited shipping to and from the GULF throughout the conflict. During the war, fears of oil depletion sparked U.S. government interest in the resources of Saudi Arabia. Although plans for the U.S. government to buy all or part of CASOC were eventually shelved, in late 1943 steel and other rationed materials were allocated to the company to construct a tank farm, refinery, and marine terminal at Ra's Tanura, along with a submarine pipeline to the BAPCO refinery on Bahrain.

CASOC was noted for the unusually close relationship between host government and operating company, and the extent of the efforts its personnel made to be good guests in the kingdom. CASOC also protected its conception of Saudi interests within its parent corporations, primarily by opposing any move that would restrict production. SOCAL and Texaco were equally committed to a long-term relationship with the kingdom. In January 1944, at the suggestion of State Department

adviser Herbert Feis, who had taken part in the negotiations over government participation in CASOC, SOCAL and Texaco changed the name of the operating company to the Arabian American Oil Company (ARAMCO). The Saudi king grew to view ARAMCO as a means to achieve his goals. ARAMCO became the conduit that carried Saudi Arabia's interests to its parent corporations and to the U.S. government.

ARAMCO's rapid growth was assured once the RED LINE AGREEMENT was canceled and the company was able to acquire two new partners, Standard Oil of New Jersey and Socony Vacuum, in December 1948. The infusion of capital fueled the rapid development of Ra's Tanura and the construction of the TRANS-ARABIAN PIPELINE. That, along with continuing exploration and development efforts, transformed ARAMCO into the largest oil-producing company in the world. In 1978, forty years after oil was discovered in commercial quantities in Saudi Arabia, ARAMCO's cumulative total production exceeded 30 billion barrels.

The concern for and protection of one another's interests by Saudi Arabia and ARAMCO's parent companies were remarkable. A notable instance of efforts made on behalf of Saudi Arabia's government took place in 1973 when the parents mounted an intensive campaign in the United States to convince policymakers and the public that the continued failure of efforts to resolve the Arab–Israel conflict could lead to an oil embargo if another war broke out. The success of the oil embargo imposed by the ORGANIZATION OF PETROLEUM EXPORTING COUNTRIES (OPEC) during the ARAB–ISRAEL WAR OF 1973 was underpinned by ARAMCO's decision to observe its conditions to the letter. The government of Saudi Arabia supported ARAMCO particularly through its oil pricing policy. In the early 1980s, the government kept prices below the OPEC average, thus enabling the ARAMCO partners to earn huge profits through purchase of cheap Saudi oil, some of which was deliberately produced in excess of the OPEC-established quota.

Before the oil revolution of 1970–1973, the ARAMCO parents might have hoped to retain some of their equity in ARAMCO's operations, even though "participation" as a concept was developed by the oil minister of Saudi Arabia and a participation agreement reached between the Gulf producers and their concession holders in 1972. In June 1974, Saudi Arabia took over 60 percent of ARAMCO under that participation agreement. By the end of the year, the government told the ARAMCO parents that it wanted 100 percent of the company. The parents fought this demand but in the end were forced to agree to it. In 1976, arrangements for the transfer were worked out, and in 1980 the government of Saudi Arabia paid compensation to the parent companies for all of ARAMCO's local holdings.

However, the government did not sign the agreement transferring the ownership of ARAMCO to itself until 1990. Between 1980 and 1990, ARAMCO was preserved as it was, and its corporate interests were protected as much as possible given conflicting demands from OPEC and the exigencies of a profoundly depressed market. During this decade ARAMCO made agreements with several major oil companies for joint ventures, including an overseas marketing company, Star Enterprises, established by ARAMCO and Texaco. By the mid-1990s, Saudi ARAMCO was fast becoming a fully integrated multinational oil company.

BIBLIOGRAPHY

ANDERSON, IRVINE H. *Aramco, the United States, and Saudi Arabia: A Study of the Dynamics of Foreign Oil Policy, 1933–1950.* Princeton, N.J., 1981.

MILLER, AARON DAVID. *Search for Security: Saudi Arabian Oil and American Foreign Policy.* Chapel Hill, N.C., 1980.

NAWWAB, ISMAIL I., PETER C. SPEERS, and PAUL F. HOYE. *Aramco and Its World: Arabia and the Middle East.* Dhahran, 1980.

TÉTREAULT, MARY ANN. *Revolution in the World Petroleum Market.* Westport, Conn., 1985.

YERGIN, DANIEL. *The Prize: The Epic Quest for Oil, Money and Power.* New York, 1991.

Mary Ann Tétreault

Arabian Gulf

See Gulf

Arabian Horses

Small horses bred in Saudi Arabia.

Arabian horses stand approximately fifteen hands tall and weigh up to 1,000 pounds. Considered a gentle and intelligent horse, the Arabian has a small head, silky hair and mane, and a shorter back than other horses. Although the origins of the horse are uncertain, Arabians were historically bred in Saudi Arabia. Today they continue to be bred in the

The Arabian horse is commemorated in this postage stamp from Egypt. (Richard Bulliet)

Najd region of Saudi Arabia as well as around the world.

Shimon Avish

Arabian Mission

Mission for Protestant proselytization in Arabia; established in 1889.

The mission was founded by James Cantine and Samuel Zwemer, students at the New Brunswick Theological Seminary, under the guidance of Prof. John G. Lansing. Initially independent, it came under the Reformed (Dutch) Church's Board of Foreign Missions in 1893 but remained nondenominational.

By 1902, missions had been established at Basra, Bahrain, and Muscat, and in 1910 another was started in Kuwait. Despite the distribution of a considerable amount of Christian literature, the missionaries' objective of winning converts made little headway against the conservative Islam of Arabia. Many people were reached, however, through the work of dedicated teachers and medical doctors and received modern education and health services for the first time. Between 1889 and 1938, eighty missionaries went to Arabia, and, in the years between the world wars, tens of thousands of patients were treated each year in the Arabian Mission's seven hospitals.

The missionaries' work left a legacy of goodwill that has persisted to this day, and the sons of missionaries later played a significant role as American diplomats in the Arab world.

BIBLIOGRAPHY

MASON, ALFRED DEWITT, and FREDERICK J. BARNEY. *History of the Arabian Mission.* New York, 1926.

ZWEMER, SAMUEL M., and JAMES CANTINE. *The Golden Milestone: Reminiscences of Pioneer Days Fifty Years Ago in Arabia.* New York, 1938.

Malcolm C. Peck

Arabic

Language of Islam, the Qur'an, and about 185 million people.

Arabic is a SEMITIC LANGUAGE and the major language of the modern Middle East; it is spoken by an estimated 185 million people. It spread throughout the region during the seventh century C.E., replacing Aramaic in the Levant—as well as non-Semitic languages—as ISLAM began its conquest and conversion. The Arabic language went as far east as Iran and as far west as all North Africa, crossing Gibraltar to the Iberian peninsula in the early eighth century.

Arabic is related to two Semitic languages still used in the Middle East, chiefly HEBREW in its ancient liturgical and modern (nineteenth/twentieth century) revival forms but also Amharic, the official language of Ethiopia. Arabic is classified as South Central Semitic, sharing features not only with Amharic but also with the ancient languages Geez and Akkadian. Some countries that are now home to predominantly Arabic speakers also have speakers of traditional, non-Semitic languages, such as Berber, Nubian, Kurdish, and Coptic.

Arabic has a special relationship to Islam; it is considered the divine language of Allah by Muslims. The language has therefore been constrained by reverence, with the liturgical or classical Arabic (called *fusha,* the "purest" style) remaining basically unchanged since the revelation of the QUR'AN in the seventh century. Today's spoken Arabic is, however, considered corrupt, with diverse local vernacular versions used throughout the region.

ARABIC SCRIPT is written in phonetic symbols similar to Hebrew letters in that each symbol represents a letter and words are written and read from right to left. A feature of Arabic script is its use as an Islamic art form, since there is a religious pronouncement against rendering figures in art. Such CALLIGRAPHY decorates books, buildings, banners, and jewelry; most words are so stylized that they cannot be read, but as they are often taken from the Qur'an, their sources are recognized by most Muslims.

Arabic Dialects. The most noticeable linguistic situation in the Arab world is termed *diglossia,* which literally means "twin vocabularies," referring to the fact that every speaker of Arabic knows a local spoken vernacular and learns the formal fusha in addition to it. Because of the historical spread of Islam and, with it, Arabic, the language has today been spoken for more than 1,300 years over a wide territory that includes parts of Europe, North Africa and the Levant. Despite the freezing of the literary grammatical style of Arabic, the colloquial versions, like all spoken languages, changed unfettered by normalized rules or classical prescriptions of correctness. Often speakers from one end of the region cannot understand speakers from another without difficulty, although they can understand the versions spoken in adjacent areas.

At the same time Arabic is said to be the uniting factor of the modern Arab world—the one institution all Arabs share regardless of the culture or subculture of the countries they now inhabit. Where Arabic is the nation's official language, the classical style is used for government, religion, and schooling. No pressure seems to exist for adopting a type of "Esperanto" Arabic or even agreeing on one dialect as the standard for all sophisticated communication.

With the advent of radio, television, and the broadcasting of news in literary Arabic, comprehension of that form has increased. Knowledge of other dialects has also been spread by the motion picture industry. For example, Egyptian Arabic (Cairene) has been used in the scripts of many movies, and television soap operas produced in Cairo have helped familiarize many non-Egyptians with that dialect.

Of the large number of Arabic dialects, only a few have been given names and studied in any detail: Egyptian and Iraqi Arabic refer to the colloquial dialects of the educated classes of Cairo and Baghdad, respectively. Media broadcasts from country capitals have also become comprehensible to rural and nomadic speakers with access to radios, televisions, or video- and audiocassette recorders. Uneducated or rural vernacular dialects differ, though, sometimes dramatically, since many have developed in relative isolation. Nevertheless, speakers of similar backgrounds understand one another over short geographic distances.

The difference between dialects are mostly confined to vocabulary and the shifting or loss of some sounds. The Egyptian use of *giim* for *jiim* or even *djiim* is one of the best examples of a sound shift. Greater shifts have affected the entire sound of a dialect; for example, in North Africa, most short vowels have been lost and the stress of most words moved from the medial to the last syllable. This produces many words that start with consonant clusters. In contrast, the dialects of Cairo and those farther to the east have maintained most of the short vowels and lost mostly those at the end of the word, keeping the stress, as in Fusha, on the next-to-last syllable. Consonant clusters are generally limited to word-final positions and are no more than two consonants in length. In addition, word borrowing from other languages has occurred in both Fusha and the dialects. In some cases older Arabic words are used to meet the needs of modern life, but in others a borrowed word is used—the word for "telephone" might be written *haatif* (one who calls out), and it might be spoken as *telefon*.

Arabic language academies exist—in Cairo, Damascus, and Baghdad—each attempting to minimize the use of borrowings. They publish lists of desired usages, but it is difficult to legislate language change.

Classical Arabic. Fusha, the high style, is characterized by a complicated system of conjugations that change the case of words, which are composed of three consonants (s-l-m, for example). Using prefixes, infixes, and suffixes, as well as a change of vocalization according to rules, is basic to all Semitic languages—and formal Arabic demonstrates this practice to a greater extent than any of the others. None of these case markings has survived in the dialects; however, the Qur'an and children's books are published with them written in place so that they will not be read aloud incorrectly. Nevertheless, even the pronunciation of Fusha varies with the colloquial background of the speaker. Fusha is used in all writing that does not attempt to represent casual speech. In most novels, the characters speak in Fusha, but cartoon characters speak in vernacular Arabic, as do actors in most modern plays; and some modern novels are written in dialect. The Arabic version of *Sesame Street* uses Fusha, since it is the language style that children must learn to read.

Rise and Development of Arabic. The early history of Fusha is not clear. Before the appearance of Islam there are very few traces of Arabic in the Arabian peninsula, but it is clear from the language of the Qur'an that an oral tradition of poetical style was well established before the revelation of that holy book. The language of the Qur'an is not just a reflection of the dialect of the Hijaz (western Arabia, the original center of Islam); it is a style reflecting the koine of the poets, used for sophisticated performances of oral poetry at the markets to which the nomads came at least once a year. It is probably a combination of both language usages, which is why it is said to have been unique and miraculous at the time of Muhammad's reception of it.

Arabic script was already in use before the codification of the Qur'an, but it was unified and provided with diacritical marks to resolve ambiguities in the holy text. As the Islamic conquests began in the seventh and eighth centuries, the language of formal usage was being standardized by grammarians in the towns of Basra and Kufa (Iraq). By the ninth and tenth centuries, this linguistic work was completed, and these rules became the standard by which to measure all future literary Arabic output. To this day, "correct" Arabic is measured by these rules, and they are maintained in the belief that to change them is to offend Allah, who produced them.

BIBLIOGRAPHY

BATESON, MARY C. *Arabic Language Handbook.* Washington, D.C., 1967.
BERGSTRASSER, GOTTHELF. *Introduction to the Semitic Languages,* trans. by Peter Daniels Eisenbrauns. Winona Lake, Ind., 1983.
KILLEAN, CAROLYN G. "Classical Arabic." *Current Trends in Linguistics.* Vol. 6, *Linguistics in South West Asia and North Africa.* Mouton, 1971.
OMAR, MARGARET. *From Eastern to Western Arabic.* Washington, D.C., 1974.

Carolyn Killean

Arabic Script

Used to represent the Arabic language, as well as certain non-Arabic and non-Semitic languages.

The Arabic script is an alphabet in which each written symbol represents a single sound. It is Semitic and, thus, a near relative of the Hebrew alphabet but also historically related to the Roman alphabet. The Arabic alphabet is second only to the Roman in use today. It is used by over 185 million first-language speakers of Arabic. As the medium in which the Qur'an was revealed and much Islamic learning was recorded, Arabic is a second or liturgical language for Muslims worldwide. In addition, the Arabic alphabet has been adapted for use in other non-Arabic and non-Semitic languages, among them Persian, Urdu, and Ottoman Turkish.

The Arabic script is written from right to left. It is cursive, so that each letter in a word is joined to the following letter (exceptions to this rule are the letters *'alif, dāl, dhāl, rā, zāy,* and *wāw*). The alphabet is consonantal, consisting of twenty-eight consonants

Table 1
Arabic Alphabet

Numerical Value	Name	Letter
1	'alif	ا
2	bā'	ب
400	tā'	ت
500	thā'	ث
3	jīm	ج
8	ḥā'	ح
600	khā'	خ
4	dāl	د
700	dhāl	ذ
200	rā'	ر
7	zāy	ز
60	sīn	س
300	shīn	ش
90	ṣād	ص
800	ḍād	ض
9	ṭ.ā'	ط
900	ẓā'	ظ
70	'ayn	ع
1,000	ghayn	غ
80	fā'	ف
100	qāf	ق
20	kāf	ك
30	lām	ل
40	mīm	م
50	nūn	ن
5	hā'	ه
6	wāw	و
10	yā'	ى

and semivowels. Other signs or diacritical marks indicate short vowels and other sound changes, but these do not typically appear in written texts. In theory, at least, the lack of written vowels causes a certain ambiguity when it comes to deciphering the written word. To take one example, the word كتب or *ktb* can be read in several ways: *kataba,* "he wrote"; *kutiba,* "it was written"; *kattaba,* "he dictated"; *kuttiba,* "he was made to take dictation"; *ktab,* "[the act of] writing"; *kutub,* "books." In practice, however, context plays a considerable role in clarifying meaning. In a sentence such as "he wrote five *ktb* on this topic, *ktb* could only mean "books." Where lack of ambiguity is necessary or desirable, as in the written text of the Qur'an, in classical Islamic or literary texts, and in writings for children, the diacritical marks are written as a matter of course.

The Arabic alphabet is not simply a vehicle for written communication but is the medium for one of the most highly developed art forms of the Arab and Islamic world, the art of calligraphy. For the Arabic language, calligraphy recognizes two principal types of Arabic script, *kufi* and *naskhi,* where the former is generally more square in shape and the latter more rounded. This binary division, however, hardly reflects the tremendous diversity of scripts, from the tiny Turkish *ghubari,* or "dust," script, to the large *jali* scripts that decorate the walls of certain mosques, from the severely "squared" *kufi,* with right angles rather than curves, to the elaborate "tied" scripts, in which the capitals are linked to form knotted arabesques.

In the Arab world and elsewhere, Arabic script is a powerful symbol of ethnic and religious affiliation. Its significance does not make it inviolable, however, at least not in this century. The Arabic alphabet was replaced by the Roman alphabet in Turkey in 1929 and by the Cyrillic alphabet in a number of republics in the former Soviet Central Asia, to name two examples. Proposals to Romanize the Arabic alphabet in the Arab world have been advanced since the late nineteenth century. To date, however, only in Malta, which was conquered by the Sicilians in the eleventh century, is any variety of Arabic regularly written in other than the Arabic script.

Elizabeth M. Bergman

Arab Iron and Steel Company (AISCO)

Manufacturing facility in Bahrain known as AISCO.

Established by the government of BAHRAIN in 1981 in an attempt at diversification, AISCO had shareholders from Bahrain, Kuwait, Jordan, and the United Arab Emirates. Its first iron-pelletizing plant was built in 1984; in 1985, AISCO halted production because of a drop in demand. It was adversely affected by the IRAN–IRAQ WAR and by competition from other countries. In 1987, it was sold to a subsidiary of the Kuwait Petroleum Company.

BIBLIOGRAPHY

The Middle East and North Africa, 1991, 37th ed. London, 1991.

Emile A. Nakhleh

Arab–Israel Conflict

Conflict over the post–World War I mandated territory of Palestine.

In PALESTINE, the conflict began at the end of the nineteenth century, more than fifty years before the

State of ISRAEL was established in 1948. The crux of the conflict has been between Jewish Nationalism (called ZIONISM) and Palestinian Arab nationalism for political control over the area that, in the peace settlement after World War I (1914–1918), became the League of Nations mandated territory of Palestine—held by Britain from 1922 to 1948. When Israel was established, the struggle became known as the Arab–Israel conflict.

Soon after the first late nineteenth-century Eastern European Jewish settlers arrived in Palestine (whose population as of 1882 consisted of about 450,000 Arab and 25,000 Jews), they sporadically clashed with local Arabs over land and grazing rights—although the Jewish settlers bought their land or lived on land bought from Arabs for Jewish communities. During 1920 and 1921, in 1929, and from 1936 to 1939, Palestinian nationalist demonstrations frequently led to violence and casualties.

By the 1920s, Palestinian Arab opposition to Jewish settlement and to the Zionist movement became widespread. Arabs demanded that the British mandatory authorities halt further Jewish immigration into Palestine; that sale of Arab and government lands to Jews cease; and that immediate steps be initiated by the British government toward granting Arab Palestinian independence.

The 1929 uprising in JERUSALEM, capital of the British mandate, were officially called "disturbances." They arose over prayer rights at the TEMPLE MOUNT, where the sacred Western (or Wailing) Wall stands—believed by pious Jews to be the last remnant of the Second Temple (destroyed in 70 C.E.). Because the wall adjoins the third-most-sacred site in ISLAM, the Haram al-Sharif (Sacred Enclosure, containing two important mosques, al-Aqsa and Omar), it has been a source of continuing conflict. Many Muslims believed then and continue to believe that Jews seek to destroy the mosques and replace them with a new temple.

By 1936, Palestine's Jewish community, the YISHUV, had increased to 384,000, mainly from European immigration; the number of Jewish cities and towns, industries, and agricultural settlements extended widely through the territory, raising fears among Palestinian Arabs that they would soon become a minority in their native land. The 1936 to 1939 uprising, called the PALESTINE ARAB REVOLT, galvanized most of the Arab community to oppose the British authorities and continued Jewish immigration and settlement.

Zionist attempts to assuage Arab fears were unsuccessful. Even proposals by a small group of Jewish intellectuals in favor of BINATIONALISM—calling for the establishment of a binational Arab–Jewish state based on political parity between the two communities—received only a faint response from Arab leaders.

Both Arabs and Jews rejected proposals by the 1937 British Royal Commission under Lord Peel (the so-called PEEL COMMISSION) to partition Palestine between its two communities, although some Zionist leaders accepted the partition principle, if not specific details. Massive British force and internecine Arab quarrels ended the Arab Revolt in 1939, just as the British military became involved in World War II (1939–1945). Focus on Europe then kept the Arab–Jewish conflict quiescent until the end of the war.

With international postwar pressure on Britain to remove all restrictions on Jewish immigration and land purchases in Palestine—because of the HOLOCAUST in Europe—and for the establishment of a Jewish commonwealth, tensions between the Yishuv, the mandatory government, and the Arab community brought Palestine to the brink of civil war.

Britain appealed to the UNITED NATIONS, which recommended that Palestine be partitioned into Arab and Jewish states with an international enclave containing the Jerusalem area. The mainstream of the Zionist movement accepted the proposal (but a nationalist minority continued to insist on a Jewish state on both banks of the JORDAN RIVER).

Palestine Arabs, supported by leaders throughout the Arab world, rejected the principle of partition. Clashes then occurred between Palestinian Arabs demonstrating against violation of their right to self-determination and Jews celebrating their coming independence, which soon turned into a full-scale civil war. Since Britain's mandate was to end on May 14, 1948, a rather disorderly withdrawal of British troops began from disputed areas. By May 1948, as the Yishuv organized its military force, Palestinian Arabs retreated, fled, or were expelled from Israel despite military assistance to them from the Arab world, which continued until 1949. After Israel was established on May 15, 1948, the term *Palestinians* referred to members of the Arab community while Palestinian Jews were called *Israelis*.

The first ARAB–ISRAEL WAR lasted until Egypt, Lebanon, Jordan, and Syria signed armistice agreements with Israel early in 1949. As a result of that war, Israel was able to extend its frontiers approximately two thousand square miles (5,200 sq km) from the UN partition borders to those of the armistice agreements. Over 700,000 Palestinians became refugees, unable to return to their homes in Israel; many lived in refugee camps in the surrounding Arab countries, but some moved to North Africa, Europe, and North America. Territory intended as part of the Arab state in the UN PARTITION PLANS became controlled by Israel, Jordan, and Egypt. Jerusalem was divided between Jordan and Israel.

Since the end of the first Arab–Israel conflict there has been continuing dispute between Israel and the surrounding countries over borders, refugee rights to return or to compensation, the status of Jerusalem, the equitable division of Jordan river waters, and Arab recognition of Israel.

The United Nations dealt with these issues through several organizations. An armistice regime was established with the UNITED NATIONS TRUCE SUPERVISION ORGANIZATION to oversee the 1949 agreements between Israel and Egypt, Lebanon, Jordan and Syria. In 1948, the UNITED NATIONS PALESTINE CONCILIATION COMMISSION was named to achieve a peaceful settlement by dealing with the refugee problem, Middle East economic development, and equitable distribution of water resources.

The establishment of Israel and Israel's victories in the ensuing wars with the Arab states created turmoil in the surrounding countries. Arab opinion was so strongly anti-Israel, that defeats sparked antigovernment uprisings in several countries and led to the assassination of a number of Arab political leaders. Egypt's setbacks in the 1948 war, for example, contributed to its 1952 revolution.

The Arab states refused to enter direct negotiations with Israel for a final settlement unless Israel withdrew to the UN partition borders and permitted the refugees to return. U.S. and UN proposals for refugee resettlement in the context of the broad economic development of the Middle East were also rejected without the resolution of the issues relating to refugees, borders, and Jerusalem.

In Israel, tensions heightened after 1952, when Egypt's new ruler Gamel Abdel NASSER (who had led the coup that overthrew Egypt's monarchy) was perceived as a growing threat, and relations with Egypt deteriorated. Israeli agents set off a series of bombs in Cairo, and there was an increase of infiltrations and attacks into Israel by Palestinians from Egyptian-held GAZA across the armistice border. The situation sparked an arms race; Egypt acquired large amounts of military equipment from the USSR and the Eastern bloc while Israel obtained advanced aircraft from France. By 1956, relations between Egypt and Israel had become part of the larger conflict between Egypt and the West over control of the SUEZ CANAL.

Israel formed a secret alliance with Britain and France to overthrow Nasser after Egypt nationalized the Suez Canal in July 1956. As Israel attacked Egypt in October, Britain and France occupied the northern Canal Zone. This tripartite scheme was stymied by U.S. and Soviet intervention at the United Nations and by Moscow's threat of military action.

In November 1956, the General Assembly established the UNITED NATIONS EMERGENCY FORCE (UNEF) to supervise the withdrawal of the invaders' troops and to act as a peacekeeping body between Egypt and Israel. Egypt–Israel frontiers were relatively quiet until the 1967 ARAB–ISRAEL WAR.

Incidents erupted along other Israeli borders. Continued Palestinian refugee infiltration and guerrilla attacks from Jordan plus clashes with Syria over Israeli projects to divert the Jordan river created obstacles to a peace settlement. In 1960, the Arab League (officially, the LEAGUE OF ARAB STATES) called Israel's Jordan river-diversion scheme "an act of aggression" and in 1963 adopted its own diversion blueprint, which would have greatly diminished Israel's access to WATER. Both Israel and its neighbors continued to build up their military machines; French experts helped Israel set up a nuclear reactor, which was widely believed to be the beginning of a nuclear-weapons program.

The tensions caused by the Jordan river dispute, the escalation of border incidents, the Middle East arms race, and increasingly bitter rhetoric led to several border clashes in 1967. Both sides appeared to be on the brink of war. When President Nasser threatened to blockade Israel's passage through the Strait of TIRAN (at the southeast SINAI peninsula), ordered UNEF to leave the Sinai, and massed his troops on the border, Israel's leaders responded with a preemptive strike in June 1967 against Egypt and its allies Syria and Iraq. After firing on Israel-controlled Jerusalem, Jordan was also involved in the fighting.

Israel emerged from the 1967 Arab–Israel War as the dominant power, with the Arab states thrown into disarray. Israel had conquered the Sinai peninsula and the Gaza Strip from Egypt, the GOLAN HEIGHTS from Syria, and East Jerusalem and the WEST BANK from Jordan. The war intensified competition in the Middle East between the United States, supporting Israel, and the Soviet Union, backing Egypt, Syria, and Iraq. It led to another escalation of the arms race, the closing by Egypt of the Suez Canal, and an additional 300,000 West Bank and Golan Heights refugees who went to Jordan and to Syria.

Although defeated, the Arab states refused direct negotiations with Israel, demanding that Israel first withdraw to the 1967 armistice lines and permit the return of refugees. Efforts to end the conflict through the United Nations were blocked by disagreements between the United States and the Soviet Union. The Soviets supported resolutions condemning Israel and called for the return of territories. The United States supported Israel's insistence that territory be returned only through direct negotiations and a peace settlement.

The stalemate was somewhat eased by UN Security Council compromise Resolution 242, in November 1967. It called for the "withdrawal of Israeli armed forces from territories" occupied in the war, termination of belligerency, "just settlement of the refugee problem," and "the need to work for a just and lasting peace."

The parties disagreed over the interpretation of Resolution 242. The Arab side insisted it meant Israel's withdrawal from *all* territory seized in 1967; Israel and its supporters insisted that the resolution did not mean total withdrawal. Most Arab states no longer demanded that Israel withdraw to the 1948 partition lines, only to the 1949 armistice frontiers; they also recognized that a just solution of the refugee problem would have to include alternatives to total repatriation of the Palestinians and their descendants to their original homes, since twenty years had passed.

After the 1967 war, Palestinian nationalists brought several guerrilla factions into the PALESTINE LIBERATION ORGANIZATION (PLO)—an umbrella group established in 1964. Israeli and Palestinian forces clashed along the borders, and Palestinian guerrillas attacked Israeli civilians at home and abroad. After King HUSSEIN IBN TALAL of Jordan put down a Palestinian-initiated civil war and drove guerrilla factions from the protection of his country in 1970/71, several factions set up bases in south Lebanon to attack northern Israel.

With the failure of diplomacy, Egypt and Syria decided to regain territories lost in 1967 through a two-front surprise attack in Israel in October of 1973. Initially, Egypt recaptured large sectors of the Sinai, and Syria, the Golan; but within a few days, Israel had recovered. Nevertheless, the 1973 Arab–Israel War shattered the myth of Israeli invincibility.

An attempt by the United States and the Soviet Union to end the conflict at a Geneva, Switzerland, conference during December 1973 ended after two days. Instead, the United States initiated a "step-by-step" process, leading to disengagement agreements in which Egypt regained parts of Sinai, and Syria reoccupied al-Kuneitra in the Golan region.

In November 1977, the visit to Jerusalem by Egypt's President Anwar al-SADAT made direct negotiations possible—a new phase in Arab–Israel relations. As the talks faltered, U.S. President Jimmy CARTER convened a conference of Egypt's and Israel's leaders at the presidential retreat of Camp David, Maryland, where they eventually agreed on Israel's withdrawal from Sinai and autonomy for the Palestinians. After some communication difficulties, but the continued mediation of President Carter, a peace treaty was signed by Egypt and Israel in Washington,

D.C., on March 26, 1978, which provided for mutual recognition and normalization of relations.

Relations remained strained by differing interpretations of the CAMP DAVID ACCORDS and the treaty terms and by continued hostilities between other Arab states and Israel. In June 1982, Israel invaded Lebanon to uproot an entrenched PLO, force Lebanon into a peace agreement, and remove Syrian's troops from that country. Of these objectives only one was attained—PLO headquarters and its infrastructure were uprooted, with relocation in other Arab states. After several months of Israeli occupation, Lebanese militia attacks forced Israel to withdraw to a narrow southern border strip—an Israeli "security zone"—which Israel continued to occupy.

Twenty years of Israeli occupation of Gaza and the West Bank caused increasing unrest among the Palestinian inhabitants, which led to the uprising, or INTIFADA, begun in December 1987. Unlike previous occasions, demonstrations did not die down but escalated into a full-scale civil resistance. Palestinian demands to end the occupation galvanized the PLO to revise its political program—in November 1988, it proclaimed an independent Palestinian state and for the first time accepted UN Resolution 242, recognized Israel, and renounced terrorism.

International attention on the intifada and the Palestine problem and the GULF CRISIS that led to war in 1990/91 also led to the Middle East Peace Conference convened in Madrid, Spain, in October 1991 by the United States and the Soviet Union. The conference initiated a series of bilateral, direct negotiations between Israel and the Syrian, Lebanese, and Jordanian-Palestinian delegations, with multilateral discussions on Middle Eastern refugees, security, environment, economic development, and water. After secret negotiations in Oslo, Norway, in September 1993, Israel and the PLO signed an agreement providing for mutual recognition as well as Palestinian self-government to begin in Gaza and the town of Jericho in the West Bank during a five-year transition period, leading to the solution of the dispute between Israel and the Palestinians.

BIBLIOGRAPHY

FLAPAN, SIMHA. *Zionism and the Palestinians*. New York, 1979.

GERNER, DEBORAH J. *One Land, Two Peoples: The Conflict over Palestine*. Boulder, Colo., 1991.

KHOURI, FRED J. *The Arab–Israeli Dilemma*, 4th ed. Syracuse, N.Y., 1985.

LAQUEUR, WALTER, and BARRY RUBIN. *The Israel–Arab Reader: A Documentary History of the Middle East Conflict*, 4th ed. New York, 1985.

PERETZ, DON. *Intifada: The Palestinian Uprising.* Boulder, Colo., 1990.

SMITH, CHARLES D. *Palestine and the Arab–Israeli Conflict.* New York, 1988.

Don Peretz

Arab–Israel War (1948)

The first conflict between the Arabs and the new state of Israel.

The Arab–Israel war of 1948 culminated half a century of conflict between the Arab and Jewish populations in Palestine. It began as a civil conflict between Palestinian Jews and Arabs following announcement of the UN decision in November 1948 to partition the country into a Jewish state, an Arab state, and an international enclave encompassing the greater Jerusalem area. While the majority of the Jewish population approved the plan, Arabs in Palestine and surrounding countries vehemently objected, considering it a violation of Palestinian Arabs' self-determination. In Palestine, Arab demonstrations against the UN decision and Jewish celebrations welcoming it met head-on and quickly erupted into violent clashes between the two communities. Within a few days armed Arab and Jewish groups were battling each other throughout the country.

Palestinian Arab guerrillas received weapons and volunteers from the neighboring states and were assisted by unofficial paramilitary units from Syria and Egypt. However, the Arabs were not as effectively organized as the Jewish forces. The latter consisted of three principal groups: the Haganah, the defense organization of the mainstream Jewish community, and two dissident factions, the Irgun Zva'i Le'umi (IZL or Etzel; National Military Organization) and Lohemei Herut Yisrael (Lehi; Fighters for the Freedom of Israel), also known as the Stern Gang. The latter two were associated with Revisionist Zionism.

Following the partition resolution, casualties mounted on both sides. Arabs attacked Jewish settlements and bombed such urban targets as the *Jerusalem Post* and the headquarters of the Jewish Agency. Retaliatory and preemptive Jewish attacks against the Arab population—such as the Etzel raid on Dayr Yasin, which has been viewed by some as an instance of ethnic cleansing—set off a mass flight and military expulsion of the Arab population from areas seized by the Jewish forces.

By the end of the mandate in May 1948, when the British army left Palestine, Jewish forces had seized most of the territory allocated to the Jewish state in the UN partition plan as well as land beyond the partition borders.

With departure of the British and Israel's declaration of independence on 15 May 1948, the struggle became an international conflict between the Jewish state and the regular armies of Egypt, Transjordan, Syria, Lebanon, and Iraq. Saudi Arabia sent a token unit, and Yemen was nominally involved.

Arab states other than Transjordan intervened to preempt the plans of Emir Abdullah, developed in accord with Israel, to take over the largely Arab-inhabited parts of Palestine. In an attempt to gain Transjordan's cooperation in the war against Israel, the other Arab combatants agreed to appoint Abdullah commander in chief of the invading forces. The Arab military plans called for Egypt's units to move north along the Mediterranean coast toward Tel Aviv; for Syria's, Lebanon's, and Iraq's troops to come through Galilee and move to Haifa; and for Transjordan's Arab Legion to approach the coast after occupying central Palestine. However, the Arab Legion did not cross the UN partition line, and the other Arab forces were blocked from their objectives. Despite appointment of a commander in chief, the Arab armies failed to coordinate their plans, each operating under its own generals without integrating its actions with those of its allies. Except for the Arab Legion, the Arab armies were poorly trained and badly equipped, and morale was low. By June 1948 their offensive lost its momentum. Both sides accepted a twenty-eight-day truce ordered by the UN Security Council that went into effect on 10 June.

With resumption of fighting on 8 July, Israel's forces, now consolidated and equipped with heavy weapons, took the offensive. Arab areas including Nazareth in Galilee were seized, although attempts to capture the Old City of Jerusalem failed. Efforts to break through Egypt's lines to reach Jewish settlements in the Negev also were unsuccessful.

A second truce, initiated on 19 July, was broken several times when Israel's forces attempted to break Egypt's blockade of the Negev; Israel captured Beersheba in October and isolated most of Egypt's units south of Jerusalem. By the end of the year, Egypt's forces were either driven from Palestine or besieged in the south. In the north, another offensive extended the area under Israel's control to Lebanon's territory adjoining upper Galilee.

On 5 January 1949, Egypt agreed to accept a Security Council call for a new truce and negotiations for an armistice. Negotiations opened on 13 January 1949, on the island of Rhodes, under the chairmanship of Ralph BUNCHE. The General Armistice Agreement signed on 24 February 1949 served as a model for similar armistices with Lebanon on 23 March, with Jordan on 3 April, and with Syria on 20 July. Iraq refused to participate in armistice negotiations.

The armistice agreements were considered preliminary to permanent peace settlements. They established frontiers between Israel and its neighbors that remained in effect until the ARAB–ISRAEL WAR of 1967. A UN Truce Supervisory Organization with four MIXED ARMISTICE COMMISSIONS, comprised of Israel and of Egypt, Lebanon, Jordan, and Syria, was established to deal with disputes between the signatories.

Israel's casualties in the war, which it called the War of Independence, were heavy—over forty-five hundred soldiers and two thousand civilians killed (about 1 percent of the Jewish population). The Arab regular armies lost two thousand; there were no reliable figures for Palestinian irregulars, although some estimates ran as high as thirteen thousand.

Israel extended territory under its control from the fifty-four hundred square miles (13,986 sq km) allocated to it in the partition plan to eight thousand square miles (20,720 sq km), including land allocated to the Arab state and to what became Jewish West Jerusalem; Jordan occupied the old city and Arab East Jersalem and the West Bank. Israel emerged from the war as a regional power equal in strength to any of its Arab neighbors.

A major consequence of the war was the Palestine Arab refugee problem. Although there was no accurate census of the refugees, their number was estimated by the United Nations to be over 700,000—more than half the Arab population of mandatory Palestine. Failure to prevent establishment of the Jewish state was considered a major disaster in the Arab world; loss of the war, the flight of the Palestinians, and the establishment of Israel were called by many the *nakba*, a disaster that was to intrude into inter–Arab politics, affect Arab relations with the West, and color Arab self-perceptions for decades to come.

BIBLIOGRAPHY

BEGIN, MENACHEM. *The Revolt: Story of the Irgun.* New York, 1951.

KHOURI, FRED. *The Arab–Israeli Dilemma,* 3rd ed. Syracuse, N.Y., 1985.

MORRIS, BENNY. *The Birth of the Palestine Refugee Problem 1947–1949.* Cambridge, 1987.

SHLAIM, AVI. *Collusion Across the Jordan: King Abdullah, the Zionist Movement and the Partition of Palestine.* Oxford, 1988.

Don Peretz

Arab–Israel War (1956)

A war, which lasted from October 29 to November 6, 1956, waged by Britain, France, and Israel against Egypt. Its objective was to reestablish British and French control over the Suez Canal and to topple Gamal Abdel Nasser of Egypt.

NASSER's accession to power in 1952 was initially viewed as a positive development in the Middle East. Secret contacts between ISRAEL and the FREE OFFICERS had occurred, giving rise to some optimism concerning possible negotiations over borders. The Anglo–Egyptian treaty, signed on June 18, 1954, provided for the evacuation of British troops from the SUEZ CANAL in return for the right of reentry in the event of an attack on the Arab states or Turkey.

However, Nasser's subsequent policies of Egyptian/Arab nationalism and nonalignment were seen in the West as direct threats to British and French hegemony in the area. The Soviet (Czech) arms deal in 1955, Nasser's recognition of the People's Republic of China and his opposition to a Western-sponsored alliance in the Middle East assured his ascendancy among the newly emergent nations. The French were alarmed at Egyptian support for Algerian (FLN) nationalists.

In Israel a series of events—the Egyptian blockade of Eilat and the Gulf of Aqaba since 1951, the 1955 arms deal with Czechoslovakia that provided Egypt with planes, tanks, armored cars, artillery and self-propelled guns, the formation of a joint command with Syria and later Jordan, and increased FIDA'IYYUN incursions from Gaza into Israel—were seen as signs that Egypt was preparing for war. Israeli prime minister David BEN-GURION had already considered and rejected a preemptive strike against Egypt.

Nasser's nationalization on July 26, 1956, of the Suez Canal Company—in which the British government held a majority of the shares, though its headquarters were located in France—gave the British and French a rationale for war.

Nasser's action was in retaliation for the July 19 American refusal and the subsequent British refusal of Egypt's requests for government-to-government support or for loans from the World Bank for construction of the Aswan Dam and the implementation of economic development programs. His stand against the West generally and against Israeli raids into Gaza was seen as a challenge to western dominance in the region and to Iraqi pretensions for leadership in the Arab world.

Throughout the summer of 1956, Israel, England, and France planned for war along parallel but independent lines. Israel negotiated with France for arms and developed operations to open the Strait of Tiran to Israel shipping (Operation Kadesh). The British moved ships to Cyprus and to Malta with the aim of seizing the canal and bringing down Nasser (Operation Musketeer). The French then initiated overtures to the Israelis for joint planning and participation in the operation against Egypt. Exploratory meetings began in early September. In October (22–24), at the invitation of the French, Ben-Gurion, Shimon Peres, and Moshe Dayan met with French Prime Minister Guy Mollet and British Foreign Minister Selwyn Lloyd at Sèvres to plan the joint campaign where Israeli forces were to cross the Sinai and link up with the British and the French in the area of Port Sa'id. It was understood that the Anglo-French intervention was to be seen as an "impartial" separation of combatants and that Israel was to be able to withdraw its troops if England and France did not carry out their military missions. The allies also counted on the fact that the Soviet Union (involved in Poland and in Hungary) and the United States (in the midst of presidential elections) would be too busy to interfere. Tensions on the Israeli–Jordanian border gave the impression that Israel was preparing to invade Jordan rather than Egypt.

As British and French troops were massing on Cyprus and Malta in August, Nasser anticipated an attack on Egypt and redeployed much of the Egyptian Sinai garrison to the delta region, leaving only thirty thousand men in the northeast triangle of al-Arish, Rafah, and Abu Ageila under the eastern command of Major General Ali Amr, headquartered at Isma'ilia. The troops consisted of one Egyptian division and one poorly trained and lightly armed Palestinian division commanded by Egyptian officers and supported by field artillery and antitank guns, three squadrons of Sherman tanks, and a motorized border patrol. In addition, Amr commanded two infantry divisions and an armored division just west of the canal that could be used in the Sinai. The garrison at Sharm al-Shaykh was directly under the control of headquarters at Cairo. Of Egypt's 255 aircraft, only 130 were operational; these included MiG-15s, Vampires, and Meteors. Despite intelligence reports of Israeli mobilization, Amr was on an official visit to Syria and Jordan and returned to Egypt on the morning of October 29.

By the evening of October 28, Israel had mobilized: twelve mobile field-force brigades, or forty-five thousand men, were assigned to the southern command and six brigades held in reserve in the north. Divided into three groups, the Northern Task Group, commanded by Brigadier General Haim Laskov, with infantry and armored brigades was to advance along the coastal road through al-Arish. The Central Task Group, commanded by Colonel Yehudah Wallach, was to proceed to the canal via the two central Sinai routes, supported by a paratroop brigade under Colonel Ariel SHARON. The Southern Task Group, commanded by Colonel Avraham Yoffe, was to proceed from Eilat to Sharm al-Shaykh. The objective was to threaten the canal by securing the Mitla pass (thirty miles from the canal) and to achieve the flexibility either to advance—if the British and French carried out their part of the agreement—or to withdraw if necessary.

On October 29, Israeli parachutists, commanded by Rafael EITAN, landed east of the Mitla pass and encountered heavy Egyptian resistance. This action was followed by a high-speed dash by Sharon's mobile column, which met up with the Israelis at the pass. The next day, the British and the French issued an ultimatum calling for the withdrawal of forces from both sides of the canal in order to allow their troops to establish themselves along its length. Israel accepted, but Nasser rejected the ultimatum and began to issue orders for an Egyptian withdrawal from the Sinai to the delta. The British and the French vetoed UN-sponsored cease-fire resolutions. They began their air attacks on Egypt on October 31. Nasser subsequently sank ships (November 4) in order to block passage through the canal. By November 2 Israel had taken Abu Ageila and opened up a supply route to the Mitla pass, cutting the Egyptians off from Gaza. On November 5, Sharm al-Shaykh was taken and Ariel Sharon's troops reached the canal. Speed and mechanized transport, combined with tank warfare and air superiority, enabled the Israelis to outmaneuver the Egyptian forces sent to defend Sinai, who had no air cover for their troops due to the destruction of more than two hundred aircraft on the ground.

The British, anticipating heavy opposition by the Egyptian forces, set sail from Malta only on November 1, delaying their landing in Egypt. The delay permitted the buildup of negative reactions to the mission both at home and in the international community. The allies tried to speed up the process, landing paratroops at Port Sa'id on November 5 and taking the city on the next day just as hostilities ceased.

By then, both the United States and the Soviet Union threatened to take military action, and the newly reelected American President Dwight D. Eisenhower ordered a global alert of American armed forces. The British, in the midst of the biggest crisis in Anglo-American relations since World War II, fearful of Soviet intervention, and worried about the falling pound sterling (later shored up by a line of credit from the U.S. Export-Import Bank), accepted a cease-fire. France and Israel followed suit.

On December 4 United Nations Emergency Force (UNEF) troops moved into Sinai, and on December 22 Britain and France withdrew from Egypt.

Israeli troops withdrew from the Gaza Strip and the Strait of Tiran on March 7 and 8 as a result of heavy pressure from the United States and in the wake of the stationing of UN troops at the entrance of the Gulf of Aqaba and the U.S. assurance that it would uphold the right of innocent passage of Israeli and all other shipping through international waters. Although Egypt did not acknowledge Israel's right of passage, it allowed UNEF forces to remain in Sinai until 1967.

The war marked the end of an active British role in the region. It resulted in the development of modern armed forces in Israel, the beginnings of U.S. support for Israel, and the emergence of Nasser as victor and hero of not only the Arabs but the Third World as well.

BIBLIOGRAPHY

BAR-ON, MORDECHAI. *The Gates of Gaza: Israel's Road to Suez and Back, 1955–1957.*
DUPUY, TREVOR N. *Elusive Victory: The Arab–Israeli Wars, 1947–1974.* McLean, Va., 1984.
HAIKAL, M. *Cutting the Lion's Tail.*
LOUIS, WILLIAM ROGER, and ROGER OWEN, eds. *Suez 1956: The Crisis and Its Consequences.* New York, 1991.
LOVE, K. *Suez: The Twice-Fought War.*

Reeva S. Simon

Arab–Israel War (1967)

Rapid and decisive victory by Israel over the combined forces of Egypt, Syria, Jordan, and Iraq.

The third major military conflict between Israel and the Arab states, the Arab–Israel War of 1967 between Israel and Egypt, Syria, Jordan, and Iraq continued the century-old confrontation by Zionists and Arab nationalists over Palestine. The war erupted because of the failure to settle issues left unresolved by the wars of 1948 and 1956 and by the establishment of Israel in 1948. These issues included the problem of Palestinian refugees, disputes over water rights and the borders between Israel and the Arab states, the Middle East arms race, the rising tide of Arab nationalism, and the question of Israel's right to exist.

Efforts to peacefully resolve the Arab–Israel conflict had been unsuccessful since 1948; despite the defeat of the Arabs in 1948 and 1956, the state of war continued and it intensified many of the problems it caused. As the number of Palestine refugees increased, their infiltration from the Egyptian-occupied Gaza Strip and from the West Bank of Jordan created incidents leading to repeated border skirmishes. In re-

taliation for FIDA'IYYUN raids, Israel attacked Egyptian and Jordanian outposts.

Disputes over the demilitarized zone (DMZ) between Israel and Syria erupted in battles that escalated into air warfare in which six Syrian MIGs were shot down two months before the 1967 war broke out. Israel's insistence on proceeding with land development in the DMZ and its unilateral diversion of the Jordan River headwaters following the failure by the Arabs to ratify the Eric Johnson Jordan Valley Development project led to the decision by the Arab League to begin its own water-diversion scheme. The conflict over the Jordan River was a major cause of rising tensions and repeated border incidents.

The confrontation between Israel and the Arab states became a factor in the Cold War between the Soviet Bloc and the West, with the Soviet Union providing arms to Egypt, Syria, and Iraq and with France and the United States helping to supply Israel. Israel continued to resist demands by the Arabs that it permit the return of the Palestinian refugees and that it withdraw to the borders established in 1947 by the UN Partition plan.

Hostility to Israel, intensified by the Palestinian refugee problem, increased nationalist fervor throughout the Arab world, and this sentiment was rallied by Egypt's President NASSER. After the air battles between Syria and Israel in April, a military pact was drawn up (under Egyptian leadership) whose purpose was to confront Israel. Egypt and Syria signed the agreement on May 4, Jordan on May 30, and Iraq on June 4. The pact was backed by the Soviet Union, which supported Egypt's military buildup along the borders with Israel in Sinai, Gaza, and the Gulf of Aqaba.

Responding to the challenge by militant Arab nationalists that he take a more confrontational position, in May Nasser ordered the withdrawal of the UN Emergency Force from its post along the Egyptian-Israeli border. Despite Egypt's heavy military involvement at the time in the Yemen civil war, Nasser deployed thousands of troops along the Israeli border and ordered a blockade of Israeli shipping in the Gulf of Aqaba.

These actions created a sense of crisis in Israel, which led to the formation of a national unity government that for the first time included Menachem BEGIN and his right-wing Herut party. Efforts to mediate the crisis through the United Nations and the Western nations failed, and proposals to form an international naval flotilla to protect shipping in the Gulf of Aqaba were rejected. While negotiations to ease tensions were still being discussed in the United States, the Israel cabinet decided to initiate preemptive surprise strikes in Egypt, Syria, Jordan, and Iraq, and early on June 5, 1967, Israeli warplanes bombed airfields in these countries. Simultaneously, Israeli forces attacked Gaza and quickly advanced into Sinai. After three days, the Egyptian army was routed, and Israel seized the Gaza Strip, Sinai up to the Suez Canal, and Sharm al-Shaykh at the entrance to the Gulf of Aqaba.

Shortly after Israel attacked Egypt, Jordanian forces fired on the Jewish sector of Jerusalem, despite warnings to King Hussein not to intervene in the fighting. However, Hussein entered the war as a result of mass pressure to join forces with Egypt in expectation of a decisive victory. Within three days, Israel captured Jordanian East Jerusalem and most of the West Bank. On June 7, the UN Security Council called for a cease-fire, which Syria refused to accept. Shelling of Israeli settlements in northern Israel led Israel to attack and then capture the Golan region, and to Syria's acceptance of a cease-fire on June 10. In the six days of combat, Israel destroyed over four hundred Arab aircraft (mostly on June 5), destroyed or captured more than five hundred tanks, and demolished 70 percent of Egyptian, Syrian, and Jordanian military equipment. Egyptian casualties included over 11,000 men killed and 5,600 prisoners of war; Jordan lost 6,000 men and Syria about 1,000. Israel lost more than 20 planes and 60 tanks, and 700 of its soldiers were killed.

As a result of the war, Israel occupied territory equivalent to more than three times its pre-1967 area, including the Gaza Strip, the Sinai peninsula, Jordan's West Bank and East Jerusalem, and the Golan Heights. The routing by Israeli forces and flight of some 300,000 Palestinian and Syrian civilians increased the refugee problem and further intensified Palestinian nationalism. The defeat led to the discrediting of most Arab leaders and to a new phase in the Palestine national movement, which ultimately resulted in the formation of the PALESTINE LIBERATION ORGANIZATION.

Immediately after the war, efforts to establish peace were renewed through the United Nations and passage of SECURITY COUNCIL RESOLUTION 242, which called for Israel's withdrawal from occupied territories and peaceful resolution of the conflict. Resolution 242 became the basis of most attempts to settle the conflict for the next quarter century. Although the Arab states passed a resolution at a summit meeting in Khartoum in September 1967 that called for no peace, no negotiations, and no recognition of Israel, they eventually moderated their demands for a settlement from a return to the 1947 UN partition borders to an Israeli withdrawal from territories occupied in 1967—that is, to the 1949 armistice lines. They also no longer insisted on the repatriation of refugees to their original homes within Israel.

In Israel, the war reinforced those militant nationalists who called for unification of the "whole land of Israel" and led to formation of the Likud party, which opposed withdrawal from territory acquired in June 1967. Arab East Jerusalem was for all practical purposes annexed by Israel soon after the war, and the Golan area was subjected to Israeli law in 1981. Israel's victory polarized politics between those who favored a peace settlement based on return of territory in exchange for secure borders and those who opposed any territorial concessions. Occupation and imposition of military government in the territories stimulated Palestinian nationalist sentiment and led to the Intifada in December 1987.

BIBLIOGRAPHY

ABU-LUGHOD, IBRAHIM, ed. *The Arab-Israeli Confrontation of June 1967: An Arab Perspective.* Evanston, Ill., 1970.
BRECHER, MICHAEL. *Decisions in Crisis.* Berkeley, Calif., 1980.
LAQUEUR, WALTER. *The Road to War, 1967.* London, 1968.
PARKER, RICHARD B. *The Politics of Miscalculation in the Middle East.* Bloomington and Indianapolis, 1993.

Don Peretz

Arab–Israel War (1973)

War in October 1973 between Israel and Egypt and Syria; the fourth major military confrontation between Israel and the Arab states.

The 1973 war resulted from failure to resolve the territorial disputes arising from the ARAB–ISRAEL WAR OF 1967. Despite UN Resolution 242, calling for Israel to withdraw from territories occupied in June 1967, little progress was made in its implementation. Efforts by President Anwar al-SADAT of Egypt to obtain the return of Sinai through diplomacy included extending the Rogers plan and offering to reopen the Suez Canal if Israel would withdraw to the Mitla and Gidi passes in the Sinai peninsula. He also offered to resume diplomatic relations with the United States, declare a cease-fire, and sign a peace pact with Israel based on full implementation of Resolution 242. Israel informed UN mediator Gunnar Jarring that it would not withdraw to the pre-June 5, 1967, armistice lines.

While making diplomatic approaches to the conflict, Sadat was preparing for war. He contacted President Hafiz al-ASAD of Syria to plan a two-front attack on Israel. Egypt, however, still depended on the Soviet Union for modern weapons. Angered by the Soviet Union's failure to respond to his demands for an assured supply, Sadat surprised the international community in July 1972 by expelling all 21,000 Soviet military advisers and personnel in Egypt. Although many in the West believed that the gesture would delay moves toward war, the Soviet Union responded by stepping up arms deliveries to both Egypt and Syria, in an attempt to regain Sadat's favor.

In a last attempt at a political settlement, Sadat persuaded eight members of the UN Security Council to introduce a resolution reiterating the call for Israel's withdrawal from Sinai and underscoring Palestinian rights in July 1973. The United States vetoed the proposal, maintaining that it undermined Resolution 242, "the one and only agreed basis" for a settlement.

In Israel, positions on the conflict had hardened since the victory in 1967. The governing LABOR PARTY generally accepted the principle of "territory in exchange for peace," but it adamantly opposed return of *all* the occupied lands, asserting that for security reasons, Israel would have to continue occupation of substantial areas. Sadat's failure to follow through after his proclamations about the "year of decision" in 1971, and again in 1972, led Israel's general staff to conclude that the country was safe from an Arab attack for the indefinite future and that the BAR-LEV LINE along the Suez Canal was impenetrable. Thus Israel's army commanders were unprepared for the October attack of Egypt and Syria. Israel's intelligence misinterpreted the buildup of forces along the canal before the war as military exercises unlikely to escalate into a full-fledged attack.

The two-front war began on 6 October 1973, the Jewish Day of Atonement (Yom Kippur); hence, in Israel it was called the Yom Kippur War. It also was the Muslim month of fasting, Ramadan; thus the conflict was called the Ramadan War by the Arabs. Egypt's forces quickly crossed the Suez Canal and overran the Bar-Lev line. In the north, Syria moved into the GOLAN HEIGHTS, nearly reaching the 1967 border with Israel. Because Israel had not fully mobilized, it was outnumbered almost twelve to one when the fighting began. Within the next few days, however, rapid mobilization of reserves redressed the balance.

The fighting was the heaviest since 1948, with major losses of manpower and matériel on both sides. The numbers of tanks, planes, and artillery pieces destroyed was larger than in any battle fought since World War II. Each side had to be rearmed in the midst of the fighting, Egypt and Syria by the Soviet Union, and Israel by the United States.

During the first days of the war, there was great consternation in Israel and fear that Arab forces, es-

pecially those of Syria in the north, might succeed in penetrating the pre-June 1967 borders. Within a week, however, Israel's counteroffensives turned the tide of battle. Syria was beaten back on the Golan Heights, and Israel's forces crossed the Suez Canal and began to push toward Cairo.

The war precipitated an international crisis when the Soviet Union responded to an urgent appeal from Egypt to save its Third Army, surrounded by the Israel Defense Forces (IDF) in Sinai. Despite the Security Council cease-fire orders, Israel's troops continued to attack. When the Soviet Union threatened to send troops to assist Egypt, the United States called a worldwide military alert. The crisis ended when all parties agreed to negotiate a safe retreat for the Egyptians.

When the combatants accepted a cease-fire on 22 October, Israel's forces had regained control of Sinai and crossed to the west side of the Suez Canal. Most of the Golan was recaptured, and the IDF occupied some 600 square kilometers (240 sq. mi.) of Syrian territory beyond the Golan Heights. Both Egypt and Israel claimed victory: Egypt, because it drove Israel's forces back into Sinai; and Israel, because it finally defeated the Arab forces. However, the price of victory was steep. Nearly 3,000 of Israel's soldiers and more than 8,500 Arab soldiers were killed. Wounded numbered 8,800 for Israel and almost 20,000 for the Arabs. Israel lost 840 tanks; the Arabs, 2,550. The cost of the war equaled approximately one year's GNP for each combatant. Israel became more dependent on the United States for military and economic aid, and the Arabs turned to the Soviet Union to restock their arsenals.

The October War also had severe international economic repercussions. It emboldened the ORGANIZATION OF PETROLEUM EXPORTING COUNTRIES to double prices for its oil, and the Arab members to insist on tying the sale of oil to support from consuming nations in the war against Israel. Saudi Arabia placed an embargo on shipments to the United States in retaliation for U.S. arms supplied to Israel. Gasoline shortages in the United States resulted, and the rise in oil prices began a spiral of worldwide inflation and a recession in 1974–1975.

Attempts to resume the peace process began with SECURITY COUNCIL RESOLUTION 338, passed at the same time as the cease-fire ordered on 22 October. The resolution called for immediate termination of all military activity, implementation of Resolution 242, and the start of negotiations "aimed at establishing a just and durable peace in the Middle East." Resolution 338 subsequently became a companion piece to Resolution 242 as the basis of proposals for a peace settlement.

In December a Middle East peace conference was convened in Geneva under the cochairmanship of the Soviet Union's foreign minister, the U.S. secretary of state, and the UN secretary-general. Egypt, Jordan, and Israel attended. Syria refused to participate. After opening speeches and two days of wrangling over procedure, meetings were suspended; the conference failed to reconvene.

Collapse of the peace conference provided U.S. Secretary of State Henry KISSINGER with the opportunity to bypass the United Nations and the Soviet Union in striving for a settlement. The first step was a cease-fire agreement providing for relief of Egypt's besieged Third Army and return to the lines of 22 October. This was the first bilateral accord signed between Israel and Egypt since the 1949 armistice. In January 1974, Kissinger began another round of SHUTTLE DIPLOMACY, persuading Egypt and Israel to sign a disengagement agreement calling for Israel to withdraw its forces back across the Suez Canal.

It was much more difficult to attain the disengagement agreement between Syria and Israel. After several trips between Damascus and Jerusalem, Kissinger finally persuaded Israel to withdraw from territory seized in Syria during October 1973 and from the town of Quneitra in the Golan region. A buffer zone patrolled by United Nations Deployment of Forces (UNDOF) was established between forces of Israel and Syria in the Golan Heights, and President Asad agreed to prevent Palestinian guerrilla forces from using Syria as a base from which to attack Israel.

The disengagement agreements, which represented the diplomatic climax of the 1973 war, were the major accomplishment in Israel–Arab relations for the next several years. Egypt's military "accomplishments" opened the way for receptivity to Kissinger's diplomatic approaches, and they were a prelude to Sadat's startling peace initiative in 1977.

Despite Israel's ability to recoup militarily after the first few days of the war and its occupation of additional territory that had belonged to Egypt and Syria, the long-term consequences were disastrous. Casualties exceeded those of the two previous wars, and military intelligence was discredited for not having predicted the attack. Israel's setback broke through a psychological barrier to territorial concessions and the belief in Israel's invincibility against any combination of Arab forces. While it enhanced Arab self-confidence, it shook Israel's belief that no concessions were necessary and that the territories could be held indefinitely. The Agranat Commission, established in November 1973 to probe the reasons for the setback, blamed the mistaken IDF assessment of Egypt's war prowess for Israel's failures and recommended removal of the chief of staff and other high-

ranking officers. Its report led to a major shake-up of the Labor government, the resignation of Prime Minister Golda Meir, and a new cabinet led by Yitzhak Rabin in June 1974. The 1973 setback and the Agranat Report were among the major factors leading to Labor's defeat in the 1977 Knesset election.

BIBLIOGRAPHY

AMOS, JOHN W., II. *Arab Israeli Military/Political Relations: Arab Perceptions and the Politics of Escalation.* New York, 1979.

ARURI, NASSER H., ed. *Middle East Crucible: Studies on the Arab–Israeli War of October 1973.* Wilmette, Ill., 1975.

EL-BADRI, HAZZAN, TAHA EL-MAGDOUB, and MOHAMMED DIA EL-DIN ZHODY. *The Ramadan War.* Fairfax, Va., 1978.

HERZOG, CHAIM. *The War of Atonement, October 1973.* Boston, 1975.

LAQUEUR, WALTER. *Confrontation: The Middle East and World Politics.* New York, 1974.

Don Peretz

Arab–Israel War (1982)

War that began with Israel's invasion of Lebanon in 1982.

The fundamental purpose of the Israeli invasion on June 6, 1982, was to destroy the infrastructure and leadership of the PALESTINE LIBERATION ORGANIZATION (PLO) and to install a Maronite-dominated government, led by the Phalange party, which would ally itself with ISRAEL. Defense Minister Ariel SHARON persuaded Prime Minister Menachem BEGIN, Foreign Minister Yitzhak SHAMIR, and Chief of Staff Rafael EITAN that the elimination of the PLO would convince West Bank and Gaza Palestinians to seek an accommodation on Begin's terms of limited autonomy and thereby preempt the establishment of a Palestinian state, an idea that was gaining international support.

The timing of the invasion favored Israel. The Arab world was in disarray. The most powerful Arab country, Egypt, had made peace with Israel under terms of the CAMP DAVID ACCORDS. Support for Israel in the Reagan administration was strong. Israel's border with Lebanon had been quiet since July 1981 when U.S. emissary Philip Habib negotiated a cease-fire between Israel and the PLO. The invasion, however, was triggered not by a border incident but by the attempted assassination on June 3 of the Israeli ambassador in London. This was a pretext, though, because the attacker belonged to the anti-PLO Abu Nidal group, and PLO officials were also on the hit list.

The invasion might have been regarded in Israel and the West as a preemptive, defensive invasion (Israel called it Operation Peace for Galilee) if it had been confined to "surgical" action against PLO forces within the twenty-five-mile belt south of the Litani river, as Sharon had declared. However, once the invasion began on June 6, Sharon and Eitan ordered the Israel Defense Forces (IDF) to proceed to Beirut, when they defeated Syrian forces in the air and on the ground and drove the PLO forces back to Beirut. The IDF reached Beirut in mid-June, where it laid siege to and shelled West Beirut for seven weeks and linked up with Israel's Lebanese allies, the Phalange.

Originally, Sharon had hoped that the Phalange forces (rather than the IDF) would enter PLO strongholds in West Beirut. Phalange leader Bashir JUMAYYIL and his aides had sought Israel's intervention and shared Sharon's goal of eliminating the PLO, especially from South Lebanon and West Beirut. Sharon's advisers, who lacked confidence in Phalange military ability, rejected such an operation; but fearing a high level of Israeli casualties, they also counseled against an Israeli assault. The result was a stalemate, and heavy Israeli bombardments and air strikes against West Beirut led to heavy civilian casualties. The nightly television pictures of death and destruction caused disquiet in the West. While U.S. Secretary of State Alexander Haig seemed to acquiesce, the White House in fact disapproved of the bombing of civilians. Haig shortly thereafter resigned, and the U.S. government sent Philip HABIB to Beirut to try to reach an agreement on PLO withdrawal. An accord was reached wherein a multinational force, including U.S. Marines, would supervise an orderly PLO evacuation and safeguard civilians in the refugee camps. By September 1, about 14,420 PLO fighters and officials had departed West Beirut for various Arab locales—particularly Tunis, which became PLO headquarters. About three thousand Syrian troops were withdrawn from the city; U.S. troops were also removed. The same day, the United States announced the Reagan Plan, which opposed Israel's annexation of the West Bank and Gaza and called for a freeze on Israeli settlements there. The plan also declined to support the establishment of a Palestinian state. Instead, it supported Palestinian autonomy in association with Jordan, which the United States urged to begin negotiations with Israel. Some of the Arab states, the PLO, and Israel rejected the plan.

Much of Sharon's grand design seemed to have been realized, including the election in late August of Bashir Jumayyil as president of Lebanon. However, Jumayyil resisted Begin and Sharon's demands for an immediate Lebanese–Israeli treaty and rejected Israeli insistence that their proxy in the South, Sa'd HADDAD and his troops, remain under Israeli authority. Then, on September 14, Jumayyil was assassinated—according to some, with Syrian help. Two days later, Sharon and Eitan ordered the IDF into West Beirut, in violation of the U.S.-brokered truce agreement. They approved the entry of Phalange forces into the SABRA AND SHATILA REFUGEE CAMPS and provided them with flares. The Phalange proceeded to kill between eight hundred and fifteen hundred Palestinian civilians from September 16 to 18.

An Israeli commission of inquiry, the KAHAN COMMISSION, found that Israeli officials, in particular Sharon and Eitan, were indirectly responsible for the killings. An international commission chaired by Sean MacBride charged that Israel was directly responsible because it had been the occupying power and had facilitated the actions of its ally. In late September the IDF evacuated Beirut and were replaced by the multilateral force that included the U.S. Marines.

The Arab–Israel War of 1982 was costly for all involved. According to Lebanese authorities, 17,825 Lebanese and Palestinians were killed, 84 percent of whom were civilians. Israel lost about six hundred soldiers, and spent three billion dollars on the three-month operation. The war hurt Israel's international image and divided its own people, of whom 400,000 (8 percent of the population) demonstrated against the war. Even the United States, which had sent the Marines to help fill the vacuum left by the Israeli departure from Beirut, got mired in Lebanese politics. On May 17 the new secretary of state, George Shultz, engineered a security agreement between Israel and Lebanon that ignored Syria's interests in Lebanon, ratified Israel's control of South Lebanon, and hinted at U.S. support for Maronite primacy. Lebanese Muslims responded by bombing the U.S. embassy in Beirut, and after the White House approved naval shelling of Druze villages, a suicide bomber attacked the Marine-naval barracks, killing 241 marines. U.S. forces were withdrawn four months later, and the Lebanese–Israeli agreement was aborted on March 5, 1984. Similar attacks took place against the French and the Israelis, who finally withdrew from Lebanon in 1985 after establishing a six-mile security zone patrolled by Haddad's army.

BIBLIOGRAPHY

KHALIDI, WALID. *Conflict and Violence in Lebanon: Confrontation in the Middle East.* Cambridge, Mass., 1979.

SCHIFF, ZE'EV, and EHUD YA'ARI. *Israel's Lebanon War.* New York, 1984.

SMITH, CHARLES D. *Palestine and the Arab Israeli Conflict.* New York, 1988.

TESSLER, MARK. *A History of the Israeli-Palestinian Conflict.* Bloomington, Ind., 1994.

Philip Mattar

Arabization Policies

Algeria's efforts to adopt the Arabic language following independence.

By the time Algeria became independent in 1962, written communication, except in the religious sector, was almost exclusively conducted in French. Algeria's first constitution declared Arabic to be the only official language of the country, though French remained de facto the operative language of government and industry.

Beginning in 1964, a process of gradual Arabization of the educational system was inaugurated. By the 1970s the secondary school system featured an Arabic track and a bilingual French–Arabic track. But the shortage of openings for non-French speakers in most scientific, technical, and managerial fields caused frustration among the Arabized and led to increasing unrest on university campuses. In response, the government in 1979 accelerated the Arabization of education and totally Arabized the judicial system, creating overnight significant new outlets for that track. By the end of the 1980s, most curricula, except in physical sciences, had been Arabized, and the parliament passed a law calling for total Arabization of the administration.

BIBLIOGRAPHY

ENTELIS, JOHN. *Algeria: The Revolution Institutionalized.* Boulder, Colo., 1986.

John Ruedy

Arab League

See League of Arab States

Arab League Collective Security Pact

Arab cooperation treaty.

The original seven members of the Arab League (Jordan, Syria, Iraq, Saudi Arabia, Lebanon, Egypt, and Yemen) concluded the Joint Defense and Economic Cooperation Treaty, the treaty's official name, in 1950; it was ratified by all members by 1971. The treaty arose from the Arab world's experience in the ARAB–ISRAEL WAR of 1948, from the league's desire to adapt to United Nations security arrangements, and as a response to the formation of the North Atlantic Treaty Organization. The signatories to the treaty "confirm their desire to settle their international disputes by peaceful means" (article 1), agree to individually and collectively repel aggression against any member state (article 2), and agree to coordinate their armed forces and economic activities (articles 4 and 7). A Joint Defense Council of league foreign and defense ministers and an Economic Council of economic affairs ministers are the main deliberative bodies operating under the treaty.

BIBLIOGRAPHY

HASSOUNA, HUSSEIN A. *The League of Arab States and Regional Disputes: A Study of Middle East Conflicts.* Leiden, 1975.

Charles U. Zenzie

Arab Legion

Transjordan/Jordan military force under British command.

In September 1923, after Britain recognized Transjordan, the Reserve Mobile Force, commanded by Cap. Frederick G. PEAKE, was reorganized and merged with all other forces in Transjordan, and given the name *al-Jaish al-Arabi* (Arab Army), Arab Legion in English. ABDULLAH IBN HUSAYN promoted Peake to brigadier general in 1923; he held that rank until 1939.

The Arab Legion began as a small, elite armed force of a little over a thousand. Peake organized it to high efficiency, recruiting Arab volunteers from Transjordan, Palestine, Syria, Iraq, and Hijaz. Most recruits were village peasants; some were townsmen. None were bedouins. By 1926, Peake had fifteen hundred men. He also had opened training schools, mostly for noncommissioned officers.

Between 1923 and 1926, the Arab Legion was able to fight bedouin raiders, repulse incursions by the Wahhabi Ikhwan, and assure order and security in the countryside. By virtue of its controlled use of force, it introduced tribesmen, bedouins, and townsmen to the notion of discipline and to the acceptance of order imposed by a central administrative authority.

The creation of the TRANSJORDAN FRONTIER FORCE (TJFF) in April 1926, to protect the borders from Saudi Arabia's territorial ambitions, resulted in a reduction in the Arab Legion's strength. It did not recover fully from this until Capt. John Bagot GLUBB arrived from Iraq, in November 1930, to be second in command to Peake. Glubb created the DESERT MOBILE FORCE, composed mainly of bedouins, and provided it with fast transport and communications facilities. This force was able to shore up the Arab Legion's diminished functions and was the nucleus of the striking force of the Jordan Arab Army.

The Arab Legion was further strengthened in the 1936–1939 period with augmentation of manpower, arms, and equipment. Glubb succeeded Peake as commander of the Legion at the outbreak of WORLD WAR II in 1939. During the war, the Arab Legion's main task was to hold the ground in line with British policy and to help thwart any attempt by the Axis powers to encroach on British or French interests in the mandated areas. In May 1941, the Legion reinforced British troops who had been rushed from Palestine to crush Rashid Ali al-Kaylani's rebellion in Iraq. The Desert Mobile Force won a battle at Falluja and, in cooperation with the BASRA-based British–Indian military contingent, entered Baghdad at the end of May.

When Jordan gained full independence in 1946, the Arab Legion was transformed into a regular army under Glubb's command. It participated in the ARAB–ISRAELI WAR of 1948, acquitting itself well despite its small size, and resisting assaults on East Jerusalem. At the end of hostilities, it was in complete control of the area that later came to be known as the WEST BANK, formally incorporated into the Kingdom of Jordan in April 1950.

Further expansion occurred in the period between 1948 and 1956, including the creation of the National Guard (1948), trained by the Arab Legion and under its command, to patrol and guard the border. Glubb was dismissed by King Hussein on March 1, 1956, followed shortly thereafter by all the British officers in the Legion, who were replaced by Jordanian officers.

BIBLIOGRAPHY

DANN, URIEL. *Studies in the History of Transjordan, 1920–1949: The Making of a State.* Boulder, Colo., 1984.

KIRKBRIDE, SIR ALEC. *From the Wings: Amman Memoirs, 1947–1951.* London, 1976.

VATIKIOTIS, P. J. *Politics and the Military in Jordan: A Study of the Arab Legion, 1921–1957.* New York, 1967.

Jenab Tutunji

Arab Liberation Army

Military force of the Arab League in Palestine, 1947–1949.

After the UNITED NATIONS voted to partition PALESTINE, in November of 1947, the Arabs resisted the partition and went to war against Israel in the ARAB–ISRAEL WAR of 1948. The Arab League (LEAGUE OF ARAB STATES) sponsored a military force after the 1947 vote, which was composed of PALESTINIANS and non-Palestinian Arab volunteers, headed by a former Iraqi officer, Fawzi al-QAWUQJI. This force was separate from the armies sent in by the five surrounding Arab states and the Palestinian forces under the command of Abd al-Qadir al-HUSAYNI.

The first contingents of the Arab Liberation Army reached Palestine in January 1948. Between February and May, they suffered a string of defeats in northern Palestine. Between May and October, the Arab Liberation Army controlled parts of western Galilee but by October were completely defeated by Israel's forces.

BIBLIOGRAPHY

HIRST, DAVID. *The Gun and the Olive Branch.* London, 1984.

LESCH, ANN MOSELY. *Arab Politics in Palestine, 1917–1939: The Frustration of a Nationalist Movement.* Ithaca, N.Y., 1979.

SHLAIM, AVI. *Collusion across the Jordan: King Abdullah, the Zionist Movement, and the Partition of Palestine.* New York, 1988.

Steve Tamari

Arab Liberation Front

Faction of the Palestine Liberation Organization (PLO).

The Arab Liberation Front was established in 1969 in Baghdad, Iraq, by the Iraqi Ba'th party to counter the formation of the Syrian Ba'th party's al-Sa'iqa faction. The Front opposed a separate Palestinian state and in 1974 joined the REJECTION FRONT against the al-FATH faction's diplomatic initiatives. It also fought in the Lebanon war (ARAB-ISRAEL WAR, 1982). In the late 1980s, the Front's four hundred members were led by Abd al-Rahim Ahmad, a member of the Palestine Liberation Organization's executive committee.

BIBLIOGRAPHY

COBBAN, HELENA. *The Palestinian Liberation Organization.* New York, 1984.

QUANDT, WILLIAM B., et al. *The Politics of Palestinian Nationalism*. Berkeley, Calif., 1973.

Elizabeth Thompson

Arab Liberation Movement

Syrian political organization.

The Arab Liberation Movement (ALM) was founded by Syria's President Adib SHISHAKLI in 1952 to bolster his following among the populace and imbue his leadership with democratic legitimacy.

Gathering "the good elements from all parties and all classes" (according to Shishakli), the party's 31-point program asserted an Arab national home from the Taurus to the Persian Gulf, from the Mediterranean to the Atlantic. It called for land reform, full employment, compulsory military service, women's rights, and settlement of nomads. Party offices were formed in Damascus on August 25, 1952, and in Aleppo on October 24, 1952. ALM candidates won sixty out of eighty-two seats in the first elections under a new constitution on October 9, 1953. The ALM continued to operate through the 1950s.

BIBLIOGRAPHY

SEALE, PATRICK. *The Struggle for Syria*. London, 1965.

Charles U. Zenzie

Arab National Fund

Fund-raising body of the Palestinian national movement.

Ahmad HILMI created the Arab National Fund, whose main period of activity was between 1944 and 1947. By investing large sums in the purchase of land from indebted Palestinians, it aimed to prevent land sales to Zionists and European Jewish refugees from World War II. It was also used by ISTIQLAL rivals of Hajj Muhammad Amin al-HUSAYNI to gain political influence.

BIBLIOGRAPHY

HUREWITZ, J. C. *The Struggle for Palestine*. New York, 1968.
KHALAF, ISSA. *Politics in Palestine: Arab Factionalism and Social Disintegration, 1939–1948*. Albany, N.Y., 1991.
SMITH, PAMELA ANN. *Palestine and the Palestinians: 1876–1983*. New York, 1984.

Steve Tamari

Arab National Movement (ANM)

Organization dedicated to the unification of the Arab world.

The Arab National Movement (ANM) was established by Palestinian students at the American University of Beirut in the 1950s. In Kuwait it found a spokesman in Dr. Ahmad al-KHATIB, a member of the National Assembly since 1963. The ANM also had some impact in Bahrain, but not elsewhere in the Gulf, and as of the mid-1990s was an almost wholly spent force.

BIBLIOGRAPHY

KELLY, J. B. *Arabia, the Gulf and the West*. New York, 1980.
PETERSON, J. E. *The Arab Gulf States: Steps toward Political Participation*. New York, 1988.

Malcolm C. Peck

Arab Nationalism

Ideology that Arabs are a nation.

The ideology that has dominated the Arab world for most of the twentieth century, Arab nationalism, evolved, much as did other nationalisms in the developing world, out of a reaction to the prospect (and later the reality) of European domination and under the influence of European ideas about nationalism. The emerging ideology, whose core premise was that the Arabs are and have been a nation unified by language and a shared sense of history, but long divided and dominated by outside powers, drew on elements of the Arab and Islamic heritages. It incorporated them into a new narrative of Arab history and pride in the Arab past that was disseminated through the press and in novels, poetry, and popular histories.

By the 1920s, Arab nationalism was the hegemonic ideology of the eastern Arab world—the *mashriq*—and its influence continued to spread in succeeding decades. By the 1950s and 1960s, thanks to the espousal of Arab nationalism by the charismatic Egyptian leader Gamal Abdel NASSER, and the capacities for mobilization, organization, and clandestine action of parties such as the BA'TH and the Movement of Arab Nationalists, it appeared to be ascendant throughout most of the more than twenty independent states of the Arab world. Its decline in succeeding decades has been just as rapid, with nation-state nationalist tendencies and Islamic radicalism filling the apparent vacuum.

The first stirrings of Arab nationalism have been detected by some historians as early as the 1860s, but it is more commonly accepted that as a sustained political movement it began early in the twentieth century. This followed the reimposition of the Ottoman constitution in 1908, and the greater freedom of the press and of political expression that resulted throughout the Arab provinces of the Ottoman Empire. A tendency that has since come to be known as "Arabism" rapidly appeared: it stressed the ethnic identity of the Arabs and emphasized their common cultural roots. It also called for equality for Arabs with other national groups within the empire. As well as being influenced by European models and by reinterpretations of the Arab and Islamic past, Arabism was strongly affected by the rise of nationalism among the TURKS, ARMENIANS, and other peoples of the Ottoman Empire at this time.

The Arabist tendency built on the work of several groups of writers and thinkers, including the pioneers of the renaissance of the Arabic language, the NAHDA. Starting in the mid-nineteenth century, this group produced new printed editions of the classics of Arabic literature, as well as encyclopedias, dictionaries, and works of history and literature, mainly in Beirut and Cairo. Another group, whose work was influential in a different way, was the Islamic reformers known as *salafis*, most of them from Syria and Lebanon, who argued for a return to the practices of the earliest days of Islam, and thus emphasized the period of Islamic history when the Arabs were dominant. Among them were the writers Rashid RIDA, Abd al-Rahman al-KAWAKIBI, Tahir al-Jaza'iri, Jamal al-Din al-Qasimi, and Abd al-Razzaq al-Bitar. In addition, there were authors and publishers who traveled to Egypt to escape the censorship that increasingly afflicted the rest of the Ottoman Empire after 1876, and remained to publish newspapers, journals, and books. All these groups contributed to the growth of the Arabist idea.

The Arabist tendency identified politically with the liberal opposition to the ruling COMMITTEE OF UNION AND PROGRESS (CUP) in the Ottoman Empire. This was partly a response to strong Turkish nationalist tendencies in the CUP, and partly to its policy of tight centralization, which infringed on the autonomy of the Arab provinces. Although this Arab–Turkish tension did not erupt into open conflict until World War I, when the British helped to foment an Arab revolt in the Hijaz against the Ottoman state, it did have a lasting impact on the historiography of this and later periods. Some Arab writers reacted strongly against what they saw as Turkish suppression of Arab rights before the war, and the execution of some of the most prominent Arabist leaders during the war. This reaction engendered a version of Arab history that rendered the four

centuries of Ottoman rule very negatively, in black and white, obliterating the nuances—and with them any understanding of the fruitful political and cultural symbiosis that characterized this lengthy period. This chauvinist version of modern Arab history—which ascribed the "backwardness" that afflicted the Arabs throughout much of their history to outsiders—is still influential in Arab schoolbooks and in much writing both within the Arab world and outside it.

In the wake of World War I, the Arabist aspiration to see an independent Arab state or federation of states stretching across the Fertile Crescent and the Arabian Peninsula was frustrated by Britain and France, which carved up the region into a series of mandates, protectorates, and nominally independent states, all of which were under the strong influence of their foreign patrons. The postwar response to European rule was a sequence of revolts in several Arab countries that impelled the granting of a measure of self-rule, and sometimes nominal independence, as in Egypt in 1922 and Iraq in 1932. The end result, however, was the perpetuation of the divisions that the European powers had imposed. Thereafter, within these new borders there gradually developed both a strong de facto attachment to the new states and the interests they represented, and a powerful, unrealized, and somewhat utopian aspiration for unity among them. Although these sentiments originated during the interwar years mainly in the newly created states of the FERTILE CRESCENT—Syria, Lebanon, Jordan, Palestine, and Iraq—they were mirrored in other Arab regions in succeeding years, even in areas where the existing states had much older and more historically rooted foundations, such as Egypt, Tunisia, Morocco, Yemen, and Oman.

The tension between the contradictory sentiments of pan-Arabism and nation-state nationalism has characterized Arab politics since about 1945. On the one hand, most Arabs recognized that they had a common language, history, and culture, and that if these commonalities could find proper political expression, the Arab peoples might be able to rise above the fragmentation and weakness that have characterized their modern history. Such ideas were particularly appealing at the mass level, and long aroused the enthusiasm of the publics in many Arab countries. On the other hand, the states that have existed in the Arab world for most of the twentieth century are in some cases rooted in long-standing entities with a strong, independent administrative tradition, have all engendered a powerful network of vested interests, and in recent decades have taken on an aura of permanence. The existence of these separate Arab states was reinforced by the Charter of the LEAGUE OF ARAB STATES, established in March 1945, which reaffirmed the independence of the signatory states, provided that decisions had to be made unanimously in order to be binding, and forbade interference in the internal affairs of any Arab state by others.

In practice, most Arab governments have at most times been motivated by pragmatic varieties of *raison d'état* rather than any ideological vision. At the same time, their leaders have often clothed their actions in visionary Arabist rhetoric. Such ideological motivations were never entirely absent from the actions of most governments, if only because their respective public opinions resonated to such ideas. The result appeared to be hypocrisy, whereby governments did things for one reason while claiming an entirely different one as their real motivation. The paradoxical effect of all this was to discredit Arabism as an ideology when the failures of the various nominally Arab nationalist regimes finally exasperated their citizens and Arab public opinion generally. The ensuing bankruptcy of Arab nationalism as an ideology, and of the parties and regimes that still espouse it, would appear to be among the enduring features of modern Arab politics.

BIBLIOGRAPHY

ANTONIUS, GEORGE. *The Arab Awakening: The Story of the Arab National Movement.* London, 1938.
BUHEIRY, MARWAN, ed. *Intellectual Life in the Arab East 1890–1939.* Beirut, 1981.
DAWN, C. ERNEST. *From Ottomanism to Arabism: Essays on the Origins of Arab Nationalism.* Urbana, Ill., 1973.
HOURANI, ALBERT. *Arabic Thought in the Liberal Age, 1798–1939,* 2nd ed. Cambridge, U.K., 1983.
KHALIDI, RASHID, LISA ANDERSON, MUHAMMAD MUSLIH, and REEVA SIMON, eds. *The Origins of Arab Nationalism.* New York, 1991.
KHOURY, PHILIP. *Urban Notables and Arab Nationalism: The Politics of Damascus, 1880–1920.* Cambridge, U.K., 1983.

Rashid Khalidi

Arab Organization for Industrialization

Group formed to manufacture weapons for all Arab countries.

Originally called the Arab Military Industries Organization, the Arab Organization for Industrialization was established in 1975 through an agreement between Egypt, Saudi Arabia, Qatar, and the United Arab Emirates. The organization, which was to manufacture advanced weapons for all Arab countries, was originally capitalized with $1 billion supplied equally by the four countries. In 1979, Saudi Arabia proclaimed the dissolution of the organization in protest of the Camp David Accords. Refusing to recognize this decision, Egypt retained the title and entered into negotiations with Western companies, including an agreement with American Motors Co. to produce jeeps, and an agreement with British Aerospace to manufacture anti-tank weapons.

BIBLIOGRAPHY

NYROP, RICHARD F., ed. *Egypt: A Country Study,* 4th ed. Washington, D.C., 1983.
RICHARDS, ALAN, and JOHN WATERBURY. *A Political Economy of the Middle East: State, Class and Economic Development.* Boulder, Colo., 1990.

David Waldner

Arab Revolt

Uprising of Arab nationalists against the Ottoman Empire during World War I.

Although many Arabs had reached the highest positions in the Ottoman government by the end of the nineteenth century, opposition to Turkish authority was spreading through the empire's Arabic-speaking provinces of the Ottoman Empire. A separatist nationalist movement had followers in many Arab towns and cities, including Damascus, Cairo, Baghdad, and Jerusalem by the early 1900s. Members formed secret cultural and political organizations, including groups of Arab officers in the Ottoman military. Prominent secret societies were al-Qahtaniya and al-FATAT; the former sought to establish a dual Arab–Turkish monarchy similar to the Austro–Hungarian Empire. Al-Fatat wanted to establish Arabic as the official language in the Arab provinces, where it would be taught in all schools.

Efforts by the YOUNG TURK regime that seized power in 1908 to repress Arab nationalism intensified opposition to the government and increased demands for separation from the empire. The arrest for treason in 1914 of Maj. Aziz 'Ali al-Masri, an Ottoman staff officer of Arab origin, brought opposition to the regime among Arab officers to a head.

Among the ardent nationalists was the SHARIF OF MECCA, HUSAYN IBN ALI, a Hashimite descendant of the Prophet Muhammad, and his four sons, Ali, ABDULLAH, FAISAL, and Zaid. Because the authorities suspected their loyalty, they were forced to live in Constantinople (now Istanbul) from 1893 until 1908. After they returned to Mecca, Husayn began to rally surrounding tribes against attempts to conscript Arabs into the Ottoman armed forces. Although the Turkish governor-general of Mecca backed down from the conscription order, Husayn sought an alliance with an outside power against further Ottoman attempts to undermine his authority.

In February 1914, Husayn sent one of his sons to negotiate with the British agent and consul general in Cairo, Lord KITCHENER, but Great Britain was not yet ready to support an Arab uprising against the Ottomans. With Turkey's entry into World War I on the side of Germany (October 1914), the British authorities reconsidered the sharif's offer to revolt in return for guarantees of Arab independence after defeating the Turks.

Ottoman efforts to rally support among Muslims throughout Asia for a jihad against the Allies failed to win over many Arab subjects. Rather, most Arab notables were sympathetic to the growing demands for independence, and many looked to Husayn for leadership. As relations between the Arab provinces and Constantinople continued to deteriorate due to poor economic conditions, mass arrests of suspected Arab nationalists, and resentment of conscription, Husayn attempted to reestablish contact with the British.

In 1915 he reopened negotiations through Lord Kitchener's successor in Cairo, Sir Henry MCMAHON. In an exchange of ten letters known as the HUSAYN– MCMAHON CORRESPONDENCE, the sharif offered assistance to Great Britain against the Turks in return for a British promise to recognize the independence of what was to become Syria, Lebanon, Palestine, Iraq, and most of the Arabian peninsula, and to endorse proclamation of an Islamic Arab caliphate. The British, however, refused to accept so precise a definition of the area for Arab independence because of conflicting promises and obligations regarding the territory. McMahon eventually replied that Britain would recognize the territory demanded by the sharif except for certain areas "not purely Arab." The imprecision of British promises was the cause of postwar quarrels between Great Britain and Arab nationalists, particularly with regard to Palestine.

Following the exchange of correspondence with McMahon, Ottoman authorities initiated a massive crackdown on Arab nationalists. In May 1916, twenty-one leading Arab citizens of Damascus and Beirut were arrested and executed by public hanging. These events undermined what little loyalty remained among Arab subjects of the sultan, and sparked widespread support for open revolt against the Ottomans. Opposition to the government was further intensified by famine resulting from destruction of crops by a locust plague in 1916. In retaliation

for Arab opposition, the Turkish authorities refused to permit outside relief supplies into the region; as a result, some 300,000 people died of starvation.

Sharif Husayn gave the order to tribes in the Hijaz to strike at Ottoman garrisons and proclaimed Arab independence in May 1916. After three weeks the Ottoman garrison in Mecca fell, followed shortly thereafter by most others in the main towns of the peninsula. Arab forces were supplied by Britain, and British officers served as military advisers. The most prominent was Colonel T. E. LAWRENCE, an adviser to Faisal.

The Arab revolt against the Turks ended in October 1919 when Faisal's armies captured Damascus, and an Arab regime was established with Faisal as king. At the end of the war, Husayn alienated many of his Arab neighbors when he proclaimed himself "king of the Arab countries." Although the British government refused to recognize him as more than "king of Hijaz," he persisted in the grander title, leading to confrontation with IBN SA'UD and eventual defeat by the latter, followed by the annexation of the Hijaz into the Saudi kingdom.

The Arab revolt played an important and controversial role in postwar negotiations, and in the decisions taken by Great Britain and France about the territorial divisions of the former Arab provinces in the Ottoman Empire.

BIBLIOGRAPHY

ANTONIUS, GEORGE. *The Arab Awakening: The Story of the Arab National Movement.* New York, 1965.

KEDOURIE, ELIE. *In the Anglo–Arab Labyrinth: The McMahon–Husayn Correspondence and Its Interpretation. 1914–1939.* Cambridge, U.K., 1976.

LAWRENCE, T. E. *Seven Pillars of Wisdom.* London, 1935.

ZEINE, ZEINE N. *The Emergence of Arab Nationalism, with a Background Study of Arab–Turkish Relations in the Middle East,* 3rd ed. New York, 1973.

Don Peretz

Arab Riots

See Palestine Arab Revolt

Arab Socialism

Political philosophy advocating governmental and collective ownership of the means of production and distribution.

Arab socialism emerged as a result of COLONIALISM in the Middle East coupled with the corruption and underdevelopment characteristic of Arab societies at the beginning of the twentieth century. It was not until the late 1940s that Arab thinkers began writing about the socialist option. Among the major parties and movements that emerged as a result of this effort were the Arab Renaissance Socialist party (al-BA'TH) and the movement called the FREE OFFICERS, led by President Gamal Abdel NASSER of Egypt (Nasserism).

The aims of Arab socialism were to free the Arab world from Western colonial rule and to establish pride and social justice within Arab societies. Another aim was the unification of the Arab world. Historically, Arab socialism emerged during the period of the liberation movements of third-world countries, so self-determination and tight controls against multinational corporations and their exploitation of local resources became a major priority. Arab socialism rejects Marxism and class struggle as basic tenets; it promotes cooperation between classes for the welfare of the entire community. The community must be based on the principles of justice and the equal distribution of wealth, with government provisions for the poor and underprivileged.

Agrarian reform and land redistribution were important goals. The nationalization of industries provided the government with funds, but some forms of private property were retained if they were in the national interest. (In some countries, such as Libya and Algeria, the teachings of ISLAM have also been included.)

In foreign policy, Arab socialism advocated a constant struggle against IMPERIALISM and ZIONISM. Support for the Palestinians' cause became a major battle horse, especially for Nasser in Egypt. He and other Arab "revolutionary" leaders used the PALESTINE problem to enchance their own power and legitimacy. Nonalignment and support for liberation movements were also goals of Arab socialist regimes. From 1967, following the defeat of Arab armies by Israel, after Nasser's death in 1970, and after the bitter rivalry between the two sections of the Ba'th party—the one in Syria and the other in Iraq—Arab socialism lost much of its appeal. Lack of democracy, corrupt and huge bureaucracy, and the emergence of a new class composed of bureaucrats and army officers all contributed to the end of Arab socialism.

In the Middle East, a few political parties and regimes still remain that claim inspiration by Arab socialism. These are the ARAB SOCIALIST UNION in Egypt; the Sudanese Socialist Union in Sudan; the People's General Congress of the Socialist Jamahiriya of Libya; the National Liberation Front of Algeria; the Ba'th party in Syria and in Iraq; the Revolutionary Socialist Party in Somalia; the Socialist parties of Yemen, including the People's Socialist party; and the DESTOUR PARTY of Tunisia.

BIBLIOGRAPHY

GOODE, STEPHEN. *Arab Socialism in the Modern Middle East.* New York, 1975.
SULEIMAN, MICHAEL. *Political Parties in Lebanon.* Ithaca, N.Y., 1967.

George E. Irani

Arab Socialist Action Party

Former Lebanese branch of the Popular Front for the Liberation of Palestine (PFLP).

The party was founded in 1967, when the Movement of Arab Nationalists decided to become a Marxist–Leninist party; the branch of the movement within each Arab country was expected to become a separate party. The party never had much success, being considered an extremist Marxist–Leninist organization. It was headed for much of its existence by Abu Adnan (Hashim Ali Muhsin), an Iraqi who had headed the Arab Labor Union. The party's relationship with the POPULAR FRONT FOR THE LIBERATION OF PALESTINE (PFLP) deteriorated in the 1980s and 1990s, when it protested the hegemonic influence of the PFLP.

The party is still relatively unknown to most Lebanese and non-Lebanese. It achieved a degree of notoriety in 1976 when members assassinated U.S. ambassador to Lebanon Francis Meloy and his two aides. The party participated in the Lebanese Civil War and founded the Lebanese REJECTION FRONT to oppose Syria's intervention in Lebanon. It also was active against Israel's 1982 occupation of south Lebanon and helped found the Lebanese National Resistance Front. The party's weekly publication, *al-Thawri,* is now sold openly after years of underground status.

BIBLIOGRAPHY

TACHAU, FRANK, ed. *The Encyclopedia of Political Parties in the Middle East and North Africa.* Westport, Conn., 1994.

As'ad AbuKhalil

Arab Socialist Union

The only legal political organization in Egypt, 1962–1977.

The Arab Socialist Union (ASU) was preceded by the LIBERATION RALLY (1953–1956) and the NATIONAL UNION (1956–1962). All three organizations were used by President Gamal Abdel NASSER's regime as instruments of mass mobilization as Egypt shifted to socialism and a planned economy.

In May 1961, Nasser presented the Charter for National Action, an ideological document outlining a vision for the socialist transformation. The ASU was to symbolize "the working forces of the people," defined as workers, peasants, intellectuals, national capitalists, and the armed forces. Since workers and peasants were to be the main beneficiaries of socialism, at least 50 percent of all elected posts in Parliament and the ASU were to be occupied by them. Those whose property was nationalized or sequestered were declared "enemies of the people" and denied political rights.

The basic law of the ASU was declared on 7 December 1962. Its organization was based on place of residence and profession. Branches (basic units) were established in villages, city quarters, schools, universities, and factories. They were organized on district, provincial, and national levels; the latter included a general committee, a supreme executive committee, a secretary-general, and a president. In theory, the ASU was the supreme authority of the state. Both parliament and the cabinet were to implement the policies it decided.

In practice, the institutional development of the ASU was confused and noncumulative. Elections were not conducted on time, leaders were both elected and appointed, and for a while elected and appointed committees coexisted. In 1965, it was decided to establish an organization that consisted of cells whose members were appointed and whose activities were secret.

As in many developing countries, the single party was an organization representing broad popular consensus. It was not intended to be an active institution with decision-making powers. Indeed, it was viewed more as a means of mobilizing political support than as a vehicle for popular participation. The ASU had no real authority and was broadly seen as an appendage of the executive.

Following Egypt's defeat in the Arab–Israel War of 1967, Nasser reshuffled the ASU, but no drastic changes took place. After Nasser's death in 1970, president Anwar al-SADAT was ready to reexamine the concept of the ASU. In 1971, Sayed Mar'ei, the new secretary-general of the ASU, issued a "guide for political action" that suggested a certain measure of political liberalization.

After the Arab–Israel War of 1973, Sadat spearheaded the critique of the ASU by issuing a paper on the need to reform its structure and introduce political diversity. In 1974–1976, a nationwide debate took place on the future of the ASU. Eventually, it was decided that three platforms (*manaber*) were to be established within the ASU. They represented the right (headed by Moustafa Kamil Mourad), the center (led by Sadat), and the left (led by Khalid Mohie al-Din). In 1976, satisfied with their performance in the parliamentary elections, Sadat announced the transformation of the platforms into political parties. The law of political parties was issued in August 1977, and since then the ASU has had no legal existence.

BIBLIOGRAPHY

BAKER, RAYMOND. *Egypt's Uncertain Revolution.* Cambridge, Mass., 1978.
DESSOUKI, ALI E. HILLAL, ed. *Democracy in Egypt: Problems and Prospects.* Cairo, 1983.

Ali E. Hillal Dessouki

Arab Socialist Renaissance Party

See Ba'th, al-

Arabs of Israel

A remnant of the larger Arab community living in the parts of mandatory Palestine that became the state of Israel in 1948.

Of the approximately 900,000 Arabs who lived in this area, fewer than 170,000 (about 12.5 percent of Israel's population) remained after the ARAB–ISRAEL WAR of 1948: 119,000 Muslims, 35,000 Christians, and 15,000 Druze. About 32,000 were town dwellers; 120,000, villagers; and 18,000, nomads. Some 30,000 were refugees, having fled from one part of Israel to another during the 1948 war. Most of the community leaders and professionals had left the country (only ten Arab physicians remained); most institutions were in disarray; and nearly every family had some members in the surrounding enemy countries.

The Arab population was separated from the Jewish majority in western, central, and upper Galilee, from Nazareth north. A few thousand remained in Ramle, Acre, Haifa, Jaffa, the Negev, and several score of smaller villages—a distribution that remained basically unchanged until the 1990s. Initially most areas where the Arab minority of the new Jewish state lived were under the military authorities and subject to restrictive emergency regulations that limited freedom of movement, access to civil courts, and individual ownership of land. Many in Israel's government considered the Arabs a security risk because of the continuing state of war with the surrounding countries. The severity of these restrictions was gradually eased until the KNESSET terminated most emergency regulations during 1966. Experience had demonstrated that the number of Arabs in Israel who might be a security risk was minute.

From 1948 until the early 1990s, government policy regarding Arab citizens of Israel was coordinated by the Adviser on Arab Affairs, a special office in the Bureau of the Prime Minister. Several ministries—including Education, Religion, Minorities, Agriculture, and Social Welfare—also had special offices for Arab affairs. In the absence of most professionals, such as doctors, after the 1948 war, the government took responsibility for rehabilitating the Arab community. A social welfare network was introduced in Arab areas and welfare offices were opened. Special courses were organized to train Arab personnel, feeding centers for Arab students were opened, and clinics were established by the Ministry of Health. Village rehabilitation was organized to restore agricultural production through replanting olive groves, the introduction of farm mechanization, and agricultural loans.

Policies emphasizing security and development of Israel as a Jewish state often vitiated efforts to rehabilitate the Arabs of Israel. This was perhaps most evident in policies regarding land and other immovable property belonging to Arab citizens. Property, including homes and farms, belonging to the 30,000 internal Arab refugees and to several thousand others was taken over by the custodian of absentee property, charged with administration of possessions belonging to Arabs who left their homes during the 1948 war. Most of those affected by the Absentee Property Law had fled to surrounding countries. However, much of the agricultural land belonging to Israel's Arab citizens also was placed in the hands of the custodian. Other laws pertaining to the acquisition of land for reasons of security and for development resulted in government sequestration of about 40 percent of the land belonging to the country's Arab citizens.

These land policies resulted in a shift in the occupational pattern of the Arab community, which before 1948 had been mostly rural/agricultural, to widespread employment in the Jewish urban economy. However, the village rural social network, based on traditional *hamulas* (families), remained largely intact. The majority of those in the urban economy traveled from their villages or towns to work in centers of Jewish commerce and industry, where they were employed in unskilled or low-paid jobs at the bottom of the economic ladder.

Yet many who retained agricultural land prospered despite the overall decline in Arab farmland. Since 1949, with the assistance of the Agriculture ministry, modern farming methods, extensive mechanization, and irrigation have been introduced; Arab agricultural productivity has increased several times over. While the overall economy of the Arab community still lags behind the Jewish sector, some of those who pay the highest income tax in Israel are from the minority community.

Initially the MAPAI (labor party), which controlled the government from 1948 until 1977, organized Arab political parties headed by local notables who cooperated with the military government. These local parties elected several members to the Knesset, where they generally voted with MAPAI. Other Arab Knesset members were affiliated with the Communist party and the MAPAM (left labor party).

Government officials charged with policy for the minority communities encouraged each to develop its own institutions and organizations. Thus the system of religious courts established during the Ottoman era, and continued during the British mandate, was maintained; these included SHARI‘A (Islamic religious) courts and separate courts for each of the several recognized Christian denominations. In 1962 the first Druze religious court, separate from the Islamic courts, was organized. The Druze were initially permitted to join Israel's military forces; later they were subject to the draft. A few bedouin and Christian Arabs also have been permitted to join the armed or security forces, but government policy generally exempts the country's Muslims from serving. Not serving in the military excludes most Arabs from receiving certain family and other government allowances, and increases the difficulty of finding employment in cases where prior military service is required.

Between 1948 and the early 1990s the Arab community experienced rapid economic, social, and political development. A new generation of leaders replaced those who had fled before and during the 1948 war or had been co-opted by Israel's government. By the late 1950s, 1960s, and 1970s, the new generation of Israel's Arabs included many professionals, university-educated in Israel or abroad, who were politically active. They became increasingly dissatisfied with the position of Israel's Arab citizens. Issues that concerned them were the government's land policies; the citizenship law that gave preference to Jewish immigrants; the lack of Arabs in responsible government posts; the disparities between government allocations for Arab and Jewish education, housing, and other services; and the perception that they were not accepted as full citizens of Israel. Opposition to government policies was evidenced in a shift of Arab voting patterns from Labor and other Jewish parties to the Communist party of Israel. Attempts to organize their own Arab nationalist party or parties were blocked by government authorities or by internal dissension among potential Arab leaders.

By the 1960s, Arab nationalist sentiment increased, and many Arabs in Israel supported Egypt's President Gamal Abdel NASSER. The rise of this national consciousness was demonstrated in 1965 when Israel's Communist Party split into a Jewish faction and a largely Arab nationalist faction, the New Communist List (Rakah). Although several of Rakah's leaders were Jewish, most of its votes came from Arabs who perceived it as the principal legal vehicle for expressing opposition to government policies. A few other groups attempted to organize opposition parties, but they were either banned by the authorities or failed to galvanize sufficient support within the Arab community. By the 1970s, Rakah was winning more votes within the Arab community than any of the Jewish parties, and it became the principal voice opposed to the government's Arab policies. Rakah later was joined by organizations such as the Committee for Defense of Arab Lands and the Committee of Heads of Arab Local Councils to form the Democratic Front for Peace and Equality (DFPE).

The ARAB–ISRAEL WAR OF 1967 and Israel's occupation of the WEST BANK, East Jerusalem (formerly part of Jordan) and Gaza (formerly occupied by Egypt) constituted a watershed in the development of Israel's Arabs. For the first time since 1947–1948, they could establish direct contacts with Palestinians in the surrounding countries. From 1948 until 1967 only a small number of Christians had been permitted to cross from Israel to Jordan once or twice a year, at Christmas and Easter. After 1967, Israel's Arabs could visit the West Bank and Gaza, and Palestinians in the occupied areas could visit Israel. Thus many family relationships were reestablished, Israel's Arabs became increasingly aware of new developments in Palestinian national consciousness, and they were no longer regarded by the Arab world at large with suspicion or mistrust. Larger numbers of Israel's Arabs identified themselves not only as loyal citizens of Israel but also as supporters of the Palestinian national cause.

Significant demographic changes characterized Israel's Arab community. It grew from 12.5 percent of Israel's population in 1948 to over 18 percent by the early 1990s, mostly as a result of natural increase. However, Israel's 850,000 Arabs included over 100,000 residents of East Jerusalem (annexed by Israel in 1967). Few of them opted to become citizens of Israel, most choosing to retain passports issued by Jordan. By the 1990s, Sunni Muslims constituted 78 percent of the Arab population, the Druze, approximately 9 percent, and various Christian denominations, about 13 percent. Most Christians were Greek Catholic (32 percent), Greek Orthodox (42 percent), or Latin Catholic (16 percent).

Other changes included a substantial increase in the middle class, in professionals, and in the number of university graduates, many of whom were unable to find employment commensurate with their education. Despite the great improvement in infant mortality, average life span, literacy, and the like by the early 1990s, 92 percent of Arab workers were in the bottom half of the country's wage scale, and 60 percent of Arab children lived in poverty. Only one Arab was among the four thousand directors of the two hundred boards of state-owned companies; of over five thousand full-time professors, only twelve were Arabs. These factors were among those contributing to the growing radicalization of Israel's Arab community. It was marked by increasing demands for full equality, expressed in support for new groups such as the Democratic Arab Party, the Progressive List for Peace, and the Islamic Movement. There were also increasing tensions between the country's Jewish and Arab citizens.

BIBLIOGRAPHY

COHEN, STANLEY. *Crime, Justice and Social Control Among the Arab Sector in Israel.* Tel Aviv, 1990.
AL-HAJ, MAJID. *Education and Social Change Among the Arabs in Israel.* Tel Aviv, 1991.
AL-HAJ, MAJID, and HENRY ROSENFELD. *Arab Local Government in Israel.* Boulder, Colo., 1990.
KRETZMER, DAVID. *The Legal Status of the Arabs in Israel.* Boulder, Colo., 1990.
SMOOHA, SAMMY. *Arabs and Jews in Israel.* 2 vols. Boulder, Colo., 1989–1992.

Don Peretz

Arab Studies Society

A research center on Arab culture.

The Arab Studies Society, located in Jerusalem, is a research center dedicated to the study of Arab culture, and the cataloging and publishing of documents relevant to Palestinian history. Established in 1980 by Faisal al-Husayni, the society was the center of WEST BANK Palestinian efforts to draft plans for a Palestinian state at the time of the 1988 meeting of the PALESTINE NATIONAL COUNCIL (PNC).

BIBLIOGRAPHY

BENVENISTI, MERON, ed. *The West Bank Handbook.* Boulder, Colo., 1986.
PERETZ, DON. *Intifada: The Palestinian Uprising.* Boulder, Colo., 1990.

Steve Tamari

Arab Women's Congress

The first group of Palestinian women leaders, active during the British mandate.

Initiated in Palestine by elite Muslim and Christian women, the first Arab Women's Congress met in Jerusalem in 1929, marking the beginning of the modern Palestinian women's movement. The executive committee submitted frequent protests to British mandate authorities concerning the immigration of Jews and their land purchases, as well as general economic conditions. The congress focused on education and welfare activities.

BIBLIOGRAPHY

LESCH, ANN MOSELY. *Arab Politics in Palestine, 1917–1939: The Frustration of a Nationalist Movement.* Ithaca, N.Y., 1979.

Steve Tamari

Arab Workers Congress

Palestinian trade-union federation.

The Arab Workers' Congress (AWC), formed in 1945, was a sign of the growing strength of communists within the Palestinian labor movement. The AWC condemned Zionism but declared that Arab and Jewish workers had common interests. After Israel was established, the AWC disbanded in 1952, when the Histadrut (Israeli Federation of Labor) agreed to admit Arab workers.

BIBLIOGRAPHY

BEININ, JOEL. *Was the Red Flag Flying There? Marxist Politics and the Arab–Israeli Conflict in Egypt and Israel, 1948–1965.* Berkeley, Calif., 1990.
BUDEIRI, MUSA. *The Palestinian Communist Party, 1919–1948: Arab and Jew in the Struggle for Internationalism.* London, 1979.
HUREWITZ, J. C. *The Struggle for Palestine.* New York, 1968.

Steve Tamari

Arab World

The group of countries located in southwestern Asia and Northern Africa.

The Arab world is best defined as the group of countries located in southwestern Asia and northern Africa whose residents share a common language of Arabic and a similar culture. They do not share a common religion, nor are they restricted to any one racial group. The countries of the Arab world include Iraq, the states of the Arabian peninsula, Syria, Lebanon, Egypt, Libya, Tunisia, Morocco Mauritania, Sudan, Djibouti, and Somalia.

BIBLIOGRAPHY

The Middle East, 6th ed. Congressional Quarterly 1986.
FISHER, W. B. *The Middle East: A Physical, Social and Regional Geography,* 7th ed. London, 1978.

Bryan Daves

Arafat, Fathi   [1931/1932–   ]

Palestinian physician.

The brother of Palestine Liberation Organization (PLO) chairman Yasir Arafat, Fathi studied medicine at King Fu'ad I University (now Cairo University) and later worked in Kuwait. He was a founder and head of the medical service for the Palestinian movement al-Fath, which was renamed the Palestine Red Crescent Society (PRCS). The following year the PRCS became the medical section of the PLO and was charged with providing medical and social services to the Palestinian people. Also in 1969 it was granted observer status by the International Committee of the Red Cross.

BIBLIOGRAPHY

BRAND, LAURIE A. *Palestinians in the Arab World: Institution Building and the Search for State.* New York, 1988.

Michael R. Fischbach

Arafat, Yasir   [1929–   ]

Chairman of the PLO and the Palestiniam Authority

Between early 1969 and early 1994, Yasir Arafat (also Yasser Arafat) was transformed from a guerilla leader advocating armed struggle for the liberation of Palestine to the president of the emerging nation of Palestine after negotiations with Israel, which had long denounced him as a terrorist. Despite frequent quarrels with rivals and subordinates, no other figure has been as closely identified with the Palestine Liberation Organization (PLO) as Arafat.

Born Muhammad Abd al-Ra'uf Arafat al-Qudwa, "Yasir" originated as a nickname during his early guerilla days. He has since gone by Yasir Abd al-

Ra'uf Arafat or just Yasir Arafat, except when using the nom de guerre Abu Amar.

Arafat and his family have always insisted that he was born August 4, 1929, in his mother's family home in Jerusalem. Nevertheless an Egyptian birth registration exists suggesting he was born in Egypt on August 24, 1929. His father had been living in Egypt, but his mother may have returned to her home to give birth; others suspect that the record has been altered to give Arafat a Palestinian birthplace. He is, in any event, of old Palestinian lineage: The Qudwas (his father's line) are an offshoot of a Gaza branch of the Husayni (Husseini) family, while Arafat's mother came from the more prominent Jerusalem branch of the Husaynis. His father was a merchant trading in Gaza and Egypt, and whether Arafat was born there, he spent many of his teenage years in Egypt and long had a detectable Egyptian accent. He was the sixth of seven children.

In 1942, his father returned to Cairo, and Arafat continued his schooling there. He reportedly became an aide to the military leader of the Palestinian resistance, Abd al-Qadir al-Husayni, a kinsman on his mother's side. The young Yasir is said to have run guns to Palestine during the Arab–Israel War of 1948. Following the war, the family returned to Gaza.

In the 1950s, Arafat studied at Fu'ad I University in Cairo (now Cairo University), majoring in civil engineering. He was reportedly a member of the Muslim Brotherhood and also became active as a Palestinian student organizer, heading the General Union of Palestine Students from 1952 to 1957. He then served in the Egyptian army for about a year.

Arafat and other Palestinian activists were in Prague in 1957 when some of their colleagues were arrested in Egypt, suspected of Muslim Brotherhood activities. Arafat and the two men who were to become his closest aides until their assassinations, Khalil al-Wazir and Salah Khalaf, remained in Europe. Arafat studied engineering further in Stuttgart and then went to Kuwait. While working for the public works department, he started his own contracting firm. This engineering firm prospered, and Arafat reportedly became quite wealthy. Some accounts suggest that his personal wealth helped fund the beginnings of al-FATH. The nucleus of al-Fath had already been formed in the late 1950s, with Arafat, Wazir, Khalaf, Khalid al-Hasan, and others in Kuwait who would become lifelong colleagues.

Initially, al-Fath was one of many small Palestinian exile groups advocating armed struggle to free Palestine. Arafat received some training in Algeria, it is believed, and in Syria, where Al-Fath's armed wing, al-Asifa, was formed. He also was imprisoned in Syria for several weeks at this time.

After the 1967 war, al-Fath's prominence increased greatly. The Palestine Liberation Organization (PLO), originally created under Egyptian auspices, was overshadowed by the new guerilla groups, which increasingly won control of the Palestine National Council (PNC). In 1968 al-Fath fought off an Israeli attack on a base in Karameh, Jordan, and its prestige increased further. In early 1969, al-Fath and its allies won enough seats in the PNC to elect Arafat the new chairman of the PLO's executive Committee.

In 1970, the PLO was drawn into conflict with the government of Jordan when one of its member organizations, the Popular Front for the Liberation of Palestine (PFLP), hijacked several aircraft. In the ensuing BLACK SEPTEMBER of 1970, the PLO was driven out of its Jordanian operational base. Arafat set up his own base in Beirut, while the PLO began operations from southern Lebanon.

After the Arab–Israel War of 1973, some PLO leaders began discussing the possibility of a settlement short of the previously envisioned secular state in all of Palestine. On November 13, 1974, Arafat addressed the General Assembly of the United Nations, in a speech in which he claimed to hold both "an olive branch and a freedom fighter's gun."

But if the UN speech marked a high point, Arafat's career took another turn downward with the outbreak of the Lebanese civil war in 1975. Initially the PLO found itself fighting not only Maronite forces but also the Syrian army, though these alignments shifted as the war went on. The 1977 visit of Egypt's President Anwar Sadat to Jerusalem and the 1975 peace between Israel and Egypt were yet other blows, and then in 1982 Israel invaded Lebanon.

Having been driven from Jordan over a decade before and besieged in Lebanon by Syrians and others from time to time, the PLO had nevertheless managed to maintain its base in Lebanon. Israel not only occupied all of Lebanon up to Beirut but also (unsuccessfully) targeted Arafat personally. Arafat and ten thousand Palestinian fighters were evicted from Beirut. An attempt to form a new base in Tripoli (Lebanon) failed due to Syrian opposition, and Arafat and the PLO moved to Tunis, far from the zone of Israeli–Palestinian confrontation (though Israel did bomb PLO headquarters there).

In 1984, Arafat entered into negotiations with King Hussein of Jordan to seek a common ground for a joint Jordanian–Palestinian negotiating position—the JORDANIAN OPTION. The effort failed, with Jordan blaming Arafat for the failure.

In 1987, the Intifada or Palestinian uprising began in the occupied territories. Although Arafat's al-Fath was a major player in the Unified National Leadership of the Intifada, it was local cadres, not the Tunis leadership, who were in charge of the actual uprising. This led many analysts to once again predict that Arafat's days were numbered and the central PLO leadership had lost its relevance. As in 1970, 1982, and 1984—when earlier political obituaries had been written—they were wrong.

One of the strengths that had kept Arafat in his position for so long, despite squabbles, plots, and even fighting and assassinations among Palestinian factions, was his ability to forge a grand coalition of very differently oriented factions, left and right, communist and capitalist. Increasingly unable to hold such a broad umbrella group together, Arafat was finally willing to gamble on seizing a moderate, pro-negotiation position despite the fact that this meant the more radical factions now considered him a curse.

In 1988, the PLO leadership—now more and more Arafat and the old al-Fath elite—agreed to recognize Israel's right to exist, the principle of negotiating with Israel on peace in exchange for territorial withdrawal, and a renunciation of terrorism. After some adjustment, the formula finally met the United States' preconditions for a direct dialogue with the PLO, and this dialogue began through the US ambassador to Tunisia, Robert Pelletreau. It was subsequently suspended when Arafat failed to condemn an attack on Israeli territory by a PLO faction.

When the Madrid Peace Process was begun under the George Bush administration the U.S.–PLO talks were suspended and Israel's Likud government under Yitzhak Shamir adamantly refused to deal with the PLO, which was still denounced as a terrorist organization. This meant that the Palestinians were awkwardly represented in Madrid by a panel of moderate Palestinians, all acceptable to the PLO but none ever having been formally members of it. As long as Likud was in power, they were also technically half of a "joint Jordanian–Palestinian delegation." Once again, despite the insistence by the delegation that they were in coordination with the PLO leadership in Tunis, many analysts declared that Arafat and the PLO were no longer relevant to the search for a Palestinian–Israeli solution.

Meanwhile, in 1992, while Arafat was flying to Sudan in a private aircraft, his plane crashed in the Libyan desert, killing the pilots and several passengers. Badly injured, Arafat survived, though he required surgery to correct further problems. His friends later indicated that the survival when so many died convinced him that he had been providentially spared for some reason. The lifelong bachelor also married (the exact date was not made public), further putting his guerilla days behind him. These fac-

tors may have helped prepare him for the decision that he soon would have to make.

So long as Likud was in power, no breakthrough was possible, and the Palestinian side of the peace talks went nowhere. But Shamir was replaced by Yitzhak Rabin and the Labor party. Frustrated with the difficulties of negotiating with a Palestinian delegation that had little real authority to offer compromise, a secret back-channel negotiation began via Norwegian intermediaries. Ultimately, the result was the "Declaration of Principles on Interim Self-Government Arrangements," signed on the White House lawn September 13, 1993.

For the first time, Arafat—once denounced as a terrorist by American presidents—came to the White House to be greeted by a U.S. President. Even more dramatically, at the signing he offered his hand to Yitzhak Rabin, and Rabin accepted it, albeit with apparent reluctance. That dramatic handshake underscored the fact that Arafat had survived his enemies within the PLO as well as in Israel and the United States, to reach the White House lawn and shake Rabin's hand.

Arafat was named chairman of the Palestinian Authority, which was to take over self-government in Jericho and Gaza and, eventually, more of the West Bank as well. Although he delayed his own return to Palestine, it was clear that that return, when it came, would mark a personal vindication for Arafat, at least in his own view.

Arafat had never married during his long guerilla years, but in 1991 or early 1992 he married Suha Tawil, daughter of a PLO activist father and a lawyer mother who often represented accused Palestinians in the territories. She had served as his secretary. A Christian who reportedly converted to Islam, she is more than thirty years his junior. She has given a number of interviews to the Arab and Western press (and even the Israeli press), giving for the first time a more intimate view of Arafat. A daughter was born to the couple in 1994.

Arafat, personally, is a Sunni and is believed to practice his faith. After the 1992 plane crash, his religious convictions were reportedly strengthened. In his younger days, he was a Muslim Brother but today stands staunchly against the Islamist elements in the Palestinian movement. While much of his personal wealth was at one time invested in al-Fath, and the PLO itself is suffering from financial losses, Arafat is believed to still retain some of the profits of his business days.

BIBLIOGRAPHY

Abou Iyad with Eric Rouleau. *My Home, My Land: A Narrative of the Palestinian Struggle*. New York, 1981.

Cobban, Helena. *The Palestinian Liberation Organization: People, Power and Politics.* Cambridge and New York, 1984.

Gowers, Andrew, and Tony Walker. *Behind the Myth: Yasser Arafat and the Palestinian Revolution.* New York, 1992.

Hart, Alan. *Arafat: A Political Biography.* Bloomington, Ind., 1989.

———. *Arafat: Terrorist or Peacemaker?* London, 1984.

Kiernan, Thomas. *Arafat: The Man and the Myth.* New York, 1976.

Wallach, Janet, and John Wallach. *Arafat: In the Eyes of the Beholder.* New York, 1990.

Michael Dunn

Araj, Wasini al- [1954–]

Algerian novelist and critic.

Al-Araj was born on 8 August 1954, in the village of Sidi-bou-Jnan, near Tlemcen, Algeria. He received his Ph.D. in Arabic literature from the University of Damascus, and he is a professor of Arabic literature at the University of Algiers.

Al-Araj, who writes in Arabic, is one of the most prolific of the new generation of Algerian writers. He initiated a new trend in the structure of the novel and experimented with its language. The most striking aspect of his style is the explosion of the rigid traditional frame of the novel. The linear approach is abandoned for a more provocative and richer technique that depends on flashbacks, fragments of history, and childhood memories intermingled with folk traditions. His innovative technique has attracted the attention of critics to his novels including such works as *Waqa'i, min Awja' Rajulin Ghamara Sawba al-Bahr* (Facts from the Sufferings of a Man Who Ventured Toward the Sea [Algiers, 1983]), *Masra' Ahlam Mariam al-Wadi'a* (The Death of Sweet Myriam's Dreams [Beirut, 1984), *Joughrafia al-Ajsad al-Muhtariqa* (The Geography of the Burned Bodies [Algiers, 1979]), and *Nuwwar al-Luz* (Almond Blossoms [Beirut, 1983]).

In his collection of short stories, *Alam al-Kitaba 'an Ahzan al-Manfa* (The Pain of Writing about the Sadness of Exile [Beirut, 1980]), al-Araj presents a highly emotional text on the theme of love of homeland, which is personified as a woman. He often employs the soliloquy, a narrative form that is more an exercise in writing than in storytelling. Even in his romance novel, *Waq' al-Ahdhiya al-Khashina* (The Sound of the Rough Shoes [Beirut, 1981]), the narration is driven by literary style rather more than by events.

Al-Araj's writings criticize the shortcomings of government and its failure to fulfill the promises made during the war of independence. Some of the problems he evokes are related to the struggle of the poor and hungry to survive, a struggle that is described in his collection of short stories, *Asmak al-Barr al-Mutawahhish* (The Fish of the Wild Land [Algiers, 1986]).

Like other writers of his generation, al-Araj treats the killing of Communists who fought during the war of independence in *Ma Tabaqqa min Sirat Lakhdar Hamrouche* (Whatever Is Left of the Biography of Lakhdar Hamrouche [Damascus, 1986]). He often uses events and characters from Arab history to evoke the Algerian present, a common trend to be found among the writers of his generation. Al-Araj's latest novel (as of 1995), *Faji'at al-Layla al-Sabi'a Ba'da al-Alf* (The Tragedy of the Seventh Night after the Thousand, 2 vols. [Algiers, 1993]) conveys his interpretation of the events of the present on the basis of the characters and events of the *Thousand and One Nights*. The time frame of the novel is stretched to encompass fourteen centuries of Islamic religion, and the Qur'anic story of the People of the Cave and the last years of the Andalusian political life are used to allude to the atrocities committed in Algeria in the name of Islam and democracy. It is clear that al-Araj wants the Arab rulers of the present to learn from history in order that they might build a better future for their peoples. His pain reveals a confused man who is grappling to find a solution to a complex situation.

[*See also:* Literature, Arabic, North African]

BIBLIOGRAPHY

Bamia, Aida. "Interview with Al-Araj Wasini." *CELFAN, Review*, no. 3 (1989): 23–26.

———. "Algerian Literature." In *Encyclopedia of World Literature in the Twentieth Century.* Vol. 5, pp. 12–17. New York, 1993.

Khellas, Djilai. "Littérature algérienne d'expression arabe: Vers une deuxième génération de romanciers." *CELFAN, Review* 8, no. 3 (1992): 13–18.

Aida A. Bamia

Aral, Oğuz [1936–]

Turkish comedian and cartoonist.

Born in Istanbul and educated at the Istanbul Academy of Fine Arts, Aral first became known in the 1950s as a cartoonist. In the early 1960s, he made his name on the Turkish stage as a comic actor and pantomime artist. Aral became editor of the political comic-strip magazine *Gırgır* in 1973. Under his direction, it became one of the top-selling humor magazines in the world, reaching a circulation of 450,000 in the late 1980s. In the 1990s he established his own humor magazine, *Avni,* and returned to producing plays.

BIBLIOGRAPHY

Cumhuriyet Dönemi Türkiye Ansiklopedisi (Encyclopedia of Turkey during the Republican Period). Istanbul, 1985.

Elizabeth Thompson

ARAMCO

See Arabian American Oil Company

Arane, Zalman   [1899–   ]

Israeli minister of education and culture in the early years of statehood.

Born and educated in Russia, Arane was active in the Zionist movement from an early age. He was a member of the Central Committee of the illegal Zionist–Socialists in Russia before settling in Palestine in 1926. Arane held high offices in the Histadrut and MAPAJ, and he was the general secretary of the latter from 1948 to 1951. He served in the Knesset from its inception. He was a member of the Israeli cabinet from 1954 to 1955, and he twice served as the minister of education.

Martin Malin

Ararat, Mount

Mountain in eastern Turkey that figures prominently in the Bible.

Mount Ararat (in Turkish Ağrı Dağı) is in the province of Ağrı, eastern Turkey, near the border of Iran. First climbed in modern times in 1829, the mountain consists of two peaks—Great Ararat at 16,946 feet (5,165 m), and Little Ararat at 12,877 feet (3,927 m). According to the Book of Genesis in the Bible, Mount Ararat was the landing spot of Noah's Ark.

BIBLIOGRAPHY

Webster's New Geographical Dictionary. Springfield, Mass., 1984.

David Waldner

Aravah Valley

Valley that marks the Jordan–Israel border.

A long north–south valley beginning at the Dead Sea and ending north of the gulf of Aqaba/Eilat, the Aravah valley (also called Wadi al-Araba) is officially known in Jordan as Wadi al-Jayb. At the Dead Sea, the valley lies 1,400 feet (435 m) below sea level, rising to 1,000 feet (300 meters) above sea level some 40 miles (65 km) north of Aqaba and Eilat.

BIBLIOGRAPHY

NYRUP, RICHARD F., ed. *Jordan: A Country Study.* Washington, D.C., 1980.

Michael R. Fischbach

Archeological Museum (Istanbul)

A major museum complex of three pavilions.

The pavilions are the Çinili Köşk (Tiled Pavilion), which, as its name indicates, is where Turkish tiles and ceramics are displayed; the Museum of the Ancient Orient, which houses mostly Hittite and Mesopotamian antiquities; and the Archeological Museum building, which displays classical artifacts.

The Archeological Museum building, commissioned by the first museum director in Turkey, Osman Hadi Bey, was opened to the public in 1891. The Museum of the Ancient Orient had been first founded as the Academy for Fine Arts in 1883.

Originally the Çinili Köşk housed the Ottoman collection. However, the spectacular discovery of a large number of sarcophagi at the Royal Necropolis at Sidon, Lebanon in 1887, together with the growing Ottoman interest in the empire's antiquity-rich hinterland, necessitated the creation of a new space. These factors led to construction of the Archeological Museum, first named the Museum of Sarcophagi. Important architectural elements of the museum's design were inspired by two of its most famous sarcophagi—the Alexander Sarcophagus and the Sarcophagus of the Mourning Women.

The Archeological Museum houses some 45,000 pieces: of these, 9,000 are stone objects; 12,000 are pieces of pottery; 10,000 are terracotta figurines; 10,000 are metal objects; and 3,000 are glass objects. A shortage of space allows only a small portion of this collection to be displayed at any one time. The museum has a library that contains approximately 80,000 books covering a wide range of topics. The museum also has an enormous cuneiform tablet collection (about 75,000 pieces) and a rich coin collection (about 760,000 coins).

Karen Pinto

Roman ruins in Dougga, Tunisia. (Mia Bloom)

Archeology in the Middle East

Serious archeological inquiry in the Middle East began during the Renaissance when Europeans became interested in their Christian and classical roots.

The key sources for the Middle East's archeological past, the Bible and Homer's *Iliad,* inspired gentlemen scholars, travelers, and later, members of the various European diplomatic missions to discover sites and decipher scripts that launched the newly developing discipline of archeology. Their interest was the ancient world—the Islamic period was deemed too recent and not particularly relevant to European historical interests. Europeans collected statues, pottery, and tablets for the sake of knowledge and the glory of country and shipped them back to European metropoles, often without permission of local authorities.

Napoléon Bonaparte's Egyptian expedition (1788–1801) initiated the scramble for the acquisition of antiquities from the Middle East. The discovery of the trilingual ROSETTA STONE enabled Jean-François Champollion to decipher ancient

Egyptian hieroglyphics. French scholars continued to remain heavily involved in Egyptology on Egyptian soil until 1952. Auguste Mariette, dispatched to Egypt by the Louvre to collect papyri, received permission from Khedive Isma'il to establish the Egyptian Antiquities Service (1858) and the Egyptian Museum in Cairo in 1863. His successor, Gaston Maspero, encouraged excavation by other foreign scholars. The British established the Egyptian Exploration Fund and sent Flinders Petrie (1853–1942), who set new standards for exact recording, publishing, and the study of pottery and founded the British School of Archaeology in Egypt.

Napoleon's short sojourn in Palestine sparked new interest in the land of the Bible, which, until then, was solely the destination of religious pilgrims. Travelers found significant sites. Johann Ludwig Burckhardt (1784–1817) located Petra, and Lady Hester Stanhope (1776–1831) visited Palmyra. The field of biblical archeology was inaugurated by the work of

The Sphinx and two of the three pyramids near it. (Mia Bloom)

Roman ruins on the outskirts of Jerash, Jordan. (David Rewcastle)

Hellenistic ruins at Nemrut Daği, dating from c. 150 B.C.E. (Laura Mendelson)

Roman ruins situated at Leptis Magna, Libya. (© 1994 Yto Barrada)

Ruins of the ancient port of Bahrain. (Richard Bulliet)

Edward Robinson (1858–1931). Robinson was followed by groups of international sponsors: the American Oriental Society, the American Palestine Oriental Society, the British Palestine Exploration Fund, which began work on Jerusalem in 1867, the German Society for the Exploration of Palestine (Deutscher Plastina-Verein), the Ecole Biblique, and the Deutsche Orient Gesellschaft, which excavated Megiddo from 1901 to 1905. Maps and surveys of Jerusalem and other sections of the Holy Land were produced during the formative period in biblical archeology. Intense interest in the area by American Protestant groups led to the establishment of various Catholic and Russian (Eastern) Orthodox institutions. Jewish archeological work began with the formation of the Jewish Palestine Exploration Society shortly before World War I.

In Mesopotamia (Iraq) and Persia (Iran), the British, Germans, and French achieved the major break-throughs. The British resident of the East India Company in Baghdad, Claudius James Rich (1787–1820), surveyed Babylon and published his findings in 1818. In the 1840s, Paul Emile Botta (1802–1870), French consular agent at Mosul, worked at Assyrian Nineveh, while Austen Henry Layard (1817–1894) excavated ancient Nimrud, and the French explored areas around Basra. Most of the work was sponsored by the British Museum and ceased during the Crimean War, resuming in the 1870s.

Georg Friedrich Grotefend (1775–1853) and Sir Henry Creswicke Rawlinson (1810–1895) worked on Old Persian and deciphered cuneiform. This

The Achaemenid Treasury at Naqsh-i Rustam in Iran.
(Richard Bulliet)

could not have been accomplished without the transcriptions of Karsten Niebuhr (1733–1815) at Persepolis and Rawlinson's own painstaking copy of the inscriptions on the Behistun Rock. Cracking the cuneiform code expanded man's history to prebiblical eras, and enabled Sir Leonard Woolley (1880–1960) to work on Abraham's Ur and the pre-Akkadian Sumerians. American interest in Mesopotamia was fostered by the American Oriental Society, which included an interest in Assyria and Babylonia along with its goal of cultivating learning in the "Asiatic, African, and Polynesian languages."

The secular underpinnings of modern archeology, namely that human existence predated the Flood, the theory of evolution, and the categorization of human existence into the Stone, Bronze, and Iron ages affected the secularly oriented countries of the Middle East less than the Islamic theocratic monarchies. For the religious Muslim, the period before Islam, the *jahiliyya* was the age of ignorance, in which they had no interest.

Egyptians, both Copts and Muslims, became interested in Egypt's pre-Islamic past very early. Rifa'a al-Tahtawi, intrigued by the work on the Rosetta Stone, published a history of Egypt from the Pharoanic period and encouraged Egyptians to become involved in archeology. Ahmad Kamal (1851–1923) established Egyptology for the Egyptians.

Excavations in Syria, Lebanon, Iraq, and Palestine, were directed by Europeans. The discoveries at Byblos, Ras Shamra (Ugarit, 1929), Tall al-Hariri (Mari) in Syria, and Ebla revealed the link between ancient Semitic cultures in the Bronze Age. As a result, history was worked into pan-Arab ideology and local nationalisms. Pan-Arabism stressed the unity of pre-Islamic Semites, while Maronites in Lebanon and the Parti Populaire Syrien in Syria looked to their Phoenician and Canaanite forbears. The governments of North African countries have become interested in Carthaginians and the Romans who settled along the southern coast of the Mediterranean.

As Middle Eastern countries achieved independence or asserted their national identities, they began to control the study of their own pasts and to direct their own archeological excavations.

By 1936, Iraq, newly independent, placed legal restrictions on foreign excavations and in 1941, appointed Tahir Baqir as curator of the Iraqi National Museum in Baghdad and editor of *Sumer* (founded 1945) with the mission of investigating the Mesopotamian past. This study was continued under the Ba'th party, and Saddam Hussein, president of Iraq, has used archeology to stress the unity of ancient Mesopotamia in a country beset by ethnic and religious strife and, in pan-Arab terms, to emphasize Iraq's glorious Semitic past as opposed to Persia/Iran's later development. In spite of almost constant war since 1980, Hussein has renovated the National Museum, designated the State Organization for Antiquities and Heritage to control all excavations, renovations, and tours to sites, and has begun rebuilding Babylon, completing the Ishtar Gate, amphitheater, ziggurat, and Ishtar Temple, in order to stress the city's special significance in Mesopotamian history. To the regime, Sumer and Akkad represent the first "Iraqi internal patriotic unity in history."

Iranian competition to Mesopotamian hegemony came later. Until the early 1960s, archeology in Iran was dominated by the French, who began to excavate at Susa in the nineteenth century. In 1961, the government established a department of archeological services and the Iran Bastan Museum in Tehran. By then, under the shah, Mohammad Reza Pahlavi, Iran's Persian past was stressed almost to the exclusion of its Islamic significance. Intensive linguistic study, additional excavation at Siyalk, Tepe Yahya, and Marlik, and the lauding of the Pahlavis as successors to a long line of Persian dynasties whose capital at Persepolis was used as the setting for the 2,500th anniversary party of ancient Persian rule, angered the Islamic religious population. Since the overthrow of the shah in 1979 and the establishment of a theocratic regime in Iran, there has been little concern with the country's pre-Islamic roots. To the east, Afghanistan has begun to show interest in the Kushans as the pre-Islamic precursors of modern Afghanistan.

Biblical archeological research continued during the Palestine mandate on both sides of the Jordan River. William Foxwell Albright's work on ancient Moab in Transjordan (Jordan) and in the Dead Sea area complemented Kathleen Kenyon's excavations at Jericho. The Rockefeller Museum, after 1967 in Israeli territory, became a major repository for biblical artifacts.

Archeology in Israel remains focused on religion and history, primarily of the Jewish and early Christian periods. Excavations at biblical sites of the Megiddo of King Solomon, patriarchal Tel-Sheva at Beersheba, and at Davidic and Second Temple Jerusalem serve to authenticate Jewish claims to the land. Yigal Yadin's finds at Masada proved the existence of the heroic Jew as a counterfoil to the Holocaust victim and provided physical evidence for the histories of Jewish Roman historian Josephus Flavius, while the Dead Sea Scrolls, housed in the Shrine of the Book, focus on the origins of Christianity.

Heinrich Schliemann's excavations at Hissarlik (thought to be Troy) and Hugo Winckler's identification of the Hittite capital Hattusas at Boğazköy in 1905 sparked interest in the multi-cultural antecedents of Anatolia, only recently inhabited by the Turks. The republic of Turkey has taken pride in the fact that the fatherland provided the setting for some of the oldest inhabited and civilized settlements.

Systematic archeological investigations of the Arabian peninsula began in the late 1960s. While the government of Saudi Arabia has explored early sites on the pilgrimage routes to the Hijaz, it has only recently become interested in the significance of the Arabian peninsula in the development of human civilization. In the mid-1970s, the Saudi government sponsored surveys of pre-Islamic sites in the peninsula and scholarly work on the Nabateans and early Semitic peoples. Kuwait, Oman, and some of the United Arab Emirates have opened museums and have begun collecting Islamic antiquities.

Today, not only has virtually every country in the Middle East established its own department of antiquities, where local employees either undertake or supervise foreign work, but they have enacted strict legislation against the export of national historical treasures. Countries have also worked with international agencies to save monuments cherished by the peoples of the area and the world at large.

BIBLIOGRAPHY

LEWIS, BERNARD. *History: Remembered, Recovered, Invented.* Princeton, N.J., 1971.
REID, DONALD M. "Egyptology: The Decolonization of a Profession?" *Journal of the American Oriental Society* 105 (1985): 233–246.
SILBERMAN, NEIL ASHER. *Between Past and Present.* New York, 1989.

Reeva S. Simon

Architecture

An area of great cultural creativity.

By the nineteenth century, Middle Eastern building traditions relying on governmental or institutional patronage had undergone a metamorphosis that dramatically altered historical traditions and reflected the increasing impact of European styles and construction methods. By contrast, vernacular buildings, es-

Friday mosque in Isfahan, Iran. (Richard Bulliet)

pecially in rural areas, continued to reflect age-old traditions rooted in the materials, climate, and social structure of the local environment.

The Colonial Legacy. Even before the establishment of colonial empires in the Middle East, economic decline reduced the quantity and quality of official patronage of architecture. Simultaneously, the influence of European styles was felt in the buildings of European embassies and commercial concerns and in the way that official patronage relied upon architects and builders influenced by travel and study in Europe, by European publications on architecture, and by changing tastes in Islamic courts. In the Ottoman Empire, for example, the Balyan family provided three generations of official architects for the sultans, beginning in 1822, and produced mosques, palaces, and other official buildings reflecting a mixture of European styles. European governments, banks, commercial trading enterprises, and missionary institutions began to erect buildings in the European style. French styles prevailed in Algeria and later in the Maghrib; the style of the Balyans and later the Italian architect Montani gained currency in the Ottoman capital of Constantinople (now Istanbul); in Egypt, Muhammad Ali (ruled 1805–1848) favored buildings in a Europeanized Ottoman style,

Residences in San'a, Yemen. (© Mark Dennis)

and the Khedive Isma'il (ruled 1863–1879), who had studied in Europe, imported European architects to build his palaces and to make over modern Cairo in the image of Paris under the Second Empire. Elsewhere on the Mediterranean littoral, and to an extent in Iran, French, Italian, and British architectural ideas left their stamp on museums and government buildings.

Nationalism and Architecture. By the end of the nineteenth century, European architectural ideas had provoked a reaction both from Middle Eastern architects and from Europeans who were sensitive to local traditions. Moreover, as the neo–Islamic building style gained popularity in Europe in the nineteenth century, it began to appear in the Middle East as well. In Egypt, a substantial number of Islamic Revival buildings were erected by local and foreign architects in Cairo and in Alexandria; these used European construction methods and floor plans but were decorated with Islamic motifs. Examples include Alfonso Manescalo's Islamic Museum (1903–1904) and Mahmud

Interior of an eighteenth-century palace in Shiraz, Iran. (Richard Bulliet)

Modern residences have incorporated elements of traditional architecture in Shayikh Hamid City, Bahrain. (Richard Bulliet)

Fahmi's Awqaf Ministry building (after 1898). In the Ottoman Empire, a revival of governmental patronage in the late nineteenth century led both to an early-twentieth-century Ottoman Revival style, whose chief practitioners were the architects Kemaleddin and Mehmet Vedat, and to a new-Islamic style drawing its inspiration from Spain and the Maghrib, exemplified by the Valide Mosque (1873) by Montani, and by the mid-nineteenth-century neo-Marinid gateway to what is now Istanbul University. In Casablanca, the Law Courts and other official buildings that were built under the French protectorate reflected an attempt to understand and promote "appropriate" local styles.

Nationalist architecture in the Middle East has emerged during the twentieth century. The Ottoman Revival under the Young Turks in the early twentieth century reflected a new Turkish nationalism and sparked a tradition reflected even today in the neo–Ottoman contemporary buildings of Sedad Hakig Eldem, such as his many Bosporus villas (*yalı*) and the massive central complex of Istanbul University. After the Atatürk revolution, German architects were invited to devise a city plan for modern Ankara; public monuments both reflected European styles and often drew upon what their designers believed were the pre–Islamic Hittite and Assyrian traditions of Anatolia.

Similar attention to the pre–Islamic past was seen in Iran under the Pahlavis, where the monarchy stressed cultural continuity not only with the Safavid Islamic past but also with a Persian heritage stretching back to Cyrus the Great. The government of Muhammad Reza Pahlavi spent vast sums on restoring monuments, especially those reflecting earlier royal patronage, while largely adopting the modern international style in its institutional buildings. Its Islamic successor has produced no significant architecture reflecting its own political and religious agenda, largely because of economic decline and the demands of the war with Iraq.

Morocco's independence from the French, gained in 1956, led to a pronounced nationalism in architecture, first expressed in the tomb complex of Muhammed V in Rabat, and in the 1990s reflected in a series of laws requiring that the construction budgets for all institutional and governmental buildings allot a substantial percentage of funds to strictly defined traditional Moroccan crafts.

In Egypt, by contrast, the revolution of the 1950s led to a socialist government whose official architecture often reflected the monumental style popular in the Soviet Union, best exemplified in the massive and forbidding Central Government Building in Cairo. National revolutions thus developed architectural patronage that reflected their own ideologies.

The secularist Ba'thist regime in Iraq, for example, when it drew on the past for inspiration, often looked to the neo–Babylonian period rather than to traditional Islam, a tendency that increased under the government of Saddam Hussein; a parallel though far less pronounced tendency in Egypt has sought pharaonic inspiration for building styles and public monuments. In Central Asia, Russia first pushed its Stalinist architectural agenda, then later espoused the Soviet version of modernism. At the same time, the Soviet governments in Central Asia put significant effort into restoration of Islamic monuments, such as the giant mosque of Bibi Khanym in Samarkand, and religious monuments in Tashkent and Bukhara.

Contemporary Dilemmas. The striving throughout the Middle East to adapt modern Western technology in such areas as architecture often conflicts with a wish to bring about a renaissance of traditional architecture, or to produce a modern Islamic architecture that can keep its distinctive local or regional style while drawing upon the best of the new technology. There have been several institutional attempts to deal with this dilemma, but none has been more influential than the Aga Khan Awards, established in the late 1970s by the leader of the world's Isma'ili Muslims. Beginning in 1980, an international jury composed of architects and others from the Islamic world, Europe, and the United States has periodically awarded prizes for contemporary Middle Eastern architecture that best reflects Islamic traditions and values combined with artistic distinction. Awards have varied widely, from the neotraditionalist architecture of Hassan Fathy in Egypt, typified in his buildings for the Wissa Wassef Foundation in Harraniya, near Giza, to the technically and formally avant-garde water towers designed for Kuwait City by the Swedish firm VBB. In general, the juries that have selected the Aga Khan Award recipients have shown remarkable breadth of vision and have taken an inclusive and eclectic, rather than an ideological and purist, approach to the enormous range of distinctive modern Middle Eastern architectural styles. Awards have been given for domestic architecture, historical restoration, institutional buildings, adaptive reuse, and commercial buildings. The first group of awards was memorialized in 1983, in a handsome publication edited by Renata Holod; subsequent awards and issues of Middle Eastern architecture in general have been featured not only in similar volumes but also in a well-produced periodical, *Mimar: Architecture in Development* (up to 1994).

Three main issues confront governments, patrons, architects, and urban planners in the Middle East today. The first is how and whether there should be an ideology of architecture; the answer in Morocco has been an unequivocal yes, reflected in neotraditionalist building codes that emphasize traditional ornament and decorative crafts while utilizing modern technology to the fullest. For example, the mosque of Hassan II in Casablanca (clearly thought of as a pendant to the impressive twelfth-century ruins of the Almohad mosque in Rabat), although constructed in classical Moroccan forms and proportions with classical decoration, is an outsized reinforced-concrete giant whose skyscraper minaret is surmounted by a huge laser sending beams dozens of kilometers into the sky. Its construction has been hailed for its Islamic symbolism and condemned for its extravagance in a time of financial difficulties. Similar ideology prevailed in the reconstruction of the two major pilgrimage shrines in Mecca and Medina by the Saudi government although greatly faciliting the comfort and ease (if not the safety) of vastly increased numbers of pilgrims, these structures, lavish in size and decoration, and traditional in style, leave more questions than they provide answers for the future of Middle Eastern religious architecture.

Examples of the opposite national approach—which we might term "creative pluralism"—are found in Turkey and in Tunisia, where many different views of style, structure, and decoration exist side by side in an apparently creative mixture. The issue remains: Is "appropriate" architecture to consist of a traditional decorative veneer on what are essentially Western buildings in plan and construction, or is the new architecture of the Middle East going to be based from the ground up on the rich mosaic of social, environmental, and historical traditions? In fact, with few exceptions, local vernacular architecture is disappearing, replaced by undistinguished "modern" structures or by an equally alien homogenized "national" traditionalism that often consists of little more than employing the arch solely as a decorative device on building surfaces.

The second issue is curricula in architectural schools and colleges. The twentieth-century conflict about the role of teaching and learning the art and architecture of the past exists in the Middle East as it does elsewhere; the almost universal acceptance of Western-originated construction techniques and equipment (reinforced concrete, steel, glass, the tower crane, and so on) lends an almost surreal quality to some of these debates, and the issues often have been obscured as much as illumined by the polemics against the West used by individuals such as the late Isma'il Faruqi. The dialectic between historicism and artistic creativity is as old as art itself, however, and these debates are bound to survive as an essential part of the creative process.

The third issue is one that confronts architects and patrons everywhere. Even an examination of the record of the Aga Khan Awards demonstrates an impressive array of beautiful structures that are creative in design, and impressive in imagination and sensitivity to tradition, but for the most part, whether private houses or public monuments, expensive to construct and affordable by the few. Whether architecture in the Middle East today and in the future can fulfill its implicit role to provide decent housing and urban environments for exploding populations, while reflecting its national and local traditions, and remaining affordable, is a dilemma that will not easily be resolved.

BIBLIOGRAPHY

EVIN, AHMED. *Architecture Education in the Islamic World.* Singapore, 1986.
AL-FARUQI, ISMA'IL. "Islam and Architecture." In *Fine Arts in Islamic Civilization,* ed. by M. A. J. Berg. Kuala Lumpur, 1981.
HOLOD, RENATA, and DARL RASTORFER, eds. *Architecture and Community: Building in the Islamic World Today.* New York, 1983.
SAKR, TAREK MOHAMED REFAAT. *Early Twentieth-Century Islamic Architecture in Cairo.* Cairo, 1993.

Walter Denny

Ard, al-

A Palestinian political movement.

Founded in 1959, al-Ard (The Land) advocated nationalist goals for Arabs in Israel. It not only challenged the legitimacy of Israel; it also opposed the traditional leadership of the Palestinian community in Israel, which it accused of cooperating with the Israelis. Al-Ard tried to field a list of candidates for the Knesset elections of 1965, but the Israeli authorities refused to grant permission for the initiative, on security grounds. Eventually the Israeli government outlawed al-Ard's activities and arrested many of its leaders. Some of the leaders went on to form the Progressive List for Peace.

BIBLIOGRAPHY

LUSTICK, IAN. *Arabs in the Jewish State: Israel's Control of a National Minority.* Austin, Tex., 1980.

Bryan Daves

Ardebili, Abd al-Karim Musavi [1926–]

Politically active Iranian cleric.

Born in Ardabil in 1926, Abd al-Karim Musavi Ardebili is currently a member of the Assembly of Experts

(Najaf), the director of the Mofid Theological Seminary, and, occasionally, the conductor of Friday sermons at Tehran University. He began his religious career in 1942 in Qom, where he was a student of Ruhollah Khomeini and Ayatollah Borujerdi. In 1948, he went to Najaf, Iraq, to pursue his education further and stayed there for a year. Copublisher in the 1960s in Qom of the journal *Maktab-e Islam* (The School of Islam), Ardebili also pursued political activities in his home town of Ardabil, and in 1971 he moved to Tehran to conduct sermons at a mosque. A founder, after the 1979 Iranian Revolution, of the now-defunct Islamic Republican party, Ardebili also established the Bonyad-e Mostaz'afan (Foundation of the Oppressed). He was the prosecutor general of the Islamic Republic of Iran from 1980 to 1981 and head of the supreme judicial council and the supreme court from 1981 to 1989. Other positions held by Ardebili have included his appointment by Khomeini to the constitutional review panel and his membership in the supreme council of the cultural revolution.

BIBLIOGRAPHY

Iran Research Group. *Iran 89/90.* Bonn, 1989.

Neguin Yavari

Arens, Moshe   [1925–   ]

Israel's foreign minister, 1988–1990, and minister of defense, 1983–1984, 1990–1992.

Born in Lithuania, Arens immigrated to the United States in 1939 and to Israel in 1948. Having received his academic training at the Massachusetts and California Institutes of Technology, he was professor of aeronautical engineering at Haifa University from 1958 to 1961. He was vice president of Israeli Aircraft Industries from 1962 until 1971. Arens was elected to the Knesset in 1977 and served as chair of the Herut central committee from 1977 to 1978. From 1977 to 1982, he was also chair of the Knesset Foreign Affairs and Security Committee. Hawkish in his security views, Arens opposed the 1978 Camp David Accords in the Knesset vote. During Israel's invasion of Lebanon (1982–1983), he was ambassador to the United States. He returned to Israel to become minister of defense, replacing Ariel Sharon. In the National Unity Government (1984–1986) Arens was a minister without portfolio, and in 1986 was placed in charge of Arab affairs. From 1988 to 1990 he was foreign minister, and in 1990 once again was appointed minister of defense.

Martin Malin

Arfa, Hasan   [1895–?]

Iranian general; supporter of Pahlavi Dynasty.

Born in Tbilisi, Georgia, of an Anglo-Russian mother and Iranian father, Arfa was a career military officer in the Iranian army and retired with the rank of general. His mother, Ludmilla Jervis, was the daughter of a British diplomat and a Russian woman of the aristocratic Demidov family. His father, Reza Khan Arfa al-Dowleh, was an Iranian diplomat serving as counsul-general in Tbilisi; he later served as ambassador to Turkey and Russia. Arfa's parents divorced in 1900 after Arfa and his mother had moved to Paris; but the senior Arfa al-Dowleh provided comfortable homes in Europe for his ex-wife and son. He subsequently married a Swedish woman with whom he had a second son and a daughter. During his adult life, Hasan Arfa was close to his half siblings, especially his brother, Ibrahim, who served with him in the Iranian military.

Arfa received his early education from private tutors. His first tutor, Mohammed Sa'ed, eventually became a prominent Iranian politician who served as foreign minister and prime minister in cabinets during the 1940s. Later, Arfa attended private schools in Switzerland, Paris, and Monaco. From 1912 to 1914, he attended the Military Academy in Istanbul. After coming to his ancestral home in 1914, he joined the Imperial Guards of Iran. During the early part of World War I, the Imperial Guards sponsored his training as a cavalry officer with the Swiss army, although the guards subsequently were dissolved. Arfa returned to Iran and joined the gendarmerie in 1920, and later the army. As a cavalry officer, he campaigned against rebellious tribes in Azerbaijan, Kurdistan, Lorestan, and Turkoman Sahara during the 1920s and rose rapidly through the ranks.

Arfa first met the founder of the Pahlavi dynasty, Reza Shah (ruled 1926–1941), who was then minister of war, at the outset of the campaign against the Kurds (1921–1922). Reza Shah's forceful character left a deep impression on Arfa, who remained a loyal supporter of the Pahlavis throughout his life. Arfa also was favorably impressed by the Kurds whom he fought against, and he developed an appreciation for their culture. After he retired, he wrote *The Kurds: An Historical and Political Study* (London, 1966), which was based in part on his military experiences against Isma'il Aqa Simko, the legendary Kurdish warrior. Following the successful campaign against Simko, Arfa received a six-months' leave of absence from the military to visit his parents in Monaco. While in Europe, he met Hilda Bewicke, a British ballerina in Diaghilev's Russian Ballet. Arfa married her in 1923, and the couple returned to Iran at the end of the same year. They had one daughter, Leila.

In between military campaigns against the tribes, Arfa served a brief tour in 1926 as military attaché in London and attended the Staff College in Paris from 1927 to 1929. After his training in France, he was promoted to the rank of lieutenant colonel and placed in command of the newly formed Pahlavi Guards Cavalry Regiment. His success in creating a highly disciplined and professional unit caught the attention of Reza Shah, who also made Arfa commandant of the Military Academy and, in 1932, promoted him to the rank of colonel. In 1934, Arfa was included in the retinue that accompanied Reza Shah on his official visit to Turkey. He was appointed inspector general of the cavalry and armed forces in 1936 and promoted to general in 1939. Subsequently, he assumed additional duties as an instructor at Iran's Staff College and the Military Academy. During the joint Anglo-Soviet invasion of Iran in August 1941, the shah appointed Arfa chief of staff in charge of the defenses for Tehran. The British and Soviets speedily defeated the Iranian army, however, and forced Reza Shah to abdicate. His son and successor Mohammad Reza Shah Pahlavi (ruled 1941–1979), appointed Arfa chief of military intelligence.

Arfa became involved in national politics during the 1940s and 1950s. As chief of the general staff from 1944 to 1946, he authorized the supply of weapons to the Shahsavan tribesmen who opposed the autonomous government of Azerbaijan. At the time, the province was under Soviet military occupation (see AZERBAIJAN CRISIS, 1945–1946). In early 1946, Arfa was instrumental in gathering signatures of parliamentary deputies for a petition supporting Iran's complaint before the United Nations Security Council that Soviet forces continued to occupy northern Iran in contravention of an agreement to withdraw. Arfa's actions placed him in the camp of political leaders who tended to perceive malevolent intentions in Soviet policies but benign intentions in British policies; another camp of politicians held the completely opposite perception of British and Soviet roles in Iran. The pro-Soviet/anti-British leaders denounced Arfa in the parliament and the press. Consequently, Ahmad Qavam, who was appointed prime minister in 1946 because the shah believed he could work effectively with the Soviets, insisted that Arfa be dismissed from his post as chief of the general staff.

In April 1946, after reaching an agreement with Moscow for the evacuation of Soviet troops, Qavam ordered Arfa's arrest. The former chief of staff was imprisoned for seven months and then released on parole pending an official inquiry into his conduct. Arfa's detention, along with the imprisonment of several pro-British politicians, was interpreted as a ploy to placate the Soviets and their Iranian sympathizers. Similarly, a major shift in Qavam's policy from a pro-Soviet bias to a more neutralist position was manifested domestically by the freeing of Arfa and other pro-British figures and by the dismissal from government of pro-Soviet ministers. Eventually Arfa was exonerated of any wrongdoing, but he was summarily retired from active duty in March 1947.

Arfa blamed his successor, Gen. Ali Razmara, for his forced retirement and subsequently cooperated with his political rivals, especially after Razmara was appointed prime minister in 1950. Nevertheless, Arfa apparently was genuinely disturbed when Razmara was assassinated (1951), because he believed that the increasing levels of political violence threatened the country. He served as minister of roads and communications in the brief government of Prime Minister Hosayn Ala during the month following Razmara's assassination, before the parliament voted in Mohammad Mossadegh as premier.

Arfa distrusted Mossadegh, and he consequently formed a political group, the National Movement, that disrupted gatherings of Mossadegh supporters whom he considered to be extremists. From Arfa's perspective, Mossadegh and some of his supporters were dangerous because they opposed the continuation of the monarchy and a strong army. The National Movement's newspaper published articles, many of them written by Arfa, supporting the shah and respect for Islam. Arfa maintained contact with a variety of political activists, including Mozaffar Baqai of the Toilers' party, the fiery preacher Ayatollah Sayyed Abu al-Qasem Kashani, and Shaban Jaafari, an organizer of street mobs. His relationship with Kashani grew stronger in 1952 after the latter withdrew his support of Mossadegh. Arfa became a founding member of the secret committee of military officers, the Committee to Save the Fatherland, formed in 1952 with the objective of overthrowing Mossadegh. Following the 1953 military coup d'état that restored the shah to power, Arfa served as Iran's ambassador to Turkey (1958–1961) and Pakistan (1961–1962).

BIBLIOGRAPHY

ARFA, HASAN. *Under Five Shahs*. London, 1964.

Eric J. Hooglund

Arfa, Muhammad ibn [1877–?]

Interim puppet ruler of Morocco, 1953–1955.

A relatively unknown member of the Alawi dynasty, ibn Arfa was selected by Thami al-Glawi and other supporters of French Colonialism in Morocco to re-place Sultan Muhammed V, who was forced to abdicate in 1953. Following several attempts on his life and amid the mounting pressures of Moroccan Nationalism, ibn Arfa was removed in October 1955, to be replaced by the restored Muhammed V, who ruled as king until his death in 1961, when his son HASSAN II assumed the throne.

BIBLIOGRAPHY

ABUN-NASR, JAMIL. *A History of the Maghrib in the Islamic Period.* London, 1987.

HAHN, LORNA. *North Africa: Nationalism to Nationhood.* Washington, D.C., 1960.

Matthew S. Gordon

Argoud, Antoine   [1914–   ]

French officer during Algerian War of Independence.

Argoud was a graduate of the prestigious Ecole Poly-technique and an outstanding staff officer who became politicized to the cause of French Algeria. He supported the January 1960 settler barricades against France's President Charles de Gaulle. Argoud was also one of the French planners and participants of the April 1961 Algerian revolt against the French colonial government. After its failure, he joined the clandestine Organisation de l'Armée Secrète (Secret Army Organization, OAS). He was kidnapped from Germany in 1963 and received a life sentence but was amnestied in 1968. Since that time, he has devoted himself to writing (*La Décadence, l'imposture et la tragédiè* [memoirs; 1974]; *Les Deux missions de Jeanne d'Arc* [1988]), music, and graphology.

BIBLIOGRAPHY

HORNE, ALISTAIR. *A Savage War of Peace: Algeria, 1954–1962,* 2d ed. New York, 1987.

Phillip C. Naylor

Aridor, Yoram   [1933–   ]

Member of the Knesset and former Minister of Finance of Israel.

Aridor was first elected to the Knesset in 1969 as a Herut Party member. In 1979 he was chair of the Herut secretariat. He served as minister of finance from 1981 until 1983, when he resigned amid controversy over plans to introduce the dollar as legal currency in Israel.

Martin Malin

Arif, Abd al-Rahman   [1916–   ]

President of Iraq, 1966–1968

Arif was born in Baghdad to a poor Sunni Arab rug merchant. Graduating from the military academy in 1937, he followed an undisturbed military career, both under the monarchy and the republic of IRAQ. He joined a clandestine FREE OFFICERS organization before the revolution on 1958. After the RAMADAN REVOLUTION of 1963, he replaced his deceased younger brother Abd al-Salam Arif as president of the republic in April 1966. Under Abd al-Rahman, Iraq retained close ties with Gamal Abdel Nasser's Egypt, but carefully refrained from any unification steps (to join the United Arab Republic). A less capable leader than his brother, he lost power to the BA'TH party in July 1968; his downfall was accelerated by Iraq's ineffective participation in the ARAB–ISRAEL WAR of June 1967. He stayed in Ankara until 1980, when he was allowed to return to Baghdad, where he has lived in retirement.

BIBLIOGRAPHY

BATATU, HANNA. *The Old Social Classes and the Revolutionary Movements of Iraq.* Princeton, N.J., 1978.

KHADDURI, MAJID. *Republican Iraq.* Oxford, 1969.

Amatzia Baram

Arif, Abd al-Salam   [1921–1966]

President of Iraq, 1963–1966.

Born in al-Karkh, Baghdad, to a poor Sunni Arab rug merchant, his family had strong tribal connections in the Ramadi province (west of Baghdad) of Iraq. From 1938 to 1941, he attended military college. While he was too junior to be held responsible for the Rashid Ali pro-Axis revolt of 1941, Abd al-Salam strongly sympathized with the revolutionaries. He first met Abd al-Karim Kassem in 1942. In 1948, he participated in the Iraqi Expeditionary Force that fought in the first Arab–Israel war.

Because of Kassem's insistence, Arif was incorporated into the central organization of the FREE OFFICERS in 1957. Until the 1958 revolution, he was regarded as Kassem's protégé. On the eve of the revolution (July 14), Arif's brigade was ordered to move to Jordan through Baghdad, but in coordination with Kassem, he entered the city and took it during the early morning hours. In the revolutionary government, he became deputy prime minister of the interior, and deputy supreme commander of the armed forces. By September of 1958, he was relieved of all his posts, since he supported Iraq's unification with the United Arab Republic. In November, he was arrested and sentenced to death for attempting to kill Kassem; but he was released in early 1961, to be made figurehead president by the Ba'th regime that toppled Kassem in the RAMADAN REVOLUTION of February 8, 1963. Later that year, he ousted the Ba'th from power and became sole leader. His power base was the loyalty of the PAN-ARABIAN army officers, most of whom came from his family's region, Ramadi.

In 1964, he signed a unification agreement with Egypt's President Gamal Abdel Nasser and introduced social and economic changes designed to create a similar system to that of Egypt; these included the establishment of a Nasserite political party and wide-ranging nationalizations. Actual unification with Egypt never materialized, however. His social policy caused an economic decline, and his attempt to crush the KURDISH REVOLT failed. Arif was killed in a helicopter crash on April 13, 1966. Despite his many failures, his charisma and devotion to Islam were highly regarded by many Sunni Arabs in Iraq. The Shiites feared him, but his religiosity and tolerance for their educational autonomy enabled the two Islamic sects to coexist. He was succeeded by his older brother Abd al-Rahman ARIF.

BIBLIOGRAPHY

BATATU, HANNA. *The Old Social Classes and the Revolutionary Movements of Iraq.* Princeton, N.J., 1978.
KHADDURI, MAJID. *Republican Iraq.* Oxford, 1969.

Amatzia Baram

Arif, Arif al-   [1892–1973]

Palestinian historian, administrator, and journalist who became mayor of Arab Jerusalem in the 1950s.

Arif began his political career in his native Jerusalem as editor of the first Arab nationalist newspaper in Palestine, *Suriya al-Janubiyya,* in 1919. He was a supporter of unity with Syria and of the Emir Faisal of the short-lived Arab Kingdom in Syria (later King Faisal of Iraq). He was exiled by the British to Syria with Hajj Muhammad Amin al-Husayni in 1920, although he was allowed to return and began a career as a civil administrator under successive regimes in Palestine under the British mandate and in Jordan. He served in a variety of posts in Jenin, Nablus, Bisan, Jaffa, Beersheba, Gaza, Ashkelon, and Ramallah, and was mayor of Jerusalem from 1949 to 1955. Al-Arif was also one of the most prominent Palestinian historians. Among his most important books are *Tarikh Bir al-Sab'a wa qaba'iliha* (History of Beer-

sheba and Its Tribes) (1934), *Tarikh Ghaza* (History of Gaza) (1934), *al-Mufassal fi tarikh al-Quds* (History of Jerusalem) (1961), and the seven-volume *Tarikh al-Nakba* (History of the Disaster) (1956–62).

BIBLIOGRAPHY

PORATH, Y. *The Emergence of the Palestinian-Arab National Movement, 1918–1929.* London, 1974.
SAYIGH, ANIS, ed. *Al-Mawsu'a al-Filastiniyya.* Damascus, 1984.

Steve Tamari

Arish, Convention of al-

Agreement between France and the Ottoman Empire, providing for the French retreat from Egypt.

Napoléon Bonaparte and his troops had invaded Egypt in 1798. Besieged by British and Ottoman forces, his successor, General Jean-Baptiste KLÉBER, negotiated the terms of French withdrawal. The Convention of al-Arish, signed by Kléber and the Ottoman grand vizier Yusuf on January 24, 1800, allowed for a dignified retreat of France from Egypt.

The convention was rejected by both Napoléon and Britain and, within a year, the French were completely defeated and evicted from Egypt.

BIBLIOGRAPHY

HUREWITZ, J. C., ed. *The Middle East and North Africa in World Politics.* New Haven, Conn., 1975.
VATIKIOTIS, P. J. *The History of Egypt.* Baltimore, 1985.

Zachary Karabell

Arlosoroff, Haim   [1899–1933]

Labor Zionist leader and intellectual.

Born in the Ukraine, Arlosoroff and his family fled to Germany in the wake of the 1905 Russian POGROM. He studied economics at Berlin University and also plunged into the writings of Aaron David GORDON and the classics of LABOR ZIONISM. An economist and a social theorist, Arlosoroff became one of the main leaders of Ha-Po'el Ha-Tza'ir in Germany and editor of its journal *Die Arbeit* (Work). Elected to the Zionist Action Committee in 1923, he immigrated to Palestine in 1924 and quickly rose to a leadership position. An intellectual as well as a man of practical action, he wrote a number of books and articles on socialist and anarchist thought, Jewish social studies, and financial theory. Attempting to formulate a blueprint for a socialist Jewish state, he also helped unify the two main Labor Zionist political parties to form MAPAI in 1930. He served as head of the Jewish Agency's political department and negotiated the controversial transfer agreement with Nazi Germany in 1933, which allowed Jews emigrating to Palestine to take out of the country a fraction of their wealth in German goods. Two unknown assailants shot and killed Arlosoroff in Tel Aviv in June 1933, and although the Labor Zionist leadership accused the REVISIONIST MOVEMENT party of political fratricide, the two members tried for the murder were acquitted.

BIBLIOGRAPHY

AVINERI, SHLOMO. *Arlosoroff.* London, 1989.

Donna Robinson Divine

Armée de Libération Nationale (ALN)

The fighting force mobilized to wage the Algerian war of independence.

Beginning in 1954, the Armée de Libération Nationale (ALN; National Liberation Army) was composed of guerrilla units divided into five and later six *wilayas* (military districts within Algeria). From 1956 onward, standing armies began to emerge among expatriate Algerians in both Morocco and Tunisia, which, by 1960, came under a unified general staff.

BIBLIOGRAPHY

HORNE, ALISTAIRE. *A Savage War of Peace: Algeria, 1954–1962.* London, 1985.

John Ruedy

Armée Nationale Tunisienne

The official French-language designation for the armed forces of Tunisia.

Comprising about 38,000 men (including 26,000 one-year conscripts) distributed among the army (33,000), navy (2,600), and air force (2,500), the armed forces of Tunisia are supplemented by a 10,000-man national guard and a national gendarmerie controlled by the Ministry of the Interior. The military's primary missions are defending the nation's territorial integrity, quelling internal disorders, and promoting economic development. The minister of defense maintains operational control of the military. Tunisia's army was created in 1956; the navy in 1959; and the air force in 1960.

Since 1961, the military has acted primarily to preserve internal security and has supported United Nations missions. Military units suppressed rioting in Tunis during the Arab-Israel war of 1967, peasants who resisted collectivization in 1969, strikers at Ksar Hellal in 1977, dissidents who attacked Gafsa in 1980, rioters in Tunis in 1984, and Islamist dissidents between 1991 and 1993. UN support missions have included assistance in Zaire, Somalia, and Cambodia.

BIBLIOGRAPHY

NELSON, HAROLD D., ed. *Tunisia: A Country Study.* Washington, D.C., 1988.

Larry A. Barrie

Armenia

Member of the Commonwealth of Independent States since 1991; bordered by Georgia, Azerbaijan, Iran, and Turkey.

The Republic of Armenia is one-tenth the size of historic Armenia, which encompassed an area of eastern Turkey called Western Armenia as well as Cilicia, an area that has been the homeland of Armenians since at least the sixth century B.C.E. Armenians enjoyed protected status under the Ottoman Empire, and flourished economically and culturally.

The number of Armenians worldwide is estimated at between 6 and 7 million, of whom 3.3 million live in Armenia; the rest are scattered in the Middle East, Europe, and America. The most important communities in the Middle East were in Lebanon, Syria, and Iran where they played an important part in the local economies and in international trade.

Village scene and thoroughfare in Anatolian Armenia, 1946. (D.W. Lockhard)

Modern Armenian history has been characterized by a growth of nationalism and the struggle to gain autonomy and independence—whether under the Ottoman, Turkish, or Russian empire—at times resulting in violent suppression. The most notorious act of violence against the Armenians in central and eastern Turkey occurred in 1915, when hundreds of thousands were deported, sent in the direction of Syria and Mesopotamia, on the orders of the government. During this forced march, large numbers died from exhaustion, heat, or lack of food and water. Local officials, gendarmes, and irregulars attacked the deportees, killing large numbers of men. Some 500,000 to 600,000 were killed or died of other causes during the march, according to Turkish estimates; German sources give an estimate of 1 to 1.1 million; Armenians claim 1.5 million. Armenians maintain that the attacks took place on orders of the Turkish government, but this has been consistently denied by successive Turkish governments.

Jenab Tutunji

Armenian Community of Jerusalem

Site of the Armenian partiarchate and center of life for Armenian ethnics in Israel.

The Armenian community of Jerusalem had its beginnings in monasticism of the early Byzantine period. A few Armenian inscriptions in mosaic floors from this time are found in and around Jerusalem. The present boundaries of the Armenian quarter, covering nearly a sixth of the Old City at the southwestern corner, appear to have been in place prior to

Armenian priests march to the Church of the Holy Sepulchre in Jerusalem on Easter Sunday. (Mia Bloom)

the first Crusade (1099), with a patriarchate established in the sixth century.

After the defeat of the Crusaders, the Muslim rulers formed an alliance with the Armenians in Jerusalem since both groups were persecuted by their common enemy, the Byzantines, because of religious differences. Likewise, the Ottomans during their rule sided with the Armenians against the Greek Orthodox church—and at times the Roman Catholics—over ownership, control, or maintenance of sacred sites especially within the Church of the Holy Sepulchre and the Church of the Nativity in Bethlehem (in both churches, Armenians have nearly equal holdings with the other two denominations). Armenians in Jerusalem cherish the original edicts issued in their behalf by several Muslim rulers that abolish all taxes and reaffirm the rights of the Armenians to their possessions in Jerusalem and elsewhere. The last of these rulers was Sultan Mahmud II, whose edict of 1813 settled the long disputes with the local Greek hierarchy over ownership of St. James Monastery with its cathedral, the seat of the Armenian partriarchate. Rights to traditional holy places since then have remained unchanged by virtue of the famous *firman* (edict) issued by Sultan Abdülmecit in 1852, establishing the status quo for the various churches' control over such sites, a decree honored by all successive administrations governing Jerusalem.

The prominence of the Armenian patriarchate of Jerusalem rests on the tradition that St. James Cathedral marks the site where the Apostle James, the "brother of the Lord," had his residence. Also, therefore, this is where the Jerusalem Council was held under his leadership as recorded in Acts of the Apostles (ch. 15). Hence, the Armenian Patriarch of Jerusalem is deemed the successor of St. James. His office is much coveted by the local hierarchies who have schemed throughout history to possess the site and to appropriate the office. Also within St. James Cathedral is the traditional burial place of the head of St. James, son of Zebedee and brother of the Apostle John, whose martyrdom is likewise recorded in Acts of the Apostles (ch. 12). Thus, the St. James compound, with its traditions surrounding the two apostles named James, is one of Jerusalem's most venerated sites besides being the largest monastic center in the country. The cathedral, built in the tenth century and expanded in the twelfth, is a prized monument of Eastern Christianity.

As head of the largest Monophysite church in the Holy Land, the Armenian partiarch traditionally champions the cause of the Syriac, Coptic, and Ethiopian churches as well.

In the last few centuries, some partiarchs have played significant roles with lasting benefits for the community. Grigor V (1613–1645) expanded the community's estates beyond Jerusalem; Grigor VI (1715–1749) implemented financial reforms; Yesayi III (1865–1885) promoted publishing; and Yeghishe I (1921–1930) founded new schools. The insightful leadership of these and other patriarchs, especially in the seventeenth and eighteenth centuries, enabled the monastic community to stabilize its resources and to acquire additional properties in and around Jerusalem. These continue to provide a regular—albeit meager—income for the sustenance of the brotherhood.

Until recently, the patriarch's jurisdiction extended over all Armenians in the Arab world. With the settlement at Antelias near Beirut of the displaced catholicosate of Cilicia (a bishopric in southern Turkey), during the French administration of Lebanon (1923–1943), the patriarch's jurisdiction over Lebanon and northern Syria was ceded to Antelias. Moreover, to help that fledgling establishment, Jerusalem provided clerical administrators and instructors. Because of Communism in Armenia, where the Catholicos of All Armenians resides, Jerusalem took the lead in providing parish priests for nearly all Armenian communities in the Diaspora—a task now shared competitively with Antelias.

Unlike other ancient Armenian communities, whether in Armenia or in the diaspora, the Jerusalem community was rarely disturbed. Its continuity enabled it to flourish as a religious and learning center under the leadership of its spiritual heads, the patriarchs. Over the centuries, the monastic community was enriched by the constant flow of pilgrims, including kings and other members of the Cilician royal family, heads of the Armenian church, and scholiasts who took residence. Some of the accumulated treasures, and by no means the best, are on permanent display at the monastery.

One of the most prized possessions is the collection of ancient manuscripts housed in the Chapel of St. T'oros. The 4,000 medieval codices (manuscript books), including over a hundred works of which there are but single copies, are fully cataloged in eleven volumes. Some of these works composed by local authors and many of the others are copies made by local scribes, who, in personal comments at the end of the works, chronicled certain contemporary and near-contemporary events and encounters with other Christians as well as non-Christian entities. Except for being cataloged with brief descriptions of their contents, these manuscripts have not been sufficiently considered for their historical significance—especially when reconstructing the medieval history of Jerusalem.

In addition to the library of ancient manuscripts and a few other chapels, the St. James Monastery houses several academic establishments: a seminary largely supported by the Alex Manoogian Foundation of Detroit, a modern library supported by the Calouste Gulbenkian Fund of Lisbon, a printing press established in 1833—with nearly 500 titles published in the first hundred years of its operation (its earliest publications, including a complete concordance to the Armenian Bible, and the first issue of *Sion,* the scholarly journal of the patriarchate since 1866, are on display at the site), and a high school for the local community, built early in this century when the Armenian population of Jerusalem more than doubled as a result of the Turkish persecutions of World War I. More Armenians moved into St. James when their properties were confiscated during the Arab-Israel War of 1948. Understandably, the sharp increase of lay population brought a degree of secularism into the life of the monastic community.

The number of Armenians in Jerusalem has shrunk considerably in the last thirty years: from about 4,000 in 1960 to about 1,500 in 1990, with nearly two-thirds of them living within the compound of St. James and with ever-increasing dependence on the monastery for their livelihood. The prevailing condition is largely a result of the unification of Jerusalem under Israeli rule in 1967, affecting the population of East Jerusalem generally. The various partisan and political divisions among Armenians worldwide are represented in this small community, which until recently was further fragmented as a result of families taking sides with feuding bishops.

As one of the few minority groups with a presence for over a millennium in the Holy Land, the Armenian community of Jerusalem maintains close ties with other such groups of various faiths.

BIBLIOGRAPHY

AZARIA, VICTOR. *The Armenian Quarter of Jerusalem: Urban Life Behind Monastery Walls.* Berkeley, Calif., 1984.

HINTLIAN, KEVORK. *History of the Armenians in the Holy Land,* 2nd ed. Jerusalem, 1989.

NARKISS, BEZALEL, ed. *Armenian Art Treasures of Jerusalem.* New Rochelle, N.Y., 1979.

PRAWER, JOSHUA. "The Armenians in Jerusalem Under the Crusaders." In *Armenian and Biblical Studies,* ed. by Michael E. Stone. Jerusalem, 1976.

ROSE, JOHN H. M. *Armenians of Jerusalem: Memories of Life in Palestine.* New York, 1993.

SANJIAN, AVEDIS K. *The Armenian Community in Syria Under Ottoman Dominion.* Cambridge, Mass., 1965.

Abraham Terian

Armenian Millet

Armenian community or nation in the Ottoman Empire since the fifteenth century.

The Armenian millet (Turkish, Ermeni millet) existed in the Ottoman Empire as an institution devised by the sultans to govern the Christian population of the Monophysite churches. The millet system extended internal autonomy in religious and civil matters to the non-Muslim communities while introducing a mechanism for direct administrative responsibility to the state in matters of taxation. The reach of the Armenian millet expanded and contracted with the changing territorial dimensions of the Ottoman state. Originally the Armenian millet was defined as a broad religious group rather than narrowly as a denomination reinforcing ethnic distinction. Not only Armenians of all persuasions, which by the nineteenth century included Orthodox, Catholic, and Protestant, were treated by the Ottoman government as constituents of the Armenian millet; other Oriental Christian denominations, which were excluded from the Greek millet, also were included in the Armenian millet.

The evolution of parallel Armenian and Greek millets has led to the proposition that the Armenian community was introduced by the Ottoman government as a way of denying the Greek millet, and its leadership in the form of the Orthodox patriarch, governance over the entire Christian community in the Ottoman state. Although Ottoman political theory divided the populace along the lines of the three principal religions—Islam, Christianity, and Judaism—the Christian community was further divided to differentiate between the two branches of Christianity, Monophysite and Duophysite, and to foster competition within the sizable Christian population of the empire. From the standpoint of the overall system, the Oriental Christian communities related to the Ottoman regime through the intermediary of the Armenian leadership in the capital city of Constantinople (now Istanbul). In practice, direct communication with local Ottoman governors as the intercessors with the central authorities was more common. Nor did the system necessarily encompass the entire Armenian population as its settlements entered the Ottoman Empire during the period of expansion. In the remoter parts of the empire, the reach of the millet system was tenuous, and communities operated on the basis of interrelations traditional to the region. Only in the nineteenth century did the purview of the Armenian millet attain influence comprehensive to the Armenian population of the Ottoman Empire. However, by that point the Ottomans had agreed to the further fractionalization of the Armenian millet by extending formal recognition, in 1831 and 1847 respectively, to the Catholic and Protestant millets, both of which were predominantly Armenian.

The history of the Armenian millet as an imperial institution is more properly the history of the Armenian patriarchate of Constantinople. Though in the strictest sense an ecclesiastical office functioning within the framework of the Armenian church, the patriarchate was created by the Ottomans, and its occupant served at the pleasure of the SUBLIME PORTE (the Ottoman government). There was no precedent of an Armenian bishopric in Constantinople predating Ottoman occupation of the city. The early history of the patriarchate is barely known. Armenian tradition attributes its origins to the settlement of the Armenians of Bursa in the city upon the command of Mehmet the Conqueror and of the designation in 1461 of the Armenian bishop of Bursa, named Hovakim, as head of this community by the sultan himself. During the first 150 years of its existence, the importance of the office was restricted to the city and its environs. The rapid turnover of bishops deprived the patriarchate of political or practical significance to Armenians at large.

The patriarchate emerged as an agency central to the Armenian millet structure in the eighteenth century. Three factors appear to have contributed to the consolidation of ecclesiastical and political control by the patriarchate: growth in the Armenian population in and around Constantinople, which had been an area at some distance from the centers of Armenian demographic concentration in the Ottoman Empire—mostly eastern and central Anatolia and northern Black Sea coast; the strengthening of the economic role of the growing community in local trade, international commerce, and government finances; and finally the appearance of primates who commanded respect and expanded the role of the patriarchate in Armenian communal life. The key figure in this century was Hovhannes Kolot, whose tenure lasted from 1715 to 1741. Thereafter, the Armenian patriarch of Istanbul was regarded as the most important figure in the Armenian church despite the fact that within the hierarchy of the church itself other offices, such as that of the Catholicos at Echmiadsin in Persian (and subsequently Russian) Armenia or the Armenian patriarch of Jerusalem, could claim historical and moral seniority.

The commercial success of the Armenians was evidenced by the rise of the so-called *amira* class in Constantinople. Originally merchants, the amiras gained prominence mostly as *sarraf*s (bankers) who played a critical role in financing the empire's tax-farming system. For their services the Duzians, for example, were awarded management of the imperial mint. The Balyans held the post of chief architect to the sultan from 1750 to the end of the nineteenth century and were responsible for the construction of virtually all imperial residences and palaces. These Armenian notables put their stamp on the Armenian community of Constantinople when they also received license from their sovereign to establish educational centers, charitable institutions, hospitals, and churches.

Although their status was defined by their connection with the Ottoman system, the role of the amiras in the Armenian millet was determined by the influence they exercised over the patriarchate. A conservative oligarchy by nature, nevertheless the amira presence underscored the growth of secular forces in Armenian society, which soon derived their importance from their role in the economy of the city independent of the monarchy. Those very forces were further encouraged by the revival of interest in Armenian literature sponsored by amiras.

The TANZIMAT reforms unraveled the system of government on which the amiras depended. It also provided additional impetus to the growth of an Armenian middle class increasingly composed of smaller merchants, called *esnaf,* who demanded a voice in the management of the millet and the election of the patriarch. Soon popular sentiment called for the regulation of the election process and the adoption of a formal document prescribing the function and responsibilities of the patriarchate. A long drawn-out debate among conservative clergy and amiras, liberal-minded *esnaf,* and the press through the 1840s and 1850s resulted in the drafting of a so-called constitution for the Armenian millet. The compromise document was adopted by an assembly composed of laymen and ecclesiastics on May 24, 1860. Its formal approval by the Ottoman authorities took three more years. The Armenians called it their national constitution, and the rights and responsibilities contained in the document became the framework by which Armenians throughout the empire reorganized their communities. Placing millet leadership in the Armenian church, the national constitution also guaranteed a role for the lay community and provided specific mechanisms for its participation at all levels of management.

The constitution also elevated the office of patriarch to that of national leader with immediate responsibility in representing the concerns of the Armenian millet with the Sublime Porte. That proved a heavier burden than intended as the flock in the distant corners of the empire began to appeal more and more to the patriarch for relief from their woes at the hands of corrupt administrators and officials prone to violence. The patriarchate catalogued these problems and appealed to the resident ministers of the great powers to plead the Armenian case with the sultan. This problem of enhanced responsibility in the face of increasing unrest in the provinces while being powerless to persuade the Sublime Porte in political matters seriously compromised the patriarchate. Segments of the Armenian millet felt disfranchised; adherents turned to the Catholic and Protestant millets for protection. The Porte, in turn, closely scrutinized elections and appointments to contain the rising tide of Armenian nationalism.

The millet system remained in place until the end of the empire. The patriarchate remained in place until its suspension in 1916 by the government of the YOUNG TURKS. And although many of the later patriarchs, such as Mkrtich KHRIMIAN (1869–1873), Nerses Varzhapetian (1874–1884), Matteos Izmirlian (1894–1896), and Maghakia ORMANIAN (1896–1908), were very important figures, Armenian loyalties were already divided by the late nineteenth century. Political organizations vied for leadership in the Armenian community and the religious basis of national organization was facing serious competition from these and other sources. The patriarchate was restored in 1918 and its role reconfirmed by the Republic of Turkey. By that time, however, the Armenian bishop presided over a community whose congregants had been seriously reduced in numbers and mostly inhabited the city of Istanbul, much as when the millet system was first introduced among Armenians. As for the Armenian national constitution, it remains a living document. Armenian communities throughout the world to rely on its principles of mixed representation under ecclesiastical leadership in the organization and management of their now dispersed communities.

BIBLIOGRAPHY

BARDAKJIAN, KEVORK B., "The rise of the Armenian Patriarchate of Constantinople." In *Christians and Jews in the Ottoman Empire,* ed. by Benjamin Braude and Bernard Lewis. New York, 1982.

BARSOUMIAN, HAGOP. The Dual Role of the Armenian *Amira* Class within the Ottoman Government and the Armenian Millet (1750–1850)." In *Christians and Jews in the Ottoman Empire,* ed. by Benjamin Braude and Bernard Lewis. New York, 1982.

SANJIAN, AVEDIS K. *The Armenian Communities in Syria Under Ottoman Dominion.* Cambridge, U.K., 1965.

Rouben P. Adalian

Armenian National Movement

A movement for Armenian autonomy within the former Soviet Union; usually called the ANM.

The ANM (in Armenian, *Hayots Hamazkayin Sharzhum*) was formed in 1989 in Yerevan, Armenia, after a year of political ferment in the country growing out of the so-called KARABAGH movement. The short-term impetus for the ANM came from the arrest of the Karabagh committee, the informal leadership of the popular movement which swept the country in February 1988, and the need stemming therefrom to consolidate the movement into a political process capable of negotiating with both Yerevan and Moscow authorities.

The original Karabagh movement arose spontaneously in support of the appeal of the Nagorno Karabakh Armenians to President Mikhail Gorbachev for the transfer of jurisdiction of the Nagorno Karabakh Autonomous Oblast (NKAO) from the Soviet Socialist Republic of Azerbaijan to the Soviet Socialist Republic of Armenia. The reluctance of Moscow authorities to satisfy the Armenian demands and the violent response in Azerbaijan mobilized the population of Armenia. In the days following the devastating earthquake of December 7, 1988, as the Karabagh committee tried to lead the Armenian response to the emergency (in view of the paralysis of the government), Gorbachev ordered the arrest of the leading figures of the committee. Their incarceration and release some six months later galvanized the activists to form a popular-front type of organization. The leadership of the movement derived exclusively from the Armenian intelligentsia. Three professions seemed represented most: educators, physicist-mathematicians, and philologist-historians. Nevertheless, the movement also drew on the strong support of the urban working class and, on occasion, called upon as many as a million people in demonstrations held regularly over the course of the first two years of activity.

The ANM advocated the unification of Armenia and Karabagh and the institution of popular democracy, political pluralism, a free-market economy, and state sovereignty. Along with the Lithuanian movement Sajudis the ANM was at the forefront in pressing the Communist party to revise Soviet nationality policy and to increase republican authority. The ANM stopped short of advocating secession from the USSR while capitalizing on the changes brought about with perestroika and glasnost. In the first open elections held for the Soviet Armenian Parliament in the first half of 1990, the Communists were democratically voted out of power, and the ANM was given a plurality of seats. With the support of other nationalist parties, this proved sufficient to give the ANM control of the government, which it has retained through 1993. It quickly embarked upon the process of privatizing the economy in Armenia.

Opposing the new federal treaty proposed by Gorbachev and scrupulously following law and procedure according to the Soviet Constitution, the government organized the referendum on separate statehood held on September 21, 1991. With over 90 percent of the population voting in favor, the ANM had led the Armenians to independence.

BIBLIOGRAPHY

DUDWICK, NORA. "Armenia: The Nation Awakens." *Nations & Politics in the Soviet Successor States*, ed. by Ian Bremmer and Ray Tara. New York, 1993, pp. 261–287.
LIBARIDIAN, GERARD J. *Armenia at the Crossroads: Democracy and Nationhood in the Post-Soviet Era.* Watertown, Mass., 1991.

Rouben P. Adalian

Armenian Revolutionary Movement

Nationalist movement among Armenians of the Ottoman Empire, which lasted from 1878 to 1921.

In the 1878 Treaty of Berlin, the Ottoman government agreed to undertake reforms in the so-called Armenian provinces of the empire. Based on a track record of reforms promulgated but seldom implemented, Armenian nationalists disbelieved that any meaningful changes would be made in the Ottoman administration of the Armenian-populated regions of the Turkish state. Moderate and conservative Armenians, on the other hand, placed much stock in an international treaty signed by the great powers containing an explicit Ottoman commitment to reform. The failure of the great powers to hold ABDÜLHAMIT II to his promise as they became embroiled in the competition to carve up Africa and Asia and the sultan's recalcitrance in introducing voluntary reforms left many Armenians disillusioned with the Ottoman regime. A rising national consciousness obstructed by an increasingly despotic administration under Abdülhamit did not take long to prompt a revolutionary movement among Armenians of the Ottoman Empire.

Local self-defense units had already taken to resisting Ottoman authorities. Particularly egregious from the standpoint of rural inhabitants was the government's license and tolerance of Kurdish predation over Armenian towns and villages. In response to this predicament, the first formally organized Armenian political society made its appearance in 1885 in the city of Van. The group was quickly disbanded by Ottoman police.

The Armenian revolutionary movement acquired its real impetus in the Russian Empire. In an atmosphere of greater freedom, better education, and social advancement, the new intellectual class taking form in the Russian Caucasus spawned a group of political thinkers who began to articulate serious concern with the fate of Armenians in the Ottoman Empire. Influenced by Russian populism and radicalism, they organized two groups advocating Armenian national goals. The Armenian Social Democratic party first appeared in Geneva among Russian-Armenians studying abroad. The husband and wife team of Avetis and Maro Nazerbekian led the group. The party soon was known by the name of its publication, *Hunchak* (Clarion), selected in imitation of the Russian-language publication by the same name issued by the Russian revolutionary Alexander Herzen.

The HUNCHAK PARTY subscribed to socialism and called for the restoration of Armenian statehood. Members focused their activities on the Ottoman Armenians whom they tried to propagandize and provide with arms. Though it found adherents among Armenians in both the Russian and Ottoman empires, the Hunchak party never garnered a large following. Its ideological positions were viewed as too radical and its program infeasible in the face of the overwhelming power of the state and the absence of real political consciousness among the rural masses.

The Armenian Revolutionary Federation (ARF) had better success. Organized in Tbilisi in 1890 by a trio of ideologues known as Kristapor, Rostom, and Zavarian, the organization became known less by its acronym than by the Armenian word for federation, *dashnaktsutyun*. Its members and supporters were thus called Dashnak. The DASHNAK PARTY gained greater mass appeal as it sought to define a populist platform that was based not so much on ideological propositions as on the objective conditions of the Armenian population. In its early years it advocated reform, autonomy, and self-government, forsaking independent nationhood. The ARF emphasized the need for political organization and support for groups engaged in local struggles, which it tried to bring under one umbrella, hence the notion of federation. The object of their program remained the fate and status of Armenians in the Ottoman Empire.

After its formative years, three critical developments—the 1894–1896 violence and the 1905 and 1917 Russian revolutions—redirected the thrust of the Armenian nationalist movement. The destruction visited upon the Armenian population of the Ottoman Empire between 1894 and 1896 compelled Armenian society to rethink its condition and Armenian political organizations to reassess their course of action. The level of lethal violence unleashed by the Turkish state reached beyond anything experienced by the Armenians to that point. With hundreds of thousands affected and tens of thousands dead, the revolutionaries were confronted with a very serious dilemma. The sultan's regime used the charge of revolutionary activism against the Armenians to justify its wholesale measures. Armenians in the provinces and in Istanbul were openly challenging the state and its representatives. Demonstrations, reprisals against corrupt officials, underground publications, and revolutionary cells frightened the sultan and provided evidence of the emerging nationalism of one more minority in the empire. From the standpoint of the ruling Ottoman class, Russian tolerance of Armenian organizations advocating political change in the Ottoman Empire appeared particularly seditious.

The havoc wreaked in Armenian society by the killings alienated a large segment of the masses from political involvement. It also destroyed a good part of the Hunchak and Dashnak organizations. Thereafter, the distrust between the Ottoman regime and the Armenians was never repaired. The ARF and the COMMITTEE OF UNION AND PROGRESS cooperated in their opposition to the sultan Abdülhamit, whom even progressive-minded Turks accused of preventing the modernization of the state. After the Young Turk revolution of 1908, Armenian political organizations were legalized in the Ottoman Empire. However, the charge of sedition would be brought up again by the Unionist government during World War I, and once again measures taken against the Armenian population at large. Executions and mass deportations brought an end to the existence of Armenian society in the Ottoman Empire and with that also completely halted Armenian political and revolutionary activism in Turkey.

Events in the Russian Empire took a very different course. The 1905 revolution witnessed the intensification of radicalism all across society. Armenians were no less affected. In fact, Armenian society already had been galvanized by a measure introduced by the government that had seriously undermined Armenian loyalty to the regime. In 1903 the czar had issued an edict confiscating the properties of the Armenian church. Designed to undercut the strengthening of Armenian ethnic consciousness by depriving Armenian society of its principal means of support for its educational institutions, the edict energized the moribund revolutionary organizations and helped attract new interest and membership in them. It also compelled them to consider socialism more seriously and finally to oppose czarism as a repressive system of government. The igniting of racial animosity and virtual warfare between the Armenians and the Azeris to distract them from the revolution augmented the prestige of the ARF all the more as it took to the defense of the populace in the absence of Russian policing to contain communal violence. The repression that followed once again curbed the activities of the Armenian organizations. However, by that point the ARF had gained mass appeal and clearly had emerged as the leading political organization in Armenian society. When the Russian Empire broke up after the 1917 revolution, the ARF was in a position to assume charge of the process resulting in the establishment of the Republic of Armenia. From 1918 to 1920 during the entire duration of the independent republic, the ARF was the dominant party.

Armenian socialists, who were members of Russian organizations and opposed to specifically Armenian nationalist parties, soon gained prominence after the Bolshevik revolution. Though they were only a single strand of the Armenian revolutionary movement, the sovietization of Armenia placed the Armenian Bolsheviks at the helm of Armenian society. Calling Dashnaks and others bourgeois nationalists, the Bolsheviks excluded them from the political process in Soviet Armenia and persecuted them as counterrevolutionaries. By 1921, the momentum of the movement was spent, leaving a legacy of catastrophe in the Ottoman Empire and of successful nation-building in the Russian state.

BIBLIOGRAPHY

NALBANDIAN, LOUISE. *The Armenian Revolutionary Movement: The Development of Armenian Political Parties through the Nineteenth Century.* Berkeley, Calif., 1967.
TER MINASSIAN, ANAIDE. *Nationalism and Socialism in the Armenian Revolutionary Movement.* Cambridge, U.K., 1984.

Rouben P. Adalian

Armenians

A people of Asia Minor, long ruled by others, who became independent in 1991. Because of their location, their culture was influenced by Middle Eastern peoples and Russians.

The territory of historic Armenia covered the Armenian plateau. The Pontic range on the north, the Little Caucasus chain to the east, the Anti-Taurus range to the south, and the Euphrates river in the

Armenian church nestled in the mountains at Kharput in eastern Anatolia. (D.W. Lockhard)

west defined its perimeter. Armenian settlement in the area dates at the latest to the first half of the first millennium B.C.E. Turkish occupation and settlement from the eleventh century C.E. reduced the Armenian presence in the plateau area. A new Armenian concentration took shape in and around CILICIA on the Mediterranean coast between the tenth and fourteenth centuries. Thereafter Armenians inhabited most of the principal cities in a belt stretching from the Aegean coast of Anatolia to the Caspian Sea. Further dispersion placed Armenians across most of Eastern Europe and Western Asia as far as India. Between 1915 and 1923, Ottoman state policies eliminated the Armenians from Anatolia and historic West Armenia and drove many of them into Eastern Armenia within the zone of Russian domination. Armenian-inhabited territory at the end of the twentieth century is confined to the Caucasus region including the current Republic of Armenia, the disputed territory of mountainous KARABAGH, and the districts of Akhalkalaki and Bogdanovska in southern Georgia. The remainder of the Armenian population inhabit what are known as diasporan communities throughout the temperate zone girdling the globe.

Language. A majority of Armenians speak Armenian, an independent branch of the Indo-European family of languages. Armenian is spoken only by Armenians; however, many Armenians are bilingual so the language has absorbed a vast vocabulary of foreign words over the centuries. First recorded in the early fifth century, Classical Armenian provided the principal means of written communication until the mid-nineteenth century. By that time the spoken tongue had evolved into numerous dialects. With the rise of literacy, the dialects spoken in the two centers of Armenian cultural activity outside of historic Armenia—namely Tbilisi and Constantinople (now Istanbul)—emerged as the modern vernaculars. The development of these two vernaculars resulted in the standardization of Eastern and Western Armenian. The former was used in the Russian Empire and Iran and the latter in the Ottoman Empire. The boundary between the two dialects holds to this day. Eastern Armenian became the state language of the Republic of Armenia.

Religion. Most Armenians belong to the Armenian Apostolic church, a denomination of Eastern Orthodoxy. The church traces its origins to the evangelizing missions of the Apostles Thaddeus and Bartholomew in Armenia. Formal Christianization traditionally is dated to the year 301 with the conversion of the reigning monarch, Trdat (Tiridates) III. Political and theological differences led to the break from the Roman Catholic church by the sixth century, and a series of Armenian church councils rejected the Chalcedonian creed, which condemned portions of the Armenian beliefs. Thereafter the Armenian church was restricted by its national character and became the focal point of Armenian cultural development. Roman Catholicism returned with the Crusaders and with the growth of Mediterranean trade in the eleventh through the twelfth centuries. Protestant denominations appeared under the influence of the American missionary movement of the mid-nineteenth century. Though voluntary adherence to Islam is recorded, most Armenian conversion is believed to have occurred under duress and mainly during the period of Ottoman rule. Official atheism during the Soviet period drove religion from the Republic of Armenia. The Catholicos of All Armenians resides at Echmiadsin in Armenia, but church attendance is mostly symbolic and sparse. Religion plays a larger role in Armenian diasporan communities as a marker of Armenian identity.

Demographics. The global Armenian population is difficult to estimate as many states do not measure ethnic constituencies. In the Republic of Armenia, the most recent population figure (1993) stands at 3.7 million. The current population of mountainous Karabagh is estimated at 150,000 Armenians. About 500,000 live in Georgia, while another 800,000 are spread throughout Russia and the former Soviet republics outside Transcaucasia. Between 1988 and 1991, a forced population exchange resulted in the departure of 350,000 Armenians from AZERBAIJAN. Armenians in the diaspora are concentrated in cities throughout the Middle East, Western Europe, and North and South America. An estimated half million

live in the Middle East with the larger communities of over 100,000 found in Iran, Syria, and Lebanon. The bulk of the estimated half million Armenians in Europe are found in France, with much smaller concentrations in England, Switzerland, Italy, Austria, and Belgium. The combined North and South American population nears a million with the larger portion living in the United States.

Livelihood. Agrarian life dominated traditional Armenian society until its complete displacement during World War I. Throughout the centuries, however, dispersion helped Armenians adapt economically. Most notably they formed a strong urban commercial class eventually involved in international trade. Armenians, especially in the Middle East, occupied the role of middlemen in virtually every city. Between the seventeenth and twentieth centuries, in places such as Istanbul, Tbilisi, ISFAHAN, ALEPPO, and BEIRUT, whether through official sponsorship or individual and communal ability, Armenians dominated various sectors of the local, and in some instances the national, economy. While they tended to be traders, craftsmen, retailers, and shopkeepers in earlier centuries, the twentieth century also saw the rapid emergence of an urban professional class in the fields of medicine, engineering, banking, electronics, and computers. In the Republic of Armenia, the Soviet period was marked by rapid industrialization resulting in a country with a high density of factories involved in heavy manufacturing. The breakup of the Soviet Union has placed the entire economy of Armenia in jeopardy. It is undergoing an automatic conversion and shrinkage because of an insurmountable energy crisis. Of all fifteen former Soviet republics, Armenia, on the other hand, has proceeded the furthest toward privatization. Agricultural lands have been distributed to farmers. The Armenian parliament has legitimized private ownership, but shortages of every commodity have left private initiative hamstrung and the livelihood of the populace dependent on state subsidy.

Major Historical Figures. The 3,000-year span of Armenian history is mostly recalled in narratives recording the deeds, valor, and accomplishments of a multitude of figures among whom the names of certain kings, religious patriarchs, noblemen, and men of culture stand out. The extinction of the Armenian royal and princely families by the fifteenth century meant waiting until the early modern period for the reappearance of figures of national significance. In the absence of the men of the sword, men of the cloth and men of the pen—and often of both— began to lead the Armenian nation out of its dark ages. Mekhitar SEBASTATSI founded an Armenian Catholic monastery in Venice in 1717 and guided the cultural recovery of the Armenians. Mikayel CHAMCHIAN, a member of the Mekhitarian order, resumed the writing of Armenian history and began shaping a modern national identity. Khachatur ABOVIAN in Russian Armenia authored the first Armenian novel in 1848, while Mikayel Nalbandian in Russia advocated Armenian nationhood. Mkrtich KHRIMIAN, writer, publisher, and priest, embodied the coalescing of Armenian consciousness by the end of the nineteenth century. As Armenian patriarch of Constantinople and subsequently Catholicos of All Armenians in Echmiadsin, he allied the conservative Armenian church with the advocates of national liberation. While repression and autocracy were challenged by many locally, others took up arms, and the ARMENIAN REVOLUTIONARY MOVEMENT found its leaders among intellectuals who formulated ideology and unschooled men who fought skirmishes with the police and militia of the tsar and the sultan. ANDRANIK, the guerilla fighter, entered national lore as he escaped every snare of the sultan's police while defending the causes of the Armenian people with his own brand of resistance.

The founding of the Republic of Armenia in 1918 tested the mettle of men. While some, such as Aram Manukian and Simon VRATSIAN, defended its territories, others, such as President Avetis AHARONIAN and Prime Minister Alexander KHATISIAN, negotiated for its survival. The Soviet period reversed the role of the hero and anti-hero. The dissident, more so than the Communist party leader, captured the national imagination. In Soviet Armenia he came in the form of the poet, Yeghishe CHARENTS or Baryur Sevak, who spun with words an alternative consciousness to escape and defy totalitarian control. The national sentiment that had been preserved underground exploded in 1988 and found its guiding figure in a scholar, Levon TER-PETROSSIAN, who, with independence restored in 1991, became the first democratically elected president of his country.

BIBLIOGRAPHY

BOURNOUTIAN, GEORGE. *Khanate of Erevan under Qajar Rule.* Costa Mesa, Calif., 1992.

DER NERSESSIAN, SIRARPIE. *The Armenians.* London and New York, 1969.

HOVANNISIAN, RICHARD G. *Armenia on the Road to Independence, 1918.* Los Angeles, 1967.

MATOSSIAN, MARY K. *The Impact of Soviet Policies in Armenia.* Leiden, 1962.

WALKER, CHRISTOPHER J. *Armenia: The Survival of a Nation.* London, 1980.

Rouben P. Adalian

Armenian Secret Army for the Liberation of Armenia

A clandestine group, usually known as ASALA, that made its appearance in 1975, the sixtieth year after the 1915 mass killing of Armenians in Ottoman Turkey.

ASALA was active into the mid-1980s. The stated mission of this terrorist organization was the avenging of the mass killing of the Armenians and the liberation of the so-called occupied territories of the Armenians in eastern Turkey whence the Armenian population had been deported in 1915. ASALA was an independent organization opposed to the traditional political organizations in the Armenian diaspora. Based in Lebanon, it had close links with the Palestinian movement. A similar organization, named the Justice Commandos of the Armenian Genocide (JCAG), was organized soon after the appearance of ASALA. JCAG had the support of the ARF (DASHNAK PARTY. Although both ASALA and JCAG carried out propaganda in the Armenian diaspora, in the main their following was drawn from the Middle East. Their principal mode of operation involved the targeting of Turkish government officials for assassination or the selecting of Turkish institutions for bombing. The killing of Turkey's ambassadors in Europe and Turkey's consular officials in the United States attracted huge media attention in the late seventies and early eighties. In 1982 the terrorists even staged a suicidal attack at Ankara Airport. However, neither ASALA or JCAG succeeded in obtaining any concessions from Turkey's government nor in gaining wide support from Armenians.

When ASALA grew even more violent and began hitting non-Turkish targets, the organization split and went into rapid decline. The bombing of Orly Airport in France in 1983, where many civilians were killed, proved a turning point. With random violence directed against a non-Turkish target, Armenian terrorism ceased being a problem just for Turks. The bombing incident also resulted in popular revulsion as the campaign of political violence veered away from its initial stated objective of dealing punishment to Turkey's government for having perpetrated a mass killing against the Armenians. Better equipped with information by this point about the membership of the terrorist cells, American, European, and Turkish counterterrorist units eventually defused the movement.

From the age of members who died in terrorist operations, most participants appeared to be persons in their twenties who had been exposed to the radical politics of the Middle East. ASALA members openly expressed their alienation from the political programs of the Armenian diaspora organizations, which they charged with being internationally ineffective in advancing their stated cause of obtaining justice for the Armenian killing. Many in the leadership of ASALA and JCAG were reported to be highly educated and multilingual individuals. The most notorious of these was the shadowy figure of Hagop Hagopian, presumed to be an alias, who led ASALA during most of its active phase. He, like many of the militants, met a violent death.

One of the very few American-born members of ASALA was Monte Melkonian. He led the splinter movement against Hagopian's wing, which had been responsible for the Orly terror bombing. Melkonian was probably the most articulate of the participants in the Armenian terrorist movement. His writings constitute some of the literature central for understanding why the campaign of political violence was embarked upon and how it justified its program as a means to redress the consequences of the mass killing. Melkonian, along with others, was arrested in France. After the wave of terrorism ebbed, he was released from prison and returned underground. He resurfaced in 1991 in mountainous KARABAGH, participating in the defense of the local Armenian population during the siege of that region by Azeri forces. He was killed in the battle zone in 1993, at which time he was hailed by local Armenians for having organized and trained the Karabagh men into an effective fighting force that had gone on the offensive earlier in the year. This second career helped change people's views about him. Monte Melkonian was given a hero's burial in Yerevan, Armenia.

BIBLIOGRAPHY

GUNTER, MICHAEL M. "Pursuing the Just Cause of Their People": A Study of Contemporary Armenian Terrorism. New York, 1986.
HYLAND, FRANCIS P. Armenian Terrorism: The Past, The Present, The Prospects. Boulder, Colo., 1991.
KURZ, ANAT, and ARIEL MERARI. ASALA: Irrational Terror or Political Tool? Boulder, Colo., 1985.

Rouben P. Adalian

Armenian Soviet Socialist Republic

One of the fifteen republics of the former Soviet Union.

Armenia lies between the Black and Caspian seas, occupying part of the lands of the ancient kingdom of Armenia that were divided between Turkey, Iran, and the Soviet Union in this century. Originally ceded to Russia following the Treaty of SAN STEFANO

(1878), Armenia was reoccupied by the Communists in the 1920s and incorporated into the Transcaucasian Federation. In 1936, the federation was abolished and Armenia, Georgia, and Azerbaijan each became a republic of the Soviet Union. Beginning in 1988, the mostly Christian population of Armenia entered into a bitter dispute with the mostly Muslim population of neighboring Azerbaijan over the territory of Nagorno KARABAKH, which is situated within Azerbaijan but has a population that is 75 percent Armenian. Armenia declared its independence from the Soviet Union on August 23, 1990. The population of Armenia was 4.6 million in 1989, of which less than 2 percent were ethnic Russians. The capital of Armenia is YEREVAN.

BIBLIOGRAPHY

KURIAN, GEORGE THOMAS. The Encyclopedia of the Second World. New York, 1991.
Webster's New Geographical Dictionary. Springfield, Mass., 1984.

David Waldner

Arnita, Salvador

Lebanese musician and composer.

Founder of the American University of Beirut choir and a music teacher at the American University of Beirut, Arnita is the composer of at least three symphonies and four concertos—for piano, organ, and flute. He is recognized for his writing on music and interpretations of musical works, especially "Carte d'Identité" in 1972.

BIBLIOGRAPHY

Who's Who in Lebanon 1980–1981. Beirut, 1980.

Mark Mechler

Arseven, Celal Esat [1876–1972]

Turkish art professor and historian.

Born the son of a pasha in Istanbul, Arseven graduated from the Beşiktaş Military School in 1888 and studied drawing at fine arts school for a year before going to the war college. He continued writing and painting while in the army, from which he resigned in 1908. In the years before World War I, he worked at the humor magazine *Kalem* with Cemil Cem, one of the great early caricaturists of Turkey.

Arseven was a writer and artist of diverse talents. In 1918, he wrote a libretto for one of the first Turkish operas and went on to write several musical plays performed at the Istanbul municipal and state theaters. In addition to being an accomplished watercolorist, he was also a professor of architecture and municipal planning at the Istanbul Fine Arts Academy from 1924–1941. He published a five-volume art encyclopedia between 1943 and 1954 and many books on Turkish painting and architecture during his lifetime. Before his death, he was awarded a doctoral degree by Istanbul University. He was also a delegate to the TURKISH GRAND NATIONAL ASSEMBLY during its seventh and eighth sessions.

BIBLIOGRAPHY

AND, METIN. "Opera and Ballet in Modern Turkey." In *The Transformation of Turkish Culture,* ed. by Günsel Renda and C. Max Kortepeter. Princeton, N.J., 1986.
Yeni Türk Ansiklopedisi (New Turkish Encyclopedia). Istanbul, 1985.

Elizabeth Thompson

Arslan, Adil   [1880?–1954]

Syrian Arab nationalist politician.

Born in Shuwayfat (Lebanon), son of Emir Hamud, Adil was educated in the Maronite French Christian mission school, Madrasa al-Hikma, and at the Ottoman College in Beirut. He was also educated in France, then attended the Mülkiye (the Ottoman Empire's civil service school) but, according to one source, did not complete the course. He entered Ottoman political life under the wing of his paternal uncle, Emir Mustafa, whose tenure as leader of the Yazbaki DRUZE was just being successfully challenged by Emir Tawfiq Majid Arslan, and like his elder brother, Emir Shakib, Adil prospered as a member of the Union and Progress party.

Adil Arslan became secretary, first grade, in the ministry of the interior in 1913, director of immigration in the vilayet of Syria in 1914, *qa'immaqam* of the Shuf in 1915, and representative from Mount Lebanon (*mutasarrifiye*) from 1916 to 1918. According to some sources, he joined an Arab secret society before World War I, but older sources date his membership to the postwar period. Like many others who had served the Ottomans until the beginning or end of World War I, he joined up with Emir FAISAL ibn Husayn (who was promised a government by the British because of the effectiveness of his troops under T. E. LAWRENCE [of Arabia]). Arslan was appointed governor of the Lebanon in the fall of 1919,

then aide to the military governor of Syria and, in 1920, political counselor to Faisal, who had become the new king of independent Syria. Despite Arslan's and his cousin Amin's efforts, most Druzes in Mount Lebanon followed Nasib Jumbulat or Tawfiq Majid Arslan and accepted the French mandate over Syria—hence Faisal's short-lived kingdom fell, and Arslan fled to Transjordan, to Faisal's brother Emir ABDULLAH IBN HUSAYN, where he served as chief of the *diwan* (court staff) from 1921 to 1923. When in response to the British, Abdullah exiled the Syrian Arab nationalist expatriates, Arslan took refuge in Saudi Arabia. In exile, he was closely associated with Shukri al-QUWATLI and the Istiqlalists (independence movements). During the Syrian rebellion of 1925–1927, he was active as a fund-raiser and combat commander. Again condemned by the French, he continued his activities outside Syria, mainly in Egypt. When he was expelled from Egypt for anti-Italian activities in 1931, he went to Baghdad (since Faisal was then king of Iraq under British treaty protection). He was in Switzerland in 1937, continuing to participate in pan-Arab activities. After the Syrian National Bloc (to which Quwatli and the Istiqlalists adhered) reached agreement with France and formed a government, Arslan was appointed minister to Turkey, a post he held until 1938, when the ALEXANDRETTA territorial question reached a crisis (an Ottoman district that became a semiautonomous region of Syria in 1920, the Republic of Hatay in 1938, but was incorporated into Turkey in 1939 by agreement between France and Turkey). Arrested, then released by the French in 1940 and 1941, he fled in late 1941 to Turkey, where he spent the rest of WORLD WAR II. Like other Arab nationalist politicians, he sought support for Arab causes from the Germans, but he opposed Rashid Ali al-Kaylani and Mufti of Jerusalem Hajj Amin al-HUSAYNI, declining invitations to go to Germany.

Returning to an independent Syria after the war, he was minister of education in two NATIONAL PARTY cabinets in 1946 and 1947 and was elected to parliament from al-Jawlan in 1947. He was a member of the Syrian delegation to the London roundtable on Palestine in 1946/47. He was a member and, after April 19, 1948, chief of Syria's United Nations delegation, but he resigned on October 20, blaming the Syrian government for the Arab defeat in Palestine (Israel had declared independence in May 1948 and was fighting off invading Arab forces to remain a new state). In the volatile condition of Syrian politics, in December 1948 he twice failed to form a cabinet. Colonel Husni al-ZA'IM turned to him immediately after the coup of March 30, 1949, and made him his chief political aide. He served as foreign minister from April 16 to June 26, 1949. After Za'im's fall, Arslan was minister in Turkey from late 1949 to early 1952. He died at his home in Beirut on January 23, 1954. He was a writer and a poet, but his only books were *Dhikrayat al-Amir Adil Arslan an Husni al-Za'im* (Emir Adil Arslan's Recollections concerning Husni al-Za'im) (Beirut, 1962) and *Mudhakkirat al-Amir Adil Arslan* (Memories of Emir Adil Arslan), edited by Yusuf Ibbish, in three volumes (Beirut, 1983).

BIBLIOGRAPHY

CLEVELAND, WILLIAM L. *Islam against the West: Shakib Arslan and the Campaign for Islamic Nationalism.* Austin, Tex., 1985.

HIRSZOWICZ, LUKASZ. *The Third Reich and the Arab East.* London, 1966.

KHOURY, PHILIP S. *Syria and the French Mandate: The Politics of Arab Nationalism.* Princeton, N.J., 1987.

SEALE, PATRICK. *The Struggle for Syria: A Study of Post War Arab Politics, 1945–1958.* London, New York, and Toronto, 1965.

C. Ernest Dawn

Arslan, Faysal

Lebanese politician.

Arslan (also Arsalan) is the son of the influential Yazbaki DRUZE leader Majid ARSLAN, whose death in 1991 triggered a battle for the succession between Faysal and his half brother Talal. They claimed to represent two different political lines. Faysal made a critical mistake in the late 1970s when he aligned himself with Bashir JUMAYYIL and the LEBANESE FORCES, assuming that Jumayyil would become president. Indeed, Jumayyil had intended to appoint Faysal as a minister but was assassinated in 1982. The war of the mountains in 1983/84 discredited Faysal, and he no longer has influence within the Druze community. His half brother Talal assumed the mantle of leadership in the family, backed by his mother, Khawla.

As'ad AbuKhalil

Arslan, Majid   [1915–1991]

Lebanese politician.

Arslan was born in Shuwayfat. Uneducated and unsophisticated, he owed the success of his political career to his unwavering loyalty to the MARONITE political establishment. He served continuously in Lebanon's parliament from 1937 until his death. His election was almost automatic by virtue of his leadership of the Yazbaki confederation within the DRUZE community. After independence, he tied his political fortunes to Camille Chamoun. Lebanon, under the influence of the Maronite establishment, supported Arslan as an alternative to Kamal JUMBLATT.

Arslan is hailed as a hero of the "struggle for Lebanese independence," although his role is more myth than reality. He claimed to have served valiantly in the ARAB–ISRAEL WAR (1948), but no evidence exists to support his claims. He was a member of most cabinets after independence, mainly as minister of defense. His last wife, Khawla Arslan, became an influential politician in her own right and assumed the leadership of the family when her husband was incapacitated by age.

As'ad AbuKhalil

Arslan, Shakib   [1869–1946]

Lebanese poet, journalist, and political activist.

Shakib Arslan was a DRUZE notable from the Shuf region of Lebanon. He was dedicated to the preservation of the Ottoman Empire and to the social order of Islam. Between World War I and II, he became an anti-imperial activist and a relentless campaigner for the cause of Islamic solidarity. His voluminous writings, his well-connected network of associates, and his knack for attracting publicity made him one of the most visible Arab figures of this era.

The Arslans were a powerful Druze family whose members had the right to bear the title of emir (roughly equivalent to prince). Shakib's somewhat eclectic education—he studied at both the Maronite College and the Ottoman government school in Beirut—was designed to prepare him to carry on the family tradition of political leadership in changing times; however, his primary interest as a young man was literature. He published his first volume of poetry at seventeen and continued to engage in literary pursuits for the next several years, earning for himself the honorific title "the prince of eloquence," by which he was known throughout his life. Eventually, he assumed the role expected of an Arslan emir by serving as *qa'immaqam* of the Shuf—in 1902 and from 1908 to 1911. He was elected to the Ottoman parliament in 1914 and spent the years of World War I defending the Ottoman cause—to hold the empire together. He disavowed the Arab Revolt of 1916, branded its leader Sharif HUSAYN IBN ALI a traitor to Islam, and predicted that an Allied victory would lead to the division and occupation of the Arab provinces by the forces of European imperialism.

When this prediction was realized, Arslan became an exile, barred by British and French authorities from entering the Arab states that came under their control through League of Nations mandates. Instead of being marginalized by his changed circumstances, Arslan emerged as an international figure during the period between the world wars. His residence in Geneva, Switzerland, served as a gathering point for Arab and Muslim activists, and his position as the unofficial representative of the Syro-Palestinian delegation to the League of Nations afforded him opportunities to present the Arab case to the European community. His influence was expanded through the journal *La Nation Arabe* (1930–1938), which he founded and edited with Ihsan al-JABIRI. *La Nation Arabe* attacked all aspects of European imperialism but devoted special attention to French policies in the Maghreb (North Africa) and to ZIONISM in Palestine.

Notwithstanding his Druze origins, Arslan made his reputation as a staunch defender of mainstream SUNNI ISLAM. He contributed frequent articles to such Islamic-oriented Egyptian journals as *al-Shura* and *al-Fath*; wrote biographies of his friends Rashid Rida and Ahmad Shawqi; compiled a history of Arab rule in Spain; and authored other books on Islamic subjects. The purpose of his writing was to awaken among Muslims an awareness of their shared Islamic heritage and to summon them to action in the name of Islamic unity against the Western occupation. He believed in the primacy of an Islamic-inspired social order, and his interwar writings refuted all who challenged that belief, from the Egyptian liberal nationalists to Mustafa Kemal ATATÜRK, the founding president of the new secular Republic of Turkey.

More than any other figure of the era, Arslan endeavored to bring together the leaders of the North African and eastern Arab independence movements. He played an especially important role as political strategist and personal mentor to the group of young Moroccans associated with the Free School movement, and his orchestration of their international Islamic propaganda campaign against the French decree known as the Berber DAHIR (1930) was certainly one of the most successful Arab protest movements of this period.

Arslan's final reputation was diminished by his World War II association with the Axis powers; at the peak of his popularity, he endeavored to coordinate an Italo-German alliance with the Arab world in order to generate leverage against Britain and France. His pro-Axis stance during the war served to discredit him, and his death in Beirut in 1946 attracted little notice.

BIBLIOGRAPHY

ARSLAN, SHAKIB. *Our Decline and Its Causes*, by M. S. Shakoor, Lahore, Pakistan, 1962.
CLEVELAND, WILLIAM L. *Islam Against the West: Shakib Arslan and the Campaign for Islamic Nationalism.* Austin, Tex., 1985.

William L. Cleveland

Arslan Family

One of the two most important Druze families in Lebanon.

The Arslan family, in the Druze community for centuries, are now in competition with the JUMBLATT FAMILY to retain that position. Druze in Lebanon have historically been divided into Yazbakis and Jumblatts, and the Arslan family heads the Yazbaki confederation. Its head is now Emir Talal Arslan, who inherited the position from his father, Majid.

As'ad AbuKhalil

Arsuzi, Zaki al-   [1900–1968]

Alawite Syrian Islamic pan-Arab intellectual and political activist; a founder of the Ba'th party.

Zaki al-Arsuzi was born in Latakia (north Syria) in or around 1900. His father, Muhammad Najib al-Arsuzi, originally from the Alexandretta district, was an Alawite Islamic landowner and the leading attorney for his coreligionists. Within the Ottoman Empire, his vehemence in the courtroom resulted in a transfer to Antioch (Turkey), and during World War I, the Ottomans banished him to Konya (Turkey). He is commonly said to have been of middling circumstances, but his official biography states that the family's material wealth in Alexandretta was great. Zaki attended the primary school in Antioch and completed his secondary education in Konya. He studied at the French lay mission school in Beirut (Lebanon) after World War I and the demise of the Ottoman Empire. He taught mathematics in the secondary school at Antioch, 1920/21, was director of the Arsuz nahiya (county), 1924/25, and served as secretary of the department of education, 1926/27. After studying philosophy in Paris from 1927 to 1930, he taught philosophy and history in the secondary schools, briefly in Antioch, and then in Aleppo and Deir-ez-Zor from 1930 to 1934. He built up a following among his students, in whom he instilled pan-Arabism, including the need for Arab resurrection (*ba'th*). He was an early member of the League of National Action (Asaba al-Amal al-Qawmi). He resigned or was forced out of his post in 1934 and returned to Antioch, where he was head of the Alexandretta province branch of the league. From 1936, his campaign to keep Alexandretta a part of Syria became violent and resulted in his expulsion in late 1938. He continued his protests from Damascus, but he broke with the league as well as the National Bloc. An agreement with Michel AFLAQ, Salah al-Din al-BITAR, and three others to form a political party was fruitless, as was his own effort to organize a party that he called the Arab Nationalist Party (al-Hizb al-Qawmi al-Arabi). After experiencing disappointment as a teacher in Baghdad during 1939/40, he resided in Damascus without employment, living with a group of students, fellow refugees from Alexandretta, but he continued to attract students from throughout Syria.

On November 29, 1940, he and six students formed al-Ba'th al-Arabi (which later became the ruling BA'TH party). The peak membership was twelve within the university, with a few more from the high school. Meanwhile, a similar group, calling itself at different times al-Ihya al-Arabi or al-Ba'th al-Arabi, gathered around Aflaq and Bitar. Most members of Arsuzi's group were students of Aflaq and Bitar, and members of their group frequently visited Arsuzi, but there was rivalry. Arsuzi disliked Aflaq intensely. Arsuzi was undeniably the more prominent. He had presided over the most successful branch of the League of National Action and won the acclaim of nationalist students throughout Syria. The head of the Italian Armistice Commission in Syria sought a meeting, but Arsuzi declined because he thought the British were about to occupy Syria. On similar grounds of military realism, he opposed Rashid Ali al-Kaylani's action in Iraq; his position was unpopular. Arsuzi, became progressively unwilling to brook dissent; he was biting and sarcastic in his sessions with followers and opponents. His followers diminished, while Aflaq's group grew. The group dwindled, then broke up in 1944. In the same year, Arsuzi moved first to Latakia, then to Tartus, a Syrian coastal town. The members of his group, led by Wahib GHANIM, joined the Aflaq–Bitar organization in 1945/1946, but Arsuzi refused urgings to reenter politics. Accepting a teaching appointment secured through the intercession of his followers, he taught in Hama (1945–1948), Aleppo (1948–1952), and at the Dar al-Mu'allimin al-Ibtida'iyya in Damascus until retirement in 1959. He published books and articles on cultural and philosophical subjects and Arab nationalism and gave frequent lectures to army units. In the 1960s, as Alawite officers increased their influence in the Ba'th party and Syrian government, Arsuzi's reputation and influence rose as Aflaq's position declined.

Arsuzi died in Damascus on July 2, 1968. His collected works were published in six volumes by the Political Administration of the Army and the Armed Forces (*al-Mu'allafat al-Kamila*, Damascus, 1972–1976). His writings have received little attention in the published scholarship of Western languages, but his concept of the Arab nation, its mission, predicament, and future, is close to that of other writers of the 1920s and 1930s. His use of the Islamic theological term *ba'th* was not unprecedented, but he gave it unusual emphasis.

BIBLIOGRAPHY

DEVLIN, JOHN F. *The Ba'th Party: A History from Its Origins to 1966.* Stanford, Calif., 1976.
OLSON, ROBERT W. *The Ba'th and Syria: The Evolution of Ideology, Party and State, from the French Mandate to the Era of Hafiz al-Asad.* Princeton, N.J., 1982.
RABINOVICH, ITAMAR. *Syria under the Ba'th, 1963–66: The Army–Party Symbiosis.* Jerusalem, 1972.

C. Ernest Dawn

Art

[*This entry includes the following articles:* An Overview; Arab Art; Iranian Art; Israeli Art; and Ottoman and Turkish Art.]

An Overview

In the Middle East today, due to the homogeneity of national populations, the deep social embeddedness of traditional art forms, the tenuous relationship between figural art and Islamic theology, the powerful example (if not outright influence) of the West, and the great interest of governments in visual art as an expression of political ideologies, painting, sculpture, architecture, and traditional applied arts have more than a relatively marginal status. Historical art and contemporary art together help to define the concept of nationhood or of religious identity, and thus, art is deemed important not only as a means of establishing national identity and cultural accomplishment, but also as a definition of social and religious standing.

Since 1800, art has existed in an atmosphere bounded, on the one hand, by the glorious accomplishments of the past, which are seen not only as aesthetic creations but also as emblems of a time when Middle Eastern countries were at the height of their political, economic, and cultural development, and, on the other hand, by the media and styles of Western art, which by the end of the twentieth century had become a secular, industrial world culture that respected neither political or cultural boundaries. But it is a mistake to characterize the resultant blending of cultures in the Middle East simply as the degraded by-product of Western cultural imperialism; moreover, the entire issue is further complicated by the Western notion of the strict separation and hierarchical ranking of the socially embedded and often humble "traditional" or "applied" arts—which reached their zenith under the powerful Islamic polities of the past—and the more highly regarded upper-class "fine arts" of easel painting and sculpture, essentially public artistic forms, that were virtually unknown in traditional Islamic societies.

Further complicating the issue is the schizophrenic attitude of traditional Islamic civilization toward *taswir*—representational painting—which forms the central focus of most Western art. Condemned as potentially idolatrous by traditional theologians, works of art depicting people and animals nevertheless flourished from earliest Islamic times under royal patronage. The efforts of some modern theological commentators to reinterpret or eliminate the theological ban on taswir by a revisionist view of the important HADITH on the subject, although intellectually creative, seem unlikely to have a profound effect on the acceptance of such art. Far more important in this regard is the influence of television, film, and advertising, which provide public images that are highly figural, pervasive, and popular. Representational images, once the private preserve of the royal court, are today avidly followed by the broad public in most Islamic countries, Wahhabi Saudi Arabia being somewhat of an exception. In Iran, where there has been strict censorship of public art by the clerical regime, there also has been a widespread use of political images, and the Ayatollah Khomeini's austere visage appeared on public posters with the same frequency as had the face of the secularist shah under the Pahlavi regime. Thus the theological issue of images is, to say the least, highly confused.

Artistic Responses. The artistic, as opposed to the ideological, response to this charged atmosphere has been very interesting. Since the seventeenth century, as European prints became known in the Middle East, techniques such as modeling and linear perspective have had an impact on Islamic painting, but the perceived "decline" of Islamic painting after 1700 is primarily the result of the changing economics of patronage rather than of "corruption" imported from the West. Painting with oils on large

canvases or panels led to genres once deemed unfortunate anomalies; some of these, such as the nineteenth-century Qajar oil paintings, are now recognized as bold innovations within the Iranian painting tradition. To be sure, some imports from the West proved disastrous—for example, the use of aniline industrial dyestuffs in carpet weaving in the second half of the nineteenth century resulted in fading, running colors that diminished the status of the carpets. The development among Islamic elites of a taste for European artistic media, which undermined local patronage and set local norms of taste, was a far more significant factor in the perceived decline of Islamic art in the late nineteenth and early twentieth centuries than was any direct influence of Western artistic techniques or styles.

Whether real or perceived, whether pernicious or provocative, in the twentieth century the "decline" of Islamic art and the confrontation with the West have provoked significant attempts within the Islamic world to establish an Islamic aesthetic theory, some of the most original interpretations of the history of Islamic art, and some of the most important developments in art. For example, calligraphy, the most distinctive, pervasive, and religiously embedded Islamic art form, has, due to the printing press, declined in the traditional media of pen upon paper, yet has found expression in a host of "new" media, from oil on canvas and silk-screened prints to neon-filled glass tubing and composite polymer materials. The popularity of Islamic rugs among Western collectors has led not only to a flourishing (and expensive) market that has sucked many of the best old pieces out of the Middle East and into European collections, but also to an important renaissance in production of traditionally dyed carpets in Turkey, Iran, and Afghanistan, and a new sense of pride in this popular art form. Western architectural technology, especially the use of reinforced concrete, not only has blighted the Middle East with high-rise urban slums and shiny but egregiously foreign hotels and corporate buildings; it also has allowed a return to characteristic Islamic forms—arches, molded arabesque surfaces, expressive sculptural masses—that is helping in the rebirth of Islamic architecture.

History, Criticism, Theory. The East–West dialectic has provoked an examination of the conceptual basis of Islamic art by critics and historians in the Middle East. Former Egyptian minister of culture Sarwat Okasha and the expatriate Iranian academician Seyyed Hossein Nasr, among others, have written on the essential meaning and conceptual uniqueness of Islamic art, which they see as focused on multiple levels of meaning and on an overall adherence to the central religious principle of *tawhid* (unity or oneness). Perhaps the most important factors in the disappearance of the Islamic artistic inferiority complex have been the work of art historians in the discovery and study of Islamic works of art, the gradual emergence of the Islamic artist from historical anonymity, and the growing awareness of the importance that Islamic art has had for European artists. By the time Edward Said's *Orientalism* was published in 1978, Islamic art had largely overcome most of the pejorative stereotypes and simplistic judgments passed upon it, and was an increasing source of pride to Muslims.

The uses of the artistic past are highly complex and differ from place to place. The vast expenditures of Soviet governments on restoration of Islamic monuments in Central Asia may be cynically viewed as a sop to nationalist sentiments, but the insights gained into techniques of architectural decoration and traditional construction were significant. The same judgment may be rendered for the policy of restoring royal monuments in Iran under the shah, or of King Hassan's subsidies of traditional crafts in Morocco, or of the tremendous efforts in historic preservation made in the Republic of Turkey. Whatever contemporary political agendas these may serve, they have established in the public consciousness a respect for the visual arts of the past and, by implication, a respect for the arts in the present day.

Contemporary Problems and Solutions. This does not mean that the twentieth century has not seen profound losses both in artistic freedom and in examples from the artistic heritage. As described by Samir al-Khalili in *The Monument*, the vibrant Iraqi art that had flourished in the earlier years of the Ba'thist regime declined under dictatorship into a kind of tasteless political parody of itself. Among the key demands of Islamic revivalists in many Middle Eastern countries have been the removal of figural sculptural monuments, the elimination of life drawing and nude figural studies from art school curricula, and adherence to other standards of "Islamic modesty" in the subject matter of works of art. Under the banner of "progress," the old quarters of Jidda are gone, obliterated forever or sanitized beyond recognition; religious fanaticism claimed the famous wooden pulpit (*minbar*) given by Saladin to the Aqsa Mosque in Jerusalem and threatens the Dome of the Rock; secular fanaticism resulted in the destruction by bombing of the Great Mosque of Hama and serious damage to Shi'ite shrines in southern Iraq. The artistic losses resulting from the destruction of Islamic monuments in Bosnia have been as heartbreaking as they are senseless.

Governmental responses to the issue of traditional art, with its implications for tourism and the economy, vary around the Islamic world. In Morocco the *ensembles artisanales* serve as training grounds for artists and as a government-sponsored system of marketing traditional crafts to tourists. In Kuwait the organization al-Sadu, formed by younger members of the political elite, seeks to study and preserve the artistic heritage of the country's tribal groups. Through Marmara University, Turkey's government has funded the DOBAG cooperatives, which have spearheaded the remarkable revival of traditional wool dyeing and carpet weaving.

Painting and sculpture are in a considerably more tenuous and ambiguous position in most Islamic countries, because they are largely nurtured in academic institutions and sustained by Western-oriented elites or, in the case of sculpture, by authoritarian regimes in search of legitimizing monuments. In Turkey, public sculptural monuments are highly symbolic of the secularist revolution of Atatürk; thus bronze statues of Atatürk have long been the target of vandalism by Islamic extremists. The taste for public commemorative monuments fostered by colonial or Western-oriented regimes often has transferred with a vengeance to their revolutionary successors, regardless of ideology; the large-scale public monuments to the revolution and to the losses of the Iran–Iraq War erected in Iran are of a piece with the examples of gigantism and new-Babylonianism so devastatingly chronicled by Samir al-Khalili in his discussion of Saddam Hussein's Iraq.

Education and Popularization. A central issue confronting the arts in Islam is education and popularization, especially in the face of the engulfing world popular culture. Teaching children about their cultural past is a priority in many Middle Eastern countries; art museums often are placed under the Education Ministry (and sometimes under the Ministry of Tourism and Culture as well). Popular periodicals on both traditional and contemporary art are published in most Middle Eastern countries, and film and video are being explored as vehicles for art education. Publications specifically geared to Western audiences, most published in English, also have multiplied: these include *Mimar: Architecture in Development*, published by the Aga Khan Foundation; *Aramco World*, published by a U.S.–Saudi Arabia oil consortium; *Ilgi*, published in Turkey by the Shell Oil Company; and *Arts and the Islamic World*, published in London by the Islamic Arts Foundation. The World of Islam Festival, a major undertaking centered in Britain in 1976, was a highly successful series of museum exhibitions, films, performance events, and educational programs. The World of Islam Festival Trust has overseen the publication of many important volumes that bring a Muslim perspective to the discussion of Islamic art. Increasing travel to the Middle East has created a taste for Middle Eastern art among the public in the West, which in turn has nourished artistic traditions in Middle Eastern lands.

[*See also:* Architecture]

BIBLIOGRAPHY

BURCKHARDT, TITUS. *Art of Islam: Language and Meaning.* London, 1976.
CRITCHLOW, KEITH. *Islamic Patterns.* London, 1976.
NASR, SEYYED HOSSEIN. *Islamic Art and Spirituality.* Albany, N.Y., 1987.
OKASHA, SARWAT. *The Muslim Painter and the Divine.* London, 1981.

Walter Denny

Arab Art

Art in the Arabic-speaking world encompasses a broad range of cultural traditions and artistic ideologies.

Contemporary art is immensely complex in the contemporary Arabic–speaking world, which stretches from Morocco to Iraq and from Lebanon to Sudan, and in which both traditional and "modern" forms of artistic expression are important. There is a pan–Arab ideology of art, a general pride in the artistic accomplishments of the Arabs in the past that varies from vague cultural nostalgia to an acute and bitter sense of how far Arabs have fallen from their position of dominant artistic creativity and political accomplishment. At the same time, art also constitutes a major element of national identity, something that makes an individual nation distinctive within the broader Arabic–speaking world. Under both the broader and the more restricted definitions of what constitutes "Arab art," there are traditional and modern art forms; in many respects, focusing on the former serves the nationalist agenda, whereas it is only minimally possible to make characterizations about the latter that adequately cover the broad expanse of the "Arab world."

Interest in the art of the Arab past takes several forms. In nineteenth-century Egypt and Syria, perhaps influenced by similar developments in Europe, groups of artisans attempted, with governmental backing, to re-create the greatest Islamic forms of the past by making what amounted to high-quality reproductions of famous early works of art, especially of Mamluk metalwork. Other such artistic revivals were undertaken by Europeans under colonial gov-

ernments; for example, in the late nineteenth century a member of the French Parvillée family founded a school in Marrakech that taught local youths "Islamic" crafts reflecting the Ottoman style. Since 1955, Morocco has undertaken the most ambitious governmental support of the arts anywhere in the Arab world, through extensive royal, governmental, and private patronage; through the establishment of schools and marketing centers for traditional crafts; and through laws and building codes requiring use of traditional crafts in public buildings. Today traditional arts are supported by governments to varying degrees, and for a variety of reasons, from national pride to promotion of tourism, in most Arabic-speaking countries.

Throughout the Arab world, the earlier twentieth century saw the introduction of formal artistic education, usually as the result of colonial innovation or the wish of local regimes to imitate European practices, but the only major institution on the university level until after World War II was the Academy of Fine Arts in Cairo, founded in 1908. Since the 1950s, this situation has changed explosively and dramatically. National museums and galleries throughout the Arab world regularly exhibit the works of artists who combine nontraditional media, such as painting with oil or acrylic pigments, or various printmaking techniques, with styles that reveal a wide range of inspiration, local traditions often being prominent among them. Even such small polities as the Gulf states have new art museums, ranging from the National Museum of Kuwait (housing one of the great new collections of historical Islamic art, that of Shaykh Nasir and Shaykha Hussa al-Sabah) to the small National Museum of Qatar, remodeled from an old palace structure. Art classes are a part of secondary and even primary curricula throughout the Arab world, and most countries now have art schools attached to national universities; private associations, such as the Bahrain Art Society, founded in 1983, support the practice of art and influence art education. Neotraditionalist experiments in art education include that of Ramses Wissa Wassef, who founded a school in Cairo after World War II to teach village children the art of weaving. Moved to Harraniya, near Giza, in 1952, this institution influences similar programs throughout the Arab world.

Art in today's Arab world often reflects the changing political climate, but just as often has managed to flourish despite political impediments. In the early 1950s in Iraq, artists such as the painters Fa'iq Hassan and Shakir Hassan, and the sculptor and painter Jawad SALIM, helped to found associations promoting modern art that have continued to influence art in Iraq through changes in regime and official ideology.

Other artists have pursued careers in London and Paris; the Lebanese painter Shafiq Abboud has gained distinction in Paris; the Palestinian painter Kamal Boullata, whose work incorporates traditional Islamic calligraphic themes, has achieved considerable artistic success outside the Middle East.

In recent decades, opportunities to encounter Arab art both in the Middle East and elsewhere have increased markedly. Institutions such as the Institut du Monde Arabe in Paris and Al al-Bayt foundation in Amman, regularly schedule exhibitions of contemporary as well as of traditional and historic Arab art, and journals such as *Arts and the Islamic World* (published in London by the Islamic Arts Foundation), *Aramco World* (published in Houston, Texas, by Saudi Aramco), and *Ur: The International Magazine of Arab Culture* (formerly published in London by the Iraqi Cultural Center) have helped establish an international audience for talented Arab artists.

BIBLIOGRAPHY

The three magazines mentioned above provide a wealth of information in individual articles; a cumulative index to *Aramco World*—46, no. 4 (July–August 1995)—is useful for finding articles published therein on individual artists, exhibitions, and institutions.

Walter Denny

Iranian Art

Iranian art has drawn inspiration from its traditions and cultural heritage.

Nineteenth-century Iranian art was rooted in the styles and crafts of earlier centuries. Painted pen boxes and enameled cups and vases of the Qajar period continued eighteenth-century forms but exhibited a taste for floral ornamentation and sentimental compositions, often featuring figures in clothing influenced by Europe. Though miniature painting and ornamentation of manuscripts continued, easel painting became the most important medium. Qajar court painters, continuing the late Safavid (early eighteenth century) style of Mohammad Zaman and his son, showed a zest for large compositions and royal portraiture. These large oils, echoing Western models, featured flat, brilliantly colored shapes, detailed ornamentation of jewelry and clothing, and static poses. In addition, artists began to paint landscapes in the backgrounds of their compositions and to experiment with perspective and shading.

Fath Ali Shah named Mirza Baba, a native of Isfahan, as the Qajars' first "chief painter" (*naqqashbashi*). His latest known work is dated 1810. A prominent rival, Mehr Ali, who was working as late as 1829, excelled in monumental portraits of the ruler and did murals for palaces. Both men also executed paintings in a new under-glass technique, but few such works have survived. One outstanding painter in the distinctive Qajar style during the reign of Fath Ali Shah's successor, Mohammad Shah, signed his works with the name Ahmad. He was probably a student of Mehr Ali. He was surpassed by another of Mehr Ali's students, Abu al-Hasan Khan Ghaffari, known by his honorific Sani al-Molk, who worked until around 1866. He was director of the painting department of the Dar al-Fonun school, founded by Naser al-Din Shah to promote European knowledge. Naser al-Din was also a photography enthusiast and established a school to popularize that medium.

The most eminent graduate of the painting department of the Dar al-Fonun, and the dominant figure of the late Qajar period, was Sani al-Molk's nephew Mohammad Ghaffari, who received the honorific title Kamal al-Molk in 1892. His work, entirely European in manner, belonged to the Orientalist school of academic painting. Excelling in both portraits and genre scenes, Kamal al-Molk used photographic detail in capturing scenes from everyday Iranian life. He also started an art school, the Madrasa-ye Sanae-ye Mostadrafa, after returning from Europe in 1911. Kamal al-Molk's academic realist style dominated Iranian painting even after his death in 1940.

Though some miniature painting continued to be done and a few artists worked in an Impressionist style, most of the innovations sweeping Europe in the first half of the century had no counterpart in Iran until the 1950s. Then, as art students returned from Europe, a rush began to exploit every style at once. The first Tehran Biennale (1958) featured forty-nine artists, many of them oriented toward cubism. Two years later, abstractionism made a notable appearance. Only in 1962, at the third Biennale, did a style appear that seemed to have a national rather than a European base. The critic Karim Emami dubbed it the *saqqakhaneh* school.

A *saqqakhaneh* is a fountain or cistern common in villages and older urban neighborhoods. To commemorate the thirst suffered by the martyred third imam, Husayn ibn Ali, and his family in 681, pious Shi'ites burn candles at night in the *saqqakhaneh* enclosure, display black or green flags, or embellish it with calligraphy and folk decoration. This type of pious folk art was brought to mind by the 1962 "calligraphic" paintings of Hoseyn Zendarudi (b. 1927). He had evolved his style, a complex interlacing of thousands of word fragments, after earlier painting geometric iconographic canvases. Many of the artists associated with the *saqqakhaneh* were, like Zendarudi, graduates of Tehran's School of Decorative Arts, an institution established in 1961 that was not burdened by the stylistic legacy of Kamal al-Molk. Others included Nasser Ovissi (b. 1934), an artist–diplomat who relied heavily on historical motifs and ceramics as well as calligraphy, often drawing on the works of classical Persian poets.

Another group of artists in this period were the Nature Artists. One prominent member of this school was Sohrab SEPEHRI (1928–1980), whose painting and poetry reflected his interest in East Asian art and culture. After graduating from Tehran University's School of Fine Arts, he studied in Paris and Tokyo. His landscapes were done in a spare, semi-abstract style reminiscent of Zen wash drawings.

The fifth and last Tehran Biennale was held in 1966. The number of Iranian artists was reduced to 37 from the previous exhibit's 113 to allow participation by artists from Turkey and Pakistan. In the 1970s an increasing number of galleries and private collectors supported a thriving art community, and in 1976 the Museum of Contemporary Art opened in Tehran. After the Iranian Revolution of 1979, most modern artists left the country or stayed but found few opportunities for exhibits and sales. Though most private galleries closed, the Museum of Contemporary Art mounted exhibits featuring themes of revolution and martyrdom. Calligraphy has continued to flourish as an art, and the government has sought to preserve and restore many older crafts.

BIBLIOGRAPHY

CANBY, SHEILA. *Persian Painting.* New York, 1993.
EMAMI, KARIM. "Art in Iran XI. Post–Qajar." In *Encyclopaedia Iranica,* vol. 2, pp. 640–646.
———. "Introduction." In *Modern Persian Painting.* New York, 1968.
ETTINGHAUSEN, RICHARD, and EHSAN YARSHATER, eds. *Highlights of Persian Art.* Los Angeles, 1979.
SCARCE, JENNIFER M., and BASIL W. ROBINSON. "Art in Iran X. 1–2 Qajar." In *Encyclopaedia Iranica,* vol. 2, pp. 627–640.

Nasser Ovissi

Israeli Art

Israeli art is a dialogue between expressive polarities: religious and secular, regional and universal, ideological and personal.

Though Israel was established in 1948, Israeli art traces its origins to the Yishuv's early days at the turn of the twentieth century and to the Bezalel Art Institute founded in 1906 in Jerusalem. From the beginning, there was a connection between the cultural traditions of the Jewish people and the notion of art as a conduit for education; together these two factors contributed to national self-awareness and fulfillment.

At the fifth Zionist congress, held in Basel in 1901, the philosopher Martin Buber stated that Jewish art should be based on the traditions of the Jewish people and their language, customs, folk culture, and religious rituals. Ahad Ha'am, another proponent of the idea of art as integral to the Zionist program, claimed that culture was nationality as defined by its adherents. Both Buber and Ha'am influenced the founding ideology of Bezalel and its efforts to create a modern form of art intrinsic to the Yishuv.

By the 1920s artists active in the Yishuv were questioning this perspective. Hence, the visionary elements of the original program were giving way to pragmatic, concrete challenges. The new movement, based in Tel Aviv and comprising young artists with contemporary priorities, was successfully challenging Jerusalem's status as the center of artistic production. To these rebels, traditional expressions of Judaic arts and crafts did not fit in with their vision of a reborn society, emancipated from its exilic heritage. They also aptly criticized early indigenous Zionist creative efforts for being neglectful of contemporary European trends in the fine arts, since Bezalel's emphasis ignored those developments.

Thus, the emergence of Tel Aviv as a new—and second—center of Israeli art marked a turning point. Henceforth, inspiration from contemporary European movements would be integrated with regional characteristics: the landscape—its colors, shapes, lights—and scenes of daily labor. Local art would reflect local idealism. Israeli art would incorporate a multiplicity of expressions rather than a single approach. Tel Aviv artists found in European expressionism and in the work of Henri Rousseau and Georges Rouault their dominant inspiration. Indeed, by the 1930s the Jewish expressionist school in Paris influenced Tel Aviv artists while German expressionists affected those in Jerusalem.

The period of World War II and the first Arab-Israel War of 1948 saw the development of "Canaanite" art, which dealt essentially with the roots of Israeli art. Yishuv artists had come to resent the excessive influence of Europe. The failure of European liberalism, the advent of Nazism, and the struggle for survival and national independence were clearly having an impact on the creative perspective of Israeli artists. Decisively rejecting the Diaspora, their vision encompassed an independent state whose sociocultural parameters would be the civilizations of the Nile and the Euphrates.

After 1948 a new group called *Ofakin Hadashim* (new horizons) took up abstract painting in an expressive mode combining American and European practices with Israeli nuances. Proponents of this movement were united by a vision rather than a style of abstraction. Two major trends emerged in subsequent Israeli art and lasted well into the late 1960s: the lyrical abstract and the geometric abstract. The former fused Western techniques of expressionism with vibrant Israeli colors; the latter stressed form and line. Moreover, the lyricists addressed landscape; the geometrists emphasized historical legacies and national symbols, which politicized their work.

The perennial dichotomy between Jewish art and Israeli art—the universalist and the indigenous, the representational and the abstract—continues to permeate the artistic creativity of Israel.

BIBLIOGRAPHY

Balas, Gila. *New Horizons.* Tel Aviv, 1980. In Hebrew.
Omar, Mordechai. *Essays on Israeli Art.* Jerusalem, 1992. In Hebrew.
Goodman, S., ed. *Artists of Israel: 1920–1980.* New York, 1981.

Tsilit Ben-Nevat

Ottoman and Turkish Art

Turkish art reflects both its Ottoman past and the influx of new ideas.

The normative view of Ottoman Turkish art from 1800 to the end of the empire in 1921 sees it as under the influence of Europe and exemplifying a decline from the vigor and purity of the sixteenth-century Ottoman "classical" style. There is indisputable evidence of the influence of the West: "modern" Turkish painting began in the 1830s when the Ministry of War sent military officers to Paris to study the "scientific" method of linear perspective. The Balyan family, which from 1822 provided the sultans with three generations of royal architects, promoted a Europeanized style in the decorative arts. Royal porcelain and silk-weaving establishments at Yıldız (founded by Abdülhamit II in 1890) and Hereke (founded by Abdülmecit I in 1843), and the crystal and glass establishments at Şubuklu (founded by royal decree in 1847) and Beykoz (founded around 1795; purchased by Sultan Abdülmecit I in 1846), not only continued the Ottoman tradition of *ehl-i hiref* (salaried royal artisanry) but also can be seen as a response to such European institutions as the Sèvres and Gobelins factories. Moreover, European architects (Montani) and restorers of historical monuments (Parvillée) were given broad authority over parts of the Ottoman cultural past; and the influential bureaucrat, museum director, and painter Osman Hamdi, who helped to found Turkey's first modern art school, the Sanayi-yi Nefise Mektebi (1910), was a European-trained Ottoman of markedly secularist persuasions who apparently both loved and despised his native culture.

Nineteenth-Century Developments. Despite European cultural influence and Europeanized taste, economic decline, and the devastating effect of industrialization on traditional arts such as textiles, one might argue that the nineteenth century was in many respects a time of remarkable artistic ferment and creativity in the Ottoman Empire. The art of calligraphy, for example, flourished; and important masters, such as Mustafa Rakim (1757–1826) and Mehmed Şefik Bey (1819–1880), were innovators in this most respected and religiously embedded of Islamic art forms. Before imported aniline dyestuffs and economic devastation affected Anatolian traditional rug-weaving areas, nineteenth-century Turkish weavers in villages and encampments produced pile carpets and kilims that are highly prized as major works of art. In urban centers, traditional Ottoman arts from miniature painting to embroidery were not submerged by the industrial and Western tides but often met these two challenges with fresh artistic ideas and ingenious adaptations. Because nineteenth-century Ottomans had lost a clear view of the classical past, they were denied some of the benefits of its inspiration and spared its oppressive weight on their creative impulses. Late Ottoman domestic embroideries, the glass of Beykoz, the local ceramics of Şanakkale, and Anatolian copper and brassware are increasingly regarded as significant artistic accomplishments. The first governmental antiquities collection was begun as early as 1846 under the patronage of the vizir Damad Fethi Pasha; the first museum of Islamic art, containing objects under the control of the Directorate of Pious Foundations, was founded in Constantinople (now Istanbul) in 1914. It can easily be argued that the last twelve decades of Ottoman rule saw profound and important changes in the arts that influenced the art of the Republic of Turkey throughout the twentieth century.

Art in the Early Republic. The Atatürk revolution in Turkey affected the visual arts in the same profound manner as it did other sectors of public cultural life. For Atatürk, the artistic traditions of the West were hugely symbolic; the creation of large public sculptural monuments and the establishment of the Museum of Painting and Sculpture in Istanbul were essential didactic elements of his revolution, and painting and sculpture epitomized the civilization he sought to emulate and were the ultimate symbol of his disdain for conservative aspects of traditional Islam. The figural sculptures favored by the government as political monuments (and as a sort of cultural shock therapy) are still a feature of Turkish public art, perhaps best typified by the cast bronze neo–Baroque monuments of Hüseyin Gezer. Today, public sculptures in Turkey reflect both the general familiarity with artistic developments in the West and the diversity and originality of Turkish artists, many of them graduates of art schools founded in the Atatürk years.

Unlike sculpture, an essentially public art form usually endowed with political meaning, and largely unknown in the late Ottoman Empire, easel painting in oils was flourishing in Turkey by the later nineteenth century. By 1923, artists such as Osman Hamdi, an accomplished painter who had studied under Gérome in Paris; Ahmet Ziya AKBULUT, the product of a military education; and Prince Abdülmecit, son of the last sultan and himself the last caliph, had laid the foundation on which postrevolutionary painting built. While the early days of the Republic produced quantities of political art centering on Atatürk's image and his political agenda, they also saw the emergence of the major figures in twentieth-century Turkish painting—Bedri Rahmi EYÜBOĞLU (1911–1975), Nurullah Berk (1906–1982), and Fikret Muallâ (1904–1969). These artists, who belonged to an association known as "Group D," were well versed in the new developments of painting in Europe, but also sought, through the use of Turkish imagery, to propagate a distinctively national style of painting.

Contemporary Developments. Following World War II, a virtual explosion of groups and styles in Turkish painting occurred, with many artists winning recognition outside the Republic. Turan Erol, Salih Acar, Adnan Turani, Leyla Gamsíz, and the self-taught İbrahim Balaban are among the artists whose work has molded the diverse directions of Turkish art by the end of the twentieth century. Existing side by side with the work of these "modern" artists since 1980, there has also been a return in Turkey to serious artistic endeavor in traditional media. The work of artists such as Niyazi Sayin and Feridun Özgören in *ebru* (paper-marbling); Faik Kırımlı, Ahmet Şahin, and Mehmet Gürsel in ceramics, and Belkis Balpınar in carpet design demonstrate the capacity of Turkish artists to work creatively within the matrix of the classical past as well as in respectful apposition to it.

Today the visual arts in Turkey are varied and vibrant; books and journals dealing with traditional and contemporary art are published frequently, and art is actively covered in the metropolitan press. Governmentally financed museums have been founded throughout the country, and since 1980 the private museum foundation—exemplified by the Sadberk Hanım Museum in Sariyer, near Istanbul—has made its institutional debut.

BIBLIOGRAPHY

ELIBAL, GÜLTEKIN. *Atatürk ve Resim-Heykel.* Istanbul, 1973.
GEZER, HÜSEYIN. *Cumhuriyet Dönemi Türk Heykeli.* Ankara, 1984.
GLASSIE, HENRY. *Turkish Traditional Art Today.* Bloomington, Ind., 1994.
PINAR, SALMAN, ed. *A History of Turkish Painting.* Seattle, Wash., 1988.

Walter Denny

Arya Mehr University

Iran's first institution of higher learning devoted to technical studies.

Arya Mehr Technical University, renamed after the Iranian Revolution of 1979 as Sharif Technical University, was founded in 1965 by Mohammad Reza PAHLAVI. It comprised, among others, a Faculty of Technology and Mechanics, Petroleum, and Petrochemicals. Its first president was Dr. Mojtahedi.

BIBLIOGRAPHY

AQELI, BAQER. *Ruz shomar-e tarikh-e Iran: Az mashruteh ta enqelab-e eslami* (A Chronology of Iranian History: From the Constitutional to the Islamic Revolutions). Tehran, 1993.

Neguin Yavari

As'ad, Ahmad

Leader of the influential Shi'ite family of Jabal Amil.

As'ad's family (also spelled al-As'ad), which was descended from the Saghir family of Jabal Amil, traces its origins to Arab tribes in southern Arabia. This large landowning family has monopolized the political representation of the Shi'ites of south Lebanon for centuries. Ahmad, the leader of the family in the first half of the twentieth century, was elected to parliament from 1937 to 1960; was briefly speaker of parliament; and served in several cabinets. His popularity in south Lebanon was so strong that his entire list of candidates was assured victory. People in south Lebanon joked that a stick would win a parliamentary seat if included on Ahmad al-As'ad's list. He and his son Kamil were both in the 1953, 1957, and 1960 parliaments. After Ahmad's death, his wife, known as Umm Kamil, shared political responsibilities with her son.

As'ad AbuKhalil

Asad, Hafiz al- [1930–]

Syrian air force officer and statesman, president of the Syrian Arab Republic since 1971.

Born in Qurdaha, near Latakia, Asad was the ninth of eleven children of Ali Sulayman, a peasant of Alawi origin whose strength, bravery, and chivalry made him a pillar of his village. Until his death in 1963, Ali carried on the family tradition of mediating quarrels and giving protection to the weak. Asad was one of a handful of boys in his village to receive formal education when the French opened primary schools in remote villages. From his father he acquired a lifelong determination not to submit when pressures mount.

This family legacy offers an important clue to Asad's proud and vigorous personality. While he was a student, Asad joined the BA'TH party and became one of its stalwarts in Latakia. After his graduation in 1951, he entered the flying school at Aleppo; he graduated as a pilot officer in 1955. He then plunged into the intrigues of the highly politicized and

Portrait of Hafiz al-Asad on Syrian postage stamp. (Richard Bulliet)

faction-ridden officer corps, and in 1959 he was chosen to go to Egypt for further military instruction.

Early in 1960, almost a year after his arrival in Cairo, Asad and four fellow officers who also had joined the Ba'th party through the Zaki al-ARSUZI stream, founded a secret organization they called the Military Committee. These young men had never admired the middle-class Damascene theorists of the Ba'th, Michel AFLAQ and Salah al-Din al-BITAR, who, they believed, had caused the party's demise by entering impulsively into an ill-fated union with Egypt on 1 February 1958. Egypt's president, Gamal Abdel Nasser, distrusted political parties, and as a condition for accepting union with Syria, he insisted on the dissolution of the Ba'th party.

Being Ba'thists who aspired to positions of dominance in Syrian public life, Asad and his colleagues in the Military Committee were very careful not to reveal the existence of their organization to Egyptian intelligence. Following the breakup of the Egypt–Syria union in September 1961, Asad became a low-paid clerk in the secessionist government of Lieut. Col. Abd al-Karim Nahlawi. He spent 1962 conspiring with his colleagues on the Military Committee to overthrow the secessionist government. In March 1963, he played a leading role in the coup that brought the Ba'th officers to power. Following the coup, Asad became commander of the air force, and in 1968 he was promoted to the rank of lieutenant general. From 1965, Asad was a member of the national (*qawmi*) and regional (*qutri*) Ba'th High Command.

During the seven years following the 1963 coup, Asad mastered the techniques of survival in the factional struggles that plagued Syria. Rejecting Aflaq and the social and economic order from which he came, Asad sided with the radical faction of Salah Jadid and Muhammad Umran, making in the process both lasting friendships and permanent enemies. Umran kept an eye on the government machine, Jadid ran the army, and Asad helped the Military Committee extend its networks in the armed forces by bringing every unit under its close control and by ensuring that Committee loyalists occupied the sensitive commands.

For ideological guidance, Asad sought the advice of Aflaq's early rival, the Alawite Zaki al-Arsuzi, who contributed editorials to the party and army press and provided Asad with insights until Arsuzi's death in 1968. In February 1966, following a bloody intraparty shootout, Asad secured the defense portfolio, thus moving very close to the top of the government. To get to the top, he had to neutralize or purge the leftist team of Jadid and the officers who supported it. Asad believed the radicalism of the

Jadid-led team caused Syria's isolation in the Arab world, and the army it tried to build was ill prepared to cope with Israel. In February 1969, Asad gained control of the government and party command, but agreed to keep some of his adversaries in positions of power. In November 1970, he seized full control, purging and dismissing his opponents and detaining their leaders, including President and Prime Minister Nur al-Din al-Atasi.

With Asad's advent to power, a new chapter in the domestic and foreign policies of Syria began to unfold. On the domestic front, Asad sought to establish his rule on a firm footing, primarily by building stable state institutions and by wooing the disenchanted social classes with measures of political and economic liberalization. He emphasized the need for reconciliation and national unity after the divisive years of the Jadid-led faction. To create a sense of a fresh start, Asad introduced a more liberal climate for writers and novelists, and set about courting former Ba'thists who had been generally out of favor with the previous regime. At the same time, however, Asad allowed no challenge to his rule. He ruthlessly suppressed the MUSLIM BROTHERHOOD and virtually eliminated its resistance during the Hama uprising of February 1982.

Asad also neutralized or put an end to the factional struggles within the army and the Ba'th party. The institutional pillars of his rule have been the army, a multilayered intelligence network, formal state structures, and revitalized party congresses. A People's Assembly appointed Asad president after nomination by the Ba'th command in 1971, and plebiscites have endorsed his reelection for seven-year terms, (the latest was held in December 1991).

In foreign policy, Asad called into question the radical orientation of his predecessors and the policies they pursued. Three stages of Syria's foreign policy in the Asad years can be identified. The first lasted from 1970 to 1974. During this stage, Asad moved quickly to improve relations with Egypt, which had been strained since the 1961 breakup of its union with Syria. He even joined the aborted federation of Egypt, Libya, and the Sudan. He also set about putting Syria's relations with Lebanon, Saudi Arabia, Tunisia, and Morocco on a friendly basis. To show good faith toward Saudi Arabia, he closed the Damascus-based anti-Saudi radio station.

Asad also moved very quickly to convince the Soviet Union that he was reliable, and that Syria would be a valuable regional partner. This entailed facilitating a stable Soviet presence in the region in order to curtail American influence. As for the United States, mutual hostility and mistrust kept the two countries diplomatically apart until 1990.

In the second stage, which lasted from 1974 to the end of the 1980s, there were three major alterations in Syria's foreign policy. The first was its revision of its strategy of alliance with Egypt; it now sought to isolate Egypt in the Arab world. The aim was to discredit Anwar al-Sadat and eliminate even the possibility of a Camp David kind of agreement between Israel and other Arab states, particularly Jordan and Lebanon. Thus, Asad tried to extend his influence over Jordan, Lebanon, and the Palestinians, and in 1983–84 he fought with colossal obstinacy to kill the Israel–Lebanon accord of May 17, 1983, which was brokered by U.S. Secretary of State George Shultz.

A second change concerned Asad's relations with the leader of Iraq, Saddam Hussein, who remains Asad's most implacable Arab adversary. Nonpersonal considerations notwithstanding, including the party schism and the geopolitical rivalry that divided the two countries, Asad swallowed his pride and went to Baghdad in 1978, following Egypt's entente with Israel. In June 1979 he again visited Iraq in an unsuccessful bid for a federation between the two countries. Suspecting that the federation scheme was intended to undermine his position of dominance in Iraq, Saddam did not bother to meet Asad at the airport and later accused Syria of hatching a plot to overthrow him. The following year, when the Iran–Iraq war broke out, Asad condemned Iraq and backed Iran, Gradually, Syria and Iran became close partners, to the displeasure of the rulers of Saudi Arabia and the Gulf states, who saw in Ayatollah Khomeini's revolution a potentially fatal threat to their regimes and to the territorial integrity of their countries.

The third change concerned Syria's relations with Israel. The process of change in this regard was relatively fast in getting under way. The first visible step was Syria's acceptance of United Nations Security Council Resolution 242 in March 1972. In the past, Asad had reiterated Syria's rejection of Resolution 242 on the grounds that without redressing the military and political balance with Israel, the Arabs could not force Israel to solve the Palestine question and withdraw from the Arab territories it had seized in June 1967.

A more tangible step was the May 1974 disengagement agreement between Syria and Israel, negotiated under the auspices of the U.S. government in the wake of the Arab–Israel War of 1973. The Soviet Union remained neutral except for hints in the Soviet press warning Asad not to be tricked into accepting half measures. One significant aspect of the agreement was the two sides' declaration that the disengagement of forces was only a step toward a just and durable peace based on UN Resolutions 242 and 333. Another was Asad's oral commitment not to allow any guerrilla raids from the Syrian side of the disengagement line.

The third stage relates to Syria's entente with Egypt, its participation in the U.S.-led alliance against Iraq, and its subsequent involvement in the Middle East peace process. Whereas in the previous stage Syria was adamantly opposed to Egypt, in this stage it sought to enter into an alliance with the government of President Husni Mubarak. Most significantly, these moves led to Syria's entry, for the first time, into face-to-face negotiations with Israel. Not only did Syria drop its insistence on an international peace conference under UN sponsorship, but it contributed to creating the psychological climate for successful bilateral negotiations with Israel.

In many respects, the principle that governed Asad's foreign policy was similar to the principle that governed the policy of British statesman Lord Palmerston (1784–1865), who once said, "We have no eternal allies, and we have no perpetual enemies. Our interests are eternal and perpetual, and those interests it is our duty to follow." In the execution of this principle, Asad proved himself a cautious and calculating tactician as well as a master politician.

BIBLIOGRAPHY

MUSLIH, MUHAMMAD. "Asad's Middle East Strategy." Unpublished manuscript.
SEALE, PATRICK. *Asad: The Struggle for the Middle East.* Berkeley, Calif., 1989.

Muhammad Muslih

As'ad, Kamil   [c. 1930–   ]

Lebanese political leader, son of Ahmad As'ad.

As'ad (also al-As'ad) was born in Taybah and educated in Beirut. He earned a law degree at Saint Joseph University in Beirut. As the only son of Ahmad al-AS'AD, he was prepared for a political career from an early age. As'ad served in parliament from 1957 until 1992 (but lost the 1960 election), when he failed to win a seat in the highly controversial election. As'ad was speaker of parliament in 1964, 1968, and from 1970 until 1984, when he was replaced by Husayn al-HUSAYNI. As'ad had a reputation for detesting the poor. The civil war brought an end to his political career as Shi'ites rebelled against "feudal" traditional families, who were seen as arrogant and insensitive. The rise of the left, the AMAL movement, and later HIZBULLAH brought a final end to the major role played by this family for centuries. As'ad heads the Democratic Socialist party.

As'ad AbuKhalil

Asad, Lake

Reservoir formed by the Tabaqa Dam, completed on the Euphrates river, 1973, to irrigate Syria.

The lake is 50 miles (80 km) long and contains some 40 billion cubic meters of water. When all projects are completed, the irrigated area of Syria will be doubled (by 1.6 million acres/640,000 hectares); and 600 megawatts of electricity will be generated.

BIBLIOGRAPHY

SINAI, ANNE, and ALLEN POLLACK. *The Syrian Arab Republic.* New York, 1976.

John R. Clark

As'ad Family

A prominent family of southern Lebanon.

The As'ad family claims descent from the family confederation of al-Saghir, who in turn trace their lineage to tribes in Arabia. Ahmad al-As'ad and his son Kamil have been dominant politicians in the twentieth century; both held ministerial positions and Kamil was speaker of Parliament for much of the 1970s and also in the 1960s and 1980s. His family leadership suffered from the rise of radical political parties among Shi'ites in the early phase of the civil war of 1975. In later years, the rise of AMAL and HIZBULLAH, eclipsed the influence of the family. Kamil al-As'ad failed to win a seat in the 1992 parliamentary elections.

As'ad AbuKhalil

As'ad Wali

Wali of the Vilayet of Sidon.

As'ad Wali is not to be confused with the As'ad Pasha who was a prominent Ottoman official in Istanbul. In 1843, under As'ad's rule, as *wali* of the *vilayet* (province) of Sidon, the Mount Lebanon region was divided into DRUZE and MARONITE (Christian) sections in the wake of Druze–Maronite conflict. Some historians think that he sincerely tried to reconcile the various religious factions in Lebanon, but the intensity of conflict, not only between Maronites and Druzes but also between Maronites and Greek Orthodox, for example, prevented the establishment of a harmonious political arrangement in the mountains of Lebanon. The government of the Ottoman Empire accused him of bias in favor of Christians and replaced him in 1845. His replacement ushered in an era of more bloodshed and killing.

BIBLIOGRAPHY

AL-HAKIM, YUSUL. *Memoirs.*

As'ad AbuKhalil

Asali, Faysal al-

Syrian politician.

A deputy from Zabadani, Faysal al-Asali led the small but vocal right-wing Socialist Cooperative party, founded in 1948. An outspoken critic of Husni al-ZA'IM's army leadership, he was arrested in Za'im's coup of March 30, 1949. He was re-elected to the chamber of deputies in November of 1949, after being released in the wake of Sami al-Hinnawi's coup of August 14, 1949. Al-Asali's pan-Islamist views were reflected in the papers *al-Barada* and *al-Insha.*

BIBLIOGRAPHY

SEALE, PATRICK. *The Struggle for Syria: A Study of Post-War Arab Politics, 1945–1958.* London, 1958.

Charles U. Zenzie

Asali, Sabri al-

Syrian politician.

Asali, born into an upper-middle-class, landowning family, participated in the Syrian national liberation movement beginning in the 1920s. He joined the NATIONAL BLOC in 1930, and from 1945 on, he served as minister in several cabinets; he headed four governments between 1954 and 1958. Asali was elected a deputy to the National Assembly on several occasions. During the French mandate over Syria, he was active in the League of National Action. Asali served very briefly as president of the UNITED ARAB REPUBLIC before leaving politics in 1958. With BA'TH's advent to power in 1963, Asali and other members of the ancien régime were pushed aside by a younger generation of army officers, many of humble rural origins and with a strong penchant for conspiratorial politics.

BIBLIOGRAPHY

KHOURY, PHILIP S. *Syria and the French Mandate.* Princeton, N.J., 1989.
SEALE, PATRICK. *The Struggle for Syria.* New Haven, Conn., 1987.

Muhammad Muslih

Asali, Shukri al-   [?–1916]

Syrian politician.

From a landowning family of the Maydan, Shukri al-Asali became a provincial governor in the Ottoman Empire, after receiving training in Istanbul. An early member of the Renaissance Society and editor of the newspaper *al-Qabas,* he was elected to parliament in 1911. Al-Asali worked continually against the Zionists in Palestine and was affiliated with the Ottoman Party of Administrative Decentralization; for his activities against Ottoman Turkish authority he was executed sometime in 1915 or 1916.

BIBLIOGRAPHY

KHOURY, PHILIP S. *Syria and the French Mandate: The Politics of Arab Nationalism, 1920–1945.* Princeton, N.J., 1987.

Charles U. Zenzie

Ash

Term for a traditional Persian stew.

Ash (thick soup) is made from different combinations of noodles, rice, vegetables, meat, fruits, as well as yogurt and vinegar. Usually served hot, each specific ash derives its name from its main ingredient. Persian tradition has ascribed a specific ash for different occasions; for example, *ash-e posht-e pa,* which marks farewell ceremonies, is cooked to shorten the duration of the sojourn. According to Islamic ritual, acts of charity alleviate illness, and these acts are also accompanied by the preparation of some type of ash for distribution among the needy.

BIBLIOGRAPHY

"Ash." In *Encyclopaedia Iranica,* vol 2. New York, 1989.
DABIRSIYAQI, MOHAMMAD. *Persian Lexicon,* vol. 4. Tehran, 1984. In Persian.

Neguin Yavari

Asharina Dam

On the Orontes river in Syria, providing water for irrigation since 1966.

The dam was built near the village of Asharina in Syria. The Asharina plain skirts the GHAB plain to the southeast. The Asharina is smaller than the Ghab but more elevated at 656 to 722 feet (200–220 m). Its area of 106 square miles (275 km) is separated from the Ghab by the Suqaylbiyya plateau—elevation 787 to 820 feet (240–250 m)—but it connects with the Ghab near the village of Tall Salhab to the west of it.

The dam holds water from the ORONTES RIVER (al-Asi), which traverses the Asharina plain from east to west and irrigates the Ghab. The Ghab-Asharina dam project was begun by the Syrian government in 1952. The dam was completed in 1960, and its use started in 1966. It irrigates 123,550 acres (50,000 ha). An office for the exploitation of the Ghab and the Asharina was established in 1969.

BIBLIOGRAPHY

SAFADI, CHAFIC. *Hydraulic Resources in the Syrian Arab Republic.* Typescript. Damascus, 1978.

Abdul-Karim Rafeq

Ashkenazim

European Jews whose daily language was Yiddish (often in addition to the languages of the countries and regions in which they lived during the Diaspora).

Ashkenazim is the plural of *Ashkenazi,* a term derived from the Hebrew name Ashkenaz, a great-grandson of the biblical Noah. The Ashkenazim are Jews whose Middle East ancestors migrated to Germany (called Ashkenaz by medieval Jews) and the surrounding areas, where they spoke Middle High German during the fourteenth and fifteenth centuries andwhich evolved into Jüdisch Diutsch, or Yiddish. Their liturgical Hebrew differs markedly in both rhythm and pronunciation from that of today's Middle Eastern Jews or of the Sephardic Jews of Southern Europe and North Africa.

In modern Israel, the Ashkenazim were, until recently, a minority, outnumbered by Sephardic and Middle Eastern Jews; as large numbers of refugees from the former Soviet Union arrive, however, the Ashkenazim may become the majority of the Jewish population.

Although the Hebrew language taught in Israel's public schools uses the Sephardic pronunciation, Ashkenazic Hebrew can be heard during services in East and Central European congregations. Small but strongly cohesive communities of Ashkenazic pietists—particularly in the United States, Jerusalem, and B'nai B'rak—speak Yiddish, regarding Hebrew as too sacred for secular matters and daily conversation. In the modern Middle East, outside Israel, only Turkey has a small but viable Ashkenazic community.

BIBLIOGRAPHY

BARON, SALO WITTMAYER. *A Social and Religious History of the Jews,* 19 vols. New York, 1952–1983.

Arnold Blumberg

Ashur

Islamic tithe.

Ashur, also called ZAKAT, is one-tenth of the crop or profit given by the Muslim peasant or merchant to charity. In most dialects of the MAGHRIB, it is also the name given to the month of MUHARRAM to differentiate it from ashura, which is the celebration occurring on the tenth day of this month. However, in some regions of the Maghrib, like in northern Morocco, ashur also means the celebration (ashura). The month of ashur is subject to many rituals and beliefs that have combined pre-Islamic, Islamic, and Shi'a celebrations.

BIBLIOGRAPHY

DOUTTÉ, E. *Magie et religion dans l'Afrique du Nord.* Paris, 1909.
LAOUST, E. *Les mots et les choses berbères.* Rabat, 1920.
MARCAIS, PH. "Ashura", *Encyclopedie de l'Islam,* vol. 1.

Rahma Bourqia

Asir

A geographic region in southwest Saudi Arabia bordered by Yemen and the Red Sea.

Asir is mountainous and characterized by the presence of coastal peaks rising to three thousand feet (915 m). Sufficient rainfall supports dry-farming in some places, which is being supplemented by government irrigation schemes. Asir, along with the NAJRAN OASIS, is now part of the South/Southwestern administrative district of Saudi Arabia. The towns of ABHA and Khamis Mushayt are the main population and national centers.

Eleanor Abdella Doumato

As-Is Agreement

Agreement establishing a cartel of Western oil companies, 1928.

Price wars among major oil companies in the 1920s, most significantly one in India between Standard Oil of New York and a subsidiary of ROYAL DUTCH SHELL, threatened major oil company profits, especially those from relatively high-cost production in the United States. At an August 1928 secret meeting at Achnacarry Castle in the Scottish highlands, the As-Is Agreement was devised by the leaders of the Anglo-Persian Oil Company (later BP), Royal Dutch Shell, and Standard Oil of New Jersey (later Exxon). Together with the RED LINE AGREEMENT, the As-Is Agreement formed the basis of what a U.S. Senate subcommittee in 1952 called "the international petroleum cartel."

The As-Is Agreement consisted of seven "principles" to limit "excessive competition" that had led to enormous overproduction by dividing markets, fixing prices, and limiting the expansion of production capacity. The agreement affected the development of oil production capacity in the Middle East by limiting price competition in product markets and, as a result, supporting the prices of products made from high-cost, primarily American, crude oil. This strategy was implemented as a "basing-point" system under which all sellers calculated delivered prices as the sum of FOB prices at one or more specific locations—basing points—plus a standardized freight charge from that point to the point of delivery. Such a system is very effective because it ensures that all sellers quote the same prices and that producers with low costs cannot use that advantage to expand their market shares by passing on the low costs.

The impact of the As-Is Agreement on the position of Middle Eastern oil producers was profound. It was substantially responsible for the reluctance of concession holders to expand production in this low-cost region. In 1928, when it was adopted, more than a third of worldwide production capacity was shut down due to oversupply. Owners feared that expanding low-cost capacity in the GULF would only add to their losses. The As-Is and Red Line agreements retarded the development of Middle Eastern oil resources until after World War II; at the same time they led to the depletion of reserves in what were later seen as politically "safe" areas, such as the United States and Canada. The resulting division of production shares between Middle Eastern countries and others aggravated anticolonial and anti-Western feelings among the populations of many Middle Eastern states, most notably IRAQ and IRAN. It also established a pattern for ensuring oil profits by exercising market control that the members of the ORGANIZATION OF PETROLEUM EXPORTING COUNTRIES later tried to emulate.

[See also: Arabian American Oil Company.]

BIBLIOGRAPHY

PENROSE, EDITH T. *The Large International Firm in Developing Countries: The International Petroleum Industry.* New York, 1968.
SAMPSON, ANTHONY. *The Seven Sisters: The Great Oil Companies and the World They Shaped.* New York, 1975.
UNITED STATES CONGRESS. SENATE. SELECT COMMITTEE ON SMALL BUSINESS. SUBCOMMITTEE ON MONOPOLY. *The International Petroleum Cartel: Staff Report to the Federal Trade Commission.* 82nd Congress, 2nd session. Washington, D.C., 1952.

Mary Ann Tétreault

Asiyan

Ottoman Literary magazine.

Edited by Ahmed CEVDET, *Asiyan* (The Nest) was a weekly journal covering literary and scientific issues. A total of twenty-six issues of *Asiyan* were published between September 10, 1908 and 12 March 1909. *Asiyan* featured original poetry and stories along with translations of French literature. Among the contributors to *Asiyan* were Abdülhak Hamid, TEVFIK FIKRET, and Hüseyin Cahid Yalçın.

BIBLIOGRAPHY

ÖZKIRIMLI, ATILLA. *Türk Edebiyat Ansiklopedisi.* Vol, 1. Istanbul, 1982.
Tanzimat'tan Cumhuriyet'e Türkiye Ansiklopedesi. Vol. 1. Istanbul, 1984, p. 124.

David Waldner

Askari, Ja'far al-   [1887–1936]

Arab nationalist and military leader; friend of Faisal ibn Husayn during the Arab revolt in World War I; political leader under Faisal as king of Syria, 1920, and as Faisal I of Iraq, 1921–1932.

Ja'far (also Ja'far) was born in Baghdad, the son of a military leader for the Ottoman Empire. He was educated in both military and legal affairs, graduating from the Ottoman military academy in 1904. He served in the Ottoman army and was captured by the British in Egypt during World War I. Following a dramatic escape from an Egyptian fort, he later joined the ARAB REVOLT against the Ottomans under T. E. LAWRENCE and Sharif HUSAYN IBN ALI of Mecca. Ja'far organized Husayn's army and led it, becoming the trusted friend of Husayn's son FAISAL, who in 1920 became king of Syria (before he was removed by the French mandate).

When the British supported Faisal and made him king of IRAQ in 1921, Ja'far was named first minister of defense (1920–1922) and assumed that position in 1930 and again in 1931/32. He was also prime minister of Iraq (1923, 1926–1928) and Iraq's minister of foreign affairs (1926–1928 and 1931/32).

BIBLIOGRAPHY

AL-ASKARI, JA'FAR. *Memoirs* London, 1988. (In Arabic).
BATATU, HANNA. *The Old Social Classes and the Revolutionary Movements of Iraq.* Princeton, N.J., 1978.

Ahmad Abdul A. R. Shikara

Asmahan   [1917?–1944]

Actress and singer.

Asmahan was a gifted singer known principally for her work in films. Her delicate and flexible high voice was clear, powerful, and brilliant, and she was frequently compared to UMM KULTHUM (the Arab world's most famous female singer), although their voices and musical styles were very different. Many saw her as Umm Kulthum's only serious rival.

Asmahan was born Amal al-Atrash in Jebal al-Duruz (in Syria) to Fahd al-Atrash and Aliya Husayn. The mother and the children, Amal, Farid, and Fu'ad, moved to Cairo in about 1924, to escape the fighting in Syria during the French mandate. Amal began her performing career in the music hall of Mary Mansur in Cairo around 1930 and adopted her stage name at the suggestion of one of her mentors, composer Dawud Husni. Asmahan's career was interrupted by marriage to her cousin Hasan al-Atrash in Jabal al-Duruz in 1933. They separated in 1939, and she returned to Cairo with her daughter. Asmahan subsequently appeared in two successful Egyptian films, *Intisar al-Shabab* and *Gharam wa-Intiqam,* both with music composed by her brother Farid al-ATRASH.

Asmahan performed at private parties, for radio broadcasts, and made commercial recordings. Her popular and financial success was limited, because she abhorred public concerts and preferred films. The film companies of the day typically released one film per singing star every two years; thus her performances were fewer than those of her principal competitors, notably Umm Kulthum and Layla Murad—both of whom performed extensively in public.

Asmahan's private life may have been too public: her alleged affairs with a succession of prominent men, including journalist Muhammad al-Taba'i, banker Tal'at Harb, and royal aide Ahmad Hasanayn, were topics of public conversation. In 1941, she re-turned to Jabal al-Duruz, allegedly as a British spy, an activity that did little to enhance her popularity. She was, in many respects, her own worst enemy; her habits of cigarettes, alcohol, and late nights had a deleterious effect on her voice. Asmahan died in an automobile accident in Egypt in 1944. She was equally comfortable with Arab and European singing styles. Among her most famous songs were "Dakhalt marra fi 'l-jinayna," "Ya tuyur" (in which her skills in European virtuosic singing were aptly displayed), and "Alayk salat Allah wa-salamuh."

BIBLIOGRAPHY

SAHHAB, VICTOR. *Al-Sab'a al-kibar fi 'l-musiqa 'l-arabiyya 'l-mu'asira* (The Great Seven of Contemporary Arabic Music). Beirut, 1987.
AL-TABA'I, MUHAMMAD. *Asmahan tirwi qissataha* (Asmahan Tells Her Story). Cairo, 1965.

Virginia Danielson

Asmar, Fawzi al-   [1937–   ]

Arab journalist and author.

Fawzi al-Asmar (or el-Asmar) was born in Haifa, Palestine, and grew up in Israel. He studied history and political science in the United States and received his Ph.D. from the University of Exeter, in Britain. He became a U.S. citizen in 1981.

Asmar served as managing editor of the international ARABIC-language daily *al-Sharq al-Awsat* and is bureau chief of the United Arab Emirates (UAE) news agency in Washington, D.C.; he is also a columnist for the Saudi Arabian daily *al-Riyadh*. He has authored journal articles and such books as *To Be an Arab in Israel,* which has been translated into eight languages.

Jenab Tutunji

Asnaj, Abdullah Ali

Politician of South Yemen and North Yemen.

Asnaj was the founding head of both the Aden Trade Union Council and the PEOPLE'S SOCIALIST PARTY. In the mid-1960s, he was defeated by the National Liberation Front (NLF) in his effort to head the first independent South Yemeni government after the British colonial era. Asnaj then went north to the YEMEN ARAB REPUBLIC to serve as foreign minister and adviser to four YAR heads-of-state between 1973 and 1979. He was disgraced by charges of inappropriate dealings with a foreign power, probably Saudi Arabia.

Robert D. Burrowes

Assad Family, al-

Prominent Syrian family.

The Assad family has its roots in Syria's northwestern ALAWI village of Qurdaha. Sulayman Al-Wahhish, of the Kalbiyya tribe, had a son, Ali Sulayman (1875–1963), who became respected in the region for arbitrating disputes and doing charitable works. Ali Sulayman's first wife, Sa'da, bore him five children, and his second, Na'isa, bore one daugher and five sons, among them Hafiz al-ASAD (1930), Jamil (1933), and Rifaat (1937). The family name was changed from Wahhish (savage) to Assad (lion) in 1927, when Ali Sulayman was promoted to minor notable. Many close relatives live in the area as well.

BIBLIOGRAPHY

SEALE, PATRICK. *Asad: The Struggle for the Middle East.* Los Angeles, 1988.

Charles U. Zenzie

Assassa, Muwaffaq

Syrian military officer.

Assassa, of Sunni heritage, rose in the ranks of Syria's air force to become lieutenant colonel in 1961, colonel in 1962, and chief of staff after the March 1962 coup. He was arrested and publicly reprimanded after the March 1963 coup.

BIBLIOGRAPHY

HOPKINS, ED. "Military Intervention in Syria and Iraq." Master's Thesis, American University of Beirut, 1970.

Charles U. Zenzie

Association of Algerian Muslim Ulama (AUMA)

Islamic clergymen in Algeria organized to promote Muslim and Arab values during the French colonial period.

The Association of Algerian Muslim Ulama was formed in 1931 under the leadership of Shaykh Abd al-Hamid BEN BADIS. In the Islamic reformist tradition, it affirmed Muslim values and the Arab identity

of Algerians. In 1956 its leaders dissolved the organization and rallied to the FRONT DE LIBÉRATION NATIONALE (FLN).

BIBLIOGRAPHY

MERAD, ALI. *Le réformisme musulman en Algérie de 1925 à 1940.* Paris, 1967.

John Ruedy

Assyrians

A Nestorian Christian minority.

Originating in the Hakkari Mountains of Turkey, the Assyrians resided in northern Iraq. Their position as a de jure minority was controversial because many of them had arrived in Iraq in late 1918; their refugee status, backed by the British, contributed to their isolation and stereotype as British protégés. In 1932, under the leadership of Mar SHIM'UN, the Assyrians drew up a National Pact, mirroring the Turkish National Pact, in which they defined themselves as a separate nation and culture. The authorities perceived the pact as a threat to the territorial integrity of Iraq. Since Assyrians were not a native minority, they were less entitled than other Christian minorities to special administrative privileges. The government of Rashid Ali al-Kaylani, encouraged by the British, responded by forcing the Assyrians to relinquish their weapons. The Assyrians attempted to involve the French in neighboring Syria, and clashes between Iraq's army and the Assyrians ensued. Assyrian villages were looted by Arabs and Kurds. In 1933, General Bakr Sidqi protected Iraq's "national interest" by planning and executing a systematic massacre of members of the Assyrian community in the village of Summayl.

BIBLIOGRAPHY

HUSRY, KHALDUN S. "The Assyrian Affair of 1933." *International Journal of Middle East Studies* 5 (1974): 161–176, 344–360.

LUKITZ, LIORA. *Iraq: The Search for National Identity.* New York, 1995.

Mia Bloom

Aswan

Upper Egyptian province and its capital city, health resort, and industrial center.

Originally named Syene, the city was located on the east bank, at the first cataract of the Upper NILE

View of Elephantine Island, Aswan, on the Upper Nile. (Mia Bloom)

View of a felucca on the Nile at Aswan, Egypt. (D. W. Lockhard)

The pharaonic Temple of Philae at Aswan, Egypt. (Mia Bloom)

Landscape and river view at Aswan, Egypt, on the Nile. (Mia Bloom)

RIVER; it marked the southern border of pharaonic EGYPT. About 3.5 miles (5.5 km) south of the city is the ASWAN dam, erected by British and Egyptian engineers from 1899 to 1902 and enlarged in 1912 and 1934. The dam's construction facilitated the conversion of Middle Egypt and parts of Upper Egypt to perennial irrigation. From 1960 to 1971, this process was completed with the construction of the ASWAN HIGH DAM. One of the largest public works ever built, the High Dam has enabled Egypt to reclaim some desert land for cultivation (but not the 1.2 million acres [0.5 million ha] hoped for) and to generate hydroelectric power. It has cost dearly in soil erosion, the loss of fertile alluvium from the annual flood and of nutrients that used to support marine life, and the resettlement of NUBIANS who used to live in lands flooded by the waters of Lake NASSER, created by the dam. The province had some 801,400 inhabitants in 1986.

BIBLIOGRAPHY

WATERBURY, JOHN. *Hydropolitics of the Nile Valley.* Syracuse, N.Y., 1979.

Arthur Goldschmidt, Jr.

Aswan High Dam

Dam to control Nile river waters.

The first dam on the NILE RIVER, south of the city of Aswan, Egypt, was completed in 1902 and made higher in 1912 and 1934. Its insufficient WATER-holding capacity led to construction of a larger dam and reservoir, the Aswan High Dam, constructed from 1960 to 1971.

In March of 1953, the FREE OFFICERS of Egypt's army, which had overthrown King FAROUK in a military coup, hired a firm to design a high dam on the Nile some five miles (8 km) south of the older British-built Aswan Dam. The U.S. and British governments and the World Bank agreed to finance its construction, conditional on Egypt's acceptance of the following terms: Western government control of Egypt's economy; no new Egyptian arms purchases; and open bidding for the construction contract, but the exclusion of communist countries. Despite initial reluctance, Egypt accepted these terms; then U.S. Secretary of State John Foster Dulles, alarmed at the ties to the Soviet Union of Gamal Abdel NASSER, Egypt's president, vetoed the deal. In response, Nasser ordered the nationalization of the SUEZ CANAL, with the intention of using canal tolls to pay for the dam's construction.

In 1958, the Soviet Union financed the dam, providing the equivalent of 330 million U.S. dollars, and work began in 1960. The hydroelectric power plant began operation in 1968. The reservoir formed by the dam created Lake Nasser, which extended almost 300 miles (485 km) southward and forced the relocation of the Nubians. The temples at PHILAE island and at ABU SIMBEL, dating from ancient Egypt, were flooded, although a rescue effort was attempted by UNESCO and some colossal statuary was raised to overlook the lake.

The dam's completion permitted reclamation of some 675,000 acres (273,000 ha) and the conversion of about an additional 1 million acres (420,000 ha) to perennial irrigation. Twelve electric turbines provided 60 percent of Egypt's electrical needs, but increased use of irrigation without adequate drainage has caused waterlogging and salinization of the topsoil. The dam has also caused a rise in the water table in the region.

BIBLIOGRAPHY

GOLDSCHMIDT, ARTHUR, JR. *Modern Egypt: The Formation of a Nation-State.* Boulder, Colo., 1988.
NYROP, RICHARD F., ed. *Egypt: A Country Study,* 4th ed. Washington, D.C., 1983.
WUCHER KING, JOAN. *Historical Dictionary of Egypt.* Metuchen, N.J., 1984.

David Waldner

Asyun, Fath Allah   [1899–?]

Syrian lawyer and politician.

Born in 1899 in Aleppo to an upper-middle-class Armenian Catholic family, Fath Allah Asyun received his advanced education in Cairo. He served as deputy from 1936 to 1943.

BIBLIOGRAPHY

KHOURY, PHILIP S. *Syria and the French Mandate: The Politics of Arab Nationalism, 1920–1945.* Princeton, N.J., 1987.

Charles U. Zenzie

Asyut

Large city and province in middle Egypt.

Asyut province (governorate) has an area of about 600 square miles (1,553 sq km) and a population of 2,223,000 (1986) and the highest concentration of COPTS (Christian) of any governorate in Egypt. The city, located on the west bank of the Nile river, has a population of 270,000 and is the site of Asyut University, in which Muslim societies (*jama'at*) are especially prominent. The city was shaken by religious riots after the assassination of Egypt's President Anwar Sadat in 1981, and again during the early 1990s.

BIBLIOGRAPHY

The Coptic Encyclopedia.
The Encyclopaedia of Islam, 2nd ed.

Arthur Goldschmidt, Jr.

Asyut University

Authorized in 1949 as Muhammad Ali University, Egypt's fourth modern state university opened, as Asyut University, in 1957.

Students in Upper Egypt no longer had to travel to Cairo or Alexandria for higher education, but could attend the university in ASYUT. The university drew on American models and initially emphasized science and technology. In the late 1980s it had 2,110 teachers and 42,520 students.

BIBLIOGRAPHY

QUBAIN, FAHIM I. *Education and Science in the Arab World.* Baltimore, 1966.

Donald Malcolm Reid

Atabat

Shi'a holy places in Iraq.

Atabat, literally "thresholds," are Shi'a holy places in Iraq, at Karbala, Qadimayn, Najaf and Samarra, containing the tombs of six imams revered in Twelver Shi'ism, serving also as holy sites for pilgrimage. Ali ibn Abi Talib, the first imam of Shi'ism, is buried in Najaf. His son, Husayn ibn Ali, the third Shi'a imam, Husayn's half-brother Abbas, and Husayn's son Ali Akbar were martyred and buried in Karbala, fighting the Umayyads in 680. Qadimayn is the burial site of the seventh and ninth imams, Musa al-Kazem, who died in 802, and Muhammad al-Taqi who died in 834. Samarra, which lies at a distance from the remainder of the Atabat, is the burial site of the tenth and eleventh imams, Ali al-Naqi and Hasan al-Askari, who died in 868 and 873, respectively.

The Atabat have historically served as centers of Shi'a learning. During the Iranian constitutional revolution from 1905 to 1911, the Atabat, under Ottoman suzerainity, served as a safe haven for the revolutionaries. Ayatollah Hasan Shirazi, who engineered the retraction of the Regie tobacco concession in 1870, resided in Samarra. The Atabat also played a decisive role in fostering clerical opposition in the Pahlavi period, as Ayatollah Ruhollah KHOMEINI lived in exile in Najaf from 1965 to 1978.

BIBLIOGRAPHY

ALGAR, HAMID. "Atabat." In *Encyclopaedia Iranica,* vol. 2. London, 1987.

Neguin Yavari

Atalla, Muhammad   [1929–   ]

Lebanese economist.

Born in Sidon, Atalla earned degrees from the American University of Beirut, the Institute of Social Studies at the Hague, and Rotterdam University. He taught economics at the American University of Beirut from 1959 to 1972, during which time he also served as a member of the planning board and the money and credit board. Atalla was the Lebanese government representative on the first board of directors of New Intra Bank, and president of the development and reconstruction council. He is the author of several articles on the Lebanese economy and other Arab economies.

BIBLIOGRAPHY

Who's Who in Lebanon 1980–1981. Beirut, 1980.

Mark Mechler

Atalla Family

Leading family of the Palestinian Greek Orthodox community.

Antun Atalla (1897–1988), a lawyer, was vice-mayor of JERUSALEM from 1944 to 1946. In 1954, he was elected to Jordan's parliament and served there for two years. He was involved in Greek Orthodox activities and, in the early 1960s, took the Palestinian cause to European and North American capitals.

Fu'ad Atalla (1905–1983), a Nazareth-born Palestinian, became a lawyer and defended political prisoners during the years of the British mandate over PALESTINE. In the late 1960s, he made several trips to the United States to defend the Palestinian cause before Christian groups.

BIBLIOGRAPHY

KHALAF, ISSA. *Politics in Palestine: Arab Factionalism and Social Disintegration, 1939–1948.* Albany, N.Y., 1991.
SMITH, PAMELA ANN. *Palestine and the Palestinians: 1876–1983.* New York, 1984.

Steve Tamari

Atasi, Hashim al-   [1876?–1960]

A prominent Syrian politician.

Atasi hailed from a Sunni Muslim landowning scholarly family of Ashraf from Homs, a commercial city in west central Syria, which in mandatory times was commonly referred to as al-Atasi's fief. He served three times as president of Syria (1936–1939, 1949–1951, 1954–1955) and as prime minister for a short time in 1949. Having received an advanced Ottoman education in Istanbul, he served as a district governor in the imperial bureaucracy of the Ottoman state. In 1920 he acted as chairman of the Syrian-Arab Congress. For a short time, he was also prime minister in Emir Faisal's government in Damascus. With the French occupying Syria, Atasi distinguished himself in Syria's struggle for independence. He was one of those who formed the core of the NATIONAL BLOC (al-Kutla al-Wataniyya), a nationalist organization that steered the course of the independence struggle in Syria from 1927, when its seeds were planted at the Beirut conference (held in October of that year) until the completion of the fight for independence nineteen years later. He belonged to an older generation of nationalists who subscribed to a policy of "honorable cooperation" with France—that is, a policy of collaboration based on reciprocity of interests and mutual obligations. Proponents of this policy believed that France supported the Syrian national cause and that establishing confidence through cooperation between the two nations would help the cause of independence. However, French insensitivity to Syrian aspirations exposed the fallacy of the National Bloc's assumption and made Atasi increasingly frustrated by the bloc's failure to make any meaningful progress toward independence through the policy of "honorable cooperation." In 1931 and 1932 he assumed a more radical posture, which helped him attract to the bloc council more activist Syrian nationalists, most notably the Istiqlal Party leader Shukri al-QUWATLI. Atasi headed the Syrian delegation sent to Paris in March 1936 to negotiate Syria's independence with the government of Albert Sarraut. The inflexibility of the Sarraut government's bargaining position would have caused the complete breakdown of the negotiations had it not been for the victory of a left-wing coalition (known as the Popular Front) headed by the Socialist Party leader Leon Blum in the general French elections of April 1936. The advent of a new French government, together with the subsequent appointment of a second French negotiating team headed by the enlightened and forward-looking Pierre Vienot (who viewed the French mandate in the Levant as transitory) set the stage for the signing of the Franco–Syrian Treaty of 1936. The treaty, which was never ratified by France because the right-wing French forces were able to convince the French parliament not to accept it, provided for peace, friendship, and alliance between France and Syria and defined France's military position in Syria as well as the relations of the Syrian state with Syrian minorities and with Lebanon. With factionalism plaguing the National Bloc and other nationalist organizations, and with the French government suspending the Syrian constitution and instituting almost direct French control in the country, Atasi resigned his office as president in 1939 and adopted a less activist stance in Syrian politics until August 1949, after Colonel Sami al-HINNAWI's coup against Husni al-ZA'IM. In December of the same year Atasi became a titular president, with real power concentrated in the hands of Adib SHISHAKLI, the tough pro-French colonel who overthrew Hinnawi on December 19, 1949, allegedly to save Syria from British influence and a union with the pro-British Hashimite monarchy of Iraq. It was convenient for both Hinnawi and Shishakli to have the veteran Atasi as president because he was the finest symbol of Syria's struggle against French imperialism. Differences with Shishakli, together with the chaotic Syrian politics, compelled Atasi to resign from the presidency in November 1951. He then began conspiring for the overthrow of Shishakli. In March 1954, Atasi returned to the presidency, and in September 1955 he retired from Syrian politics, disaffected by the internal struggles of officer cliques. Perhaps he was also bemused to see the door of Syria, whose allegiance remained with the West for much of the decade that followed independence, thrown open to Egyptian influence and to the flow of Soviet and East European arms and other blandishments.

Muhammad Muslih

Atasi, Jamal al-   [1922–   ]

Syrian psychologist and politician.

Atasi was born in Homs, where he completed his primary and secondary studies. In 1947, he enrolled in the School of Medicine in Damascus, where he obtained a doctorate in psychology. He was then appointed doctor in the Ministry of Health. He is one of the founding and prominent members of the Syrian BA'TH party and editor of one of its newspapers, *Al-Jamahir*. In 1963, he was appointed minister of information in the cabinet headed by Salah al-Din al-Bitar. After a long fight with the Ba'th, he left the party and became general secretary of the Nasserist ARAB SOCIALIST UNION. Atasi was also a member of the "Committee of Thirteen" which undertook the task of forming the NATIONAL PROGRESSIVE FRONT. He is considered one of the main opponents of the regime of President Hafiz al-ASAD.

George E. Irani

Atasi, Nur al-Din al-   [1929–1993]

President of Syria, 1966–1970.

Atasi was a member of a landowning scholarly family from Homs. A physician who had served as medical volunteer in the Algerian revolution, he was a leader of the second civilian generation of the BA'TH party. Two other prominent leaders of this generation were Ibrahim Makhus and Yusuf Zu'ayyin. This generation, which was composed mainly of rural Alawis, Druzes, and Isma'ilis and a sprinkling of Sunnis, imbued the Ba'th party in the early 1960s with vaguely argued ideas of class struggle and scientific socialism. Its members formed what came to be known as the neo-Ba'th. Their opponents believed them to have subordinated Arab unity to their program of revolutionary socialism. The neo-Ba'th was centered in Damascus, building up branches in other Arab countries; members of the old Ba'th (e.g., Bitar and Aflaq) were either imprisoned or escaped to operate from Beirut or elsewhere. After the Ba'th officers' coup of March 1963, Nur al-Din became minister of the interior (August 1963–May 1964), deputy prime minister (October 1964–September 1965), and a member of the Revolutionary Council and the Presidential Council in 1964. Nur al-Din's political beliefs were consistent with those of the neo-Ba'thists—fearing communism, distrusting popular movements, endorsing economic reform along socialist lines, and subscribing to the theory of popular war, especially through the Palestine resistance movement, which was developing around the mid 1960s. In the internal power struggles that were buffeting Syria, Nur al-Din sided with the hawkish faction of the group that came to power in the coup of February 23, 1966. This faction rejected the proposal of a peaceful solution with Israel and tried in vain to assert party authority over the army. Nur al-Din's alliance with the Jadid faction put him on a collision course with the more powerful, army-supported faction of Lieutenant General Hafiz al-ASAD, whose position as defense minister and commander of the Syrian air force, together with his pragmatic and calculating approach, enabled him in February 1969 to occupy strategic points in the Syrian capital and to gain full control of the Syrian state in November 1970. After Asad's semicoup of February 1969, Nur al-Din retained his posts as president, prime minister, and secretary general of the party, due in part to the weakness of Asad within the party and in part to the intervention of Algeria, Egypt, and the Soviet Union. This created a duality of power in Syria, with Nur al-Din and his colleagues in the Jadid faction controlling the regional Ba'th organization and its cadres—hence nominally the government—and Asad's faction controlling the army and intelligence—hence *practically* the government. When Asad took full control in November 1970, Nur al-Din was dismissed from all his posts and sent to jail, where he reportedly languished till he died.

Muhammad Muslih

Atatürk, Mustafa Kemal   [1881–1938]

Turkish soldier and nationalist leader; founder and first president of the Republic of Turkey, 1923–1938.

Born in Salonika, the eldest of the two surviving children of a lower-middle-class family, Mustafa Kemal Atatürk was given the name Mustafa at his birth. His father, Ali Rıza Efendi, had been a minor officer in the Ottoman customs before trying his luck in trade. Although he died when his son was only seven, Ali Rıza Efendi had a great influence on him through his adherence to secular values and his decision to send Mustafa to a secular elementary school. Like all Ottoman women in her situation, the mother,

Portrait of Mustafa Kemal Atatürk on a Turkish postage stamp. (Richard Bulliet)

Zübeyde Hanım, had to be supported by relatives after her husband's death. It is during the years of refuge in the extended family that Mustafa seems to have developed the lifelong characteristics of both the ambitious, captivating loner and the resolute, charismatic leader.

It was his decision to pursue a military career. He was an outstanding student from the time he entered military middle school in Salonika (1893), where he was given his second name, Kemal, until the staff college from which he graduated (1904) with the rank of captain. He also developed a strong interest in politics as well as literary and rhetorical pursuits during his school years. The command of late Ottoman Turkish with touches of pedantry that his writings disclose are the result of Mustafa Kemal's extensive readings in history and literature. Throughout his military and political career, his speeches and improvised harangues were marked by the eloquence and persuasiveness that he cultivated as early as his high-school years. His interest in politics developed somewhat later, when he attended the War Academy, and at a time when the negative aspects of Sultan ABDÜLHAMIT II's absolutism had become more offensive.

Mustafa Kemal served with the Fifth Army in Damascus (1905–1907), where he joined the revolutionary secret society Fatherland and Freedom. This society was soon subsumed in yet another secret society based in Salonika, the Ottoman Freedom So-

Atatürk's home in Salonika. (D.W. Lockhard)

ciety, which subsequently took the name COMMITTEE OF UNION AND PROGRESS (CUP) after its merger with the YOUNG TURK group that was active in Paris (1907). When Mustafa Kemal was transferred to the Third Army in his native city (late 1907), he joined the CUP, and for a long time thereafter he remained a frustrated member with minor influence in that society.

During the period between the Young Turk Revolution (July 23, 1908) and the end of World War I, Mustafa Kemal emerged as an outstanding soldier with remarkable organizational skills, tenacious ambition, and a quarrelsome demeanor toward superiors with whom he disagreed. He distinguished himself in Libya, where he fought the Italians in the regions of Derna and Tobruk (1911–1912), but his political career was obstructed by the CUP leaders, who disliked his vocal criticism. After an unsuccessful bid for election to the Chamber of Deputies (1912), he was sent off as a military attaché to Sofia (1913–1914). He became a hero during World War I, thanks to his successes against the armies of the Triple Entente countries (France, Great Britain, Russia), which he checked twice in the Gallipoli peninsula (1915). Promoted to brigadier general at

the age of thirty-five, he was transferred to the eastern front, where he retook Bitlis and Muş from the Russians (1916). As the commander of the Seventh Army in Syria, he was in charge of the front north of Aleppo when the Mudros Armistice was signed (October 30, 1918).

At the end of World War I, Mustafa Kemal organized a movement in Anatolia that consisted of both a constitutionalist rebellion against the sultan and resistance against the designs by Triple Entente countries to partition the Ottoman Empire. Mainly because of the support of local military authorities and of the notables whose provinces were threatened by partition, he managed to convene the SIVAS CONGRESS (September 4–11, 1919), which forced the sultan to return to the parliamentarian rule the latter had suspended in November 1918. When the new Chamber of Deputies adopted the document known as the National Pact (January 28, 1920), rejecting the dismemberment of the lands under Ottoman sovereignty at the conclusion of the armistice, the Triple Entente powers occupied Istanbul (March 16, 1920). Subsequently, Mustafa Kemal called for the meeting of an extraordinary parliament in ANKARA, thereby marking the beginning of the Turkish Revolution.

As the president of the Grand National Assembly (GNA), which opened on April 23, 1920, Mustafa Kemal successfully conducted a diplomatic and military campaign to defeat the stipulations of the Treaty of SÈVRES imposed on the Ottoman government by the Entente (August 10, 1920). After he had succeeded in checking the Greek advance on Ankara in the battle of the Sakarya (August–September 1921), he was promoted to the rank of marshal and given the title Ghazi (victorious) by the GNA. Under his command, the Turkish national forces launched an

Atatürk's mausoleum in Ankara, 1955. (D.W. Lockhard)

offensive (August 1922) that completed the liberation of practically all the territory considered Turkish homeland by the National Pact and forced the Allies to call for a new peace conference. The question of Turkish representation at the Lausanne Conference was given a radical solution by the GNA, which dissolved the Ottoman state after Mustafa Kemal's proposal to abolish the sultanate took effect on November 1, 1922.

The Treaty of Lausanne recognized an independent and fully sovereign Turkey (July 24, 1923). Having gained complete control of the GNA through his newly founded People's party, Mustafa Kemal embarked on a series of revolutionary changes. First he proclaimed the Republic of Turkey on October 29,1923. The following year he instituted measures that set the republic on a secular path, including abolishing the caliphate and the ministry of SHARI'A and WAQF, unifying education under state authority (March 3, 1924), and abolishing the religious courts (April 8, 1924). These developments prompted the growth of political opposition, which came out into the open with the founding of the Progressive Republican party (November 1924). Seizing as a pretext the rebellion by Shaykh Sa'id (February 1925), Mustafa Kemal's republican regime quickly put an end to all political opposition in the country by passing the Law on the Maintenance of Public Order (March 4, 1925). In 1926, a plot to assassinate its leader gave the regime the opportunity to suppress the remnants of the CUP, whose leaders had posed a threat to Mustafa Kemal's power since the period of national resistance in Anatolia. By the time Mustafa Kemal read his famous speech in the GNA (October 1927), in which he gave his personal account of the recent history of Turkey, the country had entered the period of a de facto single-party regime, which, with the exception of the brief free party period (August–November 1930), lasted until after World War II.

In this political setting, Mustafa Kemal realized his far-reaching social-engineering program. Secularization was completed by the adoption of the Civil Code (April 4, 1926) and the amendment of Article 2 and Article 26 of the Turkish constitution (April 10, 1928), which, respectively, referred to Islam as the official religion and entrusted the GNA with enforcing the Shari'a. Latin characters were adopted in 1928, thus putting an end to a long debate on the reform of the Turkish alphabet. Citizenship rights were extended to women in 1934 with a constitutional amendment that introduced universal suffrage. A new law, passed the same year, required all citizens to have a patronym in Turkish. The revolution also employed such symbolic measures as replacing the fez with Western-style hats (1925), obliging religious authorities to wear their particular garments only when officiating (1934), and banning the use of honorific titles like pasha, bey, and effendi (1934).

In accord with the law on Turkish patronyms, Mustafa Kemal was named Atatürk (Father Turk) by the GNA (1934). Suggestive of the Roman *pater patriae*, the name reflected Mustafa Kemal's achievement and political status, but to its bearer, the connotations of "mentor" or "guide" that it had in old Turkish were probably more meaningful. The role of mentor, which his numerous remarks indicate he had assigned himself, was evidently accepted by Turks, as attested by the huge crowds that paid homage to his memory after his death in Istanbul (1938).

Mustafa Kemal's regard for modern science was conspicuous in many of his speeches but was only to a limited extent responsible for his comprehensive secularization campaign. Rather than being motivated by positivistic determinism, his policy grew out of his personal reading of the history of Islam and the vision of an astute politician. Two days before abolishing the caliphate, he told the GNA what amounted in fact to a secular rewording of the pious contention that the politics of humans tarnished Islam: "We see that the emancipation of Islam from the status of political tool that it has been constantly reduced to for centuries, and its exaltation, are really necessary" (*Parliamentary Minutes*, 2nd Session, vol. 7, pp. 3–6). Convinced of the autonomy and primacy of politics in the history of Islam in general, and of the Ottoman Empire in particular, Mustafa Kemal, in a way that was ahead of his time, was able to see that far from creating a dual society by introducing Western institutions into an Islamic polity, successive generations of Ottoman statesmen—from Sultan SELIM III (1709–1807) to the Young Turks—had Westernized an age-old, secular state tradition. The perceived dualism was only an exacerbation of the secularity of the state. Under these circumstances, if what was sought was an organic relation between state and society (that is, democracy) the society must be synchronized with the state by strictly confining religion to the sphere of the individual. Hence, it would be more accurate to attribute Mustafa Kemal's secularizing measures to the radical anticlericalism of a standard-bearer of *raison d'état* than to interpret them as a reform of Islam or as the manifestations of anti-Islamic prejudice.

Although a nation builder, Mustafa Kemal was more of a patriot than a nationalist. His interest in the cultural and ideological aspects of nation building (as manifested by the founding of the Turkish Historical Society in 1931 and the Turkish Language Society in 1932) surfaced rather late in his life, and only after the economic and political upheavals of the Great Depression had revealed an ideological vacuum in the country. His first years as president of the republic were necessarily devoted to the strengthening of the new regime against an opposition that predated its founding. Even after establishing his de facto single-party system, however, he did not proceed in a nationalistic direction. His humorous references to the excesses associated with the "Turkish historical thesis" and the "Sun-language theory"—developed, under his guidance, by the historical and language societies—also indicate his lighthearted approach to nationalist ideology and his view of such theories as a transient pedagogic device in the training of the common citizen.

Mustafa Kemal's aversion to ideological speculation is apparent in his reactions to the attempts to define his regime during his lifetime. Influenced by the proliferation of single-party dictatorships in Europe throughout the interwar period, zealous admirers tended to formulate a doctrine they called KEMALISM to describe his government. Mustafa Kemal courteously discouraged such definitions, because he did not want anything to arrest the dynamism of the regime. For the same reason, he published his book *Civic Notions for the Citizens* (in Turkish; Istanbul, 1930) as the work of his adoptive daughter, Afet. This reluctance to associate his name with the actual politics of his time can best be explained by his view of his regime as being transitory and his ultimate vision of Turkey in the future as a liberal democracy.

Although his was a personal rule in which he went so far as to select individually all the candidates for the GNA, ample evidence shows he very much disliked such dictators as Hitler and Mussolini and was genuinely offended by Western commentators and journalists who placed him in the same category as they. He rationalized that his role was exactly the opposite of theirs, in that he was trying to establish a democratic tradition in Turkey; that is why he took care to do everything through the legislature and did not envisage suspending the constitution of 1924 or altering its liberal spirit. He also refused life presidency; he preferred to be reelected by the GNA at the beginning of each term. Mustafa Kemal's dictatorial rule was in effect an apprenticeship in democracy in the paradoxical tradition of Jacobinism, and he was aware of the tragic role he was playing in Turkish history. Very early on, he told a group of journalists how objective conditions prevail over ideas: "An individual would think in a particular manner in Ankara, in a different manner in Istanbul or Izmir, and in yet another different manner in Paris" (in Turkish, 1923; edited by Arı Inan, Ankara, 1982, p. 51).

Mustafa Kemal knew that the establishment of democracy was accompanied by legal, economic, social, and ideological prerequisites, and his regime was designed to prepare the country in these areas.

BIBLIOGRAPHY

The *Bibliography of the History of Atatürk and His Reforms*, 3 vols. (Ankara, 1981–1983), compiled by MUZAFFER GÖKMAN, covers an impressive number of publications in all languages, but it is not annotated, and using it effectively requires great patience. The best biography of Mustafa Kemal Atatürk, ŞEVKET SÜREYYA AYDEMIR's *Mustafa Kemal, First and Last*, 3 vols. (Istanbul, 1963–1965), is available only in Turkish. *Atatürk: The Rebirth of a Nation* (London, 1964), by LORD KINROSS, and despite its excessive psychologizing, *The Immortal Atatürk: A Psychobiography* (Chicago, 1984), by VAMIK D. VOLKAN and NORMAN ITZKOWITZ, are the best of the multitude of biographies available in English. *A Speech Delivered by Mustafa Kemal Atatürk* (Istanbul, 1963) is the most recent translation of Mustafa Kemal Pasha's own account (1927) of the Turkish national struggle. ERIK JAN ZÜRCHER's *The Unionist Factor: The Role of the Committee of Union and Progress in the Turkish National Movement, 1905–1926* (Leiden, 1984) is an indispensable corrective for all other readings about the period. Two books, *The Emergence of Modern Turkey*, 2nd ed. (London, 1968), by BERNARD LEWIS, and *The Making of Modern Turkey* (London and New York, 1993), by FEROZ AHMAD, help place Mustafa Kemal Atatürk in a broad historical context.

Ahmet Kuyas

Atatürk University

A public university in Erzurum, Turkey.

Founded in 1957, it comprises faculties of agriculture, medicine, arts and sciences, economics and administrative sciences, education, engineering, dentistry, theology, and veterinary science (the last located in Kars), as well as the College of Education (one in Agri and one in Erzincan), the School of Nursing in ERZURUM, and the College of Vocational Education (one in Erzurum and one in Erzincan). In 1990, the university had about 850 teaching staff and about 18,000 students (about 4,500 were female). The state-funded budget of the university for 1991 was 200 billion Turkish lire, of which about 50 billion was for capital investment.

Named for Mustafa Kemal ATATÜRK, first president of Turkey (1923–1938), the university was founded in an era of increasing U.S. influence in

Turkish politics and society. While older universities in Ankara, Istanbul, and Izmir were patterned after European models—mainly German and French—Atatürk University in Erzurum was modeled on an American land-grant college. Its original emphasis was on academic areas that would have a direct bearing on the needs of eastern ANATOLIA. From its inception, Atatürk University was aided by its association with the University of Nebraska; climatic similarity, especially in relation to the development of the region's agricultural potential, was an important consideration in this association. The university's teaching and research in the humanities, too, have been in harmony with the conservative and relatively traditional outlook of eastern Anatolian provincial society.

BIBLIOGRAPHY

Higher Education in Turkey. UNESCO, European Centre for Higher Education. December 1990.
World of Learning. 1990.

I. Metin Kunt

Ataullah, Mehmed   [c. 1770–1826]

Ottoman Turkish historian and medical writer.

Known as Şanizade, Mehmed Ataullah was the son of an Islamic religious official in the Ottoman Empire. Şanizade studied at religious schools, but supplemented his traditional education with studies in medicine, mathematics, science, and European languages. After serving with his father as an army QADI (judge) and as qadi of Eyüp, he was appointed imperial historiographer in 1819.

Şanizade's advocacy of modern medical practices earned him the enmity of the sultan's physician Behçet Effendi, and in 1825 he was dismissed from this post and sent into exile, ostensibly because of his membership in the BEKTASHI religious brotherhood. Through his translation into TURKISH of an Austrian medical textbook, along with a treatise on anatomy and a translation of a work on vaccinations, Şanizade introduced to Ottoman Turkey the study of modern medicine; the medical vocabulary he created remained in use until it was replaced by recent language reforms.

BIBLIOGRAPHY

LEWIS, BERNARD. *The Emergence of Modern Turkey,* 2nd ed., London, 1961.

David Waldner

Atay, Salıh Rifki   [1894–1971]

Turkish Kemalist politician and journalist.

Born in Istanbul, Atay became a disciple of the Turkish nationalist Ziya Gökalp at an early age, joined the Committee of Union and Progress, and as a journalist wrote on NATIONALISM during the final years of the Ottoman Empire. In the 1920s, he invested in the development of radio in the new Republic of Turkey and became a leading example of language reform, known for his beautiful style in the new TURKISH LANGUAGE.

Atay became a close associate of ATATÜRK in the 1930s and 1940s and edited *Ulus* (Nation), the official newspaper of Turkey's ruling political party, the PROGRESSIVE REPUBLICAN. He was linked with the party's hard-line modernists, like Recep Peker, prime minister from 1946 to 1947. He left *Ulus* in 1947 amid intraparty intrigue and was replaced by a more moderate editor. In the 1950s, he published the newspaper *Dünya* (World), opposing DEMOCRAT PARTY rule (Turkey's new second party, which became oppressive and was removed in the coup of 1960). Atay published several books on Atatürk and the nationalist struggle, as well as a number of travel books.

BIBLIOGRAPHY

FREY, FREDERICK W. *The Turkish Political Elite.* Cambridge, Mass., 1965.

Elizabeth Thompson

Atfi, Abdullah   [1897–?]

Syrian military officer of Isma'ili descent.

The son of Muhammad Ali Atfi, Abdullah Atfi was educated at the Ottoman Military College in Istanbul and later in Paris. He rose in the ranks of the Syrian army to become chief of staff. He served as Syria's minister of defense in the 1948 NATIONAL BLOC administration and again in 1949 under the PEOPLE'S PARTY. Among other honors, General Atfi was awarded the Ottoman Military Medal and the French Military Cross and was inducted into the Syrian Order of Merit.

BIBLIOGRAPHY

Who's Who in the Middle East.

Charles U. Zenzie

Atlas Mountains

Mountain system in northwest Africa.

The Atlas mountains extend approximately 1,300 miles (2,090 km) through the Maghrib countries of Morocco, Algeria, and Tunisia—from the Atlantic Ocean, south of Agadir, to the Mediterranean Sea near Tunis. This system comprises a series of roughly parallel ranges. From west to east, these include the Anti-Atlas, High Atlas, and Middle Atlas in Morocco; the Saharan Atlas, maritime Tell Atlas (itself formed of a series of distinct massifs such as the Ouarsenis, Grande Kabylie, and Petite Kabylie), and Aurès in Algeria; and the Kroumirie, Medjerda, and Tébessa mountains in Tunisia, which are extensions of the Algerian ranges. Some authorities also include the Rif range (al-Rif), along Morocco's Mediterranean coast in the Atlas system.

The Atlas ranges dominate the landscapes of Morocco, Algeria, and Tunisia, differentiating them from the other North African countries, where desert lowlands prevail. These ranges serve as a barrier to the Sahara, sheltering the coastal lowlands of the three countries from the desert conditions to the south. They also function as orographic barriers to moisure-laden winter storms off the Atlantic and Mediterranean, causing rainfall in the coastal lowlands. Finally, they serve as vast water towers, capturing rain and snow and giving rise to numerous permanent rivers and streams. As a result, the northern portions of the three Maghreb countries are relatively well watered and have major agricultural potential. This potential has long fostered relatively dense settlement by the Berbers—indigenous Caucasoid tribal peoples—particularly in the mountains. The region's agricultural potential has attracted colonizers, beginning with the Phoenicians and Romans, then later the Arabs and French. Europeans have referred to the Maghrib highlands as the Atlas mountains since classical times, because of the Greek legend that they were the home of the god Atlas; the Arabs have referred to the entire highland area as *Jazirat al-Maghrib*, the "Island of the West," because it represented a relatively lush mountainous island jutting out of the deserts.

The most impressive range within the Atlas system is the High Atlas, which extends for some 350 miles (560 km) through the center of Morocco and has an average elevation of around 10,000 feet (3,050 m). Many High Atlas peaks are snow clad for much of the year. Jabal Toukal, south of Marrakech, reaches 13,665 feet (4,165 m) and is the highest peak in the High Atlas as well as in North Africa. The Middle Atlas range possesses the most luxuriant vegetation in the Atlas system, with extensive stands of fir and

cedar at higher elevations. Forests of various species of oak are common on the more humid slopes throughout the Atlas system, with open stands of pine and juniper typical on drier slopes. Generally, the mountains diminish in elevation from west to east and become more barren of vegetation from north to south.

Historically, the Atlas mountains have functioned as a refuge area for the indigenous BERBER peoples, helping them to preserve their distinctive languages and customs. Portions of the Moroccan Atlas and the Kabylie in Algeria remain strong bastions of Berber culture. Tribal areas in the Atlas had autonomy in the precolonial period; only occasionally did they fall under the control of rulers in the lowland capitals. This tradition of dissidence continued during the colonial period: The Atlas mountains figured prominently in the resistance and independence movements, serving as effective strongholds for rebel groups.

BIBLIOGRAPHY

GELLNER, ERNEST. *Saints of the Atlas.* Chicago, 1969.
MILLER, JAMES A. *Imlil: A Moroccan Mountain Community in Change.* Boulder, Colo., 1984.

Will D. Swearingen

Atrash, Farid al-   [1915?–1974]

Composer, singer, and oud player.

Farid al-Atrash appeared in and composed music for numerous films and wrote songs for many other performers as well. His low-pitched voice was characterized by a poignant and evocative sadness (*huzn*), and he commanded vocal styles considered to be authentic (*asil*) in Egypt as well as in the Levant.

He was born in Jabal al-Duruz (Syria) to Aliya Husayn and Fahd al-Atrash. Aliya moved to Cairo with her children Fu'ad, Farid, and Amal (later the professional singer and film star known as ASMAHAN) in about 1924, to escape the fighting against the French mandate troops, in which her husband was involved. To sustain the family, Aliya sang for private radio stations in Cairo and appeared in music halls.

Farid began his performing career in the music halls of Mary Mansur and Badi'a Masabni. Ibrahim Hamuda, then a rising star in musical theater, encouraged Farid and hired him to play the *ud* (oud; a short-necked lute) in his accompanying ensemble. Soon thereafter, Farid enrolled in the Institute of Arabic Music and studied with oud virtuoso Riyad al-Sunbati. He also worked with Dawud Husni and composer, Farid Ghusn.

Farid's reputation spread via local radio stations. He was introduced to radio audiences by Medhat Assem, one of his mentors, who was then the director of music programming for Egyptian Radio. His career as a composer blossomed in the late 1930s, and he flourished as a composer, singer, and oud player until his health began to deteriorate in the 1970s.

In his compositions, Farid, like Muhammad Abd al-Wahhab and many of his contemporaries, evinced interest in Western music and incorporated many Western instruments. He tried to modernize Arabic music while preserving its essential character. His efforts along these lines extended into harmonization, adoption of Western dance rhythms, and use of genres such as the operetta. In his vocal style, however, he cultivated local nuances, and his voice was believed to carry the flavor of authentically Egyptian and Arabic song.

He made over thirty films, for which he composed the music and appeared as the star; among them were *Bulbul Afandi, Matqulsh li-Hadd, Ayza at-Jawwiz, Lahn al-Khulud,* and *Lahn Hubbi. Intisar al-Shabab,* with his sister Asmahan, was particularly successful. Several, such as *Wa-ja al-Rabi,* closely followed Western models. He also wrote hundreds of songs, sung by himself and others. Among the most famous are "Awwal Hamsa" and "al-Rabi."

BIBLIOGRAPHY

Farid al-Atrash: Mudhakkirat, majmu'at aghanihi (Farid al-Atrash: Memoirs, Collection of His Songs). Beirut, 1975.
AL-NAJMI, KAMAL. "Fann al-Dumu" (The Art of the Tear). In *Al-Ghina al-misri* (Egyptian Song). Cairo, 1966.

Virginia Danielson

Atrash, Mansur al-

Syrian politician.

Mansur al-Atrash was the son of the Druze chieftain Sultan Pasha al-ATRASH, leader of a rebellion against the French Mandate authorities in 1925. As a member of the al-BA'TH party in Syria, Mansur was arrested in 1953 for fomenting a revolt against Adib SHISHAKLI by distributing pamphlets in the JABAL DRUZE. He was Syria's minister for social affairs and labor in 1963/64 and was chairman of the National Revolutionary Council of the al-Ba'th party in 1965.

He was arrested and exiled in the 1966 radical takeover of the party and, from then on, served as director of the al-Tali'a Publishing Company in Beirut.

BIBLIOGRAPHY

SEALE, PATRICK. *Asad: The Struggle for the Middle East.* Los Angeles, 1988.

Charles U. Zenzie

Atrash, Sultan Pasha al-

Prominent Syrian Druze chieftain.

Sultan Pasha was feared by the French because of his continued efforts to rally the Druzes against French interference in the JABAL DRUZE in Syria. He was the leader of the Jabal Druze revolt (1925–27) against French administration in Syria, during which he called on all Syrians to fight for the complete independence of Syria. Although the revolt was under Druze leadership, it assumed a truly national character and became Syria-wide. Sultan Pasha's anti-French activities compelled him to live years of exile with many of his followers. Exile, which ended with the French amnesty of May 1937, allowed new rivals to Sultan Pasha to emerge in the Jabal Druze. Sultan Pasha remained close to the faction of Abd al-Rahman SHAHBANDAR, a prominent Syrian politician who had British and Hashimite links.

Muhammad Muslih

Attas, Haidar Abu Bakr al-

Yemeni government official.

Al-Attas was a longtime second-level leader who, despite—or possibly because of—a reputation for not being political, had been prime minister of the PEOPLE'S DEMOCRATIC REPUBLIC OF YEMEN (PDRY) for nearly a year at the time of the intraparty blood bath in 1986. He then became PDRY head of state in the regime of survivors that followed that event. Al-Attas became prime minister upon the creation of the Republic of YEMEN in 1990, remaining in that post until he was forced into exile in mid-1994 as a leader of the failed attempt at secession earlier in the year. Long regarded by most as a loyal, hard-working technocrat, he is of a great learned family from WADI HADRAMAWT.

Robert D. Burrowes

Attlee, Clement   [1883–1967]

Prime minister of Britain, 1945–1951.

Attlee was prime minister of Britain at an important juncture of Middle Eastern history: the surrender of Britain's mandates over Jordan (April 25, 1946) and Palestine (May 15, 1948) after the end of World War II and renegotiation of treaties between Britain and Jordan (March 15, 1948). Major issues of contention were Jewish claims to Palestine and Arab aspirations to nationalism, which ultimately Attlee was unable to reconcile as the Arab–Israel conflict continued.

Jenab Tutunji

Auchinleck, Claude   [1884–1981]

British general.

As a young officer Auchinleck served in World War I in Egypt and Mesopotamia and was at Kut al-Amara. In World War II he was named commander-in-chief in India (1940–1941), where he was responsible for sending troops to suppress Rashid Ali al-Kaylani in Iraq in May of 1941. In July 1941 he succeeded General Sir Archibald WAVELL as commander of British forces in North Africa, which were succumbing to the German Panzerarmee (known as the Afrikakorps) under General Erwin ROMMEL.

In late 1941, Auchinleck removed General Sir Alan Cunningham from command of the Eighth Army, took command himself, and stopped the Germans at TOBRUK in Libya. By February 1942, the Germans had regrouped and counterattacked, pushing the British out of BENGHAZI and Tobruk, toward al-ALAMAYN in Egypt. That June, Auchinleck again assumed direct command of the Eighth Army to halt the new German advance.

Auchinleck's success at the first battle of El Alamein was not seen as such at the time, and Prime Minister Winston Churchill had replaced him with General Sir Harold Alexander as commander-in-chief in the Middle East and General Bernard Law MONTGOMERY as commander of the Eighth Army. After his success at the second battle of El Alamein, Auchinleck was made commander-in-chief in India from 1943 to 1946, was promoted to field marshal in 1946, and was supreme commander in India and Pakistan in 1947.

BIBLIOGRAPHY

BARNETT, CORRELLI. *The Desert Generals*. Bloomington, 1982.

Dictionary of National Biography 1981–1985. New York, 1990.

Zachary Karabell

Auspicious Event

See Vaka-i Hayriye

Austria-Hungary and the Middle East

Austria and Hungary joined to form the Austro-Hungarian Empire in 1867, under Austrian Emperor Franz Joseph, a member of the Hapsburg dynasty that had ruled since 1278.

During the fourteenth through seventeenth centuries, before Hungary joined Austria, both countries had been repeatedly attacked, first by the Turks and then by the OTTOMAN EMPIRE attempting to expand into Europe by way of the BALKAN peninsula. In the sixteenth century, western and northern Hungary accepted Austrian rule to escape Ottoman occupation. In 1683, the Ottoman armies were halted at Vienna, but fighting continued in the Balkans until a peace was signed in 1699, the Treaty of Karlowitz. After suppression of the 1848 revolt of Hungary against Austrian rule, the dual monarchy was formed in 1867, as a Christian empire, but one relatively tolerant of the religious and ethnic diversity that characterized its citizens.

Austro-Hungarian policy toward the Middle East was focused on two main concerns—preservation of the Ottoman Empire and containment of Balkan NATIONALISM, which had emerged in the Serbian revolt of 1804 against Ottoman rule. The Balkan peninsula was inhabited by both Christians and Muslims, most of them Slavs. Russia was in the process of instigating a pan-Slavic movement (in an attempt to link Russian Slavs with Poland and the Balkans and gain access to the warm-water ports of the eastern Mediterranean—crucial to Russian trade interests before aviation allowed a way around frozen northern ports). As a multinational empire encompassing several Slavic groups, Austria-Hungary was vulnerable to these same forces of Slavic nationalism and pan-Slavism that threatened the European possessions of the Ottoman Empire. Austro-Hungarian Slavs included Poles, Ukrainians, Czechs, Slovenes, Serbs, Croats, and Slavonized Bulgars. Nationalism in the Balkan peninsula was seen as the beginning of the potential breakup of both the Austro-Hungarian and Ottoman empires.

Even before the eruption of Balkan nationalism in the nineteenth century, Austrian statesmen had been concerned with the potential breakup of the Ottoman Empire and the resulting politics that would affect the Austrian Empire. Therefore, Austria-Hungary adopted a dual strategy: (1) help preserve Ottoman suzerainty over the Slavs where possible and (2) make sure that Austria, not Russia, gained when preservation of Ottoman authority was no longer possible. Toward this end, Austro-Hungarian bankers floated loans to the Ottomans and, to improve communications, sponsored the construction of the Vienna-Istanbul railroad. Under Klemens von METTERNICH, Austria's foreign minister from 1809 to 1848, and for the rest of the nineteenth century, Austria looked to expand its domain over the northwestern Balkan territories of Bosnia and Herzegovina. By the beginning of the great Eastern Crisis of 1875–1878, Austro-Hungarian Foreign Minister JULIUS ANDRÁSSY sent the Andrássy Note of December 30, 1875, calling for autonomy for Bosnia-Herzegovina and Ottoman reform of its administration of its Balkan provinces. Andrássy was simultaneously trying to curtail Russian pan-Slavism, which dictated Russian support for Serbian and Bulgarian expansion. The resulting crisis led to the defeat of the Ottomans by the Russians in the RUSSO-OTTOMAN WAR of 1877–1878 and the subsequent Treaty of San Stephano, which resulted in a vastly enlarged Bulgaria and a clear advantage for Russia in the Balkans. Andrássy sided with the British to attempt to force a revision of the treaty in Austria-Hungary's favor and, at the July 1878 Congress of BERLIN, he prevailed, when a virtual protectorate over a technically autonomous Bosnia-Herzegovina was given to Austria-Hungary.

The following years saw increasing nationalist activity in the Balkans and increasingly complex alliances among the European powers. During the height of the Macedonian crisis at the turn of the twentieth century, Austria-Hungary at times supported Serbia and at times opposed it—all with the overall goal of obtaining Austrian influence on the northern Aegean. When the Albanians revolted against the Ottomans in 1912, Austro-Hungarian pressure on the Ottomans led to the creation of an independent state, which was advantageous from an Austrian perspective, because Albania provided a buffer against Serbian expansion to the Adriatic. The Ottoman defeat in the two BALKAN WARS, fought just prior to WORLD WAR I, was disadvantageous to Austria-Hungary. Spurred by victories in the Balkan Wars, Serbia overran northern Albania to the Adriatic. Serbian ambitions in Bosnia-Herzegovina led to the assassination of the heir to the Austro-Hungarian throne, Archduke Franz Ferdinand, in July of 1914; this was used as a symbolic outrage that allowed for the beginning of World War I in August.

Ultimately, both the Ottoman and Austro-Hungarian empires were on the losing side of that war, and their territories were allowed to become independent states or protectorates of the winning European countries—mainly Britain and France—by the peace treaties and the LEAGUE OF NATIONS.

BIBLIOGRAPHY

ANDERSON, M. S. *The Eastern Question*. London, 1966.
LANGER, W. L. *European Alliance and Alignments 1871–1890*. New York, 1950.
SHAW, STANFORD, and EZEL KURAL SHAW. *History of the Ottoman Empire and Modern Turkey*. Cambridge, U.K., 1977.
TAYLOR, A. J. P. *The Struggle for Mastery in Europe*. Oxford, 1954.

Zachary Karabell

Avidan, David   [1934–1995]

Israeli poet.

Avidan was born in Tel Aviv. From 1952 to 1954 he studied at the Hebrew University in Jerusalem. Avidan was a poetic innovator who published thirty books as well as several plays and movie scripts. His titles include *Interim* (1960), *Something for Somebody* (1964), *Axiomatic Poems* (1978), and *The Last Gulf* (1991). He has won the Prime Minister's Prize as well as other prestigious literary awards.

Avidan was an important member of a small group of poets who ushered in a poetic revolution in Israel in the 1950s and 1960s. He and his peers sought to undermine the positivistic ethos of the Zionist poets of the 1940s, who generally identified with the national efforts of state building. Unlike the optimistic poems of the preceding generation, many of Avidan's poems are preoccupied with death and infused with a pervasive sense of impending doom. Although Avidan was strongly criticized early in his career for his morbidity, his poetry gained national recognition for its profundity and its impressive linguistic powers. His poems are marked by two incongruent oppositions: an unsettling sense of the speaker's omnipotence and an equally strong sense of his weakness, both of which are connected by biting irony. Avidan's poetic voice often speaks from the depth of loneliness, desperately seeking compassion while at the same time weary of the very attempt to do so. He introduced new ways of expression and greatly expanded the use of Hebrew as a poetic language, which had a profound influence on contemporary Hebrew poetry.

BIBLIOGRAPHY

AVIDAN, DAVID. *Personal Problems.* Arad, 1959. In Hebrew.

——. *Pressure Poems.* Levin-Epstein, 1962. In Hebrew.

BERNSTEIN, URI. "Adon ve-Eved la-Ivrit." *Ha'aretz* (May 19, 1995): 10.

GELLERMAN, MORDECAI. "Flirt im ha-Ye'ush." *Ha'aretz* (May 19, 1995): 10.

Yaron Peleg

Avneri, Uri [1923–]

Israeli journalist, member of the Knesset.

Born in Germany, Avneri immigrated to Palestine in 1933. As a youth he was active in the Revisionist Zionist underground, the Irgun. He joined the Haganah in 1948. In 1950, as editor of the political weekly *Ha-Olam Ha-Zeh*, he advocated severing ties with the Jewish diaspora and the development of a "Hebrew nationalism" that would allow accommodation with the Arabs. He expressed these ideas in his book *Israel Without Zionism: A Plea for Peace in the Middle East* (1968).

He was elected to the Knesset in 1965 and 1969 on the list of the Ha-Olam Ha-Zeh–Ko'ah Hadash party (This World–New Force). In 1979 he founded the Sheli Party, representing it in the Knesset until 1981. Sheli split in 1983, and Avneri was among those who established a new party, Alternative. Members of that group joined others in 1984 to form the Progressive List for Peace, of which he is cochair. Avneri has defied Israel's ban on meeting with Palestine Liberation Organization (PLO) members and since 1984 has held occasional talks with PLO leaders, including Yasir Arafat.

Martin Malin

AWACS Arms Deal

Sale of special planes to Saudi Arabia by the United States.

In 1980 the United States deployed four AWACS (airborne warning and control system) planes to Saudi Arabia to help defend it against Iran. In the same year the government of Saudi Arabia asked to purchase such planes. On August 24, 1981, the administration of Ronald Reagan formally notified the Congress of its intention to sell five AWACS planes to Saudi Arabia. Only the president's personal politicking overcame powerful opposition to the sale led by the pro-Israel lobby. A narrow Senate victory of 52–48 on October 28 enabled the sale to go through. The planes were transferred to Saudi Arabia beginning in 1985.

BIBLIOGRAPHY

CORDESMAN, ANTHONY H. *The Gulf and the Search for Strategic Stability: Saudi Arabia, the Military Balance in the Gulf, and Trends in the Arab–Israeli Military Balance.* Boulder, Colo., 1984.

Malcolm C. Peck

Awad, Louis [1914/15–1991]

Egyptian scholar and essayist.

Louis Awad was born in the village of Sharuna in the district of Mina. He studied literature at the universities of Cairo, Oxford, and Princeton. As chairman of the Faculty of Letters at Cairo University, Awad inaugurated the modern study of literary criticism based on scientific principles in Egypt. In the period from 1945 to 50, Awad took his place as one of a generation of writers calling for the total reform of Egyptian society, looking for inspiration in, among other sources, Marxism. His novel *al Anqa* (The Phoenix) expresses this orientation. His volume of poetry, *Plutoland*, introduced free verse forms to Egyptian literature and contained a scathing attack on traditionalism. Awad's unwavering critical stance continued after the 1952 revolution, and as a consequence, in 1954 he was forced to give up his position at Cairo University.

In 1960, Awad became the literary editor at *al-Ahram*. In 1964, he published a devastating critique of higher education in Egypt, arguing that students were interested in instruction, not in independent study and research. Awad's writings in *al-Ahram* made him one of the leading opinion-makers in the Arab world.

BIBLIOGRAPHY

AIS, SALAH. "Tarikh Louis Awad." *Adab wa Naqd* 57 (May 1990): 144.

KILPATRICK, HILARY. *The Modern Egyptian Novel: A Study in Social Criticism.* London, 1974, p. 65.

TARABAY, EDOUARD, ed. *Anthologie de la Litterature Arabe Contemporaine,* vol. 3: *La Poesie.* Paris, 1967, p. 61.

David Waldner

Awakened Youth

Afghan political-literacy organization.

Awakened Youth was a political-literacy group formed in 1946 or 1947, in part as a reaction to the autocratic Afghan prime minister Shah Mahmoud. One of its founders was MUHAMMAD DAUD, a future prime minister and a member of the royal family. The party advocated social change and promoted the cause of Pushtunistan. Later it became more radicalized, and many members were arrested at the end of the Seventh Afghan National Assembly in 1952 when liberal laws allowing political activity expired.

BIBLIOGRAPHY

ARNOLD, ANTHONY. *Afghanistan's Two-Party Communism: Parcham and Khalq.* Stanford, Calif., 1983.

Grant Farr

Awali, al-

Town located in the middle of the island of Bahrain.

Situated atop Bahrain's oil field, Awali lies approximately two miles (3 km) south of Rifa, the town where the ruling family of BAHRAIN resides. Awali was built during the British protectorate by the BAHRAIN PETROLEUM COMPANY (BAPCO), following the discovery of PETROLEUM in 1932, to provide housing for the company's expatriate, especially European and American, personnel. The town consists primarily of small garden homes; it offers cultural and recreational facilities for its residents.

BIBLIOGRAPHY

NYROP, RICHARD, ed. *Persian Gulf States: Country Studies.* Washington, D.C., 1985.

Emile A. Nakhleh

Awdatallah, Tu'ma al-

Syrian military officer.

An army officer loyal to Adib Shishakli, Tu'ma al-Awdatallah was one of fourteen officers sent to Cairo on January 12, 1958 to assure Egypt's President Nasser of Ba'th support in the face of the growing communist movement. He later held a ministerial post in the Syrian executive under the first Syro–Egyptian union.

BIBLIOGRAPHY

SEALE, PATRICK. *The Struggle for Syria: A Study of Post-War Arab Politics, 1945–1958.* London, 1958.

Charles U. Zenzie

Awir Oasis

Oasis east of the city of Dubai, United Arab Emirates.

Awir oasis originally provided the city with its water. Today, it is called al-Awir, a residential quarter, with a military academy. The Jabal-Ali distillation station provides the city with 85 percent of its water, while the al-Awir water plant provides another 15 percent. New artesian wells irrigate hundreds of farms in the area as well.

M. Morsy Abdullah

Awn, Michel

See Aoun, Michel

Awqaf

See Waqf

Ayan

Plural of the Arabic word ayn, *meaning notable person.*

The term *ayan* was used in the OTTOMAN EMPIRE to refer to a variety of elites, particularly landed notables in either cities or the countryside. Ayan were usually tax farmers from merchant, ULAMA, or Janissary families, although their origins differed in various regions of the empire. In the provinces of Egypt, Syria, and Iraq, the ayan were typically MAMLUKS or local Ottoman officials like governors. In eastern ANATOLIA, they were called *derebeys,* or valley lords affiliated with dominant clans.

In the late eighteenth and early nineteenth centuries, many provincial ayan amassed personal armies and control of local finances, challenging the influence of the central state. Particularly in the European provinces, the ayan were able to gain power in the late eighteenth century because they supplied crucial military support to the sultan in the several wars against Russia. Their power was formalized when the sultan granted them official status (*ayanlik*) as representatives of the people to the government in exchange for their support.

In the early nineteenth century, the ayan openly rebelled against the central state in the Serbian revolt (1803–1805) and in their refusal in the Balkans to cooperate in conscription to Selim III's new army, the NIZAM-I CEDIT. In 1807, ayan from the European provinces cooperated with opponents of reform to overthrow Selim. An attempt to negotiate a truce between Constantinople and provincial notables produced in 1808 the ineffective and largely ignored SENED-I ITTIFAK (Pact of Alliance). Mahmud II devoted the latter part of his reign to undermining the autonomy of the ayan and enlarging central power, reforms continued in the TANZIMAT era.

BIBLIOGRAPHY

GIBB, H. A. R., et al., eds. *The Encyclopedia of Islam,* new ed., vol. 1. London, 1960.
KARPAT, KEMAL H. "The Land Regime, Social Structure, and Modernization in the Ottoman Empire." In *The Beginnings of Modernization in the Middle East: The Nineteenth Century,* ed. by William R. Polk and Richard L. Chambers. Chicago, 1966.
SHAW, STANFORD J. *The History of the Ottoman Empire and Modern Turkey.* New York, 1976.

Elizabeth Thompson

Ayandegan

Iranian daily newspaper, 1967–1979.

Ayandegan was a daily morning newspaper in Iran that began publication on December 16, 1967. It was founded by Hoseyn Ahari, Mas'ud Behnud, and Daryush Homayun. *Ayandegan* was distinguished by its more professional approach to journalism, as well as its critical stance vis-à-vis government policy, in comparison to *Kayhan* and *Etella'at,* the two other dailies of import in Iran.

In 1978, the newspaper was taken over by Firuz Guran, whose leftist and pro-revolutionary leanings made their imprint on its editorials. At the outset of the Iranian Revolution of 1979, *Ayandegan* emerged as the most widely read Iranian daily, owing to its anti-clerical, liberal stance. It developed into a forum for all stripes of opposition to clerical takeover of the revolution, including the NATIONAL FRONT, the MOJAHEDIN-E KHALQ, and several marxist political groupings. The newspaper had gained such high societal standing that it took an explicit condemnation by Ayatollah Ruhollah KHOMEINI before government authorities could take measures to terminate

its publication. *Ayandegan* was officially banned in August 1979.

BIBLIOGRAPHY

ELWELL-SUTTON, L. P., and P. MOHAJER. "Ayandegan." In *Encyclopaedia Iranica,* vol. 3. London, 1989.

Neguin Yavari

Aya Sofya

Religious structure in Istanbul, now a museum.

The Aya Sofya (also known by its Greek name, Hagia Sophia) was built by the Roman Emperor Constantine from 325 to 330 C.E. during his rebuilding of the city of Byzantium as his capital. It was built as a

Aya Sofya in Istanbul, Turkey. Originally built as a Byzantine cathedral, the building has been a mosque since 1453. (Mia Bloom)

Christian church, the cathedral of Constantinople (now Istanbul), for the first Roman emperor to espouse that faith. The present structure dates from the sixth century, when the cathedral was rebuilt by the Byzantine Emperor Justinian. In 1453, the Ottomans conquered the city and transformed the church into a MOSQUE. In 1935, the new Republic of Turkey transformed it again, this time into a museum. The Aya Sofya served as the inspiration for several mosques built during the OTTOMAN EMPIRE, including SÜLEYMANIYE MOSQUE, designed by Sinan, and the Blue Mosque.

Zachary Karabell

Ayatollah

See Molla

Aydınlık

Turkish political group and journal.

As a journal, *Aydınlık* (Light) has had two incarnations in the publishing world of Turkey. First, it was the name of a group of intellectuals, who published a socialist literary journal of the same name in Istanbul between 1921 and 1925. Leaders of the group, Sefik Hüsnü and Ethem Nejat, were tied to the Turkish Workers and Peasants Socialist party. Although they had communist sympathies, they criticized the Comintern (Communist International) and advanced a gradualist vision of bourgeois democracy on the road to socialism. The group also published several strictly political journals, brochures, and books. Although it professed support for ATATÜRK, *Aydınlık* and more than ten other publications were shut down under a 1925 press-control law for criticizing the government.

The name *Aydınlık* was revived later in the 1960s for a weekly leftist journal, which was banned in 1971 when martial law was proclaimed. It resumed publication only to have several of its staff journalists jailed in 1974 for allegedly publishing state secrets during Turkey's landing in Cyprus. In 1980, Turkey's national security council finally closed down *Aydınlık*, along with other radical journals of the left and right.

BIBLIOGRAPHY

AHMAD, FEROZ. *The Turkish Experiment in Democracy.* Boulder, Colo., 1977.
KARPAT, KEMAL H. *Turkey's Politics: The Transition to a Multi-Party System.* Princeton, N.J., 1959.

Elizabeth Thompson

Ayn, al-

Originally one of six small oasis villages east of the Emirate of Abu Dhabi and adjacent to al-Buraymi oasis in the Sultanate of Oman.

In 1970, al-Ayn (Arabic, the spring) still provided Abu Dhabi with water. By the 1990s, the modern city of al-Ayn hosted the Emirates University of the UNITED ARAB EMIRATES, Zayed Military Academy, and a museum featuring the prehistoric artifacts found in the al-Ayn area.

M. Morsy Abdullah

Ayn, Ras al-

Town in northeastern Syria near the border with Turkey.

It has one of the world's largest karst springs, which are formed from Paleogenic (nummilitic) and marine Miocene limestone. The springs' average annual discharge is estimated at 1,056 gallons (4,000 litres per second) or 1,594 million cubic yards (1,219 million cu m). The springs form the Khabur river, which flows south into the Euphrates river near Dayr al-Zawr in Syria's province of Dayr al-Zawr. They have been called the "Queen of Springs" on account of their high, exceptionally steady discharge throughout the year.

BIBLIOGRAPHY

SAFADI, CHAFIC. *Hydraulic Resources in the Syrian Arab Republic.* Typescript. Damascus, 1978.

Abdul-Karim Rafeq

Ayn al-Dowleh, Abd al-Majid Mirza
[1845–1926]

Prominent Iranian political figure during Mozaffar al-Din Shah's reign, 1896–1907.

Ayn al-Dowleh, Sultan Abd al-Majid Mirza Atabak-e A'zam, was the son of Sultan Ahmad Mirza Azod al-Dowleh, Fath Ali Shah Qajar's forty-eighth son. After administering several governorates, he was given the title of Ayn al-Dowleh by NASER AL-DIN SHAH in 1893. Shah MOZAFFAR AL-DIN appointed him chief minister in 1903, and he was promoted to prime minister the following year. His vociferous opposition to the constitutional movement brought about his dismissal in 1906. He was reinstated for brief intervals in 1915 and 1917, but British disapproval and the hostility of the parliament proved insurmountable. Following the coup d'état in 1921, he was arrested and heavily fined.

BIBLIOGRAPHY

ADAMIYYAT, FEREYDUN. *The Idea of Freedom and the Origins of Constitutionalim in Iran.* Tehran, 1961. In Persian.
ALGAR, HAMID. *Religion and State in Iran, 1786–1906.* Berkeley, Calif., 1969.

Neguin Yavari

Ayni, Muhsin al-   [1932–   ]

Yemeni politician.

A Yemeni nationalist identified with republican, progressive, and unionist policies, al-Ayni was exiled from North YEMEN by Imam Ahmad in the 1950s.

He then became involved in South Yemen's politics, associated with the Aden Trade Union Congress and its political wing, the Popular Socialist party. With the military revolt and the fall of the imamate in North Yeman in 1962, he became the first foreign minister of the Yemen Arab Republic. He was also appointed prime minister four times, between 1968 and 1975. During his various tenures in that office he presided over the 1969/70 reconciliation between republicans and royalists that ended the North Yemen civil war; he also negotiated the 1972 unity agreement with the People's Democratic Republic of Yemen (South Yemen; established 1967). Because he is a controversial political figure, al-Ayni's career after 1975 was limited to overseas diplomatic posts, including that of his 1990 appointment as the first ambassador of the Republic of Yemen to the United States.

BIBLIOGRAPHY

BURROWES, ROBERT. *The Yemen Arab Republic.* Boulder, Colo., 1987.

F. Gregory Gause, III

Ayn Shams University

The second largest university in Egypt.

Ayn Shams (or Ain-Shams) University was established in Cairo in 1950 under the name Ibrahim Pasha University and comprised then the Higher Training College for secondary school teachers, the Commercial Institute, and the Agricultural Institute. In 1954, it acquired a new name, the University of Heliopolis, and is known now as Ayn Shams University. When founded in 1950, it was located in the Munira district, and in 1952 it was moved to the Za'afaran palace in Abbasiyya, its current site.

The university consists of thirteen faculties and higher institutions covering a broad spectrum of specializations including law, arts, commerce, medicine, engineering, and agriculture. One of its unique features is that it has a girls' college (faculty of women for arts, science, and education), which is almost a mini-university. Similar to other Egyptian universities, it has a governing body that consists of the president of the university; three vice-presidents for undergraduate studies, graduate studies and research, and social service; the secretary-general and his two assistants; and deans of colleges; in addition to a number of public figures.

In 1993, the university had a faculty of almost 785 professors, 605 associate professors, and 1,095 assistant professors along with 1,350 lecturers and teaching assistants. Faculties of medicine, agriculture, science, engineering, and arts employ almost 70 percent of the teaching staff. Some twenty-five research centers deal with issues ranging from computer sciences and energy researches to childhood studies.

In 1990, Ayn Shams University had a student population of almost 78,000, divided approximately as follows: Faculty of Commerce, 20,000; Faculty of Law, 14,500; Faculty of Arts, 11,600; Faculty of Education, 6,400; Faculty of Women, 6,100; Faculty of Engineering, 5,800; Faculty of Medicine: 5,000; Faculty of Agriculture, 3,000; Faculty of Science, 3,000; Faculty of Language, 2,200; and the Higher Institute for Nursing, 400.

The university library consists of the central library and the faculty libraries, which contain valuable manuscripts, maps, drawings, encyclopedias, and collections of books. Full medical care is provided for its undergraduate and graduate students. The university has a central residential campus, with various branches at different quarters. The main body of male residences, ten buildings, is situated at Khalifa al-Mamoon street near the university, whereas the main body of female dormitories, eight buildings, lies near the faculty of women.

Each faculty has a students' union, which consists of elected members. Unions cooperate with the student welfare offices of the faculties in taking care of all student activities.

BIBLIOGRAPHY

AIN-SHAMS UNIVERSITY. *Guide Book.* Cairo, 1991–1992.

Ali E. Hillal Dessouki

Ayyad, Kamal   [1901–1986]

Syrian academic and philosopher.

Born in Syria, although some sources claim that he was born in Tripoli, Libya in 1900, Ayyad was one of the first Syrians to obtain a doctorate in philosophy from a German university. In 1951, he began teaching at the University of Damascus. In the early 1940s, he became a pioneer in introducing and explaining Marxist and socialist ideas dealing with materialism and class struggle. He was one of the founders of two progressive Arabic journals: *al-Tali'a* (the Vanguard) and *al-Tariq* (the Road). He also published several articles on the relationship between society and economy, education, and socialism. He is the author of *History of the Ancient East* (2 volumes) and *The Influence of Ibn Rushd Across the Ages*, both in Arabic. With Dr. Jamil Saliba he wrote *Ibn Khaldun* (1934), *Hayy ibn Yaqzan* (1935), and *An Arab Novelist and a Soviet Novelist: Omar Fakhury and Maxim Gorky* (1946), also all in Arabic.

George E. Irani

Ayyub, Dhu al-Nun   [1908?–1988]

Iraqi novelist of the 1930s and 1940s and social critic.

Born in Mosul to a SUNNI Arab lower middle-class merchant family, Ayyub graduated from the Higher Teachers' College in Baghdad in 1928. For over a decade afterward, he worked as a high school mathematics teacher in a number of places in IRAQ. At the end of the 1930s, he became director of Baghdad's institute of Fine Arts, and between 1938 and 1944 he was chief editor of the cultural magazine *al-Majalla*. In 1941–1942, he was a member of the central committee of the Iraqi COMMUNIST PARTY from which he was expelled due to a controversy with its secretary general over Ayyub's demand for democratization in the party. Upon his expulsion, he established his own moderate left-wing party, the Congress (*al-mu'tamariyyun*). In 1944 he decided to try his luck in agriculture and leased a plot of government land. This enterprise, however, failed miserably, and he lost his investment. In 1959, he was appointed by General Abd al-Karim KASSEM as director general of guidance and broadcasts, but in June 1960 he was dismissed. For a while, he was a press attaché in the Iraqi Embassy in Vienna, but most of the time he lived off a small pension from the Iraqi government. He also tried unsuccesfully to run a restaurant. In the 1980s, due to the Iraq–Iran war, his pension was stopped. He died in Vienna.

Ayyub's first recognition as a writer resulted from a number of translations from Western prose, first published in 1933. His first, and most important novel, *Doctor Ibrahim,* was published about 1940 in his hometown. Until then, writing novels was regarded as a far less prestigious occupation than the writing of poetry. Ayyub contributed to this change in public opinion. His second book, a volume of short stories, *The Hand and the Land and the Water* (*al-Yad wa'l-Ard wa'l-ma*), reflecting his experience as a farmer, came out in 1948. Among his other writings were: *The Tower of Babylon* (*Burj Babil*), *The Toilers* (*al-Kadihun*), and *The Messengers of Culture* (*Rusul al-Thaqafa*). His novels and short stories are written in a naive, realistic style. They reflect the feeling that all good social values are the creation of simple working people, and they contain scathing criticism against the widespread corruption in Iraqi society, yet they lack a revolutionary message. *Doctor Ibrahim* portrays an ambitious and unscrupulous Iraqi politician, who some believed to be modeled after the Shi'ite politician Muhammad Fadhil al-JAMALI. Ayyub's last novel was published in Beirut in the 1970s. Six volumes of his memoirs are still unpublished, in the possession of Iraqi poet Buland al-Haydari, who lives in London.

BIBLIOGRAPHY

BARAM, AMATZIA. Introduction to chapter 1 of *Doctor Ibrahim* (trans. into Hebrew). *Hamizrah Hehadash* 30 (1981): 163.
BATATU, HANNA. *The Old Social Classes and the Revolutionary Movements of Iraq*. Princeton, N.J., 1978.

Amatzia Baram

Ayyubi, Ali Jawdat al-   [1885?–1969]

Friend and retainer of Faisal ibn Husayn during the Arab revolt of World War I; politician in Iraq, 1920s–1958.

Ali Jawdat was born in Mosul (Iraq) during the OTTOMAN EMPIRE, to a family who practiced SUNNI ISLAM. His father was a military man, chief sergeant in the gendarmerie, and Ali's education was basically military. During WORLD WAR I, he joined the ARAB REVOLT against the Ottomans under Sharif HUSAYN IBN ALI and became a trusted friend of the sharif's son FAISAL, who in 1920 became king of Syria (until the French mandate), then king of IRAQ in 1921 under the British mandate.

Ali Jawdat was appointed military governor and head of several government ministries (finance, interior, and foreign affairs) during the early years, when Iraq tried to gain independence from the British. In 1932, the British mandate was ended, but Britain kept troops there until the mid-1950s. During the 1930s, Ali Jawdat became a chief administrative and diplomatic officer, representing Iraq in London, Paris, and Washington. He was made prime minister of Iraq in 1934/35, 1949/50, and during 1957 (just before the government was overthrown by a leftist military coup in 1958, headed by Abd al-Karim KASSEM). In 1967, Ali Jawdat published his memoirs in Beirut, covering the years 1900 to 1958.

BIBLIOGRAPHY

AL-AYYUBI, ALI JAWDAT. *Memoirs of Ali Jawdat 1900–58*. Beirut, 1967. In Arabic.
AL-SUWAYDI, TAWFIK. *Faces from Iraqi History*. London, 1987. In Arabic.

Batatu, Hanna. *The Old Social Classes and the Revolutionary Movements of Iraq.* Princeton, 1978.

Ahmad Abdul A. R. Shikara

Ayyubi, Mahmud al- [1932–]

Syrian prime minister.

Married with two children, al-Ayyubi studied at the University of Damascus where he obtained a degree in literature. He joined the Ba'th Party early and was one of its regional leaders. In 1969, he was appointed minister of education and kept this post until March 1971. In April 1971, he was appointed vice president. He headed the "Committee of Thirteen," which was formed by President al-Asad to organize the NATIONAL PROGRESSIVE FRONT. In 1972, and again in 1974, he was appointed prime minister.

George E. Irani

Azadi Party

Political party in Iran.

The Azadi Party was a small party in Iran headed by the famous lawyer, journalist, and active politician Hassan Arsanjani. The youth section of the Party was assimilated by the powerful Iranian Communist party, the TUDEH party, in the mid-1940s, when Arsanjani decided to join with Ahmad Qavam's Democrat Party.

BIBLIOGRAPHY

Abrahamian, E. *Iran between Two Revolutions.* Princeton, N.J., 1982, p. 300.

Parvaneh Pourshariati

Azadi Square

See Shahyad Square

Azerbaijan

Region in northwestern Iran.

Today Azerbaijan is made up of two Iranian provinces—Eastern Azerbaijan and Western Azerbaijan. Both are separate from the newly independent Republic of Azerbaijan, which was part of the former Soviet Union until its dissolution in 1991, and which was surrendered to then Czarist Russia according to

View of a village street in the Azerbaijan Republic. (Robin Bhatty)

Rural landscape area in the Azerbaijan Republic. (Robin Bhatty)

Street scene from the Azerbaijani capital of Baku. (Robin Bhatty)

The town of Maku dwarfed by looming mountains in Iranian Azerbaijan. (Richard Bulliet)

Prospect of the city of Tabriz in Iranian Azerbaijan. (Richard Bulliet)

the provisions in the Treaties of GOLESTAN (1813) and TURKMANCHAI (1828).

In Achaemenian times, the region of Azerbaijan formed the satrap of Media Atropatene; it became a part of the Persian Sassanid Empire in the second century C.E. Azerbaijan was gradually Turkified by the end of the twelfth century through the migration of Turkic tribes from central Asia. Its spoken language, Azeri, is a Turkic language that is heavily influenced by Iranian. According to the 1986 census, the population of Iranian Azerbaijan is about five million. Under the Safawids, Ardabil, in East Azerbaijan, was the seat of government; also Tabriz, in East Azerbaijan, was the seat of the Qajar crown prince (1796–1925).

In 1945, a Soviet-backed autonomous republic, led by the Communist Ja'far Pishevari, was declared in Azerbaijan. The incident prompted the famous Iron Curtain speech (1946) by Winston Churchill, who warned of Soviet expansionist designs. The so-called Democratic Republic of Azerbaijan was defeated mainly by unrelenting U.S. opposition and the shrewd diplomacy of Ahmad Qavam, then foreign minister.

BIBLIOGRAPHY

BOJNURDI, KAZIM, ed. *The Great Islamic Encyclopaedia*, vol. 1. Tehran, 1990. In Persian.

Neguin Yavari

Azerbaijan Crisis

A clash between the USSR and Iran that presaged the Cold War.

Considered by diplomatic historians to be one of the international political disputes that initiated the Cold War, the Azerbaijan Crisis erupted in October 1945, when the newly formed DEMOCRATIC PARTY OF AZERBAIJAN in Iran's northwestern province began taking over local governments with the backing of the Soviet army, which had been occupying the area since the joint Anglo–Soviet invasion of Iran in 1941. By December 1945, the Democratic party had established an autonomous government in Tabriz, the provincial capital of Iranian Azerbaijan, and this regime threatened to resist with force any effort by Tehran to restore central authority. A similar movement emerged in Mahabad, the main town in the Kurdish area of Iranian Azerbaijan. The Soviets prevented security forces of the central government from interfering with these takeovers, thus prompting fears in Tehran that Moscow intended to separate the province from Iran and possibly unite it with the neighboring Soviet Socialist Republic of Azerbaijan. These fears intensified when the Soviet Union declined to set a date for the withdrawal of its troops from the country, in contravention of the Tripartite Treaty of Alliance (1942) stipulating that all foreign military forces were to be withdrawn from Iran within six months of the end of World War II.

The Iranian government sought diplomatic support from the United States, which encouraged Iran to submit a formal complaint to the newly created United Nations. The Azerbaijan crisis thus became one of the first issues to be considered by the Security Council. Although the Security Council discussions about the Azerbaijan crisis were not substantive in nature, the publicized manifestation of tensions between the former wartime allies Britain, the Soviet Union, and the United States probably contributed to its resolution. While the situation in Iranian Azerbaijan remained on the Security Council's agenda during the first three months of 1946, Prime Minister Ahmad Qavam of Iran negotiated an agreement for the withdrawal of Soviet troops. The agreement provided for the evacuation of all Soviet forces from Iran by May 1946, in return for Tehran's promise to withdraw the complaint it had brought before the United Nations, to negotiate peacefully with the autonomous government of Azerbaijan, and to submit for parliamentary consideration a proposal for a joint Soviet–Iranian oil company with exclusive rights to exploit any petroleum resources in northern Iran.

Following the withdrawal of Soviet troops from the country, the central government discussed economic and linguistic grievances with the Azerbaijan autonomous government, but throughout the spring and summer of 1946 the two sides were unable to resolve their political differences. Finally, in December 1946, on the pretext that nationwide security had to be reestablished prior to holding elections for a new parliament that would consider the proposed Soviet–Iranian oil company, Qavam ordered the army into Azerbaijan, including the Kurdish area around Mahabad, and the autonomy movements were crushed. Parliamentary elections were held subsequently, but in June 1947, the new parliament rejected the prime minister's proposals for creating a joint Soviet–Iranian oil company.

BIBLIOGRAPHY

ABRAHAMIAN, ERVAND. *Iran between Two Revolutions.* Princeton, N.J., 1982.
RAMAZANI, ROUHOLLAH K. *Iran's Foreign Policy, 1941–1973: A Study of Foreign Policy in Modernizing Nations.* Charlottesville, Va., 1975.

Eric J. Hooglund

Azeri Language and Literature

Language spoken in Azerbaijan and northwestern Iran by the Azeris.

Azeri is spoken by 6,770,000 Azeris (1989 census) in AZERBAIJAN and elsewhere in the former Soviet Union. Millions of additional speakers of Azeri live in northwestern Iran. Azeri (together with the closely related languages TURKISH and TURKMEN) belongs to the southwestern, or Oghuz, branch of the Turkic languages. Azeri was originally written using ARABIC SCRIPT (and in Iran is now written again in Arabic script); the Azeris of the former Soviet Union adopted Latin script in 1927 and a modified Cyrillic alphabet in 1939. There is a current move to adopt a Turkish-style Latin script.

Azeri literature enjoyed continuous close ties to Persian, Turkish, and Chaghatay literature since its beginnings in the thirteenth century. Major figures of classical Azeri literature include İsfaraini, Nesimi, Hatai, Habibi, Fuzuli, and Vakil. The founders of modern Azeri literature include Kasım Beg Zakir (1784–1857), who introduced satire, Abbas Kulı Agha Bakıhanı ("Kudsi," 1794–1848), İsmail Beg Kutkaşınlı, and Mirza Şefi ("Vazeh," 1792–1852). Mirza Feth-Ali Ahundzade (1812–1878) first introduced drama and other prose genres, and Necef Beg Vezirli (1854–1926) was another notable playwright. Mirza Ali-Ekber Sabir (1862–1911) wrote fine satire, and Celil Mehmedkulızade (1869–1932) wrote important prose.

BIBLIOGRAPHY

CAFEROĞLU, AHMET, and GERHARD DOERFER. "Das Aserbeidschanische." In *Philologiae Turcicae Fundamenta,* ed. by Jean Deny et al. Wiesbaden, Germany, 1959.

Uli Schamiloglu

Azhar, al-

Official mosque of Cairo and the center of Muslim learning in Egypt.

Jawhar the Sicilian, the general of al-Muʿizz li-Din-Allah, established al-Azhar in 970; it was to be the official mosque of the new Fatimid regime, and to serve as the center of the effort to bring the Egyptians into the Shiʿite fold. For this reason, it lost its official status under the Sunni Ayyubids but regained it under the Mamluks. The line of succession of its head, known as Shaykh al-Azhar, has been traced to Muhammad Abd Allah al-Kurashi (d. 1690). Although the shaykh was always a member of a religious elite, the occupant of this position only gradually became the chief Muslim religious official in Egypt.

Al-Azhar is the oldest school of higher learning in continuous operation in the world. Although the Islamic disciplines have dominated, it has a history of

The mosque of al-Azhar in Cairo. (Richard Bulliet)

When one had acquired a number of these certificates, and a sufficient reputation, he could compete in the informal process by which teachers were given the right to teach in the mosque.

In the late nineteenth century al-Azhar came under sharp criticism for outmoded education content and methods, not only from the secular elite but also from such Muslim reformers as Muhammad ABDUH. The curriculum had almost no secular content, its religious content was more theoretical than applied, and student performance was very low. As early as 1812, the state had intervened by appointing the Shaykh al-Azhar, and in 1895/96, Abduh, representing the government, intervened by introducing a salary law, a government salary subsidy, the Azhar Administrative Council, and the Azhar Organization Law. A conservative reaction thwarted this effort, which was followed by a new organization law in 1911, designed to introduce a bureaucratic organization and modern programs of study, examinations, and degrees. In that year, 62 percent of al-Azhar's budget was of government origin (it reached 96 percent by 1959). In 1930, under Shaykh al-Azhar Muhammad al-Ahmadi al-Zawahiri, a major reform law established a true college program with three departments: theology, Islamic law, and Arabic. For the first time diploma programs roughly paralleled the Western bachelor's, master's, and doctorate system. President Gamal Abdel Nasser promoted even more change. In 1961, under Shaykh al-Azhar Muhammad SHALTUT, a secular campus was added at a different site; it had the various degree programs of a full university, including medicine and other sciences. During the course of this development, an extensive primary and secondary system of Azhar institutes was built throughout Egypt, with a core program of secular courses, but also including a significant number of courses in the Islamic disci-

secular education as well. Moses Maimonides taught medicine there. By the middle of the nineteenth century, with over 7,000 students, it had achieved a preeminent position in Egypt and was attracting students from the entire Islamic world. In 1903, al-Azhar had 104 foreign students, mostly from Arab countries and Africa, but also from Afghanistan, India, Indonesia, and China. Although all four Sunni rites were represented there, the Maliki, Shafi'i, and Hanafi rites, each with its own shaykh, dominated. The student residential sections were endowed for specific rites or geographical groups. The only organization to integrate this segmented structure was the office of the Shaykh al-Azhar, who sided with his own group when interests conflicted. There were no formal programs of study, no degrees, and no general examination system. Students sat in circles in the mosque, each group surrounding its teaching shaykh, who sat in front of one of the numerous columns. The teacher commentated on a classical or postclassical text, which the students were to memorize. When a student was deemed to have mastered a text, the teacher wrote a note authorizing him to teach it.

Courtyard of the Mosque of al-Azhar. (D.W. Lockhard)

plines. Thus al-Azhar established a viable, comprehensive Muslim alternative to the state education system, which Egypt's *ulama* tended to view as a secular threat to Islamic society and mores.

By virtue of the increased organizational differentiation and hierarchy, some positions began to enjoy a presumption of religious authority and correctness of opinion. The 1911 law created the Corps of High Ulama, which was partly an effort to co-opt senior *ulama* who might otherwise have opposed the reform, but was also a response to a perceived need to have a group to pronounce on Islamic issues. The 1961 organization law transformed this body into the Academy of Islamic Research, specifically to research and pronounce on Islamic issues. The academy holds conferences to bring together *ulama* from most Muslim countries, to present and discuss studies. The academy, along with the non–Azhar positions of the mufti of Egypt, the minister of *awqaf* (religious properties), and the Supreme Council of Islamic Affairs, presents the state with important issues of control. To address this fact, all these positions, both in and outside al-Azhar, are filled by state appointees.

Since a number of Muslim countries have created their own centers of Muslim learning, it is a tribute to al-Azhar that it continues to enjoy the greatest prestige internationally, even if its dominance is somewhat eroded. However, both in Egypt and abroad, Muslims with differing views, including those who oppose current regimes in the Muslim world, criticize the Azharis as "official" or "government" *ulama*. It is quite true that most violent Muslim radicals in Egypt are neither Azhar *ulama* nor Azhar graduates. Yet the case of Umar Abd al-Rahman, and his relationship to the Jihad Organization that killed President Anwar al-Sadat, as well as well-known cases where Azharis oppose government policies (e.g., in the realm of family planning), indicate that Azhari autonomy of opinion and action is far from totally compromised. Today, as in the past, al-Azhar performs an essential role in the accommodation of Muslim and secular institutions and maintains continuity in the face of rapid social and cultural change.

BIBLIOGRAPHY

ARMINJON, PIERRE. *L'enseignement, la doctrine et la vie dans les universités musulmanes d'Égypt*. Paris, 1907.
CRECELIUS, DANIEL. "The Ulama and the State in Modern Egypt." Ph.D. diss., Princeton University, 1968.
ECCEL, A. CHRIS. "Alim and Mujahid in Egypt: Orthodoxy Versus Subculture, or Division of Labor?" *The Muslim World* 78 (1988): 189–208.
———. *Egypt, Islam and Social Change: Al-Azhar in Conflict and Accommodation*. Berlin, 1984.

A. Chris Eccel

Azhari, Isma'il   [1900–1969]

First prime minister of independent Sudan.

Azhari, a descendant of the nineteenth-century religious leader Isma'il al-Wali and a grandson of the mufti of the Sudan, was educated at Gordon College in Khartoum and the American University of Beirut. After teaching mathematics in the Sudan Department of Education (1921–1946), he became a major figure in the Sudanese nationalism that favored union of the Nile Valley with Egypt. It remains unclear whether his support for this union was a sincere conviction or a device to eliminate Britain's control of the Sudan.

As he became increasingly absorbed in politics, Azhari was a founder of the Graduates Congress, whose members consisted of most of the educated elite. To promote his political aims, he founded the Ashigga (Brothers) Party; its principal goal was union of the Nile Valley with Egypt. In order to broaden his political base, he became the first president of the National Unionist Party (NUP), founded in 1952. The NUP dominated the elections for parliament.

Following his election as prime minister, Azhari continued his campaign for union with Egypt until he realized that the overwhelming majority of Sudanese wanted independence without Egypt. He then declared the independence of Sudan on January 1, 1956, creating a split in the NUP that led to the fall of his government. During the subsequent military regime of Gen. Ibrahim Abbud, he held no political office and was active in the opposition to the government.

After the overthrow of the Abbud regime in 1964, Azhari again led the NUP, often in alliance with his former enemies, the UMMA PARTY. He was elected permanent president of the Supreme Council, an office he held until the military revolution of Muhammad Ja'far Numeiri.

Robert O. Collins

Azib

Land ownership in precolonial Morocco in a system similar to feudalism.

In precolonial MOROCCO, *azib* was land property owned by a SHARIF, for whom people called *azzaba* would work. Azib land is usually conceded by the Makhzan (state) to some SHORFA. Azzaba would work within a relationship of servitude toward the sharif to whom they owed respect and obedience from father to son. In case anyone wanted to leave the azib, they had to seek permission from the landowner. The most important azib were to be found in the GHARB, such as the azib of Ahl Wazzan.

Rahma Bourqia

Aziz, Tariq   [1936–   ]

Iraq's foreign minister, 1983–1991.

Tariq Aziz was born in the village of Ba'shiqa, near Mosul, to a Christian family of the lower middle class. He lost his father at the age of seven. Joining the al-BA'TH party in the early 1950s, he became one of its first members in Iraq. In 1958, he graduated from Baghdad University with a degree in English; from his first days in the party he was was one of its leading intellectuals. During most of the 1950s and 1960s, he edited the clandestine party magazines *al-Ishtiraki* and *al-Jamahir*. After the RAMADAN REVOLUTION of 1963, Aziz supported the centrist faction in the party, under General Ahmad Hasan al-BAKR.

In the mid-1960s, Aziz became very close to Saddam HUSSEIN. Since Hussein became the strongman in Baghdad in the early 1970s, Aziz has served as his close confidant and mouthpiece. Winning Hussein's trust may have been easier for a Christian than for a Muslim, since he posed no threat to the ruler. Under the Ba'th regime, Aziz served as chief editor of the party daily newspaper and as minister of information. Since 1977, he has been a member of the two highest bodies—the Revolutionary Command Council and the party's Regional Leadership. Since 1979, he has been a deputy prime minister. From 1983 to 1991, Aziz was Iraq's foreign minister, in which capacity he managed to greatly improve Iraq's foreign relations during the IRAN–IRAQ WAR (1980–1988). During the GULF CRISIS of 1990/91, however, he did not dare to oppose Hussein, and thus his contacts with the West were of no use to his country.

After the Gulf war, he was relieved of his foreign ministry but retained his position as a deputy prime minister. Due to his level of education and relations with the West, Aziz (along with Sa'dun Hammadi) remains an exceptional figure at the top of the Ba'th hierarchy.

BIBLIOGRAPHY

BARAM, AMATZIA. "The Ruling Political Elite in Ba'thi Iraq, 1968–1986." *International Journal of Middle East Studies* 21 (1989): 447–493.

Amatzia Baram

Azm, Abd al-Rahman al-   [1916–   ]

Syrian politician and diplomat.

A member of a prominent family of landowners in Hama, Abd al-Rahman al-Azm is married with four children. He completed his primary and secondary education at the preparatory school of the American University of Beirut (AUB). He then enrolled in the French law school at the Université de Saint-Joseph (Beirut) and obtained a law degree. In 1947, he was elected deputy of Hama. Between December 1949 and May 1950 he was minister of finance in the cabinet headed by Khalid al-Azm. He was reappointed to the same post in the AZM government, which lasted from March to July 1951. He again held the post of minister of finance in the Dawabili cabinet (1951) and the government headed by Sabri al-ASALI (1954). In 1956, he was appointed Syrian ambassador to Egypt.

George E. Irani

Azm, Haqqi al-   [1864–?]

Syrian politician.

Born in Damascus to a prominent Sunni Islamic family in 1864, Haqqi al-Azm received an advanced Ottoman education in Istanbul. A notable who acquiesced to French occupation, al-Azm became the first governor of the French-created state of Damascus in 1920. His administration was criticized for political corruption, nepotism, and being a puppet for the French. He served as prime minister from 1932 to 1934.

BIBLIOGRAPHY

KHOURY, PHILIP S. *Syria and the French Mandate: The Politics of Arab Nationalism, 1920–1945*. Princeton, N.J., 1987.

Charles U. Zenzie

Azm, Muhammad Fawzi al-

Ottoman Syrian politician.

Born the son of Muhammad Ali Pasha al-Azm into a powerful Damascus family, Muhammad Fawzi al-Azm became president of the Damascus municipality in 1892. He went on to become minister for the Awqaf in Istanbul and director of public works for the Hijaz Railway.

BIBLIOGRAPHY

KHOURY, PHILIP S. *Urban Notables and Arab Nationalism: The Politics of Damascus 1860–1920.* Cambridge, Mass., 1983.

Charles U. Zenzie

Azm, Rafiq al-

Early Arab nationalist writer and politician from Syria.

Born in Damascus and educated in Istanbul, al-Azm was known by 1910 as a leading anti-Zionist essayist and politician. In opposing ZIONISM he accused Jews who sought to establish their own state of treason. In 1913 al-Azm became president of the new DECENTRALIZATION PARTY based in Cairo. In 1916 the Ottomans sentenced him in absentia to death for seeking to sever the Arab provinces from the OTTOMAN EMPIRE.

BIBLIOGRAPHY

KHOURY, PHILIP. *Urban Notables and Arab Nationalism.* New York, 1983.
MANDEL, NEVILLE J. *The Arabs and Zionism Before World War I.* Berkeley, Calif., 1976.
MUSLIH, MUHAMMAD Y. *The Origins of Palestinian Nationalism.* New York, 1988.

Elizabeth Thompson

Azm, Shafiq Mu'ayyad al- [?–1916]

Arab Syrian political figure.

Azm served in the Ottoman provincial bureaucracy before 1908. After the Young Turk revolution in 1908, he was elected to the Lower Chamber of Deputies as a representative of Damascus. Between 1908 and 1914 he was a spokesman for Arab causes and developed a strong aversion to the Committee of Union and Progress (CUP), the effective power at the center of the Ottoman Empire, which he accused of pursuing a policy of Turkification in the empire. He was hanged at Damascus on May 6, 1916 by a Turkish military tribunal.

BIBLIOGRAPHY

BARRU, TAWFIQ. *Al-Arab wa al-Turk fi al-Ahd al-Dusturi al-'Uthmānī 1908–1914.* Cairo, 1960.
———. *Al-Qadiyya al-Arabiyya fi al-Harb al-Alamiyya al-Ula 1914–1918.* Damascus, 1989.

Mahmoud Haddad

Azm Family

Prominent family in Syrian politics.

Wealthy landowners from the fertile HAMA region of SYRIA, the Azms dominated Damascene (referring to Damascus, capital of Syria) politics from the eighteenth to the mid-twentieth centuries as provincial governors, OTTOMAN EMPIRE bureaucrats, and Arab nationalists. At the turn of the nineteenth century, a branch of the family migrated to Egypt, where they also achieved prominence.

In the early twentieth century, Rafiq, Haqqi, and Shafiq Mu'ayyad al-Azm were active proponents of Arab nationalism. From the 1940s to the early 1960s, Khalid al-Azm held various ministerial posts in Syria, including prime minister. Sadiq al-Azm is a noted writer on Arab politics.

BIBLIOGRAPHY

SCHILCHER, LINDA SCHATKOWSKI. *Families in Politics.* Stuttgart, 1985.
SEALE, PATRICK. *The Struggle for Syria.* New York, 1965.

Elizabeth Thompson

Azuri, Najib [?–1916]

Arab nationalist

Najib Azuri, a Christian Arab born in Azur in south Lebanon, was an Ottoman official in Jerusalem. Through his Paris-based League of the Arab Homeland, in 1904 he issued manifestos appealing to the Arabs of Iraq and Syria to overthrow the sultan of the Ottoman Empire. In his book, which was published in Paris in 1905 under the title *Le réveil de la nation arabe* (The Awakening of the Arab Nation), he posited the existence of an Arab nation that was entitled to independence from Ottoman rule. He openly advocated the secession of the Arabs from the Ottoman Empire—this was the first open demand for complete detachment of the Arab provinces.

From the perspective of Azuri, the Ottomans were barbarous oppressors who inflicted much suffering on the Arabs. His accusations against the sultan and the governor of Jerusalem, Kazem Bey, were violent and bitter. Azuri directed his most violent attack against ABDÜLHAMIT II, whom he described as a pernicious "beast," running the empire through intrigue and espionage from his "cave" in Istanbul. Azuri also ridiculed Abdülhamit's claim to the caliphate because he did not know Arabic and because, at the age of sixty-five, he still had not performed the pilgrimage (HAJJ) to Mecca.

Against this background, Azuri stated that the Arabs, with their national feelings now revived, would form an empire comprising Mesopotamia, Syria, Palestine, and the Arabian peninsula. Within these boundaries, Azuri wanted to see the emergence of an Arab nation under the protection of a European power—France having a "better right" to rule the Arabs than the rest.

Azuri's preference for France stemmed from his anti-Russian stance and his apparent belief in the right of France to protect the Catholics and their establishments in the Ottoman Empire. In his book, Azuri warned that should Russia control the Turkish Straits and penetrate the Ottoman Empire, the people of the East would never attain their national independence.

Azuri had had close connections with French political figures in Paris and Cairo. Among them were René Pinon, Edmond Fazy, and Eugène Jung. In partnership with Jung, Azuri tried to create the impression, by means of articles and periodicals, that an Arab movement was under way in the Ottoman Empire. Both men, however, were rebuffed by the French, the Italians, and the British. Their ten-year partnership, which lasted roughly from 1905 to 1916, made no progress toward their goal of raising the Arabs against the Ottomans.

Azuri was also equally famous for his anti-Zionist position and for his prediction that the Zionist movement was destined to conflict with Arab nationalism. Beyond his contribution to Arab nationalist thought, one deduces in Azuri's work a European brand of anti-Semitism that was typical of other writings by Arab nationalists in this period. It is probable that Azuri had developed his anti-Semitic sentiments during the DREYFUS AFFAIR, at which time he was a student in Paris.

Muhammad Muslih

Azzam, Abd al-Rahman al-   [1893–1976]

First Secretary General of the Arab League.

Azzam was appointed by the League Council in 1945 when the pact of the league was signed by member countries. He served as Secretary General until 1952, when he was replaced by Abd al-Khaliq Hassouna. Before becoming the League's secretary-general, Azzam served in a number of diplomatic positions and carried numerous diplomatic missions on behalf of Egypt to many Arab capitals.

Azzam started his political life as an anti-British Egyptian nationalist. Although he was a Wafdist in the first phase of his political life, he became associated with King Farouk and the anti-Wafdist prime minister Ali Maher from the mid-1930s on. He was pan-Arabist and pan-Islamist at the same time. When Italy conquered Libya, then an Ottoman province in 1911, Azzam volunteered against the Italian invaders. During World War I, he left Egypt and fought alongside Sanusi forces in Cyrenaica (east Libya today) and the Egyptian western desert.

From 1934 on, Azzam called for the formation of an Arab Bloc since, according to him, there was no place in the present age for small countries with limited resources. He also believed closer Arab ties would bring Egypt political, economic, and strategic advantages.

BIBLIOGRAPHY

GOMAA, AHMED. *The Foundation of the League of Arab States: Wartime Diplomacy and Inter-Arab Politics 1941 to 1945.* London, 1977.

MACDONALD, ROBERT. *The League of Arab States: A Study in the Dynamics of Regional Organization.* Princeton, N.J., 1965.

Mahmoud Haddad

B

Ba'albak

City in Lebanon famous for its archeological remains.

Located in the BIQA' VALLEY some fifty-three miles from Beirut, Ba'albak, or Ba'albek, is the foremost tourist site in Lebanon. Perhaps a center of the cult of the great Semitic god Baal, it owes its fame today to its Roman temples, which date to the late second century and the beginning of the third century. The Temple of Bacchus is the best-preserved Roman temple of its size in the world.

Prior to the Lebanese civil war (1975–1990), Ba'albak was known for its annual international festivals, which offered a typical Lebanese blending of Eastern and Western cultures. The present city, the capital of one of the least Westernized districts of Lebanon, had an estimated 150,000 inhabitants in the early 1990s, with a strong Shi'ite majority and a Christian minority. The political significance of the city was heightened in 1982–1983, when it became the base for a contingent of REVOLUTIONARY GUARDS sent by the Iranian regime to help build, organize, and train the militant group ISLAMIC AMAL, which provided the nucleus for the better-known HIZBUL-LAH. In the early 1990s, Hizbullah's headquarters were in Ba'albak.

BIBLIOGRAPHY

ALOUF, MICHEL. *A History of Ba'albek.* Beirut, 1914.
RAGETTE, FRIEDRICH. *Baalbek.* Park Ridge, N.J., 1980.

Guilain P. Denoeux

Corinthian columns at Ba'albak, Lebanon. (Richard Bulliet)

Bab, al- [1819–1850]

Charismatic leader of an Iranian religious movement that began in 1844.

275

Sayyid Ali Mohammad Shirazi was born on October 20, 1819, in Shiraz (southwestern Iran). His father, a clothier, had married into a clan of long-distance merchants. His family had adopted the Shaykhi school of SHIʿISM, as had his elementary teacher, Shaykh Abid. Sayyid Ali Mohammad had an uneven education and rebelled against dry scholasticism and the minutiae of ARABIC grammar. He engaged in the family trade, spending 1835 to 1840 in the Iranian port city of Bushehr on import–export affairs. But his real interests were religious devotions and SHAYKHI-style dreams and visions of the IMAMS (the holy figures of Shiʿism). He settled his accounts and left for the shrine cities of Iraq in 1841, in part to meet Sayyid Kazim Rashti, leader of the esoteric and millenarian Shaykhi school of Shiʿism. He spent eleven months there, but appears to have spent little time in seminary study, concentrating on devotions at the shrines. His family put pressure on him to return to Shiraz, which he did in 1842, where they married him off to Khadija Khanom and set him up once again in business. He continued to think and write about esoteric religious subjects and began to have a following as a charismatic figure.

When Rashti died in Karbala, in early 1844, a section of the Shaykhis, convinced that the appearance of the Muslim *Mahdi* (messiah) was near, set off in search of him. One of these, Molla Hosayn Bushru'i, stopped in Shiraz on his way to Kirman and accidentally met Sayyid Ali Mohammad, who put forward a charismatic claim. When Molla Hosayn became his disciple on May 22, 1844, followed by other Shaykhi seminarians in his circle, he was recognized as *al-Bab*, "the Gate"—an ambiguous term implying divine inspiration. Belief in his spiritual leadership spread rapidly among urban craftspeople and merchants, as well as some peasants.

The Bab went on pilgrimage later in 1844 to proclaim his mission to the sharif of Mecca but proved unable to get his attention. In the summer of 1845, he returned to Shiraz, but the municipal authorities, alarmed by his claims, put him under house arrest. In 1846 and 1847 he resided in Isfahan, gaining the protection of the Qajar governor there, who attempted to arrange an interview with the shah for him. The chief minister, however, thwarted this meeting, and ordered the Bab to be imprisoned in Maku, in Azerbaijan. There the Bab openly claimed to be the Mahdi and a manifestation of God and wrote his book of laws, the Bayan, intended to supplant the QURʾAN. In July 1848, he was interrogated by a group of clerics and pronounced a heretic. He spent the last two years of his life imprisoned in the even more remote fort of Chihriq. In 1849/50, sev-

eral outbreaks of violence occurred between Shiʿites and Babis, and the state began to feel the need to act decisively. On July 8, 1850, the government ordered the Bab executed in Tabriz. He was taken during a conversation with a disciple, then suspended against a wall with ropes. The first firing squad missed him, severing his ropes and allowing him to disappear, which many in the crowd took as a divine sign. He was found completing his words to the disciple. Another firing squad had to be commissioned to complete the execution.

The religion he founded was brutally persecuted in Iran and driven underground. From the late 1860s, most Babis became BAHAʾI, which remains Iran's largest non-Muslim religious community.

BIBLIOGRAPHY

AMANAT, ABBAS. *Resurrection and Renewal: The Making of the Babi Movement in Iran, 1844–1850*. Ithaca, N.Y., 1989.

Juan R. I. Cole

Babaghanush

The name of a well-known Arab dish.

Translated as "la coquette," the dish is reputedly an invention of an Arab girl in an Ottoman harem. It consists of eggplant, flavored with garlic, lemon juice, and tahini paste, garnished with pomegranate seeds, chopped mint, and paprika. Babaghanush is best eaten as a dip or an appetizer.

Cyrus Moshaver

Bab al-Mandab

The narrow waterway separating Asia and Africa.

Because of its place on the sea-lanes between Europe and the Indian Ocean and points east, the Bab al-Mandab straits have been assigned considerable strategic importance over the centuries, particularly with the building of the SUEZ CANAL, the flowering of the British empire, and the more recent dependence of Europe on oil from the Persian/Arabian GULF. The two Yemens meet on the Asian side of the strait, and Ethiopia and Djibouti meet on the African side. This geography helps explain Yemeni interest in the politics of the Horn of Africa.

Robert D. Burrowes

Baban, Ahmad Mukhtar   [1900–?]

Iraqi politician.

Born in Baghdad, his father was Hasan Beq and his mother was a member of the Baban family. Baban graduated from the Law College of Baghdad and served as a royal palace official in the 1920s. In 1942, he was governor of the Karbala district and minister of social affairs. He became deputy prime minister in 1954. Baban was opposed to the attempts to unite the Fertile Crescent that took place in the wake of Adib Shishakli's overthrow in Syria. He was later present at the spring 1956 meetings in Baghdad, where a plan to rehabilitate Shishakli in Syria, with Iraqi support, was discussed. He became the last prime minister of the Royal regime in 1958 and died in Bonn, Germany.

BIBLIOGRAPHY

Who's Who in the Middle East, 1967–1968.

Charles U. Zenzie

Baban, Jalal Rustam   [1892–1970]

Iraqi statesman.

Born in Baghdad, Jalal Rustam Baban was the son of Rustam Baban, the assistant governor of Suwara. He graduated from the Military Academy of Istanbul in 1912 and took part in World War I as an Ottoman officer. He occupied seven cabinet posts, including that of minister of defense and of minister of education. He resigned his last position, as minister of economics and transportation, in 1949 and immigrated to Lebanon, where he died in 1970.

Mamoon A. Zaki

Baban, Jamal Rashid   [1893–1965]

Iraqi politician.

Born in Baghdad, Jamal Rashid Baban graduated from the Lam College in 1914 and was recruited by the Ottoman army during World War I. Between 1924 and 1926, he served five times as a deputy in the Iraqi parliament. He was a minister in eight governments, until the coup of 1958, after which he immigrated to Lebanon, where he died in 1965.

Mamoon A. Zaki

Baban Family

Prominent Iraqi family.

The oldest known ancestor of the family is Mufti Ahmad, who was granted a huge lot of land by the Ottoman authorities in the north of Iraq. His son Sulayman Baba established himself as a powerful ruler and, in 1670, became the governor of the SANJAK (an administrative unit smaller than a governorate) of Baban, from which the family derived its name. The most well-known ancestor of the family is Sulayman Pasha al-Kabir, who was called Abu Laila.

Mamoon A. Zaki

Bab-ı Âli Tercüme Odası

See Bureau of Translation

Babis

A millenarian religious movement developing out of Iranian Shi'a Islam, begun by the Bab, Sayyid Ali Mohammad Shirazi, in 1844.

By 1849 there may have been 100,000 Babis in Iran and Iraq. The movement spread chiefly to cities, towns, and large villages, attracting the middle and lower-middle classes. Middle-ranking clerics, seminary students, urban artisans, laborers, and small landowners appear to have been its principal constituents, along with some influential merchants and retailers. The movement spread throughout Persia (Iran), with an especially strong showing in Khurasan to the northeast, as well as in Mazandaran, Fars, and Iraqi Ajam.

Between the beginning of the BAB's mission in 1844 and his execution in 1850, most Babis probably knew relatively little about his doctrines, and were attracted to him for charismatic and millenarian reasons. The Bab's works, many in Arabic, are abstruse and inaccessible except to the highly literate among his followers. The main emphases of mature Babi belief were that the Bab was the returned Mahdi (messiah), the hidden Twelfth IMAM, and that the judgment day had symbolically occurred; that the Bab had the authority to reveal a new divine law; that he and his disciples possessed esoteric knowledge; that martyrdom was noble and that holy war could be declared by the Bab; and that a future messianic figure, "He whom God shall make manifest," would appear. The Bab allowed the taking of interest on loans and was favorable toward middle-class property; slightly improved the position of women by limiting polygamy; and admired what he had heard of Western science.

The rise of this new religion was attended by violence, as it was rejected by the Shi'a clerics and by the state. The Babi movement often became implicated in the quarter-fighting that was typical of QAJAR cities. A major clash took place in Mazandaran in 1848/49, at the shrine of Shaykh Tabarsi, where several hundred Babis, including prominent disciples of the Bab, like Molla Hosayn, having raised the black banner of the Mahdi, were besieged by government troops and finally defeated, and killed or captured. In some small cities Babi quarters developed, with their own clerics and notables, and came into conflict with conservative neighborhoods. The Babis defended their quarters, withstanding sieges, until finally government troops intervened to crush them (Zanjan, 1850/51 and Nayriz, 1850–1853).

In 1850, the Bab was executed in Tabriz; in 1852, a faction of about seventy notable Babis in Tehran plotted to assassinate the monarch, NASER AL-DIN SHAH, in revenge for his execution of the Bab. The attempt failed, and in response the Qajar state ordered a nationwide pogrom against the Babis. By the middle 1850s perhaps five thousand had been killed, and most of the rest had gone underground.

Most Babis recognized Mirza Yahya Sobh-i Azal (1830–1912) as the successor to the Bab. After the failed attempt on the shah, he followed his elder half-brother, Hosayn Ali Baha'ullah, into exile in Baghdad in 1853. From 1853 to 1864 he faced a number of regional challenges to his authority, but appears to have retained at least some loyalty among the furtive and much reduced Babi community. In the late 1860s, however, Baha'ullah asserted that *he* was the messianic figure foretold by the Bab, and in the space of a decade most Babis had gone over to him, becoming BAHA'I. The Babis who remained loyal to Azal were called Azalis, and by 1900 they numbered probably only two to four thousand.

The small Babi community remained determinedly anti-Qajar and was open to Western ideas and culture. It produced radical intellectuals, such as Aqa Khan Kermani and Shaykh Ahmad Ruhi (both became atheists and were executed in 1896 in connection with Naser al-Din Shah's assassination); and Yahya Dawlatabadi, Mirza Jahangir Khan, Malik al-Mutakallimin, and Sayyid Jamal al-Din Isfahani (all activists on the constitutionalist side in Iran's CONSTITUTIONAL REVOLUTION that began in 1905). In the twentieth century, the Babi community shrank to negligible size and influence.

BIBLIOGRAPHY

AMANAT, ABBAS. *Resurrection and Renewal: The Making of the Babi Movement in Iran, 1844–1850.* Ithaca, N.Y., 1989.

Juan R. I. Cole

Baccouche, Hedi

See Bakkush, Hadi

Badakhshan

Province in northeastern Afghanistan.

The most northeastern province of Afghanistan, Badakhshan includes the Wakhan corridor and is, for the most part, situated at an elevation of over 10,000 feet. The province, whose capital is Faizabad, borders on Tajikistan in the north and has a population of about 600,000. Most of the people are ethnically TAJIK, although other groups also live in the province, including Kyrgyz nomads in the Wakhan corridor and Pushtun nomads.

BIBLIOGRAPHY

DUPREE, LOUIS. *Afghanistan.* Princeton, N.J., 1980.

Grant Farr

Badghis

Province in northwest Afghanistan.

The capital of this Afghan province in northwestern Afghanistan is Qala Naw. Although Badghis borders on the Turkmen Republic, 70 percent of its people are Persian speaking. Before 1979, Badghis had a population of nearly 300,000, but during the war of resistance (1978–1992), over half of this population fled to Iran. Some refugees have returned to Badghis, but it is not known how many have been repatriated.

BIBLIOGRAPHY

EIGHMY, THOMAS. *Afghanistan's Population Inside and Out.* Peshawar, Pakistan, 1990.

Grant Farr

Badr, Muhammad al-   [1926–1978]

Ruler and 111th Zaydi imam of Yemen, 1962.

Muhammad al-Badr (also called Imam al-Badr) was the son of Imam AHMAD IBN YAHYA HAMID AL-DIN, who ruled YEMEN following his election to the imamate on March 13, 1948. In October 1961, Muhammad al-Badr was designated by his father as successor despite earlier disagreements. He became the ruler and the 111th IMAM after his father's death on September 9, 1962. Imam al-Badr was the last ZAYDI imam of the Rassid dynasty to hold the title. This dynasty of Shi'ite Muslims was established in northern Yemen (San'a) in the final decade of the ninth century. The Zaydi imams traced their origin to Ali ibn Abi Talib, the Prophet Muhammad's cousin and fourth caliph. They base their absolute rule on their claim of descent from the Prophet and on the allegiance given them by individual tribes—who, at least in Yemen, were the mainstay of the imamate.

Imam al-Badr was educated in Egypt and in the 1950s presented himself as interested in NATIONALISM and liberal reform. He admired Gamal Abdel NASSER during his presidency of Egypt; he also supported the nonalignment movement and advocated a neutral role for Yemen in world affairs. In the 1950s, al-Badr traveled to the Soviet Union and Eastern Europe and tried to establish friendly relations with the communist world. In Yemen, he consolidated tribal support for himself and supported the South Yemen (Aden) political struggle for independence from Britain.

Upon assuming power, Imam al-Badr proclaimed social and economic reform in Yemen. He announced the establishment of a forty-member advisory council, of which half would be elected, and he appointed himself prime minister. Egyptian, Soviet, and Chinese leaders believed he was implementing a policy of socialism and sent him their best wishes.

Nevertheless, dissatisfaction with al-Badr emerged immediately among the military and within the tribes seeking revenge for the execution of some of their leaders by al-Badr's father, Imam Ahmad. Within a week, a group of army officers formed the FREE OFFICERS movement and sought Egypt's support for a coup. Egypt encouraged them to move against al-Badr quickly, since he had not yet consolidated his power; the British were preoccupied with the problems of federating South Yemen, and the Saudi ruling family had its internal problems. Within a month, a republic was declared by General Abdullah al-SALLAL.

On September 27, 1962, Radio San'a announced that a coup was in progress; it also announced, erroneously, that al-Badr had been killed. The YEMEN CIVIL WAR was under way; Imam al-Badr was overthrown and Egyptian forces entered Yemen in large numbers to support the new regime. Saudi Arabia, where Imam al-Badr had fled, and Jordan supported the royal forces. The civil war continued until 1970.

In 1968, however, a split developed within the royalist ranks that resulted in al-Badr relinquishing the imamate in favor of the new Imamate Council, headed by Muhammad ibn Husayn. Al-Badr died in 1978.

BIBLIOGRAPHY

Area Handbook for the Yemens. Washington, 1977.
BURROWES, ROBERT D. *The Yemen Arab Republic: The Politics of Development, 1962–1986.* Boulder, Colo., 1987.
WENNER, MANFRED. *The Yemen Arab Republic.* Boulder, Colo., 1991.

Emile A. Nakhleh

Badran, Mudar   [1934–   ]

Prime minister of Jordan 1976–1979, 1980–1984, and December 1989–June 1991.

Before becoming prime minister of Jordan in 1976, Mudar Badran had risen through the ranks as a public security (intelligence) officer. He was asked to form a government at a time when security was a high priority in the kingdom. He was known not to be on friendly terms with Syria, even supporting the Muslim Brotherhood rebellion in Syria in 1978/1979, and may have been the target of a Syrian-backed assassination attempt. During the 1980s, he supported the development of a close relationship with Iraq. During the Iran–Iraq War of 1980–1988, Iraq was given access to the port of Aqaba, providing it with a vital supply line and providing Jordan with the economic benefits that ensued. In December 1989, Badran headed the cabinet formed after the first general elections to be held in Jordan in twenty-two years.

BIBLIOGRAPHY

GUBSER, PETER. *Jordan: Crossroads of Middle Eastern Events.* Boulder, Colo., 1983.

Jenab Tutunji

Baghdad

Capital city of Iraq.

Baghdad is situated centrally in Iraq, about 350 miles (563 km) from the northern, southern, and western borders, at a point in the Tigris river where the Euphrates is only twenty-five miles (40 km) to the west. Baghdad is on an alluvial plain about 110 feet (34 m) above sea level. It has cool, damp winters and

View of Baghdad from an airplane, circa 1930. (Royal Air Force Official Photo)

hot, dry summers; winter-temperature lows are 29 to 31°F, and summer highs are 114 to 121°F. Rainfall is sparse, mainly from December to April, averaging six inches (150 mm) per year.

In 762 C.E., al-Mansur, the second caliph of the new Abbasid dynasty, chose the site for his administrative center. It was called Madinat al-Salam (City of Peace) but was known as the Round City, since it was built in circular form; its three concentric walls had a deep surrounding moat and four gates opening

The tomb of Sitt Zubayda, the wife of Harun al-Rashid, the Abbasid Caliph, in Baghdad. (Richard Bulliet)

A street in Baghdad, circa 1930. (Richard Bulliet)

toward Basra, Syria, al-Kufa, and Khorasan. The site was chosen for its strategic location, a meeting place on the caravan routes on the road to KHORASAN. With an adequate water supply and relative freedom from malaria, it grew into a cosmopolis of the medieval world, with districts on both banks of the Tigris. The population reached some 500,000 by the ninth century, with international trade in textiles, leather, paper, and other important goods from the Baltic to China.

Baghdad was sacked in 1258 by the Mongols and again in 1401 by Tamerlane. Successive Persian and Turkish dynasties then controlled the city. It was taken by Shah Isma'il of Persia in 1508 and later by the Ottoman Turks under Süleyman the Magnificent in 1556. It remained basically under Ottoman rule until the dismemberment of the Ottoman Empire after World War I.

During the early Ottoman period, Baghdad lost its importance as a center for trade and learning. The caliphs of Islam shifted their center to Istanbul, and so Baghdad became a provincial town with doubtful authority over even the neighboring districts. A succession of plagues, famines, floods, and other disasters destroyed thousands of people, and the population was reduced, according to one report in the sixteenth century, to less than fifty thousand.

In the nineteenth century, Baghdad received some attention from both its Ottoman rulers and the Western powers. Two Ottoman governors, DA'UD PAŞA (1816–1832) AND MIDHAT PAŞA (1869–1872) made some serious attempts to improve the conditions of the city. Da'ud tried to control the tribes and restore order and security. He cleared up irrigation canals, established textile and arms factories, and encouraged local industry. He built three large mosques and founded three *madrasas* (schools). He organized an army of twenty thousand, trained by a French officer. Midhat Paşa laid telegraph lines, built a horse tramway to Qadimayn, and built several government schools and other useful institutions. He started a Turkish steamboat line between Baghdad and Basra. Western powers, particularly Britain, showed some interest in Baghdad for commercial purposes and as a land route to India; Britain established a consulate in Baghdad in 1802, and the French, soon after.

Late in the nineteenth century, Baghdad became the terminal rail station on the line from Constantinople, which later was extended to Basra. In 1917, during World War I, Baghdad was occupied by the British, and in 1921 it became the capital of a new country, Iraq.

Since 1921, Baghdad has grown in both size and population. From an area of less than 4 square miles, it grew to about 39 square miles in 1950, to 312 square miles in 1965, to more than 780 square miles in the 1990s. The population has grown from 200,000 in 1921, to 515,000 in 1947, to 1.5 million in 1965, to about 5 million in 1990.

In the early 1900s, Baghdad was surrounded by dikes in several directions to protect it from the unpredictable floodwaters of the Tigris. These dikes then limited the city's outward expansion. In 1956, a dam was completed at Samarra, north of the city, so expansion occurred to the east and west. To the north, expansion absorbed the medieval townships of al-A'zamiyya on the east bank and al-Kazimiyya on the west bank.

Bridges connect both banks of the Tigris. The east-bank settlement is called al-Rusafa and the west, al-Karkh. From the Tigris, the city's central core runs eastward to the inner dike, called the bund, built by Ottoman governor Nazim Pasha in 1910. In this core are the government buildings, the financial district, the copper, textile, and gold bazaars, as well as the shopping, dining, and entertainment facilities. Luxury hotels, the commercial district, and ultramodern housing are also here. Older middle-class residential areas are adjacent to the center, such as al-Sulaykh to the north, al-Wizariyya to the west, and al-Karrada to the south, all densely settled. A fashionable residential area and Baghdad University

are located on al-Jadriyya, a peninsula in the Tigris. The 1950s saw eastward expansion beyond the bund, with planned middle-class neighborhoods between the bund and the army canal, which connects the Diyala river to the Tigris. A low-income housing development is at the eastern edge of the city beyond the canal, inhabited by more than one million urban migrants.

The west bank has some residential quarters, including the oldest, al-Karkh, and several upper- and middle-class districts with walled gardens around villas. Among these is the prestigious al-Mansur, surrounding the racetrack, with boutiques, fast-food restaurants, and sidewalk cafes. In the 1970s, highrise apartment blocks were built, mainly to comply with government policy to curb the horizontal expansion of the city.

Since World War II, Baghdad's population has been mainly Muslim and ARAB, with the Muslims divided into the two main sects of Islam, Sunni and Shi'a. Other ethnic and linguistic groups include Kurds, Armenians, and Turks. A significant number of Persian speakers departed for Iran in the 1970s and 1980s, in the midst of the Iran–Iraq War. Several eastern-rite Christian communities exist, notably Chaldeans and Assyrians, and a small Jewish community has ancient roots in Mesopotamia (although most of the Jews left for Israel in the early 1950s). A large community of foreign Arabs lives in Baghdad, consisting of hundreds of thousands of Egyptian workers and Palestinians.

Traditionally, people of the same sect, ethnic group, or craft lived together in city districts or quarters; with oil wealth and massive migration from poor rural areas to the city, however, new neighborhoods resulted in socioeconomic stratification.

Baghdad is the center of Iraq's transportation system, with Saddam International Airport serving numerous international airlines. The state-owned railway lines meet at Baghdad, connecting the capital with Basra and Umm Qasr near the Gulf, with Kirkuk and Irbil in the northeast, with Mosul in the north, and with al-Qa'im near Syria in the northwest. Overland roads and highways connect the city with Turkey, Syria, Jordan, Iran, Kuwait, and Saudi Arabia. A 1980s expressway project within the city relieves traffic congestion and links the city center with the suburbs.

The cultural life of the city was traditionally centered on its religious sects. Many mosques and minarets exist in every quarter, but the tombs of the two imams and the adjacent mosque at Qadimayn are among the important places of Shi'ite pilgrimage. Collections of Arabic history and literature are included in the major libraries of al-Awqaf and at the

University of Baghdad. Other cultural institutions include museums; learned societies in the arts and sciences; and educational facilities such as al-Hikma University, al-Mustansiriyya University, the Higher Technical Institute, and the Institute of Fine Arts, as well as other colleges. The capital was provided with new hospitals and clinics, health and welfare services, electric power plants and water-supply facilities.

In 1958, Iraq's monarchy was overthrown and was replaced by a politically modern, socialist, pan-Arab ruling party, following about ten years of political turbulence and a succession of military regimes and coups. In 1968, the Arab Socialist BA'TH party came to power and achieved relative stability and internal development, especially after 1973 when oil prices rose and greatly increased government revenues. During the 1980s, however, Baghdad's development was curtailed by the war with Iran and, with the 1991 Gulf War, the city was bombed by Coalition forces. Since the end of the war, much of the city and its infrastructure has had to be restored.

BIBLIOGRAPHY

ELLIS, WILLIAM, "The New Face of Baghdad." *National Geographic* 167 (1985).
HITTI, PHILIP K. *Capital Cities of Arab Islam.* Minneapolis, Minn., 1973.

Ayad al-Qazzaz

Baghdadi, Abd al-Latif al- [1917–]

Egyptian officer, politician, and cabinet minister.

A graduate of Egypt's military academy, Abd al-Latif al-Baghdadi led FREE OFFICERS, who plotted the 1952 revolution, and later of the REVOLUTIONARY COMMAND COUNCIL. He was the inspector general for the liberation rally in 1953 and defense minister under Muhammad Naguib in 1953–1954.

When Gamal Abdel NASSER took power, Baghdadi went to municipal affairs and later became minister of planning. He became the first president of the National Assembly in 1957 and, after the formation of the United Arab Republic in 1958, he became vice-president for economic affairs and minister of planning. After Syria seceded in 1961, he became minister of finance and economic planning. In September 1962 Baghdadi became one of Egypt's vice-presidents and resumed the chair of the assembly.

Removed in 1964 from the vice-presidency, he also left the Assembly and has not been active in politics since that time. Poor health and differences with Nasser over Yemen war policy and ARAB SO-CIALISM have been offered as reasons for his mysterious early retirement, but the deciding factor was probably the rise of his rival, General Abd al-Hakim AMIR, to Egypt's second highest political post in March 1964. He criticized Egypt's friendship treaty with the Soviet Union in 1971 and its peace treaty with ISRAEL in 1979. His memoirs, *Mudhakkirat Abd al-Latif al-Baghdadi,* were published in 1977.

BIBLIOGRAPHY

SHIMONI, YAACOV. *Biographical Dictionary of the Middle East.*

Arthur Goldschmidt, Jr.

Baghdad Law College

The Faculty of Law at the University of Baghdad.

In 1908, the Ottoman Empire founded the College of Law in Baghdad (Iraq). In 1957, the College of Law became part of the University of Baghdad. The law school has produced scores of Iraqi lawyers, government ministers, journalists, diplomats, and civil servants. Prominent Iraqi political figures, such as Rashid Ali al-Kaylani and Abd al-Rahman al-BAZZAZ taught there. The curriculum, mainly secular, was based on French law—originally, with a teaching staff educated mainly in France or Egypt. Since the early 1970s there has been an increasing emphasis on BA'TH party ideology and views in courses taught at the Law College.

Louay Bahry

Baghdad Museum

Museum promoting Iraqi-centered pan-Arab ideology

Established in 1969, this unusual museum was part of a new trend in Iraq under Ba'th rule, which began in 1968. It presented Iraq as the future leader of all the Arabs and sought to preserve, even strengthen, the Iraqi identity rather than allow it to dissipate in an all-Arab melting pot. Alongside Mesopotamian and Islamic archaeology, folklore brought out Iraq's uniqueness and seniority among the Arabs. The museum traces Baghdad's history to its establishment by al-Mansur in the eighth century C.E. and highlights its splendor during the Abbasid golden age. Just as importantly, however, it focuses on the traditional way of life in "old Baghdad": crafts, apparel, models of living quarters, domestic equipment and utensils, and scenes of social life.

BIBLIOGRAPHY

BARAM, AMATZIA. *Culture, History and Ideology in the Formation of Ba'thist Iraq, 1968–1989.* London, 1991.

Amatzia Baram

Baghdad Pact

Anti-Soviet agreement and security pact of the late 1950s.

After the failure of the Middle East Defense Organization (MEDO), the United States, Great Britain, Turkey, Iran, Pakistan, and Iraq continued their efforts to create a regional (Northern Tier) security pact along the lines of the North Atlantic Treaty Organization (NATO) as a bulwark against the Soviet Union.

In April 1954, Turkey and Pakistan signed a mutual assistance pact, which Iraq then signed on February 24, 1955, forming the core of the Baghdad Pact. Its most forceful Middle Eastern proponent, Nuri al-SAʿID of Iraq, championed the agreement because it tied Iraq more closely to the West and provided the Iraqi leader with potential leverage against his rival, Egypt's President Gamal Abdel NASSER. Lebanon and Syria did not join the pact, succumbing to Egyptian influence. Over the course of 1955, Britain, Pakistan, and Iran signed the pact, and a Middle East Treaty Organization (METO) was formed with headquarters in Baghdad.

The United States, while heavily involved in the various security guarantees, did not become an official member. It feared alienating Egypt and driving Nasser into the Soviet orbit. The United States also felt that formal membership in the pact would force it to choose sides in Middle East politics, since Israel could not be provided with comparable guarantees. Nonetheless, the security agreement fit U.S. strategic interests in the region. Through Turkey, the Middle East was linked to NATO and through Pakistan to the Southeast Asia Treaty Organization (SEATO). U.S. influence continued through military guarantees and diplomatic support.

The July 1958 revolution in Iraq led to the deaths of King Faisal II and Nuri al-Saʿid. Iraq withdrew from the Baghdad Pact in March 1959 and denounced it as a vestige of Western imperialism. The group was then renamed the Central Treaty Organization (CENTO).

BIBLIOGRAPHY

AMBROSE, STEPHEN. *Eisenhower: The President.* New York, 1985.

CAMPBELL, JOHN C. *Defense of the Middle East: Problems of American Policy.* New York, 1958.

LENCZOWSKI, GEORGE. *The Middle East in World Affairs,* 4th ed. Ithaca, N.Y., 1980.

Zachary Karabell

Baghdad Summit

Arab summit held after the Camp David Accords.

Egypt's President Anwar al-SADAT's diplomatic overtures to Israel beginning in late 1977 came as a tremendous shock to the rest of the Arab world, which was concerned by the prospects of Egypt, Israel's strongest Arab enemy, splitting Arab ranks by signing a separate peace with the Jewish state. Iraq, emerging as a powerful force in intra-Arab politics, was instrumental in convening a summit meeting after the CAMP DAVID ACCORDS, signed by Israel and Egypt in September 1978. Leaders from twenty Arab states and the Palestine Liberation Organization (PLO) met in Baghdad between November 2 and 5, 1978, to consider the Arab world's response.

The summit acted on several major issues. It rejected the Camp David Accords and offered its own peace proposal. Based on United Nations Security Council Resolution 242, it called for Israel's full withdrawal from occupied Arab territories, the establishment of a Palestinian state, and recognition of the right of all states within the region to exist.

Second, the summit threatened Egypt with severe penalties if it followed up on the Camp David Accords by signing a formal peace treaty with Israel. Although Saudi Arabia tried to prevent such drastic steps, these threats amounted to total isolation of Egypt from the rest of the Arab world. Specific measures included expelling Egypt from the LEAGUE OF ARAB STATES, moving the league's headquarters from Cairo, breaking off diplomatic relations, and halting all economic and military aid.

Third, the summit adopted financial measures to bolster the remaining frontline states and prevent further defections from Arab ranks. Some Arab states were particularly concerned that Jordan, which had expressed guarded interest in President Sadat's diplomatic initiatives with Israel, might follow his lead. Responding to a proposal by Iraq, the summit created a $9 billion fund to provide financial assistance for Syria, Jordan, and the PLO. The action proved crucial in discouraging Jordan from going against Arab consensus.

The summit also was important in paving the way for collective action among Arab states after several years of tension. Iraq and Syria set aside their poor relations, at least temporarily, just as the summit and the financial aid it provided symbolized Jordan's improving relations with Iraq.

Representatives of the summit were dispatched to meet with Sadat on November 4, but he refused to receive them. On March 27, 1979, the day after the peace treaty between Israel and Egypt was signed, the council of the League of Arab States met in Baghdad to follow through on the reprisals promised at the November summit; representatives of Sudan, Oman, and the PLO were not present. The sanctions were applied on March 31, the final day of the meeting: all Arab states except Sudan, Oman, and Somalia terminated diplomatic relations with Egypt and halted all forms of assistance. Egypt was expelled from the League of Arab States, the headquarters of which were transferred from Cairo to Tunis.

Michael R. Fischbach

Baghdad University

Administrative unit, dating from 1957, which centralized ten of the twelve autonomous colleges in Iraq.

In Baghdad, the first institutions of modern higher education were the College of Law and the Higher Teachers' Training School. By the time steps for unification were taken, schools of medicine, pharmacy, dentistry, engineering, agriculture, commerce, arts and sciences, and veterinary science had been added. The Shari'a College (of Islamic law) was incorporated into the university in 1960.

In 1992, there were twelve colleges and seven higher institutes under the Baghdad University administration, and the colleges in Basra and Mosul originally attached to Baghdad have developed into separate universities. Student enrollment in 1985 was 44,307, with 1,346 engaged in postgraduate studies. Iraq has been ranked second to Egypt in the region for producing university graduates in the sciences; it does, however, lose many trained scientists through emigration.

BIBLIOGRAPHY

MUHAMMAD, USAMA. "A Look at Higher Education in Iraq." *Dirasat Arabiyah,* April 1988, pp. 113–114. In Arabic.

John J. Donohue

Baghlan

City and province in northern Afghanistan.

Baghlan province has a population of approximately 600,000, about 200,000 of whom fled during the war from 1979 to 1992. Approximately 75 percent are TAJIKS, 17 percent are Pushtu-speaking, and a smaller percentage, in the north, are Uzbeks. The province, which lies along the major route between Kabul and the north, saw heavy fighting in the war. The provincial capital, the city of Baghlan, has a population of approximately 100,000.

BIBLIOGRAPHY

EIGHMY, THOMAS. *Afghanistan's Population Inside and Out.* Peshawar, Pakistan, 1990.

Grant Farr

Baha'i Faith

Baha'ism is a religion founded in the second half of the 1860s by an Iranian Babi, Mirza Hosayn Ali Nuri (1817–1892), known as Baha'ullah (the Glory of God).

Baha'ism grew out of the millenarian (messianic) Babi movement that began in the 1840s. Baha'ullah,

Baha'i temple in Haifa. (Mia Bloom)

a Babi nobleman, had been exiled for his beliefs to Baghdad in the Ottoman Empire in 1853. He declared himself in 1863 to a small group of close relatives and disciples as the messianic figure promised in Babism, "He whom God shall make manifest." He was exiled to Istanbul (1863), to Edirne (1864–1868), and finally to Akka in Ottoman Syria (1868–92). From about 1864 he began sending letters back to BABIS in Iran, announcing his station. He later asserted that he was the fulfillment of millenarian hopes, not only in Babism, but in Islam, Christianity, ZOROASTRIANISM, and in other traditions as well. Within a decade or so the vast majority of Babis had become Baha'is.

Baha'ullah, in an age of Middle Eastern absolutism, advocated parliamentary democracy. His own religion lacked a formal clergy, and he put executive power in the hands of community-steering committees he called "houses of justice," which later became elective bodies. Baha'ullah preached the unity of religions, progressive revelation, and the unity of humankind. He urged peace, criticized states for engaging in arms races, and advocated a world government able to employ collective security to prevent aggression. He said all Baha'is should school their children, both boys and girls, and he improved the position of women, saying that in his religion women are as men. Baha'i women are not constrained to practice veiling or seclusion. The initial social base of the movement was the urban middle and lower-middle classes and small landowners who had been Babis. Merchant clans who claimed descent from the Prophet MUHAMMAD (Sayyids) emerged as especially important in the leadership of the Baha'i community in Iran. Substantial numbers of Shi'ites, Jews, and Zoroastrians also became Baha'is throughout Iran.

Baha'ullah was succeeded by his eldest son, Abdu'l-Baha, who presided over the religion from 1892 to 1921. By 1900, the community had recovered from the persecution of the 1850s and had reached from fifty to one hundred thousand out of a population of nine million. Shi'a clerics and notables agitated against the Baha'i faith, and major pogroms broke out in 1903 in Rasht, Isfahan, and Yazd. In 1905, the CONSTITUTIONAL REVOLUTION broke out in Iran. Abdu'l-Baha at first supported it, but later declared his community's neutrality. Nonintervention in party politics then became a Baha'i policy. The religion spread internationally. Restricted to the Middle East and South Asia in Baha'ullah's lifetime, it now spread to Europe, North America, East Asia, Africa, and South America.

From 1921 to 1957, the Baha'i faith was led by Shoghi Effendi Rabbani, Abdu'l-Baha's grandson, from his headquarters in Haifa, Palestine/Israel.

Thereafter, from 1963, the worldwide Baha'i community periodically elected a central body, the Universal House of Justice, as prescribed in Baha'ullah's writings. The religion developed close ties with the United Nations, and it is recognized as a nongovernmental observer. In Iran, the rise of the Pahlavi state, 1925–1978, and a more secular policy had both benefits and drawbacks for Baha'is in Iran. Greater security and a decreased clerical influence produced less violence toward them, although they continued to face harassment. The authoritarianism of the Pahlavi state also led to tight restrictions on Baha'i activities and publications, and occasional state persecution, as in 1955.

By an accident of history (Baha'ullah's Ottoman exile), the world headquarters of the religion since the nineteenth century, Haifa, are now in Israel, although less than a thousand Baha'is live in that country. Critics of the Baha'is in the region charge them with being Zionist agents, but Baha'is point to their principle of nonintervention in partisan politics. Israel has granted Baha'is freedom of religion, as it has other religious communities, and no evidence of political collusion has ever been produced. In the 1960s, the rise of authoritarian populist regimes stressing ARAB NATIONALISM led to the persecution of Baha'is in Egypt, Libya, Iraq, and elsewhere in the Arab world, a situation that continues to this day.

In Iran, by 1978, the Baha'i community numbered around 300,000 out of a population of 35 million. Most Baha'is were lower-middle and middle class, although they included a few prominent millionaires. The Islamic Republic of Iran launched an extensive campaign against the Baha'is from 1979 through 1988. Many Muslim clerics despised the Baha'is as heretics and apostates, whose beliefs posed a dire threat to traditional Islam. Iran executed nearly two hundred prominent Baha'is for their beliefs and imprisoned hundreds more. Baha'i investments and philanthropies were confiscated. Baha'is were denied ration cards, excluded from state schools and universities, and often forced to recant their faith. After 1988, most were released from prison but still suffer widespread official discrimination in Iran.

As the religion has grown in India and the Americas, the often persecuted and constrained Middle Eastern communities have come to represent less than 10 percent of Baha'is worldwide—estimated in 1990 at 4.5 million.

BIBLIOGRAPHY

SMITH, PETER. *The Babi and Baha'i Religions: From Messianic Shi'ism to a World Religion.* Cambridge, U.K., 1987.

Juan R. I. Cole

Bahar, Mohammad Taqi   [1886–1951]

Iran's last great qasideh (ode) poet, also a literary scholar and politician.

Mohammad Taqi Bahar was born in Mashhad. In response to a congratulatory *qasideh* he composed on the occasion of MOHAMMAD ALI QAJAR's accession to the throne, in 1907 Bahar was named *malek al-sho'ara* (king of poets = poet laureate), the last Iranian poet to have that title. In 1906, when the constitution of Persia (now Iran) was granted, Bahar joined the constitutionalists in his hometown of Mashhad. For the next decade, he wielded his pen as poet, journalist, and editor for progressive causes and suffered incarceration and banishment.

In the 1920s he was elected to the parliament. A target for assassination, he turned from politics to literary scholarship and joined the faculty at Tehran University upon its founding in 1934. His *Divan* [Collected Poems] appeared after his death, revealing Bahar as firmly traditionalist in terms of poetic form but modern in terms of poetic subjects. Among his many other books, his history of Persian Literature called *Sabkshenasi* (1942) stands out.

BIBLIOGRAPHY

Almost the only writings on Bahar in English are M. LORAINE, "Bahar in the Context of the Persian Constitutional Revolution," *Iranian Studies* 5 (1972); "A Memoir on the Life and Poetic Works of Maliku'o-Shu'ara Bahar," *International Journal of Middle East Studies* 2 (1972): 140–168; and "Bahar, Mohammad-Taqi," *Encyclopedia Iranica* 3 (1989). BOZORG ALAVI treats Bahar's role as chairperson for the First Iranian Writers Congress at the Soviet Cultural Institute in a report called "The First Iranian Writers Congress, 1946" in *Critical Perspectives on Modern Persian Literature* (1984).

Michael C. Hillmann

Baharina

Arab descendants of the original inhabitants of the island of Bahrain; mainly Shi'ites.

The Baharina consider themselves the original and rightful owners of the island of Bahrain, the main island of the State of Bahrain. They consider the KHALIFA FAMILY, who conquered the island in the 1780s, to be foreign, minority interlopers—adherents of SUNNI ISLAM. The original inhabitants were rural and coastal people who fished and dove for pearls. Today, most Baharina still live away from the capital cities of Manama and Muharraq. As adherents of SHI'ISM, they do not especially identify with other Bahraini Shi'ites—who trace their origins to Persia (now Iran) and who are known in Bahrain as *Ajamis* (Persians).

Like most of the Shi'ites in Bahrain, the Baharina believe that the country's economy has benefited the Sunnis, especially the ruling and merchant families; the Bahraini Shi'ites find themselves on the lower end of the economic scale.

BIBLIOGRAPHY

BILL, JAMES, and ROBERT SPRINGBORG. *Politics: Middle East,* 3rd ed. Glenview, Ill., 1990.

Emile A. Nakhleh

Bahariya

A group of Egyptian oases in the Western Desert, located about 217 miles (350 km) southwest of Alexandria.

These oases in Egypt's Matruh governorate were known in the early history of Islam for their excellent dates and raisins. Cereals, rice, sugarcane, and indigo were also grown there. The fertility of the oases is due to hot springs containing various chemicals. Roman temples and Coptic (Christian) churches were built in the oases, and their ancient population probably exceeded today's estimated 6,000.

BIBLIOGRAPHY

Encyclopaedia of Islam, 2nd ed.
FAKHRY, AHMED. *The Oases of Egypt.* Cairo, 1974.

Arthur Goldschmidt, Jr.

Bahdinan Family

Ruling family of northern Iraq.

Reputedly descendants of the Abbasid caliphs, highly regarded by the Kurds, and favored by the Ottomans, the Bahdinan family ruled the principality of Amadiya and its dependencies of Aqra, Dair, and Dohuk, all north of Mosul, from the late fourteenth century until its defeat by Injeh Bayraqdar, Wali of Mosul, in 1837.

BIBLIOGRAPHY

LONGRIGG, STEPHEN HEMSLEY. *Four Centuries of Modern Iraq.* Oxford, 1925.

Albertine Jwaideh

Bahnini, Muhammad   [1914–   ]

Moroccan political leader.

Educated in Fez and Rabat, Bahnini was a professor at the Imperial College, where he taught Morocco's Crown Prince Hassan, then heir apparent. Bahnini was chosen to lead the royal cabinet of Morocco's King Muhammad V in the early 1950s, just before independence from French colonialism in 1956. Following a brief exile, he rejoined the government. In 1958, he was minister of justice in the short-lived Ibrahim government.

Hassan II came to the throne in 1961, and Bahnini was then designated prime minister in 1964, a post he held for one year, resigning in the midst of a political crisis. During the next few decades, he remained a loyal member of the court, serving as minister of defense (1970–1971), minister of justice (1971–1972), minister of state for cultural affairs (1974–1979; 1980–1982), and minister of state (1972–1974; 1982–present).

BIBLIOGRAPHY

Morocco: A Country Survey. Washington, D.C., 1986.
Who's Who in the Arab World. 1990–1991.

Matthew S. Gordon

Bahrain

The State of Bahrain is an archipelago of thirty-three islands in the heart of the Persian/Arabian Gulf.

The Bahraini islands are some fifteen miles (24 km) off the northeast coast of Saudi Arabia and thirteen miles (21 km) to the northwest of the Qatar peninsula. Connected by causeway to Saudi Arabia, Bahrain, the largest, is twenty-seven miles (44 km) by ten miles (16 km). The total land area of the country, 213 square miles (554 sq km), supports a population of 354,857 (1987). Manama, on Bahrain island, serves as the capital city. The ruling family, the KHALIFA, a major branch of the Bani Utub confederation of the northern Gulf, conquered the islands in 1782 (from Arab subjects of Persia) and set up a commercial, estate-holding elite. Class distinctions between the new rulers and the indigenous population were reinforced by religious ones, as the al-Khalifa and their tribal allies were and remain adherents of SUNNI ISLAM, while the local farmers, pearl divers, and fisherfolk remain Shi'ites (see SHI'ISM). A British protectorate was formed in 1880.

Outbreaks of nationalism, unrest, and rebellion have been a recurrent feature of modern Bahraini

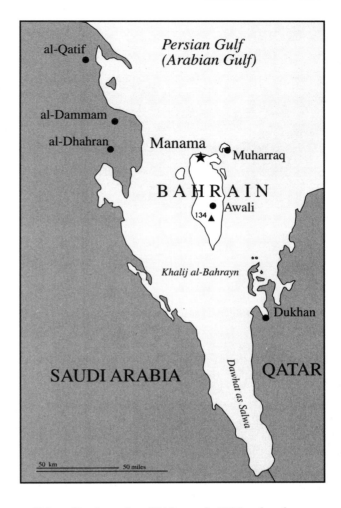

politics. During the 1910s and 1920s, local merchants, tradespeople and pearl divers rose in opposition to a number of innovative economic regulations imposed by the government of British India, which took charge of the islands' affairs at the end of the nineteenth century. From the 1930s to the 1950s, a broad coalition of merchants, intellectuals and oil workers (petroleum was discovered in 1932) demonstrated against continued British domination; against the presence of large numbers of foreign workers; in favor of allowing local labor to unionize; and in favor of establishing an elected legislature.

After the 1950s, outbreaks became increasingly localized and intermittent. Some episodes, such as the March 1972 general strike by the construction, shipyard, and aluminum-factory workers remained class based, while others began to take sectarian overtones, as when Shi'ites openly demonstrated support for the Iranian Revolution during the late 1970s and early 1980s.

Shaykh Isa ibn Sulman al-Khalifa became Emir of Bahrain in 1961, upon the death of his father, and proclaimed independence in 1971. According to the

Remains of a sixteenth-century Portuguese fort in Bahrain. (Richard Bulliet)

Street scene in Manama, the capital of Bahrain. (Richard Bulliet)

written constitution, adopted in 1973, the office of emir is to pass from father to eldest son unless the ruler chooses someone else to succeed him. Close relatives of the emir fill the most important posts in the country's cabinet of ministers. Ministers who are not members of the KHALIFA FAMILY have usually been sons of the established wealthy merchant families and have received specialized training in Western universities. Bahrain's largest industrial concerns are also managed by this group of royal family members and influential civil servants.

Political parties, like trade unions, are prohibited by the 1973 constitution. This document does, however, provide for an elected national assembly, the first elections for which were held in December 1973. College-educated professionals, shopkeepers, middle-income merchants and the country's intelli-

gentsia were the strongest supporters of the electoral system. The commercial elite remained largely noncommittal and did not participate in the elections, either as candidates or as voters. Radical groups, most notably the local branch of the Popular Front for the Liberation of Oman and the Arab Gulf, tried to convince voters to boycott the proceedings, and advocated more comprehensive freedoms of press and assembly, as well as agitating for the release of those they claimed were political prisoners and urging the adoption of laws permitting the formation of trade unions. Younger, comparatively radical delegates nevertheless emerged victorious from the balloting, although the government manipulated technicalities in the election law to block several of the newly elected delegates from taking their seats in the assembly.

Although only empowered by the constitution to give advice and consent regarding laws initiated by the cabinet, the national assembly began debating three volatile issues during 1974. The first concerned the formulation of a general labor law that would have authorized the formation of a general labor law that would have authorized the formation of trade unions and reduced the number of expatriate workers in the country. The second was the renewal of the informal arrangement whereby the United States maintained a small naval facility at the port of Jufair. And the last was the continuation of the strict Public Security Law, which had been promulgated to suppress radical organizations during the early 1960s. By mid-1975, the two largest informal groupings of deputies, the People's Bloc and the Religious Bloc, could find no common ground from which to cooperate in overturning this regulation. Consequently, the assembly became deadlocked and, in

Date palms of Bahrain. (Richard Bulliet)

August 1975, the prime minister submitted the cabinet's resignation to the emir, who dissolved the assembly but reinstated the government, giving the cabinet of ministers "full legislative powers."

Since the dissolution of the national assembly, organized opposition to the regime has come primarily from Bahrain's various Islamist political movements. Advocates of moderate reform can be found in the Sunni Social Reform Society and Supporters of the Call, as well as in the Shi'a Party of the Islamic Call. Proponents of more profound social transformation belong to the Islamic Action Organization (IAO) and the Islamic Guidance Society, both predominantly Shi'ite; demonstrations organized by these two associations erupted periodically during late 1979 and early 1980, culminating in a series of large-scale marches in support of the new Islamic Republic of Iran (1979) during April and May of 1980. State security forces broke up these demonstrations by force, killing a number of marchers.

After these events, underground groups, such as the IAO, changed their tactics—abandoning mass popular demonstrations and turning instead to isolated acts of sabotage carried out by small groups of committed cadres. This shift was buttressed by the formation of the Islamic Front for the Liberation of Bahrain (IFLB) in Tehran, Iran, at the end of 1979; the clandestine operations envisaged by the leaders of this organization were epitomized by the December 1981 plot to overthrow the Khalifa family and set up an Islamic republic on the islands. Sizable caches of small arms belonging to clandestine groups of radical Shi'ites continued to be uncovered in rural districts as late as the fall and winter of 1983/84.

Concerted efforts on the part of the Bahrain authorities to expose and destroy militant Shi'ite cells largely succeeded in disrupting the operations of the IAO and IFLB by the mid-1980s. Some 100 persons were charged in December 1987 with conspiring to assassinate the ruler and seize the country's main oil facilities, the radio and television station, the international airport, and the American embassy; this group may have been affiliated with the IFLB, but Bahraini officials refused to implicate the Iranians in the plot. Instead, the government imposed strict curfews on Shi'ite residential districts and promulgated a regulation prohibiting Bahraini Shi'ites from taking jobs in the armed forces. Police made further arrests in the days following the death of Iran's Ayatollah Ruhollah KHOMEINI, in June of 1989, and during the weeks around Ashura (see MUHARRAM) two months later. With the exception of persistent but unconfirmed reports of isolated attacks on state installations, the Islamist opposition appeared to have been firmly suppressed as the 1990s began.

BIBLIOGRAPHY

ANTHONY, JOHN DUKE. *Arab States of the Lower Gulf.* Washington, D.C., 1975.
KHURI, FUAD I. *Tribe and State in Bahrain.* Chicago, 1980.
LAWSON, FRED H. *Bahrain: The Modernization of Autocracy.* Boulder, Colo., 1989.
NAKHLEH, EMILE A. *Bahrain.* Lexington, Mass., 1976.
AL-RUMAIHI, MOHAMMED GHANIM. *Bahrain: A Study on Social and Political Changes since the First World War.* Kuwait, 1975.

Fred H. Lawson

Bahrain–Kuwait Petrochemical Industries

Joint venture of Bahrain, Kuwait, and Saudi Arabia.

In 1979, Bahrain decided to complement its petroleum industry by building the Gulf Petrochemical Industries Company, a joint venture with equal equity participation for each of the three partners. A petrochemical production complex was built at SITRA and inaugurated in 1981. It produces twelve hundred tons (1,100 metric tons) of ammonia and methanol per day and is chaired by Bahrain's ruler, Shaykh Isa ibn Ali al-KHALIFA.

BIBLIOGRAPHY

The Middle East and North Africa, 1991, 37th ed. London, 1991.

Emile A. Nakhleh

Bahrain Nationalist Movement

The effort to gain autonomy from Britain.

Nationalism has a long history in BAHRAIN, because local notables persistently resisted British influence over the rulers in the years after 1880. When British officials deposed the ruler in 1923, SUNNI ISLAMIC notables opposed to overt British interference in the country's internal affairs organized a Bahrain National Congress to demand the ruler's restoration and the creation of an advisory council to assist him in governing the country. In 1934, Shi'ite leaders (of the petite bourgeoisie and working class) unsuccessfully petitioned the ruler to promulgate a basic law and institute proportional representation on the municipal and education councils. In 1938, Sunni reformers demanded the establishment of a popular assembly (MAJLES) and an end to administrative inefficiency. When students and oil workers (petroleum was found in 1932) threatened a general strike in support of the *majles* movement in November of 1938, the regime arrested some prominent reformers and deported them to British-controlled India. Several clandestine opposition groups—including the Representatives of the People, the Secret Labor Union, and the Society of Free Youth—remained active after the suppression of the reform movement, but none posed a serious challenge to the regime during the 1940s.

Unrest emerged in 1953/54, culminating in a general strike in July of 1954. Liberal reformers from both the Sunni and Shiite communities organized a Higher Executive Committee (HEC) that October to call for greater national autonomy, the convening of a legislature, the right to form trade unions, and the creation of an appellate court. Protracted negotiations between the ruler and the HEC led to formal recognition of a Committee of National Unity, in return for the HEC's agreeing to end its demands for a national assembly. Activists in the industrial labor force responded by forming the National Liberation Front-Bahrain, pressing for more fundamental changes in the country's political structure. Anti-British demonstrations at the time of the Suez (Sinai) War of 1956 precipitated restraints on all opposition forces and the declaration of a state of emergency, which effectively terminated the nationalist movements of the 1950s. Shaykh Isa ibn Sulman al-KHALIFA succeeded to the throne in 1961; he announced Bahrain's independence on August 14, 1971.

BIBLIOGRAPHY

HALLIDAY, FRED. *Arabia without Sultans.* Harmondsworth, U.K., 1974.

LAWSON, FRED H. *Bahrain: The Modernization of Autocracy.* Boulder, Colo., 1989.

NAKHLEH, EMILE A. *Bahrain.* Lexington, Mass., 1976.

Fred H. Lawson

Bahrain National Oil Company (BANOCO)

State-owned oil company.

The Bahrain National Oil Company was established in 1976, following the decision of the government of BAHRAIN to assume a direct 60 percent interest in Bahrain's petroleum business—which previously was totally owned by Bahrain Petroleum Company (BAPCO). By 1981, BANOCO took over the complete management and operation of offshore oil exploration, producing, and refining activities.

BIBLIOGRAPHY

NYROP, RICHARD, ed. *Persian Gulf States: Country Studies.* Washington, D.C., 1985.

Emile A. Nakhleh

Bahrain Offshore Banks

Offshore Banking units (OBU) are licensed to provide all banking services outside Bahrain itself but are domiciled and operate within Bahrain.

After 1973 Bahrain, faced with declining oil production and a rapidly increasing population, sought to develop as a service center for the Gulf. The government invited large international banks to open offshore branches in Bahrain. OBUs are free of income tax and can operate without a local sponsor, as is the case for all other commercial ventures in the Gulf. The OBUs are regulated by the Bahrain Monetary Agency, the central bank of Bahrain. By 1980 seventy-two banks had OBU status. Two main groups of banks took advantage of this license: large money-center banks, such as Citibank, Bank of Tokyo, and Indosuez, and newly formed large banks owned by both private and public Arab funds.

The Arab-owned banks are registered as local banking corporations but only have activities offshore. The largest ones are the Arabian Banking Corporation (ABC), owned by the governments of Kuwait, the UAE, and Libya; the Gulf International Bank (GIB), owned by the governments of the Gulf Cooperation Council; the Arab Investment Company (TAIC), owned by the governments of the Arab League; and Investcorp, owned by the public at large, with shares traded on the stock exchanges of the region.

Between 1974 and 1987, the OBU status appealed to the money-center banks because it gave them a central base of operation to cover the booming Gulf markets, especially that of Saudi Arabia. Their main products were letters of credit (mainly advance-payment guarantees and performance bonds to contractors) and related loan facilities. They were able to use Bahrain for treasury operations. They could overlap foreign-exchange trading hours between London and Tokyo, and they could arbitrage the large Saudi riyal/U.S. dollar differentials. After 1984, however, the market for banking services declined along with the region's oil-revenue decline and the increase in services offered by the local Gulf banks. Changes in foreign-exchange practices and technology limited Bahrain's geographical advantage, and interest differentials between riyals and dollars became too small to arbitrage. Thus the money-center banks limited their activities in Bahrain. By 1993 there were forty-eight active OBUs with assets of seventy billion dollars.

BIBLIOGRAPHY

HAZZAM, HENRI. *Gulf Financial Markets*. Bahrain, 1988.
SEZNEC, JEAN-FRANÇOIS. *The Financial Markets of the Arabian Gulf*. London, 1987.

Jean-François Seznec

Bahrain Order in Council

Effort to establish Bahrain as a formal British protectorate, 1909–1913.

In response to active German interest in the Persian/Arabian GULF during the first decade of the twentieth century, Britain became concerned with protecting its trade, position, and interests there. In 1909, Britain's Committee of Imperial Defense saw the necessity for better trade and port facilities, but it rejected the India Office suggestion to issue an Order in Council delineating the jurisdiction of the British resident agent in Bahrain—thus establishing a formal British protectorate (although Bahrain had been under British protection since 1820). It was concerned that the Order in Council might create unnecessary complications, since Persia (now Iran) and the Ottoman Empire both claimed the islands. An order was drawn in 1909 but was tabled in 1911 because of Anglo-Ottoman negotiations. The Bahrain Order was prepared in 1913, but it was withheld and never formally implemented; in that year, however, Bahrain was informally placed under a protectorate status.

BIBLIOGRAPHY

BUSCH, BRITTON COOPER. *Britain and the Persian Gulf 1894–1914*. Berkeley, Calif., 1967.

Emile A. Nakhleh

Bahrain Petroleum Company (BAPCO)

The region's first American-owned oil company, now held by Bahrain.

In June 1930, Standard Oil Company of California (SOCal) was granted a fifty-five-year concession to explore for petroleum in Bahrain in return for

BAPCO worker adjusting a pipeline valve. (BAPCO)

a minimum royalty payment of 75,000 rupees ($37,500) per year. This agreement was signed over the strenuous objections of the British government, which held a protectorate over Bahrain (by treaty) since 1820 and which insisted that all concessions along the Arabian coast of the Persian/Arabian Gulf abide by the terms of the 1928 RED LINE AGREEMENT—reserving exclusive rights to market any oil produced in the former territories of the Ottoman Empire to British enterprises. As a compromise, SOCal, in partnership with Texas Oil Company (Texaco), registered their joint production company in Canada under the name Bahrain Petroleum Company (BAPCO). This technicality enabled SOCal and Texas Oil to set up the only American-owned operating company in the region.

Oil was discovered at Jabal al-Dukhan on the main island of Bahrain in May 1932, and commercial production began in 1934. By 1938, annual exports exceeded 8 million barrels and the company had constructed one of the world's largest oil refineries on the eastern shore of the main island to process both local and Saudi Arabian crude (discovered in 1936). During World War II, labor unrest at the refinery led the government to permit BAPCO to recruit sizable numbers of South Asian workers, as well as to import a wide range of goods on a duty-free basis. These trends, combined with a sharp increase in royalty payments to the state, precipitated renewed strike activity at the company's facilities in 1953/54. With the suppression of this wave of strikes, the company began purchasing food and machinery through local distributors, thereby boosting its role in the local economy.

Annual petroleum production in Bahrain peaked at around 28 million barrels in 1970 and since then has declined steadily. Bahrain became independent in 1971 and, in September 1974, took over a 60 percent share of BAPCO, effectively nationalizing the company. The following year, Bahrain transferred its interest in the company to the newly created Bahrain National Oil Company, which was put in charge of the exploration, refining, storage, transportation, and marketing of local petroleum products. A sister company, Bahrain National Gas Company, was set up to handle the production and shipment of natural gas. Despite the introduction of new techniques designed to augment output at existing wellheads, production declined to some 15 million barrels per year by the mid-1980s, with no new reserves having been discovered. As a result, Saudi oil makes up more than 75 percent of the throughput at the BAPCO refinery.

BIBLIOGRAPHY

Lawson, Fred H. *Bahrain: The Modernization of Autocracy.* Boulder, Colo., 1989.
Lenczowski, George. *Oil and State in the Middle East.* Ithaca, N.Y., 1960.

Fred H. Lawson

Bahr al-Abyad

The White Nile.

Bahr al-Abyad rises in Lake No, from which it flows one thousand kilometers (625 miles) to Khartoum and its confluence with the Blue Nile. Flowing east, it receives significant water from its major tributary, the Sobat, which originates in Ethiopia, then swings north to contribute one-third of the total mean annual flow of the Nile. Along the reach of the White Nile the land becomes increasingly arid, and the river is dotted with clusters of water hyacinth and papyrus that become islands. It forms the reservoir behind the Jabal Auliya Dam forty-seven kilometers (29 miles) south of Khartoum.

Robert O. Collins

Bahr al-Arab

River separating southern Sudan from Darfur and Kordofan.

Bahr al-Arab is more important as the frontier between the Africans of Southern Sudan and the Arab Muslims of Darfur and Kordofan than as a hydrological entity. Rising on the watershed between Sudan and the Central African Republic, it flows sluggishly east in a great arc to its confluence with the BAHR AL-GHAZAL at Gabat al-Arab, by which point it has lost most of its water through evaporation. Its lower reaches are choked with aquatic vegetation.

Robert O. Collins

Bahr al-Ghazal

Tributary of the Nile.

Bahr al-Ghazal (the Gazelle River) drains a basin the size of France, yet its contribution to the Nile is insignificant. It tributaries, which come from the Congo–Nile watershed as well as from rivers of Darfur and Kordofan, are consumed by evaporation and transpiration in the great swamps along the river. The river should not be confused with the province in southern Sudan of the same name.

Robert O. Collins

Bahr al-Jabal

Tributary of the Nile.

Bahr al-Jabal (Mountain River) begins at the outlet of Lake Albert (Lake Mobutu Sese Seko); from there to the river port of Nimule, it is frequently called the Albert Nile. At Nimule, the river turns northwest and plunges through a narrow gorge 160 kilometers (100 miles) long. At Bor the Bahr al-Jabal enters the SUDD, the world's largest swamp. It then flows 370 kilometers (231 miles) to Lake No where it joins the BAHR AL-GHAZAL to form the BAHR AL-ABYAD.

Robert O. Collins

Baida

City and administrative district (baladiyya) of Cyrenaica, Libya; population (1973) 60,000.

Baida (also called Zawiya al-Baidu) was the site of the first Sanusi ZAWIYA (Islamic lodge) in Libya in 1843. In the 1960s it was developed as Libya's new administrative capital. The project was abandoned after the 1969 revolution, because of its impracticality, remoteness, and close association with the SANUSI monarchy (although much of the infrastructure, parliament house, and government buildings had been completed).

John L. Wright

Baily Committee Report on Village Administration

Report of British mandate authorities in Palestine, completed in October 1941.

The Baily Committee Report recommended reviving and formalizing the prerogatives of village leaders and village councils in Palestine. Along with recommendations of the PEEL COMMISSION REPORT of 1937, the Baily report represents British efforts to use local political mechanisms to facilitate and legitimize colonialism and colonial rule.

BIBLIOGRAPHY

MILLER, YLANA N. *Government and Society in Rural Palestine, 1920–1948.* Austin, Tex., 1985.

Steve Tamari

Baka' Valley

See Biqa' Valley

Baker, James [1930–]

U.S. secretary of state, 1989–1992.

As secretary of state during most of the administration of U.S. President George Bush, Baker played a crucial role in U.S.–sponsored negotiations to end the Arab–Israel conflict. In late 1989 he proposed the "Baker Plan," which dealt with Israel–Palestinian talks over the future of the West Bank. Israel rejected the plan in the spring of 1990.

In the wake of the Gulf War, Baker—known as a blunt and persistent negotiator willing to pressure and cajole Arabs and Israelis alike—exerted tremendous efforts in arranging for negotiations that included not only Israel and the Arab states but Palestinian representatives as well. In the spring of 1991, he traveled to Jerusalem and met with prominent Palestinians titularly independent of the Palestine Liberation Organization (PLO), which both the United States and Israel refused to include directly in the proposed negotiations.

In October 1991, face-to-face negotiations began in Madrid, under U.S. and Soviet involvement, within a framework established by Baker: Palestinian

representatives would participate as part of a joint Jordanian–Palestinian delegation, and the various parties would engage both in bilateral talks aimed at producing peace treaties and in multilateral talks dealing with wider regional issues, such as refugee repatriation and water. Although not completely responsible for the successful Arab–Israel agreements that followed, the negotiations were the most significant diplomatic effort undertaken on behalf of a comprehensive settlement to the conflict.

Michael R. Fischbach

Bakhtar-e Emruz

Iranian daily evening newspaper, 1949–1953.

Bakhtar-e Emruz (Today's East), was a daily evening newspaper published in Iran from 1949 to 1953. Its founder, Dr. Hoseyn Fatemi, was one of Dr. Mohammad MOSSADEGH's closest associates in the National Front, and participated actively in the nationalization of the Iranian oil industry in the early 1950s. The newspaper was closed down following the fall of Mossadegh's government in 1953.

BIBLIOGRAPHY

SHIFTEH, N. *Doktor Fatemi* (Dr. Fatemi). Tehran, 1985.

Neguin Yavari

Bakhtiar Shahpur [1914–1991]

Iranian president overthrown by Islamic Revolution.

Bakhtiar's parents were committed activists during Iran's Constitutional Revolution of 1905 and his father was executed on the order of Reza Shah. He began his preliminary education in Isfahan and continued it in Beirut and later in France. In 1942, he obtained his doctorate in philosophy and political science from the Sorbonne. During World War II, Bakhtiar joined the French Resistance and fought against Nazi Germany. Upon his return to Iran, he worked for the Labor Ministry and became a member of the Iran Party, one of the constituent parties of the National Front. He worked closely with Mohammad Mossadegh and was a leader of the National Front formed in the early 1960s. He accepted the Shah's offer to form a democratic government in January 1979, but as the Iranian Revolution proceeded, Bakhtiar's 37-day government collapsed and he was forced to flee the country. He settled in Paris and established the National Resistance Movement against the Islamic government in Iran. He escaped an assassination attempt in 1980, but was finally assassinated in his house in 1991. The three assassins were said to have been directed by Tehran's government.

BIBLIOGRAPHY

CHAKERI, ALI. "The Life of Shahpour Bakhtiar." *Qiam-e Iran* 11 (1994): 4–5.
IRAN RESEARCH GROUP. *Who Is Who in Iran.* 1990, pp. 71–72.
Le Monde. August 12, 1994.

Farhad Arshad

Bakhtiar, Timur   [1914–1970]

Iranian general.

The son of Sardar Mu'azzam Bakhtiari, Timur Bakhtiar attended the French military college at St. Cyr (1930–1935). During the premiership of Mohammad MOSSADEGH, he was commander of several provincial garrisons, but he enjoyed greater success after the fall of Mossadegh (1953), because he had the same tribal lineage as Soraya Esfandiari, who was then queen of Iran. As military governor of Tehran, he was largely responsible for eradicating the opposition to the PAHLAVI DYNASTY, whether the opposition stemmed from the leftist TUDEH PARTY, the liberal National Front (see NATIONAL FRONT, IRAN), or the religious FEDA'IYAN-E ISLAM quarter. In 1958, he was appointed the first chief of SAVAK (Sazman-e Ettela'at va Zed-e Ettela'at-e Keshvar, or the National Intelligence and Counterintelligence Agency). Influenced by his premier, Ali AMINI, who feared Bakhtiar's grasp on power and resented his reported meeting with Pres. John Kennedy in Washington, DC., MOHAMMAD REZA SHAH PAHLAVI removed the general from his position. Bakhtiar joined the ranks of the opposition in exile, and he was active in Europe, Lebanon, and Iraq in contacting both Ayatollah KHOMEINI and remnants of the leftist Tudeh party. In 1970, by instruction of the shah, Bakhtiar was murdered in Iraq, close to the Iranian border, by a SAVAK agent.

BIBLIOGRAPHY

"Bakhtiar, Timur." In *Encyclopedia Iranica,* vol. 3. Ed. by Ehsan Yarshater.
Iranian Oral History Project. Cambridge, Mass., 1986.

Neguin Yavari

Bakhtiari

Luri-speaking tribal people of central Iran.

Bakhtiari LURS are members of a historically important tribal confederacy of approximately 700,000 (1990) people who reside in the central Zagros mountains of Iran. They are Shi'a Muslims. Until the mid-twentieth century, most Bakhtiari led a life of pastoral Nomadism; in the 1990s, most were settled in villages and practiced a mixed agricultural-pastoral economy.

BIBLIOGRAPHY

GARTHWAITE, GENE. *Khans and Shahs: A Documentary Analysis of the Bakhtiyari in Iran.* Cambridge, U.K., 1983.

Lois Beck

Bakhtiari, Najaf Qoli Khan Samsam al-Soltaneh   [1854–1930]

Prime minister of Iran, 1911–1913.

Born to a leading family of the Bakhtiari tribe, Najaf Qoli Khan Samsam al-Soltaneh was prime minister of Iran after Mohammad Ali Shah was deposed and the Constitutionalists assumed power in 1911 (see CONSTITUTIONAL REVOLUTION). Samsam al-Soltaneh, with the aid of his tribal army, was instrumental in militarily defeating Mohammad Ali Shah, and thus he enjoyed significant mass support during his tenure in office. As a consequence, when the Russian legation in Tehran, together with the British, issued an ultimatum to the newly founded Iranian parliament asking for his resignation, popular uprisings ensued and he retained his position until 1913. He was made prime minister again, briefly, in 1918. During his premiership, Swedish officers were charged with the founding of the pro-reform internal Iranian gendarmerie, which was modeled on the Ottoman TANZIMAT. In 1921, Bakhtiari was named governor of Khorasan, but he refused the appointment because of his support for the rebellious Colonel Mohammad Taqi Khan Pesyan, who had set up government in Mashhad. Samsam al-Soltaneh died in the Bakhtiari region in 1930.

BIBLIOGRAPHY

GARTHWAITE, GENE R. *Khans and Shahs: A Documentary Analysis of the Bakhtiyari in Iran.* Cambridge, U.K., 1983.

Neguin Yavari

Bakil Tribal Confederation

One of Yemen's two largest and most important tribal confederations.

The tribes of Yemen have traditionally been the basic unit of social, political, and military organization in the country. Until the reign of Imam Yahya (1918–1948), the vast majority of the tribes of Yemen belonged to one of four large confederations; the Bakil is one of the two largest and most important. Imam Yahya's campaign to subject the country, and more specifically the tribes, to his control, led him to undertake massive campaigns against their influence and power; in fact, his efforts succeeded in permanently eliminating all but two of the ancient confederations (the HASHID is the other one to survive).

Many writers have referred to the Hashid and Bakil confederations as the "two wings" of the ZAYDI imamate; in the sense that many of the tribes that belong to these confederations are and were strongly committed to Zaydi Islam, the Imams were recognized—to a greater or lesser degree—as the heads of the Zaydi community and could, therefore, count on a measure of support and loyalty. Not all the tribes, however, accepted the temporal and even legal role that the imams arrogated to themselves; consequently, many imams (Imam Yahya and Imam Ahmad in the twentieth century included) complained bitterly about the tribes' inordinate political power.

The member tribes of the Bakil Confederation are found primarily in the mountains of the west, northwest, and far north of the country; its leaders today are the Abu Luhum clan, of the Nihm tribe.

Manfred W. Wenner

Bakkush, Hadi [1930–   ]

Prime minister of Tunisia, 1987–1989.

Bakkush holds a degree in political science from the Sorbonne in Paris. He was chosen as prime minister by President Zine al-Abdine BEN ALI in November 1987, following the latter's overthrow of thirty-year president of Tunisia Habib BOURGUIBA; he was charged with pursuing the platform of reforms promised by Ben Ali upon his accession to office. These included the lifting of restrictions on press freedoms, the introduction of political pluralism, and reforms of the judicial system. Toward this end, and shortly after taking office, Bakkush met with leaders from the Communist and Social Democratic parties and permitted the media to report the activities of these opposition parties. Moves toward a multiparty system continued through 1988 and included a loosening of restrictions on even the Islamic Tendency Movement (MTI); in May 1988, the head of the MTI, Rashid GHANNUSHI, was pardoned by the Ben Ali government. It remained clear, however, that the dominant political institution was to remain the ruling party, the old DESTOUR Socialist party (PSD), renamed the Constitutional Democratic Rally (RCD) in 1987.

From the start of his tenure in office, Bakkush and his cabinet faced severe ecnomic problems, including a mounting payments deficit, a faltering tourist industry, and high unemployment; few gains were achieved in solving these problems. In September 1989, Bakkush was replaced by Dr. Hamid Qarwi. According to rumors, more than official sources, Bakkush is said to have been too cautious for Ben Ali's tastes in pursuing the political and economic reforms sought by the Tunisian president.

BIBLIOGRAPHY

Middle East International. 1987–1991.

Matthew S. Gordon

Baklava

A sweet pastry found throughout the Middle East.

Baklava is made with a filling of ground almond, pistachio, or walnut mixture bound with an egg white and sugar. The nut stuffing is layered with butter and wrapped in phyllo pastry. It is soaked in sugar syrup or honey flavored with rose water. Baklava is baked in several rows on large baking trays, then cut into triangles, quadrangles, or rhomboids. Baklava comes from the Turkish word for lozenge, originally a diamond-shape.

Clifford A. Wright

Bakr, Ahmad Hasan al- [1914–1982]

A senior Iraqi military officer and politician.

Hasan al-Bakr (also called Abu Haytham) was born in Tikrit, Iraq, to a family of small landowners of the Begat tribe. Upon graduation from a teachers' training high school in Baghdad in 1932, he served as a primary school teacher. In search of a more promising career, in 1938 he joined the military academy that had recently been opened for cadets from middle- and lower-middle-class backgrounds. By 1958, he was a lieutenant colonel. In the mid-1950s, he became involved in political activity as a member of the FREE OFFICERS.

Simultaneously, al-Bakr became interested in the newly formed al-BA'TH party (although he did not officially join the party until 1960). After the republican revolution of July 14, 1958, he became associated with Abd al-Salam ARIF and PAN-ARABISM, which demanded unification of Iraq and Egypt into the United Arab Republic under Gamal Abdel NASSER. As a result, when Arif lost power in October 1958, al-Bakr was dismissed from the army by the ruler, Gen. Abd al-Karim Kassem. During the following years, he became a central link between the two most potent pan-Arab opposition groups, which sought to bring down Kassem's "secessionist" regime: the civilian al-Ba'th party and the Nasserite army officers—both retired and active—chief among whom was Arif.

Al-Bakr assisted in planning the first Ba'th coup d'état on February 8, 1963. Following this RAMADAN REVOLUTION, he became a powerful prime minister, while Arif was made a ceremonial president. Throughout the nine months of Ba'th rule, al-Bakr served as a mediator between the civilian and military wings of the party as well as between its left and right factions. In September 1963, he became a member of the regional leadership of the Ba'th party and, a few months later, of the pan-Arab leadership.

On November 18, 1963, a severe rift between the party's left and right caused him to opt for a third solution: he supported President Arif and his Nasserite army officers in their coup d'état, which toppled the Ba'th from power. After a few months of cooperation, during which he served as deputy prime minister, Arif sacked him and his Ba'thi colleagues. In September 1964, most of the party leadership, including al-Bakr, were jailed for an attempted coup. Upon their release a few months later, they once again attempted to overthrow the Arif regime.

The Arab defeat in the Arab–Israel war of June 1967 presented al-Bakr and his conspirators with a golden opportunity to agitate against the regime for its failure to give adequate military support to the Arabs. On July 17, 1968, independent army officers joined the Ba'th to assume power in a bloodless coup d'état. Al-Bakr led one of the army units that participated in the takeover. He then became president of the republic and chairman of the all-powerful Revolutionary Command Council. By July 30, the Ba'th rid themselves of their partners, with al-Bakr becoming prime minister and field marshal. He also held the positions of commander-in-chief of the armed forces, secretary-general of the regional leadership for the party, and deputy secretary-general of the pan-Arab leadership under Michel AFLAQ as a

figurehead. Between 1973 and 1977, al-Bakr also served as minister of defense.

Throughout these years, al-Bakr cooperated very closely with his young relative, the civilian party and internal-security apparatchik, Saddam HUSSEIN. This cooperation stemmed from mutual interdependence. Bakr needed Hussein as a watchdog against actual and potential enemies both inside and outside the party. Hussein, for his part, could not survive on his own even when he became the strongman in Baghdad in 1970/71, because he lacked the necessary contacts with the military and sufficient support from the party old-timers—and because he was not yet known among the Iraqi public. Thus, while Bakr needed protection, Hussein needed time.

Throughout the 1970s, the two effectively purged the army of politically ambitious officers and turned it into a docile tool in the hands of the party, which sent its tentacles into every army unit. The relatives also shared their approach to politics—both were pragmatists, preferring Iraqi interests over those of Arabism, as interpreted by traditional party ideology. Yet, on a few occasions, al-Bakr showed more attachment to traditional party doctrine in terms of his commitment to Arab unity and the struggle against Israel. Differences, however, were minor, until the issue of Iraqi–Syrian relations came up in 1978/79, after the CAMP DAVID ACCORDS. Following a rapprochement, al-Bakr favored a loose federation with Hafiz al-ASAD's Syria, while Hussein objected to it for fear of losing his position.

On July 16, 1979, Hussein—who by then had complete control of all internal-security branches and through them of the party and the army—staged a bloodless coup, forcing al-Bakr to announce his resignation, caused by ill health (Bakr's health was indeed somewhat shaky). A few days later, Hussein announced that he had uncovered a [Syrian-sponsored] plot to strip away his power, and he used this excuse to execute all his remaining opponents who, until then, could hide behind al-Bakr's back. Hussein also took advantage of this opportunity to sever ties with Damascus.

Between 1979 and 1982, when his death was reported, al-Bakr was living under house arrest and was not involved in matters of state. According to a widely believed rumor, al-Bakr was murdered by poisoning because in 1982, at a low point in the IRAN–IRAQ WAR, Hussein was afraid that the retired president might become a focus of opposition against him.

BIBLIOGRAPHY

BARAM, AMATZIA. "The Ruling Political Elite in Ba'thi Iraq, 1968–1986." *International Journal of Middle East Studies* 21 (1989): 447–493.

BATATU, HANNA. *The Old Social Classes and the Revolutionary Movements of Iraq.* Princeton, N.J., 1978.

MARR, PHEBE. *The Modern History of Iraq.* Boulder, Colo., 1985.

Amatzia Baram

Ba'labakki, Layla   [1936–   ]

Lebanese journalist and novelist.

Born in southern Lebanon, Ba'labakki had to struggle hard against her traditional family to continue her education. She interrupted her university education to work as a secretary in the Lebanese parliament. In 1960, she went to Paris on a one-year scholarship from the French government. She started publishing articles and short stories at a very early age.

Ba'labakki is considered among the first Arab women writers who brought women's voices and perspectives into male-dominated mainstream Arabic literature. Her first novel, *I Am Alive* (1958, in Arabic), is translated into French and other European languages, and has been compared to the works of Françoise Sagan. *I Am Alive* is not only acclaimed for being one of the few groundbreaking novels advocating women's independence and freedom, but even more for its marked use of the first person narrative voice in Arabic women's fiction. Her second novel, *The Disfigured Deities* (1960, in Arabic), is a more complex novel with respect to narrative structure and perspective. Her third work, a collection of short stories, *Spaceship of Tenderness to the Moon* (1963, in Arabic), was confiscated and led Ba'labakki to face trial with the Lebanese authorities on obscenity charges for harming public morality.

BIBLIOGRAPHY

JOHNSON-DAVIES, DENYS, tr. *Modern Arabic Short Stories.* Oxford, 1967.

ZEIDAN, JOSEPH. *Arab Women Novelists: The Formative Years and Beyond.* Albany, N.Y., 1995.

Sabah Ghandour

Balaclava, Battle of

Battle that occurred during the Crimean War.

On October 25, 1854, a Russian field army under General Menshikov attempted to relieve Sevastopol, besieged by British, French, and Turkish forces, by driving a wedge among British units. The relative success of the attack netted some Turkish cannons, but a subsequent Russian cavalry attack was repulsed by the British Heavy Cavalry Brigade and the stubborn resistance of the 93rd Highlanders. The latter's success gave rise to the phrase "the thin red line," after their uniforms and signifying dedication against high odds.

The British Light Cavalry Brigade, in suicidal disregard for conventional military wisdom, then attacked the Russian field guns to their front. Whether Lord Lucan or Lord Cardigan, commanders respectively of the cavalry division and the Light Brigade, gave the order for the attack or whether it was the result of confusing dispatches has remained a mystery. The brigade's charge into the mile-long valley under murderous enemy crossfire from both flanks was immortalized by Tennyson's poem "The Charge of the Light Brigade." The brigade reached the guns and rode beyond them to clash with Russian cavalry. Returning through the same crossfire, the survivors were assisted by the Fourth French Chasseurs d'Afrique. Of the 673 mounted officers and men entering the twenty-minute-long charge of the Light Brigade, 247 men and 497 horses were killed. A fitting epitaph was coined by French General Bosquet, who remarked: "It is magnificent, but it is not war." The Russians retained possession of the Vorontsov ridge commanding the Sevastopol–Balaclava road while the allies kept Balaclava and the approaches to Sevastopol. Neither the battle itself nor the charge of the Light Brigade had any effect on the outcome of the campaign.

BIBLIOGRAPHY

RICH, NORMAN. *Why the Crimean War? A Cautionary Tale.* New York, 1991.

Jean-Marc R. Oppenheim

Balafrej, Ahmed   [1908–   ]

Moroccan nationalist; prime minister in 1958.

Ahmed Balafrej earned degrees from Cairo University and the Sorbonne in Paris. Active in Rabat and Paris among student groups for reform and nationalism (Morocco was under French and Spanish protectorate from 1912), he founded the newspaper *Maghreb* in 1932. In 1943, he cofounded the ISTIQLAL political party. Following independence in 1956, and as secretary-general of Istiqlal, he was made foreign minister. In 1958, he became prime minister, a post from which he resigned in December of that year. By the late 1960s, Balafrej was largely inactive politically.

BIBLIOGRAPHY

ASHFORD, DOUGLAS. *Political Change in Morocco.* Princeton, N.J., 1961.

HAHN, LORNA. *North Africa: Nationalism to Nationhood.* Washington, D.C., 1960.

Matthew S. Gordon

Balbo, Italo   [?–1940]

Governor of Libya (by then the united Italian province of Libia), 1934–1939.

Balbo was responsible for introducing state-aided settler colonization in Libya from 1938, which brought in 32,000 settlers before the outbreak of war under Italy's *Quarta Sponda* (Fourth Shore) program. This program replaced the previous scheme of allowing autonomous companies to organize sharecropping settler colonization alongside private colonization. By 1939, when Libya had been formally integrated into metropolitan Italy, there were approximately 110,000 Italians in Libya. Marshal Balbo was also an advocate of the Fascist Italianization program for Libya, in which Libyan Muslims were to become Muslim Italians. He was killed at Tobruk in June 1940.

BIBLIOGRAPHY

SEGRE, CLAUDIO G. "Italian Development Policy in Libya: Colonialism as a National Luxury." In *Social and Economic Development of Libya,* ed. by E. G. H. Joffe and K. S. McLachlan. Wisbech, U.K., 1982.

George Joffe

Balfour Declaration

A 1917 British declaration supporting the establishment of a Jewish national home in Palestine.

Few documents had such far-reaching consequences on the modern history of Palestine as did the Balfour Declaration of November 2, 1917. It was drafted by Zionist leaders, revised and approved by the British war cabinet, and forwarded by Lord Arthur Balfour, the British foreign secretary, to Baron Edmond de Rothschild, a Zionist philanthropist and one of its drafters. It consisted of a mere sixty-seven-word paragraph, as follows:

His Majesty's Government view with favour the establishment in Palestine of a national home for the Jewish people, and will use their best endeavours to facilitate the achievement of this object, it being understood that nothing shall be done which may prejudice the civil and religious rights of the existing non-Jewish communities in Palestine, or the rights and political status enjoyed by Jews in any other country.

This was one of a number of contradictory promises Britain made during World War i. Needing Arab support against the Ottoman Empire, Britain promised in the 1915/16 HUSAYN-MCMAHON CORRESPONDENCE to support the establishment of an independent Arab nation, which Arabs understood to include Palestine; and needing French and Russian support, it promised in the 1916 SYKES-PICOT AGREEMENT to rule the region, including Palestine, with its allies.

The cabinet issued the declaration for a number of reasons, both immediate and long term. It hoped thereby to enlist American and Russian Jewish help to bring America into the war and to keep Russia from abandoning the war. In addition, the cabinet sought to preempt a similar German pro-Zionist declaration and needed Jewish money for Britain's own war effort.

The climate of opinion in England favored Zionist goals for Palestine. Fundamentalist Christians, some of whom were anti-Semites, considered it their duty to assist Jews to go to Palestine so that biblical prophesy could be fulfilled. Liberals such as Balfour and Prime Minister David LLOYD GEORGE believed that the West had committed a historical injustice against the Jewish people, one that must be atoned. To this intellectual climate can be added the sociopolitical factor. Jewish contributions to British society, disproportional to their numbers, were recognized and admired. Sir Herbert SAMUEL, who later became the first high commissioner of Palestine, was a philosopher and a statesman who served in several cabinets; and Chaim WEIZMANN was a chemistry professor who assisted the British munitions industry. Both were persuasive advocates of a Jewish state. By 1917, the war cabinet accepted the view that postwar strategic advantages could be derived from a Jewish state or commonwealth allied to Great Britain.

The phraseology of the declaration was carefully chosen; even its ambiguity was deliberate. The phrase "national home" was new, with no precedence in international law; it was used in the declaration to pacify anti-Zionist Jews, who feared that creation of a state would jeopardize the rights of Jews in the DIASPORA. Lord Balfour explained the meaning of the phrase two days before the declaration was issued: "It did not necessarily involve the early establishment of an independent Jewish State, which was a matter of gradual development in accordance with the ordinary laws of political development."

Little thought was given to the indigenous Palestinian population, in large part because Europeans considered them inferior. The declaration referred to these Palestinians, who in 1917 constituted 90 percent of the population, as the "non-Jewish communities in Palestine," a phrase that accounts for every population group but conceals the identity of the majority. Yet the declaration contained a promise to guarantee the civil and religious rights of the "non-Jews," a promise that the British attempted to enforce even at the expense of Jewish religious rights. At the Wailing or WESTERN WALL (Hebrew, *ha-Kotel ha-Ma'ravi*) the British, in order to protect Muslim property and religious rights to the Wall, allowed the Palestinians to restrict Jewish visitation and prayer, even though the Wall was the holiest shrine of Judaism.

But British political support for a Jewish national home worked against Palestinian national interests. The Balfour policy, which was incorporated in the League of Nations mandate for Palestine, was backed by the European powers and by the British military. It gave the YISHUV (Jewish community) time to grow through Jewish immigration from 50,000 in 1917 to more than 600,000 by 1947 and time to develop quasi-governmental and military institutions. Palestinians, fearing domination or expulsion, protested and resisted through political violence in 1920, 1921, 1929, and 1933; each time they were put down by the British military. The Palestine Arab Revolt of 1936–1939 was suppressed by both British and Zionist forces. The Palestinians were a weak, underdeveloped society, no match for the British and, after 1939, for the Zionists. Ultimately, the 1917 Balfour policy paved the way for the establishment in 1948 of the State of ISRAEL and the exodus of some 725,000 Palestinians who left out of fear and panic or were expelled by the Israel Defense Forces.

BIBLIOGRAPHY

HUREWITZ, J. C. *The Middle East and North Africa in World Politics: A Documentary Record.* 2nd ed., rev. Vol. 2, *British-French Supremacy, 1914–1945.* New Haven, Conn., 1979.
———. *The Struggle for Palestine.* New York, 1968.
JEFFRIES, JOSEPH MARY NAGLE. *Palestine: The Reality.* New York, 1939.
MONROE, ELIZABETH. *British Moment in the Middle East, 1915–1956.* Baltimore, 1963.
STEIN, LEONARD. *The Balfour Declaration.* New York, 1961.
WEIZMANN, CHAIM. *Trial and Error.* Philadelphia, 1949.

Philip Mattar

Balkan Crises of the 1870s

Regional unrest led to independence for much of the peninsula, but no permanent solutions.

As the Ottoman Empire decayed in the nineteenth century, various crises erupted in the empire's European regions as a result of the national awakening of its Christian subjects. Religious conflict and economic oppression led the Christian peasants of Herzegovina to revolt in July 1875, and despite Ottoman promises of reform, the uprising continued and soon spread into neighboring Bosnia. Despite diplomatic intervention by the Austro-Hungarians aimed at bringing an end to the conflict in the Ottoman Empire's two western-most provinces, fighting intensified, and within nine months approximately 156,000 refugees had fled to Austria-Hungary, Serbia, and Montenegro. Public opinion in the latter two states demanded intervention on behalf of their fellow Slavs, whose rebellion was joined in May 1876 by revolutionaries in Bulgaria. In that same month, the Russian, Austro-Hungarian, and German governments, associated in the Three Emperors' League, tried to mediate the conflict. The resulting Berlin Memorandum provided that refugees be repatriated, reforms enacted, and that the great powers supervise both. However, the plan ran into opposition from the British government of Prime Minister Benjamin DISRAELI, who was determined to introduce a new, more active foreign policy and unwilling to approve a plan that his government had not cosponsored. Collective mediation thus failed and the following month, Serbia declared war on the empire and Montenegro quickly followed suit.

Britain clung to its policy of nonintervention even after news of Ottoman mass killings in Bulgaria, the BULGARIAN HORRORS, provoked outrage throughout Western Europe. Public pressure for intervention eventually caused Czar ALEXANDER II of Russia to issue an ultimatum to the Ottoman sultan demanding a six-week armistice for the SERBS. The Turks yielded and accepted the armistice on 30 October 1876, but Disraeli's refusal to accept a peace proposal that would have increased Russia's influence in the Balkans led the Turks to reject the settlement. Russia responded on 24 April 1877 by declaring war on the Ottoman Empire.

Russia's armies marched through Romania and into Bulgaria. Despite several months' delay caused by unexpectedly tenacious resistance by the Turkish garrison at Pleven (or Plevna), the Russians resumed their advance in January 1878. As Turkish defenses withered, armistice negotiations began, and Russian forces moved to within ten miles of Istanbul. Meanwhile, the British countered by sending their fleet to the Sea of Marmara as a show of support to the sultan and as a warning to the Russians. Negotiations between the Russians and the Turks ended in the Treaty of SAN STEFANO, which was signed 3 March 1878. The treaty provided that reforms be enacted in

Bosnia-Herzegovina and that Serbia and Montenegro become fully independent and receive more territory. Romania, which had entered the war against Turkey, was to receive part of the region of Dobruja, in return for giving southern Bessarabia back to Russia, which also was to receive Batum, Kars, Ardahan, and Bayazid in eastern Asia Minor. A Greater Bulgaria was to be created as an autonomous principality, with an elected prince.

However, the treaty aroused the opposition of Britain and Austria-Hungary, who feared Russian access to the Aegean and control over Istanbul, and by Greece and Serbia, who could not accept the notion of a Greater Bulgaria that included areas that they coveted especially Macedonia. The Russians recognized that the San Stefano settlement infringed upon the Peace of PARIS (1856), which had, among other provisions, guaranteed Ottoman independence and territorial integrity, and the Russians now acknowledged the right of the signatories to the Paris treaty to consider the provisions of the new settlement. Meeting at the Congress of BERLIN, those powers determined that Greater Bulgaria should be divided into three parts: an autonomous Bulgaria, still under Turkish sovereignty but with its own elected prince; Eastern Rumelia, south of the Balkan mountains, which was to have a Christian governor appointed by the sultan but approved by the powers; and Macedonia, which was returned to direct Turkish rule. Serbia and Montenegro now became fully independent and were enlarged, while Romania did receive part of Dobruja in return for ceding southern Bessarabia to Russia. Bosnia-Herzegovina and the SANJAK of Novi Pazar were placed under the political administration of Austria-Hungary, and Russia received Batum, Kars, and Ardahan, while Cyprus came under British rule.

Signed on 13 July, 1878, the Treaty of Berlin was the single most important agreement for the Balkan nations in the nineteenth century. While allowing the Ottoman Empire to maintain its presence in Albania, Macedonia, and Thrace, it left all of the Balkan peoples, with the exception of the Albanians, with independent or autonomous states. Its provisions, however, were an immediate source of frustration to them, and led to further strife and eventually World War I.

BIBLIOGRAPHY

JELAVICH, CHARLES and BARBARA, *The Establishment of the Balkan National States, 1804–1920.* Seattle, 1977.
STAVRIANOS, L. S. *The Balkans, 1815–1914.* New York, 1963.

John Micgiel

Balkans

While racially similar, the peoples of the Balkans diverge in language and religion.

Five peoples inhabit the Balkan peninsula, an area in southeast Europe that is generally considered to be bounded by the Danube river plain to the north, the Black Sea to the east, the Aegean Sea to the south, and the Adriatic Sea to the west: South Slavs, Romanians, Greeks, Albanians, and Turks.

The most numerous group, the South Slavs, comprises five nations, settled in a broad band across the central Balkans from the Adriatic to the Black Seas: the Slovenes, northeast of the Adriatic; the Croats to the southeast; the Serbs further east; the Macedonians to the south; and the Bulgarians along the Black Sea. The Slavs arrived in the sixth century and began assimilating and displacing the older inhabitants of the northern and central Balkan peninsula—the Illyrians, Thracians, and Dacians. Some Illyrians and Thracians found refuge in isolated mountain areas, and their descendants eventually became Albanians and Vlachs, respectively. The latinized Dacians were pushed north and emerged as the modern Romanians. As the South Slavs settled down, some were conquered by the Bulgars, an Asiatic people few in number and so quickly assimilated that only their name survives.

Meanwhile, the ancient Greeks inhabited the peninsula further south, as they do today. The arrival of the Ottoman Turks in the fifteenth century brought scattered Turkish settlements; with the exception of Eastern or Turkish Thrace (European Turkey), few Turks remain there. Germans came to the area as a result of Austrian defense policies that called for frontier colonization. However, few of the 1.5 million Germans in the area before World War II remain today. Jews fleeing persecution in Spain and Portugal were given refuge by the Ottomans in the sixteenth century in what later became Bulgaria, Yugoslavia, and Greece, while many Jews arrived in Romania from Russia and Poland in the seventeenth and eighteenth centuries. Of the 1.2 million Jews in the Balkans before World War II, fewer than 50,000 remain today. Gypsies arrived in the fifteenth century and today comprise a small and persecuted minority, particularly in Romania.

The Balkan peoples are predominantly Orthodox Christians. But the overwhelming majority of Slovenes and Croats are Roman Catholic, and Protestant communities exist in the northwest. Eastern Thrace is predominantly Muslim, as is 70 percent of Albania's population. Substantial Muslim minorities exist in Bosnia, Macedonia, and Buglaria.

BIBLIOGRAPHY

STAVRIANOS, L.S. *The Balkans, 1815–1914.* New York, 1963.
STOIANOVICH, TRAIAN. *A Study in Balkan Civilization.* New York, 1967.

John Micgiel

Balkan Wars

Warfare among the states of the Balkan Peninsula that affected the balance-of-power politics in Europe and contributed to the outbreak of World War I.

In the first Balkan War (October 1912–March 1913), the Ottoman Empire fought against the Balkan League composed of Serbia, Bulgaria, Greece, and Montenegro. The second Balkan War (June–July 1913) pitted the former allies against each other and also involved Romania.

The Young Turk Revolution of 1908 in the Ottoman Empire precipitated changes in the Balkan status quo. Bulgaria declared independence, and Austria annexed Bosnia-Herzegovina, reducing Ottoman control in Europe to Thrace, Macedonia, and Albania. Fear of Austro–Hungarian expansion and the vulnerability of the Ottoman Empire, at war with Italy over Libya since 1911, prompted the formation of the Balkan League with Russian blessing. The Christian Balkan states temporarily reconciled conflicting geopolitical ambitions and irredentist disputes over ethnically mixed Macedonia. They hoped for a more advantageous repartitioning of the region at the expense of the Ottoman state.

Montenegro opened hostilities against the empire over border disputes. At the same time, Bulgaria and Serbia, which had launched in March 1912 the series of alliances that led to the Balkan League, mobilized their armies. The Ottoman government hastily concluded peace with Italy and declared war against the Balkan allies on October 17, 1912. The Ottomans suffered defeats in both Macedonia and Thrace, as Albania declared its independence from the Ottoman Empire in November. On December 16, 1913, upon a ceasefire agreement and appeals from Anglophile Ottoman Grand Vizier Kâmil Paşa, ambassadors convened at the London Conference. The Ottomans surrendered Macedonia and Western Thrace but refused to yield EDIRNE, which was besieged by Bulgaria. Failure to agree on revised borders led to a Bulgarian offensive in February 1913. This action forced the Ottomans to surrender the European territories to the west of the ENEZ-MIDYE LINE, a situation formalized at the London Conference of May 30.

Disagreement about the repartitioning of Macedonia revived old rivalries. Bulgaria, dissatisfied with its allotment, surprised former allies Serbia and Greece with an attack on June 29. This led to an anti-Bulgarian realignment that also included Romania, which feared losing territory to its southern neighbor. The Ottomans exploited the disarray to recover Edirne from the Bulgarians in July. The Treaty of Bucharest of August 10, 1913, between Bulgaria and its former allies, was followed by the Istanbul Treaty between Bulgaria and the Ottoman Empire (September 29, 1913), which left Edirne in Ottoman hands. The Ottomans concluded separate treaties with Greece (in Athens on November 14) and Serbia (in Istanbul on March 14, 1914). Greece obtained the Aegean islands, except the Dodecanese, which went to Italy. The Muslims of ceded territories were given a choice of immigrating into the empire. The borders that emerged at the end of these treaties have changed remarkably little despite the shocks of World War I and later events.

In the Balkan wars, the Ottomans lost more than 80 percent of their European territory inhabited by 4 million people. The new demographic and geopolitical realities triggered domestic political and ideological change in the Ottoman Empire. On January 23, 1913, the COMMITTEE OF UNION AND PROGRESS implemented a coup against Kâmil Paşa, ostensibly because he lost Edirne. At the end of the wars, with the Ottoman relinquishment of predominantly Christian territories, the empire was largely reduced to its Muslim-dominated Asian lands. This fact was reflected in the ideological reorientation toward a distinctly Islamic Ottomanism and in the proliferation of Turkish cultural activity.

BIBLIOGRAPHY

BAYUR, YUSUF HIKMET. *Türk İnkılâbı Tarihi* (History of the Turkish Revolution). Vol. 2, part 2, *Balkan Savaşları* (Balkan Wars).
KIRÁLY, BÉLA K., and DIMITRIJE DJORDJEVIC, eds. *East Central European Society and the Balkan Wars.* New York, 1987.
STAVRIANOS, L. S. *The Balkans, 1815–1914.* New York, 1963.

Hasan Kayali

Balkh

Northern Afghan province and city; ancient Bactrian site.

Ancient Balkh was an important city in Bactria, which was originally a satrapy created by Darius the

Great (522–486 B.C.E.) Bordering in the north on Uzbekistan, the modern Afghan province of Balkh has a population of approximately 700,000, consisting mostly of ethnic TAJIKS, but with some Uzbeks and Turkomans in the north. The provincial capital is Mazār-i-Sharif.

BIBLIOGRAPHY

DUPREE, LOUIS. *Afghanistan*. Princeton, N.J., 1980.

Grant Farr

Balta Liman, Convention of

Agreement expanding British trade rights in Ottoman Empire.

Signed between Britain and the Ottoman Empire on August 15, 1838, the agreement reaffirmed and widened Britain's rights under the capitulations (privileges granted by the Ottoman government) that gave British subjects the right to trade freely in the Ottoman Empire. In a move designed to weaken the power of Muhammad Ali Pasha of Egypt, the convention also forbade the formation of commercial monopolies in the Ottoman domains.

BIBLIOGRAPHY

ANDERSON, M.S. *The Eastern Question*. London, 1966.
SHAW, STANFORD, and EZEL KURAL SHAW. *History of the Ottoman Empire and Modern Turkey*. New York, 1977.

Zachary Karabell

Baluchi

See Iranian Languages

Baluchis

An ethnic group centered in Baluchistan, an area that spans southeastern Iran and Pakistan.

Baluchis are also to be found in Afghanistan and in all the towns of the Persian Gulf, especially in Oman and the coast of eastern Arabia, where Baluchi workmen have found employment in the oil industry and on construction projects. Most Baluchis are Sunni Muslims (see SUNNI ISLAM).

Eleanor Abdella Doumato

Baluchistan

Literally "land of the Baluch"; the name given to the region of approximately half a million square miles that straddles southeastern Iran, southwestern Pakistan, and southern Afghanistan.

Although its precise boundaries are still undetermined, it is generally thought to stretch from the edge of the Iranian plateau (the Dasht-e Lut), including parts of the Kirman desert east of Bam and the Bashagird mountains, to the coastal lowlands of the Gulf of Oman, up to the rugged Sulaiman range in the East, at the edge of the western boundaries of the Pakistani provinces of Sind and Punjab. The volcano of Kuh-i Taftan (13,500 ft.) located on the Iranian side is considered Baluchistan's most spectacular peak. Its most important cities are Iranshahr (formerly Fahraj) the capital of Iranian Baluchistan and Quetta the capital of Pakistani Baluchistan.

Due to the nature of its divergent topography, Baluchistan appears to have been divided throughout its history between Iranian "highland" and Indian sub-continent "lowland" spheres of influence. Indeed, its hybrid population, comprising Baluch, Brahuis, Djats, and other South Asian elements, thought to amount to a little more than two million, reflects this. In particular, the region has been influenced greatly by the politics of the neighboring areas of Kerman, Sistan, Qandahar, Punjab, Sind, and Oman.

The Baluch are generally divided into two groups, the Sarawan and the Jahlawan, separated from each other by the Brahuis of the Kalat region. The exact origins of the Baluch are unclear. It is generally thought that they migrated to the region either from the east, beyond Makran, or from north of Kerman sometime in the late medieval period. The earliest mention of them occurs in an eighth-century Pahlavi text, while a number of the medieval Muslim geographers mention a group called the "Balus," in the area between Kerman, Khorasan, Sistan, and Makran.

When they actually began to see themselves as a distinct cultural unit is another matter of debate. The idea of a single, politically unified Baluchistan seems to date back to the eighteenth century and the time of their only successful indigenous leader, the Brahui Nasir Khan, who attempted to consolidate all the Baluch into one unified nation. This idea of a single Baluchistan was further fueled by the British—who began to take a great interest in the area in the nineteenth century and formally incorporated large sections of it into their subcontinental Empire as part of their divide-and-rule policy. Indeed, it was the British who first began extensive mapping of the area, promoted scholarship on the Baluchi tribes, and negotiated the formal international boundaries with

Iran, Afghanistan, and Pakistan in 1947, ultimately spurring Iranian and Russian interests in the area.

Regardless of the debates, it can be said with certainty that a distinct ethnic and social entity, complete with an independent language, Baluchi, and a distinctive social and political structure based on a primarily nomadic way of life, emerged in the region known as Baluchistan.

BIBLIOGRAPHY

BALOCH, MIR KHUDABUX BIJARANI MARRI. *The Balochis through the Centuries, History versus Legend.* Quetta, Pakistan, 1965.
EMBREE, A. T., ed., *Pakistan's Western Borderlands.* Durham, U.K., 1977.

Neguin Yavari

Balyan Family

Ottoman architects.

A family of nine Ottoman architects named Meremetçi—Bali Kalfa (died 1803); his sons Krikor Amira (1767–1831) and Senekerim Amira (died 1833); Krikor's son Garabet Amira (1800–1866); Garabet's sons Nikogos (1826–1858), Sarkis (1835–1899), Agop (1838–1875), Simon (1846–1894), and Levon (1855–1925)—were responsible, individually or in collaboration with each other, for the majority of the buildings for the Ottoman Empire in and near Constantinople (now Istanbul) during the nineteenth century.

Prominent among these works are the Nüsretiye (Tophane), Bezm-i Alem Valide Sultan (Dolmabahçe), Büyük Mecidiye (Ortaköy), Küçük Mecidiye (Ciragan), Pertevniyal Valide Sultan (Aksaray), Cağlayan, Teşvikiye, Hamidiye (Yıldız) mosques, Mahmud II and Abdülmecid tombs; Dolmabahçe, Beylerbeyi, Ciragan, Yıldız, Küçüksu, Ihlamur, Baltalimanı, Adile Sultan (Kandilli) palaces; Aynalıkavak, Izmit, Mecidiyeköy, Zincirlikuyu, Ayazağa, Kalender royal pavilions; the Imperial College of Medicine (now Galatasaray Lycée); the Military School (Mekteb-i Harbiye); Selimiye, Davutpaşa, Rami, Gümüşsuyu, Maçka barracks and Taş Kışla near Taksim; Gümüşsuyu hospital; the Mint (Darphane); Bahçeköy Valide and Mahmud II dams; Terkos waterworks; Bayezid fire tower, Tophane, Dolmabahçe and Yıldız clock towers.

BIBLIOGRAPHY

TUĞLACI, PARS. *Osmanlı Mimarliğinda Batılılasma Dönemi ve Balyan Ailesi* (The Era of Westernization in Ottoman Architecture and the Balyan Family). Istanbul, 1981.

Aptullah Kuran

Bamyan

Ancient Gandharan site; central Afghan province and city.

Bamyan was an important Buddhist site of the Gandhara empire. In the Bamyan valley in central Bamyan province, several large statues of Buddha remain, the oldest dating from the second half of the third century. The modern province of Bamyan is located in the high mountains of central Afghanistan in the Hazarajat. The population of 300,000 consists mostly of ethnic HAZARA, who speak Persian, belong to the Shi'a sect of Islam, and have Mongoloid physical characteristics. The provincial capital is the city of Bamyan.

BIBLIOGRAPHY

DUPREE, LOUIS. *Afghanistan.* Princeton, N.J., 1980.

Grant Farr

Bandung Conference

Assembly of twenty-nine Third World nations, including many from the Middle East, to discuss international relations, colonialism, and cooperation.

The conference was convened by prime ministers Muhammad Ali of Pakistan, Jawaharlal Nehru of India, U Nu of Burma, Sir John Kotelawala of Ceylon, and Ali Sastroamidjojo of Indonesia. Twenty-nine nations of the Third World assembled in Bandung, Indonesia, in April 1955 to discuss their role in a world dominated by the superpowers. Major issues were colonialism, economic and cultural cooperation, the legitimacy of defense pacts such as the North Atlantic Treaty Organization (NATO) and Southeast Asia Treaty Organization (SEATO), and the viability of peaceful coexistence.

The Middle Eastern states were represented by such leaders as Dr. Charles Malik of Lebanon, Dr. Muhammed Fadhel Jamali of Iraq, Gamal Abdel Nasser of Egypt, and Prince Faisal ibn Sa'ud of Saudi Arabia. The conference passed resolutions supporting the independence struggles of Algeria, Morocco, and Tunisia against France, and it called for a peaceful settlement of the issue of the Palestinians in accordance with United Nations resolutions.

The Bandung Conference saw Nasser emerge as an international leader. The ties that he established there with Nehru would lead in six years to the first Nonaligned Nations Conference in Belgrade, Yugoslavia.

BIBLIOGRAPHY

ABDULGANI, ROESLAN. *The Bandung Connection*. Tr. by Molly Bondan. Singapore, 1981.
JANSEN, G. F. *Afro-Asia and Non-Alignment*. London, 1966.

Zachary Karabell

Bani Sadr, Abolhasan [1933–   ]

First president of the Islamic Republic of Iran, 1980–1981.

Abolhasan Bani Sadr was the first president of the Islamic Republic of Iran. He was born in Hamadan to a relatively wealthy landowning family. His father, a cleric, wished for his son to pursue a religious vocation in Qom. Bani Sadr studied theology and law at Tehran University where, as a student activist with the Islamic branch of the NATIONAL FRONT, he ran into problems with the Pahlavi regime. He left Iran for France in the 1960s to pursue higher education, after having gained exposure to the ideas of Paul Vieille, the French marxist sociologist in Iran. In his anti-shah activities while in Paris, Bani Sadr was convinced that Iran's only political solution was a return to a (reformed) Islamic ideology. Some scholars believed him an anarchist, opposed to all forms of formal government.

Bani Sadr met Ayatollah Ruhollah KHOMEINI in 1972, while in Iraq for his father's funeral. Bani Sadr has often been named as the spiritual son of Khomeini, and close ties developed between the two activists. They were reunited in Paris in 1978, after Khomeini's exile from Iraq. Bani Sadr distinguished himself in the eyes of Khomeini when he steadfastly argued against any compromise with Mohammad Reza PAHLAVI, or with his National Front prime minister, Shahpur Bakhtiar, on the eve of the Islamic revolution.

After the IRANIAN REVOLUTION of 1979, Bani Sadr served as foreign minister and minister of finance before becoming Iran's first elected president in 1980. The early stages of his presidency were fraught with conflicts with two members of the Islamic Republican Party, Ayatollah Beheshti and Hashemi Rafsanjani, Bani Sadr, however, enjoyed the support of Ayatollah Khomeini and his son Ahmad Khomeini. In February 1980, he was also appointed chairman of the Revolutionary Council. In that same month, Ayatollah Khomeini appointed Bani Sadr commander in chief of the armed forces, a position secured by Khomeini as the leader of the revolution. Under Bani Sadr's influence, the government sought to restore normalcy and order in the country.

Bani Sadr's efforts to stabilize the country and curb revolutionary excesses did not bear fruit, however, with the Islamic Republican Party's candidates sweeping the first parliamentary election, and its subsequent imposition of the IRP candidate for prime minister, Mohammad Ali Raja'i. The rivalry between the president and the IRP extended to the seizure of the American Embassy in Tehran in November 1979 by student followers of Kohmeini. Bani Sadr opposed the takeover and tried fruitlessly to secure the freedom of the hostages. An attempted coup, supported by the Iranian military in July 1980, served further to undermine Bani Sadr's presidency. The armed forces were severely purged, and Bani Sadr's appointees to many of its commanding positions were executed.

Iraq's president, Saddam Hussein, attacked Iran in September 1980, and Bani Sadr was appointed by Khomeini as chairman of the Supreme Defense Council. Spending most of his time at the front and away from Tehran, Bani Sadr failed to exploit the opportunities provided by the IRAN–IRAQ WAR to bolster his power. From September 1980 to June 1981, when it was shut down by the IRP, Bani Sadr used his newspaper, *Jomhuri-ye Eslami* (Islamic Republic) to criticize the IRP and other hardline factions in the government. The IRP, on the other hand, pointed to Iran's repeated defeats at the war front and Bani Sadr's policy of favoring the regular armed forces over the Revolutionary Guards in combat.

After several showdowns with the IRP, Bani Sadr sought support from various opposition groups active in Iran, including the National Front and the MOJAHEDIN-E KHALQ. Bani Sadr was dismissed as acting commander in chief of the armed forces on June 10, 1981. Following repeated failed attempts at reconciliation, the parliament, with Ayatollah Khomeini's approval, proceeded to impeach Bani Sadr from the presidency later that month. Bani Sadr fled the country with the help of the Mojahedin-e Khalq and once in Paris, where he currently lives in exile, joined the leadership of the National Resistance Council alongside Mas'ud RAJAVI, the head of the MOJAHEDIN.

BIBLIOGRAPHY

ABRAHAMIAN, ERVAND. *The Iranian Mojahedin*. New Haven, Conn., 1989.
BAKHASH, SHAUL. *The Reign of the Ayatollahs*. New York, 1984.

BANI SADR, ABOLHASAN. *L'Espérance trahie* (Hope Betrayed). Paris, 1982.

———. *Usul-e payeh va zavabet-e hokumat-e eslami* (The Basic Principles and Criteria of Islamic Government). Tehran.

Neguin Yavari

Baniyas

One of the three headstreams of the Jordan river.

The Baniyas (in Hebrew, Nahal Hermon) flows southwest to unite with the other two headstreams, the Dan and Hasbani (Hebrew Nahal Senir). After World War I, the Baniyas became part of Syria. After the ARAB–ISRAEL WAR (1967), it came under Israel's administration.

BIBLIOGRAPHY

ORNI, EFRAIM, and ELISA EFRAT. *Geography of Israel*. Jerusalem, 1973.

Sara Reguer

Banks, Afghanistan

Afghan Banking System (Bank-e Melli).

Because of growing exchange problems in overseas trading, primarily Karakul skins to England and wool to Russia, Abd al-Majid Zabuli, a wool trader, started the Sherkat-e Sahami-ye Afghan, now known as the Bank-e Melli, or national bank, in 1932. It began first as a stock company and later became an investment bank. The bank itself opened in 1934 with 120 million afghanis. The Bank-e Melli served as a major center for capital accumulation and investment funds in the 1930s and was a major part of Afghanistan's economic development.

The bank later became part of the government monopoly system (*sherkat*), in which the Afghan government holds 40 to 45 percent of the stock. Under this system much of the stock was held by members of the royal family. While it did enrich many members of the Afghan royal family, the Sherkat and Bank-e Melli system was important in the industrialization of Afghanistan.

BIBLIOGRAPHY

DUPREE, LOUIS. *Afghanistan*. Princeton, N.J., 1980.

Grant Farr

Banks, Algeria

The financial institutions of Algeria since independence in 1962 from the French colonial empire.

Following independence in 1962, the banking system of Algeria was put under national control. It was guided by the Central Bank of Algeria, established in 1963. A small number of commercial banks were established at the same time, but these only served as credit providers, under tutelage from individual ministries, for the national enterprises and had no financial autonomy. Only since 1985 have three commercial and four savings and development banks been allowed to operate more or less freely, although they continue to implement rather than establish credit policies.

BIBLIOGRAPHY

VANDEWALLE, DIRK. "Breaking with Socialism: Economic Liberalization and Privatization in Algeria." In *Privatization and Liberalization in the Middle East,* ed. by E. Harik and D. J. Sullivan. Bloomington, Ind., 1992.

Dirk Vandewalle

Banks, Bahrain

Commercial financial institutions in the State of Bahrain.

Prior to independence from the British protectorate (1820–1971), only three major banks existed in Bahrain: the Chartered Bank, the British Bank of the Middle East, and the Bank of Bahrain (renamed the National Bank of Bahrain). By 1988, twenty commercial banks existed in the country, six of which were locally incorporated and the rest branches of foreign banks. They are regulated by the Bahrain Monetary Agency. In the mid-1970s, almost thirty offshore banking units were established in Bahrain; by 1988, they had assets of more than 5 billion U.S. dollars. Bahrain's banking was adversely affected by the Iran–Iraq War and by the Gulf War of 1990/91.

BIBLIOGRAPHY

The Middle East and North Africa, 1991, 37th ed. London, 1991.

Emile A. Nakhleh

Banks, Egypt

Financial institutions have played an important role in modern Egypt.

In the first half of the nineteenth century, a large inflow of foreign capital necessitated the creation of private foreign banks in Alexandria, Egypt's first financial center. These institutions also exploited the financial opportunities offered by the eastern Mediterranean. Egypt thus became a regional banking center whose member banks had interests both domestic and foreign.

By 1874, the banking capital available at Alexandria was estimated at $125 million—not much less than New York's. Egypt's position as a developing country came to be recognized by the European investing public, which—in two periods of intense activity, 1862 to 1875 and 1897 to 1907—placed more than one hundred million pounds sterling in government loans and in private companies operating in Egypt. Many of these banks were founded in Europe to exploit the financial opportunities that existed in Egypt; others were created in Egypt, mainly in Alexandria, with European financial connections. The banking industry grew unabated until the financial crisis of 1907, after which it stabilized, with finance remaining the preserve of Europeans and Levantine Egyptians.

The most significant Egyptian attempt at competition with foreign and foreign-resident economic hegemony was the Bank Misr. Founded in 1920 in the midst of the economic boom that immediately followed World War I, it sold shares only to the indigenous Egyptians who profited from the boom—large landowners and big merchants. Its creation led to the development of local Egyptian chambers of commerce in order to reduce the domination of British, French, Italian, Greek, and Belgian chambers, which were already solidly in place by the end of the nineteenth century. Nonetheless, attempts at redressing this equation had only limited success until after World War II when government legislation redressed somewhat the inequities present in the economic sphere.

After the Arab–Israel War of 1956, banking supremacy in the eastern Mediterranean passed to Lebanon. This development was due to Nasser's expropriation of foreign ventures and his establishment of a tightly planned economy with a nationalized banking sector. With Sadat's *infitah,* however, Western banks have once again reestablished their presence in Egypt.

BIBLIOGRAPHY

DAVIS, ERIC. *Challenging Colonialism: Bank Misr and Egyptian Industrialization, 1920–1941.* Princeton, N.J., 1983.
LANDES, DAVID S. *Bankers and Pashas: International Finance and Economic Imperialism in Egypt.* Cambridge, Mass., 1979.

Jean-Marc R. Oppenheim

Banks, Iran

Iranian banks are limited in their operations by Islamic law.

Iran has ten commercial banks and five specialized government banks. They were nationalized shortly after the revolution. The system is entirely based on Islamic principles. No interest can be paid on deposits or charged on loans. Deposits are paid according to a profit-sharing arrangement. The banks will offer a return based on expected profits for any given period. Until 1992, rates applying to deposits and loans were fixed by the Central Bank of Iran. However, practices have been liberalized, and since then percentages paid by the banks vary as they vie to attract depositors. The main instruments of lending are the mudaraba used for short-term transactions, the musharaka for medium-term ones, and the ijara for leasing. The computation of a minimum profit sharing for each instrument includes the cost of funds, the allocations for bad debt, the need to keep the minimum liquidity ratio of 8 percent set by the Central Bank, and a return for bank owners and depositors.

Consolidated Balance Sheets of Iranian Banks

| | Billions of riyals | |
	1990	1991
Reserves	6,779.5	7,764.2
Foreign Assets	203.1	188.1
Claims on Central Government	1,346	1,337.7
Claims on Private Sector	8,728.8	12,058.9
Demand Deposits	6,028.3	7,850.9
Time and Savings Deposits	10,662.7	13,341.6
Foreign Liabilities	121.5	146.1
Credit from Monetary Authorities	194.1	378.7
Capital Accounts	133.6	133.6
Other Items (Net)	(82.8)	(502.0)
$1 = Iranian Rial	65.3	64.59

Source: IMF International Financial Statistics

The regulator of the banks is the Central Bank of the Islamic Republic Iran.

Jean-François Seznec

Banks, Israel

Israeli banks are recovering from the hyperinflation of the 1980s.

In 1992, Israel had 22 so-called ordinary banks, subject to the Bank of Israel's liquidity regulations. It also had 31 other banking and financial institutions. The banks had just over 1,000 branches in Israel and about 125 abroad. Their assets came to 90 billion U.S. dollars, and they employed 31,000 people in Israel. In 1992, the five main banking groups were:

| | Millions of new shekels | | | |
	Net Profit	Capital	Credit to the public	Affiliation
Bank Leumi	210.5	3,936	37,200	Jewish Agency
Bank Hapoalim	246.8	3,890	46,300	Histadrut
Bank Discount	154.4	2,301	17,463	Recanti Family
First International Bank	97.5	1,121	8,350	Safra Bank
Bank Mizrachi	111.5	861	16,030	World Mizrachi Movement

In October 1992, the price shares of Bank Leumi, Bank Hapoalim, Bank Discount, and Bank Mizrachi collapsed on the Tel Aviv stock exchange. During the hyperinflation of the early 1980s, they had been a favorite form of investment by the public, offering very high real returns. The banks encouraged purchase of their own shares, but the speculative bubble burst in October 1982 and the government bought shares from the public in exchange for bonds. In 1992 and 1993, the government started to sell its shares in the banks, effectively ending a decade of nationalization.

BIBLIOGRAPHY

BANK OF ISRAEL, SUPERVISOR OF BANKS. *Israel's Banking System.* Jerusalem, 1992.

Paul Rivlin

Banks, Jordan

Banks currently operating in Jordan.

In the following chart, figures are expressed in millions of Jordanian dinars (JD), with JD 1 = US$ 1.46. Note that the year given is the latest year for which figures are available.

Name	Year	Paid up capital	Deposits	Reserves	Total assets
Central Bank of Jordan	1990	6	677.8	12	2,048.3
Arab Bank PLC	1989	22	5,917	230.5	7,560
Bank of Jordan PLC	1990	5.25	140.4	–	171.6
Cairo Amman Bank	1988	5	167.4	11.8	246.9
Jordan Gulf Bank SA	1988	6	126.5	–	167.6
Jordan Islamic Bank for Finance and Investment	1990	–	214.4	12.1	256.2
Jordan Kuwait Bank	1989	5	143	–	–
Jordan National Bank PLC	1990	9.1	166.7	12.8	205.1
Specialized Banks					
Agricultural Credit Corp.	1990	9.7	.25	4.1	42.4
Arab Jordan Investment	1990	5	132.8	2.9	170
Cities and Villages Development	1990	12	–	10.5	68.3
Housing Bank	1990	12	487.9	–	607.2
Industrial Development Bank	1990	6	–	–	69.5
Jordan Cooperative Org.	1990	1	9.4	.1	–
Jordan Investment and Finance Bank	1990	4.5	72.6	7.4	189.6
Social Security Corporation	NA	–	–	–	–
Foreign Banks					
ANZ Grindlays Bank	1990	5	91	–	–
Arab Banking Corp. (Jordan)	1990	10	21.8	–	41.1
Arab Land Bank	1990	5	52	3	61
British Bank of the Middle East	1989	5	83	–	106
Citibank NA	NA	–	–	–	–
Rafidain	1983	3	10.2	.55	–

Source: International Financial Statistics, The World Bank, 1991–1992.

Jenab Tutunji

Banks, Kuwait

Kuwait has eight commercial banks.

In 1960 the banks with foreign (mainly British) interests were forced to become 100 percent Kuwaiti. As of 1994, each of the Kuwaiti banks is owned by the public at large with shares traded on the Kuwait stock exchange but controlled by large minority interests held by a few major merchant families. The main products of the banks are letters of credit for imports, associated self-liquidating short-term loans, as well as performance letters of credit issued to guarantee work of local and foreign companies for the Kuwaiti government.

The banks are regulated by the Central Bank of Kuwait, which follows the general requirements for Western banks for risk accounting, and capital adequacy ratios set by the concordat of Basle.

From 1978 to 1982, most banks were involved in financing the purchase of shares on the parallel stock market secured by shares, some real estate, and personal guarantees. When the stock market crashed, the value of these assets plummeted and banks were left with seven billion U.S. dollars of bad debt supported by 4.5 billion U.S. dollars of capital. Between 1982 and 1994, the government intervened to protect the integrity of the banking system. Bad debt was bought by the Central Bank and paid for by treasury bonds, which gave the banks solid interest-earning assets and avoided large write-offs against

capital. The government also protected the liquidity of the banks by placing money with each institution. Only the National Bank of Kuwait did not suffer substantially from losses on the stock market. It now controls 30 percent of all the deposits and 70 percent of all the loans in the country.

The Iraqi invasion forced the banks to shut down most of their operations in Kuwait in 1990. However, banks had at least some duplicate records outside the country. With the support of the European central banks, they were able to open temporary outlets in the major Western capitals where they serviced their clients with liquidity provided by the Kuwait Investment Office.

Jean-François Seznec

Banks, Oman

Modern banking began in 1948.

In September 1948 the Imperial Bank, later the British Bank of the Middle East (BBME), was granted a twenty-year monopoly for banking services in the sultanate. The BBME provided limited commercial services, with offices only in Muscat and Matrah in 1963 and mobile offices in Salala and Mina al-Fahal

Consolidated Balance Sheets of Kuwaiti Banks

	Millions of dinars		
	1991	1992	1993
Reserves	33.6	46.9	48
Foreign Assets	1,707.9	1,325.9	1,400.0
Claims on Central Government	607.6	4,919.9	3,433.9
Claims on Private Sector	5,557.8	817.8	980.3
Demand Deposits	784	652.6	712.2
Time and Savings Deposits	4,087.6	4,250	4,536.6
Foreign Liabilities	303.4	561.9	509.5
Central Government Deposits	861.5	821.2	3.4
Capital Accounts	1,087.5	786.1	836.4
Other Items (Net)	843	38.8	(722.5)
$1 = Kuwait Dinars	3.5178	3.3036	3.351

Source: IMF International Financial Statistics

Commercial Banks in Oman

Bank	Founded	Branches	Assets (in millions of dollars)
Bank Dhofar al-Omani al-Fransi[1]	1992	14	n/a
Bank Muscat al-Ahli al-Omani[2]	1992	25	600
Bank of Oman, Bahrain, and Kuwait	1974	17	240
Commercial Bank of Oman	1976	17	225
National Bank of Oman	1973	51	825
Oman Arab Bank	1984	5	230
Oman International Bank[3]	1975	54	600
Omani European Bank[4]	1976	1	80

[1]Purchased the Omani assets of Bank of Credit and Commerce International.
[2]Formed by merger of Bank of Muscat and Bank al-Ahli al-Omani (chartered 1976). In 1989 the Bank of Muscat purchased the Oman Banking Corporation (chartered as the Bank of Oman and the Gulf in 1978).
[3]Chartered as Oman Arab African Bank.
[4]Chartered as Union Bank of Oman.

in 1969. BBME also operated as the central bank, administering the accounts of both the sultan and the government and the Muscat Currency Board's issuing of the first currency in 1970.

BBME's monopoly ended in 1968, but the first local commercial bank, the National Bank of Oman, did not open until 1973. Several others have since begun operations. The first banking law was promulgated in 1974, and in 1975 the Central Bank of Oman replaced BBME as administrator of government accounts and the Oman Currency Board.

Oman also has three public-service banks: the Oman Bank for Agriculture and Fisheries (1981), the Oman Development Bank (1977), and the Oman Housing Bank (1977).

Calvin H. Allen, Jr.

Banks, Palestine

All banks in British Palestine, except one local Jewish bank, were foreign-registered.

By the end of 1921, six banks were operating in mandatory Palestine: the Anglo–Egyptian Bank, the Anglo–Palestine Company; Banco di Roma, Crédit Lyonnais, the Imperial Ottoman Bank, and the Workers' Bank. Although seventy-four banks were operating by the end of 1936, hostilities during World War II reduced this number to twenty-five, twenty of which were locally registered.

By the end of 1946, the largest locally registered Jewish banks were the Palestine Discount Bank, the Workers' Bank, Ellern's Bank, Jacob Japhet & Company, and the Kupat-Am Bank. The two largest local Arab banks were the Arab Bank and the Arab National Bank. At that time, Jewish deposits constituted some 79 percent of total bank deposits; Arab deposits, 19 percent; and other deposits, 2 percent.

BIBLIOGRAPHY

A Survey of Palestine, Prepared in December 1945 and January 1946 for the Information of the Anglo–American Committee of Inquiry. Vol. 2. Jerusalem, 1946–1947. Reprint, Washington, D.C., 1991.

Michael R. Fischbach

Banks, Saudi Arabia

Saudi banks operate for the most part according to standard banking practice.

There are twelve commercial banks in Saudi Arabia. Six are wholly owned by Saudi persons and six are

Consolidated Balance Sheets of Saudi Arabian Banks

	Billions of U.S. dollars		
	1990	1991	1992
Reserves	11.64	12.68	10.65
Foreign Assets	123.46	118.95	106.37
Claims on Private Sector	65.3	73.64	87.21
Demand Deposits	57.17	75.38	83.94
Quasi-Monetary Deposits	42.82	48.69	50.55
Foreign Currency Deposits	42.9	46.29	42.23
Foreign Liabilities	30.17	27.91	32.46
Central Government Deposits	1.29	1.5	1.47
Capital Accounts	31.94	34.5	42.4
Other Items (Net)	(5.89)	(29.06)	(48.91)

Source: IMF International Financial Statistics

joint ventures with foreign banks, but majority-owned by small Saudi shareholders.

The National Commercial Bank (NCB) is the largest Saudi bank. It is privately held by two families: the al-Mahfouz, who have management control, and the al-Kaki. Only one bank is registered as an Islamic bank, the al-Rajhi Banking and Investment Corporation. Al-Rajhi is controlled by Saleh al-Rajhi who had been the largest money changer in the kingdom until 1988 when he obtained a banking license and floated shares to the public. Al-Rajhi is the third largest bank in the country. All the other Saudi banks are owned by the public at large. Bank shares are the most active on the stock market in the kingdom.

The Saudi banks were characterized until 1991 by a very low level of loans relative to their deposits. Loans to nongovernment entities have been kept to a minimum, mainly due to legal difficulties in the kingdom. The banks have not been able to obtain judgments against bad creditors as loans bearing interest clash with the principles of the SHARIʿA law. Thus, banks have limited their risk-taking to very old and safe customers. To improve the legal environment for banks, King Fahd organized a commission for the settlement of disputes in 1988, which allowed the banks to recover some of their assets, but none of their interests.

After 1991, loans relative to deposits increased. However, the increase was mainly due to heavy borrowing by government entities. The banks have also bought substantial amounts of treasury bonds from the Saudi government, which helped it finance parts of its budget deficits.

Consolidated Balance Sheets of Saudi Arabian Banks

				For 1992 in millions of Saudi riyals			
(SRmn)	Equity	Capital	Assets	Loans/ Advances	Due from Banks	Investments in Securities	Customer Deposits
NCB	6,449	6,000	63,708	25,901	15,817	3,151	48,873
Riyad Bank	6,316	2,000	50.002	14,790	19,797	6,771	29,442
Al-Rajhi	3,531	1,500	26,526	n/a	n/a	n/a	19,632
Saudi American	2,625	600	38,277	11,601	6,386	16,600	29,063
Saudi French	2,330	900	22,961	9,457	6,372	4,895	17,736
Arab National	2,246	600	28,649	10,345	9,772	5,680	19,956
Saudi Cairo	1,500	1,200	13,443	5,024	3,731	3,464	10,624
Saudi British	1,272	400	20,704	6,909	3,519	8,257	15,359
Saudi Hollandi	997	210	13,523	4,698	3,622	4,169	8,480
U.S.C.B	822	500	9,209	3,200	2,983	1,584	6,158
Bank al-Jazira	592	400	5,662	1,689	2,643	790	2,499
SIB	301	90	5,256	2,568	1,291	1,058	3,642
Total	28,981	14,400	207,940	96,182	75,933	50,419	211,464

$1 = SR3.75
Source: Middle East Economic Survey

The banks' main products are:

- Letters of credit for the import of goods into the kingdom.
- Short-term loans associated to the trade.
- Letters of guarantee for contractors issued to secure government contracts. Government regulation requires that all contracts (except certain defense-related ones) be secured by a bid bond of 1 percent, a 5 percent performance bond, and a 10 percent advance payment guarantee. Between

1973 and 1992, Saudi and approved foreign banks provided facilities to the main contractors on four hundred billion U.S. dollars worth of infrastructure contracts multiplied by backup bonding facilities required by the subcontractors. The text of the bonds drafted by the Saudi Arabian Monetary Agency (SAMA) is very precise and not negotiable.

Saudi banks will seldom consider medium-term loans, except to government entities. They are not

Selected Balance Sheets of Saudi Arabian Banks

				For first nine months of 1993				
(SRmn)	Net Profit	Oper. Exp.	Oper. Income	Assets	Loans	Invst. in Securities	Cust. Deposit	Equity
Riyad Bank	658	548	1,128	54,127	16,901	14,320	29,095	6,973
Al-Rajhi	575	376	1,083	30,490	—	—	22,541	4,106
Saudi American	691	419	1,109	40,250	12,216	18,367	30,170	3,316
Saudi British	299	242	568	21,954	7,182	9,828	16,695	2,710
Arab National	369	342	757	31,813	10,479	9,256	19,233	2,615
Saudi al-Fransi	269	263	562	26,592	10,584	8,305	17,569	2,330
Saudi Cairo	166	161	604	14,970	6,345	5,400	10,825	1,667
Saudi Hollandi	136	173	346	14,106	5,291	5,665	8,546	1,133
U.S.C.B	203	57	282	10,034	4,225	2,785	6,352	1,024
SIB	46	47	108	5,798	2,985	954	4,175	348

$1 = SR3.75
Source: MEES

entitled to use floating liens as security, nor take and enforce mortgages on property.

Banks have problems taking security interests on assets under the *Shari'a* law. Mortgages on land and buildings are subject to debate among religious scholars. Mortgages were permitted until the mid-1980s; they were then forbidden, only to be reallowed in 1992.

SAMA regulates Saudi banks following the criteria defined by the Basle Concordat in controlling banks to ensure adequate provision levels and capital ratios. SAMA is widely considered in the Western banking industry to be the most professional regulator in the Middle East.

There are two main government-owned banks: The Agricultural Bank finances the purchase of supplies, equipment, crops, and well drilling at no interest. It subsidizes up to 50 percent of the cost of supplies and equipment to the farmers. Since inception in 1974 the bank has subsidized farmers by a total of 9.1 billion Saudi riyals and provided loans of 25 billion Saudi riyals.

The Real Estate Bank lends at no interest up to 350,000 Saudi riyals to Saudis to build homes. It will provide a 20 percent discount rebate if payments are made on time. Since inception in 1973, the bank has financed the construction of 98,761 units for a total of 103,277 million Saudi riyals.

BIBLIOGRAPHY

AZZAM, HENRY. *Gulf Financial Markets*. Bahrain, 1988.

SEZNEC, JEAN-FRANÇOIS. *The Financial Markets of the Arabian Gulf*. London, 1987.

WILSON, PETER W. *A Question of Interest: The Paralysis of Saudi Banking*. Boulder, Colo., 1993.

Jean-François Seznec

Banks, Tunisia

Tunisia's banks are experiencing growth.

There are fourteen commercial banks and four government-owned specialized banks. Banks are regulated by the Banque Centrale de Tunisie (Central Bank of Tunisia). Starting in 1986, the Central Bank has acted to develop the banking system by allowing banks to set their own interest rates on loans and deposits, limiting maximum risk exposure for any one client to 40 percent of capital, and letting banks restructure nonperforming loans.

Bank facilities consist mainly of letters of credit and short-term loans. There is a small off-shore banking sector, modeled with limited success on the Bahraini Offshore Banking Units.

Consolidated Balance Sheets of Tunisian Banks

	Millions of dinars			
	1990	1991	1992	1993
Reserves	118	130	129	181
Foreign Assets	510	522	542	571
Claims on Central Government	762	793	535	536
Claims on Private Sector	5,957	6,466	7,402	7,907
Demand Deposits	1,565	1,437	1,555	1,676
Quasi-Monetary Liabilities	2,892	3,196	3,490	3,777
Foreign Liabilities	378	424	605	614
Long-Term Foreign Liabilities	253	736	785	824
Central Government Lending Funds	412	—	—	—
Credit from Monetary Authorities	1,356	1,536	1,485	1,494
Capital Accounts	592	710	885	1,053
Other Items (Net)	(104)	(128)	(196)	(244)
Post Office: Checking Deposits	100	128	157	—
$1 = Tunisian Dinars	0.8783	0.9246	0.8844	1.004

Source: IMF International Financial Statistics

The largest bank is the Banque Nationale d'Agriculture, a government-owned institution with capital of 100 million Tunisian dinars.

Jean-François Seznec

Banks, Turkey

Establishments for the custody, loan, exchange, or issue of money and credit in the Ottoman Empire and the Republic of Turkey.

Institutionalized banking in the Ottoman Empire dates from the mid-nineteenth century. Prior to that time, moneylending was done largely by *sarraflar* (money changers), many of whom were from non-Muslim minorities, although a considerable amount was also done by *vakıfs* (pious foundations).

The earliest banks in Ottoman Turkey were established mainly with foreign capital. The earliest was the Banque de Constantinople founded in 1847. In 1856, the Bank-ı Osmani (Ottoman Bank) was opened in the form of an Istanbul branch of a London-based institution. The majority of the shares of a reorganized bank of the same name that operated after 1863 were held by British and French owners. Banks established with major participation by Turkish citizens included the Şirket-i Umumiye-i Osmaniye (General Company of the Ottoman Empire) in 1864, which gave credits to government bodies, including provinces and municipalities until 1893.

An important figure in nineteenth-century financing initiatives was Midhat Paşa, the innovative Ottoman governor of some Danube provinces, who organized a fund to extend argricultural credits to farmers in 1863. His various efforts were combined into the Istanbul Emniyet Sandığı (Istanbul Security Fund) in 1868. It and similar funds could not be maintained due to Ottoman financial stringencies, however.

The first wholly Turkish bank to be established was the Ziraat Bankası (Agricultural Bank) in 1888. It remains Turkey's largest bank today.

During the YOUNG TURK period (beginning 1908), strong efforts were made to counter foreign influences by establishing Turkish banks; some twenty-four were founded during the years 1909–1923, but it was difficult to make any real inroads against the far larger European institutions (most importantly the Banco di Roma, Banco Commerciale Italiana, and the Holantse Bank), since Turkish capital was scarce due to wars, the CAPITULATIONS, and other disruptions.

Under the Republic of Turkey (established in 1923), banking was given high priority. A major advance took place when a private bank, the Türkiye Iş Bankası (Turkish Business Bank), was opened in 1924 (it remains the largest private bank in Turkey). The Turkish Central Bank (Türkiye Merkez Bankası) was established in 1931. As economic development efforts accelerated under ATATÜRK's etatist policy (state economic enterprise), several state banks were organized, each charged with serving a particular sector. The Industrial and Mining Bank (Sanayı ve Maadin Bankası), established in 1925, was replaced by the stronger Sümerbank in 1933, which not only financed but also operated many state factories. In the same year the Provinces Bank (Iller Bankası) began to finance the needs of provincial governments. The Hittite Bank (Etibank) opened in 1935 to concentrate on development of natural resources. Others included the Maritime Bank (Denizcilik Bankası) and the People's Bank (Halk Bankası), both 1938.

Private banking expanded rapidly as Turkey came out of the stringencies of World War II, coincidentally with the waning of etatism. The two private banks that are today the largest, the Building and Credit Bank (Yapı ve Kredi Bankası) and the Mediterranean Bank (Akbankası) were established in 1944 and 1948, respectively. More than thirty private banks had been opened by 1960. In the period

of "planned development," after 1961, the government again established several new banks for various sectors of the economy, including the Tourism Bank (Turism Bankası) in 1960, the Industrial Investment and Credit Bank (Sanayı Yatırım ve Kredi Bankası) in 1963, the State Investment Bank (Devlet Yatırım Bankası) specializing in import–export activities, in 1964, and the Turkish Development Bank (Türkiye Kalkınma Bankası) in 1975. Another spurt in private banking occurred during the mid-1980s when liberalized laws were enacted to attract both private domestic and foreign capital. In recent years a number of "finance houses" working on Islamic principles have been added to the scene.

As of 1990, three state, four private, and three foreign investment banks were operating in Turkey, and eight state, twenty-eight private, and seven foreign commercial banks. In addition fifteen foreign banks operated Turkish branches. The largest foreign bank, the British-French Ottoman Bank (Osmanı Bankası) has been operating since 1863. Turkish banks also had some 27 branches and 113 representative offices abroad. Some 75 percent of the banks are headquartered in Istanbul; about 56 percent of the nominal capital of all banks in Turkey belonged to state banks. The system is also highly centralized, the five largest banks (three state, two private) controlling just over 50 percent of total assets. The banks are also favored in that they face almost no competition from other financial institutions, such as independent insurance companies.

The job of generating capital was aided by the organization of a stock exchange in 1982, with the beginning of the secondary marketing of securities in 1986. It has grown extremely rapidly: the number of corporations raising capital through stock issuance has risen from 348 in 1986 to 1,090 in 1991. Demand was also stimulated significantly by the rapid appearance of numerous mutual funds.

BIBLIOGRAPHY

CENTRAL BANKS OF TURKEY. *Annual Reports.* Istanbul.
DIRECTORATE GENERAL OF PRESS AND INFORMATION. *Turkey Yearbook.* Istanbul. Issued periodically.

Walter F. Weiker

Banks, Yemen

Banking, like the rest of the economy, is undergoing major changes as the Republic of Yemen strengthens its unitary structure.

Before unification (May 22, 1990), the two Yemens (Yemen Arab Republic and the People's Democratic

Republic of Yemen) had long been separate countries with very different political philosophies. Since May of 1990, the new Republic of YEMEN has attempted to unify its economy. The Central Bank is based in the capital, SAN'A, and has established guidelines for a transitional period, which allows the two Yemens to continue to use their own currencies until a single currency will be adopted, after thirty months.

BIBLIOGRAPHY

The Middle East and North Africa, 1991, 37th ed. London, 1991.

Emile A. Nakhleh

Banna, Hasan al- [1906–1949]

The founder of the Muslim Brotherhood (the society of the Muslim Brothers), which is considered the largest Islamic movement in the Arab world in the twentieth century.

Hasan al-Banna was born in October 1906, in al-Buhayra, one of Egypt's northern Nile delta provinces, to a religious father. He was educated first at a traditional Islamic KUTTAB (religious school) and, then at the age of twelve, joined a primary school. During the early part of his life, al-Banna became involved with SUFISM and continued that association for most of his life. At the age of fourteen, he joined a primary teachers' school and two years later enrolled in DAR AL-'ULUM College from which he graduated as a teacher.

In CAIRO, during his student years, al-Banna joined religious societies involved in Islamic education. However, he soon realized that this type of religious activity was inadequate to bring the Islamic faith back to its status in the public life of Egypt. He felt that more activism was needed, so he organized students from al-Azhar University and Dar al-'Ulum and started to preach in mosques and popular meeting places. During this period, al-Banna came to be influenced by the writings of Muhammad ABDUH, Rashid RIDA, and Ahmad Taymur Pasha.

When he graduated, in 1927, he was appointed as a teacher of Arabic in a primary school in al-Isma'iliyya, a new small town with a semi-European character. It hosted the headquarters of the SUEZ CANAL company and a sizable foreign community. In Isma'iliyya, al-Banna started to preach his ideas to poor Muslim workers, small merchants, and civil servants. He kept warning his audience against the liberal lifestyle of the Europeans in the town and the dangers of emulating it—thus cultivating strong feelings of fear and anxiety in them.

In March 1928, he founded the MUSLIM BROTHERHOOD or Brethren. In the first four years of its existence, al-Banna's primary goal was to recruit membership, establishing branches along the eastern and western edge of the delta. The quick and remarkable spread of the Brethren engendered governmental resistance, especially during the cabinet of Isma'il SIDQI Pasha.

In 1932/33, al-Banna was transferred to Cairo, and his group merged with the Society for Islamic Culture, forming the first branch of the Muslim Brothers, which then became the headquarters of the society. During this period, the number of branches reached 1,500 to 2,000—most of which ran schools, clinics, and other welfare institutions. Not only that, but branches in Sudan, Syria, and Iraq were established, and the society's publications were distributed throughout Islamic countries.

At the beginning of his political career, al-Banna did not have an elaborate program; his message centered on the centrality of Islam. Gradually, he developed the notion of Islam as a religion that embraces all aspects of human life and conduct. He declared that the objective of the Muslim Brotherhood was to create a new generation capable of understanding the essence of Islam and of acting in accordance. Between 1928 and 1945, al-Banna consistently denied that the society had any political aims, asserting that it was primarily concerned with social and religious matters. However, following World War II, al-Banna assumed a greater political role. He started to call for the replacement of secular institutions by Islamic-oriented ones and asked for major reforms.

By the end of World War II, al-Banna had become an acknowledged political figure, and the Muslim Brethren emerged as a militant force presenting itself as a political alternative. The society established a military wing, which assassinated a number of its adversaries, including a judge. The Brethren reached its apogee during the Arab–Israel War (1948), in which the Muslim Brothers participated through their paramilitary organs. However, the expansion of the society, its growing influence, and its resort to violence brought it into a clash with the government. In February 1949, al-Banna was assassinated by police agents. His disappearance represented a blow to the society as he was its founder and most charismatic figure. His successor, Hassan al-Hudaybi, never enjoyed similar status or prestige.

BIBLIOGRAPHY

KHADDURI, MAJID. *Political Trends in The Arab World: The Role of Ideas and Ideals in Politics.* Baltimore, Md., 1970.
MITCHELL, RICHARD. *The Society of the Muslim Brothers.* London, 1969.

AL-SA'ID, RIF'AT. *Hassan al-Banna: Mata, Kaifa, wa Limadha* (Hassan al-Banna: When, How, and Why). Cairo, 1977.

Ali E. Hillal Dessouki

Banna, Sabri al- [1937–]

Palestinian nationalist who opposed the Palestine Liberation Organization and formed his own militant group.

Sabri al-Banna (also called Abu Nidal) worked as an agent for a series of Arab intelligence organizations, then formed his own group in 1974, called al-FATH: the Revolutionary Council. He and his followers opposed the move toward a two-state solution that was being considered then by the PALESTINE LIBERATION ORGANIZATION (PLO) under Yasir ARAFAT.

His group has assassinated Arab, Israeli, and Palestinian diplomats and has attacked Jewish institutions in Europe and in Turkey—they attacked and killed passengers at the Rome and Vienna airports in 1985; worshipers at an Istanbul synagogue in 1986; and passengers on a Greek cruise ship in 1988. Among the PLO representatives and advisers to Yasir Arafat who were killed by Abu Nidal were Sa'id Hammami in London; Ali Yassin in Kuwait; Izz al-Din Qualag in France; Na'im Khudr in Brussels; and Issam SARTAWI in Portugal.

The assassination of Israel's ambassador to Great Britain, Shlomo Argov, in 1982, triggered Israel's invasion of Palestinian bases in Lebanon. From 1974 to 1983, Abu Nidal was based in Iraq; from 1983 to 1987 in Damascus, Syria; since then in Libya. In 1989, internal conflicts seriously weakened his organization.

BIBLIOGRAPHY

SEALE, PATRICK. *Abu Nidal: A Gun for Hire.* New York, 1992.
SHAFRITZ, JAY M., et al., eds. *Almanac of Modern Terrorism.* New York, 1991.

Steve Tamari

Bannis, Mohammad [1948–]

Moroccan poet and critic.

Bannis was born in Fez, Morocco. He received his Ph.D. in modern Arabic poetry from the University of Rabat in 1989, and is a professor of Arabic literature at Muhammed V University in Rabat.

A prolific writer, Bannis has published a considerable number of books of literary criticism and poetry, as well as an Arabic translation of Abdelkabir KHATIBI's *La Blessure du Nom Propre* (*Al-Ism al-Arabi al-Jarih* [1980]). An avant-garde poet, his interests extend from poetics to graphic arts, and his writings are deeply rooted in Moroccan life and culture.

Closely involved in the political life of Morocco, Bannis favors the involvement of the individual in changing society; otherwise, the written word is equivalent to a dead word, as he suggests in his poem "Belonging to a New Family." He is among the group of poets who changed the structure of the poem and presented a new interpretation of reality, dynamic and optimistic. His latest collection of poetry, *Hibat al-Faragh* (1992; The Gift of Leisure), clearly reflects these structural and thematic changes. Another experimental technique is employed in his collection of poetry *Mawasim al-Sharq* (1986; The Festivals of the East), in which he combines poetic prose with free verse. The poems adopt the shapes of the ideas they embody.

[*See also:* Literature, Arabic, North African]

BIBLIOGRAPHY

BANNIS, MUHAMMAD. "La Poésie de langue arabe." *Europe* (June–July 1979: 37–45.
JAYYUSI, KHADRA S. *Modern Arabic Poetry.* New York, 1987.

Aida A. Bamia

BANOCO

See Bahrain National Oil Company

Banu Lam Tribe

Tribe of eastern Iraq.

Appearing in Iraq in the sixteenth century, this numerous and powerful tribe occupied lands straddling the Iran–Iraq border between the Pusht-i Kuh mountains and the river Tigris. Frequently in rebellion against Ottomon authority, tribal raids interrupted traffic on the Tigris and menaced British lines of communication during WORLD WAR I.

BIBLIOGRAPHY

LONGRIGG, STEPHEN HEMSLEY. *Iraq 1900 to 1950: A Political, Social and Economic History.* London, 1953.

Albertine Jwaideh

Banu Utub Tribe

A tribe of north-central Arabia.

The Banu Utub emigrated to the region of Kuwait on the eastern shore of the Persian/Arabian Gulf in the early eighteenth century. One branch of this tribe, the AL SABAH, are the ancestors of the present ruling family of Kuwait. The other two branches, the al-Khalifa and the Al Jalahiman, migrated to the town of al-Zubarah on the Qatar peninsula, from whence they conquered the Bahrain islands. The al Khalifa family remain rulers of Bahrain to the present day.

Eleanor Abdella Doumato

Banu Yas Tribe

A loose grouping of numerous small sharif tribes situated in eastern Arabia.

The Banu Yas were originally centered in al-Liwa Oasis in what is now the western part of ABU DHABI, a territory of the Arabian peninsula that the Banu Yas share with the Manasir tribe. Banu Yas tribespersons are also located in DUBAI and throughout the United Arab Emirates (UAE) as well as in Oman, Qatar, and Bahrain.

Eleanor Abdella Doumato

BAPCO

See Bahrain Petroleum Company

Baqri Family

Prominent Jewish family in Algeria.

The Cohen–Baqri family (not related to the Arab Bakri family) was one of three Livornese (Italy) Jewish clans (the others were the Boucharas and the BUSNACHs) that were prominent in Algerian commerce and politics throughout the eighteenth and early nineteenth centuries. Invariably it was a member of one of these three families that served as *muqaddam* (government-appointed head) of the Jewish community in Algiers.

In 1797, Joseph Baqri and his brother-in-law Naphtali Busnach went into partnership. Naphtali was the chief adviser of the newly elected Dey Mustafa, and all diplomatic and commercial contact with the regency had to go through the Baqri & Busnach firm. It was over a debt of 5 million French francs owed to the firm by the government of France since the 1780s, that the Dey Husayn insulted France's consul in 1827. This touched off an international "incident" that ended with the French invasion of 1830. The last Baqri of importance was Jacob, who was reconfirmed as "Chef de la Nation Juive" by the French in November 1830 but moved to France shortly thereafter.

BIBLIOGRAPHY

HIRSCHBERG, H. Z. *A History of the Jews in North Africa.* Leiden, Netherlands, 1981.

Norman Stillman

Barada River

Known in biblical literature as Abana, it rises in the Anti-Lebanon mountains from a height of 3,609 feet (1,100 m).

It irrigates the green belt (the Ghuta) surrounding Damascus, capital of Syria, and then pours into Utayba lake. The length of the river is about 43 miles (70 km), but 18.6 miles (30 km) from its source, the volume of its water almost doubles after the spring of Ayn al-Fija empties into it. It also receives water from other springs, notably Ayn al-Khadra. After leaving the gorge of al-Rabwa, on the outskirts of Damascus, the river is divided, on the east and the west, into six main canals, which irrigate a total area of 1,467 square miles (3,800 sq km) of arid land.

BIBLIOGRAPHY

Al-mu'jam al-jughrafi li al-qutr al-arabi al-Suri (The geographical dictionary of Syria), vol. 1. Damascus, 1990.

Abdul-Karim Rafeq

Baraheni, Reza [1935–]

First and most prominent of Iran's American-style literary critics of the 1960s and after.

Reza Baraheni trained in English at his hometown Tabriz University, completed a Ph.D. program at Istanbul University, and served on the faculty at Tehran University thereafter. Alongside his academic activities, Baraheni produced several volumes of verse in Persian in the 1960s and early 1970s, a novel called *The Infernal Days of Mr. Ayaz* (1972) that the government would not allow to be published, and several volumes of essays. Baraheni's *Story-writing* (1968) and *Gold in Copper* (1968, 2nd ed.) combined unprecedented applications of practical elements of New Criticism to Persian literature and voiced Baraheni's belief in social commitment and content as necessary features of serious literature. His literary critical writings in leading journals of the day also exhibited a characteristic directness and bluntness, contributing to the controversy that has long surrounded him.

Baraheni is the only Iranian writer to have made a name in American literary circles, as he did through his involvement with PEN and other organizations while in the United States (1972–1973, 1975–1979). In those years, he published two volumes in English that represent his interests and style: *God's Shadow Prison Poems* (1976) and *The Crowned Cannibals: Writing on Repression in Iran* (1977). A self-contained section of *The Infernal Days* appears in translation in *New Writing from the Middle East* (1978).

In the Islamic Republic since 1979, after being purged from university teaching, Baraheni published book after book, chief among them three novels called *From Well to Well* (1983), *Song of the Slain* (1984), and *Secrets of My Land* (1987/88), and such essays as *Alchemy and Earth* (1985). Expanded editions of his earlier critical guides to fiction and lyric verse were in press in the early 1990s. All this activity enabled Baraheni to make a living from writing, something no Iranian writers had accomplished in the Pahlavi era outside of hack writing, journalism, and translation.

Michael C. Hillmann

Baraka

Arabic, "blessing."

Baraka means the blessing or favor of God, frequently invoked in polite expressions in daily speech; it is also a figurative expression for luck or good fortune. *Baraka* is also the holy emanation of a saintly figure, which can be passed on in turn to successors.

Laurence Michalak

Barakzai, Afdal   [1811–1867]

Amir of Afghanistan, 1866–1866.

Mohammad Afdal Khan was one of many sons of Afghan ruler DOST MOHAMMAD, who died in 1863.

Afdal Khan seized control of Afghanistan from his half brother Sher Ali in a revolt in 1866, but he died in October 1867, having ruled Afghanistan for less than eighteen months. He was the father of Abd al-Rahman, the Iranian amir of Afghanistan.

BIBLIOGRAPHY

FLETCHER, ARNOLD. *Afghanistan: Highway of Conquest*. Ithaca, N.Y., 1965.

Grant Farr

Barakzai Dynasty

Rulers of Afghanistan.

The Barakzai dynasty of Afghanistan was created gradually. Although the Barakzai were Durrani PAKHTUNS, their advent marked a departure from the imperial mode of government that characterized the DURRANI DYNASTY and empire. Unable to preserve the empire, the Barakzai divided the country into a series of competing principalities that fought one another. This competition eventually resulted in the creation of a centralized state and the concentration of power in the hands of the Mohammadzai lineage of the Barakzai clan. The Mohammadzais faced a number of domestic and foreign challenges to their power but held on until 1978.

The Barakzai brothers rose to prominence during the reign of Shah Mahmud Durrani (1809–1818) when Fateh Khan Barakzai became chief minister and appointed several of his brothers to important governorships. In 1818, the crown prince had Fateh Khan blinded; seeking revenge, his brothers overthrew Shah Mahmud and brought about the collapse of the Durrani dynasty. They were, however, unable to agree among themselves and ended up carving three principalities around Kabul, Peshawar, and Kandahar. DOST MOHAMMAD, who gained control of Kabul in 1826, was ousted from power in 1838 in the course of the first Anglo-Afghan war. He returned in 1842 and extended his control to all Afghan provinces. During the wars of succession that followed his death, the country was again divided. Sher Ali (ruled 1863–1866; 1869–1879) succeeded in establishing a centralized state, but the second British invasion of 1878–1880 shattered the political structure he had built.

Ceding control of the country's foreign relations, ABD AL-RAHMAN KHAN (ruled 1880–1901) concentrated his efforts to consolidate yet again a centralized polity in Afghanistan. He also attended to the welfare of his Mohammadzai lineage by assigning both its male and female members a regular stipend disbursed by the state. During his reign, the country acquired its present boundaries, including the disputed DURAND LINE dividing the Pakhtuns between Afghanistan and the North-West Frontier Province of British India. He was the last Barakzai ruler to die peacefully while still in power. His son and successor, HABIBOLLAH KHAN (1901–1919), was assassinated, and his grandson AMANOLLAH KHAN (1919–1929) was overthrown.

The Barakzai briefly lost power in 1929 when a social bandit, Habibollah, became ruler for nine months. They regained control under the leadership of NADIR Shah (1929–1933), a descendant of Dost Mohammad's brother. Unable to tax land like his predecessors, Nadir Shah derived most of the state's revenue from taxes on foreign trade. In return, he conceded many privileges to the merchant class, who proceeded to establish modern financial and industrial enterprises. Following his assassination by a student, his son ZAHIR Shah succeeded him (1933–1973).

Zahir Shah reigned but, for the most part, did not rule. In a first phase, his two uncles, Muhammad Hashem (prime minister 1929–1946) and Shah Mahmud (prime minister 1946–1953), managed the affairs of the state. Then, for a decade, his cousin and brother-in-law, Muhammad Daud, exercised power, also as prime minister. Daud, taking advantage of the bipolarization of world politics, welcomed offers of foreign aid both from the Soviet Union and the United States. The shift in the financial basis of the state from domestic revenue to foreign aid reinforced the power of the Mohammadzai lineage at the expense of the merchant class. The Afghan bureaucracy was substantially expanded. A number of state-sponsored projects in irrigation and road building were initiated.

Daud was forced to resign when his policy of confrontation with Pakistan backfired in 1963. Zahir Shah promulgated a new constitution and assumed actual power, selecting prime ministers from outside the lineage. During the following decade, the country witnessed the formation of political movements and the emergence of a free press. In 1973, Daud overthrew Zahir, proclaiming a republic, yet suppressing the newly acquired freedoms. His overthrow by the Afghan Communist party, in April 1978, marked the end of the Barakzai rule in Afghanistan.

BIBLIOGRAPHY

DUPREE, LOUIS. *Afghanistan*. Princeton, N.J., 1980.

FAIZ MUHAMMAD. *Saraj al-tawarikh* (The Lantern of History), 3 vols. Kabul, 1913–15.

GREGORIAN, VARTAN. *The Emergence of Modern Afghanistan: Politics of Reform and Modernization 1880–1946*. Stamford, Conn., 1969.

Ashraf Ghani

Baramki, Gabriel [1929–]

Palestinian educator and university administrator.

Baramki ran the day-to-day affairs of BIR ZEIT UNIVERSITY, a Palestinian university located in the village of the same name, from the time of Israel's deportation of its president, Hanna NASIR, in 1974 until Nasir's return in 1993.

BIBLIOGRAPHY

Who's Who in the Arab World. Beirut, 1990–1991.

Steve Tamari

Barazi, Husni al–

Syrian prime minister and governor of Aleppo.

From a family of landowners in Hama, Al-Barazi is married with no children. He was governor of the province of Alexandretta and Homs under the reign of King Faisal I. In 1942, he formed the Syrian government and was minister of interior until 1943. In 1949, he was elected deputy of Hama. Al-Barazi was one of the founders of several Arab political parties. He was also one of the seven drafters of the Syrian constitution.

George E. Irani

Barbary Pirates

See Corsairs

Barbary States

Sixteenth-century term for states of North Africa's Mediterranean shore.

Morocco and the Ottoman Empire provinces of Algiers, Tunis, and Tripoli ranged along the southern coast of the Mediterranean Sea became known in the West as the Barbary states beginning in the sixteenth century. In the West, they became synonymous with CORSAIR raiding and the so-called Barbary pirates, who waged the BARBARY WARS against ships of Christian states until 1821.

Jerome Bookin-Wiener

Barbary Wars

Naval battles from the sixteenth century until 1821 between European powers and corsairs of North Africa who were attacking merchant shipping in the Mediterranean.

With the Christian reconquest of Spain from the Moors in the west and the rise of the Ottoman Empire in the east, the Mediterranean basin became the stage for a major, long-running confrontation between Christianity and Islam. Naval warriors (called the Barbary pirates, but more correctly CORSAIRS) based in the North African port cities of Algiers, Tunis, Tripoli, and Rabat-Salé in Morocco were among the most important frontline participants in the conflict. They began in the sixteenth century and lasted until the Treaty of Aix-la-Chapelle (1821) outlawed their activity.

The corsairs seized the ships of the Christian states whose rulers did not have treaties with their political overlords, took their goods, and sold their passengers and crews into slavery. As a result, a series of wars was fought throughout the period between the Europeans (after 1800 the newly independent United States of America also became involved) and their North African corsair adversaries. Because the corsairs served the interests of some of the Europeans, and their depredations against commercial shipping served the interests of the mercantilist policies of the time, the Christian nations never formed a common front against them.

It was only with the rise of free trade as the dominant theory in international trade that the powers banded together to quash the corsairs following Napoléon Bonaparte's defeat in 1815. The final stand of the corsairs came in 1818, with the Treaty of Aix-la-Chapelle in 1821 putting an end to the era by banning piracy, privateering, and corsairing.

Jerome Bookin-Wiener

Bardo, Treaty of

Agreement between France and Tunisia foreshadowing the establishment of a French protectorate.

The treaty of Bardo (1881) allowed Tunisian ruler MUHAMMAD AL-SADIQ Bey to retain his throne but gave the French extensive authority over Tunisia. This was based on agreements reached at the Congress of BERLIN (1878), but the French government had not acted on them, distrusting German Chancellor Otto von BISMARCK's motives. In 1881, imperialist Jules Ferry, the French prime minister, took advantage of a situation precipitated by the Italians in

North Africa (who were eager to secure gains at the expense of Austria).

French troops from Algeria entered Tunisia in April 1881, ostensibly to punish Tunisian Krumir tribes for raids across the border. The Bey, to hold his throne, permitted France to station troops and on May 12 signed the Treaty of Bardo (also known as Qsar Sa'id). It specified that the bey could no longer deal independently with foreign powers, that a French resident minister would act as the bey's foreign minister, and that the Tunisian army would be under the command of a French officer. Resistance developed in the center and south of Tunisia, but it was crushed by French troops by the end of the year. The Treaty of Bardo (named for a beylical palace in Tunis) marked the emergence of French imperialism with the expansion of the French Second Empire. It initiated a long period of Franco–Italian tension and modified the Mediterranean situation to Britain's disadvantage.

BIBLIOGRAPHY

KAROUI, HACHEMI, and ALI MAHJOUBU. *Quand le soleil s'est levé à l'ouest: Tunisie 1881—impérialisme et résistance.* Tunis, 1983.

Kenneth J. Perkins

Bardo Palace Incident

Events that led to establishment of France's protectorate in Tunisia.

The Bardo Palace incident stemmed from a meeting of France's consul, Theodore Roustan, with MUHAMMAD AL-SADIQ Bey, the ruler of Tunisia, at the bey's summer villa in the village of Qsar Sa'id. Roustan gave the bey a copy of a treaty that would impose France's protectorate over his country. Muhammad al-Sadiq received the treaty on 12 May 1881 at 4 P.M. Three hours later he signed the TREATY OF BARDO. It became the legal basis for France's protectorate, which lasted until Tunisia was granted independence, March 20, 1956.

At the Congress of BERLIN (1878), representatives of Britain and Germany encouraged France to seize Tunisia. Political pressure to convince the bey to sign a protectorate treaty with France between 1878 and 1881 failed. Thus, in early 1881, France decided to employ force.

In late April 1881, France massed troops along the frontier. On April 24, they crossed into Tunisia, and on April 26 they occupied Le Kef almost without a fight. On May 1, 1881, France's troops occupied BIZERTE. Between May 3 and 11 General Bréart landed at Bizerte and proceeded to Al-Judayyida (northwest of Tunis). These maneuvers occasioned the May 12 meeting at Qsar Sa'id.

BIBLIOGRAPHY

GUELLOUZ, E., A. MASMOUDI, and M. SMIDA. *Histoire de la Tunisie: Les temps modernes*. Tunis, 1983.

Larry A. Barrie

Barghuti Family

Prominent Palestinian family of the Ramallah area, north of Jerusalem.

Since the latter years of the Ottoman Empire, members of the Barghuti family have played prominent roles in Palestinian politics. Umar Salih Barghuti (1894–1965), a lawyer, politician, and historian, was active in ARAB NATIONALISM during Ottoman rule in Palestine. Then a shaykh of the Banu Zayd tribe of the Ramallah area, he founded al-JAMI'A AL-ARABIYYA, whose membership drew largely from his tribe. In 1952, he was appointed to Jordan's parliament.

Bashir Barghuti (1931–   ), the General Secretary of the Palestinian People's Party (formerly the Palestine Communist Party), founded Jerusalem's Palestinian weekly *al-Tali'a* in 1978. Mustafa Barghuti (1954–   ) is a physician and chairman of the Union of Palestinian Medical Relief Committees, one of the grassroots organizations that formed the social and political backbone of the Intifada.

BIBLIOGRAPHY

Palestinians in Profile. Jerusalem, 1993.
PORATH, Y. *The Emergence of the Palestinian-Arab National Movement, 1918–1929*. London, 1974.
SMITH, PAMELA ANN. *Palestine and the Palestinians: 1876–1983*. New York, 1984.

Steve Tamari

Bar-Ilan University

University in Ramat Gan, Israel, that features Jewish studies.

The university was founded in 1955 as an institution of higher learning that would fulfill the basic aims of Judaic tradition. The curriculum for both men and women includes required courses in Jewish studies, which pursue the goals of integrating Judaism and present-day reality—cultivating a respect for Jewish principles and customs. Pinkhos Churgin was the university's founder and first president. In 1993, the student body numbered approximately 12,000.

The university offers undergraduate and graduate degrees in liberal arts, social sciences, and natural sciences. There are faculties in Jewish studies, humanities, social sciences, natural sciences, and law.

BIBLIOGRAPHY

FISCH, HAROLD. "Bar-Ilan University." In *The Israel Year Book, 1971*. Tel Aviv, 1971.

Miriam Simon

Baring, Evelyn   [1841–1917]

British consul general and virtual ruler of Egypt from 1883 until 1907.

One of Britain's most illustrious pro-consular figures, he contributed profoundly through his policies in Egypt to the modern history of that country. As an administrator he stressed fiscal stability, hydraulic reform, and the cultivation and export of cotton. Critics charged him with neglecting industrialization and failing to fund vital social services, especially education. During his latter years in Egypt the nationalist movement revived, having been moribund since the Urabi revolt, and from then on became a vital force in Egyptian politics.

Lord Cromer was born as Evelyn Baring on February 26, 1841, at Cromer Hall in Norfolk, England, a son of Henry Baring, a member of the British Parliament. His father died when Baring was seven, and the youngster was raised by his mother. In 1855 he entered the military academy at Woolwich and was commissioned three years later. His first posting was to the Ionian islands; it proved formative for him. Not only did he meet his future wife there, Ethel Stanley, but he acquired an interest in ancient history—an intellectual avocation which he pursued throughout his lifetime. Upon returning to Britain, he entered the military staff college, but instead of pursuing a military career for which his education had prepared him, Captain Baring in 1872 became private secretary to his cousin, Lord Northbrook, Viceroy of India at the time. This decision cast his fate with Britain's overseas imperial interests. He quickly distinguished himself as a resourceful and skilled administrator and a person destined for high office. In 1877, at a time when the government of Egypt was endeavoring to stave off bankruptcy under the profligate rule of the viceroy, Khedive Isma'il Pasha (1863–79), Baring was selected as the British representative on a multinational financial body, called the Caisse de la Dette, or Egyptian Public Debt Commission, which looked after the interest of the European bondholders with the government of Egypt. In 1879 Baring involved himself in internal Egyptian politics and played a role in the deposition of Khedive Isma'il and the coming to power of Muhammad TAWFIQ Pasha. The next year he left Egypt to become the financial adviser to Lord Ripon's Viceroy's council in India.

Baring's absence from Egypt proved short-lived. Discontent had surfaced within the Egyptian army during the crisis of 1879. It welled up once again in 1881 and 1882. A group of young native-born Egyptian officers, led by Ahmad URABI, galvanized a movement of opposition to Ottoman Turkish rule and the growing foreign influence over the country. In September 1882, the British invaded Egypt, defeated the Egyptian army at Tal al-Kabir, exiled Urabi and other nationalists, and restored Tawfiq to power in Cairo. The British promised a swift evacuation of the country, which continued to be juridically part of the Ottoman Empire and in which numerous European powers had substantial financial and cultural interests, most notably France. The British quickly set about the task of reforming the Egyptian administration so as to facilitate their withdrawal.

In 1883 Baring was chosen to be Britain's consul-general in Egypt. Although his choice came as a surprise to many since he was relatively young (forty-two) and had not previously held such a responsible position, he was an ideal choice. He already had considerable knowledge of Egypt from having served on the Caisse de la Dette. He was familiar with the imperial administration from his duties in India, and he was a recognized expert on financial matters. At the time, Egypt's single most pressing administrative problem was financial. In 1880 the government's external debt totalled 100 million pounds, the interest on which consumed nearly half of Egypt's tax revenues. To realize its goal of withdrawal—a goal enunciated repeatedly in official pronouncements—Britain would have to tackle Egypt's budgetary problems.

Baring devoted his first decade in Egypt (1883–1892) to achieving fiscal solvency. He rightly judged that the only way Egyptian finances could be set to rights was by increasing agricultural production and thereby raising the tax base. The key to agricultural development, in his estimation, was irrigation, since Egypt, as the gift of the Nile river, was totally reliant on irrigation waters for its agricultural success. MUHAMMAD ALI, ruler of Egypt from 1805 until 1849, had first begun to transform Egyptian irrigation from a basin or flood system to what was called perennial irrigation. By digging deep canals and erecting dams

and weirs along the Nile, he had enabled parts of Egypt to receive irrigation waters year-round instead of only during the flood season. As a result, Egyptian farmers had begun to cultivate cotton, which, as a summer crop, required irrigation waters when the Nile was at its lowest. Unfortunately, in the latter years of Isma'il's reign the hydraulic system of Egypt had fallen into disrepair. Bringing some of Britain's most talented irrigation engineers to Egypt, Baring put the old system in order and then embarked upon a vigorous program of hydraulic improvement. Critical in this first decade was the repair of the Egyptian barrage—a wide dam at the bifurcation of the Nile, just south of Cairo—which had been built in pre-British days but never rendered serviceable.

Even the dramatic events in the Sudan in the 1880s were tied to Egyptian finances. Egypt had expanded steadily into the Sudan in the nineteenth century. A Mahdist movement threatened Egypt's control. Because of financial pressures the British government compelled Egypt to withdraw its forces from the Sudan and to leave the fate of that territory to the Sudanese. Baring secured the evacuation of the Sudan but not before the Mahdists had killed one of Britain's war heroes, General Charles "Chinese" Gordon, slain while defending Anglo–Egyptian interests at Khartoum.

In 1892 Khedive Tawfiq died. He had worked closely with Baring to bring fiscal stability to the country and to improve agricultural productivity. His younger son, ABBAS Hilmi II, succeeded him. In the same year Baring was elevated to the British peerage as Lord Cromer in recognition of his services to the British Empire. The political tranquility which had characterized British rule to that point was shattered soon after Abbas came to the throne. In January 1894, the new khedive made critical remarks about the Egyptian army, which he was reviewing, and about its commanding general or sirdar, Horatio Kitchener. Kitchener tendered his resignation, but Cromer, already worried by the nationalist-minded advisers whom Abbas had surrounded himself with at the palace, moved with alacrity to defeat this challenge to British authority. A British battalion was diverted from its homeward journey and marched to Cairo in a show of strength. Abbas was compelled to back down. He reinstated Kitchener as sirdar. Although Cromer had his way, the event left a legacy of bitterness between the khedive and the British consul. While Abbas never again openly challenged British authority, the palace became a patron of various nationalist parties when they first appeared on the political scene at the beginning of the twentieth century.

In Cromer's second decade in Egypt, Britain extended its authority over the country's internal affairs and effected the reconquest of the Sudan. No longer was the prospect of evacuation imminent, although the British continued to proclaim their occupation a temporary one. Now, however, British "advisers" were appointed in the ministries of justice, interior, and education. They sought to impose British cultural standards where previously Ottoman Turkish, Egyptian, and French influences had predominated. Hydraulic reform continued apace, culminating in the construction of a massive dam at ASWAN in 1902. Cotton accounted for more than 80 percent of the value of Egyptian exports at this time.

Cromer had hoped to postpone the military conquest of the Sudan until Egypt's finances were unshakable and the Aswan dam had been completed. The European scramble for African territory forced his hand. By the mid-1890s the Sudan was one of the few territories still independent of European colonial authority. The British deemed the upper Nile basin of vital importance to their African empire and feared that a hostile power in control of the area, like the French, would threaten British interests in Egypt. Hastily preparing the Egyptian army for action, Cromer despatched troops into the Sudan in 1896. Khartoum fell to an Anglo–Egyptian force in 1898. A tense moment occurred on the upper White Nile at Fashoda (now Kodok) in 1898 when Egyptian forces under General Kitchener met a small band of French soldiers under Jean-Baptiste Marchand. Both leaders claimed the territory for their countries. Only after the French had backed down and recognized Anglo–Egyptian preeminence in the Sudan did the crisis of the FASHODA INCIDENT end.

Once Cromer had engineered the military occupation of the Sudan, he set about creating its administrative system. Here he used considerable ingenuity to devise a way for Britain and Egypt to share in the governance of the Sudan. Seeking to spare the Sudan the tangle of international obligations that bedevilled Britain's rule over Egypt, he established the Anglo–Egyptian Condominium over the Sudan in 1899. By the terms of his anomalous political organization, the Sudan was exempted from the jurisdiction of the CAPITULATIONS and the MIXED COURTS, while Egypt retained its formal suzerainty over the Sudan, and Britain became the effective sovereign power.

In the latter years of Cromer's administration, anti-British, nationalist sentiments gained in strength. New political parties, like the Watani party and the Umma party, came into being, and new leaders, like Mustafa KAMIL, launched attacks against Cromer for being an autocrat. The nationalists castigated Cromer for failing to share power with Egyptians, neglecting parliamentary institutions, and starving the educa-

tional system of funds. A galvanizing nationalist event occurred in the village of Dinshaway in 1906 where the British carried out a series of public executions of villagers who had killed a British soldier while trying to protect their possessions. The severity of the sentences appalled many and came to symbolize the heavy-handedness of the British rule. Just one year after the DINSHAWAY INCIDENT, Cromer submitted his resignation. He left a country he had dominated for a quarter of a century but the affection of whose inhabitants he had failed to win.

In Britain Cromer did not completely break his ties with Egypt. Always a prolific writer, with a marked scholarly bent, he published a two-volume account of Egyptian affairs during his time there. *Modern Egypt* (1908) was for many years the standard treatment of British rule in Egypt. It is read now, however, for its insights into the imperial mentality rather than its descriptions of Egyptian society and its assessment of British rule. Subsequently, he wrote *Ancient and Modern Imperialism* (1910) and *Abbas II* (1915) and collected his many essays on diverse subjects into three volumes, entitled *Political and Literary Essays*.

BIBLIOGRAPHY

BERQUE, JACQUES. *Egypt: Imperialism and Revolution,* tr. by Jean Stewart. London, 1972.
MARLOWE, JOHN. *Cromer in Egypt.* New York, 1970.
OWEN, E. R. J. *Cotton and the Egyptian Economy, 1820–1914.* Oxford, 1970.
AL-SAYYID, AFAF LUTFI. *Egypt and Cromer: A Study in Anglo-Egyptian Relations.* London, 1968.
SCHÖLCH, ALEXANDER. *Egypt for the Egyptians! The Socio-Political Crisis in Egypt, 1878–1882.* London, 1981.
TIGNOR, ROBERT L. *Modernization and British Colonial Rule in Egypt, 1882–1914.* Princeton, N.J., 1966.

Robert L. Tignor

Barkan, Ömer Lutfi   [1902–1979]

Turkish social and economic historian who pioneered the study of the Ottoman state and society based on archival documentation.

Born in Edirne in 1902, Barkan studied philosophy at Istanbul University (1927) and social sciences at the University of Strasbourg (1931).

Barkan served briefly as lycée (secondary school) teacher in Eskişehir (1931–33) before he joined the newly organized Istanbul University in 1933. He stayed there, first in the Faculty of Letters and from 1937 in the Faculty of Economics as docent, professor (1940), dean (1950–52), and founder and director of the Institute of Turkish Economic History (from 1955) until his retirement in 1973. He married Süreyya Meriç in 1951 and had three sons. He was a member of the Turkish Historical Society and of various international organizations.

Barkan was the first historian in the Republic of Turkey to base his historiography entirely on the vast archives of the Ottoman Empire. His publication and analysis of Ottoman provincial regulations (*Kanunlar,* 1945), provincial population and production surveys (in many articles and *Hüdavendigar* [Bursa], published posthumously), and sixteenth-century Istanbul *waqf*s (1970), to name the truly seminal of his numerous important contributions, brought Ottoman historiography to the attention of non-Orientalist Western historians, especially Fernand Braudel and the Annales school. Facilitating this mutual respect must be considered his most significant legacy.

BIBLIOGRAPHY

For biographical notices and full bibliographies, see *Belleten* (Journal of the Turkish Historical Association) 44/173 (1980): 153–77; *Armagan* (commemorative issue of the Journal of the Faculty of Economics, Istanbul) 41 (1982–83): 3–38; *Türkiye'de toprak meselesi* (Land Problems in Turkey, vol. 1 of Barkan's collected works), Istanbul, 1980, pp. 9–22.

I. Metin Kunt

Bar Kochba Rebellion

Famous revolt of the Jews against Roman rule.

Few details are known about the causes and the course of the rebellion, but in approximately 132 C.E. Bar Kochba (originally probably Bar Kosiva) led a revolt in Judea against Roman rule under Hadrian. Hadrian's rebuilding of Jerusalem as a Roman city under the name of Aelia Capitolina and his erecting, on the site of the destroyed temple, a temple to praise the Roman god Jupiter were two possible causes of the revolt. Other uprisings throughout Judea had preceded the Bar Kochba Rebellion, which probably was a continuation of them.

As the last attempt to establish a Jewish commonwealth in the land of Israel before the establishment of the modern state of Israel, the revolt has an important place in Jewish history. It lasted three years, during which the Jewish people's messianic expectations were heightened when Rabbi Akiva declared Bar Kochba the Messiah (a view not universally shared by the rabbis of the time). For the duration of the revolt, the Jews regained sovereignty over Jerusalem.

There were no survivors among those who fought at the end of the rebellion at Betar, a Jewish fortification in the Judean desert. In history of the Jews and of Zionism, the Bar Kochba Rebellion serves as a symbol of supreme sacrifice for the sake of creating a Jewish commonwealth.

BIBLIOGRAPHY

Encyclopedia Judaica. New York, 1971.
Jewish Encyclopedia. New York, 1976.

Bryan Daves

Bar-Lev, Haim   [1924–   ]

Member of Israel's Knesset; chief of staff of the Israel Defense Force.

Haim Bar-Lev was born in Vienna, Austria, and in 1939 immigrated to Palestine. From 1942 to 1948, he was a member of the PALMACH. In the 1948 Arab–Israel War, he commanded an armored battalion on the Egyptian front and in 1956 commanded an armored brigade that reached the Suez Canal. Throughout the 1950s and 1960s, he held a number of high command posts in Israel's military, including head of the Northern Command (1952), commander of the Givati Brigade (1954–1955), and commander of the Armored Corp (1958–1961). After a brief hiatus from the military, in which he completed a master's degree in business and economics from Columbia University in New York City, he returned to Israel to assume the post of chief of operations in 1964. In 1967, he was appointed deputy chief of staff, serving in this capacity during the Arab–Israel War of 1967. Bar-Lev served as chief of staff from 1968 to 1972, commanding the Israel Defense Forces (IDF) during Egypt's War of Attrition and constructing the BAR-LEV LINE on the east bank of the Suez Canal, which was designed to defend Israel against an Egyptian attack on the Sinai. In the Arab–Israel War of 1973, he served as commander of the Egyptian front.

Since 1973, Bar-Lev has been a member of the Knesset (Israel's parliament) for the Labor Alignment. He was minister of commerce and industry between 1972 and 1977. In 1978, he was elected secretary-general of the Israel Labor party. He served as minister of police in 1984.

BIBLIOGRAPHY

ROLEF, S. H., ed. *Political Dictionary of the State of Israel.* New York, 1987.

Martin Malin

Bar-Lev Line

Israeli defense system built along the Suez Canal.

The Bar-Lev Line was planned by Israel's General Avraham Eden to be similar to the structure of the forward posts of Kibbutz Nirim used during the first ARAB–ISRAEL WAR of 1948. It was built after the Arab–Israel War of 1968 and modified during the period when Haim BAR-LEV was chief of staff (1968–1972). The line was made up of thirty strongholds along the eastern side of the Suez Canal, with eleven constructed after Egypt's WAR OF ATTRITION (1968-1970). The eleven additional posts were planned by Ariel Sharon.

When the Arab–Israel War of 1973 broke out, only sixteen of the forty-one positions were fully armed or staffed. Israel was taken by surprise when Egypt crossed the canal on the morning of October 6, 1973, and all but one position fell.

BIBLIOGRAPHY

O'BRIEN, CONOR CRUISE. *The Seige.* London, 1986.

SAFRAN, NADAV. *Israel: The Embattled Ally.* Cambridge, Mass., 1981.

SHIMONI, YAACOV, ed. *Political Dictionary of the Middle East in the 20th Century.* New York, 1974.

Zachary Karabell

Barmada, Mustafa

Syrian politician.

A legal expert educated in Istanbul, Mustafa Barmada resigned as governor of Aleppo on January 5, 1924, as opposition to the French high command grew among the native governments. He was a leader of the People's Parliamentary Group during the fractious 1947 elections, a faction opposed to President Quwatli's group in the National Bloc.

BIBLIOGRAPHY

KHOURY, PHILIP S. *Syria and the French Mandate: The Politics of Arab Nationalism, 1920–1945.* Princeton, N.J., 1987.

Charles U. Zenzie

Baron, Dvora   [1887–1956]

Israeli writer.

Dvora Baron was born in a small Jewish town in Lithuania. From her father, who was the rabbi of that community, Baron learned Hebrew and became versed in traditional and sacred Hebrew texts, an education unavailable to women before that time. At age sixteen she began to publish short stories in Hebrew. Baron immigrated to Palestine in 1911 and served as the literary editor of a major Zionist periodical. Although she spent most of her life in the land of Israel, the thirteen volumes of her short stories describe life in the eastern European community of her childhood, particularly the plight of women under the yolk of traditional custom and law. Regeneration through family and community, and individual victimization and human suffering, are the main themes of her work. Her style has been likened to that of Chekhov and Flaubert, authors whose works she translated into Hebrew. Some of Baron's stories were published in English in *The Thorny Path* (1969).

Zvia Ginor

Barondi, Fakhr al-   [1889–?]

Syrian politician.

Born to an Egyptian family, al-Barondi studied agriculture in Paris in 1911, after receiving secondary education in Damascus. While serving in the Ottoman army in Palestine, he was captured and sent to Egypt; there he joined King Faisal's Arab Army and became chamberlain to Faisal. A dedicated Syrian nationalist, al-Barondi joined the National Bloc party in 1928 and earned a seat that year as deputy. In 1929, he was arrested and imprisoned for his activities during the great revolt. His innovative fund-raising plans for social programs fueled his various operations, and he later contributed heavily to the Steel Shirts, a wing of the National Bloc designed to check radical sentiment.

BIBLIOGRAPHY

KHOURY, PHILIP S. *Syria and the French Mandate: The Politics of Arab Nationalism, 1920–1945.* Princeton, N.J., 1987.

Charles U. Zenzie

Barq al-Shimal

Important daily newspaper in Aleppo, Syria, 1923–1963; (in English, the Northern Telegraph).

It started publication in French in 1923 and was distributed at noon. Its owner and editor-in-chief,

Niqula (Nicolas) Janji, born in Aleppo in 1901, was a moderate politician and journalist. He was twice elected to parliament, in 1928 and 1932. In 1949, he joined the People's party based in Aleppo. After Syria became independent in 1945, *Barq al-Shimal* was published in Arabic until it ceased publication in 1963. In its later years, Abd al-Rahman Abu Qaws shared its editorship with Janji.

BIBLIOGRAPHY

ILYAS, JOSEPH. *Tatawwur al-sihafa al-Suriyya fi mi'at am, 1865–1965* (The development of the Syrian Press in One Hundred Years, 1865–1965), vol. 2. Beirut, 1983.

Abdul-Karim Rafeq

Barth, Henry   [1821–1865]

German explorer of Africa.

Employed by the British government and a contemporary of the famous English explorer Richard BURTON, Barth traveled throughout the Middle East (1845–1847), through North and Central Africa (including an 1849 mission to suppress East African slavery), and later through Greece, Asia Minor, and Turkey. He published a multivolume account of his journeys, *Reisen und Entdeckungen in Nord- und Zentralafrika* (Travels and Discoveries in North and Central Africa, 1855–1858), was a member of Britain's Royal Geographic Society, and a professor at the University of Berlin (1863–1865).

BIBLIOGRAPHY

Chambers Biographical Dicitonary. 1990.
RICE, EDWARD. *Captain Sir Richard Francis Burton.* New York, 1990.

Zachary Karabell

Baruni, Sulayman al-   [?–1940]

Muslim Ibadi Berber scholar and politician from Jabal al-Gharb, Tripolitania.

A member of the Ottoman parliament from 1908 to 1912 and a senator from 1913, this leader of the Tripolitanian resistance to Italian rule in Libya (1911–1921) was also active in the Tripolitanian state (1912–1913) and the Tripolitanian republic (1918–1921). He was the Ottoman representative in Libya during World War I.

BIBLIOGRAPHY

ANDERSON, LISA. "The Tripoli Republic, 1918–1922." In *Social and Economic Development of Libya,* ed. by E. G. H. Joffe and K. S. McLachlan. London, 1982.
PETERSON, J. E. "Arab Nationalism and Idealist Politician: The Career of Sulayman al-Baruni." In *Law, Personalities, and Politics in the Middle East: Essays in Honor of Majid Khadduri,* ed. by J. Piscatori and G. S. Harris. Boulder, Colo., and Washington, D.C., 1987.
VAGLIERI, L. VECCIA. "Sulayman al-Baruni." In *Encyclopaedia of Islam,* 2nd ed., vol. 1.

Rachel Simon

Bar-Yehudah, Israel   [1895–1965]

Israeli politician.

Born in Ukraine, Bar-Yehudah emigrated to Palestine in 1926 and became active in the socialist labor movement. He was a member of Israel's Knesset (parliament) from 1949 until his death in 1965, at first from the political party MAPAM and then from Ahdut Ha-Avodah-po'alei Zion. He was minister of the interior (1955–1959), minister of transport (1962–1965), and party general secretary (1960–1962).

BIBLIOGRAPHY

Encyclopedia Judaica. New York, 1971.
New Standard Jewish Encyclopedia. New York, 1977.
ROLEF, SUSAN HATTIS, ed. *Political Dictionary of the State of Israel.* New York, 1987.

Zachary Karabell

Barzani, Mas'ud al-   [1946–   ]

Kurdish leader.

Born in Mahabad, Kurdistan (Iran), Mas'ud is the son of General Mulla Mustafa BARZANI. Through his father, he was closely associated with the struggle of the Iraqi KURDS as early as 1968. As a refugee in Iran, following the collapse of the Kurdish resistance in 1975, he took over the leadership after his father's death, experiencing the tragedies of Halabjah in 1988 and the Gulf War in 1991. He presently serves as the chairman of the Kurdistan democratic party.

BIBLIOGRAPHY

KUTSCHERA, CHRIS. *Le mouvement national kurde.* Paris, 1979.

Chris Kutschera

Barzani, Mustafa   [1904–1979]

Kurdish leader.

Son of Shaykh Mohammad (?–1903), a NAQSHBANDI shaykh, Mullah Mustafa was born in the small village of Barzan (which gave its name to this family), in Iraqi Kurdistan. After taking part in a revolt led by his elder brother Shaykh Ahmad in the early 1930s, Mullah Mustafa was exiled to southern Iraq, then to the city of Sulaymaniya. It was in this "capital" of Iraqi Kurdistan that the young uneducated villager met the intellectuals who founded the first nationalist organizations for Iraqi KURDS and gave him his first political lectures.

After his flight from Sulaymaniya in 1943, and a new revolt in 1945, he was forced to take refuge in Iranian Kurdistan, where he was promoted by Qazi Mohammad, president of the Kurdish Republic at Mahabad. From this point on, Mullah Mustafa was known as General Barzani. After the collapse (December 1946) of the short-lived Kurdish republic of Mahabad, he sought asylum (June 1947) with several hundred of his partisans, in the Soviet Union, until 1958.

The revolution in Iraq of July 14, 1958, opened a new chapter in the history of that country—allowing General Barzani to make a triumphant return in October. He had been the revolutionary leader who had fought first against the British and then against both the Iraqi and the Iranian monarchies. Good relations with the new leader of the Republic of Iraq, Abd al-Karim KASSEM, did not last. In March 1961, Barzani, fearing for his safety, went back to his village.

Kassem was no more able to solve the Kurdish question—sharing power and wealth between Kurds and Arabs in Iraq—than was his predecessor, King FAISAL II. In September 1961, the area around Barzan was attacked—beginning a fourteen-year war marked by long cease-fires between General Barzani and the four regimes that alternated in Baghdad after violent coups.

Overcoming the 1964 crisis within the leadership of the Kurdistan DEMOCRATIC PARTY (KDP), Barzani was able to consolidate his power over both the party and the territory of Kurdistan, stretching from Syria east to Iran. With his army of several thousand guerrillas (PESH MERGA), he forced on then Vice-President Saddam HUSSEIN the 1970 agreement granting autonomy to the Kurds of Iraq. To achieve recognition for Kurdish political rights in a written document, Barzani made an alliance with the shah of Iran. This agreement had some fateful shortcomings: Its implementation was not immediate and the borders of the Kurdish region were not defined.

In March 1974, fighting erupted after the failure of negotiations focusing on the city of Kirkuk; Kurdish resistance collapsed after a year when, on March 6, 1975, in Algiers, the shah of Iran reached an agreement with Saddam Hussein that put an end to the Iranian (and secret U.S.–Israel) assistance to the Kurds. Living first in exile in Iran, Barzani died of cancer in the United States on March 2, 1979—a few days after the shah's fall.

BIBLIOGRAPHY

ADAMSON, DAVID. *The Kurdish War.* London, 1964.
KUTSCHERA, CHRIS. *Le mouvement national kurde.* Paris, 1979.

Chris Kutschera

Barzani Family

Kurdish family of religious shaykhs and nationalist leaders.

This family is rooted in the village of Barzan, in what is today Iraqi KURDISTAN (but was for centuries the Ottoman Empire). Unlike the Shemzini or the Barzinji shaykhs, the Barzanis do not claim any famous genealogy; they were uneducated and obscure mullahs until Taj ad-Din became the *khalifa* (deputy) of Mawlana Khalid (died 1826), who introduced the NAQSHBANDI *tariqa* (order) to Kurdistan. Shaykh Mohammad (died 1903), his great-grandson, was himself a half-educated mullah but had nevertheless a considerable number of followers; after the disposition of his rival shaykh, Ubaydallah of Shemzinan, he marched on Mosul, to be captured by the Ottomans.

His sons continued the family tradition: Shaykh Abd al-Salam II (1885–1914), a nationalist leader and a religious shaykh revered by his followers, was hanged by the Ottomans. Shaykh Ahmad (died 1969), the second brother, led his first revolt in 1931 and gave up politics after the collapse of the Kurdish republic of Mahabad. Mullah Mustafa (1904–1979), the third brother, became famous under the name General BARZANI. Presently, the family leadership is split between Shaykh Mohammad Khalid, son of Shaykh Ahmad, and Mas'ud al-BARZANI, son of the general, who, since the death of his brother Idris (1944–1987), claims the political heritage of his father.

BIBLIOGRAPHY

KUTSCHERA, CHRIS. *Le mouvement national kurde.* Paris, 1979.

Chris Kutschera

Bashayan, Burhan al-Din   [1915–1975]

Iraqi diplomat and politician.

Born in Basra, Bashayan completed his secondary studies at the American University in Beirut (AUB). He then enrolled in the law school of the University of Baghdad, where he obtained his law degree. In 1938, he was appointed secretary of the Iraqi consulate in Cairo and, in 1941, deputy consul of Iraq in Jerusalem. In 1949, Bashayan was elected deputy of Basra. In December 1955 and April 1958 he was appointed foreign minister in the two cabinets headed by Nuri al-SAʿID.

George E. Irani

Bashir

See Chehab, Bashir

Basic People's Congresses

Part of the Libyan political structure.

The congresses provide the second level (above village and submunicipal congresses) of popular consultation and participation in the exercise of popular power in the JAMAHIRIYA (state of the masses) of Libya proclaimed in March 1977. Each of some two hundred basic people's congresses send three delegates to the chief debating and decision-making forum—the annual GENERAL PEOPLE'S CONGRESS.

John L. Wright

Başiret

Ottoman newspaper.

Published between 1870 and 1877, *Başiret* (Insight) was an organ for popularizing new ideas concerning Muslim solidarity and union. Founded by Ali BAŞIRETCI with government financial assistance, *Başiret* was published five times a week and emphasized foreign news. In 1878, as a result of his opposition to the sultan, Ali Başiretci was arrested and exiled, and the paper was closed. The paper reappeared briefly in 1908 upon the announcement of the constitution but was quickly closed down again.

BIBLIOGRAPHY

İNUĞUR, M. NURI. *Türk Basımında "İz" Bırakanlar.* Istanbul, 1988, p. 29.

SHAW, STANFORD, and EZEL KURAL SHAW. *History of the Ottoman Empire and Modern Turkey,* vol. 2: *Reform, Revolution, and Republic: The Rise of Modern Turkey, 1808–1975.* Cambridge, U.K., 1977, p. 157.
TOPUZ, HIFZI. *100 Soruda Türk Basım Tarihi.* Istanbul, 1973, pp. 24–25.

David Waldner

Başiretci, Ali   [1838–1912]

Ottoman Turkish journalist.

Ali Başiretci was educated at the Imperial Service school but did not enter palace service. In 1863, he began to work for the finance ministry, and in 1869, he began to publish the daily newspaper *Başiret* (Insight), which popularized Jamal al-Din al-AFGHANI's ideas about Muslim unity. Accused of pro-Prussian activities during the Franco–Prussian war, Başiretci was forced into exile in Jerusalem. After being pardoned, he reentered government administration as a *qaʾimmagam* in various districts. After 1908, he attempted to reestablish *Başiret,* but it was closed soon after.

BIBLIOGRAPHY

ORAL, FUAT SÜREYYA. *Türk Basım Tarihi, 1728–1922.* Ankara, p. 257.
SHAW, STANFORD, and EZEL KURAL SHAW. *History of the Ottoman Empire and Modern Turkey,* vol. 2: *Reform, Revolution, and Republic: The Rise of Modern Turkey, 1808–1975.* Cambridge, U.K., 1977, p. 157.
Tanzimat'tan Cumhuriyet'e Türkiye Ansiklopedisi, vol. 1. Istanbul, 1984, p. 86.
Türk Ansiklopedisi, vol. 2. Ankara, 1948, p. 85.

David Waldner

Basra

City in Iraq; Iraq's only seaport, but situated some 75 miles (120 km) north of the Persian/Arabian Gulf, on the Shatt al-Arab.

Basra is an administrative and commercial center for IRAQ, with a population of some 1.4 million (according to a 1986 estimate). It is linked to BAGHDAD, the capital, by railroad and is governed by the *muhafidh,* a chief of the administrative unit who is also the representative of the central government in Baghdad.

The seaport itself is actually situated at the head of the SHATT AL-ARAB, the confluence and the lower reach of the TIGRIS AND EUPHRATES rivers, which

Port of Basra in the 1930s. (D.W. Lockhard)

Shaykh Ghazal market in Basra, 1930. (Richard Bulliet)

flows for some 112 miles (180 km) to empty into the Gulf. Basra is bounded on the north by the governate of Maysan, on the east by Iran, and on the west by the Western Desert. Basra has a desert climate with great temperature variations between day and night, summer and winter. The high temperature reaches 106°F (50°C); the low is above frost. Annual relative humidity is 44 to 59 percent; annual rainfall ranges between two and eight inches (50–200 mm). Winters are warm, with temperatures above freezing.

With its multitude of waterways, Basra has the right conditions for the successful cultivation of DATES; the incoming and outgoing tides of some 635 rivers and channels that water approximately 14 million palm trees make the region one of the world's most fertile. Despite the devastation that occurred here during the Iran–Iraq war, the orchards are still farmed in quantity. Besides the 530 kinds of dates, other crops include maize (corn), citrus, apples, and many types of vegetables.

PETROLEUM has become the leading industry of Basra. The upstream operations are carried out by the Iraq National Oil Company, beyond the areas allotted to the British Petroleum Company, according to laws passed in 1961. In 1975, Iraq nationalized the Basra Petroleum Company, and the era of oil concessions ended. The oil refineries and the petrochemical and fertilizer plants were moved out of Basra during the IRAN–IRAQ WAR, but the paper, fishing, and date industries still operate. Through Basra as a port-of-entry come imports, such as sugar, timber, coffee, and tea. The main export is crude oil and petroleum products, dates, leather, and wool.

The Saray creek in Basra City, circa 1930. (Richard Bulliet)

Ashar creek in Basra, circa 1930. (Richard Bulliet)

Although Basra was a multiethnic city, today—because of the political changes in Iraq since 1958—Muslim Arabs form the majority: Armenians, Indians, and Iranians are, for the most part, gone, as are the Jews. Arabic is the language of the city, and Shi'ism is the predominant form of Islam—although some few Christians, Jews, and Sabaeans remain.

The University of Basra and a branch of the University of Technology are the schools of higher education; some 385 primary schools, 175 secondary schools, and 15 vocational schools exist. The Center for Arab Gulf Studies was located in Basra, but it was moved to Baghdad in 1985.

Basra was founded by Caliph Umar I in 638 C.E. It is the Bassorah of the *Arabian Nights* and Sinbad. In 1534, Basra was made part of the OTTOMAN EMPIRE by Sultan Sulayman, who incorporated Iraq into his empire; along with Baghdad and Mosul, Basra was designated one of the vilayets (provinces) of Ottoman Iraq. Although the MAMLUKS ruled Iraq for several centuries, the Ottomans reestablished their authority in 1831, ousting the Mamluks and forcefully subjugating the tribal areas. British companies meanwhile established a sphere of influence, strengthening ties with tribal shaykhs and controlling the import–export market. The strategic position of Basra as a link in the overland route to Asia or the Mediterranean created a competition between the Ottomans, Germans, British, and Indians. The growth of the British and German presence in Basra during the eighteenth century awakened the Ottomans to its importance. They therefore attempted to reestablish their domination over Basra, Kuwait, and the surrounding region.

During World War I, Basra was the first Ottoman city to fall to a British-Indian occupation, on November 23, 1914, and a military governor was appointed. Britain was planning to keep Basra under permanent jurisdiction, perhaps linking it to the Indian administrative unit, but international events worked against this. Although Britain was granted a mandate over Iraq by the League of Nations in 1920, they recognized FAISAL I IBN HUSAYN as king in 1922 and dissolved the mandate in 1932, when Iraq was admitted to the League of Nations.

One of the factors that led to the Iran–Iraq War (1980–1988) was control of the Shatt al-Arab, the major waterway connecting the Gulf with Iraq's port of Basra and Iran's ports of Khorramshahr and Abadan. This had been the very issue between the Ottomans and Persia (now Iran) before World War I. Because of its location, then, Basra became central to the struggle, and the surrounding countryside suffered ecological damage, which was made worse by the destruction wrought by the Coalition forces during the GULF CRISIS of 1991.

BIBLIOGRAPHY

ALTIMIMI, HAMID. *Basra: Under British Occupation, 1914–1921.* London, 1973.

ATIYYAH, GHASSAN. *Iraq, 1908–1921: A Political Study.* Beirut, 1973.

CORDESMAN, ANTHONY H., and ABRAHAM R. WAGNER. *The Lessons of Modern War: The Iran–Iraq War.* London, 1990.

HARRIS, GEORGE L. *Iraq: Its People, Its Society, Its Culture.* New Haven, Conn., 1958.

LONGRIGG, S. H. *Iraq, 1900 to 1950: A Political, Social, and Economic History.* London, 1956.

Nazar al-Khalaf

Basri, Mir [1911–   ]

Iraqi poet and economist.

Basri, born in Baghdad, graduated in 1928 from the Alliance Israélite Universelle. For many years he was director of the Baghdad Chamber of Commerce and, from 1938 to 1945, editor of its journal. In 1948 his first collection of short stories, *Rijal wa-Zilal* (Men and Shadows), appeared in Baghdad. After the EZRA AND NEHEMIA OPERATIONS (1950–1951), he became increasingly active in the Jewish community and was elected as its head (*ra'is al-ta'ifa*) in 1971. Three years later, he left Iraq and settled in London. Since then, he has published *A'lam al-Yahud fi al-Iraq al-Hadith* (1983; History of Iraq: Jewish personalities); a volume of collected poetry *Aghani al-Hubb wa'l-Khulud* (1991; Songs of Love and Eternity); and his autobiography, *Rihlat al-Umr* (1992; English title: *Life Journey from the Banks of the Tigris to the Banks of the Valley of the Thames.*

BIBLIOGRAPHY

SEMAH, DAVID. "Mir Basri wa al-nahdat al-adab al-Iraqi al-hadith." *Al-Karmil* 10 (1989): 83–122.

Sasson Somekh

Bast

Inviolable sanctuaries in Iran used to seek protection from political or religious persecution.

Bast means sanctuary or asylum. Mosques, holy shrines, and foreign embassy compounds have most frequently been used as bast. Although the period of the Constitutional Revolution (1905–1911) is when the most famous bast were taken, instances existed in early Islamic Iran. In April 1905, pro-constitutionalist merchants, bankers, and retailers took bast at the Shah Abd al-Azim shrine in Rayy. The most celebrated bast in Iranian history took place in July 1906, when between twelve and sixteen thousand Tehrani demonstrators took bast at the British legation in Tehran, while about one thousand clergymen left the capital in protest for Qom. The bast at the British compound was instrumental in the granting of a constitution, and the creation of a national assembly by the monarch, Mozaffar al-Din QAJAR. In turn, the anti-constitutionalist cleric, Shaykh Fazlollah NURI, took bast at the Shah Abd al-Azim shrine with some followers for ninety days, to protest the granting of the constitution. At times, the inviolability of bast was breached, when for instance Sayyid Jamal al-Din Asadabadi was expelled from the Shah Abd al-Azim shrine during the reign of NASER AL-DIN SHAH. After the constitutionalist period, the *majles* (national assembly) was also considered a bast. Mohammad Mossadegh took refuge there in 1953.

BIBLIOGRAPHY

ALGAR, HAMID. *Religion and State in Iran, 1785–1906.* Berkeley, Calif., 1980.

BROWNE, E. G. *The Persian Revolution of 1905–9.* Cambridge, U.K., 1910.

Neguin Yavari

Ba'th, al-

A left-wing pan-Arab political party.

The Arab Socialist Renaissance (Ba'th) political party was founded officially in Syria in 1947 by two schoolteachers from Damascus, Michel Aflaq, an Orthodox Christian and Salah al-Din al-BITAR, a Sunni Muslim. A mixture of socialism, freedom from foreign rule, and pan-Arabism (a unified Arab state), the party's secular ideology focuses on radical change of Arab society and the achievement of Arab unity through the mechanism of the party. As each country comes under the rule of a Ba'th regional command, according to the party's plan, all will ultimately unite under the aegis of the Ba'th leadership in a national command. Strictly organized by cell, members can be elected to positions through the hierarchical party organization. Two countries, Syria and Iraq, have nominally Ba'th regimes.

In its early days, the party drew support from leftist secondary school and university students who followed the lectures of the founders. The Ba'th in Syria did not enter politics, preferring to focus attention on social and economic reform rather than political power. Party branches were established in Lebanon, Jordan, and Iraq. Syrian political instability, however, and Arab defeat in the Arab–Israel War of 1948 led to a Ba'thist merger in the early 1950s with the Arab Socialist Party of Akram al-HAWRANI. Membership in the party increased from five hundred to two thousand members. By 1956 as Egypt's president Gamal Abdel NASSER became more avowedly Arab nationalist, the Ba'th decided to work for Syrian–Egyptian unity. Egyptian domination of the UNITED ARAB REPUBLIC (UAR) (1958–1961) and Ba'th agreement to dissolve for the sake of unity, led to a military coup in Syria and the dissolution of the UAR. The Syrian Ba'th and the Hawrani went their separate ways, leaving the party open for new leadership and young recruits, primarily from the army and the ALAWI minority.

In 1963, the Ba'th took control of Syria scarcely a month after a Ba'th-supported coup in Iraq (see below). A National Command was created to direct Ba'th policy across national borders, and regional commands were established in Syria and Iraq. As the military began to dominate the Syrian command, disagreements with the party founders, ideologues Aflaq and Bitar, developed. On February 23, 1966, a neo-Ba'th coup led by Ghassan JADID ousted the Ba'th government of Bitar. The new government, with a strong Alawi base of support, nationalized industry, implemented a land reform program, and supported the Palestinians' struggle against Israel. Jadid aligned himself with the civilians in the party and was challenged for leadership by his minister of defense, Hafiz al-ASAD. Almost retired because of the overwhelming Syrian defeat in the Arab–Israel War of 1967, Asad worked to gain control of the internal security apparatus and forced his rival, Jadid, from power in November, 1970. Asad's support is derived from the Alawi minority in Syria and from family members who hold the key positions in security and the military, educated sons of peasants, minorities, and members of the rural lower class. Party cells have been established in villages, schools, and factories and are incorporated into the divisions, branches, and Regional Command, but party membership is not automatic. The party-controlled press disseminates ideology, and youth movements recruit for membership. By the mid-1980s there were 100,000 full members and 400,000 candidates for party membership.

The Ba'th ideology was brought to Iraq by Iraqi students studying in Syria. Led by a follower of Shi-'ism, the engineer Fu'ad al-Rikabi, the Iraqi Ba'th was designated a regional branch of the party headquartered in Syria. In the early 1960s membership numbered fifty to one hundred organized cells drawn from the army, secondary schools, and the universities. Unlike the Syrian party, the Iraqi Ba'th remained under civilian leadership. When Abd al-Karim KASSEM and the Iraqi Free Officers overthrew the monarchy in 1958, the party initially supported him but in 1959 ordered his assassination, fearing that Kassem was becoming too powerful. Unsuccessful, the leadership, including Saddam HUSSEIN, went into exile to Syria and Egypt, even though by this time the party had already begun to oppose Nasser's rule in the UAR.

In 1963 the Ba'th supported a military coup led by Abd al-Salam ARIF to topple Kassem, but political success was short-lived. A split in the party among the militant pragmatists and the centrists led the centrists to appeal to Damascus for mediation. The result was that, in the confusion, Arif was able to oust the Ba'th from the government.

While out of power, the Iraqi Ba'thists, led by al-Bakr, reorganized, deriving support increasingly from Iraqi Sunnis from the town of Tikrit. At the same time, they maintained their political legitimacy by remaining loyal to Aflaq. By then more politically astute and better organized, the Ba'th organized a coup on July 17, 1968. Having learned their lesson from 1963, al-Bakr and his supporters moved quickly to purge their non-Ba'thist allies and took complete control of the Iraqi government on July 31.

In 1970 the Iraqis proceeded to ensure their complete separation from the Syrian Ba'th. The new Iraqi constitution established a Revolutionary Command Council to operate as the supreme executive, legislative, and judicial institution of the state, completely separate from the Regional Command of the party. In addition, the Iraqis organized their own National Congress, officially splitting with the Syrians to the point where, during the IRAN–IRAQ war, Syria supported non-Arab Iran. Aflaq was retained as secretary-general, albeit with no power, and lived in Baghdad from 1975 until his death in 1989.

Al-Bakr, with Saddam Hussein in control of security, was able to control the government, purging the party of influential military officers. Successful negotiations with the Kurds and an oil-profit-induced boom created jobs, supported literacy programs, and generally improved the economic lot of Iraqis, especially for party members, whose numbers increased substantially throughout the 1970s. By the mid-1980s there were 25,000 full members and 1.5 million candidates for membership, organized in an elaborate hierarchical party structure similar to that of Syria.

Meanwhile, Saddam Hussein systematically removed all his own rivals and accrued enough support to urge al-Bakr to retire in 1979. Since then, as head of the government and of the party, Saddam Hussein has instituted personal authoritarian rule rather than party rule. Relying more and more on family members for important positions, he has repeatedly purged the party and the military but maintains the party structure as a means for retaining power. Saddam Hussein's miscalculations in foreign policy during the Iran–Iraq War and the GULF CRISIS wars and the serious social and economic dislocations that have followed have resulted in the elimination of economic gains for Iraqis, except for a small coterie of loyalists. Like Syria, Iraq under Ba'th rule has not developed politically through the party, but rather the party has been used to create dictatorial regimes for both Hafiz al-Asad and Saddam Hussein.

BIBLIOGRAPHY

BARAM, AMATZIA. *Culture, History and Ideology in the Formation of Ba'thist Iraq, 1968–89*. New York, 1991.
HINNEBUSCH, RAYMOND A. *Power and State Formation in Ba'thist Syria*. Boulder, Colo., 1990.
FAROUK-SLUGLETT, MARION, and PETER SLUGLETT. *Iraq Since 1958*. London, 1990.

Reeva S. Simon

Battle of

See under the place of battle

Bayar, Celal   [1884–1986]

Turkish politician and statesman; Turkey's third president.

Bayar was born in Umurbey, near Bursa, the son of a village teacher. Educated at the French school in Bursa, he worked as a clerk in a German bank there and rose rapidly in banking circles. In 1907, he joined the Union and Progress Society and became an important official in Bursa and Izmir; he was elected deputy for Saruhan (Manisa) in the last parliament of the Ottoman Empire. He was an active political leader during Turkey's war of independence, a member for Saruhan in the TURKISH GRAND NATIONAL ASSEMBLY when it was first organized by Mustafa Kemal (ATATÜRK) in 1920; later he represented Izmir in all the republic's assemblies until 1960.

In 1920, he was made minister of economics. He was also founder and longtime head of the Türkiye İş Bankası (Turkish Labor Bank), and, by 1932, his vigorous advocacy of etatism (state economic enterprise) led to his being regarded as the leading promoter of state factories. He continued as minister of economics during much of the 1920s and 1930s. In 1937, Atatürk appointed him to replace İsmet İNÖNÜ as prime minister, continuing a bitter rivalry between the two men. His tenure in office lasted until shortly after Atatürk's death and İnönü's succession as president in 1938.

Until 1946, Turkey had a one-party political system under the aegis of the REPUBLICAN PEOPLE'S PARTY (RPP); in that year Bayar became one of four RPP deputies who initiated Turkey's multiparty period by forming the opposition DEMOCRAT PARTY (DP). After only moderate success in the 1946 election, the Democrats came to power in 1950, and Bayar was elected the republic's third president. He presided over a decade that saw modifications to (but not basic reversal of) several of Atatürk's policies—which included the RPP's strong attitude of hostility toward the private sector and a relaxation of some aspects of secularism. In foreign affairs, Bayar and his associates continued a strong identification with the West, particularly the United States.

Convergence of several favorable factors enabled the Democrats to preside over a period of rapid economic growth, which together with more conservative social policies resulted in their electoral victory in 1954. Fear that the party's popularity would not continue, plus their intense dislike of the RPP and its leader İnönü, led to increasingly repressive measures. These included actions against the opposition party and the press, the partisan use of state funds, and eventually to accusations of serious election fraud in 1957, when they were returned to office but with a much reduced margin. In 1959, university students and others began violent demonstrations that led to the ouster of the DP government by the armed forces on May 27, 1960. Many Democrat officials, including all the party's assembly members, were arrested and brought to trial on the island of Yassiada, near Istanbul, on a long list of political and criminal charges. Bayar was one of four defendants sentenced

to death, but he was spared due to his advanced age. He went to prison and was released in 1973. He was constitutionally barred from returning to active politics and so confined himself to occasional statements until his death at the age of 102.

BIBLIOGRAPHY

KARPAT, KEMAL. *Turkey's Politics*. Princeton, N.J., 1959.
WEIKER, WALTER F. *The Turkish Revolution 1960–1961*. Brookings, S. Dak., 1963.

Walter F. Weiker

Bayat, Mortaza Qoli   [1886–1958]

Iranian statesman.

He was the son of a wealthy landowner of Arak, a constitutionalist during the Revolution of 1906, and a member of the E'tedali (moderate) party. He was elected to the *majlis* (national assembly) in 1922 and was reelected nine times. In 1925, the fifth *majles* deposed the QAJAR DYNASTY, voting in the Pahlavi dynasty, with Reza Shah PAHLAVI as monarch, and Bayat became minister of finance, then prime minister in 1945. He resigned in six months because he had to deal with the removal of Allied forces, especially the Soviets, who were entrenched in AZERBAIJAN. He also had to deal with the all-powerful Anglo-Iranian Oil Company and Soviet demands for oil concessions in the north.

In 1950, Bayat was elected senator and vice-president of the senate; after the nationalization of the PETROLEUM industry by Dr. Mohammad MOSSADEGH, Bayat (who was related to him) was appointed head of the new Iranian oil company. From 1955 to 1958, he headed the newly formed oil consortium.

BIBLIOGRAPHY

BAMDAD, M. *Sarh-e hal-e rejal-e Iran, dar qarn-e 12, 13, va 14, hejri* (Biographies of Iranian Notables in the 12th, 13th, and 14th Centuries A.H.), 4 vols. Tehran, 1979.

Mansoureh Ettehadieh

Bayati, Abd al-Wahhab al-   [1926–   ]

A leading Iraqi and Arab poet from the late 1940s to the mid-1970s, who broke with traditional patterns of modern Arab poetry.

Born in Baghdad to a merchant family of the largely Sunni Arab Bayat tribe north of Baghdad, al-Bayati graduated in 1950 from the Higher Teachers' College and taught the Arabic language in Ramadi, western Iraq. In 1953, he returned to Baghdad, where he taught and edited a communist intellectual magazine *al-Thaqafa al-Jadida* (though he always claimed that he was an independent Marxist and never joined the party). Due to this political affiliation, in 1954 he lost his teaching job and in 1955 had to go to Syria, then to Egypt. Following the "Free Officers" coup d'état of 1958, Bayati returned to Baghdad to become one of the leading intellectuals in the regime of Abd al-Karim KASSEM. But in 1959, following an estrangement between Kassem and the Communists, he was sent as a cultural adviser to Moscow. In 1964, he moved to Egypt, and in 1972 he returned to Baghdad, where BA'TH party officials made him cultural adviser for the ministry of information. A few years later, he was sent as a cultural attaché to Madrid, where he served in this capacity in the early 1990s.

His first DIWAN, *Mala'ika wa Shayatin* (1950), was written in a conventional romantic style. Following the example of two other Iraqi poets, Badr Shakir al-SAYYAB and Nazik al-MALA'IKA, in 1954 Bayati adopted the new style of free verse (*al-Shi'r al-Hurr*), in which the length of the line and the rhyming flow freely. Until the late 1970s, his poetry reflected most of the innovations that appeared in Arab poetry. Again, following al-Sayyab, since the mid-1960s his poetry is heavily loaded with surrealistic symbolism. Dominant among the various mythological symbols used were those borrowed from ancient Mesopotamia, chiefly Tammuz and Ishtar. Since the mid-1970s, the main tools in his poetry have been Sufi mystical motifs. In much of it, al-Bayati expresses the frustration and alienation of a secular revolutionary intellectual in a traditional society—a humanistic socialist under totalitarian revolutionary regimes that betrayed their human ideals.

BIBLIOGRAPHY

BARAM, AMATZIA. "Culture in the Service of Wataniyya: The Treatment of Mesopotamian-Inspired Art in Ba'thi Iraq." *Asian and African Studies* 17 (1983): 277–287.
MOREH, SHMUEL. *Modern Arabic Poetry, 1800–1970.* Leiden, 1976.

Amatzia Baram

Bayburtlu, Zihni [1797–1859]

Ottoman Turkish poet.

The son of a religious scholar, Zihni Bayburtlu was born in Bayburt and educated in Trabzon and Erzurum. At the age of twenty, he moved to Istanbul and entered the civil service. He composed poetry in the diwan genre, but he is better known for his folk poetry, composed in syllabic meter. His son published his diwan in 1876.

BIBLIOGRAPHY

ÖZKIRIMLI, ATILLA. *Türk Edebiyatı Ansiklopedisi,* vol. 10. Istanbul, 1982.
Yeni Türk Ansiklopedisi, vol. 1. Istanbul, 1985.

David Waldner

Baydani, Abd al-Rahman

Economist in Yemen Arab Republic.

Egyptian born and raised, Baydani had the ear of the regime of Gamal Abdel Nasser at the time of the 1962 revolution in the Yemen Arab Republic. For this reason, he immediately became Egypt's man in Yemen and gained appointment as deputy prime minister for economic affairs in the new republican government. An outsider in SAN'A, without a Yemeni power base, he soon fell victim to the parochial complexities of Yemeni politics and was dismissed.

Robert D. Burrowes

Baydh, Ali Salim al-

South Yemen revolutionary and republican leader.

An early participant in the struggle against the British and local "feudalists" in South Yemen, al-Baydh (also al-Bid) survived intraparty struggles and rose from the second rank of party leaders and ministers to become head of the ruling YEMENI SOCIALIST PARTY after the intraparty blood bath in ADEN in January 1986. By the late 1980s, al-Baydh had emerged as the most influential member of the new collective leadership. He led the PEOPLE'S DEMOCRATIC REPUBLIC OF YEMEN (PDRY) into merger with the YEMEN ARAB REPUBLIC (YAR) in May 1990, at which time he became vice president of the new Republic of Yemen. Al-Baydh declared the secession of South Yemen from the Republic of Yemen in mid-1994 and fled into exile when his forces were defeated in the short civil war that ended in July of that year. His family was from the Hadramawt, but originally of Yafi tribal origins.

Robert D. Burrowes

Bayrakdar, Mustafa   [1775–1808]

Ottoman grand vizier.

The son of a Janissary, Bayrakdar was a notable of Ruschuk (or Ruse) in Bulgaria who served as a lieutenant in Tirsinikioğlu Ismail Ağa's large provincial army. He inherited command of the army in 1806 and used it in 1807 to restore order in Constantinople (now Istanbul) after the JANISSARIES deposed SELIM III. But Bayrakdar was denied power in the new regime, and in 1808, in concert with the secret Ruschuk committee of Selim supporters, he and his army replaced the conservative new sultan MUSTAFA IV, with the reform-minded MAHMUD II.

As Mahmud II's first grand vizier, Bayrakdar used his military standing to defy opposition and resume reform efforts. He invited all important local notables to Constantinople to negotiate new relations between the sultan and provinces, producing the October 1808 Sened-i Ittifak (Pact of Alliance). But the following month, Bayrakdar's planned military reforms produced another Janissary revolt, during which he was killed. Bayrakdar's defeat postponed military reform for nearly twenty years.

BIBLIOGRAPHY

LEWIS, BARNARD. *The Emergence of Modern Turkey.* New York, 1961.

SHAW, STANFORD J. *History of the Ottoman Empire and Modern Turkey,* vol. 1. Cambridge, U.K., 1976.

SHAW, STANFORD J., and EZEL KURAL SHAW. *History of the Ottoman Empire and Modern Turkey,* vol. 2. New York, 1977.

Elizabeth Thompson

Bayram V, Muhammad   [1840–1889]

Tunisian reformer, writer, administrator, and newspaper editor.

Muhammad Bayram V was born into an illustrious family of *ulama* in Tunis. His paternal uncle Muhammad Bayram III was *bash mufti* (chief jurisconsult) at the time of his birth. His mother was the daughter of Mahmud Khujah, a MAMLUK official of AHMAD BEY; his father, Mustafa, was a farmer. His earliest recollections were of his father's laborers complaining of their situation. This, coupled with his maternal grandfather's political involvement, led him to consider a career in politics.

Upon completion of his studies at Zaytuna University, Bayram became a teacher of religion in a secondary school. When his uncle Bayram IV died in 1861, Bayram V was too young to succeed him as SHAYKH AL-ISLAM. (Apparently the designation "V" stemmed from the near assumption of this important religious office.)

The death of his uncle enabled Bayram V to establish a closer relationship with political reformers among the mamluk class, especially KHAYR AL-DIN al-Tunisi. When Khayr al-Din became prime minister in 1873, he appointed Bayram V editor of the official gazette, *Al-Ra'id al-Tunisi,* and head of the Hubus (WAQF) Administration to regulate religious trusts. The *hubus* constituted an important economic base for the *ulama.* Bayram V regularized the *hubus,* eliminating corruption, improving efficiency, and maintaining accurate records of transactions. Bayram V also directed the state printing office, organized the new library at Zaytuna University, and regulated the curriculum at SADIQI COLLEGE.

After his ministry collapsed in 1877, Khayr al-Din left the country under a cloud of suspicion and failure. Bayram remained in government service until 1879. During these years, Bayram may have conspired with Khayr al-Din, who had become Ottoman prime minister, to seek French assistance in deposing MUHAMMAD AL-SADIQ Bey, ruler of Tunisia.

Bayram was allowed to go to Mecca in October 1879. He never returned to Tunisia but went to Constantinople for four years (where he reconciled with Khayr al-Din) and then to Egypt in 1884, where he spent the rest of his life. While in Egypt, Bayram launched an Arabic-language newspaper, *Al-I'lam* (The Clarion), which became the most widely read and most influential Arabic newspaper of the 1880s. He also published a history of nineteenth-century Tunisia. He died 18 December 1889.

BIBLIOGRAPHY

ABDESSELEM, AHMED. *Les historiens tunisiens des XVIIe, XVIIIe et XIXe siècles: Essai d'histoire culturelle.* Paris, 1973.

BARRIE, LARRY A. "A Family Odyssey: The Bayrams of Tunis, 1756–1861." Ph.D. diss., Boston University, 1987.

BAYRAM V, MUHAMMAD. *Kitab Safwat al-i'tibar bi-mustawda al-amsar wa al-aqtar* (The Book of the Best Contemplation of the Repository of Cities and Regions), 5 vols. plus appendix. Cairo, 1884–1893.

GREEN, ARNOLD H. *The Tunisian Ulama, 1873–1915.* Leiden, 1978.

PERKINS, KENNETH J. *Historical Dictionary of Tunisia.* Metuchen, N.J., 1989.

TLILI, BECHIR. "L'idée d'un bon gouvernement ottoman dans la pensée de Bayram V (1840–1889)." *Les Cahiers de Tunisie* 20, nos. 79–80 (1972): 147–170.

Larry A. Barrie

Baysan

See Bet She'an

Bazaars and Bazaar Merchants

*The bazaar has long been the central marketplace
and crafts center of Iranian cities, and, together with
the mosque, it has been the principle arena for
extrafamilial sociability.*

In spite of Iran's rapid modernization in the second
half of the twentieth century, the bazaar has shown
remarkable economic resiliency and growth. It has
served, in addition, as the financial and political
power base of the Islamic religious establishment of
SHI'ISM and a bastion of nearly all popular political
protest movements, including the TOBACCO REVOLT
of 1890/91, the Constitutional Revolution of 1905–
1911, the oil nationalization movement of 1950–
1953, the urban riots of 1963, and the Islamic
IRANIAN REVOLUTION of 1977–1979.

The social hierarchy of the bazaar includes the big
merchants (*tujjar*) at the top of the pyramid; the master artisans and shopkeepers, loosely organized within
well over 100 guildlike associations (*asnaf*), at the
middle level; and apprentices and footboys, as well as
such marginal elements as poor peddlers, dervishes,
and beggars, at the lowest levels.

Functionally, three major types of bazaars have
developed in modern Iran; (1) the unique bazaar of
Tehran, functioning as a strategic center for local,
national, and international trade; (2) the provincial
bazaars engaged in wholesale and retail trade for the
central city and its hinterland; and (3) the local bazaars of small towns and large villages, in which re-

Bazaar street at Djerba. (Mia Bloom)

tailers and peasant peddlers serve primarily the town
and surrounding rural areas. The more significant
provincial bazaars also played an important role in
foreign trade. The bazaars of Isfahan, Kerman, Kermanshah, Mashhad, Shiraz, Tabriz, and Yazd were
included in this category until the mid-twentieth
century. The bazaar of Tehran, however, monopolized most of the foreign trade in the latter half of the
twentieth century and became the main center of
import, export, collection, and distribution of agricultural cash crops, modern manufactured consumer
items, and Iran's most important handicraft product,
Persian CARPETS.

The socioeconomic and morphological changes in
urban Iran since the 1960s have reduced the traditional function of the bazaar as the sole urban marketplace, supplementing it with many new shopping
centers in various parts of the city rather than replacing the bazaar's shops. In Tehran, for example, the

Bazaar shop at Tunis. (Mia Bloom)

*Small domes over the center of a covered bazaar in
Istanbul.* (Richard Bulliet)

bazaar underwent a rapid spatial expansion as its surrounding residential areas were increasingly used for commercial and small-scale manufacturing establishments. The southern sections of the bazaar became a shopping area for the lower-middle classes, the urban poor, and rural families, whereas its northern sections catered primarily to middle-class clients. As a result, in most cases, the shops' "key money" increased several times in the late 1970s, reaching as high as several hundred thousand dollars in the case of some well-located shops.

Iran's bazaars survived the blow of modernization and urbanization for two main reasons: (1) the rate of industrialization did not keep pace with the rapid growth of the urban population and urbanization, leading to the rapid expansion of the service sector, in general, and of middle-man trade activities in particular; (2) having been already established as the main locus for social, religious, and economic activities, many bazaars continued to grow with their surrounding urban centers. In Tehran, for example, the number of master artisans and shopkeepers—both within and outside of the bazaar's boundaries—increased from approximately 12,000 in 1928 to about 250,000 in 1976, as the city's population rose from 250,000 to 4.5 million over the same period.

Modernization and urban development created a socioeconomic and cultural duality in large urban areas of Iran, particularly in Tehran. This duality consists, on the one hand, of the religiously conservative merchants, master artisans, and shopkeepers who exhibit traditional urban lifestyles, living mainly around the bazaar and the old quarters of the town, and, on the other, the elites and the new middle classes living in the more modern city quarters. The traditional *bazaari* lifestyle, shared with the ULAMA, includes such elements as sitting, eating, and sleeping on rugs or *gelims,* participating in prayer congregations in mosques, taking part in or organizing Shi'ite rituals of mourning for the martyrdom of Imam Husain, and the veiling of women.

The bazaar's relationships with the state under the shah, Mohammad Reza PAHLAVI (ruled 1941–1979), were fraught with tensions and conflicts. Given the considerable material gains that the bazaaris made in the 1960 and 1970s, the threats to the bazaaris were, more often than not, in the forms of various state interventions in commercial activities and the regime's repressive policies toward them rather than the expansion of the new shopping areas. The government's arbitrary and discriminatory implementation of commercial regulations, tax laws, and a campaign against price-gouging were the major sources of the bazaaris' hostility toward the state. Another aggravating factor was the shah's and elite's thinly disguised contempt for the "fanatic bazaaris . . . [who] were highly resistant to change" (Pahlavi, *Answer to History,* New York, 1980, p. 156). Bazaaris, along with the *ulama* and the young intelligentsia, constituted a major faction in the triangle of the revolutionary coalition of 1977–1979. Many of the strategies and tactics for revolutionary mobilization were planned and carried out by the younger generation of bazaaris under the leadership of a small group of militant *ulama.* Furthermore, the bazaaris made a substantial financial contribution to the revolution. As "ordinary," pre-existing structures, the bazaar and the mosque have served as an arena for mobilizing "extraordinary" actions of collective protests and revolts. In the absence of labor unions, political parities, professional societies, and neighborhood associations, the bazaar-mosque alliance has proved to be the main vehicle for social protest.

The postrevolutionary period of the 1980s witnessed a bitter struggle of the rising radical, leftist elements within the new Islamic regime, on the one side, and the merchants and artisans' guilds and their old allies, the conservative *ulama,* on the other, over such critical policies as nationalization of foreign trade, anti-price-gouging measures, and state control over guild councils. By early 1990, with the normalization of the revolutionary situation, the government adopted a more moderate treatment of the bazaar merchants and artisans. However, arbitrary interventions of the state agencies in guild affairs and in selection of guild leaders since the early 1990s has, once again, led to alienation of many bazaar merchants and artisans from their own organizations.

BIBLIOGRAPHY

ASHRAF, AHMAD. "Bazaar-Mosque Alliance: The Social Basis of Revolts and Revolutions." *Politics, Culture, and Society* 1 (1988): 538–67.
"Asnaf." In *Encyclopaedia Iranica,* vol. 2. 1987.
"Bazar." In *Encyclopaedia Iranica,* vol. 4. 1989.
BONINE, MICHAEL. "Shops and Shopkeepers: Dynamics of an Iranian Provincial Bazaar." In *Modern Iran, the Dialectics of Continuity and Change,* ed. by Michael Bonine and Nikkie Keddie. Albany, N.Y., 1981.
SCHWEIZER, GÜNTHER. "Tabriz (Nordwest-Iran) und der Tabrizer Bazaar." *Erkunde* 16 (1972): 32–46.
SEGER, MARTIN. *Tehran, eine stadtgeographische Studie.* Vienna, 1978.
THAISS, GUSTAV. "The Bazaar as a Case Study of Religion and Social Change." In *Iran Faces the Seventies,* ed. by Ehsan Yarshater. New York, 1971.

Ahmad Ashraf

Bazargan, Mahdi [1906–]

Muslim intellectual and politician in Iran.

Mahdi Bazargan was born in Tehran. In 1931, he went to Paris to study engineering. Returning home in 1936, he taught at the college level. During the 1951 oil-nationalization movement, Bazargan worked with Prime Minister Mohammad Mossadegh and served as the director of the National Iranian Oil Company. After Mossadegh was deposed by the 1953 coup, Bazargan resumed teaching.

In the early 1960s, with the help of Ayatollah Mahmud Taleqani, Bazargan founded the Freedom Movement (Nahzat-i Azadi), which played an important role in the IRANIAN REVOLUTION of 1977–1979. After the revolution, Bazargan became the premier of the provisional government. With its fall, Bazargan lost much of his political influence but was elected, with a huge margin, as Tehran's representative to the parliament of the new Islamic Republic of Iran in the 1980 election. Throughout his career, Bazargan has been a leading advocate of democracy. He also has been a prolific writer, publishing more than twenty books and articles.

BIBLIOGRAPHY

ABRAHAMIAN, ERVAND. *Iran between Two Revolutions.* Princeton, N.J., 1982.

Mansoor Moaddel

Bazzaz, Abd al Rahman al– [1913–1971]

Iraqi jurist, politician, and writer.

Al-Bazzaz was born in Baghdad to a Sunni Muslim family. He completed elementary school and high school in Baghdad and graduated from Baghdad Law College in 1934. He completed his law studies in 1938 at King's College of London University. As a young man he was active politically. In the 1930s, he was a member of the Muthanna and Jawwal clubs, the intellectual focus of which was Pan-Arabism and promotion of Arab nationalism. In 1941 he supported the Rashid Ali uprising against the British. After the uprising's collapse and with the second British occupation of Iraq, he was interned during World War II. Shortly after the war ended, he was released from jail and appointed dean of the Baghdad Law College. In 1956 he was removed from his post for protesting the aggression against Egypt by England, France, and Israel. He and several educators signed a petition critical of Iraq's government's stand during the Suez crisis. He returned to his job as dean

of the law college in the aftermath of the July 14 Revolution.

Bazzaz's interest and activities in the Pan-Arab movement again put him in conflict with the new government of Abd al-Karim KASSEM. After the collapse of the Shawwaf uprising in 1959, he was arrested and tortured. Upon his release, he went to Egypt, where he assumed the deanship of the Institute of Arab Studies at the Arab League. He returned to Iraq after the military overthrow of the Kassem regime in 1963. This coup marked a turning point in al-Bazzaz's political career. President Abd al-Salam ARIF, a close friend, assigned al-Bazzaz to several government positions. He was appointed ambassador to the UNITED ARAB REPUBLIC, and later to England. In 1964–65, he became the secretary-general of the ORGANIZATION OF PETROLEUM EXPORTING COUNTRIES. On September 6, 1965, he was named deputy prime minister. The prime minister then tried to unseat the president and seize power. The coup failed, however, and President Arif invited Bazzaz to form a new government on September 21, 1965. Al-Bazzaz was the first civilian prime minister since the collapse of the monarchy in 1958.

President Arif died unexpectedly on April 13, 1965, in a helicopter crash. A brief power struggle for the presidency ensued. In the first joint meeting of the Defense Council and cabinet to elect a president, al-Bazzaz held a plurality of one vote over the two military candidates. However, he needed a two-thirds majority to win the presidency. A compromise candidate, Abd al-Rahman ARIF, the brother of the late president, was chosen instead. The new president asked al-Bazzaz to form a new cabinet on April 18, 1966. However, Bazzaz was forced to resign on August 6 under pressure from various political groups. Chief among them was the group of politically minded senior officers who took for granted their right to govern the country. These officers resented al-Bazzaz's outspokenness concerning the proper role of the army and his intentions to reduce military salaries and privileges.

Furthermore, the officers opposed his attempts to solve the Kurdish problem peacefully. The leftist groups, including the Communists, denounced al-Bazzaz as an agent of the imperialists. The supporters of President Gamal Abdel NASSER of Egypt and Ba'thists accused him of being an enemy of Arab socialism and paying only lip service to the proposed union of Egypt and Iraq. On January 24, 1969, he was accused by the newly established Ba'thist government of involvement in clandestine activities against the government. He was tortured and imprisoned for fifteen months. In 1970, he was released because of illness and went to London for treatment, dying there in 1971.

Several features distinguished al-Bazzaz's eleven months as prime minister. First, he strongly advocated the rule of law and an end to the erratic behavior of military officers who had dominated Iraq's politics since the Revolution of July 14, 1958. His government became increasingly civilianized. He replaced the Revolutionary Military Council with the National Defense Council and limited its function in regard to defense and internal security. The political system was open compared with previous regimes. As prime minister, al-Bazzaz held numerous news conferences and appeared on radio and television. Constructive criticism was encouraged, and he promised to restore parliamentary life and hold elections as soon as possible.

Second, in the field of economy, al-Bazzaz announced the First Five Year Plan (1965–1970). He advocated "prudent socialism," which attempted to strike a balance between the public and private sectors. He encouraged joint ventures between public and private sectors as well as between foreign and domestic investors. The doctrine of prudent socialism sought to increase production without abandoning the principle of equitable distribution. It was designed to lessen the impact of nationalization measures issued by the previous government.

A third distinguishing feature of al-Bazzaz's administration was the announcement of the twelve-point agreement in June 1966. Its purpose was to solve the Kurdish problem, the most unsettling difficulty of Iraq's government since 1960. The pact provided statutory recognition of the Kurdish nationality; recognized Kurdish as an official language, along with Arabic, in schools and local administration; and permitted the employment of KURDS in local administrative posts. The plan promised to hold a parliamentary election within the period stipulated in the provisional constitution of 1964. It provided for proportional representation of the Kurds in all branches of the government, including the cabinet, the Parliament, and the judiciary. It gave the Kurds the right to publish their own newspapers and to organize their own political parties. The plan provided general amnesty to all persons who had taken part in the Kurdish revolt and restored them to their previous posts and positions. It created a special Ministry for Rehabilitation and Reparation to pay damages incurred in Kurdish territory. It also endeavored to compensate Kurdish victims in northern Iraq. Unfortunately, al-Bazzaz was forced to resign in August 1966, and the agreement was never enacted.

In foreign policy, al-Bazzaz emphasized that Iraq needed to maintain a friendly relationship with its neighbors, including the non-Arab countries of Turkey and Iran. He visited both in order to improve relations, which had deteriorated since the 1958 revolution. As for the union with Egypt, he adhered to the pronouncement concerning the Iraqi–UAR Unified Political Command of May 25, 1965. However, he did little to advance the union because of Iraq's internal affairs, including the Kurdish problem.

Al-Bazzaz was a prolific writer. He published more than twelve books on subjects including law, Iraq's history, Arab nationalism, and Islam. In his writings, he saw no apparent contradiction between Arab nationalism and Islam. Arab nationalism was not a movement based on race or solidarity of the blood. Rather, it was based on ties of language, history, spirituality, and basic interests in life. In addition to religious belief, Islam was viewed as a social system, a philosophy of life, a system of economics and of government. It belonged to the Arabs before becoming a world religion. The Prophet was an Arab. The language of the Qur'an is Arabic, and many of the Islamic rules and customs are Arabic. For example, the pilgrimage to the KAʿBA was an ancient Arab custom before its incorporation into Islamic tradition.

BIBLIOGRAPHY

AL-BAZZAZ, ABD AL-RAHMAN. On Arab Nationalism. London, 1965.
KHADDURI, MAJID. Republican Iraq: A Study in Iraqi Politics since the Revolution of 1958. London, 1969.
PENROSE, EDITH, and E. F. PENROSE. Iraq: International Relations and National Development. London, 1978.

                                        Ayad al-Qazzaz

Beaufort, Charles-Marie-Napoléon d'Hautpoul de   [1804–1890]

Commander of the French expeditionary force to Lebanon, 1860–1861.

Because of General Beaufort's past service in Syria, Italy, Algeria, and Morocco, Napoleon III sent him with seven thousand men to stymie the massacre of the Christians in Mount LEBANON. Chanting "Partant pour la Syrie," they disembarked late, but their presence reassured the Christian population and foreshadowed the return of the French at the end of World War I. The expedition drew a geographic survey that later inspired proto–Lebanese nationalists in their quest for an enlarged and independent state.

BIBLIOGRAPHY

LAMMENS, HENRI. *La Syrie: Précis historique,* 2 vols. Beirut, 1921.

Bassam Namani

Beaufort Castle

A castle in what is now southern Lebanon.

Also known as Belfort Castle or Qal'a al-Shaqif, Beaufort Castle was built by the Templars, an order of crusading knights, in the twelfth century. The castle served as a point of support from which to attack Arab caravans to and from Egypt. It belonged to the lords of Sidon, until it fell to Saladin. It was in Muslim hands from 1190 until 1240,

Beaufort Castle and the Litani River Valley. (D.W. Lockhard)

when it was recovered by treaty; in 1260 it was sold to the Templars. In 1271 the Egyptian Mamluk sultan Baybars laid siege to the castle; the emblem of the conquerors, a carved lion, has been found among the ruins.

Recently, the castle was used as a base of operations by the Palestine Liberation Organization during the Arab–Israel War of 1982. Beaufort Castle was captured by the Golani Brigade in the battle for Tyre.

BIBLIOGRAPHY

KENNEDY, HUGH. *Crusader Castles.* Cambridge, U. K., 1994.
KHALIDI, RASHID. *Under Siege: PLO Decision Making during the 1982 War.* New York, 1986.

Mia Bloom

Bechtel Company

Large construction company based in the U.S. that built oil refineries and pipelines in the Middle East.

One of the largest construction, engineering, and contracting companies in the world, the firm was founded in 1925 as the W. A. Bechtel Company, by Stephen Bechtel in San Francisco, California. Bechtel was responsible for such U.S. projects as the Hoover Dam and the San Francisco Bay Bridge.

In the Middle East, Bechtel built oil refineries and pipelines in Iraq, Kuwait, Algeria, the United Arab Emirates, Bahrain, and most of all, Saudi Arabia. In the 1970s and 1980s, Bechtel was contracted by the Saudi royal family to oversee the construction of two cities, al-Jubayl near the Persian/Arabian Gulf and Yanbu on the Red Sea. These vast projects were capitalized at more than 20 billion U.S. dollars.

Bechtel influence has also been felt on U.S. foreign policy. Two of President Ronald Reagan's most powerful cabinet members—Secretary of State George Schultz and Secretary of Defense Caspar Weinberger—were former Bechtel executives.

BIBLIOGRAPHY

LENCZOWSKI, GEORGE. *The Middle East in World Affairs,* 4th ed. Ithaca, N.Y., 1980.
SPIEGEL, STEVEN. *The Other Arab–Israeli Conflict.* Chicago, 1985.

Zachary Karabell

Bedel-i Askeri

Tax paid by non-Muslims for exemption from Ottoman military service.

The *bedel-i askeri* essentially replaced the JIZYA (head tax) traditionally paid by non-Muslims, which was abolished with the 1856 HATT-I HÜMAYUN declaration that all subjects of the Ottoman Empire were equal and therefore obligated to serve in the military. The attempt to legislate equality among Muslims and non-Muslims, however, met opposition from all sides. In 1857, non-Muslims were once again allowed exemption from military duty. The bedel-i askeri tax of fifty liras was levied only on those theoretically required to serve, 1 out of 180 male subjects of age. It was much lower than the exemption tax paid by Muslims. In 1909 the bedel-i askeri and all other conscription-exemption taxes were abolished, and all male subjects regardless of religion were required to perform military duty.

BIBLIOGRAPHY

DAVISON, RODERIC H. *Reform in the Ottoman Empire 1856-1876.* Princeton, N.J., 1963.

Encyclopedia of Islam, vol. 1. London, 1960.

SHAW, STANFORD J., and EZEL KURAL SHAW. *History of the Ottoman Empire and Modern Turkey,* vol. 2. New York, 1977.

Elizabeth Thompson

Bedouin

See Nomadism

Beersheba

City in southern Israel.

Located in the northern NEGEV (Arabic, Naqab) desert, Beersheba (Hebrew, B'er Sheva; Arabic, Bir Sabi) is midway between the Dead Sea to the east and the Mediterranean to the west. It is one of the biggest cities in Israel, after the metropolitan centers of Tel Aviv-Jaffa, Jerusalem, and Haifa. Its principal industries are chemicals, porcelain, and textiles. Beersheba is the home of Ben-Gurion University of the Negev and the Negev Institute for Arid Zone Research.

Historically, the city has been an important trading center between a variety of ecological zones— the mountains to the east, the desert to the south, and the seacoast to the west. In biblical times, it marked the southern limit of Palestine. In 1901, the Ottoman Empire made Beersheba the administrative center for the bedouin tribes of the Negev. In 1917, it was the site of a British victory over the Turks that opened the way for the Allied conquest of Palestine and Syria. After Israel became a state in 1948, Beersheba was settled and enlarged by new immigrants. The population estimate as of 1990 is about 115,000.

BIBLIOGRAPHY

PATAI, RAPHAEL, ed. *Encyclopedia of Zionism and Israel.* New York, 1971.

SAYIGH, ANIS, ed. *Al-mawsu'a al-filastiniyyah.* Damascus, 1984.

Steve Tamari

Beg

See Bey

Begin, Menachem   [1913–1992]

Leading Israeli statesman and sixth prime minister of Israel, 1977–1983.

Menachem Begin was a leader of the nationalist HERUT PARTY and the LIKUD, and, from 1944 to 1948, he was commander of the IRGUN ZVA'I LE'UMI (IZL), an armed unit of militant Revisionists. Born and educated in Brest Litovsk and a student of law at Warsaw University, he joined the youth Zionist movement Betar in 1929 and was a leading activist in it from 1931 onward. In 1938, as a result of internal tensions in the movement, he was elected, as a compromise candidate, to the position of commissioner of Betar in Poland, the largest and most important branch of Betar. Although he belonged to the activist circles of Betar, he was not at this time a member of an IZL cell.

After the Germans invaded Poland, Begin escaped to briefly independent Vilna, and following its conquest by the Soviet army, in September 1940, he was arrested and sentenced to eight years of hard labor in the Arctic region. Since he was a Polish citizen, he was released; he then joined General Anders's Free Polish Army at the end of 1941 and came to Palestine with it in 1942. At the end of 1942, he was formally released from the Polish army and only then agreed to command the IZL, an appointment he was given in the hopes that he would unite its ranks and give it a political orientation. On February 1, 1944, Begin declared the opening of a revolt ("armed warfare," as he called it) against the British mandate and the policy of the white paper setting limits to Jewish immigration. This campaign turned into a four-year underground struggle against British rule in Palestine, designed to bring about the immediate withdrawal of the British and the declaration of a Jewish state in the entire territory of western Palestine. From the various flats in which he hid, Begin conducted the clandestine military and political operations as well as the propaganda of the underground organization. He was thus able to keep the IZL organized and active in spite of the severe blows it suffered during the so-called "open season" declared on it by the Haganah, the official Yishuv army. Begin strongly objected to the IZL taking any retaliatory actions.

At the end of 1945, Begin led the IZL when it joined forces with the Haganah and with Lehi (a dissident group more extreme than IZL), to form the Hebrew Resistance Movement. He firmly believed that the decision in 1947 by the British to evacuate Palestine was directly related to the impact of the IZL operations. Begin was on board the ALTALENA, which IZL had obtained for shipping arms and men, when it was shelled in June 1948 in skirmishes with the Israel Defense Forces; Begin claimed that the attack on the ship was also aimed at killing him. In 1948, he founded the Herut Party, which replaced the veteran Revisionist party. He became its virtually undisputed leader, despite attempts to challenge him throughout almost thirty years during which he continued his futile opposition to the governing labor party and suffered a succession of defeats in election campaigns. He bitterly opposed the popular Prime Minister Ben-Gurion and the dominant MAPAI party and led the protest in 1952 against the reparations agreement that Ben-Gurion concluded with West Germany.

From 1965 onward, Begin was active in attempts to wrest Herut from its isolation, first by establishing in 1965 through a merger of Herut and the Liberals the Gahal faction in the Knesset and later, in 1973, by establishing the Likud party. In May 1967, he was named minister without portfolio in the National Unity government, set up after neither the Labor party nor the Likud party could achieve a majority. He left the post in 1970 along with his Gahal colleagues to protest the government's acceptance of the United Nations Security Council framework for regional peace, Resolution 242, and the Rogers Plan for a cease-fire between Israel and its Arab neighbors.

Because of the political turnabout in the elections for the Ninth Knesset, in which the Likud won one-third of the seats, Begin became the head of the first right wing–Liberal coalition in 1977, and in May 1981 he won the elections for a second time, by a large majority of forty-eight seats for the Likud, twenty-six of them for Herut members.

Almost immediately after setting up his government on June 20 (in which Moshe DAYAN was foreign minister and Ezer WEIZMAN minister of defense), Begin initiated secret negotiations with Egypt, which culminated in President Sadat's visit to Israel in November 1977, the Camp David conference, and the peace treaty with Egypt in March 1979. The peace treaty was made possible by Begin's readiness to withdraw from Sinai in exchange for a full-scale peace treaty and an autonomy plan for the West Bank, but he continued to believe that the West Bank was an integral part of "historical Israel" and that in the future it should be under Israeli sovereignty.

During Begin's rule, Israel pursued an aggressive settlement policy. The peace agreement with Egypt caused an internal split within the Likud that resulted in the establishment of Ha-Techia, a new radical national party, which opposed it. At the same time, the more moderate members of Begin's Cabinet, Moshe Dayan and Ezer Weizman, resigned in protest of what they termed his hard-line policy. For his

role in the peace initiative, Begin, together with President Sadat, was awarded the Nobel peace prize on December 10, 1979.

During Begin's second term as prime minister, legislation was enacted applying Israeli law to East Jerusalem (June 1980) and to the Golan Heights (December 1981). On June 7, 1981, Israeli planes destroyed Osirak, the Iraqi atomic reactor, to prevent Iraq from manufacturing atomic weapons.

In June 1982, the Begin government launched Operation Peace for Galilee, which officially had the limited aims of destroying PLO bases but was allegedly intended to permanently destroy the PLO's fighting capability, rid the area of Syrian troops, and form an alliance with Lebanon's Maronite faction. The operation, which quickly turned into a full-scale war in Lebanon, caused a deep split in Israeli society and continues to be the subject of fierce debate. The results of the war, the findings of the commission of inquiry on the massacres at the SABRA AND SHATILA REFUGEE CAMPS, his protracted illness, and the death of his wife all caused Begin to sink into a deep depression that culminated in his resignation on September 19, 1983. From that time until his death in 1992, he remained secluded in his home and rarely appeared in public.

Begin was a controversial figure before he became prime minister, and his policies as prime minister also aroused extreme reactions. He was regarded by some people as a freedom fighter and as a statesman with a national-liberal world outlook, as well as a man of moral stature who always advocated the rule of law. Others described him as a terrorist and an extreme nationalist whose consuming vision was that of Greater Israel. His achievements in the areas of foreign and domestic policy are also controversial. To his devoted followers, Begin was the man who restored honor to the Jewish communities, whereas his critics accused him of having manipulated the feelings of these ethnic groups without solving their economic problems.

Begin's son, Ze'ev Benyamin Begin, became active in politics in the 1980s. In March 1993, he ran in the primaries for the position of head of the Likud and lost.

[See also: Camp David Accords; Settlements Policy, Israel]

BIBLIOGRAPHY

BEGIN, MENACHEM. *The Revolt.* 1964. In Hebrew.
———. *White Nights.* 1957. In Hebrew.
NAOR, AYRE. *Writing on the Wall.* 1993.
PELEG, ILAN. *Begin's Foreign Policy.* New York, 1987.
PERLMUTTER, AMOS. *The Life and Times of Menachem Begin.* New York, 1987.

PREUSS, TEDDY. *Begin: His Regime*. Jerusalem, 1984. In Hebrew.

SOFFER, SASON. *Begin: An Anatomy of Leadership*. Oxford, 1988.

TEMKO, NED. *To Win or to Die: A Personal Portrait of Menachem Begin*. New York, 1987.

Yaakov Shavit

Behar, Nissim   [1848–1931]

Zionist and educator.

Born in Jerusalem, Behar has been called the founder of modern Hebrew education. After being taught the Hebrew language by Eliezar BEN-YEHUDA, he became a teacher of modern Hebrew at the ALLIANCE ISRAÉLITE UNIVERSELLE in Jerusalem and was the school's director from 1882 to 1887.

In 1901, Behar moved to New York City, where he directed the National Liberal Immigration League from 1906 to 1924. During his years in New York, he continued to develop his method for teaching Hebrew, which became known as *Ivrit be Ivrit*. At the same time, he was an active propagandist for Zionism, calling for the return of the Jews to Palestine, and along with Baron Edmond de Rothschild tried to regain the WESTERN (Wailing) WALL for the Jewish community in Jerusalem. His methods were not always to the liking of U.S. Jewish leaders, some of whom were uncomfortable with the public meetings and protests that he organized to further the cause of the Jews of Palestine.

BIBLIOGRAPHY

New Standard Jewish Encyclopedia. New York, 1977.

ROLEF, SUSAN HATTIS, ed. *Political Dictionary of the State of Israel*. New York, 1987.

Zachary Karabell

Behesht-e Zahra Cemetery

Main cemetery of Tehran.

Behesht-e Zahra, built around the 1950s, is situated between the capital and the city of Qom. Its name is a reflection of the reverence that is accorded the Prophet's daughter, Fatima. The cemetery has become known in the last fourteen years for its symbolic use by revolutionaries and the Islamic Republic. Ayatollah KHOMEINI used it upon his return from exile (February 2, 1979) as the site from which he delivered his first public speech against the Pahlavi regime. It serves as the burial place for many of the soldiers killed in the war between Iran and Iraq (1980–1988). A custom has developed around Behesht-e Zahra in which the tombs of the "martyrs" are indicated by their photographs, and families congregate around the grave with food and memorabilia.

BIBLIOGRAPHY

ALGAR, H., ed. *Cambridge History of Iran*, vol. 4. London, 1990.

HIRO, D. *Iran under the Ayatollahs*. London, 1985.

Roshanak Malek

Beheshti, Mohammad   [1928–1981]

Iranian religious scholar and a principal figure in the founding of the Islamic Republic of Iran.

Receiving his early education in his birthplace of Isfahan, Beheshti began his specialized studies in Islam in Qom (Qum) in 1946, studying under a series of prominent scholars that included Ayatollah Ruhollah KHOMEINI. He also obtained a doctorate from the Faculty of Theology at Tehran University and took pains to learn English and German. In the early 1960s, he contributed articles on the contemporary problems of the Muslim world to the numerous Islamic periodicals that were flourishing at the time. Despite his links to Khomeini, he escaped arrest in the aftermath of the June 1963 uprising in Iran and in 1965 was permitted to leave to become director of the Islamic Center in Hamburg, Germany. He returned to Iran in 1970 and resumed his educational activities in Qom.

From 1975 on, Beheshti was active in mobilizing the religious scholars against the regime of Mohammad Reza PAHLAVI. In 1978, he met with Khomeini to assist in the planning of the revolution; early in 1979 was named to the Revolutionary Council that was intended to function as an interim legislature. After the success of the revolution, in 1979, he was appointed head of the Supreme Court and elected to the parliament as a leading figure in the Islamic Republican party. In the latter capacity, he became the leading adversary of Abolhasan BANI SADR, the first president of the Islamic Republic. He was killed on June 28, 1981, in an explosion that destroyed the Tehran headquarters of the Islamic Republican party.

BIBLIOGRAPHY

ANON. *U be tanha'i yek ommat bud* (He Was a Whole People by Himself). Tehran, 1982.

Hamid Algar

Beirut

The capital of Lebanon.

Beirut, on the coast of the Mediterranean, is LEBA-NON's center of government and finance. There are no reliable demographic statistics on the inhabitants of Beirut. The city has over a million inhabitants and greater Beirut has around 1.5 million. The city has existed since the time of the Canaanites. The origin of the name is unknown, although it is often said to be Ba'l Brit, one of the deities of the Canaanites. A variation of the name in Hebrew, Syriac, and Phoenician means "a well," referring to its rich water sources. The city's name was given to a *Vilayet* during Ottoman times and was in a jurisdiction separate from Mount Lebanon.

The association of Beirut and Lebanon is a twentieth-century phenomenon. When the French formed greater Lebanon in 1920, Beirut, along with other districts, was joined with the area of Mount Lebanon to compose a new political entity. Beirut was added for economic reasons: Mount Lebanon needed access to the sea. The people of Beirut at the time had a different demographic composition than Mount Lebanon, which was predominantly Druze and Maronite (Christian).

Beirut gradually grew in size and in political significance. The centers of administration and government were located there, as were educational institutions like the AMERICAN UNIVERSITY OF BEIRUT and the Jesuit St. Joseph University, both of which were founded in the nineteenth century. The centrality of Beirut increasingly marginalized other regions, including Mount Lebanon. This led to massive waves of migration into the city by people seeking education and jobs. This population movement changed the demographics of the city, which had been mainly Sunni and non-Maronite Christian. Maronites were in-

Civil war destruction in downtown Beirut, circa 1990. (© Yto Barrada)

creasingly present in the city, and Shi'ites began settling in large numbers as early as the 1950s.

Beirut was enlarged in the 1950s and 1960s as a result of the inflow of former rural residents who could not afford to live within the city boundaries. The "suburbs" of Beirut (as they came to be called) enlarged to include more than half a million migrants. Hundreds of thousands of Shi'ites fleeing southern Lebanon, the center of the confrontation between the PALESTINE LIBERATION ORGANIZATION (PLO) and ISRAEL, resided in East Beirut and South Beirut, in what was later called the "poverty belt." Factories in East Beirut attracted Lebanese looking for work. During the period of prosperity and glamour before the LEBANESE CIVIL WAR of 1958, Beirut was actually two cities: the old Beirut, where the rich and the middle class lived and prospered, and the suburbs, where poor Lebanese (mostly Shi'ites) lived. The poor Lebanese came into contact with Palestinians in refugee camps in and around the city. This contact revolutionized the political situation in Lebanon for much of the

Beirut skyline in 1954. (D.W. Lockhard)

1960s and 1970s. The presence of a large student population in the capital helped the efforts of the PLO and
its Lebanese allies who wanted to draw attention to
the plight of the South and the poor in general.

The primacy of Beirut was shattered by the LEBA-
NESE CIVIL WAR of 1975. The city that had symbolized
prosperity and ostentation came to symbolize bloodshed and cruelty. The war began in Beirut, in the
Maronite suburb of Ayn al-Rummanah, where a bus
carrying Palestinians was ambushed in April 1975 by
gunmen belonging to the PHALANGE party. The war
sharpened sectarian divisions in the capital and produced the GREEN LINE, a street that separated East
Beirut (predominantly Christian) from West Beirut
(predominantly Muslim). The length of the war resulted in some degree of "sectarian purity" in the two
sections, although Lebanese belonging to the "wrong
sect" continued to live—at their peril—in their customary dwelling places. Attempts at "sectarian cleansing" were relatively successful in East Beirut, when
forces loyal to the Phalange party evicted hundreds of
thousands of Shi'ites and Palestinians from their
homes. Refugee camps located in East Beirut were
demolished. Eviction of Christians from West Beirut
never reached the massive, organized proportions of
the ejection of non-Christians from East Beirut.

In the course of the civil war, the downtown area
(where the parliament and the financial district were
located) was completely destroyed. Looting of shops
in 1975 and 1976 forced businesses to relocate into
sectarian enclaves. Local militiamen controlled the
downtown area through much of the war. Although
those Lebanese who could afford to emigrate did so,
the city did not suffer from underpopulation because
many were entering the capital, seeking jobs and
education. The instability of southern Lebanon continued to send waves of migrants into the southern
suburbs of Beirut.

The end of the civil war was supposed to bring an
end to the division of Beirut. Reference to the Green
Line is now politically unacceptable. The government of Rafiq al-HARIRI is emphasizing the reconstruction of downtown Beirut, although critics
complain about the purely commercial nature of the
enterprise. Concerned economists warn that the reconstruction plans will reinforce the service sector
bias of the prewar economy, which, according to
critics, was responsible for the social injustices that
were manifested in the civil war. Repair of damage
continues in the city, and new residential and office
buildings are being constructed. However, only the
rich can afford to occupy them: residential apartments can sell for one million dollars U.S.

As'ad AbuKhalil

Beitaddin Declaration

*A 1978 attempt by six Arab countries to end the
Lebanese civil war of 1975.*

The Beitaddin Declaration was issued following a
meeting (October 15–17, 1978) in Lebanon, attended by the foreign ministers of the six Arab countries contributing troops to the Arab Deterrent Force
(Syria, Saudi Arabia, Kuwait, United Arab Emirates,
Qatar, and Sudan). The meeting took place during
the LEBANESE CIVIL WAR, amid heightened tension. A
national reconciliation document adopted by the
Lebanese parliament (April 1978) had never been
implemented. Further, Christian militias of the LEB-
ANESE FORCES and Syrian troops were involved in
heavy clashes in east Beirut. In March of 1978, Israel
had invaded southern Lebanon. The resolutions
adopted at Beitaddin (a famous residence of Lebanese emirs) included a recognition of Lebanon's independence, sovereignty, and territorial integrity; a
call for the dissolution of all armed presences in the
country; and the full implementation of the agreements adopted by Arab heads of state in Riyadh,
Saudi Arabia, and Cairo, Egypt (1976), which involved the establishment of a phased program for the
rebuilding of the Lebanese army and the creation of
a follow-up committee with delegates from Saudi
Arabia, Syria, and Kuwait.

BIBLIOGRAPHY

KHUWAYYRI, ANTOINE. *Hawadith Lubnan: 1977–1978*
(The Lebanese Events: 1977–1978). 1978.

George E. Irani

Beja

A people of the eastern Sudan.

The Beja of eastern SUDAN are a people of great
antiquity with a variety of names—Bughia, Bugiens,
Blemmyes, and Bugas; since medieval times they
have been known as the Beja. They inhabit the hills
and the coastal plain along the Red Sea. Much of
their past is uncertain, but they were known to the
pharaohs and certainly to the British in more modern
times. The latter viewed them as a people who had
survived the interest and the impact of more powerful nations without losing their character. They are
divided into the Besharin, the Amara, the Hade-
nowa, and the Beni Amer.

The Beja are characterized by a nomadic way of
life and a mental and physical toughness that has
helped them to overcome the harshness of their en-

vironment, blood feuds, and what appears as an undervaluing of the sanctity of human life. Defiantly individualistic, immune to authority, and widely dispersed in the solitary wadis of eastern Sudan, they display a freedom, strength, and individuality that enable them to survive. From the time of the pharaohs to the nineteenth century, the Beja were regarded as "the hateful Kush" or "scarcely human." The German botanist Schweinfurth described them "as repellant as the thorns and as clinging as the prickles of their native plants." These condemnations were perhaps much too harsh for a people who today remain aloof from world affairs, concerned more with their life in a harsh land but increasingly aware that to protect their interests, they must have influence in Khartoum, the capital of Sudan. This presents difficulties because the Beja traditionally live in small family groups spread over a wide area of scrub and desert. They have always had difficulty with languages, even among themselves, and certainly with strangers including the Sudanese. They remain in Western literature as Rudyard Kipling's Fuzzy Wuzzys with their "hay-rack head of hair," who broke the British army's "square" at Tamai on March 13, 1884.

Robert O. Collins

Bejerano, Maya   [1949–   ]

Israeli poet.

Bejerano was born in Haifa in 1949. She studied art, literature, philosophy, and music. In addition to writing poetry she works as a librarian. Bejerano won the Prime Minister's Prize and other literary awards.

Bejerano's poetry is concerned with the age-old journey of self-discovery, which, in her poems, takes place outside of the self. Bejerano makes frequent use of space-age terminology as metaphors for observation. In such books as *Ostrich* (1978) and *Song of Birds* (1985), she invokes technical imagery—computers, spaceships, laser light—in order to create the distance and the precision necessary for effective observation. Bejerano does not emphasize the existential emptiness and social detachment that is sometimes associated with modern scientific knowledge. Rather, she uses science to enhance and facilitate human communication. Unlike some of the somber and more iconoclastic Israeli poetry that preceded hers, Bejerano's poetic journeys emphasize the positive and humanistic. Humanity, according to Bejerano, is the center of meaning and it is only through humanity that the world around us can be intelligible. She is constantly aware of the very act of writing and uses that consciousness to infuse her poems with wit and irony. Bejerano does not promote a specific ethical or ideological message in her poems. To her, the very vacillation between conflicting choices is the basis of human existence. She muses freely in her poems without being afraid where that may take her. The focus of Berjerano's poetry is the journey itself and the inherent promise of change it holds.

BIBLIOGRAPHY

BEJERANO, MAYA. *Selected Poems*. Am Oved, Israel, 1985. In Hebrew.
LAHAV, AVNER. "A Wondrous Journey," *Achshav* 51–54 (1987): 562–569.

Yarom Peleg

Bek, Davit   [?–1728]

Leader of the first Armenian liberation effort in modern times.

Upon the fall of the Safavid dynasty and the ensuing disorder in the Transcaucasus in 1722, the Armenian *meliks* (traditional feudal lords) of mountainous KARABAGH requested assistance from the Georgian monarch in Tbilisi, who sent them one of his Armenian military officers. Davit Bek assumed command of the Armenian population, which had taken up arms in defense of the historic Armenian districts of Siunik and Ghapan, present-day Zangezur in southern Armenia and Karabagh. Expecting aid from the Russians when Peter the Great marched south along the Caspian Sea in the same year, the people in the mountainous areas of eastern Armenia organized the first liberation struggle among Armenians since the Mongol conquests.

With the support of the Armenian peasantry and the cooperation of the Armenian feudal barons whose governance of the area had long been recognized by the Persian shahs, Bek was able to muster a sufficient number of men to defend the Armenian-inhabited areas from the Muslim tribes competing for influence in the region after the collapse of the Safavid state. In a series of successful campaigns, Davit Bek held back local tribal armies until such time as the Ottomans advanced into the Transcaucasus; thereupon Shah Tahmasp bestowed upon him in 1727 the right to govern the area as a vassal Armenian principality. Bek died the following year as the Ottomans made deeper incursions into the Armenian areas. Command of the region passed to Davit Bek's lieutenant Mekhitar *Sparapet* (Armenian for commander-in-chief), who fell to the Ottomans in 1730. Mekhitar's death marked the end of the

Armenian struggle. It also marked the beginning of the breakdown of the five Armenian melikdoms of mountainous Karabagh, resulting in the interpenetration of the area with Muslim settlers, mostly derived from the local Turkic tribes.

Rouben P. Adalian

Beka'a Valley

See Biqa' Valley

Bekir Fahri

Ottoman Turkish writer.

Bekir Fahri graduated from the Mülkiye and entered the civil service. A partisan of the YOUNG TURKS, he was forced to take refuge in Egypt, returning to Istanbul after the 1908 revolution. In 1910, his novel *Jönler* (The Youngsters) was published, and he became literary editor of the journal *Piyano*. The last years of his life, like the early years, remain a mystery; all we know is that in 1914, he sent some stories to the magazine *Ruhab* from Cairo. His naturalist style was heavily influenced by the French author Émile Zola.

BIBLIOGRAPHY

ÖZKIRIMLI, ATILLA. *Türk Edebiyatı Ansiklopedisi,* vol. 1. Istanbul, 1982, p. 211.

David Waldner

Bektashis

Members of the nominally Shi'ite Ja'fari dervish order.

Originating in central Anatolia and founded, according to its members, by Hajji Bektash in the thirteenth century, this order incorporated practices and beliefs from pre-Islamic Central Asia and Anatolia. It also included some of these practices' Christian counterparts, and it always displayed intense veneration for the fourth caliph, Ali. It spread widely throughout the Ottoman Empire because of its association with the JANISSARIES and its capacity to adapt to local conditions. The characteristics of liberality, support for the oppressed, and involvement in political revolts attracted the frequent displeasure of the Ottoman establishment and the condemnation of the Sunni hierarchy. In 1826, Sultan MAHMUD II attempted to suppress the Bektashis when he annihilated the Janissaries. Members grew accustomed to operating clandestinely, and their network of lodges subsequently helped the YOUNG TURKS before the revolution of 1908. Bektashis enthusiastically welcomed Mustafa Kemal ATATÜRK's successful challenge to Ottoman rule, and, because he curbed Sunni influence, they continued to support him, despite his suppression in 1925 of all dervish orders, including their own. They survived in hiding within Turkey and openly outside—chiefly in the Balkans—with fluctuating fortunes. In Turkey, they began to reemerge in the 1960s. Their annual festival, held in mid-August in the town of Hacıbektaş, has now become a significant event. It publicly celebrates the contributions of the Bektashis to Turkish culture through their mystical poetry, music, and dancing, and never fails to attract politicians vying for Bektashi support.

Estimated in the 1990s at anywhere from five to twenty million in Turkey, devotees of Hajji Bektash are divided between those, commonly known as ALEVIS, whose leaders claim physical descent from their founder and those who assert he had no children. According to Alevis, Bektashis are born into their religion and outsiders cannot join; according to the others, people become Bektashis by choice and are eligible to rise to the progressively higher ranks of *baba, halife,* and *dedebaba.* Common to all is a deep attachment to the trinity of ALLAH, MUHAMMAD, and Ali, and to the Twelve Imams, Fourteen Innocents, and Forty Saints of the spiritual hierarchy, as well as a conviction that their interpretation of Islam is superior to the Sunni version and absolves them from the need to observe the standard obligations imposed on less enlightened Muslims. They see no necessity for mosques. They do not make the pilgrimage to Mecca, but on visits to Hacıbektaş they observe customs that include both pre-Islamic rites and copies of Meccan pilgrimage rituals. They are traditionally monogamous; the emancipation of Bektashi women is also a source of pride for the order. Their failure to fast during RAMADAN and their enjoyment of alcohol further contribute to the popular image of Bektashis as irreligious drinkers famed for the wit they have cultivated in response to disapproval or persecution. At times severe in the past, the persecution of Bektashis still occasionally recurs. Many Alevi Bektashis lost their lives when they were attacked by fervent Sunni right-wing extremists at Kahramanmaraş in 1978, and at Sivas in 1993. Since the 1980s, Alevi Bektashi villagers have been under increasing pressure to improve their material lot by abandoning their traditional support for left-wing politicians and their resistance to Sunni Islam.

BIBLIOGRAPHY

BIRGE, JOHN KINGSLEY. *The Bektashi Order of Dervishes.* London, 1937.

John D. Norton

Belgasem, Cherif [1933–]

Algerian officer and government minister.

Born in Morocco, Belgasem joined the Armée de Libération Nationale (ALN) in 1956. By the end of the ALGERIAN WAR OF INDEPENDENCE in 1962, he became a prominent general staff officer. As a member of the National Assembly, he influenced the passage of the constitution of 1963. He became minister of education and orientation (1963) and then of education (1964) under Ahmed Ben Bellah. After Houari BOUMÉDIENNE's coup (June 1965), Belgasem was assigned to the position of coordinator to revitalize the ruling one-party FRONT DE LIBÉRATION NATIONALE (FLN). He also served as minister of finance from 1968 to 1970. He resurfaced prominently in 1991 as a leader of a faction composed of former Boumédienne government ministers and officials who opposed the policies of President Chadli Benjedid.

BIBLIOGRAPHY

OTTAWAY, DAVID, and MARINA OTTAWAY. *Algeria: The Politics of a Socialist Revolution.* Berkeley, Calif., 1970.

Phillip C. Naylor

Belgrave, Charles Dalrymple [1894–1969]

Adviser to the Bahraini ruling family, 1926–1957.

Born in England, Charles Dalrymple Belgrave was a junior officer in the British Colonial Office on leave from a tour of duty in Tanganyika when, in the summer of 1925, he answered a classified advertisement in the *London Times* for the position of permanent adviser to the ruler of BAHRAIN, a British protectorate since 1820. He arrived on the islands in March of 1926 and took charge of all branches of the local administration, assisted by a small corps of British civil servants.

Under his supervision, petroleum was discovered in 1932 and the oil revenues accruing to the state were used to build the country's infrastructure and create a variety of new government departments, including those of education and public health. He gradually extended his influence over virtually all aspects of the country's fiscal and administrative affairs; by the mid-1950s, his identification with both the ruling family and British IMPERIALISM in the Persian/Arabian Gulf made him the focus of widespread popular discontent. At the urging of the ruler, Shaykh Sulman ibn Hamad al-KHALIFA, he retired as adviser in April 1957 and returned to London, where he died on 28 February 1969. Bahrain announced its independence in 1971, under Sulman's successor, Shaykh Isa ibn Sulman al-Khalifa.

BIBLIOGRAPHY

BELGRAVE, CHARLES. *Personal Column.* London, 1960.

Fred H. Lawson

Belkacem, Sherif

See Belgasem, Cherif

Belkind, Meir [1827–1898]

One of the first teachers of the modern Hebrew school system in Palestine.

Born in Logoisk, Byelorussia, Belkind emigrated to Palestine in the early 1880s. First settling in Jaffa, he later moved to Gedera where, because he was a traditional Jew, he was the rabbi for the new settlers. Belkind became the teacher for religious subjects in the first Hebrew school established by his son Israel in Jaffa in 1889. In doing so, Belkind molded the style of religious instruction in Palestine.

Miriam Simon

Bell, Gertrude [1868–1926]

British explorer and orientalist.

A graduate of Oxford, Bell traveled throughout the Middle East and wrote several popular books about her travels, including *The Desert and the Sown* (1907), about Syria, and *Amurath to Amurath* (1911), about Baghdad and Mosul.

Her skill as a linguist and her knowledge of the region brought her during World War I to Britain's Arab Bureau in Cairo, Egypt, where in 1915 she compiled information on the bedouin of Arabia. In 1916, at the request of Britain's viceroy of India, Lord Hardinge, she went to Basra in Mesopotamia (Iraq) to aid the Indian Expeditionary Force and gather military intelligence. She remained in Mesopotamia for much of the next ten years, as oriental secretary to both Sir Percy Cox and Sir Arnold Wilson, British administrators. In 1920 and 1921, she was an active partisan of FAISAL I IBN HUSAYN and helped bring him to the throne of Iraq in July 1921. Aside from her political work, Bell was honorary director of antiquities in Iraq and took part in creating the national museum in Baghdad.

BIBLIOGRAPHY

Dictionary of National Biography 1922–30. London, 1937.
WINSTONE, H.V.F. *Gertrude Bell.* New York, 1978.

Zachary Karabell

Bell Organization

See Hunchak Party

Bellounis, Mohamed [1912–1958]

Algerian nationalist and Messalist.

Bellounis was a staunch supporter of Messali al-HADJ and served in the Parti du Peuple Algérien (Party of the Algerian People, PPA), the Mouvement pour le Triomphe des Libertés Démocratiques (Movement for the Triumph of Democratic Liberties, MTLD), and particularly the Mouvement National Algérien (Algerian National Movement, MNA). The MNA (established in December 1954) disputed the claim of the Front de Libération Nationale (National Liberation Front, FLN) to be the only revolutionary voice of the Algerian people. Bellounis was charged to organize a military MNA presence within Algeria. Instead of the French forces, the MNA targeted the FLN's military, the ARMÉE DE LIBÉRATION NATIONALE (National Liberation Army, ALN). In the summer of 1955, the ALN, under the command of the fierce Colonel Amirouche (nom de guerre of Aït Hamouda), engaged Bellounis and five hundred of his MNA fighters at Guenzetin, Kabylia. Bellounis and a small number of men survived the assault and escaped to the Mélouza region of Algeria, south of Kabylia, where there was still significant Messalist support. This provoked the fratricidal Mélouza massacre on May 28, 1957, by the ALN, where about three hundred died, forcing Bellounis to turn to the French for logistical support. With French assistance, Bellounis mustered 1,500 to 3,000 men by the summer of 1957 who were given their own uniforms and flag. Bellounis named this force, which Messali did not officially embrace, the Armée Nationale Populaire Algérienne (or du Peuple Algérien, ANPA) and styled himself as a two-star general. At first, Bellounis succeeded against the ALN, but his counterproductively severe treatment of civilians and of his own soldiers forced the French to terminate this collaboration (known as Operation Ollivier). The French army tracked down Bellounis in July 1958 and executed him. His death signaled the end of the MNA's military threat to the FLN.

BIBLIOGRAPHY

COURRIÈRE, YVES. *La guerre d'Algérie.* Paris, 1970.
DROZ, BERNARD, and EVELYNE LEVER. *Histoire de la guerre d'Algérie, 1954–1962.* Paris, 1982.
HORNE, ALISTAIR. *A Savage War of Peace: Algeria, 1954–1962.* New York, 1978.

Phillip C. Naylor

Belly Dance

See Dance

Ben Aharon, Yitzhak [1906–]

Israeli politician.

Ben Aharon emigrated to Palestine from Austria in 1928. He was active in the labor movement and was one of the founders of HASHOMER Hatza'ir (a Viennese Zionist socialist pioneer youth movement). During World War II, he fought in the British army and was taken prisoner by the Germans. In 1946, he was one of the Yishuv leaders arrested by the British on Black Saturday. After Israel became independent, in May 1948, he became a member of the KNESSET (1949–1977); he helped found and led MAPAM and was instrumental in creating the LABOR PARTY in 1968. He served as secretary-general of Histadrut (1969–1973) and remained active in politics after his retirement from the Knesset.

BIBLIOGRAPHY

Encyclopedia Judaica. New York, 1971.
New Standard Jewish Encyclopedia. New York, 1977.
ROLEF, SUSAN H., ed. *Political Dictionary of the State of Israel.* New York, 1987.

Zachary Karabell

Ben Ali, Zayn al-Abidine [1936–]

President of Tunisia, replacing Habib Bourguiba in a constitutional coup, November 1987.

A member of the Destour movement since his teens, Ben Ali pursued a military career, receiving training in France (St. Cyr Academy) and the United States (Ft. Bliss, Tex.). From 1958 to 1974, he was head of military security in Tunisia. Following two periods of disfavor with the BOURGUIBA government, from about 1974 to 1984, Ben Ali was assigned several top security positions and, in 1986, was named minister of the interior. The following year, he was named prime minister as well as secretary-general of the Destour Socialist party (Parti Socialiste Destourien, or PSD).

Following his ousting of Habib Bourguiba in 1987, who had been president for thirty years (since the end of French colonialism), Ben Ali set out to reverse or reform many of the "old man's" later policies. He eased the stern political measures adopted by Bourguiba, especially as concerned opposition movements—chief among them the Social Democrat Movement (Mouvement des Démocrates Sociaux; MDS) and, to a lesser extent, the Islamic Tendency Movement (Mouvement de tendance islamique; MTI)—and pushed through reforms of the judicial system. Ben Ali also pursued strong links with other states of North Africa (the MAGHRIB) primarily through the Arab Maghrib Union founded in 1989. More challenging were the serious economic problems facing Tunisia in the late 1980s and early 1990s—among these, chronic unemployment, a balance of payment deficit, and an unwieldy state subsidy and price control system. Despite his expressed interest in a multiparty system, which led in 1988 to the signing of the so-called National Pact with opposition leaders, Ben Ali has relied almost entirely on the ruling party, the old PSD, which in 1987 was renamed the CONSTITUTIONAL DEMOCRATIC RALLY (RCD).

BIBLIOGRAPHY

HABEEB, WILLIAM MARK. "Zine El Abidine Ben Ali." In *Political Leaders of the Contemporary Middle East and North Africa,* ed. by Bernard Reich. New York, 1990. *Middle East International.* 1987–1991.

Matthew S. Gordon

Ben Ammar, Tahar

Tunisian nationalist and diplomat.

A wealthy landowner, Ben (also ibn) Ammar served as president of the Tunisian section of the Grand Council in the early 1950s. In 1955, as premier, he signed a series of six conventions on internal autonomy for Tunisia with the French government of Premier Pierre Mendès-France. In March of 1956, he was one of four Tunisian signatories to the official protocol granting independence to Tunisia.

BIBLIOGRAPHY

HAHN, LORNA. *North Africa: Nationalism to Nationhood.* Washington, D.C., 1960.

Matthew S. Gordon

Ben Arfa

See Arfa, Muhammad ibn

Ben Badis, Abd al-Hamid   [1889–1940]

Algerian nationalist and founder of the Association of Algerian Muslim Ulama (AUMA).

Born to a traditional Muslim family in Constantine, northeast Algeria (although his father had served on France's colonial *conseil supérieur*), Ben Badis received his higher education at Zaytuna mosque university in Tunis. There, he was influenced by the reformist SALAFIYYA MOVEMENT of Muhammad Abduh and Rashid Rida. Determined to apply Salafiyya principles to Algerian society, Ben Badis engaged in educating Algerians to proper Islamic practice and observance. Besides establishing schools, his ideas appeared in periodicals such as *al-Muntaqid* and *al-Shihab*. In 1931, he founded the Algerian Association of Reformist Ulama (Islamic scholars), known also as the ASSOCIATION OF ALGERIAN MUSLIM ULAMA (AUMA).

Although chiefly concerned with education, Ben Badis also entered the political arena by asserting that French assimilation was impossible. He declared: "This Algerian nation is not France, cannot be France, and does not wish to be France." This complemented his famous conviction that "Islam is my religion, Arabic my language, Algeria my fatherland." These views inevitably brought him into contact with nationalists Ferhat ABBAS and Messali al-HADJ. Ben Badis, however, preferred a cultural rather than a political role in Algerian history and NATIONALISM. If later the Front de Libération Nationale (National Liberation Front, FLN) purposely ignored the contributions of other nationalist rivals, Ben Badis's legacy was recognized and respected.

BIBLIOGRAPHY

NAYLOR, PHILLIP C., and ALF A. HEGGOY. *Historical Dictionary of Algeria,* 2nd ed. Metuchen, N.J., 1994.
QUANDT, WILLIAM B. *Revolution and Political Leadership: Algeria, 1954–1968.* Cambridge, Mass., 1969.

Phillip C. Naylor

Ben Barka, Mehdi [1920–1966]

Moroccan nationalist politician.

Mehdi Ben Barka, the son of a local Moroccan religious leader, was raised in a traditional milieu. He excelled in his studies, particularly in mathematics, entered the French system, and completed a baccalaureate. At twenty-one, he graduated from the university in Algiers. Postponing graduate study in mathematics, he taught in Rabat, for a time at the imperial college, where Crown Prince Hassan was his student.

Drawn into nationalist, anticolonialist politics, he held a number of significant ISTIQLAL party positions and various government posts following independence in 1956, culminating in King Muhammad V's appointing him president of the first National Consultative Assembly. Ben Barka devoted particular attention to party youth and the labor movement. As a second-generation Istiqlal leader, his policies of party reform often put him at odds with the senior leaders. He challenged the regime by calling for elections, a constitutional monarchy, and a greater role for labor and popular participation. Despite his progressive stance, he utilized party institutions to build a personal power base.

In 1959, Ben Barka announced the formation of a new political party, the National Union of Popular Forces (UNFP). In 1963, accused of participation in a reputed plot against King Hassan, he went into exile, where he continued to denounce the Moroccan monarchy. In October 1965, Ben Barka was abducted in Paris, possibly tortured, and killed by a conspiracy that involved the French secret service, Moroccan minister of the interior General Muhammad OUFKIR, and Ahmad Dlimi, Moroccan chief of security. General Oufkir was brought to trial in absentia and found guilty. The refusal of the Moroccan government to extradite Oufkir generated a breach in Moroccan–French relations that lasted almost four years.

BIBLIOGRAPHY

ASHFORD, DOUGLAS E. *Political Change in Morocco.* Princeton, N.J., 1961.
JULIEN, CHARLES-ANDRÉ. *Le Maroc face aux impérialistes: 1415–1956.* Paris, 1978.
LE TOURNEAU, ROGER. *Chronicle politique: Annuaire de l'Afrique du nord.* Paris, 1963–1967.
NYROP, RICHARD F., et al. *Area Handbook for Morocco,* 3rd ed. Washington, D.C., 1972.
WATERBURY, JOHN. *Commander of the Faithful.* New York, 1970.

Donna Lee Bowen

Ben Bella, Ahmed [1916–]

First premier president of Algeria, 1962–1965.

Born in Marnia near Oran, Algeria, Ahmed Ben Bella was the youngest child in a large family steeped in the ritual and custom of ISLAM. Nevertheless, Ben Bella completed a French primary education and was more comfortable in speaking French than Arabic. He was decorated during World War II after distinguishing himself in the Italian campaign. Like other young Algerians, Ben Bella was deeply moved by the massacre during the SETIF REVOLT (May 1945) and subsequent colonialist repression. He joined Messali al-HADJ's illegal Parti du Peuple Algérien (PPA) and later the paramilitary Organisation Spéciale (OS). He participated in an attack on the main post office in Oran (April 1949) but was soon captured by French police and imprisoned from 1950 until his escape in 1952 to Egypt.

Along with other radical nationalists, he prepared for armed insurrection and is regarded as one of the nine historic chiefs of the ALGERIAN WAR OF INDEPENDENCE (1954–1962) and a founder of the FRONT DE LIBÉRATION NATIONALE (FLN). During the Algerian revolution, Ben Bella sought financial aid and material in foreign capitals for the ARMÉE DE LIBÉRATION NATIONALE (ALN). He was viewed as the head of the external faction of the FLN, which began to rival the internal group over the leadership of the revolution. France's skyjacking in October 1956 of Ben Bella and three other historic chiefs—Hocine AIT AHMED, Mohamed BOUDIAF, and Mohamed KHIDER—postponed an inevitable intra-elite confrontation. Ben Bella was incarcerated in France until 1962.

After the war, he and external ALN strongman Houari BOUMÉDIENNE established the Bureau Politique in opposition to the Gouvernement Provisoire de la République Algérienne (GPRA) and seized power in August 1962. Ben Bella emerged as Algeria's first prime minister (1962/63) and then was elected president (1963–1965). Criticized for his flamboyance and demagogy, Ben Bella faced enormous problems, but he gave his country, as pointed out by Robert Merle, "purpose and direction." He restored order in Algeria, steered his country toward a socialist economy highlighted by the self-management (*autogestion*) system, and allocated considerable sums toward education. In foreign policy, he supported wars of national liberation and espoused nonalignment. Nevertheless, he also pursued a close cooperation with France, as Algeria remained profoundly dependent on the former *métropole*. Despite declarations of MAGHRIB (North African) unity, relations with Morocco deteriorated, as underscored by a border conflict—the

MOROCCAN–ALGERIAN WAR of 1962/63—that necessitated the conciliatory intervention of the Organization of African Unity.

Ben Bella became increasingly authoritarian, an expression of his own personality and in reaction to political and military perils such as the Kabyle Revolt led by Ait Ahmad (1963) and the insurrection of Colonel Mohammed Chaabani (1964). Recognizing the ambitions of Vice-President Boumédienne, Ben Bella moved against his rival's supporters in his cabinet (Interior Minister Ahmed Medeghri and Foreign Minister Abdelaziz Bouteflika). Nevertheless, on June 19, 1965, Boumédienne deposed Ben Bella in a nonviolent military coup.

Ben Bella was arrested and placed in house arrest, which prompted international concern. He was not freed until July 1979 by President Chadli Benjedid. Ben Bella promptly moved to France and, in 1984, formed an opposition party called the Mouvement pour la Démocratie en Algérie (MDA). Ben Bella and Ait Ahmed reconciled in exile (December 1985) and called for a constituent assembly guaranteeing political rights in Algeria.

In 1990, Ben Bella was allowed to return to Algeria, where he continued his opposition to the Benjedid government. For a brief period, observers believed that Ben Bella could reconcile both secular and Islamist political movements. But Ben Bella discovered that the younger generation did not even know of him.

Ben Bella was a strong supporter of Iraq's President Saddam Hussein during the GULF CRISIS and conflict of 1990/91. The replacement of the Benjedid government in January 1992 by a High Security Council presided over by his old comrade Boudiaf still left Ben Bella consigned as a marginal political figure. He remains an important, historic figure determined to remain an active rather than anachronistic participant in Algerian affairs.

BIBLIOGRAPHY

ENTELIS, JOHN. *Algeria: The Revolution Institutionalized.* Denver, Colo., 1985.

MERLE, ROBERT. *Ahmed Ben Bella.* Tr. by Camilla Sykes. New York, 1967.

NAYLOR, PHILLIP, and ALF HEGGOY. *Historical Dictionary of Algeria,* 2nd ed. Metuchen, N.J., 1994.

Phillip C. Naylor

Ben Boulaid, Moustafa   [1917–1957]

A historic chief of the Algerian revolution (1954–1962).

Moustafa Ben Boulaid (also Mostefa Ben Boulaïd) was born to a peasant family in the impoverished Aurès (Awras) mountain region. A Free French veteran, Ben Boulaid was an enterprising man who eventually owned a bus line. Colonial authorities terminated his business license due to his support of Messali al-HADJ. Like other young nationalists, Ben Boulaid grew impatient with Messali's leadership and demanded immediate action against colonialism. He played an important role in establishing the CO-MITÉ RÉVOLUTIONNAIRE D'UNITÉ ET D'ACTION (CRUA; Revolutionary Committee for Unity and Action), the parent organization of the FRONT DE LIBÉRATION NATIONALE (FLN; National Liberation Front), which earned him his reputation as one of the nine historic chiefs (*chefs historiques*) of the revolution. He unsuccessfully attempted to gain Messali's support for the FLN.

Guerrillas in the Aurès under his command opened the ALGERIAN WAR OF INDEPENDENCE with attacks on October 31 and November 1, 1954. Ben Boulaid was captured by the French in February 1955, but he escaped in November. Resuming his guerrilla command, he died in March 1957 while examining a booby-trapped field radio.

BIBLIOGRAPHY

HORNE, ALISTAIR. *A Savage War of Peace: Algeria, 1954–1962,* 2d ed. New York, 1987.

STORA, BENJAMIN. *Dictionnaire biographique de militants nationalistes algériens.* Paris, 1985.

Phillip C. Naylor

Bene Israel

Jewish community of India.

The Bene Israel lived for centuries on the Konkan coast in Maharashtra state, India. After the establishment of the State in 1948 they began to emigrate from Bombay to Israel, where fifty thousand live today. In 1964 they were recognized as "full Jews" by Israel's chief RABBINATE. The Bene Israel speak Marathi and Hebrew; some speak English. They live in development towns and are employed largely as skilled workers.

BIBLIOGRAPHY

WEIL, SHALVA. "Yom Kippur: The Festival of Closing the Doors." In *Between Jerusalem and Benares: Comparative Studies in Judaism and Hinduism,* ed. by I. Hananya Goodman. Albany, N.Y., 1994, pp. 85–100.

Shalvah Weil

Benghazi

Chief city and Mediterranean seaport of Cyrenaica (Barqa), second in Libya only to Tripoli.

Originally founded by the Greeks as Berenike on a small natural harbor on the gulf of Sidra, Benghazi (also Marsa ibn Ghazi) was refounded and renamed in the Middle Ages. Its importance was due to its position as the only port between Tripoli and Alexandria, as an outlet for the agricultural produce of northern CYRENAICA, and as a center of local administration. In the early nineteenth century, Benghazi was still an impoverished village of some five thousand people. Its prosperity and importance increased with the spread of the SANUSI ORDER in Cyrenaica and, beginning in the 1840s, in the eastern Sahara and the Sudan. It became the main Mediterranean outlet for the newly opened, Sanusi-controlled trade route to the rising sultanate of Wadai in eastern Sudan (now Chad). In the later nineteenth century, despite being the local seat of Ottoman administration, it was one of the few remaining North African shipment markets for the trans-Saharan SLAVE TRADE.

Benghazi was still largely undeveloped (with a cosmopolitan population of about 20,000) when Italy invaded in 1911. As in Tripoli, the Italians created a modern, European-style city outside the old Arab quarters, particularly after the defeat of the Cyrenaican rebellion in 1931/32. By 1937, the population was fifty thousand, but expansion was constricted by its position between the sea and an inland saltwater lagoon.

During the North African campaigns of World War II (1940–1943), Benghazi changed hands five times and suffered some two thousand air raids. Destruction was extensive and the British military administration, set up after the city's final capture by the British Eighth Army in November 1942, could not fund rebuilding. In 1949, Benghazi became the seat of the first Cyrenaican government and was later recognized as the joint capital—with Tripoli—of the independent United Kingdom of Libya (proclaimed December 1951). Over the next five years, the town and port were rebuilt, but rapid urban expansion and development only started with the oil boom of the 1950s and 1960s, with thousands of migrant families forced into shanty settlements. After the 1969 revolution, Benghazi was deprived of its joint-capital status, regaining its traditional role as chief port and city of Cyrenaica, a center of administration, industry, commerce, and education. It houses the University of Gar Younis and an international airport (at Benina). Benghazi is linked by road to Tripoli and Egypt and to the Saharan regions of eastern Libya. The 1984 population was some 485,000.

BIBLIOGRAPHY

BULUGMA, HADI M. *Benghazi through the Ages.* Benghazi, 1972.
WRIGHT, JOHN. *Libya.* London and New York, 1969.

John L. Wright

Ben-Gurion, David   [1886–1973]

Israeli politician and statesman.

David Ben-Gurion was born in October 1886 under the name of David Gruen, which he later changed to David Green, in Plonsk, Poland, then part of the Russian Empire.

He was educated at an Orthodox Hebrew school in Poland. In 1903, he helped to organize the Polish branch of the Workers for Zion movement, known as Po'alei Zion.

In 1906 he moved to Palestine. Despite contracting malaria shortly after arriving, he worked as a farmer in various Jewish agricultural settlements, where his duties included serving as an armed guard against Arab attackers. At the time, Palestine was administered under Turkish rule. He was one of the organizers of the Palestine Labor party and became the editor of its newspaper *Ahdut* (Unity) in 1910, which is when he Hebraized his name to Ben-Gurion.

In 1913 he began taking classes at the University of Istanbul, studying law. When World War I began, with Turkey fighting on the side of Germany, Ben-Gurion returned to Palestine. He suggested that a Jewish militia be created to help defend Palestine, but he was deported by the Turkish authorities in 1915, along with thousands of other Jews and Zionists, including his friend Yizhak BEN-ZVI, who later became the president of Israel. Both he and Ben-Zvi left Palestine and moved to New York City, where Ben-Gurion met and married his wife.

In the United States, Ben-Gurion helped to encourage immigration to Palestine and founded the organization *He-Halutz* (Young Pioneers) to support this goal.

Following the November 1917 BALFOUR DECLARATION of the British government, he and Ben-Zvi agreed with the speeches of Zionist leader Chaim WEIZMANN that Jewish and Zionist goals would be best furthered by supporting the British government. Accordingly, Ben-Gurion and Ben-Zvi enlisted in the British army's JEWISH LEGION to fight against the Ottoman regime. Ben-Gurion enlisted in Canada in 1918, was sent to Nova Scotia to train, and after further training in England and Cairo served with General Allenby in fighting the Turks.

Back in Palestine in 1920, Ben-Gurion and Ben-Zvi helped to create the HISTADRUT, the national labor federation; Ben-Gurion was elected its first secretary general in 1921. The Histadrut was referred to as a "state within a state," or a "government within a government," and was a major force in economics, social policy, labor policy, and housing in the Jewish community in Palestine.

In 1923 the League of Nations mandate for Palestine passed to Great Britain, and Britain took control of Palestine. In the early years of the mandate, Britain not only tolerated but actually encouraged Jewish immigration, and in 1929 the mandatory government recognized the JEWISH AGENCY as the official body representing Jewish interests in terms of immigration and settlement in Palestine. In 1930 Ben-Gurion helped to found the Israel workers' party, *Miphleget Po'alei Israel,* MAPAI, and became its head.

In 1933 Ben-Gurion became a member of the executive board of the Jewish Agency for Palestine; in 1935 he became chairman of the Zionist executive, the body that coordinated Zionist organizations around the world. Although the director of the Jewish Agency's political department, Haim ARLOSOROFF, was advocating a moderate approach to the Arab population in Palestine—specifically suggesting that neither the Arabs nor the Jews should dominate the territory—Ben-Gurion's views became increasingly inflexible in this regard. He felt that the lessons of the 1929 Arab riots against Jewish settlement required that the Jewish Agency push for the classic goals of Zionism: a Jewish majority in Palestine, and Jewish self-defense in the meantime. During this period, Ben-Gurion published three books dealing with the labor movement, the Jewish working class, and the idea of Zionism. He was a strong Zionist and, after the creation of the state of Israel, took the position that the only real Zionists were individuals who immigrated to Israel. Jewish life outside of Israel, when migration was a real option, was anathema to Zionism.

In 1936 a royal commission of inquiry—known by the name of its chairman, Lord Peel—arrived in Palestine to investigate the Arab–Jewish tensions that had surfaced there in recent years. Ben-Gurion, as chairman of the Jewish Agency's Palestine executive committee, presented a very moderate, and to some extent not wholly accurate, testimony before the PEEL COMMISSION. He explained that it was not the goal of Zionists to transform all of Palestine into a Jewish state. However, he argued, Jews had to be allowed to migrate to Palestine and to settle peacefully there. After the Peel Commission's final report was issued, Ben-Gurion continued to believe that it would be possible for Zionists to negotiate with Ar-

abs in Palestine and arrive at a peaceful resolution of the apparently irreconcilable interests of the two groups.

Ben-Gurion believed, however, that negotiations had to take place from a position of strength and was a strong advocate, with Arlosoroff and others, of Jewish self-defense. He urged that activities of the *Hagannah*—the Jewish self-defense forces in Palestine—be given support, so that Jewish settlers in Palestine would not have to worry about their safety.

In 1939, when Britain changed its fundamental attitudes toward the Middle East in general, and Zionism in particular, and adopted a strong pro-Arab line, Ben-Gurion called for the Jewish community to resist Britain and advocated the concept of "the fighting Zionist." The British WHITE PAPERS ON PALESTINE called for severely restricted Jewish immigration to Palestine over the five-year period starting in 1939 and said that all immigration would have to end in 1944.

At the outbreak of World War II, Ben-Gurion argued that Jewish forces had to work on the side of Britain, despite the existence of the 1939 White Papers. He was convinced, as were many other Jewish and Zionist leaders, that Winston Churchill deserved the loyalty and support of Zionist supporters and that once the war was over a satisfactory solution to Zionist demands would be found. Throughout the war, Ben-Gurion continued to appeal to the British to reverse the White Papers and to recognize a Jewish Palestine, but the British refused.

Ben-Gurion was pragmatic in his relations with Britain, and as late as 1940, he was still urging compromise, indicating that he would accept a partition of land in Palestine and even a binational state of Arabs and Jews in Palestine. British authorities never responded positively to his suggestions, however.

In 1947, at the end of the war, Britain announced that it was handing jurisdiction for Palestine, and consequently the Palestine problem, over to the newly created United Nations. The United Nations formed a Special Committee on Palestine (UNSCOP) to look into the problem, and in November 1947 UNSCOP voted to partition Palestine into distinct Jewish and Arab states, reserving a small territory in and around Jerusalem to be controlled by the United Nations. At that time Ben-Gurion and the Jewish Agency executive council began to focus their attention on two major goals: guaranteeing the security of the Jewish population in Palestine against Arab attacks during the transition period and defending the new state of Israel from neighboring nations once independence was declared.

In March 1948, while he was chairman of the Zionist executive, Ben-Gurion announced his opposition to a proposal from the U.S. government that an international trusteeship be created over Palestine. In April of that year, a people's council of thirty-seven members, headed by Ben-Gurion, representing all parties in Palestine, was set up to act as an unofficial provisional legislature and government after the departure of the British.

On 14 May 1948, Ben-Gurion publicly read the declaration of independence of the state of Israel; on May 16, Weizmann was named president of the provisional government. The state was attacked by Jordan, Egypt, Iraq, Syria, Lebanon, and other Arab neighbors in what became known as the War of Independence. One of Ben-Gurion's top priorities in the war was access to JERUSALEM; he felt that statehood without Jerusalem would only be a partial success for Zionist causes. In the end, access was achieved to only part of Jerusalem, the western edge of the city, a severe disappointment to Ben-Gurion and other Israeli leaders. One of Ben-Gurion's other priorities, access to the Red Sea, was achieved with conquest of the small city of Eilat.

An armistice took effect in February 1949; soon thereafter a parliament, the KNESSET, and other democratic institutions were formed. Weizmann was elected the first president of the state of Israel and served in that position until his death (1952). Ben-Gurion formed a coalition government at that time, something he was to do until 1953, and again from 1955 to 1963. He served as both prime minister and minister of defense.

One of the responsibilities of the first Knesset had been to draft a new constitution for the state of Israel, but after a relatively brief period of time Ben-Gurion and other leaders decided not to adopt the draft constitution, which had been authored by Dr. Leo Kohn, the legal adviser to the Jewish Agency. Ben-Gurion's primary arguments against the rapid adoption of the new constitution were threefold. First, he argued that no country should rush into any constitutional structure and that time should be taken to consider the implications of any particular model. This was especially true for Israel, given its heterogeneous population and the extraordinary range of constitutional backgrounds from which its population had come. Second, he argued that debate over constitutional structures would distract Israel from other, more pressing issues, including resolution of the war, rapid immigration, housing, and finding jobs for new immigrants. Third, the role of religion in the new state needed to be resolved; the extent to which the new constitution would incorporate religious dogma was a highly contentious one that could not be ignored in the quest for a rapid adoption of a constitution.

Indeed, many of the Orthodox Jewish leaders of the day were arguing that Israel already had a perfectly functional constitution in an assortment of talmudic documents that were widely known to Israel's Jewish population. Ben-Gurion strongly opposed this position, and eventually an agreement was reached to respect the religious status quo while a constitution was worked on in piecemeal fashion.

Ben-Gurion regularly had conflicts with his coalition partners over the years, primarily with the Orthodox religious parties in the coalition. The support of the Orthodox parties was necessary in order for Ben-Gurion to maintain the support of a majority of seats in the Knesset, but his socialist background and secular beliefs often disagreed with the principles espoused by the religious parties. Indeed, in 1951 his government suffered a vote of no confidence because of the desertion of religious parties from his coalition.

This happened more than once, and each time his government fell, Ben-Gurion and his cabinet would stay in office as a caretaker government until a new coalition could be assembled. Typically, he would be able in relatively short order to construct a new coalition, usually with the same partners, to demonstrate the support of a majority in the Knesset.

In 1951 Ben-Gurion had to make a difficult decision concerning Israel's relations with West Germany and whether to seek reparations from the West German government. There was a tremendous emotional outcry in Israel, and in Jewish populations around the world, about whether or not this was accepting blood money. But Ben-Gurion held to the position that this should be seen as financial aid to help Israel absorb immigrants and survivors of the Nazi regime, not as a gesture to allow Germany to forget crimes of the past. Demonstrations and acts of violence, bordering on civil war, led by opposition leader Menachem BEGIN, were unable to dissuade Ben-Gurion, and in 1952 an agreement was signed.

In 1953 Ben-Gurion resigned as prime minister, for what he cited as health reasons, and turned the position of prime minister over to his deputy prime minister, Moshe Sharett. Following his resignation, he moved to a kibbutz just outside Beersheba, Kibbutz Sde Boker.

In 1955 Ben-Gurion returned to political life by taking the portfolio of defense minister under prime minister Sharett. Later that year, following new elections, Ben-Gurion resumed the position of prime minister, with Sharett taking over as foreign minister. In 1956 Ben-Gurion asked for Sharett's resignation when Sharett failed to support Ben-Gurion's policy with regard to Israeli cooperation with Britain and France in an invasion of the SUEZ CANAL. Sharett was replaced by Golda MEIR as foreign minister.

The decision to act in the Sinai campaign of 1956 was a difficult one, but one that Ben-Gurion felt was necessary as a result of the continued hostilities with Egypt, Egypt's posturing with the threatened closing of the Suez Canal, and the newly developing Soviet policy of actively and massively arming Egypt. Britain and France were interested in regaining control of the Suez Canal for Western democratic powers; Israel was interested in a secure southern border. At the end of the 1956 Sinai War, Ben-Gurion was disappointed with Britain and France, and especially with the United States for its failure to stand up to the demands of the Soviet Union. Ultimately, Israel held out for promises by the United States that it would guarantee open passage through international waterways for Israel; these were promises that were not honored when Israel contacted Lyndon Johnson in 1967.

Ben-Gurion was a strong supporter of development in the sciences, especially atomic energy. As early as 1956, he made the decision to proceed vigorously to develop nuclear capability in Israel, primarily as a source of energy. The defense potential of the industry was not lost on him, however.

In 1963 Ben-Gurion resigned from the government for "personal reasons," and was succeeded by Levi Eshkol. Although he was officially out of power, he continued to be regarded as "the Old Man" and was kept informed of government decisions. Even the top secret decision to launch a preemptive strike in June of 1967, leading to the Six-Day War, was shared with Ben-Gurion before the fact; he gave it his blessing.

In his later years, Ben-Gurion was reported to have scaled back what were often militaristic views of Israel's security needs. Following the Six-Day War, he was a supporter of negotiating land for peace, arguing that Israel did not need any of the conquered territories, save those of Jerusalem and the Golan Heights.

Ben-Gurion retired from the Knesset in 1970 and moved back to his kibbutz in Sde Boker. He died on 1 December 1973 in the aftermath of the Yom Kippur War, yet another symbol to the people of Israel that a milestone had been passed in Israel's development.

BIBLIOGRAPHY

BAR-ZOHAR, MICHAEL. *Ben-Gurion: A Biography.* Tr. by Peretz Kidron. New York, 1978.
BEN-GURION, DAVID. *Israel: A Personal History.* New York, 1971.
GAL, ALLON. *David Ben-Gurion and the American Alignment for a Jewish State.* Bloomington, Ind., 1991.
PENKOWER, MONTY NOAM. *The Holocaust and Israel Reborn: From Catastrophe to Sovereignty.* Urbana, Ill., 1994.
SACHAR, HOWARD M. *A History of Israel: From the Rise of Zionism to Our Time.* New York, 1981.
TEVETH, SHABTAI. *Ben-Gurion and the Palestinian Arabs: From Peace to War.* New York, 1985.
———. *Ben-Gurion: The Burning Ground, 1886–1948.* Boston, 1987.
ZWEIG, RONALD, ed. *David Ben-Gurion: Politics and Leadership in Israel.* Portland, Oreg., 1991.

Gregory S. Mahler

Ben-Gurion University of the Negev

Israeli university.

Ben Gurion University of the Negev was established in 1969 by David Ben-Gurion, Israel's first prime minister, to develop the NEGEV DESERT (60 percent of Israel's land mass and 10 percent of its population). Originally called the University of the Negev, in 1973 it was renamed to honor Ben-Gurion. The center of education and research in the area, it focuses on desert research, high technology, medicine, and regional development.

Besides a medical school, there are four faculties: engineering sciences, natural sciences, health sciences, and humanities and social sciences. The student population in 1993 was eight-three hundred.

Miriam Simon

Benha

City in the Nile delta.

The city is situated on the Damietta branch of the Nile River, twenty-eight miles (45 km) north of Cairo. Benha was noted in the early history of Islam for its excellent honey; more recently for its oranges and tangerines. Muhammad Ali's grandson—Abbas Hilmi I—had a palace in Benha and died there under mysterious circumstances in 1854. The capital of Qalyubiya governorate (province), Benha had an estimated 120,000 inhabitants in 1986.

BIBLIOGRAPHY

Encyclopaedia of Islam, 2nd ed.

Arthur Goldschmidt, Jr.

Ben Hadouga, Abdelhamid   [1928–   ]

Algerian novelist and short story writer.

Ben Hadouga was born in al-Mansura, Algeria. He received a solid education in Arabic from his father, a teacher of Arabic and Islamic thought. Ben Hadouga received his secondary and higher education in Tunisia. At al-Zaytuna university in Tunis he obtained a degree in Arabic literature. While in Tunisia he also attended the Arab Drama Institute. His educational interests shifted when he went to France, where he spent three and a half years in Marseilles and Paris studying plastic transformation.

Ben Hadouga is credited with the first significant Arabic novel in Algeria, *Rih al-junub* (1971; The Southern Wind). In addition to his published novels and short stories, he wrote numerous radio and television plays in colloquial Algerian. After Algeria's independence in 1962, Ben Hadouga worked for the Algerian Broadcasting Service, eventually becoming cultural adviser at the General Administration for Radio and Television. He retired in 1987 but was soon appointed director general of the National Book Foundation and then president of the National Council for Culture.

Ben Hadouga's two collections of short stories, *Zilalun Jaza'iriyya* (1960; Algerian Shades) and *Al-Ashi'a al-Sab'a* (1962; The Seven Rays), although published during the Algerian War of Independence, generally did not concern patriotic topics. Ben Hadouga is primarily concerned with the human dimension of characters depicted in unusual situations. Another major theme of his fiction is love in its various aspects: conjugal, filial, and parental. He expressed deep compassion and concern for the meek and the wronged members of society, a feeling that stems from his socialist beliefs. He often gives the impression of being on a mission to redeem and to establish fairness in the world. This is obvious in his novel *Nihayat al-Ams* (1975; The End of Yesterday), which concerns the wife of the *Harki* and, in general, all wronged women in his society.

Ben Hadouga's writings reveal his deep affection and respect for women, although he sometimes fails to portray his feelings forcefully, particularly in his novels *Rih al-Junub* and *Bana al-Subh* (1980; The morning appeared). A more successful portrait of a feminine character is achieved in *Al-Jaziya w'a-Darawish* (1983; The Jaziya and the Dervishes); it suggests an improvement in the status of women while maintaining a respect for traditions which Ben Hadouga always demonstrates in his writings. He is critical, however, of such outdated customs as exorbitant dowries, which affect the marriage plans of young couples.

Ben Hadouga has a tendency to dramatize events, and often adopts a moralizing and didactic tone in his works. He does, however, paint a true picture of greed and hypocrisy among the ruling authorities in independent Algeria. He preaches honesty in a world and time when opportunism prevails.

The action of most of Ben Hadouga's fiction takes place in rural settings (except *Bana al-subhu,* which is set in Algiers.) The author opposes the corrupt and hypocritical life in the city to the simpler and healthier world of the country.

Ben Hadouga sees the novel as an ideal channel for the promulgation of his ideas. He uses stream of consciousness and flashback as effective means of relating the events of the war of independence.

[*See also:* Literature, Arabic, North African]

BIBLIOGRAPHY

BAMIA, AIDA. "Ibn Haduga, Abd al-Hamid." In *Encyclopedia of World Literature*. Vol. 5, pp. 304–305. New York, 1993.
———. "Le roman algérien de langue arabe depuis l'indépendence." *Annuaire de l'Afrique du Nord* 19 (1980): 1127–1133.
DÉJEUX, JEAN. *La littérature algérienne contemporaine.* Paris, 1975.

Aida A. Bamia

Beni Suef

Province (governorate) of Egypt.

This is a middle-Nile province south of Giza, with an area of some 510 square miles (1,325 sq km) and an estimated population in 1986 of 1.5 million. Its capital and principal city—also called Beni Suef—located seventy-five miles (120 km) south of Cairo, on the west bank of the Nile, had an estimated population of 165,000 in 1986. It became an important cotton and trade city during the reign of MUHAMMAD ALI (ruled 1805–1848). It is now a major agricultural center with a moderate amount of commercial and industrial activity.

BIBLIOGRAPHY

Encyclopaedia of Islam, 2nd ed.

Arthur Goldschmidt, Jr.

Benjedid, Chadli [1929–]

Third president of Algeria, 1979–1992

Benjedid was born in Bouteldja in the Annaba region of Algeria. His father was a small landholder. A veteran of the ALGERIAN WAR OF INDEPENDENCE (1954–1962) against France, Benjedid became a professional officer in the Algerian Armée Nationale et Populaire (ANP) (National and Popular Army). He was a member of the Revolutionary Council of Houari BOUMÉDIENNE and a loyal supporter of his regime. He was entrusted with the command of strategic military regions (Constantine, then Oran) and played an important role monitoring French troop withdrawals. After Boumédienne's death (December 1978), he found himself positioned as a compromise candidate for the presidency. He was selected secretary-general of the Front de Libération Nationale (FLN) (National Liberation Front) in January 1979 and was elected president in February.

Unlike his predecessors Ahmed BEN BELLA and Boumédienne, Benjedid was less ideological. Characterized as a pragmatic man, Benjedid tempered Algeria's ambitious state-planning and foreign policy. His five-year plans emphasized more balanced sectoral development (with more attention to agriculture and services). He also reorganized the large state companies and encouraged smaller enterprises. Benjedid strove to realize the shared goal of MAGHRIB unity through amity treaties with Tunisia and Mauritania (1983). Regional integration also necessitated a *rapprochement* with Morocco. Relations severed over the WESTERN SAHARA WAR were restored in 1988. Though Western Sahara's future remained unresolved, the Arab Maghrib Union was proclaimed in February 1989.

As Benjedid consolidated his power internally (marked by the removal of Boumédiennists and his reelection in 1985), he sought to "enrich" the National Charter (first proclaimed in 1976), giving it his imprint. The revised document reaffirmed Algeria's Arab and socialist identity. This particularly dissatisfied restive Kabyles (Berber groups), fearful of the future of their distinct culture and language, as demonstrated particularly by a violent outburst in 1980. The continued attachment to secular socialism also alienated populist Muslims. Chronic unemployment exasperated the disillusioned younger generation. Furthermore, the collapse of oil prices, which were indexed to natural gas prices, hurt the entire economy. These variables contributed to widespread discontent that provoked national uprisings in October 1988, resulting in a state of siege, with scores killed and wounded. Benjedid quickly promised reforms such as political pluralism and civil rights, as realized by the February 1989 constitution.

Benjedid's political survival from 1988 to his deposition in January 1992 is less a testament to his popularity than to Algerians' fearing the alternatives. He was reelected president in 1989, but he failed to galvanize political and popular support, as seen by a series of prime ministers and their governments (Kasdi Merbah [1988–89], Mouloud Hamrouche [1989–91], and Ahmed Ghozali [1991–92]).

The rise of the Islamic Salvation Front (FIS) and its stunning success in regional elections in June 1990 astonished the ruling elites. But Benjedid was determined to permit the democratic process he had inaugurated to complete its imperfect course. National legislative elections in June 1991 had to be postponed, however, given the violent protests of the FIS (in part over eleventh-hour changes by the FLN concerning electoral procedure); Benjedid ordered another state of siege. The FIS's first-round electoral success in December 1991 produced a military coup in January 1992 that established a high security council. President Benjedid was forced to resign and was placed under house arrest.

BIBLIOGRAPHY

ENTELIS, JOHN. *Algeria: The Revolution Institutionalized.* Denver, 1985.
MORTIMER, ROBERT A. "Algeria after the Explosion." *Current History* 89 (April 1990): 161–68.
———. "Algeria's New Sultan." *Current History* 80 (December 1982): 428–31; 433–34.

Philip C. Naylor

Ben Jelloun, Umar   [1933–1975]

Moroccan political activist.

Ben Jelloun, born in Oujda, studied law and telecommunications in Paris, and was president of the Association of Muslim North African Students. In the late 1950s, he was among Mehdi Ben Barka's supporters within ISTIQLAL, and joined him in the breakaway from it and the formation of the UNION NATIONALE DES FORCES POPULAIRES (UNFP). He was a member of the UNFP's national committee and political bureau and director of its newspaper, *al-Muharrir*. His duties led to clashes with trade union leaders over their alleged corruption and advancement of their personal interests. Ben Jelloun served several prison terms, underwent torture, and was sentenced to death in 1963 (pardoned in 1965). He was tried again in 1973 for plotting to overthrow the government and acquitted on August 30, but was held and charged with another offense. In 1974 he received a limited pardon. Ben Jelloun was murdered by unknown assailants on December 18, 1975, in Casablanca. Clement Henry Moore described Ben Jelloun as a major casualty of a political system whose rules he rejected.

Bruce Maddy-Weitzman

Ben Khedda, Ben Youssef   [1920–   ]

President of the Gouvernement Provisoire de la République Algérienne, 1961–1962.

Ben Khedda, born in Berrouaghia, Algeria, worked as a pharmacist and was an active member of Messali al-HADJ's Parti du Peuple Algérien (People's Party, PPA). He rose to secretary-general of its successor organization, the MOUVEMENT POUR LE TRIOMPHE DES LIBERTÉS DÉMOCRATIQUES (Movement for the Triumph of Democratic Liberties, MTLD), but he sided with the centralists in opposition to Messali.

Ben Khedda joined the revolutionary Front de Libération Nationale (National Liberation Front, FLN), earning a reputation as an ideologist. He co-drafted the Soummam Congress Platform and wrote for the FLN's newspaper, al-MOUDJAHID. In 1958, he was selected as minister for Social Affairs in the first Gouvernement Provisoire de la République Algérienne (Provisional Government of the Algerian Republic, GPRA) and also served as an FLN diplomat before replacing Ferhat Abbas as the GPRA's president (August 1961). Ben Khedda supported the conclusion of the Evian Agreements (March 1962), which gave Algeria its independence.

That summer, Ahmed BEN BELLA and Houari BOU-MÉDIENNE, who had the support of a trained external army, took over the leadership of the government. Ben Khedda returned to private life until 1976 when he cosigned a manifesto criticizing the policies of Boumédienne. After the October 1988 riots and the constitutional reforms of 1989, Ben Khedda formed an Islamic party called Oumma.

BIBLIOGRAPHY

STORA, BENJAMIN. *Dictionnaire biographique de militants nationalistes algériens.* Paris, 1985.

Phillip C. Naylor

Ben Lounis, Mohamed

See Bellounis, Mohamed

Ben M'hidi, Muhammad Larbi
[1923–1957]

Algerian revolutionary leader.

Muhammad Larbi Ben M'hidi was born to a farming family in Ain M'Lila near Constantine. A follower of Messali HADJ, he joined the Parti du Peuple Algérien (PPA; Algerian People's Party) and the paramilitary Organisation Spéciale (OS; Special Organization), which was affiliated with the Mouvement pour le Triomphe des Libertés Démocratiques (MTLD; Movement for the Triumph of Democratic Liberties). Like other members of the younger elite, Ben M'hidi grew impatient with the venerable nationalist Hadj and collaborated in the founding in 1954 of the Comité Révolutionnaire d'Unité et d'Action (CRUA; Revolutionary Committee for Unity and Action) and subsequently the Front de Libération Nationale (FLN; National Liberation Front). He is regarded as one of the nine historic chiefs (*chefs historiques*) of the Algerian revolution against French colonialism.

During the ALGERIAN WAR OF INDEPENDENCE (1954–1962), Ben M'Hidi initially commanded Wilaya I (the military district in the Oran region) and played an important role at the FLN's Soummam conference in August 1956. Ben M'hidi believed that the revolution should be directed by "internal" rather than "external" revolutionaries. During the Battle of Algiers (1956–1957), he headed FLN operations until his capture in February 1957. The French announced in March that Ben M'hidi had committed suicide in his cell. This account was disputed by others, who have contended that he was in fact tortured and murdered.

BIBLIOGRAPHY

NAYLOR, PHILLIP C., and ALF A. HEGGOY. *The Historical Dictionary of Algeria,* 2nd ed. Metuchen, N.J., 1994.

Phillip C. Naylor

Ben Porat, Mordechai   [1923–   ]

Israeli politician and community leader.

Ben-Porat, a native of Baghdad, emigrated to Palestine in 1945 and joined the Haganah in 1947. During the War of Independence he fought in the battles of Latrun and Ramla-Lud.

Ben-Porat was sent to Iraq in 1949 to organize emigration of Jews to Israel; he remained there until June 1951, while EZRA AND NEHEMIA OPERATIONS were proceeding at full speed. He escaped arrest three times but was ultimately caught and tortured.

In 1965 Ben-Porat was a founding member of the RAFI PARTY established by David Ben-Gurion. He was a member of the KNESSET and its deputy speaker in 1965; deputy secretary-general of the Labor party from 1970 to 1972; and a member of Israel's mission to the United Nations in 1977. Ben Porat was reelected to the Knesset on the list of

Telem, the party founded by Moshe Dayan, in 1982; he resigned in 1984.

Ben Porat founded the TEHIYAH (revival) movement, the World Organization of Jews from Arab Countries, and the Babylonian Jewry Heritage Center, of which he is chairman.

Nissim Rejwan

Ben Salah, Ahmed   [1926–   ]

Tunisian political and labor leader.

Born in Moknine, he attended Sadiqi College in Tunis and began his political career as a DESTOUR student leader at the University of Paris. Neo-Destour was the Tunisian political party that led the nationalist struggle against French colonial control. Returning to Tunisia in 1948, he remained active in the party but became involved with the Union Général des Travailleurs Tunisiens (UGTT), the General Union of Tunisian Workers. From 1951 until 1954, he worked with the International Confederation of Free Trade Unions in Brussels. Following his election as general secretary of the UGTT in 1954, he advocated the introduction of socialist economic concepts.

In 1955, Tunis was granted autonomy by France; Ben Salah's success in maintaining UGTT loyalty to Habib BOURGUIBA, leader of Destour and first president of the Republic of Tunisia (1957–1987), when he was threatened by a radical movement within the party headed by Salah Ben Yusuf, assured Ben Salah of an influential political role. Although Bourguiba initially rejected Ben Salah's socialist approach, the deterioration of the new republic's economy led to his appointment as minister of planning in 1961.

Ben Salah introduced a ten-year plan built around socialist development projects, intending to promote self-sufficiency and raise living standards. His ideas generally met with success in the industrial sector, but his insistence on organizing state-run agricultural cooperatives and his intention to bring all cultivable land under state management provoked widespread rural antagonism. Accusations of corruption and mismanagement followed and, in 1969, fearful that popular opposition to these policies would undermine the entire government, Bourguiba renounced Ben Salah, who was arrested and imprisoned but escaped in 1973. In exile, he organized the opposition party MOUVEMENT DE L'UNITÉ POPULAIRE, embodying the socialist principles he had tried to use while in office. In 1988, President Zayn al-Abidine Ben Ali allowed him to return to Tunisia, but Ben Salah refrained from playing an active role in post-Bourguiba politics. His economic views are summarized in "Tunisia; Endog- enous Development and Structural Transformation," in *Another Development: Approaches and Strategies,* edited by Marc Nerfin (Uppsala, 1977).

BIBLIOGRAPHY

MOORE, CLEMENT HENRY. *Tunisia since Independence: The Dynamics of One-Party Government.* Berkeley, Calif., 1965.
PERKINS, KENNETH J. *Tunisia: Crossroads of the Islamic and European Worlds.* Boulder, Colo., 1986.

Kenneth J. Perkins

Ben Seddiq, Mahjoub   [1925–   ]

Cofounder of the Moroccan Labor Union.

In 1955, following jail sentences for having organized a general strike, Ben Seddiq and Tayyib Bouazza founded the UNION MAROCAINE DU TRAVAIL (UMT). Since 1960, Ben Seddiq has been its secretary-general. The UMT, which initially was closely affiliated with the ISTIQLAL PARTY, was the original—and for a time the most important—all-Moroccan trade union. Ben Seddiq is considered to be one of the founders of the UNION NATIONALE DES FORCES POPULAIRES (UNFP; National Union of Popular Forces), which broke away from the Istiqlal in 1959. He formally disassociated himself from the UNFP in January 1963, while remaining associated for a time with "loyal opposition" politics. Ben Seddiq was sentenced to eighteen months of imprisonment in July 1967 for undermining the respect due to the authority of the state, after he sharply criticized the government's decision to block the firing of Jewish employees in state-owned firms in the aftermath of the ARAB–ISRAEL WAR of 1967.

In more recent years, the UMT has become less confrontational, especially in comparison to the two other competing labor confederations—the Confédération Démocratique du Travail (CDT), affiliated with the Union Socialiste des Forces Populaires (USFP), and the Union Générale des Travailleurs du Maroc (UGTM), affiliated with the Istiqlal party—and Ben Seddiq himself has adopted a lower public profile. He is currently secretary-general of Royal Air Maroc, the Moroccan national airline.

Bruce Maddy-Weitzman

Ben Simeon, Raphael Aaron   [1848–1928]

A leading Sephardic legal scholar and modernist.

Born in Rabat, Morocco, and raised in Jerusalem, Raphael Aaron Ben Simeon avidly studied foreign languages, read modern Hebrew literature, and kept abreast of scientific and technological developments in addition to learning traditional rabbinics. In 1891, Ben Simeon was appointed Hakham Bashi in Cairo. Together with his liberal colleague, Elijah Bekhor HAZZAN, the chief rabbi of Alexandria, Ben Simeon made Egyptian Jewry the most progressive in the Middle East and the MAGHRIB (North Africa). His many responsa (writings and interpretations) show his openness to modernity, which he understood brought with it an unprecedented measure of freedom of choice to the individual.

He retired to Palestine in 1923 and lived his remaining years in Tel Aviv. His voluminous writings include *Nehar Mizrayim* (Alexandria, 1908), a work on Egyptian Jewish customary legal practice; *Tuv Mizrayim* (Jerusalem, 1908), a biographical dictionary of the Egyptian rabbinate; and *Umi-Zur Devash* (Jerusalem, 1911/12), his collected responsa.

BIBLIOGRAPHY

STILLMAN, NORMAN A. *The Jews of Arab Lands in Modern Times.* Philadelphia, 1991.

Norman Stillman

Bentov, Mordekhai

Israeli politician.

Born in Poland, Bentov settled in Palestine in 1920 and was active in the labor and kibbutz movements. He was minister of labor and reconstruction in Israel's 1948-1949 provisional government, and he sat in the KNESSET as a MAPAM (United Workers' party) deputy after 1949. He was minister of development (1955–1961) and minister of housing (1966–1969). Also he was the founding editor of the MAPAM daily, *Al ha-Mishmar.*

BIBLIOGRAPHY

Encyclopedia Judaica. New York, 1971.
New Standard Jewish Encyclopedia. New York, 1977.

Zachary Karabell

Bentwich, Norman   (1883–1971)

First British attorney general in mandate Palestine; legal scholar and author.

Bentwich, an English Jew, was first trained as a classicist and then in law. He entered the Egyptian Ministry of Justice in 1912 as inspector of native courts.

In 1918, he became legal secretary to the British military administration in Palestine and, after the establishment of the mandate government in 1922, he became attorney general. As the conflict in Palestine between the Arabs and Jews escalated, the presence of a Jewish attorney general became an embarrassment to the British. Bentwich was recalled in 1929 to the Colonial Office in London and retired in 1931. In 1932, he became professor of international relations at the Hebrew University of Jerusalem. During the 1930s, he took an active role in welfare efforts for German Jewish refugees. He was the author of more than thirty books on Judeo-Greek civilization, international law, and Israel.

BIBLIOGRAPHY

BLAKE, LORD, and C. S. NICHOLLS, eds. *The Dictionary of National Biography, 1971–1980.* Oxford, 1986.

Steve Tamari

Benvenisti, Meron   [1934–   ]

Israeli reformer.

Formerly deputy mayor of Jerusalem (1967–1978) and Knesset member, Benvenisti became head of the WEST BANK DATA PROJECT, a group formed to monitor and evaluate Arab–Israeli relations. He has been one of the most vocal critics of Israeli policy toward the Palestinians and the West Bank. In 1981, he put forth the "Benvenisti Prognosis," which foresaw a continued stalemate over the occupied territories (the West Bank and Gaza Strip) and predicted that inertia, religious beliefs, and Israeli "imperialism" would prevent the Israelis from withdrawing in the near future.

BIBLIOGRAPHY

O'BRIEN, CONOR CRUISE. *The Siege.* London, 1986.
ROLEF, SUSAN HATTIS, ed. *Political Dictionary of the State of Israel.* New York, 1987.
SHIPLER, DAVID. *Arab and Jew.* New York, 1986.

Zachary Karabell

Ben-Yehuda, Eliezar   [1857–1922]

Author and editor; pioneer in the restoration of Hebrew as a living language.

Born in Lushky, Lithuania, where he received both a Jewish traditional and a secular education, Eliezar Ben-Yehuda was impressed by the nationalist struggles in the Balkans (1877–1878) against the Ottoman Empire and became interested in the restoration of a Jewish homeland in Palestine and the revival of the HEBREW language. In 1881, he settled in Palestine, working as an editor for various Hebrew periodicals and establishing his own, *Ha-Tzvi,* in 1884. In 1889, he established the Hebrew Language Council, among whose tasks was the coining of new Hebrew words. He served as chairman of the council until his death.

Ben-Yehuda's greatest work was the compilation of a comprehensive dictionary of the Hebrew language, several volumes of which were published in his lifetime. The complete edition of seventeen volumes was published in 1959.

BIBLIOGRAPHY

LAQUEUR, WALTER. *A History of Zionism.* New York, 1976.

Martin Malin

Ben Yusuf, Salah [1910–1961]

Tunisian lawyer, political activist, and leader of a radical group within the anticolonial movement that challenged Neo-Destour party leader Habib Bourguiba on the eve of independence.

Born on the island of Djerba (Jerba), Ben Yusuf was an early associate of Habib BOURGUIBA (who became president of Tunisia, 1957–1987) and was a member of the Neo-DESTOUR political party, which was led by Bourguiba and which challenged French colonial control. The French had formed a protectorate in 1883, after the LA MARSA CONVENTION, and had suppressed first the Destour and then the Neo-Destour attempts to modify Tunisia's political status.

In 1937, Ben Yusuf was named to the Destour political bureau; in 1945, he became secretary-general of the party. At a congress of Tunisian opposition groups in 1946, he expressed the frustration of many politically conscious Tunisians by calling for immediate and unequivocal independence—a demand that Bourguiba had never voiced and one that invited a split between party radicals and moderates. Anxious to prevent the radicals from dominating the party, the French permitted Bourguiba to return from exile in 1949.

In 1950, Ben Yusuf accepted the post of minister of Tunisian justice in a government pledged to explore the possibility of internal autonomy. When French-settler protests caused the abandonment of political reforms in 1952, Ben Yusuf traveled to Paris to place the Tunisian case before the United Nations Security Council. Amid a campaign of repression of the Neo-Destour, the resident general ordered his return, but Ben Yusuf fled to Cairo. Influenced there by PAN-ARABISM, Ben Yusuf continued to insist on Tunisia's complete break with France and its establishment of ties with other Arab states.

In April 1955, Bourguiba negotiated an agreement with France granting Tunisia home rule, but allowing France to retain considerable influence in many important areas. Although this Franco-Tunisian convention enjoyed widespread support within the Neo-Destour, Ben Yusuf regarded it as a betrayal both of Tunisian national interests—by withholding the full sovereignty he sought—and of pan-Arabism—by allowing France to concentrate on the suppression of nationalist uprisings in Algeria and Morocco. Thus, he returned to Tunisia in September, determined to block the party's endorsement of the convention. Ousted from the political bureau because of his opposition, Ben Yusuf turned to the party membership for support. In addition to the backing of many small businessmen (especially fellow Djerbans who dominated the retail grocery trade), he also had the support of old aristocratic families and conservative religious leaders, both traditionally opposed to Bourguiba. But Ben Yusuf's efforts to mobilize a broader following were thwarted by Neo-Destour loyalists. In November, the party congress voted overwhelmingly to accept the convention.

Unwilling to admit defeat, Ben Yusuf and his aides set about creating rival Neo-Destour branches throughout the country. His most militant supporters resorted to a campaign of terrorism that resulted in a police crackdown in January 1956. Ben Yusuf fled to Egypt, but violence continued in his name until mid-1956. His denunciations continued even after Tunisian independence in March, with criticisms not only of Neo-Destour's undemocratic tendencies, but also of Bourguiba's decision to concentrate on resolving domestic problems before committing himself to pan-Arab concerns. In 1961, Ben Yusuf died at the hands of an unidentified assassin in Cairo.

The vehement opposition of this once-trusted colleague undoubtedly shaped Bourguiba's views on political dissent. For the rest of his career, Bourguiba refused to tolerate an opposition element, no matter how benign, within his party.

BIBLIOGRAPHY

MOORE, CLEMENT HENRY. *Tunisia since Independence: The Dynamics of One-Party Government.* Berkeley, Calif., 1965.
LE TOURNEAU, ROGER. *Evolution politique de l'afrique du nord musulman, 1920–1961.* Paris, 1962.

Kenneth J. Perkins

Ben-Zvi, Yizhak [1884–1963]

Journalist; Labor Zionist leader; second president of Israel, 1952–1963.

Born in Poltava, in the Ukraine, into a family active in Zionism, Yizhak Ben-Zvi served as second president of Israel until his death. He assumed the role of chief theoretician of Labor Zionism from his arrival in Palestine in 1907.

As a childhood friend of Ber Borochov, Ben-Zvi had attended the founding conference of the Po'alei Zion (Workers of Zion) movement in Russia in 1906. He lived near the center of Russian revolutionary activities and the site of major pogroms. Committed to socialism and Zionism, Ben-Zvi's intellectual and political activities had one overwhelming purpose—to bridge the gap between Labor Zionist theory and conditions in Palestine. One of the founders of the Po'alei Zion party in Palestine, he also organized a clandestine Jewish defense society called Bar Giora (a name associated with one of the Jewish leaders fighting the Romans in 66–70 C.E.). Bar Giora's members aimed at replacing the Arab guards usually hired to secure outlying Jewish agricultural settlements. Hoping to raise class consciousness among Palestine's Jews, Ben-Zvi edited his party's newspaper and opened a small school in Jerusalem with a curriculum appropriate to the needs of a modern Jewish society.

With the restoration of the Ottoman Empire's constitution after the YOUNG TURK Revolution in 1908, Ben-Zvi and one of his closest friends and party comrades, David Ben-Gurion, traveled to Constantinople (now Istanbul) to study law as an avenue of entry into Ottoman politics. With the outbreak of World War I in Europe, he and Ben-Gurion returned to Palestine but were unable to remain. Exiled by Ottoman authorities as potential troublemakers, Ben-Zvi and Ben-Gurion lived and lectured, on behalf of the Po'alei Zion movement, in the United States. Ben-Zvi returned to Palestine as a soldier in the Jewish Legion.

Ben-Zvi's commitment to the fundamental principles of Labor Zionism never wavered. The possibilities opened by the advent of British rule altered the perspective of many Labor Zionists and the positions adopted by the political parties and institutions. Ben-Zvi maintained his close personal friendship with Ben-Gurion despite the latter's departure from such Labor Zionist strictures as the inevitability of class struggle. As Ben-Zvi saw it, only a clear Labor Zionist ideology and program would unify Jews in Palestine and create the foundations for a humane society. Sensitivity to the differences between Zionist and Palestinian national interests led Ben-Zvi to devote considerable effort to uncovering the history of Ottoman Palestine. As a prolific journalist, he also undertook research of ancient and remote Jewish communities. Elected to the Jerusalem municipality several times, he established ties with the council's Arab representatives. He participated in the National Council first as a member and then later as its chair. He became a link between the British mandate government and the organized Labor Zionist leadership. He founded the Institute for the Study of Jewish Communities in the Middle East, later renamed the Ben-Zvi Institute. As president of Israel until his death in 1963, he lived in a simple house in a quiet Jerusalem neighborhood, personifying the original egalitarian impulse of Labor Zionism. He is the author of *The Jewish Yishuv in Peki'in Village* (1922); *Eretz-Israel under Ottoman Rule* (1955); *The Exile and the Redeemed* (1958); and *The Hebrew Battalion Letters* (1969).

BIBLIOGRAPHY

FRANKEL, JONATHAN. *Prophecy and Politics.* Cambridge, U.K., 1981.
HALPERN, BEN, and JEHUDA REINHARZ. "The Cultural and Social Background of the Second Aliyah." *Middle Eastern Studies* 27 (July 1991): 487–517.

Donna Robinson Divine

Berber

Person(s), language(s), and culture of North African groups descended from the pre-Arab Mediterranean-type indigenous populations.

The term *Berber* was first applied centuries ago by foreign conquerors. Modern-day Berbers generally prefer their own designations—*amazigh* (male Berber) and *tamazight* (female Berber or Berber language/dialect)—or the local variants of these. Speakers of Berber languages, those to whom we now refer as Berbers, are most numerous today in western North Africa, but they can be found as far east as eastern Libya and even western Egypt (Siwa) and as far south as the Sahara Desert, northern Saharan regions of Niger, Mali, and Burkina Faso. The nation of Senegal takes its name from a Berber-speaking group, the Zenaga, who live in an area of southwestern MAURITANIA.

No Berber race can be distinguished, rather the variety of features found throughout the MAGHRIB (North Africa) are essentially those associated with Mediterranean peoples generally. There seems always to have been a considerable mixture and, at present, one is confronted with Berbers having a

Berber woman from the Aurès Mountains in Algeria. (Richard Bulliet)

wide spectrum of skin colors, statures, cranial and facial proportions.

Several of the largest groups of Berbers that are characterized by linguistic and cultural distinctiveness are referred to using terms of non-Berber origin, usually from Arabic—the Kabyles in Kabylia (Djurdjura mountains, east southeast from Algiers); the Chawia (Aurès mountains in eastern Algeria, south of Constantine); the Tuareg (Saharan Algeria, Mali, Niger, Burkina Faso); the Chleuh (High Atlas and Anti-Atlas mountains, Sous valley in southern Morocco); and the Braber (also called simply *imazighen*, plural of *amazigh*) of the Middle Atlas mountains of Morocco. Virtually all other Berbers go by terms referring to the name of their place or region of origin: Nefusi, Djerbi, Mzabi, Rifi, and so on.

North African countries have not chosen to include native language data in their census process—but taking Berber speakers as constituting between 30 percent and the commonly cited 40 percent of Morocco's population, around 20 percent of Algeria's, adding several tens of thousands each from Tunisia, Libya, Niger, Burkina Faso, and Mauritania, one could very roughly assess the total to be somewhere around 12 million in the mid-1990s.

The overwhelming majority of Berbers have their homes in rural environments, far from the urban centers. In general, they can be found on the least productive lands—the mountains, the high plateaus, the pre-Saharan *hammada,* and in the Sahara desert. Although the Tuareg—camel nomads of the central Sahara—more vividly capture our imagination by their fascinating aspect and institutions, their lifestyle is not particularly representative. Most Berbers are—and have been throughout recorded history—sedentary agriculturalists. Along the mountains bordering on the high plateaus and desert, some Berbers practice forms of seminomadism, or transhumance, during part of the year to maintain their flocks (especially in the Aurès mountains and the southern part of the Middle Atlas).

Sedentary Berbers typically live in villages and eke out a meager peasant existence from small irrigated gardens, dry cereal culture, arboriculture, and small flocks of sheep and goats, occasionally a cow or two. In today's world, it is necessary for many of the most able-bodied men to export, for a time, their most marketable asset, their labor. It is not uncommon to find villages largely devoid of men between the ages of sixteen and forty. They emigrate temporarily, usually without families, both to North African cities and to European industrial centers and, from there, send home the money that, by living frugally, they are able to accumulate. Without their support, these villages and areas simply could not survive.

In many instances, by virtue of a natural tendency of younger emigrants to follow their elder family members, a village or even a whole area becomes specialized in a particular vocational field to the extent that they hold a near monopoly on one or another activity or commercial enterprise. Interestingly, this has happened in the grocery trade in all three of the main Maghribian countries. In each case, Berbers from a specific area have come to dominate to such an

Berber Twaregs in market at Tamanrasset, Algeria. (Richard Bulliet)

extent that, in the towns and cities, one typically does not go to the grocer's: in Tunisia one goes to the Djerbi's (from the island of Djerba), in Algeria to the Mzabi's (pre-Sahara), in Morocco to the Sousi's (Sous river valley and Anti-Atlas mountains). It is a significant instance of very successful adaptation to nontraditional ways, but it should be noted that its purpose, for the overwhelming majority, is precisely to permit the maintenance of the traditional homeland and lifestyle.

Art. The forms of Berber artistic expression, at least in the modern period, are primarily linked to utilitarian objects—pottery, weaving, and architecture—and to jewelry. All are characterized by predominantly geometrical, nonrepresentational patterns. Neither the forms and patterns nor the techniques appear to have changed significantly since ancient times, and they can be related directly to forms found in the Mediterranean basin from as early as the Iron Age. While they are not especially original or exclusive to Berbers, one is struck by the extraordinary persistence and continuity, in Berber country, of the tradition. Some of the most remarkable examples of Berber artistic expression are: (1) the fortified architecture of the southern Moroccan *ksars,* massive but majestic rammed earth and adobe-brick structures with intricate decorative patterns seemingly chiseled into their towers and facades; (2) Kabyle and Chawia pottery, extraordinary for the variety and elegance of its modeled forms as well as the composition and proportion of its applied patterns; (3) silver jewelry, embossed and inlaid with stones as well as with enameled cloisonné, especially—but by no means exclusively—that represented by the Kabyle tradition; (4) textiles throughout North Africa, but particularly in southern Tunisia and in central and southern Morocco.

Social Organization. Traditional social organization is family based and therefore quite segmentary. Relations between extended families—or, if need be, between clans or villages—have in the past been (and continue to some extent to be) mediated by an assembly of heads of family, or elders, called the DJEMA'A. In today's more centrally administered bureaucratic world, many of the traditional competencies of the assembly have been taken over by government agencies. Nonetheless, a number of issues—those concerning local resources of common interest and responsibility: maintenance of paths, irrigation canals, mosques, and Qur'anic schools; hiring of the Qur'anic teacher; usage of forests and pastureland; setting of plowing and harvest dates; protection of crops; cooperative support (usually in

the form of labor) of disadvantaged families; collective meat purchasing; hospitality for outsiders; organizing local religious or secular celebrations; and so forth—continue to require consensus decisions and the shared provision of labor and material resources. While the term *democratic,* which has often been applied to Berber institutions, does not appear appropriate, one is struck by their profound egalitarianism, less as a moral imperative than one born of a distrust of power concentrated in the hands of one segment or another. This is often summarized in the terms *balance* and *opposition:* balance of power maintained by a constant resistance to the other segments' natural self-interest and by vigilance to assure that all segments bear burdens and reap benefits equally.

Berbers seem always to have had, and earned, a reputation of fierce independence, of inclination to rebellion, of resistance to any imposition of control over their lives. North African history is extremely fragmented, constantly jostled by new revolts, realignments, and alliances. Every schismatic movement seems to be welcomed against the previous orthodoxy, Donatism when the Berbers were being Christianized, Kharidjism in the early years of Islamization. As often as not, the not yet entrenched conqueror is joined with to throw off the previous tyrant—whether either or both were Berber or not. Each time that a choice was to be made, it was seemingly made in the direction of greater local control and independence. Only on rare occasions in their history did the Berbers put together something like a Berber nation, uniting for a time over a vast territory to create a state or empire. In the two most important instances, the Almoravid and the Almohad dynasties of the eleventh and twelfth centuries, they were drawn together by the ideal of reform of the previously dominant regime(s), seen as having fallen into corrupt ways. This search for ever purer forms is, along with their deep cultural conservatism, one of the most constantly recurring themes throughout their history.

Religion. Virtually all Berbers today are Muslims and, like most North Africans, are of SUNNI ISLAM orthodoxy. In the Mzab and in Ouargla in Algeria, on the island of Djerba in Tunisia, and in the Nefusa mountains of Libya, there subsist Ibadite communities—all essentially Berber-speaking—who trace their history back to the Kharidjite schism of the seventh/eighth century.

Little reliable detail can be given as to the nature of the Berbers' pre-Islamic religious beliefs and practices. There is evidence from archeology, from the remarks of observers in antiquity, and also from popular practices that have survived into the present in North Africa, of a generally animistic set of beliefs manifested in sacralization of promontories, outcroppings, caves, trees, and water sources. The usages seem to have been highly varied and local in their expression but widespread and reflective of the quasi-universal need to assuage the spirits to which the vicissitudes of everyday life can be—and are still—attributed. Much of the North African fondness for the veneration of local saints, so-called MARABOUT-ism, tolerated by the central tradition of Islam as somewhat deviant and marginal, can be understood as deriving in large part from this substratum: saints' "tombs" are often situated next to trees, caves, topographical features, or water sources that give evidence of cultic activity going back well before the life of the nominal vessel of *baraka* (blessedness, protection, God's power made present).

Language and Literature. Berber languages constitute together one branch of the Afro-Asiatic (or Hamito-Semitic) language family, whose other four branches are Semitic, Egyptian, Cushitic, and Chadic. Berber languages show a high degree of homogeneity in their grammar, somewhat less in their phonology. The differences that one notes between them are fewer and less considerable than those within the Semitic, Cushitic, or Chadic branches (Egyptian is manifested as essentially homogeneous at any historical moment). In a number of important respects, Berber bears a closer resemblance to Semitic languages than to the other branches: (1) the sound system employs contrasts of consonant "length" and pharyngealization (emphatics); (2) there are three basic vowels *a, i, u* with an archaic contrast of short versus long vowels found in the important set of Tuareg languages; (3) the morphological system is highly complex, characterized by a prevalence of tri-radical roots (less than Semitic, however), and considerable use of both consonant length and intraradical vowel alternation to express grammatical categories such as verb aspect and noun number; (4) the verbal system is based on a fundamental contrast of perfective versus imperfective aspect, with tense being secondary; (5) word order is predominantly V(erb) S(ubject) O(bject), though SVO is very frequent in main clauses.

Some noteworthy features peculiar to Berber include the following: (1) as reflected in the words *amazigh, tamazight* (cf. supra), as well as many place names on maps, masculine nouns begin with a vowel and feminine nouns begin with *t* + vowel and most often end in *t* as well (the vowel is *a* in 80% of nouns); (2) a special form of the noun (the annexed or construct form), characterized by an alteration of the vowel of the first syllable (*amazigh* > *umazigh, tamazight* > *tmazight*), is used for the subject noun after its verb, after prepositions, and as the second element in a noun-complement construction; (3) the subject markers of finite verb forms are both prefixed and suffixed to the stem (with the prefix elements being clearly identifiable with those of the Semitic prefix conjugation); (4) pronominal objects of the verb basically go immediately after the verb but must precede it in a number of conditions (essentially those of subordination); (5) particles can be used with the verb to "orient" the verbal action: *d* = "toward speaker" and *n* = "away from speaker."

Berber languages are generally only spoken, seldom written. Among the Tuareg, however, there subsists an alphabet, the *tifinagh,* which descends from the Libyan alphabet that is found in ancient inscriptions throughout much of North Africa (but principally present-day Tunisia and eastern Algeria). This alphabet, which like Arabic is essentially consonantal, can be written right to left or left to right, occasionally vertically. Among the Tuareg, it is used primarily for short inscriptions on rocks and for brief messages but does not seem to be employed for the recording of stories, documents or history, those uses for which writing is basic in our Western cultures. Some efforts have been made by advocates of Berber cultural affirmation, to adapt the *tifinagh* to such functions and to broaden its use to other Berber-speaking groups, as in Kabylia and in Morocco. These efforts have had only very limited success and those publications (several in Algeria and in Morocco) written in the Berber language generally use the Latin-based transcription system employed by the French.

Berber literature is then essentially oral. It includes many traditional stories—tales of animals, marvelous tales with ogres and monsters, tales of kings and princesses (à la *Thousand and One Nights*), hagiographic legends, and myriad other stories that hand down the moral and ethical base of Berber society. As for poetry, among the Berbers it goes with music and is—unlike the tales and stories—constantly regenerated around a wide spectrum of subjects. There are extremely traditional forms, such as the often bantering repartee in the context of celebratory line dances in Morocco. There are more lyrical forms, songs of the heart and its joys and pains. There are the elaborate and often quite lengthy commentaries by troubador-like itinerant singers who hold forth, often quite bitingly, on all subjects, including the political scene. And, of course, one cannot fail to mention Berber popular music, which constitutes the richest and most fertile field of Berber literary expression today.

Of the languages with which Berber has shared North Africa at different times and places—among them Phoenician, Latin, Germanic (German and English), Turkish, Italian, Spanish, and French—none has had the profound effect that the Arabic dialects have had. Most Berber languages have a high percentage of borrowing from Arabic, as well as from other languages (these often indirectly through Arabic, however). Least influenced are the Tuareg languages; most influenced, those that are near urban centers and from whose areas there has traditionally been much temporary emigration for work.

Berber languages survive because children learn their first language from their mothers and it continues to be the language of the home, of the private world, long after they become adults and the men become bilingual. Berber women continue, in most areas, to have little education and little contact with the Arabic-speaking world around them, so their children will doubtless continue to learn and to perpetuate Berber languages. The movements to preserve Berber culture, most developed in Kabylia and somewhat in Morocco, will also doubtless have a conservative effect. Where Berber is spoken only in a village or two surrounded by Arabic speakers, it is disappearing. In the larger Berber-speaking regions, however, it is quite resistant, and the numbers of speakers are growing at nearly the same rate as that at which the population increases.

In postindependence North Africa, Berber languages and cultures have been neglected and even repressed by the agencies of the central governments. This seems to have been caused by a perceived need to discourage cultural differences in the building of the nation-state—cultural differences that, it was felt, had been exploited by the French colonial regimes to divide the colonized and impose their authority. On occasion, the reaction to this repression has been violent, as in 1980 in Kabylia. Not surprisingly, political movements have grown up around the issues of cultural expression and autonomy. In both Algeria and Morocco, there exist official political parties made up essentially of Berbers with Berber cultural preservation as one of their highest priorities.

BIBLIOGRAPHY

BASSET, ANDRÉ. *La langue berbère*. London, 1952.
"Berbers," *Encyclopedia of Islam*. Leiden, Neth., 1960.
CAMPS, GABRIEL. *Berbères: Aux marges de l'histoire*. Toulouse, France, 1980.
EICKELMAN, DALE. *Moroccan Islam: Tradition and Society in a Pilgrimage Center*. Austin, Tex., 1976.
Encyclopédie berbère. Aix-en-Provence, 1984.
GELLNER, ERNEST. *Saints of the Atlas*. London, 1969.
GELLNER, ERNEST, and CHARLES MICAUD, eds. *Arabs and Berbers: From Tribe to Nation in North Africa*. Lexington, Mass., 1972.
PRASSE, KARL G. *Manuel de grammaire touarègue*. Copenhagen, 1972–1974.
WESTERMARCK, EDWARD. *Ritual and Belief in Morocco*. London, 1926.

Thomas G. Penchoen

Berber Dahir

The sultan's order that in 1930 removed Morocco's Berbers from the jurisdiction of Islamic law.

The Berber Dahir, a decree issued by Morocco's sultan at the instigation of French colonial authorities on May 16, 1930, created courts in Berber-speaking regions that decided cases by codified local custom (*urf*) instead of Islamic law (SHARI'A). The mass urban protests against the decree served as a catalyst for Morocco's nationalist movement and drew support from Muslims worldwide.

BIBLIOGRAPHY

BROWN, KENNETH. "The Impact of the Dahir Berbère in Salé." In *Arabs and Berbers,* ed. by Ernest Gellner and Charles Micaud. London, 1973.

Dale F. Eickelman

Berihah

Underground mass movement, both organized and spontaneous, of Jewish Holocaust survivors fleeing Eastern Europe for Palestine.

Functioning from about 1944 through 1948, the Berihah (Hebrew for flight) organization was officially established in Lublin, Poland, in January 1945, under the leadership of Abba Kovner. Among the founders were Jewish resistance fighters, partisans, and ZIONIST underground groups, all of whom had had previous experience in smuggling Jews across hostile borders in Nazi-occupied Europe during the Holocaust. The key transit points were Czechoslovakia, Hungary, Yugoslavia, Italy, and U.S. army-controlled zones in Germany and Austria.

The height of Berihah activity was in 1945 and 1946, when about 180,000 Jews fled or migrated. In 1946 the USSR closed its borders; in early 1947 Poland halted its lenient policy of allowing Jews to cross freely; in April 1947 the U.S. army declared that it was no longer accepting Jews in D.P. (displaced persons) camps. By 1948 Berihah activity was winding down, although some crossing points remained on the borders of Eastern Europe.

From 1944 through 1948, Berihah helped approximately 200,000 Jews to flee Eastern Europe. The organization's ideology was Zionism, and its importance lay not only in helping these Holocaust survivors flee lands of persecution, but, by bringing masses of Jews to Palestine, it also played a key role in the establishment of the State of ISRAEL.

BIBLIOGRAPHY

ROLEF, S. H., ed. *Political Dictionary of the State of Israel.* New York, 1987.

Ann Kahn

Berkowitz, Yizhak [1885–1967]

Hebrew and Yiddish writer and editor.

Born in Belorussia, Berkowitz won a prize in a 1904 literary contest sponsored by the Warsaw Jewish newspaper *Ha-Zofeh* for his story "Moshkele Hazir." By 1905, his writings appeared in most of the contemporary Hebrew and Yiddish journals. From 1905 to 1928, Berkowitz served as editor of numerous Hebrew and Yiddish journals in Eastern Europe and the United States, among them *Ha-Zeman, Di Naye Velt, Ha-Toren,* and *Miklat.*

He reached Palestine in 1928 and became an editor of the weekly *Moznayim.* He translated into Hebrew and published the collected works of Sholem Aleichem, his father-in-law. Berkowitz is recognized as a master of the short story, many of which are set in turn-of-the-century Russia. They deal with the social upheavals that confront Eastern European JEWS.

Ann Kahn

Berlin, Congress and Treaty of

Treaty that ended the Russo–Turkish War, redividing the countries of southeastern Europe that had belonged to the Ottoman Empire.

In March 1878, following the Russian victory over the Ottoman Turks in the Russo–Turkish War of 1877–1878, the Treaty of San Stefano was imposed. The principal feature of that pact was the creation of a large Bulgarian state, possessing coastal territory on the Mediterranean as well as on the Black Sea. The new Bulgaria also included the bulk of Macedonia, denying Austria–Hungary any avenue for advancement south to the coveted Mediterranean coast. Britain disliked the treaty, because it could allow the Russians to become a naval power in the Middle East, using the Mediterranean ports of the newly created Bulgarian puppet state. A grave danger existed that Austria and Britain would make war rather than tolerate such Russian aggrandizement.

Prince Otto von Bismarck, chancellor of the new German Empire (1871–1890), realized that such a major war might provide France with allies and a chance to avenge Germany's 1871 conquest. He therefore proffered his services as an "honest broker" who sought peace disinterestedly, since Germany had no ambitions in the Balkans or Middle East. Thus, the Congress of Berlin was convened in June–July 1878, attended by the plenipotentiaries of Turkey and all the major powers. Benjamin Disraeli, prime minister of Great Britain (1874–1880), and Count Gyula Andrássy, foreign minister of Austria-Hungary (1871–1879), made their advance preparations carefully, offering African territory to France and Italy and slashing the size of Bulgaria by returning most of it to the Ottomans, so that Russia's satellite would no longer claim Macedonia or a Mediterranean coast line. The Austrians gained a protectorate over Bosnia-Herzegovina and prepared for a future thrust southward to the Mediterranean by leaving their intended avenue of advance, the Sanjak of Novi Bazar, in Ottoman hands. Even Russia, deprived of a Mediterranean base, received compensations on the Asian Caucasus frontier. In a separate treaty, the Ottomans yielded the valuable island of Cyprus to Britain for ninety-nine years, in return for guaranteeing the Ottomans possession of their Asiatic lands for that period. Only afterward did the Ottomans realize that they had surrendered a valuable naval base in exchange for a British guarantee that neither could be nor would be fulfilled.

The Congress of Berlin is, therefore, the point at which Britain ceased to be Ottoman Turkey's great defender and Germany gradually took on that role. In the next generation, Germany, which had had no major Middle Eastern interests, was to become the principal protector of the Ottoman Empire and of Islam.

In the long term, by supporting Britain and Austria against Russian claims, Bismarck threatened that perfect harmony among the Great Powers—his chief instrument in keeping France isolated. To his credit, Bismarck "kept the telegraph lines open to St. Petersburg" as long as he held office. Nevertheless, Russian fears of an Austro–German alliance came to fulfillment in 1879, and those fears led to the Franco–Russian alliance, consummated from 1892 to 1894.

BIBLIOGRAPHY

JASZI, OSCAR. *The Dissolution of the Habsburg Monarchy.* Chicago, 1964.

JELAVICH, BARBARA. *The Habsburg Empire in European Affairs, 1814–1918.* Chicago, 1969.

Arnold Blumberg

Berlin–Baghdad Railway

Begun in the Ottoman Empire in 1903, it was to extend the existing Anatolian railway from Konya, in south-central Anatolia, to Baghdad and the Persian/Arabian Gulf.

In 1886, Sultan Abdülhamit II, desirous of greater economic control over his empire, proposed a railway from the Bosporus to the Persian/Arabian Gulf. It would extend Baron Maurice de Hirsch's Oriental Railway, which linked Berlin to Istanbul at its completion in 1888. In the same year, the Ottoman government granted the Anatolian Railway Company, a syndicate dominated by the Deutsche Bank, the concession to construct a railway from the Bosporus to Ankara, in order for Germany to pursue its economic penetration of the Ottoman Empire. This railway line, completed in 1893, was extended to Konya by 1896.

Developing Ottoman–German political and economic cooperation induced the Ottomans to grant the Anatolian Railway Company the concession to extend the railway from Konya to Baghdad and beyond. The Baghdad Railway Company, dominated by the Deutsche Bank and other German interests, was formed in 1903.

Construction was hampered by technical and financial difficulties, Anglo–French–Russian fears of German penetration of the region, and World War I. The Ottoman and German governments agreed to Britain's demand that the railway end in Basra, and not extend to the Gulf. The lines from Istanbul to Nusaybin, and from Baghdad to Samarra in the south, were not completed until 1917. Track laying and tunnel construction continued throughout the war, as late as September 1918. The Nusaybin–Mosul–Samarra gap was finally closed in 1939–1940, and the first train set out from Istanbul to Baghdad in 1940.

BIBLIOGRAPHY

EARLE, EDWARD M. *Turkey, the Great Powers and the Baghdad Railway.* New York, 1923.

WOLF, JOHN B. *The Diplomatic History of the Baghdad Railway.* Columbus, Mo., 1936.

Francis R. Nicosia

Bermuda Conference

International conference held in Bermuda by the Allies during World War II to consider the refugee problem in Nazi-occupied areas.

The conference was convened by the United States and Britain in April 1943. It had been proposed by Britain in late 1942 to diffuse public protests after it was revealed that Nazi Germany had established a policy of systematic liquidation of Jews. The conference became the high point of Allied efforts to thwart official rescue efforts for European Jewry during World War II. No government was opening doors to the refugees at that point.

A number of remote islands were discussed as possible asylums, but PALESTINE was not considered. Only one definite action was authorized—the removal to North Africa of 21,000 refugees who had found refuge in neutral Spain; of them some 5,000 Jews were considered stateless or of enemy nationality. The conference also revived the UNITED NATIONS Intergovernmental Committee on Refugees, but both the committee and the conference accomplished nothing—except to convince the world that there was no hope for the Jews of Nazi-occupied areas. The final report of the conference, published nine months later in December, inflamed public protest but inspired no official rescue efforts.

BIBLIOGRAPHY

GUTMAN, I., ed. *Encyclopedia of the Holocaust.* New York, 1990.

MORSE, ARTHUR D. *While Six Million Died.* New York, 1968.

SACHAR, HOWARD M. *History of Israel: From the Rise of Zionism to Our Time.* Oxford, 1979.

Miriam Simon

Bernadotte, Folke   [1895–1948]

Swedish diplomat; UN mediator between Arabs and Israel in 1948.

Count Bernadotte, a Swedish diplomat, was appointed United Nations (UN) mediator to watch over the creation of the State of Israel following the end of Britain's mandate over Palestine, May 15, 1948. When the first Arab-Israel War broke out, he negotiated several cease-fires between June and September of 1948, at which time he was assassinated along with UN observer André-Pierre Serot by the Stern Gang, a Zionist extremist organization.

After the June cease-fire, Count Bernadotte had made territorial recommendations favorable to the

Arabs, which angered some Israelis. He proposed that Palestinian refugees be allowed to return to their homes in the new state.

BIBLIOGRAPHY

HIRST, DAVID. *The Gun and the Olive Branch*. London, 1984.

Steve Tamari

Berrada, Mohammad   [1938–   ]

Moroccan novelist and literary critic

Berrada, born in Rabat, Morocco, studied in Rabat and Cairo, and received his *Doctorat 3eme Cycle* from the Sorbonne in 1973. Although he is bilingual, his creative writing is in Arabic; he also has translated books from French into Arabic. Berrada is professor of Arabic literature at Muhammad V University in Rabat. He was the editor in chief of the journal *Afaq* during his presidency of the Union of Moroccan Writers.

Berrada is an accomplished short story writer who relies on symbols to convey his ideas. His short story "Qissat al-Ra's al-Maqtu'a" (The Story of the Cut-off Head) is an excellent illustration of his technique; the absence of free expression in Morocco is portrayed through the surrealistic journey of a cutoff head. He also can be extremely realistic and direct, as in his short story "Dolarat" (Dollars). Berrada is concerned with the human quest for an answer to the questions of life and a solution to the dilemmas encountered.

Berrada's novel *Lu'bat al-Nisyan* (1987; The Game of Forgetfulness) adopts a philosophical approach to human memory. While relating the childhood memories of the characters from different sources, the author aims at demonstrating the workings of memory by sifting and discarding the events of the past. This process reveals the thin line that separates reality from imagination and casts doubt on a person's conscious recollection of the past. The only reality remains the city of Fez, a sign of immutable truth and a symbol of the cherished souvenirs and elating emotions, regardless of their truth. A respect for reality is achieved through the dialogue of the various narrators of the novel, each of whom speaks the language that denotes his or her cultural level. Thus, Si Brahim, who is illiterate, speaks only colloquial Moroccan.

The eye of the literary critic that Berrada revealed himself to be in *Muhammad Mandour wa Tandhir al-Naqd al-Arabi* (1975; Muhammad Mandour and the Theorizing of Arabic Literary Criticism) is visible in the background of the creative writings but does not overwhelm them.

[*See also*: Literature, Arabic, North African]

BIBLIOGRAPHY

BARAKAT, HALIM, ed. *Contemporary North Africa*. Washington, D.C., 1985.
TOUIMI, MUHAMMED B., KHATIBI ABDELKABIR, and MUHAMMED KABLY. *Ecrivains marocains, du Protectorat à 1965. Anthologie*. Paris, 1974.

Aida A. Bamia

Berri, Nabi   [1938–   ]

Politician in Lebanon.

Berri came to prominence in the political life of Lebanon in the late 1970s when the "disappearance" of Imam Musa SADR thrust him, as a key leader of the AMAL movement, into the forefront of political activity. He was born in Sierra Leone and received his law degree from the Lebanese University. He subsequently became a close associate of Musa Sadr and assumed the presidency of AMAL in 1980. He has held several ministerial posts since 1984. His charismatic personality has helped his political fortunes, but it is his political deference to the government of Syria that has been primarily responsible for his ability to limit the influence of his rivals within the Shi'ite community. Berri transformed the AMAL movement from an organization loyal to the legacy of Musa Sadr into one under his political control. He headed the "Liberation List" in the 1992 election and formed the largest bloc in parliament, thereby becoming its speaker. Although Berri is not from a traditional political (*zu'ama*) family he has not refrained from forming coalitions with traditional landowning families.

As'ad AbuKhalil

Betar

See Revisionist Movement

Bethlehem

City in the West Bank important to Christianity and Judaism.

This small city is a center of Christian pilgrimage to the birthplace of Jesus and to the site of the Church of the Nativity, built in the fourth century. Greek Orthodox, Armenian, and some Latin-rite churches also exist. In Judaism, it is the setting for most of the biblical Book of Ruth; King David lived there when it was called Judaea and was anointed king of Israel there by the prophet Samuel.

Bethlehem is five miles (8 km) southwest of Jerusalem. It was part of the territory that brought the Crusaders to fight the Muslims; became part of the Ottoman Empire; then, with the dismemberment of the empire after World War I, became part of the British mandate territory of Palestine. With the independence of the State of Israel in 1948, Jordan annexed it after the first Arab–Israel War. Israel occupied the WEST BANK and has controlled it since the Arab-Israel War of 1967.

In addition to being a center of tourism and pilgrimage, Bethlehem is now an agricultural market and trade center, with an estimated population of some twenty thousand (1984).

Encyclopaedia of Zionism and Israel.

Bet She'an

Town in northeastern Israel bordering the Jordan Valley to the east and just south of Lake Tiberias.

Bet She'an (Arabic, Baysan) is the site of one of the oldest inhabited cities in Palestine. Excavations at Tell al-Husn reveal settlement as early as the fourth millennium B.C.E. Remains of a Roman amphitheater and bridge, a Byzantine monastery, and the tomb of the Muslim conqueror of Syria, Abu Ubayda ibn al-Jarrah, remain.

In May 1948, the Palestinian inhabitants were expelled in the Arab–Israel War by Jewish forces and the town was destroyed. In 1949, it was resettled largely by recent Jewish immigrants to Israel from the Arab countries. It became the center of Israel's chief cotton-growing region, and the estimated population (1993) was some 14,800.

SAYIGH, ANIS, ed. *Al-Mawsu'a al-filastiniyya: al-am,* vol. 1. Damascus, 1984.
Statistical Abstract of Israel. Jerusalem, 1994.
The New Encyclopaedia Britannica, 15th ed. Chicago, 1987.

Bevin, Ernest   [1881–1951]

Foreign secretary of Great Britain (1945–1951).

Bevin was associated with the Bevin–Bidault agreement of December 1945, which provided for the evacuation of Britain's and France's troops from Syria and Lebanon. He was also responsible for the abortive Bevin–SIDQI agreement, signed between Britain and Egypt in October 1946, and the equally unsuccessful 1949 BEVIN–SFORZA PLAN concerning Libya.

It was Bevin's involvement with the Palestine problem for which he is best known. When the affairs of the Palestine mandate came under the jurisdiction of the Foreign Office, Bevin took an active role in the formulation of British policy during the crucial years of the Arab–Jewish struggle for Palestine. In November 1945, Bevin announced the formation of the Anglo-American Committee of Inquiry on Palestine. Although he desired the United States to become involved in the resolution of the Palestine problem, he envisaged a dominant role for Britain in the Middle East.

Although Bevin pursued a policy that closely followed the aims of the British white paper of 1939—which restricted the number of Jewish immigrants from Europe to Palestine—it became clear that Britain could not resolve the differences between the Zionists and the Palestinians. In April 1947, Bevin decided to pass the Palestine problem to the United Nations. When the United Nations recommended partitioning Palestine into Arab and Jewish states, he refused to allow the British mandate authorities to participate in the implementation of the agreement. Instead, he ordered them to dismantle their administration and withdraw British forces by May 1948.

Many Zionists suspected Bevin opposed the creation of a Jewish state in Palestine, but recent revisionist scholarship has shown that he tacitly cooperated in implementing the partition plan. According to new accounts based on declassified documents from Israel's archives, Bevin met secretly with Transjordan officials in London and privately sanctioned King ABDULLAH IBN HUSAYN's plans to seize the West Bank. This plan had been arranged by Abdullah and Golda MEIR, a prominent Zionist leader.

SHIMONI, YAACOV. *Political Dictionary of the Arab World.* New York, 1987.
SHLAIM, AVI. *The Politics of Partition: King Abdullah, the Zionists and Palestine, 1921–1951.* New York, 1990.

Bevin–Sforza Plan

A post–World War II plan to administer former Italian colonies in North Africa.

After World War II, Italy was forced to relinquish its African colonies by the terms of its February 1947 peace treaty with the Allies. Libya was made the temporary responsibility of the United Nations, although Britain and France continued to administer it. Partly to protect their interest and partly to avoid Soviet interference, the British foreign secretary, Ernest Bevin, and the Italian foreign minister, Count Carlo Sforza, promulgated a joint plan on May 10, 1949, for the United Nations to grant trusteeships to Britain in Cyrenaica; Italy in Tripolitania; and France in the Fezzan, for a ten-year period, after which Libya would become independent. The plan, which met massive hostility in Libya itself, was rejected by the United Nations General Assembly eight days later.

BIBLIOGRAPHY

WRIGHT, JOHN. *Libya: A Modern History.* London, 1982.

George Joffe

Bey

A Turkish honorific title.

The title imparts nobility or princeliness to the possessor. In the Ottoman empire the title generally applied to positions of political and military authority; whether obtained from a ruler, by election, or by usurpation. Holders of administrative positions may also acquire the title, hence meaning a distinguished man of noble rank. Today in Turkey, the title is commonly suffixed to a man's first name as a form of address.

Cyrus Moshaver

Beyoglu Protocol

Terms reorganized administrative structure of Lebanon as province of Ottoman Empire.

Following the massacres by the Druze of thousands of Lebanese and Syrian Christians in the summer of 1860, the Ottoman sultan, ABDÜLMECIT I, sent Mehmed Fuad Paşa, foreign minister, to Syria to resolve the crisis. Fuad had two goals: to restore order and to prevent the European powers from intervening. Though France landed troops and Britain sent a fleet, Fuad was thorough and provided them with no excuse to intervene further. In June 1861 the French withdrew their forces, and on June 9 the sultan issued the Beyoglu Protocol, which reorganized the administrative structure of Lebanon. Under the terms of the protocol, Lebanon was given a new Organic Law that established Lebanon as a privileged province headed by a non-Lebanese, Ottoman Christian governor (*mutassarrif*) appointed by the sultan after consultation with European governments. The predominantly Christian mountain region was detached from the coastal district of Beirut and Tripoli as well as from the inland Biqa Valley. It was a smaller, more homogenous province, but it survived intact without major disruptions until World War I.

BIBLIOGRAPHY

HUREWITZ, J.C., ed. *The Middle East and North Africa in World Politics.* New Haven, Conn., 1975.
SHAW, STANFORD, and EZEL KURAL Shaw. *History of the Ottoman Empire and Modern Turkey.* New York, 1977.

Zachary Karabell

Bezalel Academy of Arts and Design

School located in Jerusalem.

The former Bezalel School of Arts and Crafts was founded in 1906 by the sculptor Boris Schatz and named for the biblical architect of the Tabernacle, Bezalel ben Uri. Within the Ottoman Empire, Schatz wanted to establish a cultural center and craft industry in Jerusalem's yishuv (Jewish settlement). The Bezalel Museum was founded as part of the school.

From the outset, efforts were made to preserve a uniquely Jewish artistic style. Funding for the project was provided by wealthy Zionists in Germany. During World War I, the school was destroyed but later rebuilt. It closed in 1932 but soon reopened as Jewish refugees fled Hitler's Germany (1933–1945). The "new" Bezalel, independent of the museum, opened in 1935. In 1955, it began training teachers and, in 1970 became an academy, with its diploma recognized as a B.A. equivalent. Under the directorship of Dan Hoffner, it was modernized, emphasizing design.

Ann Kahn

Bialik, Hayyim Nahman   [1873–1934]

Towering figure of modern Hebrew poetry, "national poet," essayist, storywriter, and editor.

Bialik lived his first six, impressionable years in the countryside near Zhitomir (Ukraine), where his father engaged in business before becoming impoverished. This early immersion in nature became a symbol of lost paradise and fountain of creation in poems like "Zohar" (Radiance), "Ha-Berekhah" (The Pool), and "Ehad, Ehad Uve'en Ro'e" (One by One). Only late in life did Bialik dare write of his traumas: moving to Zhitomir, his father's humiliating alehouse and, later, his death; and his mother entrusting the seven-year-old Bialik to a strict, pious, and scholarly grandfather.

Bialik first studied in a traditional religious school (heder) and then continued, on his own, to delve into the Talmud. During this time he encountered HASKALA (enlightenment) texts which directed him towards modern, European education.

His generation's dominant conflict between the old faith and modernity was played out for Bialik in Volozhin's yeshiva, where he gained insight into the power of the former and the pull of the latter. He began to write, studied Russian and German, and read European literature. But the division between the old and the new, echoed later in "Levadi" (Alone) and "Ha-Matmid" (The Talmud Student), continued to haunt Bialik for decades after having abandoned the yeshivah.

AHAD HA-AM's essays offered Bialik and his tortured contemporaries some reconciliation—a modern, rational Jewish existence. Bialik sought Ahad Ha-Am out in Odessa and became his lifelong disciple. Bialik's first poem, "El ha-Zippor" (To the Bird, 1892), was published in *Ha-Pardes* with Ahad Ha-Am's recommendation. Returning to his dying grandfather and his brother in Zhitomir reawakened Bialik's "inner pendulum," but in 1893 he married, and joined his wife's family timber business until its decline in 1896.

Before the First Zionist Congress (1897), Bialik supported Ahad Ha-Am's spiritual Zionism against HERZL's political Zionism. In a poem of prophetic vision, which began to establish him as national poet, he reproached Jewish apathy.

His first volume appeared in 1901 in Odessa, the center of Jewish culture at that time and Bialik's home for the next twenty years. There he wrote his great epic "Metei Midbar" (The Dead of the Desert, 1902), in which boundaries between self and nation are blurred, a hallmark of his poetics. The epic's failed rebels may symbolize unleashed psychic energies, cosmic powers, or a national uprising.

Bialik's message is painfully unequivocal, however, in the prophecies of wrath and doom found in "On the Slaughter" and "In the City of Slaughter," written after the 1903 pogroms in Kishinev. Bialik went with a commission to investigate, but wrote poems calling for Jewish self-defence. With Vladimir

JABOTINSKY's translations into Russian, Bialik's words became a call to action and organizing.

A year's stay in Warsaw (1904) and contact with its neoromantic Hebrew writers produced rare lyrical and tender poems. Upon returning to Odessa, Bialik, striving to revitalize Hebrew, created a publishing house, rediscovered, and collected, and edited classical texts. He dominated the Hebrew literary scene as literary editor of *Ha-Shilo'ah* (1904–1909), *Keneset* (1917), and *Reshumot* (1918–1922), and expressed his views on the state of Hebrew culture in several monumental essays (1907–1917).

In 1921, Gorki helped Bialik and other Hebrew writers leave Soviet Russia. After three years in Berlin, Bialik settled in Tel Aviv where he founded a new Hebrew genre: children's poetry, and worked as publisher and scholar of medieval poetry. Until his death he acted as a cultural leader, enjoying superior spiritual and national authority.

When Bialik appeared, modern Hebrew poetry was conventional and collective; it imitated biblical diction and old European models. Bialik transformed this poetry, showing how to subordinate the entire linguistic and conceptual inventory of tradition to modern verse. He uprooted biblical text from its religious framework and infused its strength into the alternative secular culture. Bialik's verse, like the Bible's, is both a powerful, lyrical, human, universal expression and a dense, rich essence of the specific Jewish culture that produced it.

With Bialik for the first time in Hebrew Literature, the "I" of the individual became the central entity, and poetry became the arena of the self, its depths and turmoil. His poetic voice is that of a Jewish individual who holds the pains of his national culture in his heart while living an intense, personal inner life.

Bialik solved most of the aesthetic dilemmas which confronted Hebrew poetry in the 1890s and prepared the provisions needed for the creation of a modern Hebrew literature equal to the best literatures of the world.

Nili Gold

Bible

The Judeo-Christian scriptures.

The word *Bible*, derived from the Greek for "book," connotes both the Hebrew Bible—twenty-four books written in Hebrew, consisting of the five books of Moses, usually called the Law (Torah); the Prophets (Nevi'im); and the Writings (Ketuvim)—and the Christian Bible. While the Christian Bible includes the whole of the Hebrew Bible, several of the twenty-four books are divided, making a total of thirty-nine.

The Christian Bible includes the Hebrew Bible (the Old Testament) and the New Testament, twenty-seven books that cover the life, ministry, and death of Jesus Christ and the development of the early church. When the Hebrew Bible was translated into Greek (a version called the Septuagint) during the third century B.C.E., it included some writings—often termed the Apocrypha—that were added to what would become the Christian canon. Eastern Orthodox Greek, Syriac, and Armenian Christians and Roman Catholics use the Septuagint version as the basis of their Old Testament text.

Reeva S. Simon

Bidonville

One of many shantytown communities in French colonial North Africa, situated near cities and towns.

A form of living space in colonial France's MAGHRIB possessions—the other two being the traditional Arab MEDINA, which formed the nucleus of precolonial cities and towns, and the *villeneuve,* its Western counterpart that was designed by Europeans and built during colonial times. Bidonvilles in their original sense referred to the flimsy shacks and shantytowns that emerged in the nineteenth century at the margins of North African cities and towns—often built from "*bidons à pétrole,*" tin containers used to distribute kerosene. The emergence of bidonvilles across North Africa was both directly and indirectly linked to the colonial presence. In several instances bidonvilles emerged as entire villages and populations were displaced, as in Algeria during so-called CANTONNE-MENTS and *regroupements*—policies that were aimed at either providing agricultural land to colonial settlers or to keep the local populations away from what were considered by the colonial authorities to be strategic areas. What contributed to the physical growth of a population that could no longer be incorporated into the confines of the precolonial city or town included: The growth of the North African coastal cities, linked to their new and intermediary role in the French economy; the impoverishment of the rural areas either through neglect or their incorporation into wider economies; the burgeoning population as a result of the introduction of health, sanitary, and hygienic standards; and the creation of an urban salaried class employed by France. As a result of this uncontrolled and more often than not hasty growth, bidonvilles contrast sharply both with the planned *villeneuves* of

North African towns and the carefully integrated design of the traditional *medinas*; as a result, they have often been described by French colonial observers as monotonous and unpleasing.

At the time of independence of the North African countries in the 1950s and 1960s, and in the two decades that followed, bidonvilles became firmly established features of the urban landscape. Often, they possess only rudimentary sanitary systems, water, or electricity. The conditions that had contributed to their creation or existence in the colonial period were continued and often exacerbated by the economic and development strategies of the new governments. In several cases, substantial portions of city populations—in some instances up to 40 percent—found themselves temporarily but more often than not permanently in bidonvilles that often remained for years without the amenities enjoyed by other citizens. Perhaps not surprising, as bidonvilles became permanent fixtures throughout North Africa, they often were the focal points for riots and violent demonstrations against local governments—forcing them to devote considerable resources to upgrading and incorporating the bidonvilles into their towns and cities, providing water and electricity, sanitation and transportation. Despite this, one of the unavoidable and seemingly enduring sights of the Maghrib remains that of bidonvilles that physically, socially, and economically are literally at the margins of each country's society.

BIBLIOGRAPHY

DESCLOITRES, ROBERT. *L'Algérie des bidonvilles: Le tiers monde dans la cité.* Paris, 1961.

Dirk Vandewalle

Bilad, al-

Newspaper of Saudi Arabia.

Al-Bilad was established in 1934, under the name *Sawt al-Hijaz,* as a literary and religious periodical. In 1941 it was suspended along with all other newspapers. By 1953 it had reemerged under its current name and had become Saudi Arabia's leading newspaper. It is published daily in Arabic, at JIDDA.

Les Ordeman

Bilhayr, Abd al-Nabi   [?–1930]

Local leader of the powerful Warfalla tribal group located to the south of Misurata during World War I.

He participated in the Council of Four, the ruling body of the short-lived Tripolitanian Republic, although, as the republic collapsed under Italian pressure, he also fell out with its most important leader, Ramadan al-Suwayhli. Eventually he retired to southern Tripolitania and Fazzan, where he continued to resist Italian occupation. In 1927 he retired to southern Algeria, where he died in 1930.

BIBLIOGRAPHY

ANDERSON, LISA S. "The Tripoli Republic, 1918–1922." In *Social and Economic Development of Libya,* ed. by E. G. H. Joffe and K. S. McLachlan. Wisbech, U.K., 1982.

George Joffe

Bilkent University

Private university in Ankara, Turkey.

Established in 1986 as a privately endowed foundation, with English as the language of instruction, it comprises the faculties of economics and social sciences, management studies, engineering, natural sciences, fine arts and architecture, humanities, and music and performing arts, as well as schools of applied language study and tourism and hotel management, vocational schools of tourism and hotel service, computer technology and office management, and the Preparatory School of English. In 1990, it had about 350 faculty members and 4,400 students (1,700 were female). As a private university, it has high tuition and room and board charges, at least by Turkish standards: for the 1991/92 academic year tuition was 14 million Turkish lire ($2,000). The university is also eligible for state support.

Bilkent, in Ankara, was the only privately endowed university in Turkey until 1993, when several more universities of private foundations were to be established. It was founded by Prof. Ihsan Doğramacı; the anomaly of the chairman of the Council of Higher Education (YÜKSEK ÖĞRETIM KURULU) being at the same time the benefactor of his own university has recently received substantial adverse comment. Its relatively high charges, its luxuriously appointed and well-equipped facilities, and its policy of using English as the language of instruction mark it as an elite establishment.

BIBLIOGRAPHY

Higher Education in Turkey. UNESCO, European Centre for Higher Education. December 1990.
World of Learning, 1990.

I. Metin Kunt

Biltmore Program

Resolutions adopted at a Zionist conference held at the Biltmore Hotel in New York City, May 9–11, 1942.

About 600 American Zionists were joined by a number of visiting Zionist leaders at the Biltmore Hotel, including the organization's president, Dr. Chaim Weizmann, and the Jewish Agency chairman, David Ben-Gurion, to call for "the fulfillment of the original purpose of the Balfour Declaration and the Mandate."

Well before news reports confirmed the wholesale and systematic extermination of European Jews, the Zionist conference at the Biltmore Hotel offered "a message of hope and encouragement to their fellow Jews in the Ghettos and concentration camps of Hitler-dominated Europe" and strongly denounced the British White Paper of May 1939 as "cruel and indefensible in its denial of sanctuary to Jews fleeing from Nazi persecution."

Other resolutions paid tribute to the "steadfastness" and "pioneering achievements" of the Yishuv (Jewish community of Palestine), and reaffirmed previous Zionist Congress resolutions "expressing the readiness and the desire of the Jewish people for full cooperation with their Arab neighbors." The conference also called for recognition of the rights of Palestinian Jews to form "a Jewish military force fighting under its own flag and under the high command of the United Nations."

In its final resolutions, the Biltmore Program declared that "the new world order that will follow victory cannot be established on foundations of peace, justice and equality, unless the problem of Jewish homelessness is finally solved." To that end, the program was clearer and went further than any previous official Zionist statement in risking a breach with Britain and orienting the movement's fate toward American sponsorship. The conference "urged that the gates of Palestine be opened; that the Jewish Agency be vested with control of immigration into Palestine and with the necessary authority for upbuilding the country, including the development of its unoccupied and uncultivated lands; and that Palestine be established as a Jewish Commonwealth integrated in the structure of the new democratic world."

The Biltmore Program was to serve as an important weapon in the Zionist struggle against the White Paper's restrictions on Jewish immigration and land purchase. The resolutions also formed part of an unsuccessful diplomatic campaign that aimed at obtaining from the Allied powers a strong, pro-Zionist declaration regarding Palestine in the postwar era.

The debates during and after the Biltmore conference reflected internal Zionist disputes between gradualists and radicals—a struggle personified, somewhat simplistically, as one between Weizmann, the pro-British diplomat, and Ben-Gurion, the uncompromising activist. The Biltmore Program's call for the establishment of Palestine "as a Jewish Commonwealth" was interpreted by many as equivalent to the maximalist demand for a Jewish *state* in *all* Palestine and, hence, aroused some internal controversy.

Biltmore was rejected outright by the minority of Zionists who favored binationalism and was an embarrassment to those Jews who preferred to work behind the more flexible "Jewish national home" phraseology of the Balfour Declaration. The Biltmore Program was subsequently endorsed by authoritative Zionist and Yishuv bodies and remained official policy until late 1946, when a Jewish state in *part* of Palestine became the new operative goal of the movement's leadership.

BIBLIOGRAPHY

BAUER, YEHUDA. *From Diplomacy to Resistance: A History of Jewish Palestine, 1939–1945.* Philadelphia, 1970.
FLAPAN, SIMHA. *Zionism and the Palestinians.* New York, 1979.
HUREWITZ, J. C. *The Struggle for Palestine.* New York, 1950. Reprint, 1968, 1976.
LAQUEUR, WALTER, and BARRY RUBIN, eds. *The Israel–Arab Reader: A Documentary History of the Middle East Conflict,* 4th ed. New York, 1984.

                                        Neil Caplan

BILU

See Aliyah

Binationalism

Political theory for Palestine, current during the British mandate, 1922–1948.

Binationalists asserted that Palestine belonged equally to Arabs and Jews and that its ultimate political disposition should be based on this principle—that Arabs and Jews are equally entitled to national self-determination within the full territory. Constitutional arrangements for any binational state would be based on parity, regardless of the relative numbers of each group, to assure equal representation for both in all the institutions of the national government.

The original supporters of binationalism formed a small but articulate minority within the political spectrum of the Yishuv (Palestine's Jewish community). Among the leading proponents of binationalism were idealists and humanists, rather than political

tacticians: Dr. Judah I. Magnes, president and chancellor of the Hebrew University of Jerusalem; world-renowned philosopher Martin Buber; and land-purchase agent Chaim Kalvaryski. The most notable of the associations formed to advance binationalism during the mandate period were Brit Shalom (Covenant of Peace: founded 1925), the League for Jewish–Arab Rapprochement and Cooperation (founded 1939), and Ihud (Unity: founded 1942). Two left-wing workers' parties, Poalei-Zion-Smol (Left Faction, Workers of Zion) and ha-Shomer ha-Za'ir (the Young Watchman), also took an active part in advocating a binational solution.

Binationalism never became a strong force within the Zionist movement, within the Yishuv, or among any Arab political groups. The idea seems to have reached a high point in the year 1946, when the arguments advanced by Magnes and Buber before the Anglo–American Committee of Inquiry influenced the committee's report, which proposed that "Jew shall not dominate Arab and Arab shall not dominate Jew," and that "Palestine shall be neither a Jewish state nor an Arab state." But the committee's recommendations soon proved unworkable and, subsequently, the United Nations opted for the partition of mandatory Palestine. Faced with the reality of the State of Israel after May 14, 1948, Magnes reluctantly abandoned binationalism and began advocating instead a confederation between the new Jewish state and a Palestinian Arab state-to-be-created. Thereafter, the concept of binationalism surfaced from time to time (e.g., following the 1967 Arab–Israel war), usually in academic discussions of alternative approaches to resolving the Arab–Israeli–Palestinian dispute.

Binationalists were opposed to the partition of Palestine into separate Arab and Jewish states on the grounds that it would fragment the integral unity of the small country and would give rise to irredentism (where a territory ethnically related to one political unit comes under the control of another). Likewise, they rejected as unjust and/or unworkable the mutually exclusive quests for either an Arab or a Jewish state, each with its recognized minority. Finally, binationalism—with its essential stress on the rights and status of Arabs and Jews as coequal but autonomous national communities—should not be confused with recent Palestinian proposals based on a nonsectarian, secular democratic state.

BIBLIOGRAPHY

COHEN, AHARON. *Israel and the Arab World.* New York, 1970.
FLAPAN, SIMHA. *Zionism and the Palestinians.* New York, 1979.

GOREN, A. A., ed. *Dissenter in Zion: From the Writings of Judah L. Magnes.* Cambridge, Mass., 1982.

HATTIS, SUSAN LEE. *The Bi-National Idea in Palestine during Mandatory Times.* Haifa, 1970.

HUREWITZ, J. C. *The Struggle for Palestine.* New York, 1950. Reprint, 1968, 1976.

Neil Caplan

Bin Ayad Family

Large, wealthy tax-collecting family of Tunisia.

Originally from Spain, the Bin Ayad family were hereditary governors of the island of Djerba. Mahmud Bin Ayad (c. 1805–1880), financial adviser to AHMAD BEY HUSAYN, fled to France in 1852 and cashed notes exceeding the holdings of the Tunisian bank, almost bankrupting Tunisia.

BIBLIOGRAPHY

Notice sur le Général Mansour Benaïad: Sa famille et son administration à Tunis. Paris, 1876.

Laurence Michalak

Bin Diyaf, Muhsen   [1932–   ]

Tunisian novelist and short story writer.

Bin Diyaf, born in Tunis, received a B.A. in Arabic language and literature. Although he is bilingual, he writes in Arabic. Bin Diyaf has published two novels—*Al-Tahaddi* (1972; The Defiance) and *Yawm min al-Umr* (1976; A Certain Day in a Life)—and a collection of short stories, *Kalimat ala Jidar al-Samt* (1977; Words on the Wall of Silence). His writings reflect a concern with human beings and the quality of life in political and social contexts.

[*See also:* Literature, Arabic, North African]

BIBLIOGRAPHY

FONTAINE, JEAN. *La littérature tunisienne contemporaine.* Paris, 1990.

Aida A. Bamia

Bint

Patronymic prefix used in Arabic female names.

Bint is a word of Arabic origin meaning daughter, girl, or maiden. It is the functional equivalent of the male form, "ibn."

Cyrus Moshaver

Bint al-Shati   [1913–   ]

Egyptian academic and writer.

Bint al-Shati was born Aisha Abd al-Rahman in Dumyat to a religious conservative family. Her father sent her to a *kuttab* to study the Qur'an. With the help of her mother, Bint al-Shati was able to continue her education. She got her first degree from Cairo University in Arabic in 1939 and her Ph.D. in 1950. She held various university posts in Egypt and Morocco and also served as inspector of the teaching of Arabic language and literature for the Egyptian Ministry of Education.

Aisha Abd al-Rahman started publishing articles and poetry in women's magazines. In 1933, she adopted her pen name. Bint al-Shati (the daughter of the shore), when she started publishing in more widely circulated magazines and daily papers like *Al-Ahram,* for which she is still a contributor. A prolific writer, Bint al-Shati has published more than thirty books on various topics. Her first two books, which deal with issues of peasantry in Egyptian villages, appeared in 1936 and 1938.

Although her contribution to Arabic fiction is modest, she is known for her literary studies which include books such as *New Values in Arabic Literature* (1961), *Contemporary Arab Women Poets* (1963), *Al-Khansaa* (1963), and *Abu al-Ala al-Ma'arri* (1968). Her numerous books on famous women related to Muhammad are well regarded: *The Daughters of the Prophet* (1963), *The Mother of the Prophet* (1966), and *The Wives of the Prophet* (1959), which was translated into English (Lahore, Pakistan, 1971).

BIBLIOGRAPHY

ZEIDAN, JOSEPH. *Arab Women Novelists: The Formative Years and Beyond.* Albany, N.Y., 1995.

Sabah Ghandour

Biqa' Valley

Fertile region between the Lebanon and Anti-Lebanon mountain ranges.

Running parallel to the Mediterranean coast, the Biqa' valley throughout the eighteenth and nineteenth centuries enjoyed close ties to Damascus, whose populace constituted a ready market for its agricultural produce. Nevertheless, in August 1920, French mandatory authorities incorporated the Biqa' into the newly created state of Lebanon. Thereafter, it served as the breadbasket for the rapidly expanding port city of Beirut.

Lush fields of the Biqaʻ valley. (D.W. Lockhard)

After the outbreak of the Lebanese civil war in 1975, the towns of the Biqaʻ provided strongholds for a number of militant Shiʻite organizations. These included not only HIZBULLAH and ISLAMIC AMAL, headquartered around Baʻlabah, but also a detachment of Revolutionary Guards seconded from the Islamic Republic of Iran. Neither Syrian troops, who controlled the Beirut-Damascus highway beginning in the the summer of 1976, nor Israeli forces, which raided the area by air and land on numerous occasions, succeeded in dislodging the militants, who supported their activities by producing opium and other drugs for export.

Fred H. Lawson

Birth Control

Limiting of births, often for population reduction.

Both the term "birth control" (in the sense of limiting births) and the concept of population reduction are controversial in the Middle East. Population issues touch on tensions inherent in the change and development being experienced by the area. Population growth affects patterns of urbanization, labor, and immigration, and strains the provision of education, health, and social services in resource-poor countries. For many, birth control symbolizes the negation of such traditional values as the importance of marriage and family, and the necessity for women to be chaste and remain in the home. Others view contraceptive technology as an important tool in areas ranging from national development policy to a woman's safeguarding of her health.

Although the region shares a common culture and a dominant religion (Islam), accidents of geography and resource allocation have generated different policy responses to population growth. Whereas some countries seek to limit their populations, others seek to increase theirs. Egypt, Iran, Turkey, Tunisia, Lebanon, and Morocco, lacking a sufficient resource base to support their growing populations, have supported family planning programs designed to reduce population growth. Saudi Arabia, Kuwait, Libya, and the Gulf oil states, on the other hand, lack sufficient population to supply their labor needs.

Overall, the rapid growth of population in the Middle East is a matter of concern. In 1993 the population of the Middle East was approximately 360 million, and by 2025 is expected to reach 747 million. This population is a young population; 41 percent are under fifteen years of age. Fears that resources may not stretch to support their populations have prompted governments to make contraceptive use an integral part of their public health programs and to mount campaigns to encourage use.

Demographic evidence suggests that disease and warfare combined to keep population figures relatively level until the beginning of the twentieth century. Population of the central Middle East (excluding North Africa) is estimated to have been around 40 million at the beginning of the twentieth century. By 1950 it had doubled to 80 million (1993, 265 million). Explosive growth followed the end of World War II, when greater emphasis upon public sanitation and health care reduced the death rate while the birth rate remained high. In the early 1960s, Gamal Abdel Nasser of Egypt and Habib Bourguiba of Tunisia were the first national leaders to realize the negative relationship between unrestricted population growth and socioeconomic development, and feared that the resulting pressure could spur political unrest. The family planning programs they initiated encountered opposition, but since about 1970 the programs of Egypt and Tunisia, along with those of Lebanon, Turkey, Morocco, and Iran, have achieved limited success.

Opposition has come from political, military, religious, and cultural quarters. Both the culture of the Middle East and the religions of the area—Islam, Christianity, and Judaism—encourage marriage and family. The term "birth control" (*tahdid al-nasl*) is considered highly perjorative because it connotes preventing the birth of children. Less objectionable terms are *tanzim al-usra* and *takhtit ala'la* (family planning), which connote organization and ordering rather than limitation of progeny. Nations of the Middle East have historically sought to augment their strength against enemies by increasing their numbers. To many, birth control connotes Western imperialism; family planning programs are often considered

Western impositions designed to weaken the Middle East, even though Western development organizations have introduced contraceptive technology and programs throughout the developing world. The idea that the West was attempting to limit the size of nations and to prevent the birth of children fueled political opposition to family planning programs in the Middle East.

Political parties and nationalist groups throughout the Middle East have deemed spurring population growth a national necessity in order to supply a large population base for military endeavors. Following heavy military losses, Iran and Iraq, at the end of the Iran–Iraq war in 1988, emphasized pro-natalist policies. Competition among Middle Eastern nations for regional prominence have led them to discourage family planning and advocate high birth rates. National, ethnic, or religious factionalism often augurs lack of support for family planning as each group seeks to enlarge its numbers. European Community governments have decided to attack root problems of immigration from the Middle East by initiating programs supporting family planning in North Africa.

Most of the major religious traditions of the area believe contraception is permitted. Christians are divided on its permissibility. The traditions of Judaism differ, but largely consider it permissible. Islamic jurisprudence condemns a pre-Islamic form of birth control, *wa'd* (exposure of female infants) but, reasoning from hadith texts, permits contraceptive use as analogous to coitus interruptus (*azl*). This is a personal, mutual decision of the husband and wife. Muslim opponents of contraception see it as murdering a creation of God and as a denial of the will (*irada*) and sustaining power (*rizq*) of God.

The importance of family in the Middle East has proved to be the largest obstacle to family planning. Because the status of both spouses, particularly the wife, depends upon the birth of children, family planning programs have had difficulty encouraging both men and women to consider contraceptive use. One important support has been the Qur'an's injunction to nurse children for two years, and most women appreciate the harm of becoming pregnant while nursing. That spacing children is important for a mother's health is becoming better understood. Children have traditionally been seen as providing economic support for the family and, in the absence of social security programs, are considered guarantees of parents' financial security in their old age. Finally, children are loved and valued as a true blessing and a rare good. Another obstacle has been rumors claiming medical dangers from using various contraceptive methods.

The most popular methods of contraception in the Middle East are used by women: pills and IUDs.

Concern over sexually transmitted diseases and AIDS has increased publicity for and availability of condoms. Much interest has been shown in injectable or implantable contraceptives. Nonreversible sterilization for men or women is prohibited by Islam, as is abortion (although qualifications exist). However, tubal ligations are increasingly common, and because new medical technology makes the procedure reversible, they can be considered religiously permissible. The majority of states ban abortion except when the health of the mother is endangered, at which point responsibility falls on the doctor. Tunisia permits abortion.

BIBLIOGRAPHY

Bowen, Donna Lee. "Islam and Family Planning." World Bank, *EMENA Technical Papers* 1, no. 1 (February 1991).
Musallam, Basim. *Sex and Society in Islam*. Cambridge, U.K., 1983.
Omran, Abdel-Rahim. *Family Planning in the Legacy of Islam*. London, 1992.
———. "The Middle East Population Puzzle." *Population Bulletin* 48, no. 1 (July 1993).
———. "Population Problems and Prospects in the Arab World." United Nations Fund for Population Activities, *Population Profiles* (July 1984).
Warwick, Don. *Bitter Pills: Population Policies and Their Implementation in Eight Developing Countries*. New York, 1982.
Weeks, John R. "The Demography of Islamic Nations." *Population Bulletin* 43, no. 4 (December 1988).

Donna Lee Bowen

Bir Zeit University

Palestinian university.

Founded in 1924 as a primary school on the WEST BANK, the school began to offer secondary education in 1930. In 1942, the institution became known as Bir Zeit College, and provided instruction above secondary level in the 1950s. In 1972, the name of the institution officially became Bir Zeit University, and offered it degrees in sciences, literature, physical education, economics, sociology, and other fields.

Bir Zeit University became a center of anti-Israel activism in the 1970s and 1980s, with student groups becoming increasingly involved in Palestinian politics. After the outbreak of the INTIFADA in December 1987, classes were disrupted, and the university closed during curfews imposed by Israel's military authorities.

[*See also:* Palestine; Palestinians]

BIBLIOGRAPHY

KIMMERLING, BARUCH, and JOEL S. MIGDAL. *Palestinians: The Making of a People.* New York, 1993.

Lawrence Tal

Bishara, Abdullah   [1936–   ]

Kuwaiti diplomat.

Bishara, born in Kuwait, was educated in Cairo, Oxford, and St. Johns University. From 1971 to 1981 he was ambassador and permanent representative to the United Nations; during this period he was also Kuwait's ambassador to Argentina and Brazil. His next post was secretary-general of the GULF COOPERATION COUNCIL (1981–1993). Since April 1993 Bishara has been special adviser to the deputy prime minister and minister of foreign affairs at the Home Office in Kuwait.

BIBLIOGRAPHY

The International Who's Who of the Arab World. 1983.

Les Ordeman

Bisitun

Important archeological site in western Iran (also Behistun; Bagestana; Bisutun).

On a limestone cliff in Lorestan province, IRAN, is a ruined town and a monument to Darius the Great (550–486 B.C.E.), consisting of sculpture and cuneiform inscriptions that are considered the "Rosetta Stone of Asia" (its deciphering by Henry Rawlinson in 1846 led to our knowledge of Assyrian and Babylonian). Carved in 520 B.C.E., it shows Darius and two companions facing nine defeated rebels, accompanied by an inscription in Elamite, Old Persian, and Babylonian describing Darius's restoration of the Persian monarchy.

Besides this, the site contains remains of various epochs, notably Hellenistic and Parthian rock reliefs and a rock-cut terrace (called *Teras-e Farhad*) of Kosrow I and three capitals from his palace. A modern village of the same names exists at the base of the cliff.

BIBLIOGRAPHY

HINZ, W. "Die Behistun-Inschrift Darius' des Grossen." In *Texte aus der Umwelt des Alten Testaments* (Elamite). Gütersloh, Germany, 1984.

SCHMITT, R. *The Bisitun Inscriptions of Darius the Great* (Old Persian text). London, 1991.

VOIGTLANDER, ELIZABETH N. VON. *The Bisitun Inscription of Darius the Great* (Babylonian). London, 1978.

A. Shapur Shahbazi

Bismarck, Otto von   [1815–1898]

German statesman; first chancellor of the German Empire, 1871–1890.

Prince Otto Eduard Leopold von Bismarck pursued a domestic and foreign policy, after German unification, to preserve German gains in Europe by avoiding new wars. After the Russo–Turkish War, he served as the "honest broker" at the 1878 Congress of Berlin, which ended the war and redivided southeastern Europe, especially the Balkans.

He experienced a brief period of colonial enthusiasm, for motives that are still not understood, and gained colonies for Germany in Africa and the Pacific. He also encouraged France and England to pursue colonial adventures in North Africa to increase the tensions between them, thus relieving pressure on Germany.

[*See also*: Russo-Ottoman Wars]

BIBLIOGRAPHY

EYCK, ERICH. *Bismarck and the German Empire.* New York, 1968.

Jon Jucovy

Bitar, Salah al-Din al-   [1912–1980]

Syrian politician.

Born to a prosperous Damascene family, Salah al-Din Bitar studied physics at Damascus University and in Paris. While in Paris, he founded the Ba'th al-Arabi (Arab renaissance) in 1940 with Michel Aflaq. He was elected to parliament in 1954 and served as foreign minister in 1957. In these capacities, Bitar, along with other Ba'th colleagues, played a key role in the forging of the United Arab Republic. He was appointed minister of state for Arab affairs and minister of national guidance in the United Arab Republic. After Syria's secession from the United Arab Republic in 1961, Bitar became prime minister. After the Ba'th coup in 1963, he became foreign minister.

As the military began to dominate the party more and more, Bitar gradually lost influence and was arrested. He was expelled from the party when the leftist faction seized power in 1966. Exiled to Lebanon, he distanced himself from the pro-Iraqi faction led by Aflaq, who was also expelled from the faction then in power. Bitar was sentenced to death in 1969 but subsequently pardoned. He was assassinated in Paris in 1980.

BIBLIOGRAPHY

SHIMONI, YAACOV. *Political Dictionary of the Arab World.* New York, 1987.

Charles U. Zenzie

Bitat, Rabah   [1927–   ]

Algerian revolutionary, government minister, and president of Assemblée Nationale Populaire (ANP).

Bitat was a founder of the FRONT DE LIBÉRATION NATIONALE (FLN) and is regarded as one of the nine historic chiefs of the Algerian revolution. The French captured Bitat, and he remained in detention until the end of the ALGERIAN WAR OF INDEPENDENCE in 1962.

Bitat first supported, then opposed Ben Bella. He held the transportation portfolio under Houari BOUMÉDIENNE before becoming the first president of the ANP (by the constitution of 1976). Bitat served as acting president (December–February 1978/79) after Boumédienne's death in December 1978. Bitat returned to the ANP following Chadli BENJEDID's election. After the October 1988 riots, Benjedid's accelerated reforms compounded by a declining dinar alienated Bitat, who resigned in protest in 1990. Since then he has remained a critic within FLN circles. His wife is Zohra Drif, a heroine of the Battle of ALGIERS.

BIBLIOGRAPHY

NAYLOR, PHILLIP, and ALF HEGGOY. *Historical Dictionary of Algeria,* 2nd ed. Metuchen, N.J., 1994.

Phillip C. Naylor

Bittari, Zoubida   [1937–   ]

Pseudonym of Louise Ali-Rachedi.

Bittari, an Algerian, has written a single autobiographical novel. She was born in Algiers, to a Muslim family of modest means who withdrew her from school at age twelve in order to marry her to a man of their choice. After her divorce at age fourteen, she left Algeria to work for a French family in France. While there she wrote *O Mes Soeurs Musulmanes,*

Pleurez! (1964; Oh! My Muslim Sisters, Weep!). The book relates the story of a young married woman at odds with her in-laws. She sees her dreams of freedom crushed as a result of her marriage. The highly melodramatic book analyzes the situation of women from the colonial position.

BIBLIOGRAPHY

BADRAN, MARGOT, and MIRIAM COOKE, eds. *Opening the Gates: A Century of Arab Feminist Writing.* Bloomington, Ind., 1990.
GORDON, DAVID. *Women of Algeria: An Essay on Change.* Cambridge, U.K., 1968.

Aida A. Bamia

Bizerte

Northern Tunisian seaport situated between a large inland lake and the Mediterranean Sea.

Although a settlement had existed on the site of Bizerte since Phoenician times, the town first attained significance in the sixteenth century when an influx of Moorish and Jewish refugees from Roman Catholic Andalusia (Spain) spurred both agricultural and artisanal development. Like other North African seaports, Bizerte served as a base for Barbary Corsairs of the Barbary states and their raids against European ships. In retaliation, Spanish forces seized and fortified the city in 1535. Troops of the Ottoman Empire recaptured it briefly in 1572, but definitively only in 1574 when its garrison was sent to defend the more important Spanish positions at TUNIS. Throughout the seventeenth century, Bizerte's economy continued to depend almost exclusively on the raiding of its corsairs.

France set up a trading post at Bizerte in 1738 as one of a string of such establishments along the Algerian and Tunisian coasts. Although poor relations between French merchants and the Tunisian government led to the post's temporary closing in 1741/42, it operated until Ali Bey evicted the French in 1770. This, plus French anger over corsair forays staged from Bizerte, led to a naval bombardment that badly damaged the city. A similar attack by a Venetian fleet in 1785 all but destroyed Bizerte. Despite these hostilities, Marseilles merchants continued to import wheat from Bizerte, especially during the French Revolution and the Napoleonic Wars. In 1789, a French consulate opened there.

The Tunisian government's renunciation of corsair activity in 1819 hurt Bizerte, but the silting up of the port was an even more serious problem, causing a steady decline in commercial activity in the first half of the nineteenth century. At the same time, however, TUNISIA was being drawn into a more extensive relationship with Europe. A telegraph line linking Tunisia with Algeria and France passed through Bizerte in the 1850s, and the city was the starting point for a submarine cable that opened communications with Italy in 1864.

Following the Treaty of BARDO (1881), which established a strong French presence in Tunisia, the canal connecting the lake with the sea was improved. This, and other extensive French public-works projects in Bizerte in the 1880s and 1890s, made its harbor and port facilities among the finest in the Mediterranean. Much of this work revolved around the creation of a French naval base and arsenal, which, by the turn of the century, were widely regarded as among the largest and most powerful in the Mediterranean. During World War II, this base, and its proximity to the narrow channel between Sicily and Africa joining the eastern and western Mediterranean basins, gave Bizerte great strategic importance. The city was occupied by the Axis immediately following the Anglo-American landings in Morocco and Algeria in 1942. Allied air raids destroyed 70 percent of Bizerte prior to its liberation in the following year, but the canal remained intact and the base became a jumping-off point for the successful Allied invasion of Sicily.

France retained control of the naval facilities at Bizerte after Tunisian independence (1955/56) and refused to accede to demands for their evacuation in 1961. France's attempts to break a blockade of the base led to violent confrontations with hastily mobilized Tunisian civilians and paramilitary units. Tunisia appealed to the United Nations, which called for negotiations on the base's future. Only after lengthy delays, did France agree to abandon the installation in late 1963.

In the years since Tunisian independence, Bizerte and other cities around its lake have become major industrial centers, while the port remains the country's primary import-export terminal.

BIBLIOGRAPHY

GINESTOUS, PAUL. "Bizerte et l'histoire." *Bulletin économique et social de la Tunisie* 100 (May 1955): 89–117.

Kenneth J. Perkins

Bizerte Crisis

Tunisian blockade of French naval base at Bizerte.

Tunisia imposed a blockade on France's naval base at Bizerte in July 1961, hoping to force its evacu-

ation. French soldiers broke the blockade and gained control of most of the city in fierce fighting with hastily mobilized Tunisian civilians and paramilitary units. Tunisia appealed to the United Nations, which called for a negotiated settlement. French troops remained in occupation of the city until autumn, while the base itself was not abandoned until late in 1963, following the conclusion of the Algerian War.

BIBLIOGRAPHY

RUF, WERNER. "The Bizerte Crisis: A Bourguibist Attempt to Resolve Tunisia's Border Problem." *Middle East Journal* 25 (1971): 201–211.

Kenneth J. Perkins

Bizri, Afif al-

Syrian military officer.

Afif al-Bizri was arrested by French mandate authorities in Syria in 1941 as he fled Rashid Ali al-KAYLANI's failed revolt against the British. He served in the Arab–Israel War of 1948 and rose to command the cartography division of the Syrian army. He presided over the January 8, 1957, military trial of Adib SHISHAKLI and became chief of staff of the army in August 1957.

Bizri led a delegation of military officers to Cairo to pledge Syrian al-BA'TH support to Egypt's President Gamal Abdel Nasser in January 1958 when Syria and Egypt formed the UNITED ARAB REPUBLIC (UAR).

BIBLIOGRAPHY

SEALE, PATRICK. *The Struggle for Syria.* London, 1965.

Charles U. Zenzie

Black Friday

See Jaleh Square

Black Letter

See MacDonald Letter

Black Panthers

An Israeli protest movement of second-generation Middle Eastern immigrants, mostly Moroccan.

The Black Panthers aimed at improving material conditions in ISRAEL in Middle Eastern Jewish communities (EDOT HA-MISRAH). Erupting briefly as street demonstrations in Jerusalem and Tel Aviv, in 1971, the movement attracted publicity. The name, taken from the U.S. black-pride movement, was chosen to shock Israelis out of complacency. The movement led to improved community services and some activists began their political careers.

Shlomo Deshen

Black Sea

Large inland saltwater sea between Turkey on the south and Ukraine on the north, connected to the Mediterranean Sea.

About 180,000 square miles (466,000 sq. km.), the Black Sea is connected to the Aegean Sea, the northeast arm of the Mediterranean Sea, by the Turkish STRAITS (the Dardanelles, the Sea of Marmara, and the Bosporus). Until the late eighteenth century, the Black Sea was controlled almost entirely by the Ottoman Empire, but the sea was opened to Russia in the Treaty of KUÇUK KAYNARJA (1774). Over the next century and a half, the Russians and the Ottoman Turks vied for control of the Black Sea. The Ottoman EMPIRE attempted to keep Russia from establishing a military presence in the Black Sea, and the Russians attempted to push the Ottomans ever southward and prevent access to the Black Sea by the other European powers through the Turkish straits. Control of the straits remained a live issue well into the twentieth century. After World War II, Josef Stalin, USSR premier, unsuccessfully pressured Turkey to revise the 1936 MONTREUX CONVENTION, which barred belligerents from the straits and hence limited the ability of the USSR to use the Black Sea as a naval base. The Black Sea is also a major commercial shipping region. It is thus a vital economic link between Eastern Europe, Russia and other states of the former USSR, Turkey, and the states of western Central Asia, as well as a link between these states and the countries of the Mediterranean and the world.

BIBLIOGRAPHY

LENCZOWSKI, GEORGE. *The Middle East in World Affairs,* 4th ed. Ithaca, N.Y., 1980.
SHAW, STANFORD, and EZEL KURAL SHAW. *History of the Ottoman Empire and Modern Turkey.* Cambridge, U.K., 1977.

Zachary Karabell

Black September

A Palestinian commando movement that grew out of the defeat of Palestinians in the 1970/71 civil war in Jordan.

Black September was established in the autumn of 1971 by Palestinian followers of Salah KHALAF (Abu I'yed), intelligence chief of the mainstream al-FATH organization. Their first targets were aimed against Jordan, including the assassination of the Jordanian Prime Minister Wasfi al-TAL in November 1971.

Black September's most dramatic attack was the capture of eleven Israeli athletes at the September 1972 Olympic Games in Munich, Germany. All the athletes and five of the commandos were killed when German security forces stormed a plane the commandos and their hostages were preparing to board. Black September was also at the forefront of an underground war between the Israelis and the Palestinians that was carried out in Europe and the Middle East.

BIBLIOGRAPHY

COBBAN, HELENA. *The Palestinian Liberation Organization: People, Power, and Politics.* Cambridge, U.K., 1984.
COOLEY, JOHN. *Green March, Black September.* London, 1973.

Steve Tamari

Black Thursday

Tunisian riots between government forces and striking workers over a sagging economy.

On January 26, 1978, demonstrations organized by the General Union of Tunisian Workers (Union Générale de Travailleurs Tunisiens; UGTT) in Tunis led to clashes between state security forces and striking workers. Scores of demonstrators were killed and injured, and hundreds of UGTT members, including its leadership under Habib ACHOUR, were arrested. The demonstrations were organized to protest a worsening economic crisis in TUNISIA brought on by state policies as framed in the Five-Year Plan of 1973–1977.

BIBLIOGRAPHY

PERKINS, KENNETH. *Tunisia: Crossroads of the Islamic and European Worlds.* Boulder, Colo., 1986.

Matthew S. Gordon

Bled al-Siba/Bled al-Makhzan

A theory recognizing the pragmatic governance of a multicultural society.

French colonial theorists developed the idea that pre-colonial Morocco consisted of two areas, *bled al-makhzan,* the land of government, where the sultan ruled over plains and cities and collected taxes more securely, and *bled al-siba,* the many Berber mountainous areas where the Sultan was relatively powerless. The use of the term *makhzan* (treasury) for the government clearly showed the relationship between taxation and authority. The sultan's authority over *siba* areas, they said, was confined to his religious role. The *makhzan-siba* division laid the theoretical basis, under the protectorate, of a system of "indirect rule," under which the Berber areas would be administered separately from the Arab-speaking areas, supposedly in accordance with their customary law. Arabic-speaking nationalists saw this as an attempt to "divide and rule." Nationalist historians pictured the sultan not as a powerless figurehead but as an arbitrator who stepped in to settle disputes in the mountainous and Berber areas, but who was otherwise content to allow these more remote and poor areas to use local systems to maintain order.

BIBLIOGRAPHY

BERNARD G. HOFFMAN's *The Structure of Traditional Moroccan Rural Society* (The Hague and Paris, 1967) is a restatement of the French colonialist view, while GERMAIN AYACHE's "La fonction d'arbitrage du makhzen," *Bulletin Economique et Social du Maroc* (179), and "Société rifaine et pouvoir central marocain," *Revue Historique* (1985), express the nationalist and revisionist viewpoint; they are reprinted in AYACHE's collection *Etudes d'Histoire Maghrébine* (Rabat, 1979).

C. R. Pennell

Bliss, Daniel   [1823–1916]

The American University of Beirut's first president.

Born in the United States, Reverend Daniel Bliss came to Beirut in 1856, as one of a group of American Protestant missionaries sent to what was then called Syria. When in 1862 the mission decided to create a college in Beirut, he was given responsibility for raising money for the project in England and the United States. His success in doing so was one of the factors that made possible the establishment in Beirut in 1866 of the Syrian Protestant College, which later was renamed the AMER- ICAN UNIVERSITY OF BEIRUT. He became the college's first president and retained that position until 1902, when he retired and was succeeded by his son, Howard Bliss.

BIBLIOGRAPHY

BLISS, DANIEL. *Letters from a New Campus.* Beirut, 1993.
BLISS, FREDERICK. *The Reminiscences of Daniel Bliss.* New York, 1920.
SALIBI, KAMAL S. *The Modern History of Lebanon.* New York, 1965.

Guilain P. Denoeux

Bliss, Howard   [1860–1920]

Minister and educator.

Bliss earned degrees from Amherst College and Union Theological Seminary; he also studied in Oxford and Berlin, but he returned to the United States to be ordained in the Congregational ministry in 1890. Bliss served as pastor of the Christian Union Congregational Church in New Jersey but left in 1902 to become president of the Syrian Protestant College in Beirut, Lebanon.

BIBLIOGRAPHY

Who Was Who 1916–1928. London, 1929.

Mark Mechler

Bloc d'Action Nationale

The first Moroccan nationalist party.

Established in 1933–1934, and often known simply as the *kutla* (bloc), the bloc is another name for the COMITÉ D'ACTION MAROCAINE (CAM).

Bruce Maddy-Weitzman

Blood Libel

Anti-Semitic ritual murder accusation.

The allegation that the Jews murder Christian children to use their blood for ritual purposes first appeared in Norwich, England, in 1144, then spread rapidly to the Continent. Despite repudiation by popes and kings, it captured the popular imagination and was the pretext for massacres and expulsions of Jews.

The blood libel first appeared in Muslim lands soon after the expulsion of the Jews from Spain, generally instigated by Ottoman Christians around Easter. Sultan Süleyman the Magnificent issued an imperial decree (*firman*) in 1553 requiring that ritual murder accusations be adjudicated by the sultan and his imperial council.

Blood libels increased during the nineteenth century as Western influence grew among Ottoman Christian subjects. The 1840 libel of Damascus inspired an international campaign of defense by Western Jews and inaugurated a new era of Jewish involvement in foreign affairs. Although Sultan Abdülmecit denounced the libel as "pure calumny" in 1840, it nevertheless increased in both Christian and Muslim lands, wreaking havoc among Ottoman and European Jewish communities.

BIBLIOGRAPHY

DUNDES, ALAN. *The Blood Libel Legend. A Casebook in Anti-Semitic Folklore.* Madison, Wis., 1991.

Jane Gerber

Bludan Conference

Arab conference in 1937 that rejected the partition of Palestine, also known as the National Arab Congress.

The conference, held from September 8 to 10, 1937, at a Syrian resort, Bludan, was attended by more than three hundred delegates from the Arab world. They passed a resolution rejecting the PEEL COMMISSION's July 1937 proposal to split Palestine, then under British mandate, into Arab and Jewish states.

The delegates rejected the establishment of a Jewish state and threatened Britain that they would ally with other European powers if it did not change its policy. They called for an independent Arab Palestinian state that would honor British rights in a treaty.

BIBLIOGRAPHY

HUREWITZ, J. C. *The Struggle for Palestine.* New York, 1950, 1976.
MATTAR, PHILIP. *The Mufti of Jerusalem.* New York, 1988.
SACHAR, HOWARD M. *A History of Israel.* New York, 1982.

Elizabeth Thompson

Blue Mosque

See Sultan Ahmet Mosque

Blue Shirts

See Wafd

Blum–Viollette Plan

French legislation that intended to give Algerian Muslims full citizenship rights.

Influenced by ex–Governor General and then Minister of State Maurice Viollette, Pierre Viénot, and historian Charles-André Julien, France's Premier Léon Blum submitted a bill to Parliament in 1936 that aimed at giving approximately 30,000 Muslims in Algeria full rights without the loss of their Muslim status. The Senate defeated it in 1938 and the legislation was never brought to the floor of the Chamber of Deputies. This was a terrible blow to the ÉVOLUÉS (assimilated Algerians) and convinced many of them (including Ferhat ABBAS) to pursue other directions of reform. It has been called a "lost opportunity" that might have prevented the savage ALGERIAN WAR OF INDEPENDENCE (1954–1962).

BIBLIOGRAPHY

GORDON, DAVID C. *The Passing of French Algeria.* London, 1966.

Phillip C. Naylor

Blunt, Wilfrid Scawen   [1840–1922]

British poet, explorer, and writer.

Blunt and his wife, Lady Anne, traveled throughout the Middle East and published accounts of their adventures. In 1881–1882, Blunt was in Egypt and became friends with Muhammad ABDUH, an Egyptian scholar and reformer, who inspired him to write *The Future of Islam* (1882). Blunt attempted to forestall Britain's occupation of Egypt, and he later denounced it in his *Secret History of the Occupation of Egypt* (1907). Among his other works were *Gordon at Khartoum* (1911) and *Atrocities of Justice Under British Rule in Egypt* (1906).

BIBLIOGRAPHY

Dictionary of National Biography 1922–1930. London, 1937.
HOURANI, ALBERT. *Arabic Thought in the Liberal Age, 1789–1939.* New York, 1983.
LONGFORD, ELIZABETH. *A Pilgrimage of Passion.* London, 1979.

Zachary Karabell

B'nai Brak

City located in central Israel, 3.1 miles (5 km) from Tel Aviv, between Ramat Gan and Petah Tiqwa.

The new Israeli city (also known as Bene Beraq) founded in 1924 by Hasidic Jews from Warsaw, is situated in the vicinity of the ancient city of B'nai Brak (mentioned in the Bible [Joshua 19:45] and in the Talmud). B'nai Brak has retained a special religious character, with a population of about 98,000, and is a major center of Orthodox Jewish sects; as the majority of the city's population, they control it. It is also the site of a growing number of yeshivas (Jewish religious schools), religious organizations, and courts of Hasidic rabbis. It has many industries, including major bottling and food-processing companies and a variety of other factories.

BIBLIOGRAPHY

CARTA. *Kol makom ve-atar* (Israel—Sites and Places). Jerusalem, 1980.
SURASKI, AHARON. *Hevlei yozer* (Pains of a Creator). B'nai Brak, 1974. A biography of the founder of B'nai Brak, Rabbi Isaac Gershtenkorn.

Chaim I. Waxman

B'nai B'rith

The oldest and largest international Jewish fraternal and service organization.

B'nai B'rith (Hebrew, Sons of the Covenant) was founded in the United States in 1843, and in 1881, the first European lodge was established in Germany. Middle Eastern branches were founded not long afterward.

The first of these were in Egypt, where a considerable number of ASHKENAZIM and Europeanized Sephardic Jews were living. The Maimonides Lodge was opened in Cairo in 1887 and the Eliahu Hanabi Lodge in Alexandria in 1891.

Lodges in Istanbul and Edirne were established in Ottoman Turkey in 1911. That same year, the Arze ha-Levanon Lodge was opened in Beirut (Lebanon). The B'nai B'rith lodges attracted the modernizing elites of the Levantine Jewish communities and became the principal centers for communal activism, reform, and philanthropy. In the 1920s, the B'nai B'rith lodges in the new Republic of Turkey led the campaign for Jews there to adopt Turkish as their primary language. In Egypt, in 1933, the powerful B'nai B'rith lodges organized mass demonstrations against German anti-Semitism and established the Ligue Contre l'Antisemitisme Allemand (LICA), and in 1935 a boycott of German products and films.

BIBLIOGRAPHY

STILLMAN, NORMAN A. *The Jews of Arab Lands in Modern Times.* Philadelphia, 1991.

Norman Stillman

B'nei Akivah

See Gush Emunim

Bodenheimer, Max   [1865–1940]

German Jewish lawyer and a German Zionist leader.

Head of the Zionist group founded in Cologne, Germany, in May 1887, Bodenheimer was also the president of an independent society of Cologne's Hovevei Zion, which became the German Zionist Federation.

Bodenheimer outlined a plan for the establishment of a Zionist bank and central fund. In 1897, at the First Zionist Congress in Basle, Switzerland, he outlined the organizational program of ZIONISM. He was chairman and one of the first directors of the JEWISH NATIONAL FUND, resigning in 1914.

BIBLIOGRAPHY

LAQUEUR, WALTER. *A History of Zionism.* New York, 1972.
VITAL, DAVID. *Origins of Zionism.* Oxford, 1975

Miriam Simon

Bodrum

Resort town located on the Anatolian shore of the Aegean Sea on a peninsula of the same name, opposite the Greek island of Kos.

It is said that Bodrum, which in Turkish means "underground vault" or "cellar," got its name from the vaultlike ancient ruins that abound in the area. Originally, however, it was called Halicarnassos—a name it acquired from its first settlers, the Dorians from the Peloponnese (1000 B.C.). Bodrum's claim to fame in ancient times stems from the fact that it was the birthplace of a number of famous Greek intellectuals, in particular Herodotus (ca. 484–ca. 420 B.C.), who in his *Histories* chronicled the city's fortunes and the struggle for control of it between Greece and Persia. In 1402 the Knights of Saint John came from Rhodes and built one of the most famous landmarks of Bodrum, the Castle of St. Peter. The peninsula was finally brought back into the Ottoman fold when in 1523 Süleyman the Magnificent ousted the Knights of St. John from Rhodes, and consequently from Bodrum.

Today, Bodrum is part of the Turkish Riviera. It is well known for its historic sites, its clement weather, its colorfully decorated jazz bars, its picture-postcard whitewashed houses, its marina and yachting facilities, and its resident artist community. The most famous artist is the novelist Cevatsakir Kabaa-ğaçlu, better known as the "Fisherman of Halicarnassos," who immortalized the lore and legends of the local seafarers in a collection of short stories.

The 1990 census taken by the Turkish government listed the resident population of Bodrum as 20,931. However, the town is renowned for its seasonal population fluctuations. In the summer, at the height of the tourist season, its population can easily be ten or twenty times the winter figure.

BIBLIOGRAPHY

Encyclopaedia of Islam, 2nd ed.

Karen Pinto

Boğaziçi (Bosporus) University

Public university in Istanbul, Turkey.

Founded in 1863 as Robert College, an American missionary school, it maintains English as the language of instruction even though it was transferred to the Turkish state in 1971. It comprises the faculties of engineering, arts and sciences, economics and administrative sciences, and education, as well as the School of Foreign Languages and the College of Vocational Education. In 1990 it had about 600 teaching staff and 7,600 students, (3,300 female). Its state-funded budget for 1991 totaled 92 billion Turkish lire, of which slightly more than 23 billion was for capital investment.

Robert College in Istanbul, was the first and most famous of the many schools founded by American missionaries in the nineteenth-century Ottoman Empire. Being a missionary establishment, it did not attract any Muslim-Turkish students for its first forty years; Greeks, Armenians, and Bulgarians were the main students before the era of the republic of Turkey began in 1923. Robert College had an academy (lower) division as well as the college. Just before World War I, the School of Engineering was added.

In 1958 the institution was substantially reorganized to bring it in line with changes in the Turkish school system, allowing a full-scale college to be established at the same level as the School of Engineering. This enlargement and upgrading benefited from the post–World War II influence of the United States

in Turkey. Turkish governments that had tolerated but restricted foreign schools in the country then made an exception and allowed Robert College to add new buildings to accompany the enlarged academic program. The college responded well to the government's expectations: its new School of Administration provided well-educated managers for the booming private sector, and its innovative common-core curriculum set a high standard for other educational institutions.

Financial difficulties, even more than the campus militancy of the 1960s, forced Robert College's American trustees to turn over the college division to the Turkish state in 1971. Meanwhile, the high school continues to exist (at a nearby campus which had been a girls' college) as the coeducational Robert Lycée, still the most prestigious school in the country.

At the time of the turnover, the college division had barely a thousand students. In the 1970s Boğaziçi University grew steadily to become a well-rounded and academically superior institution. In the 1980s, however, the university was forced to increase its student intake at an unrealistic rate, as was the case in all other universities; in the near future it will face a serious challenge to its elite status from BILKENT and other private universities that emerged in 1993. For the moment, Boğaziçi University remains the most prestigious academic institution in Turkey in management, social sciences, and humanities, and probably also in engineering, though there it faces more serious competition, notably from the ISTANBUL TECHNICAL UNIVERSITY and the Middle East Technical University in Ankara. Boğaziçi continues to have very close ties with Istanbul business circles; at the same time many of its graduates have taken up academic positions throughout the country, in the Middle East, and in the United States.

BIBLIOGRAPHY

Higher Education in Turkey. UNESCO, European Centre for Higher Education. December 1990.
World of Learning. 1990.

I. Metin Kunt

Boğazköy

City in Turkey on the site of the probable Hittite capital in central Anatolia.

Known as Hattushash (or Pteria, in Greek), today's Boğazköy was built over a site first inhabited by Hittites in the third millenium B.C.E. It was a major trading town and became the Hittite capital in the second millenium B.C.E. Thousands of clay tablets impressed with cuneiform writing have been excavated. The Hittite kingdom was extended into Syria, where a famous battle was fought with the Egyptians at Qadesh (near today's Homs) in 1285 B.C.E. By 1200 B.C.E., the Hittite empire was destroyed by migrating tribes known as the "sea peoples."

BIBLIOGRAPHY

Cambridge Encyclopedia of the Middle East and North Africa. New York, 1987.

Elizabeth Thompson

Bonaparte, Napoléon

French general and emperor.

The ascendancy of Egypt on the modern world stage can be traced to the period of French occupation, 1798 to 1801. French armies under the command of Gen. Napoléon Bonaparte landed at Abuqir Bay on July 1, 1798, stormed Alexandria the next day, and proceeded to Cairo. On July 21, 1798, outside the city, the French, although less than thirty thousand strong, defeated a MAMLUK army twice their number and occupied the city. Bonaparte's initial reason for the Egyptian expedition was to threaten Britain's supply line to India. However, once in Egypt, he realized the advantage to France that an occupation would ensure and set about structuring a system of local government to that end.

Suggesting that he himself was intent on becoming a Muslim, Bonaparte tried to convince the Egyptians of the sincerity of his intentions regarding their country. Among his claimed intentions were the liberation of Egypt from the stranglehold of the Mamluks, the introduction of enlightened government responsive to local needs, and respect for Egyptian religious traditions. Not surprisingly, the Egyptians were quite wary of his conversion, although given his intellectual makeup, he may very likely have found in Islam appealing characteristics.

He appointed *diwans,* or councils, composed of *ulama* (Muslim legal scholars), to stabilize local government by giving French policies the sanction of the country's notables. Having established relatively good relations with the local population, Bonaparte set about threatening the Ottoman Porte and Britain through an expedition to Palestine. Defeated and decimated by cholera, his troops returned to Egypt. Bonaparte, informed of the changes in the French political winds, left his army in Egypt in the care of Gen. Jacques Menou and returned to France in August 1799. Menou was forced to capitulate to an Anglo–Ottoman force in 1801; he and the army returned to France.

Though historians considered it a failure from a military perspective, Bonaparte's occupation of Egypt had great impact on the world of learning. One member of the expedition was Jean-François CHAMPOLLION, whose discovery of the ROSETTA STONE in the Nile delta permitted the deciphering of hieroglyphics and the development of Egyptology. The expedition also included dozens of artists as well as hundreds of social and natural scientists representing most of the academic disciplines. Their task was to catalog all the flora, fauna, and architecture—ancient and contemporary—of Egypt as they discovered it. To that end, once he established himself in Cairo, Bonaparte founded the Institut d'Egypte, whose purpose was to store and structure the immense body of newly discovered information. Between 1808 and 1829, the institute published the *Description de l'Egypte* in twenty-three enormous volumes of narrative and accompanying plates.

Certain recent scholarship has credited Bonaparte's expedition to Egypt with a development of dubious honor: orientalism. Originally considered the study of the Orient, "orientalism," in the postmodernist view, represents the textual deconstruction of the non-Western cultural heritage. The *Description de l'Egypte,* for instance, in laying bare the structure of Egyptian culture, may be seen as making that structure "vulnerable" to what such critics call Western "imposition."

BIBLIOGRAPHY

HERROLD, J. CHRISTOPHER. *Bonaparte in Egypt.* London. 1962.
AL-JABARTI, ABD AL-RAHMAN. *Napoleon in Egypt: Al-Jabarti's Chronicle of the French Occupation, 1798.* Tr. by Shmuel Moreh. Princeton, N.J., 1993.

Jean-Marc R. Oppenheim

Boneh

A term used for collective agriculture in Iran.

Boneh (plough teams) was a term used for collective agriculture in QANAT-irrigated regions of Iran, in which farmers used four to six oxen, and in some villages up to eight, to plough the land. The members of boneh included laborers as well as the owners of oxen, seed, water, and, at times, land. Each member's contribution determined his share of the produce. Cultivating the land by pooling their resources, the boneh members then collectively paid in kind for their daily necessities, such as the services of the carpenter, bath attendant, coppersmith, and barber. Any resident of a village where boneh was practiced was entitled to membership in the boneh system. The boneh member was given not only a share of the produce, but also access to the wells, pastures, and woods of the village. The boneh system was functioning, more or less intact, until the second half of the twentieth century, at which time tremendous population growth rendered the system dysfunctional.

BIBLIOGRAPHY

ABRAHAMIAN, E. *Iran between Two Revolutions.* Princeton, N.J., 1982, pp. 113–115.

Parvaneh Pourshariati

Boratav, Pertev Naili   [1907–   ]

Turkish scholar, folklorist, translator, and editor.

Boratav was born in Gümülcine (now Ziotigrad in Bulgaria), then under the jurisdiction of Edirne, where his father was qa'immaqam (lieutenant governor). He received his elementary education in Istanbul, to which the family immigrated upon the outbreak of the Balkan War (1912), and in various provincial towns to which his father was later assigned. After four years at the Kumkapı French School in Istanbul, he was graduated from the Istanbul Lycée (1927), continuing his studies at the Istanbul Faculty of Letters (Turkish language and literature) and the Teachers Training College (1927–1930). He taught at Istanbul University, the Konya Lycée, and the Teachers Training College, then spent 1936–37 on a government scholarship in Germany. On his return, Boratav worked one year in the library of the School of Political Science before becoming associate professor of Turkish folk literature at Ankara University, gaining promotion to professor of folklore in 1946.

A former student describes Boratav the professor as exhibiting "revolutionary behavior," introducing a new teacher–student relationship based upon mutual respect, care, and equality. Boratav also spoke out for academic freedom, freedom of the press, and human rights at a time of transition to multiparty democracy. But there were still limits to the new liberalism in Turkey, especially where fear of communism was involved. Thus in 1948 four professors at Ankara University, considered to be spreading Marxist views, lost their posts. Boratav was among them. In 1952 he joined the Centre Nationale de la Recherche Scientifique (National Center for Scientific Research) in Paris and from 1963 also taught Turkish folklore at the École Pratique des Hautes Études. Officially retired in 1974, he continued his research and writing and, from 1975, taught a seminar on Ottoman paleography at the school.

Publishing extensively, Boratav produced translations and wrote on the general literature of the Turks, contributing, for example, to *Turcica* and to the three-volume *Histoire Générale des Litteratures* (Paris, 1961). He is best known, however, as a folklorist. Under his leadership, folklore studies functioned as an independent intellectual discipline at Ankara University. He also encouraged interest in folklore at the local level, editing *Halk Bilgisi Haberleri* (News of Folk Culture), turning it into "a major instrument of research into social and religious groups, nomadic tribes, agricultural methods and other matters of interest to the villages." His own publications in Turkish include general studies on folklore and folk literature, collections of various folk genres, and studies on individual works and figures.

He also brought Turkish folklore and literature to world attention, becoming a highly respected figure in international folklore circles. With Wolfram Eberhard, he compiled *Typen Türkischer Volksmärchen* (Wiesbaden, 1953), an index of Turkish folktales following the Aarne and Thompson standards. This supplied Turkologists with important material, filled "a great gap in our knowledge about folktales of the world," and was "welcome as a milestone of scholarship." Other works in Western languages include *Contes Turcs* (Paris, 1955) and his contributions in French on folk literature in *Philologiae Turcicae Fundamenta, II,* edited by Jean Deny et al. (Wiesbaden, 1965).

Living in Paris, Boratav maintains a close interest in the Institute of Turkish Studies and has been working on a major study of the NASRUDDIN HOCA material.

BIBLIOGRAPHY

BAŞGÖZ, ILHAN. *Studies in Turkish Folklore in Honor of Pertev N. Boratav,* ed. by Ilhan Başgöz and Mark Glazer. Bloomington, Ind., 1978.
KARPAT, KEMAL. *Turkey's Politics.* Princeton, N.J., 1959.
SHAW, STANFORD J., and EZEL KURAL SHAW. *History of the Ottoman Empire and Modern Turkey,* vol. 2. Cambridge, U.K., 1977.
WALKER, WARREN S., and AHMET E. UYSAL. *Tales Alive in Turkey.* Lubbock, Tex., 1990.

Kathleen R. F. Burrill

Borek

The name of a specialty pastry of Turkish or Balkan origin, served fried or baked.

The paper-thin pastry is rolled, then filled with savory flavored meat or cheese. The most popular boreks are usually thin and long, shaped like a cigarette, or square, resembling a cushion. Boreks are best taken with cocktails or as an appetizer.

Cyrus Moshaver

Borochov, Ber [1881–1919]

Pioneer Labor Zionist.

Ber Borochov was born in Poltava (Ukraine) and died in Russia. *The National Question and the Class Struggle,* which he published in 1905, served as one of the founding texts to LABOR ZIONISM—a synthesis of socialism and Zionism.

He was a founder of Po'alei Zion and argued that socialism would not remove Anti-Semitism as long as Jews had no state of their own; he advocated their return to ERETZ YISRAEL and the building of a national economy based on a Jewish working class. He insisted that for Jews the class struggle and nationalism could not be separated; this viewpoint added new categories to Marxian analysis and influenced the organization and direction of Labor Zionism for decades.

BIBLIOGRAPHY

AVINERI, SHLOMO. *The Making of Modern Zionism.* New York, 1981.

Donna Robinson Divine

Borujerdi, Hosayn [1865–1962]

Religious leader and teacher; director of the Feyziyeh in Qom, 1944–1962.

Ayatollah Hosayn Borujerdi was director of the religious teaching institution in QOM, the Feyziyeh, for seventeen years, and for fifteen years the most prominent *marja' al-taqlid* (source of emulation) for Shi'a communities throughout the world. He was born in Borujerd, Iran, to a family of scholars; and at least five marja' al-taqlid appear in his ancestry. He received his formal religious training in Isfahan and Najaf. In the early 1900s, Borujerdi moved to Najaf, to study with the famous Akhund Molla Mohammad Kazem Khorasani. In 1910 he returned to Iran. In 1944, he was appointed as head of the Feyziyeh religious seminary in Qom. The institution flourished considerably under his supervision, rivaling older such establishments of Najaf. Borujerdi's tenure both as marja' al-taqlid and head of the Feyziyeh was marked by his apolitical, compromising, and quietist stance. He actively pursued a Sunni-Shi'a rapprochement and was in constant correspondence with the director of al-Azhar, his Sunni counterpart, in Egypt. In the 1950s, when the radical Islamic group Feda'iyan-e Eslam (Devotees of Islam) embarked on a series of political assassinations, Borujerdi repeatedly denounced their actions, and he distanced himself and the Feyziyeh from any confrontation with the government of Mohammad Reza PAHLAVI. He in fact expelled the Feda'iyan-e Eslam from their headquarters at the Feyziyeh. In 1955, Borujerdi involved himself with the anti-Baha'i campaign of another prominent cleric, Abu al-Qasem Falsafi, grounding his opposition in religious rather than political motivations. Borujerdi also denounced the land reform program of the Shah, launched in 1951, on the grounds that it was contrary to Islamic law. Borujerdi's public denouncement of the bill was the first instance of open confrontation between the clergy and the government of Mohammad Reza Pahlavi. In 1953, when Mohammad Mossadegh, the prime minister of Iran, moved to nationalize the oil industry, Borujerdi distanced himself from the activist stance of Ayatollah Abu al-Qasem Kashani, who, together with the Feda'iyan-e Eslam, opposed Mohammad Reza Pahlavi in support of Mossadegh. In that same period, he was steadfast in his conviction in the autonomy of Qom, and the unacceptability of any government interference in its religious and financial affairs. When the government tried to impose its representative in Qom's office for religious endowments, Borujerdi flatly denounced the move. Borujerdi was closely associated with Ayatollah Ruhollah KHOMEINI, who had worked as Borujerdi's special assistant. But Borujerdi died in March 1962, before the clerical uprisings of 1963 led by Khomeini, along with several other clerics, his successor as marja' al-taqlid. Borujerdi's death also paved the way for the coming to power of the more radical, reform-minded *ulama* in Qom, who sought to preserve Islam's sociocultural hegemony by direct participation in the political life of the country, and later criticized Borujerdi's conservative, apolitical policies. During his lifetime, Borujerdi was one of the few Iranian, Qom-based, marja' al-taqlid who enjoyed considerable support and financial backing by Shi'ites outside Iran, notably in Najaf and Karbala, Iraqi centers of Shi'ite learning that tend to emulate their own clerical leadership.

BIBLIOGRAPHY

ABRAHAMIAN, ERVAND. *Iran Between Two Revolutions.* Princeton, N.J., 1982.

AKHAVI, SHAHROUGH. *Religion and Politics in Contemporary Iran*. Albany, N.Y., 1980.
FISCHER, MICHAEL M. J. *Iran from Religious Dispute to Revolution*. Cambridge, Mass., 1980.

Neguin Yavari

Bosporus

See Straits, Turkish

Bost

Afghan city; ancient Ghaznavid site.

The city of Bost, later renamed Lashkar Gah, was a Ghaznavid palace and soldiers' bazaar near the confluence of the Helmand and Arghandab rivers built by Sultan Mahmud of Ghazni around the year 1000. The city is now the capital of Helmand province and has a population of about twenty thousand inhabitants. In the 1950s and 1960s, this area became part of the Helmand Valley project, in which the HELMAND RIVER, which drains over half of the Afghan watershed, was damned and a series of canal projects diverted water for irrigation. Afghan farmers were resettled from other areas of Afghanistan to farm this new agricultural area. Although many eventually left and the project was viewed by some as a failure because of the technical problems encountered and the salinization of the soil, many thousand acres of arable land were reclaimed from the desert.

BIBLIOGRAPHY

DUPREE, LOUIS. *Afghanistan*. Princeton, N.J., 1980.

Grant Farr

Bouabid, Abderrahim   [1920–   ]

Moroccan diplomat and opposition party leader.

As a student, Abderrahim Bouabid joined the movement for Moroccan nationalism, which sought independence from the French and Spanish protectorates imposed in 1912. In the 1950s, he joined the Istiqlal party.

In 1956, France and Spain recognized the independence and sovereignty of Morocco, and Bouabid was put in charge of economic planning in the first independent government. He played a leading part in the political crisis of 1958/59, which led to a split in the Istiqlal. With Mehdi BEN BARKA and others, he formed a new progressive party, the National Union

of Popular Forces (UNFP); in the mid-1970s, he helped form an offshoot party called the Socialist Union of Popular Forces (USFP), which emerged as the leading opposition to King Hassan II. In 1981, following riots in Casablanca, Bouabid and others were jailed, although he remained at the head of the party through the 1980s.

BIBLIOGRAPHY

ASHFORD, DOUGLAS. *Political Change in Morocco*. Princeton, N.J., 1961.
ZARTMAN, I. WILLIAM, ed. *Man, State and Society in the Contemporary Maghrib*. New York, 1973.

Matthew S. Gordon

Boucetta, Muhammad   [1925–   ]

Moroccan lawyer and political figure.

Boucetta was educated in Fez and at the law faculty at the Sorbonne in Paris. After joining the movement for nationalism in the 1940s, he became a leading member of the ISTIQLAL political party by the early 1950s. Morocco became independent of French colonialism in 1956; during the 1958/59 split of Istiqlal, Boucetta remained in the more conservative wing, under Allal al-Fasi. As secretary-general of the party (1974; then 1978–present), Boucetta held a series of government posts, including minister of state for foreign affairs (1977; then 1981–1983).

BIBLIOGRAPHY

ASHFORD, DOUGLAS. *Political Change in Morocco*. Princeton, N.J., 1961.
WATERBURY, JOHN. *The Commander of the Faithful*. New York, 1970.
Who's Who in the Arab World. 1990–1991.

Matthew S. Gordon

Boudiaf, Mohamed   [1919–1992]

Algerian revolutionary; head of High Security Council (1992).

Born in M'Sila, Boudiaf was drafted in 1943 into the French Army, where he tried to organize nationalist cells in the Algerian ranks. He supported the nationalist ideals of Messali al-Hadj and joined the paramilitary Organisation Spéciale (OS). He eluded French authorities and later became a party organizer for the Mouvement pour le Triomphe des Libertés

Démocratiques (MTLD) in France. Aligning with the restive younger Messalist elite, Boudiaf played an important role in launching the Comité Révolutionnaire pour l'Unité et l'Action (CRUA) which led to the formation of the Front de Libération Nationale (FLN). He is regarded as one of the nine "historic chiefs" of ALGERIA's revolution. He served in the "external" faction of the FLN until the controversial French skyjacking in October 1956 resulting in his capture along with historic chiefs Ahmed Ben Bella, Hocine Ait Ahmed, Rabah Bitat, and Mohamed Khider. He spent the rest of the war in prison.

Boudiaf supported neither Ben Bella or the Gouvernement Provisoire de la République Algérienne (GPRA) in the power struggle after the war. He founded instead an organization called the Parti de la Révolution Socialiste (PRS). Boudiaf was arrested in 1963 and condemned to death. He was subsequently sent into exile. After Ben Bella's deposition in June 1965, he continued his opposition to Houari BOUMÉDIENNE's regime.

Unlike Ben Bella and Ait Ahmed, Boudiaf did not return to Algeria soon after the October 1988 riots and the subsequent political liberalization. Nevertheless, with the electoral crisis of 1991 and the replacement of President Chadli Benjedid in January 1992 by a High Security Council (HSC), Boudiaf returned to prominence by accepting the titular leadership of this new government. His presence was viewed as historical and symbolic. He attempted to mobilize the Algerian "silent majority" to support the HSC and its goals. Boudiaf claimed to serve no party except the Algerian nation, and this was reflected in the HSC's initiative to establish a new national assembly that would have no former FLN or Islamic Salvation Front (FIS) politicians. Boudiaf was assassinated in Annaba in June 1992.

BIBLIOGRAPHY

IBRAHIM, YOUSSEF M. "President of Algeria Assassinated; Officials Blame Muslim Fundamentalists." *New York Times,* June 30, 1992.
STORA, BENJAMIN. *Dictionnaire biographique des militants nationalistes algériens.* Paris, 1985.

Phillip C. Naylor

Boudjedra, Rachid   [1941–]

Algerian novelist.

Boudjedra was born in Aïn Beïda in Algeria and attended secondary school in Tunis. He later earned a philosophy degree at the Sorbonne in Paris. He was wounded while serving in the Armée de Libération

Nationale (ALN; National Liberation Army) during the Algerian revolution. Boudjedra earned his literary reputation from his novels *La répudiation* (1969) and *L'insolation* (1972), which dramatically questioned contemporary social conventions and traditions through psychologically complex characters. Other novels include *Topographie idéale pour une agression caractérisée* (1975); *L'escargot entêté* (1977); *Les 1001 années de la nostalgie* (1979); and *Le vainqueur de coupe* (1981). Boudjedra then announced in June 1982 that he would no longer write in French. He did translate, however, his Arabic novel, *Ettafakouk* (1982) into French as *Le démantèlement al-Tafak* (1982) and wrote the essays *La vie quotidienne en Algérie* (1971) and *Naissance du cinéma algérien* (1971).

BIBLIOGRAPHY

DÉJEUX, JEAN. *Dictionnaire des auteurs maghrébines de langue française.* Paris, 1984.

Philip C. Naylor

Boulam, Benaïssa   [1906–1982]

Algerian native governor and leader.

Boualam was born in Souk-Ahras, Algeria, and was promoted during the era of French colonialism to the title of *bachaga* (native governor). He was a veteran officer in the French army and became the most prominent *harki* (an Arab leader in the French military) during the Algerian War of Independence (1954–1962). Along with several hundred of his harkis, Boualam fled to France and to exile. He worked arduously for France to recognize harki service and sacrifice through his writings (e.g., *Mon pays, la France,* 1962; My Country, France) and his leadership of the Front National des Rapatriés de Confession Musulmane (National Front of Muslim Repatriates). Boualam also served in the National Assembly as vice president and was a member of the Legion of Honor.

BIBLIOGRAPHY

DÉJEUX, JEAN. *Dictionnaire des auteurs maghrébines de langue française.* Paris, 1984.

Phillip C. Naylor

Boumahdi, Ali   [1934–]

Algerian novelist and educator.

Boumahdi, born in Berrouaghia, Algeria, studied English literature in London and Paris. He lives in

France and is the principal of a college in the region of Seine Saint-Denis. Boumahdi, who writes in French, has published two novels: *Le Village des Asphodèles* (Paris, 1970) and *L'Homme-cigogne du Titteri* (Paris, 1987). The first is highly autobiographical and deals with the colonial period. The second deals with the end of the French occupation and the early years of independence, which he criticizes. Boumahdi uses descriptive narrative in his writings, in the tradition of the early ethnographic Algerian novels.

BIBLIOGRAPHY

ACHOUR, CHRISTIANE. *Anthologie de la littérature algérienne de langue française.* Paris, 1990.

Aida A. Bamia

Boumédienne, Houari   [1927?– 1978]

First vice-president of Algeria, 1962; second president of Algeria, 1965–1978.

The son of a small farmer whose family originated in the Kabylia (BERBER) region of Algeria, Houari Boumédienne was born Mohammed Ben Brahim Boukharouba at Clauzel (now al-Hussainiya), a small village near Guelma in the Constantinois region of the country. As a young man, he spent his school years attending both Qur'anic and French primary schools in Constantine and, at one point, a conservative *madrasa,* or religious school. After finishing his studies, he returned to his native village and became a teacher at the local school. Active early on in student politics, Boukharouba, as many of his generation, became interested in the growing nationalist sentiments and the emerging struggle against the French. His early involvement culminated in his participation in the 1945 SETIF REVOLT and, later, in the ALGERIAN WAR OF INDEPENDENCE (1954–1962). In the aftermath of the insurrection, he joined the Parti du Peuple Algérien (Algerian People's party, PPA), headed for a short while by Messali al-HADJ. To avoid forced enlistment in the French army, Boukharouba left Algeria in 1952.

During his years in exile in Cairo, he attended al-Azhar, the famous Islamic university. Although he remained a secularist throughout his years in power, he adhered to a secularism that was always tempered by respect for the Islamic/Arab heritage that Algeria had experienced. He infiltrated back into Algeria in 1955 and joined the *mojahedin* (fighters) of Wilaya V (the Oranie region) where he assumed his nom de guerre—Houari Boumédienne—a name he would keep after the Algerian War of Independence. As an assistant to Abd al-Hafid Boussouf, commander of

Wilaya V at the time—the best organized and disciplined of the military apparatus in the interior of Algeria—Boumédienne was put in charge of the Moroccan wing of the Armée de Libération Nationale (National Liberation Army, ALN). He slowly rose to the top of the external army structure between 1957 and 1960 and became the chief of the western general staff in September 1958, then located in Oujda, Morocco, where most of the important army commanders of postindependence Algeria were gathered at one time or another.

In February 1960, he was again promoted—this time to chief of the united general staff, headquartered in Ghardimaou, Tunisia. His position as one of the most prominent officers and powerbrokers within the future Algerian army was confirmed in 1959 when Boumédienne was put in charge of a military court that prosecuted a number of ALN colonels in Tunisia who had plotted the overthrow of the Provisional Government of the Algerian Republic (GPRA).

In time, however, Boumédienne himself grew disenchanted with the GPRA and resigned as the second round of the Evian agreements (the negotiations between France and representatives of the Algerian leadership) limped to a halt. Although Boumédienne cited disagreement with the Algerian participants at the Evian agreements on a number of issues, the real dispute centered on the power of the ALN versus the GPRA as independence grew nearer. At that point Boumédienne received the support of Ahmed BEN BELLA, whose visibility, despite his incarceration in France, had steadily grown among Algerian participants in the struggle for independence. Ben Bella's help became crucial in 1961 and 1962 when Boumédienne wanted to remove a number of old-time revolutionaries and politicians from the GPRA. Boumédienne then returned to the provisional government, but the internal battle for power was far from settled and would resurface once independence was achieved.

After independence in 1962, Houari Boumédienne, as a key member of the Algerian military, became minister of defense and first vice-president of the republic under the presidency of Ahmed Ben Bella. His primary task was to convert the internal and external units of the Algerian army that had emerged during the war of independence into a unified force. Disenchanted with the lack of direction of the newly independent government, faced with lingering internal political battles, and resentful of the foreign ideologues rather than local nationalists who helped determine Ben Bella's outlook on politics, Boumédienne deposed the first president of independent Algeria in June 1965 and assumed the presidency of the Council of the Revolution, the ruling body of the country, calling the coup a "historic rectification" of the Algerian revolution.

The 1965 coup, however, was not an indication of the personal power of the new president but reflected the political power of the armed forces whose independence Boumédienne had attempted to preserve. This would largely explain the collegial rule Boumédienne instituted after assuming power, a careful balancing act that he would be forced to maintain until his death.

Self-effacing, austere, pragmatic, and imbued with the ideals of the anticolonial struggle for which he had fought for almost two decades, Boumédienne after 1965 charted a political and economic future for his country that would slowly yield grudging admiration both abroad and at home. Its political and economic principles were described in detailed fashion in the 1976 national charter that became the guiding document for Algeria's socialist experiment.

The basis for his internal economic policies was a commitment to a socialist strategy that was simultaneously less draconian than that of his predecessor but still managed to put the Algerian state in charge of virtually all economic enterprises in the country. Boumédienne held the conviction that only coherent and centralized decision-making would allow the country to overcome both the disastrous economic effects of the eight-year struggle for independence and the lingering factionalism within the country. Businesses were grouped into a number of state enterprises, forming the basis of what was called an "industrializing industry" strategy. This contained the notion that, with direct and consistent state intervention, Algeria would build a heavy industry base—fueled by the income from petroleum and natural gas—that would serve as a platform for creating intermediary and eventually consumer products. The ultimate aim, according to Boumédienne, was greater economic self-sufficiency.

In foreign policy, Boumédienne steered Algeria toward a policy of neutrality in international affairs while committing the country to increased solidarity with Third World concerns. Under Boumédienne, Algeria became one of the original sponsors of the New International Economic Order at the United Nations and remained one of the most vocal members of the nonaligned movement. Boumédienne's cautious approach in international politics paid off as Algeria became, in several instances, a valuable interlocutor in mediating conflicts, with a corps of skilled diplomatic representatives at its service. Internally, however, Boumédienne increasingly relied on a coalition of technical experts and professional military advisers, particularly after an attempted coup by a fellow officer, Col. Tahar Zbiri, in 1967. The out-

come was that the FRONT DE LIBÉRATION NATIONALE (National Liberation Front, FLN), the country's single party, lost much of the legitimacy and the mobilizing potential it had possessed. The long-term result of this increasingly technocratic/military alliance was a gradual loss of popular confidence in the single party and a further narrowing of the political base during the remainder of Boumédienne's tenure.

Boumédienne's economic strategy also was not as successful in the long run as he had hoped. The heavy state intervention had created an enormously inefficient public sector by the mid-1970s, exacerbated further by the easy borrowing privileges that Algeria enjoyed when oil prices rose after the ARAB-ISRAEL WAR (1973), and made worse by the one-party system where patronage and favoritism rather than personal capability provided criteria for recruitment. By the end of Boumédienne's life in December 1978, there was substantial disagreement over his economic strategy. This potential struggle had been kept in abeyance because of the personal respect Boumédienne enjoyed, and it reflected the crucial role he had played in Algeria's factional politics, which had never truly been resolved after independence.

After his death, the succession was not settled until 1980 at a special party congress but according to institutionalized procedures—a testimony in part to Boumédienne's political skills but also to the stranglehold the one-party system and the ALN, its most powerful defender, had on the country. The newly elected president, Chadli BENJEDID, abandoned his predecessor's economic strategy and embarked on a more market- and Western-oriented development that would have been anathema to Boumédienne and many of his advisers. Algerian socialism died along with its enigmatic second president.

BIBLIOGRAPHY

ENTELIS, JOHN. *Algeria: The Revolution Institutionalized.* Boulder, Colo., 1986.
RUEDY, JOHN. *Modern Algeria: The Origins and Development of a Nation.* Bloomington, Ind., 1992.

Dirk Vandewalle

Bourboune, Mourad [1938–]

Algerian author.

Born in Jijel, Algeria, Bourboune studied in Constantine, Tunis, and Paris. After the Algerian War of Independence (1954–1962), he helped organize the Union des Ecrivains Algériens (Union of Algerian Writers) and served as cabinet director for Bachir Boumaza, the minister of labor and social affairs during Ahmed Ben Bella's government. He wrote *Le*

Mont des genêts (1962), but his most famous work is *Le Muezzin* (1968), whose hero is a religious and revolutionary apostate. Bourboune has questioned the social legacy of the revolution.

BIBLIOGRAPHY

DÉJEUX, JEAN. *Dictionnaire des auteurs maghrébines de langue française.* Paris, 1985.

Phillip C. Naylor

Bourguiba, Habib   [1903–   ]

Leader of Tunisia's independence movement and first president of the Tunisian republic, 1957–1987.

The seventh child of a former army officer, Habib Bourguiba was born August 3, 1903, in Monastir, a small village in the Sahil, Tunisia's fertile coastal region. He was an intelligent youngster and won admission to Sadiqi College, a Tunis secondary school that had been established before the 1881 imposi-

President Habib Bourguiba of Tunisia (wearing a hat) with President Chadli Benjedid of Algeria. (© Chris Kutschera)

tion of the French protectorate to provide a superior education in both Arabic and French to the sons of the Tunisian elite. He then went on to study law at the Sorbonne in Paris from 1924 to 1927, where he met and married a French woman, the mother of his only child, a son named Habib Bourguiba, Jr. (He later married Wassila Ben Ammar, the daughter of a powerful Tunis family.) In Paris, Bourguiba encountered other North African intellectuals and activists as well as French liberals, and his interest in politics deepened. Upon his return to Tunisia, he opened a law office and became active in the Tunisian nationalist party, which was known as DESTOUR (Constitution).

By the early 1930s, as the economic crisis of the Great Depression deepened, Bourguiba grew impatient with the inability of the predominantly bourgeois Destour leaders to address the disproportionate burden borne by Tunisian peasants and farmers while French settlers were being given special dispensations by protectorate authorities. He founded a French-language newspaper in 1932 to give voice to his demands on behalf of the predominantly rural Tunisian population, and in 1934, he led a secession from the Destour, establishing what became known as the Neo-Destour party.

Openly agitating for independence with Bourguiba at its helm as secretary-general and later president, the Neo-Destour methodically organized a countrywide network of branches, turning the nationalist cause, previously an elite campaign, into a genuinely mass movement. Moreover, although Bourguiba was clearly the principal figure in the movement, his willingness to encourage other leaders within the party ensured that his colleagues were able to sustain the momentum of the movement in the face of French repression. Many Neo-Destour leaders were repeatedly imprisoned or exiled, including Bourguiba himself, who was in detention for nearly ten years between 1934 and 1955.

By 1954, in the face of rising local agitation, the French government decided that it had no alternative but to open negotiations with the Tunisian nationalists. In April 1955, the French granted Tunisia autonomy, reserving control of foreign affairs and defense, and within a year Bourguiba concluded a treaty granting the country full independence. In 1957, the Tunisian monarchy was abolished and Bourguiba elected president of the new republic. It was not until 1963, however, and at the cost of nearly one thousand Tunisian lives, that the French evacuated the last of their military bases.

Bourguiba's willingness to pursue a gradualist approach to negotiations with the French enhanced his reputation in the West as an artful, pragmatic leader, but it earned him enemies at home. In fact, the autonomy agreements nearly precipitated a civil war, as Bourguiba was opposed by other nationalist leaders, such as Salah BEN YUSUF, who argued that Bourguiba had conceded too much. Although Bourguiba won the war and eventually independence as well, he took the challenge very seriously, ultimately arranging Ben Yusuf's assassination in exile in 1961.

Similarly, Bourguiba's policies in the early years of independence demonstrated an independence of mind that only some of his fellow statesmen, both at home and abroad, appreciated. During the 1960s, like many Third World rulers, Bourguiba embraced socialism, declaring the Neo-Destour the sole political party, nationalizing much of Tunisia's trade and industry, and establishing cooperative farms. By the end of the decade, however, the policy was meeting increasing domestic resistance, particularly among the coastal farmers who were Bourguiba's most important supporters in his battles with the French and later with Ben Yusuf. In 1969, in a dramatic reversal, Bourguiba dismissed the prime minister associated with the policy, Ahmed BEN SALAH (later to accuse him of treason), and became one of the Arab world's earliest proponents of economic liberalism as the surest path to development.

Bourguiba's ideological independence—the pragmatism that became known in Tunisia as "bourguibisme"—was also evident elsewhere. During the 1960s, at a time when such a resolution was virtually unimaginable, he called openly for a negotiated settlement of the Arab–Israeli dispute. This placed Tunisia on the fringes of inter-Arab politics. Similarly, although Tunisia was described in its constitution as an Islamic country, Bourguiba had little patience for what he viewed as the anachronisms of religious observance. Thus, he advocated abandoning the obligatory fast during the month of Ramadan, arguing that the consequent loss of worker productivity interfered in the country's development. He also engineered Tunisia's family code, one of the most far-reaching personal-status laws in the Muslim world, to outlaw polygamy and to make access to divorce, support, child custody, and the like more equitable among men and women.

While many of these positions won him great esteem abroad, by 1975, when the National Assembly declared him president for life (a position he had previously refused), Bourguiba's command of the Tunisian political scene had begun to weaken. Health problems that began to appear in the late 1960s recurred periodically, and although he proved not to be nearly so frail as his admirers feared (or his detractors hoped), his remarkable political insight and intellectual agility began to diminish. By the late 1970s, his government was drawing increasing crit-

icism for failing to accompany its economic liberalism with political reform. The architect of the economic policy, Prime Minister Hedi Nouira, was openly contemptuous of multiparty politics, but it was not until he suffered a stroke in 1980 that Bourguiba saw fit to replace him.

Nouira's successor, Mohammed MZALI, initially lived up to his more liberal reputation, authorizing a number of opposition parties and calling for contested elections, but he was soon consumed by the jockeying for position among the political elite precipitated by Bourguiba's increasingly erratic behavior. Bourguiba was said to be out of touch with most daily events, often preoccupied with plans for his own state funeral, yet unwilling to surrender any of his virtually absolute authority. By the middle of the 1980s, however, the country needed a strong hand; it faced serious economic problems, a growing Islamic political movement (whose participation in Tunisian politics was anathema to the secularist Bourguiba), and a political elite divided by a preoccupation with its own political future. Although Bourguiba had designated Mzali his successor, he dismissed him in 1985, appointing in his place General Zayn al-Abidine BEN ALI, the first military officer ever to serve in a Tunisian cabinet.

As Bourguiba, long an advocate of a small and apolitical military establishment, might well have predicted, it was Ben Ali who ended his political career. After a Tunisian court failed to hand down death sentences to Islamists convicted on charges (probably trumped-up) of attempting to overthrow the state, Bourguiba demanded they be executed anyway. Instead, Ben Ali arranged to have several doctors certify that the president was too ill and too senile to govern effectively, and Bourguiba was deposed in a constitutional coup November 7, 1987. He retired to live in seclusion in the palace he had earlier built for himself in Monastir.

BIBLIOGRAPHY

ANDERSON, LISA. *State and Social Transformation in Tunisia and Libya, 1830–1980.* Princeton, N.J., 1986.
BEESIS, SOPHIE. *Bourguiba.* Paris, 1988. In French.
HOPWOOD, DEREK. *Habib Bourguiba of Tunisia: The Tragedy of Longevity.* New York, 1992.

Lisa Anderson

Bourse

The name of the stock market in Lebanon.

The Bourse was established by the French high commissioner in 1920. In the early 1950s, the financial market became prominent in an economy dominated by the service sector. The market continued to prosper until 1969, when the collapse of the INTRA BANK, among other events, caused its performance to suffer. By 1974 it had returned to its profitable status, and forty registered companies were members. The LEBANESE CIVIL WAR (1975) halted its activities, and it was officially closed in 1983. In the summer of 1994, Lebanese authorities and financial officials were preparing to reactivate the Bourse.

As'ad AbuKhalil

Boussouf, Abd al-Hafid   [1926–1982]

Algerian revolutionary military commander.

Boussouf was born in Mila, Algeria, and joined Messali Hadj's Parti du Peuple Algérien (PPA) and its successor, the Mouvement pour le Triomphe des Libertés Démocratiques (MTLD). He believed in direct confrontation with French colonialism, as disclosed by his association with the Organisation Spéciale (OS) and later the Centralists after the MTLD split (1953). During the Algerian War of Independence (1954–1962), Boussouf rose to the Armée de Libération Nationale's (ALN) highest rank (colonel) and was in charge of Wilaya V (ORAN region). He became minister for liaison and communications (1958) in the Gouvernement Provisoire de la République Algérienne (GPRA). He opposed Ramdane ABANE and was involved in his murder. After the war, Boussouf withdrew from active politics and pursued a shipping business.

BIBLIOGRAPHY

STORA, BENJAMIN. *Dictionnaire biographique des militants nationalistes algériens.* Paris, 1985.

Phillip C. Naylor

Bouteflika, Abdelaziz   [1937–   ]

Algerian government minister.

Bouteflika, born in Morocco, was educated in his native Oujda and then at Tlemcen, Algeria. During the Algerian War of Independence (1954–62), he served in the Armée de Libération (ALN) as a political officer (in Wilaya V) and became a confidant of the powerful Houari BOUMÉDIENNE. He served as minister for youth sports and tourism before becoming foreign minister under President Ahmed Ben Bella. Ben Bella's moves against Boumédienne sup-

porters, especially against Bouteflika, contributed to the June 1965 coup in which Boumédienne deposed Ben Bella.

Under Boumédienne, Bouteflika continued Algeria's foreign policy of support for revolutionary movements and nonalignment. He especially championed the rights of the less developed countries, highlighted by his chairmanship of the United Nations special session on north-south relations in 1974. He played important roles in negotiating the Algiers agreement of 1975 with France and in nationalizing French hydrocarbon concessions in 1971. However, Bouteflika misperceived Morocco's territorial intentions and ambitions concerning Western Sahara, formerly Spanish Sahara. He subsequently lobbied with success for the international recognition of POLISARIO's Sahrawi Arab Democratic Republic (SADR).

Bouteflika delivered the eulogy at Boumédienne's funeral and was viewed as a prominent presidential candidate. When Chadli Benjedid became president in 1979, Bouteflika served as a minister without portfolio and as adviser. In 1981, however, he was suspended from the FRONT DE LIBÉRATION NATIONALE (FLN) political bureau and central committee. Bouteflika began a self-imposed exile the following year and was charged with corruption and embezzlement in 1983. His return to Algeria in 1987 was viewed as an effort for intraparty reconciliation. After the Third Extraordinary Congress of the FLN (1989), Bouteflika became a member of the expanded central committee. Though associated with the anti-Benjedid faction of the FLN he campaigned for the FLN in local elections in 1990.

BIBLIOGRAPHY

GRIMAUD, NICOLE. *La politique extérieure de l'Algérie.* Paris, 1984.

STORA, BENJAMIN. *Dictionnaire biographique des militants nationalistes algériens.* Paris, 1985.

Phillip C. Naylor

Boutros-Ghali, Boutros   [1922–   ]

UN diplomat and Egyptian political leader.

Boutros-Ghali was born in Egypt, the son of a former minister of finance and the grandson of Boutros Pasha Ghali, who served as prime minister from 1908 until he was assassinated in 1910.

Boutros-Ghali earned an LL.B. from Cairo University in 1946 and a Ph.D. in international law from the University of Paris in 1949. He was a Fulbright scholar at Columbia University from 1954 to 1955. He started his career as a professor of international law and international relations at Cairo University, where he also served as chairman of the political science department and as head of the Center for Political and Strategic Studies. He was a founder of *Al-Siyasa al-Dawli* and the economic weekly *Al-Ahram al-Iqtisadi*.

When President Anwar Sadat decided to launch his peace initiative with Israel, Boutros-Ghali was appointed Sadat's minister of state for foreign affairs after Isma'il Fahmy, then foreign minister, resigned in protest to Sadat's peace moves. He accompanied Sadat on his historic trip to Jerusalem.

Throughout the negotiations with Israel that eventually led to the CAMP DAVID ACCORDS (1978) and the subsequent Egyptian–Israeli peace treaty, Boutros-Ghali was one of the principal Egyptian negotiators. In 1991 he was appointed deputy prime minister for foreign affairs.

Javier PÉREZ DE CUÉLLAR decided in 1991 to step down as secretary general of the United Nations after two terms. Boutros-Ghali immediately began actively campaigning for the position, something that had never been done before. He was elected on the first ballot. During his term as secretary general, the United Nations went through a transition from a world dominated by the U.S.–Soviet rivalry to a more multipolar political environment. This has meant a greater role for the world body in peace-keeping and peacemaking. Boutros-Ghali has attempted to expand the mission of the United Nations to make it more relevant in solving ethnic conflicts and to redefine the use of UN forces in solving inter- and intranational conflicts. The transition has not been easy, as the difficulties the UN faced in brokering peace in Somalia and the former Yugoslavia demonstrated. Nor has there been consensus on what the role of the United Nations should be in the post–Cold War world. Moreover there have been criticisms over waste and abuse in the UN bureaucracy. Principal among the critics has been the United States, which has regularly withheld financial contributions. Boutros-Ghali has pleaded that without the necessary resources, the United Nations cannot fulfill its historic mission.

Bryan Daves

Bowman, Humphrey   [1879–1965]

British educational administrator in the Middle East.

Educated at Eton and at New College, Oxford, Bowman began his career as an adviser to Egypt's ministry of education (1903–1925). During that time, he also served as an inspector for the Sudan's education department (1911–1913); performed war service in France, India, and Mesopotamia; and was temporary director of education in Iraq (1918–1920). After Bowman was director of education in Palestine (1920–1936), he was reassigned to special duty at the Foreign Office (1941–1945) and published his autobiography and memoirs, *Middle East Window* (London, 1942).

Peter Sluglett

Brahimi, Abdelhamid   [1936–   ]

Algerian prime minister, 1984–1988.

After serving as an Armée de Libération Nationale (ALN) officer during the Algerian War of Independence, he became director of the Organisme de Coopération Industrielle, an institution established after the Algiers agreement of 1965 to stimulate French–Algerian cooperation. He also represented the national hydrocarbon enterprise, SONATRACH, in the United States during a crucial period in Algerian–American natural gas relations.

Under President Chadli Benjedid, he became minister of planning and organization of the national territory (1979) and then served as prime minister (1984) until being replaced by Kasdi Merbah after the October 1988 riots.

BIBLIOGRAPHY

NAYLOR, PHILLIP, and ALF HEGGOY. *Historical Dictionary of Algeria,* 2nd ed. Metuchen, N.J., 1994.

Phillip C. Naylor

Brami, Joseph   [1881–1924]

A modernist rabbi, journalist, and educator in Tunis.

Joseph Brami was a strong proponent of modern-Hebrew education. In 1910, he cofounded with Alfred Valensi and Rabbi Jacob Boccara the Zionist Agudat Sion society. Three years later, Brami brought out and edited a monthly Judeo-Arabic newspaper *Kol Sion*. Until his untimely death, he was one of the leading figures of the Tunisian Zionist movement.

BIBLIOGRAPHY

BARAD, SHLOMO. *The Zionist Movement in Tunisia.* Tel Aviv, 1980. In Hebrew.

Norman Stillman

Brandeis, Louis Dembitz   [1856–1941]

Justice of the U.S. Supreme Court and Zionist leader.

He was born in Louisville, Kentucky, to parents who had fled from Bohemia to the United States in 1848. Brandeis was appointed to the Supreme Court by President Wilson in 1916 and served until his retirement in 1939. He played a leading part in American Zionism. Brandeis was honorary president of the ZIONIST ORGANIZATION OF AMERICA from 1918 to 1921, and of the WORLD ZIONIST ORGANIZATION between 1920 and 1921. He resigned after a difference of opinion with Chaim WEIZMANN.

BIBLIOGRAPHY

DAWSON, NELSON L., ed. *Brandeis and America.* Lexington, Ky., 1989.
UROFSKY, MELVIN I. *A Mind of One Piece: Brandeis and American Reform.* New York, 1971.

Mia Bloom

Brenner, Yosef Hayyim   [1881–1921]

Hebrew and Yiddish writer.

Born in Novi Mlini in the Ukraine and educated in Yeshivot, Brenner moved to Bialystok in 1900 and served in the Russian army from 1901 to 1904. At the onset of the Russo-Japanese War he fled to London where he worked in a printing shop. While in London he became active in the Po'alei Zion movement and founded the periodical *Ha-Me'orer* in 1906. He moved to Lemberg in 1908 and served as editor of another Hebrew periodical, *Revivim*. At that time he also wrote, in Yiddish, a brief biography of the writer Avraham Mapu. He left for Eretz Yisrael in 1909 where he first worked in Hadera before moving to Jerusalem. He became an Ottoman citizen during World War I to avoid deportation. In 1915, he moved to Jaffa and taught Hebrew literature and grammar at the high school in Herzliyya. He left Jaffa when the Turkish authorities drove out the Jews and returned after the British assumed control of the area.

Brenner was a contributor to the major periodicals of the Second ALIYAH: *Ha-Po'el ha-Zair and Ha-Ahdut.* He continued publishing *Revivim* (1913–1914) and edited a monthly, *Ha-Adamah* (1920). Brenner was also a founder of the HISTADRUT in 1920. While returning from the Galil to Jaffa on May 2, 1921, Brenner was murdered in the Abu Kabbir district during the Arab riots.

Brenner, a major figure in the modern Hebrew literary world, was a product of a generation whose life had been turned upside down and which, consequently, lost its sense of direction. His approach to literature was introspective and psychoanalytical and he distinguished minimally between creativity, art, and life. Stylistically he was a follower of M. J. Berdyczewski and his social outlook reflected that of Mendele Mokher Sefarim. Like other contemporary Hebrew writers, Brenner was also strongly influenced by the literature of Russian writers such as Tolstoy and Dostoevski.

His first story, *Pat Lehem* (A Loaf of Bread, 1900), was published in *Ha-Meliz. Me-Emek Akhor* (From Valley of Trouble, 1901) is a collection of short stories reflecting the literary style and social content of the Hibbat Zion era. A short novel, *Ba-Horef* (In Winter, 1902), established Brenner as an independent writer whose work reflected his life experiences. This novel deals with a young boy who attends a yeshiva in a large town and then moves to a city where he becomes secularized and a member of the Jewish intelligentsia—echoing the experiences of Brenner himself. In *Shanah Ahat* (One Year, 1908), Brenner writes about military service, and in *Min ha-Metzar* (Out of the Depths, 1908–1909) he deals with Jewish workers in London. *Aggav Orha* (1909) describes the Second Aliyah, while *Ben Mayim le-Mayim* (Between Water and Water, 1910) depicts life in the settlements of Eretz Yisrael.

Brenner's fiction is always concerned with society and its problems. The first-person narrative style of his stories reinforces the authenticity of his works. Nomadic existence is a theme which runs throughout his stories, and his characters are constantly wandering from place to place in the hope of ameliorating their unhappy destiny. These wanderings are multidirectional: from town to city in *Ba-Horef: Mi-Saviv a-Nekudah;* from eastern to western Europe in *Min ha-Mezar;* from Diaspora to Eretz Yisrael in *Aggav Orha, Azzabim;* and within Eretz Yisrael itself.

Brenner's linguistic style attempted to capture spoken Hebrew, then in its inchoate stages. He frequently resorted to Yiddishisms or German and Russian words and phrases to compensate for words lacking in Hebrew. Brenner disagreed vehemently with Ahad ha-Am's concept of *galut* (exile) which he viewed as fostering a life of idleness rather than work.

As a critic, Brenner wrote about the foremost writers of Hebrew literature such as P. Smolenskin (1910), J. L. Gordon (1913), Mendele Mokher Sefarim (1907 and 1914), and others. His critical criterion was whether an author succeeds in creating harmony between experience and expression. He opposed pompous writing and the tendency of various writers to over-glorify life in Eretz Yisrael. Brenner was also a translator. He translated works such as G. Hauptmann's *Di Weber* (1900), Dostoevski's *Crime and Punishment* (1924), and Tolstoy's *The Landlord* (1919).

Brenner received mixed reviews from his contemporary critics. Later critics focused on the complex inner life created in his works. Modern critics point to his simple, direct, and authentic style. Brenner served as a role model for the many young writers who, after Israeli independence, preferred an existential approach to literature to the then in-vogue patriotic perspective that was espoused by so many of his contemporaries.

Ann Kahn

Brezhnev, Leonid Ilyich   [1906–1982]

Soviet politician; president of the USSR 1960–1964 and 1977–1982; premier 1964–1982.

Son of a Russian metalworker in the Ukraine and a factory worker himself, Brezhnev went on to study land management and reclamation. He joined the Communist party in 1931 and was appointed secretary of the Dnepropetrovsk (industrial center in Ukraine) regional party committee in 1939. After World War II, Brezhnev became first secretary of the Dnepropetrovsk party organization and, subsequently, of the Moldavian Soviet Socialist Republic. In 1954, he was promoted to the leadership of the Kazakhstan party organization and placed in charge of Khrushchev's "virgin land" campaign. Recalled to Moscow in 1956, Brezhnev was appointed Central Committee secretary in charge of heavy industry and capital construction and, in 1957, was graduated to full membership in the Politburo. In 1964, having led the group that ousted Khrushchev, he became secretary-general of the CPSU, remaining in that position until his death in 1982.

In his foreign relations, Brezhnev adhered to many of the policies initiated by Khrushchev while introducing some changes of his own. Thus, he rejected the notion of superpower conflict and insisted that differences between Moscow and Washington be settled by peaceful means. Brezhnev did, however, allocate considerable resources to achieving relative nuclear parity with the United States. In this task he was successful. Like Khrushchev, Brezhnev insisted on superpower competition in the Third World. While Khrushchev distributed Soviet largesse virtually for the asking, however, Brezhnev picked his clients with care. The determining factor was their ability to provide the USSR with tangible benefits (such as naval and air bases) or political advantages in its global competition with the United States. In the

Middle East, in particular, the Soviets required naval and air bases to counter the U.S. Sixth Fleet and Polaris submarines. Khrushchev's efforts to obtain the bases failed. Brezhnev succeeded, but only temporarily. Nasser's "war of attrition," waged against the Israeli positions along the Suez Canal, led to Israeli deep-penetration raids against Egyptian targets. In desperation, Cairo asked Moscow for help. Brezhnev obliged but on the condition that Soviet naval and air bases be established on Egyptian territory. These important gains, made in 1970, did not last. In 1972, Sadat ordered the Soviet military advisers and the air force to leave Egypt; the navy followed in 1976. Nevertheless, the USSR had stood by its clients: Moscow backed the Arabs during the wars of 1967 and 1973. In the late 1970s, however, relations with Egypt and Iraq deteriorated sharply. Syria and South Yemen (or the PDRY) remained friendly but, by 1980, the Soviet position in the Middle East had grown much weaker than it had been a decade earlier.

In 1968, upset by the Communist reform movement in Prague, Brezhnev ordered Soviet troops into Czechoslovakia. The move was subsequently explained by Moscow's obligation to "protect socialism" in countries where it was being endangered by "anti-Communist elements." This Brezhnev Doctrine was invoked only once in the Middle East: in 1979, Soviet troops crossed into Afghanistan to back its Communist regime against powerful antigovernment rebels (*mujahidin*). A quick victory did not materialize and, by 1982, Soviet forces were bogged down in a stalemated conflict with the anti-Communist opposition, finally withdrawing in 1989.

BIBLIOGRAPHY

DAWISHA, KAREN. *Soviet Foreign Policy toward Egypt.* New York, 1979.
FREEDMAN, ROBERT O. *Soviet Policy toward the Middle East since 1970,* 3rd ed. New York, 1982.

Oles M. Smolansky

Britain and the Middle East up to 1914

Britain's engagement in Middle East affairs has a long and troubled history.

In the Middle East, Great Britain is remembered most for its interlude of paramountcy. The political–geographical concept of the Middle East was coined early in the twentieth century, several decades after Britain entered the region. In a review of Britain's relations with the region before then, and how it rose to the top, this must be kept in mind. Most of the territory that composed its Middle East empire from the end of World War I to the end of World War II had once been under Ottoman rule. Before the ratification in 1924 of the peace settlement with the Turkish Republic, the Ottoman Empire's lineal successor, the inspiration and rationale for adding each politically identifiable unit, with the arguable exception of Sudan in 1899, had come from the perceived need to defend British India.

On India's north (Afghanistan) and northwest (Persia—Iran after 1935—and the Ottoman Black Sea coastline and its interior), Russia's southward thrust stirred anxiety among Britain's empire builders. In the southern Mediterranean, France's tenacious pursuit of influence in Egypt made both Britain and India, as guardians of the imperial routes to the subcontinent, nervous. The anxiety dated from Napoleon's dramatic appearance in the self-governing Ottoman province of Egypt in 1798, through the opening in 1869 of the French-built Suez Canal, to the long-lived yet contested British presence that began in 1882.

In the the first half of the twentieth century, to confirm its regional primacy, Britain served in effect as Europe's imperial coordinator in the Ottoman succession. Later, in the crisis of its global imperial mobilization in World War II, Britain was the region's unifier, after 1941 in close harmony with the United States. In retrospect, if the port of Aden (even including its insular appendages, it encompasses little more than 100 square miles [260 sq. km.]) is set aside, the rise and fall of Great Britain's regional preeminence lasted less than a century (1878–1971). This is not to suggest that the Ottoman sultan's Asian Arab and adjacent northeast African provinces were available earlier for easy European plucking. They were not.

The Levant and East India Companies. Napoléon's appearance in Egypt in 1798 with a massive armada and the declared aim of shortening the sea route to India, in order to reconquer the empire there that France had lost to Britain over the preceding half-century, marked a change in Britain's relations with the Sublime Porte from commercial to political imperialism and diplomacy. During Britain's monopoly of commerce under successively renewed royal charters (1581–1825), the Levant Company had cultivated trade with the Ottoman Empire's eastern Mediterranean territories from Greece to Egypt. As late as 1798 the company, at its own expense but in the name of Britain, handled all formal diplomatic and consular relations with the Ottoman Empire. It also paid the salaries of the British ambassador and the consul general in Constantinople (now Istanbul), and

of other British consular officials in Aleppo and selected Ottoman ports. Beginning in the mid-eighteenth century, the ambassadors, though still on the company payroll, were gradually integrated into the regular diplomatic service. The Foreign Office did not begin paying their salaries until 1804 (five years after Britain entered into its first formal alliance with the Sublime Porte). The consuls remained employees of the Levant Company until just before its dissolution in 1825.

Once the industrial revolution had taken hold in Britain late in the eighteenth century, the Levant Company faced no serious competition from Western European rivals. With few exceptions, even during the French Revolution and the Napoleonic wars (1789–1815)—indeed, until 1825—the company enjoyed the most profitable phase of its 244 years of Anglo–Ottoman monopoly trade. Given the long head start before the industrial revolution crossed the English Channel, Britain captured and held first place in the external Ottoman trade until World War I. In the middle decades of the nineteenth century, the Ottoman Empire was Britain's third-best foreign customer.

Early on, the Levant Company yielded to the reality that the deep interior of its assigned zone lay beyond reach and released the privileges to the East India Company (1600–1858). The oldest charters of the two companies, both issued under authority of Queen Elizabeth I, were mirror images. But in the pursuit of monopoly commerce in the allotted areas, the prospects for each differed sharply. The East Indies titled not a fixed state, like the Ottoman Empire, but a zone in South Asia lacking precise geographic definition. At its height the Mogul Empire (1526–1857) ruled much, but not all, of the subcontinent and lacked diplomatic ties to Europe. Although the East India Company (EIC) trade centered on the Indian subcontinent, that sphere spread over more than a single suzerainty.

EIC agents moved freely, seizing commercial opportunities, including those in the Islamic empires (Ottoman, Persian, and Omani) and self-ruling shaykhdoms around the Gulf, with half the Gulf's littoral. Persia lay beyond the Levant Company's assured circuit. But in theory that circuit did embrace the Ottoman Gulf littoral, which varied in the seventeenth, eighteenth, and nineteenth centuries. Beyond Ottoman reach, and thus freely claimed for EIC trade, sprawled Oman (variously known as Muscat or as Muscat and Oman) and the "independent" shaykhdoms along the lower Gulf and the Arabian Sea as far as the entrance to the Red Sea.

Despite its exercise of Britain's diplomatic and consular duties, the Levant Company remained to the end a trading association. The EIC, by contrast, had become the primary instrument for conquering India and integrating it into the British Empire. In 1757 it rose from a decade-long war with its French rival as the governing agent for Britain. Within a dozen years the French company expired. After yet another war with France (1778–1783), the EIC absorbed the remaining Mogul provinces and districts until the Islamic empire passed out of existence in 1857. (By the 1780s French India had shriveled into the Union of Pondichéry, comprising four disconnected enclaves in the subcontinent's southeast with a total area of 143 square miles [372 sq. km.].)

Not until the shock of Napoléon's lightning entry into Egypt (July 1798) and his stealthy personal departure (August 1799), leaving behind for two years a large French military and civilian body of occupation, did British India begin building a durable political presence and strategy in the Gulf. At the EIC's request, the sultan of Oman signed a pledge—not honored by his successors—that nationals of France and the Netherlands, Britain's Gulf rivals in the preceding two centuries through their own East India companies, would be shut out of his realm. Oman was then more substantial than a shaykhdom yet less than a suzerain state (on European criteria). Thus, the true meaning of a second agreement, early in 1800, that looked like a provision for the Gulf's first permanent, if only quasi-diplomatic, mission, was that it reflected the dramatic structural transition of the EIC, which since 1757 had blossomed into the government of British India.

Parliament toughened its supervision of the EIC. In 1784, following the second and virtually complete rout of French rivals from the subcontinent, Parliament passed the Government of India Act, laying down strict rules of accountability. The president of the company court (board) of directors was given a nonvoting seat in the British cabinet, to serve as the channel for guiding the EIC's governance of India. To carry out the new duties of protecting and promoting British interests, the company began reorganizing its own administrative structure. Starting in the 1820s, the EIC changed its former commercial residencies into political residencies and agencies at key ports in the Gulf, broadly interpreted to include Basra and Baghdad, which could be reached by vessel via the Shatt al-Arab and the Tigris and Euphrates rivers.

Relations of Britain and British India with Persia in the eighteenth century had been the least satisfactory in the Gulf, because of the domestic political chaos in the decades between the effective end in 1722 of the Safavid dynasty and the rise of its Qajar successor, which in 1794 reunited the shahdom. As part of the strategy of defense in depth against Napoleonic France, in 1801 the EIC signed commercial and political agreements with the new dynasty designed to establish continuous diplomatic links. However, Fath Ali Shah (1797–1834) repudiated both agreements because British India had dallied for six years before returning the ratifications. The Foreign Office in London and the EIC unknowingly had separately framed plans in 1808 for fresh exchanges with Persia—the Foreign Office, out of anxiety about Russia; the EIC, about France. Their emissaries met for the first time in Tehran. In stages, from 1809 to 1814, a treaty of defensive alliance emerged, laying the base for Britain's permanent diplomatic relations with Persia. From then on, Persia fell into the diplomatic jurisdiction of the Foreign Office, with only two lapses (1823–1835, 1858–1859) when the Asia-focused Political and Secret Department of the Bombay Presidency managed Britain's interests in Tehran.

Britain and the Arabian Peninsula. In 1858, after the last vestige of Mogul rule had vanished, the EIC charter was revoked. Responsibility for governing India passed from Calcutta—and for managing British affairs in the Gulf, from Bombay—to London. In London the secretary of state for India, with full voting rights in the cabinet but no longer attached to a nongovernmental company, presided over the India Office and thus over framing imperial policy. Even then, anxiety over India's defense colored all major decisions on the Middle East until World War II. By then, British India had to share the center of imperial concern with Britain's interest in Gulf oil, which at that time still came largely from Iran, with a modest supplement from Iraq.

Against this background it becomes possible to chart the origins, rise, and style of British Middle East imperialism east of the Red Sea and the complementary yet reactive diplomacy and imperialism in the Ottoman Empire. During the century-long conquest of the Mogul Empire, British India was distracted enough not to plan simultaneous expansion beyond the subcontinent. The distraction went far to explain India's nervous yet cautious reply to inflated fear of perils looming in and around the Gulf, reaching back to 1798. From time to time (1806, 1809, 1819), the EIC deployed in the lower Gulf, chiefly for service along the coast of the Arabian Peninsula, vessels of the Bombay Marine to suppress what the Anglo-Indian monitors labeled a rampant tribal piracy that "even preyed upon" vessels flying the Union Jack.

In 1820 the coastal shaykhs and their neighbors as far as the Bahrain archipelago were forced to sign a general treaty banning piracy and the slave trade.

The pact was renewed semiannually until 1835 by all (except Bahrain), and then annually until 1843, when it was prolonged for a decade and finally hardened into a permanent maritime truce. By then the EIC had come to view the Persian Gulf as an Anglo–Indian lake. Upon authorization by Tehran, the EIC named the British consul at Bushehr on the Persian coast as the EIC political resident, with the duty of observing the execution of the truce and guarding against piracy. He was assisted by the political agent for the Trucial Coast (at Sharja) and, at the turn of the century, by political agents named to the other pact signatories. In 1822, for the resident's service, British India deployed vessels of the Bombay Marine and, after 1879, of the Indian navy, berthed at the rented Basidu based on Persia's Qeshm Island, at the entrance to the Persian Gulf.

However, it was the port of Aden, lying outside the Gulf, that became Britain's first onshore presence in the Middle East. By the beginning of the second third of the nineteenth century, new anxieties had arisen. As seen in Britain and in India, the benefits of the dramatic shrinkage between the two of distance and time in transport and communication were risks when they served an imperial rival such as France. By the 1830s the EIC had developed a regular route between India and England via the Mediterranean and Red seas, with overland transfer in Egypt of passengers, goods, and mail between Alexandria and Suez in both directions.

In the Mediterranean, which had British bases at Gibraltar and Malta, there were no bunkering problems. East of Suez, the company chose Aden as the site for resupply of fuel and other needs of increasingly larger and more modern oceangoing ships. After six years of talks with the sultan of Lahij, punctuated by forcible occupancy, two treaties and a bond defined the terms of the Anglo–Indian use of the harbor at Aden, for an annual rent of £1,300 ($6,500). By handling its first onshore presence in the Middle East as a quasi-commercial station with a modest rental, British India minimized the likelihood of tribal hostility.

In 1854, the five virtually unpopulated Kuria Muria islets, east of Aden on the southwest coast of Oman, were given to Britain by the sultan of Oman for a telegraph station. The experiment (1859–1860) in the Red and Arabian seas with submarine cables to tie into the European lines failed. Britain finally built alternative routes to British India via the Ottoman Empire as well as Russia and Persia. Attached by conquest to Aden in 1857 was the strategic islet of Perim, not quite in the center of the Bab al-Mandab Strait, then the only water entrance to the Red Sea. All the islands annexed by Britain were virtually uninhabited. Aden remained Britain's first and only dependency in the Middle East until 1878. Even with the port's enlargement by the addition of Little Aden in 1868 and its further enlargement by British India's purchase of the adjacent promontory belonging to Shaykh Uthman in 1862 and 1888, Aden's total area, islets and all, barely exceeded 100 square miles (260 sq. km). Until 1937, it was administered as if it were the Bombay Presidency's private colony.

Britain and the Eastern Mediterranean. Also in the 1830s, Britain's primary Middle East attention, still inspired by India, moved from the Gulf and the periphery of the Arabian Peninsula to the eastern Mediterranean, and basic policymaking, from the Political and Secret Department in Bombay to the Foreign Office in London. With Viscount Palmerston as foreign minister (1830–1834, 1835–1841, 1846–1851) and as prime minister from 1855 until his death in 1865, Britain dug in its heels to deny France economic and strategic domination of the key link between Western Europe and South Asia. In 1840 and 1841 Palmerston framed a strategy that rested on an Anglo–Ottoman alliance and committed the major powers to preserve the European balance by upholding the territorial sovereignty and integrity of the Ottoman Empire. By consensual diplomacy the powers, with Britain serving as the balancer, prevented the overthrow of Mehmet Ali, the self-made governor of Egypt, by internal revolt (in 1839–1841); the shrinkage of the Ottoman Empire by European conquest (by Russia in 1854–1856 and by France in 1860–1861); and the unilateral revision of a concert agreement (by Russia of its 1856 Straits Convention with the Ottoman Empire, in 1871). In each European–Ottoman dispute, Britain kept France and Russia apart by forming temporary great-power coalitions that isolated the would-be offender.

Despite Palmerston's precautions, Anglo–French rivalry in and over Egypt deepened. In the 1840s French engineers began framing feasible designs for linking the Mediterranean and Red seas by canal, to assure uninterrupted ocean travel from Britain and Western Europe to the African and Asian rims of the Indian Ocean, as well as Australia and New Zealand. In the mid-1850s, once Ferdinand de Lesseps pocketed a ninety-nine year concession for building and running the waterway, French magnates and bankers promptly oversubscribed the operating company. But at the height of the Anglo-Ottoman alliance (1841–1879/82), Palmerston's diplomacy had interrupted the canal's construction for more than a decade. At his urging, in order to escape an imperial contest for dominance in Egypt, British investors put their sterling into an Alexandria–Suez railroad via Cairo, completed in the 1850s.

In November 1869, four years after Palmerston's death, the French promoters finally opened the Suez Canal. As might have been expected, ships flying the Union Jack made up 70 percent or more of the traffic in the first years. However, the absence of British shareholders denied British users a voice in canal policy. Even the secret purchase in 1875 of the 44 percent interest in the company owned by Egypt's khedive, making Britain the largest single shareholder, proved inadequate to modify rates and other rules of use. Nor did the boost to Egypt's treasury long delay Khedive Isma'il's fiscal collapse. In 1876 he accepted a Dual Control, the working title of the Anglo–French Public Debt Commission, to manage Egypt's finances. Two years later, after the dual controllers reported continuing breach of the commission's rules, the khedive installed a cabinet government, with the Briton as finance minister and the Frenchman as minister of public works. When Isma'il tried to restore direct rule by abolishing the cabinet in June 1879, British diplomacy in Constantinople brought his son Tawfiq to the governorship.

Occupation of Cyprus and Egypt. While Anglo–French rivalry in and over Egypt was turning explosive, a crisis in the north had led Russia to declare war against the Ottoman Empire in April 1877; eleven months later it imposed a humbling peace on the Sublime Porte that was promptly ratified. Britain saw its eastern Mediterranean interests squeezed yet again between renewed threats from Russia and continuing ones from France. Disraeli's cabinet cobbled together a strategy of detaching Austria from its alliance with Russia, wooing France with an offer not to oppose its conquest of Ottoman Tunisia, and coercing the reluctant sultan into allowing Britain to occupy Cyprus, purportedly to inhibit further intrusion by Russia into the Islamic realm.

After deliberate delay, with the secret deal on Cyprus in hand, Disraeli finally agreed to attend the Berlin Congress (13 June–13 July 1878), called by Chancellor Bismarck of Germany to cool the overheated diplomacy in Europe through top-level accord. Only toward the close of the congress did Disraeli divulge the text of the Cyprus convention for integration into the collection of approved actions. The congress modified Russia's crippling terms and sorted out the imperial rivalries, thus avoiding wider war in Europe. However, the Ottoman Empire paid the price by having to make major land transfers to Russia in northeastern Anatolia and, to Russia and its Balkan allies, in southeastern Europe; placement of Cyprus under Britain's occupation

without fixed time limit; and—unmentioned—Britain's promise to France of diplomatic support in assimilating Ottoman Tunisia. In the Ottoman view, the congress, by annulling the ban on European expansion into the Ottoman Empire, had erased the essence of its durable alliance with Britain. Britain's replacement by Germany came four years later.

Once on Cyprus, Britain added two other Ottoman provinces—Egypt and Sudan—to the western portion of its future Middle East empire. It is far from clear, however, that the island was originally meant to be the first such unit. Occupation by formal, if also forced, agreement without time limit was intended as notice that Cyprus had been taken over only temporarily. The island's administration, without transfer of ownership title, was simply handed to Britain for such use as might serve its immediate imperial interest and, it was claimed, that of the Sublime Porte, which received a British pledge to stop deeper penetration by Russia into Antolia. Britain had already denied Russia possession of the Turkish Straits and Constantinople. Without the Turkish Straits, Russia could not become a Mediterranean power. To buttress the notion of a rental contract, the Disraeli government assured the Sublime Porte that all public revenue, beyond administrative needs, would revert to the sultan along with a fixed annual payment of £5,000 ($25,000).

More important, yet unmentioned in the convention, Britain saw Cyprus as a convenient military base to shore up its political and military stance in the eastern Mediterranean as a deterrent to both France and Russia. Within a fortnight of the outbreak of the Russo–Ottoman war in April 1877, Britain had warned Russia against blockading the Suez Canal and/or the Turkish Straits or occupying Egypt and/or Constantinople. The security planners in London felt a gnawing need for a nearby military presence to defend the Suez Canal, which they had come to see as the lifeline to India and to Britain's widening empire along the rim of the Indian Ocean and beyond. In this scheme, Cyprus "would enable us without any act of overt hostility and without disturbing the peace of Europe, to accumulate material of war and, if requisite, the troops necessary." This observation was embodied in Foreign Minister Salisbury's instructions to the British ambassador in Constantinople, charged in mid-May 1878 with imposing on the Sublime Porte the convention for Britain's open-ended occupation of Cyprus. (Egypt, though unmentioned, also was firmly in mind.)

Britain finally occupied Egypt in 1882 to quiet the long-standing fear of French conquest. The war in Europe that the British action threatened did not break out, even though the major powers withheld de facto recognition of the reality for nearly a quarter-century. After the British invasion, six years elapsed before the European maritime powers initialed a convention to assure free transit through the Suez Canal in peace and war, and seventeen more passed before its ratification. France kept goading Britain to fix a date for military withdrawal; Britain, no less stubbornly, insisted on recognition as the canal's sole defender for the duration of its military presence in Egypt.

Together with Russia, France did not stop condemning Britain for its occupation of Egypt, and particularly its refusal to share the Suez Canal's protection with the convention's signers. Nonstop collaboration against Britain in Egypt contributed to a Franco–Russian entente on European imperial issues in 1894. Ten years later, France and Britain finally signed their own Entente Cordiale in a trade-off: Britain's free hand in Egypt in return for France's free hand in Morocco. Within a year, the Suez Canal convention finally went into effect, carrying with it European de facto recognition of Britain's occupation of Egypt and, for its duration, as the waterway's exclusive guardian.

Conquest of Sudan. Lacking any document in its files to verify an unqualified Ottoman surrender of legal titles to Cyprus and to Egypt, Britain did not seriously seek the Sublime Porte's recognition of the conquest of Sudan in 1896 through 1898. Judged by the record, Britain seems to have concluded that without legal confirmation, it would be best to continue needed imperial expansion on the Mediterranean side of the Middle East by means of temporary tenancy. For this, given the Ottoman denial of legitimacy, the search for European recognition seemed the logical course of action.

The political status of Sudan had been complicated ever since 1885, when all British and Egyptian troops were pulled out after defeat by the self-proclaimed Mahdi (Messiah), Muhammad Ahmad, and his *mujahidin* (religious warriors). The mahdi did not long survive his declaration of Sudan's independence. But the independent Mahdiyya of Sudan survived under his dynastic *khalifa* (successor) for more than a decade, until Maj. Gen. Horatio Herbert Kitchener, commanding a modest Egyptian force, reclaimed the province in the name of Egypt (1896–1898). The victory was capped by an Anglo–French standoff at Fashoda (19 September–3 November 1898), micromanaged by the Foreign Office in London and the Foreign Ministry in Paris.

Kitchener was pitted against Maj. Jean Baptiste Marchand, a desert explorer who for more than two years had trekked some three thousand miles (4,800 km) from the Atlantic seaboard of French Equatorial Africa, with a small band of infantry volunteers, before arriving at the southern reaches of the White Nile. Fifteen months before Marchand and his commandos set out in June 1896, the undersecretary of state for foreign affairs, Sir Edward Grey, announced in Commons that the entire Nile (White and Blue) basin, from sources to mouth, formed a British sphere of influence. Any intrusion would be viewed as an unfriendly act. En route from the Atlantic to the White Nile, Marchand and company received little public notice, less the result of planned secrecy than of crude communications.

At Fashoda, one of the few rural towns along that stretch of the White Nile, Marchand subdued the *mudir,* who surrendered the patch of well-watered desert that made up his *mudiriyya* (municipality). On that basis, Marchand, as instructed, claimed for France all of southern Sudan, as yet without boundaries and thus undefined. The situation was formally resolved not by Marchand and Kitchener, on the bank of the White Nile, but by the foreign secretaries on the banks of the Thames and the Seine. Indeed, a confident Kitchener reached Dover on 27 October 1898 (before France had officially backed down) for weeks of national celebration.

The decision on how to factor Sudan into Britain's burgeoning Middle East empire was left to Lord Cromer, the British agent and consul general in Cairo. He rationalized a complex arrangement to establish Britain's right to rule Sudan at its pleasure, yet leave no more than a nominal role for Egypt, and to do so without seeking the Sublime Porte's approval. Cromer devised a formula to assure British supremacy while calming France and denying European powers capitulatory privileges.

The British claim to dominance in governing the Anglo–Egyptian condominium rested on the right of conquest, in the name not of the Ottoman sultan but of his viceroy, the Egyptian khedive, though the occupation had nullified the khedive's subordination to the sultan. In Cromer's scheme, except for the low-level civil and military service, Egypt had little more to show than its flag. Even that had to fly below the Union Jack. Though run as an undeclared British colony, Sudan was governed by the Foreign—not the Colonial—Office, which prided itself on installing a paternalistic regime. Until 1914, however, Sudan's public revenues came primarily not from local sources or Britain's Exchequer but from interest-free loans granted by Egypt.

In Sudan, as in Cyprus and Egypt, the Sublime Porte was infuriated by the denial of a policy voice or even of a nominal administrative role. In all three cases, the Foreign Office was pressed into an unaccustomed Colonial Office role by having to recruit and supervise senior administrative personnel. The makeshift handling of Cyprus had set the precedent for the later assimilation of Egypt and Sudan into the expanding western sector of Britain's Middle East empire. Named custodian of such borrowed territory was the Foreign Office, the branch of the British government best equipped to cope with problems of international law and diplomacy, but one of the most poorly equipped for colonial administration.

In Cyprus, Egypt, and Sudan, Britain did not stray from the fiction that the Foreign Office's exercise of Britain's de facto sovereignty had introduced neither legal nor political change into the former Ottoman provinces. The Ottoman Empire responded with an absolute refusal to surrender the title of ownership. Thus, the western sector of Britain's rising Middle East empire still lacked legal solidity at the outbreak of war in Europe in 1914—indeed, for a decade longer, until the peace settlement with the Turkish Republic.

Humbling the Gulf. In contrast with the political tenancies that Britain imposed on the Sublime Porte, British India continued to devise its own forms of British primacy along the periphery of the Arabian peninsula. This activity must be seen in the context of India's progressive intrusion into the Gulf in the nineteenth century. The office of resident was a title that the EIC had used, ever since its arrival in South Asia, to identify its factors (merchants) at chosen commercial posts. The step-by-step politicization of the office traced back to the 1820 maritime truce and reflected the slow conversion after 1757 of the EIC from a merchants' monopoly into Britain's formally recognized empire-building and governing agency in the subcontinent. As early as 1822, the Bombay Presidency began appointing a "resident in the Persian Gulf" at Bushehr, on Persia's upper Gulf Coast, to oversee the truce, with instructions to take action against violators and advise on policy. Commonly a middle-level officer of the Indian army or navy, the resident was authorized to call upon the Indian navy (known as the Bombay Marine until 1830), which from 1822 deployed a token squadron at the rented base of Basidu on Qeshm Island, near the Gulf entrance. Soon after the EIC lost its charter in 1858, the Indian navy's facilities and manpower were folded into the Royal Navy.

The long-delayed 1841 British commercial treaty with Persia had reaffirmed the right of the resident to keep his office at Bushehr. Not much later, Persia grudgingly allowed Britain to confer on the incumbent a second and separate title of consul general for the coastal provinces, thus formally assuring that his jurisdiction embraced the Gulf's entire rim except for the Ottoman segment. Nominated through 1872 by the Bombay Presidency and thereafter by the governor-general and viceroy in Calcutta, the political resident, as he had been formally designated for some time, was still British India's senior official and policy coordinator in the Gulf. He also served as envoy at large to the Arab tribalities, shaykhdoms, and ministates on the coast of the Arabian Peninsula. As necessary, British India delegated political agents to selected shaykhdoms growing into ministates; and by the turn of the twentieth century, political officers were delegated to troublesome tribalities. Meanwhile, from the start of the truce, Indian naval officers who served on patrol duty at times doubled as surveyors to map the Gulf and its bed for navigation, pearl fisheries, and other marine sources of commercial value.

By 1880, British India's presence rested on a system of control by an experienced and informed bureaucracy that steadily deepened its knowledge of the Gulf and its rim's inhabitants. With such proved interests, British India was ready to fend off aspiring European rivals. The Anglo–Indian custodians of the British Empire then, and for some time to come, persisted in viewing the Persian Gulf and the Arabian Peninsula not as part of the Middle East (a term not yet invented) but as a region that fell into the subcontinent's influence sphere. Still, British India's uncontestable presence remained offshore.

The Sublime Porte inadvertently sparked the growth of British India's onshore presence. On reabsorbing al-Hasa in 1871, the Ottoman Empire had reentered Gulf politics. Hasa's governor later gave asylum to a disgruntled faction of the Al Khalifa, the clan that ruled the Bahrain archipelago. To British India's political resident, the Sublime Porte appeared to be testing a rediscovered political option in 1879, when Hasa's governor and Isa ibn Ali, Bahrain's ruler, explored the rental of a coaling bunker on one of his islands. The action was seen as a likely Ottoman first step in claiming Bahrain, lying off Hasa's coast.

In December 1880, India undertook to protect Isa and his heirs as the shaykhdom's governing dynasty, assuring it full domestic sovereignty and a guaranteed safeguard against local opponents. In return, the ruler surrendered to Britain, and to India acting in Britain's behalf, the archipelago's external sovereignty. He agreed to an absolute ban on relations with other governments, the nearby shaykhdoms excepted, expressly disallowing the creation on his territory of "diplomatic or consular agencies or coaling depots . . . unless with the consent of the British Government." In March 1892, Shaykh Isa more explicitly reaffirmed his original surrender of external sovereignty by adding a general nonalienation clause that he would "on no account cede, sell, mortgage or otherwise give for occupation any part of my territory save to the British Government." Thus Bahrain became the model for what British India later called a system of independent states in special treaty relations with Great Britain.

In 1887 a first version of parallel exclusionary pacts with the shaykhs of the six tribalities of the Trucial Coast proved porous. Defying the Anglo–Indian ban, French agents appeared in 1891, seeking to open formal relations with the Trucial six by tempting them with such promises as the revival of slave trading under the French flag. India finally plugged the leak in 1892. In the next twenty-four years India, in Britain's name, absorbed the external sovereignty of Kuwait (1899) and, in World War I, of Najd (1915) and Qatar (1916). In the Trucial Coast, Fujayra broke away from Sharja in 1902 but did not receive Britain's formal recognition until a half-century later. Between 1913 and 1932, starting with Kuwait's shaykh, British India won explicit pledges from the rulers of Bahrain and each Trucial shaykhdom never to grant an oil concession to anyone except an official British governmental nominee. In the accords with Najd and Qatar, such commitments were assumed in promises to issue no concessions whatsoever without British consent.

Meanwhile, in 1891, Sayyid Faysal ibn Turki of Oman also had placed himself in nonalienation bondage. Clearly, Oman still had not been reduced to the status of a shaykhdom. It persisted in styling itself a sultanate, and as such it remained larger than eighty thousand square miles (208,000 sq. km), nearly nine-tenths the size of Great Britain and Northern Ireland. Oman still flaunted imperial pretensions with the residual possession of Gwadar, a port on the Baluchi coast with some three hundred square miles inland that was not returned to Pakistan until 1958. Indeed, in earlier decades of the nineteenth century, Oman had held long-term leases on the island of Qeshm and the nearby port of Bandar Abbas, issued by Persia's Fath Ali Shah and renewed by his successor. Until 1856 it also comprised the African islands of Zanzibar and Pemba and the coastal towns of Mombasa and Dar es-Salaam, which collectively had served as the major conduit of the once thriving slave trade in the Gulf. For that commerce the realm's capital, Muscat, served as the entrepôt.

The key to understanding Oman's vague ties to the system of protected ministates was Britain's inability to gain full command over the sultanate's foreign relations. By the time British-India began

moving to tighten its hold on the ministates, Oman had long since entered into capitulatory treaties with the United States (1833), France (1844), and the Netherlands (1877). Its ruler could not unilaterally cancel such instruments, even if he had wished to. Nor did Britain, in the exercise of its treaty rights in the sultanate, ever vigorously challenge the capitulatory powers, with the occasional exception of France.

Britain's management of its affairs in the Persian Gulf after 1858 was settling slowly and not always happily into the joint duty of the Foreign and India offices. Through World War I, the top administrator was recruited from the British officer cadre of the Anglo–Indian Army at the rank of lieutenant (or full colonel) and held appointments from both offices. In the overseas hierarchy of the Foreign Office he was the consul general at Bushehr, attending to Anglo–Indian and British interests in Persia's coastal provinces of Fars and Khuzistan and its islands in the Gulf. At the India Office and in India he was titled political resident in charge of Ango–Indian affairs along the Gulf peninsular coast. Accountable to him in that role by 1914 were political agents for Bahrain and Kuwait, and political officers for the Trucial Coast and later also Qatar, all drawn from British India's political service. The political resident in the Persian Gulf was thus responsible to the Anglo–Indian government and ultimately to the India Office in London for basic policy, at first with advice from the Foreign Office, largely regarding interactive Gulf politics of Persia and the Arab ministates. But the Foreign Office's influence steadily increased as the Gulf was drawn, issue by issue, into European imperial politics after Britain's occupation of Cyprus and Egypt.

Sole Policeman in the Gulf. An immediate effect of abandoning the long-lived alliance with the Sublime Porte was that Britain lost its leverage in the European imperial rivalry over Ottoman territory. That loss promptly encouraged Russia and France to cooperate against Britain on Ottoman issues. No less important, it opened the way for Germany's belated entry into the competition. Germany, in fact, replaced Britain as the Porte's durable ally, a friendship that lasted until the armistice ending World War I in 1918. At first, Chancellor Bismarck still discouraged official promotion of German interests in the Ottoman Empire despite the Porte's receptivity. In 1881, when Germany sent its first military mission to Constantinople on Ottoman invitation, the chancellor cut the mission's formal national ties. By the time of Kaiser Wilhelm II's accession in 1888, the new friendship came into the open. German industry had made such striking advances after the nation's unification in 1870 that it sought new markets. Between 1886 and 1910, Germany vaulted from fifteenth to second place in Ottoman foreign trade, surpassed only by Britain.

Much of this upturn could be attributed to the kaiser's enthusiastic response to Sultan Abdülhamit II's national goal of building railroads across his Asian domains to underpin their economic expansion, unity, and defense. With official encouragement, investors in France centered their projects in Palestine, Syria, and the latter's adjacent zone in southern Anatolia. The sultan's chosen enterprise was a trans-Anatolian railroad linked to Europe via its international railway complex. The sultan coaxed the new kaiser, on his first visit to Constantinople, to arouse interest in the plan among German bankers and entrepreneurs. An initial segment was promptly begun that would link Constantinople to Europe's international railway complex. By 1896 the German-built segment (with limited French investment) had pierced western Anatolia as far as Eskişehir with a spur to Konya.

There the venture stalled. On a second visit to Constantinople in 1898, the kaiser's zeal was re-honed. But ahead, between Konya and Basra, lay the mountains of eastern Anatolia and Mosul province, where it would be far more expensive to build each kilometer of roadbed than it had been in the plains of west Anatolia. Also envisaged were four spurs along the way: to Aleppo, Urfa, and Khanaqin (on the Persian side of the Ottoman border, some 90 miles [154 km] north of Baghdad), and from Zubayr (9 miles [14.5 km] south of Basra) to a point on the Persian Gulf "to be agreed upon." Wilhelm II enlisted the aid of Georg von Siemens, director of the Deutsche Bank, to promote the project as a German national interest, and the sultan issued a preliminary concession in 1899. Limiting its concern largely to the venture's commercial side, the bank did not agree to the definitive concession until 1903, after having canvassed banks of other nations—notably France and Britain—to invest in the project. In March 1903 the Deutsche Bank finally signed a ninety-nine year concession for the Berlin–Baghdad Railway.

The quickening of European interest in the Persian Gulf, especially the confirmation of the Berlin–Baghdad Railway concession on 5 March 1903, led Britain to update its defensive strategy. Precisely two months later, on 5 May 1903, Foreign Secretary Lord Lansdowne disclosed the commercial and strategic principles that would guide Britain's government in the future. Although high priority would be given to "protect and promote British trade" in the inland waters, Lansdowne ruled out the notion of excluding "the legitimate trade of other Powers." Yet he left no doubt that Britain would "regard the establishment of a naval base, or of a fortified port, in the Persian Gulf by any other Power as a very grave menace to British interests and we should certainly resist it with all the means at our disposal."

The British strategy of depriving other European powers of a military presence in the Persian Gulf, never seriously disputed, remained fixed through World War II and, with the exception (from 1949) of a modest U.S. naval station in Bahrain, lasted until Britain's final withdrawal in 1971.

Unlike the British-occupied Ottoman provinces, which European powers recognized but the Sublime Porte did not, the protected ministates in the Gulf won the approval of neither. Still, the European governments—not even Germany, the latest entrant into the contest—did not effectively dispute Britain's exercise of rights in the shaykhdoms. In the decade before the eruption of war in 1914 the Gulf's guardians, particularly in British India but also in Britain, perceived a mounting threat from Germany, which was enlarging its trade with Ottoman Asia and opening markets in the Gulf. In 1906 the Hamburg–Amerika Line began calling on a fixed monthly schedule at promising ports, offering lower rates and better banking services that those of the entrenched Anglo–Indian and British shipping firms.

In 1911, less concerned than British India, Britain finally responded to the persistent overtures of Germany and the Ottoman Empire to reconsider the differences over completing a railway with a terminal at the head of the Gulf. Britain felt the least pressure, since the Porte depended on British assent to increase the tariff rates, the only reliable funding source for Ottoman subsidies to the railway builders. Britain insisted on preserving its role as the Gulf's sole policeman to safeguard Anglo–Indian commercial and maritime primacy. On these terms Britain consented to pursue, with the Ottoman Empire and Germany, a multilateral settlement by weaving together three bilateral accords: British–Ottoman, British–German, and German–Ottoman.

From the outset the Sublime Porte had challenged the legality of Britain's protected ministate of Kuwait so as to reassert the sultan's suzerainty in the shaykhdom. Instead, the convention initialed in July 1913 gave the Porte only the symbols of political ownership. Although obliged to fly the Ottoman flag (with the inscription "Kuwait"), the shaykh was assured of "complete administrative autonomy." The Ottomans also conceded the validity of the shaykh's agreements with Britain. The purpose of the accord—whether, when, and under what terms the railroad might build its terminal in Kuwait—was described and the decision deferred. Beyond assuring Britain membership on the Berlin–Baghdad Railway directorate and guaranteed equal rates for all users, the British–German convention, initialed in June 1914, stated that the Baghdad–Basra extension would be built and run by a separate Ottoman company with an assured 40 percent British interest and a pledge of no extension to the Gulf without full prior approval by Britain, Germany, and the Ottoman Empire.

A fourth bilateral accord, framed by the Deutsche Bank and the French-dominated Imperial Ottoman Bank, was reached and initialed in February 1914. It was essentially designed to protect the special position of France's railroad entrepreneurs in Syria and Alexandretta, as well as their planned branches in western Anatolia, all to be linked to the German trunk line.

Ratification of the bilateral instruments awaited the drafting of the Ottoman–German convention. Preliminary talks, begun in June 1914 but interrupted by war in August, ended in a secret treaty of defensive alliance. The Sublime Porte became an active ally of Germany and Austria late in October. Early in November, Britain amplified the existing territorial guarantees to Shaykh Mubarak by declaring Kuwait, together with its islands and the ruler's date groves in the Fao district of the Basra *vilayet,* "an independent Government under British protection" as a reward for his pledged cooperation in the war effort.

Aden: Settlement and Protectorates. Reshaping the British protected shaykhdoms in the Gulf into potential ministates had run parallel with dividing Aden's upcountry, between 1880 and 1914, into projected tribalities that remained politically frozen in that condition until after World War II. The two imperial initiatives were sparked by perceived threats to Anglo–Indian security. Also, both Arabian coastal zones were recurrently infused with tribal migrants from the interior. Some tribal groups in each zone had passed in and out of the Ottoman Empire. This occurred for the last time in the early 1870s, when the sultan's troops reannexed Hasa, on the Gulf, and Yemen, on the Red Sea. In both retaken provinces, the Ottoman Empire did not simply seek recognition for its new international borders. The Sublime Porte clearly hoped to regain more of the land lost and to reintegrate tribal groups on the southern edges of Hasa and Yemen.

British India's imperial process in the southwestern Arabian Peninsula differed from that in the Gulf. Under the Gulf's enforced maritime truce, adjacent shaykhdoms gradually began to settle their common borders. However, except for Aden itself, few upcountry tribalities had mutually defined borders before the eve of World War I. Instead, the process was essentially limited to those blending into unmarked edges of Yemen on the north. In this period British India had not yet negotiated Aden's upcountry periphery alongside Oman on the east or the suitably named Rub' al-Khali (Empty Quarter) at the southern rim of the vast Arabian Desert. On neither of the two frontiers did the British face obstructions comparable with those in Ottoman Yemen.

Until January 1873, the Bombay Presidency had served as British India's ultimate custodian of the Gulf. Thereafter, it became accountable to the viceroy in Calcutta; beyond that, to the India Office; and, within the British cabinet after 1882, increasingly to the Foreign Office. Yet in regard to running Aden and its interior until 1932, the Bombay Presidency seems largely to have slipped through the net of accountability. From the outset, the Bombay Presidency treated the town of Aden as a private colonial trust. Even Aden's bureaucracy, below the top level, was almost wholly recruited in Bombay, joined in time by a swelling number of Indian settlers, mostly immigrant shopkeepers.

The presidency also kept watch on Aden town's hinterland, which widened eastward from slightly more than thirty miles (48 km) at the harbor to about two hundred miles (320 km) and a total length close to five hundred miles (800 km), for possible Ottoman or European intrusion. By 1902 Aden's administration in the interior covered some twenty-five to thirty local rulers with a wide range of titles—sultan, amir, sharif, naqib, shaykh. Even after agreements with the presidency, their number kept changing as a result of tribal fission and fusion in what finally compassed a thinly populated expanse of 112,000 square miles (291,200 sq. km). Its eastern two-thirds was largely desert; its western sector, partly desert and partly hill country. Frequent regime changes reflected the absence of Anglo–Indian dynastic guarantees and stabilizing boundaries, and they revealed the rulers' loss of much domestic as well as all external sovereignty. They thus resembled less the Gulf's shaykhdoms than the contemporary European colonies on the nearby Horn of Africa.

In 1900 Aden town was renamed the Aden Settlement, to sharpen its distinction from the inland protected tribalities it administered. The resident was accordingly retitled governor. Nature roughly fixed the frontier with the Rub' al-Khali. Like most boundary lines separating ownership claims to deserts that seem to have little or no commercial prospects, a straight line sufficed. That was also true, for the most part, of the eastern border with Oman.

In 1902/05, when it came to marking the boundaries of Yemen, once again an Ottoman province after 236 years, the issue could not be resolved by British India in exchanges with Yemen. Only Britain could deal with the Sublime Porte. Because of Ottoman delays, the accord was not ratified until 1914, too close to the outbreak of war to take solid effect. Indeed, in 1915 Ottoman troops occupied a few adjacent British-protected tribalities and stayed for the duration of the war. The unresolved problem of legal title was thus left for renegotiation with the sovereign imamate of Yemen, which after World War I because an Ottoman successor state.

Persia and Afghanistan. The Anglo–Russian imperial rivalry over Persia, which traced back to the Napoleonic wars, grew menacing after the 1860s. It was then that Russia completed the conquest of Central Asia, thus extending its border with Persia to its full length (the formal line was not confirmed until 1885). Russia's territorial advance coincided with Britain's continuing effort to consolidate its strategic control of the Persian Gulf—in the case of Persia, by locking in its coast, the longest national segment on the Gulf's rim. Simultaneously, the tension roused by the imperial competition in and over Persia enveloped Afghanistan, which in the south looked to India, and in the north, to Russian Central Asia. The two Asian countries had thus become trapped between expansion by Russia and by British India. For the security planners in Britain and India at the turn of the century, Russia's designs on Persia appeared more threatening than those on Afghanistan.

To underpin eventual imperial claims to Persia, the contenders began laying the groundwork in the last quarter of the nineteenth century. They extracted military and fiscal privileges from the shah that trimmed his power. An 1879 agreement provided for a Persian Cossack Brigade, which enlisted Persians to serve under Russian officers chosen by Russia and paid by Persia. It remained a nominal brigade even after the murder of Nasir al-Din Shah in 1896, when it was upgraded to an imperial guard for protecting the monarch and the dynasty, and even a decade later, when the Persian Cossacks, joined by a contingent of the regular Russian Army, failed to prevent adoption of the new constitution and the inauguration of a parliamentary regime—both realized with the implied blessings of Great Britain. (Only in 1916 did Russia finally transform the Cossacks into a fighting division and pay fully for its upkeep.) British India did not start responding until 1911, when it recruited and financed a gendarmerie or provincial police under Swedish officers. (In November 1916, the gendarmerie, without the Swedes, was integrated into the newly raised South Persia Rifles, trained and commanded by British officers.)

Less concealed and in most respects far more effective were the encroachments on the shah's fiscal sovereignty. In 1889, Baron Julius de Reuter, backed by the Foreign Office and the British legation in Tehran, procured a sixty-year concession to open the Imperial Bank of Persia, the first such institution in Persia. Its branches, in all the cities and larger towns, introduced the country to modern banking services. More significantly, the Imperial Bank received the exclusive right to serve as the fiscal agent of Persia and had the authority to issue banknotes. Two years later, Russian nationals, with active endorsement of their government, procured a parallel concession to launch the Banque de Prêts, originally designed to provide small-scale loans to Persians. Russia's Ministry of Finance bought the bank in 1894 and, under its new name, Banque d'Escompte de Perse, it pursued a deliberate policy of offering generous mortgages to rich landowners.

Russia's Foreign Ministry opened consulates not only in Mohammerah (present-day Khorramshahr), at the lower end of the Shatt al-Arab, but also in the major gulf ports of Bushehr and Bandar Abbas, where it sought to build coaling bunkers. In 1901/02 the Banque d'Escompte issued personal loans to the shah totaling £3.4 million ($17 million). As surety, Russia's Finance Ministry won the pledge of customs, without explicitly omitting those collected in the Gulf ports. The Finance Ministry also lowered the customs rates on Russian imports while doubling them on those from Britain and British India, thereby violating their entitlement to most-favored-nation treatment under an 1841 commercial treaty. After briefly trying to soften Britain's rigid stance against such a meddlesome presence on the Gulf coast, Russia ended its discriminatory practice. Soon thereafter the customs service was transferred to Belgian officials employed by Persia.

Even more clearly in Afghanistan, Britain's imperial thrust was driven by strategic rather than economic concerns. Before 1747 Afghanistan had never formed a united independent state. It had passed back and forth, in whole or in part, between Persia and the Mogul Empire. From the mid-eighteenth century, the ruling dynasties came from tribesmen in the Kandahar area. Yet even after tearing itself away from the neighboring Asian empires, Afghanistan did not remain united. In the middle of the nineteenth century, rival khanates or principalities once again were struggling for supremacy.

While the outcome of the Russo–Ottoman War and the search for a renewed consensus in Europe at the Congress of Berlin in 1878 fully engrossed Britain, a small Russian force entered Afghanistan, seeking to round out Russia's recently captured Central

Asian provinces. Anglo-India refused to tolerate such a prospect. In the early fall of 1878, the Russian mission and its Afghan puppet fled before advancing Anglo–Indian troops. Amir Shir Ali named his eldest son, Ya'qub, regent at Kabul. In the treaty of peace of May 1879, Ya'qub Khan surrendered Afghanistan's external sovereignty to Britain, accepted a resident Anglo–Indian mission at Kabul, and ceded the Khyber Pass and other strategic districts to British India. Ya'qub abdicated five months later.

Not until the midsummer of 1880 did British India finally inaugurate a new regime that took three years to put in place. The authority of Abd al-Rahman Khan, Ya'qub's cousin, at first did not reach beyond the district of Kabul. After demonstrating his ability to rule and his loyalty to British India, in 1883 he was finally allowed, with Anglo–Indian financial and military support, to take over the districts of Qandahar and Herat, thereby reuniting the country. In June 1883, Abd al-Rahman reaffirmed the status of Afghanistan as a British protectorate, in return receiving assurance that he and his dynasty would be insured against external aggression and that he would receive a monthly subsidy of £10,000 ($50,000) to cover the costs of his troops and related expenses.

The border with British India was drawn in 1893 at a line, traced under the supervision of the foreign secretary in Calcutta, Sir Henry Mortimer Durand, that confirmed the cession to the British of the Khyber Pass and adjacent areas. Two years later, the Amu Darya River was accepted as Afghanistan's northeast boundary with Russia's Central Asian Tajik province.

Given the mutual fears aroused by the hardening rival positions, the European imperial strategies had been shaped to shut the adversary out. With boundaries fixed by the turn of the century, Afghanistan was removed temporarily from the zone of British–Russian contention. After the close of the Victorian era in 1901, Britain favored the division of Persia into mutually recognized spheres of imperial influence: Russia's in the north and Britain's in the south, with the two separated by a buffer. The Russo–Japanese war (1904–1906) interrupted exploratory talks that were resumed in the spring of 1906 and concluded in the summer of 1907. The convention divided Persia as originally agreed. Russia recognized Afghanistan as a British protectorate, won equal commercial opportunity, and gained the right to conduct local, nonpolitical frontier relations with Afghanistan.

The Coming of the Oil Age. Baron Julius de Reuter's 1889 bank concession in Persia included—as had his aborted railway concession more than a quarter-century earlier—the exclusive right to search for and develop mineral resources, including oil. To this end, he founded the Persian Bank Mining Rights Cor-

poration, which never seriously pursued oil exploration. A decade later the Persian government canceled the mineral privileges. In 1901, William Knox D'Arcy, a wealthy British speculator with gold-mining experience in Australia, won the sole right to a sixty-year concession to explore for and extract oil across Persia except for the five northern provinces. The first commercial well in Persia was drilled in 1908, in the southern province of Khuzistan. A year later D'Arcy founded the Anglo–Persian Oil Company (APOC) to activate the concession. By 1912, on Abadan Island in the Shatt al-Arab, APOC put into operation the first units of its refinery to distill crude oil into fuel.

APOC's discovery of oil coincided with the British Admiralty's shift from coal to oil as the fuel for its war vessels. "In the year 1909," First Lord of the Admiralty Winston Churchill reported to the House of Commons on 17 July 1913, "the first flotilla of ocean-going destroyers wholly dependent upon oil was created, and since then, in each successive year, another flotilla of 'oil only' destroyers has been built. There are now built or building more than 100 [such] destroyers. . . . Similarly, during the last five years, oil has been employed in coal-burning battleships and cruisers, to enable them to realise their full powers in an emergency."

Churchill's statement prepared Parliament for the British government's partnership in APOC, so as to assure both British India and the Admiralty access to much of their oil needs at reduced cost. In an agreement of 20 May 1914, Britain bought 51 percent of APOC's shares and amended the company statutes to empower the government to veto any policy inconsistent with the national/imperial interest. As a further precaution, British India obtained explicit pledges from the shaykhs of Kuwait (1913) and Bahrain (1914) "never [to] give a[n oil] concession . . . to any one except a person appointed from the British Government."

Oil also figured prominently in the Anglo–German talks of 1913/14. By then three groups were pursuing oil concessions in the Ottoman provinces of Mosul and Baghdad: the Deutsche Bank, APOC, and the Anglo-Saxon Oil Company (a subsidiary of Royal Dutch–Shell, an Anglo–Dutch combine). The Deutsche Bank's claim rested on a 1904 option that had been allowed to lapse; APOC's, on a series of appeals to the Sublime Porte after 1906, with the active backing of the British embassy in Constantinople; and that of Royal Dutch–Shell, on "the good offices of Mr. C. S. Gülbenkian, an Ottoman subject of considerable influence and ability, sometimes called the Talleyrand of oil diplomacy." Britain insisted that APOC be given the largest share. When the two other groups acceded, a deal was framed at the Foreign Office in London on 19 March 1914. APOC procured a 47.5 percent interest in the Turkish Petroleum Company; the Deutsche Bank, 25 percent; the Anglo-Saxon Oil Company, 22.5 percent; and Gulbenkian, "a beneficiary five percent . . . without voting rights." On 28 June 1914, the Sublime Porte promised Britain and Germany that it would issue an oil concession in the Mosul and Baghdad *vilayets*.

The 1914 agreement etched the guidelines that, with appropriate adjustments to reflect the evolving postwar realities, assured Britain the largest share of the output of an international consortium that became operative in 1928, with a French company taking over the German allotment and a group of American companies, half of APOC's.

Postage stamps from Bahrain, Cyprus, Gibraltar, Kuwait, Palestine, and the Sudan, during the period of British imperial rule. (Richard Bulliet)

BIBLIOGRAPHY

BULLARD, SIR READER. *Britain and the Middle East from Earliest Times to 1952.* London, 1952.

BUSH, BRITON COOPER. *Britain and the Persian Gulf, 1894–1914.* Berkeley, Calif., 1967.

CHAUDHURI, K. N. "East India Company." In *Encyclopedia of Asian History,* vol. 1. New York, 1988.

HALLBERG, CHARLES WILLIAM. *The Suez Canal: Its History and Diplomatic Importance.* New York, 1931.

HUREWITZ, J. C. *The Middle East and North Africa in World Politics: A Documentary Record,* vol. 1, *European Expansion: 1535–1914.* New Haven, Conn., 1975.

KELLY, J. B. *Britain and the Persian Gulf, 1795–1880.* Oxford, 1968.

LANGER, WILLIAM LEONARD. *European Alliances and Alignments, 1871–1890.* New York, 1931. Reprint, 1960.

LEE, DWIGHT IRWIN. *Great Britain and the Cyprus Convention Policy of 1873.* Cambridge, Mass., 1934.

SHIBEIKA, MEKKI. *British Policy in the Sudan.* New York, 1952.

VATIKIOTIS, P. J. *The Modern History of Egypt.* London, 1969.

WILKINSON, JOHN C. *Arabia's Frontiers: The Story of Britain's Boundary Drawing in the Desert.* London, 1991.

WOOD, A. C. *A History of the Levant Company.* London, 1935.

YERGIN, DANIEL. *The Prize: The Epic Quest for Oil, Money and Power.* New York, 1991.

J. C. Hurewitz

Britain and the Middle East from 1914 to the Present

Britain's short-lived Middle East empire was a product of economic interests and strategic imperatives.

British involvement in the region long antedated WORLD WAR I, but Britain's "moment" in the Middle East, as it has been called—the period in which it was the dominant power in much of the area—lasted from 1914 to 1956. The axis of Britain's Middle Eastern empire stretched from the SUEZ CANAL to the Persian Gulf. At its height between the two world wars, Britain's supremacy was almost unchallenged either by other powers or by indigenous forces. Yet after 1945, British dominance quickly crumbled, leaving few relics of any kind.

The initial impetus toward deeper British involvement in the Middle East arose from the entry of the OTTOMAN EMPIRE into World War I on the side of the Central powers at the end of October 1914. The British did not seek conflict with the Turks, seeing it as a diversion from the primary task of defeating Germany; they nevertheless moved quickly both to confront Turkey in the battlefield and to plan postwar dispensation in the Middle East. The "Eastern question" in its traditional form terminated abruptly, and a new phase began in which the Allied powers struggled over the postwar partition of the Ottoman Empire among themselves.

The British cabinet decided on 2 November that "after what had happened we ought to take a vigorous offensive." In a public speech at Guildhall in London on 9 November, the prime minister, H. H. Asquith, declared: "It is the Ottoman government, and not we who have rung the death knell of Ottoman dominion not only in Europe but in Asia." The next month Britain severed the formal constitutional link between Egypt and the Ottoman Empire, declared a protectorate over the country, deposed the anti-British Khedive Abbas Hilmi II, and installed a successor, Hussein Kamel, as sultan.

Despite misgivings in the High Command, which favored concentration of Britain's limited military resources on the western front against Germany, an onslaught against the Ottoman Empire was launched on three fronts: at the Dardanelles, in Mesopotamia, and on the border between Egypt and Palestine; Russian forces, meanwhile, engaged Turkey from the north.

The attack on the Straits resulted in one of the great catastrophes of British military history. An initial naval attempt to force the Dardanelles was easily repulsed. Subsequent landings on the Gallipoli peninsula by British and empire troops gained no significant military objective and led to a bloodbath. Turkish forces led by Mustafa Kemal (later known as ATATÜRK) repelled the invaders, causing many casualties. The reputation of Winston CHURCHILL, then first lord of the admiralty, who had been the chief political patron of the operation, was damaged.

In Mesopotamia, too, the British were humiliated. An army was dispatched from India to invade the country, from the Persian Gulf. But in April 1916 Gen. Charles Townshend's Sixth Division was forced to surrender at Kut al-Amara. The British nevertheless brought in new forces, which advanced to conquer Baghdad by March 1917.

On the Egypt–Palestine front, Turkish raids on the Suez Canal led to British occupation of the Sinai peninsula. Thereafter, a stalemate developed, partly because of lackluster leadership but mainly because of British inability to commit large forces to a front that was regarded as peripheral to the outcome of the war. In 1917, however, the advance resumed under Gen. Edmund Henry ALLENBY who entered Jerusalem in triumph in December 1917. He moved on the following autumn to win the battle of Megiddo and to conquer Syria. This was the last great cavalry victory in the history of warfare. By the time of the Turkish armistice on October 30, 1918, British forces were thus in control of most of the FERTILE CRESCENT.

Meanwhile, the British had sponsored and financed a revolt of tribesmen in the Arabian peninsula against their Ottoman Turkish overlords. Organized by a Cairo-based group of British Middle East experts known as the Arab Bureau, the revolt began in June 1916. It engaged, in particular, the followers of the Hashimite ruler of the HIJAZ, Sharif of Mecca (Husayn), and his sons. Among the British officers who advised the rebels was T. E. LAWRENCE, who fought with bands of Arab guerillas against targets in Arabia. They blew up Turkish installations along the Hijaz Railroad, captured Aqaba in 1917, and harassed the enemy on the eastern flank of Allenby's army as it advanced north toward Damascus. In recognition of their efforts, and as a sop to Arab nationalist feeling, Allenby stage-managed the capture of Damascus on October 1, 1918, allowing the Arab army to enter the city in triumph, though the victory had been chiefly the work of Australian cavalry commanded by Gen. Sir Harry Chauvel.

The parade fitted into larger British schemes. During the war, the British had given benevolent but unspecific encouragement to Hashimite aspirations toward the creation of a unified Arab state under their leadership. Later Arab claims made much of alleged promises made in correspondence in 1915–1916 between the British high commissioner in Egypt, Sir Henry McMahon, and Sharif Husayn, though the exchanges were vague and inconclusive on both sides and never resulted in a formal treaty.

Britain entered into more specific obligations to other allies. In April 1915, it signed a secret treaty promising Constantinople to Russia, thus explicitly jettisoning Britain's long-standing reservations about Russian control of the Straits. (In fact, British governments since the time of Lord Salisbury at the turn of the century had resigned themselves to eventual Russian control of Constantinople.) At the same time, as part of the price of persuading Italy to enter the war on the Allied side, Britain agreed in the Treaty of London that, in a postwar carve-up of the Ottoman dominions, Italy would receive southwest Anatolia. Under an agreement negotiated in 1916 between Sir Mark Sykes and François Georges-Picot, Britain promised France most of Syria, Cilicia, and the oil-bearing region around Mosul in northern Mesopotamia. Most fraught with evil consequence for the British was the BALFOUR DECLARATION of November 1917 in which Britain undertook to facilitate the establishment of a national home for the Jewish people in Palestine—with provisos protecting the "civil and religious rights of the existing non-Jewish communities" and the rights of Jews in other countries. All of these engagements were designed to serve urgent wartime objectives rather than long-term interests.

These overlapping (many said conflicting) claims came home to roost at the PARIS PEACE SETTLEMENTS in 1919, at which all parties presented their claims. Both the Zionists and the Arabs were represented by pro-British leaders: the Zionists by Chaim WEIZMANN, the Arabs by a Hijazi delegation headed by Emir Faisal (FAISAL I IBN HUSAYN). T. E. Lawrence acted at the conference as adviser to Emir Faisal, who conformed to British desires in all matters—even to the extent of making friendly gestures toward Zionism. The French, however, proved less amenable. They spoke darkly of "a new Fashoda" and vigorously asserted their territorial demands in the Levant and Anatolia.

In large measure, Britain, as the power in possession, was able to impose its own design on the region. Its forces, commanded by Allenby, were in occupation of the Fertile Crescent and Egypt. Although Allenby's army included French, Italian, and other national units, these were too weak to form a counterweight to British military might. The Bolshevists had in the meantime published the text of the Constantinople convention and renounced their predecessors' claim to the city. The implosion of Russian power and the outbreak of the Russian civil war eliminated Britain's great historic fear of Russian movement south toward the Mediterranean, the Persian Gulf, and India.

Overwhelming military power also enabled the British to dispose of indigenous challenges to their authority. Rebellion in Egypt in 1919 was repressed by Allenby with a dextrous mixture of force and diplomacy. Revolt in Iraq in 1920 was put down by Gen. Arnold T. Wilson with an iron fist. Riots in Palestine in April 1920 and May 1921 were suppressed, in the latter case by bombarding villages from the air, and succeeded by political concessions.

The Paris Peace Conference did not, in fact, achieve a resolution of territorial issues in the Middle East. In August 1920, the Treaty of SÈVRES, by which Turkey gave up all its non-Arab provinces as well as parts of Anatolia, was signed by the Allied powers and representatives of the Ottoman government, which by this time was little more than a diplomatic ghost. Simultaneous secret agreements among the Allies provided for an additional carve-up of much of what remained of Turkish Anatolia. The treaty never came into effect. As a result of the Kemalist revolt, it was disavowed by the Turks and fell into abeyance.

Following the peace conference, France continued to squabble with Britain over a division of the Middle East spoils. The British conceded control of Syria and Lebanon to their erstwhile ally. They were dismayed, however, when the French, in July 1920, unceremoniously ejected Emir Faisal from Damascus, where his enthusiastic supporters had proclaimed him king of Syria. Faisal arrived in British-controlled Palestine as a refugee with a large entourage. A harried British governor of Haifa complained that they were "in and out like a swarm of bees" and warned that "they cannot stay here indefinitely." There was no disposition, however, on the part of his British patrons to seek to reinstall Faisal in Damascus. As a kind of consolation prize, the British arranged for his "election" by cooperative Mesopotamian notables as king of Iraq.

The British successfully resisted broader French territorial aspirations. The northern oil-bearing region of Mesopotamia, inhabited mainly by Kurds, was assigned to British-controlled Iraq. This departure from the wartime agreement had been informally agreed to at a meeting of the British prime minister, David Lloyd George, and the French prime minister, Georges Clemenceau, in November 1918, but the French continued for some time to grumble about the arrangement. French aspirations to a role in Palestine, where they saw themselves as historic protectors of Christian interests, were thrust aside by the British.

Meanwhile, in Transjordan, Faisal's brother, ABDULLAH IBN HUSAYN, had suddenly appeared in October 1920 at the head of a motley army, threatening to attack the French in Syria and to reclaim his brother's "kingdom" there. The British government saw little advantage in taking over the unfertile hollow of the Fertile Crescent. On the other hand, they could not permit Abduallah to drag them into a war with the French. The foreign secretary, Lord George Nathaniel Curzon, reluctantly sanctioned the dispatch of some British officers to the territory, ostensibly to prevent its "relapse into anarchy"—in reality to restrain Abdullah from adventures against the French.

In March 1921, Churchill, then colonial secretary, convened a conference in Cairo of British officials in the region. This meeting set out broad lines of British administration in the Middle East that were to endure for the next decade. Under this arrangement, Abdullah was established as emir of Transjordan; the territory was to form part of the British mandate over Palestine without, however, being open to Jewish settlement. While Abdullah formally ruled the country, the British resident and a small number of other officials discreetly steered policy in directions compatible with British interests.

Having established their paramountcy, the British rapidly reduced their military establishment in the Middle East. In the early 1920s, the conservative press in Britain, particularly newspapers owned by Lords Northcliffe and Beaverbrook, agitated against large military expenditures in the region and called for a British exit from recent acquisitions there. In a general climate of demobilization and budget cutting, the government felt obliged to withdraw the bulk of its troops. Henceforth, except in times of crisis, the British did not maintain a large standing army in any part of the Middle East except at the strategically vital Suez.

For the rest of the period between the wars, the British maintained security in the Middle East mainly with locally recruited forces financed by locally collected revenues. Riots, disturbances, and other challenges to British authority were suppressed by the new tactic of aerial bombardment, demonstrative shows of strength, and limited political concessions.

In the age of Gordon and Kitchener, Middle East empire building had a jingoistic tinge, but after 1914 this tendency disappeared. Unlike other parts of the empire—notably, regions of white settlement—Middle East imperialism had no significant popular constituency in Britain. (France, where there was a strong pressure group on behalf of Roman Catholic interests in Syria, was very different.)

At the same time, the legend of Lawrence of Arabia, stimulated first by public lantern shows in Britain and America and later by T. E. Lawrence's writings on the ARAB REVOLT, encouraged the growth of public interest in Arabia. Although the Arab revolt had only minor military significance, it formed the basis of myth and countermyth. The myth was of a natural affinity between the British empire and Arab desert warriors. The countermyth was of the betrayal of Arab nationalism by duplicitous British diplomacy. Both myths exercised a powerful subliminal influence on Anglo–Arab attitudes over the next generation. The Arab vogue was further encouraged by the writings of Middle Eastern explorers, travelers, and administrators, such as Freya Stark, Gertrude Bell, and Ronald Storrs. The great Victorian classics of Arabian exploration by writers such as Charles Doughty and Richard Francis Burton were revived and achieved a certain réclame.

The official mind of British imperialism, however, was shaped less by sentimental considerations than by hardheaded, realistic calculation of national interest. More than anything, official thinking was predicated on concern about India—specifically, about the security of routes to the subcontinent and the Far East and the possible effects of Middle East developments on internal security in India. With the growth of aviation as well as sea traffic, the need for a string of secure air bases was seen as vital. Indian priorities also lay behind British officials' anxiety about the inflammatory threat, as they saw it, of growing pan-Islamic feeling on the large Muslim minority in India. As it turned out, such fears proved exaggerated: Indian Muslims were not greatly preoccupied by Middle Eastern concerns.

The resurgence of Turkey under Atatürk caused some anxiety in Britain and led to a momentary crisis at Chanak (near Constantinople) in the autumn of 1922. As the revived Turkish army advanced on Constantinople, British and French forces, in occupation of the city, prepared to resist. Lloyd George, who had given encouragement to the disastrous Greek invasion of Anatolia, was at first inclined to order British forces to stand and fight. But there was no enthusiasm in Britain for such a war. The episode led to the withdrawal of Conservative support for Lloyd George and his fall from power. With the evacuation of British and French forces from Constantinople, the crisis passed. The new Turkish regime signed the Treaty of LAUSANNE in July 1923, giving up any claim to the Ottoman Empire's former Arab provinces—but holding on to the Turkish, Kurdish, and former Armenian regions of Anatolia.

With the settlement in 1923 of differences over the border between Palestine and Syria, British diplomatic conflict with the French diminished. Disputes with the United States over oil concessions were settled in 1925 with a division of interests in the northern Iraqi petroleum industry. For the next decade, Britain could control the region without worrying about any significant great-power competitor.

British policymaking in the Middle East was not centralized in any one government department. The foreign, colonial, India, and war offices all held responsibility at certain periods for different parts of the region. Broadly speaking, the foreign office was responsible for Egypt, the India office for the Persian Gulf, and the colonial office (from 1921) for the mandates in Palestine, Transjordan, and Iraq. Each of these departments refracted its specific angle of vision and concerns in its formulation of policy. Aden, for example, whose importance to Britain was primarily as a coaling station for ships en route to India, was ruled until 1932 directly from Bombay; after that, responsibility was taken over by the central government in Delhi, and, beginning in 1937, Aden became a crown colony. In some cases, diffusion of responsibility led to conflict between departments: Palestine, over which the colonial and foreign offices clashed repeatedly, was a case in point.

Britain's favored method of rule in the Middle East was indirect and inexpensive: this was a limited liability empire. The model was not India but Egypt, where British advisers had guided government policy since the start of the British occupation. Hardly anywhere did direct rule by a British administration survive intact until after WORLD WAR II. Typical of British attitudes throughout the region during the period was the comment of the colonial secretary, Lord Cranborne, in 1942: "We not only disclaim any intention of establishing direct rule, but also quite sincerely and genuinely do not wish to do so." Warning against direct British administration of the tribal hinterland of Aden colony, Cranborne added: "We must keep steadily in front of us the aim of establishing in Aden protectorate a group of efficient Arab authorities who will conduct their own administration under the general guidance and protection of His Majesty's government." The characteristic tone of British governance was set by Sir Percy Cox in Iraq and by Allenby in Egypt: benevolent paternalism in time of peace; readiness to resort to brute force in reaction to civil unrest.

The British did not believe in large public investment in this new empire. They nevertheless greatly improved the primitive economic infrastructure bequeathed them by their Ottoman predecessors, established sound public finances, built solid judicial and (though slowly) educational systems, rooted out corruption, and protected minorities. Efficient government was not the primary purpose of imperial rule, but the British installed it almost by reflex.

The mandatory system in Palestine, Transjordan, and Iraq was a constitutional innovation. Formally, the British ruled these territories not as a colonial power but under the ultimate authority of the LEAGUE OF NATIONS. Mandatory government was to last for a limited period with the specific goal of preparing the countries for self-rule. All this, in the eyes of most observers, was merely a fig leaf to cover the nakedness of imperial acquisition. Although Britain was ultimately responsible to the league for its conduct of affairs in the mandated territories and was obliged to render account annually of its administration, the league exercised little influence over policy. In effect, Britain ruled the mandated territories as if they were colonies, though here too they sought to establish limited local self-government.

As in other parts of the empire, British power ultimately rested on a collaborative equation with local elements. Its exact form varied depending on local contingencies. In some places, the British practiced a variant of the politics of notables inherited from the Ottomans. In others, they established mutually beneficial alliances with minorities—as with the Jews in Palestine for a time. Elsewhere, they combined these policies with patronage of dynastic rulers, particularly with the family of Sharif Husayn.

Britain's patronage of the Hashimites was dealt a blow in 1925 when Sharif Husayn was driven out of the Hijaz by the resurgent Wahhabi army of Ibn Sa'ud, ruler of Najd. Husayn escaped in a British ship bound for Cyprus. Although Ibn Saud had been granted a British subsidy in 1916, he had not joined in the Arab revolt and had remained jealous of his Hashimite neighbor. Compelled to accept realities, the British quickly came to terms with Ibn Saud. In 1927, they signed a treaty with him that recognized his sovereignty over the Hijaz and, as a result, his leading position among native rulers in the Arabian peninsula.

Although Ibn Sa'ud employed a freelance British adviser, Harry St. John Bridger PHILBY, a convert to Islam, the Saudi regime's relations with Britain were never intimate. In the kingdom of Saudi Arabia, which Ibn Sa'ud proclaimed in 1932, U.S. rather than British companies were favored in the scramble for oil concessions. At the time, this seemed of minor importance; later, when vast oil reserves were discovered, the British regretted the failure. Oil production on a large scale, however, did not begin in the country until after World War II.

Until the late 1930s, the limited liability system survived more or less intact. The independence granted to Egypt in 1922 and Iraq in 1932 did not fundamentally affect Britain's paramountcy. In each case, Britain retained effective control over vital strategic and economic interests. The continuation of this "veiled protectorate," as it became known in the Egyptian case, exacerbated nationalist frustrations and resentments, but these posed no imminent threat to Britain. Independence in Iraq was followed by the mass killing of members of the Nestorian Christian community, known as ASSYRIANS. Thousands fled overseas. Like other minorities, they had looked to the British for protection; the failure to assure their security left a dark stain on Britain's imperial record in the country.

From 1936 onward, Britain's dominance in the Middle East was increasingly threatened from within and without. Mussolini's determination to create an Italian empire around the Mediterranean and the Italian conquest of Ethiopia in 1935 posed a sudden danger to Britain. The powerful Italian broadcasting station on the island of Bari began broadcasting anti-British propaganda to the Middle East. The Italian dictator wooed Ibn Sa'ud and other Middle Eastern rulers and gave covert support to anti-British elements in the region, including the anti-British leader of the Palestine Arab nationalist movement, Mohammad Amin al-HUSAYNI. The PALESTINE ARAB REVOLT between 1936 and 1939 tied down large numbers of British troops at a time when, with the Nazi threat looming in Europe, the British could ill afford such a diversion.

Conscious of their limited resources, particularly of military manpower, the British faced unpalatable policymaking dilemmas in the final months of the peace and felt compelled to subordinate all other considerations to the imperatives of imperial security: hence, the WHITE PAPERS ON PALESTINE of May 1939, which reversed the Balfour Declaration policy of support for a national home for the Jewish people and restricted Jewish immigration to Palestine at a time of mounting danger to Jews in Europe.

During World War II, the Middle East played a vital part in British strategic calculations. As prime minister from May 1940, Churchill placed a high priority on bolstering British power in the region. At a critical phase in the war, he insisted on dispatching large numbers of tanks and men to reinforce British forces confronting the Italians, and later the Germans, on the border between Egypt and Libya.

The British could no longer afford the luxury of a piecemeal bureaucratic approach to the Middle East. Economic planning and supply questions for the entire region were coordinated by the MIDDLE EAST SUPPLY CENTER in Cairo. A British minister resident was sent to Cairo to take charge of overall policymaking. (One incumbent, Lord Moyne, a close friend of Churchill, was murdered in November 1944 by Zionist terrorists as a protest against British policy in Palestine.)

After Italian entry into the war in June 1940, the danger of attack in the Mediterranean precluded use of the SUEZ CANAL by British ships carrying supplies to and from India and the Far East. Ships carrying reinforcements to British forces in Egypt had to take the Cape of Good Hope route before passing through the canal from south to north.

Except in Egypt, where they built up their forces to confront the Italians and later the Germans, the British could not afford to maintain more than a thin crust of military control in most of the region during the war. Yet by a mixture of diplomacy, guile, and occasional demonstrative concentrations of force, they succeeded in averting serious challenge from nationalist opponents. The two most dangerous threats came in Iraq and Egypt. A pro-Axis coup erupted in Iraq in April 1941, headed by Rashid Ali al-Kaylani, aided by Italian and Nazi agents and by the ex-mufti of Jerusalem. With pro-Vichy forces in control of Syria and Lebanon, British power throughout the Fertile Crescent seemed for a moment on the verge of toppling. But in May, a small British force from the Habbaniya air base moved into Baghdad. Al-Kaylani and the ex-mufti fled to Germany where they devoted themselves to anti-British propaganda. The following month, British and Free French forces, operating from Palestine, advanced into Syria and Lebanon and installed new French administrations sympathetic to the Allied cause.

The other threat appeared in Egypt, where nationalist elements, particularly in the Egyptian army, were impressed by Axis military successes and sought to take advantage of Britain's moment of weakness. The British reacted firmly. In February 1942, British tanks surrounded the royal palace as a weeping King Farouk was forced by ultimatum to appoint a prime minister acceptable to the British, Mustafa al-Nahhas, head of the Wafd party. From the British point of view, the Abdin palace coup, as the episode became known, gave a salutary demonstration of British resolve at a time of acute military pressure from the Germans in the western desert.

The battle in the western desert swung to and fro. In the initial phase, between June 1940 and February 1941, a British army under Gen. Archibald Wavell beat back an offensive by Italian forces under Marshal Rodolfo Graziani and advanced into Cyrenaica. In the spring of 1941, however, Axis forces were bolstered by the arrival of the German Afrika Korps commanded by Gen. Erwin Rommel, a brilliant strategist. The tide was reversed: the British were routed from Libya, and the British garrison at Tobruk was besieged and captured. By mid-1942, the Germans had advanced deep into Egypt. Government departments in Cairo began burning secret documents, and emergency evacuation plans were prepared.

In November 1942, the critical battle of the campaign was fought against Rommel at al-ALAMAYN by the British Eighth Army under Gen. Bernard Montgomery. Months of careful planning coupled with imaginative mobile tactics, intelligent exploitation of ultra signals intelligence, as well as British superiority in numbers of men and machines, brought a decisive victory. This was, in Churchill's phrase, "the end of the beginning." Thereafter, the British strategic position in the region eased. Almost simultaneously in Morocco and Algeria, Operation TORCH, the landing of U.S. and British forces commanded by General EISENHOWER, had opened a new front against the Axis. By May 1943, the Germans and Italians had been cleared out of northern Africa.

Churchill's preoccupation with the Mediterranean led him up some blind alleys. He tried repeatedly to draw Turkey into the war on the Allied side but without success. Turkey remained neutral until early 1945, when it declared war on Germany at the last moment in order to qualify for membership in the United Nations. The United States opposed Churchill's Mediterranean strategy both on military grounds and because the United States did not wish to give the appearance of propping up British imperial interests. Ibn Saud, too, remained neutral until the last moment, though he received handsome subsidies from the British and the United States and made some gestures of support for the Allied cause.

Britain did not seek territorial acquisition in the Middle East in World War II. It nevertheless found itself drawn into new responsibilities. Following the German attack on the Soviet Union in June 1941, Britain joined the USSR in occupying Iran. Arms and other supplies to the Soviet Union were sent by rail through Iran. With the expulsion of the last Axis forces from Libya in 1943, that country was placed under military administration—French in the Fezzan and British in Tripolitania and Cyrenaica. British forces also occupied the former Italian possessions of Eritrea, Abyssinia, and Italian Somaliland. Abyssinia was restored to its indigenous imperial ruler. Eritrea remained under British rule until 1952 when it was annexed by Abyssinia. Italian Somaliland was returned to Italy as a UN trusteeship in 1950. Libya became independent in December 1951, though Britain was granted the right under the Anglo–Libyan Alliance Treaty of 1953 to maintain military installations there.

During the war, large reserves of oil in the Arabian peninsula had come onstream. Because of the closure of the Mediterranean to British commercial shipping, British use of Middle East oil during the war was mainly restricted to the area east of the Suez. Elsewhere, Britain mainly relied on imports from the Americas. After the war, the balance changed. Over the next three decades, Britain became steadily more dependent on oil imports from the Middle East, especially Kuwait.

In the later stages of the war, the British government, seeing the nationalist mood in many Arab countries, tried to move toward a new relationship with the Arabs. Following a speech by the British foreign secretary, Anthony Eden, in which he indicated British sympathy for the idea of Arab unity, a conference of Arab states at Alexandria in October 1944 approved the foundation of the LEAGUE OF ARAB STATES. The effort to ride the tiger, however, had only limited success; the British soon found that Arab nationalism turned strongly against them.

During the war, the Soviet Union had cautiously raised its diplomatic profile in the Middle East. After 1945, the region became a secondary arena of great-power conflict in the Cold War. In 1945 and 1946, the USSR signaled its newly aggressive posture by attempting to establish pro-Soviet administrations in northern Iran. Eventually British and American, as well as Russian, forces withdrew from Iran and a pro-Western regime was consolidated under Muhammad Reza PAHLAVI.

Elsewhere, Soviet influence was exercised by propaganda and subversion rather than direct military intervention. Although Communist parties remained weak in the region, Soviet sponsorship of Arab nationalist movements posed a growing threat to Western interests in general and the British in particular.

The end of British rule in India in 1947 lessened the strategic argument for a major British military commitment in the Middle East. But oil—both investments and supply—and the security of the Suez Canal remained central British concerns. British policy now faced acute difficulties in the Middle East: on the one hand, Britain retained vital interests there; on the other, its postwar economic debilitation left it unable to muster the military forces required to meet any serious challenge to control those interests.

As a result, Britain was increasingly overshadowed by the United States in the Middle East. Under the Truman Doctrine, enunciated in 1947, the United States replaced Britain as the main provider of military and economic assistance to Greece and Turkey. The United States had already begun edging the British out of monopolistic control of oil concessions. Now, the United States became the dominant ex-ternal diplomatic power, particularly in Saudi Arabia. It established a large air base in Saudi Arabia, built the Trans-Arabian Pipeline, and became the major external source of arms and other aid. Saudi relations with Britain were meanwhile clouded by the BURAYMI OASIS DISPUTE (claimed by Abu Dhabi and Oman, which were both under British protection). The dispute flared into military conflict in 1952 and again in 1955; it led to a breach in Anglo–Saudi diplomatic relations between 1956 and 1963.

British military and political weakness was damagingly demonstrated to the world by the collapse of the British mandate in Palestine. In spite of the presence of substantial British forces and the experience gained in crushing Arab insurgency between 1936 and 1939, the mandatory government proved unable to assert its authority in the face of a revolt by the half million Jews in the country.

The international ramifications of the Palestine conflict created serious difficulties for the British between 1945 and 1948. In the British-occupied zones of Germany and Austria, the military authorities were faced with growing numbers of Jewish displaced persons, the majority of whom demanded to be allowed to proceed to Palestine. In the United States, on which Britain depended for economic aid, the assertive and electorally significant Jewish community pressed Congress and President Harry Truman to secure a pro-Zionist outcome in Palestine. Meanwhile, British diplomats throughout the Arab Middle East reported that the Palestine question had become a central mobilizing issue for Arab nationalists and anti-British agitators.

Although the colonial office remained formally responsible for Palestine, these international complications led the foreign office to take effective control of British policymaking on the issue after 1945. The Labour Government's foreign secretary, Ernest BEVIN, adopted an anti-Zionist position, which at times tipped over the edge into anti-Semitism; his undiplomatic outspokenness secured applause from frustrated officials but was bitterly resented by many Jews. In the final stages of the crisis (1947–1948), the British publicly washed their hands of the matter, professing to leave it to the decision of the United Nations. Yet, following the decision of the UN General Assembly on 29 November 1947 to partition Palestine into Jewish and Arab states, the British barely cooperated in implementing the decision. Privately, Bevin encouraged the government of Transjordan to reach a modus vivendi with the Zionists on the basis of a different kind of partition, one in which the Transjordanians would take over the Arab-inhabited hill regions of the country and coexist with a Jewish state in the rest of Palestine. In the end this was, broadly speaking, the outcome.

The ARAB–ISRAELI WAR, which lasted from 1947 to 1949, tightened the British connection with Transjordan. Although the country had been granted independence in 1946, it remained under British tutelage. In March 1948, an alliance treaty was concluded in which the two countries promised each other military assistance and Transjordan agreed to the stationing of British forces in the country "until such a time . . . that the state of the world renders such measures unnecessary." Britain was the only country in the world to recognize the Jordanian annexation of the West Bank.

The Zionists' feat in driving the British out of Palestine in 1948 depressed British prestige throughout the region. The British government after 1945 made strenuous efforts to dissociate itself from Zionism; Arab nationalists for the next generation nevertheless attributed the creation of Israel in large measure to Britain's earlier support of a national home for the Jewish people.

After Palestine, the second significant test of British political will in the Middle East came in Iran. In 1951, the ANGLO–IRANIAN OIL COMPANY, in which the British government owned 51 percent of the shares, was nationalized by legislation in the Iranian parliament. A nationalist government, headed by Mohammad MOSSADEGH, defied British attempts to secure a reversal of the nationalization. With the support of major international oil companies, the British government organized a boycott of Iranian oil. Diplomatic relations between the two countries were broken. The departure of foreign oil exports led to closure of the Abadan oil refinery. As the oil companies refused to process, ship, or purchase Iranian oil, the entire petroleum industry in the country ground to a halt. At the height of the crisis in 1953, the Shah, who strongly opposed Mossadegh, fled the country.

Meanwhile, in November 1952, the British had approached the United States about the possibility of organizing a joint covert operation to protect western interests in Iran. Shortly afterward, an Iranian army coup, engineered by the U.S. Central Intelligence Agency with British help, overthrew Mossadegh and brought about the return of the Shah. The Iranian oil industry was reorganized: the British granted formal recognition of Iranian ownership of the oil industry in exchange for the lease of its operations to a multinational consortium. The British share in this consortium was reduced to under a half, with the remainder held mainly by U.S. companies.

Of even greater concern to British governments was the deterioration of the British position in Egypt. Egyptian nationalists, chafing under what was seen as continued behind-the-scenes British influence, demanded the renegotiation of the Anglo–Egyptian treaty of 1936 and the closing of British bases. There was also conflict with Britain over the Sudan, which was ruled by Britain though it was formally an Anglo–Egyptian condominium; the Egyptian government now sought to annex the country to Egypt. In January 1952, anti-British riots broke out in Egypt and paved the way·for the revolution of July 1952 in which a group of military officers, headed by Muhammad Naguib and Gamal Abdel NASSER, seized power, deposed the king, and declared a republic.

The British now began to consider moving the center of gravity of their Middle East operations to a more secure point. A first step was the decision in December 1952 to move the Middle East headquarters of the British armed forces from Egypt to Cyprus.

In the hope of constructing a bulwark against Soviet subversion and of limiting the growth of anti-Western influences in the region, Britain and the United States had proposed in October 1951 the creation of the MIDDLE EAST DEFENSE ORGANIZATION. Turkey, which was concerned about Soviet pressure for a new regime at the Straits, expressed willingness to join such an alliance; but Egypt rejected it, and no other Middle Eastern state expressed interest, whereupon the scheme was abandoned.

Other such proposals met similar fates. The BAGHDAD PACT of 1955 represented a final attempt by the western powers, with the United States by this time playing the leading role, to create a regional framework under their auspices. The core of the scheme was a multilateral military aid treaty signed by Britain, Iraq, Turkey, Iran, and Pakistan, with the United States acting as an interested outside party. No Arab state apart from Iraq could be induced to join the pact, and Egypt, in particular, opposed it vigorously. The failure to attract Arab members was seen as a further sign of the decline of British authority in the region.

In Jordan, the young King HUSSEIN IBN TALAL, educated at Harrow and Sandhurst, became the most pro-British of postwar Middle East rulers. His cultural formation was as much British as Arab; he maintained a home in Britain and was the one Arab ruler who was a popular public figure in Britain (his second wife was British). Such personal predilections, however, could not overcome the larger forces shaping events. Hussein, whose long career was marked by frequent shifts of policy consummated with supreme maneuvering skill, found himself compelled to bend to the anti-British wind. In March 1956, responding to external and internal political pressures, he dismissed the British commander of his army, Sir John Bagot Glubb. Since the formation of the Transjordanian emirate in 1921, the state's army, the ARAB LEGION, had always been commanded by a British officer. In his ability to reconcile loyalties to the British and to his Arab employer, Glubb had been characteristic of a fading type of British officer in the Middle East. While commanding the Arab Legion he had routinely supplied the British government with secret copies of Jordan's war plans. The dismissal of "Glubb Pasha" was generally regarded as the end of an era and a telling sign of the decline of British influence.

The supreme crisis of British power in the Middle East came later that year, appropriately at the focal point of Britain's interests in the region and the reason d'être of its presence there—the Suez Canal. In spite of its gradually diminishing economic position relative to other powers, Britain remained the world's foremost shipping nation, and the British merchant fleet was by far the largest user of the canal. With the growth of motor transport and the switch from coal to oil as the main industrial fuel, Britain had become overwhelmingly reliant on the importation of Middle East oil carried through the canal in tankers. Pressure from the Egyptian government for a British evacuation of the Suez Canal zone, therefore, encountered stiff resistance.

In October 1954, Britain had promised to withdraw all its force from the canal zone by mid-1956. However, the agreement was hedged with several provisos reminiscent of the veiled protectorate, among them a stipulation that Egypt continue to offer Britain "such facilities as may be necessary to place the Base [in the canal zone] on a war footing and to operate it effectively" if any outside power attacked a member of the Arab League or Turkey. In November 1955, British troops withdrew from the Sudan as the country moved toward full independence in January 1956. The following July, in accordance with the 1954 agreement, Britain withdrew the last of its troops from the canal zone.

Hardly had the last British soldiers packed their bags, however, than the Egyptian president afforded the British a pretext to return. On 26 July, Nasser, infuriated by the withdrawal of an offer by the United States, Britain, and the World Bank to finance the construction of a new dam at Aswan, announced the nationalization of the Suez Canal Company, which operated the canal. The British *locus standi* in the matter was doubtful. The British government owned a minority stake in the company, but nationalization in itself was no offense against international law, provided compensation was paid, and the Egyptians insisted that they would continue to operate the canal as before.

The nationalization was, nevertheless, regarded by the British prime minister, Eden, as an intolerable affront. When diplomacy failed to secure an Egyptian retreat, the British prepared for war. They were joined by France, which had its own reasons for opposing the Nasser regime on account of Egypt's support of Algerian rebels. Israel, which had suffered a series of border incursions from Egypt, was also drawn into military and diplomatic planning. Conspiratorial discussions among representatives of the three countries at a villa in the Paris suburb of Sèvres from 22 to 24 October culminated in a secret treaty. The agreement mapped out a scenario for war with Egypt. Israel would attack first across the Sinai peninsula. The British and French would then enter the conflict, ostensibly to secure the Suez Canal, in fact to destroy Nasser's regime.

The Israelis attacked on 29 October, and the British and French duly issued an ultimatum the next day calling on Israel and Egypt to withdraw to positions ten miles east and west of the Suez Canal (the Israelis had not yet, in fact, reached the canal). In the absence of Egyptian acquiescence, British and French planes began bombing Egyptian military targets on 31 October. On 5 November, the two powers landed paratroops. The next day, however, British policy went into reverse as a result of U.S. opposition to the invasion and of growing market pressure on sterling. Britain and France were humiliatingly obliged to agree to a cease-fire, and by Christmas they had withdrawn their forces from Egypt.

Britain's collusion with France and Israel in the events leading to the Suez war became the subject of bitter controversy in Britain. The issue is said to have divided the nation more than any foreign-policy question since Munich. The Labour party, a small part of the Conservative party, some foreign office officials, and most enlightened opinion were hostile to Eden's policy. For the British government, Suez was an unmitigated catastrophe—not least in the severe strains it placed on relations with the United States. Eden resigned a few weeks later, complaining of ill health.

Although Suez is generally regarded as a watershed in British history, heralding a wider imperial withdrawal, Britain continued for another decade to maintain a substantial military presence in the Middle East and to be ready on occasion to use it forcefully in defense of its interests.

The next flashpoint was Jordan. In March 1957, a nationalist government in Jordan abrogated the Anglo–Jordanian Treaty. In July 1958, the Jordanian regime was severely shaken by the revolution in Iraq, in which the Hashimite regime was ousted and the young King Faisal II and the pro-British Prime Minister Nuri al-Sa'id were both murdered. British paratroops were sent, at the request of King Hussein, to prevent a similar revolution in Jordan. Two aspects of this intervention, code-named Operation Fortitude, illustrated the changed political environment within which the British, perforce, now operated. First, the cabinet refused to commit British forces until the approval of the U.S. government had been secured. Second, the British requested and received permission from Israel to overfly Israeli territory in order to transport troops from bases on Cyprus. The British force succeeded in bolstering the Hashimite monarchy without firing a shot. The pro-British Jordanian monarchy survived, but Britain lost its bases in Iraq as well as its oil interests there.

In 1961, when Kuwait, hitherto a British protectorate, secured independence, the military regime in Iraq threatened a takeover of the oil-rich principality. As at the time of the intervention in Jordan in 1958, the British made sure that they had U.S. approval before taking military action. Eight thousand British troops were sent to Kuwait and remained there as a deterrent against Iraqi invasion until 1963.

In Aden in the mid-1960s, British forces conducted a miserable campaign against nationalist insurgents supported by Egypt. The British military headquarters at Aden were evacuated in November 1967 when the Federation of South Arabia achieved independence as the People's Democratic Republic of Yemen. Although the writing was on the wall for what remained of British power in the Middle East, there was no complete pullout yet. With the liquidation of the base at Aden, Britain expanded its military presence in Bahrain and other Gulf principalities.

In the crisis prior to the outbreak of the Arab–Israel War of 1967, the British government of Harold Wilson briefly considered participating in the dispatch of an international naval flotilla to assert the right of passage to Israel through the Strait of TIRAN, which the Egyptian government had declared closed against Israeli and Israeli-bound ships. But no other country was prepared to join in the effort, and the idea was dropped. Although both Wilson and his foreign secretary, George Brown, were sympathetic to Israel, their attitude was not governed by any pro-Zionist altruism. The British remained vitally interested in free passage through the Suez Canal. Upon the outbreak of war with Israel in June 1967, Nasser closed the canal to all shipping; it did not open again until 1975. The closure severely affected the British balance of payments. The British economy was blown off course, and the government was compelled, against its wish, to devalue sterling in November of that year.

Only in 1968 did the Wilson government abandon pretensions to world-power status by dropping the east-of-Suez defense policy. In March 1970, the revolutionary government in Libya, headed by Col. Muammar al-QADDAFI who had attended an officers' training school in Britain, ejected the British from their bases in the country. British forces withdrew from Bahrain in 1971, but retained naval facilities there. Also in 1971, British forces left Abu Dhabi, whereupon the seven Trucial Coast shaykhdoms formed the federation of the UNITED ARAB EMIRATES. The British retained troops in Oman, where they helped suppress a leftist rebellion in the Dhufar region. Although British forces were formally withdrawn in 1976, many senior British officers remained on individual contracts as commanders of the Omani army. Only in 1984 was the British commander in chief of the country's armed forces replaced by an Omani. After that, the sole remaining permanent British military presence in the Middle East was in the sovereign bases on Cyprus.

With the elimination of its military power in the region, Britain found itself relegated to a secondary role in Middle Eastern politics. More and more, Britain was buffeted and unable to deflect ill political and economic winds blowing from the Middle East.

During the 1970s, the exploits of Palestinian Arab terrorists and the anti-Western rhetoric of Middle East leaders like Qaddafi evoked some admiration on the radical left of the political spectrum in Britain as elsewhere in Europe. Episodes such as the hijacking by Palestinian terrorists of two planes to a desert aerodrome in Jordan—the episode that occasioned the Black September conflict between the Jordanian government and the Palestine Liberation organization in 1970—riveted television audiences in Britain. In that instance, the government of Prime Minister Edward Heath decided to give way to terrorist demands and released an imprisoned Palestinian, Leila Khaled, who became a folk hero of the revolutionary left.

The Arab–Israel War of 1973 and the ensuing international energy crisis had dramatic and damaging effects on the British economy. The sudden huge increase in the price of oil and the restriction of supply by the oil producers' cartel, the ORGANIZATION OF PETROLEUM EXPORTING COUNTRIES (OPEC), were the major causes of the stagflation that afflicted Britain in the mid-1970s. The coal miners' union attempted to seize the opportunity offered by the general rise in energy prices to secure a large increase in wages paid by the nationalized coal industry. The miners' strike ushered in a bitter confrontation with the Conservative government of Heath, which called a general election on the issue in February 1974 and narrowly lost to the Labour party.

As a member of the European Economic Community (EEC) from 1973 onward, Britain generally sought to adjust her diplomacy in the Middle East to conform to a consensus of EEC members. In the aftermath of the 1973 and 1979 oil crises, this resulted in a suddenly humble attitude by former imperial powers to sometime protégés such as Iran and the Gulf emirates. A case in point was the Venice Declaration, issued by the EEC in June 1980, which marked a significant shift in diplomatic posture toward the Arab position in the conflict with Israel.

The power of OPEC enabled the producing states at last to seize effective control over their oil industries. During the 1970s and 1980s, they moved toward vertical integration of the industry, nationalizing the extraction installations, establishing refineries and petrochemical industries, investing in their own transportation of products by tanker or pipeline, and creating their own marketing mechanisms. The power of the international oil companies in the region consequently dwindled. The British government's direct interest in Middle East oil evaporated in the 1980s when the government of Prime Minister Margaret Thatcher sold off government share holdings in British Petroleum and Anglo–Dutch Shell.

Unlike most western industrial countries, however, Britain enjoyed fortuitous good fortune in the discovery and successful development of indigenous oil resources. Its dependence on Middle East oil imports ended after 1980 with the arrival onstream of large oil reserves from the North Sea. As Britain's oil production grew, it was able to play a major role in weakening and ultimately destroying the effectiveness of OPEC. Although oil production costs were much higher in the North Sea than in the Middle East, the British, in concert with other non-OPEC producers, proved able to undercut the floor prices set by OPEC. Several OPEC members, desperate for revenues to sustain their commitments to large expenditures on armaments or social programs, broke cartel discipline and secretly sold at lower prices. With demand flagging, this led in 1986 to a sudden collapse in oil prices.

In the 1980s, Middle Eastern politics spilled over onto the streets of London with a spate of terrorist incidents, including assassinations, bombings, and embassy seizures. In 1984, a British policewoman was murdered in the street during a demonstration in front of the Libyan People's Bureau in Saint James's Square in London. The gunshots were fired by a Libyan diplomat from within the embassy. There were also attacks on several Israeli and Zionist targets in Britain, as well as on Jewish institutions that had nothing to do with Israel. The most shocking terrorist incident was the midair explosion in 1988 aboard a Pan Am plane over Lockerbie, Scotland, in which all the passengers and crew members were killed. Scottish and U.S. prosecutors sought to secure the extradition of two Libyan citizens suspected of responsibility for planting the bomb. But the Libyan government refused to yield up the men, in spite of the imposition of economic sanctions by the United Nations in 1992.

Perhaps the most bizarre of all these episodes was the *fatwa* (legal opinion) issued in 1989 by the leading Iranian cleric, Ayatollah Ruhollah KHOMEINI, pronouncing a death sentence against the British novelist Salman Rushdie, who is of Indian Muslim background. Rushdie's novel *The Satanic Verses* was held by some, but not all, devout Muslims to contain blasphemous libels against Islam. Rushdie was forced to live in hiding for several years, protected by the British security services. In spite of pressure, at first private and discreet, later public and emphatic, from the British and other western governments, the Iranian theocracy proclaimed itself unable to rescind the decree even after Khomeini's death in 1989.

By the 1990s, the Middle East occupied a relatively lower place in British diplomatic preoccupations than in any other decade since World War I. British economic interest in the region became focused primarily on trade rather than investment. But with their reduced purchasing power following the collapse of the oil cartel, the Middle East oil producers no longer offered such abundant markets. British arms and engineering exports to the Middle East assumed greater importance as the balance of oil imports decreased. During the long-drawn-out Iran–Iraq war between 1980 and 1988, Britain, like other western countries, sold arms to both sides.

This policy rebounded against the British government in 1990 when Iraq invaded and occupied Kuwait. The British joined the United States and twenty-six other countries in sending forces to the Gulf to eject the Iraqis from Kuwait in 1991. Although Britain played only a secondary role in the war, the crisis lit a slow-burning fuse in British internal politics in the shape of a scandal concerning the authorization of earlier British arms sales to Iraq. The Conservative government was gravely discredited by the affair and several senior politicians and civil servants were strongly criticized by a committee of inquiry in 1995.

The cultural and social residue of Britain's Middle East empire was slight. Unlike France, Britain left behind no significant network of religious or educational institutions. Anglican Christianity had found few adherents in the region. Its mainly British clergy in the Middle East was gradually replaced at all levels by indigenous priests. The British Schools of Archaeology in Jerusalem, Ankara, and Baghdad continued to make a central contribution to excavations; but the one in Baghdad was defunct by the 1990s, and the Jerusalem school was largely inactive after the 1967 War (it later opened an Amman branch). In the Sudan, the Christian population in the south retained some links with the Church of England, but the University of Khartoum (formerly Gordon College) no longer looked to the English university system as a model. In Jordan, the royal court and the army maintained intimate links with Britain and copied British styles. Elsewhere, few relics of British cultural influence remained. Unlike most other parts of the former British empire, the imperial language did not survive into the postcolonial era in the Middle East as the primary means of communication. Insofar as English continued to be spoken, this was a reflection of new American, not old British, influence. Probably the most significant British cultural export was the World Service of the BBC: its broadcasts in English, Arabic, and other languages commanded a wide audience in the region.

At no time in the twentieth century did the Middle East take priority over the rest of the world in British diplomatic or strategic preoccupations. Yet the most striking land victories of British arms in both world wars were won respectively at Megiddo in 1918 and at al-Alamayn in 1942; the resignations of three British prime ministers (Lloyd George, Eden, and Heath) were occasioned by Middle East conflicts; and Britain's most severe economic recession after the 1930s came about as a direct result of the interlinked political and energy crises in the Middle East in 1973. For all these reasons, the Middle East occupies a central position in the history of British external relations in the twentieth century.

BIBLIOGRAPHY

For the diplomatic record, the best source is J. C. HUREWITZ's The Middle East and North Africa in World Politics, 2 vols. (New Haven, Conn., 1975). GEORGE ANTONIUS's The Arab Awakening (London, 1938) is the classic statement of the Arab nationalist case against Britain's allegedly duplicitous diplomacy in the Middle East during and after World War I. ELIE KEDOURIE's In the Anglo–Arab Labyrinth (Cambridge, U.K., 1976) amounts to a scholarly rebuttal of Antonius's argument. The same author's The Chatham House Version and Other Middle Eastern Essays (London, 1970) presents provocative revisionist readings of several key episodes and themes. BRITON C. BUSCH's Britain, India, and the Arabs, 1914–1921 (Berkeley, Calif., 1971) focuses, in particular, on the Indian element in imperial policymaking. T. E. LAWRENCE's Seven Pillars of Wisdom (London, 1935), once admired as a masterpiece of English style, now reads like a bloated exercise in self-glorification. JOHN DARWIN's Britain, Egypt, and the Middle East (London, 1981) explores the hidden preoccupations of policymakers in the wake of World War I and elegantly disposes of some more cynical interpretations. ELIZABETH MONROE's Britain's Moment in the Middle East, 2nd rev. ed. (London, 1981) is a crisp, opinionated account of the period from 1914 to 1956. Her Philby of Arabia (London, 1973) is a biography of the idiosyncratic British imperialist, explorer, and adventurer. MARY WILSON's King Abdullah, Britain, and the Making of Jordan (Cambridge, U.K., 1987) analyzes the relationship between the British and their ebullient, difficult protégé. SIR RONALD STORR's Orientations (London, 1937) is a sparkling autobiography by one of the most knowledgeable British officials (and greatest snobs) in the region. YEHOSHUA PORATH's In Search of Arab Unity (London, 1986) uncovers the origins of the Arab League. WILLIAM ROGER LOUIS's The British Empire in the Middle East, 1945–1951 (London, 1984) recounts the postwar Labour government's travails in the region on the basis of massive archival documentation. The best account of the Suez adventure, taking account of the now-open British public papers, is KEITH KYLE's Suez (London, 1991). Britain's subordinate role in the 1991 Gulf War is outlined in LAWRENCE FREEDMAN's The Gulf Conflict (London, 1993). SARAH SEARIGHT's The British in the Middle East (New York, 1970) and Tales of Empire, edited by Derek Hopwood (London, 1989), afford insights into imperial social relationships. A subtle exploration of literary images and collective psychologies is KATHRYN TIDRICK's Heart-Beguiling Araby (Cambridge, U.K., 1981).

Bernard Wasserstein

British East India Company

See East India Company

British Federation of Zionists

British organization that supports and promotes Zionism.

Founded in 1899, the federation is an umbrella organization for more than five hundred affiliated Zionist groups and synagogues in Britain. The official organ of the federation is the weekly Jewish Observer and Middle East Review.

Martin Malin

British–French Oil Agreement

Established rights to Middle East oil for Britain and France upon the breakup of the Ottoman Empire.

At the SAN REMO CONFERENCE of April 1920, Philippe Bertholet of France and Sir John Cadman of Britain confirmed France's 25 percent share in the oil of Mesopotamia (now Iraq) as stipulated by the LONG-BERENGER AGREEMENT (1919). The COMPAGNIE FRANÇAISE DES PÉTROLES (CFP) was formed later to handle this French share of the Turkish Petroleum Company. Cadman and Bertholet also established guidelines for the oil rights of their respective countries in Romania, Asia Minor (or Anatolia), and various British and French colonies.

BIBLIOGRAPHY

HUREWITZ, J. C., ed. *The Middle East and North Africa in World Politics*. New Haven, Conn., 1979.
YERGIN, DANIEL. *The Prize*. New York, 1991.

Zachary Karabell

Brit Shalom

See Binationalism

Brookings Report

Report on peace in the Middle East.

In late 1975, the Brookings Institution, a liberal think tank in Washington, D.C., issued a report titled *Towards Peace in the Middle East*. It endorsed SECURITY COUNCIL RESOLUTION 242 but went beyond it in speaking of Palestinian self-determination. When one of the signatories of the report, Zbigniew Brzezinski, became President Jimmy Carter's national security adviser, hopes were raised in the Arab world, but little came of it.

Jenab Tutunji

Browne, Edward Granville   [1862–1926]

British Iranologist.

Born of a wealthy Gloucestershire family, E. G. Browne was educated at Eton and Cambridge, England, where he qualified as a physician. In 1877, his interest stimulated by the Russo-Ottoman War, he began a largely informal study of Turkish, followed by Persian and Arabic. Elected a fellow of Pembroke College at Cambridge, he spent the year 1887/88 in Iran, which he described in *A Year amongst the Persians* (London, 1893, reprint 1926). On his return he was appointed university lecturer in Persian, then in 1902 Sir Thomas Adams Professor of Arabic. He married in 1906 and remained in Cambridge until his death.

As a rich man holding a virtual sinecure, Browne was able to direct his enormous energy and phenomenal memory into an almost virgin field. In Britain, Middle East studies had formerly been concerned mainly with Arabic. Persian studies, a legacy via the "back door" from the Mogul Empire (of India, which had become part of the British Empire following the Sepoy mutiny of 1857), had been confined to the few literary classics used in examinations for the Indian Civil Service. Browne unlocked the "front door" to post-Islamic Persia (now Iran) and to the full range of New Persian studies—including the modern spoken and literary language, religious history, and politics.

His most important contribution is the four-volume *A Literary History of Persia* (1902, 1906, 1920, 1924), still a valuable resource for scholars. It quotes extensively from original sources and from information provided by his Iranian friends and correspondents, including major writers and scholars of the time such as Ali Akbar DEHKHODA and Mohammad Qazvini. Apart from his large scholarly output, Browne also promoted Oriental studies at Cambridge by attracting prospective diplomats and administrators to an academic training; these included later historians of the Middle East, such as Laurence Lockhart and Sir Reader Bullard.

Even before his journey to Iran, Browne had taken a sympathetic interest in the BABIS movement (c. 1844–1853) and its successors, the Azali and BAHA'I faiths. He wrote a detailed account of these for the Royal Asiatic Society in 1889, met with leading adherents of the sects (especially Azalis), and published some of their works. He is best remembered in Iran for his active support of the constitutional movement from 1905 to 1911, which was characteristic of his liberal sympathies with all aspirants to self-determination. In 1908 he helped found the Persia Committee, composed of prominent members of the British Parliament (MPs); through this pressure group, in lectures, and in letters to the press, Browne sharply criticized his own government's and Russia's machinations in Iran. His book *The Press and Poetry of Modern Persia* (1914) is not merely a supplement to his *Literary History* but an avowedly partisan promotion of the democratic ideals he saw in the vigorous free press of constitutionalist Iran.

Browne was awarded the Persian Order of the Lion and Sun and, on his sixtieth birthday, he received accolades from his Iranian admirers and his British colleagues. Both as a scholar and an activist, he did much to present a sympathetic picture of Iran's people and culture to a Western public, whose view of the Middle East was already being shaped chiefly by the dictates of geopolitics, and petroleum.

BIBLIOGRAPHY

ARBERRY, A. J. *Oriental Essays*. London, 1960.
Encyclopaedia Iranica, Vol. 4. Costa Mesa, Calif., 1989.

John R. Perry

Bruce, Thomas   [1766–1841]

Thomas Bruce, seventh earl of Elgin, British diplomat.

In 1799 Elgin was appointed envoy to the Ottoman Empire's sultan in Istanbul. Elgin had a passionate interest in Greek antiquities, and with the permission of Sultan SELIM III, he sent an expedition in 1800 to Athens, Greece, then part of the Ottoman Empire, to make drawings of the various monuments. In 1801, the sultan granted Elgin the right to remove, for purposes of preservation, any stones he might wish from the Athenian Acropolis. Elgin left Istanbul in 1803, taking with him the first of many shipments of sculpture from Athens. Of particular import were the friezes and metopes that had adorned the Parthenon. Now known as the Elgin marbles, they are in the British Museum. In recent years the Greek government has demanded their return, contending that these treasures of Western civilization were unlawfully conceded to Elgin.

BIBLIOGRAPHY

Dictionary of National Biography. New York, 1908.
HOOPER, FINLEY. *Greek Realities*. Detroit, 1982.

Zachary Karabell

Buber, Martin   [1878–1965]

Jewish philosopher and influential thinker of the twentieth century.

Buber was born in Vienna, during the Austro-Hungarian Empire. He attended the university there, in Leipzig and Berlin, Germany, and in Zurich, Switzerland. He was active in Zionism and, in 1901, became editor of the zionist journal *Die Welt* (The World). From 1924 to 1933, he was professor of Judaism at the University of Frankfurt, Germany; after Hitler came to power in 1933, Buber directed Jewish adult education and teacher training until stopped by the Nazis; in 1938, he emigrated to Palestine and became professor of religion at Hebrew University in Jerusalem. From then until his death in 1965, Buber was one of the main proponents of binationalism for an Arab–Israeli state; he strove to ameliorate the distrust between the two peoples.

Recognizing the difficulties of assimilation faced by immigrants to Israel, Buber helped train teachers. During the 1950s, Buber lectured throughout the United States and became famous as a political philosopher, as a spokesperson for the problems facing the post–World War II Middle East, and most of all, as an advocate of compromise. His philosophy drew on sources ranging from mysticism to modern psychology—holding that there was a bond between the human relationship with God and the ensuing bond between people. His philosophic doctrine is published in two major works, *I and Thou* (English translation, 1937) and *Between Man and Man* (English translation, 1947). In *I and Thou*, he contrasts the relationship of I–it (the world as object) with I–thou (the world as subject); in *Between Man and Man*, he explores the application of the method of I–thou to the broader community and to education. Buber interpreted the Bible in these terms in *The Prophetic Faith* (English translation, 1949) and in *Moses* (English translation, 1946). When he discovered the Hasidic masters, he realized that the dialogic principle of Judaism, which he was exploring along modern philosophical and psychological paths, had been carried on by them in this recent development of Jewish tradition; he published these points in *Tales of the Hasidim* in 1961.

Buber's greatest hope was that his dialogic principle might be applied to the problems of Israel, as well as to the broader canvas of social and political organization in the modern world.

BIBLIOGRAPHY

EDWARDS, PAUL, ed. *The Encyclopedia of Philosophy*. New York, 1967.
Encyclopedia Judaica. New York, 1971.
New Standard Jewish Encyclopedia. New York, 1977.

Zachary Karabell

Bubiyan Island

Island at the head of the Persian/Arabian Gulf, off the north coast of Kuwait and west of the Shatt al-Arab.

Separated from Kuwait by a narrow waterway, Bubiyan is Kuwait's largest island. Along with al-Warba island, it lies at the mouth of Iraq's GULF port, Umm Qasr. Both islands have been the focus of Iraq's territorial claims. In 1990, before invading Kuwait and announcing an annexation of Kuwaiti territory, Iraq's President Saddam HUSSEIN demanded that Kuwait cede its sovereignty over both islands. Following Iraq's defeat in spring of 1991 by a United Nations coalition of forces, and the restoration of Kuwait's ruling AL SABAH family, this boundary dispute cooled but has not been settled. Iraq may yet raise the issue, if it develops the political and/or military means to do so.

BIBLIOGRAPHY

ADAMS, MICHAEL, ed. *The Middle East.* New York, 1988.

Emile A. Nakhleh

Bucharest, Treaty of (1812)

Treaty ending the Ottoman–Russian war by which Russia returned territory to the Empire.

After six years of war between the Ottoman Empire and Russia, the Treaty of Bucharest was concluded between May 16 and May 18, 1812. With Napoléon Bonaparte, emperor of France, prepared to attack Russia, Tsar Alexander I renounced Russian rights to the Romanian principalities and evacuated most of the Black Sea coast territory that Russia had won during the war, excepting Bessarabia. The treaty also contained a provision for autonomy of the Serbs, who had rebelled against the Ottomans.

BIBLIOGRAPHY

ANDERSON, M. S. *The Eastern Question.* London, 1966.
SHAW, STANFORD, and EZEL KURAL SHAW. *History of the Ottoman Empire and Modern Turkey.* New York, 1977.

Zachary Karabell

Bucharest, Treaty of (1913)

Ended Second Balkan War; Bulgaria ceded territory to Ottoman Empire.

Ending the Second Balkan War (1913), the Treaty of Bucharest was signed on August 10, 1913, by badly defeated Bulgaria and the victors—Serbia, Greece, Romania, and the Ottoman Empire. Bulgaria conceded Salonika and part of Thrace to Greece; part of Macedonia to Serbia, thus doubling Serbia's size; some territory to Romania; and Edirne and eastern Thrace to the Ottomans. The ceded lands had been won by Bulgaria from the Ottomans during the First Balkan War (1912–1913).

BIBLIOGRAPHY

ANDERSON, M. S. *The Eastern Question.* London, 1966.
SHAW, STANFORD, and EZEL KURAL SHAW. *History of the Ottoman Empire and Modern Turkey.* New York, 1977.

Zachary Karabell

Budapest Convention

Agreement between Austria and Russia regarding Russia's planned war against Ottoman Empire.

Determined to amend the decisions made by the 1876 ISTANBUL CONFERENCE, Russia made plans for war against the Ottoman Empire. By the Budapest Convention of January 15, 1877, Austria agreed to remain neutral in the coming war in return for the provinces of Bosnia and Herzegovina. Provision was also made for the partition of the Balkans in the event the Ottoman Empire collapsed.

BIBLIOGRAPHY

SHAW, STANFORD, and EZEL KURAL SHAW. *History of the Ottoman Empire and Modern Turkey.* New York, 1977.

Zachary Karabell

Bugeaud de la Piconnerie, Thomas-Robert [1784–1849]

French military officer; governor-general of Algeria, 1841–1847.

In the early nineteenth century, North Africa was under the Ottoman Empire, but local rulers sponsored Corsairs, pirates, and the Slave Trade in their coastal towns. The Europeans tried to salvage Mediterranean shipping from attack and end the taking of Christian sailors as slaves. In 1830, a French force took Algiers, but by 1832, local leader ABD AL-QADIR of Mascara defeated the French and was recognized as dey of Mascara. Abd al-Qadir repeatedly defeated French forces from 1835 to 1837.

Marshal Bugeaud was sent to negotiate the Treaty of Tafna between France and Abd al-Qadir (May 30, 1837), which abandoned most of Algeria to Abd al-Qadir. In 1839, the French broke the treaty, and in 1841 Bugeaud led a large force on the offensive against Abd al-Qadir. Bugeaud served as governor-general from 1841 to 1847. He was recalled to France and forced to resign in 1847 for disobeying orders; ironically that was the year that Abd al-Qadir surrendered to the French.

BIBLIOGRAPHY

SULLIVAN, ANTHONY. *Thomas-Robert Bugeaud, France, and Algeria, 1784–1849: Politics, Power, and the Good Society.* Hamden, Conn., 1983.

Kenneth J. Perkins

Bu Hamara   [1865–1909]

The nickname of al-Jilali ibn Idris al-Zarhuni, a Moroccan pretender to the Alawi throne.

Initially a minor official in the ALAWITE DYNASTY in Morocco, Bu Hamara (Arabic, "the man with the she-ass") was imprisoned in 1894 on charges of forgery. Between 1901 and 1903, passing himself off as a brother of the sultan Abd al-Aziz, he rallied the forces of the Ghiyata tribal confederation in the middle Atlas mountains. His activity can be understood as one in a series of rural movements opposed to heavy-handed policies by the makhzan government. Bu Hamara effectively controlled northeastern Morocco until his defeat and execution in 1908/09 by the new sultan, Mulay HAFID (Abd al-Hafiz).

BIBLIOGRAPHY

ABUN-NASR, JAMIL. *A History of the Maghrib.* Cambridge, U.K., 1976.
BURKE, EDMUND, III. *Prelude to Protectorate in Morocco.* Chicago, 1976.

Matthew S. Gordon

Buhayra

Egypt's westernmost delta province (governorate).

This province has existed as an administrative unit since Fatimid times. Nearest of Egypt's rural provinces to Alexandria, it was known while under the MAMLUKS and under the Ottoman Empire as a center of rebellious bedouin Arab tribes. Its capital is DAMANHUR. The estimated 1986 population of Buhayra was 1.8 million. Of its entire area, some 4,000 square miles (10,150 sq km) are in the Nile delta.

BIBLIOGRAPHY

Encyclopaedia of Islam, 2nd ed.

Arthur Goldschmidt, Jr.

Bu Janah Family

See Busnach Family

Bulgarian Horrors

Phrase coined by British politician Gladstone to describe the atrocities perpetrated by the Turks in putting down the revolt of the Bulgarians in 1876.

In 1875, a revolt began in Bosnia and Herzegovina that spread to neighboring Bulgaria the next year. Public opinion in Serbia and Montenegro soon caused them to declare war against the Ottoman Empire in an effort to intervene on behalf of their fellow Slavs. Meanwhile, eyewitness reports revealing that over 10,000 Christians had been slaughtered in Bulgaria by Turkish irregulars reached England, which had fought the Crimean War to preserve the Ottoman Empire and was intensely interested in the conflict. A wave of moral indignation swept over the country, fired by the revelations of the liberal press, the high point of which was an indictment by William Ewart Gladstone of Turkish rule in his pamphlet, "Bulgarian Horrors and the Question of the East." In it he argued passionately in favor of autonomy for the empire's Christian subjects, with little effect.

Although Gladstone was successful in rallying public opinion in Western Europe on behalf of the Bulgarians, the situation there was not resolved until after Russia attacked Turkey in 1877. In the following year, the treaties of San Stefano and Berlin established Bulgaria as an autonomous principality under Turkish sovereignty.

BIBLIOGRAPHY

HARRIS, D. *Britain and the Bulgarian Horrors of 1876.* Chicago, 1939.

John Micgiel

Bulgarians

South Slavs who inhabit the area in the Balkan peninsula bounded by Romania, the Black Sea, Turkey, Greece, Macedonia, and Serbia.

Having settled the area in the sixth and seventh centuries, the Slavs joined forces against Byzantium in 679 with the newly arrived Asiatic Proto-Bulgars led by Khan Asparukh. By the end of the reign of Boris I (852–893), the Proto-Bulgars had been completely absorbed by the Slavs, and Christianity was accepted as the official religion of the state.

Bulgarian is a distinct South Slavic language spoken by the approximately 9 million inhabitants of Bulgaria. Old Bulgarian, also known as Old Church Slavonic, was the first Slavic language to be written, through the efforts of two monks in the ninth century, Cyril and Methodius. A great flowering of literature and culture followed under Boris's son, Simeon, who enlarged the state to include most of Serbia, Albania, and Macedonia. In 1018, however, the Byzantine Empire defeated the Bulgars, who achieved independence through rebellion in 1185. Bulgaria passed under Turkish rule in 1396, and for the next five hundred years, the Bulgarians were ruled as a subject people. Bulgaria achieved autonomy in 1878 and full-fledged independence in 1908.

Ethnic Bulgarians today account for over 85 percent of the population and 9 percent are Turkish. Some two-thirds of the population are adherents of the Eastern Orthodox faith and 9 to 10 percent are Muslim. Traditionally an agricultural country, industrialization in the postwar period has caused manufacturing to become the leading employer with 46 percent of the working population, followed by agriculture with 21 percent. Major historical figures of the modern period include Georgi Rakovski, a nineteenth-century literary figure and revolutionary; Alexander Stamboliski, Peasant party leader and prime minister (1920–1923); and Todor Zhivkov, first secretary of the Bulgarian Communist party from 1954 to 1989.

BIBLIOGRAPHY

STAVRIANOS, L. S. *The Balkans since 1453*. New York, 1958.

John Micgiel

Bulgur

Cracked hard-wheat.

Bulgur is a parched and cracked hard-wheat (*Triticum durum*) food product, high in nutritional value. The wheat kernels are boiled until soft and about to crack, then drained, sun-dried, and finally ground into fine or coarse particles. This process dissolves some of the vitamins and minerals in the bran; the water soaks into the endosperm, bringing the dissolved nutrients with it to the inside of the grain. Coarse bulgur is used in stews and PILAF, while fine bulgur is used in *kibbeh* and *tabbouleh*.

Clifford A. Wright

Bull, Odd

Swedish general who served the United Nations in Lebanon.

In 1958 Bull was assigned by the United Nations Security Council to head an observation team that was to determine whether there was any evidence to support the accusations of the Lebanese Christian government that the United Arab Republic was infiltrating armed men into Lebanon. The accusations were the foundations of President Camille Chamoun's policies, which sought Western support against "Communist" infiltration. The mission of the team was rendered obsolete with the deployment of U.S. Marines in Lebanon the following month.

As'ad AbuKhalil

Bunche, Ralph J.   [1904–1971]

American educator and diplomat.

Born in Detroit, Bunche was an assistant professor of political science at Howard University before working for the United Nations. Following Folke BERNADOTTE's assassination in 1948, Bunche became chief UN mediator in Palestine and was responsible for drafting the June 1948 PARTITION PLANS. Bunche was awarded the Nobel Prize for Peace in 1950 for negotiating armistices between Palestinian Arabs and Jews in 1949. In 1964, he directed UN troops on Cyprus to keep peace between Greeks and Turks.

BIBLIOGRAPHY

O'BRIEN, CONOR CRUISE. *The Siege*. London, 1986.
Chambers Biographical Dictionary. 1990.

Zachary Karabell

Bund

Yiddish and German term for a political association.

The Bund was a Jewish socialist organization founded in Vilna (now Vilnius, Lithuania) in 1897. There, Bundists attacked Zionists for trying to flee from oppression instead of fighting it. The Bund advocated cultural autonomy for Jews in the Russian Empire and the end to the economic exploitation of the Jewish lower classes. After the Bolshevik Revolution (1917), government repression led to the Bund's demise in the Soviet Union. The Bund continued to play an influential role in Poland until the Nazi invasion of 1939 and the beginning of World War II. After the war, the remnants of the Bund in Europe and the United States continued to oppose vigorously the establishment of a Jewish state.

BIBLIOGRAPHY

TOBIAS, HENRY J. *The Jewish Bund in Russia: From Its Origins to 1905*. Stamford, Conn., 1972.

Jon Jucovy

Buraymi Oasis Dispute

Dispute involving Saudi Arabia, several emirates, and Western powers, 1800–1974.

In 1800 forces from Saudi Arabia seized the Buraymi Oasis (actually a cluster of oases of which Buraymi is one) from Oman, and controlled it for much of the nineteenth century. Abu Dhabi and Oman later established their authority there, and Britain, as protectorate power for both states, supported their claims. The issue of sovereignty flared when British and American oil companies began exploring the area after World War II. A United States-proposed "standstill agreement" averted conflict between Saudi Arabia, on one side, and Oman and Abu Dhabi, on the other, and led to the creation in 1954 of an international tribunal to adjudicate the conflicting claims. The tribunal's proceedings ended abruptly in 1955 when Britain's member resigned, claiming improprieties by Saudi Arabia. The rulers of Oman and Abu Dhabi sent Trucial Omani Scouts, led by British officers, to occupy Buraymi. Ties between Saudi Arabia and Britain were severely strained, and relations between Britain and the United States soured, because the U.S. government backed Saudi Arabia, where the Arabian American Oil Company (ARAMCO) represented a vital American interest. Bitterness driven by a strong sense of historical right led Saudi Arabia to withhold diplomatic recognition from the United Arab Emirates (UAE) when it was established in 1971. In 1974 Abu Dhabi ceded to Saudi Arabia a territorial corridor to the Gulf south and east of Qatar in exchange for recognition of the Abu Dhabi-Omani claim to Buraymi.

BIBLIOGRAPHY

KELLY, J. B. *Arabia, the Gulf and the West*. New York, 1980.
PECK, MALCOLM C. *The United Arab Emirates: A Venture in Unity*. Boulder, Colo., 1986.

Malcolm C. Peck

Burckhardt, Johann Ludwig   [1784–1817]

Swiss explorer; known in the Arab world as Ibrahim ibn Abd Allah.

Born in Switzerland to an Anglophile father, Burckhardt was educated at Leipzig University in Germany, then hired by the London-based Association for Promoting the Discovery of Africa. To perfect his disguise as a Muslim traveler, he gained their approval to study Islam in the Middle East. In this manner, he became the first European to produce detailed eyewitness accounts of Mecca and Medina and rediscovered Petra in 1812. Burckhardt wrote *Travels in Syria and the Holy Land* (1822), *Travels in Arabia* (1829), and *Notes on the Bedouins and Wahabys* (1830).

BIBLIOGRAPHY

SIM, KATHERINE. *Desert Traveller: The Life of Jean Louis Burckhardt*. London, 1969.

Benjamin Braude

Bureau of Translation

Ottoman agency (Bab-ı Ali Tercüme Odası) that also served as a training ground for diplomats and government officials.

Having long employed Greeks as translators, in 1821 the Ottoman Empire reacted to the GREEK WAR OF INDEPENDENCE (1821–1830) by dismissing the last Greek translator of the Imperial Divan, appointing a Bulgarian convert to Islam to replace him. In 1821, MAHMUD II created the translation office, which led an obscure existence for the next twelve years—serving more as a school than as a translation bureau, because few Muslims then knew European languages well enough to translate. Upgraded during the Ottoman-Egyptian diplomatic crisis of 1832/33 (during which MUHAMMAD ALI of Egypt demanded all Syria as a reward for his aid in Greece), the translation office assumed an important role in preparing young men to serve abroad as embassy secretaries; some of these later became ambassadors, foreign ministers, even grand viziers. Primarily a diplomatic translation bureau, the office became part of the Foreign Ministry (*Hariciye Nezareti*) when it was organized in 1836.

For a generation, the translation office was one of the best sources of Western education in Istanbul, and men trained there dominated the ranks of reforming statesmen, Westernizing intellectuals, and opposition ideologues. Patterns of bureaucratic mobility changed within the Ottoman CIVIL SERVICE, but this office kept its prestige as a place to begin a career, and it continued to function until the end of the empire (1922).

BIBLIOGRAPHY

FINDLEY, CARTER VAUGHN. *Bureaucratic Reform in the Ottoman Empire: The Sublime Port, 1789–1922.* Princeton, N.J., 1980.
———. *Ottoman Civil Officialdom: A Social History.* Princeton, N.J., 1989.

Carter V. Findley

Bureaux Arabes

French military administration in Algeria, 1830–1847.

The expansion of French power and influence in ALGERIA after the July 1830 conquest of ALGIERS necessitated intermediaries besides interpreters to deal with both Arab and Berber tribes. A systematic administration run by specially trained military officers was structured by Governor-General Thomas-Robert BUGEAUD DE LA PICONNERIE and established by decree in 1844 to execute this service. These bureaux arabes provided the governor-general with mediation and intelligence. The officers viewed their operations as a civilizing mission and were often paternalistic and protective of native rights. The civilian COLONS (European settlers in Algeria) resented this flaunted example of "rule by the sabre." After Bugeaud's departure (1847), the personnel and performance of the bureaux arabes declined. A French decree in October 1870 restructured the administration, which effectively ended the system though an analogous organization continued in south Algeria. The military resumed a similar political and social mission with the Sections Administratives Spécialisées (SAS) during the Algerian War of Independence (1954–1962).

BIBLIOGRAPHY

JULIEN, CHARLES-ANDRÉ. *Historie de l'Algérie contemporaine: La conquête et les débuts de la colonisation (1827–1871),* 2nd ed. Paris, 1979.

Phillip C. Naylor

Burg, Yosef   [1909–   ]

Israeli politician.

Burg was born and educated in Germany; there, he was ordained as a rabbi and received a doctorate from the University of Berlin before emigrating to Palestine in 1939, where he was a teacher. From 1945 to 1949, he worked in Paris, caring for Holocaust survivors. He was elected to the Knesset (Israel's parliament) in 1949, and soon after helped found the National Religious Party (NRP). From 1951 to 1986, Burg served in every Israeli government; he was minister of health (1951–1952), minister of social welfare (1959–1970), minister of interior (1970–1984), and minister of religious affairs (1981–1986). Burg has been relatively moderate on Arab–Israel relations. As a key member of Menachem BEGIN's 1977 Likud government, he participated in negotiations with Egypt following the Camp David Accords on autonomy for the West Bank and the Gaza Strip. Burg resigned from the national unity government in October 1986, to make way for younger leadership when Yitzhak SHAMIR succeeded Shimon PERES as prime minister.

BIBLIOGRAPHY

New Standard Jewish Encyclopedia. New York, 1977.
ROLEF, SUSAN HATTIS, ed. *Political Dictionary of the State of Israel.* New York, 1987.

Zachary Karabell

Burj al-Barajna

Palestinian refugee camp in West Beirut, Lebanon.

Along with two other Palestinian Refugee Camps, Sabra and Shatila, Burj al-Barajna was subjected to massive attacks by AMAL, a Shi'ite group, in 1985 as AMAL was attempting to consolidate its control over West Beirut. Despite heavy losses, the besieged Palestinians retained control of the camp.

Benjamin Joseph

Burla, Yehuda   [1886–1969]

First modern Hebrew writer of Middle Eastern Jewish descent.

Burla was born in Jerusalem, the child of a family of Turkish rabbis and scholars who settled in Ottoman Palestine in the eighteenth century. He was educated at yeshivas (Hebrew schools) and at the Jerusalem Teachers' Seminary. He served as an interpreter for the Ottoman Empire during World War I. After the war, during the British mandate over Palestine, he directed and taught at various Hebrew schools. From 1930, he headed the Arab department of HISTADRUT, was envoy of Keren Hayesod to Latin America, was director of Arab affairs in the ministry of minorities, and served as president of the Hebrew Authors' Association.

After reading the works of modern Hebrew writers, Burla realized that they dealt exclusively with Ashkenazim. He was therefore determined to present the rich world of Middle Eastern Jewry. His first novella, *Lunah* (1918), is a love story among Sephardim in old Jerusalem. His first novel, *Ishto ha-Senu'ah* (1928, His Hated Wife), concerns a man who hates his wife but, fearing economic ruin, does not divorce her. He also wrote about bedouins in *Beli Kochav* (1937, Without a Star). Burla was a realist; his style is narrative and the mood evoked is romantic.

Ann Kahn

Burnoose

The name of a garment worn in parts of North Africa.

The burnoose consists of a large woolen mantle covering other attire and having a hood. The burnoose is generally white, though tribes adopt different colors to distinguish themselves from others. This garment has long been known in Spain and parts of France under the name Albornoz.

Cyrus Moshaver

Bursa

Fourth largest city of Turkey, in northwest Anatolia.

Bursa was the first major conquest of the early Ottomans in 1324. A modest Byzantine provincial market town, it quickly developed as the first capital of the growing Ottoman state, featuring many of the finest examples of early Ottoman architecture. Positioned on the northern foothills of Ulu Dağ (Bithynian Mt. Olympus) close to the Sea of Marmara, with easy access to the Mediterranean and on the natural extension of Anatolian routes, it became the major Ottoman international commercial center where European, mainly Genoese, merchants bought silk and other eastern goods. Abundant hot springs and magnificent baths made it a favorite spa center, famous also for its peach orchards in the plain just below the city.

Even after the conquest of Constantinople (now Istanbul) in 1453 when it became the definitive capital of the empire, Bursa remained an imperial city and a thriving international market, with significant manufacture of cotton and silk textiles, in addition to its long-established role as terminus for long-distance Asian caravan trade. With a population of about 40,000 in the sixteenth century, it was the largest city in Anatolia. Bursa's growth was hampered in the seventeenth century as a result of the Ottoman policy of promoting IZMIR as the major port for Asian and European trade, but the city retained its position as a prominent, if less prosperous, cultural, manufacturing, and commercial center. In the TANZIMAT age of free trade, with competition from industrialized Europe, Bursa's silk and cotton textile manufacture suffered significantly, but both Ottoman policy of industrialization and private investment in steam-powered plants allowed recovery of local production before the end of the century. Bursa became the seat of an enlarged province incorporating several northwest Anatolian districts: ABDÜLHAMIT II's efforts to glorify the early Ottoman heritage also contributed to the city's growing fortunes.

Bursa was occupied by the Greek army after World War I, and the city suffered during the ensuing Turkish War of Independence, especially with the destructive retreat of the Greek army in 1922 and the loss of its non-Muslim population. During the Republican era of étatist industrialization, Bursa recovered its textile manufacturing prominence, its population reaching 130,000 in 1955. But its real growth came in the 1960s, with the establishment by private enterprise first of large-scale canning and food processing, and then of the automotive industry, till Bursa reached its present population of over a million. Alongside this rapid industrial transformation, Bursa still maintains its traditional role as a spa and a heritage center; Ulu Dağ has recently become a favorite winter resort and its highland pastures have regained their early-Ottoman importance for summering. Ulu Dağ University, opened in 1975, aims to recover the city's traditional position of cultural and intellectual prominence.

Main square in Bursa, 1948. (D.W. Lockhard)

BIBLIOGRAPHY

Yurt Ansiklopedisi (Encyclopedia of Turkey). Istanbul, 1982-83.

I. Metin Kunt

Burton, Richard Francis   [1821–1890]

British explorer, Orientalist, author, and consul.

Born in England to a gentleman army officer and raised in Europe, Burton was sent to Oxford University but was quickly expelled. Despite a lack of formal education, he did go on to learn as many as forty languages and dialects during his explorations and years of service to the British Empire.

His pilgrimage in disguise to Mecca and Medina, and his voluminous publications about Islam, Arabic LITERATURE, and non-Western sexuality constitute his most notable achievements. His most enduring work is *Personal Narrative of a Pilgrimage to Al-Madinah and Meccah* (London, 1855/56). He was a British consul beginning in 1861, consul in Damascus (1869–1871), and he explored or spent time in India, Africa, Brazil, the United States, and Italy, where he died.

BIBLIOGRAPHY

BRODIE, FAWN M. *The Devil Drives, A Life of Sir Richard Burton.* London, 1967.

Benjamin Braude

Bush, George Herbert Walker   [1924–   ]

U.S. president, 1989–1993.

During Bush's presidency, the United States undertook two major initiatives in the Middle East. The first was to lead the military coalition that expelled Iraq's occupation forces from Kuwait in 1991. Following Iraq's defeat, Bush decided to take advantage of the new regional climate to convene the first face-to-face Arab–Israel peace negotiations since the 1979 Israel–Egypt peace treaty. Following months negotiations, the United States and the Soviet Union presided over both bilateral and multilateral talks among Israeli and Arab delegations, including, for the first time, Palestinians (as part of joint Jordanian–Palestinian delegation).

[*See also:* Baker, James.]

Michael R. Fischbach

Busnach Family

Prominent Jewish family of Algeria.

The Busnach (in Arabic, Bu Janah) family was one of three Livornese (Italy) Jewish families (the others were the Boucharas and the Cohen–Baqris) that were prominent in Algerian commerce and politics throughout the eighteenth and early nineteenth centuries. The patriarch of the clan, Naphtali Busnach, established a shipping business in Algiers in the early 1720s. He was also involved in the ransoming of European captives of the CORSAIRS (Barbary pirates).

His grandson Naphtali II was the right-hand man of Mustafa Bey of Constantine. When Mustafa was chosen dey in 1797, Naphtali became his chief courtier. At about the same time, Naphtali went into partnership with Joseph BAQRI, with whom he was related by ties of marriage, and the firm of Baqri & Busnach came to hold a virtual monopoly on trade with the regency. Naphtali was appointed *muqaddam* (chief) of the Jewish community by the dey in 1800. Naphtali, who had survived one attempt on his life during a failed coup in 1801, was assassinated by a janissary in 1805. The incident touched off anti-Jewish riots among the Ottoman troops. Most of the Busnachs fled to Livorno at this time, although their relatives, the Baqris, remained in Algiers.

BIBLIOGRAPHY

HIRSCHBERG, H. Z. *A History of the Jews in North Africa.* Leiden, 1981.

Norman Stillman

Bustani, Butrus al-   [1819–1883]

Ottoman writer and intellectual.

Butrus al-Bustani was born in the village of Dubbiya, north of the city of Beirut during the Ottoman Empire. Although initially a Maronite Christian and educated at the Maronite seminary of Ayn Waraqa, in 1840 he converted to Protestantism after coming into contact with missionaries from the United States. He then taught Arabic at their seminary school. From 1848 to 1851, al-Bustani—with his compatriot Nasif YAZIJI and the American missionary Eli Smith—engaged in translating the book of Genesis into Arabic to produce the first printed edition of this first book of the Bible. Since he was not interested in holding clerical office, al-Bustani concentrated on literary work and on his work as DRAGOMAN (interpreter) for the American consulate in

Beirut (Lebanon), a post that he held from 1851 to 1862, when he passed it on to his son Salim.

Al-Bustani's main contributions to the Arabic literary world's interest in Western literary forms include his Arabic dictionary *Muhit al-Muhit* (produced also in an abridged form as *Qutr al-Muhit*), his Arabic encyclopedia *Da'irat al-Ma'arif*, and his editorship of the periodical *al-Jinan*, which appeared in 1870. During the 1860 civil war in Mount Lebanon, he also published an irregular newsletter under the title *Nafir Suriyya* (The Clarion of Syria).

Al-Bustani changed his orientation after he distanced himself from the American missionaries at the end of the 1850s and started to emphasize the need for national, not communal, education. To this end, in 1866, he established in Beirut al-Madrasa al-Wataniyya (The National School). Politically, he stressed his allegiance to both the Syrian *Watan* (fatherland) and the Ottoman state. He abhorred sectarian loyalties and projected a secular outlook that called for equality for all within the Syrian–Ottoman political framework.

BIBLIOGRAPHY

ABU MANNEH, BUTRUS. "The Christians Between Ottomanism and Syrian Nationalism: The Ideas of Butrus al-Bustani." *International Journal of Middle Eastern Studies* 2 (1980): 287–304.

TIBAWI, A. L. "The American Missionaries in Beirut and Butrus al-Bustani." *Middle Eastern Affairs*, no. 3, *St. Antony's Papers*, no. 16, ed. by Albert Hourani. London, 1963.

Mahmoud Haddad

Bustani, Emile al-   [1909–?]

Lebanese army officer.

Bustani was born to a Maronite (Christian) family in Junyah. He entered the military academy in Damascus in 1931. After graduation, he rose through the ranks of the Lebanese army to become commander in chief in 1965. Much of his success was made possible by his mentor, Fu'ad Shihab. He is perhaps best known for the Cairo Agreement—signed by him, Egypt's President Gamal Abdel Nasser, and Yasir Arafat—which governed the relationship between Lebanon and the Palestine Liberation Organization (PLO) and recognized the military rights of the PLO within Lebanon.

Bustani's Maronite critics accused him of forfeiting Lebanon's sovereignty in return for promises of Egypt's support for his 1970 candidacy for the presidency of Lebanon. While head of the army he also controlled the military-intelligence apparatus and the Shihabi political machine. Contrary to all expectations, Bustani did not run for the presidency. He withdrew from the political world after President Sulayman Franjiyya (1970–1976) replaced him as commander in chief with Iskandar Ghanim.

As'ad AbuKhalil

Bustani, Sulayman   [1856–1925]

Ottoman writer and government official.

Born to a Maronite Christian family in the village of Bkashtin in the Shuf region of Mount Lebanon, Sulayman Bustani was educated from 1863 to 1871 in the National School (al-Madrasa al-Wataniyya) in Beirut (founded by his relative Butrus al-BUSTANI). There he studied English and French in addition to Arabic and Turkish. He traveled extensively in the Arab provinces of the Ottoman Empire and beyond, to Persia and India. He assisted Butrus al-Bustani and his sons, Salim and Najib, in writing and editing the first Arabic encyclopedia, *Da'irat al-ma'arif,* and contributed to the periodical *al-Muqtataf*, published in Cairo, Egypt. In 1904, he published his most important contribution to the interaction between Arabic culture and Greek literature—the first Arabic translation of Homer's *Iliad.*

In 1908, after the coming of the YOUNG TURKS to power in Istanbul and the beginning of the second Ottoman constitutional period, Bustani published *Ibra wa Dhikra aw al-Dawla al-Uthmaniyya Qabla al-Dustur wa Ba'dahu* (A Lesson and a Memory, or the Ottoman State before the Constitution and after It), which implicitly criticized the autocratic rule of Sultan ABDÜLHAMIT II and sang the praises of liberal policies in all aspects of political, social, economic, and religious life. He hammered away at the theme of allegiance to the Ottoman state and criticized Western educational institutions in the country, which undermined that allegiance. Bustani also believed that the best way to eradicate religious fanaticism was to make the Christians serve alongside the Muslims in the Ottoman army. Further, he thought the best way to eradicate ethnic conflict was to spread the Turkish language among the population by making it mandatory in all the empire's schools.

In 1908, Bustani was elected to serve as deputy for the province of Beirut in the lower chamber of deputies in Istanbul; in 1911, he became a member of the upper chamber. In 1913, he was appointed minister for commerce, agriculture, forests, and mines—however, he resigned at the end of the following year when the COMMITTEE OF UNION AND PROGRESS, the effective Ottoman power, decided to enter World War I on the side of Germany. Bustani then belonged to a group of Ottoman officials who held that a policy of neutrality would serve the empire best.

BIBLIOGRAPHY

BUSTANI, SULAYMAN. *Ibra wa dhikra aw al-dawla al-Uthmaniyya qabla al-dustur wa ba'dahu.* Ed. by Khalid Ziyadah. Beirut, 1978.
HOURANI, ALBERT. "Sulayman al-Bustani (1856–1925)." In *Quest for Understanding: Arabic and Islamic Studies in Memory of Malcolm H. Kerr,* ed. by Samir Seikaly et al. Beirut, 1991.

Mahmoud Haddad

Butayna Tribe

One of two major factions within the Siba'a (also Asbi'a) tribe of Syria.

Siba'a is a major tribe of the ANAZA confederation of tribes. The other faction is al-Abda tribe. Both factions were divided into clans. Those clans spend the summer season north of al-Salamiyya in Syria to the east of Hama, and also east of Homs.

The Siba'a tribe as a whole numbered about 4,000 households (*bayt*) in the early 1930s. A bayt or *khayma* (tent) numbered about 5 persons, according to the Ottoman *Salname.* Thus the Siba'a would total 20,000 persons. It is not known what percentage of this total the Butayna tribe represented.

BIBLIOGRAPHY

KAHHALAH, UMAR RIDA. *Mu'jam qaba'il al-Arab al-qadima wa al-haditha* (A Dictionary of the Old and Recent Arab Tribes). 5th ed, 5 vols. Beirut, 1985.
ZAKARIYYA, AHMAD WASFI. *Asha'ir al-sham* (The Tribes of Syria). 2nd ed., 3 vols. Damascus, 1983.
————. *Jawla athariyya* (An Archaeological Tour), 2nd ed. Damascus, 1984.

Abdul-Karim Rafeq

Büyük Millet Meclisi

See Turkish Grand National Assembly

Buzo, Ali

Syrian politician.

A member of the People's party, Ali Buzo served as minister of agriculture under Nazim al-Qudsi in 1950; later in that year he was minister of national economy under Ma'ruf al-Dawalibi. He was arrested in Adib Shishakli's preemptive coup in the face of growing Druze dissent in late January 1954. He became minister of the interior late in 1954, after Shishakli's downfall; he was moved to the justice ministry and then back to the interior ministry in 1955.

BIBLIOGRAPHY

SEALE, PATRICK. *The Struggle for Syria: A Study of Post-War Arab Politics, 1945–1958.* London, 1958.

Charles U. Zenzie

C

Caid

See Qa'id

Cairo

The capital of Egypt, the largest city in the Middle East and Africa, and a major political, religious, and cultural hub for the Arab, Islamic, and African worlds.

A city with fertile hinterland and a crossroads location for river, sea, and land trade has flourished near the juncture of the Nile valley of Upper Egypt and the delta of Lower Egypt for five thousand years. In 640

Aerial view of Cairo, the Nile, and Tahrir Bridge at the lower right. (Laura Mendelson)

Midan al-Tahrir, the main square of Cairo, by the Nile river. (D.W. Lockhard)

C.E., the conquering Muslim Arabs founded al-Fustat (now Old Cairo to Westerners), which superseded the Babylon of the Romans and its predecessor, the Memphis of the pharaohs. In 969, the invading Fatimids founded al-Qahira (the Victorious), and Cairo resumed its ancient role as an imperial center. (In Arabic, Misr has long been used interchangeably for both Egypt and Cairo.) The Fatimids established the renowned mosque-university al-AZHAR, and Salah al-Din (Saladin) of the Ayyubid dynasty built the hilltop Citadel, which remained the seat of power until the mid-nineteenth century.

Its population weakened by epidemics and the ruling Mamluks' internecine warfare, Cairo fell to the Ottomans in 1517. By the seventeenth century, the

433

Tal'at Harb Square in Cairo. (Mia Bloom)

Street scene near al-Azhar Mosque. (Mia Bloom)

Cape of Good Hope route had deprived Cairo (reduced once more to the status of a provincial city) of much of its spice trade. Europeans no longer spoke with awe of the city Egyptians called the Mother of the World. In 1798, the cartographers of Napoleon's military expedition found a city of a quarter of a million people, half of the population of Cairo at its fourteenth-century peak. The narrow, irregular streets of the preindustrial city served pedestrians, riders, and pack animals well enough, and balconies provided welcome shade. Gates that closed at night and dead-end alleys marked off city quarters, which were defined mainly along religious, ethnic, and occupational lines. WAQF endowments supported mosques, schools, Sufi lodges, baths, fountains, and hospitals.

The innovation introduced during Muhammad Ali's reign (1805–1848) left few external marks on Cairo, and the city's population, checked by epidemics and competition from burgeoning Alexandria, remained stagnant until the middle of the century. After 1850, however, the population grew because of lower

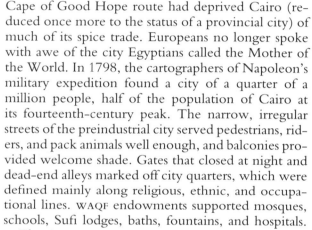

Part of the 6th October Bridge in Cairo. (Laura Mendelson)

mortality rates, an influx of people from the countryside, and the immigration of European and Levantine entrepreneurs. The Alexandria-Cairo railroad and the Suez Canal, whose construction was completed respectively in 1855 and 1869, quickened the pace of life in Cairo. The city's share of Egypt's total population, which had dipped from 5.8 percent in 1800 to a low of 4.7 percent in 1865 (when Alexandria was in full bloom), rose to 6.9 percent in 1897. Today it accounts for over 20 percent of the total population.

Under Muhammad Ali's grandson Isma'il (ruled 1863–1879) and the British occupation (1882–1922), the unused space between Cairo and its river ports Bulaq and Old Cairo was developed. Inspired by the municipal improvements effected in Paris by George Haussmann and determined to impress the Europeans at the ceremonies celebrating the Suez Canal's completion, Isma'il instructed engineer Ali Mubarak to equip the suburb Ismai'liyya with Parisian-style boulevards, traffic hubs, gardens, palaces, and even an opera house. Isma'il had two boulevards created for vehicle traffic through the old city before the bankruptcy of Egypt intervened and cost him the throne. European connoisseurs of "Oriental Cairo" persuaded his successor to found the Comité de Preservation des Monuments de l'Art Arabe (1881), and preservationists still fight to save some monuments and neighborhoods in Cairo from relentless overpopulation, decay, and demolition.

Under the British, Cairo's European population (30,000, or 6 percent of the city's population in 1897) dominated big business and filled the fashionable new quarters of HELIOPOLIS, Garden City, Ma'adi, and Zamalek with their Western-style villas. European concessionaires developed the water, gas, electricity, telephone, and tramway services and built the bridges across the Nile. Bridges made accessible the first artery to the West Bank in 1872. By 1914, the access provided by additional bridges to more arteries to the

Qasr al-Aini Street in Cairo. (Mia Bloom)

West Bank and to the islands of Rawda and Gazira resulted in rapid development. Between 1896 and 1914, electric tramways (soon replaced by motor vehicles) revolutionized transportation within the city and made possible the swift development of suburbs to the northeast (Abbasiyya, Heliopolis), the north (Shubra), and the west (Rawda, Zamalek, GIZA).

Between 1922 and 1952, the domination by Europeans of economic and political life in Egypt ebbed. In 1949, the closing of the MIXED COURTS put an end to special privileges for Westerners, and Cairo belatedly acquired a municipal government that was distinct from the national ministries. Life in the old city deteriorated (see the masterful portrayal of this time by novelist Najib MAHFUZ). Well-to-do Egyptians left for the suburbs, Egyptians from rural parts of the country crowded in, and the overflow of tens of thousands of inhabitants spilled over into the cemeteries of the City of the Dead.

Under NASSER (ruled 1952–1970), there was an acceleration of both planned and unplanned urban development. Private utility and transport concessions reverted to the state, waqf reform freed land for development, a new airport opened, and a revamped road network briefly alleviated some of the traffic congestion. The Corniche exposed Cairo to the river, and Maydan al-Tahrir became the city center. The Nile Hilton and the new Shepheard's were the first of many luxury hotels built to cater to the expanding tourist trade. Heavy industry was set up in suburban Helwan and Shubra al-Khayma. The 1956 Master Plan for Cairo recommended that the city limit its population to 3.5 million (a maximum that had already been exceeded) and advocated planned satellite communities and development on desert rather than on agricultural land. The resulting Nasr City—with government offices, housing blocks, schools, a 100,000 seat stadium, and a new campus for al-Azhar—was a success, but Muqattam City, perched on the desert cliffs, was not.

Since 1970, al-Marj Helwan metro line has been opened in Cairo, sewer and telephone systems have been upgraded, and more satellite cities have been built in the desert (Sadat City, 10th Ramadan, 6th October). The population crush nevertheless threatens to dwarf such efforts. The runaway sprawl into agricultural lands in the delta and Giza continues, while the problem-plagued desert satellite cities sit half empty and a purple cloud of polluted air regularly hangs over Cairo. Yet opportunities in regard to jobs, schooling, housing, and health care are better in Cairo than in the teeming countryside, and for that reason people from rural areas keep coming. One out of every five Egyptians lives in this third-world megalopolis of eleven million to twelve million people.

Cairo, moreover, remains the cultural capital of the Arab world. Its assets include al-Azhar and four modern universities, twenty-odd museums, a movie industry and playhouses, a radio and television industry, bookshops and publishing houses, *al-Ahram* and other periodicals, a zoo, a new opera house, the headquarters of the Arab League, and the Academy of the Arabic Language.

View of Zamalek Island, the 6th October Bridge, a Cairo broadcasting tower, and the Nile River. (Charles Issawi)

Cairo Population Estimates			
1798	264,000	1947	2,048,000
1846	257,000	1960	3,416,000
1897	590,000	1970	7,000,000
1927	1,065,000	1991	10,099,000

Sources: Janet Abu-Lughod. *Cairo, 1971;* Daniel Panzac, "The Population of Egypt in the Nineteenth Century" (*Asian and African Studies* 21 [1987]:11–32); *World Almanac, 1994.*

BIBLIOGRAPHY

Le Caire, by ANDRÉ RAYMOND (Paris, 1993), is the most up-to-date, authoritative study. In English, JANET ABU-LUGHOD's *Cairo: 1,001 Years of the City Victorious* (Princeton, N.J., 1971) is excellent, though now dated. SUSAN JANE STAFFA's *Conquest and Fusion: The Social Evolution of Cairo A.D. 642–1850* (Leiden, 1977), though loosely focused and omitting the modern period, is also useful. *Cairo: A Life-Story of 1,000 Years, 969–1969* (Cairo, n.d.) includes a good range of photographs. The article "al-Qahira" (pp. 424–444, 2nd ed., vol. 4, *Encyclopedia of Islam,* Leiden, 1978) provides a summary view; the section by J. JOMIER on modern Cairo is on pages 441 to 444. The Blue Guide *Egypt* (3rd ed., London, 1993) is valuable, and JAMES ALDRIDGE's *Cairo* (Boston, 1969) provides a readable though dated popular account.

Donald Malcolm Reid

Cairo Conference

Meeting of Middle East experts to decide on administration of British mandates Iraq and Transjordan.

The conference was convened by Winston Churchill, then Britain's colonial secretary. With the mandates of Palestine and Iraq awarded to Britain at the SAN REMO CONFERENCE (1920), Churchill wished to consult with Middle East experts, and at his request, Gertrude BELL, Sir Percy COX, T. E. LAWRENCE, Sir Kinahan CORNWALLIS, Sir Arnold T. WILSON, Iraqi minister of war Ja'far al-ASKARI, Iraqi minister of finance Sasun Effendi (Sasson HESKAYL), and others gathered in Cairo, Egypt, in March 1921. The two most significant decisions of the conference were to offer the throne of Iraq to Emir Faisal ibn Husayn (who became FAISAL I) and the emirate of Transjordan (now Jordan) to his brother ABDULLAH IBN HUSAYN. Furthermore, the British garrison in Iraq would be substantially reduced and replaced by air force squadrons, with a major base at Habbaniyya. The conference provided the political blueprint for British administration in both Iraq and Transjordan, and in offering these two regions to the Hashimite sons of Sharif Husayn ibn Ali of the Hijaz, Churchill believed that the spirit, if not the letter, of Britain's wartime promises to the Arabs would be fulfilled.

BIBLIOGRAPHY

FROMKIN, DAVID. *A Peace to End All Peace.* New York, 1989.
KLIEMAN, AARON. *The Cairo Conference of 1921.* London, 1970.

Zachary Karabell

Cairo University

Cairo University's early founding and location made it a model for later universities throughout the Arab world. Opened as the small, private Egyptian University in 1908 and taken over as a state university in 1925, it became Fu'ad I University in 1940 and Cairo University in 1954.

The retirement in 1907 of Britain's consul general, Lord Cromer, who opposed a university for fear of Egyptian nationalism, allowed the plan to proceed. Egypt's minister of education Sa'd ZAGHLUL, Qasim AMIN, and others insisted that Egypt needed a Western-style university to complement its state professional schools and the Islamic religious university of al-Azhar. Europe provided the models and a number of the professors when the university opened with Prince Ahmad FU'AD as rector in 1908.

In 1925 Fu'ad, by then king, transformed the Egyptian University into a major state institution, with colleges of arts, science, law, and engineering—the latter two being formed from existing higher schools. Other schools were similarly brought in later: engineering, agriculture, commerce, veterinary science, and the teachers college of DAR AL-'ULUM. The university now has fourteen colleges and six institutes in Cairo and several provincial branches. ALEXANDRIA (then Farouk I) UNIVERSITY split off in 1942; today Egypt has a dozen universities.

During the quarter-century after 1925, the British beat out the French for influence at the university but slowly lost out themselves to pressures to Egyptianize the faculty. The battle for coeducation was won, with the first women graduating in 1933. In the 1930s Ahmad Lutfi al-SAYYID as rector and Taha HUSAYN as dean of arts fought for university autonomy from palace and cabinet interference, while the students were inevitably caught up in turbulent national politics.

At serious cost in quality, Nasser opened Cairo and other universities more widely to provincials and the poor. His purge of 1954 crushed student and professorial opposition until after the 1967 war. President Sadat initially encouraged Islamist groups on campus to counter the left, and campus Islamists remain a major challenge to the Mubarak regime. Cairo University still has its pockets of excellence, but it is desperately underfunded and overcrowded and continues churning out thousands of poorly educated graduates onto a glutted job market.

BIBLIOGRAPHY

REID, DONALD MALCOLM. *Cairo University and the Making of Modern Egypt.* Cambridge, U.K., 1990.

Donald Malcolm Reid

Caliphate

The caliph was the temporal and spiritual ruler of Islam until the office was abolished in 1924.

On March 3, 1924, the Grand National Assembly of the young Republic of Turkey passed legislation to abolish the Ottoman caliphate, which also marked the end of the caliphate as an Islamic institution. The Ottoman dynasty's claim to the office had been recognized in the Muslim world in the nineteenth century, even though its historical basis was controversial. This claim was based on an alleged transfer of caliphal authority to the HOUSE OF OSMAN after Ottoman armies conquered Mamluk Egypt. There, an Abbasid caliph with descent from the Quraysh tribe of the Prophet Muhammad had been maintained as a dependent figurehead.

Ottoman SULTANs advanced their role as caliph in the nineteenth century, when the Muslim world was falling under imperialist domination. The caliphate served as a psychological rallying point for colonized Muslims against imperialist rule. Even though the Ottoman government failed to reap practical gains from the title during World War I (see ARAB REVOLT), the impending collapse of the empire mobilized Muslims worldwide to campaign for the retention of the caliphate as a locus of strength and unity. The India Khilafat Congress was especially active in this cause during the peace negotiations of 1919, because Indian Muslims sought self-determination based on allegiance to the caliph.

After the Ottomans were defeated in the war, the Anglo–French occupation of Constantinople (now Istanbul), the seat of the caliphate, further compromised the authority of Sultan-Caliph MEHMET VI VAHIDETTIN. Mustafa Kemal (ATATÜRK) and other leaders of the Anatolian independence movement declared that a principal objective was to liberate the sultanate and the caliphate from occupation forces. At the same time, Vahidettin denounced the resistance on Islamic grounds. Political and military circumstances, however, gradually transformed the nationalists' attitude toward the caliphate. In view of the successes of the independence struggle and the complicity of Vahidettin with the occupying powers to undermine the movement, the rival Ankara government promulgated in January 1921 the Fundamental Law that established the nation's sovereignty. On November 1, 1922, it passed legislation to abolish the Ottoman monarchy, while separating the sultanate from the caliphate, maintaining it as a vague spiritual authority. On November 16, Vahidettin sought asylum with British authorities and left Constantinople for Malta and later, the Hijaz.

The new law authorized the Turkish Grand National Assembly to select a meritorious member of the Ottoman dynasty as caliph. As the Muslim world debated the legitimacy of a caliphate without political authority, the assembly conferred the title of caliph on ABDÜLMECIT II (1868–1944), son of Sultan Abdülaziz. Rescuing the caliphate from the defunct monarchy was a tactical step toward abolishing the House of Osman and soothing domestic and international Muslim public opinion.

Foreign reaction was apathetic as the Khilafat Congress recognized the new caliph. In Turkey, though, the caliph quickly became the focus around which the proponents of the constitutional monarchy rallied. In October 1923, Mustafa Kemal declared the Turkish republic. The designation of the president of the republic as the head of state further compromised the caliph's position.

In December 1923, Indian Muslim leaders Amir Ali and Aga Khan, the IMAM of the ISMA'ILI sect, wrote a letter to the Turkish prime minister İsmet İNÖNÜ and urged retention of the caliphate. Pro-constitutional-monarchy Turkish newspapers publicized the letter, which led to the arrest and trial of the editors in the Independence Tribunals. The Indian plea only accelerated the end. The Kemalists denounced the intervention of the two Muslim leaders as interference in the affairs of the new state and discredited them as Shi'a British proxies. Indian religious scholars called for an international conference to determine the status of the caliphate. On March 3, 1924, the assembly passed legislation eliminating the office as part of a string of secularizing measures, including the abolition of religious education. The Kemalists argued that the caliphate was superfluous because the governments of Muslim countries should administer to both temporal and religious affairs. The subsequent policy of the Kemalists to regulate religious life precluded the separation of state and religion in Turkey.

Abdülmecit left Turkey for Switzerland and later France. Since Turkey had emerged as the strongest independent country in the Muslim world, its abandonment of the caliphate elicited concern and disapproval from colonized Muslims, while in Turkey and other independent Muslim countries there was relative indifference. There was no Muslim consensus on how to respond to the Turkish fait accompli. The SHARIF OF MECCA, Husayn, immediately put forward his claim, which was sanctioned by Vahidettin. While Husayn had a legitimate claim due to his prestige and descent from Quraysh, by 1924 he lacked any political authority. In fact, Indian Muslims were inclined toward his rival ABD AL-AZIZ IBN SA'UD of Najd. Also as possible candidates emerged King Fu'ad of Egypt and Imam Yahya of Yemen as well as the Moroccan and Afghan kings. Others advocated the continued recognition of Abdülmecit as the legitimate caliph.

There could not be agreement on a single candidate, when there was not even consensus on the continuation of the office. A Caliphate Congress (*mu'tamar al-khilafa*) convened in Cairo in May 1926 with the participation of ULAMA (Islamic clergy) from several Muslim countries. At this conference King Fu'ad hoped to promote his claim, but the relative apathy toward the meeting and disagreement about eligibility requirements resulted in its adjournment with only the group's affirmation of the requirement for a caliph. Not only did the caliphate emerge as an ever-more incongruent political institution in a Muslim world that was becoming increasingly fragmented, but also the issue of caliphal succession became embroiled in the nationalist rivalries and inward-looking struggles of the Muslim countries.

BIBLIOGRAPHY

ARNOLD, THOMAS W. *The Caliphate.* London, 1965 (in particular the concluding chapter by Sylvia Haim).
TOYNBEE, ARNOLD J. "The Abolition of the Ottoman Caliphate by the Turkish Great National Assembly and the Progress of the Secularization Movement in the Islamic World." In *Survey of International Affairs, 1925*, vol. 1: *The Islamic World since the Peace Settlement.* London, 1927.

Hasan Kayali

Calligraphy

Fine Islamic writing as an art form.

In the Islamic context, calligraphy refers to the artistic writing of the ARABIC SCRIPT, either in the Arabic language or in other languages transcribed with the Arabic script. Originally, Islamic calligraphy was an expedient to ensure legibility. It soon became the primary visual art in the realms of Islamic religious influence and remained so at least until the nineteenth century.

Islamic calligraphy shares the characteristics of other fine arts: a long and well-documented history, an extensive roster of renowned practitioners, an elaborate educational protocol, a wide selection of acknowledged masterpieces, a variety of media that are peculiar to it, and a wide range of accepted techniques and styles. In addition, there are religious and cultural regulations that pertain to the teaching, production, and display of Islamic calligraphy. There are also ancillary professionals and amateurs who produce the tools and materials used in the production of the art works, such as inks, marble paper, and pens. Finally, a well-developed body of literature deals with the criticism and appreciation of Islamic calligraphy.

From the beginning of the Islamic period, and possibly substantially before it, two types of writing were used, according to occasion, in the Hijaz region of the Arabian peninsula. One was a simple, loose, and informal script for everyday use. The other—reserved for special purposes, especially religious uses that demanded a spectacular presentation—was the "dry" or stiff style of writing commonly, albeit incorrectly, called Kufic. In Islamic times, this became the favored style for Qur'anic transcriptions, due to its gravity, legibility, grace, and sheer visual impact.

By the tenth century, new scripts had taken shape from the earlier, informal writing and had gained in popularity. Because the shapes and sizes of the letters were calculated geometrically, these scripts were called "the proportioned scripts." They include the Thuluth, Naskh, and Muhaqqaq scripts. These are commonly referred to as Naskhi (supposedly meaning cursive), a name that has no basis in history.

Four important calligraphers, working in Baghdad during the Abbasid caliphate, founded the modern trend in Islamic calligraphy. These were Muhammad ibn Muqla (d. 940), his brother Abu Abdullah ibn Muqla (d. 939), Ali ibn Hilal, called Ibn al-Bawwab (d. 1022), and Yaqut al-Musta'simi (d. 1298). Through the works and teachings of these masters, the art of calligraphy radiated to other important Islamic cultural centers.

By the sixteenth century, the center of Islamic calligraphy was to be found in the Constantinople (now Istanbul) of the Ottoman Empire. There the pivotal Şeyh Hamdullah (1429–1520), a lifelong calligrapher, completely revised the structure of the basic scripts of Thuluth and Naskh in particular, giving them a more precise, lighter, and more dynamic

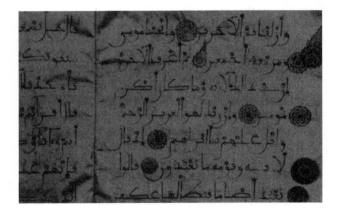

Handwritten page of the Qur'an. (Government of Saudi Arabia)

look. Since the life and teaching of this great master, the Ottoman Turkish method has been paramount. This method is distinguished by its special teaching protocols, its attention to detail, and its insistence on the highest standards.

Another Ottoman master, Mehmet Asat Yesari (d. 1798), took the Persian style Nasta'liq and, while maintaining its basic rules, transformed it into a powerful visual instrument, especially in its large (Celali) version.

Other trends in Islamic calligraphy of significant historical and artistic merit have existed continuously in the Maghrib-Andalusian orbit, in the Persian orbit, and in China. Although Islamic calligraphy reached its apogee in the late nineteenth century, it is experiencing a revival today, in particular due to the efforts of the Research Centre for Islamic History, Art, and Culture in Istanbul (IRCICA). The art continues to reign supreme in its ability to convey in the most emphatic way the written Islamic texts.

BIBLIOGRAPHY

The best early sources on Islamic calligraphy are in Arabic and Persian; the best on later developments are in Turkish.

DÉROCHE, FRANÇOIS. *The Abbasid Tradition of Qur'ans of the 8th to the 10th Centuries A.D.* Oxford, 1992.

JAMES, DAVID. *The Decorated Word: Qur'ans of the 17th to 19th Centuries.* Oxford, 1993.

LINGS, MARTIN. *The Qur'anic Art of Calligraphy and Illumination.* London, 1976.

SAFADI, Y. H. *Islamic Calligraphy.* London, 1978.

SAFWAT, NABIL. *The Art of the Pen: Calligraphy of the 14th to 19th Centuries.* Oxford, 1996.

ZAKARIYA, MUHAMMAD. "Islamic Calligraphy: A Technical Overview." In *Brocade of the Pen: The Art of Islamic Writing,* ed. by Carol Garret Fisher. East Lansing, Mich., 1991.

Muhammad Zakariya

Cambon, Jules   [1845–1935]

French governor-general of Algeria, 1891–1897.

Cambon entered the cabinet of the director-general of Algerian Civil Affairs in 1874 and served as prefect of Constantine in 1878 and 1879, after Algeria had been placed by France under civil government instead of military rule. As governor-general, Cambon's attempts to slow the integration of Algeria into France's metropolitan administrative structure won him the enmity of the settlers, who forced his resignation. He later held the post of French ambassador to the United States, Spain, and Germany.

BIBLIOGRAPHY

TABOUIS, GENEVIÈVE R. *The Life of Jules Cambon.* London, 1938.

Kenneth J. Perkins

Cambon, Paul   [1843–1924]

Resident general of France in Tunisia, 1882–1886.

Cambon's efforts to consolidate French colonialism in Tunisia led to the establishment of the protectorate, made formal in 1883 with the LA MARSA CONVENTION. Cambon's residency was also marked by an unresolved dispute with the French military command over their respective areas of jurisdiction in the province.

BIBLIOGRAPHY

ABUN-NASR, JAMIL. *A History of the Maghrib in the Islamic Period.* London, 1987.

CAMBON, HENRI. *Histoire de la régence de Tunis.* Paris, 1948.

Matthew S. Gordon

Cambon–Lansdowne Agreement

Pact between France and Great Britain affecting each country's activities in Egypt and Morocco.

After having been rivals for a long time, France and Great Britain mutually agreed to desist. According to the agreement, France had total freedom of action in Morocco; meanwhile France would stop interfering with English financial activities in Egypt, as it had since 1882. The English enjoyed immediate but limited advantages. As for the French, it meant getting potential interests and indicated the end of an obsessional opposition. The agreement took place on April 8, 1904, in a general atmosphere of mutual reconciliation, for the two countries were worried about Germany's growing power.

Rémy Leveau

Camels

Domesticated ruminant of central Asia, Arabia, and North Africa.

A domesticated animal, with one or two humps, that is used as a mode of transportation in the Middle East, the camel is a survivor of an almost vanished

Camels in Judean Desert. (Mia Bloom)

Group of camels at a way station in a Sudanese village. (D.W. Lockhard)

group of ungulates (hoofed mammals) that once populated all the large land masses of the world except Australia. Its close relatives are the South American llama, alpaca, guanaco, and vicuña. The only camels existing today are two domesticated species: the Arabian dromedary, *Camelus dromedarius* (or *ibil*), which has one hump and is used for riding; and the two-humped Bactrian camel, *Camelus bactrianus,* which has shorter legs and is more heavily built. A few survive in the Gobi desert.

Traditional belief has it that one-humped camels do not adapt well to cold or moist climates nor the two-humped camel to extremely hot climates. Both store fat in their humps, have long necks suitable for feeding on bushes and trees, and have padded feet suited for travel on sand but ill-suited for travel on mud. Both have the capacity to go long intervals without water. Camels do not store water as some folk stories allege. Rather, they conserve it through

highly efficient kidneys that allow them to process water with a high concentration of impurities; they also have the capacity to absorb heat by allowing their blood temperature to rise, without ill effect. The horn of Africa constitutes the largest and most abundant camel territory in the world and today Somalia alone has a camel population exceeding four million. Camel milk is a dietary staple in Somalia. Camels exist as a form of wealth and nourishment and form part of the traditional bride-price.

BIBLIOGRAPHY

BULLIET, RICHARD. *The Camel and the Wheel.* New York, 1990.

Mia Bloom

Arab tribe migrating in Jordan. (D.W. Lockhard)

Cameri

Tel Aviv's municipal theater.

In 1944, a group of actors led by Josef MILLO founded the Cameri to establish a young, modern, avant-garde theater in Palestine. It created a forum for works of native Hebrew playwrights. Its first successful production was a translation of Goldoni's *A Servant of Two Masters* (1945). Its first indigenous Israeli stage character was presented by Moshe Shamir's play *Hu Halakh Besadot* (1948; He Walked in the Fields).

During the first twenty-five years, the Cameri staged 160 productions. By the 1970s, it had become established and was no longer considered a vanguard of innovative theater. Nevertheless, in 1988, the Cameri theater appointed the controversial and avant-garde dramatist Hanoch LEVIN as its playwright-in-residence.

Ann Kahn

Camp David Accords

Agreements signed by Egypt, Israel, and the United States on September 17, 1978.

The Camp David Accords were a major step in the Middle East peace process initiated by the dramatic visit of Egypt's president, Anwar al-SADAT, to Israel from November 19 to 20, 1977, and culminating in the peace treaty between Egypt and Israel, signed in Washington, D.C., on March 26, 1979. Sadat's visit to Jerusalem began a series of direct negotiations that bogged down over Israel's withdrawal from and demilitarization of Sinai, the future status of Gaza and the West Bank (occupied by Israel in June 1967), and terms of normalization between Israel and Egypt. When it appeared that the negotiations would collapse, U.S. President Jimmy CARTER invited President Sadat and Prime Minister Menachem BEGIN of Israel to the presidential retreat at Camp David, Maryland.

The Camp David conference, beginning on September 5, ended with two accords signed by Egypt, Israel, and the United States: "Framework for Conclusion for Peace in the Middle East" and "Framework for Conclusion of a Peace Treaty Between Egypt and Israel." Participants included President Carter, President Sadat, Prime Minister Begin, their foreign and defense ministers, and a large number of top civilian and military officials. The acrimonious relationship between Sadat and Begin threatened to disrupt the conference, but President Carter's personal intervention and moderating influence saved it from failure. Later, Sadat and Begin received the Nobel Peace Prize.

The framework for an Egypt–Israel peace called for a treaty, in which both parties would apply the principles of UN SECURITY COUNCIL RESOLUTION 242, within three months. Terms would be implemented between two and three years after signing the document. Israel's armed forces were to withdraw from Sinai, and Egypt's sovereignty up to the international border was recognized. The right of free passage for Israel's ships through the Suez Canal, the Strait of Tiran, the Gulf of Suez, and the Gulf of Aqaba was guaranteed. A highway was to be constructed between Sinai and Jordan through southern Israel, with guaranteed free passage by vehicles from Egypt and Jordan. Arrangements were to be made for demilitarized zones and limitations on military forces along the border, under surveillance of UN observers. Following the signing of a peace treaty and completion of interim withdrawal by Israel, normal relations would be established between Israel and Egypt, including "full recognition . . . diplomatic, economic and cultural relations;

termination of economic boycotts and barriers to the free movement of goods and people; and mutual protection of citizens."

The framework for Middle East peace focused on arrangements for Palestinian self-rule in Gaza and the West Bank. It, too, was based on Resolution 242, stating that "Peace requires respect for the sovereignty, territorial integrity and political independence of every state in the area and their right to live in peace within secure and recognized boundaries free from threats or acts of force." This framework was "to constitute a basis for peace not only between Egypt and Israel, but also between Israel and each of its other neighbors."

With this objective in mind, Egypt, Israel, Jordan, and representatives of the Palestinians were to negotiate a three-stage plan for the future of Gaza and the West Bank. First, in a transitional period not to exceed five years, full autonomy would be provided to the inhabitants of the West Bank and Gaza, followed by withdrawal of Israel's military government and its civilian administration. Second, Egypt, Israel, and Jordan were to agree on modalities for election of a self-governing authority; Palestinians in the Egyptian and Jordanian delegations, or other Palestinians mutually agreed upon, could be included in the negotiations. The parties were to reach agreement on powers and responsibilities of the self-governing authority. Following withdrawal of its troops, Israel's remaining forces would be "redeployed . . . into specified security locations." "A strong local police force," which could include Jordanians, was to be established. Israelis and Jordanians would participate in joint patrols to assure border security. Third, the five-year transitional period was to begin following establishment of the self-governing authority (administrative council); no later than its third year, final status negotiations were to start, leading to a peace treaty with Jordan by the end of the period. "The solution . . . must . . . recognize the legitimate rights of the Palestinian people and their just requirements."

During the transitional period, representatives of Egypt, Jordan, Israel, and the Palestinian self-governing authority were to constitute a continuing committee to agree on readmission of persons displaced from the West Bank and Gaza during and after the ARAB–ISRAEL WAR of 1967.

Egypt and Israel agreed that the following principles and provisions should apply to peace treaties between Israel and Egypt, Jordan, Syria, and Lebanon: full recognition, abolition of economic boycotts, and guaranteed protection of each other's citizens.

Continued disagreement between Israel and Egypt over interpretation of the two framework agreements prolonged the three-month period within which a peace treaty was to be signed. It took several more rounds of negotiations, mediation by the U.S. secretary of state, and a Middle East visit by President Carter before the treaty's terms were accepted by both sides. The treaty was signed, more than six months later, on March 26, 1979.

There was strong opposition to the Camp David Accords. In Israel's 120-member KNESSET, 84 members voted in favor of the agreements, 19 against, and 17 abstained. Sixteen members of Begin's LIKUD party either abstained or voted against the agreements, and a third of his sixty-nine-member government coalition abstained or opposed. A far higher percentage of the opposition than of his own coalition supported the prime minister.

Those who failed to support Begin argued that he had betrayed basic principles of the Likud, which opposed any territorial concessions for peace and adamantly rejected recognition of the Palestinian people as a party to negotiations.

In Egypt, opposition elements including Islamic, Nasserist, and other Arab nationalist groups protested the peace negotiations and agreements with Israel. Most members of the Arab League broke ties with Egypt, and the Arab League headquarters were removed from Cairo. The chain of events from Sadat's initiative to the 1979 peace treaty led to Egypt's isolation from the Arab world for several years. It would be nearly a decade before its position as a leader was reestablished and League headquarters were returned to Cairo.

Although the Israel-Egypt peace process did lead to the normalization of relations, including the establishment of embassies in each country, many regarded it as a "cold peace" with low-level trade exchanges, few Egyptian visitors to Israel, and a failure to implement several provisions of the Camp David Accords, especially those in the Middle East peace framework related to Jordan and the Palestinians.

BIBLIOGRAPHY

BAR-SIMAN-TOV, YAACOV. *Israel and the Peace Process, 1977–1982: In Search of Legitimacy for Peace.* Albany, N.Y., 1994.

DAYAN, MOSHE. *Breakthrough: A Personal Account of the Egypt–Israel Peace Negotiations.* London, 1981.

KAMEL, MOHAMMED IBRAHIM. *The Camp David Accords: A Testimony.* London, 1986.

QUANDT, WILLIAM B. *Camp David: Peace Making and Politics.* Washington, D.C., 1986.

TELHAMI, SHIBLEY. *Power and Leadership in International Bargaining: The Path to the Camp David Accords.* New York, 1990.

Don Peretz

Camus, Albert   [1913–1960]

French Algerian author.

Camus was born in eastern Algeria at Mondovi near today's Annaba. His father represented grape-growing and wine-making interests and also served as a Zouave, an Algerian member of a French infantry unit. He died in 1914 from wounds received at the Battle of the Marne in France. His mother was illiterate and of Spanish descent. Camus grew up with her and her extended family in the poor Belcourt neighborhood of Algiers. He received a degree in philosophy from the University of Algiers. During the 1930s, he publicized Kabyle deprivations and briefly joined the Algerian Communist party. He distinguished himself in the Resistance by editing *Combat*. He associated with French existentialists Jean-Paul Sartre and Simone de Beauvoir. While his writings have "existentialist" themes, he claimed that he did not subscribe to that philosophy. His novels include *The Stranger* (1942), *The Plague* (1947), and *The Fall* (1957). His most important essays are *The Myth of Sisyphus* (1942) and *The Rebel* (1951). He also wrote short stories and plays. He received the Nobel Prize for literature in 1957. During the war of independence, Camus proposed a French–Algerian federation that was rejected by both sides. He died in an automobile accident.

BIBLIOGRAPHY

LOTTMAN, HERBERT. *Albert Camus: A Biography.* Garden City, N.Y., 1979.

Phillip C. Naylor

Canning, Stratford   [1786–1880]

The most influential European diplomat in the Ottoman Empire during the first half of the nineteenth century.

While still an undergraduate at Cambridge, Canning (Viscount Stratford de Redcliffe) joined the British Foreign Office then headed by his cousin, George Canning. His first posting to Constantinople (now Istanbul) as secretary to the British mission occurred in 1808 in the midst of the Napoleonic Wars. Upon his superior's departure, Stratford Canning became the acting chief. Despite his inexperience and with even less than the usual guidance from home, he secured the Treaty of BUCHAREST in 1812. By ending the war between the Russian and the Ottoman Empires, this treaty freed the Russians to repel the invasion of Napoléon Bonaparte. He then left for other assignments, but from 1825 to 1827, Canning returned to Constantinople to confront two problems: the Greek revolt and the deprivatization of the British consular service in the Levant (countries of the eastern Mediterranean).

Despite Canning's best efforts, he failed to mediate an end to the Greek conflict. As for the second, until the beginning of the nineteenth century, British affairs in the Ottoman Empire—commercial, consular, and diplomatic—had been managed by the Levant Company, which had been granted a monopoly to trade with the eastern Mediterranean by British royal charter in 1581. The transformation of British interests in the East, particularly the growth of political and military concerns as a result of the Napoleonic Wars, undermined the old arrangement. The British government took over direct responsibility for the embassy in 1804 and the consular posts in 1825; Canning's skill in overseeing this transition helped established Britain's diplomatic preeminence.

After his Ottoman tour had ended, Canning embarked upon an unremarkable parliamentary career, which quickly revealed that his skills were far greater as a diplomat than as a politician. Consequently, in 1831/32 he returned to Constantinople on a successful mission to fix a more favorable frontier for the Kingdom of Greece, which was newly independent of Ottoman rule.

His last period of service in Constantinople was the most important and the longest, from 1842 to 1858, occasionally interrupted by efforts to resign. Canning played a key role in the major events of the era: Russian intervention in the region culminating in the CRIMEAN WAR and the TANZIMAT reforms—most notably the Islahat Fermanı (Reform Decree) of 1856. He also succeeded in removing from the Ottoman realm to the British Museum such archeological discoveries as the Bodrum frieze and the winged lions of Nineveh.

Although Canning began his career by promoting peace with Russia, he spent much of it as the Romanov empire's implacable foe. Ottoman weakness in the face of the Russian threat forced ever greater dependence on Britain's diplomatic and military support, which Canning offered at a price—a program of internal reform that insisted upon the equality of the empire's Muslim and non-Muslim subjects. Canning's experience and personality backed by Britain's dominant position enabled him to secure Ottoman assent, at least on paper, to the effective annulment of Islamic law on this question.

Although he maintained close personal ties with the then-reigning sultan, ABDÜLMECIT I, his deepest sympathies were reserved for the Christian subjects of the empire, whose improved status, he hoped,

would maintain Ottoman integrity in the face of Russian ambition. Later in his life, when that hope proved false, he welcomed the end of Ottoman control in the Balkans.

BIBLIOGRAPHY

LANE-POOLE, STANLEY. *The Life of the Right Honourable Stratford Canning, Viscount Stratford de Radcliffe,* 2 vols. London, 1888.
TEMPERLY, HAROLD. *England and the Near East: The Crimea.* London, 1936.

Benjamin Braude

Cantonnement/Refoulement

French colonial policies.

These French policies were meant—first in the mid-nineteenth century and then in the years just before independence—to confine sections of the Algerian population to areas that could be supervised by the colonial army. This was to prevent access to agricultural land by the local population or to areas judged strategically important by the French. By the independence of Algeria in 1962, an estimated three million rural Algerians had been displaced, thus adding considerably to the extremely high urbanization rates the new government faced as a result of these earlier cantonnement and refoulement policies.

BIBLIOGRAPHY

RUEDY, JOHN. *Modern Algeria: The Origins and Development of a Nation.* Bloomington, Ind., 1992.

Dirk Vandewalle

Capitulations

Term derived from capitula (chapter or paragraph, in Italian) that refers to the clauses of an international treaty, particularly between a Muslim state and a European state.

The term *capitulation* was originally a "privilege" given by a powerful Middle East government, such as the Ottoman Empire, to a weaker government in Europe. An early Ottoman treaty of this type was negotiated between Sultan Selim I and Venice in 1517. Formerly Venice had enjoyed exclusive trade privileges with Mamluk Egypt in order to expedite the profitable spice trade. There is a similarity between this type of privilege (and the accompanying attitude) and the type of privileges the Chinese emperors accorded to lesser lands of Asia that wished to trade with China. The traditional attitude might be stated as follows: "Our realm is self-sufficient and superior; thus we have no need to trade with you. But because we are a civilized people, we show our beneficence in this manner."

Next consider the types of privileges accorded by such treaties. The most important clause dealt with mutual trade relations. Both governments agreed to provide, in their respective countries, a place for warehousing items to be traded; protection for those goods from theft or damage; and on the amount of tariff to be charged ad valorem for each item. Protection was also accorded to the vessels delivering the merchandise, and the flag under which these vessels could enter territorial waters was carefully controlled. For example, France obtained an *imtiyaz* (capitulation) early in the sixteenth century; thereafter, until Britain received its own *imtiyaz* about 1580, British ships entering Ottoman waters had to fly the flag of France (and doubtless pay for the privilege). In case of shipwreck, the capitulation provided for protection, docking, and repair.

To these general commercial clauses were gradually added legal clauses dealing with the right of extraterritoriality, protection of foreign personnel working in the trade facility, and specification of the court that held primary jurisdiction in case of a dispute. Generally speaking, if the trading company was established in a country where a diplomatic representative of its home country was in residence, the primary jurisdiction over, say, a foreign merchant committing a crime in the host country would be the merchant's own consular court. Often, however, in the case of a capital crime, such as the rape or murder of a Muslim subject, the primary jurisdiction would be the Muslim court.

These were provisions of what might be called the ordinary capitulation-type treaty. This arrangement underwent important changes in the eighteenth and nineteenth centuries as certain European countries, and the United States, grew much more powerful than their counterparts in the Middle East. First, foreign businesses selling their goods in the Middle East, as a means to save costs, often sought out local Muslims, Christians, or Jews to assist in their transactions: interpreters and expediters to speed wares through customs, longshoremen, workers, secretaries, managers, agents, and sales personnel. Gradually these persons were placed officially under the protection of the company or the foreign government consular service by a device known as a *berat* (minor government decree). A bearer of such protection was known as *beratlı* (bearer of a privilege). At first these berats were issued under the auspices of the grand vizier or his subordinates. Later, some embassies issued berats from their own chanceries.

Because the Muslim populations often were more interested in learning Arabic, Persian, or Turkish, it fell to the Christian and Jewish minorities to learn the languages of western Europe. Hence, many minority families came to be closely associated with Western firms and their governments. Often this relationship proved very advantageous financially. These subject peoples' *beratlı* status extended to them, and often to their relatives and family, the privileges of extraterritoriality and the protection of a powerful foreign country; thus, in the nineteenth century, Muslim government officials began to harbor doubts about their loyalty. The *beratlı* held a kind of dual citizenship. Thus, capitulations, originally straightforward trade agreements, became intertwined with issues of national sovereignty for Muslim governments, and for powerful governments of Europe, with the protection of their property, trade agreements, missionaries, and "beratlı agents" for powerful governments of Europe. For some members of minority communities, the berat had become a cover for illegal activities. In the case of outright disagreement, the governments of Europe and the United States often resorted to gunboat diplomacy or "showing the flag" to coerce states of the Middle East. If this did not have the desired effect, such states as imperial Russia often resorted to open warfare. Thus, the Ottoman government and other states of the Middle East in the nineteenth century could not protect locally made crafts or manufactures from cheap imports because foreign powers blocked the raising of tariffs, nor could they directly punish violations of law within their own borders.

Various states of the Middle East, in the twentieth century, sought to abolish these trade treaties that had been turned into major tools of imperialist intervention and control by foreign powers. Ottoman Turkey, upon entering World War I on the side of Germany in 1914, announced the abolition of the capitulation agreements, a move that was not fully approved by Germany. The capitulations had become so burdensome that they constituted grounds for nations of the Middle East to join with a friendly power like Germany against the exploiting states of Europe. True to their own attitudes toward weaker states, when the Allied powers of Europe won the war, they quickly declared the capitulations once again in full force. Only after Turkey's war of independence (1919–1922) were they forced to accept the end of these lopsided trade treaties under the terms of the LAUSANNE Treaty of 1923. At the CAIRO CONFERENCE in 1921, establishing the semi-independence of Egypt from Britain, the powers of Europe agreed to lift most clauses of the capitulations, but the mixed courts, where foreign litigation had taken place, were left in place.

BIBLIOGRAPHY

INALCIK, HALIL. "Imtiyazat." In *Encyclopaedia of Islam,* 2nd ed., vol. 3.

C. Max Kortepeter

Capsali Family

Prominent Jewish family from Crete.

The Capsali family attained high positions both in Crete and in Istanbul under the Ottomans. Moses ben Elijah Capsali moved to Byzantine Constantinople and became a rabbi in the fifteenth century, serving as the first chief rabbi in the city after the Ottoman conquest in 1453. He became a powerful Jewish figure throughout the Ottoman Empire. Elkanah Capsali was a rabbi and constable (head of the Jewish community) in Candia (now Iráklion), Crete, who assisted Sephardic refugees arriving from Spain in 1492/93. His son, Elijah Capsali, was also a rabbi in Candia and, beginning in 1523, the constable. He was also a noted historian.

Michael R. Fischbach

Carlowitz, Treaty of

Ended Austria–Ottoman war; Ottoman Empire conceded much of Hungary to Austria.

After an unsuccessful siege of Vienna in 1683 and sixteen years of war with Austria, the Ottomans conceded defeat and signed the peace of Carlowitz on January 26, 1699. Austria received all of Hungary except the Banat of Temişvar, Transylvania, Croatia, and Slavonia. The treaty marked the first time the Ottoman Empire was forced to surrender territory to a European power.

BIBLIOGRAPHY

LEWIS, BERNARD. *The Emergence of Modern Turkey.* New York, 1961.

Zachary Karabell

Carmel, Moshe   [1911–   ]

Israeli general and politician.

Born in Poland, Carmel emigrated to Palestine in 1924 and became a member of the Kibbutz Naan in 1939. He was a leading general in the Haganah and commanded the northern district during the Arab–Israel War of 1948. A prominent MAPAM member, Carmel served in the Knesset (parliament) for many years and was minister of communication during two periods (1955–1959, 1965–1969).

BIBLIOGRAPHY

New Standard Jewish Encyclopedia. New York, 1977.

Zachary Karabell

Carmel, Mount

Mountain in northern Israel.

Mount Carmel is the northwest projection of the Samarian mountain range in Israel, culminating in a Mediterranean coastal promontory reaching 1,800 feet (549 m) above sea level. Since prebiblical times its conspicuous shape has made the Carmel a base for religious worship of many different kinds. In modern times the mountain was sparsely populated until the expansion of the port city of HAIFA up its northern slope. Most areas of Mount Carmel are currently designated nature and forestry reserves by the government of Israel.

Zev Maghen

Carpets, Persian

Heavy woven floor coverings with traditional patterns; considered works of art today.

The twentieth century witnessed unparalleled expansion of Persian pile carpet weaving (*qalibafi*) in Iran. Gone were court manufactories and extensive weaving by nomadic tribal peoples. In their place came commercialization of the craft, the gradual introduction of quality controls and standards, and an unprecedented availability of a wide variety of Persian carpets of tribal, village, town, and city provenance for sale in the bazaars and abroad. Throughout the Iranian plateau, Persian carpets generally appear on the floor of all rooms except for the kitchen and bathroom. Often they constitute a room's main or only art, taking the place of a mural or large painting on the wall in Western homes.

Thus, Persian carpets achieved quite a high point in the twentieth century, although Persian pile carpet weaving is generally thought to have experienced its golden age with the curvilinear "city" designs of the Safavid period (1501–1736 C.E.) and with the rectilinear "tribal" carpets of the QAJAR DYNASTY (1796–1925). Art historians, oriental carpet experts, and scholars generally think twentieth-century Persian carpets inferior because of their commercial production circumstances and less intricately designed patterns.

Early in the century, Isfahan and then Qom and other new production centers joined such famous traditional weaving centers as Kerman and Tabriz in producing carpets, almost all with traditional designs, but with synthetic dyes, mechanically spun yarn, and often the help of trained designers. Earlier CAUCASUS design traditions were continued in Ardabil and surrounding towns. Throughout Iran, classical medallion, garden, hunting, and prayer carpet designs continue to be produced, along with hybrid designs exhibiting the mutual influence of cartoon-prepared city patterns of the medallion sorts and the memory-produced repeat patterns typical of tribal weaving—Afshar, BAKHTIARI, QASHQA'I, and TURKMEN.

All the major twentieth-century Persian carpet design types appear to pay tribute in a decorative or symbolic way to springtime or paradise gardens, important culture-specific images in Persian art since PERSEPOLIS (begun in 518 B.C.E.); they feature columns, representing a sacred, or paradisial, grove of trees. The existence of the Pazyryk Carpet (at the Hermitage Museum in St. Petersburg) is evidence that pile carpet weaving existed in Central Asia and on the Iranian plateau from at least the Achaemenid period (559–330 B.C.E.), although few Persian carpets or even fragments have survived from before the sixteenth century C.E.

In the 1960s and after, Iranian scholars began paying attention to Persian carpets from technical, sociological, and cultural perspectives, which resulted in the shifting of predominant scholarship in this field from Europe to Iran. In particular, as nomadic and seminomadic communities have dwindled in size, Iranian scholars have provided records of their textile traditions, especially for Turkmen, Qashqa'i, Shahsavan, and Kurdish carpets.

In the Islamic republican era, beginning in 1979, carpet production continued unabated, although the U.S. embargo on Iranian goods in the 1980s changed the export market for Persian carpets. The same decade also witnessed a dramatic increase in the production of flat-weave products called *gelim* (Turkish, *kilim*) with their mostly uncomplicated geometric patterns. The Carpet Museum of Iran, inaugurated in 1979, the last year of the PAHLAVI DYNASTY (1925–1979), remains the world's best showcase for carpets in the 1990s.

BIBLIOGRAPHY

A. C. EDWARDS, *The Persian Carpet: A Survey of the Carpet Weaving Industry of Persia* (1953; reprint, 1975), surveys the field with its author's eyewitness account of the industry as of the early 1950s. P. R. J. FORD, *The Oriental Carpet: A History and Guide to Traditional Motifs, Patterns, and Symbols* (1981), describes and illustrates all extant Persian carpet designs according to provenance and pattern. M. HILLMANN, *Persian Carpets* (1984), suggests cultural dimensions of typical Persian carpet designs, including assorted symbolic features. The articles "Pahlavi Period" and "Post-Pahlavi Period," under the entry "Carpets" in *Encyclopedia Iranica*, vol. 4 (1991), treat production and marketing.

Michael C. Hillmann

Carter, Jimmy   [1924–   ]

Thirty-ninth president of the United States (1977–1980); founder of the Carter Center in Atlanta, Georgia.

James Earl Carter, Jr., was born on October 1, 1924, in Plains, Georgia. After serving as governor of Georgia for one term, from 1971 to 1975, he rose from relative obscurity to win the Democratic nomination and then defeat incumbent President Gerald Ford in 1976.

Carter ended the highly personal diplomacy of Henry Kissinger and stressed the role of human rights considerations in guiding U.S. foreign policy. His crowning achievement was the signing of the CAMP DAVID ACCORDS in 1978 between Egyptian President Anwar al-Sadat and Israeli Prime Minister Menachem Begin. Sadat initiated the peace process with his 1977 visit to Jerusalem. When negotiations between Egypt and Israel became tense over the issue of Palestinian self-determination, Carter invited Sadat and Begin to the presidential retreat at Camp David. After thirteen days of intense discussions, mediated by Carter, the three heads of state signed the Camp David Accords on September 27, 1978.

The accords consisted of two documents. The first set the conditions for the Egyptian–Israeli peace treaty. The second document endorsed UN Security Council Resolution 242 as a basis for a comprehensive settlement of the Middle East conflict. Palestinian autonomy was to be realized in planned stages covering five years. But the wording of the treaty—a victory for Begin and a defeat for the Palestinian cause—was vague enough to permit various interpretations, and the plan for Palestinian autonomy was never implemented, in spite of Egyptian protests. As a result of signing the Camp David Accords, Egypt was expelled from the Arab League,

league headquarters were transferred from Cairo to Tunis, and all Arab states, except Oman and the Sudan, broke off diplomatic relations with Egypt. The oil producing states canceled their subsidies, making Egypt economically dependent on the United States.

On March 26, 1979, Sadat and Begin signed a formal treaty in Washington, D.C. The two countries exchanged ambassadors the following year, and Israel started to withdraw from the Sinai, a process completed in 1982.

On November 2, 1979, militant Islamic students seized the U.S. Embassy in Tehran and took fifty-two American hostages. Carter broke off diplomatic relations with Iran on April 8, 1980, when Iran refused to negotiate the hostages' release, claiming that they were being held in retaliation for U.S. support of the deposed shah. A commando attempt to free the hostages failed when U.S. helicopters crashed in the desert two hundred miles outside Teheran. Carter continued to negotiate, and the hostages were released on January 20, 1981 (the day Ronald Reagan took the oath of office, succeeding Carter in the presidency), in return for a U.S. pledge of nonintervention and a promise to release frozen Iranian assets.

Despite losing the 1980 presidential election, Carter actively continued his public career. He wrote two books on the Middle East: *The Blood of Abraham* (1985) and *The Blood of Abraham: Insights into the Middle East* (1993), as well as other books of a more general nature: *Keeping Faith: Memoirs of a President* (1982) and *Always a Reckoning and Other Poems* (1995). He established the Carter Presidential Library at Emory University in Atlanta. He founded The Carter Center, dedicated to questions of international relations, and has continued to be an active statesman, helping to mediate a peaceful resolution of several international crises in the Middle East, North Korea, and Haiti.

BIBLIOGRAPHY

SPENCER, DONALD S. *The Carter Implosion: Jimmy Carter and the Amateur Style of Diplomacy.* New York, 1988.

Mia Bloom

Casablanca

Largest city in Morocco.

As of 1991, Casablanca (al-Dar al-Baida in Arabic) had a population of 2,980,000. The *wilaya* (province) of Greater Casablanca, which covers 1,615 square kilometers (646 sq mi), is composed of twenty-three urban districts and six prefectures. Situated on the Atlantic coast, the city is the principal maritime and air transport hub and the major industrial center of the country.

The site of modern Casablanca was occupied by Anfa, a commercial center in the thirteenth century. After being held briefly by the Portuguese, who called it Casa Branca (White House), it was abandoned in ruins about 1468. The village was rebuilt in 1770 by Sultan Muhammad III (1757–1790), who translated the name into Arabic as *al-Dar al-Baida*. It was later retranslated into Spanish as Casablanca.

Muhammad III hoped to encourage trade with Europe through the port of Essaouira (Mogador); thus Casablanca remained small and inactive. When the tribes of the Shawiya district around Casablanca revolted in the 1790s, Sultan Sulayman (1792–1822) closed Casablanca and several other ports to European commerce. It began to revive under Sultan Abd al-Rahman (1822–1859), who reopened it to commerce in 1831. Trade slowly grew from 3 percent of Moroccan maritime trade in 1836 to 10 percent in 1843. The port handled mainly agricultural produce: hides, wool, and grain. The population was estimated at fifteen hundred in the late 1850s and perhaps four thousand a decade later as European merchants set up agencies, and steamship services started to call. By the late 1880s the population had increased to around nine thousand. Although the port still had no proper wharves, it was important enough for French agents to take control of the customhouse following the Act of Algeciras (1906). European attempts to construct a modern port in 1907 led to an attack on the work site by people from the surrounding countryside. A French warship bombarded the port, local people looted the town, and French and Spanish troops then occupied it.

The population grew quickly after the imposition of the French protectorate in 1912. It rose from perhaps 40,000 in 1914 to around 250,000 in 1930. The first French resident general, Louis-Hubert Gonzalve Lyautey, decided to make Casablanca the main port and the commercial center of Morocco; Rabat became the political capital. The port relied in particular on the export of phosphates, which became Morocco's largest and most valuable export.

European speculators quickly bought up land, and the city began to grow haphazardly. In 1914 Lyautey gave the French architect Henri Prost the task of designing the city. Prost developed an overall master plan for a European city surrounding the old Muslim *madina* and Jewish *mellah*. Public buildings were required to harmonize with traditional Moroccan styles; the post office, the city hall, and the Palais de Justice made particular use of Islamic architectural elements within a European-style structure. The commercial district was dominated by the kilometer-long Boulevard de la Gare (now Boulevard Mohammad V). The European suburbs spread quickly with little control. To the rapidly growing European population was added an explosive growth in the Moroccan population. This led to the emergence of shantytowns (BIDONVILLES) in the early 1930s. By the mid-1930s some seventy to eighty thousand Moroccans lived in bidonvilles.

European working-class immigrants brought French socialist politics with them, and Moroccan workers were soon involved. In June 1936 a series of strikes began in state enterprises and spread to commercial enterprises in Casablanca; both European and Moroccan workers took part.

After the Allied landings in North Africa in November 1942, Sultan MUHAMMED V had two meetings with U.S. President Franklin Roosevelt. This assured the sultan of American interest and support for Moroccan independence and raised his reputation in the eyes of the Moroccans. After the war, the political movements in Casablanca became increasingly militant for independence. This was reinforced by an incident on 7 April 1947, when Senegalese troops in France's colonial army fired on a crowd in Casablanca, apparently after an argument over the molestation of a Moroccan woman. French officials did little to stop the massacre, in which several hundred people were reported killed.

Following Morocco's independence in 1956, Casablanca's population continued to grow and to become predominantly Moroccan as the Europeans left. By 1960 the population was nearly 1 million, and by 1970, 1.8 million. Although some attempt was made to house the new residents, most of whom moved in from the countryside, the apartment blocks that were built were woefully insufficient. This led to continued political radicalization in Casablanca, and there were riots in the poorer districts in 1965, in which large numbers of people were killed. A state of emergency was declared and remained in force for five years. Tension continued throughout the 1970s, and there were more, and very serious, riots in June 1981. In the 1980s and 1990s Ali YATA, the leader of the Party of Progress and Socialism (Parti du Progrès et Socialisme, the renamed Communist party) repeatedly won election for a Casablanca constituency. There has been some Islamist activity as well. The importance of Casablanca politically was graphically shown when King Hassan II chose it as the site of the world's biggest mosque (the Hassan II Mosque), which was opened in 1993.

[See also: Communist Party, Morocco]

BIBLIOGRAPHY

ISSAWI, CHARLES. *An Economic History of the Middle East and North Africa.* London, 1982.
MIÈGE, JEAN-LOUIS. *Le Maroc et l'Europe.* Paris, 1961–1964.
WRIGHT, GWENDOLYN. *The Politics of Design in French Colonial Urbanism.* Chicago, 1991.
ZARTMAN, I. WILLIAM, ed. *The Political Economy of Morocco.* Westport, Conn., 1987.

C. R. Pennell

Casablanca Conference

Conference on the conduct of World War II, held at Casablanca, Morocco, January 14–23, 1943.

This was the first in a series of conferences in 1943 and 1944, in which the leadership of the Allied powers developed the strategy for the conduct of World War II. At Casablanca, President Franklin D. Roosevelt of the United States met Prime Minister Winston S. Churchill of the United Kingdom. Also attending were the military chiefs of staff of the two nations and Generals Henri-Honoré Giraud and Charles de Gaulle of France.

The U.S. military had been anxious to establish a second front against Germany, via a cross-channel invasion of France. Churchill favored striking at the "soft underbelly" of Hitler's Europe from North Africa. The conferees agreed that an invasion of France in 1943 was not feasible, but that Sicily would be vulnerable to an Allied strike once North Africa came under Allied control. The invasion of France would have to wait another year.

Other agreements at Casablanca included unconditional surrender of Germany, Italy, and Japan as a conclusion to the war, announced by Roosevelt at a press conference; around-the-clock bombing of Germany as a prelude to an eventual cross-channel invasion of France; and an operation in East Asia, code named Anakim, to reopen supply lines to China through Burma, with a drive by the Chinese to the coast. The first two continued to be Allied strategy, but the offensive in China was later abandoned when it became apparent that American forces in the Pacific would reach the Chinese coast before British or Chinese forces advancing from the interior.

The two French representatives at Casablanca were bitter political enemies, neither having any significant control over events. Roosevelt and Churchill delighted in contriving to have both Giraud and de Gaulle photographed shaking hands together during a press conference, an event to which Churchill later referred as one that "cannot be viewed even in the setting of these tragic times without a laugh." The conference did, however, provide a boost to de Gaulle's standing, and he later became the primary leader in France's liberation movement.

BIBLIOGRAPHY

KEEGAN, JOHN. *The Second World War.* New York, 1989.

Daniel E. Spector

Casbah

In Arabic qasba; generally a capital city, metropolis, or citadel.

In North Africa, a casbah is a citadel that is attached to a town but remains sufficiently independent to constitute a keep capable of continuing the resistance, even after the fall of the town. In the colonial era, this word came to mean the native part of the town as distinct from that of the Europeans.

Stuart J. Borsch

Caspian Sea

The largest inland salt lake in Asia.

The Caspian Sea is bordered by Iran in the south and surrounded by the territories of the former Soviet Union in the north. The name Caspian is derived from the ancient Latin name Caspium Mare, named for the Caspi people of Transcaucasia. The sea is about 730 miles long and 180 miles wide. It is fed exclusively by rivers and tributaries, the most important being the Volga and the Ural rivers. The shallow northern part of the sea is important for sturgeon fishing, but the southern deeper portion, where the fish go to spawn, produces the best caviar in the world. The three main species of caviar are beluga, osetra, and sevruga, of which Iran exports in excess of sixty-six tons annually.

The waters of the Caspian are saline in composition but are fresh enough to allow for freezing in the northern reaches, thus preventing shipping during the winter. By far the most important commodity carried by Caspian shipping is petroleum. Crude oil is carried from Baku to Astrakhan, where it is transshipped along the Volga for industrial and commercial use in Northern Europe. The major ports of the sea are the Russian Baku and Astrakhan, as well as Bandar-e-Pahlavi and Khorrema in Iran.

Cyrus Moshaver

Castel-Bloom, Orli   [1960–   ]

Israeli author.

One of the originators and leaders of the newest wave of Israeli literature, Castel-Bloom's prose style and alienated urbanism is considered the Israeli voice of postmodernism. She studied film at Tel Aviv University, and her works reflect the pulse and language of mass media. Her works provoked critical controversy both on the ideological and stylistic levels.

Castel-Bloom published three novels and three short story collections in fifteen years. Her works were translated into Dutch, French, German, and English. Most of her protagonists are women, and her central issue is that of women trapped in myths of motherhood, societal expectations, and suppressed needs. Her works express piercing political satire, parody, and wit mostly achieved by the employment of defamiliarization both in plot and language. The synthesis of literate, literal and colloquial Hebrew, and anticonventional, often absurd, plots place her in the literary tradition of Kafka and Agnon.

Dolly City (1992) is a dystopian novel which bitterly mocks the Great Mother motif, the Jewish Mother stereotype, and the corruption of Zionist ideology in modern day Israel. Set in a fictitious city which strongly resembles Tel Aviv, the protagonist moves in a frenzy of macabre activities, grotesquely portraying the crumbling of Western civilization and its values. *The Mina Lisa* (1995) is a witty novel based on a central metaphor: a suburban housewife whose scriptwriting talents are abused by a grandmother-in-law who subsists by devouring as many manuscripts as the protagonist manages to produce.

Zvia Ginor

Castro, Léon   [1881–?]

Egyptian Zionist politician and journalist.

Castro was born in Constantinople and settled in Egypt during the first decade of the twentieth century. He studied law in France, later joining the popular Egyptian Wafd party headed by Sa'd Zaghlul. In the early 1920s, Castro promoted the pro-independence ideology of the Wafd in Europe, advocating the need for Britain to withdraw completely from Egypt. In 1922, he founded the Wafdist journal *La Liberté*.

In the late 1920s, Castro was won over to Zionism and, in the 1940s, headed the Zionist movement of Egypt. In 1933, he was instrumental in founding a branch of the anti-Nazi *Ligue internatio-nale contre l'antisémitisme allemand* (LICA) in Egypt; it called for the restriction of German propaganda in Egypt and promoted the boycott of Germany's products.

BIBLIOGRAPHY

KRÄMER, GUDRUN. *The Jews in Modern Egypt, 1914–1952.* Seattle, Wash., 1989.
LASKIER, MICHAEL M. *The Jews of Egypt, 1920–1970: In the Midst of Zionism, Anti-Semitism and the Middle East Conflict.* New York and London, 1991.

Michael M. Laskier

Catholics

See Roman Catholicism and Roman Catholic Missions

Catroux, Georges   [1877–1969]

French general, governor-general, minister, and ambassador.

A graduate of the military college at Saint-Cyr, Catroux served in Algeria, Indochina, and Morocco before he was wounded and imprisoned during World War I; after the war he was a political delegate of the high commissioner in Damascus and subsequently a military attaché in Turkey. He returned to Morocco in 1925 and held several commands there and then in Algeria. In 1940 he joined Charles de Gaulle in London and was dispatched to rally Syria and Lebanon to the Free French cause. He negotiated an agreement between Henri Giraud and de Gaulle concerning the leadership of the Free French.

Catroux was governor-general of Algeria in 1943 and minister of North Africa in 1944. Catroux understood that France must ultimately heed the rising expectations of the colonized. He demonstrated this view in the delicate negotiations that returned Mohammed V to Morocco in 1955. His appointment as resident minister of Algeria in 1956 provoked the outrage of European settlers, forcing Catroux's resignation and his replacement with Robert Lacoste.

BIBLIOGRAPHY

LERNER, HENRI. *Catroux.* Paris, 1990.

Phillip C. Naylor

Cattan, Henry   [1906–   ]

Palestinian lawyer and writer.

Born in Jerusalem, Cattan was educated at the University of Paris and the University of London. After becoming a licensed barrister, he was a lecturer at the Jerusalem Law School from 1932 to 1942, a practicing lawyer in Palestine and Syria, and a member of the Palestine Law Council until 1948. Cattan testified before the ANGLO–AMERICAN COMMITTEE OF INQUIRY on Palestine in 1946. On behalf of the Arab Higher Committee, he presented the Palestinian case to the UN General Assembly in 1947 and 1948. Cattan later negotiated with Count Folke Bernadotte, the UN mediator for Palestine.

Cattan's best-known publications include *Palestine, the Arabs and Israel*; *Palestine: The Road to Peace*; *Palestine and International Law*; *The Evolution of Oil Concessions in the Middle East and North Africa*; and *The Garden of Joys*.

BIBLIOGRAPHY

Who's Who in the Arab World, 1988–1989, 9th ed. Beirut.

Lawrence Tal

Cattaoui Family

Prominent Jewish family of scholars, businessmen, and politicians who settled in Egypt in the seventeenth century.

The Cattaoui were descendants of Sephardic *megorashim* (Jews expelled from Spain in 1492). The earliest recorded member was Yusif ben Ishaq Sambary Cattaoui (1640–1703), author of a history of humankind in two volumes, copies of which are found in the library of Oxford University. His descendants, Jacob (1801–1883) and Moïse (1849–1924), were dynamic financiers who were close to the Egyptian khedives and instrumental in financing and managing the railway systems of Upper Egypt as well as the public transportation systems in Cairo. Moïse also served as president of Cairo's Jewish community from 1883 to his death in 1924.

The best-known member of the family was Joseph Aslan Cattaoui Pasha (1861–1942). In addition to his functions as one of the chief entrepreneurs of Egypt's sugar industry and in engineering, he helped found the Misr Bank, which financed more than thirty industrial, commercial, and agricultural enterprises. After independence from Britain, in 1922, he was elected to the new parliament as deputy of the constituency of Kom-Ombo. In 1924, he served as finance minister in the Egyptian government; he was appointed minister of communications in 1925. In 1927, he was named senator, a position he held until his death. He succeeded Moïse Cattaoui Pasha as president of Cairo's Jewish community, and one of his sons, René (born 1896), succeeded him.

BIBLIOGRAPHY

KRÄMER, GUDRUN. *The Jews in Modern Egypt, 1914–1952.* Seattle, Wash., 1989.
LANDAU, JACOB M. *Jews in Nineteenth-Century Egypt.* New York, 1969.
LASKIER, MICHAEL M. *The Jews of Egypt, 1920–1970: In the Midst of Zionism, Anti-Semitism and the Middle East Conflict.* New York and London, 1991.
MIZRAHI, MAURICE. "The Role of Jews in Economic Development." In *The Jews of Egypt: A Mediterranean Society in Modern Times,* ed. by Shimon Shamir. Boulder, Colo., and London, 1987.

Michael M. Laskier

Caucasus

Multiethnic region of southern Russia.

Several ethnic groups emigrated from the Caucasus to the Middle East, including the CIRCASSIANS, the Shishans (Chechens), and the Jewish populations of Georgia. The majority of the Circassians and Shishans emigrated to Jordan, whereas the Jews emigrated to Palestine. The Muslims of the Russian Federal Republic are concentrated in the Caucasus.

Mia Bloom

Cave, Stephen

British member of Parliament who investigated Egypt's debt problem in 1875.

With Sir John Stokes, Cave headed a mission, known as the Cave Mission, which went to Egypt in 1875, at the request of Khedive Isma'il Pasha, viceroy of Egypt, to investigate Egypt's growing debt problem. Cave judged Egypt solvent based on the country's level of resources. His report recommended placing Egyptian state finances under the control of an international commission of creditors and rescheduling the repayment of debts. Egypt's European creditors rejected this proposal.

BIBLIOGRAPHY

VATIKIOTIS, P. J. *A History of Modern Egypt,* 4th ed. London, 1991.

WUCHER KING, JOAN. *Historical Dictionary of Egypt.* Metuchen, N.J., 1984.

David Waldner

Cavit, Mehmet [1875–1926]

Ottoman government minister.

Mehmet Cavit, the son of a merchant, was born in Salonika into a family of *dönme,* or members of a Judeo-Islamic syncretist sect. After graduating from the *Mülkiye* (civil service school) in Istanbul in 1896, he worked briefly for the Agricultural Bank before being appointed to the finance ministry. In 1902, he returned to Salonika where he taught economics and law. He joined the COMMITTEE OF UNION AND PROGRESS (CUP) and, in 1908, was a member of the COMMITTEE OF SEVEN, sent by CUP to Istanbul to represent it immediately following the 1908 revolution. During the Young Turk period, he was a CUP member of parliament and also taught economics at the Mülkiye. In 1912, he joined the cabinet of Sait Paşa as minister of finance. He served in the same position in the cabinet (formed in October 1918) that signed the Treaty of Mudros with Britain. In 1926, he was arrested and accused of conspiring against Mustafa Kemal Atatürk; found guilty by the independence courts, he was executed in Ankara on 26 August 1926.

BIBLIOGRAPHY

SHAW, STANFORD, and EZEL KURAL SHAW. *Reform, Revolution, and Republic: The Rise of Modern Turkey, 1808–1975,* vol. 2: *History of the Ottoman Empire and Modern Turkey.* Cambridge, U.K., 1977.
Türk Ansiklopedisi, vol. 10. Ankara, 1960, pp. 37–38.

David Waldner

Caylak [1843–1893]

Turkish Ottoman writer and journalist.

Born Mehmet Tevfik in Istanbul, he was the son of an Ottoman official. After working as a civil servant and attempting poetry, Tevfik found fame as a journalist and folklorist; he was called Caylak after the newspaper in which he wrote humorous pieces. He also wrote for the newspapers *Geveze* and *Letaif-i Asar.* Worried that Turkish customs and traditions were vanishing, he devoted himself to gathering folk stories. Among his publications is a three-volume collection of the stories of Nasruddin Hoca.

BIBLIOGRAPHY

ÖZKİRİMLİ, ATILLA. *Türk Edebiyati Ansiklopedisi*, vol. 2. Istanbul, 1982.

David Waldner

Cebesoy, Ali Fuat

Turkish military and political leader.

As army commander in Ankara, beginning in March 1919, Cebesoy lent critical support to the nationalist military campaign organized by Mustafa Kemal Pasha (Atatürk). Relieved of command of the army facing the Greek invaders in 1920, he was appointed ambassador to the Soviet Union. He joined the opposition to Kemal's accumulation of personal political power and his radical secularizing reforms; with several military colleagues, he formed the PROGRESSIVE REPUBLICAN PARTY late in 1924. Forced into political retirement in 1925 when the party was shut down, Cebesoy returned to politics after Atatürk's death, joining the cabinet in 1939 and becoming speaker of the Grand National Assembly (parliament) in 1947. Shortly before the 1950 election, he resigned from the Republican People's Party and was seriously considered as a nonpartisan candidate for president of the republic in that year.

BIBLIOGRAPHY

AHMAD, F. *The Turkish Experiment in Democracy, 1950–1975.* Boulder, Colo., 1977.
KARPAT, K. *Turkey's Politics.* Princeton, N.J., 1959.
SHAW, S. J., and E. K. SHAW, *History of the Ottoman Empire and Modern Turkey,* vol. 2. New York, 1977.

Frank Tachau

Cem

Ottoman humor magazine.

Following the success of the magazine *Kalem, Cem* was founded in September 1910 by the cartoonist CEMIL CEM. Refik Halid was the head writer. Like *Kalem, Cem* was published weekly, half in French and half in Turkish, and featured caricatures, short stories, and articles, all characterized by a sophisticated wit that appealed to the educated classes. *Cem* was ordered closed in September 1911, reappeared in 1927, and was closed again in May 1929, following the publication of a series of caricatures of prominent people.

BIBLIOGRAPHY

Tanzimat'tan Cumhuriyet'e Türkiye Ansiklopedisi, vol. 1. Istanbul, 1984.
Türkiye'de Dergiler Ansiklopediler, 1849–1984. Istanbul, 1984, p. 72.

David Waldner

Cemal Paça   [1872–1922]

Ottoman general, statesman, and influential leader of the Committee of Union and Progress.

Ahmed Cemal Paça was born May 6, 1872, in Mytilene, Greece, the son of a military pharmacist. He graduated from the War Academy (Mekteb-I Harbiye) in 1895 as staff officer and was appointed to the General Staff in Constantinople (now Istanbul). He transferred to the Second Army unit of construction works stationed in Edirne and in 1898 to the Third Army in Salonika. As military inspector for railways and later staff officer in the Third Army headquarters, he contributed to the regional organization of the underground resistance movement to Abdülhamit II. He joined the COMMITTEE OF UNION AND PROGRESS (CUP), and during the Young Turk Revolution in July 1908 emerged as a prominent committee leader. He took part in the first delegation that the Salonika CUP dispatched to Constantinople and received promotion to lieutenant colonel.

After July 1908 Cemal went to Anatolia with a reform commission. When a counterrevolutionary uprising broke out in Constantinople in April 1909, he rejoined the Third Army units (the Army of Deliverance) that suppressed the uprising. Subsequently, he accepted the district governorship of Üsküdar, Istanbul-in-Asia (May 1909). Armenian riots in Adana and the threat of foreign intervention led to his appointment as governor of Adana (August 1909). In 1911, he became governor of Baghdad. Upon the outbreak of the Balkan War in 1912, he engaged in active duty in Thrace as commander of reserve units and was promoted to colonel. Following the CUP's coup against the Kamil government (January 1913), which Cemal helped engineer, he was made general and commander of the First Army in Constantinople as well as military governor of the capital. He consolidated the CUP's position in the capital by suppressing the Ottoman Liberty and Entente party's opposition and sending its leaders to the gallows. In the CUP-dominated cabinets of 1913–1914, he served first as minister of public works and later minister of the navy. He is credited with the modernization of the Ottoman fleet.

Known for his pro-French proclivities, Cemal went to Paris in June 1914 to seek a wartime alliance with France. He returned empty-handed, except for the Legion of Honor. During World War I, he served as the commander of the Fourth Army and governor of Syria, while maintaining his portfolio as minister. He led the ill-fated expeditions against British military positions along the Suez Canal in February 1915 and August 1916.

As wartime governor in Syria, Cemal Paça gained notoriety for executing Arab leaders for their foreign sympathies and alleged nationalist aims and also for his draconian measures in the management of grain supplies. He undertook construction and preservation projects designed to improve material conditions in Syria. He resigned in December 1917 and returned to Constantinople.

Together with other CUP leaders, he fled abroad at the end of the war (November 1918). Cemal went first to Berlin, via Odessa, then to Switzerland. He also went to Russia and had contacts with the Bolshevik leaders. He entered the services of the Afghan king, Afdal Barakzai, to reorganize his army against the British. In 1922 he returned to Moscow and went to Tbilisi, where he hoped to monitor the independence movement led by Mustafa Kemal, possibly with an eye to return to Anatolia. He was assassinated in Tbilisi July 21, 1922, most likely by Armenian terrorists. He is buried in Erzurum, Turkey.

Cemal Paça authored a tract to justify his stern policies in Syria, which was published in Turkish, Arabic, and French (*La Vérité sur la Question Syrienne;* Istanbul, 1916). His memoirs were published posthumously. He commissioned a study of old monuments in greater Syria, *Alte Denkmäler aus Syrien, Palästina und West-Arabien* (Berlin, 1918).

As a senior and most versatile member of the Central Committee, Cemal had a strong following in the CUP. He has been implicated in conspiring against the other members of the Young Turk trio, ENVER PAŞA and MEHMET TALAT, and even for attempting to establish a state in Syria as base to supplant the leadership in Constantinople. His disagreements with other influential members notwithstanding, Cemal's political ambitions remained consistent with the broader goals of the CUP as a political organization.

BIBLIOGRAPHY

PASHA, DJEMAL. *Memories of a Turkish Statesman, 1913–1919.* New York, 1922.

Hasan Kayali

Cemil Cem   [1882–1950]

Ottoman Turkish cartoonist.

Cemil Cem was born in Istanbul and graduated from Galatasaray Lycée. Considered the most important cartoonist of the constitutional period, Cem's illustrations and caricatures first appeared in 1908 in the magazine *Kalem*. In 1910, he founded the humor magazine *Cem*. Both of these magazines were closed down in 1911.

BIBLIOGRAPHY

Tanzimat'tan Cumhuriyet'e Türkiye Ansiklopedesi. Istanbul, 1984.
Türkiye'de Dergiler Ansiklopediler, 1849–1984. Istanbul, 1984.
Yeni Türk Ansiklopedisi. Istanbul, 1985.

David Waldner

Cenap Sehabettin   [1870–1934]

Ottoman Turkish doctor and poet.

In 1891, Ahmet İhsan To'kgoz founded the journal *Servet-i Fünün* (The Wealth of Sciences) in Istanbul. Along with Tevfik Fikret, Cenap Sehabettin was one of the most prominent contributors to the journal, and his poems formed part of the corpus which became known as the *Servet-i Fünün* School. Sehabettin and the others of this school wrote in ornate and even anachronistic prose, thereby glorifying art, disdaining the present, and avoiding the censor of the sultan, Abdulhamit II. Sehabettin wrote for an elite audience, and he was heavily influenced by French culture of the Third Republic, in particular by French symbolists. Though he avoided political criticism, his poetry conveyed French cultural values and reflected on the ennui prevalent among the educated elite of Constantinople (now Istanbul) in the late Hamitian period.

BIBLIOGRAPHY

LEWIS, BERNARD. *The Emergence of Modern Turkey.* New York, 1961.
SHAW, STANFORD, and EZEL KURAL SHAW. *History of the Ottoman Empire and Modern Turkey.* Cambridge, U.K., 1977.

Zachary Karabell

Census

See Population

Central Command

Division of the Israel Defense Forces.

The Central Command is an army division assigned to the regions of Israel facing the border of Jordan and since 1967 has had civilian and military control over the West Bank. The Northern and Southern commands have jurisdiction over the frontier areas near Lebanon and Egypt. The commands constitute the Ground Forces Command, whose chief is on the General Staff of the Israel Defense Force (IDF).

The Central Command, along with all of the IDF, was idolized by Israeli society, particularly after the 1967 Six-Day War (Arab-Israel War). But that image became tarnished after 1973, and particularly with the controversial role that the Central Command played in the Intifada, the Palestinian uprising begun in 1987. Jewish settlers in the West Bank publicly criticized the Central Command for not allowing them to establish citizen militias. The militias were eventually formed, but the Central Command chief, Major General Amram Mitzna, restricted them to the Jewish settlements. Settlers, Likud party members, and their ally, General Ariel Sharon, also repeatedly accused Mitzna of being too soft in disciplining Palestinians. On the other hand, Palestinians, their supporters, and the press condemned the Central Command (and the Southern Command in Gaza) for the hundreds of Palestinian deaths caused by harsh repressive measures used to control the Intifada.

BIBLIOGRAPHY

PERI, YORAM. *Between Battles and Ballots.* New York, 1983.
SCHIFF, ZE'EV. *A History of the Israeli Army.* New York, 1985.
SCHIFF, ZE'EV, and EHUD YA'ARI. *Intifada.* New York, 1989.

Elizabeth Thompson

Central Intelligence Agency

Agency of the executive branch of the U.S. government; principal U.S. agency for collection and assessment of worldwide intelligence data.

The Central Intelligence Agency (CIA), established in 1947, is responsible directly to the president of the United States and carries out functions ordered by the president and the president's staff. The agency and its director, in his capacity as head of the U.S. intelligence community, are charged not only with collecting and analyzing intelligence data but also with coordinating the activities of other U.S. intelligence agencies, including those attached to the military services and those of the state and defense departments.

The agency is divided into three principal directorates: for clandestine collection of foreign intelligence and the conduct of covert actions; for analysis of political, military, and economic developments outside the United States; and for collection and analysis of technical and scientific intelligence.

In the Middle East, the CIA is best known for having organized the overthrow in 1953 of Iranian Prime Minister Mohammad MOSSADEGH and having returned Reza Shah PAHLAVI to the Peacock Throne in a covert operation. Mossadegh, although widely seen throughout the Middle East as a nationalist, was viewed by the Eisenhower administration as a tool of the Soviet Union who threatened U.S. interests.

Other CIA covert actions in the Middle East have included providing arms to rebel groups. For example, the CIA provided arms and covert support to the Kurds in Iraq in the early 1970s; to the Afghan guerillas following the Soviet invasion of Afghanistan in 1979; and to Chad's forces opposing a Libyan invasion in 1980.

Lebanon was for some time the center of much CIA activity in the Middle East. According to the newspaper accounts, during the 1970s and the early 1980s, the CIA and the PALESTINE LIBERATION ORGANIZATION (PLO) had a cooperative arrangement, centered in Beirut, to insure Americans security against terrorist attacks. Apparently in the hope of gaining diplomatic advantage, the PLO warned of any impending attack on U.S. citizens and provided physical protection to U.S. diplomats and installations. The principal PLO reference point in this arrangement, Ali al-Salama, was killed in what is believed to be an Israel-engineered car bombing in 1979, but the security cooperation continued until the PLO left Beirut in the aftermath of Israel's 1982 invasion of Lebanon.

The following year saw a marked upsurge in attacks on U.S. installations and large numbers of American deaths. According to one account, following bombings of the American embassy and a U.S. Marine barracks in Beirut in 1983 and 1984, all believed to be the work of the Shi'a group, HIZBULLAH, under Shaykh Husayn Fadlallah, the CIA arranged to have Fadlallah stopped. A car bomb was detonated in March 1985 at his apartment building; Fadlallah was not harmed. The CIA denied involvement, and the House Permanent Select Committee on Intelligence, following an investigation, concluded that no direct or indirect CIA involvement could be shown.

Although not responsible for maintaining diplomatic relationships with other countries, the CIA often provides a vehicle by which the U.S. government can solidify a relationship through unofficial contacts or cooperate with another country covertly on operations of joint interest. This often occurs through regular meetings between a CIA official and a foreign leader. Liaison between the CIA and the intelligence services of friendly nations provides another means of cooperation. This liaison—involving cooperation on counterterrorist operations, coordination on other specific operations, and the exchange of intelligence data—has been conducted with many Middle East countries, most particularly Israel.

BIBLIOGRAPHY

COLBY, WILLIAM, and PETER FORBATH. *Honorable Men: My Life in the CIA.* New York, 1978.

MARCHETTI, VICTOR, and JOHN D. MARKS. *The CIA and the Cult of Intelligence.* New York, 1974.

TURNER, STANSFIELD. *Secrecy and Democracy: The CIA in Transition.* Boston, 1985.

WOODWARD, BOB. *Veil: The Secret Wars of the CIA, 1981–1987.* New York, 1987.

Kathleen M. Christison

Central Planning Ministry

The Saudi Arabian governmental body responsible for economic development.

Development efforts in Saudi Arabia were carried out on an ad hoc basis until the financial crisis of 1957. The realization that some coordination was necessary led to the creation of the Economic Development Committee (1954), which identified and ranked projects for implementation. In 1960, the Supreme Planning Board (SPB) was created to supervise development planning throughout the country. However, the SPB functioned as little more than a subcommittee of the Council of Ministers, refereeing competing budget requests from the ministries. The Central Planning Organization (CPO) replaced the SPB in 1965 and was given the mandate of drawing up the kingdom's first five-year plan. To provide more authority, the CPO was transformed into the Central Planning Ministry in 1975, and it has supervised all subsequent five-year plans. Hisham NAZIR was appointed president of the CPO in 1968 and became the first minister of planning in 1975, a position he held until 1991.

John E. Peterson

Central Planning Organization

Development agency of the Yemen Arab Republic.

Created in 1972 and headed from 1973 to 1977 by Dr. Abd al-Karim al-Iryani, the Central Planning Organization (CPO) became the vital center of the rapidly expanding development activities of the Yemen Arab Republic (YAR). This government agency, the YAR's model modern institution, authored a succession of five-year development plans. By the 1980s, the CPO had declined in importance despite periodic revitalizations.

Robert D. Burrowes

Central Treaty Organization (CENTO)

Mutual-defense group of Middle Eastern countries and Britain, 1959–1979.

After the Iraqi revolution of July 1958, Iraq withdrew from the BAGHDAD PACT in March 1959. With its patronymic city now in a hostile country, the pact was renamed the Central Treaty Organization (CENTO). Its membership included Iran, Turkey, Pakistan, and Great Britain, with the United States as an associate member. CENTO, like its predecessor, was initially conceived as a defense organization on the lines of the NORTH ATLANTIC TREATY ORGANIZATION (NATO); the northern tier of Middle Eastern countries that formed the southern boundary of the USSR were

Iranian stamp from 1960 honoring the Central Treaty Organization. (Richard Bulliet)

strategically important to the cold warriors of the West. While not officially part of CENTO, the United States was an active supporter, and it obtained the use of military bases and intelligence outposts in each of the northern-tier countries. By the late 1960s, CENTO had become more important as an economic bloc, though it remained a crux of American military planning. CENTO became defunct after the 1979 Iranian revolution.

BIBLIOGRAPHY

BILL, JAMES. *The Eagle and the Lion.* New Haven, Conn., 1988.

LENCZOWSKI, GEORGE. *The Middle East in World Affairs,* 4th ed. Ithaca, N.Y., 1980.

Zachary Karabell

Ceramics

Among the glories of Islamic art, particularly in Persia and Anatolia.

The earliest examples of Islamic-style ceramics have been found at Samarra, the Abbasid caliphate's ninth-century capital on the east bank of the river Tigris (now in Iraq). Although influenced by the Chinese tradition, Muslim artisans by the tenth century were producing peculiarly Islamic styles and motifs. Persian artisans, in such cities as Rayy, Neyshabur (or Nishapur), and Isfahan, created a variety of plates, jars, and ornaments that often featured lively human and animal figures. They also produced beautiful architectural tiles to decorate mosques.

After the twelfth century, the Seljuks carried the ceramic arts to Anatolia, and eventually Iznik became the center of the industry in the Ottoman Empire. The Ottoman Turks introduced new floral motifs and colors, particularly red, green, and purple. In 1545, Ottoman Turkish artisans used highly developed polychromed tiles to restore the famed Jerusalem mosque, the Dome of the Rock. In the seventeenth century, European demand for Turkish ceramics rose as Chinese ports were closed. In the nineteenth century, the Ottomans industrialized their ceramics industry, but it failed to compete with imported European china. Egypt, North Africa, and Muslim Spain have also produced highly crafted ceramics.

BIBLIOGRAPHY

Encyclopaedia of Islam, 2nd ed.

Elizabeth Thompson

Ceride-i Havadis

Ottoman newspaper.

The second Turkish-language newspaper, *Ceride-i Havadis* (The Register of News), was established through permission of the Ottoman government in 1840 by William CHURCHILL, a businessman and correspondent for the English newspaper, *The Morning Herald.* Planned as a weekly, the paper was published on average every ten days. Initially, the paper was distributed for free but had only 150 readers: financial solvency was secured through a regular subvention by the Ottoman government. In 1851, paid advertisements began to appear in the paper. *Ceride-i Havadis* emphasized foreign news and translations. Among the Turkish writers for the paper were EBÜZZIYA TEVFIK and AHMET RASIM. *Ceride-i Havadis* ceased publication shortly after the death of Churchill in 1864.

BIBLIOGRAPHY

İNUĞUR, M. NURI. *Türk Basımında "İz" Bırakanlar.* Istanbul, 1988, pp. 3–4.

ORAL, FUAT SÜREYYA. *Türk Basim Tarihi, 1728–1922.* Ankara, pp. 77–78.

TOPUZ, HIFZI. *100 Sonruda Türk Basim Tarihi.* Istanbul, 1973, pp. 8–10.

David Waldner

Çerkes Hasan Incident

Assassination of Hüseyin Avni and Rasit Paşa.

Çerkes Hasan was a Circassian infantry captain, a brother-in-law of Ottoman Sultan ABDÜLAZIZ, and a member of the personal staff of Prince Yusuf Izzeddin. On June 15, 1976, he entered a meeting of cabinet ministers being held in the house of MIDHAT PAŞA and assassinated Chief of Staff HUSEYIN AVNI and Foreign Minister Rasit Paşa, while wounding several others. Çerkes Hasan was swiftly tried and convicted, and on June 18, he was executed. Though Çerkes Hasan claimed that he was taking revenge against Hüseyin Avni for a personal affront and against Raşit Paşa for his supposed role in the death of Abdülaziz on June 4, 1876, conservative politicians viewed the incident as a plot manipulated by Midhat Paşa to remove the only rival minister in the cabinet, paving the way for cabinet approval of the new constitution. Sultan MURAD V, who was already showing signs of mental unhealth, was so disturbed by the incident that he was unable to continue in his position.

BIBLIOGRAPHY

LEWIS, BERNARD. *The Emergence of Modern Turkey,* 2nd ed. London, 1961, pp. 162–163.

SHAW, STANFORD, and EZEL KURAL SHAW. *Reform, Revolution, and Republic: The Rise of Modern Turkey, 1808–1975.* Vol. 2 of *History of the Ottoman Empire and Modern Turkey.* Cambridge, U.K., 1977, p. 164.

David Waldner

Ceuta

Spanish enclave and port city on the Moroccan shore of the strait of Gibraltar.

Ceuta is a Spanish possession with a population in 1991 of 70,864 and an area of seven square miles (18 sq km). It commands the strait of Gibraltar and was settled by Carthaginians, Romans, Vandals, and Byzantines. Taken by the Arabs in 711, it was the base for the invasion of the Iberian peninsula. Under Muslim rule, Ceuta (Arabic, *Sibta*) was disputed by the various Spanish and Moroccan dynasties, interspersed with periods of autonomy. During the thirteenth century, Ceuta was a rich port, linking the trans-Saharan trade with the Mediterranean. In 1415, it was taken by Portuguese King John and abandoned by its Muslim inhabitants. After the union of the Spanish and Portuguese crowns in 1580, Ceuta became Spanish, which it has remained. Until the mid-nineteenth century, it was frequently besieged by Moroccan government and tribal forces, and in 1860 this led to war between Spain and Morocco, following which the boundaries were expanded in favor of Spain. The independent Moroccan government has repeatedly demanded that Ceuta be handed over by Spain. Fishing and food processing are important economic activities.

BIBLIOGRAPHY

GORDILLO OSUNA, MANUEL. *Geografía urbana de Ceuta.* Madrid, 1972.

EL-MALKI, HABIB, ed. *Le Maroc méditerranéen, la troisième dimension.* Casablanca, 1992.

C. R. Pennell

Cevdet, Abdullah   [1869–1932]

Ottoman Kurdish writer, political activist, poet, and doctor.

Cevdet was born in Arapkir, in eastern Ottoman Turkey, the son of an Islamic religious official and physician. After attending a provincial military school, he went to Istanbul at the age of fifteen to study at the army medical school. While at the medical school, Cevdet participated in a growing movement calling for liberal reform of the Ottoman Empire. In 1890 he and three colleagues, all non-Turks, formed a political society which, after a succession of name changes, became known as the COMMITTEE OF UNION AND PROGRESS (CUP).

Along with other members of the CUP, Cevdet was arrested in 1892. In 1896, he was sent into exile in Tripoli, where he served as the eye doctor for the military hospital. Continuing his political activities, he was forced to flee to Tunisia and from there to Europe. In 1900, Cevdet agreed to become the medical officer of the Ottoman Embassy in Geneva, Switzerland, in exchange for the release of political prisoners in Tripoli. For this compromise with Abdülhamit II, the sultan, Cevdet was branded a traitor and never attained high office once the CUP came to power.

Cevdet, however, never ceased his agitation for reform and, in 1905, was sentenced in absentia to life imprisonment. Between 1905 and 1911, he lived in Cairo, where he joined the YOUNG TURKS group which became the DECENTRALIZATION PARTY. In 1911, following the abdication of Sultan Abdülhamit, he returned to Istanbul. There his freethinking ideas, especially his atheism, led to frequent clashes with the new government. Cevdet's opposition to the empire's entry into World War I also aggravated his relationship with the regime. Although after the war he was appointed director of public health, his writings on religion led to charges of heresy. His trial started during the empire and continued into the early period of the new Republic of Turkey. The case was finally dismissed in December of 1926, but he was prohibited from publishing political works.

While in Geneva, Cevdet had founded the journal *Osmanlı,* in which he published articles in French and Turkish opposing the absolute rule of Sultan Abdülhamit. After this journal was closed, the principal vehicle for Cevdet's political writings was the monthly newspaper he published and edited, *Ictihat* (Interpretation). *Ictihat* was founded in 1904 and continued until his death in 1932, although it was shut down several times, particularly during World War I. Alongside attacks on despotism, *Ictihat* published articles attacking theocracy, tradition, and religion but advocating secular modernism.

In 1885, while a medical student, he met the poet Abdülhak Hamit and began writing poetry. His four volumes of poetry, published in the 1890s, were influenced by Hamit and two other Ottoman Turkish poets, NAMIK KEMAL and Mahmud Ekrem, as well as by French poets.

Two books strongly influenced Cevdet's intellectual orientation: Felix Isnards's *Spiritualisme et Matérialisme* (Paris, 1879), which presented a skeptical outlook toward religion, and Ludwig Buchner's *Force et Matière,* which provided the intellectual basis for a radical critique of religion. This orientation informed his political writings as well as his writings on sociology, psychology, science, and philosophy. Two important collections of his essays are *Science and Philosophy* (1906) and *An Examination of the World of Islam from a Historical and Philosophical Viewpoint* (1922). In addition, he translated into Turkish and wrote the preface to the mid-nineteenth-century book *Histoire des Musselmans* (History of the Muslims) by Reinhart Dozy—which created a furor on its publication.

BIBLIOGRAPHY

Encyclopaedia of Islam, supplement. Leiden, 1938.
MITLER, LOUIS. *Ottoman Turkish Writers: A Bibliographical Dictionary of Significant Figures in Pre-Republican Turkish Literature.* New York, 1988.
Yeni Türk Ansiklopedisi. Istanbul, 1985.

David Waldner

Cevdet, Ahmed [1822–1895]

Ottoman Turkish scholar-statesman.

Born at Lofça (Lovech, Bulgaria) to an Ottoman Turkish family, Ahmed Cevdet, at the age of seventeen, went to Istanbul, capital of the Ottoman Empire. During seven or eight years of study in *medrese* (higher schools of religious studies), he also found ways to learn other subjects—Persian, astronomy, mathematics—that were not taught in these schools. Mixing with learned company in dervish (SUFI religious fraternity) halls and literary men's homes, he formed important contacts. He began writing verse, and one of his literary benefactors, the poet Süleyman Fehim Efendi, gave him the pen name Cevdet. In the 1840s, he took the examination required to become a QADI, thus beginning his career as a member of the ULAMA (Islamic religious scholars).

Cevdet's work in administration began with MUSTAFA REŞID Paşa's first appointment as grand vizier in 1846. Seeking an expert on the SHARI'A (law of Islam) to consult about laws and regulations he planned to issue, Reşid Paşa asked the Şeyh ül-Islam to send him a broadminded *alim* (singular of *ulama*), and Cevdet was assigned. He remained close to Reşid Paşa for the rest of the latter's life, settling into his household and tutoring his children. There, Cevdet came under the influence of Reşid Paşa's efforts to simplify the Ottoman Turkish language and make it an effective means of mass communication; he also began to study French. In 1850, Cevdet collaborated with the future grand vizier Keçecizade Fu'ad Paşa in writing an Ottoman grammar. In the same year, he became a member of the council on education (Meclis-i Maarif) and director of the teachers' college Dar ül-Maarif, founded in 1848, playing a major role in organizing the college. Serving the education council as its first secretary, he had an important role in founding the Academy of Sciences (Encümen-i Daniş, 1851), which published his coauthored grammar, the *Kavaid-i Osmaniye,* as its first publication. When the Academy of Sciences decided to produce a history of the Ottoman Empire, Cevdet was asked in 1852 to write on the period from 1774 to 1826. So began the *Tarih-i Cevdet* (Cevdet's History).

Writing the first three volumes during the Crimean War, Cevdet was named official historian (*vak'anevis*) in 1855. Over the next few years, he continued his *History* and studied the medieval Arab historian Ibn Khaldun, finishing the Ottoman translation of Ibn Khaldun's *Muqaddima* in 1860 (begun by Pirizade Sahib, 1674–1749). Based on European as well as Ottoman sources and emphasizing the importance for the empire of developments in Europe, Cevdet's twelve-volume *History* was completed over thirty years. The work distinguished Cevdet not as an old-style chronicler but as a standard-setter for later historians.

In the 1850s, Cevdet also began to work in legal reform. Following his appointment to the High Council of Reforms (Meclis-i Âli-i Tanzimat) in 1857, Cevdet presided over the commission that drew up the land law (*arazi kanunnamesi*) of 1858. He inaugurated the publishing of laws in a volume, subsequently a series, which continues still—the *Düstur.*

When Mustafa Reşid Paşa died in 1858, and Âli Paşa became grand vizier, Cevdet was offered the governorship of Vidin province. He was not yet ready to change from the religious to the civil service, a move he deferred until 1866. The incident indicates, however, Cevdet's emergence, following Mustafa Reşid's death, into the top bureaucratic echelons—where statesmen rotated among ministerial positions and provincial governorships. This Cevdet did for the rest of his career.

Although he held many high offices, the emphasis of Cevdet Paşa's career thereafter was on law and justice. He served as minister of justice five times. He had a critical part in developing the empire's civil (*nizamiye*) courts, especially in introducing—with the Divan-i Ahkâm-ı Adliye—an appeals instance in 1868. The Ottoman Law School (Hukuk Mektebi) opened in 1880, while he was minister, and he gave its first lecture. His greatest legal contribution, however, emerged from a controversy over whether the Ottoman Empire should adopt the French civil code. Cevdet Paşa successfully championed the opposing view that a compendium of *hanafi* jurisprudence should be adopted. In 1869, he chaired a committee of Islamic legal scholars that produced the *Mecelle-i Ahkâm-ı Adliye,* a pioneering attempt to codify Islamic law. He had a hand in preparing all the *Mecelle*'s sixteen books, placed in effect by imperial decree between 1870 and 1876 as the civil code for both Islamic and secular courts. The *Mecelle* remained in force until the Turkish republic adopted the Swiss civil code in 1926; in some successor states of the Ottoman Empire, it served much longer. The *Mecelle* constitutes a unique case of successful resistance to the Ottoman tendency toward adopting European law.

Close to the palace and reluctant about the constitutional movement, Cevdet Paşa was politically very conservative. As his transfer from the *ulama* to the civil hierarchy and his close association with reformist statesmen suggest, however, he was intellectually broad-minded. He also founded an extraordinary family. He took part personally, to an unusual degree, in educating his children, in addition to hiring private tutors. His son Ali Sedad (1859–1900) authored several books on logic. His daughter Fatma Aliye (1862–1936) became the first Turkish woman novelist and a leading figure in the women's movement. His younger daughter, Emine Semiye (1864–1944), was allowed to study psychology and sociology in France and Switzerland, before returning to Turkey as an educator, writer, and political activist.

Cevdet Paşa's writings contributed to several fields. In history, he wrote not only his *History* (*Tarih-i Cevdet,* revised edition, Istanbul, 1891–92) but two sets of historical "memoranda" (*tezâkir, ma'ruzat*) that historians value as sources; he also completed the Ottoman Turkish translation of Ibn Khaldun's *Muqaddima.* In law, the *Mecelle* is largely his monument. He wrote, too, various pedagogical works, especially his multivolume *Kısas-ı Enbiya ve Tevarih-i Hülefa,* presenting accounts of the prophets and Islamic rulers, down to Sultan Murad II.

BIBLIOGRAPHY

CEVDET PAŞA, AHMED. *Tezâkir: 40—Tetimme,* ed. by Cavid Baysun. Ankara, 1967.
CHAMBERS, RICHARD L. "The Education of a Nineteenth Century Ottoman Alim, Ahmed Cevdet Paşa." *International Journal of Middle East Studies* 4 (1973): 440–464.
FATMA, ALIYE. *Ahmed Cevdet Paşa ve Zamanı.* Istanbul, 1914.
ÖLMEZOĞLU, ALI. "Cevdet Paşa." *Islam Ansiklopedisi,* vol 3. Istanbul, 1940–1988.

Carter V. Findley

Chad

Landlocked African state of 770,400 square miles (1.28 million sq. km), thinly populated by 5.1 million people.

A good part of Chad's problems stem from its enormous size. The nearest ports are in Nigeria and Cameroon, more than fifteen hundred miles (2,500 km) away. Its neighbors are two Arab states, Libya and Sudan, and five black African nations, Niger, Mali, Nigeria, Cameroon, and the Central African Republic. Chad sits uneasily between the two traditions—the violent conflicts in recent Chadian history reflect the competition between Arab North Africa and francophone black Africa. Chad's official languages are French and Arabic.

Chad is divided by the Chari river. The north—subdivided into the Saharan Borkou-Ennedi-Tibesti (BET) region and dry Sahel region—is populated almost completely by Muslims. The south—geographically a rainy forest savanna—is populated by equal numbers of Christians and believers in traditional religions. In the north, a good part of the population is nomadic or semisedentary; the population of the south is entirely agrarian and sedentary. The economy of the north is based on livestock; the economy of the south is based on cotton cultivation, earning 80 percent of Chad's export income. Chad is one of the world's least developed countries, with an annual per capita income of $105 (1990). While the north comprises 80 percent of Chad's territory, only 50 percent of the population resides there—mostly in the Sahel, where the capital, Ndjamena (formerly Fort Lamy), is located. Other towns of importance are Bardai, Faya Largeau, and Abeche in the north, and Moundou and Sarh in the south.

The ethnic map of Chad is complex and consists of dozens of peoples, each with its own territory, history, language, and culture. In the Saharan north, the dominant ethnic groups are the Toubou nomads, who are closely related to the Toubous in Libya and Niger. In the Sahel, the most important groups are the Kanembou, the Hadjerai, and the various Ouaddaian and Arab tribes. The south is dominated by the Sara, the largest ethnic group in Chad.

In precolonial times, the south was segmentary and stateless; the Saharan north was tribal; and the

Sahel was dominated by the strong Muslim kingdoms of Kanem, Ouaddai, and Baguirmi. For centuries, the northern tribes and kingdoms raided the Sara south, participating in the lucrative slave trade. In the nineteenth century, tens of thousands of southern slaves were sold each year to Arab North Africa. The historical division of Chad into the northern *Dar al-Islam* (House of Islam) and the southern *Dar al-Abid* (House of Slaves) is crucial to understanding Chad's modern history.

The French began their conquest of Chad in the late nineteenth century. They were welcomed as liberators by the African south because they put an end to the slave-raiding expeditions of the Muslim north. The French subjugation of the north was, however, violent and cruel; it was fiercely resisted well into the 1920s. French rule reversed the traditional commercial routes—the trans-Saharan slave trade was suppressed and new commercial links between "Cotton Chad" and Europe, via the ports of Nigeria and Cameroon, were established. During French colonial rule, the Sara south modernized relatively quickly—schools were established by Christian missionaries, commercial crops were introduced, and Africans were recruited to the colonial bureaucracy and the army. French rule dramatically reversed historical relationships—the former slave-raiding north stagnated, while the former enslaved south acquired the skills to rule Chad after independence.

Chad's first political parties were established after World War II. The southern Parti Progressiste Tchadien (PPT) became the leading party, and Chad became independent under its leadership in 1960. In 1962, its leader, François Tombalbaye, dissolved all opposition parties, creating a single-party state. Tombalbaye's rule, notorious for its corruption and brutality, lasted until 1975. In April 1975, Tombalbaye was killed during an army coup led by his fellow Sara—Army Chief of Staff Felix Malloum.

From 1965 to 1978, northern Muslim guerilla movements fought against Tombalbaye's and Malloum's southern governments, which they regarded as oppressive and "colonial." The major guerilla movement FROLINAT (Front Libération Nationale du Chad) was supported in its struggle against the southern "Christian" government by neighboring Libya. Libyan involvement intensified, especially after Qaddafi's rise to power in 1969. In 1972, the Libyans occupied and annexed the uranium-rich AOZOU STRIP in the north of Chad.

FROLINAT disintegrated into several groups in the 1970s. One, the FAP (Forces Armées Populaires), commanded by Goukouny Woddeye and supported by regular Libyan troops, occupied the whole Saharan BET in 1977 and threatened Malloum's government in Ndjamena. This led Malloum to form a coalition with another northern force, the FAN (Forces Armées du Nord), led by Hissen Habré in August 1978. This first north–south coalition was fiercely opposed by the Libyans and their Arab allies in Chad, led by the CDR (Conseil Démocratique de la Révolution). The Malloum–Habré alliance broke up in February 1979 when northern Muslims and southern Saras fought a ferocious battle in Ndjamena. The slaughter of thousands of Sara, the flight of Malloum and his entourage, and the exodus of all Saras to the south meant the end of southern predominance in postcolonial Chad. Between March 1975 and March 1980 a shaky northern coalition between Goukouny and Habré was formed. This coalition was opposed by the Libyans and their CDR allies. Although Muslim, it was Chadian-nationalist, anti-Libyan, and opposed to the Libyan occupation of the Aozou Strip and other areas in northern Chad. In March 1980, Libya's efforts to destabilize the Goukouny–Habré coalition bore fruit. The coalition fell apart and a year-long intranorthern civil war between Goukouny's FAP and Habré's FAN began. Initially, Goukouny remained in power with the help of the CDR and the Libyans, and Habré led his guerilla forces against the Goukouny–Qaddafi alliance. In the summer of 1980, tens of thousands of Libyan troops invaded Chad, conquered the whole north, and by December 15, 1980, Libyan tanks had rolled into Ndjamena. On January 6, 1981, Goukouny was forced by Qaddafi to agree to a "unification" of Chad and Libya. Popular anti-Libyan demonstrations in Chad and an almost unanimous hostile reaction throughout black Africa forced Libya to retract its intention to annex Chad. Qaddafi, who wanted to become OAU (Organization of African Unity) chairman, even agreed to withdraw his troops from Chad in November 1981.

Qaddafi's reversal weakened Goukouny's rule in Ndjamena and on June 6, 1982, Habré's FAN conquered the capital and formed a new government. Now it was Goukouny's turn to wage a guerilla war against Habré's government. During the 1980s, Habré's government, supported by France, the United States, and Egypt, fought opposition forces and Libyan troops that reentered Chad in 1982/83. Until 1987, the north was occupied by Libya, which appointed Libyan governors, introduced Libyan currency, and issued Libyan identity cards. In 1986/87, Libyan "colonialism" caused large-scale defections from the opposition guerilla movements. In the spring of 1987, Habré's FANT (Front Armée Nationale du Tchad), aided by the bulk of FAP, which had deserted Goukouny, and French air and ground forces, succeeded in defeating the Libyan army and liberated the entire north from Libyan occupation. The Libyans, who suffered heavy losses, succeeded in retaking the Aozou Strip in the summer of 1987, but the BET of the Sahara remained under government control.

In September 1987, Libya and Chad signed a ceasefire agreement; in August 1989 the Algiers Agreement between the two countries called for Libya to withdraw from Chad and for the Aozou Strip dispute to be resolved by the International Court of Justice. Despite these agreements, Libyan-supported opposition forces continued to fight Chad government forces. One such opposition group, the Mouvement Patriotique du Salut (MPS), established in April 1989 and led by former FANT commander Idriss Deby, was supported mainly by the Zaghawa and Hadjerai tribes and managed to defeat Habré's forces in December 1990. After the capital was conquered, a new government sympathetic to Libya was established. Habré's defeat was made possible because the French forces, which had supported Habré from 1982 to 1989, decided to regard the struggle as an internal affair and to remain neutral. In December 1991, supporters of former President Habré launched an attack on Chad from across the Nigerian border. They were soundly defeated by Deby's army and presidential guard, assisted by French Foreign Legionnaires sent from the Central African Republic.

BIBLIOGRAPHY

BUITENHUIS, R. *Le Frolinat et les guerres civiles du Tchad.* Paris, 1987.

DECALO, S. *Historical Dictionary of Chad.* Metuchen, N.J., 1977.

KELLY, S. *A State in Disarray: Conditions of Chad's Survival.* Boulder, Colo., 1986.

NEUBERGER, B. *Involvement, Invasion and Withdrawal: Qadhdhafi's Libya and Chad, 1969–1981.* Tel Aviv, 1982.

THOMPSON, V., and R. ADLOFF. *Conflict in Chad.* London, 1981.

Benyamin Neuberger

Chader, Joseph [?–1975]

Member of parliament in Lebanon.

An Armenian Catholic who for decades served in parliament as a member of the PHALANGE Party, Chader was a close associate of the party's leader, Pierre JUMAYYIL. He was chair of the parliamentary budget committee and held ministerial posts in various cabinets. He died shortly after the outbreak of the Lebanese Civil War of 1975.

As'ad AbuKhalil

Chadirchi, Kamil [1897–1968]

Iraqi politician.

Born in Baghdad, the son of Rifat Pasha al-Chadirchi, Kamil Chadirchi was thwarted in his attempt to earn a law degree by the eruption of World War I. He became a prominent member of the Ikha party, which was led by Yasin al-HASHIMI. Kamil had some differences with al-Hashimi and became a minister in the cabinet of General Bakr SIDQI, the leader of the coup of 1936. Kamil Chadirchi established and became chairman of the NATIONAL DEMOCRATIC PARTY in the 1930s and was editor in chief of the party newspaper *al-Ahali.* In 1954 he was elected by a landslide to be a representative of the National Front to the Iraqi parliament. Before it had been formed, however, the parliament was aborted by Prime Minister Nuri al-Sa'id.

After the revolution in 1958, Kamil Chadirchi faded away as a political figure. He died in Baghdad in 1968.

Mamoon A. Zaki

Chador

A large, shawl-like cloth outer garment worn by women in Iran and other Middle Eastern countries to cover the body, head, and face except for the eyes.

In the Islamic period the term *chador,* or *chadar* (veil), applied to the loose, sleeveless outer garment worn by women in the Middle East in order to cover the body. Contrary to common assumptions, however, the veil was not a novelty introduced to the Middle East by Islam. Veiling of women, and in rare circumstances men, was common in pre-Islamic Iran, especially among the nobility.

Islamic injunctions for veiling are based on two verses from the Qu'ran, 24:31 and 33:59. These are not concrete in their language; the first stipulates that "women should not display their ornaments" and the second that "when venturing outside the home, women should draw their outer garments around them." Through time, however, these Qur'anic verses came to be interpreted strictly, and various forms of veiling prevailed in Iran.

On January 7, 1936, Reza Shah Pahlavi banned the veil in Iran. This law forced many women to remain in their houses and roused the hostility of many religious scholars. After the removal of Reza Shah in 1941, many women readopted the chador. After the Iranian Revolution of 1978/79, the covering of the head, but not veiling, was gradually made compulsory for women.

BIBLIOGRAPHY

YARSHATER, EHSAN, ed. *Encyclopaedia Iranica*, vol. 1. London, 1985.

Parvaneh Pourshariati

Chalabi, Fadhil al- [1929–]

Iraqi oil official.

Born in Baghdad in 1929 to Ja'far Muhammad al-Chalabi, he received his B.A. in Muslim law from Baghdad University in 1951, his D.E.S. in economics from the Université de Poitiers, France (1956, 1958), and a Ph.D. in economics from the Université de Paris. He was the director general of oil affairs in the Iraqi Ministry of Oil between 1968 and 1973, permanent undersecretary to the Minister of Oil between 1973 and 1976, and the assistant secretary of the ORGANIZATION OF ARAB PETROLEUM EXPORTING COUNTRIES (OAPEC), based in Kuwait, from 1976 to 1978. Since 1978, he has been deputy secretary general of the ORGANIZATION OF PETROLEUM EXPORTING COUNTRIES (OPEC). His publications include *OPEC and International Oil Industry: A Changing Structure* (London, 1980).

Mia Bloom

Chaldean Church

See Christians in the Middle East

Challe, Maurice [1905–1979]

French air force general and commander in chief of French forces in Algeria, 1958–1960.

Born in Le Pontet, Vaucluse, France, Maurice Challe was a Saint-Cyr graduate and, in 1953, was commandant of the Ecole de Guerre Aérienne (School of Air War). In 1956, he assisted in the planning of France's operation to retake the Suez Canal after Egypt's nationalization of it. France's President Charles de Gaulle appointed Challe as commander in chief of the French forces in Algeria in December 1958. Challe responded by initiating highly effective aerial tactics (Challe Plan) against the nationalist ARMÉE DE LIBÉRATION NATIONALE (National Liberation Army, ALN).

Although reassigned in 1960 to the NORTH ATLANTIC TREATY ORGANIZATION (NATO), Challe was deeply affected by his Algerian experience and had become disaffected with de Gaulle's policy of decolonization—especially with the plight of Algerian loyalists (HARKIS). In February 1961, he resigned; in April, he and three other generals staged a revolt in Algiers against Paris, which failed to mobilize the anticipated support. Challe gave himself up and was interned until 1966 and then amnestied in 1968. He authored *Notre Révolte* (1968), which recollected his Algerian experiences and especially the April 1961 insurrection.

BIBLIOGRAPHY

HORNE, ALISTAIR. *A Savage War of Peace: Algeria, 1954–1962*, 2nd ed. New York, 1987.

Phillip C. Naylor

Chambers of Commerce

Associations of business people that promote commercial and industrial interests.

Beginning in the late nineteenth century, Middle Eastern chambers of commerce were established by monarchies and colonial regimes that wanted modernization for their countries. They viewed the formal and hierarchical organization of private business as indispensable to expanding state control over the domestic economy and foreign trade. Today's chambers of commerce are hybrid structures blending features of the Ottoman Empire's guilds with European corporatist models imported from France and Italy. The corporatist roots of Middle Eastern *chambers* of commerce are evident in the Turkish and Arabic words—*oda* and *ghurfa*—for the French *chambre* and the Italian *camera*.

The typical chamber of commerce is a semiofficial extension of the state bureaucracy. Its structure, finances, and daily activities are defined by detailed legislation and closely supervised by parent ministries. Its member businesses are compelled by law to join and pay annual dues. Its leaders are selected through a combination of election and government appointment. Chambers of commerce are forced to perform two inherently contradictory functions—to defend their members' interests and to implement the directives of state planners and technocrats.

Chambers of commerce often find it difficult to act as effective interest groups, because generally they must accommodate diverse constituencies with irreconcilable conflicts of interest. In many countries, chambers of commerce are expected to be the chief speaker for merchants and industrialists, importers and exporters, large monopolists and small craftsmen, technologically advanced firms in prosperous regions and self-employed shopkeepers in the provinces.

Although chambers of commerce originally were intended to regulate businesses rather than to express their demands, in one country after another their roles in policymaking and in politics have expanded steadily, along with the growth of the private sector as a whole. Chambers of commerce fashion compromises between business leaders and economic ministries over many key issues, such as import quotas and licenses, market shares, export subsidies, price and quality controls, labor relations, and joint ventures with foreign investors. Several governments such as Turkey, Egypt, and Morocco have forged long-term partnerships with chambers of commerce to implement ambitious policies of import substitution and state-led industrialization.

In the Middle East, both authoritarian and democratic regimes have relied on chambers of commerce to organize the private sector into a reliable base of social support, cooperating with the ruling coalition. Chambers of commerce have become key political actors because they are the largest associations that seek to represent diverse private-business interests. Other organizations may be more effective speaking for the interests of wealthier subsectors, such as industry, banking, or exporting, but chambers of commerce enroll the widest group of businesses from every economic category and geographic region.

In many countries, the provincial organizations of the ruling party overlap the local chambers of commerce; leadership positions in party and chamber branches frequently are interchangeable. At the national level, party chairmen often interfere in the elections of the confederation of chambers of commerce—the largest business association in the country. Party leaders draw up mixed lists of candidates from rival chambers, hoping to moderate regional jealousies in the private sector before they produce splinter parties that might cut into the ruling coalition's electoral support. Particularly in countries with multiparty systems, chamber of commerce leaders have become valued allies who are courted by politicians in power and by the opposition. Thus, over time, many chambers of commerce have become influential representatives of the very constituencies they were supposed to regulate.

BIBLIOGRAPHY

LANGER, WILLIAM L. *An Encyclopedia of World History.* Boston, 1948.

Robert Bianchi

Chamchian, Mikayel   [1738–1823]

Armenian intellectual, regarded as the first modern Armenian historian.

Chamchian was born in Istanbul to an Armenian family of the Roman Catholic faith. He was trained as a jeweler in the employ of the Armenian *amira* Mikayel Chelebi Diuzian, the imperial jeweler (*see* ARMENIAN MILLET). Abandoning secular life, Chamchian joined his brother in Venice at the monastery of the Armenian Mekhitarian Order in 1762. Upon completion of his education and training, he was sent as a preacher among the Armenians of Aleppo and Basra. In 1774 he was appointed instructor of Armenian language and grammar at the monastery, and in 1795 he was assigned to Istanbul as the resident Mekhitarian representative. He died there after a long and productive life.

Chamchian was more than a missionary and educator. As grammarian, theologian, and historian, he was the intellectual giant of his age. His *Kerakanutiun Haykazian Lezvi* (Grammar of the Armenian Language, 1779) is a landmark in Armenian linguistic studies. It was the first descriptive grammar of the Armenian language, though still of classical Armenian. His theological studies were defenses of Roman Catholicism, which, however, did not pass the censor at Rome for their attempt to reconcile Roman Catholic theology with Armenian Orthodoxy.

He made his most important contribution, however, as a historian. He wrote *Patmutiun Hayots i Skzbane Ashkharhi Minchev tsam diarn 1784* (Armenian History from the Beginning of the World to the Year 1784, 3 vols., 1784–1786.) Writing a universal history, in these volumes Chamchian developed a continuous narrative depiction of the Armenian people from the Creation to his own time. Though grounded in the biblical framework of the origin of humankind and of nations, Chamchian nevertheless, crossed a number of important thresholds from a medieval worldview. His interpretation of events suggests more modern practices of historiographic methodology: he familiarized himself with current scholarship; he contextualized Armenian history by studying the classical historians; he examined all the extant Armenian historial works; and he constructed a comprehensive history of the Armenians. As a result, Chamchian's *Patmutiun Hayots* is regarded as the first work in modern Armenian historical scholarship.

BIBLIOGRAPHY

ADALIAN, ROUBEN P. *From Humanism to Rationalism: Armenian Scholarship in the Nineteenth Century.* Atlanta, 1992.

Rouben P. Adalian

Chamoun, Camille [1900–1987]

President of Lebanon, 1952–1958; one of the most charismatic and influential Maronite politicians of the post–World War II period.

Born in Dayr al-Qamar, a predominantly Christian village located in the mixed Druze-Maronite district of the Shuf, in southern Mount Lebanon, Camille Chamoun (also Sham'un) graduated from the Faculty of Law of Saint Joseph University in Beirut in 1925 and was elected to Lebanon's parliament in 1934. A member of Bishara al-Khuri's Constitutional Bloc, he rapidly rose to political prominence and became minister of finance in 1938.

In the late 1930s and early 1940s, he developed a close connection with the British and American governments and repeatedly headed Lebanese missions overseas. It was then that he began to acquire the reputation of being one of Lebanon's most cosmopolitan and most sophisticated politicians. After playing an important role in the events that led up to the gaining of independence by Lebanon (1943), he was a minister in several of President Khuri's governments. He nevertheless broke with Khuri in May 1948, when the latter sought to have the constitution amended to allow for his reelection. In 1951, he created the so-called Socialist Front with Druze leader Kamal JUMBLATT and Maronite leaders Pierre JUMAYYIL and Raymond EDDÉ. The members of the socialist front accused President Khuri of corruption, nepotism, and violations of the law, and they sought to obtain his resignation. In the summer of 1952, they organized a successful countrywide general strike that forced Khuri to step down, and soon afterward, on September 23, 1952, Chamoun was elected president.

His presidency can be credited with several achievements. He increased the independence of the judiciary, induced Parliament to grant women the right to vote, and took measures to liberalize trade and industry that greatly contributed to the subsequent period of economic expansion and prosperity in Lebanon. He was criticized, however, for many of the very same practices he had accused his predecessor of fostering, particularly corruption and abuses of his authority. The political establishment distrusted his authoritarian leanings and his attempt to undercut the influence of traditional leaders. The Sunni Islam community especially felt alienated by his effort to undermine the authority of the premiership, which by convention was reserved for a Sunni, and by his unabashedly pro-Western foreign policy. During the 1956 crisis, for instance, he had refused to heed Muslim pressures to break off relations with France and Britain. As the pan-Arab rhetoric of Egyptian President Gamal Abdel Nasser became increasingly popular among the Sunni masses of Lebanon, he defiantly intensified the alignment of Lebanon with the United States, and, in 1957, he was the only Arab leader to publicly endorse the Eisenhower doctrine. Such open hostility to the rising tide of Arab nationalism in Lebanon made him very unpopular among Sunni Muslims. More generally, his heavy-handed, provocative style alienated many, including those within the Christian community. As a result, during his last two years in office, the people of Lebanon became increasingly polarized and discontented with his administration.

In 1957, Chamoun rigged the parliamentary elections to weaken his rivals and permit parliament to approve a constitutional amendment that would have enabled him to be reelected for a second term. Several of the country's most prominent political bosses thus failed to regain their seats in the Chamber of Deputies, which was then dominated by Chamoun loyalists. Such a blatantly illegal but effective maneuver to undermine their power led Chamoun's rivals to rise up against him during what came to be known as the 1958 Lebanese Civil War. Although Chamoun was allowed to remain in office until the end of his term, September 1958, he had to abandon any ambition of being reelected.

He never again exerted as much power as he had between 1952 and 1958, but he remained active in public life and continued to display his skills as a populist, pragmatic politician. In 1959, he founded the NATIONAL LIBERAL PARTY (NLP), which, of all parties, became the most consistent advocate of free enterprise and close ties with Western countries. He also rapidly emerged as a determined opponent of President Chehab and his policies, and in 1967 he formed the so-called Tripartite Alliance with the other chief opponents of Chehab, Raymond Eddé of the National Bloc and Pierre Jumayyil of the Phalange Party. He thus was instrumental in electing Sulayman Franjiyya to the presidency in 1970 and remained a behind-the-scenes power broker in the years that followed.

As Lebanon slowly drifted toward civil war in the early 1970s, Chamoun proved himself to be one of the most hawkish voices within the Christian community. He was determined to maintain Christian domination over state institutions and to resist calls to end the confessionalism. During the first phase of the civil war, from 1975 to 1976, he was minister of the interior. In the course of the hostilities, he and his followers were rapidly overshadowed by Bashir Jumayyil and his Lebanese Forces. In July 1980, the Lebanese Forces destroyed the military infrastructure of the Tigers, NLP's small militia. Although Chamoun joined the Government of National Unity formed in 1984, he was then no longer in a position to influence the course of national politics. He died of a heart attack in August 1987.

BIBLIOGRAPHY

CHAMOUN, CAMILLE. *Crise au Moyen Orient*. Paris, 1963.
COBBAN, HELENA. *The Making of Modern Lebanon*. Boulder, Colo., 1985.
HUDSON, MICHAEL C. *The Precarious Republic: Political Modernization in Lebanon*. New York, 1968.

Guilain P. Denoeux

Chamoun, Dany   [1934–1990]

Leader of Lebanon's National Liberal Party.

Son of former President Camille CHAMOUN, Dany Chamoun became active in Lebanese politics during the 1975 civil war, when he assumed the leadership of the Tigers, the small militia of his father's NATIONAL LIBERAL PARTY (NLP). After the Tigers were thoroughly defeated by the Lebanese Forces in July 1980, Dany Chamoun was forced into exile in Paris. When his father died, in August 1987, he inherited the leadership of the NLP and returned to Beirut. From 1989 to 1990, he backed Gen. Michel Aoun and opposed Syrian influence in Lebanon. He was assassinated in his Beirut apartment on October 21, 1990, together with his wife and two of their young children.

BIBLIOGRAPHY

HIRO, DILIP. *Lebanon: Fire and Embers*. New York, 1992.
RANDAL, JONATHAN C. *Going All the Way: Christian Warlords, Israeli Adventurers, and the War in Lebanon*. New York, 1983.

Guilain P. Denoeux

Champollion, Jean-François   [1790–1832]

French linguist and historian whose breakthrough in 1822 in deciphering hieroglyphics made him the founder of modern Egyptology.

The availability of the Rosetta Stone (uncovered in 1799) and other inscriptions, and Champollion's mastery of Coptic were prerequisites to success. The Rosetta Stone's text was inscribed in two languages (Egyptian and Greek) and three writing systems—Greek, hieroglyphics, and demotic (a form of ancient Egyptian cursive writing). Having started studying Eastern languages as a child, Champollion recognized that the scriptural language of the Coptic Christian church was the latest form of ancient Egyptian.

As conservator of Egyptian antiquities at the Louvre museum in Paris, Champollion arranged the impressive Egyptian galleries, which opened in 1827. In 1828/29, he and Ippolito Rosellini led a French–Tuscan expedition to Egypt to copy inscriptions from the ancient monuments. Champollion died at forty-two, leaving his elder brother Jacques-Joseph Champollion-Figeac to publish many of his manuscript works.

BIBLIOGRAPHY

DAWSON, WARREN R., and ERIC P. UPHILL. *Who Was Who in Egyptology*, 2nd ed., London, 1972.
LACOUTURE, JEAN. *Champollion: Une vie de lumières*. Paris, 1988.

Donald Malcolm Reid

Chamran, Mostafa   [1931–1981]

Iranian political activist.

Born in Tehran, Mostafa Chamran was an engineer by training, having earned a Ph.D. in electromechanics from the University of California at Berkeley in 1962. While studying in the United States, he cofounded, with Sadeq Gotbzader and Ibrahim Yazdi, the Muslim Students Association, which opposed the shah. He entered political life, during the days of the nationalization of the Iranian oil industry and the premiership of Mohammad MOSSADEGH (1951–1953) as a member of the National Resistance Movement, the more religiously inclined branch of Mossadegh's National Front (see NATIONAL FRONT, IRAN). In the 1970s he moved to Lebanon and joined the AMAL group led by the Shi'ite cleric Imam Musa Sadr. After the Iranian Revolution of 1979, Chamran was assistant to the prime minister and a member of parliament, until his mysterious death on the front line during the war between Iran and Iraq. In addition to being a political activist, Chamran was also the author of several collections of mystical poetry.

BIBLIOGRAPHY

ECHO OF IRAN. *Iran Almanac 1987 and Book of Facts*. Tehran, 1987.

Neguin Yavari

Chancellor, John [1870–1952]

British soldier and civil servant.

After serving as the British military governor in Mauritius, Trinidad and Tobago, and Southern Rhodesia, Chancellor was British High Commissioner for Palestine from 1928 to 1931. He opposed Zionist aspirations in Palestine and was reportedly involved in the drafting of the Passfield White Paper (1930), in which Britain seemed to back off from its commitments to the Jews, as set forth in the BALFOUR DECLARATION, thus foreshadowing the restrictions on immigration and land transfers that followed.

BIBLIOGRAPHY

WASSERSTEIN, BERNARD. *The British in Palestine: The Mandatory Government and the Arab–Jewish Conflict (1917–1929).* New York, 1982.

Bryan Daves

Charents, Yeghishe [1897–1937]

Soviet Armenian poet.

Originally named Soghomonyan, Yeghishe (also, Eghishe) Charents was born in Kars, Russian Armenia, of Iranian-Armenian parents; he was killed by the KGB (Soviet Committee of State Security) during the Stalinist purges, in Armenia's capital, Yerevan. His first poems, in a romantic-symbolist vein, were published at Tbilisi (Tiflis), Russian Georgia, in 1912. His only prose work of any length, the novel *The Land of Nairi,* is in large part a memoir of the world of his childhood. Long poems such as "The Crazed Masses," "Brigadier Shavarsh," and "A Dantesque Legend" describe, often in harsh and strident tones, the subsequent horrors he experienced during the Armenian genocide, World War I, the Russian Revolution, and the chaos of the short-lived Republic of Armenia (1918–1921). As an ardent Communist and Red Army fighter, he bitterly opposed the republic and its nationalist rulers.

In the 1920s, Charents wrote a number of poems extolling the revolution and Soviet values, frequently in the style of a Russian poet contemporary to him, Vladimir Mayakovsky. Charents was fluent in Russian and a frequent visitor to Moscow, where the first, two-volume edition of his works was published. He worked as an editor at Haypethrat, the Armenian state publishing house, introducing and encouraging young writers. He translated Goethe, Heine, and other German poets into Armenian and was a boisterous entertainer and drinker. But he was also

melancholy and mystical: In his poem "Vision of Death," he offers himself as a blood sacrifice for the Armenian people; and "The Cats and I" is a tortured confession of a lonely voyeur, jealous of spring and of animal sexuality. Charents was a heroin addict, and in his study, with its Persian furnishings (he wrote with nostalgia of the roses of Shiraz, and, in imitation of Iranian forms, composed a *Charents-nameh*), there was a portrait of Dante and a statue of the Buddha. Both figure in the manuscript of a play that is set entirely in the author's imagination. His "Song-Book" (*Tagharan,* 1920), one of his best works, is a series of GHAZELS written in the style of the eighteenth-century polyglot bard of Tiflis (now Tbilisi), Sayat Nova ("Hunter of Songs"), in which Charents portrays himself as an inspired minstrel whose poems are sung at feasts but who stands outside in the snow, barefoot, lonely, and starving. Virtually every Armenian schoolchild can recite by heart the poem "I love my Armenia's sun-steeped fruit" (*Yes im anush Hayastani*) from the cycle.

Charents was a friend of Russian poet Osip Mandelshtam; and at the first Congress of the Union of Soviet Writers at Moscow he defended Russian author Boris Pasternak. He was also a friend of the Armenian Communist Party secretary Aghassi Khanjian (killed by Stalin's chief secret policeman Lavrenti Pavlovich Beria in Tbilisi in 1936). None of this endeared him to the Stalinist authorities; and after his "Book of the Journey," an epic mass of poems on the historical path trodden by the Armenians, was published—and savagely attacked—in 1934, he withdrew into himself, writing elegiac verses on autumn, meditations with God, praises of statues and of female loveliness—the very kind of poetry he had sometimes criticized as a young Bolshevik. Many of these manuscripts were buried by friends in tin cans in back gardens at the time of his arrest and have been published only in recent years, although the poet's published works were rehabilitated in 1954.

BIBLIOGRAPHY

Charents's poems have been translated into numerous languages, including English, by this writer, in the journal *Ararat,* 1978–present; by RALPH SETIAN and GARIG BASMADJIAN in various periodicals; and by DIANA DER HOVANESSIAN, *The Land of Fire.* The six-volume critical edition, *Erkeri zhoghovatsu* (Yerevan, 1962–1967) has been supplemented by studies of rediscovered fragments—notably the work by the poet's daughter ANAHIT CHARENTS, *Ch'arents'i dzerragreri ashkharhum* (In the World of Charents's Manuscripts [Yerevan, 1978]).

James R. Russell

Charikar

Afghan City.

The provincial capital of Parwan province, Charikar is approximately 25 miles (40 km) north of Kabul on the major north–south highway and has a population of about 20,000. Most of the people are Tajiks, although there are Hazara in the surrounding regions. The city's importance lies in the fact that the various roads over the Hindu Kush, especially the paved road through the Salang pass, come together in Charikar, which, in 1839, was a major British outpost.

BIBLIOGRAPHY

ADAMEC, LUDWIG. *Historical Dictionary of Afghanistan.* Metuchen, N.J., 1991.

Grant Farr

Chefferie

A French word meaning a specific area under control of a forest ranger.

Chefferie is used in anthropological literature to mean a territory inhabited by a group of people or a tribe under the authority of a chief. In traditional societies, "chefferie" implies the existence of leadership over a social group such as a tribe or subtribe sharing the same territory. The leader is politically responsible for his chiefdom. He has internal functions such as leading meetings of the tribal council, which is the highest political authority in the chiefdom, and external functions such as leading war against other chiefdoms or making peace or alliances with other tribes. In the French ethnography of Morocco and Algeria, the notion of chefferie conceptualizes the phenomenon of leadership of the AMGHAR (the Berber chief) or that of the QA'ID over a tribe.

Rahma Bourqia

Chehab, Bashir   [1767–1850]

Early nineteenth century ruler in Lebanon.

Chehab (sometimes Shihab) born in Ghazir, was converted to Christianity with the rest of his family. Growing up in poverty, he may have received some elementary education at home. He subsequently went to Bayt al-Din, where land had been left to him by his father. Chehab's rise to power was not accidental. He first became wealthy by marrying the widow of a relative, and he cultivated good relations with al-Jazzar in Acre. When the rule of his relative Prince Yusuf became intolerable, Ahmad al-Jazzar chose him as his replacement in 1789 with the support of the Jumblatts. When Yusuf went to Acre to regain his throne, he was briefly reappointed ruler of Lebanon. However, Chehab was able to convince al-Jazzar to reverse his decision, and Yusuf was arrested and executed.

But Chehab's rule remained precarious, depending on the whims of al-Jazzar. In 1793, 1794, and 1798, al-Jazzar appointed Yusuf's sons as princes of Lebanon. The occupation of Egypt by Napoléon and his advance toward Palestine secured Chehab's position for a while. When the French besieged Acre, al-Jazzar asked for Chehab's help; Chehab declined, citing the instability of the situation. He also refused to aid the French, fearing the wrath of the Druzes if he did so, because the French were supported by the Maronites. When the French withdrew, al-Jazzar, intent on punishing Chehab, appointed five different people to challenge his authority. Chehab fled Lebanon and sought support from the Ottoman Empire. He remained in fear of al-Jazzar until the latter died in 1804.

Beginning in 1804, Chehab focused on consolidating his rule. Al-Jazzar had turned the Druze landlords against him, and he punished the latter by curtailing their economic and political power. Even members of his own family were not spared—many were killed and their holdings confiscated. By 1806, Chehab was promoting himself as the undisputed emir, and he built an opulent palace at Bayt al-Din that is now a tourist attraction. Chehab was secure in his position until 1819, when Abdallah Pasha took over as *wali* of Acre and demanded additional taxes from Chehab. The resulting protests and turmoil forced Chehab to abandon his emirate in 1820 and flee to Hawran. The resulting chaos alarmed Abdallah, who allowed Chehab to return in 1821. Chehab quickly reestablished order, for which he was rewarded with Abdallah's support of his claims against the *vilaye* of Damascus. When Abdallah was removed by the sultan, Chehab went to Egypt. There he befriended Muhammad Ali, who secured his reappointment.

Chehab's return to Lebanon marked the beginning of the disintegration of the emirate. Intoxicated with the backing of Muhammad Ali, Chehab assumed that a crackdown against Jumblatti Druzes would be safe; he had Bashir Jumblatt, the leader of the Druze community, killed. The Druzes never forgave him. The advance of Ibrahim Pasha to Acre in 1831 forced Chehab to provide help—against the wishes of the Druzes and to the delight of the Maronites. Fighting broke out between Druzes and Maronites. When Ottoman and European forces landed in Lebanon to expel Ibrahim Pasha from Syria, Chehab was evacuated on a British ship. He died in Istanbul.

As'ad AbuKhalil

Chehab, Fu'ad   [1902–1975]

The most important Lebanese statesman of the twentieth century.

Chehab (sometimes Shihab) was born to a Maronite family. During the French Mandate, he served in the Special Forces of the Levant, established by the French government to legitimize their presence in Lebanon, and rose to the rank of lieutenant colonel. In 1946, with the official withdrawal of all French troops from Lebanon, Chehab was appointed the first commander in chief of the Lebanese army. He transformed the French-created force into a small national army, modernized the forces, and introduced Western-style military academies.

Chehab's name first appeared in a political context in 1952, when he refused to obey the orders of President Bishara al-KHURI to suppress demonstrators expressing their outrage at the corruption of Khuri's regime. Chehab strongly believed that the army should be kept out of internal political disputes. He also feared that any attempt to politicize the army would encourage a coup d'état. When al-Khuri resigned, Chehab was appointed prime minister (in effect, interim president) because the Maronite establishment did not want to leave the country in the hands of a Sunni prime minister. Chehab led a smooth transition of power and oversaw the democratic election of Camille CHAMOUN as president.

When a civil war broke out in 1958, amid signs that Chamoun desired a second term (contrary to the provisions of the constitution and the wishes of the Lebanese) and wanted to use the army to crush the rebels, Chehab again refused to commit troops to support the president. His stance won him the backing of Lebanese Muslims. He feared that the deployment of troops would aggravate the social tensions in the country. His neutral position in those critical times made him the logical choice for the presidency, and with the support of Egypt (Nasserist) and the United States, Chehab was elected president in July 1958.

As president, Chehab initiated reforms to create an efficient and noncorrupt bureaucracy. He wanted to promote representatives of the professional middle class in order to end the monopolization of political

power by traditional *zu'ama* (land holding elites). He also furthered social concord at home by transcending the sectarian interests of most politicians. Unlike other presidents of Lebanon, he was aware that political radicalism among Muslims was deeply rooted in socio-economic dissatisfaction. He initiated a program of development in poor Muslim areas, although it did not, according to critics, go far enough. His presidency was not without problems. So disgusted was Chehab with the petty considerations and interests of the traditional political class that he tried to undermine their power by consolidating the security apparatus, which was accountable only to him. The rule of the Deuxième Bureau instilled fear and intimidation among civilians (especially Palestinians) and politicians.

The term "Chehabism" came to denote the political movement that pledged allegiance to the president. Unlike other political movements of the twentieth century, his power base cut across sectarian lines. Uninterested in power and politics, Chehab tried to resign before the end of his term, but was not allowed to do so by the deputies in parliament. He was succeeded in the presidency by his protégé Charles HILU. Chehab shunned the limelight and rarely gave interviews. He died in seclusion.

As'ad AbuKhalil

Chehab, Khalid   [1892–1978]

Former Lebanese prime minister (1937, 1952–1953), minister of finance (1927–1928), deputy, and speaker of parliament (1936–1937).

Born in Hasbeya, Lebanon, Khalid Chehab was first elected to the Lebanese parliament in 1922. A member of Bishara al-Khuri's CONSTITUTIONAL BLOC, he was minister of finance from 1927 to 1928. Following a short tenure as speaker of Parliament, he was appointed prime minister in 1937. Although he was one of the most influential Lebanese politicians under the French mandate, he is best remembered for the seven months during which he served as President CHAMOUN's first prime minister (September 30, 1952, to April 30, 1953). Camille Chamoun, who had been elected with a mandate to modernize the administration, entrusted him with this important task. As head of a four-man cabinet, Khalid Chehab wielded emergency powers and issued several dozen decrees that consolidated the administration by defining much more clearly than before the responsibilities of civil servants and of the administrative departments. Other significant accomplishments of his cabinet included giving women the right to vote, changing the electoral system in a way that weakened the power of traditional patrons, substantially reforming the judiciary, and liberalizing the press law. Well-established persons who had been hurt by his policies acted in coordination with radical critics to force his resignation.

BIBLIOGRAPHY

HUDSON, MICHAEL C. *The Precarious Republic: Political Modernization in Lebanon.* Boulder, Colo., 1985.
LONGRIGG, STEPHEN H. *Syria and Lebanon under the French Mandate.* London and New York, 1958.
Who's Who in Lebanon. Beirut, 1964.

Guilain P. Denoeux

Chehab Family

A politically influential family in Lebanon.

The Chehab (also Shihab) family can be traced to Arab tribes from Hawran, Syria, who settled in southern Lebanon. The power of the family was established in 1697, when it inherited the leadership of the Mount Lebanon area from the last Ma'nid prince, who had no heirs. Originally a Sunni Muslim, Bashir II converted to Maronite Christianity, which displeased the Druze population in the mountains. Family members continued to occupy important positions in government and administration in the twentieth century. Its best-known member is Gen. Fu'ad CHEHAB, one of the most powerful and popular presidents in twentieth-century Lebanon.

As'ad AbuKhalil

Cheikho, Louis   [1859–1929]

Contributor to the renaissance of Arabic literature in Lebanon in the late nineteenth century.

A Chaldean native of Mardin, Turkey, Louis Cheikho was educated in Lebanon and Europe. He then returned to teach Arabic literature at the Saint Joseph Jesuit University in Beirut. He edited the university's monthly journal, *al-Mashriq,* and published over thirty literary works.

BIBLIOGRAPHY

HITTI, PHILIP K. *Lebanon in History: From the Earliest Times to the Present.* London, 1957.

Bassam Namani

Chelow

Chelow is a Persian-style steamed rice preparation.

Long-grain rice is soaked in cold water and drained. The rice is poured into boiling water and cooked for a few minutes, drained, and rinsed. The rice is then sauteed in butter and steamed in small amounts of water until done. Some cooks add saffron and yogurt.

Clifford A. Wright

Chenik, Muhammad

Tunisian businessman and political figure.

During World War II, as a member of the Grand Council, Chenik was chosen in 1942 by the BEY, Muhammad al-Munsif, to lead a pronationalist government. The effort was suppressed by the FREE FRENCH the following year. In 1950, with the campaign for the independence of Tunisia in full swing, Chenik was picked to head a new government that featured a Tunisian majority. In 1952, during a French repression of the nationalist movement, Chenik and his cabinet, along with Habib BOURGUIBA and other leading activists for nationalism, were arrested.

BIBLIOGRAPHY

HAHN, LORNA. *North Africa: Nationalism to Nationhood.* Washington, D.C., 1960.

Matthew S. Gordon

Cherkes

See Circassians

Chesney, Francis   [1789–1872]

British explorer of the Ottoman Empire.

In 1830, Chesney surveyed the isthmus of Suez and concluded that a canal was feasible. Chesney surveyed the Euphrates river (in modern Turkey, Syria, and Iraq) in 1831 and again in 1835/1837 along with the Tigris (in modern Turkey and Iraq) in order to determine their use as a trade link with India. Finally, in 1856, he surveyed Antioch (in modern Turkey) as a possible railroad terminus along the inland trade route to India.

BIBLIOGRAPHY

Dictionary of National Biography, vol. 4.
Webster's Biographical Dictionary, 1988.

Zachary Karabell

China and the Middle East

China and the Middle East have been in contact since before the spread of Islam into East Asia.

From antiquity, China's ties with the Middle East were based on trade, with both shipping and overland caravans going from the Middle East to what was then called the Far East. Chinese merchants and ships' captains met the Middle Easterners at China's western border, led them to their trading points and then back out of Chinese territory.

After the establishment of the People's Republic of China (October 1, 1949), China made its presence felt in the Middle East as a member of the nonalignment movement, wining diplomatic recognition in 1956 by Egypt; Syria soon followed. As the European powers withdrew from the Middle East, China gradually increased its diplomatic presence. In the 1960s, however, China was undergoing its Cultural Revolution, which left few resources for diplomacy. The major role it played in the Middle East then was an alternative model to Soviet communism, inspiring various Middle Eastern revolutionary movements.

The 1970s ushered in a new period of Chinese diplomacy, in which the rulers in China's capital, Beijing, increasingly opted for improving relations with established governments in the Middle East, rather than with those who sought to topple such governments (as in Iran and Oman). The intensification of the Sino-Soviet conflict in the late 1960s and the 1970s was probably at the root of this position. In other words, China resorted to its own version of the containment of Soviet expansion by strengthening ties with the ruling regimes, regardless of their politics.

As Sino-Soviet relations improved, however, from the 1980s on, China's interest seemed to shift from geopolitics to economics. China has carved out a share in the lucrative Middle East arms-buying market as an important supplier of weapons, including missiles to such countries as Iran and Saudi Arabia.

BIBLIOGRAPHY

EMBREE, AINSLIE T., ed. *Encyclopedia of Asian History.* New York, 1988.

SHICHOR, YITZHAK. *The Middle East in China's Foreign Policy, 1949–1977.* Cambridge, U.K., 1979.

Kazuo Takahashi

Cholera

Easily transmitted intestinal disease.

The causative agent, *Vibrio cholerae,* is transmitted by contaminated water or food, usually in poverty-stricken, overcrowded areas with inadequate water supplies and sewage disposal facilities. Not endemic to the Middle East, cholera can be spread through international travel. It is characterized by diarrhea and vomiting in severe cases, leading to rapid dehydration, followed by death. The most serious cholera epidemic in the Middle East during the twentieth century occurred in Egypt in 1947; over 50 percent of those infected died.

Jenab Tutunji

Chraibi, Driss [1926–]

One of Morocco's most prominent, prolific novelists writing in French.

Born in al-Jadida, to a Muslim Berber family, Driss Chraibi studied at the French lycée Lyautey in Casablanca. He received a college degree in chemistry in 1950 and went on to study neurology and psychiatry. Two months before qualifying for his doctorate in science, he gave up his studies and decided to travel in Europe while working at various jobs.

In his early novels, *Le Passé Simple* (1954; *The Simple Past*), and its sequel *Succession ouverte* (1962; *Open Sequence*), Chraibi drew on his own life to depict the generational conflict and culture shock experienced by Moroccan youth. Other novels draw on his experiences in Europe. *Les Boucs* (*The Goats,* 1955) describes the harsh living conditions of the Maghribi workers in France (see MAGHRIB). In his next novels, *L'Ane* (1956; *The Donkey*) and *La Foule* (1961; *The Mob*), Chraibi conveys his views as a Muslim Maghribi vis-à-vis the West, whose civilization and philosophy he had acquired through education. A more biting tone was set through the author's sense of cynical amusement in *La Foule* and much lighter humor in *La Civilisation, ma mère* (1971; *Civilization, My Mother*). In *De tous les horizons* (1958; *From All Horizons*) a book described as narration (*récits*), Chraibi again tapped his personal experiences in relation to his parents and as a Maghribi in France.

The novel *Une enquête au pays* (1981; *An Inquiry in the Country*), marked a turning point in Chraibi's interests. He indicated in this novel that he was embarking on a quest for his Berber identity. This new direction led to an exploration in his writings of pre-Islamic times and an emphasis on the ties of Berbers with the land of the Maghrib and on the relatively recent Arabization and Islamization of North Africa. He continued the quest in *La Mère du Printemps L'Oum-er-Bia* (1982; *The Mother of Springtime*). As a consequence of his concerns, Chraibi found himself in the delicate position of trying to dissociate himself from Arabic and the Arabs, without rejecting the Islam brought to the Maghrib by the Arabs. A few of Chraibi's novels focus on more general topics—for example, the condition of the emancipated woman in *Un Ami Viendra Vous Voir* (1967; *A Friend Will Come to See You*) and the story of a man and woman's struggle to establish a relationship in *Mort au Canada* (1975; *Dead in Canada*). More recent works include the novels *Naissance à l'Aube* (1986; *Birth at Dawn*) and *L'Inspecteur Ali* (1991; *Inspector Ali*), and the nonfiction work *Une Place au Soleil* (1993; *A Place in the Sun*).

BIBLIOGRAPHY

DÉJEUX, JEAN. *La littérature maghrébine de langue française.* Ottawa, 1973.

KADRA-HADJAJI, HOURIA. *Contestation et révolte dans l'œuvre de Driss Chraibi.* Algiers, 1986.

Aida A. Bamia

Chrakian, Artin [1804–1859]

An Armenian, minister of commerce and foreign affairs in Egypt, 1844–1850.

Artin Chrakian was born in Istanbul. His father, Sukias Chrakian, managed the commercial affairs of Tosun Pasha, one of the older sons of Muhammad Ali, the *vali* of Egypt. Sukias emigrated to Egypt in 1812, and two years later, his family followed him there. Artin Chrakian, his brother Khosrov, and a third Armenian, Aristakes Altunian, were allowed to attend school in the palace, where the young prince Abbas, later to inherit the governorship of Egypt, was one of their classmates. Sent to Paris, Artin Chrakian studied civil administration. His education completed, he returned to Egypt and began working at the war ministry at the mundane chore of translating French military manuals into Turkish. In succeeding years, however, Chrakian, along with other Armenian colleagues, was entrusted with the responsibility of reorganizing the educational system in the country. In May 1834, he opened the School of Engineering at Bulak, and in September of the same year, in conjunction with another Armenian, Stepan Demirjian, he opened the School of Translation in the citadel of Cairo. In 1836, he was appointed a member of the school council, which subsequently became the ministry of education.

By this time, Chrakian was a full-fledged member of the administrative machinery governing Egypt. His appointment as a member of the *majles al-ali,* the council for civil affairs, brought him in direct contact with the viceroy. From then on, his promotion was rapid. Muhammad Ali chose him as his first secretary

in 1839 and sent him as an envoy to Paris and London in 1841. Upon the death of Boghos Bey in 1844, Chrakian succeeded as minister of commerce and foreign affairs. He remained in that post during the regency of IBRAHIM IBN MUHAMMAD ALI. Along with many other Armenians in the employ of the Egyptian government, he fell out of favor after Abbas assumed the post of viceroy. He was removed from office in 1850 and went into exile in Europe. He returned after Sa'id, the succeeding viceroy, invited him back to Egypt. Chrakian may have been the first Armenian in Egypt to receive the hereditary title of pasha.

BIBLIOGRAPHY

ADALIAN, ROUBEN. "The Armenian Colony of Egypt during the Reign of Muhammad Ali (1805–1848)." *Armenian Review* 33, no. 2 (1980): 115–144.

Rouben P. Adalian

Christians in the Middle East

Originally a Jewish offshoot, Christianity has been present in the Middle East since the first century C.E.

Christianity is based on the spiritual and ethical teachings of Jesus of Nazareth, who lived and preached in Judea during the first century C.E. and was crucified by the Roman authorities; adherents of the faith believe he rose from the dead. To Christians, Jesus was the awaited Messiah of the Jewish people (*christos,* "the anointed one," is a Greek translation of "Messiah"). His teachings were compiled in the Gospels, which, together with the teachings of his earliest followers, the Apostles, form the corpus of the New Testament. These twenty-seven books, along with the Jewish Bible and the books of the Apocrypha, make up the Christian Bible.

Although the earliest Christians were all Jews, some time around 45 C.E. some of the Apostles—especially Paul and Barnabas—began to preach to the Gentiles throughout the Near East. Antioch, Edessa, and Alexandria emerged as early centers of Christianity.

By the fourth century the spread and influence of Christianity were such that it had become the official religion of the Roman Empire, whose capital had been moved by the Emperor Constantine from Rome to Constantinople. At that time, too, the religion underwent a series of theological disputes centered primarily on the relationship of the divine and human nature of Christ. At the Council of Chalcedon (451), those that stressed the unitary nature of Christ (the Monophysites) were deemed heretical. (They constituted the Oriental Orthodox family of churches.) The EASTERN ORTHODOX (Greek) Church, centered at Constantinople, remained the official imperial church of the Byzantine Empire. With the expansion of the Latin-based, western-rite church centered at Rome and looking west to Europe, the theologies, languages, and rituals of the two centers of Christianity—Constantinople and Rome—developed in their distinctive fashions, leading ultimately to the formal split of 1054.

Throughout the formative period of Christianity, the Middle Eastern churches—Coptic, Armenian, Chaldean (centered in Iraq), Assyrian, and Syrian Orthodox (Jacobite)—drew their followers from the indigenous population, most of whom eventually converted to Islam after the invasions of the seventh century. The Western, Roman Catholic church became interested in the region once again after the period of the Crusades (eleventh to fourteenth centuries). (The churches of the Protestant Reformation [sixteenth century] were not yet in existence.)

European economic and political penetration of the Ottoman Empire began in the sixteenth century with the issuance of capitulations to France; missionary work was initiated, as were attempts to reconcile the Eastern churches with Rome. The Catholic and Uniate churches in the Middle East (Syrian Catholic, Armenian Catholic, Chaldean Catholic, and Greek Catholic [Melkite] churches) that looked to Rome for authority date from the seventeenth and eighteenth century, except for the Maronite church, whose union with Rome was initiated in the twelfth century. The Uniate churches, eastern-rite churches that acknowledged the pope's authority, retained only a minority of Christianity's adherents. Protestantism came into the region through the efforts of, primarily, American and British missionaries in the nineteenth century.

European strategic interests and the "Eastern Question" dovetailed with renewed religious interest in the Holy Land. Protection of Christian minorities by the European powers and the installation of Anglican and Roman Catholic institutions in Jerusalem were part of a growing European agenda to represent the interests of the various Christian minorities. Altercations over Christian holy sites led to the outbreak of the Crimean War. The fact that there are only four historical patriarchates and many contenders for their leadership has led to intercommunal acrimony. For example, Monophysite COPTS, Catholic Copts, and Greek Orthodox Copts claimed the patriarchate of Alexandria, and Maronite, Greek, and Syrian Catholics, as well as the Greek Orthodox and the Jacobites, claimed the patriarchate of Antioch.

Christian communities were a part of the MILLET system of the Ottoman Empire, which in turn was an elaboration of the *dhimmi* status given to Christians and Jews in early Islamic times. This system provided a measure of toleration, freedom of worship, and self-governance for the Christian communities, but always under the Islamic umbrella. Under this system Christians were barred from certain public offices and suffered certain legal disabilities vis-à-vis their Muslim neighbors. Proselytism was prohibited, as was conversion to Christianity from Islam.

It is, therefore, not surprising that Christians were among the more enthusiastic advocates of secular nationalist ideas at the turn of the twentieth century. They were also influenced by foreign mission schools, where such ideas were taught and discussed. Christians thus became prominent among the secular Palestinian and Lebanese leadership, and a Christian, Michel AFLAQ, was one of the theorists of the Ba'th movement that provided the ideology for modern Iraq and Syria. An important exception to this tendency has been a sector of Lebanon's Maronite population, which has favored the creation in Lebanon of a Christian enclave.

The challenge posed to secular nationalism by Islamist movements has led some Christians to reexamine their advocacy of secularism, but it remains the most attractive option for the majority of Christians in the region.

Census figures for Middle Eastern countries, particularly as they reflect religious affiliation, are notoriously unreliable or, in some instances, nonexistent. An educated estimate, however, would put the number of Christians in the region at 8 to 12 million. Emigration, however, has been a growing trend in recent decades. The Christian population of Jerusalem, for example, has shrunk from 26,000 in 1948 to an estimated 9,000 in 1992. The number of Syrian Orthodox people in southeast Turkey has dwindled from about 30,000 in 1980 to 7,500 in 1992. There are no reliable figures for Christian emigration from Lebanon, but anecdotal evidence suggests that the proportion of Christians there has dropped from roughly 50 percent to 30 or 35 percent during the course of Lebanon's sixteen-year civil war. Reasons frequently cited for emigration are war, including the Gulf War, poor economic prospects, and anxieties about the future.

Despite the deteriorating situation of Christians in the Middle East—or perhaps in response to it—Christian churches in the region have reached a historically unparalleled degree of unity in recent years. In 1974 the Middle East Council of Churches, based in Beirut, brought together the two Orthodox families and the Protestants for common witness and service. In 1987 the Catholic family joined this council.

The Eastern (Greek) Orthodox Church. The EASTERN ORTHODOX CHURCH in the Middle East developed around the four patriarchates of the early church: Jerusalem, Antioch, Alexandria, and Constantinople. During the Ottoman period the Eastern Orthodox *millet* (community) was represented before the sultan by the patriarch of Constantinople, the ecumenical patriarch, who was considered *primus inter pares* among the patriarchs. Of the other patriarchates, which serve predominantly Arab parishioners, only one—that of Antioch—has an Arab serving as patriarch. The patriarchs of Alexandria and Jerusalem are Greeks who preside over Greek hierarchies. Particularly in the see of Jerusalem, this has created a gulf between Palestinian and Jordanian parishioners and their leadership.

Of the four patriarchates the largest, both geographically and numerically (about 760,000), is Antioch. This patriarchate includes Syria, Israel, Iraq, Iran, and Kuwait, with a few parishes in southern Turkey. The smallest is Constantinople—the Greek Orthodox population in Turkey has dwindled to about 3,000. The ecumenical patriarchate, however, continues to exercise leadership for the Greek Orthodox diaspora outside the Middle East.

The Oriental Orthodox Churches. The Oriental Orthodox family in the Middle East includes three other churches: Coptic Orthodox, Armenian Apostolic Orthodox, and Syrian Orthodox (Jacobite). The largest of the three—indeed, the largest denomination in the Middle East—is the Coptic Orthodox, numbering perhaps 5.5 to 6 million. The Armenian Apostolic Orthodox church includes four jurisdictions in the Middle East: the patriarchates of Jerusalem and Constantinople and the catholicates of Cilicia (based in Beirut) and Etchmiadzin, Armenia. The Syrian Orthodox church—whose patriarch presides from Damascus, just a few buildings away from the Greek Orthodox patriarchate of Antioch—had its heartland in what is now southeastern Turkey, northern Iraq, and northern Syria. In recent years disturbances in Turkey (related both to the Kurdish question and to the Gulf War) have contributed to the emigration of many members of this community to Syria and Lebanon or to Europe and North America. The Syrian Orthodox people, locally called Suryanis, continue to speak their ancient Syriac dialect and use it in their liturgy.

Eastern Rite and Latin Catholics. The eastern-rite Catholic churches owe their origins to Roman Cath-

olic missionary activity in the sixteenth through the nineteenth centuries. These churches follow in general the rites of the orthodox churches from which their membership was drawn, but they acknowledge the primacy of the Pope.

The Greek Catholic (or Melkite) church drew from Greek Orthodox membership. The patriarch of this church—the largest of the Middle East eastern-rite Catholic churches at about 450,000 members—presides in Damascus. The largest concentrations of Greek Catholics are found in Lebanon, Syria, Israel and the West Bank, and Jordan.

The Coptic Catholic, Armenian Catholic, and Syrian Catholic churches are related historically to the three corresponding Oriental Orthodox churches. The largest is the Coptic Catholic, with about 100,000 members. The patriarch of this church resides in Cairo. The Syrian Catholic church was reorganized by the Ottoman authorities in the nineteenth century. The Syrian Catholics, unlike their Orthodox brethren, use the Latin liturgy instead of the Syriac. Today, Syrian Catholics number about 80,000. The patriarchal sees of both the Syrian and Armenian Catholic churches are located in Beirut.

The Chaldaean Catholic church, whose head is the patriarch of Babylon, historically drew its membership primarily from the Assyrian church of the East. Chaldaean Catholics constitute roughly 75 percent (250,000) of the Iraqi Christian population.

The two other Middle Eastern Catholic churches are the Maronite and Latin Catholic churches. The early history of the Maronites is clouded in legend, but it is generally agreed that their origin had to do with the fifth-century dispute over the human and divine natures of Christ. The forerunners of the Maronites, seeking to find a compromise between the contending parties, proposed a "monothelite," or "one will," position. By the thirteenth century the Maronites, who four centuries earlier had sought refuge in the mountains of Lebanon, had concluded an agreement with the Church of Rome, whereby the primacy of the Pope was acknowledged. Like the Eastern Orthodox patriarch in Antioch and the Greek Catholic and Syrian Catholic primates, the Maronite patriarch bears the title Patriarch of Antioch and All the East. The Maronites remain the largest of Lebanon's recognized Christian sects, numbering some 500,000.

The Latin Catholic patriarchate was first established in Jerusalem in 1099 and subsequently moved to Acre. Effectively terminated in the latter part of the thirteenth century, it was reestablished in Jerusalem in 1847. The Latin Catholics in the Middle East are, for the most part, expatriates from Europe and North America—with the important exceptions of Israel and the occupied territories and Jordan, where the approximately 50,000 Latin Catholics are predominantly Palestinian. The election of Michel Sabbah, a Palestinian from Nazareth, as Latin patriarch in 1987 represented the first such election of an indigenous Middle Easterner.

Protestants. Protestants make up a tiny minority within the overall Christian minority in the Middle East. Their influence has been substantial, however, both in the fostering of the ecumenical movement in the region and in the areas of education—secondary schools, colleges, and seminaries—medicine, and publishing.

[*See also:* Copts; Eastern Orthodox Church; Missionary Schools; Protestantism and Protestant Missions; and Roman Catholicism and Roman Catholic Missions]

BIBLIOGRAPHY

The best source for the demographics of contemporary Middle Eastern Christianity is NORMAN A. HORNER, *A Guide to Christian Churches in the Middle East* (Elkhart, Ind., 1989). For a historical review of Middle Eastern Christianity, the reader is directed to KENNETH CRAGG, *The Arab Christian: A History in the Middle East* (Louisville, Ky., 1991); ROBERT B. BETTS, *Christians in the Arab East* (Atlanta, Ga., 1978); and ROBERT HADDAD, *Syrian Christians in Muslim Society* (Westport, Conn., 1981).

Dale L. Bishop

Chubak, Sadeq   [1916–]

Iranian novelist, short-story writer, playwright.

Sadeq Chubak was born in Bushehr, the son of a wealthy merchant. Chubak published his first collection of short stories, *Khaymah shab bazi* (*The Puppet Show*) in 1945. His novel *Tangsir* (*A Man from Tangestan*) was first published in 1963 and translated into English as *One Man with His Gun* together with four short stories and a play in *Sadeq Chubak: An Anthology* (1982). This novel was later turned into a popular movie by Amir Naderi in 1974. Chubak's other major novel, *Sang-e sabur* (*The Patient Stone*, 1966) is also translated into English. One of the most prominent "Southern" writers, Chubak resides in California.

BIBLIOGRAPHY

MOAYYAD, HESHMAT, ed. *Stories from Iran. A Chicago Anthology, 1921–1991.* Washington, D.C., 1991.

Pardis Minuchehr

Churchill, William   [?–1864]

Newspaper publisher.

An Englishman affiliated with the Tory party, Churchill went to Constantinople (now Istanbul) in 1832, where he worked for the British embassy as a merchant and as a newspaper correspondent, particularly for the *Morning Herald*. In 1840, he founded the first private Turkish-language newspaper in the Ottoman Empire, CERIDE-I HAVADIS (Journal of Events). This broke the monopoly of the Ottoman state's official paper, *Takvim-i Vekayi,* published since 1831. Churchill's lively coverage of the Crimean War (1854–56) attracted a new audience to newspaper reading. *Ceride-i Havadis* was published irregularly, roughly every one or two weeks, until 1860, when it began daily publication. The paper closed when Churchill died in 1864, although his son Alfred revived it for one year.

BIBLIOGRAPHY

LEWIS, BERNARD. *The Emergence of Modern Turkey.* New York, 1961.

Elizabeth Thompson

Churchill, Winston S.   [1874–1965]

British statesman; prime minister, 1940–1945 and 1951–1955.

Churchill's connections with the Middle East were based on two concepts—the national interest of Great Britain and what he called "the harmonious disposition of the world among its peoples." These concepts were not necessarily contradictory. Thus, in advocating British support for the establishment and maintenance of independent Arab states in Transjordan, Iraq, Saudi Arabia, and Syria after World War I and the breakup of the Ottoman Empire, his objective was to produce a satisfactory harmony of local Arab needs, in the hope of creating states that would be well-disposed toward Britain and its defense and petroleum needs.

As a young soldier serving in India at the turn of the century, Churchill had seen the importance of Egypt and the Suez Canal for the maintenance of Britain's sea link with India and Asia. He had participated in the reconquest of the Sudan, where he had been repelled by the cruel attitude of the British commander in chief toward wounded Sudanese soldiers, and he had expressed his disgust in a book published in 1900. While British control of Egypt was something he took for granted (although nationalist movements were already a problem for Britain), at the same time, he was insistent that the British connection should be beneficial for the well-being and advancement of the Egyptian people.

At the time of the Young Turk revolution in 1909, Churchill not only supported the modernization efforts of the YOUNG TURKS for the Ottoman Empire, but met several of their leaders during a visit to Constantinople (now Istanbul) that same year and remained in contact with them. In August 1914 when World War I began, he appealed directly to the Turkish minister of war, Enver Paşa, to keep Turkey neutral and thereby preserve the integrity of the Ottoman Empire. Two months later, when Turkey committed itself to the Central powers (against the Allies) and began the bombardment of Russia's Black Sea ports, it fell to Britain's First Lord of the Admiralty, Churchill, to direct naval operations against Turkey. These culminated in the attack on the Dardanelles (Turkish Straits), the failure of which led to Churchill's own temporary eclipse from politics.

In 1915, Churchill suggested that once the Ottoman Empire had been defeated, Palestine should be given in trust to Belgium, since Germany had violated Belgian neutrality and overrun most of the country. As compensation for this, Churchill wanted Belgium to be made the European overseer of the establishment of a Jewish national home.

Once the war ended in 1918, Churchill became secretary for war and air (1919–1921). In 1919, at a time when Britain herself had assumed the responsibility for Palestine, Churchill encouraged the Zionist leader Dr. Chaim WEIZMANN to consider the southern desert region of the Negev as an area of potential Jewish settlement (in 1949, David Ben-Gurion, Israel's first prime minister, was to urge this same policy on his fellow citizens). Churchill's own instinct was, at first, to keep Britain clear of all Palestine responsibilities and even to reject the League of Nations mandate for Palestine—on the grounds, he warned the cabinet in 1920, that "the Zionist movement will cause continued friction with the Arabs." Nor were his feelings entirely supportive of Zionism: Writing in a cabinet memorandum in 1919 of those who stood to gain from the collapse of the Ottoman Empire, he declared: "Lastly there are the Jews, whom we are pledged to introduce into Palestine, and who take it for granted that the local population will be cleared out to suit their convenience."

As colonial secretary in 1921 and 1922, it then fell to Churchill to fix the terms of the Palestine mandate. His attitude on Zionism had changed. In a public article in 1920, he stated: "If, as may well happen, there should be created in our own lifetime by the banks of the Jordan a Jewish State under the protection of the British Crown which might comprise three or four millions of Jews, an event will have occurred in the history of the world which would from every point of view be beneficial, and would be especially in harmony with the truest interests of the British Empire."

Having made the link of Jewish national aspirations and British interests, Churchill was also impressed by the ideological convictions of the Zionists and by their determination to create a flourishing world for themselves in a region that had been their home many centuries earlier. During a visit to Palestine in 1921, he was impressed by the Jews' success at cultivation and by the labor Zionist work ethic—the redemption of the land through toil. Henceforth, he encouraged the Jews to enter the region, stating in the terms of the mandate, as presented to the League of Nations in 1922, that the Jews were in Palestine "of right, and not on sufferance." He also gave the Zionists monopoly rights over the development of the hydroelectric power of the country.

During this same visit to Palestine, Churchill encouraged the development of a JEWISH AGENCY for Palestine, through which the Jews would acquire virtual autonomy over health, education, and communal life, as well as participation in the political and diplomatic discussions concerning their future. At the same time, he urged the Palestinian Arabs to accept the fact of Jewish immigration and settlement and to recognize the economic benefits that the Jews would bring to the country.

When a Palestinian Arab delegation asked Churchill to suspend all future Jewish immigration, he replied (on March 28, 1921): "It is manifestly right that the Jews, who are scattered all over the world, should have a national centre and a National Home where some of them may be reunited. And where else could that be but in this land of Palestine, with which for more than 3,000 years they have been intimately and profoundly associated? We think it will be good for the world, good for the Jews and good for the British Empire. But we also think it will be good for the Arabs who dwell in Palestine, and we intend that it shall be good for them, and that they shall not be sufferers or supplanted in the country in which they dwell or denied their share in all that makes for its progress and prosperity."

At the CAIRO CONFERENCE in 1921, Churchill agreed to the establishment of Arab self-government in Iraq and Transjordan and to the exclusion of Jewish settlement in Transjordan (now Jordan). He also argued in favor of a national home for Kurds in northern Iraq but was overruled by his officials.

During the 1930s, Churchill resented the pressure of the Arab states of the Middle East to curtail Jewish immigration into Palestine. He was an opponent of the WHITE PAPERS ON PALESTINE (1939), by which the British government gave the Palestinian Arabs an effective veto over any eventual Jewish majority in Palestine. He also opposed the restrictions on Jewish land purchase in Palestine. These restrictions were introduced in 1940, shortly after Churchill had re-entered the government as first lord of the admiralty, and as such he opposed the use of Royal Navy warships to intercept illegal Jewish immigrant ships heading for Palestine. As prime minister in 1940, he rejected Arab calls for the deportation of illegal Jewish immigrants.

During World War II, while he was prime minister (1940–1945), Churchill had to take steps to defend the Middle East from German encroachment. Although in 1942 he failed to persuade Turkey to enter the war on the side of the Allies, he did encourage Turkish neutrality. He also secured the basing of British military experts on Turkish soil, to immobilize oil pipelines and facilities crossing Turkey from Iraq, should German troops try to cross Asia Minor in any attack through Palestine to the Suez Canal. During the war, the pro-German revolt of Rashid Ali in Iraq was thwarted and the pro-German Vichy French government in Syria was ended by British initiatives. Throughout 1940, 1941, and the first half of 1942, Egypt and the Suez Canal were defended by Allied troops against continuous Italian and German military threats. Later in the war, Palestinian Jews were encouraged to volunteer not only for British military tasks but for clandestine parachute missions behind German lines in Europe.

As wartime prime minister, Churchill watched sympathetically over Zionist aspirations. In 1942, he warned a personal friend "against drifting into the usual anti-Zionist and anti-Semitic channel which it is customary for British officers to follow." A year later, he told his cabinet that he would not accept any partition plan for Palestine between Jews and Arabs "which the Jews do not accept." Even the murder of his close friend Lord Moyne by Jewish terrorists did not deflect Churchill from his belief that a Jewish state should emerge after World War II, and he called upon the Jewish Agency for Palestine to take action against the terrorist minority in their midst.

In 1945, during a meeting in Egypt, Churchill tried to persuade King Ibn Saʿud of Saudi Arabia to become the leader of a Middle East federation of independent states, in which a Jewish state would form an integral part. Only Churchill's defeat in the general election five months later prevented him from setting up a Middle East peace conference and presiding over it, with a view to establishing such a

federation. In 1946, as leader of the opposition, he told the House of Commons, after a Jewish-extremist bomb in Jerusalem had killed ninety people, including many Jews, at the KING DAVID HOTEL: "Had I the opportunity of guiding the course of events after the war was won a year ago, I should have faithfully pursued the Zionist cause, and I have not abandoned it today, although this is not a very popular moment to espouse it." In 1948, Churchill pressed the Labour government to recognize the State of Israel. As prime minister for the second time, from 1951 to 1955, he argued in favor of allowing merchant ships bound for Israeli ports to be allowed to use the Suez Canal—which had been taken from British control by Egypt's military in 1952 during the revolt that ended in FAROUK's abdication and the establishment of the republic.

Churchill's sympathies for Zionism were public and pronounced, alienating many Arabs. Yet he was not without understanding of Arab aspirations and of the vast potential of the Middle East. "The wonderful exertions which Israel is making in these times of difficulty are cheering for an old Zionist like me," he wrote to the first president of the State of Israel, Dr. Chaim Weizmann, in 1951, and he added: "I trust you may work with Jordan and the rest of the Moslem world. With true comradeship there will be enough for all."

BIBLIOGRAPHY

GILBERT, MARTIN. *Churchill: A Life.* New York, 1991.
———. *Winston Churchill: The Stricken World,* vol. 4. London and Boston, 1980.

Martin Gilbert

Churchill White Paper

A 1922 British statement of policy regarding Palestine.

Drafted by the first high commissioner of Palestine, Sir Herbert SAMUEL, the white paper (also called the Churchill memorandum) was issued in the name of Colonial Secretary Winston CHURCHILL in June 1922. A year earlier the Palestinians participated in political violence against the Jews, which a British commission found to have been caused by Arab hostility "connected with Jewish immigration and with their conception of Zionist policy." Samuel therefore urged Churchill to clarify to both communities the meaning of the BALFOUR DECLARATION of November 1917 and to reassure the Palestinians.

The Churchill statement reaffirmed British commitment to the Jewish national home. It declared that the Jews were in Palestine "as a right and not on sufferance" and defined the Jewish national home as "the further development of the existing Jewish community [YISHUV], with the assistance of Jews in other parts of the world, in order that it may become a centre in which the Jewish people as a whole may take, on grounds of religion and race [sic], an interest and a pride." In order to fulfill the Balfour policy, "it is necessary that the Jewish community in Palestine should be able to increase its numbers by immigration."

At the same time, the memorandum rejected Zionist statements "to the effect that the purpose in view is to create a wholly Jewish Palestine," which would become "'as Jewish as England is English.' His Majesty's Government regard any such expectations as impracticable and have no such aim in view." It assured the indigenous Palestinians that the British never considered "the disappearance or the subordination of the Arabic [sic] population, language, or culture in Palestine" or even "the imposition of Jewish nationality upon the inhabitants of Palestine as a whole." In addition, the allowable number of Jewish immigrants would be limited to the "economic capacity of the country."

The Zionist leaders regarded the memorandum as a whittling down of the Balfour Declaration but acquiesced, partly because of a veiled threat from the British government and partly because, off the record, the Zionists knew that there was nothing in the paper to preclude a Jewish state. (Churchill himself testified to the Peel Commission in 1936 that no such prohibition had been intended in his 1922 memorandum.) The Palestinians rejected the paper because it reaffirmed the Balfour policy. They were convinced that continued Jewish immigration would lead to a Jewish majority that would eventually dominate or dispossess them. Both Zionist and Palestinian interpretations of the memorandum were largely valid: The British did pare down their support for the Zionist program, but the Balfour policy remained intact long enough to allow extensive Jewish immigration and the establishment of semiautonomous Jewish governmental and military institutions.

BIBLIOGRAPHY

HUREWITZ, J. C. *The Middle East and North Africa in World Politics: A Documentary Record,* 2nd ed. Vol. 2, *British-French Supremacy, 1914–1945.* New Haven, Conn., 1979.
———. *The Struggle for Palestine.* New York, 1968.
LESCH, ANN MOSELY. *Arab Politics in Palestine, 1917–1939: The Frustrations of a Nationalist Movement.* Ithaca, N.Y., 1979.

Philip Mattar

Cilicia

Valley in southern Turkey situated between the Taurus mountains and the Mediterranean Sea, bordering Syria.

Cilicia is an important agricultural region. Adana is its largest city, and Alexandretta and Mersin are its major ports. In the late nineteenth century, Cilicia's growing cotton industry attracted large numbers of Muslim refugees from the Balkans and Russia. Cilicia's centuries-old Armenian population, descended from the eleventh century Kingdom of Little Armenia in Cilicia, was largely exiled or killed in the revolts and wars of the early twentieth century. The French occupied Cilicia from 1918 to 1921, when it was incorporated by the FRANKLIN–BOUILLON AGREEMENT into the Turkish Republic.

BIBLIOGRAPHY

Encyclopaedia of Islam, vol. 2. London, 1965, pp. 34–39.
SELTZER, LEON E., ed. *The Columbia-Lippincott Gazetteer of the World.* New York, 1962.
SHAW, STANFORD J., and EZEL KURAL SHAW. *History of the Ottoman Empire and Modern Turkey,* vol. 2. New York, 1977.

Elizabeth Thompson

Çiller, Tansu   [1944–   ]

Turkey's first female prime minister, 1993–

Tansu Çiller was born in Istanbul, Turkey, on October 23, 1944. Her father, Hüseyin Necati Çiller, a member of Muğla's well-known Telegrafçılar family and editor of the newspaper *Akyol* in Muğla (1925–1927), was forced to leave Muğla in 1928 because of his liberal views. He moved to Istanbul. His career as governor of Bilecik ended in 1953. After his retirement, he sought election as a member of parliament from Muğla (1954) but failed.

Çiller completed her high school education in Istanbul at the Arnavutköy Girls College, an English-language school founded by American missionaries. She entered Robert College (now Boğaziçi [Bosporus] University), from which she received the B.A. in economics in 1967. In 1963 she married a fellow student, Özer Uçuran; she retained her maiden name and had her husband adopt it. In 1968 she was awarded a scholarship, and she and her husband went to the United States. There she completed an M.A. at the University of New Hampshire, then went on to receive a Ph.D. from the University of Connecticut in 1978. Her dissertation was titled "Strategy of Development Finance." After teaching for a year at

Franklin and Marshall College, the couple returned to Turkey.

Çiller began her academic career in Turkey at Boğaziçi University, where she became an associate professor. She was promoted to full professor in 1980, based on her study "National Income Distribution on the Provincial Level." Her articles and reports in English include "Public Enterprise Deficits and Inflation in Turkey," "Concept and Classification of Public Enterprise," "Determination of the Energy Shortage Impact on Business," "Economics of Financing Higher Education," and "The Turkish Investment Allocation in Developing Economy." During her university years, Çiller served as consultant to the Istanbul Chamber of Commerce (ITO), the Istanbul Chamber of Industry (ISO), and the Turkish Industry and Business Association (TÜSİAD).

Before joining Süleyman DEMIREL's Right Path party (DYP), she served as his economic adviser. Anxious to modernize his party and refurbish its image, Demirel convinced Çiller to join the DYP. At the third convention of the party, on November 24, 1990, Çiller was elected its vice-president. During the election campaign of 1991, she promised all Turkish citizens two keys—one to a home and the other to a car. The general elections of 1991 resulted in the formation of a coalition government of Demirel's Right Path and Erdal İNÖNÜ's Social Democrat (SHP) parties.

Çiller became minister of economy on November 20, 1991. Following the sudden death of President Turgat Özal (April 18, 1993) and Süleyman Demirel's election as president of the Republic of Turkey, the DYP's extraordinary convention on June 13, 1993, chose Çiller as its leader by a large majority. Consequently she was named by the president to form a government. She opted to continue the coalition between the DYP (moderate right) and the SHP (moderate left). On July 4, 1993, she presented the program of her government to the TURKISH GRAND NATIONAL ASSEMBLY. Her platform was based on three priorities: fighting against secessionist terrorism, combating inflation and unemployment, and promoting democratization and respect for human rights.

Çiller is a staunch supporter of monetarist policies. Privatization is a definite priority of her government. One of her major goals is the suppression of the armed forces of the Kürt Komünist Partisi (PKK), a Marxist–Leninist secessionist terrorist organization. In some of her political statements, Çiller has declared that she has no objection to education and mass communication in the Kurdish language, provided they are carried out through private institutions.

Although Çiller's attractive, youthful appearance conveys the image of a secular, modern Turkey, she frequently uses Islamic symbols in her political speeches. The financial activities of her family have aroused much criticism. Çiller's personal wealth, about 60 million U.S. dollars, includes real estate and other investments in the United States. A parliamentary motion regarding the sources of her personal fortune has been converted into a general investigation of the sources of financial assets of all political leaders since 1983.

Nermin Abadan-Unat

Circassians

Sunni Muslim people living in the Caucasus and in Arab countries of the former Ottoman Empire.

The Circassians came originally from the Caucasus, a region ceded to Russia by the Ottoman Empire in 1829. Many Circassians emigrated to the Ottoman Empire after Russia expanded its control over this region. Some reached Thrace, in European Turkey, while most settled in the Arab populated parts of the empire—Syria, Iraq, Transjordan, and Palestine—where they were assimilated by the Arabs. The Circassians maintained their language for several generations, but in recent decades they have been fully Arabized. Efforts exist to revive the language and start teaching it in schools.

In Jordan, 25,000 Circassians are descendants of the families who emigrated from the Caucasus in the 1880s. By encouraging the Circassians to settle in northern Jordan, the Ottoman sultans attempted to provide an element loyal to the sultan to counterbalance the existing bedouin population. Circassians originally settled in Jerash. Despite their small numbers, they were historically influential in the government, business, and security apparatus and constituted a disproportionate number of the officer corps. While they remained a small segment of the population, by 1938 they constituted 7.3 percent of the non-British officials in Transjordan. Twenty-six of the thirty-three cabinets between 1947 and 1965 contained one or more Circassian minister. They were known to be loyal to the regime and thus were not perceived as a political threat. They remained loyal supporters of the king even during times of crisis (1957). Their relative cultural and economic importance and influence were diminished by the increasing predominance of the Palestinians in Jordan, although Circassians remained influential in the military and the security services. Circassians now speak Arabic, and the rate of intermarriage between Circassians and Arab Jordanians is high. King Husayn's eldest daughter married a Circassian. The migrating Circassians were joined, in the nineteenth century, by a number of Shishans (Chechens from Russia), who also originated in the Caucasus. Over time, the differences between the two groups in Jordan disappeared as the Shishans were assimilated by the Circassians.

In Syria there are approximately 100,000 Circassians. Half of them are concentrated in the province of al-Kuneitra. The city of al-Kuneitra, destroyed and captured by the Israelis during the ARAB–ISRAEL WAR (1973), was regarded as the Circassian capital in Syria. After 1973, those Circassians who did not stay in the territory occupied by Israel moved to Damascus. Circassian village dwellers, organized tribally, primarily cultivate grain crops. In addition to farming, they maintain herds of cattle, sheep, and goats, while others are engaged in the local crafts industry. The Circassians maintain many customs that differentiate them from their Arab neighbors. Until recently, they only spoke their own language, although most now speak Arabic. In the past some have demanded autonomy, but the majority have remained faithful to the state. They are, nevertheless, distrusted by Syrian Arabs because they served as troops for the French during the mandate period. Despite their cultural differences, the Circassians are being integrated and assimilated into Syrian culture.

Certain Circassian villages in the Golan Heights were abandoned after the Israeli occupation in 1967. Additional Circassian settlements were captured as a result of the Arab–Israel War of 1973. Those Circassians that did not flee to Damascus lived under Israeli administration. In Israel, two Circassian villages exist in Galilee (Kafr Kama and Rihaniyya) and maintain good relations with their Jewish neighbors. Like the Druze people, they are conscripted into the Israeli military (the IDF). Many remain loyal to the Israeli state, and Circassians generally have not participated in the Palestinian struggle against Israel, whether in 1948 or in subsequent years.

BIBLIOGRAPHY

COLLELO, THOMAS, ed. *Syria: A Country Study.* Washington, D.C., 1987.

METZ, HELEN CHAPIN, ed. *Israel: A Country Study.* Washington, D.C., 1990.

———. *Jordan: A Country Study.* Washington, D.C., 1989.

Mia Bloom

Circumcision

Cutting away of part of the genitalia.

The practice is ancient and widespread, especially in Africa and the Middle East. Male circumcision in-volves cutting away the foreskin of the penis; female circumcision involves cutting away the clitoris and/or some tissue surrounding the clitoris.

Circumcision rituals are most often part of the puberty rite in tribal religions; there, males are circumcised more often than females. Female circumcision is performed in many parts of Islamic Africa, usually to keep women from desiring out-of-marriage sex. In JUDAISM, male babies are circumcised on their eighth day at a ceremony called a *brit* (*bris, brith*). Male circumcision does not usually develop into a medical problem, but female circumcision frequently leads to infection, recutting, and associated urogenital problems.

Benjamin Joseph

Civil Code of 1926

The civil laws of the Republic of Turkey, a secular body of laws that covers all citizens—Muslims and non-Muslims.

Turkey's civil law was enacted in 1926; unlike the gradual evolution of European civil codes, the transition from the OTTOMAN EMPIRE to the Republic of Turkey brought a new code that has undergone relatively few changes until today.

Prior to the foundation of the Turkish republic, from 1869 to 1926, Ottoman legislators promulgated private (civil) law—rules derived from the SHARI'A (Islamic law), comprising 1,851 articles and called *Mecelle-i Ahkâmi Adliye* (Compilation of Legal Rules). It had no laws concerning family and inheritance matters. Near the end of World War I, in 1917, a decree on family law, *Hukuku Aile Kararnamesi,* was promulgated by the sultan. In 1919, the pressure of organized religious forces abrogated this decree.

The Ottomans had been allied with the losing Central Powers in World War I. With the dissolution of the Ottoman Empire, the founders of the Turkish republic committed themselves to Western institutions; and they decided to undertake, in the shortest possible time, radical changes in Turkey's legal system. For Mustafa Kemal (ATATÜRK) and his colleagues, the major tools of social change were education and legal reform. An additional factor forced them to act swiftly: According to the peace of Lausanne (of July 24, 1923), the Kemalist government was pledged to adopt—under the supervision of the League of Nations—a legal statute protecting their non-Muslim minorities. Turkey obliged by introducing a general code and juridical system that would be acceptable to all citizens—Muslim and non-Muslim. The secularization of the legal system became one of Mustafa Kemal's major goals.

KEMALISM used a number of Swiss and other European codes with relatively few amendments as models. In 1926, the Kemalists produced the new civil code, the code of obligation, and the trade code; in 1927, the code of civil procedure; in 1929, the sea trade code. With these steps they realized very quickly two of Mustafa Kemal's goals while depriving the conservative Islamic clergy and others of time to organize resistance: (1) the domestic scene was free of all remnants of the Ottoman-Islamic legal system, and (2) their international relations had been freed from the obligations of the treaty of Lausanne.

The Swiss civil code was used as a model because it is based on twenty-five-year community studies of existing norms and mores in Swiss cantons where French, German, Italian, and Romansh were spoken. The Swiss code seemed best to accommodate the needs of a country with diverse cultural and linguistic groups. Turkey's Minister of Justice Mahmut Esat Bozkurt had studied law in Switzerland, and Swiss law professor G. Sausser-Hall was engaged to act as legal counsel to the government of Turkey. On February 17, 1926, the modified version was adopted in a single session of the TURKISH GRAND NATIONAL ASSEMBLY; it entered into force on October 4, 1926. Some attempts to modify the code began in 1951—concerning human rights, family law, adoption, and divorce. Although the acceptance of the code has not been universal, and Islamic law is used in some remote rural regions, the civil code has served Turkey well.

BIBLIOGRAPHY

ANSAY, T., and D. WALLACE. Introduction to Turkish Law. Dobbs Ferry, N.Y., 1978

Nermin Abadan-Unat

Civil Rights Movement (CRM)

An Israeli political party founded as an expression of dissatisfaction with the conduct of the 1973 war.

The most prominent leader of Israel's CRM was leftist, social-liberal activist Shulamit Aloni. The party won three seats in the KNESSET election of 1973 and briefly joined the LABOR PARTY government in 1974 but left when Yitzhak Rabin accepted the National Religious Party as a coalition member. The CRM was reduced to one seat in 1977 by the popularity of the Democratic Movement for Change. At various times it negotiated with other left-wing groups, such as Shinui and Ya'ad, but no mergers resulted. In 1984 CRM rebounded to win three Knesset seats and grew to five seats in 1988. It refused to join the 1984 National Unity Government on matters of principle regarding cooperation with Likud. CRM's platform has centered around freedom of religion and culture; complete equality of all Israelis without regard to religion, nationality, race, or gender; full opposition to religious coercion; and negotiation with representatives of Palestinians and recognition of their right to self-determination. In 1992 many of its members joined the combined left-wing MERETZ party, which became a coalition partner of Labor.

BIBLIOGRAPHY

ROLEF, SUSAN, ed. Political Dictionary of Israel. New York, 1987.

Walter F. Weiker

Civil Service School

Established to train civil servants to administer the Ottoman state of the mid-nineteenth century.

Established on February 12, 1859, the Civil Service School (Turkish, Mektebi-i Mülkiye) of the Ottoman Empire trained administrators in accordance with the new TANZIMAT reforms. (The term *mülkiye* refers to the civilian—the nonmilitary and nonreligious—branches of government.)

The school offered courses in humanities, social sciences, and foreign languages, as well as special courses on public administration. In 1877, the curriculum was expanded and modernized. The first graduating class had 33 members; by 1885, there were 393. Graduates often filled the provincial posts of QA'IMMAQAM (district governor). In 1935, the name was changed to School of Political Science; as the Faculty of Political Science, it is now located in Turkey's capital, Ankara.

BIBLIOGRAPHY

LEWIS, BERNARD. The Emergence of Modern Turkey, 2nd ed. London, 1961.
SHAW, STANFORD, and EZEL KURAL SHAW. History of the Ottoman Empire and Modern Turkey. Cambridge, U.K., 1977.

David Waldner

Clapp Report

The 1949 report of the United Nations Economic Survey Mission for the Middle East headed by Gordon Clapp of the U.S. Tennessee Valley Authority.

The UN Economic Survey Mission aimed to develop a long-range plan for Palestinian refugees from the new State of Israel during and after the Arab–Israel war. It had become clear that peace in the region and repatriation were not imminent. Among its recommendations were that direct relief end within a year, that Palestinian refugees be offered public-works projects, and that the responsibility be transferred to the host governments as soon as feasible. This program was endorsed by the UN General Assembly in 1949.

Benjamin Joseph

Clark–Darlan Agreement

Armistice agreement ending Vichy French resistance to Allied invasion of French North Africa.

During World War II, after the Allies invaded North Africa in November 1942, the Vichy French commander in chief, Admiral Jean Francois Darlan, signed this agreement on November 22 with General Mark Clark of the United States in Algiers, capital of Algeria, then under French control. Darlan ordered an end to French resistance, was made high commissioner of French North Africa, and severed ties with Vichy France. Because of Darlan's reputation as a Fascist, the deal aroused intense criticism.

BIBLIOGRAPHY

AMBROSE, STEPHEN. *Eisenhower*, vol. 1. New York, 1983.
HUREWITZ, J. C., ed. *The Middle East and North Africa in World Politics*. New Haven, Conn., 1979.

Zachary Karabell

Clayton, Gilbert   [1875–1929]

British officer and administrator in Egypt, Palestine, and Iraq.

After serving under Lord KITCHENER in Sudan, Clayton received a commission in the Royal Artillery (1895); he was subsequently private secretary to Sir Francis Reginald Wingate, commander of Egypt's army and governor-general of the Sudan (1908–1913). He was Sudan agent in Cairo and director of intelligence of Egypt's army from 1913 to October 1914, when he was promoted to head of all intelligence services in Egypt, a post in which he remained until 1917. Clayton rose to the rank of brigadier general in the General Staff, Hijaz Operations, in 1916, and became chief political officer to General Allenby of the Egyptian Expeditionary Force in 1917. He was adviser to the Ministry of the Interior in Egypt (1919–1922), replaced Wyndham Deedes as chief secretary in Palestine (April 1923–1925), and was high commissioner and commander in chief in Iraq (1929).

In September 1914, Clayton wrote a secret memorandum to Lord Kitchener suggesting that Arabs could be of service to Britain during World War I and that an Arab leader friendly to Britain should be made caliph in place of the Ottoman sultan. This sparked the Abdullah–Storrs correspondence, which led to the HUSAYN–MCMAHON CORRESPONDENCE. Clayton and his fellow officers convinced Sir Mark Sykes that the Arabs in the Ottoman Empire might split from the Turks and join the Allies.

Clayton, who had reservations about the Balfour Declaration, supported Zionism within a limited definition whereby the Yishuv would serve merely as a cultural center for Jews in a multinational Palestine under Britain's administration. Although he believed Britain ought to continue to govern the Arabs, he attempted to reconcile Britain's interests and Arab nationalist aspirations while chief secretary in Palestine. He allowed his political secretary, Ernest T. Richmond, to expand the authority of the SUPREME MUSLIM COUNCIL and increased Palestinian Arab appointments to government positions. Clayton helped negotiate the borders between Transjordan, Najd, and Iraq in the Hadda Agreement, signed in November 1925. He argued against giving Syria to France under the SYKES–PICOT AGREEMENT and wanted Britain to take control of both Syria and Palestine.

BIBLIOGRAPHY

CLAYTON, GILBERT. *An Arabian Diary*. Berkeley, Calif., 1969.

Jenab Tutunji

Clemenceau, Georges   [1841–1929]

French statesman.

In the 1880s, early in his political career, Clemenceau attacked the Colonialism of France in both Tunisia and Indochina. In his second term as premier (1917–1920), he headed the French delegation at the 1919 Paris Peace Conference that followed World War I and produced the Treaty of Versailles. There, Clemenceau insisted on French rights in Syria and Lebanon (in the Ottoman Empire), as stipulated by the Sykespicot agreement of 1916. At the request of David Lloyd George, prime minister of Britain, however, he did concede French claims to Palestine and to Mosul, a city now in Iraq.

BIBLIOGRAPHY

Chambers Biographical Dictionary. New York, 1990.
COBBAN, ALFRED. *A History of France, 1871–1962.* New York, 1955.
FROMKIN, DAVID. *A Peace to End All Peace.* New York, 1990.

Zachary Karabell

Climate

Middle Eastern climatic conditions vary greatly, depending on the season and the geography.

The Middle East and North Africa are perceived as both homogeneous and intensely arid, but the region is best characterized by its climatic variation. Although the hot arid, or desert, climate predominates in the region, the well-watered highlands of Turkey and the mountains of Iran and Ethiopia are important as sources of the region's major rivers. Climatic variation finds further expression in the temperature regimes of the northern and southern parts of the area. Average July maxima for inland locations near 30° north latitude are as high as 108°F (42°C), while summer maximum temperatures in northern locations like Ankara, Turkey, do not exceed 86°F (30°C). Black Sea coastal stations' (e.g., Trabzon, Turkey) average summer maxima may be as low as 79°F (26°C). January average minimum temperatures fall to 50°F (10°C) in Aswan, but reach 10°F (−12.5°C) in Erzurum on the Anatolian plateau.

Desert conditions are primarily the result of the subtropical zone of high pressure that coincides with 30° north latitude. In this area, cold, subsiding air warms as it approaches the earth, thus increasing its ability to hold moisture. This results in extreme evaporation from all surfaces, and under such conditions, very little rain falls. During the summer solstice, the sun is directly overhead at 23° 30′ at north latitude (e.g., at Aswan, Egypt). Annual periods of high sun in combination with clear skies through much of the year allow intense solar radiation with subsequent extreme *evapotranspiration* demands.

Evapotranspiration refers to the water needed by vegetation to withstand the energy of incoming solar radiation. This is accomplished through the mechanism of heat transfer by means of evaporation from inert surfaces and transpiration from stomata (pores) on leaf surfaces. Total demands made upon an individual plant are termed *potential evapotranspiration* (PE). *Actual evapotranspiration* (AE) is the amount of water actually available and used by the plant and reflects climatic conditions rather than optimal plant requirements. The difference between PE and AE defines the degree of aridity or drought and also the amount of irrigation water that would have to be applied for such vegetation to survive.

In the deserts of North Africa and Southwest Africa, total annual precipitation is between two inches (50 mm) and fourteen inches (350 mm). The area from Aden to Baghdad receives from less than two inches (50 mm) annually to about six inches (150 mm). More than thirty-nine inches (1 m) of water would be required in those places to sustain rain-fed agriculture. Under such conditions, sparse natural vegetation allows animals some seasonal grazing at best. Hyperarid areas, which seldom if ever receive rain, have no vegetation at all. Rainfall variability within the area of desert climate exceeds 40 percent, reducing to 20 percent on the moist margins of the semiarid zone, which forms a transition between the true desert to the south and the more humid areas farther north.

Precipitation on the semiarid margins of Middle Eastern deserts ranges from fourteen inches (350 mm) to thirty inches (750 mm) annually. Dry farming of grains employing alternate years of fallow can be carried out with sixteen inches (400 mm) or more of rain. It should be remembered that, while rainfall variability is greatest in the desert, this also means that aridity there has high predictability. Thus, the semiarid transition between regions of predictable aridity and predictable rainfall is one where rain-fed agriculture is possible but has a high chance of failure. This is biblical country—years of plenty followed by years of famine—and one to which pastoral nomadism was a practical adaptation.

The Black Sea coast of Turkey receives from 78 inches (2000 mm) to 101 inches (2600 mm) per year, although the transition from the windward, watered side of the Pontic range to the leeward, dry side can be very abrupt due to the topography. The Mediterranean climate, which is limited to a narrow coastal strip reaching from Gaza to Istanbul and from Tunis in the west to the Atlantic, is marked by mild winters with ample rain and long, hot summers when Saharalike conditions prevail.

Precipitation results from three different processes. *Orographic* precipitation occurs on the Pontic and Taurus mountains of Turkey; the Elburz and Zagros mountains of Iran; the peaks of Lebanon and the hills of Israel, the West Bank, and Jordan; the highlands of Ethiopia; and the Atlas and Anti-Atlas mountains of northwest Africa. Such precipitation occurs as warm, moisture-bearing winds are forced to higher elevations over the mountains. When the air cools, it loses its ability to hold moisture, and rain or snow falls on the windward sides of those ranges.

The Anatolian plateau and the steppes of northern Syria experience small quantities of rain in the form of *convectional* summer showers from thunderstorms. Equatorial convectional rains provide the waters of the White Nile.

A third cause of precipitation, particularly in the wintertime, is the passage of *frontal systems* from west to east across the region bringing alternating high and low pressure cells with associated cold, clear, or moist warm air masses. Frontal systems are propelled eastward by the subtropical jet stream, the position of which varies latitudinally by as much as fifteen° from a winter position in the north to its summer position in the south. Summer months find the path of the jet stream located from central Turkey northeastward to central Asia. Six months later the jet stream is at its maximum along a path traced across the Gulf of Suez to the head of the Gulf of Aqaba and beyond. This shift accounts for the changes in temperature and precipitation noted above.

Surface winds in the Middle East have distinctive qualities and have received local names famous throughout the region. The cold northern wind blowing from the Anatolian plateau to the southern Turkish shore in the winter is the *Poyraz* (derived from the Greek: *bora,* i.e., north); the warm onshore wind in the same location is known as the *meltem.* Searing desert winds are infamous: The Egyptian *khamsin,* which blows in from the desert, is matched by the *ghibli* in Libya and the *simoon* in Iran.

BIBLIOGRAPHY

BEAUMONT, PETER, GERALD H. BLAKE, and J. MALCOLM WAGSTAFF. *The Middle East: A Geographical Study,* 2nd ed. New York, 1988.
BLAKE, GERALD, JOHN DEWDNEY, and JONATHAN MITCHELL. *The Cambridge Atlas of the Middle East and North Africa.* Cambridge and New York, 1987.
GOUDIE, ANDREW, and JON WILKINSON. *The Warm Desert Environment.* London, 1977.
GRIGG, DAVID. *The Harsh Lands.* London, 1970.

John F. Kolars

Clot, Antoine Barthélémy   [?–1860]

French doctor who started first medical school in Egypt in 1827.

Known as Clot Bey, Dr. Clot was one of a group of European experts recruited by Muhammad Ali Pasha, viceroy of Egypt, to introduce European technology into Egypt. Clot Bey established the first medical school in Egypt in 1827, as well as Qasr al-Ayni hospital. The aim of the school was to train doctors and medical aides for the Egyptian army. Abbas I, who ruled from 1848 to 1854, dismissed Clot Bey along with most of Muhammad Ali's European advisers. Clot Bey returned to Egypt in 1856 and retired in 1857.

BIBLIOGRAPHY

VATIKIOTIS, P. J. *A History of Modern Egypt,* 4th ed. London, 1991.
WUCHER KING, JOAN. *Historical Dictionary of Egypt.* Metuchen, N.J., 1984, pp. 232–233.

David Waldner

Club National Israélite

A Zionist association.

The Club National Israélite (Arabic, al-Nadi al-Qawmi al-Isra'ili) was founded in Syria in June 1924 by Tawfiq Mizrahi, a Jewish journalist and director of the Bureau de Presse et Publicité advertising agency in Damascus, and Dr. Sulayman Tagger, the chief rabbi of Beirut, together with seven other provisionary committee members. The group's name was chosen in obvious imitation of the Arab Club, which was the focal point of Syrian and pan–Arab nationalism (see PAN-ARABISM).

The Club National Isráelite set out a nine-point program that, in addition to moderate Zionist goals, included working for friendly ties with other religious and ethnic communities in Syria. The club shifted its headquarters to Beirut in the late 1920s when the atmosphere in Damascus became increasingly hostile to any form of Zionism. It did not continue to be active for long, and most of its members joined other Jewish organizations with Zionist orientations.

BIBLIOGRAPHY

STILLMAN, NORMAN A. *The Jews of Arab Lands in Modern Times.* Philadelphia, 1991.

Norman Stillman

Code de l'Indigénat

Law code in French colonial Algeria.

Imposed by France on the native Muslim population of Algeria in 1881, the Code de l'Indigénat (Code of the Indigenous People) was exercised summarily, covering a vast array of offenses. Its arbitrary application was tempered in 1914 and 1919 by the CLEMENCEAU and Jonnart reforms. Nevertheless, the colonial lobby in France kept the intimidating code in effect until General Charles de Gaulle issued the ordinance of March 7, 1944, which gave Muslims French rights. Discrimination and prejudice, however, continued to prevent the full enjoyment of these new privileges. Summary rule resumed during the Algerian War of Independence (1954–1962).

BIBLIOGRAPHY

NAYLOR, PHILLIP, and ALF HEGGOY. *Historical Dictionary of Algeria,* 2nd ed. Metuchen, N.J., 1994.

Phillip C. Naylor

Coffee

A drink popular in the Middle East and worldwide.

The first mention of coffee appears to be from a tenth-century pharmacological work by the Persian physician Rhazes (Muhammad ibn Zakariyya al-Razi). The coffee bean (the seed from pods of the *Coffea arabica* tree) is believed to have originated in Ethiopia, traveling to Yemen by way of Arab trade routes. The Yemeni town of Maqha gave its name to a type of coffee, mocha. It had arrived in Mecca by 1511 when it was forbidden by the authorities, and by 1615 it had reached Venice. The popularity of coffee spread throughout the Islamic world, where it gave rise to the coffee houses that have enduring popularity in the Middle East and elsewhere.

Arabic or Turkish-style coffee is always prepared to order. The coffee beans are roasted in large frying

Coffee, Yemen's most important export, is commemorated on this postage stamp. (Richard Bulliet)

pans and ground very fine. The ground coffee and water are brought to a gentle boil in small long-handled pots called *rakweh*. The coffee is poured into demitasse cups without handles. After the grounds have settled, the coffee is drunk without being stirred. Sugar, cardamom, orange-blossom water, rose water, or saffron may be added to the coffee during the brewing process. Coffee is always served as part of social interactions in the Middle East.

Clifford A. Wright

Cohen, Ge'ula   [1925–   ]

Lehi radio announcer and politician.

Ge'ula Cohen was one of nineteen members of the LOHAMEI HERUT YISRAEL (Lehi) who were arrested when the British seized Lehi's radio transmitter on February 19, 1946, as part of a crackdown on Jewish terrorist groups. She was sentenced to nineteen years in prison but escaped and resumed the illegal broadcasts. As a journalist in Israel, she was an active participant in the militant struggle on behalf of Soviet Jewry. In 1970, she joined the Likud party. She was elected to a parliamentary seat in the Knesset (1973–1992), serving first as a member of the Likud and then as a member of the Ha-Techiya, a party she helped found that was to the right of the Likud. After the defeat of the Ha-Techiya party in the 1992 elections, she rejoined the Likud party. A leading oppo-

A bedouin man roasting coffee beans over an open flame. (Mia Bloom)

nent of Israel's peace agreement with Egypt and its withdrawal from the Sinai, she is associated with the ideology of the hard-liners who espouse the vision of a GREATER ISRAEL. She has published her autobiography, *A Story of a Warrior* (Tel Aviv, 1962; in Hebrew), and she regularly writes articles for daily newspapers.

Yaakov Shavit

Collège des Frères

A private elementary, middle, and high school with branches in a number of Arab capitals.

It was originally founded as a missionary institution by the Roman Catholic Franciscan order in the 19th century. The school's focus on languages, particularly English and French, has made it a favorite choice of families who like their children to speak, read, and write several languages.

BIBLIOGRAPHY

ARIF, ARIF AL-. *Al-muffassal fi ta'rikh al-quds.* Jerusalem 1961.

Muhammad Muslih

Colonialism

The settlement of a new area by individuals from a parent country.

In the ancient world, Greek city-states sent out segments of their population to establish new cities elsewhere; in the 1600s, the Spanish, Portuguese, Dutch, and British colonized North and South America. In the modern Middle East, while the French actively colonized Algeria and the Italians sent settlers to Libya, on the whole, Europeans did not attempt to colonize. In common usage, however, the term *colonialism* has come to signify the entire process of European imperialism, and thus it is common to speak of European colonialism in the Middle East when referring to the economic and political domination that Europe exercised over most of the region in the nineteenth and early twentieth centuries. It is worth remembering that only Egypt, Morocco, Algeria, Tunisia, and Libya experienced de jure direct rule by a European nation, while Palestine, Jordan, Iraq, Syria, and Lebanon each experienced a measure of de facto direct rule under the MANDATE SYSTEM between the two world wars.

Zachary Karabell

Colonial Office, Great Britain

British government service that administered colonies of the British Empire, including those in the Middle East.

Until 1854, the colonies of the British Empire were managed by the secretary of state for war and the colonies. As colonial affairs grew in importance, a separate Colonial Office with its own secretary was established, responsible for administration of Britain's colonies and for the recruitment of colonial civil servants (who comprised the Colonial Service, as of 1854). The lines of Colonial Office authority often overlapped and conflicted with those of the India Office and the Foreign Office. In the Middle East, the India Office administered the Persian/Arabian Gulf (including the Trucial Coast emirates that later became Bahrain, Qatar, and the United Arab Emirates), the Indian Ocean (including Musqat, which is part of present-day Oman), and parts of Afghanistan. The Foreign Office oversaw certain areas of informal British rule, such as Egypt.

With the League of Nations creating mandate territories after World War I, the Colonial Office and the Colonial Service were significantly enlarged, especially under the tenure of Colonial Secretary Leopold Amery (1924–1929). In the Middle East after 1920, the Colonial Office administered mandatory Iraq until 1932, Palestine including Transjordan (now Jordan) until 1948, and Aden/Yemen until 1967. In addition to Amery, who actively supported the aims of Zionism in Palestine while he was secretary, other important colonial secretaries have included Joseph Chamberlain (1895–1903), the leading voice behind British expansion in southern and western Africa; Alfred Milner (1919–1921), instrumental in negotiating with Sa'd ZAGHLUL and the Egyptian Nationalists in 1919 (the MILNER MISSION); and Sir Oliver LYTTLETON (1951–1954), the last colonial secretary of an intact British Empire in Africa.

The secretary who most heavily influenced the Middle East was unquestionably Winston CHURCHILL, later famous as prime minister. Between February 13, 1921, and October 24, 1922, Churchill drew the maps of the present-day Middle East countries of Iran, Jordan, Israel, and Iraq. He formulated policy for Iraq as the base for the British Royal Air Force in the Middle East, and he helped secure the election of Faisal I as king of Iraq in 1922. After World War II, the Colonial Office became the administrative organ for decolonization. In 1966, it merged with the Commonwealth Relations Office and soon disappeared, the vestige of an empire that no longer existed.

BIBLIOGRAPHY

BELOFF, MAX. *Britain's Liberal Empire, 1897–1921.* London, 1987.
FROMKIN, DAVID. *A Peace to End All Peace.* New York, 1989.
PORTER, BERNARD. *The Lion's Share.* London, 1984.
Steinberg's Dictionary of British History. London, 1970.

Zachary Karabell

Colons

European settlers (mostly French) who lived in Algeria during France's colonial rule.

When the ALGERIAN WAR OF INDEPENDENCE broke out in 1954, the country's colon population stood at 984,000. Only 11 percent of the population, the *colons* dominated economic life, held a monopoly of political power, and comprised the majority of the professionals, managers, and technicians who kept the country functioning. Their per capita income was roughly seven times that of Muslim Algerians.

The first colons came to ALGERIA directly on the heels of the French invasion of 1830, mainly because the collapse of the Turkish power structure left large amounts of property available on attractive terms. By the 1840s, it became official French policy to encourage settlement on the land to ensure the permanence of French conquests and to provide a tax base that could put the colony on a self-supporting basis. Demographic pressures inside France, where population was growing more quickly than the economy, added momentum to the colonization movement. Similar pressures in Italy and particularly in Spain led to large immigration from these two countries as well.

Starting in the 1850s and the 1860s, Algeria also attracted significant amounts of French capital because large amounts of state land became available to corporate interests, and opportunities for investment in rails and other infrastructure were lucrative. The earliest colonial vision saw an Algeria peopled by thousands of small European freeholders. However, the outcome by the mid-twentieth century was that most agricultural land was held by large landholders who mainly employed cheap native labor, while 80 percent of Europeans lived in cities and towns, employed in industry and, particularly, in services.

From the 1840s onward, colons realized that their ability to maintain and improve their economic status depended upon access to political power. In 1848 they won for the first time the right to elect municipal councils, and in these they were assured two-thirds majorities. Until the last years of colonial rule,

the settlers were guaranteed two-thirds or three-fourths majorities in all municipal and departmental bodies. Legislation under the Second Empire in 1865 provided that Europeans were citizens of France, while Muslims were subjects. On numerous occasions during the nineteenth century, the Algerian government attempted to intervene in defense of indigenous rights, which were regularly threatened by expanding settler hegemony. Colons were usually able to foil such attempts by invoking republican principles and condemning what they called government authoritarianism. By the twentieth century, however, republican rhetoric quieted; most colons were increasingly out of tune with the more liberal political discourse of the *métropole*. In each decade of the century, they mounted vigorous movements to block native attempts at improving their status and sharing meaningfully in the political process.

When, during the Algerian war of independence, colons began to fear that the government might make unacceptable concessions to the revolutionaries, they allied increasingly with disillusioned elements of the military to challenge civil authority. While the Evian Agreement of March 18, 1962, which provided the framework for Algerian independence, also included specific guarantees of colon rights, many of them, in the last months of French rule, joined with the Organisation Armée Secrète (OAS; Secret Army Organization) in attacks upon Muslims and in systematic destruction of the country's infrastructure. At the same time, unable to countenance minority status, they packed bags and trunks and headed for the ports and airports. By the end of 1962, not more than 30,000 colons remained in Algeria, mostly elderly, or among the minority who had favored the Algerian cause. Their numbers progressively declined in the years that followed.

BIBLIOGRAPHY

AGERON, CHARLES-ROBERT. *Histoire de l'Algérie contemporaine,* vol. 2. Paris, 1979.
DEMONTÈS, VICTOR. *Le peuple algérien: Essai de démographie algérienne.* Algiers, 1906.
JULIEN, CHARLES-ANDRÉ. *Histoire de l'Algérie contemporaine,* vol. 1. Paris, 1964.
RUEDY, JOHN. *Modern Algeria: The Origins and Development of a Nation.* Bloomington, Ind., 1992.

John Ruedy

Comité d'Action Marocaine (CAM)

The first Moroccan nationalist party, established in 1933/34, also known as the Bloc d'Action National, or simply kutla (bloc).

The CAM was the largest of three organizations created during the early 1930s by young urban nationalists to advance their aims; the two smaller bodies, the ZAWIYA and the *taifa*, were clandestine. The most important of the initial cells of the *zawiya*, based in Fez, was led by Allal al-FASI and Muhammad Hassan al-WAZZANI (Ouezzani). Along with five others from the Fez cell, and Ahmed BALAFREJ and Ahmad Muhammad LYAZIDI of the Rabat cell, they constituted the core leadership of the budding nationalist movement. Fasi was *primus inter pares* owing to his capabilities as a thinker and organizer, and to his personal charisma.

Their platform was disseminated through the Paris-based magazine *Maghrib*, and various Moroccan-based French and Arabic periodicals. Formally compiled and published in 1934 as the *Plan des réformes*, the CAM's program argued for comprehensive reform of the French protectorate—politically, administratively, judicially (mixing Western and Islamic legal codes), economically, and educationally—so as to achieve the protectorate's stated goal: the moral and material revival of Morocco with the aid of France. The plan was explicitly reformist. It did not contain any demand for discontinuing the protectorate or achieving independence.

The CAM made little headway from 1934 to 1935 in persuading the French authorities to respond to their demands. The ascent of Popular Front governments in France and Spain in the first portion of 1936 temporarily gave them new hope; the subsequent lack of progress led the CAM leadership to convene a series of mass meetings in order to mobilize wider public support. In response, in November 1936, the French authorities arrested al-Fasi, al-Wazzani, Lyazidi, and others but released them a month later. The CAM then adopted a more vigorous strategy of broadening its ranks. By early 1937, it had expanded its official membership to about 6,500 (excluding the Spanish zone), had established thirty-two sections throughout the country, and was demonstrating mass appeal among urban workers, artisans, and unemployed rural migrants to the cities.

Alarmed by its success, the French authorities dissolved the CAM on March 18, 1937. However, the CAM leadership quickly managed to reconstitute itself a month later as the National Party for the Realization of the Plan of Reforms (PARTI NATIONAL). Concurrently, a rupture occurred between a majority of the leadership, led by al-Fasi, and al-Wazzani, who formed the PARTI DÉMOCRATIQUE CONSTITUTIONEL (PDC).

Bruce Maddy-Weitzman

Comité de Coordination et d'Exécution

The executive cabinet of Algeria's FLN, 1956–1958.

The Comité de Coordination et d'Exécution (CCE; Committee of Coordination and Implementation) was created by the Soummam Valley Congress of the Front de Libération Nationale (FLN; National Liberation Front) in September 1956. It was composed of five leaders of the spreading guerrilla movement in colonial Algeria. Revamped and enlarged in 1957, it lasted until September 1958, when it gave way to the new Gouvernement Provisional de la République Algérienne (GPRA; Provisional Government of the Algerian Republic).

BIBLIOGRAPHY

RUEDY, JOHN. *Modern Algeria: The Origins and Development of a Nation.* Bloomington, Ind., 1992.

John Ruedy

Comité Juif Algérien d'Etudes Sociales

A Jewish antidefamation organization.

The Comité Juif Algérien d'Etudes Sociales (Algerian Jewish Committee for Social Studies; CESA) was founded in 1917 by Dr. Henri ABOULKER to function as a kind of antidefamation league in the face of continued, virulent *pied noir* anti-Semitism in Algeria. CESA's expressed goal was "to be on the alert that the free exercise of the Jews' rights as citizens not be violated or ignored."

The group lobbied through French political channels to achieve fuller social and civil rights for Algerian Jews, not as Jews, but as Frenchmen. One of its first campaigns was to remove the barrier preventing Jews from being accepted into the Algerian General Association of Students. As part of its public relations, CESA published and distributed to French military and public figures the *Gold Book of Algerian Jewry*, which listed all Algerian Jews who were killed in action during World War I and all who received military decorations and citations.

Having achieved most of its goals, the group became inactive after several years but revived as the leading voice of Algerian Jewry during the late 1930s.

BIBLIOGRAPHY

STILLMAN, NORMAN A. *The Jews of Arab Lands in Modern Times.* Philadelphia, 1991.

Norman Stillman

Comité National pour la Défense de la Révolution

Algerian opposition movement founded in July 1964.

The Comité National pour la Défense de la Révolution (CNDR; National Committee for the Defense of the Revolution) was a front uniting a spectrum of historic leaders frozen out by Ahmed Ben Bella's consolidation of power. It collapsed inside Algeria the same year. In Paris, however, Mohamed BOUDIAF continued to use the name for his own opposition movement for some years.

BIBLIOGRAPHY

OTTAWAY, DAVID, and MARINA OTTAWAY. *Algeria: The Politics of a Socialist Revolution.* Berkeley, Calif., 1970.

John Ruedy

Comité Révolutionnaire d'Unité et d'Action (CRUA)

The body that planned the 1954 Algerian insurrection and gave birth to the FLN.

The Comité Révolutionnaire d'Unité et d'Action (CRUA; Revolutionary Committee of Unity and Action) was a clandestine organization that kept few formal records. The details of its origins and development have been the subject of dispute among several participants and scholars.

During the early 1950s, frustration grew within the nationalist Mouvement pour le Triomphe des Libertés Democratiques (MTLD; Movement for the Triumph of Democratic Liberties). That frustration resulted from the failure of political participation to produce tangible results for the Algerian people and also from the political infighting within the party leadership, particularly that which pitted the Central Committee against followers of Messali al-HADJ. In March 1954, Mohamed BOUDIAF, an activist from M'Sila, called together a group of young militants, many of whom, like himself, had been members of the revolutionary Organisation Spéciale. Other founders identified with the MTLD Central Committee. It appears that the initial goal of the CRUA was to mediate between the Messalists and the centralists and bring about the reunification of the party. By the summer, when it became clear that the MTLD was irretrievably split, a Committee of Twenty-two decided that direct action was the only solution to Algeria's predicament and named an executive committee to take concrete steps toward armed action.

Boudiaf was to be the coordinator. The committee also included a leader for each of the *wilaya*s, or military districts into which the national territory was divided. These were Moustafa BEN BOULAID of the Aurès and Nemencha, Mourad DIDOUCHE of the northern Constantine, Rabah BITAT of the Algiers region, and Larbi BEN M'HIDI of the Oran. Later a Kabylia wilaya was recognized, and its leader, Belkacem KRIM, became the sixth member of the executive committee. In October, three exiled militants, Hocine AIT AHMED, Mohamed KHIDER, and Ahmed BEN BELLA were also named part of the executive committee. These nine men were considered the historic chiefs (*chefs historiques*) of the Algerian revolution. But it was the six militants inside Algeria who made the critical decisions.

At an October meeting or meetings, the exact date or dates of which are debated by the participants, the internal CRUA leadership decided to create the FRONT DE LIBÉRATION NATIONALE (FLN; National Liberation Front) and drew up a proclamation calling Algerians of all classes and political persuasions to join them in a war of national liberation. The insurrection broke out in the early morning hours of 1 November 1954.

BIBLIOGRAPHY

HARBI, MOHAMMED. *Le F.L.N.: Mirage et réalité.* Paris, 1980.
HORNE, ALISTAIRE. *A Savage War of Peace: Algeria, 1954–1962.* London, 1985.

John Ruedy

Commercial and Navigation Treaties

Allowed European merchants special privileges in trading with the Ottoman Empire; regulated passage of ships through the Dardanelles.

Beginning in 1352, the OTTOMAN EMPIRE granted special privileges to the merchants of Genoa, Venice, and Florence. These privileges, known as the CAPITULATIONS, placed European merchants under the direct jurisdiction of their own consular representatives—who judged the civil and criminal cases that involved their own citizens. In addition, the capitulations granted Europeans the right to travel and trade freely within the empire and to pay low customs duties on imports and exports. The capitulations allowed European merchants to organize almost all trade between the empire and Europe.

The first commercial treaty with a maritime state of western Europe, the Draft Treaty of Amity and Commerce, was negotiated with France in 1535.

Based on the model of the earlier capitulations, this treaty, which was never confirmed by Sultan Süleyman (reigned 1520–1566), stated that French merchants would be permitted to move and trade freely within the empire and to pay only the taxes and duties paid by Turkish merchants. These privileges were eventually granted in 1569. In 1580, a similar treaty was concluded, granting these privileges to Britain, to English merchants who until this point had been required to conduct business with the empire under the French flag. In 1581, the English Levant company was chartered: All English consular and diplomatic officials became employees of the company, which supervised the execution of the capitulations.

These treaties governed commerce between the empire and western Europe until 1809, when the Treaty of Peace, Commerce, and Secret Alliance (the DARDANELLES treaty) was signed between the empire and Great Britain. This treaty, which followed a brief period of British–Ottoman enmity, reaffirmed the capitulations while granting limited reciprocal privileges to Ottoman merchants. More importantly, the treaty granted the empire the right to close passage through the Bosporous and Dardanelles straits (the Turkish STRAITS) to foreign warships during times of war. The issue of free passage through the Straits would be a subject of diplomacy for the next 150 years. On May 7, 1830, the United States signed its first commercial and navigation treaty with the Ottoman Empire. This treaty extended to the United States the same privileges granted to European merchants.

Following British assistance to the sultan in defeating the army of IBRAHIM IBN MUHAMMAD ALI of Egypt, the Commercial Convention of Balta Lima was signed on August 16, 1838. This treaty, a renewal of the Commercial Convention of 1820, was a decisive defeat for the Ottoman government, which had sought to ease its fiscal constraints by raising the duties paid by British merchants. The negotiated increase from 3 to 5 percent *ad valorem* on imports was offset by a large reduction of duties paid on the internal movement of goods. The benefits accruing to Britain were strengthened by the 1861–1862 Convention, which raised the external tariff to 8 percent in exchange for the gradual reduction of duties on exports to 1 percent; this convention transformed the empire into a virtually free-trading country. The 1838 and 1861 conventions expressed the political incapacity of the Ottoman government to substitute for the capitulations a new mode of organizing trade, and it signaled the continuing economic subordination of the empire to Western states.

After the dissolution of the Ottoman Empire in the aftermath of World War I, the LAUSANNE Treaty of Peace with Turkey and the accompanying Straits Convention was signed at the conclusion of the Turkish War of Independence, dated July 24, 1923. It reestablished the principle of freedom of navigation through the Straits by demilitarizing the shores; it also established an international supervisory commission, under the permanent presidency of Turkey, to execute this agreement. In addition, the treaty bound the Republic of Turkey to maintain the prewar level of tariffs at their low rates.

Angered by the restrictive clauses of the treaty's Straits Convention, Turkey pushed for revisions, resulting in the MONTREUX CONVENTION on the Turkish Straits, dated July 20, 1936. This conferred on Turkey all the duties and powers previously granted to an international commission, while permitting the remilitarization of the Straits. The passage through the Straits of warships that threatened Turkey was left to the discretion of the Turkish government, subject to ratification by the League of Nations.

In 1945, after World War II, the USSR demanded that unilateral Turkish control over the straits granted by the Montreux Convention be replaced by joint Turkish–Soviet responsibility; the Soviets also demanded the right to establish military bases in Turkey for the defense of the straits. These veiled threats were countered by the admission of Turkey into the North Atlantic Treaty Organization (NATO).

BIBLIOGRAPHY

HUREWITZ, J. C. *The Middle East and North Africa in World Politics: A Documentary Record,* 2nd ed. New Haven, Conn., 1975 and 1979.

OWEN, ROGER. *The Middle East in the World Economy, 1800–1914.* London, 1981.

PURYEAR, VERNON JOHN. *International Economics and Diplomacy in the Near East: A Study of British Commercial Policy in the Levant, 1834–1853.* Reprint, Palo Alto, Calif., 1969.

SHAW, STANFORD, and EZEL KURAL SHAW. *History of the Ottoman Empire and Modern Turkey.* Cambridge, U.K., 1977.

David Waldner

Committee for Defense of Freedom and Human Rights

The first independent human rights organization in Iran's history.

The Iranian Committee for the Defense of Freedom and Human Rights was established in Tehran in fall

1977. It was founded by twenty-nine members of the opposition to the government of Mohammad Reza PAHLAVI, including Shahpur Bakhtiar and Mahdi BAZARGAN, both future prime ministers of Iran. Their first act was to draft a letter of protest to the secretary general of the United Nations, decrying human rights abuses in Iran. The committee's various activities contributed to the onset of the Iranian Revolution of 1979.

BIBLIOGRAPHY

ABRAHAMIAN, ERVAND. *Iran between Two Revolutions.* Princeton, N.J., 1982.

Neguin Yavari

Committee for Imperial Defense

Former British cabinet committee responsible for coordinating all matters concerning the security of the British empire.

Officially established in 1904, the committee was absorbed by Britain's war cabinet during World War I between 1914 and 1919. The Committee for Imperial Defense discussed such Middle East concerns as preserving the neutrality of the Turkish Straits and the strategic position of Iraq in defending access to India.

BIBLIOGRAPHY

BELOFF, MAX. *Britain's Liberal Empire, 1897–1921.* London, 1987.
FROMKIN, DAVID. *A Peace to End All Peace.* New York, 1989.

Zachary Karabell

Committee of Seven

Representatives of the Committee of Union and Progress to the sultan's government in Istanbul.

After the 1908 revolution, the reins of government initially remained in the hands of Sultan Abdülhamit II and his ministers. The Committee of Union and Progress (CUP), which orchestrated the revolution from its headquarters in Salonika, sent the Committee of Seven to Istanbul to oversee the establishment of a new government and elections. The CUP intended to influence the government indirectly through the committee, which enforced reforms in several ministries before withdrawing behind the scenes in late 1908.

BIBLIOGRAPHY

SHAW, STANFORD J., and EZEL KURAL SHAW. *History of the Ottoman Empire and Modern Turkey,* vol. 2. New York, 1977, pp. 274–275.

Elizabeth Thompson

Committee of Union and Progress

The principal Young Turk organization that left its mark on the politics of the Ottoman state from the 1890s to 1918.

The Turkish name translates literally as the "Society of Union and Progress," although reference to it as *komite* is common in its conspiratorial phases. Its members are referred to as unionists. Its precursor was the Ottoman Union Society, a secret circle of liberal-minded students in the imperial military medical school in Constantinople (now Istanbul) who aspired to overthrow the autocratic regime of Sultan ABDÜLHAMIT II. The founders were İbrahim Temo (Albanian), İshak Sükuti, Abdullah CEVDET (both Kurds), and Mehmed Reşid (Circassian). Despite its clandestine organization modeled along the Italian Carbonari, Abdülhamit's police discovered and suppressed the society as its cell spread among higher schools in Constantinople.

After 1895, the society established contact with Ottoman liberals in European exile. Its name changed to Committee of Union and Progress (CUP) under the influence of positivist AHMET RIZA, who became the president of the first European branch of the committee and represented the centralist camp in the Young Turk movement abroad. The first issue of Rıza's "Meşveret" on December 3, 1895, publicized the CUP's program. The internal and external branches of the CUP differed on the appropriateness of use of force against the regime. Over this issue, the gradualist Ahmet Rıza forfeited his leadership temporarily to Murad Bey, a revolutionist exile from the Constantinople organization. After two unsuccessful coup attempts in 1896 and 1897, the domestic leadership, which now included high officials and officers, was imprisoned. In Europe, rivalries between Young Turk groups and within the branches weakened the committee.

After 1906, underground revolutionary activity intensified in the empire, particularly in Macedonia. Two groups, Patrie and Liberty and the Ottoman Liberty Society, merged in Salonika and contacted Ahmet Rıza, who had reorganized with Bahattin Şakir the exile community under the name Progress and Union. The Macedonian and the external branches agreed to cooperate under the more familiar name of Committee of Union and Progress around the revised program of forcing Abdülhamit to submit to constitutionalist demands. The leadership of the domestic branch used the organizational tactics of Macedonian nationalist committees, masonic lodges, and Sufi brotherhoods to expand membership. Committee army officers had ready access to arms and disaffected men, whom they led in July 1908 to rebellious acts that triggered the revolutionary wave.

The 1908 revolution brought an end to the secrecy of the CUP. However, its central committee, dominated by ethnic Turks and still in Salonika, remained exclusive and its proceedings clandestine. The administrative inexperience and social insecurity of its leaders (among them civilians Talat, Bahattin Şakir, Midhat Şükrü; and officers CEMAL PAÇA and ENVER PAŞA kept the committee from taking charge of the government. After securing a decisive majority of approved candidates in parliament, the CUP established a parliamentary group. It redefined itself as a political party only in 1913. The headquarters of the committee moved to Constantinople at this juncture, and decision making was broadened with the institution of a General Assembly next to the Central Committee.

The society exercised more direct control over government after the counterrevolutionary attempt of April 1909 by placing its men in key cabinet positions. Its main objective was to unify all ethnic and religious groups around an Ottomanist allegiance. The CUP cultivated friendly relations with the great powers, while seeking the abolition of the CAPITULATIONS. The centralist policies it imposed in the name of preserving the territorial integrity of the empire at a time when large territories were breaking away, strengthened the CUP's decentralist rivals. Its manipulation of the 1912 elections through its control over the state machinery gave the society a Pyrrhic victory. It was forced to give up power to the leaders of the old regime in 1912.

Alarmed by losses in the Balkan War and fearful of the government's suppression of their clubs, the unionists carried out a coup on January 23, 1913, to topple Kamil Paşa and replace him with Mahmut ŞEVKET Paşa. The assassination of Mahmut Şevket later in 1913 gave the excuse to the society to crush its opposition and come to uncontested power. Wartime emergency after 1914 facilitated the establishment of single-party rule. The disastrous outcome of World War I discredited the unioninst leadership. In November 1918, as the three strongmen—Talat, Enver, and Cemal—fled abroad, the Committee of Union and Progress dissolved itself.

Both as society and party, the Union and Progress had a diverse membership and grassroots political organization. Its clubs sponsored cultural and educational activities. It co-opted the notables in the countryside, even though the latter did not always favor its policies. Its constituency included the officialdom, army officers, workers, and younger professionals and small merchants (especially in the Turkish provinces).

BIBLIOGRAPHY

AHMAD, FEROZ. *The Young Turks: The Committee of Union and Progress in Turkish Politics, 1908–1914*. London, 1969.
RAMSAUR, ERNEST E. *The Young Turks: Prelude to the Revolution of 1908*. Princton, N.J., 1957.
TUNAYA, TARIK ZAFER. *Türkiye'de siyasal partiler* (Political Parties in Turkey), vol. 3: *İttihat ve Terakki* (Union and Progress). Istanbul, 1989.

Hasan Kayali

Communication

Because of the Middle East's central location and the relatively high percentage of its people who engage in commerce, ease and speed of information transmission have long been major concerns.

Early Muslim dynasties, including the Abbasids, the Zengids, and the Mamluks, used carrier pigeons to convey military intelligence or vital state information. Messengers mounted on camels or mules carried official information throughout the Umayyad and Abbasid realms. Although this service (*barid*) was unavailable for private or commercial use, unofficial couriers (*fuyuj*) carried mail on land and sea, and some merchants used private messengers. The Ottoman and Safavid states had postal and courier services. Modern postal service began in the Ottoman Empire as early as 1823 and was extended to most cities by 1856. Private courier services existed in Egypt by the 1830s; the government post office, founded in 1865, carried mail from the outset and money orders from 1868.

France's occupation of Egypt in 1798 and the spread of European commerce in the Middle East in the early nineteenth century led to the introduction of new courier services and communication devices, including semaphores and heliographs. The electric telegraph first came to Constantinople (now Istanbul) in 1839; Sultan Abdulmajid authorized a telegraph line from the capital to Edirne in 1847 (it was not completed until 1855); and the first cable was laid under the Black sea, from Varna to the

Crimea, in 1854. Companies based in Britain vied to extend telegraph lines across the empire to Egypt and the Persian Gulf, but the Ottoman government undertook the task; the lines reached Baghdad by 1861. A telegraph line was built between Alexandria and Cairo in 1854, at the same time that Egypt's first railway was built. Under Saʿid (1854–1863) and Ismaʿil (1863–1879), telegraph lines were extended to all inhabited parts of Egypt.

The Sepoy Mutiny (1857), news of which took forty days to reach London, made Britain aware of its need for telegraphic communication with India. After an abortive attempt to lay an underwater cable from ADEN to Bombay, Britain's government negotiated with the Ottomans and the government of Iran for the right to extend lines across their territories. The Indo-European Telegraph Department of the government of India began to string lines across Iran in 1863; two years later the telegraph was operational from Baghdad to Baluchistan, although problems arose from both attacks by nomads and official obstructionism. The Indo-European Telegraph Company, which was formed in 1867, built a more efficient line across Iran and Russia to Germany that began service in 1870. Telegraph operators, whether French-speaking Turks and Armenians in the Ottoman Empire or English-speaking Indian officers in Iran, soon became potent agents of Westernization and of tighter state control over provincial and local government.

The telephone was introduced into Constantinople and Alexandria in 1881. Used at first by European merchants, this new medium of communication was soon adopted by Egypt's government and later by businesses and households. The telephone's spread in the Ottoman Empire was held up by Sultan Abdülhamit II (1876–1909), who was fearful of electricity, then accelerated by the Young Turks (1909–1914). Wireless telegraphy was introduced into the Ottoman Empire and Egypt in 1913.

World War I accelerated public familiarity with modern means of communication. After 1918, the governments of the states in the Middle East, new and old, set up ministries to manage the postal, telegraph, and telephone services for both official and private use. Radio broadcasting began in Egypt in 1932 and soon spread to most other countries in the area, which established transmission facilities and radio stations under government auspices. During World War II, and later during regional conflicts, such as the Arab–Israel War of 1948, extensive state censorship was imposed on all communications and has been maintained in some countries until the present time. Television broadcasting began in Iraq in 1958 and soon spread to all other countries of the Middle East, gen-

erally under state control. In recent years, governments have expended large sums of money to update their communications systems, replacing telegraphs with telex facilities and augmenting telephones with fax machines.

BIBLIOGRAPHY

DAVISON, RODERIC. "The Advent of the Electric Telegraph in the Ottoman Empire." In *Essays in Ottoman and Turkish History*. Austin, Tex., 1990.
HERSHLAG, Z. Y. *Introduction to the Modern Economic History of the Middle East,* 2nd ed. Leiden, 1980.
SHAW, STANFORD J., and EZEL KURAL SHAW. *History of the Ottoman Empire and Modern Turkey*, vol. 2. New York, 1977.

Arthur Goldschmidt, Jr.

Communism in the Middle East

Soviet foreign policy influences regional Communist parties.

The Communist revolution in Russia inspired Arab intellectuals with the hope that communism might be a tool to overthrow both their feudal (or bourgeois) ruling classes and, after World War I, the imperial control of Britain and France, which took over Syria, Lebanon, Palestine, Jordan, and Iraq after the war. The Communist party of Egypt was formed in 1921. In Palestine, an anti-Zionist offshoot of the Jewish Socialist Workers Party formed the Communist party of Palestine in 1922. The Communist party of Syria and Lebanon was formed from an amalgam of parties in 1925. Communism came later to Iraq—a Communist party there was not formed until 1934—and still later to the Sudan, where a party was formed in 1946 as an offshoot of Egypt's Communist party. In Jordan the Communist party was officially founded in 1951; it had conducted clandestine activities since 1949.

From 1921 to 1955, the Communist parties were hampered by problems, including the presence of large numbers of minorities (Jews, Kurds, etc.), the absence of a strong base in the peasantry, periodic conflict with nationalist parties (such as the Wafd in Egypt), and, above all, the requirement to follow the dictates of the Soviet Union despite the many reverses in position, such as the Comintern's 1928 decision to fight the national bourgeois, the 1935 decision to cooperate with the national bourgeois in a united front against fascism, the 1939 Nazi–Soviet pact, and especially, the Soviet decision to support the partition of Palestine, which was universally unpopular in the Arab world. Meanwhile,

Soviet support for Kemal Atatürk even as he was attacking Turkish Communists led to the near decimation of Turkey's Communist party, while heavy-handed Soviet diplomacy in Iran (1945–1946) cost Iran's Communist party any chance of seizing power.

The Soviet Union emerged onto the Middle East stage in 1955 through an arms deal with Egypt. Egypt's Communist party, having been outlawed by President Gamal Abdel Nasser in 1954, could not have been overjoyed to see its mentors in Moscow cooperating with its jailer in Cairo. This situation was exacerbated in 1958 when, with the union of Egypt and Syria in the United Arab Republic, Syria's Communist party, one of the most powerful in that country, was declared illegal. A similar fate befell Iraq's Communist party. After cooperating with the Communists against the Nasserites in his country in 1958 and 1959, Iraq's leader, Abd al-Karim Kassem, turned on the Communists with great brutality. This posed yet another dilemma for Moscow, which courted Kassem, as it did Nasser, because Iraq and Egypt had adopted anti-Western positions. Throughout this period, the Soviet Union preferred to have good relations with the one-party regimes of the Middle East instead of working for their overthrow by Communist parties.

In an effort to remove the suspicion and hostility with which Arab leaders viewed the Communist parties in their states, the Soviet leadership adopted a number of tactics. In the latter part of Nikita Khrushchev's rule, they encouraged the Communist party of Egypt to dissolve and join the Arab Socialist Union (ASU) to work for socialism (and good Soviet–Egyptian relations) from the inside.

By 1971, however, it had become clear that this policy had failed, and the Soviet leadership began to encourage "national fronts" in which the Communists would participate as parties, although as clearly junior parties. By stressing Communist recognition that the Arab nationalist parties were the dominant force in each national front, the Soviets hoped to allay the fears of the Arab nationalists that the Communists would use their positions to overthrow the nationalist regimes. At the same time, however, Soviet leaders clearly hoped that the presence of Communists within the national front would help steer the Arab nationalist leaders away from the West and counter the wave of anticommunism and anti-Sovietism that resulted from the failure of the Communist-supported coup attempt in the Sudan in July 1971. By 1974 the Communist party of the Soviet Union (CPSU) had established party relations with the Front de Libération Nationale in Algeria, with the ASU in Egypt, and with the Ba'th parties of Iraq and Syria.

These policies were not particularly successful. Indeed, it appeared that the Arab regimes, especially those in Syria and Iraq, had established party relations with the CPSU and allowed Communists into their governments, in nominal positions, primarily to extract more economic and military assistance from the Soviet Union. To make matters worse for the Soviet leadership, a number of Arab Communists had been angered by the Soviet policies; and the Communist parties of Sudan and Syria had chosen to split rather than follow them.

In any case, the end of the 1980s witnessed the rise of Islamic radicalism rather than Arab communism, as the dominant opposition movement in the Arab world. In 1991 the Soviet Union collapsed, which left Arab Communists adrift; a number turned to Islamic radicalism.

Robert O. Freedman

Communist Party, Algeria

Algerian communists found themselves caught between ideology and practicality regarding Algeria's independence.

While the Communist party and its affiliates in France gave early support to the émigré workers who were the pioneers of Algerian Nationalism, the party in Algeria found itself in an ambiguous position. Until the early 1930s, the Communist federations of Algeria were extensions of the French Communist party and were predominantly European in membership. The French party, like the Communist International, generally viewed independence movements as secondary to class struggle. Also, since the French party, beginning in 1936, was frequently a member of French governments, support for colonial secessionist movements was usually problematic. Therefore, even when a technically independent Algerian party was created, it was increasingly associated with reformist rather than with revolutionary elements of the political spectrum. After the outbreak of the war of independence, the Algerian Communist party attempted to negotiate a coalition relationship with the Front de Libération Nationale (FLN; National Liberation Front). Failing this, it finally recommended that its members join the FLN and went out of existence on July 1, 1956.

BIBLIOGRAPHY

SIVAN, EMMANUEL. *Communisme et nationalisme en Algérie, 1920–1962.* Paris, 1976.

John Ruedy

Communist Party, Egypt

Marxist movement founded in the early twentieth century.

Egyptian Marxism can be traced to the early twentieth century and to leaders as diverse as Joseph Rosenthal, a Jewish jeweler of Italian nationality, and Mahmud Husni al-Arabi, of Egyptian descent. Soon after the formal Communist party was founded in Egypt in the early 1920s, however, it was outlawed and driven into clandestine activities. Because it was separated from the workers and peasants it hoped to represent, the party was isolated from the main currents of political activity. Eventually, the party disappeared, leaving a vacuum in Egyptian Marxism from the mid-1920s to the mid-1930s.

In the latter part of the 1930s, the communist movement reemerged in response to the global rise of fascism. At this stage, the communist movement was made up of diverse and competing organizations and drew its cadres largely from middle- and upper-class students and intellectuals, with a disproportionately large ethnic-minority involvement. After World War II, the communist movement sought to widen its base, making some successful alliances with trade unionists. Among the leaders of the various Marxist groups were Henri CURIEL, Ahmad Sadiq Sa'ad, Muhammad Sid Ahmad, Fu'ad Mursi, and Isma'il Sabri Abd Allah.

After Egypt's monarchy was overthrown in 1952, the military regime tolerated no oppositional views from the Marxists. They were subdued and at times co-opted. Today, the left is still grappling with the fundamental problems of organizing, recruiting, and reaching out ideologically to the Egyptian masses.

While the Egyptian communist movement never became a mainstream political force, its importance and influence were larger than its small numbers imply. Marxists had significant ideological impact on Egyptian society and were present at key moments of nationalist, trade unionist, and student militancy.

BIBLIOGRAPHY

BOTMAN, SELMA. *The Rise of Egyptian Communism, 1939–1970.* Syracuse, N.Y., 1988.

Selma Botman

Communist Party, Iran

See Tudeh Party

Communist Party, Iraq

Iraqi political party founded in 1938.

The Communist party of Iraq came to prominence by organizing strikes and demonstrations in 1948 and playing a major role in the labor movement. It suffered a blow when Secretary-General Yusuf Salman YUSUF was executed in 1949. It recovered to play an important role in the revolution of 1958.

The Communists generally supported Abd al-Karim KASSEM. After his overthrow in February 1963 by Ba'thists and nationalists, thousands of party members and sympathizers were rounded up and killed.

The party regrouped in the mid-1960s and was still strong when the BA'TH regained power in 1968. The Communists were responsible for many of the more radical policies adopted by the Ba'th. By 1973 the party had formed a front with the Ba'th, a step that lost it much credibility and support. By 1978 the Ba'th was able to manage without the Communists and turned against them once more. Although still highly influential, the Communists had ceased to be major players by 1979, when Saddam HUSSEIN established his personal dictatorship.

Marion Farouk-Sluglett

Communist Party, Israel

Political party that embraces Marxist-Leninist principles of government, economics, and social structure.

Under the general name Miflagah Komunistit Yisraelit (Maki), communist parties in Palestine and Israel date back to at least 1919 and have undergone many metamorphoses. Ideology of class warfare and affiliation with international communist movements resulted in their generally being seen by some Jews as anti-Zionist, and they were therefore excluded from participation in YISHUV affairs. After establishment of the state of Israel, there were attempts by Maki, the mainly Jewish Communist party, to unify Jewish and Arab communists. They were successful until 1964 when an irreconcilable split over policy toward Arab nationalism and pan-Arabism resulted in the formation of an Israeli Arab Communist party, which took the name of Rakah. Since 1973, only Rakah has borne the name Communist. Jewish communists have carried on their activity in other structures, such as the Democratic Front for Peace and Equality. One or more Communist parties have had seats in every Israeli KNESSET, but they have never been included in the coalition governments by which Israel has always been governed.

BIBLIOGRAPHY

ROLEF, SUSAN, ed. *Political Dictionary of Israel.* New York, 1987.

Walter F. Weiker

Communist Party, Jordan

Jordanian political party.

Established in the early 1950s, the Jordanian Communist party was long headed by Ya'qub Zayadin. Zayadin ran successfully for a seat in parliament, representing Jerusalem (although he was from Karak himself) but was later expelled. The party predictably opposed the Anglo–Jordanian treaties, the BAGHDAD PACT, and other pro-Western sentiment. The party was represented by one cabinet minister in Sulayman al-Nabulsi's cabinet of October 1956. Banned in 1957 along with all other political parties, the Communist party of Jordan has been reconstituted since the ban was lifted in June 1991.

BIBLIOGRAPHY

GUBSER, PETER. *Jordan: Crossroads of Middle Eastern Events.* Boulder, Colo., 1983.

Jenab Tutunji

Communist Party, Lebanon

Lebanese political party advocating governmental reform as part of the solution to the Lebanese civil war.

Founded in 1924, the Lebanese Communist party (LCP) claims 20,000 members; however, the Central Intelligence Agency (CIA) estimates 2,000 to 3,000 members. Legalized in 1970, the LCP is led by a politburo of eleven members and a central committee of twenty-four members. Auxiliary organizations include the Communist Labor Organization, the World Peace Council in Lebanon, and some student unions and movements.

Since the beginning of the civil war in Lebanon in 1975, the LCP has advocated political reforms as a fundamental condition to stopping the bloodshed. Further, the LCP has constantly denounced Israel's occupation of southern Lebanon and advocated active resistance against Israel's army and its proxies, namely the SOUTH LEBANON ARMY (SLA). The LCP

has strongly supported Syria's involvement in Lebanon. Following the adoption of the Ta'if Accord (October 1989), and given its dwindling influence, the LCP was not invited to join the Lebanese government. Throughout its existence, the LCP has expressed its solidarity with the PALESTINIANS and the PALESTINE LIBERATION ORGANIZATION (PLO). It has also had a close relationship with the former Soviet Union and the communist parties of Eastern Europe.

BIBLIOGRAPHY

SULEIMAN, MICHAEL W. *Political Parties in Lebanon: The Challenge of a Fragmented Political Culture.* Ithaca, N.Y., 1967.

George E. Irani

Communist Party, Morocco

Political party also referred to as PCM, known in its current incarnation as the Parti du Progrès et du Socialisme (PPS).

Founded in 1943, the PCM's small membership was initially almost entirely of European origin. It supported the broader nationalist movement only after 1945. The party then began to recruit Moroccans, particularly through the newly legalized trade unions. The French authorities banned the PCM in 1952; the newly independent government of Morocco did the same in 1960, and its head, Ali YATA, was detained for several months. In 1968, Yata founded a new party, the Parti de Libération et du Socialisme; but, in 1969, it too was proscribed and Yata served another prison term.

In 1974, Yata founded the PPS (Parti du Progrès et du Socialisme). Its platform embraced land reform; nationalization of banks, industry, insurance companies, and foreign trade; the Arabization of education; amnesty for political exiles; and the freeing of political detainees. The party's support of the king's policies on the WESTERN SAHARA question was an important factor in its ability to avoid the imposition of another ban. For the next twenty years, the PPS remained a small opposition faction in parliament. In 1992–1993, it was nominally affiliated with the parliamentary opposition's "Democratic Bloc," which pressed for constitutional and electoral reform. In 1993, the parliamentary election results gave the PPS six seats in the direct voting (up from two seats in 1984) and four seats in the indirect elections (up from none in 1984).

Bruce Maddy-Weitzman

Communist Party, Palestine

Political party in Palestine.

The Palestine Communist Party (PCP) emerged in the 1920s as a Jewish underground group with strong anti-Zionist inclinations. It provided ideological backing for Palestinian and Arab nationalism and opposed Zionist plans to "colonize" Palestine. By the early 1930s, the PCP had an Arab wing. During the Palestinian revolt of 1936–1939, despite the PCP's support for the Palestinian nationalists under the leadership of Radwan al-Hilou, the party split. Palestinian Communists remained active in trade unions (organized mainly by the ARAB WORKERS CONGRESS) and other organizations (chiefly the League for National Liberation).

In 1947–1948 the PCP was the only significant Palestinian group not opposing the UN partition plan for Palestine. However, many Arab leaders of the party opposed the creation of a Jewish state and had difficulty reconciling left-wing ideology with their pro-Palestinian sympathies.

The Arab–Israel War of 1948 led to the exodus of the bulk of the Arab population of Palestine, the PCP was the only Palestinian organization with its structure intact. It had its own leaders—including Tawfiq TOUBI, Emile Habibi, and Emile Touma—and its own party organ, the weekly paper *al-Ittihad*. The birth of Israel led to the formation of a united COMMUNIST PARTY, ISRAEL. During the five elections between 1949 and 1961, the party obtained 2.5 to 4.5 percent of the total vote and 3 to 6 seats in the 120-member Knesset. Among Arab voters it garnered 11 to 22 percent of the vote. In 1965 the party split over the continuing Arab–Israel conflict and the question of Palestinian loyalty to the Jewish state. The Jewish groups merged with other leftist groups, and the Arab groups formed the New Communist list.

After 1977, the Arab Communists were represented in elections as the Democratic Front for Peace and Equality. Among the Arab population of Israel, support for the Communists has not been consistent. In 1965, for example, the Communists received 23 percent of the Arab vote. This figure reached 50 percent by 1977 but dropped to 23 percent in 1984. Support for the Communists also has varied from place to place. In areas like Nazareth, the party has traditionally dominated municipal elections, while in other areas support has been more sporadic.

[*See also:* Palestinians, Zionism]

BIBLIOGRAPHY

HILTERMANN. *Behind the Intifada: Labor and Women's Movements in the Occupied Territories*. Princeton, N.J., 1991.

SHIMONI, YAACOV. *A Political Dictionary of the Arab World*. New York, 1987.

Lawrence Tal

Communist Party, Syria

Political party supportive of the former Soviet Union.

Founded in Beirut in 1924, the Syrian Communist party (Hizb al-Shuyu'i al-Suri) separated from its Lebanese base in 1944 and has remained a clandestine party for most of its existence. Under the leadership of Khalid Bakdash, the pro-Soviet party became important in the Syrian political struggles of the 1950s and aligned with the BA'TH to suppress the SYRIAN SOCIAL NATIONALIST PARTY. It was outlawed under the United Arab Republic but reemerged when the radical wing of the Ba'th party took control of Syria in 1966. Under the Hafiz al-Asad regime, the party joined the Ba'th-dominated NATIONAL PROGRESSIVE FRONT. Although somewhat marginalized, the party fields candidates legally during legislative elections as part of the regime-dominated NPF and won seats in the People's Assembly in 1977 and in 1986. It has supported Asad's policies against the Muslim Brotherhood and condemned the Camp David Accords.

BIBLIOGRAPHY

TACHAU, FRANK, ed. *Political Parties of the Middle East and North Africa*. Westport, Conn., 1994.

VAN DAM, NIKOLAOS. *The Struggle for Power in Syria*. New York, 1979.

Reeva S. Simon

Communist Party, Turkey

Marxist-inspired political parties since the 1920s.

Several parties and groups have advocated communist doctrines in the Republic of Turkey. Since communism has been illegal during most of the period of the republic, they were usually unofficial, underground, or existing under other names. Often they did not advocate communist tenets as such. An unofficial TCP first appeared soon after World War I (as the Russian Revolution was under way), led by Mehmet Mustafa Suphi; it continued through the 1930s but was carefully watched by the Turkish government.

Communist-related ideas gained particular exposure from 1932 to 1934, when an intense ideological debate occurred on social and economic reforms. During World War II, the TCP urged Turkey to side with the Allies (but it remained neutral until February 1945, declaring war on Germany and Japan but not entering the fight). After the war, under the leadership of Şefik Hüsnü Değmer, it organized a Front for the Struggle Against Fascism and Profiteers, with an elaborate social and economic program. A TCP-in-exile existed for many years in the former Soviet Union.

Communist ideology has mainly influenced the ideas of other leftist groups, the most prominent of which was the Labor Party of Turkey (Türkiye Işçi Partisi), which operated between 1961 (when radical leftist parties were legalized) and 1971 (when the party was closed on the grounds that it was a communist organization). Leading intellectuals of this ideology have included Zekeriya Sertel, Behice Boran, and Mehmet Ali Aybar.

BIBLIOGRAPHY

Harris, George S. *The Origins of Communism in Turkey.* Stamford, Conn., 1967.

Landau, Jacob. *Radical Politics in Modern Turkey.* Leiden, 1974.

Walter F. Weiker

Compagnie Française des Pétroles

A company, usually called CFP, formed to handle French share of Mesopotamian oil.

Formed in 1923–1924, the CFP was organized to handle the 25 percent French share of the Turkish Petroleum Company. This percentage of oil from Mesopotamia (now Iraq) was stipulated by the LONG–BERENGER AGREEMENT of 1919 and confirmed by the BRITISH–FRENCH OIL AGREEMENT of 1920. Owned in part by the government of France, CFP cosponsored the 1928 RED LINE AGREEMENT, and after World War II, it was part of the Iranian oil consortium.

BIBLIOGRAPHY

Hurewitz, J. C., ed. *The Middle East and North Africa in World Politics.* New Haven, Conn., 1979.

Yergin, Daniel. *The Prize.* New York, 1991.

Zachary Karabell

Conciliation Commission for Palestine

See United Nations Palestine Conciliation Commission

Condominium Agreement

The 1899 pact that conferred and described joint British–Egyptian dominion over the Sudan.

The concept of condominium in international law refers to a joint dominion over a certain territory by two or more states, which jointly exercise their sovereignty over it. A unique feature of the condominium is that the territory in question belongs simultaneously to two or more states and is in this sense a part of the territory of each of them. Hence, each state is entitled to implement its authority in accordance with the condominium agreement.

In the context of Egyptian–Sudanese relations, the Condominium Agreement refers to the Anglo–Egyptian agreement on the Sudan signed January 19, 1899, by Lord Cromer, the British counsel-general in Egypt, and Butros GHALI Pasha, the Egyptian minister of foreign affairs. Since Egypt itself was occupied by the British, the agreement legalized British control of the Sudan and framed it as an Anglo–Egyptian rule and administration. The Condominium Agreement was meant to offset potential Ottoman and European opposition to British expansionism.

The Condominium Agreement referred to "certain provinces in the Soudan [*sic*] which were in rebellion against the authority of the Khedive, but which had now been reconquered by the joint military and financial efforts of Britain and Egypt." The first two articles defined the Sudan by reference to territories south of the 22nd parallel that had previously been administered by Egypt and had now been reconquered or that might in future be reconquered by Anglo–Egyptian forces or that had never been evacuated by Egyptian troops. Therefore, according to the agreement, the territories of the Sudan included both Wadi Halfa, a town in northern Sudan, and Suakin, a city on the Red Sea.

The third and fourth articles dealt with executive and legislative matters in the new joint administration. The supreme military and civil command of the Sudan was to be vested in one officer, termed the governor-general, who was appointed by a khedival decree on the recommendation of the British government and could be removed only by a khedival decree with the consent of the British government. The Condominium Agreement also dealt with judicial matters in the Sudan and stressed the independence of the Sudanese judicial system and the prohibition of slave trade. With the new arrangements, Lord KITCHENER, who was the commander of the Anglo–Egyptian forces, was appointed as the first governor-general of the Sudan.

The Condominium Agreement lasted until 1954 when Sudan gained its independence.

BIBLIOGRAPHY

HOLT, P. M. *A Modern History of the Sudan*. London, 1961.
SHIBEIKA, MEKKI. *British Policy in the Sudan, 1882–1902*. London, 1952.

Ali E. Hillal Dessouki

Confédération Démocratique du Travail

Moroccan trade union confederation usually referred to as CDT.

Affiliated to the UNION SOCIALISTE DES FORCES POPULAIRES (USFP), the CDT was organized in 1978 in opposition to the largest labor confederation, the Union Marocaine du Travail, whose leadership it accused of corruption and stagnation. Its membership in the mid-1990s is about 300,000, making it the smallest of the three trade unions (the third is the Istiqlal-affiliated UNION GÉNÉRALE DES TRAVAILLEURS MAROCAINS [UGTM]). Following widespread riots and student unrest in 1981, the CDT was accused of helping to foment the troubles; all offices were closed, and many of its activists were imprisoned. It was allowed to reopen in April 1987.

During the early 1990s, the CDT and the other labor federations pressed the authorities for improved wages and working conditions. With the UGTM, the CDT led a one-day general strike in late December 1990 that resulted in a number of fatalities. The CDT's secretary-general, Noubir Amaoui, was sentenced to two years' imprisonment, in the spring of 1992, for "libel and insult" in his criticism of the government published in a Spanish newspaper. He was released in July 1993. The CDT received four seats in the 1993 indirect elections for parliament, an increase of one from the 1984 elections.

BIBLIOGRAPHY

NELSON, HAROLD D., ed. *Morocco: A Country Study,* 5th ed. Washington, D.C., 1986.

Bruce Maddy-Weitzman

Confederation of Arab Republics

A federal union of Egypt, Libya, and Syria, planned but never implemented.

In April of 1971, Libya, Syria, and Egypt signed an agreement establishing the Confederation of Arab Republics. The agreement was intended to be the basis for a federal union of the three countries. In August of 1971, a constitution was signed and approved by referendum in the three countries. Cairo, Egypt, was designated the capital of the new federation, and Anwar al-Sadat, president of Egypt, selected as the first president. The plan was never implemented, however, and by 1973, a feud between Sadat and Libyan leader Muammar al-QADDAFI led to the suspension of the project.

BIBLIOGRAPHY

WUCHER KING, JOAN. *Historical Dictionary of Egypt*. Metuchen, N.J., 1984, pp. 292–93.

David Waldner

Confederation of Iranian Students

An Iranian student group opposed to the government; the confederation (CIS) coalesced out of various student groups abroad around 1960.

The Confederation of Iranian Students was, throughout its history, under considerable leftist influence, especially that of the TUDEH PARTY, one of the main Communist parties in Iran. With Tudeh's loss of popularity, after the rapprochement of Iran and the USSR in the 1970s, however, some members of the CIS inclined toward the pro-Chinese group that had been formed as an offshoot of the Tudeh party. But when, in the 1970s, the shah, Mohammad Reza PAHLAVI, recognized the People's Republic of China, and relations between the two countries also became amicable, the CIS became increasingly radicalized and included within its ranks members of various guerilla groups with bases in Iran. Among the most important of these groups fighting for Communism were the Marxist Feda'iyan-e Khalq and the Mojahedin-e Khalq.

BIBLIOGRAPHY

ABRAHAMIAN, E. *Iran between Two Revolutions*. Princeton, N.J., 1982, pp. 235–236.

Parvaneh Pourshariati

Confederation of Turkish Trade Unions

The largest labor confederation in Turkey.

The Confederation of Turkish Trade Unions, known as Türk Iş, was founded in 1952. Its history has reflected the increasing importance of industrial labor in a developing economy in which political regimes have been uneasy about voluntary associations whose appeal is bound to involve class interests.

During the 1950s, the confederation played cat and mouse with the government, which sought to extend control over the organization, which, in turn, appealed to the opposition for support. The right to strike was finally legalized in 1963, opening the way for genuine trade unionism. The confederation's efforts to solidify its dominant position, however, were resisted by rival organizations. In 1966, the Revolutionary Confederation of Labor Unions (DISK) broke away and aligned itself with the socialist TURKISH WORKERS PARTY. This split strengthened Türk Iş's relations with the ruling conservative JUSTICE PARTY, which tried to solidify the confederation's dominance of labor through new legislation. The proliferation of often politically motivated strikes and lockouts, increasingly accompanied by violence, was a factor in bringing on the military intervention of 1980. Ironically, the coup finally made possible the achievement of the confederation's goal of obtaining a monopoly in labor organization, since all other labor unions were simply banned by the military regime. This drastic measure was followed by a series of restrictive conditions written into the constitution that was adopted by popular referendum in November 1982.

BIBLIOGRAPHY

BIANCHI, B. R. *Interest Groups and Political Development in Turkey.* Princeton, N.J., 1984.
DODD, C. H. *The Crisis of Turkish Democracy,* 2nd ed. Huntingdon, U.K., 1990.

Frank Tachau

Conference of Non-Aligned Nations in Cairo

Meeting of countries not aligned with Communist or non-Communist blocs.

The nonaligned movement was officially founded at the September 1961 Belgrade Conference. The leading lights of the movement were President Josef Tito of Yugoslavia, Prime Minister Jawaharlal Nehru of India, and President Gamal Abdel Nasser of Egypt. The second nonaligned meeting was held in Cairo, Egypt, in October 1964, and Nasser presided over the proceedings. Forty-seven full members attended the meeting, along with ten observer nations; the African nations were by far the largest contingent. The major themes of nonalignment—peaceful coexistence, anticolonialism, the problem of nuclear weapons—were discussed and disputed at length, and the participants were divided over how they defined the issues and what they perceived to be viable so-

lutions. Nonetheless, the Cairo Non-aligned Conference signified to the world that the movement had become firmly entrenched in the international politics of the third world.

BIBLIOGRAPHY

CRABB, CECIL. *The Elephant and the Grass.* New York, 1965.
JANSEN, G. H. *Afro-Asia and Non-Alignment.* London, 1966.

Zachary Karabell

Confessional System

See Lebanon

Confrontation States

Arab opponents of Sinai II.

In December 1977, Arab opponents of the second disengagement agreement between Egypt and Israel, Sinai II—Algeria, Iraq, Libya, South Yemen, Syria, and the Palestine Liberation Organization—met in Tripoli, Libya as the REJECTION FRONT. They convened again at Damascus in September 1978, and adopted the name Arab Steadfastness and Confrontation Front.

Jenab Tutunji

Congress of Ottoman Liberals

Forum for opposition groups.

Organized by Prince SABAHETTIN to reconcile differences among various groups opposed to the unconstitutional rule of Sultan ABDÜLHAMIT II, the first Congress of Ottoman Liberals was held in Paris between February 4 and 9, 1902. Participants included Young Turk liberals living in exile in Europe and representatives of minority national groups. A renewed attempt to coordinate opposition movements resulted in a second congress, held in Paris December 27–29, 1907, chaired by Sabahettin, AHMET RIZA, and K. Maloumian of the Armenian Revolutionary Federation (Dashnaks).

BIBLIOGRAPHY

SHAW, STANFORD, and EZEL KURAL SHAW. *Reform, Revolution, and Republic: The Rise of Modern Turkey, 1808–1975,* vol. 2: *History of the Ottoman Empire and Modern Turkey.* Cambridge, U.K., 1977.

David Waldner

Conseil National de la Révolution Algérienne (CNRA)

The parliament of the Algerian revolution, September 1956 to July 1962.

The Conseil National de la Révolution Algérienne (CNRA; National Council of the Algerian Revolution) was created by the Soummam Valley Congress of the FRONT DE LIBÉRATION NATIONALE (National Liberation Front) to accommodate the broadening of the revolutionary movement that occurred during 1955 and 1956. The first CNRA, which for logistical reasons never formally met, included seventeen members of the founding COMITÉ RÉVOLUTIONNAIRE D'UNITÉ ET D'ACTION, members of the former UNION DÉMOCRATIQUE DU MANIFESTE ALGÉRIEN, THE MOUVEMENT POUR LE TRIOMPHE DES LIBERTÉS DÉMOCRATIQUES, and the ASSOCIATION OF ALGERIAN MUSLIM ULAMA.

The first formal meeting of the CNRA took place in Cairo in July 1957 and formalized the growing authority of the external militants over the internal. The second and third meetings, held at Tripoli from December 1959 to January 1960 and during August 1961, reshuffled the membership of the Provisional Government, dealing with internal power struggles between civilian and military leaderships. The final session, held in Tripoli in May and June 1962, adopted the TRIPOLI PROGRAMME, a statement of leftist ideological orientation. But, as Algeria faced independence, the CNRA was unable to agree on fundamental political arrangements.

BIBLIOGRAPHY

RUEDY, JOHN. *Modern Algeria: The Origins and Development of a Nation.* Bloomington, Ind., 1992.

John Ruedy

Constantine

One of Algeria's major cities.

Constantine is located about 330 miles (530 km) east of the capital, Algiers, near the coast, with a population of 335,100 (1990). While known as a trading center, Constantine is best known for its association with the so-called Constantine plan, an attempt announced by the French in 1958 to tie Algeria economically to the métropole (the French nation) through a number of rural and industrial development plans. After independence in 1964, Constantine became an important educational center with the country's only Islamic university.

Dirk Vandewalle

Constantinople Agreement

Secret plan for dividing Ottoman Empire after World War I.

First of the secret agreements between the Entente allies—Russia, Britian, and France—in World War I, this was actually a series of diplomatic exchanges sent between March and April, 1915. The agreement established Russian claims to Constantinople (now Istanbul), French claims to Cilicia and Syria, and British claims to Persia (now Iran), the Arabian peninsula, and parts of Anatolia.

BIBLIOGRAPHY

ANDERSON, M. S. *The Eastern Question.* London, 1966.
HUREWITZ, J. C., ed. *The Middle East and North Africa in World Politics.* New Haven, Conn., 1979.

Zachary Karabell

Constitution

For discussion of national constitutions, see main entry on the particular country.

Constitutional Bloc

Twentieth-century parliamentary bloc in Lebanon.

The Constitutional Bloc was formed in 1936 to call for the restoration of the constitution in Lebanon after its suspension by French mandate authorities. It was headed by Bishara al-KHURI, who championed the cause of Lebanon's independence. Although the bloc cannot be considered a political party, it did not differ from other political organizations in Lebanon in terms of its personality-oriented structure. Its members were drawn from the commercial and political elite, who did not agree with the views of Emile EDDÉ, a supporter of French policies in Lebanon. It was most active in Mount Lebanon and Beirut, among Maronites and Druze. After 1941, the bloc became identified with British policy in the Middle East. The cohesiveness of the bloc, which was based on the shared goal of independence, quickly splintered after al-Khuri was elected president in 1943. He continued to use the bloc as a tool against his well-organized enemies. It continued to operate as a political force, with limited influence and appeal, into the 1960s. After al-Khuri retired, his son Khalil al-KHURI assumed leadership of the bloc. With the outbreak of the Lebanese civil war in 1975, the bloc ceased to exist, and Khalil retired to France.

As'ad AbuKhalil

Constitutional Democratic Rally

Tunisian government political party.

The name Ralliement Constitutionnel Démocratique (RCD) was adopted in 1988 by the party originally known as the Neo-Destour and since 1964 as the Parti Socialiste Destourien (Socialist Destour Party, PSD). Habib BOURGUIBA founded the Neo-Destour in March 1934 as a breakaway party from the original DESTOUR. He transformed the Neo-Destour into a grassroots populist party grounded in the Sahel middle class. Many of its members had studied at Western-oriented Sadiqi College in Tunis or at mainland French universities. The party's first president was Tahar SFAR. Bahri Guiga was another prominent member, along with Bourguiba and his brother Muhammad.

Neo-Destour cadres worked with the union movement represented by the General Confederation of Tunisian Workers (Confédération Générale des Travailleurs Tunisiens, CGTT; later the UNION GÉNÉRALE DES TRAVAILLEURS TUNISIENS, UGTT). Their collaboration enabled the party to generate massive anti-protectorate demonstrations.

After World War II, Bourguiba adopted a gradualist policy that incensed his main rival, Salah ibn YUSUF. Their political rivalry dominated the years from 1949 to 1956 and continued until Yusuf's assassination in 1961. Yusuf was probably killed on Bourguiba's orders.

Neo-Destour party structures were revamped and expanded after independence. The cell structure was retained for local party activities. To coordinate the cells, regional committees were established. Party congresses chose delegates for a central committee that decided policy. The political bureau, the highest party authority, was chosen from central committee members. In all practical respects, party and state fused in Tunisia as party members dominated the political machinery of the state.

In the 1960s, Bourguiba's socialist planning led the party to change its name to the Parti Socialiste Destourien. These policies generated opposition and confrontation with farmers in the late 1960s.

By the early 1980s, discontent with the nation's restrictive political atmosphere and PSD domination led to the growth of Islamist influence in Tunisia. By 1981, Islamist dissidents had formed the Mouvement de Tendance Islamique (Islamic Tendency Movement, MTI). Bourguiba underestimated the strength of Islam in Tunisia and failed to see that his secularism and Islam-bashing actions had alienated a large proportion of the masses. As a result, there was continual confrontation with the Islamist movement that reached fever pitch in

1986/87. On November 7, 1987, Minister of the Interior Zayn al-Abidine BEN ALI had a team of doctors declare Bourguiba mentally incapacitated and incapable of ruling, then utilized constitutional authority to remove the aging president.

Ben Ali promised a "regime of change," and "change" became so associated with the new regime that the PSD was enjoined to change its name in 1988 to Ralliement Constitutionnel Démocratique. In the 1989 elections the RCD won every seat in the Chamber of Deputies. Most independent observers asserted the elections were fair. Since 1989, the RCD has continued to dominate Tunisia's politics. At its congress in late July–early August 1993, the party expanded its political bureau, eliminated much of the old guard, and elected a number of young delegates in accordance with Ben Ali's wishes for youthful reinvigoration of the party cadres.

BIBLIOGRAPHY

NELSON, HAROLD D., ed. *Tunisia: A Country Study,* 3rd ed. Washington, D.C., 1986.
PERKINS, KENNETH J. *Historical Dictionary of Tunisia.* Metuchen, N.J., 1989.
SALEM, NORMA. *Habib Bourguiba, Islam, and the Creation of Tunisia.* Dover, Del., 1984.
ZARTMAN, I. WILLIAM, ed. *Tunisia: The Political Economy of Reform.* Boulder, Colo., 1991.

Larry A. Barrie

Constitutional Revolution

Movement in opposition to the shah's rule that led to the convening of the majles.

Iran's Constitutional Revolution began in April 1905 when a group of merchants from Tehran sought sanctuary in the Abdal-Azim shrine south of the capital to protest against foreign control of the country's customs administration, the government's economic policies, and the repressive political regulations of the Qajar monarch MOZAFFAR AL-DIN QAJAR (ruled 1896–1906). The merchants who led this demonstration belonged to a secret society that had formed several weeks earlier to oppose oppression and seek the establishment of a house of justice. Their protest—effectively a business strike—attracted the support of other secret societies with similar grievances. The demonstration was defused after two weeks when the shah agreed to discuss the complaints of the protesters, but he soon left for a prescheduled private tour of Europe and forgot about his promises. The secret society of merchants, as well as other clandestine political groups in Tehran and in Tabriz, the capital of Azerbaijan province and the official residence of the crown prince, circulated pamphlets calling for fulfillment of the shah's promises and the implementation of other reforms. By December 1905, when the shah had returned to the country and it seemed obvious that he would not honor his commitments, a much larger group of two thousand merchants, joined by two of the city's leading clergy and their theology students, again took sanctuary in the Abd al-Azim shrine and demanded, in addition to action on their earlier requests, that the government create a house of justice.

The second protest had been sparked by the arbitrary arrest and beating of two respected sugar merchants, whom the government tried to blame for the inflationary rise in sugar prices. Popular indignation over this incident was widespread. In addition to the merchants who sought sanctuary, artisans and laborers in the capital went on strike to register their sympathy with the merchants demanding justice. Unable to force an end to the general strike in Tehran, the shah agreed in January 1906 to dismiss the Belgian national who was director of customs and to establish a house of justice. In subsequent months, however, Mozaffar al-Din Qajar again failed to fulfill his promises, thus prompting a third round of demonstrations during the summer of 1906.

The demonstrations of 1906 were ignited by the arrest of a fiery Shi'ite preacher who had denounced the shah's government during religious ceremonies and the arrest of several other critics of the regime. A crowd gathered outside the police station to demand their release; in the ensuing confrontation, the police killed a protester. A huge crowd attended the funeral the next day, and demonstrators clashed with the Russian-officered Cossack Brigade; twenty-two persons were killed and more than one hundred injured. The incident transformed the antigovernment protests into a mass movement. In July 1906, most of Tehran's Shi'ite clergy demonstrated its disapproval of the government by departing in a group for Qom, a shrine city about ninety miles south of the capital, thereby leaving Tehran without spiritual direction. In addition, more than ten thousand merchants took sanctuary in the British embassy's summer property in the mountains a few miles north of the city.

By mid-July 1906, most of the capital was on strike; even women organized demonstrations in front of the shah's palace. The growing opposition movement spread to several provincial centers, including Iran's second most important city, Tabriz; committees sent telegrams from all over the country to express sympathy with the protesters and their demands. The main intellectual ferment and negotiations took place among the 10,000 protesters who had camped out for three weeks in the British legation. Their most important decision was to change the former request for a house of justice to a new demand for an elected, constitutional assembly, or *majles*. The crisis forced the shah to accede to the popular demands, and on August 5, 1906, he signed a decree convening a constituent assembly.

The constituent assembly met immediately, drew up an electoral law, divided the country into electoral districts, and scheduled elections. The country's first elected *majles* met in October 1906. It drafted a fundamental law, based on the Belgian constitution, which provided for a parliamentary form of government. Special features that were incorporated into the constitution included articles authorizing the establishment of provincial assemblies and the creation of a body of senior Shi'ite clergymen to judge the conformity of legislation with Islamic law; these two provisions, however, were never implemented. Since the constitution limited the powers of the monarch, Mozaffar al-Din Shah indicated his opposition to the document by denouncing its main architects as religious heretics. His ploy not only failed, but, instead, incited mass demonstrations in favor of the constitution in the capital and several other cities, including Isfahan, Kermanshah, Mashhad, Rasht, Shiraz, and Tabriz. The disturbances climaxed with the assassination of the shah's prime minister, the public suicide of the assassin in front of the *majles* building, and a mass funeral procession for the assassin. Deeply distressed by these developments, the shah reluctantly signed the fundamental law in December 1906, a few days before his death. A supplementary fundamental law was signed by his son and successor, MOHAMMAD ALI QAJAR, in 1907. These two documents made up the Iranian constitution, which remained in force until 1979, when it was replaced by a new constitution.

To some historians, the Constitutional Revolution refers only to the events of 1905 to 1907, but other historians also view the struggles over the constitution during 1907 to 1909 as part of the Constitutional Revolution. Although Mohammad Ali (ruled 1906–1909) disliked the limits the constitution placed on his authority, the united opposition to the court within the *majles* initially forced him to abide by the new constraints. Factions of conservatives, moderates, liberals, and radicals soon emerged in the *majles,* however, and their differences over policies throughout 1907 provided the opportunity for the shah and his supporters to make political alliances with the conservatives and some moderates. By June 1908, the shah, feeling strong enough to mount a coup against the *majles*, ordered the Russian colonel of the Cossack Brigade to attack the volunteer militia defending the *majles* building and to arrest the deputies who had not escaped. After the bombardment, in which more than 250 persons lost their lives, the shah dissolved the *majles* and suspended the constitution.

Mohammad Ali's coup effectively put the capital under his control, but not the rest of the country. In Isfahan, Rasht, Tabriz, and other cities, volunteers took up arms to defend the constitution. For a year, constitutionalists and royalists waged a civil war for control of Iran's provincial centers, with the constitutionalists gradually gaining the upper hand. Constitutional forces finally advanced on Tehran from Rasht in the north and from Isfahan in the south. A mass uprising against the government opened the city to the constitutionalists in July 1909. Mohammad Ali, who had fled to the Russian embassy, was deposed; his twelve-year-old son, Ahmad (ruled 1909–1925), was installed as the new shah; the constitution was reinstated; and elections for a new *majles* were scheduled.

BIBLIOGRAPHY

ABRAHAMIAN, ERVAND. *Iran between Two Revolutions.* Princeton, N.J., 1982.
BAYAT, MANGOL. *Iran's First Revolution: Shi'ism and the Constitutional Revolution of 1905–1909.* Oxford and New York, 1991.
LAMBTON, ANN K. S. *Qajar Persia.* Austin, Tex., 1988.

Eric J. Hooglund

Constitutional Union Party

See Morocco, Political Parties in

Convention

See under the geographic term associated with the convention or under its popular name.

Cooper, Anthony Ashley   [1801–1885]

Seventh earl of Shaftsbury.

Lord Shaftsbury was renowned as an advocate of social and labor reform in Britain. He was also a supporter of Evangelicalism and headed the evangelical wing of the Church of England. As president of the Society for Promotion of Christianity Among the Jews (later known as the London Jews' Society), he encouraged Protestant missionary work throughout the Middle East. His close friendship with Lord Palmerston was instrumental in promoting the establishment of a British consulate in Jerusalem (1838), the Anglican Bishopric of Jerusalem (1841/42), and British protection of the Jewish minority in the Middle East.

BIBLIOGRAPHY

Dictionary of National Biography. New York, 1971.
TUCHMAN, BARBARA W. *Bible and Sword: England and Palestine from the Bronze Age to Balfour.* New York, 1956.

Reeva S. Simon

Coptic Museum

Cairo museum of antiquities from the Roman and Byzantine eras.

Founded in 1908 by Marcus Simaika, the Coptic Museum in Cairo has the world's greatest collection of antiquities reflecting the various cultures that flourished in Egypt after the introduction of Christianity in the first or second century. Although "Coptic" is a problematic term that usually denotes Egyptian monophysite Christianity, the museum possesses many items that attest to the survival of the various pharaonic cults (Osirian, Isiac) long after Christianity was established in the Nile valley. Among the categories of approximately fourteen thousand antiquities are textiles, sculpture, relief, icons, woodwork, metalwork, glass, ceramics, ivories, and manuscripts. Perhaps the most famous works in the collection are the Coptic gnostic texts known as the Nag Hammadi Gospels, named after the town in southern Egypt near their site of discovery between 1945 and 1948.

Stone carving in a courtyard at the Coptic Museum. (Mia Bloom)

BIBLIOGRAPHY

BASTA, M. "Coptic Museum." In *The Coptic Encyclopedia*, ed. by A. S. Atiya. New York, 1991.

GABRA, GAWDAT, and A. ALCOCK. *Cairo: The Coptic Museum and Old Churches.* Cairo, 1993.

Donald Spanel

Copts

Adherents of Egyptian Orthodox Church, the largest Christian denomination in Egypt today.

The frequent misuse of the words "Copt" and "Coptic" is unfortunate but understandable because their complicated and at times contradictory etymology has rarely been the subject of thorough discussion. Nonetheless, even if the misinterpretations are venial, they are regrettable because they falsify both historical and contemporary realities. Thus, "Copt" and "Coptic" are recurrent and erroneous labels for not only any Egyptian Christian regardless of denomination but also for the congregations of the Syrian Orthodox and Armenian Apostolic Churches. A better case can be made for the Ethiopian Orthodox Church, which is largely, though not completely, Coptic in organization and liturgy. A brief description of the origins and development of the word "Copt" will help to elucidate both the true meaning of the word and the reasons for the continuing confusion.

When the Arabs conquered Egypt between 641 and 643 C.E., they used a word similar to "Copt" as a designation of the country's inhabitants. "Copt" surely arose from an Arabic pronunciation (probably *Kpt*) of the Greek word *Aigyptos,* which means "Egypt" and is itself derived from the ancient Egyptian name for Memphis, a capital of the pharaohs. The Greeks called the native inhabitants Aigyptoi (Egyptians). Memphis (outside of modern Cairo) was well known to the Greeks because it was at the base of the Nile delta in which some Greeks had settled during the seventh century B.C.E. Therefore, the Greeks no doubt used the native word for Memphis, the capital, as a synecdoche to describe the whole country.

The original sense was thus purely geographic or ethnic. Because most Egyptians were Christians, however, "Copt" and "Coptic" soon acquired a religious value. This sense underlies the word "Copt" today, although "Coptic" retains its geographical/ethnic denotations in certain contexts.

"Copt" is not a term of general reference for any Egyptian Christian. In theological parlance, it describes an adherent of the Egyptian Orthodox church, which is one of several Eastern churches that refused to accept the controversial definition of Christ's nature formulated at the Council of Chalcedon (451 C.E.). In the following decades, the Eastern churches slowly developed a complex theology known as monophysitic. A brief digression about the council and monophysiticism is necessary because it will assist in the clarification of "Copt."

The Council of Chalcedon, assembled on the eastern side of the Bosporus, across from Constantinople (now Istanbul), was the decisive moment for Eastern Christianity. Although the meeting was convened by the imperial family of Constantinople, Marcian (emperor 450–457) and his wife Pulcheria (empress 450–453), to resolve the doctrinal disputes that had hindered the unity of the Eastern and Western dioceses, it resulted in a major schism that persists. At issue was the definition of Christ's individuality.

The patriarchs and bishops of several Eastern churches, particularly those of Alexandria in Egypt and Antioch in Syria, refused to accept what has been called the Chalcedonian Definition of Faith. By this exposition, Christ existed after the Incarnation "in two natures," divine and human, "unconfusedly, unchangeably, indivisibly, inseparably." The Western church with its two great seats at Rome and Constantinople favored this declaration of belief. To the Eastern clergy, however, it was unacceptable because the phrase "in two natures" admitted the existence of two separate persons and supposedly implied a diminution of Christ's divinity. The patriarchs of Alexandria and Antioch insisted that Christ may have come into being "out of two natures" but that after the Incarnation he existed in a single, indivisible divine nature although he had assumed manhood from the Virgin. Both the content of and the differences between the Eastern and Western Christology are often exceedingly difficult to understand. The theology that slowly developed among the Eastern dioceses has been called "monophysite," from the Greek words for "single" and "nature."

Outside of Egypt, the most important contemporary monophysitic churches are found in Ethiopia, Syria, and Armenia. Although these churches developed distinct theologies in reaction to the Chalcedonian Definition of Faith, many of their ecclesiastical officials reject the term "monophysite." Nowhere does it appear, for example, in the constitution of the Ethiopic Orthodox Church revised in 1955.

The misuse of the words "Copt" and "Coptic" usually results from either ignorance of their doctrinal meaning or from Egypt's historical demography. The words have been misapplied to both early and contemporary Egyptian Christianity. Egyptian Christians living before the Council of Chalcedon cannot be called Copts because the schism had not occurred, and even after 451 monophysiticism was a very gradual development, not taking hold until eighty years later. Furthermore, even if the majority of Egyptians were Christians, some were not. Both pre-Christian cults and Judaism existed. Some Egyptian Christians (the so-called Melkites) remained loyal to the Western church and had their own patriarch at Alexandria.

Another source of confusion lies in the word "orthodox" as applied to Copts. Perceiving themselves as upholders of the true faith, Copts have always referred to themselves as orthodox, as in the name of their denomination: Coptic Orthodox. The problem is that several other churches that are in communion with Rome also have "orthodox" as part of their names.

In two important contexts, the word "Coptic" retains its original geographical and ethnic value as a description of the art and written language of Egypt between the second and seventh centuries. Although Christian themes certainly appear in Coptic art, both pharaonic and especially classical themes and motifs are also prominent. Likewise, several non-Christian texts survive in the language known as Coptic. Obviously neither the art nor the language was exclusive to monophysitic Egyptian Christians.

Today, Copts are by far the most numerous of all Egyptian Christians, who can be divided into about fifty denominations. Taking them all into account, Egypt has the largest Christian community in the Middle East. Of the other Christian denominations in Egypt, at least two have the word "Coptic" in their names, for example, the two largest—the Coptic Catholic Church and the Coptic Evangelical Church—but they are not truly Coptic because they are not monophysitic. The result of a partial reconciliation of true Copts with Rome, the Coptic Catholic Church came into being in the late nineteenth century, drawing many of its communicants from Coptic parishes. Furthermore, six other Catholic communities exist in Egypt, each with a distinctive liturgy and ethnic composition reflecting the country's diverse population: Melkite (Greek), Maronite (Lebanese), Syrian, Armenian, Latin-rite (primarily Italian), and Chaldaean (Iraqi). The Coptic Evangelical Church was established in 1854 by American Presbyterian missionaries. The great majority of the many other Christian denominations in Egypt are also the result of American and European missionary activity, often evangelical and fundamentalist. These churches and congregations are quite small; among them are the Jehovah's Witnesses, Pentecostal Church of God, Baptists, Church of God of Prophecy, Seventh Day Adventists, Anglicans, Church of

Christ (Scientist), Free Methodist church, and the German Evangelical Mission. Obviously, "Copt" and "Coptic" completely lose their doctrinal heritage when applied to so many diverse Christians.

Any attempt at an estimate of the number of Copts must be performed with extreme caution because population counts for Egypt as a whole differ widely, and those of the Copts in particular are marked by a vast divergence between Egyptian government and church calculations. In 1975, the Egyptian government put the number of Copts at 2.3 million, but the Coptic church suggested the much greater figure of 6.6 million. Likewise, a United Nations population estimate for Egypt in the year 2000 reckons the total inhabitants at 64,588,000. Of this number, 3,128,000 persons are estimated to be Copts who openly acknowledge their faith. Because many more Copts are registered in church records (baptisms, marriage, death, etc.) than those who are active in the church, the actual sum of all Copts for the year 2000 is predicted to be much higher: 9,817,000. Underlying the discrepancy is the reluctance of many Copts to confess their belief publicly. An undisguised prejudice toward Copts exists in predominantly Islamic Egypt. Despite the guarantee of religious equality before the law contained in Article 40 of the Egyptian constitution, Copts suffer employment discrimination both in hiring and promotion, particularly concerning governmental positions.

The Coptic Orthodox Church may be the largest branch of Christianity in the Middle East, but the Ethiopic Orthodox Church has the most adherents of all monophysitic congregations. Ethiopia is largely Christian. The United Nations population estimate for Ethiopia in the year 2000 puts the number of Christians at 32,199,000 or 60 percent of the inhabitants.

The Ethiopic Orthodox Church is commonly called Coptic with some justification. It has always had close ties with the Coptic Orthodox Church of Egypt, especially in its recognition of the Coptic patriarch, but it is now a separate entity. The liturgy of the Ethiopic Orthodox Church derives much from its Coptic counterpart, although significant differences give it a distinct identity. Nevertheless, many adherents of the Ethiopic Orthodox Church refer to themselves as Copts.

BIBLIOGRAPHY

ATIYA, A. S. *A History of Eastern Christianity,* rev. ed. Millwood, N.Y., 1980.
BARRETT, D. B., ed. *World Christian Encyclopedia: A Comparative Study of Churches and Religions in the Modern World, AD 1900–2000.* Nairobi, 1981.

BOUTROS-GHALI, M. "Ethiopian Church Autocephaly."
    In *The Coptic Encyclopedia,* vol. 3, ed. by A. S. Atiya.
    New York, 1991.
DU BOURGUET, P. "Copt." In *The Coptic Encyclopedia,* vol.
    2, ed. by A. S. Atiya. New York, 1991.
FREND, W. H. C. "Monophysitism." In *The Coptic Ency-
    clopedia,* vol. 5, ed. by A. S. Atiya. New York, 1991.
PENNINGTON, J. D. "The Copts in Modern Egypt." *Mid-
    dle Eastern Studies* 2 (1982): 158–179.
TAMURA, A. "Ethnic Consciousness and Its Transforma-
    tion in the Course of Nation-Building: The Muslim
    and the Copt in Egypt, 1906–1919." *Muslim World* 75
    (1985): 102–114.

Donald Spanel

Corcos Family

A Jewish family of Morocco.

The Corcos family was one of the premier families of
Morocco's Sephardim from the sixteenth through
the twentieth centuries. They produced many rab-
binical scholars.

Members of the Corcos family also held posts as
court advisers, bankers, and *tujjar al-Sultan* (commercial agents of the ruler). Several acted as British and
American consular representatives. Straddling the
traditional and modern worlds, the Corcoses were a
classic example of the Jewish comprador class.

BIBLIOGRAPHY

SCHROETER, DANIEL J. *Merchants of Essaouira: Urban Society
    and Imperialism in Southwestern Morocco, 1844–1886.*
    Cambridge, U.K., 1888.

Norman Stillman

Cornwallis, Sir Kinahan   [1883–1959]

British diplomat; ambassador to Iraq.

In 1906, Cornwallis entered the Sudan civil service,
and he was attached to the Arab Bureau during
World War I. Instrumental in the negotiations leading to the accession of FAISAL I in Iraq, Cornwallis
remained in Iraq throughout Britain's mandate period (1920–1932) and after its 1932 independence.
In February 1941, he became ambassador to Iraq and
organized the successful British countercoup against
the prime minister, Rashid Ali al-Kaylani, which resulted in the return of the regent ABD AL-ILAH.

BIBLIOGRAPHY

Dictionary of National Biography, 1951–1960. New York,
    1971.

FROMKIN, DAVID. *A Peace to End All Peace.* New York,
    1990.
SLUGLETT, PETER. *Britain in Iraq, 1914–1932.* London,
    1976.

Zachary Karabell

Corsairs

*Naval freebooters (often mistakenly called pirates) of
many nations.*

The corsairs sailed under the colors of the so-called
Barbary states of North Africa from the early sixteenth century until the European naval powers suppressed their activity after the end of the Napoleonic
Wars. The North African corsairs attacked commercial ships sailing the Atlantic Ocean and Mediterranean Sea of those Christian powers that did not have
treaty relations with their political masters, seized the
vessels, cargoes, and crews, and sold them in their
home ports—Algiers, Tunis, Tripoli, Rabat-Salé,
and other smaller coastal towns. In Algiers, and to a
lesser extent in Tunis and Tripoli, the corsairs came
to control the (nominally) Ottoman Empire's political systems in the latter part of the sixteenth century,
while in Morocco the Alawi (of the Alawite Dynasty) sultans used them as a tool of their foreign
policy after their rise to power in the 1660s. The
corsairs were chief participants in the BARBARY WARS
that ended in 1821.

Jerome Bookin-Weiner

Cossack Brigade

*Iranian cavalry unit that became the basis for the
Iranian national army under Reza Shah.*

Nasir al-Din Shah established the Iranian Cossack
Brigade in 1879. Hoping to emulate the ruthless reputation of Russia's Cossacks, he solicited the czar's
assistance in contracting for a few Russian instructors
to create a similar six-hundred-man mounted force.
Reduced in its early years to two hundred, the so-
called brigade (normally a 5,000-troop unit) was almost disbanded. In 1896, it helped maintain order in
the streets after the shah's assassination; notoriety
came when the shah used the unit to shell and in-
timidate the *majles* (parliament) in 1908.

With only Russians in command until 1920, the
unit, which was reorganized as a division in 1916,
served as a visible manifestation of Russian influence
in northern Iran. The departure of all czarist officers
in 1920 permitted Reza Khan, who had risen

through the ranks, to take command of the division. In February 1921, his Cossacks supported the coup that led to the overthrow of the QAJAR dynasty and transformed Reza Khan into Reza Shah PAHLAVI by 1925. Under his control, the Cossack division became the nucleus of the forty-thousand-man national army he demanded as his first priority.

BIBLIOGRAPHY

KAZEMZADEH, FIRUZ. "The Origin and Early Development of the Persian Cossack Brigade." *American Slavic and East European Review* 15 (Oct. 1956): 351–363.

Jack Bubon

Cotton

A valued fiber crop.

An important fiber crop in the Middle East from the early Islamic period onward, cotton acquired new significance in the nineteenth century as the region's paramount export crop and most important raw material link to the world of European industrial capitalism. Egypt took pride of place in the development of the cotton industry as the earliest and long the largest producer of cotton for export. Traditionally, Egyptians had grown several different short-fiber varieties for domestic use, but under Muhammad Ali the government experimented with a locally discovered long-fiber variety of the sort preferred by European textile manufacturers. The first large harvest, overseen at every stage by experts from Syria and Anatolia, was realized in 1822. It brought a good price in Europe, where specialists appraised it as second in quality only to American Sea Island cotton from Georgia.

Farming cotton in Turkey, 1952. (D.W. Lockhard)

Harvesting cotton in the Sudan in the early 1950s. (D.W. Lockhard)

Poor agricultural practices and quality control, stemming partly from the Egyptian government monopoly's reluctance to reward peasant farmers for following the advice of the experts, led to a decline after initial success. After the mid-1830s, the frustration of Muhammad Ali's ambitous industrialization efforts, which had included textile factories for producing military uniforms, contributed to the decline. Recovery was unexpectedly prompted by the American Civil War, which made it difficult for European mill owners to acquire high-quality raw materials. Exports soared from 25,000 tons, the plateau reached in the 1850s, to 125,000 tons in 1865. After a postwar readjustment, exports resumed their increase, hitting a record 374,000 tons in 1910. By that time, cotton, to which almost a quarter of all cropped land was dedicated, accounted for 80.1 percent of Egypt's total exports, up from 66.6 percent in 1884. Later, nationalist critics charged the British, in control of Egypt since 1882, with turning the country into a giant cotton farm for the benefit of British manufacturers.

The American Civil War stimulated cotton exports from Syria and Anatolia, as well; but the postwar slump in prices drove production back down. Iran, too, shared in the wartime boom; but there the postwar fall in prices was eventually countered by a twelvefold expansion in general trade with Russia, particularly from the 1880s on. By World War I, Russia received 70 percent of Iranian exports, with cotton the most important product. Volume was 25,000 metric tons in 1913, amounting to some 95 percent of all cotton exports. In the 1930s, the Iranian government entered on an industrialization drive that increasingly exploited cotton for domestic manufacturing. By the end of the decade, production had grown to 38,000 metric tons, of which only one-seventh was being exported; and Iranian mills were supplying half the domestic market for cotton cloth.

Cotton developed as the major cash crop of the Sudan from 1925 onward with the development of new irrigation projects. Turkish production expanded after World War I and boomed in the 1950s when the Korean War raised world commodity prices. The same circumstances turned cotton into Syria's biggest cash crop. Israeli and Afghan production expanded in the 1960s, much of the latter country's cotton being destined for export to the Soviet Union. By the late 1970s, 11.6 percent of the world's cotton production came from the Middle East, and the region encompassed 7 percent of the total world acreage devoted to cotton. The largest outputs, in thousands of metric tons, were those of Turkey (522), Iran (490), Egypt (413), Sudan (166), Syria (150), Israel (65), and Afghanistan (50). Much smaller amounts were produced in Morocco, Iraq, Jordan, and Yemen.

Cotton is the fabric of choice for clothing in much of the Middle East. Its lightness and absorbency particularly suit it to hot climates. Terms of Middle Eastern origin pertaining to types of cotton cloth—damask from Damascus, gauze from Gaza—testify to the long history of cotton textiles and are a reminder of a time when many cities of the area were known for their distinctive weaves and patterns. The transition from hand-woven cotton fabrics to factory-made products initially favored the export of raw fiber and the import of inexpensive finished goods. This led, in turn, to disarray in the domestic textile industry, largely based on small workshops. Though tens of thousands of workers were still using hand-looms at the end of World War I, and distinctive local fabrics like the block-printed cottons of Iran and the embroidered tablecloths of Damascus survive to this day as choice products of national handicraft industries, most cotton textile production now takes place in modern spinning and weaving mills.

In 1977 the region produced 500,000 metric tons of cotton yarn, with the highest output from Egypt, Turkey, and Syria. It also produced 2,640 million square meters of cotton fabric, with production concentrated most heavily in Egypt, Iran, and Syria. These figures represent approximately 5 percent of total world production from a region then comprising roughly the same proportion of the world's population.

BIBLIOGRAPHY

EHLERS, ECKART, AHMAD PARSA, HASAN HAKIMIAN, and DANIEL BALAND. "Cotton." In Encyclopaedia Iranica, vol. 6. Costa Mesa, Calif., 1993.

ISSAWI, CHARLES. An Economic History of the Middle East and North Africa. New York, 1982.

OWEN, E. R. J. Cotton and the Egyptian Economy. Oxford, 1969.

RIVLIN, HELEN ANNE B. The Agricultural Policy of Muhammad Ali in Egypt. Cambridge, Mass., 1961.

TIGNOR, ROBERT L. Modernization and British Colonial Rule in Egypt, 1882–1914. Princeton, N.J., 1966.

Richard W. Bulliet

Council for Development and Reconstruction (CDR)

The CDR was to assess the extent of damages resulting from Lebanon's civil war and allocate international and Lebanese financial aid for reconstruction purposes.

Established in 1977 by the government of Lebanon, the Council for Development and Reconstruction (CDR) enjoyed wide powers and was directly accountable to the office of the prime minister. In 1978, 454 million U.S. dollars were committed by the CDR for road repairs, housing, transportation, and the rebuilding of Beirut International Airport. In 1983, following Israel's invasion of southern Lebanon to rout Palestinian militants—and its devastating results—the CDR could only raise 571 million U.S. dollars of the 15 billion U.S. dollars necessary for the rebuilding of Lebanon's infrastructure. International and Arab pledges of financial support were never totally forthcoming; some countries did not make good on their pledges. Between 1985 and 1988, the activities of the CDR were undermined by government paralysis, rampant inflation, financial crisis, and the growing violence inside Lebanon.

In 1990, following the Ta'if Accord and the formation of a new government in Lebanon, the CDR was reinstated.

BIBLIOGRAPHY

AMERICAN TASK FORCE FOR LEBANON. Working Paper: Conference on Lebanon. Washington, D.C., 1991.

George E. Irani

Couscous

A staple food of North Africa.

Couscous is the husked and crushed, but unground, semolina of hard wheat (*Triticum durum*), although the preparation of the same name can be made with barley, millet, sorghum, or corn. Semolina is the hard part of the grain of hard-wheat, which resists the grinding of the millstone. The word "couscous" derives from the Arabic word *kaskasa,* to pound small, but the word is also thought to derive from the Arabic name for the perforated earthenware steamer pot used in steaming the couscous, called a *keskes* in Arabic (*couscousière* in French). Another theory is based on onomatopoeia—from the sound of the steam rising in the couscousière. In any case, the Arabic word derives from a non-Arabic, probably Berber, word. Couscous is also the general name for all prepared dishes made from hard-wheat or other cereals. In fact, it would not be incorrect to call couscous a kind of pasta.

Couscous is a staple food in the Maghrib (North Africa). Hard-wheat couscous was probably invented by Arabs or Berbers in the twelfth century based on techniques possibly learned from Saharan Africans. This is suggested by Ibn Battuta's description of a millet couscous he ate in Mali in 1352. One of the first written references to couscous is in an anonymous thirteenth century Hispano-Muslim cookery book, *Kitab al-Tabikh fi al-Maghrib wa al-Andalus.*

The Berbers call this food *sekrou* (or *seksou*), while it is known as *maftoul* or *mughrabiyya* in the countries of the eastern Mediterranean and *suksukaniyya* in the Sudan. In Algeria it is called *tha'am* or *kesksou.* In Tunisia it is called *keskesi.* Very large couscous grains are called *m'hammas,* and very fine grains, usually used for sweet couscous dishes, are called *mesfouf.*

Couscous is processed from a fine and coarse grade of semolina. The fine grain affixes to the coarse grain by sprinkling water and salt by hand (although mechanization is used for mass production). The grains are rolled and rubbed with the palms and fingers until the desired size is formed. The couscous may be dried and stored, or it may be steamed over water or broth in a couscousière. Couscous is served in a pile on a large platter with meat, chicken, or fish and vegetables and spices. It is also served in bowls as a loose stew with similar ingredients included.

Clifford A. Wright

Cox, Percy [1864–1937]

British diplomat and colonial administrator.

After six years (1884–1890) in the British and Indian armies, Sir Percy Cox entered the Indian Political Department, where he was to spend most of the rest of his professional life. At this time, the government of India controlled British diplomatic relations with much of the coast of East Africa and with the shaykh-doms of the Persian/Arabian Gulf. After postings at Zailaand and Berbera (Somalia), Cox was appointed British consul and political agent at Musqat (now a part of Oman), his first major post, in 1899. His knowledge of Arabic was crucial in enabling him to restore the relationship between the sultan, Faysal ibn Turki Al Bu Sa'id, and the British and Indian governments, which had become strained as France attempted to replace British influence. By 1903 Faysal's subsidy had been restored, Faysal's son Taymur had attended the Delhi Durbar, and Lord Curzon, the viceroy of India, had visited Musqat and invested Faysal as Grand Commander of the Order of the Indian Empire (GCIE).

Cox spent most of the rest of the period before World War I in the Gulf, first as acting political resident and political resident, then as consul general (under the British minister in Tehran) for southwestern Persia (now Iran) including the Gulf islands, at a time when British trade with the area was rapidly increasing. In 1914 Cox, who had been knighted in 1911, was appointed secretary to the Foreign Department of the government of India. But a few months later, at the outbreak of World War I, he became chief political officer to Indian Expeditionary Force 'D,' which landed at Iraq's Fao peninsula at the end of 1914. Apart from two years as acting British minister to Tehran (1918–1920), the rest of Cox's career was spent in Mesopotamia/Iraq. In the early part of the war, he also played a crucial role (although at a distance) in ensuring the neutrality of the Saudi ruler of Najd, Abd al-Aziz ibn Abd al-Rahman (Ibn Sa'ud), and postponing, if not ultimately preventing, the differences between the former and Britain's other protégé, the Sharif of Mecca, from breaking out into open conflict.

Southern Mesopotamia was invaded in the last few weeks of 1914; British imperial troops reached Baghdad in March 1917 and Mosul a few days after the 1918 armistice that ended the war. One of the consequences of the fact that British authorities conducted the Mesopotamia campaign from India and the campaign in Egypt and Palestine from London and Cairo was that Cox, head of Iraq's civil administration, was not informed of the details of the SYKES-PICOT AGREEMENT until May 1917. As neither Cox nor his subordinates (notably Arnold Wilson) were kept abreast of London's thinking on possible future developments in the Middle East, they proceeded to set up an administration on the lines of the British Indian provinces with which they were familiar. When it became clear, toward the end of the war, that this kind of old-style colonialism was no longer acceptable (in the new international atmosphere that engendered the League of Nations), the result was a period of great uncertainty for British officials in the field.

Lord Curzon had asked Cox to go to Tehran to negotiate a new Anglo–Persian treaty, but the turbulent political circumstances in Persia made this impossible. By June 1920, when he was appointed British high commissioner in Iraq, after spending nearly two years in Tehran, the situation had become extremely volatile, especially since the award of the Iraqi mandate to Britain at the SAN REMO CONFERENCE in April. During the summer, a rebellion broke out that threatened the whole future of the British connection with the country; Cox advised firmly against the lively "Quit Mesopotamia" campaign in the British press. He went to Iraq in the autumn and managed to secure the candidature of Faisal ibn Husayn (whom the French had ousted from Syria) for the throne of Iraq. In October 1922, Cox forced through the signature of the ANGLO–IRAQI TREATIES (which replaced the mandate in form while maintaining its substance) and fixed the borders between Kuwait, Saudi Arabia, and Iraq over the next two months. After his retirement from Iraq in May 1923, he acted as British plenipotentiary in the negotiations over the Anglo–Iraqi frontier with Turkey in 1924.

BIBLIOGRAPHY

GRAVES, PHILIP. *The Life of Sir Percy Cox.* 1941.

Peter Sluglett

Crane, Charles R.

U.S. industrialist opposed to Zionism and the Jewish state.

A Chicago valve manufacturer and influential contributor to the Democratic Party, Crane later became an ardent Anglophile and anti-Zionist. He was sent by President Wilson to the Middle East after the 1919 Paris Peace Conference to investigate the interests of the people of the region. The KING–CRANE COMMISSION returned and made its report to the president, arguing that the French should not be given a mandate. The commission also questioned the propriety of creating a Jewish homeland in the face of Arab opposition.

BIBLIOGRAPHY

KHALIDI, WALID. *From Haven to Conquest: Readings in Zionism and the Palestine Problem until 1948.* Beirut, 1971.

Mia Bloom

Creech-Jones, Arthur

British colonial secretary.

Creech-Jones, responsible for Palestine after World War II, was involved in discussions and negotiations over termination of the British mandate over Palestine, handing over responsibility to the United Nations, partitioning Palestine between Jews and Arabs, and the resettlement of European Jewish refugees in Palestine. Although mildly pro-Zionist, he supported Ernest BEVIN's position of maintaining good relations with Arab nations while advocating Jewish–Arab understanding.

Jenab Tutunji

Crémieux Decree

French legislation that granted full French citizenship to the Jews of French colonial Algeria.

Named for Adolphe Crémieux, France's minister of justice, the decree was one of a series of acts affecting the political organization of Algeria that were issued by the French republic on October 24, 1870, shortly after it had come to power. Since the French occupation in 1830, Algerians had been French subjects, but not French citizens. Only a handful had applied for naturalization, primarily because doing so necessitated acknowledging the primacy of French law and renouncing the right to be judged in accordance with religious statutes—a step almost no Muslims and very few Jews were prepared to take.

Because the Crémieux Decree accorded Jews—a religious minority in Algeria—a right denied to the country's religious majority, it angered Algerian Muslims. Further alienating Muslims was the decree's automatic application to the entire Jewish community, without conditions concerning their acceptance of the French legal system. Moreover, many of the European settlers in Algeria were opposed to the decree, because it permitted Algerian Jews to vote with them for local officials as well as for Algeria's seats in the French parliament.

Shortly after the passage of the Crémieux Decree, revolts erupted in the Algerian countryside, which threatened French settlers rendered especially vulnerable by the withdrawal of significant portions of the French army for service in the Franco–Prussian War. Asserting that Muslim anger over the Crémieux Decree had directly inspired these challenges to French authority, many settlers demanded its abrogation before it caused further troubles.

The settler reaction against the naturalization of the Jews was so vehement that the government did consider withdrawing the decree, but refrained from doing so to avoid antagonizing European Jewish financiers whose support it badly needed. It became clear in the light of subsequent evidence that the decree had played little, if any, role in sparking the rebellions. Rather, the rural Algerian Muslims involved in them had seized the opportunity presented by the decrease of French military power to challenge the newly constituted republican government—which, they were convinced, would sacrifice their interests while promoting those of the French settlers.

Settler opposition to the decree—and the deliberately deceptive attempt to tie it to the revolts—revealed a pervasive strain of anti-Semitism that continued to recur among lower-class Europeans in Algeria throughout the late nineteenth and early twentieth centuries. In 1940, during World War II, the German-sponsored French Vichy government abolished the Crémieux Decree when it took control of Algeria, but the provisions were reinstated after the war and remained in effect until the end of French rule in Algeria, in 1962.

BIBLIOGRAPHY

JULIEN, CHARLES-ANDRÉ. *Histoire de l'Algérie contemporaine: La conquête et les débuts de la colonisation (1827–1871).* Paris, 1964.

POSENER, S. *Adolphe Crémieux: A Biography.* Philadelphia, 1940.

Kenneth J. Perkins

Crete

The second largest island in the eastern Mediterranean.

Covering 3,189 square miles and situated between the southern Greek mainland and Egypt, Crete has been part of Greece since 1913. It had previously, ever since its capture from the Venetians in 1669, belonged to the Ottoman Empire. The island's population—502,165 according to a 1981 census—is almost entirely Greek Orthodox. A community of a few hundred Jews were killed by the Nazis, who occupied the island during World War II. About 32,000 Muslims were exchanged for about the equivalent number of Greek Orthodox people during the Greco–Turkish transfer of populations in 1923. Rather than constituting one separate administrative unit, Crete consists of four regional departments (named in all but one case after the largest city in each department: Iráklion, Canea, Rethymnon, and Lasithion, whose largest town is Hagios Nikó-

laos). The island's economy is primarily dependent on agriculture, and there is only a little industry, in the vicinity of Iráklion, the largest city. Since the 1960s, however, tourism has developed significantly.

The immediate effects of Ottoman rule in Crete included widespread conversions from Christianity to Islam; a revival of the agrarian economy, which had stagnated under Venetian feudalism; and a strengthening of the role of the church under the MILLET SYSTEM for the Greek Orthodox population, but a decline in the poetic and literary traditions that had been established under the Venetians. The flourishing of Cretan painting that had occurred under the Venetians came to an end, although the artistic tradition survived, transformed into a more decorative, Orient-influenced genre. Travelers' accounts have made it possible to estimate that in the late eighteenth century the island held about 350,000 inhabitants, of whom almost 200,000 were Greek Orthodox, 150,000 Muslims, and a few thousand Jews. The establishment of a French consulate in the eastern port city of Canea in 1679 signaled a growing French interest in the island's produce. By the late 1700s, Crete was an important exporter of olive oil and other agricultural products that were shipped to Marseilles, Alexandria, Constantinople, and Smyrna. Soap began to be produced and exported in the mid-eighteenth century.

Beginning in the mid-nineteenth century, the prominent role it played in the EASTERN QUESTION brought Crete a half century of strife, marked by successive Christian uprisings in support of uniting the island with Greece. A Christian uprising that broke out in 1858 was contained by the Ottomans, but the subsequent revolt of 1866 to 1869 required the involvement of the great powers, who mediated between Greece and the Sublime Porte, persuading the Greek government to stop assisting the rebels in return for the Porte's allowing the Christians a greater role in the administration of the island's affairs. In 1878, an elected assembly was established in Crete, but sporadic agitation continued in the 1880s as the consuls of the powers sought to mediate between the demands of the Greek population and the Ottoman administrators. Serious clashes in early 1897 prompted the powers to declare that rather than favoring Crete's union with Greece, they supported self-government for the island, which would remain under the nominal rule of the Porte. This initiative, which did not appease Greece, led to the short-lived GRECO–TURKISH WAR (1897).

Despite Greece's defeat in the war, the powers imposed on Crete a Greek high commissioner, Prince George of Greece, while placing the island under their own military control. This situation was regarded by the Greek inhabitants of Crete as an interim arrangement pending full union with Greece, and they proclaimed this expectation in two uprisings (1905, 1908). After a period of de facto self-governance, the island was finally incorporated into Greece upon the signing of the London Treaty (1913), which formalized the Ottoman Empire's territorial losses following the 1912–1913 Balkan war. The Muslim inhabitants of the island were removed to Turkey in 1923 in accord with the exchange-of-populations agreement reached between Greece and Turkey.

Crete has played an important role in Greek history since 1912. The birthplace of the liberal politician Eleuthérios VENIZÉLOS (1864–1936), who dominated Greek politics for several decades, the island has provided a strong electoral base for centrist and center-left political parties. In the twentieth century, the island remained an important strategic post in the eastern Mediterranean. The Germans occupied it during World War II, thereby provoking into action a local guerilla resistance movement. The site of major U.S. and NATO military installations, Crete remained strategically important to the West during the Cold War.

BIBLIOGRAPHY

CHRISTOPOULOS, GEORGE, ed. *History of the Greek Nation.* University Park, Pa., 1975.

Alexander Kitroeff

Crime

Traditional Islamic law and modern law codes have both represented societal responses to crime and punishment.

Approaches to crime and punishment in the Middle East and North Africa during the past two centuries have swung between two poles: the tradition of Islamic law (*Shari'a*) and the codification of criminal law that took place in Europe in the nineteenth century. In recent decades, the political call by various groups for implementation of the *Shari'a* has been popularly symbolized, particularly by adversaries, in terms of amputation of hands, death by stoning, and public flogging, punishments specified as *hudud* (sing., *hadd*), meaning "hindrance, impediment, or limit." The offenses punishable by *hudud* are unlawful sexual intercourse, false accusation of unlawful intercourse, wine drinking, theft, and highway robbery. On the basis of Qur'anic verses, medieval legal specialists affirmed death by stoning as the maximum penalty for unlawful intercourse and crucifixion or decapitation as the punishment for highway robbery with loss of life. Cutting off the hand or foot is the hadd penalty for theft or nonlethal highway robbery. One hundred lashes is the lesser penalty for unlawful intercourse and eighty lashes the penalty for false accusation of unlawful intercourse and for drinking wine. The legists further specified that repentance should be taken into account in instances of theft and highway robbery, that false accusations of adultery should be vigorously investigated to minimize executions for that offense, that confessions requiring severe punishments could be retracted, and that the most rigorous standards of moral qualifications should be set for witnesses.

Given the limitations hedging the application of the hudud, and the comparatively limited range of offenses they covered, most acts included in modern criminal codes were left to the state to decide according to its own criteria. The legists termed the punishments meted out by the state for such offenses *ta'zir* (deterrence) rather than hudud. The jurisdiction of the state was not systematically defined, however. Though documents appointing religious judges (*qadi*) to office did not emphasize criminal jurisdiction, religious courts sometimes exercised broader authority than at other times. Other alternatives varied. Market-related offenses that fell into the category of *hisba*, for example, such as short measures, could be brought before the market inspector (*muhtasib*) in regimes where this official existed. Certain other crimes might be handled by police authorities (*shurta*) or by state officials charged with adjudicating administrative infractions (*mazalim*).

By the eighteenth century, the terms *siyasa shar'iya* (political law) and *qanun* (fiat law) were generally used to refer to legal matters over which the state asserted legislative authority on the premise that they fell outside the purview of the *Shari'a*. On this basis, nineteenth century legal reformers considered criminal law to be open to fundamental revision. In 1840 the Ottoman Empire, for example, adopted a new penal code (*Ceza Kanunnamesi*) that embodied the word *qanun* and presented itself as an exercise of the secular legislative prerogative of the sultan. The new code continued the earlier Ottoman practice of supplementing the *Shari'a* by stipulating punishments for offenses outside the category of hudud, but it also included aspects of French law. A more radical revision of the Ottoman penal code, based heavily on French models, was promulgated in 1858. When Iran adopted a penal code in 1925, it was also closely patterned on a French model. As Middle Eastern and North African countries fell under imperialist control, European views of crime and penal law prevailed there also.

In contrast to the narrowness of the category of criminal activity enshrined in the concept of the hudud, the reformed criminal codes of European inspiration were broad and flexible. Belonging to a communist party or criticizing a monarch, for example, might be classified as a criminal offense. Crime became less a matter of sin than a matter of offending society or the current government. In Iran, this gap was narrowed, to some degree, after the 1979 revolution when the religious offense of "corruption on the earth" (fasad fi al-ard) gained prominence as a criminal category of loose definition and substantial flexibility. Though this offense was based on Qur'anic verse, its application as a means of purging opponents of the new regime was a distinctly modern innovation. As such, it is representative of the fluidity of the current ideological struggle between secularism and political Islam. Despite the prominence given to the hudud, there is no consensus on how the Shari'a should be applied in the area of penal law. While Saudi Arabia adheres to a comparatively strict interpretation of the Islamic legal tradition, including its corporal punishments, Muslim modernists have often disagreed with that approach.

Because of inconsistencies in how crime has been defined and in systematic record keeping, a reliable survey of the incidence of various offenses across the region is not available. A frequently stated generalization, however, maintains that crime rates in the eighteenth century, prior to any reform or systemization of penal law, were low by European standards. Historian Abraham Marcus, for example, writes of eighteenth-century Aleppo:

> Crimes against life and property . . . were relatively rare. Every year a few fell victim to physical assaults and even murders. Money and belongings were stolen from some homes and shops. In 1754 a mosque was the target of a thief, who escaped with three prayer rugs. Some residents lost their donkeys, mules, and horses, which were tempting targets when left unattended in public places. For a large metropolis, however, the overall number of such crimes was low indeed. Only a dozen or so complaints reached the Shari'a court every month; although not inclusive of all incidents, they attested to the generally low crime rate. (p. 102)

How to compare such appraisals with figures from later periods remains a problem. In 1948, Turkey reported 2,348 convictions for murder, 9,816 for robbery, and 110,529 for other offenses. However, the Turkish Criminal Code of 1926 (Article 163) included penalties for those "who, by misuse of religion, religious sentiments, or things that are religiously considered as holy, in any way incite the

people to action prejudicial to the security of the state, or form associations for this purpose." This offense against secularism clearly would not have been considered a crime in Aleppo two centuries earlier.

The question of how or whether the contradictions and inconsistencies embodied in the comparison of crime and punishment in the Shari'a with penal codes of European inspiration will be resolved remains unanswered. The reality of the situation in various countries is often much more complex than the stereotypes purveyed in political debate. In Iran, criminal statistics for 1971 included such violations of the penal code as strikes, crowding and conspiracy, distribution of "harmful" papers, opposition to monarchy, professing communism, and insulting public officials and members of parliament. A decade later, under the Islamic Republic of Iran, which ostensibly had adopted the Shari'a as its legal basis, a nearly identical set of crimes was reported, with retail sale of alcohol in restaurants and false accusation of adultery added and crimes against monarchy and being a communist deleted.

BIBLIOGRAPHY

COULSON, N. J. A History of Islamic Law. Edinburgh, 1964.
MARCUS, ABRAHAM. The Middle East on the Eve of Modernity: Aleppo in the Eigtheenth Century. New York, 1989.
TYAN, EMILE. Histoire de l'organisation judiciaire en pays d'Islam. Leiden, 1960.

Richard W. Bulliet

Crimean War

The Crimean War developed out of a basic misunderstanding between Great Britain and imperial Russia over fundamental aims regarding the disposition of the territories of the greatly weakened Ottoman Empire.

About 1830, a Russian war against the OTTOMAN EMPIRE had assured the independence of Greece. Until that time, the British, a close trade partner of Russia, had largely acquiesced to Russian acquisition of protector status over certain of the Ottoman Empire's Orthodox Christian territories, such as Serbia and the Romanian principalities.

There had always been Russophobes among British leaders, including William Pitt, the Younger, and George Canning. But it was only when Lord Palmerston was appointed secretary of state for external affairs that a clear British policy concerning the Middle East was conceived. The Treaty of HUNKÂR-ISKELESI, following Egypt's invasion of Asia Minor in

1833, appears to have been the catalyst. Apart from awarding to Muhammad Ali Pasha control of Syria and the island of Crete, a secret clause recognized Russia's right to intervene in Turkish affairs to "protect" the interests of Orthodox subjects. Palmerston made it clear to Parliament that this arrangement must be undone. He proposed that, to protect Britain's lifeline to India, Britain must either station soldiers in the Middle East at strategic points or energetically assist the Ottoman leadership to reform its armed forces and liberalize its system of government.

Britain chose the less expensive route of assisting such pro-British Viziers as Mustafa Reşid Paşa and their protégés to reform the Ottoman system. Upon the accession of Sultan Abdülmecit I in 1839, the Ottoman government launched the so-called TANZIMAT reform, which would culminate in the first Ottoman constitution of 1876. Also in 1839, the combined European powers forced Muhammad Ali, who was on the verge of usurping further powers from the Ottoman sultan, to withdraw his forces from Syria and the Sudan in exchange for the conciliatory gesture of receiving Egypt as his hereditary kingdom.

Despite this heightened British interest in the Mediterranean region, apparently Russia missed the message. When Czar Nicholas I (1825–1855) paid a state visit to Britain in 1842, he queried the British about the disposition of "the Sick Man of Europe." In typical British fashion, officials in London failed to give the czar a direct answer; consequently, he and his delegation concluded that if Russia strengthened its hold over Ottoman Turkey, Britain would not be upset.

A clash of interest and a cause célèbre was not long in developing. Sultan Abdülmecit, after consulting the powerful and popular British resident ambassador, Stratford Canning, decided to award to France the traditional function and title of Protector of the Holy Sepulchre in Jerusalem. Imperial Russia, which annually sent thousands of pilgrims to the Holy Land and had recently invested sizable funds in Jerusalem for churches and pilgrim hostels, took grave offense at not receiving the honored designation. After long drawn-out bickering over the issue, Russia issued an ultimatum. With the Ottomans supported by the British ambassador, who now ordered the British fleet into the Black Sea, Russia declared war and marched on the Balkans, where the Turks put up a stiff resistance. Meanwhile, the British and French landed troops in the Crimea in 1853 and 1854 and besieged Russian fortifications at Inkerman and Sebastapol. Ill-equipped and ravaged by cholera, the Russians capitulated in 1855, and Czar Nicholas abdicated to be replaced by Czar Alexander II.

In the Peace of Paris (1856), Ottoman Turkey, France, Britain, and Austria—the latter not having been an active participant—forced upon Russia a humiliating settlement. Russia was to cease its meddling in Ottoman affairs, including Romania, and it was not permitted to fortify any point on the Black Sea. Her naval vessels also were placed under strict control of the allies.

This embarrassing result was an important factor in forcing Czar Alexander to declare the liberation of the serfs in 1861. Moreover, the heavy commitment by Britain in the war and the great loss of life, in spite of heroic medical assistance by Florence Nightingale's field hospital in Istanbul, played a major role in Britain's decision twenty-five years later to occupy Cyprus and then Egypt to assure its lifeline to India without recourse to Ottoman Turkey.

C. Max Kortepeter

Cromer, Lord

See Baring, Evelyn

Crossman, Richard   [1907–1974]

British statesman and journalist.

Crossman was appointed in 1946 to the ANGLO-AMERICAN COMMITTEE OF INQUIRY into the question of Jewish refugees from Europe after World War II by Britain's foreign secretary, Ernest Bevin. Among that committee's recommendations was to allow 100,000 Jews to enter Palestine. Crossman was favorably disposed toward ZIONISM and Israel. As a Labor party member of Parliament after serving on the Committee of Inquiry, Crossman sought to move British policy in the Middle East in a direction more favorable to Israel.

BIBLIOGRAPHY

Encyclopedia of Zionism and Israel. New York, 1971.
SACHAR, HOWARD M. *A History of Israel.* New York, 1979.

Benjamin Joseph

Çukurova

See Cilicia

Çukurova Holding Company

Turkish business conglomerate.

Established by the Eliyeşil and Karamehmet families, two wealthy landowning families from the cotton-growing region of Turkey on the Mediterranean Sea, the Çukurova Holding Company is one of the largest private-sector enterprises in Turkey. The group was active in importing machinery for agriculture in the 1950s. Today, the company owns several banks, including Yapı ve Kredı Bankasi and Pamukbank, a large export-import company, and several factories, including the giant manufacturer of electrical products, Çukurova Elektrik.

BIBLIOGRAPHY

SÖNMEZ, MUSTAFA. *Kırk Haramiler: Türkiye'de Holdingler.* Istanbul, 1987.

David Waldner

Cumhuriyet

Daily newspaper in Turkey.

Cumhuriyet (The Republic) is the oldest newspaper in Turkey and, with *Hürriyet* and *Milliyet,* one of the country's three major dailies. Although after 1990, a new breed of sensationalist newspapers began capturing the larger share of the 2.8 million Turkish newspapers sold daily, the three remained the most influential of the print media based in Istanbul. In fact, the three compete for the country's top journalists, who often spend some part of their careers at each of the publications.

Originally published in Arabo-Persian script, the paper was launched in May 1924 by journalist and publisher Yunus Nadi Abalioğlu, soon after the founding of the Republic of Turkey. It was given its name by the father of modern Turkey, Mustafa Kemal Atatürk, a friend of the publisher. Although not directly affiliated with the new government, *Cumhuriyet* was an ardent defender of the regime and its concept of the democratic republic; it remains basically Kemalist today. Abalioğlu had previously supported and covered the Turkish war of independence through his Ankara paper, *Yenigün.*

Cumhuriyet is the only noncolor Turkish newspaper, using exclusively black and white photographs and graphics. It is unique in that it uses no cheesecake photos. Its tone is consistently serious, rejecting the tabloid style that other Turkish papers use at least in part. It is considered the paper of record for the country. At its peak in the late 1980s, the paper claimed 125,000 readers, mostly from the more educated and more affluent in Turkey. According to a house survey done at that time, more than 44 percent of *Cumhuriyet*'s readers were university educated, and more than 63 percent spoke English as a foreign language. The paper provides the most complete source of art, cultural, and entertainment news; it also publishes weekly science and technology and book review supplements.

Although *Cumhuriyet* has never been associated with a political party, it has remained slightly left of center. One exception may have been during the early stages of World War II, when it carried some editorials favorable to Germany, perhaps in defense of government allies. (Germany had been Turkey's ally in World War I. In 1939, however, Turkey signed a mutual assistance pact with France and Britain and remained neutral during most of World War II.)

Abalioğlu was publisher of the paper until his death in 1945. His son, Nadir Nadi, then took over the post, with one brief interruption, until his death in 1991. Descendants have held various management positions at the paper, and the family retains a controlling share of the company. In 1991, as in 1971, the paper was seriously shaken by a defection of writers and a boycott by readers when it was viewed as becoming too centrist.

The newspaper's morale and readership were strengthened, however, in the wake of the assassination on January 24, 1993, of Uğur Mumcu, the paper's respected investigative columnist. The fifty-year-old, Ankara-based writer was killed in a car-bomb explosion at his home. The Islami Hareket (Islamic Movement), a radical religious organization, took credit for the murder, as did other groups. Mumcu, trained as a lawyer, had written extensively against Islamic fundamentalism. At the time of his death, he also was writing a book about alleged links between the Kurdistan Workers Party (PKK) in Turkey, under the leadership of Abdullah Ocalan, and Turkey's National Intelligence Organization (MIT).

Mumcu's death sparked broad public protests against the Islamic fundamentalist movement. His funeral, with one million attending, was one of the largest in Turkey's history and was followed by large, pro-secular demonstrations in the country's major cities. One year after the murder, the police had not charged anyone with the crime.

BIBLIOGRAPHY

Interviews with Hasan Cemal, former editor in chief at *Cumhuriyet,* and Haluk Şahin, former columnist at *Güneş,* now defunct.

Stephanie Capparell

Cumhuriyet Halk Partisi

See Republican People's Party

Curiel Family

Family of European Sephardim and Marranos who became active in Jewish life in Egypt in the nineteenth century. Most were Italian nationals who entered the banking profession.

The most noted family member was Henry Curiel (1914–1978), who joined Marxist groups during the years between the two world wars. In 1941, he opened a bookshop in Cairo, where Marxist and antifascist elements engaged in political discussions. As a fervent proponent of Egyptianization despite his communist leaning, Curiel was instrumental in creating the Egyptian Movement for National Liberation (al-Haraka al-Misriyya lil-Taharrur al-Watani, MELN) during World War II to promote the idea among Marxists. In 1946, Curiel's MELN and Hillel Schwartz's pro-Communist ISKRA merged to become the Democratic Movement for National Liberation (al-Haraka al-Dimuqratiya li'l-Taharrur al-Watani, HADITU), and membership quickly rose to several thousand.

HADITU enjoyed an ephemeral existence, for in May 1948, in the wake of the Palestine war, many of its activists were arrested along with the Zionists. HADITU was organized into sections of students, workers, women, and even army officers. Pursuing the Soviet line, HADITU advocated the creation of a secular democratic state in Palestine integrating Jews and Arabs. Subsequently, however, it advocated the two-separate-states solution—Arab and Jewish. In 1950, following the emergence of Egypt's Wafdist government, noted Communists, either interned or under surveillance, were expelled from Egypt. Henry Curiel spent the rest of his life in Europe, promoting revolutionary movements. In 1978, he was assassinated in France.

BIBLIOGRAPHY

BOTMAN, SELMA. *The Rise of Egyptian Communism, 1939–1970.* Syracuse, N.Y., 1988.
KRÄMER, GUDRUN. *The Jews in Modern Egypt, 1914–1952.* Seattle, 1989.
LASKIER, MICHAEL M. *The Jews of Egypt, 1920–1970: In the Midst of Zionism, Anti-Semitism and the Middle East Conflict.* New York and London, 1991.
PERRAULT, GILLES. *Un homme á part.* Paris, 1984.

Michael M. Laskier

Curzon, George Nathaniel   [1859–1925]

English statesman who stressed Iran's strategic importance to Britain.

Born in Britain, Curzon, the Viscount of Keddelston, was emerging as a British authority on the Middle East when he traveled to Iran in 1889 as a newspaper correspondent. During the six months he spent traveling throughout the country on horseback, he became impressed with Iran's importance to the strategic defense of British India. Russia had become Britain's principal imperial rival in central Asia, and Curzon perceived Russian interests in the region as being inimical to those of Britain. In his monumental work, *Persia and the Persian Question,* he argued that Britain should protect Iran, the gateway to India, from European (and especially Russian) encroachments. The book also contained insightful descriptions of Iran's politics and society at the end of the nineteenth century.

Following his tour of Iran, Curzon was appointed foreign office undersecretary for India and subsequently viceroy of India. As the de facto British ruler of India from 1899 to 1905, he played a major role in shaping policy toward Iran, which fell under the purview of the India office. In 1903, Curzon made a ceremonial naval visit to the Persian Gulf that he viewed as intended to convey to Russia the extent of British power in the area.

Curzon was appointed to the House of Lords after he returned home in 1905. He distrusted efforts by the government to establish an understanding with Russia and opposed the ANGLO–RUSSIAN AGREEMENT (1907), which he criticized for abandoning British interests in Iran to Russia. After World War I, he was appointed foreign secretary. He was the architect of the ANGLO–PERSIAN AGREEMENT (1919), which would have made Iran a virtual British protectorate; much to his disappointment, the Iranian parliament failed to approve the controversial treaty.

BIBLIOGRAPHY

CURZON, G. N. *Persia and the Persian Question.* London, 1892.

Eric J. Hooglund

Cuza, Alexander   [1820–1873]

Romanian prince.

In 1859, the Ottoman Empire principalities of Wallachia and Moldavia elected the Moldavian minister of war, Alexander Cuza, prince of the united principalities (Romania). After seven troubled years, Cuza was ousted in 1866 and succeeded by the prince who became King Carol I in 1881.

BIBLIOGRAPHY

ANDERSON, M. S. *The Eastern Question*. London, 1966.
SHAW, STANFORD, and EZEL KURAL SHAW. *History of the Ottoman Empire and Modern Turkey*. New York, 1977.

Zachary Karabell

Cyprus

The largest island in the eastern Mediterranean.

The Cyprus Republic was established as a sovereign independent state in 1960. It is a presidential republic in which the president is elected by popular vote to a five-year term and the legislature consists of the unicameral House of Representatives. Covering 9,251 square kilometers (3,700 sq mi.), Cyprus lies south of the Turkish mainland and east of Syria. Prior to 1960, Britain ruled Cyprus, after having annexed it from the Ottoman Empire in 1878.

Cyprus has been divided since 1974 when Turkey invaded and occupied the northern part of the island. Turkey's troops control this territory, which makes up about a third of the island. The Turkish occupation of 1974 caused 200,000 Greek Cypriots to move southward and 50,000 Turkish Cypriots to relocate to the occupied territories. In 1983, a Turkish Republic of Northern Cyprus was established but has not been recognized by any country besides Turkey.

The last census to survey the entire island, in 1973, recorded a population of 631,788, of whom about 80 percent are Greek-speaking Orthodox, 18 percent Turkish-speaking Muslims, and the remaining 2 percent Maronites and Armenians. A 1986 census found the population in nonoccupied Cyprus to be 677,200, whereas that in the north was estimated to be about 160,000 (not including about 65,000 people from mainland Turkey who had settled in northern Cyprus). An official estimate for the population of the entire island in 1991 came to 708,000.

The capital of Cyprus, Nicosia, was divided by a "green line" that separated the northern occupied part from the rest of the city and effectively closed the

Postage stamps from Greek Cyprus (1987) and Turkish Cyprus (1983). (Richard Bulliet)

city's international airport. The other major cities are Larnaca (where the international airport was relocated), Limassol, and Paphos; in occupied Cyprus, the largest towns are Kerynia, virtually deserted since the invasion in 1974, and Famagusta. With the exception of Nicosia, all the major towns are seaports. Two mountain ranges on the island run east to west, one in the north and the higher Troödos range in the south.

After Cyprus gained independence in 1960, its economy changed dramatically. Within the next three decades, the formerly agrarian character of the island was transformed as domestic manufacturing and international trade were developed vigorously, in the process raising the per capita income from 350 dollars in 1960 to 7,500 dollars in 1986. The development of tourism was also a significant factor in this period.

The MILLET SYSTEM, which operated in Cyprus during the period of Ottoman rule (1570–1878), allowed the Greek Orthodox church of Cyprus to play an important role in the affairs of the majority Greek-speaking population of the island. The leader of the church, Archbishop Kyprianos, and a group of notables supported the Greek war of independence (1821) and were executed by the authorities. The Tanzimat reforms of 1839 and especially the HATT-I HÜMAYUN reforms introduced in Cyprus in 1856 improved living conditions for the Greek Orthodox inhabitants and enhanced their commercial and educational opportunities.

Cyprus was awarded to Britain at the Berlin Congress (1878), and Britain took over its administration. The island, however, remained formally part of the Ottoman Empire until 1914, when it was annexed by Britain as a consequence of the Ottoman Empire's siding with the Central powers in World War I. British rule brought a greater degree of self-government for the population and a Western-based judicial system but also much higher taxation, imposed to finance the compensation Britain had undertaken to pay the Ottomans after 1878.

The disaffection of the local Greek Orthodox population with British rule served to encourage sentiment in favor of union with Greece. During an uprising in support of enosis (union with Greece) in Nicosia (1931), the British Government House was burned down. The authorities retaliated by suspending the island's legislative council. The pro-enosis movement grew again in the late 1940s after the referendum—organized by the all-party Ethnarchic Council under the new Greek Orthodox Archbishop MAKARIOS III—that decided overwhelmingly in favor of union with Greece.

The Greek Cypriots took their case to the United Nations and Archbishop Makarios traveled to the United States to publicize the movement, but the

UN assembly declined to take up the issue and more anti-British demonstrations occurred on Cyprus. On April 1, 1955, attacks on British installations signaled a new phase in the island's anticolonial struggle. The campaign was led by the National Organization of Cypriot Fighters (EOKA), a Greek Cypriot guerrilla organization headed by Georgios Theodoros GRIVAS, a colonel of the Greek army who used the nom de guerre Dighenis. In retaliation, Britain exiled Archbishop Makarios and his close collaborators to the Seychelles (1956). While diplomatic initiatives began to resolve the Cyprus crisis at the United Nations and in London (1957), the minority group of Turkish Cypriots on the island, fearing the consequences of enosis, declared themselves to be for either a federation or partition.

Diplomatic negotiations between the British, Greek, and Turkish governments led to the Zurich Agreement between Greece and Turkey and the London Agreement between Britain, Greece, Turkey, and the Greek and Turkish Cypriot leaderships. The series of arrangements brought about the establishment of an independent state, the Cyprus Republic, whose sovereignty was to be guaranteed by Britain, Greece, and Turkey. Small garrisons of Greek and Turkish forces were to be stationed on Cyprus, and the rights of the Turkish Cypriot minority were enshrined in the constitution, which provided for the office of a Turkish Cypriot vice president of the republic with extensive veto powers. In December 1959, Makarios was elected president and Fazıl Kuçuk vice president. Elections for the legislative assembly were held in 1960, and in August of the same year the last British governor, Sir Hugh Foote, announced the end of British rule on the island (Britain retained two military bases under its sovereignty), thereby paving the way for the formal proclamation of the Cyprus Republic.

After a breakdown in Greek Cypriot and Turkish Cypriot relations led to intercommunal fighting in 1963, the areas populated by Turkish Cypriots were separated administratively by a so-called green line. When the situation continued to be tense in 1964, the Greek Cypriots began fearing a military invasion from mainland Turkey. Through a series of negotiations held under the aegis of the United Nations, diplomats sought a more practical resolution of the intercommunal conflict. Their proposals ranged from a reaffirmation of the original constitutional structure to either union with Greece or division of the island, but none of these measures was acceptable to both sides. The arrival of a UN peacekeeping force (1964), however, helped to reestablish peace. By remaining committed to preserving the Cyprus Republic, Makarios incurred the opposition of the Greek Cypriot nationalists and their leader, Colonel Grivas. Aided by the Greek dictatorship established in 1967, Grivas, working through an organization named EOKA-B, led a renewed struggle for enosis from 1971 till his death in 1974.

Growing conflict between Makarios and the Greek dictatorship culminated in the latter's support of Makarios's overthrow and the imposition of a dictatorship headed by Greek Cypriot nationalist Nikos Sampson (July 1974). Makarios survived an assassination attempt and left the island. Claiming to be exercising its rights as a guarantor of the sovereignty of Cyprus, Turkey launched a military invasion and eventually placed the northern third of the island under its control. The Greek dictatorship and the Sampson regime collapsed, and Glafkos Clerides was made acting president, pending the return of Makarios in December 1974.

After 1974, the two sides undertook numerous negotiations and held many meetings under the auspices of the United Nations, whose General Assembly called for the withdrawal of the Turkish occupying forces and the return of all the refugees to their homes. Several plans designed to resolve the crisis were submitted and although the Greek Cypriots agreed to a number of successive concessions, no overall arrangement has been acceptable to both sides.

Makarios died in 1977. His successor, Spyros Kyprianou, was president until 1988. As the candidate of the Democratic party, he then lost the presidential elections to George Vasileiou, who was supported by, among others, the large Communist party (AKEL). Vasileiou's tenure ended in 1993, when Glafkos Clerides won the presidential elections. In the meanwhile, Turkish Cypriot leader Rauf Denktash had declared the establishment of the Turkish Republic of Northern Cyprus (TRNC) in 1983. He was elected president of TRNC in 1985 and reelected in 1990.

BIBLIOGRAPHY

ATTALIDES, MICHAEL A. Cyprus Nationalism and International Politics. New York, 1979.
IOANNIDES, CHRISTOS P., ed. Cyprus Domestic Dynamics, External Constraints. New Rochelle, N.Y., 1992.
NECATIGIL, ZAIM M. The Cyprus Question and the Turkish Position in International Law. Oxford, 1989.

Alexander Kitroeff

Cyprus Convention

Agreement to let the British occupy Ottoman-held Cyprus in return for promise of military aid.

The Russian–Ottoman War of 1877 to 1878 ended with the Treaty of SAN STEFANO, forced on the defeated Ottoman Empire by Russia's czar and his minister Nikolai IGNATIEV. However, San Stefano was not to the liking of Britain's prime minister, Benjamin Disraeli. He offered to support the Ottomans and seek a revision of the treaty. In return, he demanded the island of Cyprus. The British had been looking for a naval base in the eastern Mediterranean, and Cyprus was ideally situated. By the Cyprus Convention of June 1878, the Ottoman sultan allowed the British to occupy Cyprus in return for a British guarantee of military aid if Russia refused to withdraw from the eastern Anatolian provinces occupied during the war. It took some time for the details to be arranged to the satisfaction of both parties, and the final terms of the convention were not settled until February 3, 1879. With the tentative agreement in hand by June 4, 1878, however, Britain engineered a drastic revision of the San Stefano treaty in favor of the Ottoman Empire at the Congress of BERLIN in July 1878.

BIBLIOGRAPHY

HUREWITZ, J. C., ed. *The Middle East and North Africa in World Politics.* New Haven, Conn., 1975.
SHAW, STANFORD and EZEL KURAL SHAW. *History of the Ottoman Empire and Modern Turkey.* New York, 1977.

Zachary Karabell

Cyrenaica

Former province of eastern Libya.

The province of Cyrenaica (also Barqa) bordered the Mediterranean, Egypt, Sudan, Chad, and the former Libyan provinces of Tripolitania and Fezzan. The administrative areas have been changed during the twentieth century. Today the main city and port in this region is Benghazi.

John L. Wright

Cyril IV [1816–1861]

110th Coptic patriarch of Egypt, 1854–1861.

Despite his short tenure, Cyril IV was the father of reform in the Egyptian Coptic church, both in the laity and the clergy; he remains one of the greatest modern Coptic patriarchs. Concerned for education in its broadest sense, Cyril established many schools throughout Egypt, promoted basic literacy, advanced theological training, and published new editions of important Coptic documents. The most famous institutions founded by the patriarch were the Coptic Orthodox College for clerics and Egypt's first women's college, both in Cairo. Empowered by the tuition received at these new schools, Copts attained important governmental positions in unprecedented numbers. Cyril's aggressive reform of church administration, particularly in land management, made him unusually popular among the laity, which had long sought a more equitable balance of power with the clergy. Unfortunately, Cyril's successors had no interest in continuing the enfranchisement of the laity and thus created a tension that has been played out even in recent times. Cyril fostered Coptic nationalism through an aggressive campaign of restoring ancient churches and building new ones, his greatest achievements being the construction of Saint Mark's Basilica in Azbakiya. A skillful negotiator, Cyril successfully mediated a dispute between Egypt and Ethiopia from 1856 to 1858. His dream of closer ties with the Russian Orthodox Church and the Church of England led to a conflict with Khedive Sa'id Pasha, who feared foreign interference. Cyril's assassination (by poison) was rumored to have been ordered by the khedive.

[*See also:* Copts]

BIBLIOGRAPHY

ATIYA, AZIZ S. *A History of Egyptian Christianity,* rev. ed. Millwood, N.Y., 1980.
STROTHMANN, R. *Die koptische Kirche in der Neuzeit.* Tübingen, Germany, 1932.

Donald Spanel

Cyril V [1824–1927]

112th Coptic patriarch of Egypt, 1874–1927.

Cyril V enjoyed the longest tenure of any Coptic patriarch but had a relatively insipid career. Even his admirers commented upon his simple-minded disinterest in matters foreign to his conservative, clerical background. Like his predecessor, DEMETRIUS II, Cyril supported education. In 1894, he established the Coptic Clerical College in Cairo. Nonetheless, Cyril lacked Demetrius's zeal, and he even closed some schools. To his credit, Cyril fostered Coptic nationalism by restoring ancient churches and building new ones, although he was unconcerned for the most crucial issue confronting his church, the sharing of power with the laity, which had enjoyed a promising but abortive start under Cyril IV.

The neglect by Cyril V further widened the gap between the progressive populace and the more conservative clergy. As a former monk, Cyril was solidly entrenched in that tradition. He especially infuriated the populace by reneging on his promise of cooperation in the administration of the *waqfs* (religious endowments). Worse still, he refused to attend the sessions of the Community Religious Council (Majlis Milli), which had come into existence shortly before his patriarchate, to empower the Coptic laity in the areas of church property, personal rights, and social welfare. Cyril's nonparticipation led to the suspension of the council and had serious consequences for the equitable adjudication of marriage, divorce, and inheritance, thus worsening the rift between ecclesiastical and secular factions within the church. Despite parliamentary restoration of the council in 1883 and 1891, Cyril's continued noncompliance left both assemblies powerless. The khedive acquiesced reluctantly to the council's petition for Cyril's banishment because he had enjoyed good relations with the patriarch. The action proved highly controversial; even many of Cyril's foes found his punishment unfair. Nevertheless, Cyril was exiled in 1892/93 for his stubborn opposition to the council. Ironically, when restored, he enjoyed widespread support from friend and foe alike.

[*See also:* Copts]

BIBLIOGRAPHY

ATIYA, AZIZ S. *A History of Egyptian Christianity,* rev. ed. Millwood, N.Y., 1980.
SHOUCRI, MOUNIR. "Cyril V." In *The Coptic Encyclopedia,* ed. by Aziz S. Atiya. New York, 1991.
STROTHMANN, R. *Die koptische Kirche in der Neuzeit.* Tübingen, Germany, 1932.
WAKIN, EDWARD. *The Copts: A Lonely Minority.* New York, 1963.

Donald Spanel

Cyril VI [1902–1971]

116th Coptic patriarch of Egypt, 1959–1971.

Cyril became pope of the Coptic church amid a long and bitter controversy between the Holy Synod of bishops and the Coptic Community Council, which consisted of laypersons. At issue was the appropriate field of candidates for the office. Until the twentieth century, the patriarch had been chosen from the monks. Beginning with the tenure (1927–1942) of JOHN XIX, however, the selection had shifted to provincial bishops. Yusab (Joseph) II, bishop of Girga in southern Egypt, served as acting patriarch from 1942 to 1944. After the brief tenure of another bishop, MAKARIUS III, as pope (1944–1945), Yusab II was elected to the office and served from 1946 to 1956. Following his death, Athanasius, bishop of Beni Suef,

became acting pope from 1956 to 1957. Because all four pontiffs had undistinguished and even disastrous (in the case of Yusab II) terms of office, both the government of Gamal Abdel Nasser and the populace generally favored a monk. In a confusing inversion of preference, however, the assembly of bishops favored a monk and the community council sought a monk. So divided was the church over the selection of a new pontiff that the government temporarily suspended the papal election in 1957. The choice of Cyril, a monk from Baramus in the Nile delta, represented a victory for the Nasser regime and the laity.

Cyril's name, adopted at the time of the papal election, honored several illustrious predecessors, particularly Cyril I (patriarch 412–444), a preeminent early Alexandrian theologian widely regarded as one of the fathers of the Coptic church. The true first name of Cyril VI was Mina. As a monk, he had enjoyed wide renown as an ascetic and a mystic. For many years he had sought unsuccessfully to rebuild the ancient monastery of his namesake, St. Menas (Mina), near Alexandria and lost no time as patriarch in realizing this project. At his behest, more than forty other churches and monasteries were excavated, restored, or built anew. These endeavors attracted criticism as well as praise. To many, Cyril was aloof, more interested in antiquarian and monastic concerns than with either the country's or the church's pressing needs. This complaint was repeated throughout Cyril's administration. Nonetheless, even Cyril's detractors admired his piety, which had been honed through his years as a monk.

Cyril's efforts at reform met with some success. He sought closer relations with the other Christian churches of the Near East. Coptic missionary activity flourished in many parts of Africa, and numerous African divinity students received scholarships to study at the Coptic Theological College and the Institute of Coptic Studies in Cairo. Of all African countries outside Egypt, Cyril was especially interested in Ethiopia because its primary Christian church had for centuries been under the jurisdiction of the Coptic patriarch and, in more recent years, had demanded autonomy. One of Cyril's first acts as patriarch was to convene a council that addressed the Ethiopians' demands. The historic accord of 1959 remains the foundation upon which the relations between the Coptic and Ethiopic orthodox churches are grounded. Although the Coptic pontiff retained his position as head of the Ethiopic church, the Ethiopians could henceforth participate in papal elections. Furthermore, the Ethiopians could now elect their own leader. Heretofore, the Ethiopians had had a metropolitan or archbishop but no patriarch. The new patriarch or *abuna* of the Ethiopian church was to be an Ethiopian, not an Egyptian. The abuna could consecrate his own clergy. Ethiopians could participate in all synods convened by the Coptic pope. Several other important privileges were granted to the Ethiopians.

In other areas, Cyril's achievements were more limited. In 1960, the government placed the handling of WAQF property (endowments given to the church) under a special committee composed of Copts. This move was hailed by some as an efficient administrative reform because the high clergy and the Coptic Community Council had clashed for decades over the handling of the *waqfs,* and it was condemned by others because the action took away much responsibility from both the clergy and the community council. The latter was left with responsibility for little more than administration of the Coptic centers for theological education and for building various projects.

Cyril's struggle to alleviate the discrimination toward and persecution of COPTS tolerated by the Islamic regime was similarly inspired but fruitless. Believing that close cooperation with the Islamic government would foster better relations between Muslims and Copts, Cyril joined with Muslim leaders in denouncing Israel on several occasions. Furthermore, through wider participation in international religious conferences and meeting with leaders of other churches, Cyril reckoned that oppression of the Copts would abate if the rest of the world was watching. Although the plight of the Copts is now more widely recognized, unfortunately it has not improved.

BIBLIOGRAPHY

ATIYA, AZIZ S. *A History of Eastern Christianity,* rev. ed. Millwood, N.Y., 1980.

MEINARDUS, OTTO. *Christian Egypt: Faith and Life.* Cairo, 1970.

SHOUCRI, MOUNIR. "Cyril VI." In *The Coptic Encyclopedia,* ed. by Aziz S. Atiya. New York, 1991.

WAKIN, EDWARD. *A Lonely Minority: The Modern Story of Egypt's Copts.* New York, 1963.

Donald Spanel